DIRECTORS' DISQUALIFICATION & INSOLVENCY RESTRICTIONS

THIRD EDITION

DIRECTORS' DISQUALIFICATION & INSOLVENCY RESTRICTIONS

THIRD EDITION

ADRIAN WALTERS
MALCOLM DAVIS-WHITE Q.C.

SWEET & MAXWELL

Published in 2010 by Thomson Reuters (Legal) Limited
(Registered in England & Wales, Company No 1679046.
Registered Office and address for service:
100 Avenue Road, London, NW3 3PF) trading as
Sweet & Maxwell

For further information on our products and services, visit
www.sweetandmaxwell.co.uk
Typeset by LBJ Typesetting Ltd of Kingsclere
Printed in the UK by CPI William Clowes Ltd, Beccles, NR34 7TL

A CIP catalogue record for this book is available from the British Library

ISBN 978-1-84703-333-8

No natural forests were destroyed to make this product, only farmed timber was used and re-planted.

DEDICATION

To Rachel and Alice
And to Sarah and . . . the Bear, the Bat and the Beaver

CONTENTS

CHAPTER 3

DISQUALIFICATION FOR UNFIT CONDUCT: PRELIMINARY MATTERS

CHAPTER 4

ESTABLISHING UNFIT CONDUCT (1): GENERAL PRINCIPLES

CHAPTER 5

ESTABLISHING UNFIT CONDUCT (2): SPECIFIC INSTANCES OF UNFIT CONDUCT AND PERIOD OF DISQUALIFICATION

CHAPTER 6

COMPETITION DISQUALIFICATION ORDERS

CHAPTER 7

PROCEDURE AND EVIDENCE IN CIVIL DISQUALIFICATION PROCEEDINGS

CHAPTER 8

PERMISSION TO COMMENCE SECTION 6 PROCEEDINGS OUT OF TIME AND THE IMPACT OF DELAY IN CIVIL DISQUALIFICATION PROCEEDINGS

CHAPTER 9

CIVIL DISQUALIFICATION CASES: TERMINATION WITHOUT A FULL TRIAL

CHAPTER 10

ALTERNATIVE GROUNDS FOR DISQUALIFICATION: SECTIONS 2 TO 5 AND 10 OF THE CDDA

CHAPTER 11

BANKRUPTCY, INSOLVENCY RESTRICTIONS AND COUNTY COURT ADMINISTRATION ORDERS

CHAPTER 12

DISQUALIFICATION ORDERS AND UNDERTAKINGS

CHAPTER 13

PROCEDURE IN CIVIL DISQUALIFICATION PROCEEDINGS AFTER JUDGMENT OR ENTRY INTO A DISQUALIFICATION UNDERTAKING: REVIEWS, VARIATIONS AND APPEALS

CHAPTER 14

THE LEGAL EFFECT OF DISQUALIFICATION

CHAPTER 15

PERMISSION TO ACT NOTWITHSTANDING DISQUALIFICATION

CHAPTER 16

THE INTERNATIONAL DIMENSION

APPENDICES

PREFACE TO THIRD EDITION

While doubts may be expressed in some quarters from time to time about the efficacy of disqualification as a regulatory tool, in the five years since the publication of the second edition of this book under the title *Directors' Disqualification & Bankruptcy Restrictions*, its place in the law has continued to expand. Moreover, its role in the sanctioning and deterring of misconduct in such diverse areas as competition and health and safety continues to be emphasised by regulators and lawmakers. The recent call by the Business and Enterprise Committee of the House of Commons for the Insolvency Service to be provided with sufficient funding to meet increasing need for its investigation and enforcement activities, including disqualification under the CDDA and the imposition of insolvency restrictions (on which see further below) in respect of errant debtors, reflects this continuing emphasis on disqualification in policy discourse. In the realm of personal insolvency, the introduction by the Tribunals, Courts and Enforcement Act 2007 of debt relief orders—a new form of administrative bankruptcy for the financially excluded in England and Wales—has spawned the debt relief restrictions regime, an analogue to the bankruptcy restrictions regime, designed to deal with misconduct on the part of debtors who have accessed it. This has led us to extend further the chapter on bankruptcy and bankruptcy restrictions and caused us to change the title of this third edition to *Directors' Disqualification & Insolvency Restrictions*, "insolvency restrictions" serving as a convenient way of referring collectively to bankruptcy restrictions orders, bankruptcy restrictions undertakings, debt relief restrictions orders and debt relief restrictions undertakings. We have also added a new final chapter on the international dimension, which considers the extraterritorial scope of disqualification powers and prohibitions, the framework for recognition of foreign disqualifications introduced by the Companies Act 2006 with effect from October 1, 2009 and, in overview, the analogous directors' disqualification provisions in force in the Crown Dependencies, namely the Channel Island bailiwicks of Guernsey and Jersey and the Isle of Man. As a result of these, and a series of other case law and statutory developments that have occurred in the intervening period since the second edition, not least the enactment and staggered introduction of the Companies Act 2006, the size of the book has once again expanded.

It is not possible in the space available to mention by name all those who have helped us during the preparation of this edition. However, special thanks go to Donna McKenzie Skene of Aberdeen University for invaluable advice on the position in Scotland and to our publishers, Sweet and Maxwell, in particular, Katherine Milburn and Laura Wood, who successfully piloted this edition through the production process. We are also grateful to our publishers for preparing the tables and index. Adrian Walters acknowledges and thanks the following for their help and unstinting support: John Armour; David Burdette; Graham Ferris; Keith Gaines; Tom Lewis; David Milman; Paula Moffatt; Rebecca Parry; Mary Seneviratne; Gary Wilson; his friends and colleagues (past and present) at Geldards LLP; his parents, Anne and Allan; and (last but by no means least) his wife, Rachel and daughter, Alice. Malcolm Davis-White thanks everyone who has contributed to his knowledge of, and practice in, the subject and to the wider class of persons who, through their encouragement, forbearance and support, have enabled him to complete the task, and most of all thanks his family. He now looks forward to spending more time with the Bear, the Bat and the Beaver.

Finally, the usual disclaimer applies: the views expressed in this book and any errors are those of the authors alone. We have sought to state the law as at October 1, 2009.

AJW
MDW

Nottingham and
Lincoln's Inn
November 2009

TABLE OF ABBREVIATIONS

BRO	Bankruptcy Restrictions Order
BRU	Bankruptcy Restrictions Undertaking
CCR	County Court Rules 1981
CDDA	Company Directors Disqualification Act 1986
CPR	Civil Procedure Rules 1998 as subsequently amended
Disqualification Practice Direction	The Practice Direction entitled "Directors Disqualification Proceedings"
Disqualification Rules	The Insolvent Companies (Disqualification of Unfit Directors) Proceedings Rules 1987 (SI 1987/2023) as subsequently amended
DRO	Debt Relief Order
DRO debtor	A person to whom a moratorium period under a debt relief order applies
DRRO	Debt Relief Restrictions Order
DRRU	Debt Relief Restrictions Undertaking
ECHR	The European Convention for the Protection of Human Rights and Fundamental Freedoms (opened for signature on November 4, 1950)
RSC	Rules of the Supreme Court 1965

TABLE OF CASES

TABLE OF STATUTES

UNITED KINGDOM

ALDERNEY

AUSTRALIA

GUERNSEY

JERSEY

1861 Loi sur les Sociétés avec Responsabilité Limitée .. 16–74
1861—1968 Companies (Jersey) Laws 16–74
1968 Companies (Supplementary Provisions) (Jersey) Law 16–74
1990 Bankruptcy (Désastre) (Jersey) Law
art.24 .... 16–74, 16–78
(7) 16–77
art.43 .... 16–74, 16–76, 16–77
1991 Companies (Jersey) Law 16–74
Pt X 16–76
art.1(1) 16–74
art.78 .... 16–74—16–78
(4) 16–75
art.79 .... 16–74, 16–75
2002 Companies (Amendment No.6) (Jersey) Law 16–74, 16–75
2003 Parish Rate (Administration) (Jersey) Law 16–78
2005 Companies (Amendment No.8) (Jersey) Law 16–74
2006 Bankruptcy (Désastre) (Amendment No.5) (Jersey) Law 16–76

SINGAPORE

Companies Act
ss.148—149A 16–53

SOUTH AFRICA

2008 Companies Act
s.69 16–53
s.162 16–53

UNITED STATES

2005 Bankruptcy Abuse Prevention and Consumer Protection Act (US) 11–09

TABLE OF STATUTORY INSTRUMENTS

TABLE OF RULES

CHAPTER 1

COMPANY DIRECTORS DISQUALIFICATION ACT 1986: INTRODUCTION AND OVERVIEW

INTRODUCTION

1–01 In the last 20 years, the number of disqualifications imposed under the Company Directors Disqualification Act 1986 ("CDDA") has ebbed and flowed. From a high point of some 1,929 disqualifications in 2001–02, the numbers have decreased year on year and as at 2005–06 were running at some 1,197 per year.[1] Although insolvency is not the only trigger to disqualification, in practice it is one of the largest drivers of the disqualification process.[2] The decrease in the overall number of disqualifications is therefore due, at least in part, to the decreasing number of company insolvencies experienced during the benign economic conditions of the decade or so between 1995 and 2007. The available budget is another factor. In 2006–07, due to other funding pressures on what is now the Department of Business Innovation and Skills ("BIS"), the enforcement and investigation budget of the Insolvency Service, the executive agency that instigates civil disqualification proceedings under CDDA s.6, was cut by some £3.3 million. This appears to have led to the suggestion that the Insolvency Service was only targeting cases involving more serious misconduct that would attract a period of disqualification in excess of five years.[3] However, from April 1, 2007 and as regards compulsory winding up orders and bankruptcy orders made after that date, insolvency case administration fees were increased to ensure that the cost of investigation work carried out by Official Receivers and previously met from BIS funding could be recovered from fees. This has allowed BIS to restore budget cuts made in 2006–07. It was hoped that this would lead to an increase in enforcement output.[4] In fact in 2007–08 the Insolvency Service secured some 1,145 disqualification orders and undertakings against directors of failed companies, compared to 1,200 in 2006–07.

[1] See the Department of Trade and Industry, *Companies in 1990–1991* through to *Companies in 2005–2006* inclusive. The numbers are of those disqualification orders and undertakings notified to the Secretary of State.

[2] A. Neal and F. Wright, *A survey of the use and effectiveness of the Company Directors Disqualification Act 1986 as a legal sanction against directors convicted of health and safety offences*, Health and Safety Executive, Research Report RR597 (HSE Books, 2007), *http://www.hse.gov.uk/research/rrhtm/rr597.htm* [Accessed August 10, 2009].

[3] See S. Frieze, "Insolvency Intelligence—20 Years Old" (2008) 21(1) Insolv. Int. 10 at p.11.

[4] See the Insolvency Service, *Annual Report and Accounts 2006–2007* H.C. 752 (London: The Stationery Office, 2007), pp.15–23. As at July 2008 the Insolvency Service was operating against a target of achieving a year-on-year increase of 7% in the number of enforcement outcomes (director disqualifications, bankruptcy restrictions and criminal prosecutions): see the Insolvency Service, *Annual Report and Accounts 2007–2008* H.C. 800 (London: The Stationery Office, 2008), p.5.

Of the 1,145 disqualifications 897 (78 per cent) were achieved by way of an undertaking given by directors compared to 954 (80 per cent) in 2006–07.[5] As the numbers of corporate insolvencies increase in the much harsher economic climate that has arisen in the wake of the global "credit crunch" and banking collapses of 2007–08, it may be thought that the number of disqualifications will once again start on an upward trend. However, while the number of disqualifications did increase in 2008–09 to 1,252 (with undertakings back at 80% of the total),[6] the Insolvency Service again faces the prospect of reduced funding from BIS for its investigation and enforcement activity, a matter that has attracted criticism from the House of Commons Business and Enterprise Committee.[7]

1–02 Although insolvency enforcement activity has been in relative decline in recent years,[8] disqualification of directors remains a significant force shaping the development and practical application of the law relating to directors' duties. The increase in disqualifications between 1986 and the early years of the current century was accompanied by the growth of a considerable volume of judicial pronouncements concerning the standards of conduct to be expected of the modern company director. Thus, disqualification has not only become one of the principal means by which the general law of directors' obligations is enforced, it has also generated a significant body of law that has articulated the standards of conduct required of directors by law in the late twentieth and early twenty-first century. In consequence, the case law on the CDDA can properly be regarded as a major driver of developments in the modern law of directors' duties.[9] It may be thought that its influence as a source of development and visible enforcement of directors' duties will be eclipsed by the landmark statutory reforms brought in by the Companies Act 2006, notably the codification of general duties in ss.170–177 of that Act and the statutory derivative action. However, given that it receives the backing of the state and is not dependent on the vagaries (and pockets) of private litigants, the disqualification regime can be expected to play a continuing role especially in times of greater economic uncertainty and regulatory vigilance such as those prevailing at the time of writing. That said, as

[5] The Insolvency Service, *Annual Report and Accounts 2007–2008* H.C. 800 (London: The Stationery Office, 2007) at p.14.

[6] The Insolvency Service, *Annual Report and Accounts 2008–2009* H.C. 623 (London: The Stationery Office, 2009) at p.22.

[7] *The Insolvency Service—Sixth Report of Session 2008–09* H.C. 198 (London: The Stationery Office, 2009) at pp.18–20. The Committee noted the Secretary of State's decision to scrap the Service's target of increasing the number of successful enforcement outcomes by 7% each year imposing instead a target for 2009–10 of maintaining enforcement outputs at the same level that was achieved in 2008–09. Rather than targeting a higher number of enforcement outputs, the Service has indicated that it will take a rigorous approach to prioritising cases in the public interest.

[8] Contrast the encouragement to prosecutors in the health and safety field: see A. Neal and F. Wright, *A survey of the use and effectiveness of the Company Directors Disqualification Act 1986 as a legal sanction against directors convicted of health and safety offences*, Health and Safety Executive, Research Report RR597 (HSE Books, 2007), *http://www.hse.gov.uk/research/rrhtm/rr597.htm* [Accessed August 10, 2009] and the trickle of competition cases under CDDA s.9A which are beginning to come through the pipeline.

[9] See A. Walters, "Directors' Duties: The Impact of the Company Directors' Disqualification Act" (2000) 21 Co. Law. 110; L. Sealy, "Directors' Duties Revisited" (2001) 22 Co. Law. 79.

noted in 1-01 above, the Insolvency Service faces the prospect of cuts in public funding. It therefore seems unlikely that there will be any significant expansion of its investigation and enforcement activity over the medium term unless BIS is able to respond to calls from the House of Commons Business and Enterprise Committee to provide the Service with sufficient funding to meet increasing demand.

1–03 Following reforms introduced by the Insolvency Act 2000, it is now possible in many cases for directors to be disqualified by administrative means. The main consequence of this, as was intended, is that fewer disqualification cases now reach trial.[10] Nevertheless, CDDA case law continues to be an important source of guidance to directors, practitioners and regulators alike.[11] Such case law has also influenced the development of the bankruptcy restrictions regime established by the Enterprise Act 2002[12] which itself is now under increasing scrutiny, given the exponential growth in personal insolvencies in England and Wales since the turn of the century.

1–04 The Enterprise Act 2002, as well as shortening the period of bankruptcy, introduced a new concept of bankruptcy restrictions.[13] Bankruptcy restrictions may be imposed by the court in circumstances where the court "thinks it appropriate" having regard to the conduct of the bankrupt, which encompasses conduct before or after the making of the bankruptcy order. There is also power for the Secretary of State to accept a bankruptcy restrictions undertaking and thus avoid the need for a court order. The purpose of these provisions was to deal with the dishonest, reckless or irresponsible bankrupt. In addition, it was envisaged that many restrictions on conduct or on the holding of certain offices and positions which flowed from the status of bankruptcy would be removed and that instead the vast majority of restrictions previously applicable to undischarged bankrupts would apply solely to "culpable" bankrupts who were subject to the bankruptcy restrictions regime. The bankruptcy restrictions regime is very similar to the disqualification regime.[14] As such, it is a regulatory device shaping the development of the standards to be expected of individuals, primarily in the financial sphere.[15] It can be

[10] See generally Ch. 9 on disqualification undertakings. According to recent figures, about 78 to 80% of disqualifications under CDDA s.6 are imposed without a court order: see the Insolvency Service, *Annual Report and Accounts 2006–2007* H.C. 752 (London: The Stationery Office, 2007), p.15 and the Insolvency Service, *Annual Report and Accounts 2007–2008* H.C. 800 (London: The Stationery Office, 2008), p.15.

[11] Given the continuing expansion of the regulatory state within the commercial arena, especially in relation to matters such as financial services, it will be interesting to see the extent to which concepts from disqualification law will fertilise other areas of regulation. Compare, for example, the "unfit conduct" test in CDDA s.6 and the "fit and proper" test in the Financial Services and Markets Act 2000 (see, in particular, Sch.6 to the 2000 Act).

[12] On which see 1–04 and Ch.11.

[13] By the insertion of a new Sch.4A to the Insolvency Act 1986.

[14] See e.g. *Randhawa v Official Receiver* [2006] EWHC 2496 (Ch), [2007] 1 W.L.R. 1700.

[15] In this respect the position of the trader bankrupt is likely to be different to the position of the consumer bankrupt. The trader bankrupt is likely to be regulated in the manner of his trading well beyond solely the financial sphere (for example, in relation to health and safety matters). The consumer bankrupt is more likely to be regulated in the manner in which he conducts his or her financial affairs.

seen as complementary to the disqualification regime in that both regimes focus on persons whose conduct is dishonest, reckless or irresponsible. The disqualification regime focuses on certain types of business and corporate organisation. The bankruptcy restrictions regime focuses on the individual, whether as trader or as regards the management of his personal (non-business) financial affairs. Bankruptcy restrictions can only be sought in relation to a bankrupt's conduct after April 1, 2004. In 2006–07 and 2007–08 the number of bankruptcy restrictions orders and undertakings secured was 1,867 and 1,827 respectively. Of these, approximately 90 per cent were bankruptcy restrictions undertakings rather than bankruptcy restrictions orders.[16] More recently the Tribunals, Courts and Enforcement Act 2007 has introduced a new form of moratorium on the enforcement of debts, the debt relief order, primarily for those debtors who cannot afford to invoke the bankruptcy regime. As a concomitant of that regime, the 2007 Act also introduced the concept of debt relief restrictions, playing a similar role in relation to debt relief orders as bankruptcy restrictions play in relation to bankruptcy.

1–05 The aim of the present chapter is to consider the history and evolution of directors' disqualification legislation culminating in the enactment (and subsequent amendment) of the CDDA. Chapter 2 is also introductory in nature and seeks to analyse the rationale and purpose of disqualification as a form of regulatory sanction.

COMPANY DIRECTORS DISQUALIFICATION ACT 1986

1–06 Despite its name, the Company Directors Disqualification Act 1986 does not solely involve the disqualification of directors, nor is any disqualification under it limited solely to a legal restriction on acting as a director. It is a single piece of consolidating legislation which governs the disqualification of directors and other persons who act improperly in the course of managing companies and which triggers a series of disqualifications and restrictions. The enactment of the CDDA brought down the curtain on a wider process of legislative reform that also led to the enactment of the Insolvency Act 1986.[17] Seen in that context, the CDDA was merely one part of a connected series of general reforms in the field of company and corporate insolvency law.

1–07 Disqualification under the CDDA is essentially a legal response to misconduct. The CDDA sets out a number of grounds that, if established, trigger the sanction of disqualification. These triggering events (which are discussed in outline further below) range widely and include, for example, criminal offences, defaults under

[16] See the Insolvency Service, *Annual Report and Accounts 2007–2008* H.C. 800 (London: The Stationery Office, 2008), pp.17 and 18.

[17] The CDDA and Insolvency Act 1986 were enacted on the same day, July 25, 1986. "The provisions of the Disqualification Act are part of the same body of law as the Insolvency Act 1986": *Re Pantmaenog Timber Co Ltd* [2003] UKHL 49, [2004] 1 A.C. 158 at [87] (Lord Walker). See also at [60] (Lord Millett) to the same effect.

companies legislation and breaches of the general law relating to the duties of company directors. The concept of "unfit conduct", which lies at the heart of the CDDA[18] and is its most important concept, rests to a considerable extent on obligations imposed on directors by specific provisions of companies and insolvency legislation and by the general law.[19] As a regulatory technique, disqualification therefore provides an additional and ancillary response to various forms of misconduct, which also now include breaches of competition law,[20] over and above the sanctions already provided for by the ordinary criminal and civil law. As a process, disqualification is ancillary to other forms of legal process. In some cases, it is ancillary to criminal or civil proceedings in court.[21] In other cases, it is ancillary to formal corporate insolvency processes such as winding-up or administration.[22] It is also ancillary to investigatory processes.[23] It should be noted that disqualification under the CDDA triggers the operation of restrictions imposed by other pieces of legislation (such as charities legislation) that have little or nothing to do with companies per se. As such, disqualification under the CDDA does more than simply prohibit the disqualified person from acting as a company director or from taking part in the management of companies and it therefore represents a broader regulatory endeavour. An overview of the scheme of the CDDA containing a synopsis of the main powers and provisions is set out below. The remainder of the chapter considers the history and legislative evolution of the main substantive powers of disqualification.

1–08 In order to understand the operation of its provisions, it is important to appreciate the historical genesis of the CDDA. Whilst the prominence of disqualification as an enforcement tool since the mid-1980s has undoubtedly been caused, in large part, by a governmental resolve to pursue regulation through this mechanism and to commit financial resources to it, there is a wider context that has also shaped its development. A number of provisions now found in the CDDA have their legislative origins in the late-1920s. A further point that cannot be overlooked is that the CDDA is an intrinsic element of the insolvency legislation and one that is concerned, in particular, to advance insolvency law's public interest goals. The Cork Committee observed that: "The law of insolvency takes the form of a compact to which there are three parties: the debtor, his creditors and society"[24] and that, as a consequence, insolvency proceedings:

[18] CDDA ss.6–9A.

[19] This is not exclusively so. See, e.g. *Re Bath Glass Ltd* [1988] B.C.L.C. 329 which establishes that trading while insolvent to the detriment of creditors can make a director unfit for the purposes of CDDA s.6 even in circumstances where his conduct would not attract liability for wrongful trading under s.214 of the Insolvency Act 1986. This particular point is discussed further from 5–05.

[20] See CDDA ss.9A–9E and Ch.6.

[21] See, e.g. CDDA ss.2 and 5 for powers that are ancillary to criminal proceedings and CDDA ss.9A and 10 for powers that are ancillary to other forms of civil proceeding.

[22] CDDA ss.4, 6–7.

[23] CDDA ss.8 and 9C.

[24] Report of the Review Committee, *Insolvency Law and Practice*, Cmnd.8558 (London: HMSO, 1982), para.192.

"have never been treated in English law as an exclusively private matter between the debtor and his creditors; the community itself has always been recognised as having an important interest in them."[25]

The same point was developed by Lord Walker of Gestingthorpe in *Re Pantmaenog Timber Co Ltd*:

"[W]hat I might call the public element in winding up has changed a good deal in the course of a century and a half. That is not surprising. The development of the law has responded to major social changes, including the establishment of prosecuting authorities, the emergence of a body of skilled and responsible professionals undertaking work as insolvency practitioners, and the recognition that the protection of the public against reckless or dishonest businessmen may be better attained by civil procedures (in particular disqualification of persons unfit to act as company directors) rather than by criminal proceedings. But although the practice and procedure has varied over the years the need to protect the public against the abuse of limited liability is a clear and constant theme."[26]

The need to protect the public is constantly echoed in the authorities. In *Re Grayan Building Services Ltd, Secretary of State for Trade and Industry v Gray*, Henry L.J. made the following observations:

"The concept of limited liability and the sophistication of our corporate law offers great privileges and great opportunities for those who wish to trade under that regime. But the corporate environment carries with it the discipline that those who avail themselves of those privileges must accept the standards laid down and abide by the regulatory rules and disciplines in place to protect creditors and shareholders. And, while some significant corporate failures will occur despite the directors exercising best managerial practice, in many, too many, cases there have been serious breaches of those rules and disciplines, in situations where the observance of them would or at least might have prevented or reduced the scale of the failure and consequent loss to creditors and investors. Reliable figures are hard to come by, but it seems that losses from corporate fraud and mismanagement have never been higher. At the same time the regulatory regime has never been more stringent—on paper even if not in practice. The parliamentary intention to improve managerial safeguards and standards for the long term good of employees, creditors and investors is clear. Those who fail to reach those standards and whose failure contributes to others losing money will often both be plausible and capable of inspiring initial trust, often later regretted. Those attributes may make them attractive witnesses. But as section 6 [of the CDDA] makes clear, the court's focus should be on their conduct, on the offence rather than the offender. The statutory corporate climate is stricter than it has ever been, and those enforcing it should reflect the fact that Parliament has seen the need for higher standards."[27]

Thus, in its proper historical context, the CDDA can be seen as a scheme of corporate regulation and discipline that is intimately linked to the public interest

[25] Cmnd.8558, para.1734. Both passages were cited by Lord Millett in *Re Pantmaenog Timber Co Ltd* [2004] 1 A.C. 158 at [52].

[26] [2004] 1 A.C. 158 at [78].

[27] [1995] Ch. 241 at 257–258.

aspect of insolvency law. Having said that, the legislation is not confined to the insolvency sphere. Various provisions provide the court with powers to impose disqualification in circumstances where insolvency may not have intervened and even in the insolvency context, disqualification may be imposed for misconduct that has no particular causal link with the ultimate insolvency of a company.

Overview of the CDDA

1–09 The main provisions of the CDDA can usefully be grouped under four broad headings namely, disqualification by court order or undertaking, automatic disqualification, consequences of disqualification, and permission to act notwithstanding disqualification. Not every provision of the CDDA is covered in this outline. There are a number of other miscellaneous provisions. These are tackled at appropriate points in the rest of the book. The CDDA applies to England, Wales and Scotland but not to Northern Ireland.[28] However, the Company Directors Disqualification (Northern Ireland) Order 2002[29] applies to Northern Ireland a disqualification regime which is the same in all material respects to that under the CDDA and the CDDA gives effect to Northern Ireland disqualifications within England, Wales and Scotland treating them as if made within the Act's territorial jurisdiction.[30]

Disqualification by court order or undertaking

1–10 Section 1 defines the scope of a disqualification order made by the court under any of ss.2 to 6, 8, 9A and 10. A disqualification order imposes a wide prohibition. Broadly speaking, it prohibits the disqualified person from being a company director or from engaging generally in the promotion, formation or management of companies, in each case without the permission of the court, and it absolutely prohibits the disqualified person from acting as an insolvency practitioner. Section 1A defines the scope of a disqualification undertaking in the same terms as a disqualification order. Disqualification undertakings in the competition law context are defined by s.9B. First introduced by the Insolvency Act 2000, disqualification undertakings are a means by which disqualification can be imposed under CDDA ss.6, 8 or 9B without the need for a court order. The making and commencement of disqualification orders and undertakings is dealt with in Ch.12 while the legal effect of disqualification orders and undertakings is discussed in Ch.14.

1–11 Section 2 gives the court power to make a disqualification order against a person convicted of an indictable offence in connection with the promotion, formation, management, liquidation or striking off of a company, with the receivership of a company's property or with his being an administrative receiver of a company.[31] The maximum period of disqualification is 15 years (save where

[28] CDDA s.24.
[29] SI 2002/3150 (NI 4).
[30] CDDA ss.12A and 12B.
[31] Administration, perhaps surprisingly, has not been included in this section.

the order is made by a court of summary jurisdiction in which case the maximum period is five years).[32]

1–12 Section 3 gives the court power to make a disqualification order against a person where that person has been persistently in default in relation to the provisions of companies legislation requiring returns, accounts, documents or notices to be filed with the Registrar of Companies. The maximum period of disqualification is five years.

1–13 Section 4 gives the court power to make a disqualification order against a person if, during the course of the winding-up of a company it appears either that he has been guilty (whether convicted or not) of an offence of fraudulent trading under the Companies Act 2006 s.993 (formerly Companies Act 1985 s.458), or he has otherwise been guilty while acting as an officer or as liquidator of the company, receiver of the company's property or administrative receiver of the company, of any fraud in relation to the company or of any breach of duty in any of those capacities.[33] The maximum period of disqualification is 15 years.

1–14 Section 5 gives the court power to make a disqualification order where a person is convicted of a summary offence in consequence of a contravention of, or failure to comply with, any provision of companies legislation requiring returns, accounts, documents or notices to be filed with the Registrar, and in the previous five years he has received or been made the subject of not less than three convictions or default orders counting for the purposes of the section. The maximum period of disqualification is five years. Although the criteria are not identical, the power in s.5 is essentially directed at the same mischief as s.3, namely persistent default in the filing of accounts and returns. The main difference is that the power in s.3 is only exercisable by the civil courts whereas that in s.5 is exercisable by the criminal courts and, in particular, the magistrates' courts. Sections 2 to 5 inclusive are discussed in Ch.10.

1–15 Section 6 requires the court to make a disqualification order against a person where satisfied that he is or was a director (or shadow director) of a company which has become insolvent and that his conduct as a director of that company (taken alone or taken together with his conduct as a director of any other company or companies) makes him unfit to be concerned in the management of a company. The court must disqualify an individual whose conduct is found to make him unfit in accordance with s.6 for a minimum of two years. The maximum period of disqualification is 15 years. Section 6 differs from the various discretionary powers in ss.2 to 5 (see above) and ss.8, 10 and 12 (see below) in that it imposes a duty on the court to disqualify a person for at least two years where the requirements of the section are made out.

1–16 Section 7 sets out various procedural matters that relate to applications under s.6. Section 6 proceedings can only be brought by the Secretary of State (or the

[32] It is interesting to compare this provision with the Australian Corporations Act 2001 s.201B which provides for automatic disqualification on conviction for certain types of offences.

[33] The offence of participating in fraudulent business carried on by a sole trader etc., created by s.9 of the Fraud Act 2006, has not yet been included as a ground of disqualification but perhaps it should be.

official receiver if the Secretary of State so directs in the case of a person who is or was a director of a company which is being wound up by the court in England and Wales). Section 7(2) imposes a two-year time limit for the commencement of proceedings, after which proceedings can only be commenced with the permission of the court. Section 7(3) requires licensed insolvency practitioners who are appointed as office-holders to provide reports on the conduct of directors of insolvent companies (meaning companies that enter voluntary liquidation, administration or administrative receivership) to the Secretary of State. The same provision requires the official receiver to report on the conduct of directors of companies that are being wound up in England and Wales. In the early stages these reports are used to determine whether or not the Secretary of State should contemplate disqualification proceedings in a particular case. The various requirements in s.7 concerning the reporting procedures and the commencement of proceedings are discussed in Chs 3, 7 and 8.

1–17 Section 8 gives the court power to make a disqualification order against a director (or shadow director) of a company on the application of the Secretary of State made following the receipt of information obtained as a result of certain specified types of statutory investigation or inspection. The court may exercise this power if it is satisfied that the director's conduct in relation to the company makes him unfit to be concerned in the management of a company. The maximum period of disqualification is 15 years.

1–18 Section 7(2A) empowers the Secretary of State to accept a disqualification undertaking from a person instead of applying, or proceeding with an application, for a disqualification order under s.6. Section 8(2A) confers an identical power on the Secretary of State in relation to s.8. Disqualification undertakings are considered in Ch.9.

1–19 Section 9 and Sch.1 set out a number of non-exhaustive criteria to which the court must pay particular regard in determining, on an application under either s.6 or s.8, whether an individual's conduct as a director (or shadow director) makes him unfit to be concerned in the management of a company. The maximum period of disqualification is 15 years. The provisions on unfit conduct in ss.6 to 9 are the core provisions of the CDDA. Most of the disqualifications to date have been imposed either by order or undertaking under these provisions.[34] As a consequence, the vast majority of the reported cases are concerned with substantive and procedural aspects of proceedings brought on grounds of unfit conduct. The central significance of these provisions within the overall scheme is reflected in the structure of this book given that Chs 3 to 8 are devoted principally to an exposition of law and practice under ss.6 to 9. For all that, it is important that these provisions are not viewed in isolation from the other substantive provisions in the CDDA. One of the principal themes of this book is that the CDDA should properly be regarded as a legislative scheme with common features and objectives in which the concept of unfit conduct forms a central and unifying part.

[34] For evidence over the period 2001–02 to 2005–06 see the Department of Trade and Industry, *Companies in 2005–2006* H.C. 1534 (London: the Stationery Office, 2006), p.23.

1–20 Sections 9A to 9E were introduced by the Enterprise Act 2002 and extend the scope of the CDDA into the realm of competition law. Section 9A requires the court to make a disqualification order against a person where satisfied, on the application of the Office of Fair Trading or another specified regulator, that the company of which the person is a director has committed a relevant breach of competition law and that his conduct as a director makes him unfit to be concerned in the management of a company. Section 9B empowers the relevant regulator to accept a disqualification undertaking from a person instead of applying, or proceeding with an application, for a disqualification order under s.9A. The maximum period of disqualification that can be imposed is 15 years. There is no minimum. The competition disqualification regime is considered generally in Ch.6.

1–21 Where a civil court orders a person to make a contribution to a company's assets under either the fraudulent or wrongful trading provisions in ss.213 to 214 of the Insolvency Act 1986, CDDA s.10 gives the court power, of its own motion, to disqualify that person. The maximum period of disqualification is 15 years. Further coverage of s.10 can be found in Ch.10.

1–22 Where, in accordance with its powers set out in s.429(2) of the Insolvency Act 1986, a county court revokes an administration order made under Part VI of the County Courts Act 1984, it may direct that s.12 of the CDDA shall apply to that person for a specified period not exceeding one year. Section 12 simply records that where this power under the insolvency legislation is exercised, the person is disqualified from acting as a company director or liquidator or from taking part generally in the promotion, formation or management of companies without the permission of the court. This provision is discussed further in Chs 11 and 14.[35]

Automatic disqualification

1–23 Section 11 automatically disqualifies undischarged bankrupts, persons who are subject to a bankruptcy restrictions order or undertaking, or a debt relief restrictions order or undertaking and persons to whom a moratorium period under a debt relief order applies from being company directors or from engaging generally in the management of companies without the permission of the court. This applies without the need for a court order under the CDDA and is the only provision of its type in the legislation. Section 11 is considered in Ch.11. Chapter 11 also contains a comprehensive discussion of the bankruptcy restrictions order regime and the virtually identical debt relief restrictions order regime,[36] including coverage of the sorts of misconduct that may be regarded as relevant for the purposes of those regimes.

Consequences of disqualification

1–24 The CDDA imposes both criminal and civil penalties on those who act while disqualified. It is a criminal offence under s.11 for an undischarged bankrupt; a

[35] At the time of writing the amendments to s.12 effected by the Tribunals, Courts and Enforcement Act 2007 had not come into force.

[36] Introduced by the Tribunals, Courts and Enforcement Act 2007.

person subject to a bankruptcy restrictions order or undertaking; a person subject to a debt relief restrictions order or undertaking; or a person to whom a moratorium period under a debt relief order applies to act in breach of the automatic ban. Sections 13 and 14 also impose criminal penalties on those who act in breach of a disqualification order or undertaking (or, in the case of s.14, those who are accessories to such a breach). Furthermore, s.15 provides that an individual is personally liable for certain debts of a company if he is at any time involved in the management of that company in breach of either a disqualification order, a disqualification undertaking or the automatic ban in s.11.

1–25 Section 15 also renders an individual personally liable for certain debts of a company if, while being involved in the management of that company, he acts or is willing to act on the instructions of another individual whom he knows to be the subject of a disqualification order or undertaking or to be an undischarged bankrupt.[37] The penalties imposed by these various provisions and other wider consequences of disqualification are discussed in Ch.14.

1–26 Section 18 requires the Secretary of State to maintain a register of disqualification orders and undertakings which is open to public inspection. The connected issues of registration and the publicising of disqualification orders are canvassed in Ch.12. The registers in relation to personal insolvency are dealt with in Ch.11.

Permission to act notwithstanding disqualification

1–27 With the exception of the ban in CDDA ss.1(1)(b), 1(1A)(b) and 9B(3), (4) on disqualified persons acting as an insolvency practitioner, which is an absolute prohibition, it is clear on the face of the statute that a disqualified person may apply to the court for permission to act in certain prohibited capacities. Section 17 is the main procedural provision of the CDDA governing applications for permission to act. The court's power to grant permission has considerable significance within the overall scheme of the legislation, a point that is emphasised throughout this book and developed, in particular, in Chs 12 and 15.

Extension of the CDDA to other forms of organisation

1–28 By virtue of ss.22A to 22D the CDDA applies expressly to building societies, incorporated friendly societies, NHS foundation trusts and open-ended investment companies. As a result of various amendments made in 2009, the Act also applies in relation to bank insolvency and administration and in relation to building society insolvency and special administration as it applies in relation to liquidation.[38] By virtue of other legislation, the CDDA also applies to insolvent

[37] Rather oddly accessory liability under s.15 is confined to those who were accessories to a breach of the s.11 prohibition by undischarged bankrupts and does not encompass accessories to a breach of the s.11 prohibition by reason of the person being subject to insolvency restrictions or a moratorium under a debt relief order.

[38] CDDA ss.21A-21B, inserted by the Banking Act 2009, and CDDA s.21C, inserted by The Building Societies (Insolvency and Special Administration) Order 2009 (SI 2009/805), made pursuant to the Banking Act 2009.

partnerships, limited liability partnerships, European Economic Interest Groupings registered in Great Britain and European Companies (SE) provided that the head office of such body is situated in the United Kingdom. The scope of the CDDA is further expanded by CDDA s.22 which, among other things, provides that with the exception of s.11, the expression "company" in the CDDA includes any company which may be wound up under Part V of the Insolvency Act 1986. Thus, the scope of the CDDA and the prohibitions that can be imposed are not confined to companies registered under the Companies Acts. The width of the CDDA jurisdiction and prohibitions is considered further in Chs 2, 3, 14 and 16.

Territorial extent and international dimension

1–29 Sections 12A and 12B extend the effect of Northern Ireland disqualifications to England, Wales and Scotland by treating them, for enforcement purposes, as if made within the territorial scope of the CDDA (which only extends to Great Britain). However, the Northern Ireland High Court retains exclusive power to relieve from the effect of Northern Ireland disqualifications under the terms of the Company Directors Disqualification (Northern Ireland) Order 2002.[39] By art.17 of the 2002 Order, a person disqualified in Great Britain by order or undertaking made pursuant to the CDDA is disqualified to the same extent in Northern Ireland. Insofar as a CDDA disqualification imposed in Great Britain takes effect in Northern Ireland, art.17 confers jurisdiction on the Northern Ireland High Court (and not the relevant court in Great Britain) to grant permission to act notwithstanding disqualification.

1–30 Part 40 of the Companies Act 2006 (ss.1182 to 1191)[40] provides for a regime whereby disqualifications imposed outside the United Kingdom may be recognised and given effect within the United Kingdom. The workings of the regime will largely be determined by statutory instrument. Section 1184 empowers the Secretary of State to make regulations which may provide either that the foreign disqualification will automatically result in a UK disqualification or that a UK disqualification may be imposed by the relevant UK court. There is scope for a regime similar in all main respects to the scheme of the CDDA to be established by regulations, including provisions for permission to act notwithstanding disqualification, the imposition of disqualification by undertaking and the creation of criminal and civil liability for breach of the UK disqualification. In addition regulations may provide for a person subject to foreign restrictions, but not disqualified in the UK, to notify the Registrar of Companies if he does anything that, if done by a person disqualified in the UK, would be in breach of the disqualification.

1–31 The territorial scope of the CDDA and trans-jurisdictional issues both within and outside the United Kingdom are considered further in Chapter 16.

[39] SI 2002/3150 (NI 4).

[40] These provisions were brought into force on October 1, 2009 by The Companies Act 2006 (Commencement No.8, Transitional Provisions and Savings) Order 2008 (SI 2008/2860). However, the secondary legislation required to bring the Pt 40 regime fully into operation had not been enacted at the time of writing.

Regulatory responsibility in relation to CDDA disqualification

1–32 Prior to June 2007, the Department of Trade and Industry was the regulator having principal responsibility for companies.[41] From June 2007, following the creation of the Department for Business, Enterprise and Regulatory Reform ("BERR"),[42] regulatory responsibility was taken over by the new department. Regulatory responsibility moved from BERR to the Department of Business, Innovation and Skills ("BIS") on the creation of the latter in June 2009 by the merger of BERR and the Department for Innovation, Universities and Skills. Pending the making and coming into force of a transfer of functions order, existing proceedings continue in the name of the Secretary of State for Business, Enterprise and Regulatory Reform but new disqualification proceedings are commenced in the name of the Secretary of State for Business, Innovation and Skills. While the Secretary of State for Business, Innovation and Skills is not the only person who can commence disqualification proceedings under the CDDA,[43] in practice, the majority of disqualification proceedings (including prosecutions of disqualified persons who act in breach of the prohibition) are initiated by the Secretary of State or his agents. So for example, responsibility for the initiation of s.6 proceedings rests with the Insolvency Service, a BIS executive agency, acting by its Enforcement Directorate. The one area in which the Secretary of State does not have regulatory responsibility is disqualification on competition law grounds under CDDA ss.9A–9E. This is a matter for the Office of Fair Trading or, where appropriate, one of the other specified regulators listed in s.9E(2).

HISTORY AND EVOLUTION OF THE DISQUALIFICATION REGIME[44]

1–33 This section provides an outline of the origins and evolution of the various powers in the CDDA. Disqualification provisions relating to bankruptcy and fraudulent trading were first enacted in the Companies Act 1928 implementing reforms earlier proposed by the Greene Committee.[45] Since then there has been a sporadic process of consolidation and extension culminating in the reforms of the mid-1980s. There are roughly six strands in the evolution of the various substantive powers of disqualification that can conveniently be given the following headings: (a) bankruptcy; (b) fraud during winding-up and associated criminal offences; (c) persistent non-compliance with filing obligations under companies legislation; (d) unfit conduct; (e) insolvency restrictions; and (f) international recognition.

[41] A point further demonstrated by the Secretary of State's responsibility in relation to applications for the grant of permission to act following disqualification, even where the disqualification is imposed by the criminal courts: see CDDA s.17.

[42] Full responsibility for all matters passed to BERR after the coming into force of the relevant part of the Secretaries of State for Children, Schools and Families, for Innovation, Universities and Skills and for Business, Enterprise and Regulatory Reform Order 2007 (SI 2007/3224).

[43] On the proper claimant in civil disqualification proceedings see generally Chs 7 and 10.

[44] For a useful summary and discussion of the CDDA's historical evolution see *Re Pantmaenog Timber Co Ltd* [2004] 1 A.C. 158.

[45] Report of the Company Law Amendment Committee (the Greene Committee), Cmd. 2657 (1926), especially paras 56–57 and 61–62.

Each of these is considered in turn. They should not be seen as entirely discrete, either in terms of chronology or substance. However, they can be conveniently separated for the purposes of exposition and analysis.

Bankruptcy

1–34 One concern of the Greene Committee, which reported in 1926, was the ease with which bankrupt individuals were able to continue trading through the medium of a limited company before obtaining their discharge. It has long been an offence for an undischarged bankrupt to attempt to obtain credit without disclosing his personal status.[46] Thus, it was considered objectionable that an individual who had previously incurred liabilities in his own name that he had been unable to meet could, through incorporation, obtain further credit in the name of a company while also enjoying the benefit of limited liability. The Greene Committee's recommendation that an undischarged bankrupt should automatically be prohibited from acting as a director or from taking part in the management of a company without permission, first enacted as s.84 of the Companies Act 1928, reflected these concerns. The provision was extended in 1981 to prevent an undischarged bankrupt from taking part in company promotion or formation as well as management.[47] That change apart, there is little to distinguish the original provision governing undischarged bankrupts from its current incarnation which, after several consolidations and re-enactments, is now found in s.11(1)(a) of the CDDA. Section 11 has now been further extended in England and Wales to impose automatic disqualification on persons who are the subject of bankruptcy restrictions or debt relief restrictions under (respectively) Schs.4A and 4ZB of the Insolvency Act 1986 and to persons to whom a moratorium period under a debt relief order applies.[48]

Fraud during winding-up and criminal offences in connection with the management of companies

1–35 A comprehensive provision imposing civil and criminal liability for fraudulent trading was first introduced as s.75 of the Companies Act 1928 on the recommendation of the Greene Committee and then consolidated as s.275 of the Companies Act 1929. It created a range of sanctions, including a power to disqualify anyone held liable under its terms for a maximum period of five years. However, it only applied once the company was being wound up and so was limited in scope. As conceived by the Greene Committee, the main object of this provision (and thus, the power of disqualification) was to curb "security filling": a practice whereby a controller of a private company lends money to the company in return for security by way of floating charge and subsequently, knowing that the company is insolvent, "fills up"

[46] Report of the Review Committee, *Insolvency Law and Practice*, Cmnd.8558 (London: HMSO, 1982), para.132. See now, Insolvency Act 1986 s.360.

[47] Companies Act 1981 Sch.3, para.9.

[48] Enterprise Act 2002 s.257 and Sch.21, para.5; Tribunals, Courts and Enforcement Act 2007 s.108(2) and Sch.20, para.16. See further from 1–47 below and, generally, Ch.11. The application of s.11 in Scotland is considered in Ch.16.

his security by obtaining goods on credit before putting the company into liquidation. The power in s.275 of the 1929 Act is the forerunner of the modern civil disqualification provisions in CDDA ss.4(1)(a) and 10 and is the earliest example of a power of criminal disqualification following conviction in the corporate context.[49]

1–36 At the same time, a further power was introduced in s.76 of the Companies Act 1928 (consolidated as s.217 of the Companies Act 1929). As conceived, the power in s.217 of the 1929 Act was essentially ancillary to the investigative functions of the official receiver and was directed at fraudulent misconduct. In the case of any company which went into compulsory liquidation, the official receiver was at that time under a statutory obligation to provide a preliminary report to the court explaining the causes of the company's failure.[50] It was also open to the official receiver, if he thought fit, to make a further report to the court stating that, in his opinion, a fraud had been committed by a person in the promotion or formation of the company, or by any director or other officer of the company in relation to its affairs since its formation.[51] Faced with such a report, the court had power under Companies Act 1929 s.216 to summon the relevant person to be publicly examined by the official receiver or the company's liquidator and, in addition, it could disqualify such person for up to five years under Companies Act 1929 s.217.[52] Section 217 is perhaps the earliest example of a disqualification provision based entirely on a public interest rationale, namely the public interest in exposing and explaining corporate failure and in calling delinquent directors to account.[53] On this point, it is also interesting to note that the structure of the core provisions in the CDDA relating to unfit conduct (discussed further below) is similar to s.217 in that locus standi is conferred exclusively on agents of the state, and the decision to proceed is usually based on a report on the company's affairs prepared and delivered to the Secretary of State in satisfaction of a statutory reporting obligation.[54] The power in s.217 of the 1929 Act is the forerunner of CDDA s.4(1)(b).[55]

1–37 Following the process of reform and consolidation that took place during 1947 and 1948,[56] the fraudulent trading provision in s.275 of the 1929 Act emerged as

[49] Companies Act 1929 s.275(4) provided that the power of disqualification vested in either the civil court that made a declaration of fraudulent trading under s.275(1) (as is now the case under CDDA s.10) or the criminal court that convicted for an offence of fraudulent trading under s.275(3) (as is now the case under CDDA s.2).

[50] Companies Act 1929 s.182(1).

[51] Companies Act 1929 s.182(2).

[52] The concepts of public investigation and examination in compulsory liquidation survive: see now, Insolvency Act 1986 ss.132–133 and s.218. For general background, see Report of the Review Committee, *Insolvency Law and Practice*, Cmnd.8558 (London: HMSO, 1982), paras 74–85, 653–657.

[53] Cmnd.8558, especially paras 191–194, 1734–1736. Note also, the Cork Committee's attempt to restore the link between public examination and disqualification at para.1819(b), a recommendation that was not taken up by Parliament.

[54] CDDA ss.7(3), (4) and 8(1).

[55] The 10-day notice requirement now to be found in CDDA s.16 also has its origins in Companies Act 1929 s.217(2).

[56] For general background, see the Report of the Committee on Company Law Amendment (the Cohen Committee), Cmd. 6659 (1945), especially paras 150–151.

s.332 of the Companies Act 1948. However, the court's power of disqualification was modified and separately re-enacted as part of a more extensive provision that emerged as s.188 of the 1948 Act. Section 188 created two powers:

(1) Section 188(1)(a) gave the court power to disqualify a person convicted on indictment of any offence in connection with the promotion, formation or management of a company for a maximum period of five years. This greatly extended the original power of disqualification conferred on the civil and criminal courts by s.275 of the 1929 Act which had been confined in scope to fraudulent trading. Section 188(1)(a) was the earliest version of the broad power currently found in s.2 of the CDDA.[57]
(2) Section 188(1)(b) gave the civil court power to disqualify a person who was found during the course of a winding-up to have been guilty (whether convicted or not) of an offence of fraudulent trading under the Companies Act 1948 s.332, or of any fraud in relation to the company or breach of duty perpetrated while acting as its officer for a maximum period of five years. Again, this went beyond the original scope of the powers in ss.217 and 275 of the 1929 Act in that as long as the fraud came to light in the course of a winding-up, the court was not restricted to acting on an official receiver's fraud report as had previously been the case. The modern version of the s.188(1)(b) power can now be found in s.4 of the CDDA.[58]

1–38 The final stage under this heading was the enactment of s.16 of the Insolvency Act 1985 which subsequently became s.10 of the CDDA. This empowers a civil court to disqualify an individual against whom it has made a fraudulent or wrongful trading declaration. This separate power was created broadly for reasons of convenience. As was seen above, the civil courts originally had power in s.75 of the 1928 Act and s.275 of the 1929 Act to impose disqualification on the back of a fraudulent trading declaration. In effect, this power was carried through into what became s.188(1)(b)(i) of the 1948 Act because the official receiver or liquidator, who had standing to bring proceedings for fraudulent

[57] Section 188(1)(a) was extended by Companies Act 1981 s.93(1) to cover indictable offences in connection with the liquidation of a company or with the receivership or management of a company's property. The provision (as amended) was subsequently consolidated as Companies Act 1985 s.296 before re-enactment as CDDA s.2. The maximum period of disqualification for a relevant conviction on indictment was increased from five years to 15 years by Companies Act 1981 s.93(1). The provision was further amended to include striking off by the Deregulation and Contracting Out Act 1994 s.39 and Sch.11, para.6 and to include reference to administrative receivers by Insolvency Act 2000 s.8 and Sch.4, para.3.

[58] Section 188(1)(b) was extended to cover fraud or breach of duty committed by persons acting as liquidators or as receivers or managers of a company's property by Companies Act 1981 s.93(1). Criminal liability for fraudulent trading was also extended by Companies Act 1981 s.96 to enable a person to be convicted whether or not the company had been or was in the course of being wound up: see now, Companies Act 2006 s.993 (formerly Companies Act 1985 s.458). Section 188(1)(b) (as amended) was then consolidated as Companies Act 1985 s.298 and finally re-enacted as CDDA s.4. The maximum period of disqualification was increased from five years to 15 years by Companies Act 1981 s.93(1). The provision was further amended to include specific reference to administrative receivers by Insolvency Act 2000 s.8 and Sch.4, para.4.

trading under s.332 of the 1948 Act, also had standing to apply under s.188(1)(b) for disqualification of a person who was guilty of an offence of fraudulent trading under s.332. The composite fraudulent trading provision in s.332 was subsequently divided into two separate provisions, one imposing criminal liability and the other imposing civil liability.[59] The wrongful trading provision, which is structured along the same lines as the civil provision on fraudulent trading, was introduced for the first time in 1985.[60] In light of these developments it made sense to make separate provision to that now contained in CDDA s.4(1)(a), to enable the court making a fraudulent or wrongful trading declaration to impose a disqualification order in the same proceedings without the need for a separate, free-standing application.

Persistent non-compliance with filing obligations under companies legislation

1–39 The court's power to disqualify for persistent breaches of companies legislation now contained in s.3 of the CDDA was first introduced in 1976,[61] although it derives originally from a proposal of the Jenkins Committee made some 15 years earlier.[62] The related power in s.5 was originally introduced in 1981.[63] The aim of what is now s.5 was to make it easier to obtain a disqualification order for persistent default by enabling the convicting magistrates' court to make an order. An order under what is now s.3 can only be made by a court having winding-up jurisdiction. These powers were introduced to widen the range of sanctions for enforcing compliance with the disclosure and publicity requirements of companies legislation.

The development of the provisions relating to unfit conduct

1–40 The principle that the directors of an insolvent company should be called to account for the company's failure in the public interest is long-established in insolvency law.[64] In this vein, the Companies Act 1929 made provision for the court, on the application of the official receiver, to disqualify a company director or officer who had committed fraud.[65] However, it was only comparatively recently that provisions were enacted empowering the court to disqualify an individual, without proof of fraud or commission of a criminal offence, on the ground that his previous conduct as a director of a company that had become insolvent rendered him unfit to be concerned in the management of companies

[59] See now, Companies Act 2006 s.993 (formerly Companies Act 1985 s.458) and Insolvency Act 1986 s.213.

[60] Insolvency Act 1985 s.15. See now, Insolvency Act 1986 s.214.

[61] Companies Act 1976 s.28. The provision was subsequently carried back into Companies Act 1948 s.188 by Companies Act 1981 s.93 before further re-enactment, without material amendment, as Companies Act 1985 s.297.

[62] Report of the Jenkins Committee, Cmnd.1749 (1962), paras 80, 85. See further, the White Paper, *Company Law Reform*, Cmnd.5391 (1973), paras 36–37.

[63] Companies Act 1981 s.93.

[64] See generally Report of the Review Committee, *Insolvency Law and Practice*, Cmnd.8558 (London: HMSO, 1982) and *Re Pantmaenog Timber Co Ltd* [2004] 1 A.C. 158.

[65] See 1–36.

generally. The long and often controversial process that culminated in the enactment of the present unfit conduct provisions in CDDA ss.6 to 9 is outlined below.

Insolvency Act 1976

1–41 When it reported in 1962, the Jenkins Committee was critical of the narrow scope of the powers in s.188 of the Companies Act 1948 described above. Accordingly, the Committee recommended that the court should be given a broad power to disqualify any person who was shown, when acting as a director or when otherwise concerned in the management of a company, to have acted in an improper, reckless or incompetent manner in relation to the company's affairs. It is clear that this recommendation was driven, in part, by the feeling that something needed to be done about individuals who had presided over a series of corporate failures. As the Committee's report puts it:

> "We recognise that it may be difficult to decide in any particular case whether a company director has acted so recklessly or incompetently that he should no longer be allowed to remain a director. But in serious cases, where, for example, a man has succeeded in steering a series of companies into insolvency, we think that the court should be able to put a stop to his activities."

This concern was eventually given statutory expression in the form of s.9 of the Insolvency Act 1976.[66] Section 9 (later consolidated as s.300 of the Companies Act 1985) had three key elements:

(1) Locus standi to apply for a disqualification order was conferred exclusively on the Secretary of State and (in cases where a relevant company was in compulsory liquidation) the official receiver.
(2) The court's power to disqualify was only triggered where the person had been a director (or shadow director) of at least two companies that had gone into insolvent liquidation within five years of each other.
(3) Subject to the requirement in (2), the court could, in its discretion, disqualify the director for up to five years[67] if satisfied that his conduct as a director of any of the relevant companies made him unfit to be concerned in the management of companies generally.

However, very few orders were made under this provision. There are no figures available before 1983. Between 1983 and the repeal of the provision in 1985 a mere 23 orders were made.[68]

The Cork Committee

1–42 The Cork Committee reviewed the operation of the disqualification provisions in the Companies Act 1948 and s.9 of the Insolvency Act 1976 as part of its

[66] Following on from the White Paper, *Company Law Reform*, Cmnd.5391 (1973).
[67] Extended to 15 years by Companies Act 1981 s.94.
[68] Three orders in 1983, eight orders in 1984 and 12 orders in 1985.

exhaustive enquiry into the workings of English insolvency law that led ultimately to the enactment of the Insolvency Act 1985.[69] One of the reasons that the Cork Committee gave to explain why there were so few applications under s.9 was that the Department of Trade and Industry had formed the narrow view that an application grounded on unfit conduct could only be made in a case where the director had been convicted of a criminal offence.[70] In keeping with its approach to the reform of insolvency law generally, the Cork Committee was driven by the view that harmonisation of the law of personal and corporate insolvency was both necessary and desirable. It was felt that there should be at least some degree of automatic restriction on the future activities of directors of failed companies just as there was an automatic ban on undischarged bankrupts from acting as a director or taking part in corporate management.[71] Accordingly, the Cork Committee recommended strengthening s.9 so that the court would be obliged to disqualify a person for at least two years (and up to a maximum of 15) where it appeared that his past conduct as a director of an insolvent company made him unfit.[72] This was roughly the formula eventually adopted in what is now s.6 of the CDDA. There would no longer be a requirement for the director to have been involved in two corporate failures within five years. The insolvent liquidation of a single company would suffice. Furthermore, disqualification would become mandatory once unfit conduct was established to the satisfaction of the court. To that extent, disqualification on the ground of unfit conduct would no longer be a matter within the court's discretion. The Cork Committee also recommended that the court should be empowered, but not required, to disqualify a person where it appeared to the Secretary of State, in consequence of a report received from inspectors appointed to conduct an investigation into the affairs of a company under companies legislation, that it was expedient in the public interest that the person concerned should be prohibited from being concerned (without the permission of the court) in the management of a company or a public company as the case may be.[73] This recommendation formed the basis of what is now the discretionary power of disqualification for unfit conduct in s.8 of the CDDA.

The White Paper: A Revised Framework for Insolvency Law

1–43 In its Insolvency Law White Paper which preceded the enactment of the Insolvency Act 1985, the Department of Trade and Industry saw the principal role of

[69] Report of the Review Committee, *Insolvency Law and Practice*, Cmnd.8558 (London: HMSO, 1982). For general background see I.F. Fletcher, "The Genesis of Modern Insolvency Law—An Odyssey of Law Reform" [1987] J.B.L 365; B. Carruthers and T. Halliday, *Rescuing Business: The Making of Corporate Bankruptcy Law in England and the United States* (Oxford: Clarendon Press, 1998), pp.266–283.

[70] Report of the Review Committee, *Insolvency Law and Practice*, Cmnd.8558 (London: HMSO, 1982), para.1763.

[71] Cmnd.8558, paras 1764–1766.

[72] Cmnd.8558, paras 1817–1818. Note also the Committee's recommendations at paras 1822–1823 (which led to the introduction of the personal liability provisions now found in CDDA s.15).

[73] Cmnd.8558, para.1819(c).

legislation in the context of directors' conduct and insolvency law as providing a statutory framework to encourage directors to pay careful attention to their company's financial circumstances so as to recognise difficulties at an early stage before the interests of creditors are seriously prejudiced, and to deter and penalise misconduct on the part of those who manage a company's affairs.[74] The Cork Committee's approach to disqualification was eventually followed in the Insolvency Act 1985, but only after a controversial attempt by the then Conservative government to push a more radical and draconian measure through Parliament. In the White Paper, the government took up the Cork Committee's recommendation but proposed additionally that the directors of any company that went into compulsory liquidation should be automatically disqualified from company management for three years unless they could satisfy the court that they should be exonerated.[75] This additional proposal, which would have shifted the onus onto the individual to demonstrate why he should not be disqualified, was embodied in the Insolvency Bill. However, the government was ultimately forced to abandon its original clause in the face of fierce parliamentary opposition.

1–44 Several objections to automatic disqualification were raised during the parliamentary debate and the government was defeated on a division in the House of Lords.[76] The main objections to the proposal can be summarised as follows:

(1) Unscrupulous directors could easily have evaded automatic disqualification by putting the company into voluntary liquidation.[77]
(2) Automatic disqualification would be widely seen as a stigma.[78]
(3) Automatic disqualification would deter skilled individuals from taking up non-executive directorships or consultancy positions in ailing companies where their expertise might most be needed.[79]
(4) Automatic disqualification would hamper the activities of the honest and stifle enterprise.[80]
(5) Automatic disqualification would amount to a denial of natural justice by placing an unfair onus on the individual to establish his "innocence"[81] and the courts would become congested with rebuttal or leave applications as a result.[82]

[74] *A Revised Framework for Insolvency Law*, Cmnd.9175 (1984).
[75] *A Revised Framework for Insolvency Law*, Cmnd.9175 (1984), paras 46–51.
[76] Hansard H.L. Vol.459, col.628.
[77] Hansard H.L. Vol.458, cols 909, 919; H.C. Vol.78, cols 155, 210.
[78] Hansard H.C. Vol.78 col.190.
[79] Hansard H.L. Vol.458, cols 884, 895, 898, 905–906, 918; H.C. Vol.78, cols 185–186, 210.
[80] Hansard H.C. Vol.78, col.173.
[81] Hansard H.C. Vol.78, col.210.
[82] Hansard H.L. Vol.458, col.918; H.C. Vol.78, col.186. On a comparative point, it is interesting to note that two automatic disqualification provisions enacted in Singapore during the 1980s were the subject of relentless criticism on similar grounds. For a general account of the Singapore experience see, A. Hicks, "Taking Part in Management (the Disqualified Director's Dilemma)" [1987] Malaysian L. J. lxxiv and "Disqualification of Directors (Forty Years On)" [1988] J.B.L. 27. For a theoretical critique of automatic disqualification provisions not confined to the specific case of company directors see A. von Hirsch and M. Wasik, "Civil Disqualifications Attending Conviction: A Suggested Conceptual Framework" [1997] C.L.J 599. For criticism by the Irish courts of a similar provision see *Re Tralee Beef and Lamb Ltd (In Liquidation), Kavanagh v Delaney* [2008] IESC 1, [2008] 3 I.R. 347.

1–45 In the light of this opposition, a Cork-inspired mandatory disqualification provision was reintroduced and, after re-enactment, now appears as CDDA ss.6 to 7. The onus remains firmly with the Secretary of State (or, where appropriate, the official receiver) to establish unfit conduct. A schedule of matters to which the court must have regard in determining whether a person's conduct as a director makes him unfit was introduced for the first time in the Insolvency Act 1985 and carried through into Sch.1 to the CDDA. The prevailing view within both the executive and the legislature was that some form of "highway code" was needed to assist insolvency practitioners in complying with their reporting obligations[83] and the Secretary of State in deciding whether or not to apply for an order, as well as to assist the courts.[84] The contents of the Schedule reflect the pre-CDDA experience both of the Insolvency Service and insolvency practitioners in their dealings with the directors of poorly managed companies that had ended up in formal insolvency proceedings. They include such matters as breach of fiduciary duty, misapplication of company funds and default in filing accounts and returns. As such, the Schedule might be described as a statement of basic minimum standards.[85] The substantive power in CDDA s.6 captures the spirit of the Cork recommendations. A director involved in a single corporate insolvency is exposed to the risk of disqualification and, if the court finds that his conduct as a director makes him unfit to be concerned in the management of a company under that provision, it must disqualify the individual concerned for at least the minimum period of two years.[86]

Competition disqualification

1–46 The Enterprise Act 2002 added a further power to the core provisions on unfit conduct in CDDA ss.6 to 9. This power, which is found in CDDA s.9A, requires the court, on the application of the Office of Fair Trading or another specified regulator, to disqualify a person for up to 15 years if it is satisfied that a company of which the person is a director has committed a relevant breach of competition law and his conduct as a director makes him unfit to be concerned in the management of a company. The creation of this new power looks set to extend the concept of unfit conduct beyond the confines of the corporate insolvency and company

[83] See now, CDDA s.7(3).

[84] See, e.g. Hansard, H.L. Vol. 461, cols 724, 732–733, Vol. 467, cols 1123–1124.

[85] Hansard H.L. Vol.467, col.1124. For a full discussion of the contents of the Schedule see Ch.4. The idea that the disqualification legislation is concerned with setting and promoting standards of conduct for directors is canvassed further in Ch.2.

[86] Section 6 is more unfavourable to the individual than comparable provisions in Australia: see, e.g. Corporations Act 2001 (Cth) s.206F. That provision confers a discretionary power to disqualify for up to five years on the Australian Securities and Investment Commission. The power arises where, within seven years immediately prior to the ASIC giving notice to show reason why the person should not be disqualified, he has been an officer of two or more corporations and while such officer (or within 12 months after him ceasing to be an officer) each of the corporations was wound up and a liquidator lodged a relevant report about the corporation's inability to pay its debts. See also the analogous power of the court in Corporations Act 2001 (Cth) s.206D. This provides that a person may be disqualified from managing corporations for up to 20 years if certain conditions are met. The conditions are, that within the last seven years a person has been an officer of two or more corporations when they failed and the court is satisfied (a) that the manner in which the corporation was managed was wholly or partly responsible for the corporation failing and (b) the disqualification is justified.

investigation contexts that provide the background to proceedings under CDDA ss.6 and 8. Section 9A is best viewed as creating a new gateway to disqualification. Breach of competition law is capable of forming a ground for disqualification under other sections of the CDDA. The significance of s.9A is that it provides circumstances in which breach of competition law can itself trigger a regulatory response in the form of disqualification proceedings without the necessity of, for example, a prior criminal conviction, insolvency or relevant investigation. The competition disqualification regime is considered further in Ch.6.

Bankruptcy restrictions and debt relief restrictions orders

1–47 The bankruptcy restrictions regime found in Sch.4A to the Insolvency Act 1986 was also introduced by the Enterprise Act in England and Wales[87] as a means of discriminating between non-culpable and culpable debtors. Disqualification from acting in relation to companies under the CDDA is a "knock on" effect of a bankruptcy restrictions order or undertaking made under Sch.4A. Such an order or undertaking has various other legal consequences. The CDDA and bankruptcy restrictions regimes are closely analogous in that, under both regimes, conduct that is found to fall sufficiently below the standards set by the court can result in disqualification from management of companies for up to 15 years as well as a significant number of other disabilities. It is also important to recognise that, in certain key respects, the bankruptcy restrictions regime closely follows the model of the CDDA in terms of the process by which an order or undertaking is obtained. As such, the bankruptcy restrictions regime can be seen not so much as a new concept peculiar to bankruptcy but rather as the extension of a CDDA-type regime into the province of personal insolvency and therefore as a further example of the harmonisation of corporate and personal insolvency law. The fact that bankruptcy restrictions do more than simply prohibit the restricted individual from acting in the management of companies does not dilute the point. As is made clear in Ch.14, disqualification under the CDDA also has extensive "knock-on" consequences under other legislation such as charities and pensions legislation.

1–48 The Tribunals, Courts and Enforcement Act 2007 introduced in England and Wales a form of administrative bankruptcy process, debt relief orders, designed to offer debt relief to so-called "no income, no asset" debtors who cannot afford to pay the mandatory official receiver's deposit which is required in order to enter into bankruptcy. Following the logic of the Enterprise Act reforms of personal insolvency, the 2007 Act also introduced a debt relief restrictions regime as Sch.4ZB to the Insolvency Act 1986, which, while tailored to the specific workings of the debt relief order procedure, is identical in all material respects to the bankruptcy restrictions regime applicable in bankruptcy.[88] The automatic ban on undischarged bankrupts contained in s.11 of the CDDA is extended in England and Wales to persons who are subject to a moratorium under a debt relief order and to

[87] Inserted by the Enterprise Act 2002 s.257 and Sch.20.

[88] See Tribunals Courts and Services Act 2007 s.108, Schs 17–19.

persons who are subject to bankruptcy restrictions or debt relief restrictions (which in this book are referred to collectively as insolvency restrictions). These regimes are considered further in Ch.11.

International recognition

1–49 The first step in the recognition of overseas disqualifications was very modest. Scottish disqualifications were already recognised and given effect to in England and Wales (and vice versa) under the CDDA as enacted, because that legislation applies both in England and Wales and Scotland. However, Northern Ireland disqualifications were not recognised until later. Recognition of Northern Ireland disqualifications under the law of England and Wales (and Scotland) was effected by the mechanism of automatically extending the effect of such disqualifications as if they were made under the law of England and Wales (and Scotland). The relevant changes were made by the insertion of ss.12A and 12B into the CDDA. These insertions were effected respectively by the Insolvency Act 2000 s.7(1) and by the Insolvency Act 2000 (Company Directors Disqualification Undertakings) Order 2004.[89] Disqualifications made under the CDDA (applicable in England and Wales and Scotland) are given recognition in Northern Ireland under art.17 of the Company Directors Disqualification (Northern Ireland) Order 2002.[90] However, the manner in which disqualifications are recognised is not symmetrical. As regards Northern Ireland disqualifications, it is the Northern Ireland High Court which retains exclusive power to grant permission to act notwithstanding disqualification, throughout the United Kingdom.[91] However, as regards Great Britain disqualifications which are recognised and given effect to within Northern Ireland, it is the Northern Ireland High Court, and not the courts of Great Britain, which is given the exclusive power by art.17 of the 2002 Order to grant permission to act in Northern Ireland notwithstanding disqualification.

1–50 A more far reaching change was made by Part 40 of the Companies Act 2006 (ss.1182–1191).[92] These sections are enabling provisions which empower the Secretary of State to establish by statutory instrument a regime by which effect can be given to foreign disqualifications, or foreign restrictions as they are defined by the 2006 Act, within the United Kingdom. They were enacted to "close the gap" in the law, whereby persons subject to foreign disqualification were still able to operate, without restriction, in relation to UK companies.[93] Part 40 is considered further in Ch.16.

[89] SI 2004/1941.

[90] SI 2002/3150 (NI 4).

[91] On the effect of Northern Ireland disqualifications in Great Britain and the retained jurisdiction of the Northern Ireland High Court to grant permission to act see CDDA ss.12A(a) and 12B(b).

[92] These provisions were brought into force on October 1, 2009 by The Companies Act 2006 (Commencement No.8, Transitional Provisions and Savings) Order 2008 (SI 2008/2860). However, the secondary legislation required to bring the Pt 40 regime fully into operation had not been enacted at the time of writing.

[93] See Explanatory Notes to the Companies Act 2006, para.1506.

SUMMARY AND CONCLUSION

1–51 The various substantive powers now to be found in the CDDA have evolved gradually and a number of strands of historical development are discernible. The process of evolution has not gone on in isolation and, at least up to the original enactment of the CDDA, it should be considered as part of a wider process of legislative reform in the spheres of company and insolvency law culminating in the great reforms of the mid-1980s. It might be argued that the enactment of the CDDA served merely to bring a ramshackle collection of unconnected powers derived from companies and insolvency legislation together in one place. However, it is preferable to see the CDDA as a single legislative scheme in which the various disqualification provisions are harmonised. The Insolvency Act 1986 is generally treated as if it were a piece of codifying legislation. The prevailing judicial view of the insolvency legislation is that it should not be construed too narrowly solely by reference to the law as it stood before its enactment.[94] Given that the CDDA was enacted broadly in the same period, and that its core provisions on unfit conduct were originally part of the Insolvency Act 1985, it is suggested that it should be treated more as a codifying than a consolidating statute. Further support for such a view derives from the structure of the CDDA itself. A striking feature of the CDDA is that conduct that triggers jurisdiction under ss.2 to 5 and 10 is equally capable of constituting unfit conduct under ss.6 to 8 and that unfit conduct under s.9A may also be capable of falling within other sections of the Act. The legislation is therefore bound together by the core provisions relating to unfit conduct that were originally enacted as part of the Insolvency Act 1985. Moreover, this view of the CDDA reflects the overall thrust of the historical process, in particular, the gradual shift of emphasis away from the early provisions based on fraud and bankruptcy in favour of the modern concept of unfit conduct, a concept that is not exclusively concerned with fraud or with behaviour that is criminally culpable. To a limited extent, the introduction of competition disqualification in CDDA s.9A changes the picture. However, it is suggested that its introduction is consistent with the general view stated above. As a piece of legislation, the CDDA is best seen as establishing a coherent system of regulation that provides a series of gateways to the exercise of disqualification jurisdiction, all of which are based on some form of "unfit" conduct.

1–52 Disqualification is now recognised as being firmly at the heart of the corporate insolvency process and, along with criminal proceedings and civil misfeasance proceedings, as being one of the three principal tools for the protection of the public from misconduct in relation to companies.[95] It remains to be seen whether

[94] See, e.g. *Re MC Bacon Ltd* [1990] B.C.L.C. 324 at 335, *Re a Debtor (No.1 of 1987)* [1989] 1 W.L.R. 271 (a case on statutory demands in personal insolvency); *Smith v Braintree District Council* [1990] 2 A.C. 215, 237–238 (a case on s.285 of the Insolvency Act 1985) and *Re Jeffrey S Levitt* [1992] B.C.L.C. 250.

[95] *Re Pantmaenog Timber Co Ltd* [2004] 1 A.C. 158 at [79].

bankruptcy restrictions and debt relief restrictions will develop in a similar manner so as to take an equivalent place within the personal insolvency regime. In that context, much will depend on the resources that are devoted to such proceedings, the willingness of the state to take proceedings and the approach of the courts in setting the standards which, if not met, will expose the individual to a bankruptcy restrictions order or a debt relief restrictions order. Early indications are that the two regimes are indeed operating in a complementary manner to each other.[96]

[96] See, e.g. *Randhawa v Official Receiver* [2006] EWHC 2946 (Ch), [2007] 1 W.L.R. 1700.

CHAPTER 2

THE NATURE AND PURPOSE OF DIRECTORS DISQUALIFICATION

INTRODUCTION

2–01 Chapter 1 traces the historical evolution of directors disqualification legislation from its earliest origins in the 1920s to its final culmination in the CDDA. In broad terms, the enactment of the CDDA brought about two developments in the law concerning disqualification of directors. First, it pulled together various long-standing disqualification provisions scattered through companies and insolvency legislation into a single legislative scheme. Secondly, it marked the effective launch of a new regime, in the form of CDDA ss.6 to 9, which, among other things, made provision for the disqualification of directors on the ground of unfit conduct following either corporate insolvency or a relevant investigation. While it is true to say that the provisions in ss.6 to 9 had originally been enacted in the Insolvency Act 1985, they were barely in place a year before being re-enacted in the CDDA. With that in mind it makes sense to regard the CDDA as their de facto point of commencement.[1]

2–02 If the provisions of the CDDA are taken as a whole, the following common schematic features can be identified:

(1) The CDDA contains a number of separate jurisdictional "gateways" all of which lead potentially to the same result, namely the possible imposition by the court of a disqualification order or, as an alternative in the case of ss.6, 8 and 9A, the imposition of disqualification by means of a voluntary undertaking in the same terms as a disqualification order.[2] Automatic disqualification under CDDA s.11 can also be seen as a "gateway" to disqualification although it does not require the imposition of a disqualification order or undertaking.

(2) A disqualification order amounts to a comprehensive ban in the terms of s.1 that, for a specified period, prohibits the disqualified person, amongst other things, from acting as a company director or from taking part in the promotion, formation or management of a company without the permission of the court or from acting as an insolvency practitioner. In terms of the prohibitions imposed, a disqualification undertaking accepted by the Secretary of State in

[1] The short title of the CDDA "an Act to consolidate certain enactments relating to the disqualification of persons from being directors of companies, and from being otherwise concerned with the company's affairs" while strictly accurate, can be a little misleading. Before the CDDA came into force the new powers in what are now CDDA ss.6 to 8, together with the criteria for determining whether a director's conduct made him unfit in Sch.1, were untested by the courts.

[2] On disqualification undertakings, see generally Ch.9.

a s.6 or s.8 case is, by virtue of s.1A, identical to a disqualification order.[3] The prohibitions imposed by CDDA s.11 are similarly comprehensive.

(3) All of the various jurisdictional "gateways" (with the exception of CDDA s.11) focus primarily on *individual* conduct within companies as opposed to the *collective* conduct of the board of directors. The courts only have jurisdiction to disqualify persons on the basis of their own conduct as individuals.[4] It is not open to the courts to impose a collective disqualification on a board of directors for what amounted to a collective failure. In cases involving directors, the conduct of each individual member of the board must be considered and their personal contribution to that collective failure assessed.[5]

(4) The court's power to disqualify under the "gateways" in CDDA ss.2 to 6, 8, 9A and 10 is triggered by some *defined past misconduct* on the part of the individual (certain criminal offences in s.2, persistent filing defaults in s.3, unfit conduct in ss.6, 8 and 9A etc.) referable to a specified company or companies. Automatic disqualification of persons who are the subject of bankruptcy restrictions or debt relief restrictions under CDDA s.11(1)(b) is also premised on past misconduct, namely the misconduct that triggered the imposition of the relevant order or undertaking. Even the automatic disqualification of undischarged bankrupts[6] under CDDA s.11(1)(a) can be linked to misconduct in that it amounts to a statutory presumption that an undischarged bankrupt is prima facie unfit to be involved in the management of companies.[7]

(5) Disqualification does not amount to an absolute, perpetual ban. It is not possible under the CDDA for anyone to be disqualified for a period in excess of 15 years.[8] Moreover, the courts have statutory power to grant a disqualified person permission to act as a director or to take part in the management of a company during the currency of the disqualification. However, it should be noted that the prohibition on acting as an insolvency practitioner cannot be relaxed during the currency of a disqualification order, disqualification undertaking, bankruptcy, bankruptcy restrictions order, bankruptcy restrictions undertaking, debt relief order, debt relief restrictions order or debt relief restrictions undertaking.[9]

(6) Breach of a disqualification order or undertaking has the same legal consequences regardless of whether the disqualification was imposed under CDDA

[3] On the scope of the ban imposed by a disqualification order or undertaking, see generally Ch.14. On the issue of permission to act notwithstanding disqualification, see generally Ch.15. Competition disqualification undertakings also impose a comprehensive ban although, somewhat anomalously, it is not identical in scope to that set out in CDDA ss.1 and 1A: see CDDA s.9B(3)–(4) and discussion in Ch.12 at 12-07 to 12-08.

[4] "Persons" here includes companies which are also susceptible to disqualification under the CDDA: see *Official Receiver v Brady* [1999] B.C.C. 258.

[5] On the approach of the court to the apportioning of responsibility see Chs 4 and 5.

[6] Now extended to persons who have the benefit of a moratorium under a debt relief order by the Tribunals, Courts and Enforcement Act 2007.

[7] See further 11–22 to 11–24.

[8] Where disqualification orders are made under CDDA ss.2 or 5 by a court having summary jurisdiction there is a lower limit of five years. Note that under the Australian Corporations Act 2001 (Cth) the maximum period of disqualification in some cases now stands at 20 years.

[9] See variously CDDA ss.1(1)(b), 1A(1)(b), 9B(3)(d) and Insolvency Act 1986 ss.389, 390(4), (5).

ss.2, 3, 4, 5, 6 to 7, 8, 9A to 9B or 10. This is also broadly true of a person who breaches the automatic bans in CDDA ss.11, 12A and 12B.

(7) Disqualification (as is also the case with bankruptcy, debt relief orders and insolvency restrictions) carries with it not just disqualification from relevant involvement with companies but a myriad of other disqualifications and inhibitions.[10]

Thus, the CDDA contains a range of powers that enable (and in the case of ss.6 and 9A oblige) the court to disqualify persons based on their previous misconduct, the logic being that the previous misconduct raises serious questions over their fitness or suitability to participate in the management of companies. Similarly, automatic disqualification under CDDA s.11 rests on a presumption of unfitness in the case of undischarged bankrupts and persons subject to debt relief orders or on the previous misconduct that formed the factual basis of an order or undertaking imposed under Sch.4A (bankruptcy restrictions) or Sch.4ZB (debt relief restrictions) to the Insolvency Act 1986. While all of the various "gateways" have their own particular jurisdictional requirements, none are completely exclusive in scope. So, for example, a persistent failure to file accounts or annual returns can trigger disqualification under CDDA s.3 but can also be taken into account (and, in practice, is more likely to be considered) in determining whether a person is unfit within the meaning of CDDA ss.6 or 8. The scope of the disqualification imposed is identical whichever "gateway" is used[11] and breach of the terms of the disqualification attracts common legal consequences.[12] In the light of these unitary features, the CDDA can justifiably be regarded as a coherent legislative scheme.[13]

2–03 The aim of this chapter is to explore two difficult and related issues. First, the rationale of the CDDA is considered, in an attempt to discern its overall purpose and scope. Secondly, and in the light of that discussion, the nature of the CDDA jurisdiction is explored. The second issue flows from the first and is essentially one of classification. Should directors' disqualification be classified as a form of civil regulatory process or, as some have sought to argue, should it properly be regarded as a quasi-criminal process even though the jurisdiction is, for the most part, conferred on and exercised by the civil courts? If neither of these classifications is appropriate, should it be classified in some other way? These questions are important because the way in which they are answered may have implications for law and practice, especially in relation to matters of procedure and evidence and, also, for example, in relation to the rights of the individual to a fair trial under art.6 of the

[10] See generally, Ch.14.

[11] Although each of an undischarged bankrupt, a person in relation to whom a moratorium under a debt relief order applies, a person the subject of bankruptcy restrictions and a person the subject of debt relief restrictions is not expressly prohibited by CDDA s.11 from acting as an insolvency practitioner or as a receiver of company property (contrast the scope of CDDA ss.1(1) and 1A(1)), such persons are prohibited from so acting by Insolvency Act 1986 ss.31, 389 and 390(4)(a), (5). See further Ch.14.

[12] Although it should be noted that accessory liability under s.15 of the CDDA only arises in relation to undischarged bankrupts who act in breach of s.11 prohibition.

[13] It should, however, be noted that other "knock on" effects are not common to all forms of CDDA disqualification.

ECHR.[14] A number of important general points emerge from this discussion that provide a useful context for the detailed exposition of disqualification law contained in the rest of this book. At the level of judicial rhetoric, there is a broad consensus that the main objective of the CDDA is not primarily to punish miscreant directors but rather to protect the public from those who have acted improperly in the management of a company or companies. It will be seen that this distinction between "punishment" and "protection" may well reflect a generalised attempt on the part of the higher courts to justify the view that, for practical purposes, disqualification is best regarded as a civil regulatory and/or quasi-disciplinary process. However, as the jurisdiction has been considered over time by the courts, any clear distinction between "punishment" and "protection" has effectively been abandoned. As Lord Woolf has recognised, the exercise that the civil courts engage in when determining the appropriate period of disqualification is little different to a criminal sentencing exercise. In each case, the court will be concerned with the protection of the public, not just in the sense of keeping the disqualified person "off the road" but also in the sense of deterring the disqualified person, and others who occupy similar positions, from engaging in behaviour that falls below the standards of conduct required by Parliament and/or the courts, thereby raising standards of corporate governance and management generally.[15] However, it will be suggested that the use of the criminal sentencing analogy does not necessarily mean that disqualification should be classified as a criminal process.

WHAT WAS PARLIAMENT'S INTENTION IN ENACTING THE CDDA?

Disqualification and abuse of the privilege of limited liability

2–04 In the light of the history and evolution of the directors' disqualification regime, it is justifiable to take as a starting point the basic premise that disqualification is targeted at those who abuse the so-called privilege of limited liability. Abuse of limited liability is often referred to in the case law though this often reflects the particular background with which the court in question is dealing: namely insolvent companies or financial mismanagement. Moreover, disqualification is not exclusively concerned with abuse of limited liability.[16] It also seeks to promote

[14] See, e.g. *R. (on the application of McCann) v Crown Court at Manchester* [2002] UKHL 39, [2003] 1 A.C. 787.

[15] *Re Westmid Packing Services Ltd, Secretary of State for Trade and Industry v Griffiths* [1998] 2 All E.R. 124 at 131–132. In the context of sentencing by the criminal courts, the difference between the punitive element of a sentence and the protective (i.e. future protection of the public) element can on occasion be more clearly drawn: see, e.g. *R v Considine* [2007] EWCA Crim 1166, [2008] 1 WLR 414 in relation to Criminal Justice Act 2003 s.229. The difficulty with the CDDA regime is that disqualification impacts on the freedom of the individual to pursue the restricted activities as well as containing protective and deterrent elements. Thus, the balance drawn between these various aspects can affect the manner in which the legislation operates.

[16] This is explicit in the competition disqualification provisions in CDDA ss.9A–9D. That perceptions still need to be changed is clear, for example, from the use, or non-use, of the disqualification regime in the context of breaches of health and safety legislation: see, e.g. A. Neal and F. Wright, *A survey of the use and effectiveness of the Company Directors Disqualification Act 1986 as a legal sanction against directors convicted of health and safety offences*, Health and Safety Executive, Research Report RR597 (HSE Books, 2007), *http://www.hse.gov.uk/research/rrhtm/rr597.htm* [Accessed August 19, 2009].

and uphold wider notions of probity, competence and commercial morality. Nevertheless, there can be no doubt that the need to address abuse of limited liability forms a significant element of the underlying policy and so it makes sense to consider it at the outset.

Origins of limited liability

2–05 In the case of a company limited by shares the liability of the shareholders who provide it with investment capital is limited to the amount, if any, unpaid on their shares.[17] This means that a shareholder cannot generally be required to contribute towards payment of the company's debts once he has paid for his shares in full. Thus, on the company's insolvency, each shareholder has no further liability for the company's debts and stands to lose only the amount of his initial investment. Statutory limited liability has been available in this form since the mid-nineteenth century.[18] Limited liability was originally intended to encourage widespread private investment in business and so enable entrepreneurs to raise the capital needed to fund their activities. The nascent limited company emerged primarily as a medium for raising capital from investors who had no active involvement in the running of the company's business. In its earliest form, limited liability therefore went in tandem with what would now be recognised as the publicly-quoted limited company which continues to perform broadly that same economic function. By the end of the nineteenth century, however, the limited company had emerged as a popular medium for small business. Erstwhile sole traders and partners were incorporating their businesses in increasing numbers so that they could trade with the benefit of limited liability. The limited company therefore became a trading mechanism for owner-managed businesses as well as performing its earlier function as a financing mechanism. This transition was effectively sanctioned by the House of Lords decision in *Salomon v Salomon & Co Ltd* which paved the way for the mass incorporation of small, owner-managed businesses as private companies that has occurred during the last century.[19] Official policy in the United Kingdom continues to rest firmly on the assumption that limited

[17] Companies Act 2006 s.3(2) (formerly Companies Act 1985 s.1(2)(a)).

[18] For brief accounts of the history and origins of limited liability see P.L. Davies, *Introduction to Company Law* (OUP, 2002) and *Gower and Davies: Principles of Modern Company Law*, 8th edn (London: Sweet & Maxwell, 2008); B. Pettet, "Limited Liability—A Principle for the 21st Century? (1995) 48 (II) *Current Legal Problems* 125; A. Hicks, "Corporate Form: Questioning the Unsung Hero" [1997] J.B.L. 306 and *Disqualification of Directors: No Hiding Place for the Unfit* (A.C.C.A Research Report No.59, 1998).

[19] [1897] A.C. 22. The lower courts in *Salomon* imposed personal liability on the sole director and principal shareholder for the debts of an insolvent company. This decision was reversed in the House of Lords where it was held that a company lawfully incorporated by process of registration under the Companies Acts has a legal existence distinct from that of its members who are generally only liable to contribute personally to the company's assets to the extent provided by the legislation. When the case was decided, the idea of an owner-managed company in which investment and management functions could be combined was novel. Thus, it is perhaps not surprising that the lower courts resisted the notion that one man could invest in a company and manage its affairs while at the same time enjoying the benefits of limited liability. The "one-person" company is now formally recognised by statute following implementation of the Twelfth Company Law Directive: see Companies Act 2006 s.7(1) (formerly Companies Act 1985 s.1(3A)).

liability benefits the community at large by facilitating enterprise and, in particular, by encouraging entrepreneurs to start up in business without them being forced to put their entire personal wealth on the line. Moreover, the limited company continues to be exalted as an appropriate vehicle for small, owner-managed businesses. This is borne out by the deregulatory "think small first" principle that emerged from the Company Law Review[20] which was subsequently implemented in the Companies Act 2006.[21]

Abuse of limited liability

2–06 Despite this prevailing emphasis on the facilitative aspect of company law, it has always been recognised that limited liability has disadvantages, the main one being that it transfers the risk of business failure to the company's creditors. The House of Lords in *Salomon* acknowledged that the refusal to impose personal liability on the principal shareholder for the insolvent company's debts had serious implications for unsecured creditors, although this did not sway their Lordships from their basic view that anyone complying with the registration formalities of the Companies Acts could lawfully trade with the benefit of limited liability. Nevertheless, this risk, which is inherent in the concept of limited liability, is regarded as acceptable given the concern of company law to encourage enterprise. At the same time, however, the recognition that limited liability confers benefits but also creates risks has given rise to the idea, commonly expressed in legal discourse, that limited liability is a privilege conferred by the state which should be used responsibly and not abused.[22] As such, there is a consensus that company law should have a regulatory, as well as a facilitative, function. In particular, it is generally accepted that company law should provide some means of regulating companies in the interests of shareholders, investors, employees,[23] and, of particular relevance in the present context, creditors, one of the principal aims of such regulation being to control abuse of limited liability. The enactment of the CDDA should be seen as part of this regulatory response. However, it is important to recognise that abuse of limited liability is but one example of conduct that the

[20] See the Company Law Review Steering Group, *Final Report*, (June 2001) and the White Paper *Modernising Company Law*, Cm. 5553 (2002).

[21] See, e.g. Companies Act 2006 Pt 13, Ch.2 (simplified meeting procedures); Companies Act 2006 ss.381–384, 398 (formerly Companies Act 1985 ss.246–249) (simplified accounting procedures); Companies Act 2006 ss.477–479 (formerly Companies Act 1985 ss.249A–249E) (audit exemption).

[22] This influential notion is a variant of the concession theory of company law. Concession theory holds that a limited company can only be created by an act of the state so that when the state allows individuals to incorporate their business it confers a privilege that should be used in the public interest. The "privilege" idea has exerted a powerful influence in disqualification cases: see V. Finch, "Disqualifying Directors: Issues of Rights, Privileges and Employment" (1993) 22 Industrial L.J. 35 and *Corporate Insolvency Law: Perspectives and Principles,* 2nd edn (Cambridge University Press, 2009), Ch.16 from p.716. For a flavour of the "privilege" rhetoric that was used in the parliamentary debates accompanying the passage of what became the Insolvency Act 1985 to justify, inter alia, the introduction of more stringent disqualification powers see, e.g. Hansard H.C. Vol.78, cols. 145, 154 and the report of the proceedings of House of Commons Standing Committee E, Vol.4 (Session 1984–85) commencing at cl.54 which is peppered with references to "the privilege of limited liability".

[23] See Companies Act 2006 s.172(1)(b) (formerly Companies Act 1985 s.309).

CDDA is designed to regulate and deter. A core feature of the Act is that it is directed at the conduct of those responsible for management, be it management of companies, limited or unlimited, or management of certain other specified entities and such persons need not necessarily be shareholders or directors to fall within its compass. The point is taken up further below.

2–07 A study of the available parliamentary materials suggests that the disqualification provisions now to be found in the CDDA were originally conceived to address a number of quite specific concerns and abuses as follows:

2–08 **Security filling.** It is clear from the following statement found in the report of the Greene Committee[24] that the fraudulent trading provision introduced originally in 1928 was directed primarily at "security filling":

> "Our attention has been directed particularly to the case (met with principally in private companies) where the person in control of the company holds a floating charge and, while knowing that the company is on the verge of liquidation, 'fills up' his security by means of goods obtained on credit and then appoints a receiver."[25]

This practice is objectionable as, unless regulated, the director who knows that his company is insolvent is able to top up the value of any security for the company's liabilities on his loan account at the expense of trade creditors. The legislative response (in the form of the fraudulent trading provision) was to introduce a mixture of civil and criminal liability for conduct of this nature while also making such conduct a ground for disqualification.[26] It would seem that the more extensive power in s.2 of the CDDA to disqualify persons convicted of an indictable offence in connection with the promotion, formation or management of a company was originally introduced to deal with other comparable misuses of limited liability.

2–09 **Under-capitalised companies.** Private companies are not subject to any minimum capital requirements and so it is perfectly lawful for a private company to be incorporated with an initial subscribed share capital of as little as £1 or £2.[27] The lack of a minimum requirement reflects the cultural transition away from the idea that the limited company was exclusively a medium for raising capital, a transition accelerated by the House of Lords decision in the *Salomon* case. As a consequence, the benefits of limited liability can be purchased easily and cheaply. The corollary, in theory, is that an individual can incorporate a limited company without personally injecting any working capital and trade at the risk of the

[24] Report of the Company Law Amendment Committee (the Greene Committee), Cmd. 2657 (1926).

[25] Greene Committee, para.61.

[26] Greene Committee, para.61 and see from 1–35. Retention of title by the suppliers of goods can be seen as one self-help response to the practice described.

[27] See Department of Trade and Industry, *Companies in 2005–2006* H.C. 1534 (London: the Stationery Office, 2006), Table A7 showing that the vast majority of companies on the register at Companies House as at March 31, 2006 were small private companies having a share capital of £5,000 or less.

company's creditors. Concerns about the risks that under-capitalised companies pose for creditors and consumers are voiced periodically. The following extract from the report of the Jenkins Committee provides a good illustration:

> "The Board of Trade have referred in their evidence to the irresponsible multiplication of companies, particularly of 'one-man' companies; to the dangers of abuse through the incorporation with limited liability of very small, undercapitalised businesses . . . We are satisfied that this proliferation of small companies can and does lead to abuse . . ."[28]

Similar points were made in the report of the Cork Committee[29] and during the parliamentary debate that preceded the enactment of the Insolvency Act 1985. The Cork Committee recommended that the disqualification regime should be strengthened as a means of "severely penalising those who abuse the privilege of limited liability by operating behind one-man, insufficiently capitalised companies . . .".[30] This recommendation led ultimately to the enactment of the unfit conduct provisions now found in CDDA ss.6–9 and the introduction of the provision (now CDDA s.15) that renders a person who takes part in the management of a company while disqualified personally liable for that company's debts.

Failure to comply with disclosure obligations. In return for the benefit of limited liability, the limited company and its directors are required to comply with extensive publicity requirements imposed by companies legislation. Of particular importance to creditors and shareholders alike are the recurring obligations requiring up-to-date accounts and annual returns to be filed with the Registrar of Companies. Any member of the public is entitled to carry out a search of the records at Companies House in order to access information filed on behalf of a limited company in accordance with these obligations. Disclosure is one of the main techniques used in company law for safeguarding the interests of investors and creditors.[31] The CDDA reinforces the importance of a number of these obligations by adding powers of disqualification to the range of criminal and other default sanctions imposed by companies legislation.[32] **2–10**

Trading to the detriment of creditors/wrongful trading. Wrongful trading, as conceived by the Cork Committee, occurs when the directors of a limited company allow it to continue to trade and to incur fresh liabilities at a time when they know or ought to know that the company has no reasonable prospect of survival. This practice is detrimental both to new creditors, who are persuaded to give credit to the company with no prospect of being paid, and also to the **2–11**

[28] Report of the Jenkins Committee, Cmnd.1749 (1962).

[29] Report of the Review Committee, *Insolvency Law and Practice*, Cmnd.8558 (London: HMSO, 1982).

[30] Cmnd.8558, para.1815.

[31] See P.L. Davies, *Gower and Davies: Principles of Modern Company Law*, 8th edn (London: Sweet & Maxwell, 2008), Chs 21–22, 26.

[32] See, in particular, CDDA ss.3 and 5 (discussed more fully in Ch. 10). Non-compliance with filing obligations can also be taken into account in determining whether a person is unfit for the purposes of CDDA ss.6 and 8: see, e.g. *Secretary of State for Trade and Industry v Ettinger, Re Swift 736 Ltd* [1993] B.C.L.C. 896.

company's existing creditors whose own prospects of recovering what they are owed are diminished further given the overall increase in the company's net liabilities. The Cork Committee offered this summary:

> "The essence of wrongful trading is the incurring of liabilities with no reasonable prospect of meeting them; whether by incurring debts with no reasonable prospect of paying them, or by taking payment in advance for goods to be supplied with no reasonable prospect of being able to supply them or return the money in default."[33]

The Committee also suggested that trading through an under-capitalised company could come within the concept of wrongful trading.[34] A combination of the wrongful trading provision now to be found in the Insolvency Act 1986 s.214 (which empowers the court, on the application of a liquidator, to order the errant director to contribute personally to the company's assets) and the enactment of the CDDA (in particular, ss.6–9 and 15) was intended to address this practice by creating legal incentives for directors to respond in a timely fashion to problems of financial distress.[35] Civil liability for wrongful trading and disqualification are explicitly linked in the legislation. Thus, a court imposing personal liability on a director under s.214 of the Insolvency Act may also disqualify that director in the same proceedings under CDDA s.10.[36] Conduct of this nature may also be relevant in the context of proceedings under CDDA ss.6 or 8.[37]

2–12 **Phoenix companies and multiple insolvencies.** The "phoenix syndrome" is shorthand for a practice, much castigated in official reports, that takes the following form. The directors of a limited company trade the company into insolvency, place it into voluntary liquidation and then acquire its assets and business from a "friendly" liquidator at a knock-down price using a new, clean "phoenix" company as the vehicle for the purchase. The new company is said, like the phoenix, to rise from the ashes of the old. The directors and shareholders of both companies are the same and, in order to preserve any goodwill, the new company will adopt a name which is similar to that of the old company before trading is recommenced. By this process the directors succeed in recycling the assets of the business while shedding its liabilities.[38] It was stated in the report of the Jenkins Committee that the court should be given powers to curb the activities of individuals who succeed "in steering a series of companies into insolvency".[39] Parliament responded belatedly

[33] Report of the Review Committee, Cmnd.8558, para.1784.

[34] Cmnd.8558, para.1785. Wrongful trading also embraces the specific abuse of security filling described above in 2–08.

[35] The Cork Committee and the subsequent White Paper, *A Revised Framework for Insolvency Law*, Cmnd.9175 (1984) both proposed this mixed bag of civil liability combined with an extended disqualification regime, an approach ultimately taken up in the Insolvency Act 1985. Note that there was an earlier attempt by the Jenkins Committee, Cmnd.1749 (1962), paras 499, 503 to introduce a "reckless trading" provision along similar lines to the provision in the Insolvency Act 1986, s.214.

[36] See Ch. 10 from 10–69.

[37] See Ch. 5 from 5–05. See also the Fraud Act 2006 s.9.

[38] For a colourful description of the practice see I.F. Fletcher, "The Genesis of Modern Insolvency Law—An Odyssey of Law Reform" [1987] J.B.L. 365.

[39] Report of the Jenkins Committee, Cmnd.1749 (1962), para.80.

by introducing discretionary disqualification for unfit conduct in the Insolvency Act 1976. This provision had little tangible impact and it was replaced, on the recommendation of the Cork Committee, by what is now s.6 of the CDDA.[40] It is clear that this reform was inspired to a considerable extent by the Cork Committee's preoccupation with the phoenix syndrome. This is confirmed by the following extract taken from Ch. 45 of the Cork Committee's report, the main chapter setting out its proposals for strengthening the disqualification regime:

> "We have received many proposals for increasing the severity with which the directors of insolvent companies should be treated. It has been made evident to us that there is a widespread dissatisfaction at the ease with which a person trading through the medium of one or more companies with limited liability can allow such a company to become insolvent, form a new company, and then carry on trading much as before, leaving behind him a trail of unpaid creditors, and often repeating the process several times. The dissatisfaction is greatest where the director of an insolvent company has set up business again, using a similar name for the new company, and trades with assets purchased at a discount from the liquidator of the old company."[41]

Again, the CDDA should be seen as one aspect of the legislative response to the phoenix syndrome, operating in tandem with other reforms introduced in the mid-eighties such as the compulsory licensing of insolvency practitioners (under Part XIII of the Insolvency Act 1986) and the prohibition (in s.216 of the same Act) on the re-use of a company's name where that company has gone into insolvent liquidation.[42] Contemporary concerns about phoenix sales have been voiced in the light of the rise in usage of pre-packaged administrations or "pre-packs".[43]

Enterprise, regulation and the wider objectives of the CDDA

2–13 As has been seen, much of the rhetoric in the official reports is directed at abuses of limited liability that occur within owner-managed and so-called "one-man" private companies. It can be concluded from this that one of the main objects of the CDDA as originally conceived (along with a series of other measures now to be found in the Insolvency Act 1986) was to protect creditors of small, owner-managed, limited companies. The disqualification regime is therefore in part designed to address problems that have emerged in the wake of the phenomenon of

[40] See from 1–40. The limited impact of the 1976 Act provision can probably be attributed, at least in part, to the absence of government funding for the taking of appropriate proceedings.

[41] Report of the Review Committee, Cmnd.8558, para.1813.

[42] For the operation of s.216, which, in practice, captures more than just the "phoenix" behaviour described see, e.g. *Thorne v Silverleaf* [1994] 2 B.C.L.C. 637 ;*Ricketts v Ad Valorem Factors* [2003] EWCA Civ 1706, [2004] 1 All E.R. 894; *Archer Structures Ltd v Griffiths* [2003] EWHC 957 (Ch), [1994] 1 B.C.L.C. 201. The provision has been used aggressively by Revenue and Customs: see also *Inland Revenue Commissioners v Nash* [2003] EWHC 686 (Ch), [2004] B.C.C. 150; *Revenue and Customs Commissioners v Walsh* [2005] EWCA Civ 1291, [2006] B.C.C. 431; *Revenue and Customs Commissioners v Benton-Diggins* [2006] EWHC 793 (Ch), [2006] 2 B.C.L.C. 255. On the regulation of insolvency practitioners see V. Finch, "Insolvency Practitioners: Regulation and Reform" [1998] J.B.L. 334 and *Corporate Insolvency Law: Perspectives and Principles,* 2nd edn (Cambridge University Press, 2009), Ch.5. The Company Law Review Steering Group proposed further reforms to tackle the issue: see *Final Report* (June 2001), paras 15.55–15.77 and discussion in Ch. 5 at 5–51.

[43] See, e.g. P. Walton, "Pre-packaged administrations—trick or treat" (2006) 19(8) Insolv. Int. 113.

mass incorporation of private companies during the last century.[44] The CDDA's response to the trader who abuses the privilege of limited liability is to remove that trading privilege. The disqualified trader is prohibited from running a limited company and under CDDA s.15 he is personally liable for the debts of any company which he runs during the period of his disqualification in breach of the prohibition. At the same time, however, it is notable that disqualification operates as an ex post facto measure. It is directed at those who have taken the opportunity to trade with the benefit of limited liability but who have then been found wanting in some respect. In seeking to strike a balance between the facilitative and regulatory aspects of company law, Parliament has administered a dose of regulation while continuing to trumpet the virtue of the limited company as a vehicle for business and the necessity of preserving relatively free access to limited liability as a means of encouraging enterprise. For all the complaints in official reports about the evils of under-capitalised companies,[45] proposals to curb abuse by increasing the price payable for the benefit of limited liability on incorporation, or through the imposition of some other form of entry requirement have been routinely rejected. One illustration of this is the short shrift consistently given to proposals to introduce a minimum share capital requirement for private companies.[46] Thus, the CDDA can be seen as a legislative attempt to regulate abuse of limited liability within an overall legal framework which offers limited liability "on tap" and thereby continues to encourage the proliferation of private limited companies.[47] The underlying policy assumption is that limited companies are more of a "good thing" than a "bad thing" and that the purpose of regulation is to encourage the responsible use of limited liability without in any way discouraging enterprise.[48]

[44] The impression that the CDDA is primarily a mechanism to regulate malpractice in small private companies is confirmed by the rhetoric of enforcement used in government press releases in which references to "rogue" or "cowboy" directors who take advantage of limited liability to "rip off" creditors and consumers predominate. A former senior judge expressed a similar view of the CDDA extra-judicially: see Lord Hoffmann, "The Fourth Annual Leonard Sainer Lecture" (1997) 18 Co. Law. 194. For adverse judicial comment on a "gung ho" press release issued by the old Department of Trade and Industry see *Re Uno Plc and World of Leather Plc, Secretary of State for Trade and Industry v Gill* [2004] EWHC 933 (Ch), [2006] B.C.C. 725 at [172]–[174].

[45] See para.2–09 above.

[46] See, e.g. Report of the Committee on Company Law Amendment (the Cohen Committee), Cmd. 6659 (1945), para.57; Company Law Review Steering Group, *The Strategic Framework* (February 1999), para.5.2.12. The UK's lack of a minimum capital requirement has made it an attractive location for businesses based in other parts of the European Union to incorporate offshore, a practice sanctioned by the ECJ on grounds of freedom of establishment. See, in particular, Case C-212/97 *Centros Ltd v Erhvervs- og Selskabsstyrelsen* [1999] E.C.R. I-1459 and discussion in R. Drury, "The 'Delaware Syndrome': European Fears and Reactions" [2005] J.B.L. 709.

[47] See A. Hicks, "Corporate Form: Questioning the Unsung Hero" [1997] J.B.L. 306 and *Disqualification of Directors: No Hiding Place for the Unfit* (A.C.C.A Research Report No. 59, 1998). Limited liability is also embedded within more recently developed forms of business organisation such as limited liability partnerships.

[48] There was considerable emphasis in the parliamentary debates on what became the CDDA on the need to encourage directors to monitor closely the financial circumstances of their businesses in the interests of creditors. See, e.g. Hansard H.C. Vol. 78, cols 142, 145. Indeed, the CDDA also reinforces various provisions of company law which already carry criminal sanctions, e.g. the requirement to keep proper books of account and financial records, a point taken up in Ch. 5.

2–14 The impression that the legal framework is weighted in favour of enterprise over regulation is confirmed by the structure of the CDDA itself. Not surprisingly, the CDDA does not condemn business failure per se. This is entirely in keeping with the modern view, reflected in the insolvency provisions of the Enterprise Act 2002, that business failure should not be stigmatised and the current emphasis of policy on business rescue and debtor rehabilitation.[49] Instead, the CDDA focuses on issues of individual misconduct within companies and business failure is merely one context in which that enquiry is carried out.[50] The Act also confers statutory power on the courts to grant a disqualified person permission to act as a director of a specified company or companies. The courts, therefore, have scope to balance the risk to the public of allowing the disqualified person to remain involved in the management of companies against the risk that, if he is not so involved, beneficial economic activity may be stifled.[51] Another point that illustrates the careful balance being struck is the absence of any re-entry requirement once the period of disqualification expires. When a CDDA disqualification lapses, the previously disqualified person is immediately free to recommence corporate activity unconditionally and without having to demonstrate that he has learned his lesson.[52] In summary, it is clear from its historical background and development that one of the main purposes of the CDDA is to combat abuse of limited liability and promote a culture of responsibility (in which limited liability is regarded as a privilege) within an overall legal framework which seeks to preserve open and broadly unqualified access to limited liability.

2–15 However, the CDDA is not exclusively concerned with regulating abuse of limited liability in the interests of creditors of limited companies. Two important points can be made. First, as a scheme of regulation, the CDDA is capable of embracing the protection of a number of company stakeholders such as shareholders, consumers and employees as well as creditors. Secondly, it is apparent from the structure of the legislation and the decided cases that the CDDA is a

[49] See, e.g. *Bankruptcy: A Fresh Start* (Insolvency Service, 2000); the White Paper, *Productivity and Enterprise—Insolvency: A Second Chance*, Cmnd.5234 (2001) and the Company Law Review Steering Group's discussion of phoenix companies in *Completing the Structure* (November 2000) from para.13.102 and in Volume I of the *Final Report* from para.15.55.

[50] Automatic disqualification for directors involved with failed companies was categorically rejected by Parliament: see 1–43 to 1–44. Furthermore, the Secretary of State must be satisfied that the public interest will be served before bringing disqualification proceedings: see, e.g. CDDA s.7(1). This reflects the point that while business failure should not be condemned, the investigation of its causes is a matter of public interest: see discussion in Ch. 1 and *Re Pantmaenog Timber Co Ltd* [2003] UKHL 49, [2004] 1 A.C. 158.

[51] On permission to act generally, see Ch.15.

[52] This is true even of a person who has been disqualified by the courts more than once. Thus, there is some emphasis in the law on encouraging entrepreneurs to try again in the hope that they have learned the lessons of previous business failures, an emphasis that is also reflected in modern bankruptcy law: see further Ch. 11. The assumption that a director deemed unfit to act at the point of disqualification should automatically be deemed fit to act at the point when the period of disqualification expires has been questioned by the courts: see, in particular, obiter comments of Warner J. in *Re Western Welsh International System Buildings Ltd* (1988) 4 B.C.C. 449 at 451; *Re New Generation Engineers Ltd* [1993] B.C.L.C. 435 at 440–441; *Re Moorgate Metals Ltd, Official Receiver v Huhtala* [1995] B.C.C. 143 at 154.

broad-based regulatory scheme that seeks to raise standards of probity, competence and commercial morality, not just in companies, but across a range of organisations and institutions.

The CDDA and the protection of wider constituencies

Shareholder/investor protection

2–16 The unfit conduct provisions in CDDA ss.6–9 seek, in part, to protect shareholders. In determining whether a director is unfit for the purposes of ss.6 and 8, the court must have regard (among other things) to any misfeasance or breach of any fiduciary or other duty by the director in relation to the company and any misapplication or retention by the director of, or any conduct by the director giving rise to an obligation to account for, any money or other property of the company.[53] Such duties operate to protect shareholders as well as creditors. Furthermore, it is a prerequisite to proceedings under s.8 that information or documents have come into the possession of the Secretary of State following the exercise of one or more specified inquisitorial powers contained in companies and financial services legislation. These powers (which include the powers of company investigation still to be found in Pt XIV of the Companies Act 1985 now further reinforced by the Companies (Audit, Investigations and Community Enterprise) Act 2004) are broad in scope and their rationale embraces the protection of shareholders as well as creditors.[54] The power in CDDA s.2 has also been directed at misconduct, the impact of which is felt principally by investors, such as insider dealing.[55]

Consumer protection

2–17 The unfit conduct provisions in CDDA ss.6–9 have, to some extent, a consumer protection rationale. This is because, in determining whether a director is unfit for the purposes of s.6 (and s.8, if the relevant company is insolvent), the court must have regard to the extent of the defendant director's responsibility for any failure by the company to supply any goods or services which have been paid for (in whole or in part).[56] The acceptance of customer deposits or pre-payments or the failure to safeguard the same are, in appropriate circumstances, capable of amounting to unfit conduct under the CDDA.[57] Disqualification on competition law grounds under CDDA s.9A aims to protect the public, including consumers, from anti-competitive practices. Many of the offences created by consumer protection legislation are also capable of falling within the scope of CDDA s.2.[58]

[53] CDDA s.9, Sch.1, Pt I, paras 1–2.

[54] For cases which illustrate the use of disqualification for purposes of shareholder protection, see, e.g. *Re Godwin Warren Control Systems Plc* [1993] B.C.L.C. 80 and *Re Looe Fish Ltd* [1993] B.C.L.C. 1160.

[55] See Ch.10, especially 10–22 and 10–37.

[56] CDDA s.9, Sch.1, Pt II, para.7.

[57] See 5–56.

[58] See Ch. 10, especially paras 10–31 to 10–32.

Employee protection

2–18 The unfit conduct provisions in CDDA ss.6–9 are capable of being used for the purposes of employee protection. Section 172 of the Companies Act 2006[59] requires directors, in connection with their duty to promote the success of the company, to have regard to (among other things), the interests of the company's employees. The duty is circumscribed, in that it is owed to the company rather than to employees directly, and by the overall terms of the statement of the duty itself. However, a breach of the duty can be taken into account in disqualification proceedings under ss.6 and 8. This is because the court is required in such proceedings to have regard to "any . . . breach of any fiduciary or other duty by the director in relation to the company"[60] which would clearly encompass a breach of s.172, as regards employees. CDDA s.2 also provides an additional tool of enforcement in the context of health and safety at work. The apparent failure in the past to use CDDA s.2 as an additional sanction following successful health and safety prosecutions, and the encouragement to use it in the future, was highlighted by the work of Alan Neal and Frank Wright of the University of Warwick in 2005, subsequently published by the Health and Safety Executive in the form of a report in 2007.[61]

The CDDA and protection of the public: raising standards of probity and competence

2–19 As discussed further below, the strong consensus that emerges from the case law is that the CDDA is concerned broadly with public protection and that protection is achieved: (a) by prohibiting the defendant from taking part in the management of companies; (b) by deterring the defendant from future misconduct; and (c) through general deterrence, i.e. by encouraging other directors to behave properly.[62] Clearly, public protection, in this sense, is capable of extending beyond creditor protection to encompass the protection of the other constituencies mentioned above, namely, shareholders, consumers and employees. Moreover, it is clear from high profile cases such as *Re Atlantic Computers Plc, Secretary of State for Trade and Industry v Ashman*[63] and *Re Barings Plc (No.5), Secretary of State for Trade and Industry v Baker*[64] that, while many disqualifications are of small traders who abuse limited liability, the concerns of the CDDA do extend beyond abuse of limited liability and creditor protection to encompass wider

[59] Formerly s.309 of the Companies Act 1985.

[60] CDDA s.9, Sch.1, Pt I, para.1.

[61] A. Neal and F. Wright, *A survey of the use and effectiveness of the Company Directors Disqualification Act 1986 as a legal sanction against directors convicted of health and safety offences*, Health and Safety Executive, Research Report RR597 (HSE Books, 2007), *http://www.hse.gov.uk/research/rrhtm/rr597.htm* [Accessed August 19, 2009].

[62] See, in particular, *Re Westmid Packing Services Ltd, Secretary of State for Trade and Industry v Griffiths* [1998] 2 All E.R. 124 at 131–132 (cited in 2–28 below).

[63] June 15, 1998, Ch. D, unreported.

[64] [1999] 1 B.C.L.C. 433. See also *Re Continental Assurance Co of London Plc* [1997] 1 B.C.L.C. 48; *Re Landhurst Leasing Plc, Secretary of State for Trade and Industry v Ball* [1999] 1 B.C.L.C. 286.

notions of probity and competence. *Atlantic* and *Barings* make clear that, in an appropriate case, the courts will disqualify a director who is incompetent in discharging his functions.[65] The upshot is that the application of the CDDA is not necessarily confined to cases involving "abuse of limited liability" in the sense that that phrase is usually understood (i.e. misconduct by directors in small, owner-managed companies that causes harm to creditors) nor to cases involving "commercial immorality" if that term is taken to encompass some want of probity or culpable misconduct but to exclude serious incompetence.[66] Although one may quibble with the use of the phrase "limited liability", it is interesting to note the words of the Comptroller and Auditor General in his report on the operation of the CDDA published in 1999:

> "The disqualification arrangements help to promote confidence and risk-taking in the market, by assuring those who do business with limited liability companies that directors who are unfit will be disqualified from being involved in the management of those companies. If unfit directors were able to continue in business without the sanction of disqualification, confidence in the market would be undermined."[67]

2–20 Nevertheless, there is considerable justification for the view that the disqualification regime is not concerned solely with abuse of limited liability in the CDDA itself. A number of points can be made about the scope and wording of the legislation:

(1) The meaning of "company" in the CDDA is not confined to private limited companies but clearly encompasses all forms of registered companies including public companies, companies limited by guarantee and unlimited companies. A wide variety of misconduct affecting companies of all shapes and sizes is therefore capable of being considered. Given that unlimited companies are within its scope, the CDDA clearly contemplates that there may be circumstances in which the director of an unlimited company could be liable to disqualification. The disqualification of such a person cannot be based on abuse of limited liability and must therefore be based on some broader failure of stewardship/management including (without limitation) lack of probity and/or incompetence.

(2) The meaning of "company" in the CDDA is not confined to registered companies but is expressly extended by primary and secondary legislation to a wide range of different organisations and institutions.[68] So, for example, disqualification jurisdiction can be exercised over directors or officers

[65] See further Chs 4 and 5.

[66] On the general approach of the courts in determining whether relevant conduct makes a person unfit, see discussion in Ch.4.

[67] Comptroller and Auditor General, *Company Director Disqualification—A Follow-up Report*, H.C. 424 (London: HMSO, 1999).

[68] On the wide meaning of the term "company" in the CDDA see, in particular, Chs 3 (from 3–73) and 14 (from 14–10). The width of the term has implications both for the scope of the disqualification jurisdiction and the scope of the prohibitions that are imposed on a disqualified person.

of building societies, incorporated friendly societies, NHS foundation trusts, limited liability partnerships, open-ended investment companies and insolvent partnerships. Of these, only limited liability partnerships are designed to confer limited liability on the owner-managers of a business. It is also significant to note that where an ordinary trading partnership is wound up as an unregistered company, the court has power to disqualify a partner on the grounds that his conduct as an officer of the partnership makes him unfit to be concerned in the management of a company.[69] Again, such disqualification would have to be based on misconduct other than abuse of limited liability.

(3) The wider concerns of the CDDA are illustrated further by the competition disqualification provisions contained in ss.9A to 9E. The enquiry in s.9A is an enquiry as to whether the director's conduct, in relation to a breach of competition law, is such as to make him unfit to be concerned in management of a company.

In the light of these points, it is clear that the CDDA is directed not merely (as its history and evolution might indicate) at those who abuse the privilege of limited liability but broadly at those who act improperly in the management of companies and other entities.

2–21 The notion that disqualification should be regarded as a broad regulatory technique for setting and raising standards of managerial conduct is further reinforced by the bankruptcy restrictions regime in Sch.4A of the Insolvency Act 1986. A person who is the subject of bankruptcy restrictions is prohibited, amongst other things, from acting as a director or taking part in the management of a company without the permission of the court. Bankruptcy restrictions can be imposed on the basis of a wide range of conduct occurring before or after the making of the bankruptcy order. Such conduct could, for example, include trading at a time before the commencement of the bankruptcy when the bankrupt knew or ought to have known that he was unable to pay his debts.[70] It may be argued that such conduct is, in a sense, an abuse of limited liability in that once bankrupt, an individual is released from his bankruptcy debts and the claims of creditors can only lie against the bankruptcy estate. At the same time, however, the manner in which disqualifications are imposed through the bankruptcy restrictions regime reflects the more general point that the conduct of individuals who trade without limited liability may cause as much harm to the public as the conduct of those who trade through the medium of a limited company. The same points apply as regards the debt relief restrictions regime introduced by the Tribunal, Courts and Enforcement Act 2007 which extends the bankruptcy restrictions model to debtors who have the benefit of a moratorium by virtue of a debt relief order made under Part 7A of the Insolvency Act 1986 (ss.251A–251X).

[69] See 3–83 and 4–44.
[70] See Insolvency Act 1986 Sch.4A, para.2(2)(g) and, generally, Ch. 11.

THE NATURE OF THE DISQUALIFICATION PROCESS

The regulatory technique

2–22 In what follows, attention is turned to the nature of disqualification as a regulatory process. The starting point is to consider the form of regulatory technique employed in the CDDA. As framed, the CDDA creates a series of civil powers of disqualification which give rise to a civil remedy by way of an injunction restraining the disqualified person from acting in particular capacities.[71] The prohibition is not formally a criminal sanction but if the disqualified person breaches the prohibition in any way the breach can be visited by the criminal penalties in CDDA ss.13–14. This type of legislative technique—namely the provision of a civil remedy by way of statutory injunction backed by criminal penalties for breach—is now used to tackle a number of pressing social problems such as domestic violence, football hooliganism, trespassory assembly and anti-social behaviour. As a matter of domestic law, the process employed in all of these forms of proceeding, including directors' disqualification, is a civil process and the prohibition imposed as a result of such proceedings does not of itself amount to a criminal conviction. The development of the process has been conveniently explained, with particular reference to anti-social behaviour orders, by Lord Steyn:

> "[17] . . . Before 1998 Parliament had, on a number of occasions, already used the technique of prohibiting by statutory injunction conduct deemed to be unacceptable and making a breach of the injunction punishable by penalties. It may be that the Company Directors Disqualification Act 1986 was the precedent for subsequent use of the technique. The civil remedy of disqualification enabled the court to prohibit a person from acting as a director: section 1(1) of the 1986 Act: *R. v Secretary of State for Trade and Industry, ex. parte McCormick* [1998] B.C.C. 379, 395C-F; *Official Receiver v Stern* [2000] 1 W.L.R. 2230. Breach of the order made available criminal penalties: sections 13 and 14 of the 1986 Act. In 1994 Parliament created the power to prohibit trespassory assemblies which could result in serious disruption affecting communities, movements, and so forth: see s.70 of the Criminal Justice and Public Order Act 1994 which amended Part II of the Public Order Act 1986 by inserting section 14A. Section 14B which was introduced by the 1994 Act, created criminal offences in respect of breaches. In the field of family law, statute created the power to make residence orders, requiring a defendant to leave a dwelling house; or non molestation orders, requiring a defendant to abstain from threatening an associated person: sections 33(3), (4) and 42 of the Family Law Act 1996. The penalty for breach is punishment for contempt of court. The Housing Act 1996 created the power to grant injunctions against anti-social behaviour: section 152; section 153 (breach). This was, however, a power severely restricted in respect of locality. A broadly similar technique was adopted in the Protection from Harassment Act 1997: section 3; section 3(6) (breach). Post-dating the Crime and Disorder Act 1998, which is the subject matter of the present appeals, Parliament adopted a similar model in sections 14A and 14J (breach) of the Football Spectators Act 1989, inserted by section 1(1) of and Sch.1 to the Football (Disorder) Act 2000: *Gough v Chief Constable of the Derbyshire Constabulary* [2002] Q.B. 459. In all these cases the requirements for the granting of the statutory injunction depend on the criteria specified in the particular statute. The unifying element is, however,

[71] This is true even where the powers of disqualification in CDDA ss.2 and 5 are exercised by the criminal courts: see 2–30 and from 10–79.

the use of the civil remedy of an injunction to prohibit conduct considered to be utterly unacceptable, with a remedy of criminal penalties in the event of disobedience.

[18] There is no doubt that Parliament intended to adopt the model of a civil remedy of an injunction, backed up by criminal penalties, when it enacted section 1 of the Crime and Disorder Act 1998. The view was taken that the proceedings for an anti-social behaviour order would be civil and would not attract the rigour of the inflexible and sometimes absurdly technical hearsay rule which applies in criminal cases. If this supposition was wrong, in the sense that Parliament did not objectively achieve its aim, it would inevitably follow that the procedure for obtaining anti-social behaviour orders is completely or virtually unworkable and useless. If that is what the law decrees, so be it. My starting point is, however, an initial scepticism of an outcome which would deprive communities of their fundamental rights: see *Brown v Stott* [2003] 1 A.C. 681, per Lord Bingham of Cornhill, at p.704E-F; per Lord Hope of Craighead, at pp.718G, 719B-C; my judgment, at p.707G-H."[72]

Classifying disqualification proceedings: protection of the public or punishment of the individual?

2–23 An enduring question that surfaces from time to time in the case law is whether the primary purpose of disqualification is to protect the public from those who act improperly or to punish such persons for their past misconduct. In this context, the use of the terms "punishment" and "protection" as mutually exclusive terms, to some extent begs the question and conceals the heart of the issue. In jurisprudential terms, it is usual to discuss "punishment" by reference to a range of societal objectives such as retribution, deterrence and the protection of the public in the sense of keeping the person "punished" out of circulation, for example, by imprisonment (or in the disqualification context, away from company management).[73] In order to address the question of whether disqualification is "punitive" or "protective", as if the two were mutually exclusive, it is important to identify what is meant by "punitive". If by that term what is meant is "retributive", then it may be fairly easy to draw the conclusion that the legislation is not "punitive". This assumes that the legislation does in fact fulfil a "deterrent" function.[74] However, it is not clear that this takes matters much further forward. As Lord Steyn has observed:

> "The aim of the criminal law is not punishment for its own sake but to permit everyone to go about their daily lives without fear of harm to person or property."[75]

2–24 The "punishment/protection" debate in the context of disqualification has essentially been concerned with the question of whether, in substance and rather than form, disqualification functions as a criminal process or a "quasi-criminal" process

[72] See *R. (on the application of McCann) v Crown Court at Manchester* [2002] UKHL 39, [2003] 1 A.C. 787 at [17]–[18]. The case itself was concerned with the admissibility of hearsay evidence on an application for an anti-social behaviour order under the Crime and Disorder Act 1998 s.1.

[73] On the rationales for criminal sentencing, see generally A. Ashworth, *Sentencing & Criminal Justice*, 4th edn (Cambridge University Press, 2005), Ch. 3; M. Maguire, R. Morgan and R. Renier (eds.), *The Oxford Handbook of Criminology*, 4th edn (2007).

[74] On the judicial claim that the CDDA has deterrence objectives see further from 2–26 below.

[75] See *R. (on the application of McCann) v Crown Court at Manchester* [2003] 1 A.C. 787 at [17].

that just happens to be administered by the civil courts. Within the terms of the protection/punishment distinction, if it can be said, on balance, that disqualification is a form of quasi-criminal process and sanction, concerned primarily with punishing the individual, a number of legal consequences may flow. In particular, there would be implications for such matters as the formulation of the allegations or "charges",[76] the standard of proof, the admissibility of certain types of evidence (such as hearsay evidence, character evidence and compelled evidence), the construction of the legislation (especially the scope of the prohibitions)[77] and costs.[78] Moreover, any differences of judicial opinion as to whether disqualification should be classified in substance as a civil regulatory or quasi-criminal process may lead to difficulties and inconsistencies in the application of the CDDA.[79]

2–25 The practical impact of different approaches to classification is illustrated by *Re Cedac Ltd, Secretary of State for Trade and Industry v Langridge*.[80] This case was concerned with a short point arising from the Secretary of State's failure to comply with the procedural requirements of CDDA s.16(1). Section 16(1) requires the Secretary of State to give the prospective defendant in disqualification proceedings under s.6 at least 10 days' notice of his intention to commence such proceedings.[81] In *Cedac*, the defendant had received the 10-day notice on April 11, 1989 and the proceedings were subsequently issued on April 21, 1989. However, it was established in the earlier case of *Re Jaymar Management Ltd*[82] that the period of 10 days must be calculated by excluding both the day on which the notice is given and the day on which proceedings are to be commenced: i.e. the requirement is for a period of 10 days' clear notice. Accordingly, the notice

[76] See, e.g. *Re Finelist Ltd, Secretary of State for Trade and Industry v Swan* [2003] EWHC 1780 (Ch), [2004] B.C.C. 877.

[77] On the principle that penal legislation should be strictly construed in favour of the defendant see, e.g. *R. v Allen* [1985] A.C. 1029 at 1034 and *R. v Clarke* [1985] A.C. 1037 at 1048, 1053.

[78] See, e.g. A. Walters, "Directors' Disqualification: The Vice-Chancellor's Address to the Chancery Bar Association" (2000) 21 Co. Law. 90 (discussing the view expressed extra-judicially by Scott V.C. as he then was to the effect that the costs rules applicable in criminal litigation should be applied to civil disqualification proceedings) and, generally for arguments in favour of a quasi-criminal classification, J. Dine, *Criminal Law in the Company Context* (Dartmouth, 1995), "Wrongful Trading—Quasi-Criminal Law" in H. Rajak (ed.), *Insolvency Law: Theory and Practice* (London: Sweet and Maxwell, 1993), "The Disqualification of Company Directors" (1988) 9 Co. Law. 213 and "Punishing Directors" [1994] J.B.L. 325.

[79] See further V. Finch, "Disqualification of Directors: A Plea for Competence" (1990) 53 M.L.R. 385, "Disqualifying Directors: Issues of Rights, Privileges and Employment" (1993) 22 Industrial L.J. 35 and *Corporate Insolvency Law: Perspectives and Principles,* 2nd edn (Cambridge University Press, 2009), Ch.16 from p.716. Finch draws a distinction between a "rights" approach and a "privilege" approach to disqualification. On the "rights" approach, disqualification amounts to a serious interference with the individual's right to carry on business through the medium of a limited company which can only be justified on grounds of culpable (i.e. deliberate, reckless or grossly negligent) conduct and should be attended by the procedural safeguards typically associated with the criminal process. On the "privilege" approach, the ability to incorporate and manage a company (especially a limited company) is seen as a privilege to be exercised in the public interest. Accordingly, disqualification amounts to a withdrawal of the privilege by means of civil process that can be justified by the need to protect the public.

[80] [1991] Ch. 402.

[81] On s.16(1) generally, see Ch.7.

[82] [1990] B.C.C. 303.

should have been served no later than April 10, 1989. The short question was: did this failure to comply strictly with s.16(1) invalidate the proceedings or, alternatively, was it merely a procedural irregularity that could be overlooked?[83] The question received two different answers. A majority of the Court of Appeal held that s.16(1) was directory rather than mandatory and that, as a consequence, the failure to comply did not render the proceedings a nullity. In a powerful dissenting judgment, Nourse L.J. took the opposite view. What is clear is that these two opposing conclusions stemmed from differing views about the nature of the disqualification process itself. The emphasis in the majority judgments is firmly on the idea that disqualification is a non-penal process primarily concerned with protecting the public and withdrawing the privilege of limited liability from those who abuse it.[84] Thus, while the majority accepted that the object of s.16(1) was to provide some form of protection to the individual, they gave much greater priority to the broader public interest than to the issue of individual rights in striking an overall balance. Taking this approach, Legatt L.J. was content to characterise the 10-day notice as one which was "intended to inform of intentions rather than protect rights".[85] By way of contrast, Nourse L.J. regarded disqualification as "a substantial interference with the individual's freedom to do the job which he has chosen to do".[86] It followed that he was unhappy to reach a conclusion which in any way diminished the protection potentially afforded to the individual by s.16(1).[87] The Court of Appeal decision in *Cedac* shows how the question of classification can influence the way in which cases under the CDDA are decided. The court's conclusion about the status of the s.16(1) requirement and the weight to be given to procedural safeguards turned ultimately on Balcombe and Legatt L.JJ.'s view of disqualification as essentially non-penal. It follows that there may be scope for subtle differences in judicial approach arising from different conceptions of disqualification and its impact.

Protection of the public through incapacitation and deterrence

2–26 Taken as a whole, the authorities (and, in particular, those on CDDA ss.6 and 8) suggest that there is a judicial consensus in favour of the view that disqualification is primarily protective rather than penal. At the same time, the courts generally concede that disqualification does have potentially serious consequences for the disqualified person. The following oft-cited passage from

[83] In the immediate context of the case, this was an important question. If the proceedings were invalid, the Secretary of State could only have then commenced fresh proceedings with the permission of the court as the two-year time limit in s.7(2) for the commencement of proceedings under s.6 had long since expired.

[84] For a flavour, see the extract from Balcombe L.J.'s judgment cited below in 2–27.

[85] [1991] Ch. 402 at 420.

[86] [1991] Ch. 402 at 422.

[87] Nourse L.J. would, however, have been prepared to give permission for fresh proceedings to be commenced out of time. Note that in deciding the case at first instance, Mummery J. had adopted a similar line to that taken by Nourse L.J.: see [1990] B.C.C. 555. For criticism of the majority view, see Dine, "Wrongful Trading—Quasi-Criminal Law?" in H. Rajak (ed.), *Insolvency Law: Theory and Practice* (London: Sweet and Maxwell, 1993), pp.175–176.

Browne-Wilkinson V.C.'s judgment in *Re Lo-Line Electric Motors Ltd* reflects the point well:

> "The primary purpose of [s.6 disqualification] is not to punish the individual but to protect the public against the future conduct of companies by persons whose past records as directors of insolvent companies have shown them to be a danger to creditors and others. Therefore the power is not fundamentally penal. But if the power to disqualify is exercised, disqualification does involve a substantial interference with the freedom of the individual. It follows that the rights of the individual must be fully protected."[88]

Although *Lo-line* was decided under the Companies Act 1985 s.300, the statutory predecessor of CDDA s.6, it has been referred to with approval in several s.6 cases.[89] Thus, there is clear acceptance, if any be needed, that disqualification is essentially protective but involves an interference with the liberty of the person. However, as *Cedac* demonstrates, there may be less agreement about the extent and seriousness of the interference and the weight to be given to "individual rights".[90]

2–27 According to the cases, the CDDA seeks to protect the public in broadly two ways. First, the imposition of disqualification legally incapacitates the disqualified person. This is well captured in the following extract from Balcombe L.J.'s judgment in *Cedac*[91]:

> "In my judgment the scope and purpose of the [CDDA] is clear. The ability to trade through a company with the protection of limited liability and with the use of capital subscribed by third parties, is of great economic advantage and confers considerable privileges upon persons so enabled. These privileges involve corresponding responsibilities and the public—in the form of creditors, shareholders and employees—the order in which I place them is of no significance) needs to be protected from persons whose conduct has shown that they have abused those privileges . . . Accordingly the purpose of the [CDDA] is to protect the public and its scope is the prevention of persons who have previously misconducted themselves in relation to companies, or have otherwise shown themselves as unfit to be concerned in the management of a company from being so concerned."

Secondly, disqualification is said to protect the public because it serves to deter the disqualified person from future misconduct and, through general deterrence, to encourage other directors and managers to behave properly, thereby raising standards of management. The emphasis on deterrence is evident in leading

[88] [1988] Ch. 477 at 486.

[89] See, e.g. *Re Crestjoy Products Ltd* [1990] B.C.L.C. 677; *Re Sevenoaks Stationers (Retail) Ltd* [1991] Ch. 164; *Re Cedac Ltd, Secretary of State for Trade and Industry v Langridge* [1991] Ch. 402; *Re Gibson Davies Ltd* [1995] B.C.C. 11; *Re Living Images Ltd* [1996] B.C.C. 112; *Re Amaron Ltd, Secretary of State for Trade and Industry v Lubrani* [1998] 1 B.C.L.C. 562.

[90] In *Lo-Line*, Browne-Wilkinson described the consequences of disqualification as "penal": [1988] Ch. 477 at 486 and in *Cedac*, Nourse L.J. expressed the view that there is "no inconsistency between a primary purpose of protecting the public and a subsidiary purpose of protecting the individual against whom the order is sought: [1991] Ch. 402 at 422. See also the extra-judicial observations of Lord Hoffmann, "The Fourth Annual Leonard Sainer Lecture" (1997) 18 Co. Law. 194.

[91] [1991] Ch. 402.

authorities such as *Re Grayan Building Services Ltd, Secretary of State for Trade and Industry v Gray* where Henry L.J. had this to say:

> "The concept of limited liability and the sophistication of our corporate law offers great privileges and great opportunities for those who wish to trade under that regime. But the corporate environment carries with it the discipline that those who avail themselves of those privileges must accept the standards laid down and abide by the regulatory rules and disciplines in place to protect creditors and shareholders . . . The Parliamentary intention to improve managerial safeguards and standards . . . is clear. The statutory corporate climate is stricter than it has ever been, and those enforcing it should reflect the fact that Parliament has seen the need for higher standards."[92]

2–28 In the same case, Hoffmann L.J. advanced the view that disqualification for unfit conduct had been made mandatory under CDDA s.6 with the object of general deterrence in mind:

> "The purpose of making disqualification mandatory was to ensure that everyone whose conduct had fallen below the appropriate standard was disqualified for at least two years, whether in the individual case the court thought that this was necessary in the public interest or not. Parliament has decided that it is occasionally necessary to disqualify a company director to encourage the others."[93]

In similar vein, Woolf L.J. made it clear in *Re Westmid Packing Services Ltd, Secretary of State for Trade and Industry v Griffiths* (again, in the context of s.6 proceedings) that the court can make a disqualification order solely for purposes of deterrence:

> "In *Re Lo-Line Electric Motors Ltd* . . . Browne-Wilkinson V.-C. said that the primary purpose of section 300 of the Companies Act 1985 was to protect the public against the future conduct of companies by persons whose past records as directors of insolvent companies showed them to be a danger to creditors and others. That statement has often been approved by this court. But there is often a considerable time lag between the conduct complained of, its discovery and the disqualification proceedings actually coming to the court . . . One result of delay when it does occur is that there are occasions when disqualification must be ordered even though, by reason of the director's recognition of his previous failings and the way he has conducted himself since the conduct complained of, he is in fact no longer a danger to the public at all. In such cases it is no longer necessary for the director to be kept 'off the road' for the protection of the public, but other factors come into play in the wider interests of protecting the public, i.e. a deterrent element in relation to the director himself and a deterrent element as far as other directors are concerned."[94]

Like Henry and Hoffmann L.JJ. in *Grayan*, Nicholls V.C. also laid emphasis on protection of the public through general deterrence in the earlier case of *Re Swift 736 Ltd, Secretary of State for Trade and Industry v Ettinger*. Passing judgment on the defendant's repeated failure across several companies to comply with the

[92] [1995] Ch. 241 at 257.
[93] [1995] Ch. 241 at 253.
[94] [1998] 2 All E.R. 124 at 131–132.

Companies Act requirements to keep proper accounting records and to file accounts and returns, he said:

> "Those who make use of limited liability must do so with a proper sense of responsibility. The directors' disqualification procedure is an important sanction introduced by Parliament to raise standards in this regard. Those who take advantage of limited liability must conduct their companies with due regard to the ordinary standards of commercial morality. They must also be punctilious in observing the safeguards laid down by Parliament for the benefit of others who have dealings with their companies. They must maintain proper books of account and prepare annual accounts; they must file their accounts and returns promptly . . . Those who persistently fail to discharge their statutory obligations in this respect can expect to be disqualified, for an appropriate period of time, from using limited liability as one of the tools of their trade. The business community should be left in no doubt on this score."[95]

It is interesting to note that the Court of Appeal in *Swift* relied on this general approach as a basis for increasing the period of disqualification imposed by the trial judge from three to five years. Several other cases can be cited in support of the view that the CDDA is intended primarily to offer dual protection to the public by incapacitating those who have acted improperly (keeping them "off the road" to use Lord Woolf's phrase) and by encouraging everyone else to act responsibly with a view to raising the overall standard of management within companies.[96]

2–29 The law does not impose any entry requirements on directors. No qualifications are required for becoming a director and directorship is not strictly a profession in the accepted sense. The lack of entry requirements is entirely in keeping with the policy of facilitating enterprise described earlier[97] which promotes easy access to the corporate form and to limited liability. Accordingly, there is considerable cultural resistance, especially in the context of private companies, to the professionalisation of directorship by means of ex ante regulation.[98] The CDDA along with the general law of directors' duties is therefore an important source of managerial standards and discipline, a view reinforced by the repeated emphasis in the cases on public protection and, in particular, on the deterrence aspect of disqualification. Whether disqualification, imposed ex post, does actually deter is

[95] [1993] B.C.L.C. 896 at 899–900.

[96] See, e.g. *Re Blackspur Group Plc, Secretary of State for Trade and Industry v Davies* [1998] 1 W.L.R. 422; *Re Morija Plc, Kluk v Secretary of State for Business, Enterprise and Regulatory Reform* [2007] EWHC 3055 (Ch), [2008] 2 B.C.L.C. 313. A similar view was expressed by the Public Accounts Committee in its critical review of the performance of the Insolvency Service's Disqualification Unit: see *The Insolvency Service Executive Agency: Company Director Disqualification* (London: HMSO, 1993) and the subsequent, more favourable, follow up by the Comptroller and Auditor General, *Company Director Disqualification—A Follow-up Report*, H.C. 424 (London: HMSO, 1999).

[97] See text from 2–04.

[98] *In extremis*, Lightman J. has suggested extra-judicially that directors should be subject to some form of licensing requirement: see "The Challenges Ahead: Address to the Insolvency Lawyers' Association" [1996] J.B.L. 113. The Institute of Directors, an organisation established by royal charter, does offer training programmes leading to the award of "Chartered Director", a qualification described on the Institute's website as "the professional qualification for directors". However, such training is, of course, voluntary rather than mandatory.

a separate and empirical question. There is no conclusive evidence that it does. The use of an ex post deterrence mechanism as a means of imposing managerial discipline has also been questioned on other grounds.[99] Nevertheless, as the passages cited above bear out, the idea that disqualification operates as a deterrent as well as a form of legal incapacitation is engrained in judicial conceptions of disqualification as a regulatory process and it will therefore be of practical importance whenever an issue of classification arises.

Disqualification under CDDA ss.2 and 5

2–30 The authorities discussed thus far have generally been concerned with the civil power to disqualify directors under CDDA s.6. Given that s.6 is merely one gateway to disqualification for improper conduct,[100] there is no reason, in principle, why disqualification under any of the other substantive powers should be distinguished from disqualification under s.6. However, a question arises as to whether powers of disqualification imposed by the criminal courts under CDDA ss.2 and 5 should be classified differently. In his ex tempore judgment in *R. v Young*,[101] Brooke J. stated that disqualification under s.2 (and, by inference, s.5) was "unquestionably a punishment" and that a criminal court exercising disqualification jurisdiction was in "a quite different situation" from a civil court exercising jurisdiction under s.6. These premises can be questioned on the following grounds:

(1) When a criminal court considers disqualifying a person under s.2 or s.5, it is first and foremost exercising jurisdiction under the CDDA. It just so happens that within the scheme of the legislation, this jurisdiction is ancillary to the court's primary criminal jurisdiction. Given the history and evolution of the CDDA and its overall focus on the regulation of misconduct in the corporate context, there seems little justification for saying that disqualification by a criminal court is somehow qualitatively different from disqualification by a civil court. A common approach to disqualification founded primarily on principles of public protection seems more appropriate. This criticism of *Young* can be supported with reference to the unitary features of the legislation identified at the beginning of this chapter. Disqualification by the court under s.2 (and, for that matter, ss.3, 4, 5, 9A and 10) has exactly the same legal consequences as disqualification by the court under s.6. The provisions

[99] See, e.g. A. Hicks, *Disqualification of Directors: No Hiding Place for the Unfit* (A.C.C.A Research Report No.59, 1998) criticising (at pp.76–77) the lack of any requirement to publicise directors' obligations under the law in a systematic way when a director takes up office and the absence of any positive ex ante standards against which directors could be judged in disqualification proceedings. Concerns about the clarity and transparency of directors' obligations also lie at the heart of the Company Law Review Steering Group's proposal for a statutory statement of directors' duties now implemented in Part 10 of the Companies Act 2006. For a further expression of concern about the apparent imbalance between ex ante and ex post mechanisms for regulating managerial conduct see Lord Hoffmann, "The Fourth Annual Leonard Sainer Lecture" (1997) 18 Co. Law. 194.

[100] See 2–02 above.

[101] [1990] 12 Cr. App. Rep.(S.) 262.

should therefore be seen as operating for broadly similar ends. Moreover, the fact that the criminal courts have been given jurisdiction in s.2 (and also s.5) can be seen simply as a device designed to save the necessity of further free-standing civil proceedings. Thus, it is strongly arguable that CDDA powers should properly be classified as civil powers that, for reasons of convenience, can be exercised by criminal courts in limited circumstances.[102]

(2) The power in s.2 is exercisable by the criminal and civil courts. If the principle in *Young* were correct, it would follow that a criminal court exercising the power would be doing something quite different from a civil court exercising the same power. This would be an odd result.[103]

(3) Support for the view that the s.2 power should be regarded as protective rather than punitive can be derived from Commonwealth jurisdictions. Australia, for example, has a provision under which directors are automatically disqualified on being convicted of certain criminal offences. This equivalent to s.2 is regarded by the courts in that jurisdiction as being primarily concerned with protection of the public.[104]

R. v Young is considered further from 10–87. For now it should just be noted in passing that there is no other overt support in the authorities for the notion that the principal purpose of disqualification is to punish directors, notwithstanding the view expressed by Brooke J. in *Young*.

2–31 It is not only in the disqualification context that the exercise of statutory powers is treated as primarily protective or preventative rather than punitive. For example, the same description has been applied to the imposition of anti-social behaviour orders under s.1 of the Crime and Disorder Act 1998.[105] However, and as discussed above, the distinction between "punishment" and "protection" cannot be taken too far. For a start, in practical terms, punishment and protection are not mutually exclusive objectives. Violent criminals are locked up not only to "punish" them and express society's disapproval of their crimes, but also to protect others from their violent tendencies and to deter the criminal, and others, from committing acts of violence in the future. As was effectively acknowledged in *Lo-Line*,[106] the need to protect the public will invariably involve some interference with the freedom of

[102] See *Re Westminster Property Management Ltd (No.1), Official Receiver v Stern (No.1)* [2000] 1 W.L.R. 2230 and, by analogy, *R. v Field & Young* [2002] EWCA Crim 2913, [2003] 1 W.L.R. 882.

[103] This criticism is echoed in more recent cases where it has been suggested that the criminal and civil courts should adopt a common approach to disqualification: see, e.g. dicta in *R. v Cole, Lees & Birch* [1998] 2 B.C.L.C. 234; *Re Land Travel Ltd, Secretary of State for Trade and Industry v Tjolle* [1998] 1 B.C.L.C. 333. See also *R. v Evans* [2000] B.C.C. 901 in which the Court of Appeal (Criminal Division) accepted a submission that "the purpose of disqualification is primarily to protect the public from the dishonest operations of those unfitted to take part in the management of companies, rather than to punish."

[104] See J. Cassidy, "Disqualification of Directors under the Corporations Law" (1995) 13 Company and Securities L.J. 221 and A. Hicks, "Disqualification of Directors—Forty Years On" [1988] J.B.L 27.

[105] See *R. (on the application of McCann) v Crown Court at Manchester* [2003] 1 A.C. 787.

[106] See 2–26 above.

the individual on essentially utilitarian grounds. It would therefore be a fallacy to assume that the exercise of a protective jurisdiction cannot operate punitively. Furthermore, the disqualification process contains elements that are clearly analogous to the imposition of punishment under the criminal law. The point has been explicitly acknowledged by the Court of Appeal in *Re Westmid Packing Services Ltd, Secretary of State for Trade and Industry v Griffiths* where Lord Woolf said:

> "Despite the fact that the courts have said that disqualification is not a 'punishment', in truth the exercise that is being engaged in is little different from any sentencing exercise. The period of disqualification must reflect the gravity of the offence. It must contain deterrent elements. That is what sentencing is all about, and that is what fixing the appropriate period of disqualification is all about."[107]

Within the disqualification process, it may be possible to identify elements of retribution, deterrence and denunciation.[108] A tariff is applied which seeks to tailor the length of the disqualification to the seriousness and degree of the misconduct.[109] As has been seen in cases such as *Grayan* and *Swift*, there are circumstances in which the courts are under a duty to disqualify a person on the basis of past misconduct even though the person no longer presents a risk to the public.[110] It follows that a court may be forced to disqualify a defendant who has learned the lessons of a previous business failure and built a new company which is being run properly and successfully at the date of the hearing. Such disqualifications can be seen as both deterrence-based and denunciatory.[111] Some support for a quasi-criminal classification can therefore be derived from the *Westmid Packing* sentencing analogy.[112] Moreover, few would doubt that other forms of disqualification, such as disqualification from driving a motor vehicle, are essentially penal. *In extremis*, the analogy between civil disqualification and criminal process has led some to argue that disqualification proceedings should be classified for all

[107] [1998] 2 All E.R. 124 at 132.

[108] On these terms, see generally A. Ashworth, *Sentencing & Criminal Justice*, 4th edn (Cambridge University Press, 2005), Ch.3; M. Maguire, R. Morgan and R. Renier (eds.), *The Oxford Handbook of Criminology*, 4th edn (2007).

[109] See, in particular, *Re Sevenoaks Stationers (Retail) Ltd* [1991] Ch. 164, C.A. and discussion in Ch.5 from 5–102. This could be seen as retributive (the "punishment" being tailored to fit the "crime") or it could simply reflect the view that the more serious the misconduct the greater the risk from which the public need protection.

[110] See 2–27 to 2–28. The same logic has been followed in the context of bankruptcy restrictions: see *Randhawa v Official Receiver* [2006] EWHC 2946 (Ch), [2007] 1 W.L.R. 1700.

[111] See further V. Finch, *Corporate Insolvency Law: Perspectives and Principles,* 2nd edn (Cambridge University Press, 2009), Ch.16.

[112] Supporters of the quasi-criminal view might also point to the fact that disqualification imposes wide prohibitions (on which see further Ch.14) on the basis of a public interest justification and the concern that many directors may simply be coerced into accepting disqualification because of their exposure to liability for costs under the civil system. On the latter point see A. Walters, "Directors' Disqualification: The Vice-Chancellor's Address to the Chancery Bar Association" (2000) 21 Co. Law. 90 and Lord Hoffmann, "The Fourth Annual Leonard Sainer Lecture" (1997) 18 Co. Law. 194. For judicial comments on the potential oppressiveness of disqualification as a litigation process see, e.g. *Re Rex Williams Leisure Plc, Secretary of State for Trade and Industry v Warren* [1994] Ch. 350; *Re Land Travel Ltd, Secretary of State for Trade and Industry v Tjolle* [1998] 1 B.C.L.C. 333 and *Re Barings Plc, Secretary of State for Trade and Industry v Baker* [1998] Ch. 356.

purposes as criminal proceedings. Professor Dine, the principal exponent of this view, has found the logic to be irresistible:

> "What is clear from the cases is that the courts regard disqualification as a serious matter. It is therefore disturbing that the classification of disqualification orders is unsettled. If they are akin to criminal sanctions as a number of indications . . . appear to show then the director involved should be entitled to all the protections afforded to defendants in a criminal court, including the presumption of innocence, exact determination of the *mens rea* required, the criminal standard of proof, and the inability of the court to make 'assumptions' about behaviour in the absence of direct evidence."[113]

2–32 However, just because the disqualification process can be likened to criminal sentencing, it does not necessarily follow that disqualification proceedings should be treated for all purposes as if they were criminal proceedings. The process is not only analogous to the exercise of criminal jurisdiction. It can also be likened to an administrative process which, much like a professional body exercising a disciplinary function over its members, operates to remove a trading privilege or licence in the public interest. There is a lot to be said for this civil/regulatory and/or administrative/disciplinary classification. Many areas of business and professional life are regulated by administrative or disciplinary bodies that discharge public law functions. The notion that disqualification is akin to the administrative removal of a trading privilege on public interest grounds is therefore a powerful one even though directorship is not a profession as such. This is a fortiori given that the majority of disqualifications are now imposed, in effect, by administrative fiat, by means of the Secretary of State's powers in CDDA ss.7(2A) and 8(2A) to accept disqualification undertakings in lieu of a disqualification order in proceedings under ss.6 and 8. Moreover, the width of the prohibitions and the impact of disqualification on the disqualified person—points that at first blush seem to favour a criminal classification—may be overstated. Disqualification does not prevent the disqualified person from carrying on in business either as a sole trader or partner, a point that has been emphasised by the courts.[114] Within the scheme of the legislation, it is also possible for the court to grant a disqualified person permission to act in some of the prohibited capacities.[115] So, for example, in a case where the court is obliged to disqualify a person under CDDA s.6 on the basis of his previous misconduct to promote general deterrence even though the individual concerned may no longer pose any risk to the public, it is likely that an application by that person for permission to act in certain prohibited capacities in relation to a specified company or companies will be treated favourably.

[113] J. Dine, "The Disqualification of Company Directors" (1988) 9 Co. Law. 213 at 218.

[114] See, e.g. *Re Chartmore Ltd* [1990] B.C.L.C. 673 at 675; *Re Probe Data Systems Ltd (No. 3), Secretary of State for Trade and Industry v Desai* [1991] B.C.C. 428 at 434; *Re Southbourne Sheet Metal Co Ltd* [1991] B.C.C. 732 at 734.

[115] See generally, Ch. 15. There is no comparable facility where an individual is disqualified from driving a motor vehicle.

2–33 It has already been seen that domestic law classifies disqualification proceedings as civil proceedings.[116] Under the CDDA, a disqualification order or undertaking is a civil injunction rather than a criminal conviction. In a number of cases, the European Court of Human Rights has ruled that CDDA disqualification proceedings affect "civil rights and obligations" but do not involve a "criminal charge" for the purposes of art.6 of the ECHR.[117] This is significant because, while the fair trial guarantee under art.6(1) applies to both criminal and civil proceedings, the additional protections set out in art.6(2) and (3) are generally only applicable to criminal proceedings.[118] In determining whether a particular proceeding involves a criminal charge, the European Court considers three criteria: (a) the classification of the proceedings in domestic law, (b) the nature of the offence and (c) the severity of the penalty which may be imposed.[119] The domestic law classification is never decisive and greater weight is therefore given to the second and third criteria.[120] In applying these criteria, the European Court has consistently ruled that disqualification is a regulatory rather than a criminal matter noting that the penalty is neither a fine nor a prison sentence but rather a prohibition on acting in various capacities without the permission of the court. Although it avoids the logical procedural consequences of the quasi-criminal classification in terms of the presumption of innocence, standard of proof, admissibility of certain forms of evidence, etc. acceptance of the civil regulatory classification does not deprive the director completely of procedural safeguards. Given that disqualification is premised on a public interest justification, the rules of natural justice apply.[121] The director is, of course, also entitled to a fair trial in the determination of his civil rights and obligations under art.6(1) of the ECHR.

2–34 It is suggested that disqualification is a hybrid proceeding[122] that in some respects resembles a criminal process but has been clearly (and deliberately) cast in the form of a specialised civil process. As has been seen, the domestic law classification has been respected by the European Court. There are powerful reasons for upholding the civil regulatory classification. The logic of the quasi-criminal view should be resisted as the importation of criminal process could well undermine the effectiveness of directors' disqualification as a regulatory system bearing in mind the possible impact on such matters as information-gathering and evidence. This concern may well explain why the courts have consistently emphasised the protective aspects of the

[116] See 2–22.

[117] See, e.g. *EDC v United Kingdom* [1998] B.C.C. 370; *Wilson v United Kingdom* (1998) 26 E.H.R.R. CD195; *DC, HS and AD v United Kingdom* [2000] B.C.C. 710; *WGS and MSLS v United Kingdom* [2000] B.C.C. 719. See also *R. v Secretary of State for Trade and Industry Ex. p. McCormick* [1998] B.C.C. 379.

[118] Though see further 2–35.

[119] See, e.g. *Engel v The Netherlands (No. 1)* (1976) 1 E.H.R.R. 647; *Ozturk v Germany* (1984) 6 E.H.R.R. 409; *Schmautzer v Austria* (1996) 21 E.H.R.R. 511.

[120] See, e.g. *Ozturk v Germany* (1984) 6 E.H.R.R. 409; *Steel v United Kingdom* (1998) 28 E.H.R.R. 603.

[121] See *Re Cedac Ltd, Secretary of State for Trade and Industry v Langridge* [1991] Ch. 402.

[122] See *Re Southbourne Sheet Metal Co Ltd* [1991] B.C.C. 732 at 734; *Re Westminster Property Management Ltd (No. 1), Official Receiver v Stern (No. 1)* [2000] 1 W.L.R. 2230 at [27].

jurisdiction. Indeed, in the field of anti-social behaviour orders Lord Steyn specifically adverted to this point as follows:

> "[A]n extensive interpretation of what is a criminal charge under article 6(1) would, by rendering the injunctive process ineffectual, prejudice the freedom of liberal democracies to maintain the rule of law by the use of civil injunctions."[123]

At the same time, however, the peculiar nature of civil disqualification proceedings and the impact of disqualification on the disqualified person may demand a certain degree of procedural subtlety. So, for example, in this respect, the courts have stressed that in some circumstances care may be needed in applying the basic civil standard of proof[124] and that, as a matter of general practice, care should also be taken to avoid the making of hindsight judgments about directorial conduct.[125]

2–35 The classification of disqualification proceedings as a form of "regulatory" proceeding has now been embraced by the courts in England and Wales, which have also stressed that an all or nothing "criminal"/"civil" classification for, by way of example, the purposes of art.6 of the ECHR is too inflexible. Thus in *Re Westminster Property Management Ltd (No. 1), Official Receiver v Stern (No. 1)*,[126] the Court of Appeal accepted that whilst disqualification proceedings were "civil" proceedings for the purposes of art.6, this did not of itself necessarily answer the question that the court might have to face. Some of the requirements of a fair trial spelled out in art.6(2) and (3) could still be brought into play in civil cases. In this context, it was appropriate to regard proceedings as falling within a spectrum, or as representing a hierarchy, with private civil litigation at one end and full-blown criminal proceedings at the other end. Civil proceedings involving the imposition of a penalty by a public authority occupy a position somewhere between these two end stops. The precise requirements of a "fair trial" may vary depending on where the relevant proceedings fall within the spectrum or hierarchy. This point was echoed by Lloyd J. on a later application by Mr Stern for permission to act notwithstanding disqualification:

> "I accept that the purposes for which a disqualification order is made, and is required to be made, include not only the protection of the public, but also deterrence for the respondent and other directors, and in those ways improving standards of corporate management. I do not accept, in response to a submission of Mr Stern, that the deterrent element makes the matter punitive. It seems to me that this is all within the ambit of the regulatory purpose of the legislation, as has been considered by the courts in particular on the preliminary issue in the present case."[127]

[123] *R. (on the application of McCann) v Crown Court at Manchester* [2003] 1 A.C. 787 at [31]. The House of Lords decided that the public interest in curbing anti-social behaviour enshrined in s.1 of the Crime and Disorder Act 1998 would be undermined if evidence obtained from anonymous sources who wished to protect their identities were excluded under the hearsay rule, as would have been the case had the proceedings been classified as "criminal".

[124] See further 7–120.

[125] See further 4–28 and 7–121.

[126] [2000] 1 W.L.R. 2230.

[127] *Re Westminster Property Management Ltd (No. 2). Official Receiver v Stern (No. 2)* [2001] B.C.C. 305 at 358G–H.

2–36 The recognition that "regulatory" proceedings carry with them more protection for a defendant than ordinary private civil proceedings is, at least to some extent, reflected in domestic law by the requirements lying on the Secretary of State as a public authority, for example, the requirement to conduct litigation "fairly".[128] As Henry L.J. put it in the *Stern* case, in the context of the use of compelled evidence:

> ". . . the human rights implications of compelled evidence are not a new or alien importation but are already a familiar issue for judges whose duty it is to safeguard a fair trial."[129]

It is respectfully suggested that the same is true of the human rights implications of disqualification proceedings generally.

SUMMARY AND CONCLUSION

2–37 The first two chapters have provided a background and context for the detailed exposition which follows in the remainder of this book. Three main points have emerged. First, while it is true to say that the directors' disqualification regime has not evolved in a particularly systematic way, the CDDA contains what appears to be a relatively coherent legislative scheme. Secondly, although it appears that directors' disqualification legislation was originally conceived primarily as a creditor protection measure concerned with abuse of limited liability in private companies (a point reflected in the fact that a disqualified person who breaches the prohibition on acting as director of a company is deprived by CDDA s.15 of the protection of corporate personality and limited liability), the CDDA is not restricted to cases involving abuse of limited liability but is directed, in a broad sense, at those who act improperly in the management of companies and other entities. Furthermore, the CDDA is not concerned merely with keeping wrongdoers "off the road", but also with the setting and raising of standards of conduct in the management of companies generally. Finally, it has been seen that the issue of whether disqualification should be classified as a civil regulatory or quasi-criminal process is one that has important ramifications for practice and procedure under the CDDA. Although, for now, the point seems settled firmly in favour of the civil regulatory classification, the question of what procedural safeguards are required in any given case is one that is rarely far from the surface given the hybrid quality of disqualification proceedings.

[128] See, e.g. *Re Finelist Ltd, Secretary of State for Trade and Industry v Swan* [2004] B.C.C. 877 and discussion in Ch.7.
[129] [2000] 1 W.L.R. 2230 at [41].

CHAPTER 3

DISQUALIFICATION FOR UNFIT CONDUCT: PRELIMINARY MATTERS

INTRODUCTION

3–01 The next three chapters examine the core provisions relating to disqualification for unfit conduct contained in CDDA ss.6, 8 and 9. As the majority of disqualification orders are made under CDDA s.6 on the application of either the Secretary of State for Business, Innovation and Skills or the official receiver,[1] these chapters concentrate principally on the elements that must be made out before the court is obliged to make an order under that provision. The present chapter is concerned with the background to, and inception of, disqualification proceedings under CDDA ss.6 and 8 and with a number of preliminary matters of substance that must be established before the court turns to consider the substantive issue of unfit conduct in such proceedings. The most significant element of ss.6 and 8—one that goes to the heart of the CDDA—is the concept of unfit conduct itself. Chs 4 and 5 are devoted to this area of the law.

THE INCEPTION OF SECTION 6 PROCEEDINGS: REPORTING BY OFFICE HOLDERS

Statutory reporting obligations: CDDA s.7(3)

3–02 As will be seen further below, jurisdiction under CDDA s.6 is only triggered where a relevant company or companies[2] "becomes insolvent" (that is, becomes the subject of a prescribed insolvency regime).[3] CDDA s.7(1) provides that an application for a disqualification order under CDDA s.6 can only be made by the Secretary of State or, in the case of a company in compulsory liquidation, by the official receiver if the Secretary of State so directs. In practice, the Insolvency Service discharges the Secretary of State's responsibilities in relation to the commencement and conduct of proceedings brought under s.6.[4] In gathering information about directors of insolvent companies who may be unfit, the

[1] In the context of s.6 proceedings, any reference hereafter to the Secretary of State should be read as including a reference to the official receiver.

[2] "Company" is not restricted to registered companies and includes, inter alia, partnerships, limited partnerships and limited liability partnerships: see from 3–73.

[3] See from 3–98.

[4] The Insolvency Service is an executive agency of the Department of Business, Innovation and Skills Reform. Further details concerning the Insolvency Service's role and responsibilities can be found by visiting its website: *http://www.insolvency.gov.uk/* [Accessed August 19, 2009].

Insolvency Service's Investigations and Enforcement Services division[5] depends substantially on the co-operation of insolvency practitioners and the official receiver.[6] Indeed, in *Re Pantmaenog Timber Co Ltd*, Lord Millett observed that:

> "It has never been the function of the Secretary of State to conduct an investigation or to gather information. He relies on information obtained by others; hence the investigative and reporting duties imposed on the official receiver and the responsible officeholder."[7]

To bring potential unfit conduct to the attention of the Secretary of State, CDDA s.7(3)[8] requires the relevant office holder of a company in liquidation, administration or administrative receivership[9] to report to the Secretary of State forthwith if it appears, as respects a person who is or has been a director of that company, that the conditions mentioned in s.6(1) are satisfied. In other words, the mandatory obligation to report a director arises if it appears to the office holder that the court would be likely to make findings of: (a) insolvency within the meaning of s.6(2);[10] (b) directorship within the meaning of s.6(1)(a); and (c) unfit conduct against the director in the terms of CDDA s.6(1)(b). Thus, the office holder performs an extremely important screening and alerting function that underpins the entire disqualification process.[11] However, the view of the insolvency practitioner is not decisive. It is for the Secretary of State to consider the available evidence and form a view as to whether proceedings should

[5] Created on January 1, 2009 by a merger of the former Investigations and Enforcement directorates and the Companies Investigations Branch. The latter branch had for many years been located within the Department of Trade and Industry but formally became part of the Insolvency Service on April 1, 2006: Insolvency Service, *Annual Report and Accounts 2006–2007* H.C. 752 (London: The Stationery Office, 2007).

[6] The relevant insolvency practitioner will not necessarily be the only source of information. In the disqualification proceedings which followed the administration of Barings Plc, the primary information came from the reports of inspectors appointed in Singapore and the Report of the Board of Banking Supervision H.C.673 (1994–95): see generally *Re Barings Plc (in administration), Secretary of State for Trade and Industry v Baker (No.2)* [1998] 1 B.C.L.C. 590 sub nom. *Re Barings Plc, Secretary of State for Trade and Industry v Baker (No.3)* [1999] B.C.C. 146. In other cases, the Secretary of State may also have the benefit of information and documents obtained pursuant to a power in Pt XIV of the Companies Act 1985, especially in circumstances where the exercise of such a power is a precursor to the compulsory winding up of the relevant company on public interest grounds under the Insolvency Act 1986 s.124A.

[7] [2003] UKHL 49, [2004] 1 A.C. 158 at [68]. Though cf. *Re Launchexcept Ltd, Secretary of State for Trade and Industry v Tillman* [2000] 1 B.C.L.C. 36.

[8] As amended by the Enterprise Act 2002 s.248 and Sch.17, para.42.

[9] Section 7(3) is applied, with necessary modifications, to partnerships and limited liability partnerships: see Insolvent Partnerships Order 1994 (SI 1994/2421) reg.16 and Sch.8; Limited Liability Partnerships Regulations 2001 (SI 2001/1090) reg.4(2).

[10] In the case of liquidation, the s.6 solvency test is different to the solvency test applying when the question is whether the company can or should be put into any of the various forms of liquidation. Even the liquidator of a company in members' voluntary liquidation, usually thought of as "solvent" liquidation, may therefore have to make a report or return.

[11] See further discussion in A. Hicks, *Disqualification of Directors: No Hiding Place for the Unfit* (A.C.C.A. Research Report No.59, 1998), especially Chs 4 and 5.

be commenced.[12] For the purposes of mandatory reporting the relevant office holder is:

(1) The official receiver in the case of a company, an insolvent partnership or a limited liability partnership,[13] which is being wound up by the court in England and Wales.
(2) The liquidator in the case of a company which is being wound up voluntarily.
(3) The liquidator in the case of a company which is being wound up by the court in Scotland (where there is no equivalent of the official receiver).
(4) The administrator in the case of a company which is in administration.[14]
(5) The administrative receiver in the case of a company which is in administrative receivership.

The form of report is prescribed by statutory instrument and is dealt with further below. The supervisor of a free standing corporate or partnership voluntary arrangement is not subject to the mandatory reporting regime. This mirrors the definition of "becomes insolvent" in CDDA s.6(2), the effect of which is that the court has no s.6 disqualification jurisdiction in relation to companies simply because they have entered free standing corporate voluntary arrangements. That directors should be allowed to escape the clutches of s.6 simply because they manage to avoid some other insolvency process seems questionable. A possible justification for the CDDA not conferring s.6 disqualification jurisdiction in relation to corporate voluntary arrangements may be that to do otherwise would undermine the relationship between the directors and the insolvency practitioner and thereby reduce the effectiveness of voluntary arrangements as a medium for corporate rescue. However, the same can be said of administration and yet s.6

[12] See discussion in *Re Launchexcept Ltd, Secretary of State for Trade and Industry v Tillman* [2000] 1 B.C.L.C. 36; *Re Pinemoor Ltd* [1997] B.C.C. 708; *Re Park House Properties Ltd, Secretary of State for Trade and Industry v Carter* [1997] 2 B.C.L.C. 530. In the *Barings* proceedings, at least one of the defendants was disqualified by the court even though the administrators were of the view that his conduct was not such as to make him unfit under s.6. Equally, an insolvency practitioner may form the view that a director's conduct is such as to make him unfit only for the Secretary of State to arrive at a different view. In practice, the Insolvency Service applies a vetting procedure to determine whether a case should be considered for further investigation and possible proceedings: see the guidance issued by the Insolvency Service in *Dear Insolvency Practitioner*, Ch.10, available online at *http://www.insolvency.gov.uk/insolvencyprofessionandlegislation/dearip/dearipindex.htm* [Accessed August 19, 2009] and in *Company Directors Disqualification Act 1986: Guidance Notes for the Completion of Statutory Reports and Returns* (December 1999) available online at *http://www.insolvency.gov.uk/pdfs/guidanceleafletspdf/dusguide.pdf* [Accessed August 19, 2009]. See also T. Wilkin, "IS policy on SIP4 and disqualification" Recovery (Spring 2008) p.3.

[13] For the purposes of the CDDA generally references to "company" are treated as extending to limited liability partnerships: see Limited Liability Partnerships Regulations 2001 (SI 2001/1090) regs 2 and 4(2)(a). CDDA ss.6 to 9 are modified for insolvent partnerships by the Insolvent Partnerships Order 1994 (SI 1994/2421) (as subsequently amended) art.16 and Sch.8: see 4–44. Hereafter in this chapter and save where the context otherwise requires, references to "company" should be treated as including limited liability partnerships and partnerships.

[14] The current wording of CDDA s.7(3)(c) was introduced by the Enterprise Act 2002 s.248 and Sch.17, para.42 to reflect the fact that administration is no longer an exclusively court-based procedure.

disqualification jurisdiction and the statutory obligation on the office holder to report both apply. As a result, where a company uses the shelter of administration to propose a voluntary arrangement, the insolvency practitioner is obliged to report on the directors' conduct in his capacity as administrator if he determines that the conditions in CDDA s.6(1) are satisfied.[15]

Insolvent Companies (Reports on Conduct of Directors) Rules 1996

3–03 The manner in which office holders are to make reports is governed by the Insolvent Companies (Reports on Conduct of Directors) Rules 1996.[16] The rules apply where the company[17] has gone into voluntary liquidation, administration or administrative receivership but not compulsory liquidation.[18] There are a number of requirements under the rules:

(1) Any report made under CDDA s.7(3) should be made in prescribed Form D1 set out in the Schedule or in a form which is substantially similar (r.3).
(2) If a s.7(3) report has not been submitted before the expiry of six months from the "relevant date", the office holder must submit a return in prescribed Form D2[19] set out in the Schedule, or in a form which is substantially similar, in relation to every person who:
    (a) was, on the "relevant date", a director or shadow director of the company; or
    (b) had been a director or shadow director of the company at any time in the three years immediately preceding the "relevant date" (r.4).
(3) The "relevant date" for the purpose of (2) means:

[15] It is now possible for an eligible company, meaning a small company within the meaning of Companies Act 2006 s.382(3) (formerly Companies Act 1985 s.247(3)), to obtain a moratorium pending consideration by the creditors of a proposal for a corporate voluntary arrangement: see Insolvency Act 1986 s.1A and Sch.A1 (inserted by Insolvency Act 2000 s.1 and Sch.1). This is a free standing arrangement and the supervisor has no reporting obligation under CDDA s.7(3).

[16] SI 1996/1909 as amended by the Insolvent Companies (Reports on Conduct of Directors) (Amendment) Rules 2001 (SI 2001/764) and the Enterprise Act 2002 (Insolvency Order) 2003 (SI 2003/2096). As originally enacted, these rules which were made pursuant to the Insolvency Act 1986 s.411, came into force on September 30, 1996 and replaced the earlier Insolvent Companies (Reports on Conduct of Directors) No.2 Rules (SI 1986/2134). An equivalent set of rules applies in Scotland also with effect from September 30, 1996: see SI 1996/1910 as amended by SI 2001/768. For the reporting rules applicable in Northern Ireland, see the Insolvent Companies (Reports on Conduct of Directors) Rules (Northern Ireland) 2003 (SRNI 2003/357).

[17] Equivalent provisions apply in the case of limited liability partnerships and partnerships which enter relevant insolvency procedures: see Limited Liability Partnerships Regulations 2001 (SI 2001/1090) reg.10 and Sch.6 and Insolvent Partnerships Order 1994 (SI 1994/2421), art.18 and Sch.10. As regards bank insolvency or administration under the Banking Act Pts 2, 3: see the Banking Act 2009 (Parts 2 and 3 Consequential Amendments) Order 2009 (SI 2009/317), art.3 and Schedule.

[18] In the case of compulsory liquidation in England and Wales, the obligation to submit reports under s.7(3) lies with the official receiver. In practice, such reports are currently presented in the form of the draft evidence that the official receiver would anticipate deploying in any disqualification proceedings were the Secretary of State to decide that proceedings should be brought.

[19] The trigger to the making of a return is that it appears to the officeholder that the company has at any time become insolvent within the meaning of CDDA s.6(2): see r.4(1).

(a) the date on which the resolution for voluntary winding up was passed in the case of a creditors' voluntary winding up; or
(b) the date on which the liquidator formed the opinion that the company's assets were insufficient to meet its debts, other liabilities and the expenses of winding up in the case of a company in members' voluntary liquidation, or
(c) the date of the receiver's appointment in the case of an administrative receivership; or
(d) the date that the company entered administration in the case of an administration.[20]

(4) If the office holder vacates office earlier than one week before the expiry of six months from the "relevant date" as defined and he has not already submitted a D1 report or a D2 return, he must submit a D2 return in accordance with (2) above within 14 days after vacating office (r.4(5)).

Failure to make returns as required under the 1996 Rules is punishable by fine (r.4(7)).

3–04 The effect of these rules, in practice, is that within six months of taking office the office holder must submit at least a D2 return in respect of every director and shadow director of a company that goes into voluntary liquidation, administrative receivership or administration. The D2 return can be used either as an "interim return" or a "final return".[21] An interim return is submitted in circumstances where the office holder expects to be able to submit either a full D1 report or a final return at a later date. A final return is submitted where the office holder has not become aware of any matters which would require him to submit a D1 report concerning a particular director. Office holders are encouraged by guidance notes and industry standards to submit D1 reports and D2 final returns as quickly as they possibly can given that proceedings for an order under s.6 can only be commenced without the permission of the court within two years of the company becoming insolvent.[22] The overall position is that the office holder must submit either a D1 report pursuant to s.7(3) or a final return in relation to every director and shadow director of the insolvent company. In a company where more than one insolvency practitioner has held office, whether consecutively (for example, a liquidator following an administrator) or

[20] Rules 3(1)(c) and 4(4)(d) were amended by the Enterprise Act 2002 (Insolvency) Order 2003 (SI 2003/2096) to reflect the fact that under Sch.B1 of the Insolvency Act 1986 administration may now be commenced without a court order.

[21] See *Company Directors Disqualification Act 1986: Guidance Notes for the Completion of Statutory Reports and Returns* (December 1999) available online at *http://www.insolvency.gov.uk/pdfs/guidanceleafletspdf/dusguide.pdf* [Accessed August 19, 2009]; Statement of Insolvency Practice 4: Disqualification of Directors England and Wales (September 1998) para.5 available online at *http://www.r3.org.uk/publications/default.asp?page=2&i=402&id=228#SIPStory* [Accessed August 19, 2009].

[22] CDDA s.7(2) and see Chs 7 and 8. For examples of industry standards see the materials referred to in the previous footnote and the guidance issued by the Insolvency Service in *Dear Insolvency Practitioner* Ch.10.

concurrently (for example, an administrative receiver where a company is already in liquidation), a D1 report or D2 return is required from each office holder under r.4(5).[23] However, in a case where joint office holders are appointed (for example, joint liquidators) the Insolvency Service only requires one report or return to be submitted for each director rather than one from each of the office holders.[24] Failure to submit either a D1 report or a D2 return within the six-month period is a criminal offence punishable by fine under r.4(7). Moreover, the Insolvency Service's Insolvency Practitioner Unit will report persistent non-compliance to the relevant office holder's authorising body.[25] The smooth operation of the system therefore depends heavily on the professional discipline of insolvency practitioners within the private sector. The office holder's costs in preparing reports and returns forms part of his ordinary remuneration and is an expense of the insolvency process. The costs are therefore borne by the insolvent estate (and therefore the company's creditors).

Insolvency Service procedures

3–05 On receipt of a s.7(3) Report, or a D1 Report as it is sometimes known (reflecting the name of the prescribed form), the Insolvency Service has to evaluate its contents. Procedures within the Insolvency Service change over time. The following account summarises the position as at the date of writing.[26] As from September 1, 2008 the Insolvency Service teams formerly known as Case Targeting and Initial Investigations were combined. The new team, "Conduct and Complaints" deals with all D1 Reports from receipt to allocation to an investigator. As explained by the Insolvency Service in guidance that it has issued, it is this combined team that carries out an initial vetting and review process with a view to identifying those cases that are appropriate for further investigation and consideration by the Insolvency Service:

> "Each review includes a detailed consideration of the conduct report, supporting documentation, any other available information and usually includes telephone contact with the practitioner and searches of Companies House and other databases. The decision whether or not to target a case for investigation takes account of the seriousness and timing of the alleged misconduct, the reasonableness and impact of the alleged misconduct on the solvency and failure of the company, the profile of those who have lost as a result of both the misconduct and the insolvency, the human rights and ability of the directors to defend themselves, and government policy towards both encouraging enterprise and detecting and deterring fraud and other misconduct."[27]

[23] See further *Company Directors Disqualification Act 1986: Guidance Notes for the Completion of Statutory Reports and Returns* (December 1999) at para.5.4.

[24] *Company Directors Disqualification Act 1986: Guidance Notes for the Completion of Statutory Reports and Returns* and Statement of Insolvency Practice 4 (E & W), para.6.

[25] *Dear Insolvency Practitioner* Ch.10. It is also expected that insolvency practitioners will disclose copies of D reports and returns when requested to do so by those carrying out monitoring visits on behalf of their professional body. For an insight into the possible impact of professional monitoring on the office holder's decision whether to submit a report or a final return see S. Wheeler, "Directors' Disqualification: Insolvency Practitioners and the Decision-Making Process" (1995) 15 Legal Studies 283.

[26] See the evolving description set out in *Dear Insolvency Practitioner* Ch.10.

[27] *Dear Insolvency Practitioner* Ch.10.

If it is decided that a D1 report merits further investigation it will then usually be allocated to an "investigator". Investigation work may also be outsourced to solicitors in private practice. Following such investigation, the case (including draft written evidence) will be submitted to the "Authorisation Team" which will take the decision as to whether the conditions of s.6 are met and whether it is in the public interest to issue proceedings. If the decision is affirmative in both respects, thereafter it is for the "Defendant Liaison Team" to progress matters to completion of the case. The Defendant Liaison Team will negotiate disqualification undertakings and, where appropriate, instruct Solicitors to bring court proceedings.

The Insolvency Service will pay the office holder separately for work done by way of further investigation that goes beyond the basic work that is regarded as falling within the scope of his reporting duty, including work involved in agreeing and swearing affidavits and attending court where the case is to proceed. However, the extent and likely cost of any additional work should be discussed with the Insolvency Service before it is undertaken and separate payment will only be made where the costs were authorised in advance.[28] It should be noted that where the company is in liquidation, the liquidator is under a further obligation to report a director to the appropriate authorities if it appears to him that the director has been guilty of a criminal offence in relation to the company.[29]

Material to be provided by office holders to the Insolvency Service

3–06 Guidance issued by the Insolvency Service[30] indicates the documents, or types of documents, that the Insolvency Service will expect to see accompanying any D1 Report. These include: (1) a copy of the Statement of Affairs or, where none has been submitted, an estimate of the financial position of the company by listing known assets and liabilities; (2) a copy of the office holder's report to creditors or, if this is not available, a report detailing the company's history; (3) a copy of

[28] Insolvency Service, *Company Directors Disqualification Act 1986: Guidance Notes for the Completion of Statutory Reports and Returns* (December 1999) available online at *http://www.insolvency.gov.uk/pdfs/guidanceleafletspdf/dusguide.pdf* [Accessed August 19, 2009] at 5.3; Statement of Insolvency Practice 4. If the reporting insolvency practitioner is authorised to incur costs in connection with the proceedings, these will form part of the Secretary of State's costs and will therefore fall to be assessed if an order for costs is made against the director. For attempts to control the costs incurred by insolvency practitioners in this context see *Dear Insolvency Practitioner* Ch.10. See also T. Wilkin, "IS policy on SIP4 and disqualification" Recovery (Spring 2008) p.3 (confirming that officials have increasingly taken the role of the principal witness in disqualification with a consequent reduction in the need for insolvency practitioners to review and swear affidavits and reports, or to attend court as a witness). This change in the manner in which cases have been presented to the courts has also been applied in Scotland from April 1, 2008: see *Dear Insolvency Practitioner* Ch.10, so far as it deals with changed Insolvency Service procedures regarding Scottish cases.

[29] Insolvency Act 1986 s.218 (as amended by the Insolvency Act 2000). As regards the role of the Criminal Investigations and Prosecutions team within the Department of Business, Innovation and Skills see: *http://www.berr.gov.uk/whatwedo/businesslaw/criminal-investigations/index.html* [Accessed October 17, 2009] and text from 10–106.

[30] See *Company Directors Disqualification Act 1986: Guidance Notes for the Completion of Statutory Reports and Returns* (December 1999) Appendix 2 available online at *http://www.insolvency.gov.uk/pdfs/guidanceleafletspdf/dusguide.pdf* [Accessed August 19, 2009].

any notes issued to creditors for the purposes of the creditors' meeting and of any record taken of the proceedings at the meeting; (4) a copy of the last two sets of audited or statutory accounts and any draft or management accounts for periods thereafter; (5) copies of any questionnaires which have been completed by the directors at the office holder's request; (6) the present position of the insolvency proceedings and dividend prospects; (7) copies of specific documents referred to which provide evidence of the unfit conduct reported (if there are many documents they need not all be provided at the time of reporting, but full details of what is available and where it is located should be given); (8) an aged creditors' analysis (if readily available from the company's records). The body of the report should also fully cover: (a) the position in relation to any civil recovery actions, including statements of claim, legal advice etc; (b) details of the nature of evidence available in support of insolvent trading; (c) references to professional advice taken by the directors, and to specific correspondence which sheds light on directors' conduct, for example with banks, solicitors, accountants or creditors. This list immediately raises the issue of the use that can be made of material obtained by virtue of, or under threat of, the use of the compulsory powers under ss.235 and 236 of the Insolvency Act 1986.

Material obtained pursuant to Insolvency Act 1986 ss.235 and 236

3–07 It appears from the decision of Vinelott J. in *Re Polly Peck International Plc Ex p. the joint administrators*[31] that an office holder can disclose transcripts of private examinations conducted under the Insolvency Act 1986 s.236[32] to the Secretary of State even if he has given an assurance that the transcripts would only be disclosed for the purposes of the relevant insolvency process. The same applies to information derived from such transcripts. The reason for this is that the purposes of liquidation, administration and administrative receivership include the gathering of information as to the conduct of the company's directors and the obligation to report on such matters to the Secretary of State.[33] The official receiver, in his capacity as such, also has a further regulatory role over and above that conferred on other office holders.[34] By the same reasoning, it appears that the Secretary of State or the official receiver could request production of the transcripts under CDDA s.7(4).

In the light of *Soden v Burns, R. v Secretary of State for Trade and Industry Ex p. Soden*[35] and *British and Commonwealth Holdings (in administration) v Barclays de Zoete Wedd Ltd (No.1), Re Atlantic Computers Plc*,[36] a question arises as to whether notice should be given to a person who has been compelled to provide information or documents under s.236 of the Insolvency Act before the

[31] [1994] B.C.C. 15; effectively approved by the House of Lords in *Re Pantmaenog Timber Co Ltd* [2004] 1 A.C. 158 at [11], [65].

[32] Or information obtained under Insolvency Act 1986 s.235.

[33] See also *Re Pantmaenog Timber Co Ltd* [2004] 1 A.C. 158 especially at [7], [11], [45], [51], [52], [65]–[67].

[34] See Insolvency Act 1986 s.132.

[35] [1996] 1 W.L.R. 1512.

[36] [1998] B.C.C. 200.

office holder passes any such information or documents to the Secretary of State under CDDA s.7(4). It is suggested that notice is not required. As explained above with reference to the *Polly Peck* decision, the subsequent use by the Secretary of State of such compelled material for the purposes of considering and/or bringing disqualification proceedings is inherent in the statutory purpose of s.236. The position is analogous to that where powers of investigation are exercised under Pt XIV of the Companies Act 1985.[37] In such cases, there is a statutory gateway in ss.451A and 449 of the Companies Act 1985 which permits the Secretary of State to make use of any information or documents obtained in the course of an investigation under Pt XIV for the purposes of disqualification proceedings.[38] In relation to Pt XIV, the Secretary of State's practice is not to give notice of the potential use of compelled information to the person who was compelled to provide it, in circumstances where its use is permitted by the statutory gateway. In *Soden v Burns* and *Atlantic Computers*, the relevant information had been obtained under compulsion by inspectors appointed pursuant to the Companies Act 1985 s.432. However, there was no statutory gateway permitting the information to be used either for the purposes of the insolvency of the relevant companies (as s.236 of the Insolvency Act does not come within the gateway in ss.451A and 449 of the Companies Act 1985) or for private litigation. Hence, when the court was considering whether to compel further dissemination of the information (in *Soden v Burns* by way of an order under s.236 and in *Atlantic Computers* by way of an order for disclosure), the persons who had been compelled to provide the information had to be notified first in order to give them an opportunity to object to its use for a purpose falling outside the scope of ss.451A and 449 of the Companies Act 1985. As such, the cases of *Soden v Burns* and *Atlantic Computers* can be distinguished from a case where compelled information is used for a purpose expressly contemplated by statute, in which case notice is not required. A further question is whether prior permission of the court to disclose s.236 material to the Secretary of State is always required.[39] It is suggested that as the information will have been acquired, at least in part, for the regulatory reporting purposes of the relevant insolvency procedure then, unless the court has itself expressly limited the disclosure that can be made,[40] such permission is not needed.[41]

[37] On company and other forms of investigatory powers which provide a gateway to disqualification proceedings under CDDA s.8 see further text from 3–117. Part XIV of the Companies Act 1985 remains in force notwithstanding the enactment and bringing into force of the Companies Act 2006 because its provisions do not apply exclusively to companies.

[38] See further text from 3–117.

[39] See *Re Arrows Ltd, Hamilton v Naviede* [1995] 2 A.C. 75.

[40] As was the case in *Re Arrows Ltd, Hamilton v Naviede* [1995] 2 A.C. 75, where the court making the original s.236 order had expressly provided by its order that there was to be an application to the court by the liquidators for directions in the event that the Serious Fraud Office gave notice of intention to serve a notice under s.2 of the Criminal Justice Act 1987 (in effect seeking delivery up of s.236 material): see [1995] 2 A.C. 75 at 97G. In that case the court was concerned with the regulatory reporting requirements recognised by s.218 of the Insolvency Act 1986.

[41] This is confirmed by the reasoning in *R. v Brady* [2004] EWCA Crim 1763, [2004] 1 W.L.R. 3240, a case that deals with the question of disclosure by the official receiver of Insolvency Act 1986 s.235 material to the criminal authorities.

Section 7(4): power to obtain information from officeholders

3–08 A further power of information gathering is vested in the Secretary of State and official receiver by CDDA s.7(4). This enables the Secretary of State and official receiver[42] to require the relevant office holders to provide further information and to permit inspection of books and records relevant to the conduct of the director in question.[43] The subsection is wide-ranging. It enables the Secretary of State (or the official receiver) to seek information from current or former office holders for the purposes of deciding whether to exercise, or of exercising, any function under the CDDA. Subject to this test of relevance, the power is limited by the overall restriction that the information or inspection sought must be "reasonably required".

3–09 A number of issues arise. First, the power can be invoked either before or after proceedings are commenced. This follows from the wording of s.7(4) which states that the power can be invoked "for the purpose of determining whether to exercise, or of exercising, any function" under s.7 as a whole. The continuation of proceedings under s.6 (commenced in accordance with s.7(1)), is an exercise of the function under s.7(1). That function does not cease once proceedings are issued, but continues until the proceedings are drawn to a close. Thus, if in the course of proceedings a defendant raises a particular line of defence, the Secretary of State would be entitled to call for relevant ancillary papers or explanations from the office holder. This is a point of jurisdiction under the CDDA and so the Disqualification Practice Direction[44] cannot itself confer a wider power than that conferred by s.7(4). Nevertheless, it is interesting to note that para.18 of the Disqualification Practice Direction proceeds on the assumption that s.7(4) can be invoked even after substantive disqualification proceedings have been commenced.

3–10 So far as a former office holder is concerned, his statutory powers of seeking information end with the termination of his office[45] and accordingly s.7(4) can only be used to seek information, or access to books and records, within the former office holder's possession.[46] However, as regards office holders who are still in office, it appears from the *Pantmaenog* case that the information (or access

[42] Note that the official receiver may be seeking information in relation to a potential "collateral" company of which he is not the official receiver: see *Re Pantmaenog Timber Co Ltd* [2004] 1 A.C. 158 at [14] and [70]–[74].

[43] For circumstances in which disqualification proceedings may be jeopardised if the Secretary of State does not avail himself of the power see dictum of Clarke L.J. in *Re Launchexcept Ltd, Secretary of State for Trade and Industry v Tillman* [2000] 1 B.C.L.C. 36 at 70. The existence of the power in s.7(4) does not necessarily mean that the Secretary of State can be compelled to disclose documents that are in the custody of an office holder to the defendant. In *Re Lombard Shipping and Forwarding Ltd* [1993] B.C.L.C. 238 it was held that documents in the custody of joint administrative receivers were not within the control of the Secretary of State for the purpose of ordering disclosure because the court has a discretion whether or not to order an office holder to comply with a request on an application under s.7(4) and the Secretary of State therefore has no absolute right to insist on production.

[44] On which see further text from 7–28.

[45] See *Re Kingscroft Insurance Co Ltd* [1994] 1 B.C.L.C. 80 where it was held that a s.236 order becomes inoperative if the office holder in whose favour it was made ceases to hold office.

[46] *Re Pantmaenog Timber Co Ltd* [2004] 1 A.C. 158 at [14].

to books and records) that can be sought under s.7(4) is not limited to information (or books and records) already within the knowledge or possession of the relevant office holder and that it may be reasonable for the Secretary of State (or the official receiver) to require the office holder to seek such information (or books and records) using his statutory powers, for example, those under ss.234–236 of the Insolvency Act 1986. This confirms the view expressed in the first edition of this book. As an office holder has both a right and a duty to obtain the books and records of the relevant company, it should follow that he ought not to be able to resist an order to produce them under s.7(4) on the basis that he has not taken steps to obtain them from the company's directors. If this is correct, there would seem to be no reason why, as a matter of jurisdiction, in a case where the office holder has neither obtained the company's books and records nor invoked the powers in ss.234–236 of the Insolvency Act, the court should not require the office holder to seek an order for production under those powers on an application under CDDA s.7(4).

It is, however, at this stage that the "reasonable requirement" limitation of s.7(4) comes into effect. What is "reasonable" will turn on the relevant circumstances. For example, if the office holder does not have within his possession the relevant information or books and records, it may not be a "reasonable" requirement that the office holder invoke his statutory powers in circumstances where the Secretary of State (or official receiver) is not prepared to offer some form of indemnity (so that the costs of invoking the office holder's statutory powers are not borne by the company's assets or by the office holder personally).[47] In considering the question of whether, on particular facts, it is "reasonable" to require statutory powers to be invoked, the court will no doubt take into account all the circumstances, including: (a) the prospects of success of such powers being invoked in the particular circumstances[48]; (b) the ability of the claimant, or potential claimant, in s.6 proceedings to obtain the information through another route (such as a disclosure order under CPR Pt 31)[49]; (c) whether the information is likely to be of potential benefit to the relevant insolvency procedure and to further

[47] See *Re Pantmaenog Timber Co Ltd* [2004] 1 A.C. 158 at [14] and [69]. As regards the costs falling on the office holder personally, this may flow from the risk that an application for a s.236 order will fail or from the fact that the company is so insolvent that there are no available assets to fund the application.

[48] In deciding whether to grant a s.236 order, the court has to carry out a balancing exercise and, in particular, consider potential oppression to the person against whom the order is sought (or a person interested in the information sought): see, by way of example, *British & Commonwealth Plc v Spicer and Oppenheim* [1993] A.C. 426; *Cloverbay Ltd v Bank of Credit and Commerce International SA* [1991] Ch. 90; *Shierson v Rastogi* [2002] EWCA Civ 1624, [2003] 1 W.L.R. 586. In *Pantmaenog Timber* the House of Lords considered only the question of jurisdiction under s.236. They sounded warning notes about the exercise of discretion.

[49] In the *Pantmaenog Timber* case, HH Judge Weeks Q.C. subsequently made an order for third party disclosure which had the same effect as the s.236 orders that he had previously set aside and that were the subject of the appeal to the House of Lords. The defendants had been disqualified by the time the House of Lords hearing on the point of principle took place.

its completion[50]; and (d) the offer of any costs indemnity.[51] As regards the second of these points, it is suggested that the court would not automatically refuse to make an order under s.7(4) on the basis that the Secretary of State could achieve the same or a similar result by issuing a witness summons under CPR Pt 31. On any attempt to invoke the office holder's statutory powers, the person against whom they are invoked (or the director to whom their exercise is directed) would undoubtedly be in a position to resist their use. A practical difference is likely to arise when disqualification proceedings are actually on foot, compared with the position when they are simply in prospect. Once proceedings are on foot, the Secretary of State can normally be expected to use the powers available in the substantive proceedings under rules of court (whether by way of orders for disclosure, requests for further information or, in the case of third parties, by way of witness summonses) to obtain information, rather than the power in s.236.[52] Before disqualification proceedings are commenced, the Secretary of State could have recourse to the wide pre-action disclosure powers in ss.33–34 of the Senior Courts Act 1981. However, it is suggested that, at that stage, the court would not necessarily refuse an order under s.7(4) on the ground that the information could be obtained under the Senior Courts Act 1981. Quite simply, the power in s.236 of the Insolvency Act is much wider and is likely to be of much greater use. Furthermore, the position is analogous to that in the *Polly Peck* case discussed in 3–07 above. In other words, the Secretary of State would merely be seeking, through an application under s.7(4), to exploit the statutory purpose of s.236 and enable the relevant office holder to report fully on the conduct of any of the company's directors that falls below appropriate standards.

3–11 The Secretary of State may seek to remedy any non-compliance, or inadequate compliance, with a request under s.7(4) by applying to the court under r.6 of the Insolvent Companies (Reports on Conduct of Directors) Rules 1996. On such an application, the court may make an order directing compliance within such period as may be specified. The court may provide in the order that all costs of and incidental to the application shall be borne by the relevant office holder. Although

[50] See *Re Pantmaenog Timber Co Ltd* [2004] 1 A.C. 158 at [88] where Lord Walker noted that the official receiver had conceded that the sole purpose of seeking the s.236 orders in that case was in aid of the disqualification proceedings, a somewhat surprising concession given that a liquidator had been appointed to consider possible civil recovery proceedings in relation to the matters of misconduct alleged.

[51] In this context, it is a moot point whether, and to what extent, the court might take into account the "law enforcement" nature of the powers being exercised by the Secretary of State together with the obligation of the office holder to report fully and fairly under CDDA ss.7(3) and 7(4), and not require the Secretary of State to provide an indemnity. See, by analogy, the position with regard to cross-undertakings in damages where an interim injunction is sought in a law enforcement context: *Hoffmann-La Roche v Secretary of State for Trade and Industry* [1975] A.C. 295; *Re Highfield Commodities Ltd* [1985] 1 W.L.R. 149.

[52] See, by analogy, the ordinary position where office holders seek to invoke the power in s.236 after the commencement of litigation: *British & Commonwealth Plc v Spicer and Oppenheim* [1993] A.C. 426; *Re Sasea Finance Ltd* [1998] 1 B.C.L.C. 559; *British and Commonwealth Holdings (in administration) v Barclays de Zoete Wedd Ltd (No.1), Re Atlantic Computers Plc* [1998] B.C.C. 200; *Joint Liquidators of Sasea Finance Ltd v KPMG* [1998] B.C.C. 216; though cf. *Shierson v Rastogi* [2003] 1 W.L.R. 586.

para.18 of the Disqualification Practice Direction provides that applications under s.7(4) may be made under CPR Pt 8 or by application notice (under CPR Pt 23) in existing disqualification proceedings, or by application under the Insolvency Rules in the relevant insolvency, if the insolvency practitioner against whom the application is made remains the office holder, this permissive provision has now to be read subject to the revised terms[53] of r.2(5) of the Insolvent Companies (Disqualification of Unfit Directors) Proceedings Rules 1987. That rule provides that in relation to an application to enforce any duty arising under s.7(4) of the CDDA made against a person who at the date of the application is acting as liquidator, administrator or administrative receiver, the application is to be made under the Insolvency Rules 1986, presumably as an application within the relevant insolvency. In such cases the other options provided for by the Disqualification Practice Direction, namely an application in the disqualification proceedings or by way of CPR Pt 8 Claim Form, are not available.

Disclosure of office holders' reports

3–12 An important question is whether the Secretary of State can be compelled to disclose a copy of a D1 report to the defendant in the course of disqualification proceedings. Orders for discovery and inspection were refused in two reported cases on the grounds that a D report amounted to a privileged communication.[54] However, an order for inspection of an administrator's s.7(3) report was granted by Scott V.C. in *Re Barings Plc, Secretary of State for Trade and Industry v Baker*[55] and, pending any guidance from any higher court, this should now be regarded as the definitive authority on the point. There were two separate questions facing the court. The first question was whether an order for inspection should be made in the instant case on the ground that inspection was "necessary either for disposing fairly of the cause or matter or for saving costs" within RSC Ord.24, r.13. The second question was whether, in any event, the D report was privileged in the hands of the Secretary of State. Scott V.C. decided that inspection of the report was "necessary" under RSC Ord.24, r.13 and that it was not protected by legal professional privilege. His reasoning and conclusions can be summarised as follows:

(1) While most of its factual contents could be extracted from other documents that were available to the defendant, the D report should be made available for

[53] Inserted by the Insolvent Companies (Disqualification of Unfit Directors) Proceedings (Amendment) Rules 2007 (SI 1906/2007), r.3 from August 6, 2007 (other than in relation to applications commenced prior to that date).

[54] *Secretary of State for Trade and Industry v Sananes* [1994] B.C.C. 375; *Secretary of State for Trade and Industry v Houston (No.2)* 1995 S.L.T. 196. In *Houston* discovery was also refused on the grounds of public interest immunity. Under the former rules of court applicable prior to the CPR, it was important to distinguish "discovery" (disclosure of the existence of a document) and "inspection" (the process of making the contents of the document available to the other side). Different rules governed these two separate processes although unfortunately, as a matter of nomenclature, "discovery" was commonly used when it was "inspection" that was in issue. Disclosure and inspection of documents is now governed by CPR Pt 31.

[55] [1998] Ch. 356.

inspection because its production would save the defendant the time and expense of trawling through the source material in order to produce his own organised analysis of the facts. In the judge's view, as the Secretary of State had enjoyed the benefit of the report it was only fair that it should also be made available to the defendant. The threshold test that an order for inspection should only be made if the court is of the opinion that the order is necessary either for disposing fairly of the matter or for saving costs was therefore satisfied.[56]

(2) It was not remotely arguable that the D report was immune from disclosure in order to protect the inviolability of communications between the Secretary of State and the Secretary of State's legal advisers (i.e. to protect the confidentiality of legal advice). That was because the D report did not in any sense represent legal advice given to the Secretary of State. This ground of legal professional privilege was therefore not available.

(3) That part of legal professional privilege known as "litigation privilege", which confers immunity on documents brought into existence for the purposes of litigation, should not be regarded as a species of privilege wholly distinct from legal professional privilege. Originally, litigation privilege applied only to documents that might cast light on the client's instructions to the lawyer or the lawyer's advice to the client regarding the conduct of the case or the client's prospects. More recent cases have dispensed with the connection originally required between the claim to privilege and the principle that communications between a party and his lawyers should be immune from compulsory disclosure.[57] While he regarded the removal of such a connection as wrong in principle, Scott V.C. was bound by these authorities to hold that privilege can be claimed in respect of a document provided that the document has been brought into existence for the dominant purpose of use in litigation.

(4) It was clearly arguable that the administrators had produced the D report for the dominant purpose of enabling the Secretary of State to decide whether or not to commence disqualification proceedings. However, it did not follow that the report was privileged. The usual rule in (3) above does not apply to reports that are required to be produced pursuant to a statutory duty. In such cases, it is not appropriate to examine the purpose of the office holder in making the report or the purpose of the statutory reporting obligations. Instead, the question is whether there is a public interest in the non-disclosure of the report's contents which is sufficient to override the administration of justice rationale reflected in the usual right of a litigant to inspect his opponent's documents. There being no claim of public interest immunity (nor any ground for such a claim) and there being no need to protect the D report as bearing on communications between the Secretary of State and the Secretary of State's legal advisers, there was no public interest weighing in the balance against inspection.

[56] RSC Ord.24, r.13(1). See now CPR Pt 31.

[57] See, in particular, *Re Highgrade Traders Ltd* [1984] B.C.L.C. 151; and *Guinness Peat Properties Ltd v Fitzroy Robinson* [1987] 1 W.L.R. 1027.

It is clear from the tenor of the judge's concluding remarks in *Barings* that, in his view, disqualification proceedings should be regarded as having more in common with criminal proceedings than ordinary civil proceedings concerning private rights. Indeed, he went so far as to make the point that in criminal proceedings the report would have had to have been disclosed to the defence. This tension between the idea of civil "public interest" litigation (analogous to criminal proceedings) and "ordinary" civil litigation to which the "ordinary" rules of civil procedure governing disclosure, costs, evidence, etc. should apply is a familiar one in the context of disqualification proceedings under the CDDA.[58]

3–13 There are undoubtedly difficulties with the legal analysis of litigation privilege and the application of the relevant principles in the *Barings* case.[59] A statutory D report is not a "public" document in the sense of a document that is published and made available in the public domain. Moreover, the view (summarised in (4) above) that litigation privilege does not apply to statutory reports is problematic. Such documents are clearly produced (and required to be produced) for the purposes of prospective litigation. However, it must be assumed for now that D reports are not the subject of legal professional privilege.[60] This does not necessarily mean that the court will always make an order for inspection of a D report. The *Barings* case was exceptional in a number of respects. Whether the production of the D report will really save costs in the ordinary case is open to question. Furthermore, there is no obvious justification in disqualification proceedings for the court to order inspection on grounds of fairness, provided that any points made by the office holder in favour of the defendant are fairly set out in the office holder's affidavit.[61] It is suggested in the light of these matters that inspection of D reports will not be ordered with any great frequency. Such a view is likely to be consistent with the overriding objective of the CPR and also reflects the fact that the views of an office holder as to whether reported conduct constitutes unfitness carry little or no weight in proceedings.[62] At the same time, to avoid creating the impression that he has something to hide, the Secretary of State may feel that voluntary disclosure of D reports is appropriate,[63] even in a case where disclosure would not necessarily be ordered by the court. In its current guidance[64] the Insolvency Service has indicated that in disqualification proceedings its stance is that legal professional privilege will not be claimed, that public interest immunity will rarely be claimed,[65] and that

[58] See discussion in Ch.2.

[59] See discussion in *S County Council v B* [2000] 2 F.L.R. 161.

[60] Even if they were so subject, the Secretary of State could waive the privilege. This was purportedly done in the *Barings* case prior to the delivery of the Vice-Chancellor's judgment.

[61] A requirement confirmed by *Re Moonlight Foods (UK) Ltd, Secretary of State for Trade and Industry v Hickling* [1996] B.C.C. 678.

[62] See *Re Pinemoor Ltd* [1997] B.C.C. 708; *Re Park House Properties Ltd, Secretary of State for Trade and Industry v Carter* [1997] 2 B.C.L.C. 530.

[63] Subject to an express undertaking regarding further use in equivalent terms to the undertaking that would apply on disclosure pursuant to CPR Pt 31.

[64] *Dear Insolvency Practitioner* Ch.10.

[65] Presumably by reference to the particular contents of a D1 report rather than by reference to what used to be called a "class claim".

disclosure to a defendant will usually be made but only on the basis that it is not conceded that the test for disclosure of the D report in legal proceedings is met and provided that an express undertaking is given to the effect that the D report will only be used for the purpose of the disqualification proceedings. It may be doubted whether it would necessarily be right for D reports to be disclosed so readily in the context of other civil proceedings (i.e. non-disqualification proceedings). This is particularly so if the Secretary of State has decided not to commence disqualification proceedings. In such a case, it is suggested that the contents of the report should only be made available if the interests of the effective administration of justice demand it. Moreover, consideration has to be given to the position of other directors who may also be the subject of the D report in question. The Secretary of State has successfully resisted, on appeal, an application for disclosure by the defendants to a liquidator's recovery proceedings on the basis that the report was not relevant to the action and merely reflected the liquidator's personal view.[66] The Insolvency Service guidance makes clear that circumstances may arise in which disclosure of D Reports may also be made to licensing bodies, regulators and investigating authorities such as the Police and Revenue and Customs. Details of relevant statutory and other gateways are beyond the scope of this book.

3–14 The guidance issued by the Insolvency Service[67] stresses that direct requests to insolvency practitioners about any decision to report to the Insolvency Service and any requests for copies of returns or reports should be referred, in the first instance, to the Insolvency Service. It also stresses that as the disclosure of a D1 report is more likely than not in cases where proceedings are contemplated the report:

> "should contain only facts, not speculation, and only contain relevant and pertinent information and should not be a means for passing secret or dubious information."

A chief concern for officeholders will be whether or not the contents of a D1 report may open them up to claims in defamation or at common law for negligence. In this respect it remains to be seen whether the courts will hold there to be an absolute immunity from suit, as regards both defamation and negligence.[68]

SECTION 6(1): SUBSTANTIVE PRELIMINARIES

3–15 CDDA s.6 provides:

> "The court shall make a disqualification order against a person in any case where, on an application under this section, it is satisfied—
>
> (a) that he is or has been a director of a company which has at any time become insolvent (whether while he was a director or subsequently), and

[66] *Re Harris Adacom Ltd*, September 19, 2000, Ch.D., unreported.

[67] *Dear Insolvency Practitioner* Ch.10.

[68] See, e.g., by analogy *Al-Fayed v United Kingdom* (1994) 18 E.H.R.R. 393; *Mond v Hyde* [1999] Q.B. 1097; *Mond v United Kingdom* [1993] B.P.I.R. 1347; *Taylor v Director of the Serious Fraud Office* [1999] 2 A.C. 177; *Taylor v United Kingdom* (2004) 38 E.H.R.R. CD35.

(b) that his conduct as a director of that company (either taken alone or taken together with his conduct as a director of any other company or companies) makes him unfit to be concerned in the management of a company."

The onus is on the claimant (who for these purposes is either the Secretary of State or the official receiver) to establish that the requirements of s.6(1) are made out.[69] Where the case proceeds to trial, it is for the court to decide whether the defendant's conduct makes him unfit, not the Secretary of State nor any other party.[70] If the provision is broken down into its component parts, it is clear that the court must be satisfied on all of the following points before it is obliged to make a disqualification order under s.6:

(1) that the defendant is or has been a director of a company;
(2) that the company has "become insolvent"; and
(3) that the defendant's conduct as a director of that company (either taken alone or taken together with his conduct as a director of any other company or companies) makes him unfit to be concerned in the management of a company.

In most cases points (1) and (2) are not disputed and the principal question before the court is whether the relevant conduct makes the defendant unfit. Nevertheless, there are cases in which an issue under (1) or (2) is raised. These issues are dealt with in this chapter. The critical question as to what constitutes conduct which makes a director unfit is addressed in Chs 4 and 5. A number of these matters involve the construction of particular terms (such as "director" or "company") which are used throughout the CDDA. As a result, the material in this chapter does occasionally range beyond the particular context of CDDA ss.6 to 9 and is cross-referenced to other chapters that also deal with core concepts. After considering some of the core concepts expressly set out in s.6, this chapter goes on to consider the extension of these concepts, and of the jurisdiction to disqualify, to cover other entities, such as limited liability partnerships, partnerships, building societies and so on.

DIRECTOR

3–16 "Director" is a core term of the CDDA and its importance is twofold. First, the court has no jurisdiction under CDDA s.6 unless the relevant conduct is "conduct as a director".[71] Secondly, and more generally, the term is relevant in determining the scope of any disqualification imposed under the CDDA as a disqualified person is prohibited

[69] *Re Verby Print for Advertising Ltd, Secretary of State for Trade and Industry v Fine* [1998] 2 B.C.L.C. 23. On the burden and standard of proof generally see text from 7–120.

[70] *Re Carecraft Construction Co Ltd* [1994] 1 W.L.R. 172; *Re Park House Properties Ltd, Secretary of State for Trade and Industry v Carter* [1997] 2 B.C.L.C. 530; *Re Blackspur Group Plc* [1998] 1 W.L.R. 422. It should be noted that the source of disqualification is no longer exclusively the court given the Secretary of State's power to accept disqualification undertakings: see further, Ch.9.

[71] The position is the same under CDDA s.8. Members and officers of partnerships and limited liability partnerships are considered separately below.

(amongst other things) from being a director of a company without the court's permission.[72] There is no exhaustive statutory definition of the term "director". The Companies Act 2006 simply requires all companies to have directors[73] and to provide the Registrar of Companies with basic details about them, including their signed written consent to act.[74] Furthermore, there is no statutory machinery governing the mode of appointment.[75] This matter is left for the company to determine by its articles of association though ultimate control over appointments is commonly reserved to the members. A director who has been formally appointed in accordance with the appropriate procedure set out in the relevant company's articles of association and has consented to act is known as a de jure director.[76] There is no doubt that de jure directors fall within s.6(1)(a). However, the scope of the term "director" in the CDDA is not confined to de jure directors. The CDDA also applies to what have become known as de facto directors (that is, persons who are directors "in fact" although they have not been formally appointed) and, for the purposes of jurisdiction under s.6, the term also embraces shadow directors.[77] Thus, anyone falling within these extended categories is potentially vulnerable to disqualification under s.6. As the case law has developed in this area it has become clear that de facto and shadow directors share many features in common and that any consideration of one also requires consideration of the other.

As discussed below, CDDA ss.6 and 8 are extended in their operation to entities other than limited companies and, in such cases, the equivalent office or position to that of director is utilised in place of "director". In some such cases, the concept of "shadow director" is also adapted and applied, but in others it is not.[78] The discussion below of former and de facto directors will apply to these equivalent offices or positions.

Former directors

3–17 It is also clear on the wording of s.6(1)(a) that the provision catches former directors. A director (be that a de jure, de facto or shadow director) cannot automatically escape liability to disqualification simply by resigning or otherwise withdrawing from his position. Resignation will not prevent a disqualification

[72] CDDA ss.1(1)(a) and 1A(1)(a). See further Ch.14.

[73] Companies Act 2006 s.154 (formerly Companies Act 1985 s.282). A public company must have at least two directors. A private company need only have one director.

[74] Companies Act 2006 ss.12(1)(a), (2), (3), 163–167 (formerly Companies Act 1985 ss.10 and 288). It is important to note that the appointment of a director involves two aspects: first, consent of the person concerned so to act and secondly, valid appointment under the company's constitution. Notification to the Registrar of Companies that a person has become a director under Companies Act 2006 s.167 will confirm the person's consent to act but is otherwise only circumstantial evidence of appointment.

[75] Though there is now a minimum age requirement of 16 and a modest statutory control on the appointment of two or more directors of a public company by means of a single resolution: Companies Act 2006 ss.157, 160.

[76] There may be circumstances in which a person who has apparently consented to act will be treated as not having truly consented: see *Re CEM Connections Ltd* [2000] B.C.C. 917. However, it will be very difficult for a person who has participated fully in a company's affairs to escape the conclusion that he has been appointed and has consented to act where he has signed the relevant statutory form: see *Re Mea Corporation Ltd, Secretary of State for Trade and Industry v Aviss* [2006] EWHC 1846 (Ch), [2007] 1 B.C.L.C. 618 at [77]–[81].

[77] CDDA s.6(3C).

[78] See further text from 3–44 and 3–76.

order being made on the basis of any conduct of the director up to the date of resignation which, either alone or taken together with other relevant conduct, is such as to make him unfit within the meaning of the CDDA. In some circumstances resignation may be the only option available. A failure to resign might itself open the director to criticism. In such circumstances resignation itself will not amount to conduct which will ground a disqualification order.[79] However, it is quite possible that resignation in other circumstances (for example, where a sole director and member abandons the company) may itself amount to conduct making the former director unfit and that he would be treated as bearing responsibility (for the purposes of CDDA s.6(1)) for further matters occurring after his resignation. On a separate point, a person who resigns from office should ensure that the relevant form confirming that he has ceased to be a director is properly completed and filed with the Registrar of Companies and should notify relevant parties such as the company's accountants and bank. Otherwise, in the absence of compelling evidence to the contrary, he may be treated as retaining responsibility for the company's affairs after the date of the purported resignation.[80]

De facto directors

3–18 The term "director", as defined in CDDA s.22(4), includes "any person occupying the position of director, by whatever name called".[81] This wording has received conflicting interpretations. In *Re Eurostem Maritime Ltd*,[82] it was held that a person who had been actively concerned in the administration of seven companies could be treated as "occupying the position of a director" even though he was not a de jure director. However, Browne-Wilkinson V.C. took a narrower view in *Re Lo-Line Electric Motors Ltd*,[83] stating that the words "by whatever name called" are confined to matters of nomenclature only. On this view, s.22(4) obviously covers de jure directors who take the title "director". However, beyond that, it extends only to persons who are de jure (i.e. properly appointed) and who happen to go under a different title because, for example, the company's articles provide that the running of its business is to be conducted by a board of "governors", "trustees" or "managers" rather than "directors".[84] In *Re Amba Rescue Ltd*,

[79] *Re Thorncliffe Finance Ltd, Secretary of State for Trade and Industry v Arif* [1997] 1 B.C.L.C. 34 at 46.

[80] For a salutary example, see *Re Promwalk Services Ltd, Secretary of State for Trade and Industry v Frewen* [2003] 2 B.C.L.C. 305. See also *Re Kaytech International Plc, Secretary of State for Trade and Industry v Kaczer* [1999] 2 B.C.L.C. 351 in relation to one of the appellants, Mr Solly.

[81] Adopting wording also to be found in Companies Act 2006 s.250 (formerly Companies Act 1985 s.741(1)), Insolvency Act 1986 s.251 and Financial Services and Markets Act 2000 s.417(1). This wording was first used in Companies Act 1900 s.30: see C. Noonan and S. Watson, "Examining Company Directors Through the Lens of De Facto Directorship" [2008] J.B.L. 587 at 603.

[82] [1987] P.C.C. 190.

[83] [1988] Ch. 477.

[84] [1988] Ch. 477 at 488–489. See further *Inland Revenue Commissioners v Heaver Ltd* [1949] 2 All E.R. 367 at 369–370. Browne-Wilkinson V.C.'s view is also consistent with the Companies Clauses Consolidation Act 1845 in which the expression "the directors" was originally defined to include ". . . all persons having the direction of the undertaking whether under the name of directors, managers, committee of management, or under any other name."

Secretary of State for Trade and Industry v Hollier and *Re Mea Corporation Ltd, Secretary of State for Trade and Industry v Aviss*, Lewison J. appears to have assumed that s.22(4) does encompass de facto directors.[85] However, nothing turned on the point and it was not fully argued in either case.[86] On the contrary assumption that *Lo-Line* is still good law, the definition in s.22(4) does not extend to persons who act as if they are de jure directors even though they have not been formally appointed or in circumstances where their appointment is defective in some way or has ceased to be effective.[87] It is this latter category, namely persons who act as if they are directors although not (or no longer) validly appointed as such, that are properly regarded as de facto directors. As will become clear, the question of whether or not de facto directors are within the scope of the statutory definition in s.22(4) is academic, it being settled that the term "director" in CDDA ss.6 and 8, properly construed, includes de facto directors.

3–19 Although in *Lo-Line*, Browne-Wilkinson V.C. took the view that the statutory definition of "director" did not extend to de facto directors, he accepted that the court did have the power to disqualify a de facto director under the Companies Act 1985 s.300 (the statutory predecessor of CDDA s.6). He reached this conclusion on the basis that in s.300, and as a matter of statutory interpretation, the word "director" included a de facto director. His reasoning, paraphrased below, can equally be applied to s.6 and the other sections of the CDDA:

(1) The statutory definition of "director" is inclusive, not exhaustive, and so the meaning of the term must be determined by looking at the relevant legislation as a whole and at the immediate context in which the term appears. It was clear from the Companies Act 1985 that certain provisions applicable to directors could only be referring to de jure directors. One example was Companies Act 1985 s.282 (now Companies Act 2006 s.154) which required every company to have a minimum number of directors. Equally, however, there were some sections where, in the context, the term "director" must have included a person who was not a de jure director. The best example was Companies Act 1985 s.285 (now Companies Act 2006 s.161) which validated the acts of a director whose appointment later turned out to have been defective in some way. Section 285 made no sense unless it was read as referring to a de facto director. The upshot was that the word "director" may in some legislative contexts include de facto directors, but this will not

[85] [2006] EWHC 1804 (Ch), [2007] B.C.C. 11 at [61]; [2007] 1 B.C.L.C. 618 at [82].

[86] There is also a suggestion in *Re Sykes (Butchers) Ltd, Secretary of State for Trade and Industry v Richardson* [1998] 1 B.C.L.C. 110 at 119 to the effect that a de facto director finding brings the defendant within CDDA s.22(4) as a "person occupying the position of director, by whatever name called". Compare also *Re Red Label Fashions Ltd, Secretary of State for Trade and Industry v Kullar* [1999] B.C.C. 308 at 312.

[87] For example, because of some failure to follow correct procedures under the articles or companies legislation, such as a rule governing the convening of the relevant board or general meeting, a quorum requirement or, as was the case in *Re Canadian Land Reclaiming and Colonizing Co* (1880) L.R. 14 Ch.D. 660, a share qualification.

always be so. The question of whether a given statutory provision applies to de facto directors or not will depend on the overall context of that provision.

(2) When considering disqualification on grounds of unfitness, the court is required to examine the defendant's conduct "as a director". On the view that the paramount purpose of disqualification is public protection, it was difficult to see how Parliament could have intended that the issue of a person's vulnerability to disqualification should rest on the validity of his appointment. A de facto director whose past conduct raises questions about his suitability to be involved in the management of companies should not be able to escape disqualification on the pretext that he was never formally appointed or that his appointment had been defective.[88] The argument for construing "director" narrowly in favour of the individual based on the submission that disqualification is a process with penal characteristics was accordingly rejected in *Lo-Line*.

3–20 The view taken in *Lo-Line* is clearly a sensible one. As discussed in Ch.2, the CDDA is directed broadly at those who abuse the privilege of limited liability or otherwise act improperly in managing companies. It would obviously defeat this broad purpose if a person could contrive to remove himself from the clutches of the legislation because the company conveniently failed to appoint him or his appointment was in some way defective or he had ceased to be qualified to act (e.g. by reason of some requirement such as a share qualification in the articles of association). The point is particularly germane in relation to owner-managed private companies which are rarely run at the level of formality contemplated by companies legislation, at least as regards company decision-making.[89] The basic view that the CDDA applies to de facto directors as well as de jure directors has been confirmed in several s.6 cases.[90] However, even though it is well settled that the Act applies to de facto directors, this still leaves the difficulty of how they are to be identified. What acts or characteristics constitute a person a de facto director?

[88] See also, in a different context, *Re Hydrodam (Corby) Ltd* [1994] 2 B.C.L.C. 180 at 182. It may be added that it would be odd for Parliament to make express provision bringing shadow directors within the scope of the CDDA ss.6–9 while not intending the term "director" to cover persons who act as directors without formal or valid appointment. Indeed, Parliament must be taken as having enacted the CDDA with full knowledge and approval of cases such as *Re Canadian Land Reclaiming and Colonizing Co* (1880) L.R. 14 Ch.D. 660, in light of which it has long been settled that the term "director" as regards the general obligations of directors in company law may include a de facto director by analogy with the concept of trustee or executor *de son tort*. For a comprehensive discussion of the origins of the de facto director concept and its relationship with the older doctrine of de facto officers see C. Noonan and S. Watson, "Examining Company Directors Through the Lens of De Facto Directorship" [2008] J.B.L. 587.

[89] A point reflected in the "think small first" policy that underpins the deregulatory approach taken in the Companies Act 2006 towards decision-making in private companies.

[90] See, e.g. *Re Richborough Furniture Ltd, Secretary of State for Trade and Industry v Stokes* [1996] 1 B.C.L.C. 507 and other cases discussed in the main text below.

Legal ingredients of de facto directorship

3–21 It follows from what has been said so far that a person will only be treated as a de facto director if he has in some sense been acting as a director. Millett J. in *Re Hydrodam (Corby) Ltd* offered a fuller description:

> "A *de facto* director is a person who assumes to act as a director. He is held out as a director by the company, and claims and purports to be a director, although never actually or validly appointed as such. To establish that a person was a *de facto* director of a company it is necessary to plead and prove that he undertook functions in relation to the company which could properly be discharged only by a director. It is not sufficient to show that he was concerned in the management of the company's affairs or undertook tasks in relation to its business which can properly be performed by a manager below board level."[91]

The dictum of Millett J. should not, of course, be read as if it were a statutory definition. Millett J.'s main purpose was to distinguish between de facto and shadow directors. This is clear from the passage immediately following the one cited above where the judge added:

> "A *de facto* director, I repeat, is one who claims to act and purports to act as a director, although not validly appointed as such. A shadow director, by contrast, does not claim or purport to act as a director."

On the facts of *Hydrodam*, Millett J. did not have to apply the test for de facto directors because the only arguable case against the defendants in that case was that they were "shadow directors". In *Re Moorgate Metals Ltd, Official Receiver v Huhtala*[92] Warner J. reviewed the *Hydrodam* case and qualified Millett J.'s dictum by finding that it is not a necessary condition of de facto directorship that the person concerned be held out as a director by having the label of "director" expressly attached to him. Indeed, on the facts of *Moorgate Metals*, the reason that the relevant defendant had not been appointed a de jure director (and the reason why he would not have wanted to be held out as such) was obvious: he was an undischarged bankrupt who did not have the court's permission to act as a director.

3–22 Millett J.'s dictum was adopted and applied in *Re H Laing Demolition Building Contractors Ltd, Secretary of State for Trade and Industry v Laing*.[93] In that case the Secretary of State sought disqualification orders against a de jure director and two other individuals (B and C) who were alleged to have been de facto directors

[91] [1994] 2 B.C.L.C. 180 at 183. The case concerned the applicability of Insolvency Act 1986 s.214 to de facto and shadow directors rather than the applicability of the CDDA but is of general importance. The jurisdiction of the court in relation to de facto directors and the judicial definition of a de facto director as a person who acts as a director without formal appointment has rarely been contested in disqualification cases: see, e.g. *Re Red Label Fashions Ltd, Secretary of State for Trade and Industry v Kullar* [1999] B.C.C. 308; *Re Ambery Metal Form Components Ltd, Secretary of State for Trade and Industry v Jones* [1999] B.C.C. 336. Argument tends to be concentrated much more on what constitutes "acting as a director".

[92] [1995] 1 B.C.L.C. 503 at 517.

[93] [1996] 2 B.C.L.C. 324.

of the same company. The principal ground of the application was that all three had caused the company to trade at the risk of creditors while knowing it to be insolvent. B and C were directors of another company, M Plc but were never formally appointed as directors of the company itself. M Plc entered into a conditional contract to invest in and acquire the company which had been suffering cash-flow difficulties as a result of a significant expansion in its turnover. Before the contract was completed B and C had both become signatories on the company's bank account, the terms of the mandate describing B as a "director" and C as a "manager". Furthermore, there was evidence that B had signed a contract on behalf of the company under the rubric of "director", formally witnessing the affixing of the company's seal to the relevant document. Evans-Lombe J. held that B and C's involvement in the company (the main aim of which was to oversee the completion of M Plc's acquisition rather than to manage the company's business) was not sufficient to constitute them de facto directors. Even assuming that B had held himself out as a director by signing the contract, the evidence as a whole did not suggest unequivocally that he had assumed the role of director in the terms of Millett J.'s test. The judge made the further point that, even if it was accepted that B had constituted himself a de facto director through the act of signing the contract, it remained a question of fact as to how long such a directorship could be taken to have continued. By definition, de facto directorship must be capable of ending without formal resignation and, on the facts, the judge was satisfied that B had not continued to act for a sufficiently lengthy period after signing the contract to justify disturbing his overall conclusion.[94]

3–23 This aspect of Evans-Lombe J.'s reasoning is susceptible to some mild criticism. It is arguable that if the judge was satisfied that the signing of the contract constituted B a de facto director at the time of signing, then it would have been correct to conclude that he was a director for the purposes of CDDA s.6(1)(a). This would not have altered the result as B's only identifiable "conduct as a director" under s.6(1)(b) would have been the signing of the contract and there was no allegation that this, on its own, made him unfit. Support for such an approach can be derived from *Re Ambery Metal Form Components Ltd, Secretary of State for Trade and Industry v Jones*.[95] In that case there was an allegation that the defendant had held himself out as joint managing director of the relevant company in a letter addressed to a firm of accountants. It was held by a district judge that this "holding out" was an isolated incident relating only to a period of some four days. On appeal to the High Court, Jonathan Parker J. said that the correct approach was to look at the defendant's conduct in the round to see if he had, in fact, assumed the role of a director of the company and that, as such, it was significant that the defendant was prepared to sign a letter on the company's notepaper expressing himself to be joint managing director. Thus, the appeal judge in *Ambery Metal* was prepared to draw a wide inference as to the defendant's overall role within the company based on the evidence of holding out in the letter.

[94] [1996] 2 B.C.L.C. 324 at 346.
[95] [1999] B.C.C. 336.

A more recent case where the court seems to have envisaged that a person might have been a de facto director in relation to specific acts or dealings but not more generally is *FanmailUK.com Ltd v Cooper.*[96] In that case the judge found that there were occasions on which an individual became so directly involved in making important decisions in a company that he assumed a de facto director's role in relation to those particular decisions, and would therefore have owed the company fiduciary duties in relation to those decisions on the application of the principle deriving from the judgment of A.L. Smith L.J. in *Mara v Browne*.[97] However, the judge found that much of the time the individual was doing no more than offering support, assistance and advice to other individuals, drawing on his business experience and going no further than one would expect an interested investor in the company to do. It would require detailed consideration of each incident to decide whether he had overstepped that mark and had taken responsibility for a particular decision. On the facts, the judge did not need to embark upon such an exercise. This case raises the interesting analytical question of the extent to which a person may become a de facto director at all material times, but without the full range of directors' duties applying in all circumstances, or whether he will become a de facto director only in relation to certain transactions or acts but not more generally.

3–24 It would appear from Millett J.'s test in *Hydrodam* and the manner of its application in *Laing* that the following two elements would have to be established for the court to make a finding of de facto directorship:

(1) that both the company and the defendant had represented that he was, or held him out to be, a director of the company at the relevant time;
(2) that the defendant had undertaken functions which could only be performed by a director and not by a manager or some other senior employee below board level.[98]

However, this two-limb test has since been further developed and modified. The status of the first limb as a required threshold test was questioned in *Re Moorgate Metals Ltd, Official Receiver v Huhtala*.[99] In *Re Richborough Furniture Ltd, Secretary of State for Trade and Industry v Stokes*,[100] Mr Timothy Lloyd Q.C. (sitting as a deputy High Court judge) doubted that the *Hydrodam* test amounted to an exhaustive test of de facto directorship applicable in every case. The main problem perceived by Mr Lloyd Q.C. was that, under the first limb, anyone who, on the facts of a given case, could be shown to have run the company would only

[96] [2008] EWHC 3131 (Ch).
[97] [1896] 1 Ch 199, 209.
[98] In *Laing*, the second "functional" element was not proven. As such, it is suggested that the case would have been decided the same way had the judge applied the "equal footing" test discussed below in the main text.
[99] [1995] 1 B.C.L.C. 503 at 517.
[100] [1996] 1 B.C.L.C. 507.

be exposed to disqualification if, as a threshold requirement, that person had been held out as a director and had claimed to be, and purported to act as a director. This criticism appears to have considerable force, as it is by no means clear why a person's potential liability to disqualification should turn on what essentially is a required element in establishing agency by estoppel.[101] As Professor Morse has pointed out, the concept of "holding out" is associated with the issue of corporate contractual liability (that is, whether a particular agent has the requisite authority to bind the company in contract) and the underlying policy issue of security of transaction, whereas the CDDA is concerned with broader issues of public and creditor protection.[102] As such, it would be odd if the public lost protection simply because there was no "holding out" in the sense that the concept is understood in an agency law context.[103] On the other hand, however, it can be argued that Millett J.'s reference to holding out should not be read as requiring proof that a person had authority as a matter of agency law to bind the company in its dealings with third parties for that person to be constituted a de facto director. Many individual de jure directors have only limited authority to act as corporate agents but there is no doubt that they occupy the office and carry out the functions of a director. Thus, "holding out" in the sense that the phrase was used by Millett J. may have different connotations requiring merely evidence of consent on the part of the individual to assume director functions and of acquiescence by the company rather than proof that the de facto director is a full-blown corporate agent.[104]

Concerns about the "holding out" element of Millett J.'s formulation prompted Mr Lloyd Q.C. to put forward his own description of a de facto director in *Richborough Furniture*:

> "It seems to me that for someone to be made liable to disqualification under s.6 as a *de facto* director, the court would have to have clear evidence that he had been either the sole person directing the affairs of the company . . . or, if there were others who were true directors, that he was acting on an equal footing with the others in directing the affairs of the company. It also seems to me that, if it is unclear whether the acts of the person in question are referable to an assumed directorship, or to some other capacity such as shareholder or . . . consultant, the person in question must be entitled to the benefit of the doubt."[105]

This test abandons any threshold "holding out" requirement and amounts to a reformulation of the second "functional" element of Millett J.'s definition. The decision in *Richborough Furniture* has led subsequently to the development of a looser approach in which the court considers all the relevant circumstances of the

[101] See, e.g. *Freeman & Lockyer Ltd v Buckhurst Park Properties (Mangal) Ltd* [1964] 2 Q.B. 480.
[102] G. Morse, "Shadow and De Facto Directors" in B. Rider (ed.), *The Corporate Dimension* (Bristol: Jordans, 1998).
[103] See also *Re Moorgate Metals Ltd, Official Receiver v Huhtala* [1995] 1 B.C.L.C. 503 at 517.
[104] See further C. Noonan and S. Watson, "Examining Company Directors Through the Lens of De Facto Directorship" [2008] J.B.L. 587 especially at 605–606.
[105] [1996] 1 B.C.L.C. 507 at 524.

case[106] and in which evidence of "holding out" is taken into account as a highly relevant but not necessarily decisive factor.[107]

3–25 The apparent virtue of the *Richborough Furniture* test is its emphasis on the necessity for the de facto director to have participated in directing the affairs of the relevant company or companies.[108] To this extent, it points to a threshold requirement of board level participation which is capable of flexible application in different circumstances. Where it is clear that the defendant was the only person running the company's business, there will be no difficulty in saying that he was a de facto director. Thus, cases like *Re Lo-Line Electric Motors Ltd*[109] are readily explicable. In *Lo-Line*, the defendant had been validly appointed as a director of a company. He then resigned, but subsequently resumed the sole running of the company without being formally reappointed after the only remaining de jure director had absconded to the United States. Browne-Wilkinson V.C. had no difficulty in concluding that the defendant had constituted himself a de facto director by assuming sole control of the company's business. Equally, the court will have little difficulty arriving at a de facto director finding if the evidence shows that the defendant was the main person actively managing the company's trading operations in circumstances where the de jure directors were involved to a lesser or a nominal degree.[110] Similarly, in circumstances where individuals cease to be de jure directors and procure the appointment of a company that they own, of which they are directors, as a de jure corporate director although the management of the company is carried on as before, the court may be satisfied that individuals remain de facto directors after their resignation as de jure directors.[111] Where a de jure director resigns, and where he remains involved

[106] *Re Land Travel Ltd, Secretary of State for Trade and Industry v Tjolle* [1998] 1 B.C.L.C. 333; *Re Kaytech International Plc, Secretary of State for Trade and Industry v Kaczer* [1999] 2 B.C.L.C. 351; *Re Amba Rescue Ltd, Secretary of State for Trade and Industry v Hollier* [2007] B.C.C. 11; *Re Mea Corporation Ltd, Secretary of State for Trade and Industry v Aviss* [2007] 1 B.C.L.C. 618 and further discussion below in the main text.

[107] See, e.g. *Re Sykes (Butchers) Ltd, Secretary of State for Trade and Industry v Richardson* [1999] 1 B.C.L.C. 110; *Re Ambery Metal Form Components Ltd, Secretary of State for Trade and Industry v Jones* [1999] B.C.C. 336 (considered at 3–23 above); *Re Amba Rescue Ltd, Secretary of State for Trade and Industry v Hollier* [2007] B.C.C. 11 at paras [66], [81]; *Gemma Ltd v Davies* [2008] EWHC 546 (Ch), [2008] 2 B.C.L.C. 281 at [40].

[108] *Re Amba Rescue Ltd, Secretary of State for Trade and Industry v Hollier* [2007] B.C.C. 11 at [67]–[68].

[109] [1988] Ch. 477.

[110] See, e.g. *Re Moorgate Metals Ltd, Official Receiver v Huhtala* [1995] 1 B.C.L.C. 503 discussed further in 3–21 and 3–26. A point of note arising from this case is that the de facto director had deliberately avoided formal appointment because he was an undischarged bankrupt and therefore automatically disqualified from directing or managing a company under CDDA s.11. Similarly, in *Primlake Ltd (in liquidation) v Matthews Associates* [2006] EWHC 1227 (Ch), [2007] 1 B.C.L.C. 666 a person found to be a de facto director on the basis of overwhelming evidence that he had performed the majority of management functions had avoided appointment as a de jure director for tax reasons. *Re Cargo Agency Ltd* [1992] B.C.L.C. 686 is another case in point although there it was conceded without argument that the relevant party had acted as a de facto director.

[111] Though note the requirement in Companies Act 2006 s.155 that every company must have at least one director who is a natural person and can under s.156 be directed by the Secretary of State to cure any breach on pain of criminal penalty.

in the management, the evidential burden of proof in practice moves to that individual to show that after his resignation, his role and functions did in truth change, so that he was no longer acting as a director.[112] The "equal footing" aspect of the *Richborough Furniture* test also appears to offer a means of framing more complex issues in cases where the alleged de facto director claims to have been acting in some other capacity such as a "consultant" or an "employee". The merits or otherwise of the "equal footing" test are considered in more detail below.

De facto directors: the "equal footing" test

3–26 The "equal footing" test has been considered or adopted in a number of cases with variable results. The question of whether the defendant was acting on an equal footing with the de jure directors in a given case has generally been regarded as a question of fact. In *Re Moorgate Metals Ltd, Official Receiver v Huhtala*,[113] a case decided a year before *Richborough Furniture*, there were two defendants, R and H. The company, which traded as a metal merchant, was in substance a joint venture between the two. H was a de jure director and the company secretary but had no experience of the metal trade. He took responsibility for financial and administrative matters. R, in contrast, was an experienced metal trader. R had taken sole charge of the company's trading operation but was never formally appointed as a director (he was an undischarged bankrupt). Warner J. took little persuasion to conclude that R was a de facto director and so liable to disqualification under CDDA s.6. The evidence suggested that R and H were equal joint venturers. R was the driving force behind the setting up of the business. R and H shared the responsibility of managing the company and, under this arrangement, R was left in sole control of the company's trading without any formal limit being placed on the extent of the commitments that he could enter into on the company's behalf. R and H received equal remuneration. Finally, there was in evidence a promotional brochure published by the company that described R and H repeatedly as "partners". In the judge's words, they were "equals running the company between them".

3–27 *Re Sykes (Butchers) Ltd, Secretary of State for Trade and Industry v Richardson* is another case in which the defendant was held to be a de facto director.[114] The relevant company was the subsidiary of another company called Lemoncrest. The defendant, R, was a director of Lemoncrest, but he was never formally appointed as a director of the company, although there was some evidence that this was intended. The company's only de jure director was O, who was also a director of Lemoncrest. The Secretary of State relied on several documents, including the company's bank mandates and letters on company note

[112] See *Secretary of State for Business, Enterprise and Regulatory Reform v Poulter*, April 11, 2008, Ch.D., unreported (Registrar Derrett) where the trial proceeded in the absence of the defendants.
[113] [1995] 1 B.C.L.C. 503.
[114] [1999] 1 B.C.L.C. 110.

paper that R had signed as "director" or "MD". The court also heard oral evidence from the company's bank manager, the company secretary and O to the effect that R had acted as if he were a director. On the evidence as a whole, the registrar concluded that R was a de facto director, a finding upheld by Ferris J. on appeal. The decision seems to have turned primarily on the fact that R had been held out as a director, although Ferris J. did pay lip-service to the "equal footing" test as articulated in *Richborough Furniture*. The case suggests that strong evidence of holding out may well strengthen an inference of equal participation in the management of the company's affairs between the alleged de facto director and the appointed board, even though, as was seen above, there is no threshold requirement of "holding out".

3–28 Insofar as the "equal footing" test requires the court to draw a distinction between acts that "are referable to an assumed directorship" or acts referable "to some other capacity such as shareholder or . . . consultant" it has tended to work in favour of defendants. By way of contrast with the decisions in *Lo-Line, Moorgate Metals* and *Sykes (Butchers)*, applications against alleged de facto directors in *Re Moonlight Foods (UK) Ltd, Secretary of State for Trade and Industry v Hickling,*[115] *Re Land Travel Ltd, Secretary of State for Trade and Industry v Tjolle*[116] and in *Richborough Furniture* itself were all dismissed because, on their facts, none of them was on an "equal footing" in the sense that their acts were referable to an assumed directorship. As will become clear, the decision in the *Land Travel* case also made further important modifications to the applicable test.

3–29 In *Richborough Furniture*, there were three defendants, two of who, S and Z, were de jure directors. It was alleged that the third defendant, M, was a de facto director. The relevant company was part of a group that amounted in substance to a joint venture between S, a Mr Bond (who was not the subject of proceedings) and various interests associated with Z. Z and M were married and, together with their son, they ran an unincorporated business called the Jade Partnership which provided consultancy services to small businesses. Jade invested in the group and entered into a formal consultancy agreement with it. As a result, Jade, principally through M, provided financial management, accounting and administrative services to the company. Once the company began to struggle, M regularly negotiated on its behalf with the Inland Revenue, Customs and Excise and pressing trade creditors. S's evidence was that he relied on M to perform the functions of a finance director and that M had some say in the decision to pay creditors. There was also evidence from the company's suppliers and creditors that S had introduced M to them as his "partner" and that M had referred to himself in telephone conversations as "the boss" or the "managing director". The key question was whether M had acted merely as a consultant or whether, in fact, he had assumed the role of a finance director. The position was complicated because, in effect, M was performing a dual role, acting as a consultant under the agreement while also

[115] [1996] B.C.C. 678.
[116] [1998] 1 B.C.L.C. 333.

representing Jade's interests as a shareholder in the group.[117] In keeping with the final sentence of the extract from his judgment set out in 3–24 above, the judge decided that M was entitled to the benefit of the doubt. While accepting that outsiders may have perceived that S and M were equals, he found that under the peculiar arrangement between Jade and the company, M had not been placed on an equal footing with the de jure directors.

Clearly, this was very much a borderline case. There is little doubt that within the company M was regarded as having primary responsibility for financial and accounting matters, including bookkeeping and the preparation of management accounts. He carried out tasks that were therefore consistent with directorship. However, the judge considered that these tasks could equally have been carried out by a professional adviser or an employee and that any say M had in the company derived from his position as a nominee representing Jade's interests as a shareholder. It followed that M had not unequivocally assumed the position of a director because it was possible to say that he was carrying out his functions in some other capacity, e.g. as consultant, employee or shareholder.[118]

3–30 The facts of *Re Moonlight Foods (UK) Ltd, Secretary of State for Trade and Industry v Hickling* are less complex but there are similarities in the outcome and underlying reasoning. There were three defendants: two de jure directors and, C, an alleged de facto director. C was a qualified accountant who served in the relevant company as company secretary. He was also an employee of the company's major shareholder. He acted as alternate director for one of the de jure directors and was a signatory on the bank account. Under the terms of a formal agreement between the company and its major shareholder, the shareholder provided the company with a financial management service in the person of C. C carried out functions that were consistent with those of a finance director, including the preparation of cash flow forecasts and management accounts for the board. He attended board meetings, but was always careful in the minutes, according to standard convention, to distinguish

[117] The judge expressed the view that it was legitimate for M to represent Jade as against the other shareholders and, furthermore, that in a small quasi-partnership company, decisions which are ordinarily matters of day-to-day management for the board, including who to pay and when, could reasonably be regarded as a question for the shareholders to decide, especially at a time of crisis. Given that the judge ruled in M's favour, it may be thought that a shareholder who influences company decision-making qua shareholder will not be regarded as a de facto director. However, where the evidence shows that the defendant involved himself extensively in the company's affairs with the aim of protecting or enhancing his investment, it is doubtful that the court would rule that he had not constituted himself a de facto director on the ground that he had acted qua shareholder: see *Re Kaytech International Plc, Secretary of State for Trade and Industry v Kaczer* [1999] 2 B.C.L.C. 351 at 422–423; *Re Ambery Metal Form Components Ltd, Secretary of State for Trade and Industry v Jones* [1999] B.C.C. 336 at 349–350.

[118] M maintained throughout that his role was one of offering advice and providing information to the company on behalf of Jade rather than of taking any formal decisions in relation to the running of the company. It is interesting to note that, at the relevant time, M was an undischarged bankrupt and the subject of a disqualification order made in the case of *Re Tansoft Ltd* [1991] B.C.L.C. 339. There may have been grounds for the court to draw some less favourable inferences from the evidence especially in relation to the role played by Jade. The judge did note in passing that M's involvement may have been sufficient to put him in breach of the disqualification order or the terms of CDDA s.11 as he had arguably taken part in management.

between the de jure directors, who were present, and himself as secretary, who was recorded as being merely "in attendance". Applying the approach in *Richborough Furniture* to the letter, the judge dismissed the application against C. He was not satisfied that C was on an equal footing with the two de jure directors, both of whom were active in the management of the company. Furthermore, C's acts were not necessarily referable to an assumed directorship. They were equally consistent with his role as either company secretary or as an employee of the major shareholder providing the company with services under the services agreement.

3–31 The "equal footing" test was considered further in *Re Land Travel Ltd, Secretary of State for Trade and Industry v Tjolle*. The alleged de facto director, K, was one of three defendants. She had worked her way up in the relevant company from a part-time administrative assistant to the position of a senior employee, principally responsible for sales, marketing and customer care. The dominant force in the company was its founder, T who was described in evidence as "autocratic". K had become a de jure director of the company's parent, BNE, but not of the company itself. She had some limited power to commit the company to expenditure in relation to sales and marketing but T made most of the managerial decisions. There was evidence that K had been called by various titles including "director" and "deputy managing director" to give her status in the eyes of customers and other employees. She had signed company documents, including bank mandates, using these titles. However, she had stopped using these titles and also resigned her directorship of BNE once she had realised that the group was in default in relation to its filing obligations with the Registrar of Companies. Nevertheless, she had continued to use the title "chief executive" and to attend regular meetings with T and the other de jure director. In her favour, the evidence suggested that T exercised an iron grip over the company's affairs. The company's financial records were kept locked away so that K had no access to them. There was little to suggest that she had played any real part in financial and strategic decision-making. Accordingly, Jacob J. held that K could be classified as a manager but not as a de facto director and, in so doing, he explained further the "equal footing" test and put the matter more widely:

> "For myself I think it may be difficult to postulate any one decisive test. I think what is involved is very much a question of degree. The court takes into account all the relevant factors. Those factors include at least whether or not there was a holding out by the company of the individual as a director, whether the individual used the title, whether the individual had proper information . . . on which to base decisions, and whether the individual has to make major decisions and so on. Taking all these factors into account, one asks 'was this individual part of the corporate governing structure?', answering it as a kind of jury question. In deciding this, one bears very much in mind why one is asking the question . . . There would be no justification for the law making a person liable to misfeasance or disqualification proceedings unless they were truly in a position to exercise the powers and discharge the functions of a director. Otherwise they would be made liable for events over which they had no real control, either in fact or law."[119]

[119] [1998] 1 B.C.L.C. 333 at 343–344. This passage was cited with approval by the Court of Appeal in *Re Kaytech International Plc, Secretary of State for Trade and Industry v Kaczer* [1999] 2 B.C.L.C. 351 at 423.

In the first part of the passage, the judge is not to be understood as enumerating tests which must all be satisfied if de facto directorship is to be established. On this approach, the court should consider all the relevant factors (including those matters mentioned), but recognise that the crucial question is whether the defendant has assumed the status and functions of a director so as to make himself responsible under the CDDA as if he were a de jure director.[120] Although it was clear on the facts of *Land Travel* that K was called a "director" and held out as one, she did not form part of the real corporate governance of the company, not least because she was denied access to detailed information concerning the company's financial position. The upshot is that while evidence of holding out is clearly relevant and can be taken into account, a person who takes the title "director" will not necessarily be regarded as a de facto director. It was seen above that it is not necessary for a finding of de facto directorship that the alleged de facto director was held out as a director. Conversely, it is clear from *Land Travel* that evidence of "holding out" will not necessarily be sufficient to establish de facto directorship. It is merely one of a number of relevant factors that can be taken into account. In the words of the judge:

> "[I]t is common experience that many business executives these days use (and are told to use) the title 'director' when they are no such thing . . . Titles such as 'marketing director', 'sales director' and so on are far from uncommon. It would potentially lead to injustice if all such individuals were to be treated in law as if they really were directors."[121]

However, the court may attach greater significance to evidence of holding out in other cases depending on all the relevant circumstances.[122] Thus, in *FanmailUK.com Ltd v Cooper*[123] an individual was, with his approval, held out by a company to be a non-executive director in particular, in relation to a business investment proposal but where the thrust of the relevant section in that document was held to be an indication of who would be included in the management team should an investment be made. The judge held that this and other similar statements (such as his introduction to another individual as the company's future chairman) did not amount to a declaration by the individual or anyone that he was for all purposes to be treated as a de facto director of the company and that he was

[120] *Re Kaytech International Plc, Secretary of State for Trade and Industry v Kaczer* [1999] 2 B.C.L.C. 351 at 423–424.

[121] [1998] 1 B.C.L.C. 333 at 345. This observation about the popular use of the title "director" is undoubtedly correct. It is fashionable for businesses to use such job titles as status symbols with the object of motivating staff and impressing outsiders. The converse is also true, i.e. the use of labels such as "consultant" or "manager" may be relevant but inconclusive evidence weighing against a finding of de facto directorship.

[122] See, e.g. *Re Sykes (Butchers) Ltd, Secretary of State for Trade and Industry v Richardson* [1999] 1 B.C.L.C. 110; *Re Ambery Metal Form Components Ltd, Secretary of State for Trade and Industry v Jones* [1999] B.C.C. 336; *Re Kaytech International Plc, Secretary of State for Trade and Industry v Kaczer* [1999] 2 B.C.L.C. 351; *Re Amba Rescue Ltd, Secretary of State for Trade and Industry v Hollier* [2007] B.C.C. 11 at [81]. *Kaytech* is discussed immediately below in the main text.

[123] [2008] EWHC 3131 (Ch).

not in any sense generally estopped, as between himself and the company, from denying that he was a de facto director. In each case, the critical question remains whether the defendant is, in fact, on equal terms with the appointed directors in the sense of having an equal ability to participate and share in the wider strategic or corporate governance decisions taken by those who form the company's governing structure.[124]

3–32 The flexible "in all the circumstances" test posited by Jacob J. in *Land Travel* was approved by the Court of Appeal in *Re Kaytech International Plc, Secretary of State for Trade and Industry v Kaczer*[125] and so, for now, the law appears to be reasonably settled. In *Kaytech*, the *dramatis personae* were K, P and S. K had originally run a retail mail order business selling computers but had decided to branch out of mail order and into direct retailing from shop premises. A new company, K Plc, was formed for this purpose. K's friend, P, a qualified chartered surveyor was the moving spirit behind the incorporation of the company. The trial judge found that P had been extensively involved in the company over the 18 months of its trading life. He had acquired premises for the company in different locations. He had taken sole responsibility for raising the company's initial capital (the arrangements that he claimed to have made turned out to be a fiction) and had been involved in the preparation and presentation of the company's business plan. There was evidence that P had been held out, or had held himself out, as being variously a "director", "joint founder" and "chief executive" of the company. However, P was never formally appointed as a director, although he had procured the appointment of S, an Isle of Man resident, as the second de jure director. The trial judge also found as a fact that K and P had intended K to have an 80 per cent stake in the company and P to have a 20 per cent stake. In the event, it was not clear that any share capital had ever been issued and, prior to its liquidation, the company had traded in breach of the minimum capital requirements for public limited companies. Delivering the unanimous judgment of the court, Robert Walker L.J. held that in the light of the primary findings of fact, the trial judge's conclusion that P had been a de facto director was "inevitable and incontrovertible".[126] Given the trial judge's finding that P had carried out extensive executive functions and had been held out as having such functions, the epithet seems entirely apt.

In reaching this conclusion Robert Walker L.J. saw "much force" in the approach taken in *Land Travel* because it recognised that:

> "the crucial issue is whether the individual in question has assumed the status and functions of a company director so as to make himself responsible under the 1986 Act as if he were a *de jure* director."[127]

[124] See further *Secretary of State for Trade and Industry v Elms*, January 16, 1997, Ch.D., unreported; *Re Amba Rescue Ltd, Secretary of State for Trade and Industry v Hollier* [2007] B.C.C. 11 at [68]–[81].

[125] [1999] 2 B.C.L.C. 351.

[126] [1999] 2 B.C.L.C. 351 at 423.

[127] [1999] 2 B.C.L.C. 351 at 423–424.

In a subsequent passage commenting obiter on the difference between de facto and shadow directorship, he added that a characteristic of both concepts is:

> "that an individual who was not a *de jure* director is alleged to have exercised real influence . . . in the corporate governance of a company."[128]

3–33 It is clear from the *Land Travel* test that the question of whether the alleged de facto director was part of the company's governing structure is one of degree. If the evidence suggests that the individual was regularly involved in executive decision-making, this will strengthen the case. If, however, the evidence suggests that the individual took part in only one or two key management decisions during the lifetime of the company, the case for saying that he was a de facto director exercising a "real influence" in the company's governance is likely to be weaker.

In *Re Balfour Associates IT Recruitment Ltd, Secretary of State for Trade and Industry v Becker*,[129] the company acted as a recruitment agency for a period of three years. The only issued share was held by AB. The sole de jure director was AB's son, JB. The company was financed throughout its three-year trading life by loans from AB. It ceased trading and shortly afterwards went into creditors' voluntary liquidation. The liquidator sold the company's assets to a new company of which AB was the sole director and shareholder. There was some dispute as to whether the new company had acquired the benefit of the old company's contracts under the terms of sale. However, it was clear that the new company had issued invoices in respect of the old company's outstanding contracts. The Secretary of State's case against AB was that he had been actively involved in the decision to.put the company into liquidation and had directed his son as to what should be done or, at the very least, had taken part in the decision-making process whereby he and the successor company benefited at the expense of the old company's creditors. It was not part of the Secretary of State's case that AB had played any part in the day-to-day business of the old company prior to the decision to cease trading. On appeal from the decision of Mr Registrar Baister granting the defendant summary judgment, the court had to consider whether the claimant had any real prospect of establishing that AB had been a de facto director of the old company. Taking his cue from the decision in *Re Ambery Metal Form Components Ltd, Secretary of State for Trade and Industry v Jones*,[130] Rattee J. said:

> "Of course, a sole shareholder, like anyone else, can, if he undertakes functions in relation to a company which can only be properly be discharged by a director, constitute himself a *de facto* director. There is of course no incompatibility between being a sole shareholder and making oneself by one's conduct a *de facto* director. But the question in the present case is whether there is any real prospect of satisfying the court that, by virtue of persuading his son to take the steps he did in causing the old company to cease trading and not to take any steps in seeking to prevent the new company from taking the

[128] [1999] 2 B.C.L.C. 351 at 424. See further 3–52 below.
[129] [2002] EWHC 2200 (Ch), [2003] 1 B.C.L.C. 555.
[130] [1999] B.C.C. 336.

benefit of the old company's contracts, [AB] did undertake such functions in relation to the old company."[131]

Upholding the earlier decision of Mr Registrar Baister, Rattee J. held that AB's degree of involvement was insufficient for the Secretary of State to have a real prospect of successfully establishing that he had acted as a de facto director and that, accordingly, the registrar had been right to enter summary judgment in his favour. In truth, as the registrar had pointed out, the Secretary of State's case against AB depended on the court drawing inferences about the nature and degree of his day-to-day involvement and influence during the company's three-year trading history from the liquidator's evidence of his involvement and influence at the end of the company's life. However, the court was simply not prepared to draw those inferences. As discussed in 3–23 above, the court was prepared to draw a wider inference in *Re Ambery Metal Form Components Ltd, Secretary of State for Trade and Industry v Jones*.[132] However, in that case the inference was based on direct evidence that the individual concerned had been held out as joint-managing director. There was no equivalent evidence in *Balfour Associates*.

Summary and reflections on the current law relating to de facto directors

3–34 The basic parameters of the court's approach to establishing whether or not a person is a de facto director for the purposes of the CDDA are now fairly well settled. The Court of Appeal's approval of *Land Travel* in *Kaytech* suggests that the correct test (as a matter of authority) is to ask whether in all the circumstances (no single factor necessarily being decisive) the defendant has assumed the status and functions of a de jure director.[133] The core issue is therefore whether the person assumed functions that can be equated to those of a de jure director and was in a position to participate in and exercise "real influence" (though not necessarily control) over the direction and governance of the company. As Lewison J. expressed it in *Re Amba Rescue Ltd, Secretary of State for Trade and Industry v Hollier*, "[t]he touchstone is whether the defendant was part of the corporate governing structure."[134] Moreover, it is clear that evidence that the person was held out as a director is neither necessary nor sufficient to establish de facto directorship. It is one of a range of relevant factors that can be taken into account, although it may be important evidence suggesting that to all intents and purposes the person has assumed office. The virtue of the *Land Travel* test is that it requires the court to look at the overall picture in each case to determine whether the alleged de facto director has assumed a position equivalent to that of a de jure director. It is also capable of application in cases where the alleged de facto

[131] [2003] 1 B.C.L.C. 555 at [45].
[132] [1999] B.C.C. 336.
[133] The ability to play a role in the company's management but without any such role in fact being taken up or any action being taken in relation to the company's affairs, would not constitute the person a de facto director: see *Re Mercury Solutions UK Ltd, Secretary of State for Trade and Industry v Hall* [2006] EWHC 1995 (Ch) discussed at 3–69.
[134] [2007] B.C.C. 11 at [81].

director is one of several people, including de jure directors, who took some part in the running of the company's affairs. However, within these broad parameters, difficult questions requiring fine judgments will continue to arise and much will depend on the trial judge's assessment of the evidence. Each case will turn on its own facts. This is inevitable given the highly fact sensitive and context specific nature of the enquiry that has to be undertaken. There are (at least) three areas of likely difficulty: equivalence between de facto and de jure directors; acts referable to other capacities; and standard of proof. These are considered in turn.

Equivalence between de facto and de jure directors

3–35 The "equal footing" aspect of the approach in *Richborough Furniture* and *Land Travel* begs a number of questions. It seems to rest on two assumptions. The first is that a de jure director is a straightforward comparator whose functions are readily and objectively identifiable. The second is that de jure directors necessarily take an equal, active and influential role in directing the company's affairs. The reality is that many de jure directors (admittedly, at their peril) take a nominal role and many others are in a minority or are forced to defer (for whatever reason) to the influence of a dominant personality or group on the board. More significantly, the de jure directors will often have different areas of responsibility. This will be especially obvious where there are full-time executive directors and part-time non-executive directors. It follows that the issue of equivalence should be approached flexibly and not too literally. In this respect, the approach taken by Lewison J. in *Re Amba Rescue Ltd, Secretary of State for Trade and Industry v Hollier* is instructive.

In *Amba Rescue*, Lewison J. gave this summary of the applicable principles[135]:

> "(1) The touchstone is whether the defendant was part of the corporate governing structure. (2) Inherent in that touchstone is the distinction between someone who participates, or has the right to participate, in collective decision making on corporate policy and strategy and its implementation, on the one hand, and others who may advise or act on behalf of, or otherwise for the benefit of, the company, but do not participate in decision making as part of the corporate governance of the company. Accordingly, the test is not satisfied by someone who was at all times and in all material decisions subordinate to the *de jure* directors. (3) The defendant may have been a *de facto* director even though he or she did not have day-to-day control of the company's affairs, and even though he or she was only involved in part of the company's activities."

The first matter of interest is Lewison J.'s emphasis on the *right* (or ability) to participate in collective decision making as distinct from a wholly subordinate role. This draws on a passage from HH Judge Cooke's judgment in *Secretary of State for Trade and Industry v Elms* where the judge sought to explain the "equal footing" test in *Richborough Furniture* in these terms:

> "It is not I think in any way a question of equality of power but equality of ability to participate in the notional board room. Is he somebody who is simply advising and, as

[135] [2007] B.C.C. 11 at [81].

> it were, withdrawing having advised, or somebody who joins the other directors, *de facto* or *de jure*, in decisions which affect the future of the company?"[136]

Although the context is the distinction between an advisory role and a board-level role, Judge Cooke's emphasis on the *right* or *ability* to participate reflects a finer grained approach which makes allowance for different degrees of participation in the "notional board room". In other words, it suggests that a finding of de facto directorship could not be ruled out simply because, for example, the de jure directors take the lead role in corporate decision making.

The second matter of interest is Lewison J.'s point that a person need not necessarily be involved in the running of every aspect of the company's affairs in order to assume a de facto directorship. This sensibly reflects the fact that de jure directors may have different degrees of involvement and different areas of responsibility in any given corporate setting. Lewison J. relied on the following passage from the judgment of Mr Anthony Mann Q.C. in *Secretary of State for Trade and Industry v Ashby* (an unreported case decided in 1992) to buttress the point:

> "I very much doubt that Mr Lloyd Q.C. [in *Richborough Furniture*] meant that in all respects a *de facto* director had to be on an exactly equal footing to all the other directors. For example, I would expect a *de facto* finance director to defer to the properly appointed marketing director in matters of marketing in the same way as a *de jure* appointed finance director would. I think that all Mr Lloyd was trying to do was to encapsulate the notion that, in investigating the qualities of the acts performed by the person whose status is in question, one is looking for someone who is essentially operating at the same level as the properly appointed directors, that is to say they are not in reality subordinate to them at all times."

It is suggested that this provides useful clarification insofar as it implies that rough equivalence in all the circumstances and in the relevant corporate setting is all that is required for a finding of de facto directorship.

3–36 A related point is that the duties of de facto directors may vary from the duties of de jure directors. In considering whether the conduct of a director falls below the required standards of probity and competence such as to require his disqualification under CDDA s.6, the court has to take account of this point. Whereas a de jure director has certain duties imposed by statute and almost certainly a minimum non-delegable duty to monitor and participate in the company's affairs, a de facto director may have lesser and more specific duties deriving from the precise role expressly conferred on or assumed by him.[137] However, it is suggested that as a matter of statutory construction, directors' general duties set out in the Companies Act 2006 will apply to de facto directors. The question in those cases, will be, it is suggested, whether the requirements of those duties will, as a matter of fact, require different responses of different directors, whether all are de jure or one or more is de facto only.

[136] January 16, 1997, Ch.D., unreported. See also *Re Land Travel Ltd, Secretary of State for Trade and Industry v Tjolle* [1998] 1 B.C.L.C. 333 at 343.
[137] See discussion in 3–23 of *FanmailUK.com Ltd v Cooper* [2008] EWHC 3131 (Ch).

3–37 Another aspect of equivalence which requires flexible and careful handling is Lewison J.'s touchstone requirement, derived from *Land Travel*, that the person was "part of the corporate governing structure". Language of this sort may tend to concentrate attention narrowly on the formal decision-making organs of the company, in particular, the board. This may be an appropriate approach in a large company or a company where the board functions in a formal sense and its areas of activity are clearly demarcated. However, it may not accurately reflect the position in many small or owner-managed companies where decision making is often less formal. Thus, the idea deriving from legal theory of the board as the main organ of the company, functioning formally and collectively to express the company's will, may not always capture commercial practice and reality. It is important therefore to stress the point (also made in *Land Travel* and *Kaytech*) that the court should take into account all relevant factors. When considering the issue of de facto directors, the court should consider, in particular, the specific corporate setting in which the defendant was working, taking into account factors such as the size of the company and its organisational and decision making processes (whether formal or informal). In many settings, it may be useful to frame the enquiry by reference to Judge Cooke's "notional board room" which implies that corporate decision making can be fluid and will not necessarily always operate within and through formal board structures. In *Amba Rescue*, Lewison J. showed himself to be sensitive to this point:

> "[Counsel] rightly observed that a person may properly be found to have been a *de facto* director even though there is no direct evidence of the defendant's actual participation in an occasion of collective decision making, such as a board meeting or indeed any other meeting of all or some of the other directors. The question in every case is whether it is proper to conclude, from an examination of all the facts, that the defendant did in fact participate in decision making about strategic or policy issues, including their implementation, not merely as an agent or employee or adviser, but as part of the corporate governing structure."[138]

Read in context the phrase "corporate governing structure" in this passage refers to how corporate decisions are taken *in fact* and should not be read to imply that a person must necessarily have participated in or contributed to formal board level decision making as a pre-condition to a finding of de facto directorship.

3–38 In *Land Travel*, it will be recalled that one of the factors that Jacob J. regarded as relevant in determining whether an alleged de facto director's functions were genuinely subordinate to, as opposed to equivalent with, those of the principal de jure director in that case, was whether ". . . the individual had proper information . . . on which to base decisions . . ." On the facts, it was clear that the defendant had no access to the company's financial records which were kept under lock and key and this, taken with the other evidence, led the court to conclude that she was a senior manager reporting to (and therefore subordinate to) the principal de jure director rather than a de facto director. When dealing with the defendant's lack of access to critical information Jacob J. made the following observation:

[138] [2007] B.C.C. 11 at [79].

> "... I think ... that someone who has no, or only peripheral knowledge of matters of vital company concern (*e.g.* financial state) and has no right, legal or *de facto*, to access to such matters is not to be regarded by the law as in substance a director."[139]

To the extent that this observation can be read as making access to information of "vital company concern" a necessary condition of de facto directorship, it was criticised by Lewison J. in *Amba Rescue*. In Lewison J.'s view, there may be circumstances in which the court could conclude that a person who participated in corporate decisions on policy and strategy and in the implementation of such decisions was a de facto director, notwithstanding that he or she had no right to relevant information. Moreover, unlike Jacob J., he could see no reason why, in appropriate circumstances, it would not be consistent with the policy and the purpose of the CDDA for a person to be capable of being disqualified as a director where that person, irrespective of any right to access relevant information, had in fact, alone or with others, committed the company to an unwise or improper policy or course of action, but never made any attempt or had any desire first to acquire knowledge of relevant information.[140] While, it is suggested that Lewison J.'s view is correct in principle, in fairness to Jacob J., his observations should be read in the light of the facts of *Land Travel* and of his overall emphasis on the need to take into account all relevant factors.

Acts referable to other capacities

3–39 *Richborough Furniture* and *Moonlight Foods* suggest that even where the defendant has done some acts that are consistent with de jure directorship, he will not be liable to disqualification as a de facto director if those acts are referable to some other position or capacity such as a consultant, professional adviser, employee or shareholder. One possible justification for this approach is that under CDDA s.6(1)(b), the court is required to consider the defendant's "conduct as a director" in determining whether he is unfit. Therefore, it could be argued that it is unfair for anyone who has not unequivocally assumed the position of a director to be exposed to disqualification. However, if as the authorities suggest, the primary purpose of disqualification is to protect the public, this argument becomes less compelling. The question in CDDA s.6 is whether the defendant's conduct makes him "unfit to be concerned in the management of a company". If the real purpose of the CDDA is to protect the public from those whose conduct makes them unfit to take part in company management there is an equally good argument for saying that the court's jurisdiction should extend to anyone who undertakes some acts or functions that are consistent with de jure directorship. On this analysis, the proper approach in *Richborough Furniture* and *Moonlight Foods* would have been for the court to conclude that M and C were de facto directors and then to have gone on to consider the question of their conduct and whether it

[139] [1998] 1 B.C.L.C. 333 at 344.
[140] [2007] B.C.C. 11 at para.[75].

made them unfit.[141] This approach sits better with the view that the main purpose of the CDDA is to protect the public and raise standards among those who run companies.[142] Moreover, the reference to acts done in other capacities tends to cloud the issue and allow scope for unhelpful (and possibly evasionary) recharacterisations of functions and activities. As Lewison J. put it in *Re Mea Corporation Ltd, Secretary of State for Trade and Industry v Aviss*,[143] "[i]n considering whether a person 'assumes to act as a director' what is important is not what he calls himself, but what he did." Similarly, while a person may act in a range of capacities that can be badged in a variety of different ways the focus should be on what the person actually did in the particular corporate setting taking into account all relevant factors.

3–40 Clearly, if the evidence suggests that a person is acting in some other capacity and their activities and functions are either purely advisory or subordinate to those who comprise the "notional board room" then a case of de facto directorship may not be made out.[144] However, as suggested above, there are cases where the reference to other capacities in *Richborough Furniture* may have clouded the issue. In *Re Red Label Fashions Ltd, Secretary of State for Trade and Industry v Kullar*[145] an application to disqualify the defendant was dismissed on the basis that the evidence suggesting that she had jointly-run a small company in which she was an equal shareholder with her co-defendant husband was consistent with her role as a manager and a wife and therefore not sufficient to constitute her a de facto director. Lightman J. stated that he had been taken through the relevant authorities but did not set them out in his judgment. In summary, he held simply that the authorities required him to consider whether or not the relevant defendant "assumed the role and exercised the role in management of a director". On balance and after what he described as anxious consideration, Lightman J. held that, save for a statement that the defendant was a director in the draft accounts, ". . . there was no unequivocal reference or indication that [she] was or acted as a director rather than as a manager or dutiful wife". He added that he was not satisfied:

> "that she was a *de facto* director rather than a compliant and dutiful wife willing to perform any role which Mr Kullar wanted her to perform in the hope that this might lead to the saving of their marriage and further their jointly-owned company."

It is suggested that the emphasis on the defendant's role as a "manager" and "wife" derives from *Richborough Furniture* although this is not clear from

[141] In *Land Travel*, Jacob J. covered himself by going on to decide that, even if K could be treated as a de facto director, her conduct in relation to the company did not make her unfit.

[142] See further G. Morse, "Shadow and De Facto Directors" in B. Rider (ed.), *The Corporate Dimension* (Bristol: Jordans, 1998). On the issue of public protection and the purpose of the CDDA generally see Ch.2.

[143] [2007] 1 B.C.L.C. 618 at [83].

[144] See, e.g. *Gemma Ltd v Davies* [2008] 2 B.C.L.C. 281 where on the evidence as a whole the judge accepted that while the defendant wife had performed certain clerical functions she had played no role in corporate decision making and was entirely subordinate in this respect to the wishes of her domineering husband.

[145] [1999] B.C.C. 308.

Lightman J.'s judgment. The danger with this approach is that it may deflect attention away from the role and functions which the defendant actually carried out and focus it instead on the reasons or motives behind the defendant having taken up his or her particular role (in *Red Label*, family reasons). In short, it is suggested that the test for de facto directorship turns on what role the person was carrying out and not the reasons why they may have been carrying out that particular role. On the facts as set out by Lightman J. the *Red Label* decision can properly be seen as one concerned with a managerial (but sub-directorial) and subordinate role rather than one of real influence in the company's affairs.

3–41 In the same vein, it may be difficult to distinguish acts referable to an assumed directorship and acts by a person in the capacity of a shareholder. As a practical matter, in many small private companies shareholders may well have a considerable say in the management of the company. It will frequently be the case that the distinction between director and shareholder will not be observed very carefully or formally. Shareholders may also wish to involve themselves in the running and direction of the company's business in order to protect their investment. At first instance in *Kaytech International* Rimer J. observed that the active role played by the defendant P in the running of the company could not be readily explained as having been performed by him as a shareholder because the relevant company's articles, ". . . like those of most companies, delegated its management to the directors."[146] Although the Court of Appeal upheld Rimer J.'s conclusion that P had assumed a de facto directorship, Robert Walker L.J. was unconvinced by this attempt to differentiate the roles of shareholders and directors for purposes of legal analysis and considered that the judge had been:

> "straining his reasoning at this point, probably out of deference to Mr Lloyd Q.C.'s reference in *Richborough* to 'some other capacity such as shareholder.' "[147]

Again, the point to make is that the proper approach turns on the role in fact assumed and exercised, and not the reason or motive for taking up such a role. The question is whether acts or functions which may be referable to one or more potentially overlapping capacities (director, shareholder, adviser, consultant, employee and so on) have been exercised in such a way that the person has crossed the line into de facto directorship. In this respect it is suggested that the following view expressed by Jonathan Parker J. in *Re Ambery Metal Form Components Ltd, Secretary of State for Trade and Industry v Jones* frames the issue more helpfully:

> "If a substantial shareholder in a small company—a quasi-partnership company, for example—wishes, as well he may, to take an active part in running the affairs of the company in order to protect his investment, that raises the very question whether in so doing he may not be constituting himself a *de facto* director of the company."[148]

[146] [1999] 2 B.C.L.C. 351 at 403.
[147] [1999] 2 B.C.L.C. 351 at 422–423. See further *Re Mea Corporation Ltd, Secretary of State for Trade and Industry v Aviss* [2007] 1 B.C.L.C. 618 at [90]–[91].
[148] [1999] B.C.C. 336 at 349–350.

This view was echoed and reinforced by Lewison J. in *Re Amba Rescue Ltd, Secretary of State for Trade and Industry v Hollier*:

> "Each case turns upon its own special facts. In different cases, the same facts may pull in different directions. The fact that the defendant is a relative of a *de jure* director may enable the court to conclude, as did Lightman J. in proceedings under [CDDA s.6] in *Re Red Label Fashions Ltd* [1999] B.C.C. 308, in relation to the wife of the *de jure* director, that the defendant acted as a dutiful relative rather than as a director. On the other hand, it is common ground before me that a person who participates in the affairs of a company out of family loyalty may, in appropriate circumstances, act as a *de facto* director. Similarly, the fact that the defendant has invested financially in a company, as a shareholder or otherwise, and was concerned to protect that investment, could either support or tend to negative the inference that the defendant's conduct in the company's affairs was that of a *de facto* director. It is, for example, commonplace for investors to seek information about, and often to influence, the strategy of a company, without any intention or consequence of assuming the role of a director. On the other hand, as Jonathan Parker J. observed in *Jones* at pp.349–350, if a substantial shareholder in a small company, such as a quasi-partnership company, takes an active part in running the affairs of the company in order to protect his investment, it raises the very question whether in doing so he may not be constituting himself a *de facto* director of the company."[149]

It follows that if, on the evidence, a person has exercised "real influence" over corporate decision making as part of the "notional board room" and in so doing has carried out at least some functions that one would usually expect a de jure director of the company in question (or a company of its size and type) to carry out, that person should be susceptible to the court's jurisdiction under CDDA s.6. While the focus of s.6 is on the defendant's "conduct as a director", the court should take care not to engage in too rigid an analysis of the extent to which acts and functions are referable to other capacities that may often, in practice, overlap with the acts and functions of de jure directors.

Standard of proof

3–42 The suggestion in *Richborough Furniture* that where it is unclear whether or not the relevant acts were referable to an assumed directorship or to some other capacity, defendants should be given "the benefit of the doubt" implies that a criminal, rather than civil, standard of proof should be applied. Such an approach is consistent with the view that CDDA should be regarded as quasi-penal process. However, as was seen in Ch.2, disqualification is treated by the courts as primarily protective rather than penal and, in principle and as a matter of authority, the court should apply the civil standard of proof when determining whether the defendant's acts were such as to constitute him or her a de facto director.[150]

[149] [2007] B.C.C. 11 at [80].

[150] See *Re Euro Express Ltd, Secretary of State for Trade and Industry v Deverell* [2001] Ch. 340, especially at [26], [35] and [38].

Reform

3–43 One commentator has suggested that CDDA s.6(1)(a) should be amended to give the court jurisdiction over any person who has taken part in the management of a company whether formally appointed as a director or not.[151] There is much to commend such an approach which has been taken in other jurisdictions. It would remove the need for the claimant to establish that the defendant was a director whether de jure, de facto or otherwise. Such an amendment would also have the merit of linking the test for disqualification more closely to the scope of the prohibition that flows from disqualification as well as being consistent with, for example, CDDA s.2, where disqualification flows from relevant misconduct concerning (among other things) "promotion, formation, management, liquidation or striking off" of companies rather than being limited to conduct as a director. The issue of de facto directorship is closely tied to the issue of shadow directorship. In the context of the discussion of shadow directorship, considered below, further issues regarding de facto directorship are also raised.

Shadow directors

3–44 Shadow directors are entirely creatures of statute. CDDA s.6(3C)[152] expressly provides that "director" includes a shadow director for the purposes of CDDA ss.6 and 7. Section 8 also applies to persons who have been directors or shadow directors of companies. CDDA s.22(5) provides that:

> " 'Shadow director', in relation to a company, means a person in accordance with whose directions or instructions the directors of the company are accustomed to act (but so that a person is not deemed a shadow director by reason only that the directors act on advice given by him in a professional capacity)."

The same exhaustive definition of "shadow director" is used throughout companies legislation as a whole.[153] CDDA ss.6 and 8 apply to shadow directors of building societies[154] and shadow members of limited liability partnerships,[155] but do not encompass shadow directors of incorporated friendly societies.[156] Sections 6 and 8 also apply to directors or officers of an NHS foundation trust but not shadow directors or officers of such entities.[157] The broad purpose behind this

[151] A. Hicks, *Disqualification of Directors: No Hiding Place for the Unfit* (A.C.C.A. Research Report No.59, 1998). The meaning of "take part in management" is considered in Chs 10 and 14 with particular reference to CDDA ss.1, 1A, 2, 11 and 12.

[152] Introduced by the Insolvency Act 2000 with effect from April 2, 2001 though without any alteration to the law, the effect of s.6(3C) being the same as the former s.22(4).

[153] See Companies Act 2006 s.251 (formerly Companies Act 1985 s.741(2)); Insolvency Act 1986 s.251; Financial Services and Markets Act 2000 s.417(1). See also Income and Corporation Taxes Act 1988 s.165(8)–(9). For the legislative history of the definition see further *Re Euro Express Ltd, Secretary of State for Trade and Industry v Deverell* [2001] Ch. 340 at [24].

[154] CDDA s.22A(3).

[155] Limited Liability Partnerships Regulations 2001 (SI 2001/1090) regs 2 and 4(2)(f).

[156] CDDA s.22B(3).

[157] CDDA s.22C inserted by the Health and Social Care (Community Health and Standards) Act 2003 s.34 and Sch.4, paras 67–68 with effect in England and Wales from April 1, 2004: SI 2004/759.

statutory extension of the term "director" is plain enough. It is designed to prevent persons who may have considerable influence in relation to the management of a company from avoiding exposure to disqualification (or other forms of liability under companies legislation) by declining formal appointment.[158] It used to be thought that what distinguished a shadow director from a de facto director was that the former (as the phrase seems to imply) was someone who lurked unseen in the shadows while the de jure directors danced to his tune whereas the latter acted openly and was clearly visible. There was a tendency for the two categories to be regarded as mutually exclusive, a tendency reinforced by judicial insistence that a case based on both shadow and de facto directorship should not be asserted in the alternative.[159] As will be seen, however, both the stereotypical conception of the shadow director as a figure lurking in the shadows and the view that, in any given factual situation, shadow and de facto directorship will always be mutually exclusive, need considerable revision in the light of the current law. Indeed, it is suggested that the same sort of evidential indicia are likely to be relevant to the establishing of a case of either de facto or shadow directorship. Furthermore, it is possible that, in a given factual situation, a person may from time to time be capable of being classified as a shadow director and at other times as a de facto director.

Judicial interpretation of "shadow director"

3–45 The issue of shadow directorship has arisen principally in disqualification and wrongful trading cases.[160] The broader question whether shadow directors owe the general fiduciary duties owed to a company by de jure and de facto directors has also received judicial consideration.[161] The leading authority on shadow directorship is the Court of Appeal decision in *Re Euro Express Ltd, Secretary of State for Trade and Industry v Deverell*.[162] In that case, the Secretary of State sought orders under CDDA s.6 against two defendants, D and H, on the ground that they were shadow directors of a company that had traded as a tour operator. The company was founded by D and B. B was the original shareholder and de jure director. To pursue its business the company needed as a practical matter to be a member of the Association of British Travel Agents. D had previously been a director of two failed travel businesses. Under ABTA rules, the company would not have been eligible for

[158] See Cork Report Ch. 10.

[159] *Re Hydrodam (Corby) Ltd* [1994] 2 B.C.L.C. 180 and see further 3–52.

[160] The definition of "shadow director" in the CDDA (for purposes of disqualification) and in the Insolvency Act 1986 (for purposes of wrongful trading liability) is the same. The current provisions in CDDA ss.6 to 10 and Sch.1 and the wrongful trading provision in s.214 of the Insolvency Act were originally enacted together in the Insolvency Act 1985 ss.12–16 and Sch.2 as part of a series of measures targeted against those who act irresponsibly in the management of companies. Thus, the interpretation of the term "shadow director" in wrongful trading cases is clearly applicable in disqualification cases and vice versa.

[161] *Ultraframe (UK) Ltd v Fielding* [2005] EWHC 1638 (Ch), [2006] F.S.R. 17 in which it was held that shadow directors do not owe general fiduciary duties simply by virtue of their shadow directorship. This ruling appears to survive the codification of the general duties in Pt 10 of the Companies Act 2006: see Companies Act 2006 ss.170–177, 251 noting in particular the effect of s.170(5).

[162] [2001] Ch. 340.

ABTA membership had he been appointed a de jure director because of his involvement in the earlier failures. He therefore could not be seen to be a director of the company. D claimed throughout to have acted as a consultant. However, the trial judge (HH Judge Roger Cooke) found as a fact that "in reality he was throughout the whole story senior management and a key executive".[163] It was also found that D had never had any direct or indirect interest in the company's shares.[164] The case against him did not therefore rest on any de facto control of the company exercisable through share ownership.[165] However, he had been a signatory on the company's bank account throughout the company's trading life.

The second defendant, H, who had previously been the chief executive of a tour operating company within the Granada group, was recruited to help expand the company's business on the return leg of its main route (London Gatwick to Nice). H originally acquired an indirect interest in one-third of the company's issued share capital. However, it appears that he subsequently divested himself of any beneficial interest in the shares before going bankrupt.[166] Thus, as with D, the case against H was not based on any ability to exercise control through ownership. Moreover, as an undischarged bankrupt he was subject to the prohibition in CDDA s.11 on directly or indirectly taking part or being concerned in the promotion, formation or management of a company without the permission of the court. Like D, H claimed to be a consultant. The trial judge found that H was recruited initially in a limited role that later grew substantially with the company's expansion into the market for school ski holidays. It was also found that H frequently gave advice that was accepted and acted on and that he also "tended to spill over into other matters".[167] The Secretary of State's case against D and H was based exclusively on shadow directorship. In the light of the findings of fact, it is perhaps surprising that the Secretary of State did not plead a case of de facto directorship in the alternative.[168]

3–46 The trial judge dismissed the claims against D and H on the ground that neither of them had been shown to be a shadow director. He took as his starting point the decision of Millett J. in *Re Hydrodam (Corby) Ltd.*[169] This case has been discussed above in the context of de facto directors. However, the main issue in

[163] [2001] Ch. 340 at [6].

[164] [2001] Ch. 340 at [43]–[46]. A summary of the trial judge's other main findings of fact in relation to D is at [47].

[165] As well as needing to avoid de jure directorship, it was important that D did not take up any significant shareholding as the involvement of a "principal shareholder" in previous failures would also have affected the company's eligibility for ABTA membership. In any event, the company appears to have been in breach of ABTA rules because, on the trial judge's findings, it is clear that D was "employed or concerned in the management of a member's business": [2001] Ch. 340 at [5].

[166] [2001] Ch. 340 at [55].

[167] [2001] Ch. 340 at [58] which also contains a full summary of the trial judge's findings of fact in relation to H.

[168] The Court of Appeal refused permission to allow the point to be raised on appeal: [2001] Ch. 340 at [22]. For the argument that the Court of Appeal skewed the concept of shadow directorship in order to accommodate what was really a case of de facto directorship see C. Noonan and S. Watson, "The Nature of Shadow Directorship: Ad Hoc Statutory Intervention or Core Company Law Principle?" [2006] J.B.L. 763.

[169] [1994] 2 B.C.L.C. 180.

Hydrodam was whether the directors of a parent company could be treated as shadow directors of its insolvent subsidiary for the purposes of a wrongful trading action. Having recited the statutory definition, Millett J. held that the claimant must allege and prove the following elements in order to establish that the defendant had been a shadow director:

> "(1) [W]ho are the directors of the company, whether *de facto* or *de jure*; (2), that the defendant directed those directors how to act in relation to the company or that he was one of the persons who did so; (3) that those directors acted in accordance with such directions; and (4) that they were accustomed so to act. What is needed is first, a board of directors claiming and purporting to act as such; and secondly, a pattern of behaviour in which the board did not exercise any discretion or judgment of its own, but acted in accordance with the directions of others."[170]

Two straightforward points emerge from Millett J.'s formulation that can be cleared out of the way before returning to the discussion of *Euro Express*. First, it is clear that there can only be a shadow director where the company has one or more de jure or de facto directors. A key element of the statutory definition is missing if there are no directors (de facto or de jure) for the alleged shadow director to direct or instruct. Secondly, the de facto or de jure directors must in fact act on relevant directions or instructions. As Lewison J. has pointed out:

> "There is one further point arising out of the phrase 'accustomed to act'. The operative word here is 'act'. Unless and until the board *do* something in conformity with the putative shadow director's directions or instructions, it does not seem to me that the question of shadow directorship arises. The mere giving of instructions does not make someone a shadow director. It is only when they are translated into action by the board that the question can arise."[171]

However, it should be pointed out that a decision not to act can itself be an action. The questions of whether a pattern of consistent compliance with the directions or instructions of the alleged shadow director needs to be established and whether such compliance has to be by each and every member of the board are considered further below.

Two other points from *Hydrodam* appear to have strongly influenced the trial judge in *Euro Express*. The first was Millett J.'s metaphorical description of a shadow director as one who "lurks in the shadows, sheltering behind others who, he claims, are the only directors of the company to the exclusion of himself."[172] The second was Millett J.'s suggestion in the passage quoted above that, for the directors to be "accustomed to act", there needs to be "a pattern of behaviour in which the board *did not exercise any discretion or judgment of its own*" (emphasis supplied). The influence of *Hydrodam* in these two respects is evident from the trial judge's final conclusions. In relation to D, he held:

[170] [1994] 2 B.C.L.C. 180 at 183.
[171] *Ultraframe (UK) Ltd v Fielding* [2006] F.S.R. 17 at [1278].
[172] [1994] 2 B.C.L.C. 180 at 183.

"In my judgment the facts which I have found do not support the central thesis . . . that [D] was somebody on whose directions/instructions the directors were accustomed to act. He was a prominent and powerful member of management who took part in that management on a broad and wide ranging basis on occasion on almost an equal footing with the directors. 'Consultant' certainly does not describe what he did. But this sort of open and equal participation is in my judgment the very antithesis of the 'eminence grise'/puppet-master activity (or inactivity) required of a shadow director."[173]

In relation to H, he held:

"I would accept that when [H] gave advice [the directors] usually (if not always) took it. But that . . . in my judgment is nowhere near saying that there was a 'pattern of behaviour in which the board did not exercise any discretion or judgment of its own, but acted in accordance with the directions of others'. There is no evidence which suggests that in circumstances where [H] was not giving advice that the directors did not exercise their own discretion. Nor indeed is there evidence that suggests that the acceptance of advice was mechanical as opposed to considered."[174]

3–47 The Court of Appeal held that the trial judge had adopted too strict a test. Delivering the unanimous judgment of the court, Morritt L.J. expressed his conclusions on the law in the following propositions[175]:

(1) The definition of a shadow director should be construed in the normal way to give effect to the parliamentary intention ascertainable from the mischief to be dealt with and the words used. In particular, as the purpose of the CDDA is the protection of the public and as the definition is used in other legislative contexts, it should not be strictly construed just because it also has quasi-penal consequences in the CDDA context.[176]
(2) The purpose of the legislation is to identify those, other than professional advisers, with real influence in the corporate affairs of the company. However, it is not necessary that such influence should be exercised over the whole field of its corporate activities.[177]
(3) Whether any particular communication from the alleged shadow director, be it by words or conduct, can be classified as a "direction" or "instruction" must be objectively ascertained by the court in the light of all the evidence. It is not necessary to prove the understanding or expectation of either the giver or receiver of the "direction" or "instruction". In many, if not most, cases it will suffice to prove the communication and its consequences. Evidence of such understanding or expectation may be relevant but cannot be conclusive. The label attached to the communication by the parties at the time or thereafter

[173] [2001] Ch. 340 at [48].
[174] [2001] Ch. 340 at [59].
[175] [2001] Ch. 340 at [35].
[176] On this point Morritt L.J. approved statements to similar effect in *Re Lo-Line Electric Motors Ltd* [1988] Ch. 477 at 489. For discussion of *Lo-Line* see 3–18 to 3–20.
[177] *Australian Securities Commission v AS Nominees Ltd* (1995) 133 A.L.R. 1 at 52–53.

cannot be more than a factor that is relevant to the consideration of whether the communication was a "direction" or "instruction".

(4) Non-professional advice may amount to a "direction" or "instruction". The proviso excepting advice given in a professional capacity appears to rest on the assumption that advice generally is or may be included. Moreover, the concepts of "direction" and "instruction" do not exclude the concept of "advice" for all three share the common feature of "guidance".

(5) It will, no doubt, be sufficient to show that in the face of "directions or instructions" from the alleged shadow director, the properly appointed directors or some of them cast themselves in a subservient role or surrendered their respective discretions. However, it is not necessary to do so in all cases. The imposition of such a requirement would put a gloss on the statutory requirement that the directors are "accustomed to act in accordance with . . ." directions or instructions. In looking for the additional ingredient of a subservient role or the surrender of discretion by the board, the trial judge had imposed a qualification beyond that justified by the statutory language.

(6) If the directors usually took the advice of the putative shadow director, it is irrelevant that on the occasions when he did not give advice the board did exercise its own discretion.

(7) If the board was accustomed to act on the directions or instructions of the putative shadow director it is not necessary to demonstrate that their action was mechanical rather than considered.

Morritt L.J. added these further observations:

> "[T]he use of epithets or descriptions in place of the statutory definition . . . may be very effective in graphically conveying the effect of the definition in the light of the facts of [a particular] case . . . [but may] be misleading when transposed to the facts of other cases. Thus to describe the board as the cat's paw, puppet or dancer to the tune of the shadow director[178] implies a degree of control both of quality and extent over the corporate field in excess of what the statutory definition requires. What is needed is that the board is accustomed to act on the directions or instructions of the shadow director . . . [S]uch directions and instructions do not have to extend over all or most of the corporate activities of the company; nor is it necessary to demonstrate a degree of compulsion in excess of that implicit in the fact that the board are accustomed to act in accordance with them. Further, in my view, it is not necessary to the recognition of a shadow director that he should lurk in the shadows, though frequently he may . . . Lurking in the shadows may occur but is not an essential ingredient to the recognition of the shadow director."[179]

3–48 It is suggested that the Court of Appeal decision in *Euro Express* should be read as decisively rejecting those parts of Millett J.'s judgment in *Hydrodam* that informed the trial judge's conclusions. That such a reading is justified is amply

[178] See, e.g. *Re Unisoft Group Ltd (No.3)* [1994] 1 B.C.L.C. 609.

[179] [2001] Ch. 340 at [36]. See also the obiter comments of Robert Walker L.J. in *Re Kaytech International Plc, Secretary of State for Trade and Industry v Kaczer* [1999] 2 B.C.L.C. 351 at 424, expressing the view that the influence of the alleged shadow director need not necessarily be concealed.

reflected in Morritt L.J.'s application of the law as stated to the trial judge's findings of fact. Thus, the fact that D was a prominent figure, openly involved in the management of the company's affairs rather than lurking in the shadows, did not stop him from being a shadow director, especially when the evidence showed that he had "bossed everyone around from the directors downwards".[180] Similarly, given that there was a pattern of compliance with "directions" and "instructions", the fact that the de jure directors had acted independently on occasions was not sufficient for D and H to escape the clutches of the definition.[181] Furthermore, the fact that the acceptance of H's advice had not been "mechanical" did not stop H from being a shadow director given that, on the trial judge's own findings, the directors had usually accepted and acted on that advice.[182]

3–49 An additional point that arises is whether the compliance with "directions" and "instructions" must be on the part of *all* or merely some of the de jure and de facto directors to support a finding of shadow directorship. In *Lord v Sinai Securities Ltd* Hart J. held that "all the directors, or at least a consistent majority of them" must be shown to have been "accustomed to act".[183] This view was elaborated upon further by Lewison J. in *Ultraframe (UK) Ltd v Fielding*:

> "There is, no doubt a difficulty, as a pure matter of language, in construing the phrase 'the directors of the company' as meaning '*some of* the directors of the company' or even '*a majority of* the directors of the company.' However, the policy underlying the definition is that a person who effectively controls the activities of the company is to be subject to the same statutory liabilities and disabilities as a person who is a *de jure* director. Since a *de jure* director is subject to those liabilities and disabilities even if he is non-executive, or even inactive, it would undermine the policy of the definition if the fact that an inactive director did not act on the instructions of an alleged shadow director (because he did not act at all) could prevent that person from being a shadow director, even though in reality he controlled the activities of the company. In my judgment, therefore, a person at whose direction a governing majority of the board is accustomed to act is capable of being a shadow director."[184]

Another possible analysis would be to consider whether de facto directorship could and should be expanded to cover those acting as directors indirectly, through other de facto or de jure directors, as well as those who themselves act directly (and see next paragraph).

3–50 A further component of the definition is that the directors, de jure or de facto, must be "accustomed to act" on the directions or instructions of the shadow director.

[180] [2001] Ch. 340 at [53].

[181] Note, in particular, the treatment of Mr Lyne's evidence, [2001] Ch. 340 at [48]–[52] and the criticism of the trial judge's conclusions in relation to H at [59].

[182] [2001] Ch. 340 at [59]. Morritt L.J. concluded at [63] that the only difference between D and H was that the evidence of D's participation was greater because H lived abroad. For a disqualification case in which Morritt L.J.'s approach was applied see *Re Mea Corporation Ltd, Secretary of State for Trade and Industry v Aviss* [2007] 1 B.C.L.C. 618 especially from paras [86] to [106].

[183] [2004] EWHC 1764 (Ch), [2005] 1 B.C.L.C. 295 at [27]. *Re Unisoft Group Ltd (No.3)* [1994] 1 B.C.L.C. 609 is also authority for the view that the alleged shadow director must exert influence over a majority of the board, if not the full board.

[184] [2006] F.S.R. 17 at [1272].

Clearly if there is a pattern of behaviour this test is met. However, what about the early actions of a person who throughout holds the same authority and on whose instructions the board is prepared to act, and subsequently does act?[185] At what point can it be said that the board is "accustomed" to act on directions or instructions? Will a person acting with real influence on the company's affairs and who would be a de facto director if he acted in his own right rather than by directing other directors, escape the responsibilities and consequences of being a shadow director until some pattern of behaviour is built up? There are certainly cases where the courts have held that the words "accustomed to act" mean that an occasional or "one-off" compliance by the board with directions or instructions of another will not suffice to make the giver of the same a shadow director.[186] However, as posed by Lewison J.:

> ". . . if it is shown that, over a period, the directors of a company were accustomed to act on the directions or instructions of another person, is that person a shadow director from the beginning of the period; or only from the point at which it can be said that the directors are 'accustomed' to act on his directions or instructions?"

The conclusion that the judge reached was:

> ". . . if a person becomes a shadow director as a result of the board being accustomed to act on his instructions or directions, transactions entered into before it can be said that the board is so accustomed are not retrospectively invalidated."[187]

The real problem seems to stem from the definition of shadow director requiring a pattern of behaviour to develop whereby something is "usual" before the concept comes into play. Again, it will be interesting to see whether the concept of de facto director will be able to be expanded to fill this gap. Should that concept be expanded to cover those who assume the role of director indirectly, by procuring that one or more de jure or de facto directors do what they say, as well as where they act directly? Certainly in *Mercury Solutions UK Ltd, Secretary of State for Trade and Industry v Hall*[188] Evans-Lombe J. was prepared to accept that an individual, through his control of a corporate director, can constitute himself a de facto director of a subject company (that is the company of which the other company is the corporate director) though "whether or not he does so will depend on what that individual procures the corporate director to do". If this is possible,[189] then it suggests that the same is factually possible in relation to individuals who control

[185] A classic example is in the case of companies formed in certain tax havens with resident directors, often offering such services, as the only de jure directors.

[186] For cases suggesting there must be a course or pattern of conduct: see *Re Unisoft Group Ltd (No.3)* [1994] 1 B.C.L.C. 609; and *Re Balfour Associates IT Recruitment Ltd, Secretary of State for Trade and Industry v Becker* [2003] 1 B.C.L.C. 555.

[187] *Ultraframe (UK) Ltd v Fielding* [2006] F.S.R. 17 at [1274]–[1277].

[188] [2006] EWHC 1995 (Ch).

[189] Which, where the individual acts merely in the capacity of a director of the corporate director is open to doubt: see *Re Paycheck Services 3 Ltd, Revenue and Customs Commissioners v Holland* [2009] EWCA Civ 625, [2009] S.T.C. 1639 especially the Court of Appeal's reaffirmation of orthodox company law principles from [63] (Rimer L.J.) and [115] (Elias L.J.).

or direct individuals who are de jure or de facto directors, and not just corporate directors. The danger to be guarded against would be that of widening the concept of de facto directorship to the point where all shadow directors became de facto directors, especially if there was no room for the exclusion of professional advice from the concept of de facto director, as there is for the concept of shadow director.

3–51 There seems little doubt that the Court of Appeal decision in *Euro Express* "open[s] up the concept of the shadow director for further exploitation, particularly in the context of disqualification proceedings . . ."[190] On balance, it is suggested that the decision is welcome. Millett J.'s apparent imposition of a requirement (followed by the trial judge in *Euro Express*) that the board should not have exercised any discretion or judgment of its own was always difficult to justify bearing in mind the purpose and wording of the statutory provision. Customary compliance with the directions of the alleged shadow director is all that is required. Thus, there has never strictly been any need to show that the board acted on *every* occasion in accordance with the directions or instructions of the alleged shadow director as Millett J. seemed to suggest. As long as there is customary compliance, occasional acts of independent decision making should not prevent a finding of shadow directorship.[191] A further point in favour of *Euro Express* is that there are dangers in placing too much emphasis on questions of board discretion. Such an emphasis may allow an alleged shadow director to escape liability in a case where the board claims to have taken his "advice" and exercised its discretion to act on that "advice" even though, in substance, it has always unquestioningly followed such advice. *Euro Express* suggests that the courts should treat with caution evidence that the board was free to accept or reject the alleged shadow director's "advice" and so was not acting in accordance with his directions or instructions, even though the "advice" was consistently followed.[192] At the same time, it is hard to avoid the conclusion that *Euro Express* shoehorns what looks to be a clear case of de facto directorship into shadow directorship with the result that there is now considerable overlap between the two concepts.[193]

Making mixed allegations of shadow and de facto directorship

3–52 In *Hydrodam*, Millett J. criticised the liquidator's failure to distinguish sufficiently between his two allegations of shadow and de facto directorship asserting forcefully that the two concepts are alternatives which do not overlap: "[t]hey are

[190] D. Milman, "A Fresh Light on Shadow Directors" [2000] Insolvency Lawyer 171.

[191] This view, now confirmed in *Euro Express*, has attracted academic support: see, e.g. G. Morse, "Shadow and De Facto Directors" in B. Rider (ed.), *The Corporate Dimension* (Bristol: Jordans, 1998); N. Campbell, "Liability as a Shadow Director" [1994] J.B.L. 609.

[192] See further *Australian Securities Commission v AS Nominees Ltd* (1995) 133 A.L.R. 1. Note, however, that this may have implications for financial institutions: see 3–60 to 3–65.

[193] To the point where, in the view of one commentator, the two concepts have effectively been merged: see S. Griffin, "Evidence Justifying a Person's Capacity as Either a *De Facto* or Shadow Director" [2003] Insolvency Lawyer 127; "Problems in the Identification of a Company Director" (2003) 54 Northern Ireland Legal Quarterly 43; cf. C. Noonan and S. Watson, "The Nature of Shadow Directorship: Ad Hoc Statutory Intervention or Core Company Law Principle?" [2006] J.B.L. 763.

alternatives, and in most and perhaps all cases are mutually exclusive".[194] This view received further support in *Re H Laing Demolition Building Contractors Ltd, Secretary of State for Trade and Industry v Laing*.[195] However, Robert Walker L.J. cast doubt on Millett J.'s view in *Re Kaytech International Plc, Secretary of State for Trade and Industry v Kaczer* where he said obiter:

> "Millett J.'s observations have undoubtedly had a salutary effect in discouraging the Secretary of State and his advisers from routine reliance on the two concepts in the alternative, with insufficient analysis of the real grounds of complaint. However the two concepts do have at least this much in common, that an individual who was not a de jure director is alleged to have exercised real influence (otherwise than as a professional adviser) in the corporate governance of a company. Sometimes that influence may be concealed and sometimes it may be open. Sometimes it may be something of a mixture . . ."[196]

It is suggested that the idea that shadow and de facto directorship are mutually exclusive concepts is not sustainable on the authorities or in principle. Even before *Kaytech* and *Euro Express*, the courts had accepted in interim proceedings that the claimant could advance a case both simultaneously and in the alternative that the defendant had acted as a shadow and/or a de facto director on the same evidence.[197] Furthermore, situations can be envisaged in which a person may be exercising "real influence" simultaneously as a shadow and de facto director. An obvious situation is where someone acts as a de facto managing director in the day-to-day running of the company and also instructs the de jure directors how to act.[198] The defendant, D, from *Euro Express* seems to fit this description. However, *Euro Express* was argued only on the question of shadow directorship and Morritt L.J. therefore declined to express any view on whether the two categories were mutually exclusive.[199]

3–53 In *Ultraframe (UK) Ltd v Fielding* Lewison J. observed (without anything turning on the point) that he thought it unlikely that a person would be simultaneously a shadow director and a de facto director, although he may be both in succession.[200] However, he appears to have refined this view in *Re Mea Corporation Ltd, Secretary of State for Trade and Industry v Aviss* where, in light of Morritt L.J.'s view that the role of a shadow director does not necessarily extend over the whole range of the company's activities, he reasoned that "there is no conceptual difficulty in concluding that a person can be both a shadow director and a de facto director simultaneously."[201] To illustrate the point he gave

[194] [1994] 2 B.C.L.C. 180.
[195] [1996] 2 B.C.L.C. 324 at 329.
[196] [1999] 2 B.C.L.C. 351 at 424.
[197] Oddly enough at an earlier stage in the *Laing* proceedings: see *Re H Laing Demolition Building Contractors Ltd* [1998] B.C.C. 561.
[198] See, e.g. *Re Tasbian Ltd (No.3), Official Receiver v Nixon* [1993] B.C.L.C. 297 discussed below in 3–56 to 3–57.
[199] [2001] Ch. 340 at [36].
[200] [2006] F.S.R. 17 at [1263].
[201] [2007] 1 B.C.L.C. 618 at [89].

the example of a person who assumes the functions of a director as regards one part of the company's activities (for example, marketing) and gives directions to the board as regards another (such as manufacturing and finance).

3–54 The important point for the claimant is that the two concepts should not be confused. The case under each head should be set out separately and the evidence marshalled accordingly. It should be remembered that in respect of shadow directorship (but not de facto directorship), there is a safe harbour for professional advice. At the procedural level, claimants should therefore heed Millett J.'s criticism. However, the "mutual exclusivity" point goes more to how the case is presented than to substance. Even in the manner in which a case is presented, it is important to note that the same objective facts, showing a real influence in the company's management, are likely to be relied upon in support of a case of directorship, whether shadow or de facto. Any hope that the claimant will seek to rely on both concepts sparingly, even in the alternative, is therefore unlikely to be fulfilled. Ultimately, at the level of substance the distinction between the two concepts appears to come down to a difference of degree. De facto directorship requires a person to exert "real influence" without this necessarily equating to outright control of corporate decision making. Shadow directorship requires a pattern of compliance which may be indicative of outright control but need not necessarily equate to outright control over all of the company's activities all of the time.

3–55 From the authorities it is possible to identify three non-exhaustive categories of potential shadow (or indeed de facto) director where particular problems may occur: (a) consultants and advisers; (b) financial institutions and creditors; and (c) shareholders, especially parent companies (or the directors of parent companies) in relation to their subsidiaries. These categories, and the implications of *Euro Express* for each category, are now considered in turn.

Consultants/advisers as shadow directors

3–56 CDDA s.22(5) contains a statutory safe harbour for professional advisers. Thus, a person is not deemed to be a shadow director by reason only that the directors act on advice given by him in a professional capacity. However, as discussed above, it is clear from *Euro Express* that a person who gives non-professional advice on which the directors routinely act could fall within the definition. The first issue is whether the person gave the advice "in a professional capacity". It seems clear that this protects members of recognised professions who give advice on an arms' length basis in the course of a client relationship, such as solicitors, accountants or insolvency practitioners.[202] Conversely, the fact that a person is a member of a profession will not make any difference if the "advice" is not tendered in a professional capacity. The second and crucial issue for consultants

[202] It is not clear that the safe harbour will necessarily protect members of the "turnaround" profession as some "turnaround" specialists are "company doctors" who may become actively involved in the governance of the struggling company: see discussion of *Tasbian* in the text immediately below. On the emergence of the "turnaround" profession see generally V. Finch, "Doctoring in the Shadows of Insolvency" [2005] J.B.L. 690.

and advisers is where precisely the line is drawn between the giving of "mere advice" and a higher order of involvement where the advice given may expose the adviser to liability as a shadow director. In this respect, the crucial distinction is between, on the one hand, the giving of "mere advice" and, on the other hand, the giving of "directions or instructions". It was held in *Euro Express* that the concepts of "direction" and "instruction" do not exclude the concept of "advice" as all three concepts share the common feature of guidance.[203] Moreover, if the directors accept and act on the "advice", it may take on the quality of "directions or instructions" in accordance with which the directors are "accustomed to act". In these circumstances, as was arguably the case with H in *Euro Express*, the adviser's influence is such that he has a clear role in the governance of the company. Clearly, the question of whether "advice" has become governance in the form of "directions or instructions" will be one of fact and degree.

3–57 Although it predates *Euro Express*, the Court of Appeal decision in *Re Tasbian Ltd (No.3), Official Receiver v Nixon*[204] neatly illustrates the problem that faces non-professional advisers in drawing the line between mere "advice" and involvement in governance ("directions or instructions"). The defendant, N, was a chartered accountant and an experienced "company doctor".[205] The company had never been profitable and N was enlisted to provide advice and assist in turning its fortunes around. N was formally appointed as a "consultant" to the company. He was involved in the company for around a year. At no time was he a de jure director. He resigned from his "consultancy" just before the company went into receivership. The claimant obtained permission to bring disqualification proceedings against N under CDDA s.6 out of time.[206] N applied to set aside the order giving permission on the ground that the evidence disclosed no arguable case that he had been either a shadow or de facto director. The claimant relied on the following evidence to support a case of shadow or de facto directorship:

(1) N was appointed and paid by the company.
(2) He negotiated an informal moratorium with creditors.
(3) He monitored trading and assisted the board.
(4) He negotiated with the DTI and the Inland Revenue and introduced the company to a new debt factor.
(5) He was a signatory on, and at times controlled the use of, the company's bank account.[207]

[203] [2001] Ch. 340 at [35].
[204] [1993] B.C.L.C. 297.
[205] He would probably now be a self-styled "turnaround" professional.
[206] CDDA s.7(2). On applications for permission to commence proceedings out of time see generally Ch.8.
[207] Under the bank mandate, cheques had to be signed by two of three named directors and countersigned by Mr Nixon or one of his partners, Mr Whittington. As regards being a signatory to a bank account see more recently *Ultraframe (UK) Ltd v Fielding* [2006] F.S.R. 17 at [1618] where Lewison J. said: "Signing cheques is plainly a function that can be carried out by someone below board level . . . The real question is how the account was operated; and whether it was operated in accordance with the instructions of the *de jure* directors or not."

(6) He advised on the transfer of all of the company's employees to a separate company that acted as a "labour-only" sub-contractor.
(7) The de jure directors regarded N as a shadow director or even as managing director of the company.

3–58 The Court of Appeal held that the registrar and the judge had both been right to allow the claimant to proceed against N as the evidence disclosed an arguable case. Balcombe L.J. laid particular emphasis on the fact that the company's bank account could not be operated without N's consent and that he decided which cheques drawn by the company could, and which could not, be submitted to the bank. This meant that he was concerned directly in determining which of the company's creditors were paid and in which order. Thus, it appears that he was able to exert a significant level of control over the company's affairs. (Indeed, the directors appeared to have complained to him about him exercising such control.) Clearly, *Tasbian (No.3)* cannot be regarded as a definitive ruling because the Court of Appeal only had to decide whether there was a triable issue on the facts. However, in the light of *Euro Express*, the fact that N had become a central figure in the governance of the company, suggests that a finding of shadow directorship would be likely to be made if a case like this arose now. Equally, on the facts of *Tasbian*, there would undoubtedly now be a strong case based on de facto directorship.

3–59 In the case of consultants and advisers, especially those who provide non-professional advice to struggling companies, there is a balance to be struck. Clearly, those who exert control over the governance of a company should be prime candidates for disqualification if their conduct is such as to make them unfit, regardless of whether or not they are de jure directors. Equally, however, the courts may be anxious not to expose consultants or advisers to disqualification too easily, even in the wake of *Euro Express*, if to do so may stem the flow of advice and support to companies in financial difficulties. This would be an unfortunate consequence given the potential benefits of timely advice. A well-advised board may conclude that the company should cease trading immediately and go into liquidation, which at least means that it is no longer incurring fresh debts that cannot be met. Alternatively, on proper advice, the board may be able to implement strategies that turn around the company's fortunes and advance the rescue culture. However, the case for a cautious approach should not be overstated. Professional advisers such as solicitors, accountants and insolvency practitioners can safely meet much of the demand for advice generated by struggling companies. Even so, the policy issues cannot be ignored completely as, in a climate where many of the old monopolies on the provision of advice are breaking down and the notion of what is meant by "professional advice" is itself starting to blur, cases testing the boundary between professional and non-professional advice seem likely to arise in the future.

Financial institutions and creditors as shadow directors

3–60 The position of banks and other financial institutions, such as private equity providers, that take steps to protect their financial stake in a company has been considered in a handful of cases. The difficulty for financial institutions in this context is that their incentive (and often their contractual entitlement) to assert some form of control steadily increases as the company gets deeper into financial difficulty. A particular concern for banks arises from the fact that they may only be prepared to extend loan or overdraft facilities on conditions that include the imposition of bank control over major managerial decisions. The courts have historically been reluctant to make findings of shadow directorship against banks and other financial institutions that intervene in the affairs of borrowers with a view to protecting their financial interests. However, it appears that the exposure of financiers in such circumstances has increased following *Euro Express*.

3–61 The first case to strengthen fears that banks could be treated as shadow directors was *Re a Company (No. 005009 of 1987) Ex p. Copp*.[208] The company traded profitably but got into difficulties when it lost its main customer. Once the agreed unsecured overdraft limit was reached, the bank initiated an investigation and commissioned its own financial services division to prepare a report on the company, which contained detailed recommendations. The company went into liquidation and the liquidator commenced wrongful trading proceedings against the bank under s.214 of the Insolvency Act 1986. The liquidator's case was that the implementation by the board of the recommendations contained in the report made the bank a shadow director, thus exposing it to liability for wrongful trading. The bank applied to strike out the proceedings on the ground that there was no sustainable cause of action. Knox J. refused the bank's application on the basis that a claim against the bank as shadow director was not obviously hopeless on the facts. However, the allegation was later dropped at trial, seemingly with the approval of the trial judge.[209]

3–62 After *Re a Company Ex p. Copp*, the courts continued to take a cautious line. In *Re PFTZM Ltd, Jourdain v Paul*[210] an issue arose as to whether two officers of the company's main financier had been shadow directors in the context of an application for an order for private examination under s.236 of the Insolvency Act 1986 that sought to establish this point. It had been agreed after the company got into financial difficulties that weekly management meetings would be held to discuss the company's business. The financier's officers attended these meetings, which took place for almost two years before the company went into liquidation. The liquidator argued that there was a prima facie case of shadow directorship against the officers. However, the deputy judge expressed the view strongly that the evidence established no more than that the officers were acting to protect the commercial interests of the financier as a secured creditor, and not as directors of the company. All the financier had done was to impose terms (through the medium of the weekly meetings) on which it was prepared to continue the company's facility in the light of threatened default, a level of influence entirely consistent with the normal bank-customer relationship. In the deputy judge's view,

[208] [1989] B.C.L.C. 13.
[209] *Re M C Bacon Ltd* [1990] B.C.L.C. 324.
[210] [1995] 2 B.C.L.C. 354.

the actions taken by the financier (through its officers) were simply designed to rescue what it could out of the company using its undoubted rights as a secured creditor. The board retained the power to accept or reject the financier's terms.

3–63 It is important to bear in mind that in *PFTZM* the deputy judge did not have to decide whether the financier's officers were shadow directors. The central issue in the case was whether the liquidator was entitled to an order for the private examination of the officers under s.236 of the Insolvency Act. The deputy judge found that the main object of the order sought was to elicit information from the officers that would enable the liquidator to decide whether they had acted in the capacity of shadow directors for CDDA reporting purposes.[211] The officers had already provided some information voluntarily, but the liquidator was seeking further supplementary information. The deputy judge concluded that it would have been oppressive to order the officers to provide the supplementary information under s.236.

The matter was considered further in *Ultraframe (UK) Ltd v Fielding*. Lewison J.'s comments in that case should give some comfort to lenders. He said[212]:

> "In my judgment, where the alleged shadow director is also a creditor of the company, he is entitled to protect his own interests as creditor without necessarily becoming a shadow director. [Counsel] . . . submitted that it is critical to distinguish the position of a lender (whether or not also a shareholder) from that of a director. A lender is entitled to keep a close eye on what is done with his money, and to impose conditions on his support for the company. This does not mean he is running the company or is emasculating the powers of the directors, even if (given their situation) the directors feel that they have little practical choice but to accede to his requests. Similarly with customers who may, because of their buying power, be able effectively to dictate conditions to their suppliers (or the other way around). In other words a position of influence (even a position of strong influence) is not necessarily a fiduciary position. To find otherwise would place a wholly unfair and unnatural burden on men of business. In broad terms, I accept this submission."

3–64 In the light of *Euro Express*, it will be interesting to see how the courts approach the question of what constitutes a shadow director in this sort of case. In situations like that in PFTZM, the de jure directors may have no real choice other than to accept the financier's terms if the company is to continue trading. The suggestion that the board retains a meaningful discretion may seem somewhat artificial. In any event, as discussed above, the fact that the directors retain, and from time to time, exercise their own discretion will not necessarily defeat a finding of shadow directorship if they are accustomed to act in accordance with the alleged shadow director's directions, instructions or advice. The issue of the financier's motivation—in *PFTZM*, the desire to protect its commercial interests—is not decisive. As Morritt L.J. made clear in *Euro Express*, the issue whether the words or conduct of the alleged shadow director can be classified as

[211] An office holder is obliged to report on the conduct of shadow directors to the Secretary of State: CDDA ss.6(3C) and 7(3).

[212] [2006] F.S.R. 17 at paras [1267]–[1268].

directions or instructions must be objectively ascertained and, in most cases, it will suffice to prove the communication and its consequence.[213] It does not matter that the "communication" arises as a normal incident of the bank-customer relationship if the directors regularly act in accordance with such communications. Thus, after *Euro Express*, it is possible that the role of banks and financial institutions will be subject to greater scrutiny although Lewison J.'s comments in *Ultraframe* suggest that allegations of shadow directorship in this context will continue to be approached with care.

3–65 A finding of shadow directorship is clearly justifiable in a situation where a financial institution exercises control in a real sense over the company's direction. There is a good case for saying that, where financial institutions exercise substantial control over the governance of companies, they should act responsibly. A greater willingness on the part of the courts to uphold allegations of shadow directorship may serve to reinforce such an obligation by exposing the conduct of financial institutions to scrutiny.[214] At the same time, the courts are likely to be reasonably circumspect because of fears that the increased threat of liability may encourage lenders to call in their loans at the first sign of trouble and discourage them from supporting distressed but viable companies, the fortunes of which are capable of being turned around. The courts are likely to draw a line between those cases where the financier takes steps to safeguard its investment and lays down certain minimum terms which the company's board accepts from those where the terms are such that the financier plays a real and continuing role in the management of the company and its business. Thus, the imposition of a requirement to keep within overdraft limits and even to take steps to ensure that this is so (for example, by pre-vetting cheques to ensure that payments are not improper[215] and are within the limit) are likely to be distinguished from the situation where the bank descends so far into management as to decide (in fact) which creditors should be paid and in what order.

Parent companies and parent company directors as shadow or de facto directors

3–66 The concept of shadow directorship is not easily adapted to the situation of the modern corporate group. The reality in many groups of companies is that the board of the parent company often takes decisions affecting the group as a whole. As such, the parent board may exercise greater control over the direction of its subsidiaries than the de jure directors of each subsidiary. This raises the

[213] [2001] Ch. 340 at [35]. See also *Re Tasbian Ltd (No.3), Official Receiver v Nixon* [1993] B.C.L.C. 297 where Balcombe L.J. made much the same point but cf. P. Millett, "Shadow Directorship—A Real or Imagined Threat to Banks" (1991) 1 Insolvency Practitioner 14, expressing the view that a "conscious intention" to control the board was a necessary ingredient of shadow directorship. The extrajudicial opinion of Millett J. (as he then was) can surely only prevail were the Supreme Court to get an opportunity in the future to revisit *Euro Express*. In any event, it is respectfully suggested that there is no basis in the statutory language for an enquiry into the alleged shadow director's state of mind.

[214] N.B., a finding of shadow directorship leads to *scrutiny* of the shadow director's conduct. It does not mean that the shadow director will automatically be disqualified or subjected to civil liability for breach of duty.

[215] Such as increased remuneration or loan repayments paid to directors.

possibility that the parent company or its individual directors could be treated as shadow directors (or de facto directors) for the purposes of CDDA s.6 should any of the subsidiaries become insolvent.

3–67 The leading case directly in point is again *Re Hydrodam (Corby) Ltd.*[216] Eagle Trust Plc was the ultimate parent company of Hydrodam. Hydrodam went into liquidation and the liquidator commenced wrongful trading proceedings against two directors of Eagle Trust alleging that they were liable for wrongful trading as de facto or shadow directors of Hydrodam. Millett J. struck out the application against the two directors and, in so doing, made the following points:

(1) Even assuming that the parent company has acted as a shadow director of the subsidiary, it does not automatically follow that an individual director of the parent is also a shadow director.
(2) While the individual director is someone who has a collective responsibility for the conduct of the parent, it does not follow that he has ever given instructions to the directors of the subsidiary or that they were accustomed to act on his instructions. Even assuming that the directors of the parent, acting as a board, have collectively given directions or instructions to the directors of the subsidiary, this would not turn the individuals on the parent board into shadow directors. This is because they would be acting collectively as agent for (or organ of) the parent with the result that the parent, not its individual directors, would be acting as a shadow director. Thus, the directors of the parent can only become shadow directors of the subsidiary if they issue directions or instructions to the board of the subsidiary on an individual and personal basis.

Although, in the light of *Euro Express*, there is reason to doubt certain aspects of Millett J.'s judgment as regards the definition of a shadow director,[217] the actual decision on the facts of *Hydrodam* appears to be correct as it accords with orthodox principles of company law.[218]

3–68 It follows from *Hydrodam* that it will be easier to make a case of shadow directorship against the parent company itself than against its individual directors.[219] The difficulty for the parent company, or indeed any controlling shareholder, is that in

[216] [1994] 2 B.C.L.C. 180. For the test of shadow directorship applied in this case see 3–46.
[217] See 3–46 to 3–48.
[218] For an analogous case, see *Re Mercury Solutions UK Ltd, Secretary of State for Trade and Industry v Hall* [2006] EWHC 1995 (Ch) discussed in 3–69 (controller of corporate director was not de facto director of company to which corporate director provided secretarial and administrative services). See also Companies Act 2006 s.251(3) which, for certain defined purposes falling within the scope of Pt X of the 2006 Act, provides that a body corporate is not to be regarded as a shadow director of any of its subsidiary companies by reason only that the directors of the subsidiary are accustomed to act in accordance with its directions or instructions. This safe harbour in the 2006 Act for parent companies has apparently not as yet been extended to the CDDA or s.214 of the Insolvency Act.
[219] There is comfort here too for the officers and employees of financial institutions. It appears from Millett J.'s dictum in *Hydrodam* that if an agent is acting within the scope of the authority given him by his principal, the agent will not be exposed personally to a finding of shadow directorship.

strict company law terms, the companies it controls are separate legal entities. Each entity has directors who are under a fiduciary obligation to consider the interests of that entity, which are not necessarily the same as the overall interests of the group although they may overlap. If the directors of a subsidiary simply accept and act on decisions handed down by the parent board without properly evaluating whether those decisions are in the interests of the subsidiary, the parent company is likely to be acting as a shadow director.[220] After *Euro Express*, this is a fortiori.

3–69 In *Re Mercury Solutions UK Ltd, Secretary of State for Trade and Industry v Hall*,[221] disqualification proceedings were brought against three individuals. One (Mr. N) was the de jure director of a company (LDL) which was itself a director of seven other companies. LDL provided secretarial and other administrative services to businessmen who wished to conduct their business through limited companies. One of the services was the provision of corporate directors of such companies. LDL was one such corporate director. LDL was effectively owned, run and controlled by Mr. N, through another limited company. The disqualification proceedings related to seven companies of which LDL had been corporate director. Of the seven companies, one (Mercury) went into insolvent liquidation with a deficiency of around £45,000 as a result of trading activities in respect of which, it was accepted, the company kept no adequate books or records contrary to s.221 of the Companies Act 1985. The other six companies, from time to time and during the directorship of LDL, failed to make returns to Companies House though in most cases those defaults were later remedied. LDL had been separately disqualified pursuant to CDDA s.5 as regards failures to file accounts and returns of companies of which it was a de jure corporate director and it had since been dissolved. However, the same business of providing services had continued, but with another company carrying out the same role that LDL had previously carried out. Proceedings were brought against three individuals. One of those individuals was Mr. N. The proceedings were brought against him in relation to his conduct as a director (shadow or de facto) of the seven companies, and not as director of LDL. The case against Mr. N was that he failed to be adequately involved in the affairs of Mercury with the result that there were inadequate books and records and, as regards the other six companies, that he failed to ensure accounts and returns were filed on time. The evidence was to the effect that LDL was a nominee director of the relevant client and that as part of the provision of LDL as a nominee director there was a clear understanding with the relevant client that LDL would not undertake any active management of the company and that the client would be responsible among other things for keeping proper accounts, filing those accounts and filing annual returns in a timely manner. Mr. N accepted that LDL did nothing to prevent the seven companies committing the defaults which were the grounds for disqualification against him. He played no role in their management.

[220] *Standard Chartered Bank of Australia Ltd v Antico* (1995) 131 A.L.R. 1.

[221] [2006] EWHC 1995 (Ch). See also R. Goddard, "Disqualifying the Directors of a Corporate Director" (2007) 28 Co. Law. 281.

There was no room for a finding of shadow directorship: it was accepted that Mr. N played no part in the company's management at any stage. There was no evidence that either LDL or Mr. N gave instructions on which any other directors of the seven companies were "accustomed to act". The Secretary of State's case was that Mr. N could be treated as a de facto director. Although he had not taken any positive action which demonstrated that he was acting as if he were a de jure director, it was submitted that a person in a position to control the actions of a company can constitute himself a de facto director of that company notwithstanding that he may not have ever actually exercised the powers pertinent to his position. Evans-Lombe J., on the basis of reasoning which is respectfully suggested to be flawless and which accords with the views of Millett J. in the *Hydrodam* case, decided that the mere fact that an individual was a controller of a corporate director was not sufficient to make him a de facto director of the company to which the corporate director provided secretarial and administrative services. Action was required. Inaction was insufficient. In his view:

> ". . . in order to be constituted a *de facto* director of a subject company, a director of a corporate *de jure* director must cause the corporate director to take actions with relation to the subject company as would have constituted it a *de facto* director of that company were it not already a director *de jure*."

Moreover, there was no lacuna in the legislation because LDL itself could have been disqualified for inaction or made the subject of winding up proceedings:

> "If the Secretary of State takes the view that corporate directorships are being abused by a single corporate director acquiring a mass of directorships of subject companies or by the parent company of a number of corporate directors achieving the same result, it is open to the Secretary of State to present a petition against a corporate director or its parent to wind it up under s.124A of the Insolvency Act 1986 on public interest grounds and thereafter, if appropriate, to apply to disqualify any directors of those corporate directors, or relevant parent companies, under s.8 of the CDDA."

Although the Secretary of State launched an appeal against this decision, that appeal was compromised.[222]

3–69A In a subsequent misfeasance case, *Re Paycheck Services 3 Ltd, Revenue and Customs Commissioners v Holland*,[223] Revenue and Customs sought recovery from the defendant of dividends that had been unlawfully paid by a series of companies on the basis that the defendant had been a de facto director of the companies at the time the dividends were paid. As was the case in *Mercury Solutions*, the defendant was a de jure director of the corporate director of the relevant subject companies but not a de jure director of the subject companies themselves. The trial judge relied on the passage from Evans-Lombe J.'s

[222] For a case which distinguished the Mercury Solutions case on its facts see *Secretary of State for Business, Enterprise and Regulatory Reform v Poulter*, April 11, 2008, Ch.D., unreported (Registrar Derrett).

[223] [2009] EWCA Civ 625, [2009] S.T.C. 1639.

judgment, cited above, to conclude that the defendant had been a de facto director of the relevant companies in that, insofar as he was properly to be regarded as having acted on behalf of the corporate director, he had clearly caused the latter to act in such a way as would have caused it to be treated as a de facto director were it not already a de jure director. In allowing the defendant's appeal, the Court of Appeal reaffirmed the principle (consistent with *Hydrodam*, albeit that *Hydrodam* was concerned with shadow directorship) that a director or controller of a corporate director does not become a de facto director of the subject company merely by virtue of acts in the former capacity. Rimer L.J. provided the following analysis:

> "Accepting that it is constitutionally permissible for a company to have another company as its sole director, I can see no rational basis on which a member of the board of the latter company, who at all times acts in relation to the subject company solely in his capacity as a director of the corporate director, should be regarded as a de facto or shadow director of the subject company. He may well be at the heart of the decision-making in relation to the subject company. But if he is only at such heart in his capacity as the decision-making organ of the corporate director, there is no proper basis for regarding him as a director also of the subject company. He will only become such if he steps outside the confines of his role as a member of the board of the corporate director and acts directly in relation to the affairs of the subject company … The relevant act in relation to the affairs of the subject company is an act directed by the corporate director, not one directed by the latter company's individual board members. That may be regarded as a distinction of some technicality. But so long as we have a system of company law which recognises the difference between a company and its directors, it is a distinction that must be recognised and respected."

Furthermore, insofar as the passage from Evans-Lombe J.'s judgment in *Mercury Solutions* amounted to a proposition that a director of a corporate director will be a de facto director of the subject company if he procures the corporate director to direct the subject company in respects that would make him a de facto director were he to give it such directions directly, Rimer L.J. (with whom Elias and Ward L.JJ. agreed) regarded it as wrong in principle.

Other categories of director

Foreign element

3–70 The extent to which directors who are foreign nationals or who reside outside the normal jurisdiction of the courts in Great Britain fall within the scope of the CDDA is considered in Ch.16.

Alternate directors

3–71 A company's articles of association may permit a director to appoint an alternate director to act in his place and, in particular, to attend any board meetings that he is unable to attend in person. An alternate director can only be appointed if there is authority in the articles. The status of alternate directors is not entirely clear. However, it is suggested that alternate directors who have been properly appointed under the articles should be regarded as de jure directors bringing them squarely within the scope of the CDDA. However, the key question is likely to be the extent of their duties and responsibilities in any given situation.[224]

Corporate directors

3–72 It has been seen that it is conceptually possible for one company to constitute itself a shadow director of another company. Aside from this, it has long been recognised that a company can be a de jure director.[225] Furthermore, it is clear from CDDA s.14 that a body corporate[226] is capable of committing an offence of acting in breach of a disqualification order. A body corporate that acts as a de jure or de facto director can therefore be disqualified under the CDDA. The point was confirmed in *Official Receiver v Brady*[227] where two nominee Jersey companies were disqualified from being directors under CDDA s.6.[228] In line with the reasoning adopted in the *Hydrodam* case, and as discussed above in 3–69 and 3–69A, a natural person who is a director of a corporate director will not by that fact alone be constituted a de facto or shadow director of any company for which the corporate director acts.

COMPANY

3–73 "Company" is another core term of the CDDA. Like the term "director" its scope is important in two respects. First, it operates as an outer limit on certain powers of the courts to make disqualification orders under the CDDA. Thus, for example, under CDDA s.6 the court only has jurisdiction to disqualify if the conduct complained of relates to a "company".[229] Secondly, it helps to determine the extent of the legal prohibitions that are imposed on a person who is disqualified under the CDDA. This is because a disqualified person is prohibited from engaging in various capacities and activities relating to companies.[230] The discussion in this chapter is directed solely to the question of jurisdiction to disqualify. The scope of the term "company" is revisited in Ch.14, which considers the legal effect of disqualification.[231]

[224] Note the Australian case of *Playcorp Pty Ltd v Shaw* (1993) 10 A.C.S.R. 212 which, although not a disqualification case, suggests that an alternate director will only be caught if he has participated qua director in the running of the company. This is consistent with the view expressed which goes solely to jurisdiction. If there is no relevant "conduct as a director" within the meaning of CDDA s.6(2)(b), there is no basis for a disqualification order.

[225] *Re Bulawayo Market Ltd* [1907] 2 Ch. 458.

[226] Defined to include companies incorporated elsewhere in Great Britain (i.e. Scotland) but to exclude a corporation sole: CDDA s.22(6); Companies Act 1985 s.740.

[227] [1999] B.C.C. 258.

[228] The government proposed the abolition of corporate directors in the White Paper, *Modernising Company Law* (DTI, 2002) but this proposal has not been implemented. Under Companies Act 2006 s.155(1) every company is, however, required to have at least one director who is a natural person.

[229] Subject to other provisions widening this definition as discussed further below.

[230] CDDA ss.1(1), 1A(1), 9B(3), 11, 12, 12A and 12B.

[231] Although there is considerable overlap, the "jurisdiction to disqualify" and the "scope of prohibition" questions are considered in separate chapters primarily for the convenience of the reader. A further justification for separate treatment is that there may be entities in relation to which misconduct may give rise to jurisdiction to disqualify and which can be treated as "companies" for such purposes but which are not "companies" for the purposes of the prohibition. For example, an insolvent partnership falls within the jurisdiction of s.6 but a person disqualified in the terms of CDDA ss.1(1), 1A(1), 9B(3), 11, 12, 12A or 12B is not prohibited from running an unincorporated business in partnership with others.

3–74 CDDA s.22(9) provides that expressions that are defined for the purposes of the Companies Acts have the same meaning in the CDDA.[232] The "Companies Acts" here has the meaning given to the phrase by Companies Act 2006 s.2, i.e. the company law provisions of the 2006 Act together with specified provisions of the Companies (Audit, Investigations and Community Enterprise) Act 2004, the Companies Act 1985 and the Companies Consolidation (Consequential Provisions) Act 1985. As a result of amendments introduced by the Companies Act 2006 (Consequential Amendments, Transitional Provisions and Savings) Order 2009,[233] "company" in CDDA s.22(2)(a) is defined to include "a company registered under the Companies Act 2006 in Great Britain." In the light of CDDA s.22(9), the concept of a registered company within CDDA s.22(2)(a) can only be understood by reference to Companies Act 2006 s.1(1). This defines "company" to mean the following:

(1) A company formed and registered under the Companies Act 2006.
(2) A company that immediately before the commencement of Pt 1 of the Companies Act 2006 was formed and registered under the Companies Act 1985 or the Companies (Northern Ireland) Order 1986.
(3) A company that immediately before the commencement of Pt 1 of the Companies Act 2006 was an existing company for the purposes of the Companies Act 1985 or the Companies (Northern Ireland) Order 1986 (which is to be treated on commencement as if formed and registered under the 2006 Act).[234]

3–75 It is clear from CDDA s.24(2) that the CDDA does not extend to Northern Ireland whereas the Companies Act 2006 extends to the whole of the United Kingdom.[235] As a consequence, the jurisdiction of the courts in Great Britain under CDDA s.6 will only extend to conduct in relation to a Northern Ireland registered company to the extent that such company is capable of being wound up under Pt V of the Insolvency Act 1986.[236] Otherwise, the position appears to be the same as it was before the enactment of the Companies Act 2006. Before October 1, 2009, the combined effect of the then s.22(9) of the CDDA, ss.1(1) and 2 of the Companies Act 2006 and s.735 of the Companies Act 1985 was that CDDA s.6 was to be read as applying to companies formed and registered under the Companies Act 2006 and companies formed and registered under any of its statutory predecessors on or after July 14, 1856.[237]

[232] CDDA s.22(9) substituted by Companies Act 2006 (Consequential Amendments etc.) Order 2008 (SI 2008/948), arts 3(1)(b), Sch.1 Pt 2 para.106(1), (4)(c) with effect from April 6, 2008 and further amended by SI 2009/1941 with effect from October 1, 2009.

[233] SI 2009/1941.

[234] Pt 1 of the 2006 Act came fully into force on October 1, 2009.

[235] Companies Act 2006 s.1299.

[236] CDDA s.22(2)(b); *Re Normandy Marketing Ltd* [1993] B.C.C. 879. See further Ch.16.

[237] Companies formed and registered under the Joint Stock Companies Act 1844 or in Ireland under companies legislation up to and including the Companies (Consolidation) Act 1908 were excluded from the definition of companies formed and registered under the Companies Act 1985 or the former Companies Acts: see Companies Act 1985 s.735(1)(a), (b), (3). The position appears to be the same from October 1, 2009: see Companies Act 2006 s.1(1)(b)(ii).

Accordingly, "company" for the purposes of jurisdiction under s.6 clearly encompassed all forms of registered company, i.e. guarantee companies and unlimited companies as well as companies limited by shares.[238] From October 1, 2009, by virtue of CDDA s.22(2)(a) as substituted by the Companies Act 2006 (Consequential Amendments, Transitional Provisions and Savings) Order 2009,[239] "company" includes "a company registered under the Companies Act 2006 in Great Britain". This amendment, which is consequential on the coming into force of the 2006 Act, appears to make no material change to the position before October 1, 2009 as regards companies formed and registered under earlier companies legislation.[240] There are two further points to be made about the definition of "company" for CDDA purposes. First, the definition has been expressly extended to bring a number of entities that are not directly regulated by companies legislation within the scope of the CDDA. Secondly, the term "company" not only encompasses registered companies but is also expressly defined in s.22(2)(b) to include a company that may be wound up under Pt V of the Insolvency Act 1986.[241] The scope of the term "company" is discussed accordingly under two sub-headings. Readers should be warned that the issue is a complex one and any effort to arrive at a clear interpretation is often hampered rather than helped by the way that the legislation has been drafted.

Statutory extensions and modifications

3–76 The CDDA has been expressly extended to bring those who manage the following types of organisation within the general scope of the Act and within ss.6 and 8 in particular.

Building societies

3–77 Section 22A of the CDDA provides that the Act applies to building societies regulated by the Building Societies Act 1986 as it applies to companies. The two main effects of s.22A are that directors of building societies are liable to disqualification under s.6 and that a disqualified person cannot act as a director or officer of a building society without the permission of the court. The definition of shadow director in s.22(5) also applies but with the substitution of "building society" for company.[242] The application of the unfit conduct provisions in ss.6 to 9 is expressly contemplated by s.22A(4) which provides that references to provisions of the Insolvency Act 1986, the Companies Act 1985 or the Companies Act 2006 in Sch.1 to the CDDA include references to corresponding provisions of the Building Societies Act 1986. Further changes in relation to building societies effected pursuant to the Banking Act 2009 are considered below in 3–91D.

[238] However, the court may be more minded to grant permission to a person to act in relation to an unlimited company than a limited company: see Ch.15.

[239] SI 2009/1941.

[240] See 3–74 above.

[241] From October 1, 2009 this definition applies for the purposes of the CDDA as a whole. Prior to the amendments to s.22(2) introduced by SI 2009/1941, "company" for the purposes of CDDA s.11 was separately defined and did not include all companies that, at that time, may have been wound up under Pt V: see the former CDDA s.22(2)(a).

[242] CDDA s.22A(3).

Incorporated friendly societies

3–78 Section 22B of the CDDA provides that the Act applies to incorporated friendly societies regulated by the Friendly Societies Act 1992 as it applies to companies. The effects of s.22B are broadly the same as those of s.22A in relation to building societies. Specific points to note are that references to "shadow directors" are excluded[243] and that references to "director" or "officer" are to include references to a member of the committee of management or officer of an incorporated friendly society within the meaning of the Friendly Societies Act 1992.[244] In its application to members of the committee of management of a friendly society, CDDA Sch.1 is to be read as if references to provisions of the Insolvency Act 1986, the Companies Act 1985 or the Companies Act 2006 include references to the corresponding provisions of the Friendly Societies Act 1992.[245] The CDDA did not originally apply to friendly societies. Section 22B was inserted by the Friendly Societies Act 1992 s.120(1) and Sch.21, para.8 with effect from February 1, 1993.[246] The 1992 Act makes provision for the conversion of incorporated friendly societies into registered companies in which case they fall squarely within the CDDA in any event. It should be noted that s.22B does not extend to unregistered friendly societies or friendly societies registered under the Friendly Societies Act 1974. These entities are considered below in the discussion of companies that are capable of being wound up under Pt V of the Insolvency Act 1986.

NHS foundation trusts

3–79 Section 22C of the CDDA provides that the Act applies to NHS foundation trusts as it applies to companies.[247] The effects of s.22C are broadly the same as those of ss.22A and 22B discussed above. References to "director" or "officer" are to include a director or officer of an NHS foundation trust but, as is the case with incorporated friendly societies, references to "shadow directors" are excluded.[248] In its application to the directors of an NHS foundation trust, CDDA Sch.1 is to be read as if references to provisions of the Insolvency Act 1986, the Companies Act 1985 or the Companies Act 2006 include references to the corresponding provisions of Ch.5 of Pt 2 of the National Health Service Act 2006.[249]

Open-ended investment companies

3–80 Before October 1, 2009, as under the Open-Ended Investment Companies Regulations 2001,[250] an open-ended investment company is wound up under Pt V

[243] CDDA s.22B(3).
[244] CDDA s.22B(2).
[245] CDDA s.22B(4).
[246] SI 1993/16.
[247] Section 22C was inserted into the CDDA by the Health and Social Care (Community Health and Standards) Act 2003 s.34 and Sch.4 paras 67–68 with effect in England and Wales from April 1, 2004: SI 2004/759.
[248] CDDA s.22C(2).
[249] CDDA s.22C(3).
[250] SI 2001/1228.

of the Insolvency Act 1986, these companies fell within the previous wording of CDDA s.22(2)(b) with the effect that the court's disqualification jurisdiction in the CDDA extended to conduct that related to these entities. At that time, para.5A in Sch.1 to the CDDA provided that references in Pt I of the Schedule to provisions of the Companies Act 1985 or the Companies Act 2006 should be taken to be a reference to the corresponding provision of the 2001 Regulations or any rules made by the Financial Services Authority thereunder. Thus, for the purposes of CDDA ss.6 and 8, Sch.1 was modified in such a way as to make it absolutely clear that these powers encompassed conduct in relation to open-ended investment companies. From October 1, 2009, s.22D of the CDDA[251] applies the Act directly to open-ended investment companies and para.5A of Sch.1 was removed and replaced by a provision having the same effect in s.22D(3). It is beyond doubt that open-ended investment companies are "companies" for the purposes of the CDDA and, in particular, the powers of disqualification in CDDA ss.6 and 8.

Limited liability partnerships

3–81 Limited liability partnerships ("LLPs") are formed under the Limited Liability Partnerships Act 2000, which came into force on April 6, 2001.[252] The LLP as a statutory form of business organisation is largely an adaptation of the limited company. Essentially it is a body corporate through which the members of the LLP can limit their liability. LLPs are to be distinguished from general partnerships and limited partnerships formed under the Limited Partnerships Act 1907. Regulation 4(2) of the Limited Liability Partnership Regulations 2001[253] provides, in the widest terms, that the CDDA applies to limited liability partnerships with appropriate modifications. In particular, references to a "company" in the CDDA are to include references to a LLP. Accordingly, it is clear that conduct in relation to a LLP is within the scope of CDDA ss.6 and 8.

3–82 In the case of LLPs there are, of course, no "directors" as such. Instead those open to disqualification are those who hold equivalent positions within the governing structure. Thus, the concept of "director" is replaced in the CDDA context by the concept of "member" (the concept of "officer" is also displaced by the concept of "member") and the concept of "shadow director" is replaced by the concept of "shadow member".[254] The definition of "shadow member" largely mirrors that for shadow director.[255]

[251] Inserted by SI 2009/1941.
[252] SI 2000/3316.
[253] SI 2001/1090. The 2001 Regulations have been amended to apply the relevant provisions of the Companies Act 2006 to LLPs: See SI 2008/1911 and SI 2009/1804.
[254] See the Limited Liability Partnerships Regulations 2001 (SI 2001/1090) regs 4(1)(f) and (g).
[255] Limited Liability Partnership Regulations 2001 reg.2.

Insolvent partnerships

3–83 Like companies, partnerships play an important role in the UK economy.[256] They vary greatly in size and formality. A particular type of partnership is the limited partnership formed under the Limited Partnership Act 1907. In broad terms, this entity provides a vehicle for investors who do not wish to take an active role in the management of their funds but who wish to combine to create an investment fund under the control of a general partner who alone has unlimited liability for the partnership's obligations. It has proved to be of great importance as a vehicle for venture capital and private equity funds. The limited partner is liable only to the extent of his capital contribution. However, he loses limited liability if he takes part in the management of the partnership business. The English and Scottish Law Commissions have considered partnerships and made recommendations for major reform of this area of business law.[257] After consultation, the government originally decided to take forward the recommendations for reform of limited partnerships and proposed the repeal of the 1907 Act and the introduction of new provisions about limited partnerships into the Partnerships Act 1890 by means of a Legislative Reform Order.[258] However, the 1907 Act has survived albeit with significant amendments introduced by the Legislative Reform (Limited Partnerships) Order 2009[259] designed to clarify the process for registration of limited partnerships. The recommendations for reform of general partnership law are not being taken forward. The oddity remains that under English law, partnerships are not legal entities, whereas under Scottish law they are, and that under Scottish insolvency law the insolvency model is individual insolvency whereas under English insolvency law the model is corporate insolvency.

3–84 Under English law, issues of partnership insolvency are governed by the Insolvent Partnerships Order 1994.[260] Article 16 of the Order provides that the CDDA ss.1, 1A, 6 to 10, 13–15, 17, 19(c), 20 and Sch.1 apply (with certain modifications) where an insolvent partnership is wound up as an unregistered company under Pt V of the Insolvency Act.[261] Article 3 has the further effect that references to companies in the provisions of the CDDA applied by the Order should be

[256] According to the Small and Medium-Sized Enterprise Statistics for the UK 2002 (August 2003) (and cited in the Law Commissions' Joint Report referred to below), at the start of 2002 there were some 567,955 partnerships in the United Kingdom with a combined turnover (excluding VAT) of in excess of £126,902 million.

[257] *Partnership Law*, Law Com No.283 and Scot Law Com No.192 (2003).

[258] BERR, *Reform of Limited Partnership Law: A Consultation Document* (August 2008). The government's focus on limited partnership law reflects the popularity of limited partnership as an investment vehicle.

[259] SI 2009/1940.

[260] SI 1994/2421 as amended by a series of Insolvent Partnerships (Amendment) Orders: SI 1996/1308 with effect from June 14, 1996; SI 2001/767 with effect from April 2, 2001; SI 2002/1308 with effect from May 31, 2002; SI 2005/1516 with effect from July 1, 2005; SI 2006/622 with effect from April 6, 2006.

[261] Article 16 mirrors the application of the rule-making powers in the Insolvency Act 1986 as provided for by s.21(2) of the CDDA. The Insolvent Partnerships Order was made under s.420(1), (2) of the Insolvency Act 1986 and s.21(2) of the CDDA.

construed as references to insolvent partnerships. In the context of general and limited partnerships, "director" is replaced by "officer". An "officer" is defined as meaning a "member" or a person "who has management or control of the partnership business". A "member" is defined as a member of a partnership and any person liable as a partner within the meaning of s.14 of the Partnership Act 1890.[262] It appears that the shadow director provision, modified to fit the partnership context, does apply.

3–85 Limited partnerships, formed under the Limited Partnerships Act 1907 can give rise to certain difficulties in the CDDA context. The potential point of difficulty relates to the conduct of limited partners. Under the 1907 Act a distinction is drawn between active partners ("general partners"), who are fully liable in respect of the debts of the partnership, and those partners who merely invest in the partnership ("limited partners") and who, so long as they do not engage in the management of the partnership business, are liable to third parties only to the extent of their capital contribution.[263] Limited partners are restricted from taking part in the management of a limited partnership business.[264] If a limited partner does take part in the management of the limited partnership then he will not necessarily be in breach of any statutory obligation; he will simply forfeit his limited liability status. It might be thought that it would be unusual for a limited partner who has met the requirement not to concern himself in management of a business to be the subject of successful s.6 or s.8 disqualification proceedings, the test under those sections of the CDDA (as modified by the Insolvent Partnerships Order) being focused on whether identified conduct makes the person unfit to be concerned in "management". Indeed, this is the view taken by the English and Scottish Law Commissions[265] who have suggested that the grounds for disqualification under the CDDA "presuppose some actual involvement in the management of the business".[266] However, it is important to bear in mind that the test under CDDA ss.6 and 8 is whether or not the relevant conduct is such as to make the person unfit to be concerned in the management of a company rather than the management of a company's business, though the latter may comprise an element of the former. Of course, serious misconduct or fraud as a limited partner (even if not related to a business management matter) may well, on the facts, suffice to satisfy the tests in CDDA ss.6 and 8. In the case of alleged omissions to act the position is likely to be more difficult. It is important to note that there is an uncertain boundary as to what steps a limited partner may take without breaching the

[262] See the Insolvent Partnerships Order (as amended), art. 2. Section 14 of the Partnership Act catches, in broad terms, persons who are held out as partners.

[263] These basic concepts are preserved notwithstanding the amendments to the 1907 Act introduced by the Legislative Reform (Limited Partnerships) Order 2009 (SI 2009/1940).

[264] Limited Partnerships Act 1907 s.6(1).

[265] See *Limited Partnerships Act 1907: A Joint Consultation Paper*, Law Com No.161; Scot Law Com No.118; and the Joint Report, *Partnership Law*, Law Com No.283 and Scot Law Com No.192 (2003). Insolvency was outside the terms of reference of the Law Commissions.

[266] *Limited Partnerships Act 1907: A Joint Consultation Paper*, Law Com No.161; Scot Law Com No.118 at para.2.23.

prohibition on being involved in management of the partnership business. Thus, although s.6 of the 1907 Act expressly prohibits a limited partner from taking part in the management of the partnership business without forfeiting limited liability status, it also confers a right on such a partner to inspect partnership books, to "examine into" the state and prospects of the business and to "advise with" the partners thereon. To that extent it may be said that a limited partner has some role to play in the management of a limited partnership (and indirectly in the management of the limited partnership business). Questions as to whether a limited partner has met requisite standards of conduct in respect of the areas permitted to him under the 1907 Act (and what action could properly be required of him) may well give rise to serious difficulties when considering potential disqualification proceedings.

3–86 It should be noted that CDDA s.6 has no application where the individual members of the firm present a joint bankruptcy petition under art.11 of the Insolvent Partnerships Order. In those circumstances, art.16 is not triggered because the art.11 procedure does not involve the winding up of the firm as an unregistered company. However, partners who take the art.11 route are susceptible to automatic disqualification under CDDA s.11 as undischarged bankrupts.

European Economic Interest Groupings ("EEIGs")

3–87 The EEIG is the result of a European initiative to facilitate cross-border business co-operation. It effectively enables two or more firms based in more than one EC Member State to form a grouping which is itself endowed with separate legal capacity, but not limited liability. An EEIG is not intended to operate as a holding company or joint venture profit-making entity but as an "ancillary" entity. To date it has been little used in Great Britain, and EEIG formations in the United Kingdom appear low.[267]

3–88 The CDDA ss.1, 2, 4 to 11, 12(2), 15 to 17, 20, 22 and Sch.1 expressly apply where an EEIG is wound up as an unregistered company under Pt V of the Insolvency Act. This is the effect of reg.20 of the European Economic Interest Grouping Regulations 1989.[268] For these purposes, the reference in CDDA s.6 to a director or past director of a company is taken to include a reference to a manager of an EEIG or anyone who has or has had control or management of an EEIG's business. It appears that the shadow director provision, modified to fit the EEIG context, does apply.

The European Company and the European Private Company

3–89 Since the coming into force of Council Regulation 2157/2001 of October 8, 2001 on October 8, 2004, it has been possible to incorporate a European Company (*societas*

[267] There were 185 EEIGs with a principal establishment in Great Britain in 2006: DTI, *Companies in 2005–2006* (Table E3).

[268] SI 1989/638, as amended and extended to encompass Northern Ireland disqualifications by SI 2009/2399 with effect from October 1, 2009.

europaea) ("SE") by registration in the United Kingdom. There are various means of creating such a company under art.2 of the Regulation but in all cases there must be two or more commercial bodies involved, at least two of which must be resident in different EC Member States. The SE is modelled on the public company limited by shares and there is flexibility in that the company may elect to be managed either by a two-tier board comprising a supervisory organ and a management organ (on the German model) or a single, unitary board (on the English model).[269] Although strictly a creature of Community Law, it seems clear that a SE formed and having its registered office anywhere in Great Britain will be a registered company falling within the scope of the CDDA. Article 15(1) provides that, subject to the Regulation, the formation of an SE shall be governed by the law applicable to public limited companies in the Member State in which the company establishes its registered office. Similarly, art.10 provides that, subject to the Regulation, an SE shall be treated as if it were a public limited company formed in accordance with the law of the Member State in which it has its registered office. Finally, art.9(1)(c)(ii) expressly provides that an SE shall be governed, among other things, by the provisions of domestic law that would apply to a public limited company formed in accordance with the law of the Member State in which the SE has its registered office insofar as the matter is not governed by the Regulation. It follows that the CDDA applies to an SE incorporated and having its registered office in Great Britain. Moreover, where a two-tier board structure is adopted, members of both the supervisory and management organs would be "directors" for CDDA purposes.

3–89A A further supranational corporate form, the European Private Company (*societas privata europaea*) is to be introduced and available in Member States with effect from July 1, 2010.[270] As its name suggests, the object of this proposal is to create a standard, uniform private company vehicle for small and medium-sized enterprises that wish to expand their business beyond the borders of a single Member State and provide such enterprises with an alternative to incorporating subsidiaries or establishing branches in other Member States. A European Private Company will be a creature of Community Law formed by registration in the Member State in which it has its registered office. The principal effect of the proposed Regulation is that the disqualification of a person serving as a director of a European Private Company is to be governed by the applicable national law. It follows that where the company is registered in Great Britain, the powers to disqualify directors in the CDDA will apply.

[269] Council Regulation 2157/2001, reg.38 and see now the European Public Limited-Liability Company Regulations 2004 (SI 2004/2326). For further background on the nature and constitution of a European Company see DTI, *Implementation of the European Company Statute: The European Public Limited-Liability Company Regulations—A Consultative Document* (2003) and *Implementation of the European Company Statute: The European Public Limited-Liability Company Regulations—Results of Consultation* (2004).

[270] See Proposal for a Council Regulation on the Statute for a European Private Company COM (2008) 396/3. For background see R. Drury, "The European Private Company" (2008) 9(1) European Business Organization L.R. 125; B. Mackowiz and F. Saifee, "Societas Privata Europaea: the European Private Company" (2009) 30(8) Co.Law. 227.

Not-for-profit companies

3–90 Community interest companies ("CICs") were introduced as a medium for non-charitable not-for-profit organisations and social enterprises by the Companies (Audit, Investigations and Community Enterprise) Act 2004. CICs are registered companies taking the form of either a company limited by shares or a company limited by guarantee which have opted into the special regime for which provision is made in Pt 2 of the 2004 Act. As such, CICs clearly fall within the scope of the CDDA.[271]

3–91 On the recommendation of the Company Law Review, a separate corporate medium for charitable organisations—the Charitable Incorporated Organisation ("CIO")—was introduced by the Charities Act 2006.[272] This is not a registered company under the Companies Acts but a body corporate registered by the Charity Commissioners under Pt 8A of the Charities Act 1993. The Minister is empowered by s.69N of the Charities Act 1993 to make provision by regulations about the winding up, insolvency and dissolution of CICs. At the time of writing, no regulations have been made. However, draft regulations have been published which suggest that the CDDA will be expressly applied to CIOs with appropriate modifications.[273]

Statutory extensions and modifications introduced by the Banking Act 2009

Banks

3–91A In response to the banking crisis that occurred during 2007 and 2008, Parliament introduced a statutory regime for dealing with failing banks. Initially, the Treasury was given emergency powers under the Banking (Special Provisions) Act 2008. Subsequently, a permanent statutory regime was established by the Banking Act 2009 which, inter alia, introduced a new bank insolvency procedure based on existing liquidation provisions and a new bank administration procedure. Similar regimes have also been introduced pursuant to the 2009 Act in respect of building societies.

3–91B Section 121(4) of the Banking Act 2009 introduced a new s.21A of the CDDA with effect from February 21, 2009.[274] CDDA s.21A recites that s.121 of the Banking Act applies the CDDA "in relation to bank insolvency as it applies in relation to liquidation". Section 121 provides, inter alia, that a reference in the CDDA to liquidation includes a reference to bank insolvency, a reference to winding up includes a reference to making or being subject to a bank insolvency

[271] See Companies (Audit, Investigations and Community Enterprise) Act 2004 ss.26, 32–38; Companies Act 2006 s.1, 2(1)(b).

[272] A new Part 8A, ss.69A–69Q and Sch.5B were inserted into the Charities Act 1993 by the Charities Act 2006 s.34.

[273] See the Cabinet Office and Office of the Third Sector joint consultation document, *The Charitable Incorporated Organisation (CIO)—Consultation on the new corporate form for charities* (September 2008), Annex B available online at *http://www.cabinetoffice.gov.uk/third_sector/Consultations/completed_consultations/cio.aspx* [Accessed August 19, 2009]. The draft regulations also suggest that s.72 of the Charities Act 1993 will apply for the purposes of determining whether a person subject to a CDDA disqualification, as such disqualification applies to CIOs, is disqualified from being a charity trustee.

[274] Banking Act 2009 (Commencement No.1) Order 2009 (SI 2009/296).

order and a reference to "becoming insolvent" includes a reference to becoming subject to a bank insolvency order. The main effect of these provisions is that directors of banks that enter the bank insolvency procedure are within the scope of the disqualification power in CDDA s.6 and the Secretary of State's power to accept a disqualification undertaking in lieu of a disqualification order in CDDA s.7(2A).

3–91C Section 155(4) of the Banking Act 2009 introduced a new s.21B of the CDDA with effect from February 21, 2009.[275] CDDA s.21B recites that s.155 of the Banking Act applies the CDDA "in relation to bank administration as it applies in relation to liquidation". Section 155 provides, inter alia, that a reference in the CDDA to liquidation includes a reference to bank administration, a reference to winding up includes a reference to making or being subject to a bank administration order and a reference to "becoming insolvent" includes a reference to becoming subject to a bank administration order. The main effect of these provisions is that directors of banks that enter the bank administration procedure are within the scope of the disqualification power in CDDA s.6 and the Secretary of State's power to accept a disqualification undertaking in lieu of a disqualification order in CDDA s.7(2A).

Building societies

3–91D Pursuant to powers in the Banking Act 2009, the Treasury made the Building Societies (Insolvency and Special Administration) Order 2009 ("the 2009 Order").[276] This applies the bank insolvency and bank administration regimes to building societies by means of a series of amendments to the Building Societies Act 1986.[277] Section 90E of the Building Societies Act, inserted by the 2009 Order, provides, inter alia, that a reference in the CDDA to liquidation includes a reference to building society insolvency and to building society special administration, a reference to winding up includes a reference to making or being subject to a building society insolvency order or to a building society special administration order and a reference to "becoming insolvent" includes a reference to becoming subject to a building society insolvency order or a building society special administration order. Article 12 of the 2009 Order introduced a new s.21C of the CDDA which recites that s.90E of the Building Societies Act applies the CDDA "in relation to building society insolvency and building society special administration". The main effect of these provisions is that directors of building societies that enter these forms of insolvency procedure are within the scope of the disqualification power in CDDA s.6 and the Secretary of State's power to accept a disqualification undertaking in lieu of a disqualification order in CDDA

[275] Banking Act 2009 (Commencement No.1) Order 2009 (SI 2009/296).

[276] SI 2009/805 with effect from March 29, 2009.

[277] For further modifications as regards the application of the building society special administration procedure in Scotland see The Building Society Special Administration (Scotland) Rules 2009 (SI 2009/806 (s.3).

s.7(2A). Section 90E(5) of the Building Societies Act makes identical provision as regards the scope of the disqualification regime in Northern Ireland.

Companies capable of being wound up under Pt V of the Insolvency Act 1986

3–92 CDDA s.22(2)(b) provides that in all provisions of the CDDA except for s.11, the term "company" includes "a company that may be wound up under Pt V of the Insolvency Act 1986".[278] On a literal reading, this means that the various powers of disqualification in the CDDA extend to the directors etc. of any company that is capable of being wound up as an unregistered company under Pt V. This brings the following types of company within the scope of CDDA s.6.

Unregistered companies as defined by the Companies Act

3–93 Certain provisions of the Companies Act 2006 are extended to apply to bodies corporate which are incorporated in Great Britain but are incorporated under a special Act of Parliament or by Royal Charter rather than under the Companies Acts or any other public general Act.[279]

Unincorporated friendly societies

3–94 Section 22B of the CDDA (which applies to incorporated friendly societies) does not extend to unregistered friendly societies or friendly societies registered under the Friendly Societies Act 1974. It might appear at first sight that these would be caught by the CDDA as they may be wound up as unregistered companies under Pt V of the Insolvency Act.[280] However, s.22(2)(b) of the CDDA refers to any *company* which may be wound up under Pt V. It does not expressly adopt the wider term "unregistered company" used in s.220(1) of the Insolvency Act 1986 which is there defined to include "any association and any company". It is suggested that an unincorporated association capable of being wound up under Pt V should not be treated as a "company" (i.e. a body corporate) falling within s.22(2)(b).[281]

Industrial and provident societies

3–95 An industrial and provident society is created as a body corporate by its enabling legislation,[282] and, under that legislation, is wound up under the Insolvency Act 1986 as if it were a registered company.[283] The enabling legislation does not provide for the society to be wound up as an unregistered company.[284]

[278] The current s.22(2)(b) was substituted by SI 2009/1941 with effect from October 1, 2009. The previous wording was identical in effect except that it did not extend to s.11.

[279] Companies Act 2006 s.1043 (formerly Companies Act 1985 s.718).

[280] *Re Victoria Society, Knottingley* [1913] 1 Ch. 167.

[281] The same argument is developed in Ch.14 as regards the question whether the prohibitions in CDDA ss.1 and 1A extend to general partnerships.

[282] Industrial and Provident Societies Act 1965 s.3.

[283] Industrial and Provident Societies Act 1965 s.55(a).

[284] *Re Norse Self Build Association Ltd* [1985] B.C.L.C. 219.

Accordingly, it appears that an industrial and provident society, while a corporate entity, is not "a company" capable of being wound up under Pt. V of the Insolvency Act 1986 and is accordingly not within the scope of the CDDA. It has been suggested that industrial and provident societies are also liable to be wound up under Pt V of the Insolvency Act 1986 on the grounds that s.55 of the Industrial and Provident Societies Act 1965 is "permissive" and not prescriptive.[285] The authors consider this argument to be unsound. In their view, the relevant industrial and provident societies legislation prescribes how such bodies are to be created and their relevant incidents, including the jurisdiction to wind up and the method of winding up. The winding up jurisdiction provided for is prescriptive and exhaustive and should not merely be regarded as an alternative. Indeed, the "permissive" interpretation reflects neither the basis of, nor the actual decision in, the leading authority on the point.[286]

The proposition that an industrial and provident society is not a "company" capable of being wound up under Pt V of the Insolvency Act 1986 receives further support from *Re Dairy Farmers of Britain Ltd*.[287] In that case, Henderson J. ruled that the prohibition in s.72A(1) of the Insolvency Act on the holder of a qualifying floating charge appointing an administrative receiver of a company did not apply to an industrial and provident society. His reasoning was that the definition of "company" which applied was, unless a contrary intention appeared or the context otherwise required, a company formed and registered under the Companies Acts. He held that there was nothing in the relevant legislation indicating that some other definition should be applied.

3–96 It is striking that Parliament has seen fit to extend the application of the CDDA expressly to building societies, incorporated friendly societies, NHS foundation trusts, limited liability partnerships and so on[288] but not to unincorporated friendly societies and industrial and provident societies. This also tends to reinforce the argument that unincorporated friendly societies and industrial and provident societies are beyond the scope of the CDDA.

Foreign incorporated companies

3–97 A company incorporated outside Great Britain can be wound up by the court under Pt V of the Insolvency Act 1986. The extent of the extraterritorial reach of the CDDA is considered further in Ch.16.

[285] C. Mills, "Does the CDDA Apply to Industrial and Provident Societies?" (1997) 13 Insolv. Law & Practice 182.

[286] *Re Norse Self Build Association Ltd* [1985] B.C.L.C. 219. It is clear also that an industrial and provident society is not an unregistered company for the purposes of s.1043 of the Companies Act 2006 as this provision excludes bodies incorporated by, or registered under, a public general Act of Parliament.

[287] [2009] EWHC 1389 (Ch).

[288] See text from 3–73.

BECOMES INSOLVENT

3–98 For the purposes of CDDA s.6(1)(a) it must be established that the defendant is or has been a director of a company which has at any time "become insolvent". Section 6(2) provides:

> "For the purposes of this section [6] and the next, a company becomes insolvent if—
>
> (a) the company goes into liquidation at a time when its assets are insufficient for the payment of its debts and other liabilities and the expenses of the winding up,
> (b) the company enters administration,[289] or
> (c) an administrative receiver of the company is appointed . . ."

This provision is important in two respects. First, the jurisdiction in s.6 is only triggered if the relevant company has "become insolvent". Secondly, the two-year time limit for commencing proceedings for an order under s.6 runs from the day on which the relevant company "became insolvent".[290] As regards the triggering of jurisdiction, it can be seen from s.6(2) that the company needs to have entered into one of the insolvency regimes specified. Thus, the company's *factual* insolvency—that is the company's inability to pay its debts as they fall due or an excess of liabilities over assets in the company's balance sheet—is not of itself sufficient to trigger jurisdiction.[291] Another implication of the definition is that a company that has been dissolved and struck off the register without first entering an insolvency regime has not "become insolvent" for the purposes of s.6.[292] It would have to be restored to the register and then enter one of the specified forms of insolvency regime before s.6 disqualification proceedings could be commenced.

Administration and administrative receivership

3–99 CDDA ss.6(2)(b) and (c) are relatively straightforward. If the company has gone into administration, it is treated as insolvent for CDDA purposes from the date the company entered administration for the purposes of Sch.B1 of the Insolvency Act 1986. The company "enters administration" when the appointment of an administrator takes effect. Where the administrator is appointed by means of an administration order, the appointment takes effect at the time specified in the order, or if no time is specified in the order, when the order is made.[293] Where

[289] This wording was substituted by the Enterprise Act 2002 s.248 and Sch.17 para.42 to reflect the fact that an administrator can now be appointed out of court and not exclusively by court order as was the case in the past.

[290] CDDA s.7(2). See further Chs 7 and 8.

[291] *Re NCG Trading Ltd, Official Receiver v Mansell* [2004] EWHC 3203 (Ch), [2004] All E.R. (D) 351.

[292] A different jurisdictional problem arises where a company that has entered administration (and therefore "become insolvent") is then dissolved without first being wound up and the disqualification proceedings are only commenced after dissolution: see *Re J & N International Ltd, Secretary of State for Trade and Industry v Arnold* [2007] EWHC 1933 (Ch), [2008] 1 B.C.L.C. 581 and 7–07.

[293] Insolvency Act 1986 Sch.B1 para.13(2).

the administrator is appointed out of court, the appointment takes effect when the notice of appointment and other prescribed documents are filed with the court.[294] If the company has gone into administrative receivership, it is treated as insolvent for CDDA purposes from the date of the receiver's appointment.[295]

"Goes into liquidation"

3–100 At first sight, s.6(2)(a) is equally straightforward. The Insolvency Act definition of "goes into liquidation" is expressly adopted.[296] A company "goes into liquidation" if it passes a resolution for voluntary winding up or an order for its compulsory winding up is made by the court.[297] However, the court must also be satisfied that the company was insolvent on a net asset basis (i.e. as having a deficiency of assets over liabilities) at the time it went into liquidation. This additional requirement to establish that the relevant company has gone into insolvent liquidation apparently has the effect of excluding companies that are solvent when wound up from the ambit of s.6.[298] However, in this context, insolvency has a specific CDDA meaning. As set out above, s.6 refers to the company having gone into liquidation "at a time when its assets are insufficient for the payment of its debts and other liabilities and the expenses of the winding up". To assess the company's solvency for CDDA purposes, the following matters must therefore be considered as at the date of liquidation: (a) the value of the company's assets; (b) the value of its liabilities; and (c) the amount of liquidation expenses. The value of assets will not necessarily be the same as their book value. Certain assets may appear in the company's books at historic cost but in fact be worth far more than that. Equally, certain assets may be worth less than their book value (for example, provision may have to be made for bad debts). It is also possible that value may be lost from the mere fact of liquidation, especially in respect of assets such as

[294] Insolvency Act 1986 Sch.B1 paras 19 and 31.

[295] The validity of the appointment of an administrator or administrative receiver cannot be challenged in disqualification proceedings: see *Secretary of State for Trade and Industry v Jabble* [1998] 1 B.C.L.C. 598. The proper course is for the court to stay the disqualification proceedings to enable the company to challenge the appointment in proceedings properly constituted for the purpose as illustrated by *Re Brampton Manor (Leisure) Ltd, Secretary of State for Trade and Industry v Woolf* [2005] EWHC 3074 (Ch). (For the making of the subsequent disqualification order following the unsuccessful challenge to the appointment of the administrative receivers in that case see [2009] EWHC 1796 (Ch)). The court is unlikely to stay disqualification proceedings if it considers that the challenge will fail, e.g. where the administration or receivership has long since been completed. The position would be the same if the defendant wished to challenge the validity of a resolution for the voluntary winding up of the relevant company: see *Re Kaytech International Plc, Secretary of State for Trade and Industry v Kaczer* [1999] 2 B.C.L.C. 351 at 393–396.

[296] Insolvency Act 1986 s.247(2); CDDA s.22(3).

[297] In the case of compulsory liquidation, the company "goes into liquidation" on the date of the winding up order not the date of the petition: see *Re Walter L Jacob & Co Ltd, Official Receiver v Jacob* [1993] B.C.C. 512 followed in Scotland by *Secretary of State for Trade and Industry v Campleman* 1999 S.L.T. 787.

[298] Such as companies wound up solvent on public interest grounds under s.124A of the Insolvency Act 1986 which are nevertheless squarely within the scope of CDDA s.8: compare Insolvency Act 1986 s.124A(1) and CDDA s.8(1), (1A).

work in progress and book debts. It is suggested that the valuation should be carried out on the basis that the company has entered or is immediately about to enter liquidation. This would seem consistent with the decision in *Re Gower Enterprises Ltd, Official Receiver v Moore*[299] in which the court accepted that the assets should be valued on the basis of their estimated realisation value, including interest due to the company up to the date of liquidation. It was held in that case that interest and capital gains earned after liquidation should not be taken into account in the calculation. Similarly, liabilities, including interest owed by the company, were valued as at the date of liquidation, excluding interest payable in respect of any period thereafter. If the valuation of the existing assets and such liabilities as would be provable as at the liquidation date alters (for example, because a contingency matures), it is unclear whether in the same way a proof of debt could be revised, the value of the assets and/or liabilities could be revised for the purposes of the s.6(2) test by application of the hindsight principle.[300] This issue requires consideration of the manner in which expenses are to be treated.

3–101 In determining whether the company was insolvent at the time it went into liquidation, the further question that arises is how the court should go about computing the expenses of winding up. The problem with s.6(2)(a) is that the court is being asked to take expenses into account in determining whether the company was insolvent, but at a point—the commencement of the liquidation—when those expenses have not yet been incurred. In *Re Gower Enterprises Ltd, Official Receiver v Moore*,[301] the company went into compulsory liquidation with a surplus of realisable assets over liabilities of around £100,000, according to its statement of affairs. In winding up the company's affairs, the liquidator had incurred expenses (including his own remuneration) of around £180,000. If the expenses actually incurred were taken into account under CDDA s.6(1)(a) then the company could be treated as having become insolvent with an asset deficiency of £80,000. According to Evans-Lombe J., the ostensible meaning of "expenses of the winding up" is the expenses that subsequently were incurred in the course of the winding up. He suggested that the amount of such expenses "cannot be determined at the date of the winding up". The judge was concerned that simply taking the figure for expenses actually incurred could be unjust, as this would mean that liability under the CDDA could turn on expenses that may have been improperly or ill-advisedly incurred. To avoid this possible injustice, Evans-Lombe J. held that "expenses" in s.6(1)(a) should be construed as meaning "reasonable expenses". He suggested the following two rules of thumb:

(1) What constitutes "reasonable expenses" should be those fees and expenses properly chargeable by applying the official receiver's scale fees

[299] [1995] B.C.C. 293.

[300] *MS Fashions Ltd v BCCI* [1993] Ch. 425 at 434–435; *Stein v Blake* [1996] A.C. 243 at 256; *Wight v Eckhardt* [2003] UKPC 37, [2004] 1 A.C. 147 at [32].

[301] [1995] B.C.C. 293.

under the Insolvency Fees Order 1986[302] to the realisable assets in the winding up.

(2) If the expenses can be shown to have been less than the official receiver's scale fees, the actual expenses should then be substituted for those scale fees, for the purposes of the s.6 solvency test.

The unfortunate consequence is that in rare cases like *Gower Enterprises* the court may have to hear argument on whether the expenses actually incurred were reasonably incurred. Following the judgment of Evans-Lombe J. in *Gower Enterprises*, the solvency issue had to go to an inquiry which was conducted by Blackburne J.

Blackburne J. was content to assume that book debts subsequently recovered were no greater than face value with interest up to the date of liquidation. This assumption did not affect the result. However, he pointed out that as at the date of liquidation there was considerable doubt whether book debts were then worth their full face value. As regards the expenses of the liquidation, it was accepted that certain sums, including the statutory fee payable to the DTI, were properly "expenses" but the liquidator's remuneration was challenged. It was said, and the DTI accepted, that on a time cost basis the remuneration would have been some £20,000, rather than some £102,000 or so calculated on a realisations basis. This latter figure was greater than the remuneration that would have been payable as a scale fee (which was calculated as being around £61,000) or which would have been paid to the Official Receiver had he been liquidator and all debts of the company been realised in full (calculated at around £53,000). However, remuneration had been fixed at the higher sum and approved by the creditors in accordance with the relevant statutory provisions and had not been challenged. On this basis, Blackburne J. considered that the actual sum for the liquidator's remuneration of around £102,000 was to be taken into account in the computation of liquidation expenses. As it happened, on the figures, the company was "insolvent" for s.6 purposes, which ever figure (£102,000, £61,000 or £53,000) was used. On the facts, and on the assumption he was not permitted to rely on the £102,000 figure, Blackburne J. considered that the £61,000 figure would have been reasonable as a matter of quantum.

Gower Enterprises assumes that only "actual" expenses can be taken into account. What remains to be considered is whether this assumption is correct. For example, when faced with a s.6 trial at an early stage of a complex and long insolvency are only the actual costs incurred to date to be taken into account? Alternatives might be: (a) for the court to take actual costs and estimated future costs into account (though this raises the possibility of jurisdiction coming and going under s.6(2)(a)); or alternatively (b) for the costs of the liquidation to be

[302] SI 1986/2030. Blackburne J. subsequently pointed out in his judgment on inquiry in the same case that the fees would also have to be those recoverable under the Insolvency Regulations 1986 (SI 1986/1994).

estimated as at the liquidation date as are the existence and value of the assets and liabilities. Obviously, the actual expenses may well be used as an aid in this process to the extent permitted by the authorities but no more. If anything other than actual expenses are taken account of, there is a danger that a company could move in or out of "insolvent liquidation" for s.6 purposes, depending on how far advanced the liquidation was at the time of any disqualification trial. If only actual expenses are taken into account, the company could only move into insolvent liquidation. However, this is also unsatisfactory. It is far from clear why jurisdiction should turn on this sort of point, which is not even based on the ultimate outcome for creditors, whereas, if the company enters administration or administrative receivership, there will be jurisdiction to disqualify irrespective of ultimate solvency. This conundrum was considered further in the *Lyarmo* case discussed below.

3–102 In *Re Lyarmo Ltd, Secretary of State for Trade and Industry v Glover*[303] the passage of time in disqualification proceedings[304] resulted in a situation where the liquidator had, eventually, recovered some £490,000 from the errant directors with regard to one of the matters complained of as unfit conduct in the disqualification proceedings.[305] Furthermore, large numbers of creditors for substantially small sums, originally identified in the Statement of Affairs some years before, were clearly not going to prove. By the time of the trial therefore, it appeared that the creditors proving in the liquidation of Lyarmo would be paid in full, and that there would be a distribution to members of about £250,000, 99% of which would go to one of the directors, in his capacity as shareholder. The Statement of Affairs had shown an estimated deficiency (leaving aside any expenses of the winding up) of in excess of £100,000 and did not include as an asset the claim against the directors which was subsequently realised by the liquidator. The argument put forward by the directors was that the claim against them should be included as an asset at the realisation figure, that other assets should be included at the higher figures that they had in fact realised and that the liabilities should be adjusted downwards to reflect the fact that it was known that many claims would not be proved for. Further, the requirement under s.6 was that actual expenses rather than reasonably foreseeable expenses had to be brought into the calculation. Such a test permitted the use of hindsight and there was no reason not to use hindsight when valuing assets and liabilities. The argument for the Secretary of State was that since it was agreed that the date by reference to which solvency had to be determined was the date of the winding up then what was called for was a "snapshot". Just as a conventional balance sheet for the purpose of statutory accounts is a "snapshot" of the company's financial position at the accounting date, so s.6(2)(a) required the court to ascertain the assets and liabilities as at a specific date.[306]

[303] October 21, 2005, Ch.D., unreported.

[304] The company went into liquidation in January 2000.

[305] The claim was found by the judge to have arisen as "a straightforward case of company money being used to acquire personal assets for a director of the company".

[306] See also the test in s.214(6) of the Insolvency Act 1986, and contrast with this the test required by s.89 of that Act for a members' voluntary liquidation (which requires not a "snapshot" but a "twelve month view").

Hindsight is only permitted to be used to a limited extent.[307] It was also argued that the directors were bound by the principles of approbation and reprobation[308] so that they were not permitted to resile from the Statement of Affairs to the extent that, by that document, they denied that any claims were owed by them to the company. The findings of HH Judge Norris were as follows:

(1) The question of insolvency does not arise in the abstract but in the context of deciding whether proceedings may be brought against directors who may have been guilty of misconduct and whether such directors should be disqualified. It must be approached in that setting.
(2) Section 6(2) is concerned with founding the jurisdiction to disqualify. Paragraphs (b) and (c) provide simple tests that are satisfied once and for all. Although paragraph (a) contains a more complex test, it is unlikely to be what Evans-Lombe J. described as "an indeterminative and moving test" i.e. one that causes the case to move within and without the provisions of the CDDA.
(3) The test for insolvency under s.6(2) must be one which is capable of application with reasonable certainty within the time limited for the commencement of disqualification proceedings. This makes it unlikely that the test involves a consideration of the final outcome of the liquidation. It must involve the consideration of a state of affairs which may be ascertained relatively early in the liquidation process.
(4) If (as the authorities presently demonstrate) "the expenses of the winding up" means the actual expenses so far as reasonable, then that may cause some cases to move over the solvency line, but that movement will only be one way (from solvency to insolvency), because the actual expenses reasonably incurred will never diminish but only increase. This is therefore not a warrant for the general introduction of hindsight to adjust the value of assets and the size of liabilities.
(5) The point in time by reference to which the solvency question must be answered is the time when Lyarmo went into liquidation because this is what the section says.

[307] *Buckingham v Francis* [1986] 2 All E.R. 738; *Re ESC Publishing Ltd* [1990] B.C.C. 335 and *Segama NV v Penny Le Roy* [1984] 1 E.G.L.R. 109. In brief, subsequent events may be looked at for the purpose of deciding what the position actually was on the valuation date and, where appropriate, what predictions and forecasts for the future could reasonably have been made at that date. The distinction is between, on the one hand, a fact or event later in point of time than the valuation date which enables the valuer (in this case, the court) to assess a state of affairs which actually existed at the valuation date where such a fact or event is relevant, and evidence of it is admissible in the valuation process; and, on the other hand, a fact or event which of itself influences the value of the thing to be valued only as at the date it occurs, such a change in value being irrelevant and evidence of such a fact or event being inadmissible (see *Segama*).

[308] See e.g. *Express Newspapers v News (UK) Plc* [1990] 1 W.L.R. 1320; *First National Bank v Walker* [2001] 1 F.L.R. 505; *Union Music Ltd v Watson* [2002] EWCA Civ 680, [2003] 1 B.C.L.C. 453 and, in the disqualification context, *Re Circle Holidays International Plc* [1994] B.C.C. 226. Questions of abuse of process may also have been relevant given the directors denied liability until summary judgment was obtained against them, or until just before that.

(6) It is for the Secretary of State to establish on the balance of probabilities that Lyarmo went into liquidation when it was insolvent in the technical s.6(2)(a) sense.

(7) The Secretary of State is able to discharge that burden by adducing in evidence the Statement of Affairs sworn by the directors. This is an admission by the parties against whom insolvency has to be established that Lyarmo went into liquidation at a time when it assets were insufficient to discharge its liabilities: see the effect of s.433 of the Insolvency Act 1986.

(8) The directors of Lyarmo were under a statutory duty pursuant to s.99 of the Insolvency Act 1986 to prepare a statement showing particulars of the company's assets and debts and liabilities. A statement so prepared had to include estimates (of assets yet to be realised and, to a lesser extent, of liabilities), but that is simply the same task which the directors performed for the purposes of the statutory accounts every year. The admission of insolvency, having carried out that exercise, was therefore a formal one made in the performance of a specific statutory duty.

(9) An evidential burden therefore lies on the defendant to establish that he did not perform that duty accurately and that he should be permitted to resile from the admission of insolvency contained in the Statement of Affairs.[309] Unless he does so, the evidence adduced by the Secretary of State in the form of the sworn Statement of Affairs stands and discharges the burden of proof. The defendant may, for example, demonstrate that an asset has been overlooked in the preparation of the Statement of Affairs, or that events have occurred since the making of the Statement of Affairs which would enable a valuer better to assess the position as it actually stood at the date of liquidation for the purpose of then estimating value. He may show that the admission of insolvency was based on a genuine mistake to which it would be plainly unfair to hold him. These are examples, not an exhaustive list.

(10) The doctrines of election, approbation and reprobation have more to do with choosing between *rights or remedies* than with *evidence* (though the classification of estoppel continues to be the subject of debate). The matter for consideration is one of evidence: can the directors persuade the court that their earlier admission of insolvency was wrong and that they may resile from it?

As regards one of the assets, a book debt, HH Judge Norris, having considered the factual circumstances of the creditors' meeting, the manner in which creditors had probed the relevant valuation and what was said on the directors' behalf at the meeting, said as follows:

[309] It is unclear whether some legal impediment to withdrawal was envisaged (as to which see more recently e.g. *Sowerby v Charlton* [2005] EWCA Civ 1610, [2006] 1 W.L.R. 568) or whether the judge simply decided that the evidence did not persuade him that the admission was wrongly made. The latter interpretation is somewhat problematic in the light of the fact that the civil recovery claim against the directors had been established and met and that the judge rejected an analysis based on the value of any such claim as at the date of liquidation.

> "Where directors have specifically confirmed to creditors the worth of an item on the Statement of Affairs they should not in general be permitted subsequently to assert some other value if they later consider it to their advantage to do so. Absent some demonstrable mistake at the time (or the emergence of some key fact that, if known to a valuer at the date of the s.98 meeting, would have enabled a more accurate valuation to be made, or some other such exceptional circumstance) the evidence to be given weight by the court should be the view of the directors expressed at the meeting. A subsequent attempt to substitute a value more favourable to the directors can scarcely be regarded as credible."

He was also unpersuaded, on the facts, that any higher valuation figure as at the date of liquidation would have been appropriate. As regards the omission from the Statement of Affairs of the claim against the directors, consideration was given to the argument that it was a question of valuing the claim taking into account the prospects and costs of recovery. However, the judge said:

> "Where the relevant asset is a claim against the directors making the Statement of Affairs themselves, this does not appear to me to be justified (except in cases where the directors admit the claim but assert insufficiency of assets to satisfy it). If the director admits the claim it goes on the Statement of Affairs at full value. If the director does not admit the claim it does not go on the Statement of Affairs. It must be a wholly exceptional case where the director says 'I admit the claim against me but I intend to fight it tooth and nail and put the company to great expense in pursuing me, and force the company to settle for something less than 100%. So the claim should not be entered at full value.' "

On the facts he reached the following conclusion:

> "It seems to me plain that a time when it went into liquidation Lyarmo was insolvent and did not at that time have assets sufficient to discharge its liabilities, let alone those liabilities and the costs of winding up. It has become solvent in the course of the winding up by recovering monies from the directors and despite the resistance of the directors, and they have not adduced evidence which persuades me that their initial admission of insolvency was wrong or that the DTI may not rely upon it, or which is of greater weight than the admission itself."

Moving from members' voluntary to creditors' voluntary liquidation

3–103 For a company to go into members' voluntary winding up, the directors are required to make a statutory declaration of solvency. For these purposes, the "solvency" test is a different one to that under s.6 of the CDDA. The test is a balance sheet one and relates to payment of the debts of the company (including statutory interest) in full within a 12-month period. In most cases it is likely that a company entering members' voluntary will not at that time be perceived as one that has "become insolvent" for the purposes of the CDDA. If, at a later date and notwithstanding the statutory declaration, the liquidator determines that the company is insolvent, in the sense that payment in full cannot be achieved within the statutory period, he is obliged to take steps pursuant to s.95 of the Insolvency Act 1986 to summon a creditors' meeting and convert the members' voluntary winding up to a creditors' voluntary winding up. The winding up will be deemed to have commenced from the time of the passing of the company resolution for winding up.[310] As the solvency tests for changing the liquidation to a creditors' voluntary and for making a report under s.7(3) of the CDDA or a return under r.4 of the relevant reporting rules[311] are different, a liquidator of a company in members' voluntary liquidation should keep under consideration the question of whether he should be making a s.7(3) (D1 return) or a D2 return, irrespective of whether he thinks that the company should move into creditors' voluntary liquidation.

Liquidation and insolvency: time for reform?

3–104 It is suggested that s.6(1)(a) is overdue for reform. The easiest option would be to make provision that the court's jurisdiction is triggered simply where a company goes into any form of winding up. If there is relevant misconduct it is difficult to see why a director should escape disqualification merely because the company avoids insolvency (which may be a matter of chance) or an investigation under one of the gateway provisions expressly referred to in s.8. A relevant insolvency event provides an opportunity for a company's affairs to be considered by an outsider. However, any misconduct may have nothing to do with the insolvency regime. It is also difficult to see why one form of insolvency ("cash flow" insolvency) provides a sufficient basis for a gateway to disqualification in the cases of administration and administrative receivership and yet in the case of liquidation there must be a net asset deficiency. There are two main options, with gradations in between. The first option would be to make the entry into liquidation a jurisdictional ground for disqualification under s.6 and to remove any requirement of solvency. The second option (consistent with ss.6(2)(b) or (c)) is to accept that cash flow insolvency is an appropriate jurisdictional gateway. For these purposes a rough and ready distinction could be made between compulsory winding up orders on insolvency grounds (under any of the limbs of s.123 of the Insolvency Act 1986, thus encompassing balance sheet insolvency too) and voluntary winding up. In the latter case, a convenient distinction could be made between creditors' winding up (jurisdiction under s.6) and members' voluntary winding up (no jurisdiction under s.6, unless and until converted to creditors' voluntary winding up when, for s.7(2) purposes, the entry into that process would trigger the two-year period). Either option has the benefit of simplicity.

3–105 The jurisdiction of the English courts to wind up companies under Pt IV of the Insolvency Act must now be read as being subject to the EC Regulation on Insolvency Proceedings.[312] This is directly applicable in all EC Member States with the exception of Denmark. In the case of a company incorporated in England and Wales, the English courts must decline jurisdiction unless it has at least an establishment situated here. The effect of art.3 of the Regulation is that an English-registered company having its centre of main interests elsewhere and

[310] Insolvency Act 1986 s.86.

[311] Insolvent Companies (Reports on Conduct of Directors) Rules 1996 (SI 1996/1909). See further from 3–03.

[312] Council Regulation 1346/2000 and see Insolvency Act 1986 s.117(7).

with no establishment in England and Wales cannot be wound up here and so will not "go into liquidation" for the purposes of CDDA s.6(2)(a). In the case of such a company, the jurisdiction to disqualify under s.6 will only be triggered if an English administrative receiver of the company is appointed. The appointment of an administrative receiver is outside the scope of the Regulation.

CONDUCT IN RELATION TO LEAD AND COLLATERAL COMPANIES

3–106 Under CDDA s.6(1)(b) the court must decide whether the defendant's conduct as a director of the relevant company (i.e. the one which has "become insolvent") "either taken alone or taken together with his conduct as a director of any other company or companies makes him unfit . . .". The final preliminary issue concerns the extent to which the court can take into account the defendant's conduct in relation to other companies in proceedings under s.6. In what follows the terminology used by the Court of Appeal in *Re Country Farm Inns Ltd, Secretary of State for Trade and Industry v Ivens*[313] is adopted. The main company in the proceedings, satisfying the s.6(2) test of "insolvency" and the conditions of s.7(2), is referred to as the "lead company" and other companies in relation to which complaint is made are referred to as "collateral companies".

3–107 The basic point of CDDA s.6(1)(b) is that it allows the court to take into account evidence of the defendant's misconduct in the lead company "either taken alone or taken together with" evidence of his misconduct in relation to a collateral company or companies.[314] It is clear from this wording that there must be relevant misconduct in relation to the lead company even if that misconduct is not sufficiently serious to make the defendant unfit. Beyond that, the court can rely on "collateral company" evidence to tip the balance in favour of a finding of unfitness on the evidence as a whole. Alternatively, if the court is satisfied that the evidence in relation to the lead company is enough on its own to make the defendant unfit, it can take into account the "collateral company" evidence when determining the period of disqualification.[315] Thus, "collateral company" evidence may go either to the questions of

[313] [1997] 2 B.C.L.C. 334.

[314] There may be more than one lead company: see discussion in *Re Launchexcept Ltd, Secretary of State for Trade and Industry v Tillman* [2000] 1 B.C.L.C. 36. For that to be the case, the proceedings in respect of all the lead companies would need to be commenced within the two-year time period unless the permission of the court is obtained under s.7(2) to commence them out of time. It is conceivable that the Secretary of State might commence proceedings in relation to a number of lead companies where the prospective defendant is the director of several companies in an insolvent group. It should also be noted that conduct in relation to a subsidiary of the lead company can be taken into account if it involves a breach of duty which inflicts harm on both the subsidiary and the lead company even in circumstances where the court would not have had jurisdiction over the subsidiary in isolation (i.e. where the subsidiary was not capable of being a lead company): see *Re Dominion International Group Plc (No.2)* [1996] 1 B.C.L.C. 572; *Re Helene Plc, Secretary of State for Trade and Industry v Forsyth* [2000] 2 B.C.L.C. 249.

[315] See *Re T & D Services (Timber Preservation & Damp Proofing Contractors) Ltd* [1990] B.C.C. 592 at 593.

unfitness and period of disqualification combined or just to the question of the period of disqualification. The effect is that the claimant can rely on evidence that tends to show a pattern of misconduct in relation to a series of failed companies over time. Three main questions have arisen for decision in the immediate context. The first is whether the court can take account of "good" conduct on the defendant's part in collateral companies and weigh that against misconduct in the lead company to reach an overall conclusion concerning his fitness or unfitness. The second is whether there has to be some nexus or connection between the conduct complained of in the lead and collateral companies. The third is whether "collateral company" allegations raised in one set of disqualification proceedings can be raised in a later set of disqualification proceedings against the same defendant.

Can "good conduct" in collateral companies be taken into account?

3–108 Counsel for the defendant in *Re Bath Glass Ltd*[316] submitted that it was open to the court to conclude that a disqualification order should not be made by taking into account a general record of good conduct in relation to collateral companies. This submission was based on the argument that the words "either taken alone or taken together with his conduct as a director of any other company . . ." should be treated as general words enabling the court to reach the conclusion that a disqualification order is inappropriate (on the basis that the defendant's conduct shows that he is fit to manage companies) by reference to the defendant's conduct as a director of other companies. Rejecting this argument, Peter Gibson J. concluded that CDDA s.6(1)(b) obliged the court to judge whether the defendant was unfit by looking either at his conduct as a director of the lead company alone or at his conduct as a director of the lead company and of any collateral companies. Once the court finds by either route that the defendant is unfit, it is bound to disqualify him. Counsel for the defendant's construction of s.6(1)(b) was rejected because it implied that the court has a discretion to refuse to order disqualification by allowing evidence of good conduct in collateral companies to cancel out evidence of unfit conduct in the lead company. The net result is that evidence of a general record of good conduct in relation to collateral companies is inadmissible in proceedings for an order under s.6 on the question of unfitness. Only additional evidence of misconduct can be allowed in. The broader (and related) issue of whether evidence of good conduct (in relation to any company, lead, collateral or otherwise) can be adduced on the question of unfitness is considered in Ch.4.[317] It should be noted, however, that none of this necessarily prevents the court from relying on evidence of good conduct in collateral companies to justify imposing a shorter period of disqualification than that which would otherwise have been appropriate.[318] The extent to which evidence of good conduct can be relied on to mitigate the period of disqualification is discussed further in Ch.5.

[316] [1988] B.C.L.C. 329.

[317] See, in particular, *Re Grayan Building Services Ltd, Secretary of State for Trade and Industry v Gray* [1995] Ch. 241, which adds further weight to the view put forward in *Bath Glass*.

[318] See *Re Pamstock Ltd* [1996] B.C.C. 341 at 349–350.

Does there need to be some nexus or connection between the conduct in lead and collateral companies?

3–109 The "nexus" issue was first raised by Chadwick J. in *Re Godwin Warren Control Systems Plc* where he made the following remarks:

> "There must, I think, be some nexus between the conduct in relation to other companies and the conduct in relation to the insolvent company. If this were not so, a director whose conduct in relation to the insolvent company was blameless would be at risk of disqualification because his conduct in relation to other companies (unconnected and not insolvent) was unsatisfactory. Where the position is that conduct in relation to other companies is quite independent of the conduct in relation to the insolvent company, it is not to be taken into account for the purposes of the decision which the court has to make under s.6(1)(b)."[319]

It appears, on this basis, that the judge refused to take into account evidence of the defendant's integrity in relation to companies that he had managed both before and after his involvement in the lead company in that case. Thus, all that *Godwin Warren* actually decided was that good conduct in collateral companies is irrelevant to the question of unfitness because there is no nexus between good conduct and the misconduct alleged in relation to the lead company. A similar conclusion could have been reached by following the reasoning in *Bath Glass* (discussed above) but this case was apparently not cited.[320] Chadwick J.'s dictum was subsequently interpreted in *Re Diamond Computer Systems Ltd, Official Receiver v Brown* to mean that there must be some link or connection between the alleged misconduct in relation to collateral companies and the alleged misconduct in relation to the lead company.[321]

3–110 The leading authority on the "nexus" point is the Court of Appeal's decision in *Re Country Farm Inns Ltd, Secretary of State for Trade and Industry v Ivens*.[322] In that case, the two defendants were a husband and wife and the lead company in the proceedings was Country Farm Inns Ltd. It was alleged in relation to this lead company that the husband was unfit solely on the basis that he had taken part in the company's management while an undischarged bankrupt in breach of the automatic disqualification imposed by CDDA s.11. The wife was said to be unfit because she had permitted him to act while disqualified. The Secretary of State asked the court to have regard to evidence of the defendants' conduct in relation to four other failed companies. The nature of the alleged misconduct in these

[319] [1992] B.C.C. 557 at 567.

[320] See the comments of Judge Weeks Q.C. at first instance in *Re Country Farm Inns Ltd, Secretary of State for Trade and Industry v Ivens* [1997] 2 B.C.L.C. 334 at 336–337. Chadwick J.'s suggestion that a director whose conduct is blameless in relation to a lead company would otherwise be at risk of disqualification appears to be wrong as the effect of s.6(1)(b) is that there must be some relevant misconduct in the lead company even if that misconduct alone does not make him unfit: see [1997] 2 B.C.L.C. 334 at 337, 346–347.

[321] [1997] 1 B.C.L.C. 174 at 179–180. The judge used the word "conduct" rather than "misconduct" but it is clear from the passage as a whole that he saw a need for a link to be established between the matters of complaint in the lead and collateral companies.

[322] [1997] 2 B.C.L.C. 334.

collateral companies is not spelled out in detail in the reports of the case but it is clear that it differed from the alleged misconduct in the lead company as it was said to have occurred before the husband was made bankrupt. The preliminary issue before the court was whether the defendants' conduct as a director of the collateral companies was "conduct as a director of any other company or companies" which could legitimately be taken into account for the purposes of s.6. It was common ground between the parties that there had to be some nexus in the sense that the defendant must have been a director (whether de jure, de facto or shadow) of each of the lead and collateral companies and, further, that the alleged misconduct in the lead and collateral companies must have been conduct qua director that tends to show unfitness. However, the defendants argued that misconduct as a director of collateral companies should only be taken into account where it was the same as, or similar to, the misconduct alleged in relation to the lead company or where it threw light on, explained or removed doubt about the lead company allegations. In advancing this argument, the defendants relied on Chadwick J.'s dictum from *Godwin Warren*.[323] They also pointed out that at the time the application was commenced in relation to the lead company, the Secretary of State could not have commenced proceedings based solely on the alleged misconduct in respect of the collateral companies (i.e. proceedings in which those companies would have been lead companies) without the permission of the court. This was because of the requirement in CDDA s.7(2) that proceedings for an order under s.6 should generally be commenced within two years of the day on which the relevant company became insolvent.[324] In this case the four collateral companies had all become insolvent more than two years before the proceedings were commenced in relation to Country Farm. The thrust of this argument was that unrelated conduct in collateral companies should only be taken into account where the proceedings had been commenced within two years of the collateral companies (as well as the lead company) becoming insolvent or if permission to proceed in relation to the collateral companies had first been obtained under s.7(2).

3–111 A unanimous Court of Appeal held that the defendants' conduct in relation to the four collateral companies could be taken into account in determining whether or not they were unfit. A number of important points concerning the construction of CDDA s.6(1)(b) emerge from Morritt L.J.'s leading judgment:

(1) The claimant is only required to establish a limited nexus between the allegations relating to the lead and collateral companies. The conduct complained of in respect of each company must be "conduct as a director" and conduct that tends to show unfitness. There is nothing in the CDDA to suggest that the conduct in collateral companies should be the same as or similar to the

[323] As subsequently approved by the Court of Appeal in *Re Pamstock Ltd* [1996] B.C.C. 341, a case on costs. Lindsay J. also spoke approvingly of the dictum in *Re Polly Peck International Plc (No.2)* [1994] 1 B.C.L.C. 574 at 583.

[324] On s.7(2) generally, see Chs 7–8.

conduct relied on in relation to the lead company. The court is required by CDDA s.9 to have particular regard to matters mentioned in Sch.1 when determining the question of unfitness. However, the only distinction drawn in s.9 is between solvent and insolvent companies. There is nothing in either s.9 or Sch.1 that requires the court to draw some additional distinction between the types of conduct that can be taken into account in lead and collateral companies. As long as the conduct in the collateral companies tends to show unfitness it will generally be relevant and admissible.[325]

(2) Chadwick J.'s dictum in *Godwin Warren* rested on a false assumption. The judge assumed that a defendant would be at risk of disqualification based solely on his conduct as a director of a collateral company in the absence of some wider "nexus" requirement. Morritt L.J. accepted that the judge at first instance in *Country Farm* had been correct to hold that the court can only disqualify the defendant if it concludes that his conduct as a director of the lead company, "either taken alone or taken together with his conduct as director of any other company" makes him unfit. Thus, if the defendant's conduct as a director of the lead company is in no way unsatisfactory, it is not possible for the court to disqualify him on the basis of his conduct in relation to collateral companies. On the other hand, as long as the claimant can point to some relevant misconduct in the lead company, conduct in collateral companies can be used to tip the balance towards a finding of unfitness.[326]

(3) The two-year time limit in s.7(2) only applies to the lead company. It does not apply to collateral companies. This means that as long as the proceedings in relation to the lead company are brought in time, the claimant can also rely on allegations in relation to other companies that may have become insolvent more than two years before the proceedings were commenced.[327] Although not canvassed in the Court of Appeal, this point does raise an important issue of policy. It may be argued on a narrow view of the CDDA that it is unfair for

[325] As Etherton J. put it in *Secretary of State for Trade and Industry v Green* [2006] EWHC 1739 (Ch) there must be a "probative link" and the collateral company allegations must potentially be of "probative value". To give an example, it is clearly contemplated in s.9 and Sch.1 that the court should take into account the defendant's responsibility for a company giving a preference (Sch.1 Pt II para.8) together with his responsibility for a failure by a company to prepare annual accounts (Sch.1 Pt I para.5). These can hardly be described as the same type of allegation but both are clearly relevant to the statutory question of unfitness and therefore evidence of each would potentially be of probative value.

[326] The claimant must be able to point to some element of relevant misconduct in the lead company but there is no requirement that that conduct, taken in isolation, must necessarily make the defendant unfit. The same finding was made by the Registrar of the Companies Court in the earlier *Honorbilt* proceedings referred to in the *Launchexcept* case: see *Re Launchexcept Ltd, Secretary of State for Trade and Industry v Tillman* [2000] 1 B.C.L.C. 36. See also *Re Crystal Palace Football Club (1986), Secretary of State for Trade and Industry v Goldberg* [2003] EWHC 2843 (Ch), [2004] 1 B.C.L.C. 597 at [49]–[50].

[327] The claimant has been allowed to rely on such collateral allegations in several cases: see, e.g. *Re T & D Services (Timber Preservation & Damp Proofing Contractors) Ltd* [1990] B.C.C. 592 (in this case the three collateral companies all went into liquidation before either the Insolvency Act 1985 or the CDDA came into force); *Re Tansoft Ltd* [1991] B.C.L.C. 339; *Re Melcast (Wolverhampton) Ltd* [1991] B.C.L.C. 288; *Re Pamstock Ltd* [1994] 1 B.C.L.C. 716; *Secretary of State for Trade and Industry v Green* [2006] EWHC 1739 (Ch).

the claimant to rely on matters of any great vintage. Otherwise, directors face the risk that a fresh corporate insolvency may trigger an inquiry into past failings in relation to which no proceedings were brought at the time. However, it must be remembered that the claimant is directed by s.7(1) to consider whether it is expedient in the public interest to bring proceedings for an order under s.6. Moreover, on a wider view, it is clear that the CDDA is concerned with protecting the public from (among others) those who have traded a succession of companies into the ground at the expense of creditors. Parliament must therefore have intended that the court should be able to take into account the full history of the defendant's involvement in failed companies where it might illustrate an emerging pattern of misconduct over time and this is so even though "lead company" proceedings could no longer have been commenced against some or all of those companies without the court's permission under s.7(2). Nevertheless, it is conceivable that the court may strike out "lead company" proceedings as an abuse of process in certain circumstances. It was suggested obiter by the deputy judge *in Re Diamond Computer Systems Ltd, Official Receiver v Brown* that it would be inappropriate:

> "to disqualify a director of company X for his misconduct as director of company Y in proceedings in respect of which the lead company is company X but where the essential burden of the complaint is his conduct as a director of company Y rather than company X".[328]

The judge described this as allowing "the tail to wag the dog". Thus, it is suggested that if the claimant sought to rely on conduct in relation to the lead company solely as a means to avoid an application for permission to commence proceedings out of time under s.7(2) in circumstances where the "essential burden of complaint" was the defendant's conduct in relation to other companies, the court could resort to its power to strike out the proceedings as an abuse of its process.[329]

(4) There is no requirement that a collateral company must necessarily have become insolvent. It is perfectly possible for the claimant to rely on the defendant's conduct in relation to *solvent* collateral companies as long as that conduct tends to show unfitness.[330] This point adds further force to the points in (2) and (3) above. The insolvency of the lead company is one of the crucial elements that triggers jurisdiction under s.6. As such, it must be correct to say

[328] [1997] 1 B.C.L.C. 174 at 180.

[329] The dismissal of proceedings on grounds of abuse of process is discussed further in Ch.7.

[330] It was indicated in *Country Farm* that, at least at that time, the Secretary of State was unlikely ever to rely on a defendant's conduct as a director of a solvent collateral company. However, the attitude of the Secretary of State in no way affects the construction of s.6 and indeed may well have changed over time. Breaches of s.216 of the Insolvency Act 1986 are often raised in relation to an individual's conduct as director of a phoenix company, even if the latter is solvent. There are positive reasons in the public interest (in particular, the notion that disqualification is concerned with raising standards of conduct) why reliance on conduct in relation to solvent collateral companies should not be ruled out.

that the claimant is required to point to some relevant misconduct in the lead company. Otherwise, it would follow that the defendant could be disqualified on the basis of conduct in solvent collateral companies alone, a result which cannot be reconciled with the triggering requirement that "he is or has been a director of a company which has at any time become insolvent" in s.6(1)(a). Conversely, the fact that the claimant can rely on conduct in relation to solvent collateral companies reinforces the point that s.7(2) is irrelevant to collateral companies. The two-year time limit starts to run from the date when the lead company "became insolvent". Section 7(2) thus draws directly on the wording in s.6(1)(a). As there is no absolute requirement for collateral companies to have "become insolvent" it must follow that the two-year time limit does not apply to them (subject to the point concerning abuse of process in (3) above).

3–112 It is clear from the Court of Appeal's decision that the nexus "requirement" as conceived in *Godwin Warren* is dead. However, the issue of collateral companies is not entirely free from difficulty. Morritt L.J.'s judgment does not deal with the suggestion made in *Diamond Computer* that the defendant should not be disqualified if the "essential burden of complaint" relates to his conduct in collateral companies. As indicated above, there may be circumstances in which the court is prepared to strike out disqualification proceedings based principally on allegations relating to the defendant's conduct in a collateral company as an abuse of process.[331] Nevertheless, the approach in *Country Farm* is consistent with the protective purpose of disqualification in that it allows both the claimant and the court, in an appropriate case, to reconstruct a pattern of misconduct across a number of companies over time.

When can or must allegations regarding collateral companies be raised?

3–113 In *Re Launchexcept Ltd, Secretary of State for Trade and Industry v Tillman*,[332] "lead company" proceedings were commenced against the defendant, T, claiming that his conduct in relation to Launchexcept Ltd made him unfit to be concerned in the management of a company. T had been a defendant in an earlier set of disqualification proceedings brought by the official receiver following the failure

[331] Note also the attitude of Vinelott J. in *Re Pamstock Ltd* [1994] 1 B.C.L.C. 716 and the Court of Appeal's decision on costs in that case at [1996] B.C.C. 341. The claimant must strike a balance. It is right for the claimant to draw attention to all the companies in which the defendant has been involved that have gone into insolvent liquidation. Equally, the claimant should draw attention to serious failures in the filing of returns and accounts in collateral companies even if these complaints, taken in isolation, do not justify a disqualification order, or an increased period of disqualification. However, the claimant should not put in evidence every matter that could possibly be the subject of complaint without discrimination. To do so may detain the court in dealing with matters of no substantial weight going back over a long period of time thus increasing costs. The defendant in *Pamstock* was disqualified for the minimum period of two years but he was only ordered to pay half of the official receiver's costs. This was because in the judge's view, the claimant's practice of raising every conceivable matter of complaint in relation to the collateral companies, however inconsequential, had unnecessarily increased costs. The courts are even more likely to follow this sort of robust approach in the light of the CPR.

[332] [2000] 1 B.C.L.C. 36.

of a listed company called Honorbilt Group Plc. In the *Honorbilt* proceedings, the official receiver had chosen to rely in part on T's conduct in relation to the filing of accounts and returns in respect of Launchexcept as one of a number of collateral companies. In the event, the *Honorbilt* proceedings were dismissed against T because he was not found to be responsible for any relevant misconduct in the lead company. There being no relevant misconduct in the lead company, the court could not take into account the collateral allegations relating to Launchexcept. In the *Launchexcept* proceedings, quite separate allegations of misconduct were made and the Secretary of State did not rely on the *Launchexcept* filing defaults that had been alleged in the *Honorbilt* proceedings. T sought to have the *Launchexcept* proceedings struck out as an abuse of process on the ground that the further charges in relation to Launchexcept could and should have been brought forward in the earlier *Honorbilt* proceedings. In so doing T relied on the principle in *Henderson v Henderson*[333] which requires a party to bring forward his whole case and prevents him raising in later proceedings any matter that could and should have been litigated in the original proceedings. On T's appeal against the refusal of the judge to strike out the *Launchexcept* proceedings, Chadwick L.J. said that the proper approach was to ask whether the course adopted by the Secretary of State in relation to the earlier proceedings was such that it would be manifestly unfair to the defendant to allow the later proceedings to continue against him or alternatively, whether a refusal to strike out or stay the later proceedings would bring the administration of justice into disrepute among right thinking people. On the facts of *Launchexcept* the Court of Appeal held that the later proceedings were not an abuse of process. The main points were:

(1) The matters raised in the later *Launchexcept* proceedings were not the subject of any adjudication in the *Honorbilt* proceedings.
(2) The claimant was not seeking to re-litigate the question of whether or not T's conduct in relation to Launchexcept made him unfit.
(3) The claimant was not relying on the filing defaults that had been raised in the *Honorbilt* proceedings.
(4) The matters raised in the *Launchexcept* proceedings had not come to light when the *Honorbilt* proceedings came on for trial and it was unlikely they would have done. In any event it was a sensible case management decision to include limited additional allegations in the *Honorbilt* proceedings.

The clear implication is that it may be possible for collateral allegations from earlier proceedings to be raised against the same defendant in later "lead company" proceedings if, in all the circumstances, it is fair to the defendant to allow the later proceedings to go forward on that footing. This might arise if, for example, the allegations had not been adjudicated upon in the earlier proceedings for the sort of reason that applied in the *Honorbilt* proceedings.

[333] (1843) 3 Hare 100.

"Lead" and "collateral" allegations in the context of insolvent partnerships

3–114 It was seen above in the course of the discussion concerning the meaning of "company" that proceedings for an order under s.6 can be brought against the officers of an insolvent partnership. Schedule 8 to the Insolvent Partnerships Order 1994 makes a number of modifications to the CDDA to accommodate such proceedings. The important point for present purposes is that CDDA s.6(1) is modified in the context of insolvent partnerships to read as follows:

> "The court shall make a disqualification order against a person in any case where, on an application under this section, it is satisfied—
>
> (a) that he is or has been an officer of a partnership which has at any time become insolvent (whether while he was an officer or subsequently), and
> (b) that his conduct as an officer of that partnership (either taken alone or taken together with his conduct as an officer of any other partnership or partnerships, or as a director of any company or companies) makes him unfit to be concerned in the management of a company."

Section 6(1)(b) (as modified by the Insolvent Partnerships Order) thus treats the insolvent partnership as the equivalent of a lead company and entitles the court to take into account the defendant's conduct in both collateral partnerships and collateral companies. In all other respects the position is the same as outlined above in relation to companies. It appears that evidence of misconduct in a "collateral partnership" cannot be taken into account in ordinary proceedings under s.6 (i.e. where the jurisdiction is triggered by a corporate as opposed to a partnership insolvency and the lead entity is the company). What if, for example, A, the director of X Ltd, a company which has gone into liquidation, was also previously involved in a number of failed partnership businesses? Clearly, the Secretary of State could seek a disqualification order under s.6 based on X's conduct as a director of X Ltd as the lead company. However, the court could not take into account A's conduct as an officer of the partnerships as a collateral matter to determine the question of unfitness. It would be necessary to bring proceedings in relation to at least one of the partnerships as a lead entity and, if necessary, an order under s.7(2) might have to be obtained. Although Sch.8 of the Insolvent Partnerships Order has not been amended to take account of LLPs, it is suggested that in Sch.8 to the 1994 Order references to "company" will include references to LLP. This is because art.16 of the 1994 Order takes as its starting point that it is applying the CDDA (in which "company" is to be taken as including an LLP).

SECTION 8(1): PRELIMINARIES

3–115 CDDA s.8(1) which is headed "disqualification after investigation of company" provides:

> "If it appears to the Secretary of State from investigative material that it is expedient in the public interest that a disqualification order should be made against a person who is,

or has been, a director or shadow director of a company, he may apply to the court for such an order."[334]

It follows that two preliminary requirements need to be satisfied before an order can be sought under s.8:

(1) The defendant must be or have been a director or shadow director of a company. The terms "director", "shadow director" and "company" bear the same meaning in s.8(1) as they do in s.6(1) and the commentary above applies mutatis mutandis. One consequence is that the term "director" in s.8 also includes a de facto director.[335]
(2) There must be information relating to the defendant's conduct in relation to the company deriving from "investigative material", i.e. information contained in a report made by company inspectors or information or documents obtained under the provisions discussed below.

Section 8(2A) deals with disqualification by way of undertaking in the context of investigatory material. It provides that where it appears to the Secretary of State from any report, information or documents which amount to "investigatory material", in the case of a person who has offered to give a disqualification undertaking that two conditions are met, the Secretary of State may accept the undertaking. The two conditions mirror those for the making of a disqualification order under s.8. The first is that the Secretary of State considers that it is expedient in the public interest that an undertaking should be accepted by him, rather than him applying, or proceeding with an application for a disqualification order. This mirrors the public interest trigger for s.8 disqualification proceedings. The second is that the Secretary of State is satisfied that the conduct of the person in relation to a company of which that person is or has been a director or shadow director makes him unfit to be concerned in the management of the company. This mirrors the requirement that must be satisfied in s.8 proceedings before the court can make a disqualification order under s.8.

3–116 Subject to the requirements considered above, the court may, in its discretion, make a disqualification order against the defendant where it is satisfied that his conduct in relation to the company makes him unfit to be concerned in the management of a company.[336] The relevant company need not have become insolvent for the purposes of s.8. However, it is implicit in s.8(1) that the court is not entitled to look at a person's conduct in the round, but only his conduct as a

[334] The present wording was substituted by the Financial Services and Markets Act 2000 (Consequential Amendments and Repeals) Order 2001 (SI 2001/3649) with effect from December 1, 2001.
[335] See further *Re Amba Rescue Ltd, Secretary of State for Trade and Industry v Hollier* [2007] B.C.C. 11.
[336] CDDA s.8(2). The concept of discretionary disqualification for unfitness following a company investigation, etc. originates from para.1819(c) of the Cork Report. The provision was first enacted as s.13 of the Insolvency Act 1985.

director. In other words, the requirement of being a director is not simply a jurisdictional gateway which then enables the court to consider the person's conduct generally (for example, as company secretary). Under s.8, the court can only consider the person's conduct as a director in relation to an identified company. In this respect, it is suggested that ss.6 and 8 are to the same effect. Section 6 expressly states that the relevant test is whether a person's conduct *as a director* of an identified company makes him unfit. Although s.8(2) directs the court to consider whether the defendant's conduct *in relation to* a company makes him unfit, this is qualified by s.8(1) in the manner described above.[337] Section 8(2A) in relation to disqualification undertakings must be interpreted in the same manner as s.8(2).

Investigative material

3–117 "Investigative material" is defined in CDDA s.8(1A)[338] by reference to an exhaustive list of specified statutory powers of investigation that lead either to the production of a report by company inspectors or the obtaining of information or documents. In the case of certain statutory reports the legislation has been widened to enable the Secretary of State to take into account not only the final report but material obtained by use of compulsory powers in the preparation for the making of such report. It should be noted that the investigatory powers in Pt XIV of the Companies Act 1985 have been kept in force notwithstanding the enactment and bringing into force of the Companies Act 2006 because these powers do not apply exclusively to companies. In each case the general structure of the legislation is the same. The main features can be summarised as follows:

(1) In some cases the compulsory powers do not override legal professional privilege.
(2) Generally there will be a restriction on the disclosure and use that can be made of investigative material obtained under compulsion. The restriction may be civil only or may be backed up by statutory criminal sanctions.[339]
(3) In addition, and independently of any issue of restrictions on disclosure and use flowing from the compulsory power and/or express statutory restrictions, questions of public interest immunity may arise at the stage where consideration is being given to use and disclosure of investigative material for the purpose of disqualification proceedings.[340]

[337] cf. the deputy judge's obiter comments in *Re Richborough Furniture Ltd, Secretary of State for Trade and Industry v Stokes* [1996] 1 B.C.L.C. 507 at 520.

[338] As amended by the Companies (Audit, Investigations and Community Enterprise) 2004 with effect from April 6, 2005: SI 2004/3322; the Companies Act 2006 s.1039(a), (b) with effect from October 1, 2007: SI 2007/2194 and SI 2009/1941 with effect from October 1, 2009.

[339] It should be noted that, in addition to any statutory gateway, questions of public interest immunity may arise which separately call for a balancing exercise to be carried out before the material is made use of.

[340] For example, as regards provisional criticism or so-called "maxwellisation" material.

(4) The investigative material can be used as a basis for a decision under s.8 CDDA to initiate proceedings or accept an undertaking.
(5) The power of compulsion giving rise to investigative material will either be exercisable by the Secretary of State or its product may be passed to the Secretary of State for disqualification purposes, which purposes may extend beyond proceedings under CDDA s.8. However, the use of such material in criminal proceedings is usually restricted as in (6) below.
(6) There is usually a widespread restriction on the use in criminal proceedings of investigative material obtained by use of compulsory information gathering powers.[341]

The various statutory powers that can lead to the production of "investigative material" for the purposes of CDDA s.8 are now considered.

Companies Act inspections leading to a formal report

3–118 *Sections 437 and 446E of the Companies Act 1985.* Under ss.431–432 of the Companies Act 1985, the Secretary of State has power to appoint inspectors to investigate the affairs of a company either of his own motion (in the circumstances specified in s.432(2)) or at the request of the company or its members (s.431). In addition, the Secretary of State is obliged to appoint inspectors where the court declares by order that the affairs of a company ought to be investigated (s.432(1)). Where an investigation is carried out under these powers, the inspectors are required by s.437 to make a final report to the Secretary of State on completion of the investigation. In addition they may make, and where so directed by the Secretary of State shall make, interim reports to the Secretary of State. Information and opinions in any such report, final or interim, are "investigative material" that may form the basis of proceedings under s.8 of the CDDA. Section 441 of the Companies Act provides that a certified copy of any such report is admissible in any legal proceedings as evidence of the opinion of the inspectors in relation to any matter contained in it and, in proceedings under s.8 of the CDDA, as evidence of any fact stated therein. The report may therefore be relied on as evidence in any subsequent s.8 proceedings.[342]

[341] Reflecting jurisprudence relating to the European Convention on Human Rights: see, e.g. *Saunders v United Kingdom* [1998] 1 B.C.L.C. 362.

[342] For an example of s.8 proceedings which followed an investigation under s.432(2) and the production of a report under s.437 see *Re Atlantic Computers Plc, Secretary of State for Trade and Industry v Ashman*, June 15, 1998, Ch.D., unreported. As regards relevant evidential rules see Ch.7. Important cases include *Re Rex Williams Leisure Plc, Secretary of State for Trade and Industry v Warren* [1994] Ch. 350; *Re Astra Holdings Plc, Secretary of State for Trade and Industry v Anderson* [1999] 2 B.C.L.C. 44 and *Re Queens Moathouses Plc, Secretary of State for Trade and Industry v Bairstow* [2003] EWCA Civ 321, [2004] Ch. 1. As regards compelled evidence see *Saunders v United Kingdom* [1998] 1 B.C.L.C. 362; *Re Atlantic Computers Plc, Secretary of State for Trade and Industry v McCormick* [1998] 2 B.C.L.C. 18; *R. v Secretary of State for Trade and Industry Ex. p. McCormick* [1998] B.C.C. 381; *Re Westminster Property Management Ltd (No.1), Official Receiver v Stern (No. 1)* [2001] 1 W.L.R. 2230. For further discussion of the nature and scope of the Companies Act powers of investigation see *Re Inquiry into Mirror Group Newspapers Plc* [2000] Ch. 194.

In addition to the requirements to make reports, s.437 provides that inspectors appointed under s.431 or s.432 may at any time and, if the Secretary of State directs them to do so, shall inform him of any matters coming to their knowledge as a result of their investigations.[343] Section 8(1A) of the CDDA has been extended[344] to make clear that s.8 proceedings may be instituted on the basis not just of final or interim reports under s.437 of the Companies Act 1985 but also on the basis of information or documents obtained under s.437, which also comprise "investigative material" for the purposes of s.8. This would presumably enable the Secretary of State to institute s.8 proceedings based in whole or in part on documents or information specifically provided during the course of an investigation. It is suggested that it would also enable the Secretary of State to take into account documents and information obtained in an investigation which are handed to the Secretary of State during the course of the investigation or once the investigation is completed. Section 441 of the Companies Act 1985 would not, apparently, apply to such information or documents but the material would be admissible in s.8 disqualification proceedings under the Civil Evidence Act and/or the principle established in the *Rex Williams* case.[345] Section 446E of the Companies Act 1985 enables the Secretary of State to obtain information and documents from former inspectors. Such material is also "investigative material" for the purposes of s.8 and the disqualification uses to which such material may be put would appear to be the same as in the case of information provided by inspectors to the Secretary of State, though not contained within a final or interim report.

Quite apart from the power to commence s.8 proceedings in reliance on this form of investigatory material, it is important to bear in mind the extent to which such material, otherwise subject to restrictions on use and disclosure,[346] may be used more generally in, or for the purposes of, disqualification proceedings. Section 451A of the Companies Act 1985,[347] permits the Secretary of State to make use of any information or documents obtained in the course of an investigation for a variety of purposes, including for the purposes of enabling or assisting him to exercise any of his functions under the CDDA. So far as s.8 is concerned this does not provide any jurisdictional basis for instituting s.8 proceedings, but such a basis now exists independently under s.8(1A)(b)(i). Section 451A of the Companies Act 1985 also prevents any illegality arising from the use of such material for the purposes of or in the course of any proceedings under the CDDA, whatever the provision concerned. However, it says nothing about the admissibility of such material as evidence in any legal proceedings. The admissibility of such material in any particular set of proceedings has to be considered separately. As regards criminal proceedings, there is an express limit

[343] Companies Act 1985 s.437(1A).

[344] CDDA s.8(1A)((b)(i) inserted by the Companies Act 2006 s.1039(a).

[345] [1994] Ch. 350 and see further text from 7–127.

[346] See Companies Act 1985 s.451A and the power to publish reports in Companies Act 1985 s.437(3).

[347] As amended by the Companies (Audit, Investigations and Community Enterprise) 2004.

on the use that may be made of answers to questions put pursuant to the investigatory powers in the Companies Act 1985.[348]

Other Companies Act investigations

3–119 *Companies Act 1985 ss.447 and 448*. Under s.447(2) of the Companies Act 1985,[349] the Secretary of State may at any time give directions to a company requiring it, at such time and place as may be specified in the directions, to produce specified documents[350] and/or to provide information. There is also power in s.447(3) for the Secretary of State to authorise an "investigator" to require a company to produce documents and/or to provide information. The investigator is entitled to pass that information to the Secretary of State by virtue of Sch.15C to the Companies Act 1985. The original purpose of s.447 was to allow the Secretary of State to obtain information and documents from companies under suspicion with a view to deciding whether or not to appoint an inspector and launch a full company investigation under ss.431–432.[351] It is clear from s.449 that its further purpose is to enable or assist the Secretary of State inter alia to exercise his functions under the CDDA (which include considering whether or not it is expedient in the public interest for disqualification proceedings to be commenced under s.8).[352] In practice, s.447 of the Companies Act 1985 has long been used not as a precursor to a full inspection under ss.431 or 432 but, more often than not, with a view to deciding whether or not to exercise winding up and/or disqualification powers. The vast majority of company investigations are carried out as confidential fact finding enquiries under s.447. Investigations are carried out where, for example, there are grounds for suspicion of fraud, misfeasance, misconduct, conduct unfairly prejudicial to shareholders or of failure to supply shareholders with information that they may reasonably expect to receive.[353] The power in s.447 includes power to take copies of any documents produced. Any statement made by a person in compliance with a requirement to produce documents may be used in evidence against him, but subject to widespread restrictions in the context of criminal proceedings (Companies Act 1985 s.447A)). As in the case of full company investigations (discussed above) there is a statutory gateway in s.449 which permits the Secretary of State to make use of any information or documents obtained in the

[348] See Companies Act 1985 s.434(5), (5A), (5B).

[349] The current provisions in Companies Act 1985 s.447 were substituted by the Companies (Audit, Investigations and Community Enterprise) Act 2004 s.21 with effect from April 6, 2005: SI 2004/3322.

[350] As regards the former terms of this provision, see *A-G's Reference (No.2 of 1998)* [2000] Q.B. 441.

[351] See Report of the Company Law Committee (the Jenkins Committee), Cmnd.1749 (1962), paras 214–215 and discussion in *Attorney General's Reference (No.2 of 1998)* [2000] Q.B. 412.

[352] The current provisions in s.449 were substituted by the Companies (Audit, Investigations and Community Enterprise) Act 2004 s.25(1) with effect from April 6, 2005: SI 2004/3322. The 2004 Act also inserted Schs 15C and 15D to the Companies Act 1985 which specify to whom and for what purposes information obtained under s.447 may be disclosed. See, in particular, Sch.15C para.1; Sch.15D para.9(d).

[353] See Explanatory Notes to Companies (Audit, Investigations and Community Enterprise) Act 2004.

course of the investigation for a variety of purposes including the exercise of his functions under the CDDA. In this respect, the Secretary of State is not restricted to using the information in s.8 proceedings.[354] It is clear from s.449(2) of and Sch.15D to the Companies Act 1985 that the information could be used in connection with disqualification proceedings initiated by the Secretary of State under CDDA ss.2, 3, 4 and 6 as well as s.8. Information obtained under these provisions has formed the basis of proceedings for a disqualification order under both ss.6 and 8.[355]

3–120 *Section 83 of the Companies Act 1989*. This provision confers on the Secretary of State a similar range of powers to those contained in s.447 of the Companies Act 1985. The powers are exercisable by the Secretary of State for the purpose of assisting an overseas regulatory authority that has requested assistance in connection with enquiries being carried out by it or on its behalf. A statement made by a person in compliance with a requirement imposed under s.83 may be used in evidence against him, subject to widespread exceptions in the case of criminal proceedings. The s.83 powers may also be exercised on behalf of the Secretary of State by an appropriately authorised person as provided for by s.84. It appears from s.87(1)(b) that any information obtained under s.83 could be used by the Secretary of State for the purpose of any disqualification proceedings under CDDA, and not just in relation to s.8 proceedings.[356] Similarly, disclosure can be made to the official receiver for disqualification purposes by virtue of s.87(1)(b).

Other Companies Act investigatory powers

3–121 *Section 448 of the Companies Act 1985*. This empowers a justice of the peace to issue a search warrant on the application of the Secretary of State or an investigator or inspector if satisfied that there are reasonable grounds for believing: (a) that there are on any premises documents whose production has been required (whether under s.447 or other provisions of Pt XIV of the Companies Act 1985) and which have not been produced in compliance with that requirement; or (b) that an offence has been committed for which the penalty on conviction on indictment is imprisonment for a term of not less than two years and that there are on any premises documents relating to whether the offence has been committed, that the Secretary of State, or the person appointed or authorised to obtain information under Pt XIV, has power to require the production of the documents under this Part, and that there are reasonable grounds for believing that if production was so required the documents would not be produced but would be removed from the premises, hidden, tampered with or destroyed. The product of the

[354] The material may be relied on for s.8 purposes by virtue of s.8(1A)(b)(i).

[355] See *Re Samuel Sherman Plc* [1991] 1 W.L.R. 1070; *Re Looe Fish Ltd* [1993] B.C.L.C. 1160; *Re Claims Direct Plc, Secretary of State for Business, Enterprise and Regulatory Reform v Sullman* [2008] EWHC (Ch) 3179, [2009] 1 B.C.L.C. 397 (all s.8) and *Re Rex Williams Leisure Plc, Secretary of State for Trade and Industry v Warren* [1993] B.C.L.C. 568 (Ch.D.), [1994] Ch.350 (CA) (s. 6—see [1993] B.C.L.C. 568 at 579—though, note the apparent confusion in the Court of Appeal).

[356] As provided for by CDDA s.8(1A)(b)(iv).

exercise of such compelled powers form "investigative material" for the purposes of CDDA s.8 by virtue of s.8(1A)(b)(i). Such documents may come directly to the Secretary of State as the person applying for the warrant or by way of permitted disclosure pursuant to s.449(2) of and Sch.15C to the Companies Act 1985.

3–122 *Sections 451A and 453A of the Companies Act 1985.* Section 453A of the Companies Act 1985 confers power on an inspector or investigator to require entry to premises and to remain there, if he is authorised to do so by the Secretary of State, and he thinks that to do so will materially assist him in the exercise of his functions in relation to the company. Any information or documents obtained as a result can form investigative material for the purposes of CDDA s.8. In addition, such material will fall within the statutory gateways for use and disclosure provided for by s.451A of the Companies Act 1985 and will therefore be capable of being used for the purposes of disqualification proceedings more widely (not just under CDDA s.8).

The inclusion within "investigative material" of documents and information obtained under s.451A is, at first sight, curious. That section does not set out a power of compulsion to obtain documents or information but instead provides a number of statutory gateways for the disclosure and use of information by the Secretary of State that would otherwise be prohibited. The information in question is that obtained as a result of the use of compulsory powers under ss.434 to 446E or by an inspector in consequence of the exercise of his powers under s.453A. Of these sections, to the extent that their exercise gives rise to rights to information or documents, only s.435 and the share ownership investigatory powers do not fall within the other provisions of s.8. However, s.435 material would almost certainly comprise "investigative material" as falling within ss.437 or 446E. Material discovered by reason of a share ownership investigation would be unlikely to be "obtained" by the Secretary of State under s.451A (as opposed to, say, ss.442–446), unless of course such information was passed under s.451A to another investigator and then reported back again.

Financial Services and Markets Act investigations

3–123 *Section 167 of the Financial Services and Markets Act 2000.* Under this provision, each of the Financial Services Authority and the Secretary of State has power to appoint investigators to conduct an investigation into the nature, conduct or state of the business of an authorised person or an appointed representative, a particular aspect of that business or the ownership or control of an authorised person.[357] Under s.167(4), the power may also be exercised in relation to a former authorised person. The investigators are obliged by s.170(6) to produce a report. By virtue of s.174, statements made to an investigator in the course of an

[357] An "authorised person" is a person who has permission to carry on regulated activities under Pt IV of the Financial Services and Markets Act 2000. An "appointed representative" is defined by s.39 of the Act and means essentially an employee or agent of an authorised person.

investigation under s.167 are admissible in any proceedings, other than most criminal proceedings, so long as they comply with any requirements governing admissibility. The opinions contained in any such report will be admissible in s.8 proceedings by virtue of the principle established in the *Rex Williams* case.[358] By virtue of the Financial Services and Markets Act 2000 (Disclosure of Information by Prescribed Persons) Regulations 2001[359] disclosure of information may, in certain circumstances, be made by the investigators to the Financial Services Authority. Disclosure and use is also regulated by ss.348 to 353 of the Financial Services and Markets Act 2000. A number of regulations have been made by reference to s.349 which establishes the principle of "gateways". Disclosure is permitted to the Secretary of State, including for certain disqualification purposes, by regs.3, 4 and 5 of the Financial Services and Markets Act 2000 (Disclosure of Confidential Information) Regulations 2001[360] and, in relation to the official receiver, as regards relevant companies, by reg.9 and Sch.1. The precise provisions are complex and a detailed discussion is beyond the scope of this book.

3–124 *Section 168 of the Financial Services and Markets Act 2000.* If it appears to the Financial Services Authority or the Secretary of State that there are circumstances suggesting that a person may have committed various specified offences, including an insider dealing offence under Pt V of the Criminal Justice Act 1993, or engaged in proscribed activities such as market abuse, they have power under s.168(3) (and in the case of the Financial Services Authority in relation to certain other matters specified in s.168(4) power under s.168(5)) to appoint investigators to conduct an investigation. The investigators are obliged by s.170(6) to produce a report. Statements made to an investigator in the course of an investigation under s.168 are admissible in any proceedings so long as they comply with any requirements governing the admissibility of evidence by virtue of s.174. Certain admissions are not capable of being used in a wide range of criminal proceedings. The opinions contained in any such report will be admissible in s.8 proceedings by virtue of the principle established in the *Rex Williams* case.[361] The position relating to disclosure and further use of relevant material is dealt with in the previous paragraph.

3–125 *Section 169 of the Financial Services and Markets Act 2000.* Under this provision, the Financial Services Authority has power to appoint investigators at the request of an overseas regulator. An investigator appointed under s.169 has the same powers as an investigator under s.168 and must make a report under s.170(6). Statements made to the investigator will be admissible in evidence as provided for by s.174. Certain admissions are not capable of being used in a wide range of criminal proceedings. The opinions contained in any such report will be

[358] [1994] Ch. 350 and see further text from 7–127.
[359] SI 2001/1857.
[360] SI 2001/2188 as subsequently amended by SI 2001/3437, SI 2001/3624, SI2003/693, SI 2003/2174, SI 2003/2817, SI 2005/3071.
[361] [1994] Ch. 350 and see further text from 7–127.

admissible in s.8 proceedings by virtue of the principle established in the *Rex Williams* case.[362] The position relating to disclosure and further use of relevant material is dealt with in 3–123.

3–126 *Section 284 of the Financial Services and Markets Act 2000*. Under this provision, the Financial Services Authority or the Secretary of State may appoint investigators to investigate the affairs of an authorised unit trust scheme or any other collective investment scheme (other than one operating through the medium of an open-ended investment company) and/or the affairs of the manager, trustee or depositary of any such scheme if it appears to either of them that it is in the interests of the participants or potential participants to do so or that the matter is of public concern. Sections 170 and 174 apply to such investigations as they do to investigations under ss.167 and 168. Certain admissions are not capable of being used in a wide range of criminal proceedings. The opinions contained in any such report will be admissible in s.8 proceedings by virtue of the principle established in the *Rex Williams* case.[363] The position relating to disclosure and further use of relevant material is dealt with in 3–123.

3–127 *The Open-Ended Investment Companies Regulations 2001*. Before October 1, 2009 CDDA s.8(1A)(a)(iii) included in the definition of "investigative material" a report made by inspectors under regulations made as a result of s.262(2)(k) of the Financial Services and Markets Act 2000. That definition has been moved to CDDA s.22D.[364] The relevant rules are contained in reg.30 of the Open-Ended Investment Companies Regulations 2001.[365] Regulation 30 empowers the Financial Services Authority or the Secretary of State to appoint investigators to investigate and report on the affairs of, or of any director or depositary of, an open-ended investment company if it appears to either of them that it is in the interests of shareholders or potential shareholders of the company to do so or that the matter is of public concern. Sections 170 and 174 of the Financial Services and Markets Act apply to investigations under reg.30 in the same way as they do to investigations under ss.167 and 168. Certain admissions are not capable of being used in a wide range of criminal proceedings. The opinions contained in any such report will be admissible in s.8 proceedings by virtue of the principle established in the *Rex Williams* case.[366] The position relating to disclosure (including disclosure to the Secretary of State) and further use of relevant material is dealt with in 3–123.

3–128 *Sections 165, 171, 172, 173 and 175 of the Financial Services and Markets Act 2000*. Section 165 of the Financial Services and Markets Act empowers the Financial Services Authority to require an authorised person to provide information or produce documents where such information or documents are reasonably

[362] [1994] Ch. 350 and see further text from 7–127.
[363] [1994] Ch. 350 and see further text from 7–127.
[364] Inserted from October 1, 2009 by SI 2009/1941.
[365] SI 2001/1228.
[366] [1994] Ch. 350 and see further text from 7–127.

required in connection with the exercise of the Authority's functions under the Act. An investigator appointed under s.167 has power in s.171 to require the person who is the subject of the investigation or any person connected with the person under investigation to provide information or produce documents. An investigator appointed under s.168 has similar powers in ss.172 to 173. By virtue of s.175, these powers can be exercised against a third party who is in possession of relevant documents. All information and documents obtained by this process may form the basis of a decision under CDDA s.8. The position relating to disclosure and further use of relevant material is dealt with in 3–123.

The Criminal Justice Act

3–129 *Section 2 of the Criminal Justice Act 1987.* Section 1(3) of the Criminal Justice Act empowers the Director of the Serious Fraud Office to investigate any suspected offence involving serious or complex fraud in England, Wales and Northern Ireland. By virtue of s.2(2), the Director may require a person under investigation or any other person whom it is believed has relevant information to answer questions or furnish information with respect to any matter relevant to the investigation. Such persons can also be required to produce documents and provide explanations of any document produced. However, the use to which statements made by a person in compliance with these requirements is more limited than that under s.447 of the Companies Act 1985 (see s.2(8)).[367] There is a similar range of powers in the Criminal Law (Consolidation) (Scotland) Act 1995, the only difference being that these powers are exercisable at the behest of the Lord Advocate, rather than the Serious Fraud Office, which does not have jurisdiction in Scotland. The statutory gateway in s.3 of the Criminal Justice Act 1987 permits the Serious Fraud Office to disclose information obtained under ss.1 to 2 of that Act to other competent authorities. The provision appears to be wide enough to allow information to be disclosed to the Secretary of State or the official receiver for use under the CDDA.[368]

[367] For discussion of the scope of these powers see *Smith v Director of the Serious Fraud Office* [1993] A.C. 1; *R. v Director of the Serious Fraud Office Ex p. Saunders* [1988] Crim. L.R. 837; *Re Arrows Ltd, Hamilton v Naviede* [1995] 2 A.C. 75.

[368] See *Morris v Serious Fraud Office* [1993] Ch. 372.

CHAPTER 4

ESTABLISHING UNFIT CONDUCT (1): GENERAL PRINCIPLES

INTRODUCTION

4–01 With the preliminaries out of the way, the court must decide whether the defendant's conduct as a director of the relevant company or companies "makes him unfit to be concerned in the management of a company". For present purposes it is convenient to use the shorthand description of "unfitness" for this test. The concept of unfitness is at the heart of the CDDA. It is fundamental to the operation of the key provisions in ss.6 and 8. It also encompasses many, if not all, of the specific wrongs targeted by the other substantive powers of disqualification contained in CDDA ss.2–5, 9A and 10. Unfitness is the principal criterion chosen to distinguish conduct that is acceptable from conduct (whether by way of act or omission) that is unacceptable because it demonstrates a failure to meet the standards required of directors, and thus merits disqualification. There is now a vast body of judicial pronouncements on the question of what conduct makes a person unfit. The sheer volume of the case law, most of which has arisen from applications brought in the public interest under ss.6 or 8, reflects the year on year increase in the numbers of directors that were processed by the courts in the period between 1986 and 2002.[1] The present chapter and Ch.5 attempt to distil this important area of insolvency and company law and to demonstrate the contribution that the law on unfit conduct has made to the reshaping of directors' obligations generally.[2] Issues of general principle are dealt with in this chapter. A detailed exposition of specific instances of unfit conduct and important issues such as directorial incompetence is reserved to Ch.5. Once the court has determined that a disqualification order should be made against the defendant on grounds of unfitness, it then has to determine the appropriate period of disqualification. The approach of the court in determining the length of disqualification and the factors that may be taken into account in mitigation are discussed towards the end of Ch.5.

[1] See 1–01 to 1–03. Between 2002 and 2008 the number of disqualifications has declined year on year and the introduction of the disqualification undertakings regime from April 2, 2001 has led to a significant reduction in the volume of cases that reach trial. The law relating to undertakings is covered in Ch.9.

[2] There is not space to provide a full account of the general law of directors' obligations. Nevertheless, some attempt is made in the course of the next two chapters to explore how disqualification law interrelates with the general law of directors' duties. Another prevailing theme (borne out by the detailed coverage of specific instances of unfitness in Ch.5) is the tendency for disqualification to be used as a means to reinforce core obligations in companies legislation such as the requirements to keep proper accounting records and to prepare and file audited accounts.

SECTION 6: MANDATORY DISQUALIFICATION FOR UNFITNESS

4–02 The final matter in respect of which the court must be satisfied before a disqualification order can be imposed under CDDA s.6 is that the defendant's conduct as a director "makes him unfit to be concerned in the management of a company". This is a critical requirement because once the court has determined that the defendant's conduct makes him unfit, it must disqualify him for at least the statutory minimum period of two years. Section 6 is one of only two mandatory disqualification provisions in the CDDA.[3] It differs markedly from its statutory antecedents in s.9 of the Insolvency Act 1976 and s.300 of the Companies Act 1985. Under these earlier provisions, the court only had jurisdiction to disqualify where the defendant had been a director of at least two companies that had gone into insolvent liquidation within five years of one another. Moreover, the court was not obliged to disqualify the defendant even if it was satisfied that his conduct in relation to those companies made him unfit. The question of whether or not to disqualify was a matter entirely within the discretion of the court. As such, it was open to the court to take a broad range of factors into account and weigh these in the balance before deciding that a disqualification order was appropriate.[4] So, for example, in *Re Churchill Hotel (Plymouth) Ltd*,[5] the court held that the defendant's conduct in relation to four failed companies made him unfit but declined to disqualify him on the ground that the conduct had not been dishonest and in the light of evidence that the businesses and employees of eight other companies that he was managing responsibly would have been prejudiced by the making of a disqualification order. Cases like *Churchill Hotel*, decided before the enactment of the CDDA, should be approached cautiously as they provide no sure guide as to what constitutes unfit conduct for the purposes of mandatory disqualification under s.6. A major difficulty with the old cases is that

[3] The other mandatory provision is CDDA s.9A (inserted by Enterprise Act 2002 s.204) governing disqualification for infringements of competition law. This provision is considered separately in Ch.6.

[4] The approach in Australia under ss.206D and 206F of the Corporations Act 2001 (Cth) and its statutory predecessors is comparable to that under s.300. These provisions confer discretionary powers on the court (s.206D) and the Australian Securities and Investments Commission (s.206F) to prohibit a person from managing a corporation for up to 20 and five years respectively. They are triggered broadly where the person has been a director of two companies that have failed in the previous seven years. Although the term "unfit" is not used, it is clear that the provisions are targeted at unfit conduct in the CDDA sense and it is interesting to note that the Australian courts have sometimes relied on English authorities when applying them: see *Blunt v Corporate Affairs Commission (No. 2)* (1988) 14 A.C.L.R. 270; *Dwyer v National Companies and Securities Commission* (1989) 15 A.C.L.R. 386; *Cullen v Corporate Affairs Commission* (1988) 14 A.C.L.R. 789, *Re Delonga and Australian Securities Commission* (1994) 15 A.C.S.R. 450; *Re Sheslow and Australian Securities Commission* (1994) 12 A.C.L.C. 740; *Re Agushi and Australian Securities Commission* (1996) 19 A.C.S.R. 322; *Re Iliopoulos and Australian Securities Commission* (1997) 15 A.C.L.C. 1512; *Re Healey and Australian Securities and Investments Commission* [2000] A.A.T.A. 9. The statutory predecessors of ss.206D and 206F are discussed in J. Cassidy, "Disqualification of Directors Under the Corporations Law" (1995) 13 Company and Securities L.J. 221 and A. Hicks, *Disqualification of Directors: No Hiding Place for the Unfit* (A.C.C.A Research Report No.59, 1998) pp.82–83. For an unsuccessful challenge to the constitutionality of s.206F see *Visnic v Australian Securities and Investment Commission* (2007) 234 A.L.R. 413.

[5] [1988] B.C.L.C. 341.

the courts did not always distinguish clearly between factors relevant to the question of unfitness and factors relevant to the determination of whether or not, as a matter of discretion, an unfit director ought to be disqualified. There is always the danger that a court considering these cases in s.6 proceedings may adopt too lenient a test of what constitutes unfit conduct.[6]

Mandatory disqualification for unfitness was first conceived in the Cork Report as a means of providing stronger safeguards for the public against "those whose conduct has shown them to be unfitted to manage the affairs of a company with limited liability".[7] As considered in Ch.2, mandatory disqualification is said to protect the public in a variety of ways. First, it restrains the unfit person from taking part or being concerned in the management of companies, thus keeping him "off the road". Secondly, through deterrence, it seeks to encourage both the disqualified person and others to act responsibly. Finally, and consequentially, it aims to raise standards in the conduct and responsibility of those who manage companies.[8] Indeed, the deterrent aspect is regarded as an inherent aspect of mandatory disqualification. As an illustration, let us say hypothetically that W was a director of X Ltd, which became insolvent. There is an allegation that W allowed X Ltd to trade while insolvent to the detriment of creditors and disqualification proceedings are commenced. In the period between the commencement of proceedings and trial, W is involved in the management of two successful companies, Y Ltd and Z Ltd. If the court finds that W's conduct in relation to X Ltd makes him unfit, it is required to disqualify him for at least two years, even though he has proved himself to be capable of acting responsibly in relation to Y Ltd and Z Ltd. This is because Parliament, by making disqualification mandatory, has decided that it may be necessary to disqualify a person in W's position in order to deter others.[9]

4–03 One danger with any provision of this nature is that in marginal cases (such as the example just given) there may be a tendency for the court to refuse to "convict" in the first place if it regards the mandatory "sentence" as being too harsh. Thus, while in strict theory the court has no discretion in the matter, there

[6] For other examples of cases decided under Companies Act 1985 s.300 see *Re Lo-Line Electric Motors* [1988] Ch. 477; *Re Dawson Print Group Ltd* [1987] B.C.L.C. 601; *Re Douglas Construction Services Ltd* [1988] B.C.L.C. 397; *Re CU Fittings Ltd* [1989] B.C.L.C. 556 in all of which no order was made principally on the ground that unfitness was not established. For s.300 cases in which disqualification orders were made see, e.g. *Re Stanford Services Ltd* [1987] B.C.L.C. 607 (two years); *Re Rolus Properties Ltd* (1988) 4 B.C.C. 446 (two years); *Re Western Welsh International System Buildings Ltd* (1988) 4 B.C.C. 449 (two defendants each disqualified for five years); *Re DJ Matthews (Joinery Design) Ltd* (1988) 4 B.C.C. 513 (three years); *Re J & B Lynch (Builders) Ltd* [1988] B.C.L.C. 376 (three years); *Re Majestic Recording Studios Ltd* [1989] B.C.L.C. 1 (two defendants disqualified for three and five years respectively); *Re McNulty's Interchange Ltd* [1989] B.C.L.C. 709 (18 months).

[7] Report of the Review Committee, *Insolvency Law and Practice*, Cmnd.8558 (London: HMSO, 1982), para.1808 and Ch.45. For further background on the legislative history of s.6 see text from 1–40.

[8] See *Re Swift 736 Ltd, Secretary of State for Trade and Industry v Ettinger* [1993] B.C.L.C. 896; *Re Grayan Building Services Ltd, Secretary of State for Trade and Industry v Gray* [1995] Ch. 241; *Re Westmid Packing Services Ltd, Secretary of State for Trade and Industry v Griffiths* [1998] 2 All E.R. 124; *Re Bradcrown Ltd, Official Receiver v Ireland* [2001] 1 B.C.L.C. 547 and text from 2–26.

[9] *Re Grayan Building Services Ltd, Secretary of State for Trade and Industry v Gray* [1995] Ch.241. This issue is addressed further in the discussion of the phrase "makes him unfit" in the text from 4–11 below.

is room for different judges to reach different conclusions on the same or similar facts, and provided the view reached is within a reasonable range, an appellate court will not interfere with it.[10] The self-imposed limits on the willingness of appellate courts to intervene and reverse findings made by lower courts mean, in practice, that the determination of unfitness may be viewed as involving an element of discretion, in the sense that an appeal court will allow the lower court a degree of latitude in reaching its decision and will not in all cases substitute its own view as to whether or not the misconduct in question is such as to make the defendant unfit. As such, there is scope for the court to avoid disqualifying the defendant in a borderline case by finding that his conduct falls short of unfitness. Although nothing like as wide as the discretion under s.300 of the Companies Act 1985, the latitude allowed by appellate courts to the first instance judge has the potential to create a shifting boundary between "fitness" and "unfitness" leaving room for personal and policy factors to exert some influence on the judge's decision. This is hardly surprising given the open-ended nature of the unfitness concept.[11] Mandatory disqualification has been criticised in some quarters because of the narrowness of the parameters within which the court is obliged to operate and the potential impact that this may have in marginal cases in particular. Returning to the example above, let us say that W's conduct in relation to X Ltd was a clear case of trading while insolvent to the detriment of creditors, meriting a three-year disqualification. Some would argue that to disqualify W would be punitive and unhelpful in the light of his subsequent conduct in relation to Y Ltd and Z Ltd. However, under the law as it stands, the court must confine its enquiry to W's misconduct in relation to X Ltd. It cannot say that his good conduct in the other companies outweighs his misconduct and, on balance, makes him fit.[12] This has led some to argue that mandatory disqualification should be abandoned and a discretionary power reinstated.[13] A further anomaly, noted by Chadwick J. in *Re Thorncliffe Finance Ltd, Secretary of State for Trade and Industry v Arif*, is that mitigating factors cannot be taken into account to reduce the period of disqualification below the statutory minimum of two years.[14] Thus,

[10] For appeals see Ch.13. In *Re Crystal Palace Football Club (1986) Ltd, Secretary of State for Trade and Industry v Goldberg* [2003] EWHC 2843 (Ch), [2004] 1 B.C.L.C. 597 at [14] and [327] Lewison J. described the question of unfitness as a "value judgment".

[11] For classic examples of the operation of a hidden "discretion" under s.6 see *Re Bath Glass Ltd* [1988] B.C.L.C. 329; *Re ECM (Europe) Electronics Ltd* [1992] B.C.L.C. 814; *Re Wimbledon Village Restaurant Ltd, Secretary of State for Trade and Industry v Thomson* [1994] B.C.C. 753; *Re Moonlight Foods (UK) Ltd, Secretary of State for Trade and Industry v Hickling* [1996] B.C.C. 678; *Secretary of State for Trade and Industry v Blackwood* [2003] S.L.T. 120. For further discussion see A. Hicks, *Disqualification of Directors: No Hiding Place for the Unfit?* (A.C.C.A. Research Report No.59, 1998), pp.36–37.

[12] *Re Barings Plc (No.5), Secretary of State for Trade and Industry v Baker* [1999] 1 B.C.L.C. 433 at 482–486 and, in particular, 485E–G.

[13] See generally A. Hicks, *Disqualification of Directors: No Hiding Place for the Unfit?* (A.C.C.A. Research Report No.59, 1998) and Vinelott J.'s thinly-veiled criticism of mandatory disqualification in *Re Pamstock Ltd* [1994] 1 B.C.L.C. 716 at 737.

[14] [1997] 1 B.C.L.C. 34 at 44–45. On mitigation generally, see text from 5–110.

mitigating factors that can be used to reduce what, in the absence of mitigation, would be a three-year disqualification, cannot be used to reduce a two-year disqualification.

4–04 A stock response to criticism of the harshness of mandatory disqualification is that it is always open to a person in W's position to apply for permission to act as a director of Y Ltd and Z Ltd notwithstanding disqualification. The power to grant permission to act is a structural feature of the CDDA that enables the court to mitigate the impact of disqualification. Indeed, it can be argued that, if exercised liberally, the power to grant permission may in practice serve to undermine the purposes of disqualification. Without qualitative empirical research it is impossible to gain a clear picture of the extent to which disqualification operates as a deterrent to other directors and to what extent such general deterrence is undermined by any public perception regarding the ease with which permission to act notwithstanding disqualification can be obtained.[15] However, a persuasive case can be made that the grant of permission to act in relation to companies in which the disqualified person wishes to be involved has the potential seriously to undermine any deterrent aspect of the disqualification for that person. A disqualification that does not in practice prevent the director acting in relation to those companies with which he wishes to remain involved is shorn of at least some of its force as a deterrent and may beg the question from an ordinary member of the public: "what is the point of the disqualification?" Although the deterrent aspect of disqualification is often recited as a factor to be taken into account in determining an application for permission to act, the test that the courts tend to apply is to ask whether those who deal with the company in relation to which permission is sought are adequately protected from a repetition of the previous misconduct (or other likely misconduct) of the defendant. To the extent that deterrence is ignored or downplayed as a factor, the overall policy of CDDA s.6, as articulated by the courts, is frustrated and, in practice, disqualification begins to look more discretionary than mandatory. Permission to act is considered further in Ch.15.

SECTION 8: DISCRETIONARY DISQUALIFICATION FOR UNFITNESS

4–05 In proceedings under CDDA s.8, the final matter on which the court must be satisfied before a disqualification order can be imposed is that the defendant's conduct "in relation to the company makes him unfit to be concerned in the management of a company".[16] Thus, the court's power of disqualification under s.8 turns ultimately on a finding of unfitness although, in contrast to s.6, the decision whether or not to disqualify is at the court's discretion.[17] Strictly, the

[15] A. Hicks, *Disqualification of Directors: No Hiding Place for the Unfit?* (A.C.C.A. Research Report No.59, 1998) suggests that general awareness of the CDDA may be limited thus calling into question the potential of disqualification as an effective deterrent. See also R. Williams, "Disqualifying Directors: A Remedy Worse than the Disease" (2007) 7 Journal of Corporate Law Studies 213.

[16] CDDA s.8(2). The court for these purposes is the High Court or, in Scotland, the Court of Session: CDDA s.8(3).

[17] Although the discretion must be exercised according to principle.

court must therefore engage in a two-stage process, determining first whether the defendant's conduct makes him unfit and, if so, whether it is appropriate to disqualify him for some period.[18] One practical implication of this is that the defendant may seek to adduce separate evidence on the question of unfitness and in relation to the exercise of the discretion. However, as we will see below, the approach of the courts under s.8 has been influenced by practice in relation to s.6.

4–06 The concept of discretionary disqualification for unfitness following a company investigation originates from the Cork Report[19] and the provision was first enacted as s.13 of the Insolvency Act 1985. As discussed in Ch.3, proceedings for an order under s.8 must be based on investigative material contained in a report made by inspectors or on information or documents obtained pursuant to various provisions of companies and financial services legislation. An application can be made by the Secretary of State against a person who is, or has been, a director, a shadow director,[20] or, as is also the case under s.6, a de facto director.

4–07 One issue of considerable importance is the nature of the discretion in s.8. At first sight, it may be thought that the court has the same sort of wide discretion under s.8 as it enjoyed under s.300 of the Companies Act 1985.[21] However, the courts have adopted a narrower approach to the s.8 discretion having regard to the way in which the law has developed under s.6. As discussed in Ch.2, the idea that disqualification operates to protect the public not only by prohibiting the unfit director from taking part in the management of companies but also by deterring him and other directors, thus improving standards of conduct generally, is a consistent theme of cases decided under s.6.[22] One effect of s.6 is that a disqualification order may be required by the statute, for purposes of general deterrence, even in circumstances where the director himself poses no particular ongoing risk to the public. This notion of deterrence has emerged as the rationale for mandatory disqualification under s.6 in circumstances where the defendant's past conduct has been shown on the evidence to be unfit (with the result that the court is obliged to disqualify) even though by the date of trial he has mended his ways and is running other companies successfully and properly.[23] Although s.8 confers a discretionary jurisdiction to disqualify, the courts have had regard to the s.6 cases and the underlying purpose of that jurisdiction, and have exercised their discretion under s.8 in line with those underlying purposes. It follows that the courts have sought to apply a consistent approach to the CDDA as a whole. Thus, the court will consider whether it is appropriate to disqualify the defendant in order to protect the public either by "taking him off the road" or through

[18] *Re Atlantic Computers Plc, Secretary of State for Trade and Industry v Ashman*, June 15, 1998, Ch.D., unreported.

[19] Report of the Review Committee, *Insolvency Law and Practice*, Cmnd.8558 (London: HMSO, 1982), para.1819(c).

[20] CDDA s.8(1).

[21] See 4–02.

[22] See generally *Re Grayan Building Services Ltd, Secretary of State for Trade and Industry v Gray* [1995] Ch. 241; *Re Blackspur Group Plc* [1998] 1 W.L.R. 422; *Re Westmid Packing Services Ltd, Secretary of State for Trade and Industry v Griffiths* [1998] 2 All E.R. 124.

[23] *Re Grayan Building Services Ltd, Secretary of State for Trade and Industry v Gray* [1995] Ch. 241.

deterrence (or a combination of the two), and will exercise its discretion to disqualify under s.8 accordingly. Lloyd J.'s judgment in the leading (though unreported) case of *Re Atlantic Computers Plc, Secretary of State for Trade and Industry v Ashman* provides clear authority for this approach.[24]

4–08 In *Re Atlantic Computers Plc, Secretary of State for Trade and Industry v Ashman*, Lloyd J. appears, wrongly, to have considered that there was no jurisdiction under the former s.300 of the Companies Act 1985 to grant permission to act notwithstanding disqualification.[25] Based on this misapprehension he suggested that cases such as *Re Churchill Hotel (Plymouth) Ltd*[26] would now be more likely to be decided under s.8 not by the refusal of a disqualification order, but by the making of an order coupled with the grant of permission to act notwithstanding disqualification. Despite the initial false premise, it is suggested that Lloyd J. is correct in his prediction of how the court would act in the light of judicial development of the CDDA and the recognition of an underlying coherent framework to the legislation as a whole. The judge's reasoning in *Atlantic Computers* was on firmer ground when he referred back to the following sentence from the judgment of Hoffmann L.J. in *Re Grayan Building Services Ltd, Secretary of State for Trade and Industry v Gray*:

> "Even if the court had a discretion, it would not, having formed the view that disqualification was necessary in the public interest, be acting judicially if it did not make a disqualification order."[27]

It is suggested that the purposes judicially identified as underpinning CDDA s.6, underpin all the provisions by which disqualification can be imposed and that accordingly, under CDDA s.8, the court should not simply consider the protection of the public by keeping the director "off the road" but also protection through deterrence and the public interest in the raising of standards of conduct. This also offers the prospect of a consistent approach as between the criminal and the civil courts.[28] Moreover, there will often be cases that, in terms of jurisdiction, fall within both CDDA ss.6 and 8. *Atlantic Computers* was itself a case where the preliminary jurisdictional requirements of s.6 would also have been satisfied. It is suggested that it would be unsatisfactory if defendants in such cases could be treated in a significantly different manner depending on the chance of the proceedings being brought under one jurisdictional gateway rather than another.

[24] June 15, 1998, Ch.D., unreported. See also *Re JA Chapman & Co Ltd, Secretary of State for Trade and Industry v Amiss* [2003] EWHC 532 (Ch), [2003] 2 B.C.L.C. 206; *Re Amba Rescue Ltd, Secretary of State for Trade and Industry v Hollier* [2006] EWHC 1804 (Ch), [2007] B.C.C. 11 at [48]–[60].

[25] He pointed to the lack of any statutory predecessor to CDDA s.17. However, s.17 is merely a procedural provision regulating how applications for permission to act notwithstanding disqualification are to be conducted. The disqualification from acting as a director of a company or from otherwise being involved in the management of a company has always been expressed as being subject to the grant of permission by the court: see the former s.295(1) of the Companies Act 1985 and CDDA ss.1(1)(a), 1A(1)(a).

[26] [1988] B.C.L.C. 341 and see 4–02.

[27] [1995] Ch. 241 at 253G.

[28] On CDDA disqualification in the criminal courts under ss.2 and 5, see further Ch.10.

Two further points can be made. First, in *Grayan* the Court of Appeal rejected the argument that the phrase "makes him unfit . . ." in s.6(1) was a test as to whether the director was, at the time of the hearing, currently unfit. Clearly, the words must bear the same meaning in s.8. The second point relates to the unwillingness of the courts in s.6 cases to trespass into the process by which the Secretary of State decides that it is in the public interest to bring disqualification proceedings under CDDA s.7(1). Given this unwillingness, it is likely that any discretion in the court to determine the "public interest" when deciding whether to make an order under s.8 will be regarded as narrow and the courts will not wish to see it exercised expansively in a way that could effectively overrule the view as to the public interest formed by the Secretary of State under CDDA s.8(1). In *Re J A Chapman & Co Ltd, Secretary of State for Trade and Industry v Amiss*, Peter Smith J. cited the view of Lloyd J. in *Atlantic Computers* without in any way demurring from it:

> "[A]s I have said under the power of disqualification under s.8 the court retains a discretionary power not to disqualify even if the defendant's conduct is unfit. That must be read in the light of the observations of Lloyd J. in *Re Atlantic Computers plc* . . . where he observed that it would be unusual for the court to use its discretion in this way."[29]

Amiss and *Atlantic Computers* therefore provide support for the view that the court's discretion to decline to disqualify a director whose conduct has been found to make him unfit is narrow rather than broad.

More recently, in *Re Amba Rescue Ltd, Secretary of State for Trade and Industry v Hollier*, Etherton J. described the differences between ss.6 and 8 in terms of the s.8 discretion and the lack of any minimum period of disqualification under s.8 as "significant".[30] Accordingly, he invited counsel on both sides to make submissions on whether these differences should affect the approach of the court in determining unfitness under s.8 and in making a disqualification order in the light of that determination. Counsel were agreed that the court should approach a s.8 case by applying the same approach and principles as it would in a s.6 case. Etherton J. expressed surprise at this although he did proceed to set out and follow the applicable principles from the s.6 case law.[31] It is not clear from his judgment whether *Amiss* and *Atlantic Computers* were cited to him. However, in the light of the approach in those cases, it is suggested that he was correct to adopt the course proposed by counsel.

4–09 A further issue arising from the wording of CDDA s.8(2) is whether or not conduct that can be taken into account in determining unfitness is limited to "conduct as a director". It is clear from s.6(1)(b) that relevant conduct for s.6 purposes is limited to "conduct as a director of [a] company". However, at first sight, it might appear that relevant conduct for s.8 purposes is potentially wider as s.8(2) stipulates that, in determining whether or not the defendant is unfit, the

[29] [2003] 2 B.C.L.C. 206 at [4].
[30] [2007] B.C.C. 11 at [48].
[31] [2007] B.C.C. 11 at [50]–[51].

court may take into account his "conduct in relation to the company", not merely his "conduct as a director". However, it is suggested that s.8 has to be read as a whole. Section 8(1) focuses on the relevant person's capacity as a director. It would, it is suggested, be odd if the Secretary of State had to make his decision to issue proceedings on the basis that a person was a director but that that person's conduct otherwise than as a director could subsequently be considered as a basis for disqualifying him in those proceedings. In the authors' view, s.8(2) is, in fact, limited to the person's conduct as a director.[32]

ESTABLISHING UNFIT CONDUCT

General points

4–10 A number of preliminary points can be made about the test for unfitness set out in CDDA ss.6 and 8:

(1) The test is whether or not relevant identified conduct of the defendant makes him unfit, not whether or not it is in the public interest that he be disqualified. In a number of cases the courts have expressed themselves, it is suggested wrongly, or at least confusingly, in terms of whether it is in the public interest that a person be disqualified, as if that is the test that they are obliged to apply.

(2) The conduct in question must be conduct in the capacity of a director. In this context, Lewison J. in *Re Crystal Palace Football Club (1986), Ltd Secretary of State for Trade and Industry v Goldberg* suggested, by way of example, that incompetence in providing investment advice to a prospective shareholder or in failing to control the personal financial affairs of a company's principal shareholder would not be relevant misconduct.[33] However, it is suggested that the conduct in these examples would not necessarily fall outside the scope of "conduct as a director". If, for example, the business of the company was providing investment advice and the company was acting through the director in giving that advice or, if the director, with a view to inducing someone to invest in the company, gave the investment advice, then surely such conduct would be capable of being relevant conduct? Similarly, if the company had contracted to control the personal financial affairs of the company's principal shareholder then, again, presumably the conduct of the director would be capable of being relevant conduct. In short, the examples given by Lewison J. are, it is respectfully suggested, lacking in sufficient surrounding factual material to enable a conclusive answer to be given.

(3) The test is whether the relevant misconduct makes the defendant unfit to be concerned in the management of a company, not whether or not he is unfit to be a director.

[32] See discussion at 3–116.
[33] [2004] 1 B.C.L.C. 597 at [46].

(4) The test is whether the director's misconduct, as identified, relied upon and proved by the claimant, falls below the relevant standards of probity and competence required of directors by the court and not whether or not the defendant is now (i.e. at the time of the hearing) unfit to be concerned in the management of companies.[34]

(5) The test is whether or not the defendant is unfit to be concerned in the management of "a" company. This is determined by reference to the question of whether his conduct, as found by the court, falls below the standards of probity and competence required of directors by the courts. A defendant cannot escape a finding of unfitness by demonstrating that it is possible to conceive of a management role in some other company, real or imagined, in which he would have the competence and integrity to be involved without risk to the public.[35]

(6) In applying the standard of probity and competence the court must take care to avoid hindsight judgments.[36]

(7) It is important that the words of the statute are not taken as having been given a judicial gloss. Other cases in which there were findings of unfitness are examples of cases where the court has found unfitness to be made out but the circumstances in which they made such findings are not automatically to be taken as necessary circumstances for such a finding.[37]

(8) Schedule 1 to the CDDA provides some limited guidance in determining whether or not misconduct is such as to make the defendant "unfit".[38] However, the Schedule is not an exhaustive statement of unfit conduct.

(9) In each case the court must consider the director's personal responsibility.[39]

(10) The court must consider any allegations of misconduct both individually and in the round.[40]

"Makes him unfit to be concerned in the management of a company": relevant conduct under CDDA s.6

4–11 Before the court can make a disqualification order it must be satisfied under CDDA s.6(2) that the defendant's conduct as a director of the relevant company (either taken alone or taken together with his conduct as a director of any other company or companies) "makes him unfit" to be concerned in the management of a company. The extent to which the claimant can adduce evidence of misconduct from other, so-called collateral companies is considered in Ch.3. A more

[34] See text from 4–11.
[35] See text from 4–15.
[36] See text from 4–28.
[37] See *Re Sevenoaks Stationers (Retail) Ltd* [1991] Ch. 164 and 4–22 to 4–23 below. In a different context, see the observations of Morritt L.J. cited in 3–47.
[38] See text from 4–41.
[39] *Re Westmid Packing Services Ltd, Secretary of State for Trade & Industry v Griffiths* [1998] 2 All E.R. 124 and 4–49 to 4–51.
[40] *Re Copecrest Ltd, Secretary of State for Trade & Industry v McTighe (No.2)* [1996] 2 B.C.L.C. 477 and 4–53.

general question concerning the nature and scope of the court's enquiry arises from the use of the present tense in the phrase "makes him unfit". Does this require the court to be satisfied that the defendant is, at the time of the hearing, presently unfit? If it does then the court would be entitled to assess at the date of trial whether the defendant still poses a genuine risk to the public for the future. In a broad enquiry of this nature, the court could take into account evidence of the defendant's general conduct (including responsible conduct) as a director of other companies during the period following the relevant company's insolvency up to the date of trial and/or other evidence that lessons from past failings have been learned suggesting that future repetition of the previous misconduct is unlikely. Any improvement in the standard of the defendant's conduct during the intervening period could thus be weighed against his past misconduct and indicate, as at the date of trial, his overall fitness to be concerned in the management of companies. This broad interpretation of the phrase "makes him unfit" does not, however, reflect the current state of the law.

"Tunnel vision": the narrow focus on past conduct

4–12 In *Re Grayan Building Services Ltd, Secretary of State for Trade and Industry v Gray*,[41] the Court of Appeal held that the use of the present tense "makes" means only that the court has to make a decision at the time of trial on the evidence then presently before it. Following the line taken by Peter Gibson J. in *Re Bath Glass Ltd*,[42] Hoffmann L.J. stated:

> "The court is concerned solely with the conduct specified by the Secretary of State or official receiver under rule 3(3) of the Insolvent Companies (Disqualification of Unfit Directors) Proceedings Rules 1987. It must decide whether that conduct, viewed cumulatively and taking into account any extenuating circumstances, has fallen below the standards of probity and competence appropriate for persons fit to be directors of companies."[43]

The effect of this is that the court must determine the question of unfitness solely by reference to the evidence of past conduct adduced by the claimant in relation to the lead company and any collateral companies.[44] Evidence of a more general nature concerning the defendant's present suitability, the fact that he may be running other companies successfully and responsibly at the date of trial and so on, is not admissible as evidence pointing towards his "fitness". The court makes no attempt to assess whether the defendant is likely to behave wrongly again in the future. The question is a narrow one: if accepted, does the present evidence of the defendant's past conduct make him unfit? If it does then the court must disqualify

[41] [1995] Ch. 241.

[42] [1988] B.C.L.C. 329. See also Peter Gibson J.'s decision in *Re DJ Matthews (Joinery Design) Ltd* (1988) 4 B.C.C. 513.

[43] [1995] Ch. 241 at 253.

[44] This is subject to the exception that the defendant's conduct during the proceedings can apparently be taken into account: see *Re Howglen Ltd, Secretary of State for Trade and Industry v Reynard* [2002] EWCA Civ 497, [2002] B.C.L.C. 625 and text from 4–31 where this decision is discussed and criticised.

the defendant even if it is satisfied that he is no longer a risk to the public.[45] The court is required to have "tunnel vision"[46]: it does not enquire about the defendant's current fitness or competence but concentrates narrowly on evidence of past misconduct. Once a finding of unfitness has been made, the court can, at that stage, consider wider evidence regarding his general conduct and abilities as a director in determining the appropriate period of disqualification and/or any application for permission to act. As Hoffmann L.J. put it in *Grayan*:

> "If this should be thought too harsh a view, it must be remembered that a disqualified director can always apply for [permission] under s. 17 and the question of whether he has shown himself unlikely to offend again will obviously be highly material to whether he is granted [permission] or not. It may also be relevant by way of mitigation on the length of disqualification . . ."[47]

4–13 The defendant may point to "extenuating circumstances" but evidence of extenuating circumstances is only admissible on the question of unfitness if it relates directly to the allegations of misconduct raised by the claimant.[48] An example of admissible "extenuating circumstances" can be gleaned from *Re Polly Peck International Plc (No.2)* where Lindsay J. suggested that a defendant whose defaults, after an otherwise blameless career, consisted of failing to ensure that proper accounting records were kept in accordance with what is now ss.386–387 of the Companies Act 2006 (formerly s.221 of the Companies Act 1985) might not be unfit if the defaults were wholly referable to a period of time during which his wife or child were suffering from a terminal illness.[49] Similarly, in *Secretary of State for Trade and Industry v Mitchell*,[50] the Court of Session accepted that evidence of personal circumstances applying at the time of the conduct, such as the fact that the defendant was then suffering from mental illness, could be taken into account in determining whether the conduct made him unfit.[51] However, Lord Carloway did add obiter that where a director alleges that his mental state has prompted him to act or fail to act in a particular way, it may be that the claimant could make out a case that his failure to resign in the face of his having some insight into his shortcomings (and, presumably, into the impact of the illness on his conduct) makes him unfit.

[45] *Grayan* is therefore authority for the view that there may be cases in which there is no public interest in keeping the defendant "off the road" but disqualification must nevertheless be imposed because of the public interest in encouraging others to behave properly and in raising standards: see 4–02 to 4–04 and 4–19.

[46] A phrase used by counsel and adopted by the judge in *Re Pamstock Ltd* [1994] 1 B.C.L.C. 716 at 737 and *Re Polly Peck International Plc (No.2), Secretary of State for Trade and Industry v Ellis* [1994] 1 B.C.L.C. 574 at 584.

[47] [1995] Ch. 241 at 254. See further *Re Westmid Packing Services Ltd, Secretary of State for Trade and Industry v Griffiths* [1998] 2 All E.R. 124 at 133; *Re Dawes & Henderson (Agencies) Ltd, Secretary of State for Trade and Industry v Dawes* [1997] B.C.C. 121.

[48] [1995] Ch. 241 at 254.

[49] [1994] 1 B.C.L.C. 574 at 583.

[50] [2001] S.L.T. 658.

[51] See also *Re Skyward Builders Plc, Official Receiver v Broad* [2002] EWHC 2786 (Ch) at [381] and [405].

4–14 It may be helpful to consider by way of illustration, the impact of the *Grayan* approach on the simple hypothetical raised earlier in 4–02 to 4–03. W is a director of X Ltd. X Ltd becomes insolvent and disqualification proceedings are commenced against W on the ground that he caused X Ltd to continue trading while insolvent to the detriment of its creditors. Subsequently, W becomes a director of two successful companies, Y Ltd and Z Ltd. There is clear evidence that W is running these companies in a responsible fashion without any repetition of the conduct that has attracted complaint in relation to X Ltd. On the current approach, the court will only consider the alleged misconduct in X Ltd. If the court is satisfied that such misconduct makes him unfit, it must disqualify W for at least two years even though, in the light of his subsequent conduct, he poses no ongoing threat to the public. However, the court can take into account W's responsible behaviour in relation to Y Ltd and Z Ltd if he makes an application for permission to act as a director of those companies. Equally, this evidence and any other evidence suggesting that W is unlikely to "re-offend" may be used in mitigation as a means of reducing the length of the disqualification.[52]

Unfit to be concerned in the management of "a" company

4–15 A further related point concerns the meaning of "*a* company" (emphasis added) in the phrase "makes him unfit to be concerned in the management of a company". It has been suggested that "a company" means "any company" with the effect that the claimant would be required to establish on the evidence that the defendant is unfit to manage *any* company and the court could not simply infer the defendant's general unfitness from evidence of his unfitness in relation to the company or companies that are the subject of the claim. The implication of this line of reasoning is that if the evidence of the defendant's misconduct in relation to the relevant company were not sufficiently serious to make him unfit in relation to some other hypothetical company or companies, he is not unfit within the meaning of s.6(1). In the example given above, this might mean that the claim against W would be dismissed on the ground that his misconduct in relation to X Ltd was not sufficient to establish that he is unfit to manage *any* company (in particular, Y Ltd and Z Ltd).

4–16 This reading of s.6(1) was categorically rejected by Jonathan Parker J. in *Re Barings Plc (No. 5), Secretary of State for Trade and Industry v Baker* in the following terms:

> "In my judgment it can be no defence to a charge of unfitness based on incompetence for a [defendant] to contend that even if he was grossly incompetent in discharging the management role in fact assigned to him, or which he in fact assumed, nevertheless he has not been shown to be unfit to be concerned in the management of any company, since it is possible to conceive of a management role (whether in the company or companies in question or in some other company altogether—real or imagined) which he could have performed competently—what I might call the 'lowest common denominator' approach.

[52] *Re Landhurst Leasing Plc, Secretary of State for Trade and Industry v Ball* [1999] 1 B.C.L.C. 286 at 344–345.

In the context of an issue as to unfitness it is neither here nor there whether a [defendant] could have performed some other management role competently. That is not the test of 'unfitness' for the purposes of s.6 (although of course it may be a relevant factor in the context of an application for [permission] under s.17 of the CDDA . . . Under s.6 the court is concerned only with the conduct in respect of which complaint is made, set in the context of the [defendant's] actual management role in the company. If in his conduct in that role the [defendant] was guilty of incompetence to the requisite degree, then a finding of unfitness will be made and (under s.6) a disqualification order must follow."[53]

4–17 This approach to the meaning of "a company" confirms and consolidates the view put forward in *Grayan* as to the meaning of "makes him unfit". In *Barings*, the defendants argued that evidence of their incompetence in relation to a large and complex public company did not demonstrate that they would necessarily be incompetent in relation to a small private company and that, accordingly, their conduct did not make them unfit to be concerned in the management of a company within the meaning of CDDA s.6(1). One implication of such an argument is that there is a universal minimum standard of competence based on a "lowest common denominator", namely standards of conduct within small private companies.[54] There are other wider implications. If the argument rejected in *Barings* were accepted, it would presumably follow that an incompetent director of a small insolvent company who had operated effectively as a sole trader, could successfully argue against a finding of unfitness on the basis that it would be possible to conceive of a hypothetical company with several directors where his management role would be more restricted and he would therefore be "fit" to undertake it. It is respectfully suggested that the view of Jonathan Parker J. is correct because it recognises that the standards required by the courts must be applied to the facts of each case. As Hoffmann L.J. put it in *Grayan*, the question of whether the relevant conduct falls below the appropriate standard must be adjudged "in its setting".[55] Indeed, had the argument been accepted it is likely that disqualification orders would have become very difficult to obtain and the CDDA would have been severely emasculated as a result.

4–18 In support of the argument advanced by the defendants in *Barings*, reliance was placed on a passage from the judgment in *Re Atlantic Computers Plc, Secretary of State for Trade and Industry v Ashman*[56] where Lloyd J. observed that:

". . . it does not necessarily follow that, if the director falls short of the standards of competence which might be expected, by the City or others, (whether or not by the law as regards directors' duties) of a director of a publicly listed company, that director is thereby shown to be unfit to be concerned in the management of any company, however small, private and simple its affairs may be."

[53] [1999] 1 B.C.L.C. 433 at 485 approved on the point by the Court of Appeal: [2000] 1 B.C.L.C. 523 at [35].

[54] See also *Re Polly Peck International Plc (No. 2), Secretary of State for Trade and Industry v Ellis* [1994] 1 B.C.L.C. 574 at 582.

[55] [1995] Ch. 241 at 254.

[56] June 15, 1998, Ch. D., unreported.

However, as Jonathan Parker J. pointed out, this should not be read as meaning that the conduct must be shown to be demonstrably unfit in relation to *any* company, whatever its size. Lloyd J. was merely saying that the fact that a director of a listed company may have acted, through incompetence, in ways that did not conform to City expectations, (for example, because he breached the City Code on Takeovers and Mergers or the Combined Code) may not be sufficient in all the circumstances to make him unfit.

Criticisms of Re Grayan Building Services Ltd

4–19 It may be thought that the disqualification of W in the earlier example would be a harsh result. In *Grayan*, the claimant successfully appealed against the refusal of the trial judge to disqualify the two defendants, the Court of Appeal reaching the conclusion that they should each be disqualified for two years on the basis of the approach outlined. One criticism of the approach in *Grayan* is that it sits uncomfortably alongside the general view that the purpose of disqualification is not primarily to punish the defendant for his past misconduct.[57] The fact that the court may end up disqualifying the defendant even though by the date of trial he no longer poses any threat to the public may appear punitive, a point echoed by Harman J. in *Re Crestjoy Products Ltd*, a case decided before *Grayan*.[58] The same concern prompted Vinelott J. in *Re Pamstock Ltd* to question, obiter, the merits of mandatory as opposed to discretionary disqualification.[59]

There are two principal responses to the criticism that the approach in Grayan appears primarily punitive:

(1) Parliament has chosen to make disqualification for unfitness under s.6 mandatory not discretionary. Disqualification of a defendant like W in the earlier example may appear punitive but can also be justified on the ground

[57] See Ch.2.

[58] [1990] B.C.L.C. 677 at 681. See also *Australian Securities and Investments Commission v Rich* [2003] N.S.W.S.C. 186 at [26].

[59] [1994] 1 B.C.L.C. 716 at 737. *Grayan* and *Pamstock* are in stark contrast to the wide enquiry permitted under the discretionary provision formerly in s.300 of the Companies Act 1985: see, e.g. *Re Churchill Hotel (Plymouth) Ltd* [1988] B.C.L.C. 341. The approach taken by Lindsay J. in *Re Polly Peck International Plc (No.2), Secretary of State for Trade and Industry v Ellis* [1994] 1 B.C.L.C. 574 (a case concerning an application by the Secretary of State for permission to commence proceedings out of time under s.7(2)) provides another example of judicial discomfort with "tunnel vision". Laying particular emphasis on the use of the present tense and the indefinite article in the phrase "*makes* him unfit to be concerned in the management of a company" (emphasis added), Lindsay J. held that there was an onus on the claimant to establish that the defendant was presently unfit (i.e. at the date of trial) in relation to the management of companies generally. Thus, the judge adopted a higher threshold test and refused to accept that a finding of past unfitness should result automatically in a finding of present unfitness. At the same time, he recognised that the courts face a difficulty in dealing with uncorroborated evidence suggesting that the defendant is unlikely to "reoffend". To overcome this difficulty, Lindsay J. held that a finding of past unfitness should raise a presumption that the defendant is presently unfit. The onus would then be on the defendant to satisfy the court as to present fitness with reference to his general record in managing companies and any other positive performance indicators. It is clear that this approach does not survive the Court of Appeal's approach in *Grayan* as further developed by Jonathan Parker J. in *Re Barings Plc (No.5)*.

that it may deter others from engaging in similar misconduct and lead to an improvement in standards of conduct generally. The point was made by Hoffmann L.J. in *Grayan* in the following terms:

> "If the court always had to be satisfied at the hearing that the protection of the public required a period of disqualification, there would be no need to make disqualification mandatory . . . The purpose of making disqualification mandatory was to ensure that everyone whose conduct had fallen below the appropriate standard was disqualified for at least two years, whether in the individual case the court thought that this was necessary in the public interest or not. Parliament has decided that it is occasionally necessary to disqualify a company director to encourage the others."[60]

Thus, in theory, mandatory disqualification serves the public interest not merely by taking persons whose conduct shows them to be a danger to the public "off the road", but also through general deterrence. The implication is that the negative impact suffered by the individual is a price worth paying in the pursuit of higher standards of conduct.

(2) As Hoffmann L.J. pointed out, it is always open to a disqualified person to apply for permission to act as a director of a specified company or companies. On an application for permission, a defendant in W's position would be entitled to put a case as to why he should be allowed to continue as a director of Y Ltd and/or Z Ltd despite being disqualified. Thus, in theory, the power of the courts to grant permission operates as a check and balance within the structure of the CDDA that can be used to temper the impact of disqualification on the individual.[61]

Whatever the merits of the narrow approach taken by the Court of Appeal in *Grayan*, it currently represents the law.

Standard of unfitness: judicial paraphrasing

4–20 In several cases decided in the late-1980s, including some decided under the old Companies Act provisions, there was an attempt by the judges to formulate something approaching a general threshold test. In *Re Dawson Print Group Ltd*, a s.300 case, Hoffmann J. stated:

> "There must, I think, be something about the case, some conduct which if not dishonest is at any rate in breach of standards of commercial morality, or some really gross incompetence which persuades the court that it would be a danger to the public if he were to be allowed to continue to be involved in the management of companies, before a disqualification order is made."[62]

[60] [1995] Ch. 241 at 253. It was suggested by Vinelott J. in *Re Pamstock Ltd* [1994] 1 B.C.L.C. 716 at 737 that mandatory disqualification also serves a denunciatory function. As discussed in Ch.2, it is difficult to escape the conclusion that disqualification is a hybrid form of proceeding.

[61] See further 4–04.

[62] [1987] B.C.L.C. 601 at 604. This test has been followed in Australia to determine when it is appropriate for the Australian Securities and Investments Commission to exercise its discretion to disqualify a person from managing a corporation under what is now s.206F of the Corporations Act 2001 (Cth): see *Blunt v Corporate Affairs Commission (No.2)* (1988) 14 A.C.L.R. 270.

Moreover, Hoffmann J. did not regard mere "mismanagement" on its own as sufficient to satisfy this test. A similar refrain was taken up by Browne-Wilkinson V.C. in *Re Lo-Line Electric Motors Ltd*:

> "Ordinary commercial misjudgment is in itself not sufficient to justify disqualification. In the normal case, the conduct complained of must display a lack of commercial probity although I have no doubt that in an extreme case of gross negligence or total incompetence disqualification could be appropriate."[63]

These dicta suggest that a line should be drawn with conduct amounting to either a breach of commercial morality or "gross" or "total" incompetence falling on the wrong side of the line, and mere "mismanagement" or "misjudgment" falling on the right side.[64] Furthermore, the use of phrases like "commercial morality" and "commercial probity" suggests that the courts are applying some sort of objective standard. A slightly different tack was taken by Peter Gibson J. in *Re Bath Glass Ltd*, an early s.6 case:

> "To reach a finding of unfitness the court must be satisfied that the director has been guilty of a serious failure or serious failures, whether deliberately or through incompetence, to perform those duties of directors which are attendant on the privilege of trading through companies with limited liability."[65]

4–21 It is clear from this dictum that conduct less culpable than dishonest or fraudulent conduct may be sufficient to support a finding of unfitness, a view that reflects the historical development of the unfitness provisions.[66] Again, it is implicit that there is some objective standard of competence to which the court must have regard. However, it is not clear from any of this coded language what frequently used terms such as "commercial morality", "mismanagement", "incompetence" and "serious failure", actually mean.[67] To some extent, the court can therefore set its own standard according to the facts of the particular case and

[63] [1988] Ch. 477 at 486.

[64] For other early cases with a similar flavour see, e.g. *Re Flatbolt Ltd*, February 21, 1986, unreported; *Re Wedgecraft Ltd*, March 7, 1986, unreported (two decisions of Harman J. in which acts of "commercial immorality" were said to justify disqualification); *Re Rolus Properties Ltd* (1988) 4 B.C.C. 446 (gross incompetence without dishonesty capable of amounting to unfitness); *Re McNulty's Interchange Ltd* [1989] B.C.L.C. 709; *Re Douglas Construction Services Ltd* [1988] B.C.L.C. 397 (mere mismanagement not sufficient to justify disqualification); *Re CU Fittings Ltd* [1989] B.C.L.C. 556 (defendant's conduct not justifying disqualification as there was no lack of "commercial probity"); *Re Ipcon Fashions Ltd* (1989) 5 B.C.C. 773 (conduct contrary to "commercial morality" justifying disqualification); *Re Cladrose Ltd* [1990] B.C.L.C. 204 (one of two defendants not disqualified because his conduct did not amount to "gross incompetence").

[65] [1988] B.C.L.C. 329 at 333.

[66] In particular, the general shift away from the requirement to prove fraud in directors' liability provisions towards objective standards analogous to negligence, a shift exemplified by the wrongful trading provision in s.214 of the Insolvency Act 1986, which was introduced at the same time as s.6.

[67] For an amplification of this point, see J. Dine, *Criminal Law in the Company Context* (Dartmouth, 1995), Ch.5. One problem with Peter Gibson J.'s "serious failure" test identified by Dine is that it is not clear whether it means that the conduct must have been seriously wrong (i.e. effectively contemplating a "gross negligence" standard) or simply that the conduct must have caused serious

the tastes of the individual judge. This means that in marginal cases, there is scope for a narrow approach to disqualification, laying emphasis on enterprise and individual freedom, to compete with a broader approach, emphasising the need for creditor protection and the idea that limited liability is a privilege that should be used responsibly.[68] In crude terms, a narrow approach to disqualification is likely to produce a higher threshold test than a broad, protective approach. Any judicial predisposition either way could therefore affect the standard applied.[69] Bearing in mind that disqualification on grounds of unfitness inevitably involves a trade-off between the facilitation and regulation of enterprise, it is impossible to eliminate the influence of policy on the question of where to draw the line. As such, any attempt to formulate a general, objective threshold test drawing a bright line between fitness and unfitness is beset by difficulties. Like the dicta quoted above, any broad test will tend to be so general as to be bereft of practical meaning and leave both claimant and defendant relying on some sort of judicial instinct or "sixth sense" for guidance. The main consequence of all this is that much greater guidance can be derived from the specific instances of misconduct that, time and again, have led the court to make a finding of unfitness than from any general threshold test or broad statement of principle.

---

harm in the form of substantial loss to creditors (i.e. effectively contemplating an ordinary negligence standard). A similar problem besets the dictum of Vinelott J. in *Re Stanford Services Ltd* [1987] B.C.L.C. 607 to the effect that a disqualification order is justified in the public interest where the defendant has been guilty of a serious breach of his obligations causing loss to company creditors. It is suggested that the focus of the CDDA is on the defendant's conduct and the propensity of that conduct to cause loss, not on the question of whether loss was actually suffered on the facts of the case: see, e.g. *Re Sykes (Butchers) Ltd, Secretary of State for Trade and Industry v Richardson* [1998] 1 B.C.L.C. 110 at 117–118. In other words, the focus is different to that in ordinary civil litigation (e.g. a claim in contract or tort) where the claimant will usually have to establish that the relevant misconduct caused loss in order to succeed. Nevertheless, while the focus is on conduct rather than consequences, the extent of any loss caused by the conduct is relevant in assessing the seriousness of the conduct and the appropriate period of disqualification: *Re Bunting Electric Manufacturing Co Ltd, Secretary of State for Trade and Industry v Golby* [2005] EWHC 3345 (Ch), [2006] 1 B.C.L.C. 550 at [37].

[68] Indeed, there is scope for the court to vary its approach subtly to meet the requirements of a particular case. Compare, for example, the approaches taken by Harman J. in *Re Rolus Properties Ltd* (1988) 4 B.C.C. 446 (emphasis placed on the idea of limited liability as a privilege with the consequence that disqualification was justified where the defendant was "incompetent" in the sense of his inability to discharge the statutory responsibilities that go with limited liability); and *Re Douglas Construction Services Ltd* [1988] B.C.L.C. 397 (narrower approach construing "abuse of privilege" restrictively and emphasising the need for the court to avoid stultifying enterprise with the result that no order was made). The two cases are consistent but it is interesting to note how Harman J. strived to confine the categories of "abuse of privilege" in *Douglas Construction*.

[69] Commentators who, like Dine, see disqualification as essentially a form of criminal process, insist that the courts should explicitly follow a narrow approach and only disqualify persons whose behaviour involves a high degree of criminal culpability: see Dine, *Criminal Law in the Company Context* (Dartmouth, 1995) and "Wrongful Trading—Quasi-Criminal Law" in H. Rajak (ed.), *Insolvency Law: Theory and Practice* (London: Sweet and Maxwell, 1993); "The Disqualification of Company Directors" (1988) 9 Co. Law. 213; "Punishing Directors" [1994] J.B.L. 325. Such an insistence appears to be at odds with the general shift away from directors' liability provisions based on fraud towards provisions like s.214 of the Insolvency Act based on a lesser threshold: see dictum of Hoffmann L.J. in *Re Grayan Building Services Ltd, Secretary of State for Trade and Industry v Gray* [1995] Ch. 241 at 255 confirming that the court applies a standard not just of probity, but also of competence.

The apparent rejection of paraphrasing and the move towards a standard of probity and competence

4–22 In *Re Sevenoaks Stationers (Retail) Ltd*, the Court of Appeal stated categorically that judicial statements, like those quoted above, should not be elevated to the status of legal principle at the expense of the plain words in the statute. Dillon L.J. made the following pertinent observations:

> "The test laid down in s.6 . . . is whether the person's conduct as a director of the company or companies in question 'makes him unfit to be concerned in the management of company'. These are ordinary words of the English language and they should be simple to apply in most cases. It is important to hold to those words in each case. The judges of the Chancery Division have, understandably, attempted in certain cases to give guidance as to what does or does not make a person unfit to be concerned in the management of a company . . . Such statements may be helpful in identifying particular circumstances in which a person would clearly be unfit. But there seems to have been a tendency, which I deplore, on the part of the Bar, and possibly also on the part of the official receiver's department, to treat the statements as judicial paraphrases of the words of the statute, which fall to be construed as a matter of law in lieu of the words of the statute. The result is to obscure that the true question to be tried is a question of fact—what used to be pejoratively described in the Chancery Division as 'a jury question'."[70]

4–23 The implication of *Sevenoaks Stationers* is that unfitness is simply a question of fact. The courts are not to put any wider judicial gloss on the statutory language. Furthermore, as a question of fact, any relevant judicial determination will be subject to more limited review by an appellate court compared with a question of law. The approach in *Sevenoaks Stationers* can be criticised. It will be seen below that the court is required by CDDA s.9 to have particular regard to the matters mentioned in Sch.1. However, Sch.1 is not exhaustive and the court is therefore entitled to take into account conduct that does not necessarily fall within the Schedule in order to determine whether or not the defendant is unfit.[71] On the face of the statute, the concept of unfit conduct is far from straightforward. It is arguable that the courts need to formulate some principles to enable consistency of judicial approach and to guide directors. Moreover, it is difficult to see how the question of what conduct does or does not make a person unfit can be classified purely as a question of fact. It is implicit in the concept of unfitness that the court is being asked to assess the defendant's behaviour against some objective benchmark. The difficult question of where one draws the line between conduct that is objectively fit and objectively unfit, albeit one primarily of degree, must at least in some sense be a question of law. It is preferable therefore to classify the question as one of mixed law and fact, as indeed the Court of Appeal did in *Grayan*.[72] These concerns may explain why some judges, while paying lip-service to Dillon L.J.'s dictum, have continued to provide generalised descriptions of the nature of the conduct that they

[70] [1991] Ch. 164 at 176. See also, in a slightly different context, the citation from Morritt L.J. at 3–37.
[71] See 4–46.
[72] *Re Grayan Building Services Ltd, Secretary of State for Trade and Industry v Gray* [1995] Ch. 241 at 254. See also *Re Crystal Palace Football Club (1986) Ltd, Secretary of State for Trade and Industry v Goldberg* [2004] 1 B.C.L.C. 597 at [14]; *Re Finelist Ltd, Secretary of State for Trade and*

have found amounts to unfitness.[73] At the same time, Dillon L.J.'s preference for a narrow focus on the facts and the plain words of the statute has been followed closely in several cases, which is perhaps not surprising given the status of the *Sevenoaks Stationers* decision.[74] Moreover, an approach that emphasises the autonomy of the statute and, by implication, devalues the extensive citation of decided cases while also limiting the scope for appellate review, is likely to remain attractive given the present procedural climate in which, post-Woolf, the courts in England and Wales have been forced to become increasingly costs conscious.[75]

4–24 Since *Sevenoaks Stationers* the courts have increasingly relied less on general dicta from earlier authorities such as *Dawson Print* and *Lo-Line* and there has been a shift towards a judicial language of "proper standards". In *Re Keypak Homecare Ltd*, a case decided shortly before the Court of Appeal ruled in *Sevenoaks Stationers*, Harman J. said that he preferred to use the phrase "lack of regard for proper standards" rather than "want of commercial morality" as the touchstone for unfitness.[76] A similar refrain has been taken up in subsequent cases. In *Re Pamstock Ltd*, Vinelott J. was obliged to disqualify the defendant for two years on finding that his conduct "fell short of the standard of conduct which is today expected of a director of a company which enjoys the privilege of limited

---

Industry v Swan [2005] EWHC 603 (Ch), [2005] B.C.C. 596 at [77]. In this respect the authors consider *Grayan* to be correct. There is no conflict of authority between *Grayan* and *Sevenoaks* on this point. In *Sevenoaks* the Court of Appeal interfered with the decision below and exercised its review powers in the same manner as it did in *Grayan*. On the issue of the threshold test generally see further S. Wheeler, "Re Sevenoaks—Continuing the Search for Principle" (1990) 6 Insolvency Law & Practice 174, arguing that an explanatory test is needed in the interests of establishing uniformity of approach, and D. Henry, "Disqualification of Directors: A View from the Inside" in H. Rajak (ed.), *Insolvency Law: Theory and Practice* (London: Sweet and Maxwell, 1993) in pp.182–183, exploring the problem from a regulatory perspective.

[73] See, e.g. *Re CSTC Ltd, Secretary of State for Trade and Industry v Van Hengel* [1995] 1 B.C.L.C. 545 (phrases like "grossly negligent", "totally incompetent" and "lack of moral probity" used as labels for unfit conduct although the court acknowledged that the words "unfit to be concerned in the management of a company" are ordinary English words that are simple to apply); *Re Polly Peck International Plc (No. 2), Secretary of State for Trade and Industry v Ellis* [1994] 1 B.C.L.C. 574; *Re Living Images Ltd* [1996] 1 B.C.L.C. 348 (two cases that reiterate Dillon L.J.'s dictum but go on to suggest that an order for disqualification can only be made if the defendant has acted in a way which is "serious" or "blameworthy"). For cases that refer to or echo pre-*Sevenoaks Stationers* approaches see also *Re ECM (Europe) Electronics Ltd* [1992] B.C.L.C. 814; *Re Swift 736 Ltd, Secretary of State for Trade and Industry v Ettinger* [1993] B.C.L.C. 896; *Re Looe Fish Ltd* [1993] B.C.L.C. 1160; *Re Moonlight Foods (UK) Ltd, Secretary of State for Trade and Industry v Hickling* [1996] B.C.C. 678; *Re Deaduck Ltd, Secretary of State for Trade and Industry v Baker* [2000] 1 B.C.L.C. 148; *Re Skyward Builders Plc, Official Receiver v Broad* [2002] EWHC 2786 (Ch); *Secretary of State for Trade and Industry v Blackwood* [2003] S.L.T. 120.

[74] See, e.g. *Re Samuel Sherman Plc* [1991] 1 W.L.R. 1070; *Re GSAR Realisations Ltd* [1993] B.C.L.C. 409; *Re Hitco 2000 Ltd, Official Receiver v Cowan* [1995] 2 B.C.L.C. 63; *Re Ward Sherrard Ltd* [1996] B.C.C. 418; *Re Amaron Ltd, Secretary of State for Trade and Industry v Lubrani (No.2)* [1997] 2 B.C.L.C. 115; *Re JA Chapman & Co Ltd, Secretary of State for Trade and Industry v Amiss* [2003] 2 B.C.L.C. 206; *Re Claims Direct Plc, Secretary of State for Business, Enterprise and Regulatory Reform v Sullman* [2008] EWHC 3179 (Ch), [2009] 1 B.C.L.C. 397.

[75] The "broad brush approach" to the question of unfitness and the period of disqualification called for by the Court of Appeal in *Re Westmid Packing Services Ltd, Secretary of State for Trade and Industry v Griffiths* [1998] 2 All E.R. 124 also reflects the modern procedural disposition.

[76] [1990] B.C.L.C. 440 at 444.

liability".[77] In *Re Swift 736 Ltd, Secretary of State for Trade and Industry v Ettinger* and *Re Grayan Building Services Ltd, Secretary of State for Trade and Industry v Gray*, two cases which stress the value of disqualification as a general deterrent, the Court of Appeal spoke of "ordinary standards of commercial morality"[78] and posited the idea that conduct falling below the "appropriate standard" will attract disqualification.[79] In *Grayan*, it was made abundantly clear that a major concern of the CDDA is to raise standards of conduct. Thus, in determining unfitness, the court is required, in the words of Hoffmann L.J., to:

> "... decide whether [the relevant] conduct, viewed cumulatively ... has fallen below the standards of probity and competence appropriate for persons to be fit to be directors of companies".[80]

4–25 On an application for a disqualification order under either s.6 or s.8, it is clear in the light of *Grayan* that the question of whether or not the defendant is unfit to be concerned in the management of a company should be classified as a mixed question of law and fact. In each case, the judge has to make primary findings of fact and then decide, on the facts as found, whether the defendant's conduct fell short of a standard of probity and competence fixed by the court.[81] The "standard of probity and competence" therefore amounts to an objective test used by the courts to distinguish between unfitness and conduct falling short of unfitness. The modern emphasis on standards suggests that the courts take seriously the idea that disqualification has value as a deterrent and as a means of improving directors' awareness of their legal obligations. The recourse to an objective standard fixed by the court disposes of the notion in *Sevenoaks Stationers* that unfitness is purely a question of fact.[82] Equally, however, it is fair to say that general judicial statements provide no guidance as to the substantive content of the appropriate standard. Thus, there is just as much scope for the court to vary the standard according to the dictates of policy and the circumstances of individual cases as there was with the older threshold tests. Ultimately, as discussed further in Ch.5, the detail of cases decided under ss.6 and 8 is a surer source of practical guidance on the types of misconduct that are likely

[77] [1994] 1 B.C.L.C. 716 at 736.
[78] [1993] B.C.L.C. 896 at 899.
[79] [1995] Ch. 241 at 253.
[80] [1995] Ch. 241 at 253.
[81] [1995] Ch. 241 at 253. See further *Re Landhurst Leasing Plc, Secretary of State for Trade and Industry v Ball* [1999] 1 B.C.L.C. 286 at 344; *Goldberg v Secretary of State for Trade and Industry* [2001] EWCA Civ 1237 at [29]–[30]; *Re Bradcrown Ltd, Official Receiver v Ireland* [2001] 1 B.C.L.C. 547 at [9]; *Re Structural Concrete Ltd, Official Receiver v Barnes* [2001] B.C.C. 578 at 586; *Re Finelist Ltd, Secretary of State for Trade and Industry v Swan* [2005] B.C.C. 596 at [79]; *Re Mayfair Interiors (Wolverhampton) Ltd, Secretary of State for Trade and Industry v Blunt* [2005] 2 B.C.L.C. 463 at [19]; *Re Amba Rescue Ltd, Secretary of State for Trade and Industry v Hollier* [2007] B.C.C. 11 at [52]; *Re Bunting Electric Manufacturing Co Ltd, Secretary of State for Trade and Industry v Golby* [2006] 1 B.C.L.C. 550 at [26].
[82] Implicit in the conflict between the approaches in *Sevenoaks Stationers* (unfitness as a question of fact) and *Grayan* (unfitness as a question of mixed law and fact) are deeper questions about the autonomy of the trial judge in disqualification proceedings and the extent to which an appellate court will intervene with the trial judge's findings.

to attract disqualification than any general test. In this context, Lewison J.'s rejection of a suggestion that the question of whether a person is fit or unfit should be considered under the broad headings of "competence", "discipline" and "honesty" is striking.[83] Rather like an elephant, unfit conduct tends to be immediately recognisable, even though it may be difficult to define in general terms.

Applying the standard of probity and competence

4–26 If the defendant's conduct is dishonest in the sense of being criminally culpable it will almost certainly fall short of the standard required of directors.[84] Want of probity, falling short of dishonesty but nevertheless amounting to unfitness, gives rise to difficulties when discussed in the abstract but in practice is usually easily identified.[85] However, it should be stressed that the standard fixed by the court is one of probity and competence. Accordingly, the claimant is not required to establish that the defendant's conduct was criminally culpable. Unfitness can be proved without the need to establish dishonesty or fraud. Indeed, in several cases the courts have imposed disqualification orders of five years or more while acknowledging that the defendant had not been deliberately defrauding creditors or otherwise acting dishonestly.[86] It is enough that the defendant's conduct does not measure up to the required standard of competence.

4–27 A further important aspect of the decision in *Sevenoaks* is that the Court of Appeal set the standard of competence expected from directors at a higher level than that set in previous cases. In the words of Dillon L.J.:

> "... I have no doubt at all that it is amply proved that [the defendant] is unfit to be concerned in the management of a company. His trouble is not dishonesty, but incompetence or negligence in a very marked degree and that is enough to render him unfit; I

[83] *Re Crystal Palace Football Club (1986) Ltd, Secretary of State for Trade and Industry v Goldberg* [2004] 1 B.C.L.C. 597 at [16] to [41].

[84] Dishonesty is itself a highly nuanced concept that can be tested subjectively (according to whether the defendant believed what he was doing was dishonest) or objectively (on the basis of whether a point of reference, such as the ordinary honest member of society, would have regarded the conduct as dishonest). The current preference in both the criminal and civil law seems to be for tests of dishonesty that incorporate at least some objective element: see, e.g. *R. v Ghosh* [1982] Q.B. 1053; *Royal Brunei Airways v Tan* [1995] 2 A.C. 378; *Twinsectra Ltd v Yardley* [2002] UKHL 12; [2002] 2 A.C. 164; *Barlow Clowes International Ltd v Eurotrust International Ltd* [2005] UKPC 37, [2006] 1 W.L.R. 1476; *Abou-Rahmah v Abacha* [2006] EWCA Civ 1492, [2007] 1 Lloyd's Rep. 115.

[85] *Re Crystal Palace Football Club (1986) Ltd, Secretary of State for Trade and Industry v Goldberg* [2004] 1 B.C.L.C. 597 at [38] to [41].

[86] See, e.g. *Sevenoaks Stationers* itself (defendant disqualified for seven years reduced to five on appeal where conduct not dishonest but markedly incompetent); *Re Melcast (Wolverhampton) Ltd* [1991] B.C.L.C. 288 (two defendants disqualified for seven and four years respectively despite the court finding that they had not acted dishonestly in the sense of lining their own pockets at the expense of creditors); *Re Austinsuite Furniture Ltd* [1992] B.C.L.C. 1047; *Re Thorncliffe Finance Ltd, Secretary of State for Trade and Industry v Arif* [1997] 1 B.C.L.C. 34 (in both cases one defendant disqualified for seven years despite no finding of dishonesty); *Re Linvale Ltd* [1993] B.C.L.C. 654 (two defendants disqualified for five years despite no finding of dishonesty); *Re Skyward Builders Plc, Official Receiver v Broad* [2002] EWHC 2786 (Ch) (defendant disqualified for six years where conduct not dishonest but markedly incompetent). The cases suggest that most disqualifications of less than five years are for misconduct that could not be classified as dishonest or fraudulent.

do not think it is necessary for incompetence to be 'total', as suggested by the Vice-Chancellor in *Re Lo-Line Electric Motors Ltd*, to render a director unfit to take part in the management of a company."[87]

The clear implication is that conduct falling short of "total incompetence" or "total negligence" may amount to unfit conduct attracting mandatory disqualification. As such, *Sevenoaks Stationers* marks a shift towards a more exacting judicial standard of directorial competence and a lower threshold test for unfitness. Nevertheless, where the case against the defendant is based solely on allegations of incompetence without dishonesty, the burden is on the claimant to satisfy the court that the conduct complained of demonstrates incompetence of a high degree given the serious nature of a disqualification order.[88] However, the required degree of incompetence should not be exaggerated bearing in mind the ability of the court to grant a disqualified person permission to take part in the management of specified companies.[89] The issue of disqualification on grounds of incompetence is considered further in Ch.5.

4–28 In applying the standard, the court must recognise that it is blessed with hindsight. In this respect, the following passage from Laddie J.'s judgment in *Re Living Images Ltd* is instructive:

"By the time an application comes before the court, the conduct of the directors has to be judged on the basis of statements given to the official receiver, no doubt frequently under stress, and a comparatively small collection of documents selected to support the [claimant's] and the [defendants'] respective positions. On the basis of this the court has to pass judgment on the way in which the directors conducted the affairs of the company over a period of days, weeks or . . . months. Those statements are analysed in the clinical atmosphere of the courtroom. They are analysed, for example, with the benefit of knowing that the company went into liquidation. It is very easy therefore to look at the signals available to the directors at the time and to assume that they, or any other competent director, would have realised that the end was coming. The court must be careful not to fall into the trap of being too wise after the event."[90]

In relation to allegations of incompetence, as opposed to dishonesty, it may well be that the burden on the claimant to demonstrate that the conduct was incompetent in a high degree is itself a safeguard against the operation of hindsight.[91]

[87] [1991] Ch. 164 at 184.

[88] *Re Barings Plc (No. 5), Secretary of State for Trade and Industry v Baker* [1999] 1 B.C.L.C. 433 at 483–484 approved on the point by the Court of Appeal: [2000] 1 B.C.L.C. 523 at [35]. See also *Re Cubelock Ltd, Secretary of State for Trade and Industry v Dodds* [2001] B.C.C. 523 at [50]–[53]; *Re Bradcrown Ltd, Official Receiver v Ireland* [2001] 1 B.C.L.C. 547 at [10]; *Secretary of State for Trade and Industry v Walker* [2003] 1 B.C.L.C. 363 at [48]–[50]; *Re Finelist Ltd, Secretary of State for Trade and Industry v Swan* [2005] B.C.C. 596 at [80]; *Re Amba Rescue Ltd, Secretary of State for Trade and Industry v Hollier* [2007] B.C.C. 11 at [53]–[54].

[89] *Re Barings Plc (No. 5), Secretary of State for Trade and Industry v Baker* [2000] 1 B.C.L.C. 523 at [35].

[90] [1996] B.C.L.C. 348 at 356.

[91] *Secretary of State for Trade and Industry v Walker* [2003] 1 B.C.L.C. 363 at [48]–[50].

Section 6(2): conduct connected with the company's insolvency

4–29 Where a relevant company (including a collateral company) has become insolvent, the court can expressly take into account the defendant's conduct "in relation to any matter connected with or arising out of the insolvency of that company" in determining whether or not he is unfit for the purposes of s.6. This is the effect of the closing words of s.6(2). The wording was clearly intended to cover misconduct such as a failure on the part of a director to co-operate with an office holder.[92] As such, this part of s.6(2) clearly overlaps with some of the specific criteria mentioned in Sch.1 Pt II (which include failure to submit a statement of affairs, failure to deliver up company property and failure to co-operate with an office holder).[93] The wording also makes clear that matters such as a failure to co-operate under s.235 of the Insolvency Act 1986 would be relevant in determining unfitness even if, at the time of the failure to co-operate, the person was only a former director.

4–30 However, judicial treatment of the wording has widened its scope beyond matters of non-co-operation. In *Re Bath Glass Ltd*, Peter Gibson J. suggested that it was directed at the phoenix syndrome because it would allow the court to treat the defendant's conduct in causing a new company to arise phoenix-like from the ashes of an insolvent company as conduct "connected with or arising out of the insolvency" of the latter.[94] This is one possible analysis. However, depending on the precise circumstances, it is submitted that it would be possible to rely directly upon the conduct of the defendant as a director of the successor company (assuming that he is a director of that company). This would accord more closely with s.216 of the Insolvency Act 1986 and the defendant's conduct in relation to the successor company could then be taken into account as a collateral matter to be considered together with his conduct in relation to the insolvent company, as contemplated by s.6(1)(b).[95]

4–31 A further question that has arisen is whether, and to what extent, in determining unfitness, the court can take into account the defendant's conduct during the course of the disqualification proceedings. In *Re Godwin Warren Plc*, Chadwick J. expressed the view that disqualification proceedings are themselves "matters connected with or arising out of the insolvency of the company in respect of which they are brought" with the implication that misconduct on the defendant's part in the proceedings, such as attempts to conceal evidence or otherwise mislead the court could be taken into account as additional material relevant to the issue of unfitness.[96] This reasoning was followed at first instance by Warner J. in *Re Moorgate Metals Ltd, Official Receiver v Huhtala*[97] and Laddie J. in *Re*

[92] Parliamentary Debates, H.C. Standing Committee E, Session 1984–85, Vol.IV, col.96.

[93] See paras 4–42 to 4–43.

[94] *Re Bath Glass Ltd* [1988] B.C.L.C. 329 at 331.

[95] See further Ch.3. It would not matter if the successor company was solvent and trading successfully. Moreover, it is clear that conduct as a director of one company may be criticised because of its effect on another company provided the criticisms are framed with sufficient particularity: see *Re Diamond Computer Systems Ltd* [1997] 1 B.C.L.C. 174 at 180H to 181.

[96] [1993] B.C.L.C. 80 at 91–92.

[97] [1995] 1 B.C.L.C. 503.

Living Images Ltd[98] and has subsequently been approved by the Court of Appeal in *Re Howglen Ltd, Secretary of State for Trade and Industry v Reynard*.[99]

4–32 In *Howglen*, the defendant was originally disqualified by Mr Registrar Simmonds for a period of ten years. The registrar found all the pleaded allegations of unfitness proved and also found the defendant to be "a most unsatisfactory witness in that he was disingenuous, equivocal and on some occasions untruthful". On appeal, Blackburne J. held that the registrar had been fully justified in finding that unfitness was established but reduced the period of disqualification to five and a half years. In so doing, the judge declined to take into account the registrar's finding that the defendant was an unsatisfactory witness and expressly demurred from the proposition that:

> "a director's performance in the witness box can provide a discrete head of misconduct or justify a longer period of disqualification than would otherwise have been imposed."

Blackburne J.'s conclusion turned on s.6(1)(b) and s.6(2), both of which require the court to evaluate the defendant's "conduct as a director". Accordingly, and plausibly, the judge ruled that:

> "[w]hat the court is concerned with is the director's conduct as a director, not with his conduct as a defendant in court proceedings."

He added that the notion that the defendant's conduct in the proceedings could be considered in determining unfitness was inconsistent with Dillon L.J.'s observations in *Re Sevenoaks Stationers (Retail) Ltd* to the effect that the defendant should know in advance the substance of the charges that he is required to meet.[100] This latter point is, with respect, not a good one. It has long been recognised that evidence of unfitness may emerge in the course of the proceedings, even at trial, and that, if no injustice is thereby caused, it may be appropriate to allow the Secretary of State to rely upon it.[101] In *Howglen* the Court of Appeal rightly rejected this point.

4–33 The Court of Appeal upheld the five and a half year disqualification but allowed the Secretary of State's appeal against Blackburne J.'s ruling on the point of principle on the following grounds:

(1) Section 6(2) was wide enough to include in the expression "conduct of a person as a director", his conduct in the proceedings against him for a disqualification order. The proceedings were a "matter connected with or arising out of the insolvency" of the company (a point that follows from s.6(1)(a)) and there was no reason for cutting down the width of the statutory language so as to exclude the conduct of the defendant during those proceedings. (This is essentially the same reasoning that Chadwick J. employed in *Godwin Warren*).

[98] [1996] 1 B.C.L.C. 348.
[99] [2002] EWCA Civ 497, [2002] 2 B.C.L.C. 625.
[100] [1991] Ch. 164 at 177. See further from 7–104.
[101] See discussion in 7–108.

(2) Although the defendant's conduct in the proceedings was not expressly referred to in Sch.1 as a matter to which the court must have regard in determining unfitness, the Schedule is not exhaustive. (This point of general importance is taken up later in this chapter).

(3) According to Mummery L.J. (with whom Latham and Pill L.JJ. agreed), in giving evidence on issues relating to his involvement in the management of a company, the defendant may provide the court with additional evidence of his unfitness for office. The finding of the court on his conduct as a witness on such points is therefore capable of amounting to an additional ground of unfitness and can properly be taken into account in fixing the period of disqualification.

4–34 It is helpful to separate out a number of discrete points. The first point relates to evidence given by the defendant that sheds light on the allegations of unfitness pleaded against him. Clearly, the defendant's evidence forms part of the evidence that the court is required to evaluate. So, for example, if it is alleged that the defendant caused a company to trade while insolvent to the detriment of creditors and, during cross-examination, he admits that he knew that the company was insolvent and that he caused it to continue trading contrary to professional advice, his evidence is clearly relevant to the question of whether the alleged misconduct makes him unfit.[102] A separate but related point is that the defendant's performance in the witness box, and his evidence, whether or not directly related to the matters of unfitness alleged against him, may well throw light on his credit as a witness and may therefore be relevant in assessing the weight to be given to his evidence on the matters of unfitness alleged. Furthermore, if evidence is given which discloses additional matters of misconduct unconnected to the trial then, again, and subject to whether it would be fair to permit the claimant's case to be altered to encompass the new matters, such matters would be relevant as further matters of unfitness. Such evidence may also be relevant in confirming the case against the defendant on the other allegations.[103] However, the fact that the court may take into account the defendant's conduct of his defence (including his evidence in the witness box) in the manner just described follows from the trial process and, in the view of the authors, has nothing whatsoever to do with s.6(2).

4–35 The next discrete point concerns the case where the director's conduct of his defence, including his performance in the witness box, bears upon the question of whether or not he has learned his lesson and is likely to engage in similar patterns

[102] It appears that in *Howglen* the Registrar relied on the defendant's disingenuous evidence at trial to support his findings of fact that at the time of the misconduct the director ignored warnings as to the financial state of the company and/or that he lacked sufficient business acumen to realise what was being said to him: see the last sentence of para.[15] of Mummery L.J.'s judgment.

[103] See, e.g. *Re Hitco 2000 Ltd, Official Receiver v Cowan* [1995] 2 B.C.L.C. 63 where the defendant's signing of blank cheques, which emerged from evidence given at trial, was not permitted as a new allegation of unfit conduct but was nevertheless taken into account by the judge as being relevant to the main pleaded allegation that the defendant had permitted the company to trade while insolvent having effectively abdicated responsibility for the company's affairs. It is suggested that the judge in *Hitco* treated the evidence as confirming his findings of fact on the main allegation.

of misconduct in the future. To the extent that the evidence shows that the director has learned his lesson (for example, by reference to his subsequent conduct) then clearly such evidence can be taken into account in fixing the period of disqualification. However, to the extent that his evidence shows that he is an unreformed character, it has been suggested that such evidence cannot be relied on as exacerbating the original misconduct. The reason for this is that the only misconduct which can be relied on in fixing the period of disqualification is misconduct relied on and proved as a separate matter of unfitness.[104] This is essentially the conclusion that Blackburne J. appears to have reached at first instance in *Howglen*. However, the Court of Appeal considered that this approach was too narrow. In this respect they approved the decision and approach of Chadwick J. in *Re Godwin Warren Control Systems Plc*.

In *Godwin Warren*, the company ("Systems") acquired the assets and business of another company ("Solutions") in which the first defendant had a substantial interest. The first and second defendants, who were both executive directors of Systems, concealed the first defendant's interest in the acquisition from Systems' non-executive directors, auditors and professional advisers. The second defendant told the court that he had believed that his co-defendant held only a small shareholding in Solutions and had notified the other directors of this fact. Chadwick J. rejected his evidence and found that he had deliberately sought to mislead the court. The judge continued:

> ". . . I am bound to take the view that his attempt to deceive this court . . . is an indication that he does not yet appreciate that the need for disclosure to shareholders in a public company of transactions with associates is a serious requirement and not something to be brushed aside as a technicality. I think that the vice which can be identified in his conduct in relation to the acquisition of the business of Solutions would be likely to recur if no disqualification order was made."[105]

He then went on to suggest that it would be a strange result if the court was prevented from considering under s.6(1) whether or not the director properly appreciated the vice that had brought him before the court. He ruled that the court could and should take this into account and was entitled to do so under s.6(2). It is clear that the Court of Appeal in *Howglen* accepted Chadwick J.'s analysis. The question remaining is whether the decision in *Howglen* goes wider and enables (and requires) the court to take into account, as a separate ground of unfitness, any aspect of the defendant's performance in the witness box which suggests that the defendant is unfit to be concerned in the management of a company (for example, because he lies on oath and therefore can be presumed to lack the integrity required of company directors).

4–36 Part of Pill L.J.'s judgment in *Howglen* appears to limit the extent to which conduct in the proceedings (including the witness box) can be taken into account. He expressly relied on the *Godwin Warren* reasoning but made it clear that he

[104] *Re Sevenoaks Stationers (Retail) Ltd* [1991] Ch. 164.
[105] [1993] B.C.L.C. 80 at 92.

would not have regarded it as appropriate to increase the period of disqualification "for unsatisfactory performance as a witness". It is against this background that he approved those parts of Mummery L.J.'s judgment which suggest that the director's evidence on issues relating to his involvement in the management of the company may provide additional evidence of unfitness.[106] However, his approval of the last two sentences of para.[16] of Mummery L.J.'s judgment mean that Pill L.J. expressly accepted that findings regarding conduct as a witness "is a factor capable of amounting to an additional ground of unfitness".

4–37 Mummery L.J.'s leading judgment is clearer on this issue:

> "[The director's] conduct as a defendant in the proceedings, including the giving of evidence, is a matter which is capable of being taken into account in determining his fitness to be concerned in the management of a company. The expression 'performance in the witness box' does not convey the substance of the essential point, which is that, in his evidence on issues relating to his involvement in the management of the company, the defendant may provide the court with additional evidence of his unfitness for office. The finding of the court on his conduct as a witness on such points is capable of amounting to an additional ground of his unfitness and is a factor capable of being taken into account in fixing the period of disqualification."[107]

If, for example, the director is shown to be dishonest because he lies to the court in his evidence then could this amount to a separate matter of unfitness that would justify an increase in the period of disqualification? The first sentence quoted above and the reference to "conduct as a witness . . . amounting to an additional ground of . . . unfitness" tend to suggest that Mummery L.J. would answer the question in the affirmative. However, it is suggested that the better approach would be to limit the use to which such evidence can be put.[108]

4–38 The difficulty with the *Howglen* reasoning is as follows. If a person's conduct in relation to disqualification proceedings is itself a matter "connected with or arising out of" the insolvency of the company, then why (if this is what Pill L.J. was saying) should such conduct only be taken into account as a matter of unfitness and to increase the period of disqualification if it shows, in relation to the past misconduct relied on, that the defendant has not learned his lesson and/or is unrepentant and/or still does not appreciate that what he did was unacceptable? Why is it not also relevant conduct that the director lied in giving evidence, even if the lie is only relevant to credit and not directly to the matters of past misconduct relied on by the claimant? Similarly, if, as Mummery L.J. seems to say, conduct as a witness can found a separate ground of unfitness then why should lying in giving evidence not constitute a potential separate ground of unfitness? Suppose that the original matters of misconduct are not made out but it is clear

[106] [2002] 2 B.C.L.C. 625 at [26], especially Pill L.J.'s express approval of the last two sentences of para.[16] in the judgment of Mummery L.J.

[107] [2002] B.C.L.C. 625 at [16]. Emphasis added.

[108] See, in particular, Mummery L.J.'s approval of the approach taken by Mr Registrar Simmonds, [2002] B.C.L.C. 625 at para.[15] which suggests that the manner in which the defendant gives his evidence may be relied on to support or reinforce the court's findings of fact in relation to the alleged misconduct.

that the defendant lied outrageously in the witness box; should this be capable of establishing unfitness?

4–39 The preferred analysis of the authors is that s.6(2) does not enable a court to take into account the manner of conducting the defence as a matter "connected with or arising out of the insolvency of that company". In their view, the words "conduct in relation to any matter connected with or arising out of the insolvency" are governed by the general requirement in ss.6(1)(b) and 6(2) that conduct must in essence be "conduct as a director" (essentially the position taken by Blackburne J.). When a defendant gives evidence in disqualification proceedings, he gives it on his own behalf and is no longer acting "as a director" at that point. The wording of s.6(2), it is respectfully suggested, is directed at dealing with matters where the misconduct relates to obligations that the defendant owed to, or in relation to, the insolvent company arising from his position as a director or former director. Thus, it would cover the matters expressly scheduled in Pt II of Sch.1 such as failure to co-operate with the liquidator under s.235 of the Insolvency Act 1986 or failure to account for company property. It would also (for example) cover lying as a witness in proceedings brought for the benefit of, or against, the company in liquidation. However, in his conduct of the disqualification proceedings, the defendant owes no duties to the company of which he was a director and he is not carrying out any function of a directorial nature nor any function that derives from his obligations as a former director.[109] This interpretation is further strengthened by a consideration of the position regarding proceedings brought under CDDA s.8. In s.8 proceedings the court may make a disqualification order where it is satisfied that the defendant's "conduct in relation to the company makes him unfit to be concerned in the management of a company". On the face of it, there is no extended wording in s.8(2) that would allow the court to take into account the defendant's conduct during proceedings under that provision.[110] To suggest that conduct during proceedings could amount to "conduct in relation to the company" is straining language. It is doubtful that, in enacting ss.6(2) and 8(2), Parliament intended the defendant's conduct during proceedings to be relevant to the question of unfitness under one provision but not the other. This argument can be applied with even greater force when considering the other "gateways" to civil disqualification in CDDA ss.2 to 4, 9A and 10.

4–40 The authors' approach to the interpretation of s.6(2) would avoid the sort of result that the Court of Appeal in *Howglen* (or Pill L.J. on one view of his judgment) appeared to consider to be incorrect: namely that a defendant could find himself disqualified for a longer period based simply on his performance in the witness box. However, would this mean that the court could not take into account the manner in which the defendant conducted his defence in so far as it suggests that he has not learned his lesson, which the court appears to have done in *Godwin Warren* and (apparently) *Howglen*? The authors suggest that the court can, and indeed should,

[109] The position may conceivably be different if disqualification proceedings are coupled with civil recovery proceedings under the Insolvency Act as was the case in *Official Receiver v Doshi* [2001] 2 B.C.L.C. 235.

[110] Though, against this view, it might be said that s.8 is not necessarily exhaustive.

take account of such evidence. However, the way to ensure that it is properly taken into account is for the court to refuse to discount the period of disqualification, as it would do if satisfied that the director had learned his lesson.[111] In short, the authors respectfully suggest that, in the material respects, *Howglen* and *Godwin Warren* were correctly decided on their facts but that the legal explanation given for the decisions was wrong. In the light of the approach taken in *Howglen* to the construction of s.6(2), it is very difficult to see why a defendant to s.6 proceedings is not at risk of being disqualified purely on the basis of his conduct in the proceedings and thus in a manner which the Court of Appeal appears to have rejected. The outcome in legal terms of the *Howglen* decision is, at best, confusing.

Schedule 1 of the CDDA

4–41 The starting point for the court faced with the task of determining, under CDDA ss.6 or 8, whether or not the defendant is unfit to be concerned in the management of a company is the CDDA itself. Section 9 requires the court to have regard in particular to the matters mentioned in Pt I of Sch.1 and, where the relevant company has "become insolvent",[112] also to the matters mentioned in Pt II of that Schedule. Thus, a distinction is drawn for these purposes between solvent and insolvent companies. The effect of s.6(1)(a) is that the lead company in proceedings for an order under s.6 must have "become insolvent". This means that in relation to a lead company in s.6 proceedings, the court must have regard to all the matters in Sch.1.[113] The position is the same in relation to any collateral company unless a particular collateral company has not become insolvent, in which case the court is only directed to consider the matters in Pt I of the Schedule in relation to that company.[114]

The starting point in determining unfitness under s.8 is again s.9, which directs the court's attention to Sch.1. The crucial difference between ss.6 and 8 is that under s.8 the relevant company need not have become insolvent. It is possible for the Secretary of State to commence s.8 proceedings in relation to a solvent company, in which case the court is only required to pay particular regard to the matters mentioned in Pt I of the Schedule.[115] However, a company under investigation may often be or become insolvent. If so, the Secretary of State has a choice and can apply for an order under

[111] See further paras 5–115 to 5–116.

[112] As defined by CDDA s.6(2). Section 9(2) states that s.6(2) "applies for the purposes of [s.9] and Sch.1 as it applies for the purposes of ss.6 and 7".

[113] To the extent that the claimant relies on such matters: see *Re Launchexcept Ltd, Secretary of State for Trade and Industry v Tillman* [2000] 1 B.C.L.C. 36.

[114] It was indicated in *Re Country Farm Inns Ltd, Secretary of State for Trade and Industry v Ivens* [1997] 2 B.C.L.C. 334 at 345 that, at least at that time, the Secretary of State was unlikely ever to rely on a defendant's conduct as a director of a solvent collateral company. However, the attitude of the Secretary of State in no way affects the construction of s.6 as to jurisdiction and may since have changed in any event. There are positive reasons in the public interest (in particular, the notion that disqualification is concerned with raising standards of conduct) why such an approach should not be followed. A prime example of relevant conduct that may arise in relation to a solvent collateral company is a breach of s.216 of the Insolvency Act 1986 which restricts re-use of a prohibited company name.

[115] This however does not preclude the court from taking into matters mentioned in Pt II of the Schedule even where the relevant company is solvent: *Ghassemian v Secretary of State for Trade and Industry* [2006] EWHC 1715 (Ch), [2007] B.C.C. 229 at paras [22]–[27].

either s.6 or 8. In these circumstances, the Secretary of State can choose to proceed under s.6, given that a finding of unfitness would result in mandatory disqualification.[116] However, if the decision is taken to proceed against the director of an insolvent company under s.8, it is clear that the court is directed to have particular regard to the matters in Pt II of the Schedule, that are applicable where a company has become insolvent, as well as the general matters in Pt I.[117] The key question is the same as it is in s.6, i.e. does the defendant's previous conduct make him unfit? There is no doubt that, in an appropriate case, the court can take into account many, if not all, of the specific instances of unfit conduct that have arisen in the context of s.6. As such, the fact that certain cases are decided under s.8 does little to aid understanding of the concept of unfitness. These cases are simply further factual examples of cases where unfitness was found to have been established or not. In this context, it is to be observed that s.8 cases often tend to be concerned as much with issues of investor or shareholder protection as with creditor protection.[118] The specific contents of Schedule 1 are considered in the text immediately following.

Sch.1 Pt I—Matters Applicable in all Cases

4–42 In all cases where the court is asked to decide whether the defendant's conduct makes him unfit the court must have regard, in particular, to the following matters:

(1) Any misfeasance or breach of any fiduciary or other duty by the director in relation to the company, including in particular any breach by the director under Ch.2 of Pt 10 of the Companies Act 2006 (general duties of directors) owed to the company.[119]
(2) Any misapplication or retention by the director of, or any conduct by the director giving rise to an obligation to account for, any money or other property of the company.
(3) The extent of the director's responsibility for the company entering into any transaction liable to be set aside under Pt XVI of the Insolvency Act (provisions against debt avoidance).
(4) The extent of the director's responsibility for any failure by the company to comply with any of the following provisions of the Companies Act 2006—

[116] As was the case in *Re CSTC Ltd, Secretary of State for Trade and Industry v Van Hengel* [1995] 1 B.C.L.C. 545 despite the fact that relevant evidence had been obtained pursuant to s.105 of the Financial Services Act 1986 with the consequence that proceedings could presumably also have been commenced under s.8. In other cases, s.8 may be favoured because it is not subject to the restriction in s.7(2) which prevents proceedings under s.6 from being commenced without the permission of the court later than two years from the date on which the relevant company became insolvent within the meaning of s.6(2).

[117] See *Re TMS (GB) Ltd, Secretary of State for Trade and Industry v White*, November 26, 1993, Ch.D., unreported.

[118] See text from 5–70. This is not surprising given the link between s.8 and company investigations.

[119] The reference to Ch.2 of Pt 10 of the Companies Act 2006 was inserted by SI 2009/1941 with effect from October 1, 2009.

(a) s.113 (register of members);
(b) s.114 (register to be kept available for inspection);
(c) s.162 (register of directors);
(d) s.165 (register of directors' residential addresses);
(e) s.167 (duty to notify registrar of changes: directors);
(f) s.275 (register of secretaries);
(g) s.276 (duty to notify registrar of changes: secretaries);
(h) s.386 (duty to keep accounting records);
(i) s.388 (where and for how long accounting records to be kept);
(j) s.854 (duty to make annual returns);
(k) s.860 (duty to register charges);
(l) s.78 (duty to register charges: companies registered in Scotland)[120]

(5) The extent of the director's responsibility for any failure by the directors of the company to comply with the following provisions of the Companies Act 2006—

(a) s.394 or s.399 (duty to prepare annual accounts);
(b) s.414 or 450 (approval and signature of abbreviated accounts); or
(c) s.433 (name of signatory to be stated in published copy of accounts).[121]

Sch.1 Pt II—Matters applicable where company has become insolvent

4–43 In all cases where the court is asked to decide whether the defendant's conduct makes him unfit and the relevant company or companies have become insolvent, the court must have regard, in particular, to the following matters set out in Pt II of the Schedule in addition to those in Pt I:

(6) The extent of the director's responsibility for the causes of the company becoming insolvent.
(7) The extent of the director's responsibility for any failure by the company to supply any goods or services which have been paid for (in whole or in part).
(8) The extent of the director's responsibility for the company entering into any transaction or giving any preference, being a transaction or preference—

(a) liable to be set aside under s.127 or ss.238 to 240 of the Insolvency Act 1986, or
(b) challengeable under s.242 or s.243 of that Act or under any rule of law in Scotland.

(9) The extent of the director's responsibility for any failure by the directors of the company to comply with s.98 of the Insolvency Act 1986 (duty to call creditors' meeting in creditors' voluntary winding up).

[120] The current para.(4) was substituted for the previous paras (4) and (4A) (which themselves had only been in force from April 1, 2008) by the Companies Act 2006 (Consequential Amendments, Transitional Provisions and Savings) Order 2009 (SI 2009/1941) with effect from October 1, 2009.

[121] The current para.(5) was substituted for its immediate predecessor by the Companies Act 2006 (Consequential Amendments etc.) Order 2008 (SI 2008/948) arts 3(1)(b), Sch.1, Pt 2, para.106(1), (8)(b) with effect from April 1, 2008.

(10) Any failure by the director to comply with any obligation imposed on him by or under any of the following provisions of the Insolvency Act 1986:

(a) para.47 of Sch.B1 (company's statement of affairs in administration)[122];
(b) s.47 (statement of affairs to administrative receiver);
(c) s.66 (statement of affairs in Scottish receivership);
(d) s.99 (directors' duty to attend meeting; statement of affairs in creditors' voluntary winding up);
(e) s.131 (statement of affairs in winding up by the court);
(f) s.234 (duty of any one with company property to deliver it up);
(g) s.235 (duty to co-operate with liquidator, etc.).

Power to alter the Schedule; Insolvent partnerships and limited liability partnerships

4–44 Power is delegated to the Secretary of State by CDDA ss.9(4)–(5) to make orders by statutory instrument modifying any of the provisions of Sch.1. Section 9 and the Schedule have been modified to deal with cases involving insolvent partnerships by the Insolvent Partnerships Order 1994, art.16 and Sch.8.[123] The Insolvent Partnerships Order does not amend the CDDA directly but provides that CDDA ss.1, 1A, 6 to 10, 13–15, 17, 19(c), 20 and Sch.1 apply to insolvent partnerships with the modifications set out in Sch.8 to the Order. Section 6 of the CDDA is modified to enable the court to take into account the person's conduct as an officer of the partnership (either taken alone or taken together with his conduct of any other partnership or partnerships or as a director or shadow director of any company or companies). Section 9 of the CDDA is also modified accordingly. Schedule 1 to the CDDA is adapted for use in the partnership context and there is reference, among other things, to an officer's failure to comply with certain provisions of the Limited Partnerships Act 1907. Similarly, art.4(2) of and Sch.2 Pt II to the Limited Liability Partnerships Regulations 2001[124] modifies the CDDA to deal with cases involving limited liability partnerships. One such modification is the reading of an additional para.8A into CDDA Sch.1 to enable the court, on an application to disqualify a member or shadow member of an insolvent limited liability partnership under CDDA s.6, to take into account the extent of the member's or shadow member's responsibility for events leading to a member or shadow member (whether himself or some other member or shadow member), being declared by the court to be liable to make a contribution to the assets of the limited liability partnership under s.214A of the Insolvency Act 1986.[125]

[122] See the Enterprise Act 2002 (Insolvency) Order 2003 (SI 2003/2096). Para.10(a) of the Schedule previously referred to s.22 of the Insolvency Act.

[123] SI 1994/2421 as amended by a series of Insolvent Partnerships (Amendment) Orders: SI 1996/1308 with effect from June 14, 1996; SI 2001/767 with effect from April 2, 2001; SI 2002/1308 with effect from May 31, 2002; SI 2005/1516 with effect from July 1, 2005; SI 2006/622 with effect from April 6, 2006.

[124] SI 2001/1090.

[125] The full text of the modifications made by the Insolvent Partnerships Order and the Limited Liability Partnership Regulations can be found in the appendices.

Building societies, incorporated friendly societies, NHS foundation trusts and open-ended investment companies

4–45 In relation to building societies, incorporated friendly societies, and NHS foundation trusts and open-ended investment companies to which the CDDA apply by virtue of ss.22A, 22B, 22C and 22D,[126] Sch.1 is to be read as if references to provisions of the Insolvency Act 1986 or the Companies Act 2006 included reference to the corresponding provisions of relevant legislation applying to such entities.[127]

History and legal status of Sch.1

4–46 The unfitness provisions now found in CDDA ss.6 to 9, together with the earliest version of Sch.1, were originally enacted in the Insolvency Act 1985. The idea of a detailed schedule of indicative factors appears to have first emerged during the course of the Parliamentary debates on the Insolvency Bill.[128] There was a consensus in Parliament that the term "unfit" was vague and that guidelines on the meaning of the term should be introduced into the legislation.[129] The theory was that guidelines were needed: (a) to assist the courts; (b) to provide general guidance to directors on how they should act; (c) to assist insolvency practitioners in compiling "unfitness" reports on directors of insolvent companies[130]; and (d) to assist the Secretary of State in deciding whether or not to commence proceedings in a particular case. The factors selected for inclusion in the Schedule reflected the experience of the Insolvency Service in dealing with the directors of failed companies up to that point in time and the comments of insolvency practitioners.[131] However, while there was general agreement that the Schedule ought to reinforce core statutory obligations (such as the duty of directors to keep accounting records which disclose with reasonable accuracy the company's financial position at any given moment), perhaps unsurprisingly, there was less consensus in the Parliamentary debate about what other specific factors should be included.[132]

Taken as a whole, Sch.1 reiterates a number of specific statutory obligations arising under the Companies Acts and the Insolvency Act while also bringing directors' duties generally within its scope. Sch.1 Pt 1 para.1 refers to breaches

[126] See 3–77 to 3–79.

[127] See CDDA ss.22A, 22B, 22C and 22D. The reference to the Companies Act 2006 in these provisions was first added by the Companies Act 2006 (Consequential Amendments etc) Order 2008 (SI 2008/948), arts 3(1)(b), Sch.1 Pt 2, para.106(1), (5)–(7) and further substituted by SI 2009/1941.

[128] The substantive powers in ss.6 and 8 are based on recommendations put forward in Ch. 45 of the Cork Report. Cork made no mention of a schedule of indicative factors and nor did the White Paper, *A Revised Framework for Insolvency Law*, Cmnd.9175 (1984).

[129] An amendment was introduced in the House of Lords, which eventually crystallised as Sch.1 to the CDDA: see variously, Hansard H.L. Vol.461, cols 724–725, 727, 732–733; Vol.467, cols 1123–1124.

[130] CDDA s.7(3) and 3–02 to 3–04.

[131] Hansard, HL Vol. 467, col. 1124; Parl. Deb., HC Standing Committee E, Session 1984–85, Vol. IV, cols 125–126.

[132] Standing Committee E, Session 1984–85, Vol. IV, from col. 54. Note, in particular, the attempt by some members of Standing Committee to add specific criteria requiring the court to have regard to the frequency of a defendant's involvement in corporate insolvencies and the adequacy of the relevant company's share capital.

of "any fiduciary duty or other duty by the director in relation to the company" (including in particular breach of any of the "core" duties in Companies Act 2006 Pt 10, Ch.2). On this wording alone, it is clear that the court can take into account any breach of a director's core fiduciary obligations and duty of care, skill and diligence as now set out in the Companies Act 2006 ss.170–177 as well as other duties not further itemised in the Schedule such as statutory duties arising not only elsewhere in companies legislation but also in legislation applicable to business in general such as health and safety legislation. Moreover, the concept of unfitness clearly encompasses types of misconduct that are targeted specifically by other substantive provisions in the CDDA, namely ss.2–5 and 10. The Schedule is effectively a summary restatement of existing obligations laying particular emphasis (in Pt I) on such matters as proper record-keeping and financial reporting. There is nothing in s.9 or the Schedule that serves to augment the obligations already imposed on directors by general company law or corporate insolvency law.

4–47 It is well settled that the criteria contained in the Schedule are not to be regarded as exhaustive. The court is required by s.9(1) to "have regard in particular" to the matters mentioned in the Schedule. The use of this phrase makes it clear that the contents of the Schedule are not intended to be an exclusive list. It follows that, in determining unfitness, the court is free to consider matters that fall outside the Schedule as well as the matters specifically mentioned.[133] The point is best illustrated by the decision of Neuberger J. in *Re Migration Services Ltd, Official Receiver v Webster*.[134] The issue in that case was whether the defendant's use of a prohibited name in contravention of s.216 of the Insolvency Act 1986 could be taken into account on an application to disqualify him under CDDA s.6. The defendant argued that Sch.1 para.10 contained an exhaustive list of Insolvency Act provisions and, as a consequence, a breach of s.216, which was not listed, could not be taken into account. The judge roundly rejected the defendant's argument in the light of the "have regard in particular" wording in s.9(1), reinforced by the following additional reasons:

[133] A point made during the parliamentary debate: Hansard H.L. Vol.461, cols 738, 740; Vol.467, cols 1123–1124; Standing Committee E, Session 1984–85, Vol.IV, col.90 and reiterated frequently by the courts: see, e.g. *Re Bath Glass Ltd* [1988] B.C.L.C. 329 at 132–133; *Re Samuel Sherman Plc* [1991] 1 W.L.R. 1070 at 1073; *Re GSAR Realisations Ltd* [1993] B.C.L.C. 409 at 421; *Secretary of State for Trade and Industry v Taylor* [1997] 1 W.L.R. 407 at 412, sub nom. *Secretary of State for Trade and Industry v Gash* [1997] 1 B.C.L.C. 341 at 346, sub nom. *Re CS Holidays Ltd* [1997] B.C.C. 172 at 176; *Re Amaron Ltd, Secretary of State for Trade and Industry v Lubrani (No.2)* [2001] 1 B.C.L.C. 562 at 568; *Re Sykes (Butchers) Ltd, Secretary of State for Trade and Industry v Richardson* [1998] 1 B.C.LC. 110 at 125; *Re Bradcrown Ltd, Official Receiver v Ireland* [2001] 1 B.C.L.C. 547 at [7]; *Re Skyward Builders Plc, Official Receiver v Broad* [2002] EWHC 2786 (Ch) at [384]; *Re Mayfair Interiors (Wolverhampton) Ltd, Secretary of State for Trade and Industry v Blunt* [2005] 2 B.C.L.C. 463 at [18]; *Re Bunting Electric Manufacturing Co Ltd, Secretary of State for Trade and Industry v Golby* [2006] 1 B.C.L.C. 550 at [9]. Many matters will fall within the Schedule anyway given the apparent width of para.1 pursuant to which the court must have regard to "any misfeasance or breach of any fiduciary or other duty by the director in relation to the company".

[134] [2000] 1 B.C.L.C. 666.

(1) The Schedule should be read together with the CDDA as a whole bearing in mind its purpose. It would be surprising if a potentially serious breach of the Insolvency Act, capable of attracting the sanction of imprisonment under s.216(4), could not be taken into account under CDDA s.6.
(2) If the defendant had been successfully prosecuted for breach of s.216, there was little doubt that he could have been disqualified under CDDA s.2 on conviction "of an indictable offence in connection with the . . . management of a company".[135] It would be surprising if a person could be disqualified by a criminal court for breach of s.216 under CDDA s.2 but avoid having such breach taken into account in determining whether or not he should be disqualified under CDDA s.6.
(3) Consistent with the purpose of the CDDA, the court should adopt a wide view as to what constitutes or could constitute behaviour that renders someone unfit.

In practice, the courts regularly take into account matters of alleged misconduct that are seemingly not captured by Sch.1. Two common allegations, proof of which has often been decisive in proceedings for an order under CDDA s.6, are that the defendant caused the relevant company: (a) to continue trading to the detriment of its creditors generally; and/or (b) to operate a policy of deliberate non-payment of certain creditors (such as the Crown) whilst other creditors were paid. Neither of these matters is mentioned in Sch.1 and yet they have been the central allegations in a large number of cases determined under s.6 over the years.[136]

It is also interesting to note that in proceedings for a competition disqualification order under CDDA s.9A, the court is expressly directed by s.9A(5)(c) that it must not have regard to the matters in Sch.1 when considering whether the defendant's conduct as a director (based on a specified breach of competition law) makes him unfit to be concerned in the management of a company. There are, however, no equivalent words directing the court not to have regard to competition law matters when considering whether a director's conduct makes him unfit under either s.6 or s.8. The general principle that Sch.1 is not exhaustive and the presence of the limiting words in s.9A(5)(c) suggest therefore that conduct falling within the scope of s.9A could be taken into account under ss.6 and 8 even though the converse is expressly prevented.[137]

A further issue which arose in *Ghassemian v Secretary of State for Trade and Industry*[138] is whether in a s.8 case where the relevant company is solvent, the court can take into account matters listed in Sch.1 Pt II that apply where the relevant company has become insolvent as well as those matters listed in Sch.1 Pt I. In *Ghassemian*, proceedings for a disqualification order under s.8 were commenced on the back of investigative material that had been obtained under

[135] On s.2, see generally Ch.10. A person who contravenes s.216 commits an indictable offence: see Insolvency Act 1986, s.430 and Sch.10.

[136] See further, Ch. 5, especially 5–05 to 5–35.

[137] Disqualification on competition law grounds under CDDA ss.9A to 9E is discussed generally in Ch.6.

[138] [2007] B.C.C. 229.

s.447 of the Companies Act 1985. Amongst other matters, it was alleged that the defendant had failed to co-operate with the Financial Services Authority and with the official receiver. The defendant sought to argue that neither matter could be taken into account in determining his unfitness. He took two points: (a) that the Secretary of State had "no jurisdiction" to complain on behalf of the FSA; and (b) that as the company was solvent—it had been wound up on public interest grounds rather than on grounds of insolvency—non-co-operation with the official receiver was legally irrelevant because this was one of the matters listed in Sch.1 Pt II applicable only where the relevant company has become insolvent. The first point was disposed of swiftly, Lewison J. holding that the Secretary of State's function under the CDDA is to consider whether persons are unfit to be company directors and that non-co-operation with regulators, such as the FSA, could amount to a ground of unfitness just as much "as failure to pay tax liabilities . . . or a propensity to swindle customers".[139] On the second point, Lewison J. reasoned thus:

> "[24] As a matter of language, looking at s.9, there are two points to make. The first is that s.9 refers 'in particular' to the matters mentioned in Pt.I of the Schedule or Pt.II as the case may be. It does not purport to make those matters exhaustive of the matters which the court can take into account.
> [25] The second point is that the court positively requires to have regard to the matters mentioned in the respective parts of the schedule in the respective cases to which they apply. But a positive direction to have regard in a particular case does not, in my judgment, amount to a negative injunction against having regard to those matters in a different case."

It was therefore open to the Secretary of State to rely, in part, on non-co-operation with the official receiver in the context of a compulsory winding up on public interest grounds even though the relevant company had not become insolvent. Lewison J. treated a passage in Morritt V.C.'s judgment in *Re Queens Moathouses Plc, Secretary of State for Trade and Industry v Bairstow* that appeared to support the defendant's submission as obiter and chose to disregard it.[140] The authors suggest that in the light of the weight of authority supporting the proposition that the Schedule as a whole is non-exhaustive and, as a matter of principle, Lewison J.'s approach in *Ghassemian* was correct.

4–48 While the non-exhaustive nature of the Schedule is well settled, a number of points are less clear:

(1) There has been little judicial discussion to date of whether the matters mentioned in the Schedule should be given greater weight than matters not

[139] [2007] B.C.C. 229 at [20]–[21].
[140] [2003] EWCA Civ 321, [2004] Ch. 1 at [11]. The passage reads:

> "In determining whether a person's conduct makes him unfit to be concerned in the management of a company the court is required by s.9 to have regard to the matters specified in Sch.1, Pt.II. As [the company] has not become insolvent only the matters specified in Pt.I could be relevant in these proceedings."

specifically mentioned. Neuberger J. expressed the view in *Re Amaron Ltd, Secretary of State for Trade and Industry v Lubrani (No.2)* that each allegation of unfitness should be dealt with on its merits irrespective of whether or not it falls in the Schedule.[141] However, in *Re Crystal Palace Football Club (1986), Secretary of State for Trade and Industry v Goldberg*, Lewison J. expressed the contrary view.[142] It is respectfully suggested that the view of Neuberger J. is to be preferred. The seriousness of certain misconduct must depend on the individual facts of each case and whether a particular matter is within the Schedule or not does not relate to that issue. Indeed, there are many cases where the courts have given great weight to something not within the Schedule, such as trading while insolvent to the detriment of creditors, and comparatively little weight to matters falling squarely within the Schedule, such as the completion of a statement of affairs or non co-operation with the insolvency practitioner.[143] It is clear, however, from the Court of Appeal decision in *Grayan* that s.6 should not be applied in a way that deprives the specific matters mentioned in the Schedule of any effect.[144]

(2) There is no indication in the CDDA as to the relative weight to be given to each of the matters mentioned in the Schedule. However, it is suggested that this is because everything will turn on the specific facts of each case. It is apparent from the discussion in Ch.5 on specific indicia of unfitness that a breach of s.386 of the Companies Act 2006 (Sch.1 Pt I para.4(h)) is likely to be treated as more serious than, say, a failure to file annual returns (Sch.1 Pt I para.4(j)). This approach to relative weighting has been developed entirely by the courts and is a matter of judgment in each case.

(3) The CDDA gives no general guidance as to the degree of misconduct required to make a defendant unfit. This has also been left to the courts. It is fairly safe to say that a few isolated defaults in filing accounts and returns (especially where the defaults would not reach the threshold to trigger the disqualification powers in CDDA ss.3 or 5) will probably not render a director unfit. In the *Barings* case, Jonathan Parker J. pointed out with reference to para.(a) of Pt 1 of Sch.1 that the mere fact that there is a breach of duty does not automatically lead to a finding of unfitness.[145] The same is true of any of the other matters set out in Sch.1. The drawing of the line between fitness and unfitness is ultimately a matter of judgment in each case turning on the precise facts. The task of identifying individual matters relevant to the question of

[141] [2001] 1 B.C.L.C. 562 at 568.

[142] [2004] 1 B.C.L.C. 597 at [11].

[143] See generally Ch.5.

[144] [1995] Ch. 241. See in particular the comments of Hoffmann L.J. criticising the trial judge's ruling that conduct amounting to an unlawful preference (specifically referred to in Sch.1, Pt II, para.8(a)) should be disregarded because the defendants had been proceeded against under s.239 of the Insolvency Act 1986 and this would have brought the consequences of their actions home to them. For a similar approach on the facts in the bankruptcy restrictions context see *Official Receiver v Bathurst* [2008] B.P.I.R. 1548.

[145] *Re Barings Plc (No.5), Secretary of State for Trade and Industry v Baker* [1999] 1 B.C.L.C. 433 at 486.

unfitness is a relatively easy one. It is much less easy to identify at what point a particular factor or combination of factors will take the defendant across the line.[146] This inevitably leaves some margin for the exercise of what, for present purposes, can be described as "judicial value judgments".[147]

"Extent of responsibility"

4–49 It has been seen that Sch.1 does not have any immediate impact on the law of directors' obligations. It simply restates existing aspects of the law in varying degrees of detail. However, it is important to note that the majority of the criteria in the Schedule direct the court to evaluate "the extent of the director's responsibility" for the specified failure or default. The use of this wording serves to highlight a tension peculiar to company law. On the one hand, the board of directors tends to be treated in company law as the primary organ of the company, i.e. the principal means by which the company acts, especially in relation to those outside the company. In this sense, the directors are regarded as acting collectively rather than individually. On the other hand, directors' legal obligations are owed by each director to the company individually and so, in law, the board as an entity does not owe a collective duty as such. To borrow a phrase from Lord Woolf, the board's collegiate or collective responsibility is based on individual responsibility.[148] A difficult question falling between the two stools of collective and individual responsibility is whether the duties imposed on each individual director are equivalent in character and intensity or are, in some sense, dependent on the director's function, role and expertise. Here the law has to recognise that one size does not necessarily fit all. Subject to the basic parameters established by company law, companies are generally free to adopt whatever management and organisational structure best suits their business needs. Accordingly, it would be crude for the law to treat every conceivable director in exactly the same way regardless of function and without reference to the size of the company, the nature of its business, the way it is organised and so on. So, for example, while there is no explicit distinction in company law between an executive and a non-executive director, the extent of what is, in fact, required of an executive and non-executive director in terms of determining unfitness is likely to differ. This is consistent with the current legal position in relation to the director's duty of care, skill and diligence where the test for breach is to ask in the first instance whether the director exercised the degree of care and skill of a reasonably diligent person having the general knowledge, skill and experience that may reasonably be

[146] See 4–02 to 4–03.

[147] *Re Crystal Palace Football Club (1986) Ltd, Secretary of State for Trade and Industry v Goldberg* [2004] 1 B.C.L.C. 597 at [14].

[148] See *Re Westmid Packing Services Ltd, Secretary of State for Trade and Industry v Griffiths* [1998] 2 All E.R. 124 at 130. For further discussion of the relationship between the board's collective responsibility and each director's individual responsibility see *Re Landhurst Leasing Plc, Secretary of State for Trade and Industry v Ball* [1999] 1 B.C.L.C. 286 at 345–346.

expected of a person carrying out the same functions in the company.[149] This objective standard based on the individual director's function in a given company gives the court scope to distinguish between directors according to their job descriptions such as "finance director", "sales director", "non-executive" director and so on. At the same time, the test imposes a minimum requirement on all directors regardless of function with the consequence that every director is required to participate in the management of the company to at least some minimum degree.[150] However, the precise nature and intensity of this positive obligation to participate depends on the particular context and on factors such as how the particular company was organised and the part that the director could reasonably have been expected to play.[151]

4–50 The effect of the "extent of responsibility" wording in Sch.1 is that the court is required to focus primarily on the defendant's personal responsibility. Equally, however, the use of the word "extent" suggests that the court must examine the defendant's conduct in the round, taking into account not only his own functions and responsibilities but also those of others in the company. The Schedule therefore clearly contemplates that the directors in a company may have varying degrees of responsibility. Thus, in keeping with the codified duty of care, skill and diligence in s.174 of the Companies Act 2006, the CDDA (or at least the Schedule) does not require the application of a single fixed standard to all directors. Instead, in disqualification cases, the broad tendency is for the courts to insist that every director is under an irreducible and non-delegable minimum obligation to keep himself informed of the company's affairs and, in particular, its financial position, even if he has no involvement in the day-to-day running of its business. Beyond that, what is expected of a director will depend upon his role and responsibilities and the particular manner in which the company in question is organised. The upshot is that the courts have used the CDDA to fashion minimum standards of managerial conduct and participation. However, the precise nature and intensity of a director's responsibility in relation to a given company will ultimately depend on the facts of each case.[152] These important issues of minimum standards, directors' participation and co-responsibility are considered further in Ch.5.[153]

4–51 In *Re Barings Plc (No.5)*, Jonathan Parker J. stated that the court should adopt a broad approach when evaluating the extent of a director's responsibility for the

[149] See *Norman v Theodore Goddard* [1992] B.C.L.C. 1028; *Re D'Jan of London Ltd* [1994] 1 B.C.L.C. 561; *Re Landhurst Leasing Plc, Secretary of State for Trade and Industry v Ball* [1999] 1 B.C.L.C. 286 at 344. This objective standard is drawn from the statutory test in s.214(4) of the Insolvency Act 1986 applicable in wrongful trading proceedings and is now enshrined in the general duties codified by the Companies Act 2006: see Companies Act 2006 s.174. The standard can be adjusted upwards, but not downwards, to reflect the general knowledge, skill and experience that the particular director possesses: Insolvency Act 1986 s.214(4)(b); Companies Act 2006 s.174(2)(b); *Re Brian D Pierson (Contractors) Ltd* [2001] 1 B.C.L.C. 275.

[150] *Re Brian D Pierson (Contractors) Ltd* [2001] 1 B.C.L.C. 275.

[151] See *Bishopgate Investment Management Ltd v Maxwell (No.2)* [1994] 1 All E.R. 261 at 264; and, in the disqualification context, *Re Barings Plc (No.5), Secretary of State for Trade and Industry v Baker* [1999] 1 B.C.L.C. 433 at 484, 486–489.

[152] See further the approach in *Re Barings Plc (No. 5), Secretary of State for Trade and Industry v Baker* [1999] 1 B.C.L.C. 433 at 482–486.

[153] See from 5–73.

causes of the company becoming insolvent under Sch.1, para.6, "eschewing nice legal concepts of causation".[154] It is suggested that this approach should be taken to the "extent of responsibility" wording wherever it appears in the Schedule. As a result, it is conceivable that a director could escape civil liability for breach of duty on the basis that the breach did not technically cause loss,[155] but still be disqualified because, in a broad sense, his conduct fell short of the required standard. A key aspect of this broad approach is that it does not matter that others, as well as the defendant, may also have been responsible for a specific failing either "more or less proximately".[156] Moreover, "responsibility" is not confined to direct executive responsibility for the particular misconduct and, if so alleged, may be founded, for example, on the defendant's failure to engage in proper supervision of the activities of delegates or fellow directors.[157]

Criticisms of CDDA s.9 and Sch.1

4–52 The Schedule amounts to a mixed bag of broad and narrow factors indicative of unfitness. Although it has been criticised as giving inadequate guidance, it is difficult to see how a statute could give greater guidance on how the test is to be applied given the myriad of different fact situations that are likely to arise. Past criticisms that directors have lacked a clear and accessible statement of irreducible minimum obligations and standards to which directors could refer ex ante have to a limited extent been met by the codification of general duties in ss.170–177 of the Companies Act 2006.[158] Given that one discernible purpose of disqualification is to protect the public by raising directors' standards of conduct through general deterrence, the case for clear guidance ex ante is a powerful one especially given the wide ranging sources of directorial obligations and standards on the statute book and the voluminous case law on CDDA ss.6 and 8. The 2006 Act codification is at a high level generality and does nothing to inform directors ex ante of the standards of conduct that are expected of them if they are to avoid disqualification under the CDDA.[159] Unless directors are issued on appointment with some form of supplementary, albeit non-exhaustive, guidance providing concrete examples of unfit conduct, it is likely that doubts concerning the moral legitimacy of disqualification as an ex post sanction will continue to

[154] [1999] 1 B.C.L.C. 433 at 483. The passage in the judgment was subsequently approved by the Court of Appeal: [2000] 1 B.C.L.C. 523 at [35]. See also *Re Bunting Electric Manufacturing Co Ltd, Secretary of State for Trade and Industry v Golby* [2006] 1 B.C.L.C. 550 at [59].

[155] See, e.g. *Cohen v Selby* [2001] B.C.L.C. 176.

[156] *Re Barings Plc (No. 5), Secretary of State for Trade and Industry v Baker* [2000] 1 B.C.L.C. 523 at [35].

[157] *Re Skyward Builders Plc, Official Receiver v Broad* [2002] EWHC 2786 (Ch) at [393].

[158] For background see Law Commission Paper No.153, *Company Directors: Regulating Conflicts of Interests and Formulating a Statement of Duties* (1998), especially Section B, Pt 14; Company Law Review Steering Group, *Developing the Framework* (March 2000), Ch.3 and *Completing the Structure* (November 2000), paras 3.11–3.31; the White Paper, *Modernising Company Law*, Cm. 5553 (2002).

[159] In particular, it says nothing about duties in relation to creditors: see Companies Act 2006 s.172(3).

surface.[160] Equally, there is no doubt that it is extremely difficult to provide detailed guidance bearing in mind that directorial and managerial obligations are not derived exclusively from core company law. Thus, any distillation of the extensive range of misconduct that can be taken into account under the CDDA can never hope to be comprehensive or exhaustive and therefore runs the risk of misleading directors as much as enlightening them.

The requirement to consider allegations of unfit conduct separately and cumulatively

4–53 The guidance in the statute is not exhaustive and the courts have therefore played a significant part in developing the law of unfitness. The court's basic task, having resolved any disputes of fact, is to decide whether the matters alleged and proven by the claimant make the defendant unfit. In approaching this task, the court must look at each matter of misconduct and determine whether on its own, or taken cumulatively with other matters alleged and proven, that matter is sufficient to make the defendant unfit.[161] Thus, where the defendant is faced with several allegations, it is no defence for him to show that separately and individually none of the alleged conduct is sufficiently serious to demonstrate unfitness if, taken cumulatively, the court forms the view that the conduct as a whole makes him unfit.[162] Conversely, the court is entitled to conclude that the defendant is unfit on a single ground of complaint alone if the conduct merits it and this is so even if that ground is not one of the matters specifically mentioned in Sch.1.[163] A finding of breach of duty is neither necessary nor of itself sufficient for a finding of unfitness. Thus, a person may be unfit even though no breach of duty is proved against

[160] See, e.g. Lord Hoffmann's extra-judicial comments made in the fourth annual Leonard Sainer Lecture (1997) 18 Co. Law. 194. In *Disqualification of Directors: No Hiding Place for the Unfit* (A.C.C.A. Research Report No.59, 1998) and "Director Disqualification: Can it Deliver?" [2001] J.B.L. 433 Hicks suggested that a "code for creditors" providing a positive statement of the standards to be expected should be enacted and copies distributed to new directors by Companies House as an ex ante measure. The code would restate the specific matters in Sch.1 and summarise the specific obligations to creditors and standards of proper practice established by CDDA case law. Hicks argues that this would assist the court and the law-abiding director while enhancing the moral justification for disqualification where the code is breached. One problem identified by the National Audit Office in its report of October 1993 and confirmed by Hicks' later work is that many directors are not even aware of the existence of the CDDA. This finding tends to undermine the notion that the CDDA has raised awareness of directors' duties.

[161] See dictum of Morritt L.J. in *Re Copecrest Ltd, Secretary of State for Trade and Industry v McTighe (No. 2)* [1996] 2 B.C.L.C. 477 at 485.

[162] *Re Barings Plc (No.5), Secretary of State for Trade and Industry v Baker* [2000] 1 B.C.L.C. 523 at [35]; *Re Bunting Electric Manufacturing Co Ltd, Secretary of State for Trade and Industry v Golby* [2006] 1 B.C.L.C. 550 at [27].

[163] *Re Dayglen Ltd, Secretary of State for Trade and Industry v Cachra*, July 22, 1999, Ch. D., unreported; *Re Amaron Ltd, Secretary of State for Trade and Industry v Lubrani (No.2)* [2001] 1 B.C.L.C. 562; *Re Bunting Electric Manufacturing Co Ltd, Secretary of State for Trade and Industry v Golby* [2006] 1 B.C.L.C. 550 at [27].

him or may remain fit notwithstanding the proof of various breaches of duty.[164] These mechanical statements provide only a bare framework. They say nothing about the test or standard that the court is to apply to a set of proven allegations in order to determine whether the defendant's conduct falls on the acceptable or unacceptable side of the line. In the absence of any clear statement in the CDDA, it has been left to the courts to determine the appropriate test for distinguishing between fit and unfit conduct. This they have sought to do through the development of the standards of probity and competence discussed earlier.

Armed with this account of the court's general approach to the question of unfitness, the next chapter considers the detail of individual cases decided under ss.6 and 8 and seeks to identify specific types of misconduct that, either individually or cumulatively, are liable to result in disqualification.

[164] *Re Barings Plc (No.5), Secretary of State for Trade and Industry v Baker* [1999] B.C.L.C. 433 at 486 approved on the point by the Court of Appeal: [2000] 1 B.C.L.C. 523 at [35]. See also *Re Deaduck Ltd, Secretary of State for Trade and Industry v Baker* [2000] 1 B.C.L.C. 148; *Re Crystal Palace Football Club (1986) Ltd, Secretary of State for Trade and Industry v Goldberg* [2004] 1 B.C.L.C. 597 at [21] to [28].

CHAPTER 5

ESTABLISHING UNFIT CONDUCT (2): SPECIFIC INSTANCES OF UNFIT CONDUCT AND PERIOD OF DISQUALIFICATION

INTRODUCTION

This chapter covers the following subject matter: **5–01**

(1) Specific instances of unfit conduct as they have arisen in cases decided under CDDA ss.6 and 8.
(2) Recurring themes in the law of unfit conduct, such as financial responsibility and incompetence.
(3) Periods of disqualification and mitigation.

SPECIFIC INSTANCES OF UNFIT CONDUCT

A wide variety of specific instances of unfit conduct can be derived from the reported cases decided under CDDA ss.6 and 8. This is not surprising given the width of the enquiry that can be undertaken into the director's conduct once either of the statutory gateways (corporate insolvency or a company investigation) is triggered. Accordingly, the examples that follow illustrate the wide scope of unfit conduct. In particular, it will be seen that there is considerable emphasis in the s.6 jurisprudence on the need for directors to monitor the company's financial position closely at all times and on the requirement that, where the company is in financial difficulty, they should pay proper regard to the interests of creditors. While unfit conduct clearly embraces the more egregious forms of misconduct such as fraud, the courts have also routinely disqualified defendants whose conduct (such as a failure to exercise proper financial responsibility and/or pay due regard to the interests of company creditors) can be classified as incompetent rather than fraudulent or dishonest. This reflects the general approach of the courts to the issue of unfit conduct which, as discussed in Ch.4, is based on the application of a standard not only of probity, but also of competence. **5–02**

It is natural for s.6 cases to focus on the protection of creditors because of the requirement that the relevant company must have "become insolvent". However, it should be noted that ss.6 and 8 are wide in scope and aimed at the protection of the "public" which, in appropriate circumstances, can include shareholders, investors, consumers and employees as well as creditors.[1] Moreover, once the statutory gateways are triggered the court may consider any conduct which may make the defendant unfit to be concerned in the management of a company. So, **5–03**

[1] See discussion in Ch.2.

for example, in s.6 cases, the enquiry is not necessarily restricted to an assessment of the defendant's contribution to the causes of the company's failure or his conduct in the face of the company's insolvency.[2] The question as a matter of law under CDDA s.6(1)(b) is whether the defendant's "conduct as a director . . . makes him unfit to be concerned in the management of a company".[3]

5–04 While a single instance of misconduct may, in theory, be *sufficient* for the court to make a finding of unfit conduct, it must be emphasised that proof of a single allegation falling within one of the specific heads of misconduct discussed in this chapter will not *necessarily* make the defendant unfit. The court is required to consider each alleged matter of misconduct and, having made findings of fact, determine whether on its own, or taken cumulatively with other proven instances of misconduct, that matter is sufficient to support a finding of unfit conduct.[4] Thus, the identification of *some* conduct falling within any *one* of the species of misconduct described below will not lead inexorably to the conclusion that the defendant's conduct makes him unfit. It must be emphasised that the question of whether or not the defendant's conduct makes him unfit will depend ultimately on the particular circumstances of each case. However, it is possible to identify with some precision specific instances of misconduct that are commonly raised and that, either individually or cumulatively, may result in a finding of unfit conduct.[5] This is the principal aim of the present chapter.

Trading while insolvent to the detriment of creditors

5–05 A frequent allegation raised in proceedings for an order under s.6 is that the defendant caused or allowed the relevant company to continue trading while insolvent to the detriment of its creditors (hereinafter referred to by the shorthand "trading to the detriment of creditors").[6] Moreover, there are cases where the

[2] Contrast the power in s.206D of the Australian Corporations Act 2001 (Cth). This provides that a person may be disqualified from managing corporations for up to 20 years if certain conditions are met. The conditions are, that within the last seven years a person has been an officer of two or more corporations when they failed and the court is satisfied: (a) that the manner in which the corporation was managed was wholly or partly responsible for the corporation failing; and (b) the disqualification is justified. The scope of the court's enquiry is therefore considerably narrower than that under CDDA s.6 where it may be sufficient for a finding of unfitness to demonstrative a causative link between the misconduct and the failure of the relevant company but it is not strictly necessary.

[3] The authors' position is that the scope of the enquiry is the same under CDDA s.8(2). See 3–116.

[4] See 4–53.

[5] In this respect it is worth noting the observations of Park J. in *Re Cubelock Ltd* [2001] B.C.C. 523 at [55]–[56] as to the desirability of the court taking into account the facts and outcomes of other decided cases in the interests of consistency. However, in the light of the Court of Appeal's guidance on the management of disqualification proceedings spelled out in *Re Westmid Packing Services Ltd, Secretary of State for Trade and Industry v Griffiths* [1998] 2 All E.R. 124, Park J. should not be read as giving the parties *carte blanche* to cite every first instance decision that may possibly be in point.

[6] It should be noted for these purposes that there are two types of insolvency, namely "cash flow" insolvency (where the company cannot meet its debts as they fall due) and "balance sheet" insolvency (where liabilities exceed assets): see Insolvency Act 1986 s.123(1)(e), (2). A company which is "balance sheet" insolvent may be able to trade on despite its position, and if it can meet its debts as they fall due and there is no immediate risk to creditors or prospect of collapse, the directors will not necessarily be guilty of trading to the detriment of creditors: see *Re Cubelock Ltd* [2001] B.C.C. 523 at [71]; *Secretary of State for Trade and Industry v Creegan* [2001] EWCA Civ 1742, [2002] 1 B.C.L.C. 99 at [7].

courts have found the defendant unfit on the basis of a single proven allegation of trading to the detriment of creditors in relation to one company.[7] Trading to the detriment of creditors is not specifically mentioned in Sch.1, although it appears to fall squarely within the wide wording "any misfeasance or breach of any fiduciary or other duty . . ." in Sch.1 Pt I para.1 as amounting to a failure on the part of a director to discharge his general duty to act in the interests of the company which, at common law, requires the director to take into account the interests of creditors once the company is factually insolvent.[8]

The relationship between an allegation of trading to the detriment of creditors and liability for wrongful trading

5–06 Trading to the detriment of creditors, in the context of CDDA s.6, bears some relation to the concept of wrongful trading in s.214 of the Insolvency Act 1986. On the application of a liquidator under s.214, the court can declare that a director or shadow director of a company is liable to contribute personally to the company's assets provided that:

(1) the company has gone into insolvent liquidation; and
(2) at some time before the commencement of the winding up of the company, he knew or ought to have concluded that there was no reasonable prospect that the company would avoid going into insolvent liquidation; and
(3) the defendant fails to establish that, having reached the state of knowledge referred to in (2), he took every step with a view to minimising the potential loss to the company's creditors as he ought to have taken.

If these elements are established, the court may make an order, but is not obliged to do so. The applicable standard (for the objective test of knowledge in (2), and for determining whether the defendant took "every step" in (3)) is that of a reasonably diligent person having both the general knowledge, skill and experience that may reasonably be expected of a person carrying out the same functions as are carried out by the defendant in relation to the company, and the general knowledge, skill and experience possessed by the defendant.[9]

5–07 The essential mischief of trading to the detriment of creditors and of wrongful trading is similar. Both are concerned with the director who causes or allows an insolvent company to continue incurring debts that the company is unlikely to be

[7] *Re McNulty's Interchange Ltd* [1989] B.C.L.C. 709; *Re Amaron Ltd, Secretary of State for Trade and Industry v Lubrani* [1997] 2 B.C.L.C. 115 affirmed [2001] 1 B.C.L.C. 562.

[8] See, e.g. *West Mercia Safetywear Ltd v Dodd* [1988] B.C.L.C. 250; *Facia Footwear Ltd v Hinchcliffe* [1998] 1 B.C.L.C. 218; *Colin Gwyer & Associates Ltd v London Wharf (Limehouse) Ltd* [2002] EWHC 2748 (Ch), [2003] 2 B.C.L.C. 153. See also Companies Act 2006 s.172(3). It is clear from *Re Bath Glass Ltd* [1988] B.C.L.C. 329 that the court can make a finding of unfit conduct without the need for the claimant to allege and prove that the misconduct amounted to wrongful trading as defined in s.214 of the Insolvency Act 1986, a point developed in 5–07.

[9] Insolvency Act 1986 s.214(4). See further *Re Brian D Pierson (Contractors) Ltd* [2001] 1 B.C.L.C. 275; *Re Continental Assurance Co of London Plc* [2001] B.P.I.R. 733; *Re Hawkes Hill Publishing Co Ltd* [2007] B.C.C. 937.

able to meet and that cannot under ordinary company law principles be laid at the director's own door because he is protected by the company's separate legal personality and limited liability. Significantly, however, it appears that the courts are able to find a defendant unfit under s.6 on the basis of trading to the detriment of creditors *without* the claimant necessarily being required to make out a case that would satisfy all the elements of s.214. This point was first made by Peter Gibson J. in *Re Bath Glass Limited*:

> "Take a case of wrongful trading. In proceedings brought by the liquidator under s.214 a director may be held liable under that section because for a short time before the commencement of the liquidation the director allowed the company so to trade and a small contribution might be ordered under that section . . . In contrast the test in s.6 is quite different: there is no single specified offence that is the condition to be satisfied for the court to make a disqualification order. What the court must have regard to is the director's conduct; that is a term of great generality and I do not doubt that it was deliberately so chosen . . . Any misconduct of the [defendant] *qua* director may be relevant, even if it does not fall within a specific section of the Companies Acts or the Insolvency Act . . . Even if . . . conduct *does not amount to wrongful trading within s.214, in my judgment it would still be conduct amounting to misconduct and so relevant to s.6.* Whether in any particular case that misconduct . . . proved to the satisfaction of the court, will justify a finding of unfitness will depend on all the circumstances of the case."[10]

The judge's observation to the effect that misconduct falling short of wrongful trading can amount to unfit conduct is strictly obiter as, on the facts of *Bath Glass*, it was held that the defendants' conduct, while "improper", was not sufficiently serious as to make them unfit. Nevertheless, the basic point that unfit conduct can be established without the *necessity* for the claimant to make out a case that satisfies the terms of s.214 is an important one that has subsequently been approved by the Court of Appeal.[11] The justification for this view lies in the generality of the term "unfit" and the fact that there is no specific requirement in ss.6, 9 or the Schedule to establish that the defendant engaged in wrongful trading as defined in s.214.

5–08 A related point is that the court can take into account evidence of trading to the detriment of creditors in s.6 or s.8 proceedings whether or not a liquidator has previously brought separate wrongful trading proceedings against the defendant. In a case where there are parallel wrongful trading proceedings, the defendant is doubly exposed to disqualification. If the action under s.214 succeeds, the court dealing with those proceedings may, in its discretion, disqualify the defendant for up to 15 years under CDDA s.10.[12] If it fails, or no action is taken, the claimant may still be able to put forward an allegation of trading to the detriment of creditors in proceedings for an order under CDDA s.6. Even if the court were to make a disqualification order under s.10, this does not appear to prevent the Secretary of State from seeking an additional period of disqualification under s.6 on the

[10] [1988] B.C.L.C. 329 at 333. Emphasis added. See also *Re Imperial Board Products Ltd, Official Receiver v Jones* [2004] EWHC 2096 (Ch).

[11] *Re Sevenoaks Stationers (Retail) Ltd* [1991] Ch. 164 at 183.

[12] Discussed further in Ch.10.

basis of the defendant's conduct generally, including the conduct already scrutinised in the wrongful trading proceedings. An application by the defendant to strike out the s.6 or s.8 proceedings as an abuse of process would likely be met by the argument that the two sets of proceedings were being brought for separate purposes and, while there may be a degree of overlap, the power in CDDA s.6 allows the court to take into account a much broader range of conduct than can be considered under CDDA s.10.[13]

5–09 Where there are parallel proceedings under CDDA ss.6 to 7 and Insolvency Act 1986 s.214 and the allegations and material used to support those allegations are very similar, it is conceivable that the court may arrange for both sets of proceedings to be heard together. This course can be justified on the ground that, in theory, it should avoid duplication of effort and thereby save costs. The court has followed this course of action in one reported case to date.[14]

5–10 The decision in *Bath Glass* notwithstanding, there have been cases in which the court has followed the wording in s.214 closely as a guide to determining whether a particular pattern of conduct made the perpetrator unfit, thus exposing him to disqualification.[15] However, this may simply reflect the way in which the allegations against the defendants in those cases were put, as it is clear from the authorities that a lesser test may be applied. In order to determine whether the defendant caused the company to trade to the detriment of creditors to a degree that makes him unfit on the lesser test, the court may simply ask whether the defendant took "unwarranted risks with creditors' money". This lesser test was formulated by the judge in *Re Synthetic Technology Ltd, Secretary of State for Trade and Industry v Joiner* in the following terms:

> "From the combined judgments of Dillon L.J. in . . . *Sevenoaks*[16] . . . and Peter Gibson J. in . . . *Bath Glass* . . . it is apparent that a director can permit his company to continue to trade whilst insolvent, while not exposing himself to a charge of wrongful trading under section 214 . . . but still be guilty of conduct amounting to misconduct under

[13] See, by analogy, *Re Cedarwood Productions Ltd, Secretary of State for Trade and Industry v Rayna* [2001] 2 B.C.L.C. 248, affirmed [2001] EWCA Civ 1083, [2004] B.C.C. 65.

[14] *Official Receiver v Doshi* [2001] 2 B.C.L.C. 235. The report deals only with the substantive issues and not the judge's reasons for making the order directing the proceedings to be heard in tandem.

[15] See, e.g. *Secretary of State for Trade and Industry v Taylor* [1997] 1 W.L.R. 407 at 412, sub nom. *Secretary of State for Trade and Industry v Gash* [1997] 1 B.C.L.C. 341 at 346, sub nom. *Re CS Holidays Ltd* [1997] B.C.C. 172 at 176; *Re TLL Realisations Ltd, Secretary of State for Trade and Industry v Collins*, November 27, 1998, Ch.D., unreported (Lloyd J.); *Re Cubelock Ltd* [2001] B.C.C. 523; *Secretary of State for Trade and Industry v Creegan* [2002] 1 B.CL.C. 99.

[16] [1991] Ch. 164 at 183. Per Dillon L.J.:

> "[The defendant] made a deliberate decision to pay only those creditors who pressed for payment. The obvious result was that the two companies traded, when in fact insolvent and known to be in difficulties at the expense of those creditors who . . . happened not to be pressing for payment. Such conduct on the part of a director can well, in my judgment, be relied on as a ground for saying that he is unfit to be concerned in the management of a company."

There is further citation of this passage in 5–29 below.

section 6. In the course of his submissions I was flattered by [counsel] commending to me words which I used in my judgment in the case of *Re Euromove Ltd*[17] where I sought to define such conduct as the taking of unwarranted risks with creditors' money by continuing to trade."[18]

The logic of this passage is that the taking of "unwarranted risks" may amount to unfit conduct even though it does not satisfy all the elements for wrongful trading liability under s.214. It follows that it is easier to prove an allegation of trading to the detriment of creditors couched in terms of "unwarranted risks" than an allegation framed by reference to the requirements of s.214. For example, under s.214, the liquidator must establish that *at some given moment in time* the defendant knew or ought to have concluded that the company had no reasonable prospect of survival with the (probable) consequence that, as of that date, he should have caused the company to cease trading. Thus, there is an onus on the liquidator to plead and prove (at the lowest) that there was a specific date by which the defendant knew or ought to have concluded that the company had no reasonable prospects of avoiding an insolvent liquidation.[19] In contrast, where the claimant alleges in disqualification proceedings that the defendant took "unwarranted risks", there is apparently no such onus. Indeed, it may be dangerous to frame an allegation in disqualification proceedings along the lines that the defendant knew or ought to have known at a specified date that the company was insolvent and could not survive as the court is likely to hold the claimant to the date pleaded and disallow any attempted reliance on an earlier or later date at trial.[20] Thus, if the court refuses to accept or infer that the defendant knew or ought to have known that the position was hopeless on the date specified, the allegation is not proved.

5–11 The lesser "unwarranted risks" test deriving from *Synthetic Technology* has been followed in several cases.[21] It appears that the claimant must establish at least the following:

[17] July 30, 1992, Ch.D., unreported.

[18] [1993] B.C.C. 549 at 562. The reference to "creditors' money" is not technical and carries no implication of trust or proprietary right. Indeed, the test appears to reflect the view at common law that the directors of an insolvent company are required to treat creditors' interests as paramount when discharging their fiduciary obligation to the company to act in good faith.

[19] See, e.g. *Re Sherborne Associates Ltd* [1995] B.C.C. 40; *Re Continental Assurance Co of London Plc* [2001] B.P.I.R. 733; *Re Hawkes Hill Publishing Co Ltd* [2007] B.C.C. 937 at [37] though cf. *Official Receiver v Doshi* [2001] 2 B.C.L.C. 235 where the court appears to have been less rigorous in enforcing this requirement.

[20] See, e.g. *Re Burnham Marketing Services Ltd, Secretary of State for Trade and Industry v Harper* [1993] B.C.C. 518; *Re TLL Realisations Ltd, Secretary of State for Trade and Industry v Collins*, November 27, 1998, Ch.D., unreported (Lloyd J.).

[21] See, e.g. *Re Living Images Ltd* [1996] 1 B.C.L.C. 348 at 367–368; *Re Richborough Furniture Ltd, Secretary of State for Trade and Industry v Stokes* [1996] 1 B.C.L.C. 507 at 517; *Re Moonlight Foods (UK) Ltd, Secretary of State for Trade and Industry v Hickling* [1996] B.C.C. 678 at 692; *Re City Pram and Toy Co Ltd* [1998] B.C.C. 537 at 539. A similar formulation was also used in *Re TLL Realisations Ltd, Secretary of State for Trade and Industry v Collins*, November 27, 1998, Ch.D., unreported (Lloyd J.).

(1) That the company was unable to pay its debts as they fell due.
(2) That the defendant knew or ought to have known that the company was insolvent (in a cash flow sense).[22]
(3) That the company continued to trade.[23]
(4) That the continued trading produced an increase in the company's deficit thus prejudicing creditors and/or that payment of some creditors (e.g. those not pressing for payment) was delayed or not made so that continued trading was at their risk and expense.[24]
(5) That the continued trading exposed the company's creditors (and possibly others, such as employees) to an unreasonable risk that the company would fail.[25]
(6) That the continued trading was unreasonable in all the circumstances.[26]

It is these last two elements that are crucial. Thus, while an allegation in these terms appears to have a lower threshold than one couched in terms of s.214, the claimant is still required to show that the defendant's conduct was objectively unreasonable. As Lewison J. observed in *Re Mea Corporation Ltd, Secretary of State for Trade and Industry v Aviss*, in many cases the directors will have taken the decision to trade out of insolvency and the question will be whether they were reasonable in trying.[27]

5–12 Allegations based on wrongful trading and the "unwarranted risks" test may be pleaded in the alternative.[28] As the former is regarded as more serious than the latter, there is a correspondingly greater likelihood that proof of such an allegation will result in a finding of unfit conduct. On the assumption that proof of either allegation leads to a finding of unfitness, it is anticipated that misconduct

[22] Knowledge of insolvency alone is not enough: see *Secretary of State for Trade and Industry v Taylor* [1997] 1 W.L.R. 407 sub nom. *Secretary of State for Trade and Industry v Gash* [1997] 1 B.C.L.C. 341, sub nom. *Re CS Holidays Ltd* [1997] B.C.C. 172; *Re Cubelock Ltd* [2001] B.C.C. 523; *Secretary of State for Trade and Industry v Creegan* [2002] 1 B.C.L.C. 99; *Secretary of State for Trade and Industry v Blackwood* 2003 S.L.T. 120. This is understandable as otherwise legitimate attempts by directors to trade out of difficulty and turn businesses around would be discouraged.

[23] Trading for these purposes may include the disposal of assets where the directors are effectively winding down the company's business: see *Secretary of State for Trade and Industry v Walker* [2003] 1 B.C.L.C. 363 at paras [26]–[27], [40].

[24] See *Re Sevenoaks Stationers (Retail) Ltd* [1991] Ch. 164 at 183; *Re Grayan Building Services Ltd, Secretary of State for Trade and Industry v Gray* [1995] Ch. 241 at 256; *Re Copecrest Ltd, Secretary of State for Trade & Industry v McTighe (No.2)* [1996] 2 B.C.L.C. 477; *Re Galeforce Pleating Co Ltd* [1999] 2 B.C.L.C. 704; *Re Structural Concrete Ltd, Official Receiver v Barnes* [2001] B.C.C. 578; *Re Hopes (Heathrow) Limited, Secretary of State for Trade & Industry v Dyer* [2001] 1 B.C.L.C. 575.

[25] For example, because of the level of risk or because the level of risk cannot be adequately gauged due to the absence of adequate financial information: see, e.g. *Re Grayan Building Services Ltd, Secretary of State for Trade and Industry v Gray* [1994] Ch. 241 at 257.

[26] *Re Mea Corporation Ltd, Secretary of State for Trade and Industry v Aviss* [2006] EWHC 1846 (Ch), [2007] 1 B.C.L.C. 618 at [108].

[27] [2006] EWHC 1846 (Ch), [2007] 1 B.C.L.C. 618 at [109].

[28] See, e.g. *Re TLL Realisations Ltd, Secretary of State for Trade and Industry v Collins*, November 27, 1998, Ch.D., unreported (Lloyd J.).

amounting to wrongful trading will attract a longer period of disqualification than misconduct satisfying the lesser test. Similarly, if it can be established that the defendant gained by causing or allowing the company to continue trading this will be treated as more serious misconduct.

The approach in marginal cases

5–13 The court is bound to approach marginal cases with considerable care as the court is blessed with hindsight: it knows that the company has failed. A judge must therefore be circumspect when reviewing, with hindsight, a decision to continue trading taken by a director in the heat of the moment.[29] There is some justification for such a careful approach. First, the CDDA is not directed at business failure or at trading while insolvent per se, but rather at unfit conduct. In the interests of enterprise, it may be legitimate to allow a director to try and trade out of insolvency and turn the company around or to trade with a view to selling the company's business as a going concern and/or to obtaining further necessary injections of capital. If the company still fails then it is right that the courts, with hindsight, should be slow to classify a legitimate attempt at turning the business around and obtaining a better outcome for creditors as unfit conduct even though creditors may have suffered as a result. A related justification is that the rescue of financially troubled companies and/or their businesses in the interests of preserving and perpetuating going concerns is now firmly entrenched as a desirable goal of legislative policy.[30] Some increase in the company's deficit may be inevitable while the directors put together a rescue package or negotiate the sale of the company's business to a third party.[31] Secondly, there is a danger that if the courts take a hard line and disqualify directors who fail to put their companies into liquidation at the first sign of trouble, persons with appropriate expertise will be discouraged from taking up directorships. Thus, where the case against the defendant rests principally on an allegation of trading to the detriment of creditors, the court must carry out a fine balancing exercise.[32] As Neuberger J. put it in *Re Amaron Ltd, Secretary of State for Trade and Industry v Lubrani (No.2)*:

> "It is often a difficult matter to decide the point at which an unfortunate, and in retrospect, mistaken commercial assessment goes beyond the pale and becomes a decision which is such that it is either dishonest . . . or culpable for some other reason . . . so as to justify a disqualification order."[33]

[29] See 4–28; *Re Continental Assurance Co of London Plc* [2001] B.P.I.R. 733 at [281]; *Re Hawkes Hill Publishing Co Ltd* [2007] B.C.C. 937 at [28]–[30], [38]; and A. Walters, "Enforcing Wrongful Trading" in B. Rider (ed.), *The Corporate Dimension* (Bristol: Jordans, 1998).

[30] This is borne out by the Enterprise Act 2002 which, with effect from September 15, 2003, introduced the Sch.B1 administration regime into the Insolvency Act 1986, and the policy discussion that preceded this reform: see the Department of Trade and Industry White Paper, *Productivity and Enterprise: Insolvency—A Second Chance*, Cm.5234 (2001).

[31] See, e.g. *Re Welfab Engineers Ltd* [1990] B.C.L.C. 833.

[32] The application of the "no reasonable prospects" test in s.214 is attended by similar difficulties and trade-offs: see A. Walters, "Enforcing Wrongful Trading" in B. Rider ed. *The Corporate Dimension* (Bristol: Jordans, 1998).

[33] [2001] 1 B.C.L.C. 562 at 570.

The difficulties that sometimes face the court in cases where trading to the detriment of creditors is alleged can be illustrated by contrasting the outcomes in *Re Ward Sherrard Ltd*[34] and *Re City Pram and Toy Co Ltd*[35] with those in *Re Wimbledon Village Restaurant Ltd, Secretary of State for Trade and Industry v Thomson*[36] and *Re Moonlight Foods (UK) Ltd, Secretary of State for Trade and Industry v Hickling*.[37]

5–14 In *Ward Sherrard*, the defendants were directors of a company incorporated in 1987 to carry on the business of an advertising agency. In the first year of trading the company broke even but by the end of the second year (June 1989) the company was suffering from cash flow problems caused mainly by a rapid expansion of turnover. According to the audited accounts for the second year of trading, the company was balance sheet insolvent by June 1989. Moreover, the auditors qualified these accounts by saying that the "going concern" basis on which they were prepared would prove over-optimistic unless the company was successfully refinanced. Subsequently, the defendants introduced close on £200,000 by way of directors' loans. However, in the final year and a half of trading, they withdrew some of this amount in lieu of salary with the effect that the overall net increase in the company's capital was quite small. Throughout the company's life, turnover consistently increased but increases in turnover were achieved at the expense of an increasing deficit on profit and loss account. A county court judge refused to disqualify the defendants, taking the view that their decision to continue trading was based on a genuine belief in the future viability of the company. His judgment laid emphasis on the injection of the loan monies and the continued rise in turnover following the auditors' qualification of the accounts. On the Secretary of State's appeal to the High Court, both defendants were disqualified for three years. It was held that they should have recognised that the company was in immediate need of a long term capital injection once the auditors had qualified the accounts. The funds injected by the directors had not stabilised the company's long term trading position because they had been repaid in the short term. Although turnover was increasing, there had been little prospect of financing the increase by outside borrowing on security because of the general decline in property values occurring at the time. As such, the defendants' belief that the company's business was viable was unrealistic in all the circumstances and it was held that their conduct in continuing to trade after the date of the audit qualification in the absence of a long term refinancing of the company's business made them unfit.

5–15 Like *Ward Sherrard*, the case of *City Pram* also involved an appeal by the Secretary of State to the High Court against an earlier refusal to disqualify the defendants. The company in this case was a family company, originally incorporated in 1947, which

[34] [1996] B.C.C. 418.

[35] [1998] B.C.C. 537.

[36] [1994] B.C.C. 753.

[37] [1996] B.C.C. 678. Compare also the different approaches at first instance and on appeal in *Re Grayan Building Services Ltd, Secretary of State for Trade and Industry v Gray* [1995] Ch. 241 and *Re Copecrest Ltd, Secretary of State for Trade & Industry v McTighe (No.2)* [1996] 2 B.C.L.C. 477.

traded as a retailer of prams and children's toys from various shop premises. Having lost a lucrative concession with a leading department store in the late-1980s, the company's profitability declined drastically. During the early 1990s it suffered a series of misfortunes, through no fault of the two defendants, which were compounded by a recession. The audited accounts for the year ended December 31, 1991 showed a substantial loss and contained a "going concern" qualification. The defendants signed these accounts in October 1992 by which time the company's cash flow difficulties were acute. They then sought to negotiate an increase in the company's overdraft facility in order to finance trading up to the end of 1992. The company normally achieved one-third of its yearly turnover in the two months leading up to Christmas and the defendants believed that if borrowings were increased they would be able to trade out of difficulty by the beginning of 1993, a view shared by the company's auditors. The bank agreed to extend the overdraft limit in return for the provision of fresh personal security by the defendants and their father. However, trading over the Christmas period did not produce the anticipated increase in turnover and profitability. One of the defendants suffered a nervous breakdown, further compounding the company's problems. By January 1993 the company could not hope to survive without the support of the bank and its major creditors. The bank took the view that it could justify supporting the company for a further three months. Some creditors agreed to repayment by instalments but others refused and so, on the advice of insolvency practitioners, the company entered creditors' voluntary liquidation in April 1993. The Secretary of State's principal allegation was that the defendants had caused the company to trade while insolvent to the detriment of its creditors from October 1992 onwards. The registrar dismissed the application, holding that the defendants' decision to continue trading was based on reasonable grounds. While the company was undoubtedly insolvent in October 1992, he accepted that the defendants were justified in attempting to trade out of difficulty over the Christmas period especially as their decision was supported by the bank and the auditors. Moreover, the registrar concluded that the decision to trade on while trying to rally the support of creditors for the short period after Christmas was also reasonable in the circumstances. On appeal, the judge agreed with the registrar in relation to the period up to Christmas but disagreed in relation to the period of continued trading from January to April 1993:

> "In my judgment, from January 1993, from the evidence the only conclusion which could properly be reached was that the conduct of . . . the [defendants] has to be categorised as the taking of unwarranted risks with creditors' money by continuing to trade. If the company could not be restored to profit by the Christmas trading there was no hope for it in the early months of 1993. Each [defendant] clearly permitted the company to continue to trade whilst insolvent . . . the law focuses on the offence rather than the offender, albeit that the offender is honest and does not lack commercial probity."[38]

The defendants were each disqualified for two years.

5–16 In *Ward Sherrard* and *City Pram*, the courts were not prepared to allow the defendants much margin for error. *Ward Sherrard* is a classic case of a business that over-expands in its early years and fails to control overheads. It is perhaps

[38] [1998] B.C.C. 537 at 547.

understandable that its directors saw fit to continue while turnover was increasing. In theory at least, it is not true to say that the creditors in *Ward Sherrard* were left wholly at the mercy of the defendants as they were in a position to make an informed judgment over whether to advance further credit to the company once the qualified accounts for June 1989 had been filed with the Registrar of Companies. However, it is doubtful whether, in practice, many trade creditors monitor the company's position by keeping track of filings at Companies House. The decision in *City Pram* looks even tougher. The defendants were fighting to save an established family business against the backdrop of an economic recession. The bank was consulted. The auditors were consulted. The creditors themselves were consulted and when they refused to forebear, the defendants put the company into liquidation. Creditors are always put at risk when an insolvent company continues to trade. However, the question is whether it was *unreasonable* for the defendants to take the decision to continue trading in the prevailing circumstances. It is arguable that the defendants in *City Pram* acted responsibly in difficult circumstances. That said, the court's decision can probably be justified because the defendants continued to accept customer deposits in the period from January 1993 in circumstances where there must have been serious doubt as to whether the items ordered would ever be delivered.[39]

5–17 By way of contrast, the courts in *Re Wimbledon Village Restaurant Ltd* and *Re Moonlight Foods (UK) Ltd* were prepared to allow the defendants a greater margin of error. In the first case, the Secretary of State sought disqualification orders against three directors of WVR Ltd, a company which traded in the restaurant business from March 1985 until it entered creditors' voluntary liquidation in November 1989. The company was originally incorporated by the third defendant, W, who was an experienced restaurant proprietor. Financed by bank borrowings, the company acquired the lease of some licensed premises and began trading. W gave an unlimited personal guarantee of the company's indebtedness to the bank. By the end of 1986, it was clear that the restaurant was not a financial success and W's original co-venturers decided to leave and withdrew their capital. At this point, W invited her two co-defendants, IT and GT, who were brothers, to join the company as directors. GT had an established reputation as a successful manager of wine bars and so the new board decided to reduce prices in the restaurant and open a wine bar in the basement of the premises. In order to refinance WVR Ltd, IT and GT agreed to lend the company £50,000 in return for a controlling interest. The management of the business was placed entirely in their hands and they agreed to indemnify W against any liability under her bank guarantee over and above the level of her existing exposure at the date of the takeover. W remained a director so as to monitor her personal exposure to the bank but played no further part in the management of the business. It was accepted that the company was balance sheet insolvent at the time of the takeover, but the view of the brothers, supported by professional and family advice, was that its fortunes could be turned around. Although initially they managed to

[39] See 5–56 below, though cf. *Re World of Leather Plc, Secretary of State for Trade and Industry v Gill* [2004] EWHC 933 (Ch), [2006] B.C.C. 725 discussed from 5–22.

generate an increase in turnover, the business was never profitable. By early 1989 the bank was questioning the company's continuing viability. A number of cheques had already been dishonoured by this stage. Basic accounting functions were not being carried out properly and the company's books were not up-to-date. There was no immediate prospect of selling the business because the company's lease was up for renewal and the lessor had indicated that he was not prepared to grant a new lease on the grounds that he wished to reoccupy the premises. Further cheques were dishonoured, creditors who pressed for payment were strung along with excuses and in July 1989, by which time GT had left the business, the Inland Revenue took walking possession of the company's moveable assets. The company finally ceased trading in September 1989. The deputy judge concluded that from the end of March 1989 onwards IT and GT should have realised that the company was only able to continue trading at the expense of its creditors:

> "In my judgment a dispassionate analysis at any point thereafter would have led to the conclusion that continued trading could only be justified if there was a real prospect of selling the business in the very near future. In the event no such sober analysis took place."[40]

There was never any genuine attempt either to value or market the business with a view to sale and the company was faced with the added difficulty that the lessor was refusing to renew the lease. The Secretary of State alleged that the brothers were deliberately gambling at the expense of creditors in the period after March 1989 with the objective of driving down the bank overdraft so as to reduce or eliminate their personal exposure under the indemnity that they had given to W. The judge refused to accept that there was any such conscious design but he did accept that the brothers' conduct had been unsatisfactory:

> "The picture I have is not one of a deliberate strategy to reduce the overdraft at expense of trade creditors and then to scuttle the ship, but rather one of allowing the ship to drift. Had the brothers been trading with personal liability, I doubt whether events would have taken quite the same course . . . In my judgment the way in which the business of the company was run from the end of March onwards was not the way in which such a business ought to have been run, given the possible consequences for trade creditors. I find that both [IT] and [GT] paid insufficient regard to the interests of creditors during this period. It was the responsibility of both of them to make an early and informed decision on what would be in the best interests of the company and its creditors. This did not happen . . . and, while they may have genuinely believed that they would be able to sell the business and lease . . . should the worst come to the worst, they did not have reasonable grounds on which to base such a belief. It was the product of wishful thinking."[41]

5–18 Despite this finding, the application against the brothers was dismissed. The judge emphasised that not every past impropriety necessarily makes the person responsible for it unfit and, in their favour, he took into account what he described as "the peculiar combination of family and commercial circumstances in which

[40] [1994] B.C.C. 753 at 761.
[41] [1994] B.C.C. 753 at 762.

they found themselves".[42] Left with a "significant measure of doubt", the judge decided to resolve it in the brothers' favour. W was also exonerated.

When compared with *City Pram*, the approach in this case looks generous. The judge seems to have expected the Secretary of State to establish a high degree of culpability (i.e. some conscious design) and was anxious, given the benefit of hindsight, not to apply too strict a standard.[43] Thus the approach in *Wimbledon Village Restaurant* appears to equate unfitness with lack of probity rather than some lesser threshold of culpability such as negligence or incompetence.

5–19 A similar approach was taken in *Re Moonlight Foods (UK) Ltd*.[44] In that case the company, M Ltd, ran a sandwich-making business, but traded for under two years before administrative receivers were appointed in February 1992. The company amounted in substance to a partnership between D and T. D had previously run a similar business but needed finance to expand. She was introduced to T who was the major shareholder and managing director of a building company. M Ltd was incorporated with a view to acquiring a sandwich-making business which was in the hands of receivers. T persuaded his company to invest in M Ltd (it acquired a controlling interest) and agreed to provide financial and accounting expertise. D agreed to provide her client list and experience of the business. C, the finance director of T's company was appointed as M Ltd's secretary and it was agreed that he would attend to day to day accounting matters. The business was acquired from the receivers for around £60,000 of which £10,000 was paid by M Ltd with T's company meeting the balance of £50,000. The £50,000 balance was treated as an unsecured loan by T's company to M Ltd. A secured overdraft facility was negotiated with M Ltd's bankers. It is clear from these financing arrangements that the company was highly geared from the start of its active trading life. Having lost a major contract, M Ltd was already in financial difficulty before the end of 1990. The bank agreed to increase its overdraft limit in return for a guarantee from T's company. It is clear that creditors were pressing for payment throughout the company's life. Despite regular cash injections by T's company, it was never profitable. Moreover, M Ltd's accounting records, the particular responsibility of C, were never in a satisfactory state. Several cheques were dishonoured. D and T appear to have been content to rely on profit and cash flow forecasts provided by C rather than any hard accounting information concerning the company's financial position. The auditors of T's

[42] [1994] B.C.C. 753 at 764. Among the extenuating factors taken into account were general economic conditions (with particular reference to the rise in interest rates during 1989) and the breakdown of the brothers' personal relationship. Thus economic and personal factors were said to have contributed to the situation rather than any "innate or invincible incompetence" on the brothers' part.

[43] A judge following the sort of approach taken in *Synthetic Technology* and *City Pram* might well have taken a less generous view of the evidence (especially that concerning the pressing creditors and dishonoured cheques) and imposed a short period of disqualification. It is interesting to note that the deputy judge in *Wimbledon Village Restaurants* (who became Hart J.) subsequently cast doubt on his own decision: see *Landhurst Leasing Plc, Secretary of State for Trade and Industry v Ball* [1999] 1 B.C.L.C. 286 at 346–347. Nevertheless, it has still been followed: see *Secretary of State for Trade and Industry v Blackwood* 2003 S.L.T. 120.

[44] [1996] B.C.C. 678.

company, mindful of the impact of M Ltd's business on the group as a whole, had expressed grave reservations about the company's viability and the lack of concrete accounting information from around September 1991 and, by November 1991, described the situation with regard to "problem creditors" as "dangerous". The company's salvation appears to have rested on a contract with British Home Stores. However, British Home Stores reduced their order in December 1991 and discontinued orders altogether in January 1992. The bank appointed receivers a month later. The judge held that C was principally to blame for much of what had gone wrong but declined to disqualify him as he had never been appointed a director and was not found to have acted as a de facto director. He then went on to deal with the question of whether D and T had taken "unwarranted risks":

> "It is submitted that the directors should have realised that [C's] projections were unreliable because they had not been tested against management accounts . . . No lack of probity is suggested, and in my judgment the conduct of these directors in continuing to trade on what, with hindsight, may be seen to be inadequate information is not reprehensible enough to justify a finding that either of them is unfit . . . In this case I have found no dishonesty, no breach of common standards of commercial morality, no cynical disregard for others' interests and no gross incompetence on the part of either [D] or [T]. At worst they were guilty of naivety, over-optimism and misplaced trust."[45]

5–20 The court's approach in *Moonlight Foods* was extremely circumspect. The judge accepted that it was appropriate to apply the test from *Synthetic Technology* rather than the wording of s.214. However, it appears from the passage quoted above, that the court required the claimant to establish a higher degree of culpability (e.g. dishonesty or gross incompetence) than that suggested by the "unwarranted risks" test. It may be that the court was reluctant to disqualify D and T having refused to assume jurisdiction over C on the basis that C was not a "director". It appears that the judge was anxious to avoid a result that treated D and T more severely than the person he considered to be mainly responsible for the company's downfall.[46] He may also have been influenced in D's case by the fact that she was already disqualified anyway under CDDA s.11 having been made bankrupt.

5–21 The four cases discussed illustrate the important, if trite, point that the decision in a borderline case boils down ultimately to a matter of individual judgment. The courts in *Ward Sherrard* and *City Pram* applied a lower threshold of culpability and allowed the defendants very little margin. The courts in *Wimbledon Village Restaurant* and *Moonlight Foods* applied a higher threshold of culpability and were much more prepared to make allowance for the potentially distorting impact

[45] [1996] B.C.C. 678 at 692–693.

[46] The decision not to assume jurisdiction over C is criticised in 3–30 and 3–39. A further rationalisation is that D and T were justified in delegating responsibility for the company's financial affairs to someone of C's experience and expertise. However, in several cases the courts have said that all directors have a responsibility to monitor the company's financial position. Where, as here, there has been a failure to keep adequate accounting records in accordance with the Companies Acts, even directors who are not charged with the task of overseeing the book-keeping are routinely disqualified: see from 5–36 and on the issue of apportionment of responsibility from 5–82.

of judicial hindsight.[47] This higher threshold approach is characterised by greater deference to managerial decision-making and greater willingness on the part of the court, at least implicitly, to classify the decision to continue trading as a legitimate commercial misjudgment. Thus, whereas the judge in *Ward Sherrard* dismissed as groundless a genuinely-held belief that the company could trade out of difficulty, the judge in *Moonlight Foods* was much more prepared to defer to the directors' subjective evaluation of the position. This leaves some scope for the tacit operation of variants of the discredited "sunshine" or "blue skies" test applied historically in fraudulent trading cases.[48] Even so, the counsel of perfection for the company director is to learn the lesson of the decisions in *Ward Sherrard* and *City Pram*. Where the company is insolvent, the decision to continue trading must be a well-informed one based on accurate, up-to-date financial information and a realistic, objectively justifiable evaluation of the company's prospects, preferably with the benefit of outside professional advice. Once taken, the decision must be regularly reviewed and the company's prospects continually re-evaluated. Professional advice should be heeded and unbridled optimism checked.[49] At the same time, *Wimbledon Village Restaurant* and *Moonlight Foods* show that the Secretary of State may face difficulties in making a case for disqualification based solely on an allegation of trading to the detriment of creditors. It is always possible that the court may make subtle adjustments to the burden of proof to try and counter the effect of hindsight. It is perhaps a reflection of this that few applications for orders under s.6 are brought on the basis of trading to the detriment of creditors alone. Indeed, the court is much more likely to make a finding of unfit conduct if there is evidence of other misconduct that serves to strengthen the inference of trading to the detriment of creditors or exacerbate the case. Several of the matters commonly raised as additional allegations in cases involving trading to the detriment of creditors are discussed below. The range of matters provides a useful illustration of the combinations of (often-related) misconduct that can lead to a finding of unfit conduct and mandatory disqualification. While there is nothing to prevent the claimant raising many of these additional matters in isolation, it is common for a number of them to be linked to an allegation of trading to the detriment of creditors so as

[47] For further cases where a less strict approach was adopted see, e.g. *Re Douglas Construction Services Ltd* [1988] B.C.L.C. 397; *Re CU Fittings Ltd* [1989] B.C.L.C. 556 (both decided under s.300 of the Companies Act 1985); *Re Bath Glass Ltd* [1988] B.C.L.C. 329; *Secretary of State for Trade and Industry v Blackwood* 2003 S.L.T. 120. For other cases taking a lower threshold approach see, e.g. *Re City Investment Centres Ltd* [1992] B.C.L.C. 956; *Re Amaron Ltd, Secretary of State for Trade and Industry v Lubrani (No.2)* [2001] 1 B.C.L.C. 562.

[48] See, e.g. *Re White & Osmond (Parkstone) Ltd*, June 30, 1960, Ch. D., unreported, cited in *R. v Grantham* [1984] Q.B. 675. The test is so called because the defendant who genuinely believed that the "sun would eventually shine" as far as the company's fortunes were concerned, was likely to escape liability even if the belief was groundless.

[49] On the dangers for directors who fail to follow good professional advice and plough on believing, without foundation, that the company's fortunes will turn around see *Re Synthetic Technology Ltd* [1993] B.C.C. 549; *Re GSAR Realisations Ltd* [1993] B.C.L.C. 409; *Re Living Images Ltd* [1996] 1 B.C.L.C. 348; *Re Park House Properties Ltd, Secretary of State for Trade and Industry v Carter* [1997] 2 B.C.L.C. 530.

to illustrate a general failure on the defendant's part to exercise financial responsibility.[50] Equally, some of the other matters discussed, such as breach of fiduciary duty or fraud, may well be sufficiently serious on their own to merit a finding of unfit conduct.

5–22 The foregoing has to be read in light of Blackburne J.'s decision in *Re World of Leather Plc, Secretary of State for Trade and Industry v Gill*.[51] The material facts of *World of Leather* were as follows. World of Leather Plc ("WOL") was a wholly-owned subsidiary of Uno Plc ("Uno"). The group traded as a furniture retailer through a large number of retail outlets. It did not manufacture furniture but purchased it for re-sale. The shares of both group companies were listed on the Stock Exchange. Both companies were placed in administration in mid-March 2000 with an aggregate deficiency as regards creditors in excess of £25 million. The aggregate deficiency was such that unsecured creditors, including customers who had paid cash deposits in respect of furniture ordered but not delivered, would recover nothing. The Secretary of State's case against the five defendants, all of whom it appears were directors of both Uno and WOL,[52] was based on their conduct during the four-month period from (roughly) early November 1999 to mid-March 2000 at the end of which the companies entered administration. The complaint discussed further below, related to the continued taking and using of customers deposits after November 1999. The following points emerged from the evidence:

(1) It was said to be industry practice for customer deposits to be used as working capital. In broad terms, deposits were received at a time when the companies were receiving credit from other creditors, payments by them for furniture generally not being required to be made until some time after delivery. Throughout the life of the companies, deposits provided the group with much of its working capital. No professional adviser involved (for example, the auditors) had ever commented adversely on this business practice.

(2) It was not suggested by the Secretary of State that, in the particular case, such deposits were held subject to any trust or fiduciary obligation requiring them to be segregated in any way, whether arising by way of contract or otherwise.

(3) Throughout the four-month period the cash flow problems of Uno and WOL were such that, in order to continue trading, they relied on cash deposits paid by customers for furniture in advance of delivery as a critical source of working capital. Although, overall, the company's financial position did not

[50] Even so the court will consider each distinct allegation separately (as well as cumulatively) see *Re New Generation Engineers Ltd* [1993] B.C.L.C. 435 at 438–439; *Re Copecrest Ltd, Secretary of State for Trade & Industry v McTighe (No.2)* [1996] 2 B.C.L.C. 477; *Re Barings Plc (No.5), Secretary of State for Trade and Industry v Baker* [2000] 1 B.C.L.C. 523. Moreover, the courts have on occasions made disqualification orders based exclusively on what are described in the main text as "additional matters". For an early case based exclusively on accounting defaults see *Re Rolus Properties Ltd* (1988) 4 B.C.C. 446. For a case in which the court made a disqualification order on the basis that the defendants had failed to pay Crown debts despite rejecting an allegation of trading to the detriment of creditors see *Re Verby Print for Advertising Ltd, Secretary of State for Trade and Industry v Fine* [1998] 2 B.C.L.C. 23 discussed from 5–32.

[51] [2006] B.C.C. 725.

[52] [2006] B.C.C. 725 at [15]–[31].

significantly worsen during the four-month period, the amount of customer deposits held by the group roughly doubled to about £5 million.[53]

(4) From mid-November 1999 onwards, a discount scheme was actively promoted under which customers of Uno were encouraged to pay a greater proportion of the cost of furniture ordered in advance in return for a price discount. The scheme led to increased sales.[54]

(5) The group retained the support of key creditors throughout the period and traded within the limit on its overdraft. However, cash flow was further squeezed because of the decision of a number of finance companies, with whom the group had in place arrangements for the financing of customer purchases, to modify their terms with the result that they were only prepared to fund payment of the full cash price of purchases on delivery rather than the payment of deposits at the point when orders were made.[55]

(6) It was accepted by the defendants in light of the group's cash flow projections that, in the absence of re-financing or a sale of the viable parts of the group's business, the group could not continue to trade beyond mid-2000.

(7) The defendants, on behalf of the group, sought regular advice during the period from lawyers and accountants experienced in insolvency and corporate restructuring. The central and recurring theme of the advice was that, while in an ideal world customer deposits should be paid into a separate trust account and only released into the general trading account once furniture was delivered, segregation of deposits was not essential as long as the directors reasonably and justifiably believed that a solution to the group's problems, short of formal insolvency, could be found.[56] Moreover, as immediate cessation of trading and winding up would have been unlikely to produce any return for unsecured creditors, the defendants were advised on at least one occasion that it was their duty to explore other options.[57] Unless the cash deposits had continued to be used, it is clear that the companies would have had to cease trading immediately.

(8) Throughout the four-month period, the defendants constantly monitored the company's financial position and, in particular, regularly reviewed its cash flow forecasts. They enlisted independent accountants to verify and validate the group's budgets and projections.[58]

(9) A number of possible solutions to the group's problems were actively pursued. One set of negotiations with a potential Italian purchaser of WOL's business reached the heads of terms stage and due diligence was carried out. Negotiations for a management buy-out (involving two of the defendants) backed by venture capital finance also reached an advanced stage. It is clear that these were serious offers by interested purchasers.

(10) In late February the potential Italian purchaser withdrew its offer. In early March, the management buy-out team's financial backers withdrew their

[53] [2006] B.C.C. 725 at [116], [155].
[54] [2006] B.C.C. 725 at [14].
[55] [2006] B.C.C. 725 at [3], [13].
[56] [2006] B.C.C. 725 at [46]–[48], [52]–[58], [64], [71]–[73], [81]–[85], [99]–[100].
[57] [2006] B.C.C. 725 at [72].
[58] [2006] B.C.C. 725 at [74], [78].

support. Once it became clear that a successful sale of the viable parts of the group's business would not be forthcoming, the companies were very quickly placed into administration.

5–23 The single allegation against the defendants was that they had caused or allowed the two companies to trade at the risk of its pre-paying customers at a time when the companies were insolvent.[59] Essentially, the allegation was that it had been unreasonable for the defendants to continue trading at the risk of unsuspecting members of the public. In truth, the Secretary of State's case was that the defendants had taken unfair advantage of, and/or unfairly discriminated against, those customers who had paid cash deposits in respect of furniture orders that the group, given its financial position, might not have been (and, as it turned out, was not) in a position to honour.[60] It follows that the case against the defendants was not based on an allegation that they had caused the companies to continue trading while insolvent to the detriment of creditors generally. Significantly, the Secretary of State had conceded in open correspondence that there had been a reasonable prospect of the group avoiding insolvent liquidation during the four-month period.[61] Thus, even though it was accepted that the defendants had acted reasonably in causing the companies to continue to trade for four months so as to enable a rescue strategy to be formulated and implemented, the Secretary of State's case was that the funding of such continued trading out of customer deposits was conduct which made them unfit and liable to disqualification. It is clear (see (1), (3) and (7) in 5–22 above) that the companies could not have realistically continued trading without relying on customer deposits for working capital.

5–24 In the result, Blackburne J. concluded that the defendants' conduct was not such as to make them unfit. He summarised the dilemma facing the defendants in the following terms:

> "The defendants' evidence, which was not disputed, was that if the group had ceased trading on 6 November [1999] cash-paying customers awaiting delivery of the goods they had ordered . . . would have received nothing in the event of liquidation (and would not have received the goods that they had ordered) and the group would have had to lay off several hundred employees. The judgment which the defendants had therefore to make, and keep under constant review throughout the four-month period, was whether to cease trading there and then, with the inevitable consequence of an insolvency in which the group's unsecured creditors, including in particular those who had paid cash deposits but not yet received their goods, would receive nothing and in which, in addition, there would be the loss of several hundred jobs on the part of the group's employees, or whether to continue to trade in the reasonable expectation of effecting a corporate solution which would ensure that all creditors would be paid and all customers would receive the goods for which they had provided a deposit (and many, if not all, of the employees' jobs would be safeguarded). In short, the directors were faced with an unenviable dilemma: whether, by ceasing to trade, to condemn existing cash-paying customers and

[59] On the framing of the allegation see [2006] B.C.C. 725 at [11], [117]–[121], [140].

[60] [2006] B.C.C. 725 at [149], [150]–[152]. On this type of allegation, see further from 5–27 with particular reference to Crown creditors. See also from 5–56.

[61] [2006] B.C.C. 725 at [116], [142].

> other unsecured creditors to the certainty of receiving nothing or whether, by continuing to trade and continuing therefore to receive deposits and otherwise incur credit, to subject future cash-paying customers and others extending credit to the group to the risk of loss, but to do so in the knowledge that there was a reasonable prospect of achieving a solution to the group's difficulties which would enable everyone to be paid in full."[62]

Accordingly, while mindful of the plight of the cash-paying customers, with hindsight, the judge could see no real grounds for criticising the directors.[63] Once it was accepted that the directors had acted reasonably in continuing to trade given the reasonable prospects that the companies would avoid insolvent liquidation, the trading was not at the "unreasonable risk" of creditors generally,[64] nor at the unreasonable risk of deposit paying customers. Trading could only continue if customer deposits were taken and used, as had always been the case. The Secretary of State suggested that what was improper was that unfair advantage had been taken of customers paying deposits because they, unlike the bank and other financial backers of the group, were not informed as to what was going on. However, Blackburne J. decided, correctly it is respectfully suggested, that the mere fact that customers were not informed of the position was not enough to amount to an "unfair advantage". The banks and other creditors had to be informed if the group was to continue trading. There was no evidence that the directors had tried to take advantage of customers by keeping them in the dark or that they had recklessly or negligently continued trading and taken deposits in circumstances where the risk to which such customers were thereafter exposed was unreasonable.

5–25 In the course of reviewing the authorities, Blackburne J. made some observations that could be read as suggesting that, for the purposes of an allegation of trading while insolvent to the detriment of creditors, conduct will only make a director unfit where it satisfies the test for civil liability for wrongful trading set out in s.214 of the Insolvency Act 1986. For example, at para.[144] of his judgment he expressed the following view:

> ". . . .[O]rdinarily, a director will not be at risk of a finding of unfitness, such as to lead automatically to disqualification, *merely* because he knowingly allows the company to trade while insolvent, *i.e.* he allows the company to incur credit (including, I would add, accepting a payment from a customer in advance of the supply of the relevant goods or service) even though, at the time and as he knows, the company is insolvent and later goes into liquidation. It does not add anything to the proposition to say that, in causing the company to incur credit (or accept payment in advance of the supply of the goods or service), the director was 'taking advantage' of the third party supplier of credit. If the director is to be found unfit there must ordinarily be an additional ingredient. Normally that ingredient is that, *at the time that the credit is taken (or the advance payment received, which is in essence the same), the director knows or should know that there is no reasonable prospect of his company avoiding insolvency*."[65]

[62] [2006] B.C.C. 725 at [155]. See, by analogy, *Re Continental Assurance Co of London Plc* [2001] B.P.I.R. 733 at [281].
[63] [2006] B.C.C. 725 at [164]–[165].
[64] See 5–11.
[65] [2006] B.C.C. 725 [144] (emphasis supplied) relying on *Secretary of State for Trade and Industry v Creegan* [2002] 1 B.C.L.C. 99.

It is suggested that this passage needs to be read in the context of the particular circumstances of the *World of Leather* case and of the rest of the judgment. In particular, it is clear that the judge recognised that conduct that did not satisfy the "no reasonable prospects" test for wrongful trading could nevertheless amount to unfit conduct.[66] All, in effect, that the judge did decide was that: (a) knowingly allowing a company to trade while insolvent does not necessarily amount to unfit conduct in isolation and without more; (b) merely because a director reasonably believed that the company could avoid formal insolvency proceedings does not necessarily mean that he will escape a finding of unfit conduct; and (c) on the particular facts of *World of Leather*, the defendants' conduct in causing the companies to continue accepting customer deposits in circumstances where there was a reasonable prospect of avoiding formal insolvency proceedings did not make them unfit. This does not mean that, for example, directors in a similar position who trade recklessly without professional advice and without carefully monitoring the company's financial position will escape disqualification even where it is not alleged, in addition, that the directors should have known that there was no reasonable prospect of the company avoiding insolvent liquidation.

5–26 In summary, the test is whether the defendant acted unreasonably in the knowledge of the company's insolvency to the detriment of creditors not (unless the allegation is so couched) whether the defendant knew or ought to have known that there was no reasonable prospect of avoiding insolvent liquidation. Thus, for example, in *Re Mea Corporation Ltd, Secretary of State for Trade and Industry v Aviss*, two defendants who had established a central treasury function for a group of companies were found to be unfit where monies were diverted outside of the group in order to shore up the finances of other companies in which one of the defendants was interested.[67] In *Mea Corporation*, the decision to continue trading in the knowledge of insolvency was held to be unreasonable in the circumstances. In the words of Lewison J.:

> "In many cases that come before the courts, the facts are such that the directors take a decision to attempt to trade out of insolvency; and the question then is whether they were reasonable in trying. In a typical case, the company's receipts are applied in its business, but they cannot keep up with its overheads, trade debts or tax liabilities. That is not this case. In this case the receipts of all three companies were diverted away from their respective businesses and applied for the benefit of other companies (outside the group) in which Mr Aviss had an interest. In economic terms, creditors' money was being used to attempt to shore up other companies with which they did not do business and of whose very existence they may have been ignorant. That, in my judgment, is not a reasonable decision for a responsible director to take."[68]

This chapter now turns to consider a number of other forms of unfit conduct that frequently overlap with trading to the detriment of creditors.

[66] [2006] B.C.C. 725 at [145] (citing the judgment of Peter Gibson J. in *Re Bath Glass Ltd* [1988] B.C.L.C. 329 with approval) and see further from 5–06 above.
[67] [2007] 1 B.C.L.C. 618.
[68] [2007] 1 B.C.L.C. 618 at [109].

Deliberate failure to pay Crown or other non-pressing creditors and the concept of unfair discrimination

5–27 Another specific allegation frequently raised in s.6 disqualification proceedings is that the defendant caused the company to withhold payment of sums owing to Revenue and Customs in respect of PAYE, national insurance contributions and VAT with the effect that the company was only able to continue trading at the expense of the Crown. At first sight, the non-payment of Crown debts appears merely to be one aspect of the wider allegation that the defendant caused or allowed the company to continue trading to the detriment of creditors. This is much the way in which such an allegation was approached by Ferris J. in *Re GSAR Realisations Ltd*:

> ". . . the non-payment of substantial Crown debts by a company which is in financial difficulties . . . may support an inference that the directors have made a deliberate decision only to pay those creditors who pressed for payment, with the result that the company while insolvent has unfairly been using as working capital money which ought to have been paid to creditors . . . Looked at in this way, the non-payment of Crown debts is merely one aspect of the charge . . . that he allowed the company to trade after he knew it had become unable to pay its debts. I shall deal with this complaint as part of the same general charge."[69]

It was also stated in *Re Bath Glass Ltd* that the non-payment of Crown debts is not to be regarded as significant unless the court can infer from it that the directors knew or ought to have known that the company was trading while insolvent to the detriment of creditors.[70] However, there are cases in which it is has been raised as an independent allegation.

5–28 The debate concerning the precise status and treatment of Crown debts in the context of disqualification proceedings is of long standing. The early cases decided before 1990 reveal a marked lack of judicial consensus. In a series of cases, Harman J. took the view that monies representing VAT paid by customers and deductions of tax and national insurance from employees' wages were held by the company on "quasi-trust". It followed that the company was obliged to account for these monies rather than "misapply" them for its own cash flow purposes. On this analysis the non-payment of Crown debts was regarded as more serious than the non-payment of ordinary trade debts in determining unfit conduct.[71] The justification for this approach appears to lie in the public nature of these liabilities and the Crown's status as an involuntary creditor. By contrast, in *Re Dawson Print Group Ltd*, Hoffmann J. refused to make any distinction between non-payment of Crown debts and ordinary trade debts in terms of relative seriousness.[72] Indeed, he voiced doubt over whether the failure to pay Crown debts would at that time have been regarded as sufficiently serious in the commercial world to justify a finding

[69] [1993] B.C.L.C. 409 at 412–413.

[70] [1988] B.C.L.C. 329 at 337.

[71] See, e.g. *Re Howard Davey & Co Ltd*, December 7, 1984, Ch.D. unreported; *Re Flatbolt Ltd*, February 21, 1986, Ch.D. unreported; *Re Wedgecraft Ltd*, March 7, 1986, Ch.D. unreported; *Re Cladrose Ltd* [1990] B.C.L.C. 204.

[72] [1987] B.C.L.C. 601 at 604–605.

of unfit conduct in itself. Two points can be made in support of Hoffmann J.'s approach. First, non-payment of Crown debts is not one of the specific matters mentioned in Sch.1 to which the court is directed to have particular regard. It might be inferred from this that Parliament and the Secretary of State (who has power to add further specific matters to Sch.1 under s.9(4) of the CDDA) do not currently regard such conduct as particularly heinous. However, it may be thought that this is a weak point as there is nothing in the CDDA to suggest that misconduct falling within the Schedule should automatically be regarded as more serious than misconduct falling outside.[73] Secondly, at the time when *Dawson Print* was decided (and, indeed, until recently), the Crown was protected to some extent by virtue of its preferential status in insolvency and this arguably compensated it for being in the position of an involuntary creditor.[74]

Other judges steered a middle path between the two extremes of the "quasi-trust" and *Dawson Print* approaches. In *Re Stanford Services Ltd*, Vinelott J. seems to have suggested that failure to pay Crown debts was more serious than failure to pay trade debts because of the Crown's status as an involuntary creditor. However, in reaching the conclusion that the defendant was unfit the judge laid no special emphasis on non-payment of Crown debts and simply inferred from the evidence that he had caused the company to trade to the detriment of creditors while insolvent.[75]

In *Re Lo-Line Electric Motors Ltd*, Browne-Wilkinson V.C. expressed the view, without adopting Harman J.'s quasi-trust analysis, that the use of Crown monies to finance the continuation of an insolvent company's business was more culpable than the failure to pay trade debts. However, this conclusion appears to rest on the misapprehension that failure to account for PAYE and national insurance contributions deducted from wages was somehow prejudicial to employees.[76] The emphasis apparent in *Stanford Services* and *Lo-Line* on the Crown's special status as an involuntary creditor has led the courts in some cases to treat failure to pay Crown debts less seriously where the evidence showed that Revenue and Customs had agreed to accept payment by instalments.[77] Nevertheless, with the exception of *Dawson Print*, the view that failure to pay Crown debts should be treated more seriously than failure to pay trade debts appears to have gained judicial acceptance in the period before 1990.

[73] See discussion in 4–46 to 4–47.

[74] Although this was never a complete form of protection as only limited amounts of Crown debt ranked as preferential in receivership and liquidation under the old law. The Crown's preferential status was abolished by the Enterprise Act 2002 s.251 with effect from September 15, 2003.

[75] [1987] B.C.L.C. 607 at 617.

[76] [1988] Ch. 477 at 488. The misapprehension was cleared up in *Re Sevenoaks Stationers Ltd* [1991] Ch. 164. For other cases steering a middle course see *Re Western Welsh International System Buildings Ltd* (1988) 4 B.C.C. 449; *Re J & B Lynch (Builders) Ltd* [1988] B.C.L.C. 376.

[77] See, e.g. *Re McNulty's Interchange Ltd* [1989] B.C.L.C. 709 at 536; *Re Keypak Homecare Ltd* [1990] B.C.L.C. 440 at 445; though cf. *Re Westminster Property Management Ltd (No.2), Official Receiver v Stern (No.2)* [2001] EWCA Civ 1787, [2002] 1 B.C.L.C. 119 at [58]–[62]. Note, however, that directors are not entitled to rely on the fact that the Crown has failed to take action against the company for non-payment as a justification for continuing to withhold Crown monies: see *Re Park House Properties Ltd, Secretary of State for Trade and Industry v Carter* [1997] 2 B.C.L.C. 530 at 548; *Leung v Official Receiver* [2006] EWCA Civ 3178 at [31]–[38].

5–29 The Court of Appeal decision in *Re Sevenoaks Stationers (Retail) Ltd*[78] changed the emphasis and laid the foundation for the modern approach. In this case there was evidence that substantial Crown debts had been allowed to accumulate at a time when the defendant knew that the relevant companies were in increasing financial difficulty. The Court of Appeal held that non-payment of Crown debts should not automatically be treated as evidence of unfit conduct and that the court should consider on the facts of the particular case whether to attribute any significance to the fact of such non-payment. Dillon L.J. adopted the following analysis:

> "[The defendant] made a deliberate decision to pay only those creditors who pressed for payment. The obvious result was that the two companies traded, when in fact insolvent and known to be in difficulties, at the expense of those creditors who, *like the Crown*, happened not to be pressing for payment. Such conduct on the part of a director can well, in my judgment, be relied on as a ground for saying that he is unfit to be concerned in the management of a company. But what is relevant in the Crown's position is not that the debt was a debt which arose from a compulsory deduction from employees' wages or a compulsory payment of VAT, but that the Crown was not pressing for payment, and the director was taking unfair advantage of that forbearance on the part of the Crown, and, instead of providing adequate working capital, was trading at the Crown's expense while the companies were in jeopardy. *It would be equally unfair to trade in that way and in such circumstances at the expense of creditors other than the Crown. The Crown is more exposed not from the nature of the debts but from the administrative problem it has in pressing for prompt payment as companies get into difficulties*."[79]

Thus, the Court of Appeal did not attach any special or added significance to the non-payment of Crown debts in determining whether the defendant was unfit and took a much broader approach. The implication of *Sevenoaks Stationers* is that where a company is insolvent, the deliberate practice of paying only those creditors who are pressing while withholding payment from creditors (which may include the Crown) who are not pressing is likely to result in a finding of unfit conduct. As such, the essence of the misconduct described by Dillon L.J. lies in the discriminatory impact of the practice on some of the creditors. In effect, if the directors adopt this type of practice, the company will continue to trade at the risk of its non-pressing creditors while other creditors receive preferential treatment. Discriminating between creditors in this way may be motivated by a desire to preserve the support of key creditors for possible future ventures or to reduce the directors' exposure under personal guarantees.

5–30 Following *Sevenoaks Stationers*, it is possible that the courts will treat a director who discriminates between different creditors in this way more seriously than one who simply allows the company to trade while insolvent at the expense of all its creditors. In *Sevenoaks Stationers* itself, the Court of Appeal treated the discriminatory practice as a separate ground that added weight to other findings (including a general finding of trading to the detriment of creditors) and concluded that a five-year disqualification was appropriate. Even before *Sevenoaks Stationers* there are

[78] [1991] Ch. 164.
[79] [1991] Ch. 164 at 183. Emphasis added.

some indications that the courts were starting to move in this direction. In *Re Cladrose Ltd*, Harman J. indicated that a case where all the creditors suffer would be regarded as less serious than a case where trade creditors are paid but the Crown is deliberately left unpaid with the effect that the company is using Crown monies "as a sort of piggy-bank to pay others."[80] Similarly, in *Re Keypak Homecare Ltd*, the same judge distinguished the deliberate retention of Crown monies to subsidise continued trading from a case where the Crown is merely one unpaid creditor which has suffered along with all the other creditors as a result of a corporate insolvency.[81] These dicta and several cases decided after *Sevenoaks Stationers* follow a similar line and reinforce the view that while the failure to pay Crown creditors is not unfit conduct per se, the discriminatory practice of "robbing Peter to pay Paul" is more likely to lead to a finding of unfit conduct.[82] In the majority of these cases, the failure to pay non-pressing creditors is treated simply as a form of aggravated trading to the detriment of creditors.

5–31 The claimant will be expected to establish that the defendant pursued a deliberate policy of payment that discriminated against non-pressing creditors.[83] However, the authorities suggest that the claimant is not required to prove that the defendant operated such a policy by means of direct evidence. If, for example, there is evidence that Crown monies were withheld over a sustained period, the court will usually infer that the defendant was operating a deliberate policy of non-payment. In *Re Melcast (Wolverhampton) Ltd*, where the evidence showed that Crown debts were rising consistently over a period of 18 months while amounts owing to trade creditors during the period were kept at the same level, the court readily inferred that the defendants had deliberately withheld payment from the Crown and used what money there was to keep an insolvent company temporarily afloat.[84] The case of *Re Austinsuite Furniture Ltd* suggests that the court will draw a similar inference where one company within a trading group is used as a vehicle to employ the group's workforce and during the whole of its existence it pays no PAYE or national insurance.[85] However, the court is likely to reach the opposite conclusion and attach less significance to the allegation if the evidence shows, for example, that Crown monies were withheld for only a short period just before the

[80] [1990] B.C.L.C. 204 at 211.

[81] [1990] B.C.L.C. 440 at 445.

[82] See further *Re Tansoft Ltd* [1991] B.C.L.C. 339; *Re Burnham Marketing Services Ltd, Secretary of State for Trade and Industry v Harper* [1993] B.C.C. 518; *Re GSAR Realisations Ltd* [1993] B.C.L.C. 409; *Re New Generation Engineers Ltd* [1993] B.C.L.C. 435; *Re Linvale Ltd* [1993] B.C.L.C. 654; *Re Pamstock Ltd* [1994] 1 B.C.L.C. 716; *Re Synthetic Technology Ltd* [1993] B.C.C. 549; *Re Copecrest Ltd, Secretary of State for Trade & Industry v McTighe (No.2)* [1996] 2 B.C.L.C. 477; *Re Galeforce Pleating Co Ltd* [1999] 2 B.C.L.C. 704; *Re Structural Concrete Ltd, Official Receiver v Barnes* [2001] B.C.C. 578; *Re Hopes (Heathrow) Ltd, Secretary of State for Trade and Industry v Dyer* [2001] 1 B.C.L.C. 575; *Re City Trucks Group Ltd (No.2), Secretary of State for Trade and Industry v Gee* [2007] EWHC 350 (Ch), [2008] B.C.C. 76 from [85], *Re The Premier Screw and Repetition Co Ltd, Paulin v Secretary of State for Trade and Industry* [2005] 2 B.C.L.C. 667 at [68]. Cf. *Re Vanguard Industry Ltd, Official Receiver v Dhaliwall* [2006] 1 B.C.L.C. 285.

[83] See, e.g. *Re Funtime Ltd* [2000] 1 B.C.L.C. 247 at 254–255.

[84] [1991] B.C.L.C. 288. See also *Re City Trucks Group Ltd (No.2), Secretary of State for Trade and Industry v Gee* [2008] B.C.C. 76 from [85].

[85] [1992] B.C.L.C. 1047.

company ceased trading.[86] As discussed above in relation to cases involving trading to the detriment of creditors, the court may make implicit adjustments to the threshold for unfit conduct in marginal cases.

5–32 A special case requiring separate discussion is one where the defendants have benefited personally from the company's failure to pay non-pressing creditors. A classic example of this is where the directors give personal guarantees to the company's bank and then operate a policy of repaying the bank at the expense of other creditors which has the effect of reducing their exposure under the guarantees. This type of misconduct may be classified either as a deliberate policy of unfair discrimination in favour of the bank or as a preference in favour of the guarantor. In *Re Verby Print for Advertising Ltd, Secretary of State for Trade and Industry v Fine*[87] the two defendants were the sole shareholders and directors of a company that traded in the printing business. Towards the end of 1992, the company suffered a downturn in its business and, anticipating serious financial difficulties, the defendants sought the advice of an insolvency practitioner. In March 1993, the company's creditors approved a corporate voluntary arrangement, but this collapsed before the end of April 1993 when the company lost the support of its debt factors. The defendants continued trading, but only with the aim of selling the company's business as a going concern. A buyer for most of its assets was found and the company ceased trading at the end of July 1993, before entering creditors' voluntary liquidation a month later. The company's statement of affairs revealed an estimated deficiency as regards Crown creditors of £38,000 and an overall deficiency in excess of £250,000. The Secretary of State sought disqualification orders on two grounds. The first ground was that the defendants had permitted the company to trade while insolvent with no reasonable prospect of creditors being paid. The registrar rejected this ground and held that the defendants' conduct in consulting the insolvency practitioner and in continuing to trade with a view to a going concern sale constituted an adequate and timely response to the company's financial difficulties. The second ground was that the defendants had discriminated against the Crown by using monies that could have been paid to the Crown to pay the bank and thereby reduced their own exposure under their personal guarantees. Thus, they were alleged to have taken advantage of the Crown's forbearance for their own benefit. Up to late June 1993, the registrar found that there was real uncertainty as to what, if anything, was owed to the Crown. The position was investigated by an insolvency practitioner who advised that some £37,000 was owed in respect of PAYE and national insurance. The registrar concluded that the defendants' failure to take any steps towards paying off this liability once they became fully aware of it was sufficient misconduct to render them unfit.

5–33 The registrar's decision in *Verby Print* was upheld on appeal. Neuberger J. held that the registrar had been right to conclude that the defendants should have made some attempt to reduce the outstanding liability to the Crown, especially once

[86] *Re J & B Lynch (Builders) Ltd* [1988] B.C.L.C. 376 at 379; *Re Keypak Homecare Ltd* [1990] B.C.L.C. 440 at 445; *Re Vanguard Industry Ltd, Official Receiver v Dhaliwall* [2006] 1 B.C.L.C. 285 at [25]–[31]. Compare, however, the *Verby Print* case discussed in the text immediately below.
[87] [1998] 2 B.C.L.C. 23.

they had completed the task of selling the company's assets at the end of July 1993. The judge's view of the evidence was that there was sufficient "slack" in the company's banking facilities for at least something to have been paid towards the Crown debt. In the circumstances, it could be inferred that the defendants' failure in this regard was a failure born of self-interest given their position as guarantors. It was argued on the defendants' behalf that before unfair discrimination against a creditor can justify a finding of unfit conduct, the claimant must show that there was an actual policy of discrimination and that the period under consideration in this case (one of two months) was too short to enable the court to infer that such a policy existed. Prompted by a concession from the Secretary of State, it was held that a policy of unfair discrimination between creditors must be established, following the analysis put forward by Dillon L.J. in *Sevenoaks Stationers*.[88] Neuberger J. characterised a "policy" as a decision which is conscious or unconscious taken for reasons which may be conscious or unconscious. On this analysis, the court may infer that there was a policy if, *in effect*, the company traded at the expense of a particular class of creditors, whether or not that effect was consciously intended.[89] Moreover, the judge was not prepared to introduce any threshold requirement that has to be established before the "policy" can be said to be "unfair":

> ". . . to hold that the policy should have continued for a certain minimum period, or to impose any other fetter on what has to qualify before it can be a policy of unfair discrimination, appears to me to be wrong in principle and unhelpful in practice. Clearly, the shorter the period during which the policy exists, the less grave a view the court may take of the policy, all other things being equal. However, once the court finds, as it has done in the present case, that there has been what in normal language could be called a policy of unfair discrimination, it is not, in my judgment, possible to say that it is for some reason incapable of being a policy for the purposes of deciding whether a person is unfit . . . because it continued for only a short time. In other words, once one finds a director permitting a company to engage in unfair discrimination between creditors, the only question for the court is whether, taking into account all the relevant factors relating to the policy (including the period for which the policy continued) that finding justifies the conclusion that the person concerned is unfit to be a director of a company."[90]

5–34 The striking aspect of the decision in *Verby Print* is that the defendants were disqualified on the ground that they unfairly discriminated against the Crown in circumstances where the court accepted that there was nothing illegitimate in their decision to allow the company to continue trading. Indeed, the court found that this decision was based on the reasonable view (supported by the insolvency practitioner) that continued trading for the purposes of a sale was the best way of achieving a satisfactory realisation of the company's assets. Thus, *Verby Print* is

[88] See also *Re Funtime Ltd* [2000] 1 B.C.L.C. 247 at 254–255.

[89] See further *Re Park House Properties Ltd, Secretary of State for Trade and Industry v Carter* [1997] 2 B.C.L.C. 530, a case decided by the same judge, and *Re Interim Management.com.Ltd, Secretary of State for Trade and Industry v Thornbury* [2007] EWHC 3202 (Ch), [2008] 1 B.C.L.C. 139 at [48]–[50].

[90] [1998] 2 B.C.L.C. 23 at 39. See also *Re Vanguard Industry Ltd, Official Receiver v Dhaliwall* [2006] 1 B.C.L.C. 285 at [18]–[29].

not a case of the type envisaged by Ferris J. in *GSAR Realisations* where conduct amounting to unfair discrimination was treated as an aggravated form of trading to the detriment of creditors generally. It is rather a case in which the allegations are of trading to the detriment of a particular class of creditors by preferring others. If, as in *Verby Print*, the court accepts that the defendant was acting in the interests of creditors as a whole in continuing to trade while insolvent,[91] it may seem odd that he should then be penalised for a failure to pay non-pressing creditors. Even where continued trading is regarded as *legitimate*, it is likely that some creditors will lose out if the strategy is unsuccessful and the company ends up in liquidation.[92] Moreover, if the company's business is to survive and be sold as a going concern, the directors will invariably have to pay pressing creditors first, especially if they include the bank and key suppliers. Seen in this light, the emphasis on the concept of unfair discrimination may give rise to a dilemma: the directors face disqualification for deciding to pay Creditor X because it discriminates against Creditor Y whereas if they decide to pay Creditor Y, they face disqualification for discriminating against Creditor X. Thus, in the light of *Verby Print*, it appears that the true basis of the "unfair discrimination" concept is conduct that amounts to a preference. It was found on the evidence that the company had not been pressed into reducing the sum owed to the bank. Thus, it could readily be inferred that the defendants' primary motivation in paying the bank rather than the Crown was to prefer themselves in their capacity as guarantors.[93] As such, it is necessary to be careful over treating unfair discrimination as a separate ground for disqualification uncoupled from an allegation of trading with knowledge of insolvency to the detriment of creditors. The mere fact that some creditors are, in the end, harmed more than others may be an inevitable result of a legitimate, but ultimately unsuccessful attempt, to trade the company out of its difficulties. It is another matter if the directors deliberately decide to discriminate and prefer some creditors over others in circumstances where they knew or ought to have concluded that the company was unable to pay its debts.[94] In this respect, *Verby Print* can be contrasted with *Re C.U. Fittings Ltd*, a case decided under the now repealed provision in s.300 of the Companies Act 1985. In *C.U. Fittings* the defendant had taken the decision to continue trading with the sole aim of realising some of the company's stock in the hope that a greater sum would be received for the stock in those circumstances than if the company was put straight into liquidation. The effect of this decision was that certain creditors such as the bank received payment while substantial VAT

[91] And, arguably, in the interests of the company's employees as well in accordance with their statutory duty in Companies Act 2006 s.172(1)(b) (formerly Companies Act 1985 s.309).

[92] See *Re World of Leather Plc, Secretary of State for Trade and Industry v Gill* [2006] B.C.C. 725 discussed from 5–22.

[93] For the treatment of preferences in disqualification proceedings see from 5–57. A similar allegation was treated as a preference in *Re Grayan Building Services Ltd, Secretary of State for Trade and Industry v Gray* [1995] Ch. 241. *Grayan* and *Verby Print* stand in stark contrast to the altogether more generous approach adopted in similar situations in *Re Bath Glass Ltd* [1988] B.C.L.C. 329 and *Re C.U. Fittings Ltd* [1989] B.C.L.C. 556.

[94] It must surely be a pre-requisite that the defendant knew or ought to have known that the company was insolvent and acted unreasonably in all the circumstances in preferring particular creditors. See discussion in *Leung v Official Receiver* [2006] EWCA Civ 3178 at [24]–[30].

liabilities generated by the company's sales went unpaid. Hoffmann J. characterised the defendant's conduct as a mere misjudgment and declined to make a disqualification order:

> "The company here was not using the Crown's money as working capital for a trade that should not have been carried on. It was not at the relevant time doing anything more than winding down its business. It is true that in the event the effect of its choosing to realise some of its stock rather than going into liquidation has meant that [some creditors] have received payment, whereas the VAT liabilities . . . remain unpaid. However, it seems to me that the choice as to whether to realise the stock without going into liquidation in the hope that substantially larger prices can be obtained, or to go into liquidation to preserve the preferential position of the commissioners cannot be a very easy one. Where a lack of commercial probity is required, I think that a good deal more than a misjudgment on that question must be shown."[95]

5–35 There is clearly some attraction from the State's point of view in the concept of unfair discrimination, especially in relation to Crown debts. Indeed, despite the Court of Appeal's refusal in *Sevenoaks Stationers* to treat Crown debt as a special category, it is in many cases the Crown which provides the most easily accessible source of evidence as to discriminatory treatment. The likelihood of disqualification where trading continues at the risk of some creditors, often the Crown, is well illustrated by the comments of Blackburne J. in *Re Structural Concrete Ltd, Official Receiver v Barnes*[96]:

> "Although not specifically identified in the 1986 Act as a matter determining unfitness, the non-payment of one class of debt (frequently Crown debts) as opposed to others (which are paid), often founds the basis, or one of the bases, of a disqualification order under section 6 . . . In *Secretary of State for Trade and Industry v. McTighe* . . . (an authority which was not cited to the district judge below), the respondent directors, in the course of managing three companies, had operated a policy of not paying the creditors (including the Crown as regards VAT and NIC) who did not press for payment, as that was the only way the companies could continue to trade. The sums involved were substantial. The judge below had concluded that, as there was no evidence that the directors intended never to pay the Crown debts, it was not enough for the Secretary of State to show that 'the only way to keep going was to pay the wages on time and hope that the Revenue and the DSS would be patient' or 'to put off paying Crown debts'.
>
> After quoting the passage in Dillon L.J.'s judgment in *Sevenoaks* . . . Morritt L.J. (with whom the two other members of the court agreed) said this . . . [in *McTighe*]:
>
> > 'The Secretary of State submits that the misconduct lies in the policy of not paying the debts of creditors who are not pressing when it is known that the company has insufficient reserves enabling it to trade except at the risk of such creditors. He submits that such misconduct was amply demonstrated and that the judge should have so concluded. Counsel for Mr Egan submitted that this matter should not be dealt with in isolation from all the other matters, a submission which I have already rejected, and relied on the passage in the judge's judgment, which I have already quoted, to the effect that there

[95] [1989] B.C.L.C. 556 at 560. Note that the Crown has since lost its preferential status as regards VAT. For another case involving a strategy of pre-liquidation asset realisation that gave rise to additional VAT liabilities where the defendants also escaped disqualification, see *Secretary of State for Trade and Industry v Walker* [2003] 1 B.C.L.C. 363.

[96] [2001] B.C.C. 578.

was insufficient evidence on which to conclude that the decision to continue to trade was not one which a reasonable, honest director could not have made. He suggested that this was a finding of fact from which this court should not depart. I accept the submission of the Secretary of State. The facts are not in dispute. It is quite apparent that in the management of [the three companies concerned] Mr McTighe and Mr Egan operated a policy of not paying the creditors who did not press for payment because that was the only way in which the companies in question could continue to trade. Those creditors happened to be the Crown because of the problems the Crown experienced in collecting taxes to which Dillon L.J. referred but the same objection would lie if the creditors were trade creditors generally. The result was that the three companies continued to operate at the risk of their creditors giving rise to an overall deficiency of well over £1m. In my view that is misconduct and of itself renders the directors responsible unfit to be concerned in the management of a company. The facts that in the case of [one company] the directors also lost money, that the prospect of closing down [another company] was unattractive or that the directors did not intend never to pay the debts do not seem to me to detract from this conclusion. In my view the undisputed facts constituted ample material on which to draw the conclusion that the decision to continue to trade in the case of all three companies was not one which a reasonable and honest director could reach. In my judgment the judge erred in principle in his consideration of the non-payment of Crown debts.'

There was argument as to what 'and of itself' meant in that passage. In my view Morritt L.J. was intending to say that the prolonged period of deliberate non-payment of Crown debts rendered the directors unfit to be concerned in the management of a company, irrespective of the other allegations of misconduct laid against the directors and whether those other matters amounted to unfitness. I do not think that he was intending to lay down, as a proposition applicable in all cases, that a policy of deliberate non-payment of a class of debt, whether Crown or otherwise, necessarily gives rise to a finding of unfitness although I find it difficult to envisage circumstances in which such conduct, if carried on over a lengthy period and if the non-payment is at the risk of the creditors in question, will not constitute misconduct justifying a finding of unfitness."

Failure to keep proper accounting records and the wider obligation to exercise financial responsibility

5–36 The authorities suggest that a failure by the defendants to keep adequate accounting records in accordance with what is now s.386 of the Companies Act 2006 (formerly s.221 of the Companies Act 1985) will increase the likelihood of disqualification, whether it is linked to an allegation of trading to the detriment of creditors or considered in isolation. Non-compliance with s.386 is a matter specifically mentioned in Sch.1, Pt 1, para.4(h) of the CDDA. The first three subsections of s.386 provide as follows:

"(1) Every company must keep adequate accounting records.
(2) Adequate accounting records means records that are sufficient—(a) to show and explain the company's transactions, (b) disclose with reasonable accuracy, at any time, the financial position of the company at that time, and (c) to enable the directors to ensure that any accounts required to be prepared comply with the requirements of this Act . . .
(3) Accounting records must, in particular, contain (a) entries from day to day of all sums of money received and expended by the company, and the matters in respect of which the receipt and expenditure takes place, and (b) a record of the assets and liabilities of the company."

Section 387 further provides that where a company fails to comply with any provision of s.386, every officer of the company in default commits an offence (punishable by imprisonment or fine or both), unless he shows that he acted honestly and that in the circumstances in which the company's business was carried on the default was excusable. In the context of disqualification, breach of s.386 (or its statutory predecessor) may be treated as a failure by the directors to keep themselves properly informed of the company's financial position. Moreover, if the directors have caused or allowed an insolvent company to continue trading in circumstances where they have no grasp of the company's financial position because of non-compliance with s.386 this will tend to strengthen the case for saying that the continued trading was unreasonable. Thus, the courts are more likely to make a finding of unfit conduct and less likely to make allowance for hindsight if the directors were taking decisions that were not well informed.[97] The cases discussed below illustrate the use of disqualification proceedings as a forum for fashioning a basic minimum standard of financial responsibility applicable to directors and as a principal method of enforcing what is now s.386. The emphasis on the need for directors to exercise proper financial responsibility reflects concerns expressed both in the Cork Report and during the parliamentary debates that preceded the enactment of the Insolvency Act 1986.[98]

5–37 A total failure on the part of the defendant to maintain any proper accounting records at all is the sort of misconduct that is likely to tip the balance in an otherwise marginal case. Harman J. characterised this failure in the following terms in *Re Rolus Properties Ltd*:

> "The privilege of limited liability is a valuable incentive to encourage entrepreneurs to take on risky ventures without inevitable personal total financial disaster. It is, however, a privilege which must be accorded upon terms and some of the most important terms that Parliament has imposed are that accounts be kept and returns made so that the world can, by referring to those, see what is happening. Thus, a total failure to keep statutory books and to make statutory returns is significant for the public at large and is a matter which amounts to misconduct if not complied with and is a matter of which the court should take into account in considering whether a man can properly be allowed to continue to operate as a director of companies, or whether the public at large is to be protected against him on the grounds that he is unfit, not because he is fraudulent but because he is incompetent and unable to comply with the statutory obligations attached to limited liability."[99]

On this analysis, the obligation to comply with s.386 is part of the price exacted from those who choose to trade with the benefit of limited liability. If the

[97] See *Re Grayan Building Services Ltd, Secretary of State for Trade and Industry v Gray* [1995] Ch. 241 at 252. This is true also of wrongful trading proceedings under s.214 of the Insolvency Act: see *Re Produce Marketing Consortium Ltd (No.2)* [1989] B.C.L.C. 520.

[98] See Report of the Review Committee, *Insolvency Law and Practice*, Cmnd.8558 (London: HMSO, 1982), Ch.45; Hansard, H.L. Vol.458, col.885, Vol.461 cols 712, 732–736, Vol.467, cols 1130–1131, 1133, 1137. The importance of financial responsibility is further reflected by cases where the court has been prepared to make a finding of unfit conduct based exclusively on breaches of statutory accounting obligations: see, e.g. *Re Rolus Properties Ltd* (1988) 4 B.C.C. 446; *Re Swift 736 Ltd, Secretary of State for Trade and Industry v Ettinger* [1993] B.C.L.C. 896.

[99] (1988) 4 B.C.C. 446 at 447.

company has no core accounting records the directors will be unable to ascertain the company's financial position with any certainty and will face grave difficulties when the time comes to prepare and file audited accounts. The analysis was taken forward by Chadwick J. in *Re Thorncliffe Finance Ltd, Secretary of State for Trade and Industry v Arif*[100] who attributed two distinct purposes to s.221 of the Companies Act 1985, the statutory predecessor of s.386. The first purpose is to ensure that those who trade with the benefit of limited liability maintain sufficient accounting records to enable them to ascertain the company's financial position at a given moment. Chadwick J.'s view was that directors cannot act responsibly in deciding whether or not to continue trading in the absence of proper records. The second purpose is to ensure that the directors can prepare an accurate statement of affairs should the company fail so that an insolvency practitioner who takes office can readily identify the company's assets and take steps to recover or exploit those assets in the interests of creditors.[101]

5–38 In *Arif* the three defendants, M, his son S and D were directors of a finance company, Thorncliffe Finance Ltd. Thorncliffe was acquired for the purpose of financing the businesses of four affiliated companies which were in the motor trade. M was a director of these affiliated companies. Thorncliffe was a source of hire purchase finance for customers who wished to purchase cars from the affiliated companies. It also provided the affiliated companies with the finance needed to purchase cars for resale from manufacturers or distributors. The affiliated companies ceased trading and Thorncliffe was placed in administrative receivership with an estimated deficiency as regards creditors in excess of £1.6 million. The thrust of the case against the defendants was that they had caused Thorncliffe to enter into transactions with the affiliated companies which led to the accrual of over £1 million worth of indebtedness without any proper financial controls and without security. This meant that Thorncliffe's fortunes had been inextricably tied to those of the affiliated companies. There had been some attempt by D to raise the issue of the inter-company indebtedness but no steps were ever taken to put security in place or to monitor asset levels within the affiliated companies. The inter-company indebtedness was allowed to grow unchecked with the effect that when the affiliated companies failed they brought Thorncliffe down with them. The evidence showed that the accounting records of Thorncliffe and the affiliated companies were insufficient to enable the various office holders to identify and recover any remaining assets. The defendants had been unable to prepare a statement of affairs for the purposes of the receivership. The judge held that the failure of the defendants to fulfil their statutory obligations made them unfit and all three were disqualified. The case can be interpreted as one where the defendants' general failure to act in the interests of Thorncliffe (manifested in their particular failure to protect its assets for creditors) was compounded by non-compliance with s.221 of the Companies Act 1985. *Arif* confirms that there is a minimum

[100] [1997] 1 B.C.L.C. 34.

[101] [1997] 1 B.C.L.C. 34 at 42–43. For a case in which the second purpose was given particular emphasis see *Re Galeforce Pleating Co Ltd* [1999] 2 B.C.L.C. 704.

obligation on directors to act with financial responsibility in the interests of creditors. If a decision is taken to continue trading in circumstances where the directors have no sure means of ascertaining whether the company is solvent or insolvent and trading at the expense of its creditors, the risk of disqualification on grounds of unfit conduct is increased. The case also illustrates the "cascade" effect of failure to comply with what is now s.386. If there are no proper accounting records, it is more than likely that the directors will also have failed in their obligation to prepare accounts and, where necessary, a statement of affairs. These additional matters of complaint will again increase the risk of disqualification.

5–39 The theme of proper financial responsibility has surfaced in several other cases. In *Re New Generation Engineers Ltd*,[102] Warner J. characterised the defendant's failure to comply with what is now s.386 as a failure to monitor the company's financial position that was itself indicative of unfit conduct. Part of the defendant's evidence was that he lacked accounting knowledge. The judge's response was to say that his lack of expertise made it necessary for him to have proper professional guidance in the matter of the company's accounting records and its financial position. This suggests a basic minimum standard that will not be relaxed simply because the defendant possesses no or limited financial expertise.[103] In *Re Firedart Ltd, Official Receiver v Fairall* the defendant was found to be unfit on a number of grounds including trading to the detriment of creditors and failure to keep proper accounting records. Arden J. laid particular emphasis on the latter:

> "When directors do not maintain accounting records in accordance with the very specific requirements . . . of the Companies Act . . . they cannot know their company's financial position with accuracy. There is therefore a risk that the situation is much worse than they know and that creditors will suffer in consequence. Directors who permit this situation to arise must expect the conclusion to be drawn in an appropriate case that they are in consequence not fit to be concerned in the management of a company."[104]

A notable feature of this case was that, for the purposes of the trading to the detriment of creditors allegation, the judge rejected the defendant's view that the company had first become insolvent during 1988, finding that he ought to have concluded that it was insolvent before the end of 1986. This illustrates again how a breach of s.386 may persuade the court to treat other allegations with a greater degree of seriousness.[105] Thus, it is clear that the courts take the failure to maintain

[102] [1993] B.C.L.C. 435.

[103] See further the treatment of the second defendant, Ms Zangus in *Re Richborough Furniture Ltd, Secretary of State for Trade and Industry v Stokes* [1996] 1 B.C.L.C. 507; and *Re Hitco 2000 Ltd, Official Receiver v Cowan* [1995] 2 B.C.L.C. 63.

[104] [1994] 2 B.C.L.C. 340 at 352.

[105] For further support see *Re Ask International Transport Ltd, Secretary of State for Trade and Industry v Keens*, May 5, 1992, Ch.D. unreported and *Re Bloomgalley Ltd, Secretary of State for Trade and Industry v Neophytou*, October 15, 1993, Ch.D. unreported. In *Ask International* the defendants allowed the company to continue to trade while insolvent despite a warning from the auditors concerning the inadequacy of its basic financial information. The judge found them to be unfit on the basis of "reckless or risky trading". In *Bloomgalley* the defendant's failure to keep proper stock records (a breach of what is now Companies Act 2006 s.386(4)) influenced the court to conclude that he had unreasonably caused the company to continue trading.

proper accounting records seriously and will often infer from it a lack of regard for creditors' interests sufficient to constitute unfit conduct.[106]

5–40 As well as using s.6 of the CDDA to fashion a minimum standard of financial responsibility applicable to directors based on the core obligation in the Companies Act to maintain adequate accounting records, the courts have, in several other cases, made disqualification orders on the basis of a more general failure to exercise financial responsibility not linked directly to a breach of what is now s.386. In *Re Hitco 2000 Ltd, Official Receiver v Cowan*,[107] the relevant company traded for just under two years before going into compulsory liquidation. The defendant, who was the company's sole director, had expertise in buying and selling. He delegated the task of maintaining the company's accounting records to a series of unqualified bookkeepers. His evidence was that he had no knowledge of the finer points of accounting and therefore relied on the bookkeepers to compile the books and records. Payment of the company's debts was also delegated. The defendant's practice was to sign whole cheque books in blank leaving the bookkeeper with instructions to pay as many of the company's outstanding debts as possible given available funds. The company encountered severe cash flow difficulties from the outset. No less than 84 cheques were dishonoured during its trading life and proceedings were commenced by several creditors for undisputed sums. There was no allegation of non-compliance with s.221 of the Companies Act 1985 even though a full set of accounts was never produced. Nevertheless, the fact that the defendant allowed the company to continue trading without making any realistic assessment of its prospects was sufficient to render him unfit. As the deputy judge put it:

> "The company traded for a period of a year and ten months . . . In all that period of time the business . . . was conducted without the [defendant] stopping once to make . . . an appraisal and to ask himself the question: should I stop incurring credit and cease trading? I should say immediately that there is no . . . question of want of probity on the [defendant's] part . . . But it does seem to me to be a case where trade was carried on by a sole director for the most part blind as to the true financial state of his company and thus quite unable to make an intelligent projection from time to time as to whether it was right to go on or not. In my judgment the [defendant's] greatest failing is that he did not ensure that he was provided with regular financial management information so as to enable him to answer that most difficult question which every director who trades with the privilege of limited liability is obliged to confront, especially in straitened financial circumstances, *i.e.* should I cease trading? . . . How else could any reasonable decision be made as to whether continued trading from that point of time onwards would be at the risk and expense of creditors or not?"[108]

5–41 The defendant's disqualification in *Re Hitco 2000 Ltd* illustrates that, in the case of a sole director, the basic obligation to exercise financial responsibility extends beyond ensuring that core accounting records are compiled and kept up-to-date. A

[106] This also a theme of Australian jurisprudence under the statutory predecessor of what is now the Corporations Act 2001 (Cth) s.206F: see, e.g. *Re Delonga and the Australian Securities Commission* (1994) 15 A.C.S.R. 450; *Re Agushi and Australian Securities Commission* (1996) 19 A.C.S.R. 322.

[107] [1995] 2 B.C.L.C. 63.

[108] [1995] 2 B.C.L.C. 63 at 70.

proper system of financial control must also be implemented to ensure that he receives current accounting information and can make well-informed decisions. *Hitco 2000* suggests that a sole director who abdicates control of the financial side of the business will equally be at risk of disqualification as one who fails to comply with s.386. The deputy judge added that it was incumbent on a sole director who lacked financial expertise to ensure that he had constant professional guidance whatever the cost.[109] The upshot is that a director is vulnerable to disqualification if he has maintained no books and records as the court is likely to infer that any decision to continue trading was not made on a proper basis. Even where accounting records have been maintained, *Hitco 2000* suggests that a director will be exposed to disqualification if he fails to monitor the company's financial position and allows the company to continue trading blindly against a background of persistent cash flow problems and creditor unrest. The case will be a fortiori where the defendant causes or allows the company to engage in practices such as "cheque kiting" which involves the artificial creation of credit through the making of multiple deposits in more than one bank account by means of drawings on uncleared funds.[110]

Further support for this view can be derived from *Re Grayan Building Services Ltd, Secretary of State for Trade and Industry v Gray*.[111] In *Grayan*, the Secretary of State complained, in the context of a claim of trading to the detriment of creditors, that the company's lack of management accounts was evidence of unfit conduct. This was disregarded by the trial judge on the basis that there is no statutory requirement for companies to produce management accounts. However, Hoffmann L.J. stated that the absence of up-to-date information about the company's financial position is relevant to whether it is reasonable for directors to allow a company to continue trading at a time when it is unable to pay its debts as they fall due. Thus, it is suggested that a failure to produce regular financial information in the form of management accounts may, depending on all the other circumstances, amount to a failure to monitor the company's financial position in the manner expounded in *Hitco*. Furthermore, the court is unlikely to allow a director to rely on his lack of financial expertise as a defence to disqualification proceedings. This reinforces the point that directors are expected to attain a basic minimum standard of financial responsibility.[112]

5–42 A further general aspect of the duty to exercise financial responsibility is that accounting information must be presented in a way that gives a fair impression of

[109] [1995] 2 B.C.L.C. 63 at 74. For further cases suggesting that a general abdication of financial control is likely to lead to finding of unfit conduct, especially in a small company see, e.g. *Re D.J. Matthews (Joinery Design) Ltd* (1988) 4 B.C.C. 513; *Re T & D Services (Timber Preservation & Damp Proofing Contractors) Ltd* [1990] B.C.C. 592; *Re Melcast (Wolverhampton) Ltd* [1991] B.C.L.C. 288; *Re Burnham Marketing Services Ltd, Secretary of State for Trade and Industry v Harper* [1993] B.C.C. 518; *Re Pamstock Ltd* [1994] 1 B.C.L.C. 716.

[110] *Re Finelist Ltd, Secretary of State for Trade and Industry v Swan* [2005] EWHC 603 (Ch), [2005] B.C.C. 596.

[111] [1995] Ch. 241.

[112] There are cases which suggest that a director may be less at risk where accounting functions have been delegated to someone holding appropriate professional qualifications: see, in particular, *Re Cladrose Ltd* [1990] B.C.L.C. 204.

the company's financial position. In *Re Austinsuite Furniture Ltd*[113] one of the defendants caused the lead company, A Ltd to acquire the business of B Ltd, a company of which he was also a director. Both companies were on the verge of insolvency. A valuation of £2 million was placed on the business and goodwill of B Ltd despite the fact that it was insolvent and that A Ltd had been meeting its debts for the previous six months. It appears that the principal objective of the transaction was to put a rosier complexion on the respective balance sheets of A Ltd and B Ltd. Its effect was to enhance the assets of A Ltd by the value placed on the business acquired and the assets of B Ltd by the value of the consideration. In substance, no consideration was paid to B Ltd as A Ltd simply assumed responsibility for B Ltd's debts. The judge disqualified the defendant for seven years on a number of grounds but took a particularly dim view of this transaction:

> "The position of [A Ltd] was in effect concealed by the extraordinary transaction purportedly entered into by [B Ltd] and [A Ltd]. If it had not been introduced into the accounts as filed at the Companies Registry, creditors . . . would have been alerted to the true position of [A Ltd], with the almost certain consequence that [A Ltd] would have been compelled to cease trading at a time when its liabilities would have been less than they were in . . . the following year."[114]

Not surprisingly, the auditors of A Ltd came in for considerable criticism for failing to satisfy themselves that some basis existed for the valuation placed on B Ltd's business and allowing what amounted to a fraud on creditors practiced through the accounts to pass largely unchallenged.[115] A further example, and one on a much larger scale, is provided by *Re Atlantic Computers Plc, Secretary of State for Trade and Industry v Ashman*, a s.8 case.[116] In *Atlantic Computers*, several former group executives (though not all) were found to be unfit principally on the basis that Atlantic's accounts had failed to disclose the true extent of the company's contingent liabilities. Similarly, in another s.8 case, *Re Transtec Plc, Secretary of State for Trade and Industry v Carr*,[117] the former chief executive of an engineering company was found to be unfit in circumstances where he had failed to disclose to the board or the auditors the existence of a multi-million pound claim against the company with the consequence that the company produced accounts which were materially misleading. The deliberate provision of false and misleading information as regards a company's financial position for the purposes of an acquisition was also a major factor in *Re Bunting Electric Manufacturing Co Ltd, Secretary of State for Trade and Industry v Golby*.[118]

[113] [1992] B.C.L.C. 1047.

[114] [1992] B.C.L.C. 1047 at 1060.

[115] The audit report in A Ltd's case was qualified but the judge described the qualification as one lying "at the less serious end of the possible forms of qualification set out in the accounting standards". Given that A Ltd and B Ltd had common directors it is possible that the transaction may also have required approval by both sets of shareholders under s.320 of the Companies Act 1985.

[116] June 15, 1998, Ch.D., unreported. See further 5–71.

[117] [2006] EWHC 2110 (Ch), [2007] 2 B.C.L.C. 495.

[118] [2005] EWHC 3345 (Ch), [2006] 1 B.C.L.C. 550.

Excessive remuneration

5–43 An allegation sometimes raised is that the defendant remunerated himself at a level that was unsustainable given the company's financial circumstances. Again, this is not a matter which is spelled out in Sch.1 but it amounts to a failure on the part of the defendant to pay due regard to the interests of the company (and, in particular, its creditors) which can be categorised as a breach of fiduciary duty.[119] It is important to draw a distinction between "excessive remuneration" in the popular (and pejorative) sense (in which highly remunerated executive directors are commonly described as "fat cats") and excessive remuneration that is criticised on the ground that the company was not in a financial position to afford it, even though, on an objective basis, it did not exceed the "going rate" for the services in question.[120] Reported cases decided under s.6 have only been concerned to date with the question of remuneration in the latter sense. As such, it appears that the issue is more likely to arise in cases involving owner-managers who determine their own remuneration rather than in cases of executive directors who do not own the company and whose remuneration is determined by non-executive directors or by some other independent means. Excessive remuneration is not usually relied on to establish unfit conduct in isolation. It is invariably treated as an exacerbating factor which taken in combination with related misconduct such as trading to the detriment of creditors may result in a finding of unfit conduct. For instance, if X allows a company to trade while insolvent and is only able to maintain his own remuneration at the same levels as when the company was solvent by withholding payment from non-pressing creditors, he may be liable to disqualification on the combined grounds of trading to the detriment of creditors, unfair discrimination and excessive remuneration. As with the other specific grounds discussed so far, it is a matter of fine judgment whether this ground will be established to the satisfaction of the court on the facts of a particular case. In *Re Keypak Homecare Ltd*, the company had been trading for over ten years and its annual turnover was in the region of £500,000. Aware that the company was in financial difficulties, the defendants agreed to take increased remuneration of some £25,400 between the two of them. In addition, they each enjoyed the use of a company car. Six months later the company went into liquidation. Although the defendants were disqualified on other grounds, Harman J. refused to accept that the decision with regard to remuneration amounted to unfit conduct:

> "... the Secretary of State submits that it must be wrong for directors to increase their remuneration in the face of falling profits and a business that was not doing very well. In my judgment, one cannot approach it as simply as that. I have to consider whether these [defendants] were, to use a colloquialism, 'living high on the hog' at the expense of the creditors of the company, and in my view their salaries ... are not such as in 1986

[119] See, e.g. *West Mercia Safetywear Ltd v Dodd* [1988] B.C.L.C. 250; *Facia Footwear Ltd v Hinchcliffe* [1998] 1 B.C.L.C. 218; *Colin Gwyer & Associates Ltd v London Wharf (Limehouse) Ltd* [2003] 2 B.C.L.C. 153.

[120] As well as salary, "remuneration" could also include ancillary benefits such as the provision of a company car and payments into a pension fund.

would of themselves cause any very serious eyebrow-raising for managerial people running a business with a turnover of approaching £0.5m even though the business was doing badly."[121]

5–44 In other cases the court has found that it was irresponsible for the defendants to take the "going rate" without giving any consideration to the company's financial position or its ability to pay.[122] In this regard, if the defendant is unaware of the true extent of the company's plight, a decision to maintain current levels of remuneration or increase them will compound his overall failure to exercise proper financial responsibility.[123] Similarly, the courts have said that there is no justification for a director to take increasing levels of remuneration from a company that has never made profits.[124] Not surprisingly, the courts have also castigated directors for allowing their company to pay inflated salaries to family members or co-directors who may or may not perform any function in return.[125] However, no director has yet been disqualified solely on the basis of these sorts of findings in a reported case.

Misuse of bank account

5–45 This allegation is sometimes raised to support a case based mainly on trading to the detriment of creditors and/or failure to exercise proper financial responsibility. The phrase "misuse of bank account" denotes the practice whereby the defendant allows cheques to be drawn on the company's account without any regard for whether the bank will honour them or not. If there is evidence that the company "bounced" several cheques, this may strengthen inferences of trading to the detriment of creditors and lack of financial responsibility.[126] Moreover, in cases where the defendant delegated the task of paying creditors to an employee or bookkeeper such evidence supports the contention that he abdicated responsibility for monitoring the company's financial position.[127] It was suggested obiter in *Re Hitco 2000 Ltd, Official Receiver v Cowan* that the practice of regularly drawing cheques in the hope

[121] [1990] B.C.L.C. 440 at 443–444.

[122] See *Re Stanford Services Ltd* [1987] B.C.L.C. 607 (the question is not what the director needed to draw to cover living expenses but what the company could afford to pay); *Re Cargo Agency Ltd* [1992] B.C.L.C. 686; *Re Synthetic Technology Ltd* [1993] B.C.C. 549; *Re Moorgate Metals Ltd, Official Receiver v Huhtala* [1995] 1 B.C.L.C. 503; *Re CSTC Ltd, Secretary of State for Trade and Industry v Van Hengel* [1995] 1 B.C.L.C. 545; *Re Amaron Ltd, Secretary of State for Trade and Industry v Lubrani* [1997] 2 B.C.L.C. 115, affirmed [2001] 1 B.C.L.C. 562.

[123] *Re Firedart Ltd, Official Receiver v Fairhall* [1994] 2 B.C.L.C. 340.

[124] *Re Austinsuite Furniture Ltd* [1992] B.C.L.C. 1047; *Re Ward Sherrard Ltd* [1996] B.C.C. 418; *Re Copecrest Ltd, Secretary of State for Trade & Industry v McTighe (No.2)* [1996] 2 B.C.L.C. 477. Contrast *Re ECM (Europe) Electronics Ltd* [1991] B.C.C. 268 where a defendant who drew a salary out of gross profits and reduced his level of remuneration once the company started to struggle was not disqualified.

[125] *Re Firedart Ltd, Official Receiver v Fairhall* [1994] 2 B.C.L.C. 340; *Re CSTC Ltd, Secretary of State for Trade and Industry v Van Hengel* [1995] 1 B.C.L.C. 545; *Re Skyward Builders Plc, Official Receiver v Broad* [2002] EWHC (Ch) 2786 at [404]. The directors must address their minds to whether a payment (especially a gratuitous one) serves the interests of the company by analogy with *Re W & M Roith Ltd* [1967] 1 W.L.R. 432.

[126] See, e.g. *Re Admiral Energy Group Ltd, Official Receiver v Jones*, August 19, 1996, Ch.D., unreported.

[127] *Re Pamstock Ltd* [1994] 1 B.C.L.C. 716.

that the bank account will remain within the overdraft limit when they are presented for payment is conduct capable of evidencing unfit conduct even where the cheques are ultimately met, although whether it does so in a particular case will depend on all the evidence.[128] In *Hitco*, it was also held that the practice of a director signing blank cheques and instructing employees to pay pressing creditors without exercising any proper control over their use of the cheque book amounts to a misuse of the bank account.[129] At trial, the only complaint made under this heading concerned the dishonoured cheques. The defendant argued, on appeal from a district judge, that the complaint about the use of the cheque book could not be relied on as it had not been put forward as a separate ground of unfit conduct at trial. Mr Jules Sher Q.C. (sitting as a deputy High Court judge) agreed with the defendant and held that the official receiver was not entitled in that case to rely upon the defendant's practice of leaving signed blank cheques with employees as conduct which of itself justified a finding of unfit conduct. However, such evidence was held to be relevant to the main allegation which had been properly raised against the defendant, namely his general abdication of responsibility in the realm of financial control.[130] Where there is evidence of deliberate abuse of bank accounts through practices such as cheque kiting, this will further strengthen the case for disqualification.[131]

Phoenix activity and serial failure

5–46 One of Parliament's major priorities in enacting the CDDA was to address the so-called phoenix syndrome. There is no mention of this specific abuse in Sch.1. Nevertheless, it has been suggested that the practice, whereby the directors of an insolvent company acquire its assets through the vehicle of a phoenix company on the basis of a questionable valuation and without proper regard for the company's creditors, is a matter connected with or arising out of the insolvency of the latter company for the purposes of CDDA s.6(2).[132] Whatever the technicalities, there is a strong likelihood that evidence of deliberate phoenix activity will result in a finding of unfit conduct given the amount of attention it attracted in the Cork Report and during parliamentary debate.[133] Again, however, it is the cases involving conduct falling short of deliberate phoenix activity that illustrate the complexity of the issues at stake.

5–47 The case of *Re Copecrest Ltd, Secretary of State for Trade and Industry v McTighe*[134] is at the serious end of the scale although it did not amount to a classic phoenix case. One of the allegations in *McTighe* centred on a transfer of assets

[128] [1995] 2 B.C.L.C. 63 at 69–70.

[129] The same can be said of a director who, by signing cheques, unwittingly allows corporate assets to be misapplied: see *Re Stephenson Cobbold Ltd, Secretary of State for Trade and Industry v Stephenson* [2000] 2 B.C.L.C. 614, though in that case it was held that the defendant, a non-executive director, was entitled to rely on assurances from the auditors as to the purposes for which the monies were being disbursed.

[130] See *Dorchester Finance Ltd v Stebbing* [1989] B.C.L.C. 498 and, by analogy, *Bishopsgate Investment Management Ltd v Maxwell (No.2)* [1994] 1 All E.R. 261.

[131] *Re Finelist Ltd, Secretary of State for Trade and Industry v Swan* [2005] B.C.C. 596.

[132] *Re Bath Glass Ltd* [1988] B.C.L.C. 329 at 331 and see earlier discussion in 4–29 to 4–30.

[133] See 2–12 and I. Fletcher, "The Genesis of Modern Insolvency Law" [1987] J.B.L. 365.

[134] [1996] 2 B.C.L.C. 477.

between two companies, C Ltd and L Ltd, both of which were controlled by the defendants. The assets and goodwill of C Ltd, which had consistently made losses during its recent trading history, were sold to L Ltd in 1989 for the sum of £1.4 million payable by instalments over the next five years. L Ltd provided no security with regard to the deferred consideration. Only one instalment of £185,000 was ever paid and C Ltd was put into creditors' voluntary liquidation in 1990 with a deficiency in excess of £1 million mostly made up of liabilities to the Crown. Its only asset was the unpaid debt of roughly £1.2 million owed by L Ltd. There is little doubt that the Court of Appeal regarded the transfer of C Ltd's assets to L Ltd as a device designed to put the assets out of the reach of C Ltd's creditors, enabling the business to continue free of its debts. The failure of the defendants as directors of C Ltd to obtain any security in respect of the deferred consideration payable by L Ltd was considered sufficiently serious on its own to justify a finding of unfit conduct.[135]

5–48 The pattern of conduct found in *Re Ipcon Fashions Ltd*[136] is a more direct example of phoenix activity. The defendant carried on business in the clothing trade through a succession of small, owner-managed companies. The relevant company, Ipcon Fashions Ltd was the successor to a business previously carried on at the same premises by a company called Lorenzo Fashions Ltd. Lorenzo Fashions was put into liquidation in 1985 with an estimated deficiency of over £100,000. Ipcon Fashions continued to use the trading name "Lorenzo". After a good start to its short trading life sales almost completely dried up and by mid-1986 the defendant decided, in his words, "to wind down the company's affairs with a view to paying all creditors". The business of Ipcon Fashions was transferred to a new company called Lorenzo London Ltd which carried on the same business. Although Ipcon Fashions now had no business to carry on, the defendant continued to incur liabilities through it and he and his wife each drew a salary from it without accounting for tax. A compulsory winding up order was made in respect of the company in October 1986. Hoffmann J. disqualified the defendant for five years. It is clear that the judge regarded this as a case in which the company and its creditors had been abandoned to their fate. The defendant's conduct in continuing to draw a tax-free salary and in maintaining the appearance that the company was still trading after the transfer of the business to Lorenzo London Ltd was considered "particularly reprehensible".

5–49 In *Re Keypak Homecare Ltd* the defendants' conduct was found to make them unfit on the basis that they had arranged for stock to be transferred from an insolvent company to a successor company of which they were also directors. Harman J. described the successor as being "in the most obvious of senses a phoenix company, a complete reincarnation from the ashes of the old"[137] and disqualified both defendants for three years. *Ipcon Fashions* and *Keypak Homecare* suggest that the court will come down hard on any conduct that appears to involve a deliberate

[135] [1996] 2 B.C.L.C. 477 at 232.
[136] (1989) 5 B.C.C. 773.
[137] [1990] B.C.L.C. 440 at 443.

process of sheltering assets from creditors.[138] However, the fact that the directors use a fresh company to acquire the assets and business of their former insolvent company from its liquidator will not of itself render them unfit. It is not unlawful to set up a successor company and, provided that the assets are acquired from the liquidator at a price ascertained by independent valuation, the directors will not be liable to disqualification on the ground of the acquisition alone.[139] Similarly, the phenomenon of "pre-pack" administrations in which the business and assets are sold back to the incumbent directors or owner-managers by the company in administration are lawful.[140] This is perfectly consistent with the policy associated in particular with the Enterprise Act 2002 that the law should not penalise business failure per se and should encourage business endeavour. However, it is incumbent on both the insolvency practitioner and the directors to ensure that the successor company acquires the former company's assets at market value and that the process is wholly transparent.[141] Even if the successor company later goes into insolvent liquidation as well, the directors will not automatically be liable to disqualification. It is necessary for the court to consider all the circumstances of the case.[142]

5–50 The directors must ensure that the successor company does not trade using a prohibited name in breach of s.216 of the Insolvency Act 1986. Misuse of a former company name by a successor company was raised as an allegation of unfit conduct in *Re ECM (Europe) Electronics Ltd* but rejected.[143] However, it is now settled that conduct amounting to a breach of s.216 can be taken into account under CDDA s.6[144] and where it is raised as a collateral allegation, this is so regardless of whether or not the successor company has become insolvent.

5–51 The Company Law Review Steering Group made various recommendations aimed at addressing further the problem of phoenix companies.[145] The Steering Group drew a distinction between "bad phoenix" situations that it wishes to see

[138] See also *Re Travel Mondial (UK) Ltd* [1991] B.C.L.C. 120 (defendant who engineered phoenix succession disqualified for nine years); *Re Linvale Ltd* [1993] B.C.L.C. 654 (two defendants described as reckless but honest who had attempted to carry on the same business having left its creditors behind each disqualified for five years); *Re Saver Ltd* [1999] B.C.C. 221 (defendant found to have engaged in "classic and repeated phoenix trading" disqualified for nine years); *Re Skata Ltd, Secretary of State for Trade and Industry v Zevides* [2002] EWHC 813 (Ch) (defendant found, inter alia, to have transferred assets to successor company so as to shelter them from Crown creditors disqualified for seven years); *Re Windows West Ltd, Official Receiver v Zwirn* [2002] B.C.C. 760 (defendant found to have dishonestly engineered a series of phoenix successions at the expense of Crown creditors disqualified for eleven years).

[139] *Re Douglas Construction Services Ltd* [1988] B.C.L.C. 397; *Re Pamstock Ltd* [1994] 1 B.C.L.C. 716 at 720–721; *Re Windows West Ltd, Official Receiver v Zwirn* [2002] B.C.C. 760 at [13].

[140] For court approval of a "pre-pack" administration sale in the face of majority creditor opposition see *DKLL Solicitors v Revenue and Customs Commissioners* [2007] EWHC 2067 (Ch), [2008] 1 B.C.L.C. 112.

[141] An approach reflected in the professional rules and standards applicable to the insolvency practitioner profession: see Statement of Insolvency Practice 13 (E & W), "Acquisition of Assets of Insolvent Companies by Directors" (November 1997) and Statement of Insolvency Practice 16 (E & W), "Pre-Packaged Sales in Administrations" (January 2009), *https://www.r3.org.uk/publications/default.asp?dir=professional&pag=SIPS&i=402* [Accessed August 24, 2009].

[142] See *Re McNulty's Interchange Ltd* [1989] B.C.L.C. 709.

[143] [1991] B.C.C. 268.

[144] See *Re Migration Services Ltd, Official Receiver v Webster* [2000] B.C.C. 1095; *Re Skyward Builders Plc, Official Receiver v Broad* [2002] EWHC (Ch) 2786.

[145] Company Law Review, *Final Report*, URN 01/943 (July 2001), paras 15.55–15.77.

curbed and "good phoenix" situations that it wishes to see flourish in the name of enterprise. The majority of those who responded at an earlier stage in the consultation process considered that the phoenix problem was still rife and this led the Steering Group to conclude that it remains significant despite the reforms of the 1980s, including the reform of the disqualification regime. As part of its recommendations, the Steering Group suggested that the Secretary of State should consider taking a power to apply to the court for an interim disqualification order so that directors in bad phoenix situations can be restricted at the earliest possible stage, pending hearing of full disqualification proceedings.[146] Subject to appropriate safeguards, it was argued that this procedure would not violate a defendant's rights under art.6 of the ECHR "because proceedings for disqualification are not considered to be criminal proceedings for the purpose of the Convention and because the taking of interim measures on the basis of appropriate evidence does not in any event violate the presumption of innocence".[147] Reform of the CDDA fell outside the ambit of the Steering Group's terms of reference and these proposals have not been taken forward. This is perhaps not surprising as within the present system much of the emphasis rests on the licensing and regulation of insolvency practitioners as the principal instrument for ensuring that "phoenix" sales are conducted on the basis of proper valuations with a view to maximising returns to creditors.

5–52 The phoenix syndrome aside, there are cases where directors have been disqualified following their involvement in a number of failed companies. However, this is not to say that serial failure in the absence of phoenix activity amounts to an independent ground for disqualification. It was seen in Ch.3 that the court can take into account the defendant's conduct in relation to a series of companies under s.6(1)(b). As such, where the claimant can show that the defendant has repeated the same or a similar pattern of misconduct in several companies and thus failed to learn the lessons of previous failures, there is an enhanced likelihood of disqualification.[148] It is the repetition of misconduct rather than serial business failure per se that will attract the attention of the court, an approach which reflects both the law's support for enterprise and business endeavour and the protective aspect of the CDDA.

Lack of capitalisation

5–53 The failure of directors to ensure that their companies are properly financed is not in itself a separate ground of disqualification. This is hardly surprising given that

[146] The Steering Group also recommended changes to what is now Companies Act 2006 s.190 (formerly Companies Act 1985 s.320), to deal with transfers of assets in anticipation of insolvency. This recommendation was also not taken forward. Interestingly there are powers of interim disqualification in the personal insolvency context: see Insolvency Act 1986 Sch.4A, para.5 (interim bankruptcy restrictions orders); Sch.4ZB, para.5 (interim debt relief restrictions orders) and text from 11–80 and at 11–104.

[147] Company Law Review, *Final Report*, URN 01/943 (July 2001), para.15.76. However, in the event that no cross-undertaking in damages is given, interim measures may give rise to other potential breaches of the ECHR: see further from 11–80 in connection with interim bankruptcy restrictions orders.

[148] See, e.g. *Re Majestic Recording Studios Ltd* [1989] B.C.L.C. 1; *Re Melcast (Wolverhampton) Ltd* [1991] B.C.L.C. 288; *Re Brooks Transport (Purfleet) Ltd* [1993] B.C.C. 766; *Re Admiral Energy Group Ltd, Official Receiver v Jones*, August 19, 1996, Ch.D., unreported. A defendant who has persisted in the same pattern of misconduct across several companies will commonly be disqualified for five years or more: see from 5.102.

company law does not impose a minimum capital requirement on private companies and so facilitates easy access to corporate form and limited liability. Thus, the fact that a company with a paid up share capital of £2 becomes insolvent is not itself a justification for disqualifying its directors. This is consistent with the enterprise rationale of company law discussed in Ch.2 and the dictum of Harman J. in *Re Rolus Properties Ltd* to the effect that the formation of a company with a small capital for the purposes of a speculative venture would not of itself warrant criticism.[149] Seen in this light, it is not surprising that Parliament refused to include a reference to inadequate capitalisation in Sch.1 of the CDDA and make it a matter to which the court is required to pay particular regard.[150] However, many corporate failures can be explained by lack of adequate finance and the official line is that companies trading on inadequate financial foundations pose an enhanced risk to creditors.[151] As a result, the court may be influenced in determining whether a director's conduct makes him unfit by the company's inadequate capitalisation, especially where he caused the company to trade into an increasing deficiency without making any attempt to introduce fresh capital, whether by way of share capital or long term loan. Equally, the court will not be impressed in such circumstances if the director was drawing funds out of the company for his own personal remuneration or benefit. Thus, inadequate capitalisation may surface as a further aggravating factor in cases containing a mixture of allegations including some or all of trading to the detriment of creditors, unfair discrimination, excessive remuneration and phoenix activity.[152] Moreover, the fact that a company is under-capitalised arguably enhances the obligation on its directors to exercise proper financial responsibility, especially in relation to the filing of accounts, so that potential creditors are in a position to make judgments on the basis of financial information that is reasonably current. Inadequate capitalisation is likely to be regarded more seriously in a public company than in a private company, especially in circumstances where there has been a deliberate failure to comply with the minimum capital requirement.[153]

Failure to prepare and file accounts/returns

5–54 Failure to prepare annual accounts is a matter specifically mentioned in CDDA Sch.1, Pt 1, para.5(a). The courts generally treat such failure as being less serious than a failure to maintain accounting records in breach of s.386 of the Companies Act 2006. However, where the evidence shows that the company was in a poor state

[149] (1988) 4 B.C.C. 446 at 447.

[150] Parliamentary Debates, H.C. Standing Committee E, Session 1984–85, Vol.IV, in particular cols 100–101.

[151] See 2–09 and comments made obiter by Park J. in *Re Cubelock Ltd* [2001] B.C.C. 523 at [90].

[152] See, e.g. *Re D.J. Matthews (Joinery Design) Ltd* (1988) 4 B.C.C. 513; *Re Ipcon Fashions Ltd* (1989) 5 B.C.C. 773; *Re Peppermint Park Ltd* [1998] B.C.C. 23. However, it is dangerous to assume that a so-called "aggravating factor" could never of itself lead to a finding of unfit conduct. Whether or not the defendant's conduct makes him unfit depends on all the facts of the case.

[153] See *Re Kaytech International Plc, Secretary of State for Trade and Industry v Potier* [1999] 2 B.C.L.C. 351 where one defendant, a de facto director, was disqualified for the maximum period of 15 years primarily on the basis of his false claim that the company had a paid up capital of £2.5 million.

of financial health for an extended period of time, the failure to prepare full accounts may be indicative of a more general failure to monitor the company's financial position.[154] Failure to file accounts and/or returns (especially annual returns) has been raised as a supplementary allegation. Filing obligations are important in terms of underlying policy. For instance, if the directors have not filed accounts, it is likely that none have been prepared and this may suggest a wider failure on their part to exercise financial responsibility.[155] Equally, filing defaults deprive creditors of information that might influence them in deciding whether or not to deal with a particular company. The attitude of the courts appears to depend on the frequency of default. It is unlikely that a director would be disqualified on the basis of a single default or a couple of isolated lapses.[156] This is particularly true if the company had already ceased trading at the time when the filing obligation arose as, in that case, the default could not possibly prejudice creditors.[157] However, where the evidence shows that the company was in a weak financial position throughout its trading history, the court may treat the matter more seriously.[158] Moreover, a director with professional expertise in the fields of accounting and finance stands a greater chance of being disqualified for defaults in the preparation and filing of accounts than a director who has no such expertise.[159]

In a case where there is evidence of persistent default across several companies, it is conceivable that the director responsible could be disqualified solely on the ground of failure to comply with statutory obligations. The case of *Re Swift 736 Ltd, Secretary of State for Trade and Industry v Ettinger* provides a vivid illustration. This was an appeal in which the Secretary of State contended that the three year disqualification imposed by the judge was too short. The Secretary of State argued that the judge had not attached sufficient weight to the defendant's repeated failure as a director of some 11 companies to prepare and file accounts and annual returns. The Court of Appeal agreed and increased the period of disqualification to five years. This result and the tenor of the leading judgment leave little doubt that in an appropriate case the court will treat the failure to prepare and file accounts as unfit conduct. Nicholls V.C. gave the following robust assessment:

[154] See, e.g. *Re Park House Properties Ltd, Secretary of State for Trade and Industry v Carter* [1997] 2 B.C.L.C. 530. In this sort of case, it is no defence for the defendant to rely on a dispute with the company's accountants or auditors as an explanation for the failure: see *Re Ward Sherrard Ltd* [1996] B.C.C. 418.

[155] Peter Gibson J. stated in *Re Bath Glass Ltd* [1988] B.C.L.C. 329 at 332 that failure to file accounts is "plainly a matter which can and should be taken into account".

[156] See, e.g. *Re Lo-Line Electric Motors Ltd* [1988] Ch. 477; *Re GSAR Realisations Ltd* [1993] B.C.L.C. 409; *Re Hitco 2000 Ltd, Official Receiver v Cowan* [1995] 2 B.C.L.C. 63; *Re City Pram & Toy Co Ltd* [1998] B.C.C. 537. Although not required to consider the terms of CDDA s.3, it is unlikely in practice that the court would make a finding of unfit conduct based on conduct falling short of "persistent default" as therein defined: see *Re ECM (Europe) Electronics Ltd* [1991] B.C.C. 268 at 271. On s.3 generally, see Ch.10.

[157] See, e.g. *Re Bath Glass Ltd* [1988] B.C.L.C. 329; *Re Cargo Agency Ltd* [1992] B.C.L.C. 686.

[158] See, e.g. *Re Burnham Marketing Services Ltd, Secretary of State for Trade and Industry v Harper* [1993] B.C.C. 518 at 524; *Re Pamstock Ltd* [1994] 1 B.C.L.C. 716.

[159] See, e.g. *Re Cladrose Ltd* [1990] B.C.L.C. 204 and further discussion in 5–92.

> "Limited liability is a valuable tool in the promotion of trade and business, but it must not be misused. Those who make use of limited liability must do so with a proper sense of responsibility. The . . . disqualification procedure is an important sanction introduced by Parliament to raise standards in this regard. Those who take advantage of limited liability . . . must . . . be punctilious in observing the safeguards laid down by Parliament for the benefit of others who have dealings with their companies. They must maintain proper books of account and prepare annual accounts; they must file their accounts and returns promptly . . . Isolated lapses in filing documents are one thing and may be excusable. Not so persistent lapses which show overall a blatant disregard for this important aspect of accountability. Such lapses are serious and cannot be condoned even though . . . they need not involve any dishonest intent . . . Those who persistently fail to discharge their statutory obligations . . . can expect to be disqualified . . . from using limited liability as one of the tools of their trade. The business community should be left in no doubt on this score. It may be that, despite the disqualification provisions having been in operation for some years, there is still a lingering feeling in some quarters that a failure to file annual accounts and so forth is a venial sin. If this is still so, the sooner the attitude is corrected the better it will be."[160]

5–55 It is clear from this that in cases of persistent default the courts will use the sanction of disqualification in an attempt to deter others and thus to promote compliance with core statutory obligations. A further justification for this approach is that repeated failure to prepare and file accounts will often be symptomatic of a wider failure on the part of directors to maintain any real grip on the financial position of their companies. In the majority of cases, failure to prepare and file accounts will not justify disqualification on its own. However, it may form part of a pattern of conduct or a combination of factors that lead to an overall finding of unfit conduct. The same approach is likely as regards the preparation and filing of tax returns, especially VAT returns.

Acceptance of customer pre-payments

5–56 Disqualification was clearly intended to operate in some sense as a measure for consumer protection. In the case of a company that has become insolvent, the court is directed by CDDA Sch.1 Pt II para.7 to pay particular regard to the extent of the director's responsibility for any failure by the company to supply goods or services which have been paid for in advance. If a director who allows the company to trade while insolvent causes it to continue accepting customer deposits for goods or services that the company may not be in a position to deliver and then dissipates those sums, the risk of disqualification is undoubtedly increased. It is clear from the authorities that the courts generally regard the use of customer monies to prop up ailing companies as serious misconduct.[161] This reflects the perception that consumers are in a weaker position in terms of information and bargaining power

[160] [1993] B.C.L.C. 896 at 899–900.

[161] See, e.g. *Re Western Welsh International System Buildings Ltd* (1988) 4 B.C.C. 449; *Re Austinsuite Furniture Ltd* [1992] B.C.L.C. 1047; *Re City Pram & Toy Co Ltd* [1998] B.C.C. 537. In *Re Land Travel Ltd, Secretary of State for Trade and Industry v Tjolle* [1998] 1 B.C.L.C. 333, the principal defendant was convicted of fraudulent trading after customers of his travel company lost deposits worth £6.6 million on its collapse. He subsequently consented to a maximum 15 year disqualification under the summary *Carecraft* procedure (on which see further Ch.9).

than trade creditors and therefore in greater need of protection. Disqualification orders have been made against directors of financial services companies on related grounds. In *Re City Investment Centres Ltd*[162] three directors were disqualified for periods ranging from six to ten years where the company had used client monies, which should have been used to execute dealings on behalf of clients, to make speculative loans and as working capital. Similarly, in *Re CSTC Ltd, Secretary of State for Trade and Industry v Van Hengel*[163] the principal defendant was disqualified for six years, for failing among other things, to maintain separate client accounts and for using interest accrued on client monies as working capital.

Although s.9 of and Sch.1 to the CDDA direct the court to pay particular regard to the extent of the director's responsibility for any failure by the company to supply goods or services which have been paid for in advance, it is important to note that the mere fact that a director, knowing the company to be insolvent, caused it to continue accepting customer deposits will not necessarily make him unfit.[164] All will depend on the particular circumstances of the case.

Transactions detrimental to creditors

Transactions liable to avoidance under the Insolvency Act

5–57 In contrast to wrongful trading which is not specifically referred to in the Schedule,[165] the court is directed by CDDA Sch.1 Pt II para.8 to pay particular regard to the extent of the director's responsibility for entering into transactions liable to be set aside under s.127 or ss.238 to 240 of the Insolvency Act 1986. These provisions confer various rights of action on a liquidator and also, in the case of ss.238–240, an administrator. Their overall purpose is to reverse transactions entered into by insolvent companies which benefit certain creditors at the expense of other creditors or which have the effect of unfairly reducing the pool of assets available to meet creditors' claims. There is no doubt that misconduct capable of amounting to a breach of these provisions is relevant to the question of whether a director's conduct makes him unfit. Moreover, the fact that the liquidator has successfully pursued the director in parallel civil proceedings for a remedy under these provisions does not mean that less weight should be attached to the same misconduct in any subsequent disqualification proceedings. In *Re Grayan Building Services Ltd, Secretary of State for Trade and Industry v Gray*, the judge found that conduct amounting to a preference did not make the defendants unfit because of the salutary effect on them of parallel proceedings under s.239. This finding was criticised by the Court of Appeal as depriving the reference to s.239 in Sch.1 of any effect in the worst of cases.[166]

[162] [1992] B.C.L.C. 956.

[163] [1995] 1 B.C.L.C. 545.

[164] *Re World of Leather Plc, Secretary of State for Trade and Industry v Gill* [2006] B.C.C. 725 and discussion from 5–22.

[165] See from 5–05.

[166] [1995] Ch. 241 at 256. This formed part of the Court of Appeal's attack on the notion that the claimant must show that the defendant is *presently* unfit: see from 4–11. For a case where conduct the subject of parallel civil proceedings under ss.238–239 was taken fully into account in subsequent disqualification proceedings see *Re T & D Services (Timber Preservation & Damp Proofing Contractors) Ltd* [1990] B.C.C. 592. See also, in the context of bankruptcy restrictions, *Official Receiver v Bathurst* [2008] B.P.I.R. 1548.

Conversely, the pursuit of parallel civil proceedings is not a pre-condition for a finding of unfit conduct. If the liquidator (or, where relevant, the administrator) takes no action (because, for example, he lacks funds to cover the cost of litigation), it is still open to the court to disqualify a director for misconduct falling within the ambit of the provisions.[167]

5–58 As discussed above, in the case of an allegation of trading to the detriment of creditors, the court can find unfit conduct without the claimant having to establish all the elements of wrongful trading under s.214 of the Insolvency Act 1986.[168] At first sight, it could be argued that the position is different with the provisions being considered here. By virtue of CDDA s.9 and Sch.1 Pt II para.8, the court is expressly required to take into account a director's responsibility for the company entering into transactions "liable to be set aside" under s.127 or ss.238–240 of the Insolvency Act. This suggests that the claimant may need to show that the transaction satisfies all the elements of the relevant provision and would therefore have been set aside had it been challenged in parallel civil proceedings.[169] The case of *Re Living Images Ltd*[170] seems to reflect this view but on closer analysis it probably turns on the fact that the allegation of unfit conduct was framed specifically as a breach of s.239 of the Insolvency Act 1986.[171] One allegation in that case concerned the repayment of a loan made to the company by B, a close friend of the first defendant. The Official Receiver alleged that the repayment, which was made three months before the company went into liquidation, constituted an unlawful preference. In order to succeed under s.239 of the Insolvency Act, the office holder must show (among other things) that the company giving the preference was influenced by a desire to put a creditor or guarantor in a better position, in the event of the company going into insolvent liquidation, than would otherwise have been the case. Laddie J. stuck closely to this requirement and held that a director must at least know of the desire to prefer and the fact that it has influenced the company to act for the benefit of a particular creditor before he can be disqualified on this ground. Following the guidance given by Millett J. in *Re M C Bacon Ltd*,[172] the leading case on s.239, the judge concluded that the company, through the defendants, had been influenced in repaying B by a desire to improve his position in the event of an insolvent liquidation. In disqualifying the first defendant for six years (on the basis of this and other proven allegations), Laddie J. noted that his willingness to prefer a friend at a time when the company was unable to pay its debts illustrated his indifference to the plight of the company's creditors as a whole. On this approach, a director who causes his company, in anticipation of its insolvent liquidation, to repay sums outstanding on his own loan account, is likely to have a case to answer. In this instance it is much

[167] Though note the cautious approach in *Re ECM (Europe) Electronics Ltd* [1991] B.C.C. 268.

[168] See from 5–05.

[169] For a detailed account of the main transaction avoidance provisions see J. Armour & H. Bennett (eds), *Vulnerable Transactions in Corporate Insolvency* (Oxford: Hart Publishing, 2003).

[170] [1996] 1 B.C.L.C. 348.

[171] cf. *Re Sykes (Butchers) Ltd, Secretary of State for Trade & Industry v Richardson* [1998] 1 B.C.L.C. 110.

[172] [1990] B.C.L.C. 324.

easier to satisfy the requirements of s.239 as, in the case of a preference given by a company to a connected person such as a director, there is a presumption that the company was influenced by the requisite desire to prefer.[173]

5–59 The approach in *Living Images* has not been followed in every case. In *Re Sykes (Butchers) Ltd, Secretary of State for Trade and Industry v Richardson*[174] the registrar disqualified the defendant for seven years having found him to be unfit on a number of grounds. One allegation found to be proved was that he had caused the company to extinguish its overdraft to the detriment of other creditors and to his own benefit as guarantor of the company's indebtedness to the bank. The registrar found as a fact that the defendant was influenced, at least in part by the desire to eliminate the exposure under his guarantee but rejected the Secretary of State's submission that repayment of the overdraft amounted to a statutory preference liable to be set aside under s.239. Nevertheless, the registrar allowed the Secretary of State to reformulate the case on the footing that the defendant had demonstrated a lack of probity in repaying the bank rather than trade creditors. On appeal, it was argued on the defendant's behalf that the registrar had been wrong to entertain a case based on this more general formulation, especially as the Secretary of State had originally alleged that the conduct amounted to a statutory preference. Ferris J. held that the Secretary of State had not put his case so narrowly:

> "It would . . . be surprising if the Secretary of State had been prepared to limit his case in the way suggested . . . because it is apparent from the terms of s.6 . . . that the court is to be concerned with conduct generally and not merely with contravention of specific provisions of the Companies Act . . . or the Insolvency Act . . . Moreover, although responsibility for a statutory preference liable to be set aside under . . . the Insolvency Act . . . is one of the matters to which the court, in determining unfitness, is to have particular regard . . . it is clear that these matters are not the only ones to which the court may have regard. On examination I find that the Secretary of State has not in fact limited his case in this way. The reference to 'preference' has always been made in general terms, not in terms specific to any of the statutory provisions concerning preference which I have referred to."[175]

The implication of this is that the claimant can allege that the relevant misconduct amounts either to a breach of the statutory provisions or misconduct which falls short of a specific breach[176] but is nevertheless indicative of unfit

[173] See *Re Exchange Travel (Holdings) Ltd (No. 3)* [1996] B.C.C. 933; *Wills v Corfe Joinery Ltd* [1997] B.C.C. 511; cf. *Re Hawkes Hill Publishing Co Ltd* [2007] B.C.C. 937. Even so, in disqualification proceedings the court will still need to consider the specific circumstances giving rise to the repayment of directors' loans: see *Re Keypak Homecare Ltd* [1990] B.C.L.C. 440 at 444–445. For a similar approach to that in *Living Images* applying the statutory predecessor of s.239 (i.e. the old fraudulent preference provision) in disqualification proceedings see *Re Time Utilising Business Systems Ltd* (1989) 5 B.C.C. 851.

[174] [1998] 1 B.C.L.C. 110.

[175] [1998] 1 B.C.L.C. 110 at 125.

[176] For example, the relevant conduct may take place outside the time periods applicable to transactions at undervalue or preferences. In the context of bankruptcy restrictions see *Official Receiver v Bathurst* [2008] B.P.I.R. 1548.

conduct. Thus, in a case such as *Sykes (Butchers)* where the claimant cannot establish a statutory preference, the court may still be persuaded to find that the relevant conduct makes the defendant unfit on the alternative ground of unfair discrimination.[177] This was much the conclusion reached on similar facts in the *Verby Print* case discussed in 5–32 to 5–34.

5–60 A similar approach was taken in *Re Deaduck Ltd, Secretary of State for Trade and Industry v Baker*[178] where it was alleged in the alternative, that the defendant had caused or allowed the company to make a payment to an associated company to the detriment of the general body of creditors and/or that the payment was a preference as defined by s.239 of the Insolvency Act. It was held that the allegation based on statutory preference was not established as the claimant had failed to prove that the company had been influenced in making the payment by a desire to prefer. Nevertheless, Neuberger J. ruled that the *effect* of the payment, judged both at the time it was made, and by reference to subsequent events, was to worsen the position of the company's other unsecured creditors. Moreover, once the claimant had demonstrated that the creditors were in a worse position immediately after the payment than immediately before, the onus was then on the defendant to establish, in the light of subsequent events, that the payment had not in fact been detrimental to their interests. Accordingly, the judge found that the "detrimental payment" allegation was established. It appears that it sufficed for the claimant to establish that the defendant's conduct comprised the following elements:[179]

(1) That the payment had been made at a time when the company was insolvent.
(2) That the payment had been made at a time when the defendant should have appreciated that it was insolvent and that there was a real risk of an insolvent liquidation.
(3) That the general body of creditors was, in fact, prejudiced by the payment.

Thus, it is clear in the light of *Sykes Butchers* and *Deaduck* that the claimant does not necessarily have to establish that a transaction was a *statutory* preference in order to demonstrate that the defendant's conduct in causing the company to enter into the transaction makes him unfit. Depending on the circumstances, it may be enough for the claimant to satisfy the elements set out above.[180] In a

[177] See also *Re New Generation Engineers Ltd* [1993] B.C.L.C. 435 where Warner J. appears to have treated an allegation of preference as part of a wider complaint concerning the policy adopted for payment of creditors.

[178] [2000] 1 B.C.L.C. 148.

[179] [2000] 1 B.C.L.C. 148 at 157.

[180] It should be added that, while Neuberger J. found the "detrimental payment" allegation to be proven, on the particular facts of *Deaduck*, he held that the conduct was not sufficient to make the defendant unfit. For another case where the defendant was disqualified on the basis of his involvement in a transaction that seems to have fallen short of a statutory preference see *Re Funtime Ltd* [2000] 1 B.C.L.C. 247.

similar vein, it has been suggested that even if a defendant to s.238 proceedings to set aside a transaction at undervalue could have raised a defence to those proceedings under s.238(5),[181] it would not necessarily preclude the court from considering the circumstances of the transaction in the different context of disqualification proceedings.[182]

5–61 The focus of disqualification proceedings is on the director's conduct rather than on the cause of action under the Insolvency Act 1986. It is therefore understandable that the courts do not regard it as essential to the establishment of unfit conduct that the transaction under scrutiny should necessarily satisfy all of the statutory criteria (in particular, the prescribed time periods and, in the case of s.239, the requirement to show that the company was influenced by a desire to prefer). In any event, there is an overlap between the statutory causes of action and the general fiduciary obligation of directors to consider or act in the interests of the company's creditors where the company is factually insolvent.[183] While, the precise extent and nature of this duty has yet to be clarified by the courts (it has been suggested that the common law principle amounts to a "disability" rather than a "duty" in the sense that it negates any ratification or waiver by the shareholders of the directors' actions once the company is insolvent),[184] it may provide a legal justification for the broader approach taken in *Sykes Butchers* and *Deaduck* founded on detriment to creditors. In other words, rather than being based solely on misconduct disapproved of by the court, the basis of the criticism may be a legal principle that would result in the conduct giving rise to legal consequences independently of disqualification proceedings.

Transactions in breach of fiduciary or statutory duty

5–62 There are several cases in which the court has had no trouble concluding that the defendant's conduct made him unfit based on serious breaches of fiduciary duty. The following have all been regarded in themselves as indicative of unfit conduct: diversion of assets or business away from the company whether the director benefited directly or not[185]; the siphoning off of company monies or assets for

[181] Section 238(5) provides that the court shall not make an order under s.238 if it is satisfied: (a) that the company which entered into the transaction did so in good faith and for the purpose of carrying on its business; and (b) that at the time it did so there were reasonable grounds for believing that the transaction would benefit the company.

[182] *Re Genosyis Technology Management Ltd, Wallach v Secretary of State for Trade and Industry* [2006] EWHC 989 (Ch), [2007] 1 B.C.L.C. 208.

[183] See *West Mercia Safetywear Ltd v Dodd* [1988] B.C.L.C. 250; *Facia Footwear Ltd v Hinchcliffe* [1998] 1 B.C.L.C. 218; *Colin Gwyer & Associates Ltd v London Wharf (Limehouse) Ltd* [2003] 2 B.C.L.C. 153; Companies Act 2006 s.172(3). In the disqualification context see *Re The Premier Screw and Repetition Co Ltd, Paulin v Secretary of State for Trade and Industry* [2005] EWHC 888 (Ch), [2005] 2 B.C.L.C. 667.

[184] See *Re Westminster Property Management Ltd (No.2), Official Receiver v Stern (No.2)* [2001] EWCA Civ 1787, [2002] 1 B.C.L.C. 119 at [31]–[32] and J. Armour, "Avoidance of Transactions as a 'Fraud on Creditors' at Common Law in J. Armour & H. Bennett (eds), *Vulnerable Transactions in Corporate Insolvency* (Oxford: Hart Publishing, 2003) at pp.317–319.

[185] *Re Living Images Ltd* [1996] 1 B.C.L.C. 348 (diversion of contract); *Re Mayfair Interiors (Wolverhampton) Ltd, Secretary of State for Trade and Industry v Blunt* [2005] 2 B.C.L.C. 463 (misappropriation of stock by defendant and conversion for own benefit); *Re Wedgecraft Ltd*, March 7, 1986, Ch.D., unreported (diversion of cash flow from one company to another controlled by the defendant, in the form of rent payments).

personal use by directors,[186] and illegal loans to directors.[187] A case where directors engage in misconduct of this nature at a time when the company's solvency is in doubt will undoubtedly be regarded as a serious one.[188] On the other hand, it is important to recognise that a mere technical breach of duty may not lead, in isolation, to a finding of unfit conduct.

Financial assistance

5–63 In *Re Continental Assurance Co of London Plc*[189] the first defendant allowed the funds of a subsidiary to be used in repaying sums borrowed by its parent company to finance the acquisition of the subsidiary. This amounted to financial assistance in breach of what is now ss.678–679 of the Companies Act 2006 (formerly s.151 of the Companies Act 1985). Chadwick J. took this breach of the statute into account in finding that the conduct of the first defendant and a non-executive director of the company made them unfit. Misconduct in breach of analogous statutory provisions such as the rules prohibiting payment of dividends otherwise than from distributable profits can also be such as to make the perpetrator unfit.[190]

Non co-operation with office holders and regulatory authorities

5–64 The combined effect of s.6(2) and CDDA Sch.1 Pt II para.10 is that the court must have particular regard to any failure by a director to co-operate with the relevant office holder. Non-co-operation covers a range of defaults including failure to provide a statement of affairs, failure to deliver up company records or assets and, in the case of a compulsory liquidation, failure to attend appointments with the official receiver or failure to attend a public examination at the direction of the court.[191] The importance of full co-operation from the directors of a company that has entered a formal insolvency regime cannot be underestimated. Without co-operation, the office holder's attempts to identify the company's assets and quantify

[186] *Re Tansoft Ltd* [1991] B.C.L.C. 339; *Re Copecrest Ltd, Secretary of State for Trade & Industry v McTighe (No.2)* [1996] 2 B.C.L.C. 477; *Re Park House Properties Ltd, Secretary of State for Trade and Industry v Carter* [1997] 2 B.C.L.C. 530.

[187] *Re Tansoft Ltd* [1991] B.C.L.C. 339; *Re Moorgate Metals Ltd, Official Receiver v Huhtala* [1995] 1 B.C.L.C. 503; *Re Copecrest Ltd, Secretary of State for Trade & Industry v McTighe (No.2)* [1996] 2 B.C.L.C. 477; *Re Westminster Property Management Ltd (No.2), Official Receiver v Stern (No.2)* [2001] EWCA Civ 1787, [2002] 1 B.C.L.C. 119. See also *Re Agushi and Australian Securities Commission* (1996) 19 A.C.S.R. 322, a case decided under the statutory predecessor of s.206F of Australia's Corporations Act 2001. Note now the changes embodied in Pt X of the Companies Act 2006 whereby loans to directors are only illegal if not sanctioned by the shareholders.

[188] See, e.g. *Re Westminster Property Management Ltd (No.2), Official Receiver v Stern (No.2)* [2001] EWCA Civ 1787, [2002] 1 B.C.L.C. 119, where the defendant was disqualified for 12 years in part on the basis of his unauthorised misapplication of money belonging to two insolvent companies.

[189] [1997] 1 B.C.L.C. 48.

[190] See, e.g. *Re Queens Moathouses Plc, Secretary of State for Trade and Industry v Bairstow* [2004] EWHC 1730 (Ch), [2005] 1 B.C.L.C. 136; *Re AG (Manchester) Ltd, Official Receiver v Watson* [2008] EWHC 64 (Ch), [2008] 1 B.C.L.C. 321 (illegal dividends, in excess of what the company could afford, paid without proper consideration by the board). See also *Re Bunting Electric Manufacturing Co Ltd, Secretary of State for Trade and Industry v Golby* [2006] 1 B.C.L.C. 550 (provision of false and misleading information and making of groundless statutory declaration of solvency for purposes of Companies Act ss.155–158).

[191] Insolvency Act 1986 s.133.

its liabilities may be hampered. Failure to co-operate may therefore result in further harm to creditors. In *Re Copecrest Ltd, Secretary of State for Trade and Industry v McTighe*[192] the first defendant refused to explain the background to certain items in the statement of affairs of one company, a stance he maintained throughout the liquidation. In respect of two other companies, he failed to attend appointments with the official receiver. The Court of Appeal was robust in its view that his persistent failure to co-operate was itself indicative of unfit conduct. In the majority of cases, non-co-operation is relied upon as a supplementary allegation and will be an aggravating factor rather than a matter that, in isolation, will lead automatically to a finding of unfit conduct.[193] Nevertheless, *McTighe* makes clear that, in an appropriate case, persistent non-co-operation with an office holder may of itself make the director unfit.[194] Non-co-operation with regulatory bodies such as the Financial Services Authority may be taken into account as well as non-co-operation with insolvency office holders.[195]

Breach of fiduciary and other duties

5–65 Several of the species of misconduct already discussed such as trading to the detriment of creditors and excessive remuneration could equally be characterised as breaches of the director's general fiduciary obligations. Companies Act 2006 s.172 imposes a general duty on a director to act in the way he considers, in good faith, would be most likely to promote the success of the company for the benefit of its members as a whole having regard to a number of non-exhaustive matters including inter alia the interests of the company's employees and the impact of the company's operations on the community and the environment company's best interests. To the extent that s.172 codifies and modifies the pre-existing duty of directors in equity to act in the interests of the company, it does not affect the rule that, in discharging the duty, directors should have regard to the interests of creditors in circumstances where the company is factually insolvent.[196] This is clear from s.172(3) which

[192] [1996] 2 B.C.L.C. 477.

[193] See *Re T & D Services (Timber Preservation & Damp Proofing Contractors) Ltd* [1990] B.C.C. 592; *Re Tansoft Ltd* [1991] B.C.L.C. 339; *Re City Investment Centres Ltd* [1992] B.C.L.C. 956; *Re Defence & Microwave Devices Ltd*, October 7, 1992, Ch.D., unreported; *Re Brooks Transport (Purfleet) Ltd* [1993] B.C.C. 766; *Re GSAR Realisations Ltd* [1993] B.C.L.C. 409; *Re L M Fabrications Ltd*, April 27, 1995, unreported (Northern Ireland); *Re Living Images Ltd* [1996] 1 B.C.L.C. 348; *Re Thorncliffe Finance Ltd, Secretary of State for Trade and Industry v Arif* [1997] 1 B.C.L.C. 34; *Re Skata Ltd, Secretary of State for Trade and Industry v Zevides* [2002] EWHC (Ch) 813. See also *Re Agushi and Australian Securities Commission* (1996) 19 A.C.S.R. 322 in which the defendant's failure to deliver up the company's books and records to the liquidator was regarded as being indicative of unfit conduct for the purposes of the statutory predecessor of what is now s.206F of Australia's Corporations Act 2001 (Cth).

[194] See also *Re Mayfair Interiors (Wolverhampton) Ltd, Secretary of State for Trade and Industry v Blunt* [2005] 2 B.C.L.C. 463 where the judge regarded the misappropriation of assets and the subsequent concealment of the misappropriation from the liquidator as separately meriting disqualification.

[195] *Ghassemian v Secretary of State for Trade and Industry* [2006] EWHC 1715 (Ch), [2007] B.C.C. 229.

[196] *West Mercia Safetywear Ltd v Dodd* [1988] B.C.L.C. 250; *Facia Footwear Ltd v Hinchcliffe* [1998] 1 B.C.L.C. 218; *Colin Gwyer & Associates Ltd v London Wharf (Limehouse) Ltd* [2003] 2 B.C.L.C. 153.

provides that the s.172 duty "has effect subject to any enactment or rule of law requiring directors, in certain circumstances, to consider or act in the interests of creditors of the company".

Breaches of duty affecting shareholders

5–66 Equally, however, it is open to the court under ss.6 or 8 to take into account conduct in breach of duty that, at the time, affected the interests of members rather than creditors. It is clear also that breach of duty can be taken into account regardless of whether or not it caused the company's failure. In *Re Godwin Warren Control Systems Plc*[197] the relevant company, Systems, acquired the business and assets of a company called Data Solutions Ltd. The first defendant, O, failed to disclose to the board of Systems that he had a controlling interest in Data Solutions. Moreover, he took steps to reduce his registered shareholding in Data Solutions in order to circumvent the obligation to seek shareholder approval for the transaction under s.320 of the Companies Act 1985, the immediate statutory predecessor of s.190 of the Companies Act 2006.[198] Chadwick J. held that O's deliberate attempt to conceal his interest from both the board and shareholders of Systems made him unfit and disqualified him for six years. The case was seen as being particularly serious because O was a chartered accountant and Systems was a public company. *Godwin Warren* illustrates the use of disqualification to reinforce the basic prohibition on undisclosed conflicts of interest.

Breaches of duty affecting employees

5–67 On a different note, the courts of Northern Ireland have treated breaches of the directors' statutory obligation to have regard to the interests of employees[199] as a matter indicative of unfit conduct. In *Re L M Fabrications Ltd*[200] some importance was attached to the defendant's failure to maintain compulsory employers' liability insurance. In *Re Omaglass Ltd*[201] the company was under an obligation to maintain a bonus fund for its salesmen to meet commission payments. The defendant's failure to ensure that monies were transferred into the fund was taken into account as a failure to pay due regard to employees' interests. These cases confirm that weight may be given to the interests of employees in disqualification proceedings. Breaches of health and safety legislation affecting employees could also be taken into account.[202]

5–68 It is clear from cases such as *Re Barings Plc (No. 5), Secretary of State for Trade and Industry v Baker*[203] that a director's failure to discharge his duty to

[197] [1993] B.C.L.C. 80.

[198] The transaction between Solutions and Systems would only have been caught by s.320 if O had retained either a controlling interest in Solutions or an interest in at least one–fifth of its share capital: Companies Act 1985 s.346(4), (5).

[199] Companies Act 2006 s.172(1)(b) (formerly Companies Act 1985 s.309).

[200] April 27, 1995, unreported.

[201] April 6, 1995, unreported. Both cases are discussed in A. Hoey, "Disqualifying Delinquent Directors" (1997) 18 Co Law 130.

[202] See further text from 10–25.

[203] [1999] 1 B.C.L.C. 433, affirmed by the Court of Appeal: [2000] 1 B.C.L.C. 523.

exercise reasonable care, skill and diligence[204] may be relevant in determining whether or not his conduct makes him unfit. The point is taken up below in the section dealing with disqualification on grounds of incompetence.

Fraud

5–69 It is open to the court to disqualify a director under CDDA s.6 on the basis of fraudulent conduct, and this may be so whether or not such conduct has previously been the subject of a criminal prosecution.[205] So, for example, in *Re T & D Services (Timber Preservation & Damp Proofing Contractors) Ltd*[206] there was evidence that the defendant had obtained grants from a local authority by deception. Relying on this and other proven allegations, the judge disqualified him for ten years. Similarly, in *Re Defence & Microwave Devices Ltd*, allegations that the defendants had defrauded the Revenue and appended false audit certificates to the annual accounts were found proven and treated as relevant misconduct.[207] Furthermore, a director of a public company who falsely claimed that the company had complied with the minimum share capital requirements imposed on public companies by what is now Companies Act 2006 ss.761–763 was found to be unfit in *Re Kaytech International Plc, Secretary of State for Trade and Industry v Potier*.[208] Allegations of deception and/or dishonesty, if established, commonly result in a lengthy period of disqualification.[209]

Specific instances of unfit conduct in section 8 cases

5–70 Cases decided under s.8 illustrate further the breadth of unfit conduct. Consistent with the rationale of the various specified investigatory powers that provide a gateway to s.8 proceedings, s.8 cases show that unfit conduct is capable of embracing misconduct detrimental to investors and consumers as well as to creditors. In *Re Samuel Sherman Plc*,[210] the relevant company ceased trading and,

[204] See now Companies Act 2006 s.174.

[205] In *Re Land Travel Ltd, Secretary of State for Trade and Industry v Tjolle* [1998] 1 B.C.L.C. 333 the principal defendant had previously been convicted of fraudulent trading and disqualified for ten years under CDDA s.2. Nevertheless, the Secretary of State was able to bring proceedings seeking a longer period of disqualification under s.6. It appears also that the court can take into account conduct the subject of a previous conviction even if that conviction has become spent under the Rehabilitation of Offenders Act 1974: *Secretary of State for Trade and Industry v Queen* [1998] B.C.C. 678. However, this is subject to arguments of double jeopardy and abuse of process discussed further in Ch.7.

[206] [1990] B.C.C. 592.

[207] October 7, 1992, Ch.D., unreported. See also *Re AG (Manchester) Ltd, Official Receiver v Watson* [2008] 1 B.C.L.C. 321 at [166] and text at 10–33.

[208] *Re Kaytech International Plc, Secretary of State for Trade and Industry v Potier* [1999] 2 B.C.L.C. 351.

[209] See, e.g. *Re Vintage Hallmark Plc, Secretary of State for Trade and Industry v Grove* [2006] EWHC 2761 (Ch), [2007] 1 B.C.L.C. 788 (directors who had inter alia procured subscriptions for shares in a hopelessly insolvent company through false representations concerning the value of its assets and induced purchasers to buy goods on the basis of false representations as to their resale value disqualified for the maximum period of 15 years); *Re Plazoo Pipe Systems Ltd, Kappler v Secretary of State for Trade and Industry* [2006] EWHC 3694 (Ch), [2008] 1 B.C.L.C. 120 (director who knowingly allowed false invoices to be issued in order to obtain credit on the company's invoice discounting facility disqualified for 11 years).

[210] [1991] 1 W.L.R. 1070.

at the defendant's direction its assets were sold generating a surplus of some £300,000. Without consulting the company's shareholders, the defendant used the surplus to make speculative overseas investments in the oil and gas industries. These investments were ultra vires the company's memorandum of association. The company lost money on the investments and was eventually wound up with a surplus of only £26,000. The main criticism of the defendant (who was disqualified for five years) was not that the investments were speculative in nature, but the fact that he had caused the company to change its business without having recourse to its shareholders. In *Re Looe Fish Ltd*,[211] the disqualification proceedings followed an investigation of the relevant company's affairs under s.447 of the Companies Act 1985. The defendants manipulated voting control of the company with a view to blocking a takeover bid by a rival faction. They hatched an elaborate scheme whereby the company issued sufficient extra shares to enable them to block action supported by the original majority. They then arranged for the company to repurchase these shares. Both defendants were disqualified for breach of duty despite their belief that they were acting in the company's best interests and not for financial gain or improper personal benefit.[212] Had the relevant companies become insolvent, it is clear that the misconduct in these cases could equally have led to a finding of unfit conduct through the gateway of s.6. Moreover, in *Sherman* the defendant's persistent failure to comply with statutory obligations was taken into account much as it would have been under s.6.[213] This emphasises the point that ss.6 and 8 merely provide separate gateways to the legal assessment of directors' conduct. Misconduct that will result in a finding that it makes the director "unfit" under one section, would have the same result in proceedings under the other.

5–71 One of the leading s.8 cases to date is *Re Atlantic Computers Plc, Secretary of State for Trade and Industry v Ashman*.[214] This case arose following a Companies Act investigation into the collapse of Atlantic, a computer leasing company and its parent company, British & Commonwealth Holdings Plc ("B&C"). Atlantic's shares were successfully floated on the London Stock Exchange and it was later acquired by B&C. The collapse was precipitated by the failure of Atlantic's main product, the "flexlease". Under the flexlease, Atlantic sold computer equipment to a financier at an initial profit. The equipment was then leased to the customer for a fixed term. Atlantic also entered into a parallel agreement enabling the customer either to upgrade the equipment or to walk away from the lease before the term expired. In the event that the customer exercised the so-called "walk option", Atlantic was left with a liability to pay the outstanding rental for the unexpired term to the financier. The theory underlying Atlantic's business model was that customers would favour an upgrade and therefore take fresh equipment under a new lease. Unfortunately, in

[211] [1993] B.C.L.C. 1160.

[212] There is an obvious analogy with common law authorities on improper share allotments such as *Piercy v S. Mills & Co Ltd* [1920] 1 Ch. 77 and *Howard Smith Ltd v Ampol Petroleum Ltd* [1974] A.C. 821.

[213] His defaults included the failure to lay annual accounts before general meeting. The court regarded this failure to provide basic information to shareholders as particularly serious given their lack of any obvious practical remedy: see [1991] 1 W.L.R. 1070 at 1085–1086.

[214] June 15, 1998, Ch.D., unreported.

practice, the "walk" liabilities were so large as to precipitate the collapse of the entire B&C group. Several former group executives (though not all) were found to be unfit. This finding was based principally on the failure of Atlantic to disclose the true extent of its contingent liabilities in its accounts both before it was acquired by B&C and later, after the potential magnitude of the problem became apparent. A number of other substantive points emerge from Lloyd J.'s judgment:

(1) The court can take breaches of accepted standards of financial reporting into account in addition to breaches of statutory accounting obligations. The fact that Atlantic's accounting policies did not conform to fundamental accounting principles and to certain of the Statements of Standard Accounting Practice was taken into consideration as well as failure to comply in a number of respects with Pt VII of the Companies Act 1985 (especially the requirement to maintain adequate and reasonably accurate accounting records).[215]
(2) Where a director's conduct is honest and not lacking in commercial integrity, it does not necessarily follow that, if the conduct falls short of the standards of competence which might be expected by the City or others (whether or not by the law of directors' duties), of a director of a listed company, that director is thereby shown to be unfit to be concerned in the management of a company, however small, private and simple its affairs may be. Nevertheless, where obligations of disclosure and public announcement are concerned, in the case of a listed company, issues of commercial probity do arise, even in the absence of any issue of dishonesty or personal gain.[216]
(3) Misleading statements attributable to a director in a prospectus or listing particulars can be taken into account. A statement in Atlantic's prospectus issued in the course of the company's flotation to the effect that only a small percentage of flexleases contained walk options was found to be misleading.
(4) The pursuit of a line of business (in *Atlantic*, the flexlease) which is inherently unviable does not necessarily make a director unfit. However, if a director allows the company to continue pursuing that line of business once he has been given cause to question its viability (as in *Atlantic*, once the size of the "walk" liabilities finally became apparent), this may be indicative of unfit conduct.
(5) The court must consider the extent of each defendant's responsibility for the relevant misconduct. However, as with s.6, a director cannot escape disqualification by taking no responsibility at all nor can he delegate the performance of his legal obligations entirely to someone else.[217]
(6) The court's approach to the standard of proof in s.8 cases is similar to that under s.6.

[215] See now Companies Act 2006 Pt 15.
[216] Where failure to comply with disclosure obligations is found to be dishonest then the case will be a fortiori. See, e.g. *Re Transtec Plc, Secretary of State for Trade and Industry v Carr* [2007] 2 B.C.L.C. 495 (director of listed company who concealed information that should have been disclosed to the board, the auditors and the Stock Exchange with the result that the company's accounts were materially misleading disqualified under s.8 for nine and a half years). See also *Re Claims Direct Plc, Secretary of State for Business, Enterprise and Regulatory Reform v Sullman* [2008] EWHC 3179 (Ch), [2009] 1 B.C.L.C. 397.
[217] See further from 5–73.

(7) Once a finding of unfit conduct has been made, the court must then decide whether or not to disqualify. It appears that the matters regarded by the Court of Appeal in *Westmid Packing* as relevant to determining the period of disqualification in s.6 cases (discussed below in the section on period of disqualification) may be taken into account in determining whether or not to make a disqualification order under s.8 at all.[218]

5–72 Dishonest practices have also been scrutinised in s.8 proceedings. In *Secretary of State for Trade and Industry v Amiss*,[219] the second defendant, C, caused the insurance brokerage of which he was chief executive to charge its clients inflated premiums in breach of the rules of the Lloyd's insurance market. As well as being disciplined by Lloyd's, C was disqualified under s.8 for a period of nine years. The Secretary of State's principal case against C was that he had dishonestly participated in a serious breach of the fiduciary duty owed by the company to its clients. It was suggested, on C's behalf, that in determining whether he had been dishonest, the court should apply the combined test set out by the House of Lords in *Twinsectra Ltd v Yardley*,[220] a case concerned with accessory liability for breach of trust. As understood at that time,[221] to satisfy the test it had to be shown that the defendant acted dishonestly by the standards of reasonable and honest people and that he was himself aware that, by those standards, he was acting dishonestly. On the evidence, Peter Smith J. found that C had known that the practice was "thoroughly dishonest" and therefore concluded that the *Twinsectra* test was made out. He added the following caveat:

> "I am not convinced however, that the *Twinsectra* test is required. What is required is that [C's] conduct has to be such as to make him unfit to be a director. It seems to me that even if there was not dishonesty, as the managing director, chief executive and substantial shareholder in [the company] he has participated in these transactions to such a degree that his conduct makes him unfit to be a director."[222]

This reinforces the point already made that, while unfit conduct may be premised on some form of actionable wrong, such as wrongful trading or statutory preference, the courts rely on the width of the concept to disqualify directors for conduct that would not necessarily be actionable per se under the ordinary civil law.[223]

[218] For instance, in *Atlantic* the judge considered and rejected a submission by two of the defendants that the court should refrain from disqualifying because of the length of time for which they had been in jeopardy: see 5–117. This factor and the earlier treatment of some of their co-directors were nevertheless taken into account in relation to the period of disqualification.

[219] [2003] EWHC 523 (Ch), [2003] 2 B.C.L.C. 206. For further background see DTI Press Release P/2003/178, March 20, 2003.

[220] [2002] 2 A.C. 164.

[221] See now *Barlow Clowes International Ltd (in liquidation) v Eurotrust International Ltd* [2005] UKPC 37, [2006] 1 W.L.R. 1476; *Abou-Rahmah v Abacha* [2006] EWCA Civ 1492, [2007] 1 Lloyd's Rep. 115.

[222] [2003] 2 B.C.L.C. 206 at [65].

[223] See earlier discussion from 5–05 (trading while insolvent to the detriment of creditors) and from 5–57 (transactions detrimental to creditors).

DISQUALIFICATION ON GROUNDS OF INCOMPETENCE

What level of incompetence will justify an order under s.6?

5–73 As discussed in Ch.4, the courts apply a general standard of probity and competence in order to determine whether a defendant's conduct makes him unfit. It follows that if the defendant's conduct falls short of the required standard of competence, he will be disqualified even though the conduct is not found to be dishonest or lacking in probity.

5–74 It is not necessary to show that the defendant's incompetence was "total". However, where the case against the defendant is based solely on allegations of incompetence, it must be established that he was incompetent or negligent "in a very marked degree".[224] Nevertheless, the Court of Appeal has warned that the degree of incompetence required to establish unfit conduct, whilst "high", should not be exaggerated.[225] Section 174 of the Companies Act 2006 sets out clearly the duty to exercise reasonable care, skill and competence. That section probably reflects the position that the common law had reached in any event. Although there may be cases where the duty is breached yet the breach will be found not such as to make the director unfit to be concerned in management,[226] it is suggested that in most cases where there is a breach of this duty then the relevant director's conduct will be such as to make him unfit.

What is meant by "incompetence"?

5–75 In the course of the disqualification proceedings brought against ten former senior executives following the collapse of Barings Bank, the court confirmed that "incompetence" is a basis for disqualification.[227] The court stressed that what was in issue was competence as a director and that it would be wrong to equate disqualification proceedings with a professional negligence claim. However, incompetence as a director is not an easy thing to define and, as is suggested further below, it should not be regarded as having too broad a meaning in the disqualification context. On the one hand, incompetence denotes a failure or inability to comply with basic obligations. On the other hand, it is often used, at least by the layperson, as convenient shorthand for commercial decision-making or risk-taking that goes wrong, such as an unwise investment or a decision to expand into an unfamiliar market. The courts are traditionally reluctant to intervene in cases involving commercial misjudgment or lack of business acumen. There are several reasons for this reluctance. First, the courts are not naturally equipped to deal with questions of business judgment, especially when asked to substitute their own judgment after the

[224] *Re Sevenoaks Stationers (Retail) Ltd* [1991] Ch. 164 at 184 and see further 4–27.

[225] *Re Barings (No.5), Secretary of State for Trade and Industry v Baker* [2000] 1 B.C.L.C. 523.

[226] Had the facts in *Re D'Jan of London Ltd* [1994] 1 B.C.L.C. 561 been the subject of disqualification proceedings it seems unlikely that disqualification under s.6 would have followed.

[227] See, e.g. *Re Barings Plc, Secretary of State for Trade and Industry v Baker* [1998] B.C.C. 583; and the later decision of Jonathan Parker J. in the same proceedings reported as *Re Barings Plc (No. 5), Secretary of State for Trade and Industry v Baker* [1999] 1 B.C.L.C. 433, affirmed [2000] 1 B.C.L.C. 523.

event. Secondly, the whole purpose of limited liability is to encourage commercial risk-taking. This is because it protects the entrepreneur from the consequences of business failure. Creditors and shareholders inevitably suffer in the collapse of any company. However, the exposure of directors to liability and disqualification on the basis of commercial misjudgment could discourage legitimate risk-taking. Investors and creditors must therefore shoulder some of the risk of business failure if the rationale of limited liability is to be preserved and, accordingly, it is left to them to assess the management's capabilities before investing or extending credit. Thirdly, as Hicks has pointed out, it may be difficult to construct any justification for disqualifying directors who have made commercial misjudgments given that creditors are equally exposed to the consequences of commercial misjudgments in unincorporated businesses.[228] For these reasons, a director will not be found unfit solely on the basis of commercial misjudgment.[229]

5–76 It follows that when the courts equate "incompetence" with unfit conduct they are not referring primarily to matters of business judgment or commercial acumen. At first sight, it is not obvious where commercial misjudgment ends and incompetence justifying disqualification begins. For instance, in some early cases, directors escaped disqualification because the decision to allow their insolvent companies to continue trading was treated as a commercial misjudgment or as mere mismanagement.[230] However, on further analysis, it is apparent that the notion of incompetence is closely associated with the duty to exercise financial responsibility discussed earlier and also with the general duty of a director to exercise reasonable care, skill and diligence now to be found in s.174 of the Companies Act 2006. The impression from the cases is that incompetence may justify disqualification if it is more than mere misjudgment and amounts to culpable negligence. It is suggested that some or all of the following elements are common badges of such incompetence:

(1) Failure to maintain proper accounting records and/or prepare accounts.
(2) Lack of knowledge and/or appreciation of directors' obligations, especially statutory accounting obligations.

[228] A. Hicks, *Disqualification of Directors: No Hiding Place for the Unfit?* (A.C.C.A. Research Report No.59, 1998), p.43. The argument is that questions of competence (meaning sound commercial judgment) and creditworthiness should therefore be regulated by the market. Note, however the subsequent creation of bankruptcy restrictions orders to some extent undermines this point.

[229] See, e.g. *Re Cladrose Ltd* [1990] B.C.L.C. 204 in which the court did not question the decision of the defendants to acquire a motor dealership on the basis of an agency agreement terminable on one month's notice that provided no protection for the company against termination. See also *Re Moorgate Metals Ltd, Official Receiver v Huhtala* [1995] 1 B.C.L.C. 503 (directors' reliance on a single customer and a single supplier not of itself regarded as unfit conduct) and *Re McNulty's Interchange Ltd* [1989] B.C.L.C. 709 (attempt to acquire assets and business of company in receivership not evidence of unfit conduct). In contrast, a decision to acquire an insolvent subsidiary without carrying out any proper due diligence or valuation is less likely to be treated as a mere misjudgment: see *Re Austinsuite Furniture Ltd* [1992] B.C.L.C. 1047; *Re City Investment Centres Ltd* [1992] B.C.L.C. 956.

[230] See, e.g. *Re Douglas Construction Services Ltd* [1988] B.C.L.C. 397; *Re C.U. Fittings Ltd* [1989] B.C.L.C. 556; *Re McNulty's Interchange Ltd* [1989] B.C.L.C. 709.

(3) Abdication of the responsibility to monitor the company's financial position and/or failure to maintain proper internal controls.
(4) Failure to exercise diligent supervision of the company's activities, management and delegates.

5–77 For instance, in *Re Rolus Properties Ltd*, the defendant's failure to maintain accounting records, prepare accounts and comply with filing obligations made him unfit "not because he is fraudulent but because he is incompetent and unable to comply with statutory obligations".[231] Similarly, in *Re Cladrose Ltd*, the judge equated "total incompetence" with a "failure to understand the duty of directors, or to produce any sort of proper trading record",[232] a combination of elements (1) and (2). The case against the second defendant in *Re Richborough Furniture Ltd, Secretary of State for Trade and Industry v Stokes*[233] also consisted of elements (1) and (2). The principal allegations were that the directors had allowed the company to take unwarranted risks with creditors' monies and failed to maintain adequate accounting records. The second defendant had no previous experience in the management of companies and admitted in evidence to having no financial expertise. Nevertheless, she was found to be unfit, "largely through lack of experience and knowledge", and disqualified for three years. A third example is *Re Melcast (Wolverhampton) Ltd* in which a director who seems to have regarded himself as a mere employee and who, to paraphrase the judge, had no concept of what being a director involved, was disqualified for four years. These cases provide further support for the view pressed above that the courts have fashioned a minimum standard of financial competence and stewardship based on the statutory accounting and reporting obligations. Every director is expected to exercise financial responsibility. If the company has no accounting records or up to date financial information, the court is likely to conclude that the directors were not in a position to make sensible commercial judgments.[234] Lack of financial expertise or lack of awareness and understanding of basic obligations are no defence.[235]

5–78 An example of a case involving element (3), in which the court made a finding of unfitness on the basis of incompetence is *Re Continental Assurance Co of London Plc*.[236] The company, CAL, made various loans and cash transfers to its parent company, Yorkdale Holdings Plc. Yorkdale used the monies to repay sums

[231] (1988) 4 B.C.C. 446 at 447.
[232] [1990] B.C.L.C. 204 at 213.
[233] [1996] 1 B.C.L.C. 507.
[234] See, e.g. *Re Firedart Ltd, Official Receiver v Fairhall* [1994] 2 B.C.L.C. 340; *Re Grayan Building Services Ltd, Secretary of State for Trade and Industry v Gray* [1995] Ch. 241 and discussion from 5–36.
[235] *Re New Generation Engineers Ltd* [1993] B.C.L.C. 435; *Re Linvale Ltd* [1993] B.C.L.C. 654; *Re Hitco 2000 Ltd, Official Receiver v Cowan* [1995] 2 B.C.L.C. 63; *Re CSTC Ltd, Secretary of State for Trade and Industry v Van Hengel* [1995] 1 B.C.L.C. 545 (in relation to the second defendant). These cases, together with *Richborough Furniture*, suggest that the courts will act in what Finch has described in "Disqualification of Directors: A Plea for Competence" (1990) 53 M.L.R. 385 as "a purely protective manner" and disqualify as unfit incompetent directors who fail to grasp the nature of their office and responsibilities.
[236] [1997] 1 B.C.L.C. 48.

that it had borrowed from Scanbank to fund its original acquisition of CAL. The effect was that CAL had given financial assistance for the purchase of its shares in breach of s.151 of the Companies Act 1985. The third defendant, B, was head of UK banking and, subsequently, head of UK corporate finance at Scanbank. He had responsibility for the bank's lending relationship with Yorkdale. In that capacity he was appointed as a non-executive director of Yorkdale and CAL. B's evidence was that he did not know about the inter-company transfers and he claimed that if he had known that CAL was lending money to Yorkdale to enable it to service the Scanbank loan, he would have recognised the implications and intervened. The conclusion of the court was that B, as a director of CAL, should have made it his business to know about the inter-company loans and the reason behind them. CAL was Yorkdale's only source of income. It was clear from Yorkdale's accounts, seen and approved by B, that its income was insufficient to service the annual interest charges on the Scanbank loan. It was also clear that there was a rising trend of inter-company indebtedness. B's failure to appreciate what was going on amounted to an abdication of a director's basic responsibility to familiarise himself with the company's financial position, a failure described by the judge as "serious incompetence or neglect". B was disqualified for three years.

5–79 The disqualifications made in the various proceedings brought against the senior executives of Barings Plc after the collapse of its banking group were based on a combination of elements (3) and (4).[237] The immediate cause of the bank's crash was the unauthorised trading of a group subsidiary, Baring Futures (Singapore) Pte Limited ("BFS"), on the Singapore International Monetary Exchange. The unauthorised trading was wholly attributable to Nick Leeson, the senior floor trader and general manager of BFS. Losses to the tune of £827 million, concealed by Leeson in an unnamed client account, were allowed to accrue. One part of the proceedings concerned M, the chairman of the bank's asset and liability committee. The case against M was that he had failed, despite his senior position, to monitor or control the trading activities of BFS. Over the final year of the bank's life, the level of funds transferred to BFS increased from £39 million reaching a high of £742 million on the eve of the crash. This huge outflow of funds, which ultimately precipitated the bank's collapse, was allowed to go unquestioned. The judge found that M had failed to ensure that the funding to BFS was properly understood and controlled. His conduct was said to amount to incompetence and a failure to exercise diligent supervision. Applying the dictum in *Sevenoaks Stationers*, the judge held that M was incompetent in a sufficiently marked degree to make him unfit and disqualified him for four years. Subsequently, three other former executives, B, T and G were disqualified by Jonathan Parker J. on the basis that each was guilty of serious failures of management in relation to Leeson's activities that demonstrated incompetence of such a degree as to justify a disqualification order. Again, the principal findings in the case of these executives were that they had failed to inform

[237] See, in particular, [1998] B.C.C. 583 (Scott V.C.) and [1999] B.C.L.C. 433 (Jonathan Parker J.). For a full account of the collapse and analysis of its regulatory implications see the First Report of the Treasury Committee, *Barings Bank and International Regulation*, H.C. 65 (1996).

themselves properly as to the nature of BFS's business and to exercise anything approaching effective control over its (and Leeson's) activities.[238]

5–80 A case involving elements (1), (3) and (4) is *Re Landhurst Leasing Plc, Secretary of State for Trade and Industry v Ball*.[239] The question before the court in *Landhurst Leasing* was whether the conduct of the defendants, the company's three junior directors, made them unfit for the purposes of CDDA s.6. The main instigators of the company's rise and subsequent collapse were its joint-managing directors, Messrs Ball and Ashworth. These two men were highly plausible individuals with successful track records who had been able to attract institutional funding for the company's business. However, they had engaged in a disastrous policy, systematically lending large sums of the company's money to persons best described as dubious credit risks, for a range of "exotic" purposes (including the financing of motor racing teams) that went well beyond the scope of the company's core business. The evidence suggested that much of this lending was in breach of the company's banking covenants. Ordinary loans were disguised as lease transactions. Customer exposure limits imposed by the company's bankers were evaded. Arrears on certain accounts were suspended with the effect that provisioning for bad debts was inadequate. Money was transferred to customers without documentation or proper credit enquiries. Information was withheld from the non-executive directors (appointed to represent the interests of the company's bankers) and from the auditors. It transpired that Ball and Ashworth had received bribes of approximately £500,000 from certain of the company's high risk lessees by way of inducement. Both were convicted in the criminal courts, sentenced to a term of imprisonment and disqualified under CDDA s.2. As a result, the case against the two protagonists under CDDA s.6 was not pursued.

5–81 Each of the three remaining defendants had been a director of the company for less than three years and had previously been an employee before being promoted to the board. The strong inference from the evidence was that they regarded Ball and Ashworth as "the bosses" and regarded themselves as subordinates. Even after accepting appointment to the board they were, in substance, little more than glorified employees.[240] The case against the three was that ". . . they had buried their heads in the sand in relation to various matters during their respective periods of office which greater directorial awareness would or might have prevented . . ."[241] and that, once elevated to the board, they ought to have taken some steps to question the prudence of the joint-managing directors' *modus operandi*. Two out of the three were disqualified on the basis that their conduct in failing to exercise adequate control over the management of the company's business fell short of the required standard of competence.

[238] See further A. Walters, "Directors' Duties: The Impact of the Company Directors Disqualification Act" (2000) 21 Co. Law. 110.

[239] [1999] 1 B.C.L.C. 286.

[240] Of one, the judge said, ". . . he was perfectly candid in admitting that he saw himself as acquiring no new responsibilities as a result of becoming a director . . .". For this and other comparable evidence see [1999] 1 B.C.L.C. 286 at 292, 293–294, 295–297, 313, 322–323, 325–326, 348.

[241] [1999] 1 B.C.L.C. 286 at 297.

Individual responsibility and collective failure

5–82 In company law theory the board of directors is the primary agent or organ of the company. As such, the board acts collectively. However, in the realm of directors' obligations there is no concept of collective responsibility as a basis for disqualification. Under CDDA ss.6 or 8, the court is required to consider whether the conduct of each individual director makes him unfit, and having particular regard to the matters in Sch.1, to evaluate the extent of each director's personal responsibility for a given failing. As Morritt J. put it in *Re City Investment Centres Ltd*, "the court is required to consider the extent of the responsibility of a particular director where the failure in question is of the directors as a whole".[242] Thus, it is effectively acknowledged within the scheme of the CDDA that the responsibilities of each individual director, or rather, what he must do to discharge his responsibilities, may differ in scope and degree from those of his co-directors. A further implication is that the court does not take a blanket approach where disqualification proceedings are brought against more than one director of the same company. So, for instance, if proceedings are commenced against three directors of a company, the court will not necessarily say that all of them are unfit or that they should all be disqualified for an equal period simply because they were all on the board. The board does not owe a collective duty for which all members of the board are equally answerable. In Lord Woolf's phrase, the board's collective responsibility is ultimately based on individual responsibility.[243] The purpose in this section is to examine how the courts tackle a number of pressing questions that arise in the assessment of a director's individual responsibility especially (though not exclusively) in cases where there is more than one defendant.

Is every director on the board required to participate in the company's affairs

5–83 In keeping with the spirit of the Cork Committee's recommendations, the courts have used s.6 to fashion a minimum standard of financial responsibility and competence. It has been seen that a director who fails to inform himself of his company's financial position runs the risk of disqualification under s.6 if the company becomes insolvent. This is particularly so where adequate accounting records have not been maintained. It follows that directors are expected to participate in the company's management to the minimum degree necessary for the exercise of proper financial responsibility. For some time prior to the enactment of the Companies Act 2006 and the newly formulated general duty to exercise reasonable care, skill and diligence therein contained at s.174, it was not safe for directors to assume that the court would adopt the more relaxed approach to participation evident in some of the nineteenth and early twentieth century

[242] [1992] B.C.L.C. 956 at 960. See also *Secretary of State for Trade and Industry v Taylor* [1997] 1 W.L.R. 407; sub nom. *Secretary of State for Trade and Industry v Gash* [1997] 1 B.C.L.C. 341; sub nom. *Re CS Holidays Ltd* [1997] B.C.C. 172.

[243] *Re Westmid Packing Services Ltd, Secretary of State for Trade and Industry v Griffiths* [1998] 2 All E.R. 124. See also *Re Landhurst Leasing Plc, Secretary of State for Trade and Industry v Ball* [1999] 1 B.C.L.C. 286 at 345–346.

authorities, especially in the context of an insolvent or near-insolvent company.[244] The common law's traditionally laissez faire approach paid deference to the company's shareholders: it could be left to the general meeting which, in theory, retains ultimate control over the selection and removal of board appointees, to remove incompetent directors and regulate the degree of participation required.[245] This approach also reflected the relatively undeveloped state of the law of negligence prior to the landmark decision in *Donoghue v Stevenson*.[246] The stiffer approach taken under s.6, prior to the enactment of the Companies Act 2006, not only reflected the intrusion of creditors' interests once the company's solvency is in doubt, but also a modern view of the proper scope of directors' obligations and standards of competence as reflected in Insolvency Act 1986 s.214 and now also Companies Act 2006 s.174.

5–84 It is clear from the modern authorities that, even before the enactment of the Companies Act 2006, directors had (and still have) a positive obligation to participate in the company's affairs. In *Re Barings Plc (No. 5), Secretary of State for Trade and Industry v Baker*, Jonathan Parker J. drew widely on English, Australian and United States case law to formulate the scope and content of this positive obligation. From the authorities, he derived the following three propositions:

(1) Directors have, both collectively and individually, a continuing duty to acquire and maintain a sufficient knowledge and understanding of the company's business to enable them properly to discharge their duties as directors.
(2) While directors are entitled (subject to the company's articles of association) to delegate particular functions to those below them in the management chain and to trust their competence and integrity to a reasonable extent, the exercise

[244] The position at common law rested for over three quarters of a century on the decision of Romer J. in *Re City Equitable Fire Insurance Co Ltd* [1925] Ch. 407, which suggested that a director is not bound to give continuous attention to the affairs of his company. The case of *Re Cardiff Savings Bank* [1892] 2 Ch. 100 in which a director who attended only one board meeting during his whole life escaped liability for losses of a collapsed bank occasioned by the fraud of one of its officers is perhaps the most graphic illustration of the common law's historic latitude. Hoffmann L.J. suggested that the existence of a positive obligation to participate depended on the particular context, i.e. on factors such as how the particular company was organised and the part which the director could reasonably have been expected to play: see *Bishopsgate Investment Management Ltd v Maxwell (No.2)* [1994] 1 All E.R. 261 at 264. Even so, the thrust of the approach under the CDDA was (and remains) that all directors are expected to exercise financial responsibility as a bare minimum. This is also now the position under s.214 of the Insolvency Act 1986: see *Re Brian D Pierson (Contractors) Ltd* [2001] 1 B.C.L.C. 275. The position reached at common law is now reflected in the general duty, set out in the Companies Act 2006 s.174, requiring directors to exercise reasonable care, skill and diligence. That is specified as the care, skill and diligence that would be exercised by a reasonably diligent person with: (a) the general knowledge, skill and experience that may reasonably be expected of a person carrying out the functions carried out by the director in relation to the company; and (b) the general knowledge, skill and experience that the director has.

[245] This attitude is well captured in the words of the Lord Chancellor in *Turquand v Marshall* (1869) L.R. 4 Ch. App. 376 at 386 who, exonerating the defendants from making a bad loan to one of their number, said that ". . . however ridiculous and absurd their conduct might seem, it was the misfortune of the company that they chose such unwise directors . . .". For further discussion of the traditional approach and its rationale see *Daniels v Anderson* (1995) 16 A.C.S.R. 607 at 657.

[246] [1932] A.C. 562.

of a power of delegation does not absolve a director from the duty to supervise the discharge of the delegated functions.

(3) No rule of universal application can be formulated as to the residual duty of monitoring and supervision referred to in (2) above. The extent of the duty, and the question whether it has been discharged, must depend on the facts of each particular case, including the director's role in the management of the company.[247]

5–85 The first proposition suggests that all directors who take office are under a positive obligation to inform themselves about and to participate in the company's affairs in some degree. The obligation is not intermittent, but "continuing". However, the content and intensity of the obligation will vary according to a variety of factors which may include:

(a) the size and business of the particular company;
(b) the experience or skills that the director held himself out as having in support of appointment to the office[248];
(c) how the particular business is organised;
(d) the role in the management of the company which was in fact assigned to the director or which he or she in fact assumed and his duties and responsibilities in that role[249]; and
(e) the level of remuneration which the director was entitled to receive or which he or she may reasonably have expected to receive.[250]

Thus, *Barings (No.5)* posits a universal duty of participation, the precise content and extent of which will depend on all the facts of the case.[251]

5–86 At the heart of the first proposition is a minimum requirement that a director informs himself sufficiently about the company's business to enable him to perform his functions. It is apparent from the court's treatment of one of the *Barings* defendants, T, that this requirement applies in much the same way as the first limb of the test in s.214(4) of the Insolvency Act 1986 (and see now the first limb of s.174(2) of the Companies Act 2006): i.e., it involves an objective assessment of what can reasonably be expected of a director carrying out the defendant's particular function.[252] It appears from his evidence that T regarded himself as much as a "rainmaker" as a "manager". Much of his time was spent doing

[247] [1999] 1 B.C.L.C. 433 at 489, affirmed by the Court of Appeal: [2000] 1 B.C.L.C. 523.

[248] Factors (a) and (b) derive from *Daniels v Anderson* (1995) 16 A.C.S.R. 607 at 668: see [1999] 1 B.C.L.C. 433, 488 at B5.

[249] Factors (c) and (d) derive from *Bishopsgate Investment Management Ltd v Maxwell (No.2)* [1994] 1 All E.R. 261: see [1999] 1 B.C.L.C. 433, 484 at A8. For what amounts to a working application of factor (c), see *Re Skyward Builders Plc, Official Receiver v Broad* [2002] EWHC (Ch) 2786 at [308]–[319].

[250] Factor (e) derives from *Re Barings Plc* [1998] B.C.C. 583, 586 per Scott V.C: see [1999] 1 B.C.L.C. 433, 488 at B6.

[251] [1999] 1 B.C.L.C. 433, 484 at A8–A9.

[252] See also *Norman v Theodore Goddard* [1992] B.C.L.C. 1028; *Re D'Jan of London Ltd* [1994] 1 B.C.L.C. 561; *Re Landhurst Leasing Plc, Secretary of State for Trade and Industry v Ball* [1999] 1 B.C.L.C. 286 at 344.

client work on the corporate finance side of the bank's business. The thrust of his case was that he was justified in leaving management to others. Nevertheless, the court evaluated his conduct by reference to a standard of what could reasonably be expected of the chairman of a banking corporation:

> "As chairman . . . [T] was at all times under a duty to take an active part in the management of [the bank], and that in turn meant that he was under a continuing duty to inform himself about [the bank's] affairs to the extent necessary to enable him properly to discharge that duty."[253]

Depending on the facts, the clear implication is that a director is under an active obligation to ask questions, procure information and seek enlightenment.[254] While the intensity of the obligation may vary according to status and function, the further implication is that *all* directors are required at the very least to ensure that they are kept informed about the company's business and its financial position.[255]

5–87 As a consequence of the first proposition, it would be unwise for a non-executive director who takes no part in the day-to-day management of the company to assume that his office is merely honorific. Indeed, as a consequence of developments such as the Combined Code on Corporate Governance, further reinforced by the Higgs Report,[256] non-executive directors of listed public companies are expected to play a positive role in corporate governance and the courts are now unlikely to treat them merely as adornments with no specific obligations of participation as might have been the case in the past.[257] Equally, in determining the content and intensity of the non-executive director's obligation to participate and, accordingly, the standard of competence that he can be expected to meet, the court must be careful to review the nature, scope and extent of his non-executive functions. So, for example, the court must bear in mind that a non-executive director will usually be dependent on the executive directors for the information that he receives.[258]

[253] [1999] 1 B.C.L.C. 433 at 500. See also at 502–505, 516C–D, 517A, 522C–D, 523–525, 526D, 527H, 528G–H, 529A. See further *Re Queens Moathouses Plc, Secretary of State for Trade and Industry v Bairstow* [2005] 1 B.C.L.C. 136 at [23]–[24], [34]–[35].

[254] Thus, of the other *Barings* defendants, the product manager, B, was obliged to reach an understanding of Leeson's switching business and its associated risks while the head of settlements, G, was obliged to investigate Leeson's demands for margin funding once it was apparent that these demands could not be reconciled to trading positions.

[255] See, e.g. *Re Interim Management.com.Ltd, Secretary of State for Trade and Industry v Thornbury* [2008] 1 B.C.L.C. 139 at [44]–[45].

[256] *Review of the Role and Effectiveness of Non-Executive Directors* (Stationery Office, January 2003), *http://www.berr.gov.uk/whatwedo/businesslaw/corp-governance/higgs-tyson/page23342.html* [Accessed August 24, 2009].

[257] For such an approach see, e.g. *Re Brazilian Rubber Plantations and Estates Ltd* [1911] 1 Ch. 425 and *Re Denham & Co* [1884] L.R. 25 Ch.D. 752. It was suggested at para.1.39 of Law Commission, *Company Directors: Regulating Conflicts of Interests and Formulating a Statement of Duties* (Law Com Consultation Paper No.153, 1998) that non-compliance with rules such as those contained in the Combined Code may be treated as evidence of unfit conduct. In principle, this must be correct bearing in mind that Sch.1 to the CDDA does not contain an exhaustive list of matters that can be taken into account.

[258] See *Re TLL Realisations Ltd, Secretary of State for Trade and Industry v Collins*, November 27, 1998, Ch.D., unreported (Lloyd J.).

5–88 A further consequence of the first proposition is that a director cannot safely disassociate himself from the company's affairs. The case of *Re Park House Properties Ltd* provides a graphic illustration. The principal defendant, C, was disqualified for four years for a combination of trading to the detriment of creditors, failure to exercise financial responsibility and breach of fiduciary duty. C had taken sole responsibility for the management of the company, although his wife, son and daughter were also unpaid directors. The three others were found to be unfit by virtue of their sheer inactivity. In the words of the judge:

> "... the best way in which the case against the three [defendants] can be summarised is by saying that they were three of the four directors of a company, they permitted the other director to run the company in a way which was inappropriate, they did nothing whatever to inform themselves of how the company was being managed, to what extent that management might be inappropriate, and therefore they did nothing to discourage or dissuade that director from running the company in this inappropriate way ... Directors have duties, and if, having knowingly been appointed a director, a person does nothing, he is likely to be in breach of his duties, and if the company is involved in inappropriate activity, he risks associating himself with, and taking some responsibility for, that inappropriate activity ... As a matter of principle, it appears to me that it cannot be right that a director ... can escape liability simply by saying that he knew nothing about what was going on."[259]

The upshot is that all directors, whatever their status, have a duty to make enquiries concerning the running of the company and must arrive at some appreciation of the results of those enquiries.

5–89 The second *Barings* proposition makes it clear that directors are under a positive obligation to supervise the discharge of delegated functions. Insofar as the company's articles of association allow, the board is permitted to delegate specific tasks and functions on grounds of business efficacy. Thus, delegation per se will not generally give rise to a breach of duty. However, in Jonathan Parker J.'s words, this does not mean:

> "... that, having delegated a particular function, [a director] is no longer under any duty in relation to the discharge of that function, notwithstanding that the person to whom the function has been delegated may appear both trustworthy and capable of discharging the function."[260]

Both the board as a whole and each individual director "remain responsible for the delegated function or functions and will retain a residual duty of supervision and control".[261] This amounts to saying that every director has a non-delegable duty to monitor how delegated functions are being discharged and must make at

[259] [1997] 2 B.C.L.C. 530 at 554. The effect is that "sleeping" directors who take no part at all in the affairs of the company are at grave risk of disqualification in the event that the company fails: see further *Re Kaytech International Plc, Secretary of State for Trade and Industry v Potier* [1999] 2 B.C.L.C. 351; *Re Oldham Vehicle Contracts Ltd, Official Receiver v Vass* [1999] B.C.C. 516; *Re Galeforce Pleating Co Ltd* [1999] 2 B.C.L.C. 704; and, by analogy, *Re Brian D Pierson (Contractors) Ltd* [2001] 1 B.C.L.C. 275, a wrongful trading case, and *Lexi Holdings Plc v Luqman* [2009] EWCA Civ 117, [2009] 2 B.C.L.C. 1 where there was a successful claim for breach of duty.

[260] [1999] 1 B.C.L.C. 433, 487 at B3.

[261] [1999] 1 B.C.L.C. 433, 487, at B4. See, by analogy, *Secretary of State for Trade and Industry v London Citylink Ltd* [2005] EWHC 2875 (Ch).

least some positive contribution to internal control. As such, Jonathan Parker J.'s first two propositions reinforce one another: it will be difficult for a director to exercise proper supervision without a sufficient knowledge and understanding of the delegated activity.

5–90 The non-delegable duty of supervision applies as much in relation to functions carried out by other board members as it does to delegates, such as senior managers or employees, who are not on the board. In *Re A & C Group Services Ltd*,[262] O was a director and controlling shareholder of the company. For most of his period of office (some ten years) the company made modest profits. O became ill and the company's profitability suffered as a result. O invited T to join the board and, in the contemplation that T would eventually acquire the company, allowed him to take over full responsibility for its management. Under T's management, the company engaged in a disastrous expansion resulting in trading losses of nearly £500,000. T was disqualified for six years on various grounds. Despite the fact that O's belief that T was about to buy him out was found to be genuine, he and his wife were each disqualified for two years. Citing the words of Byrne J. in *Drincqbier v Wood*,[263] the judge stated that a director who consents to be a director, has assumed a position involving duties which cannot be shirked by leaving everything to others.[264] The approach in *A & C Group Services* is reflected in a number of other cases.[265] On the facts in *Barings (No. 5)*, Jonathan Parker J. found that "delegation" had given way to "abdication".[266]

5–91 According to the third *Barings* proposition, the precise content and intensity of the non-delegable duty of supervision will depend on the facts of the case. One implication is that, in an appropriate case, the directors may be in breach of duty if the company's system of internal controls proves to be inadequate.[267] Of course, the extent of the obligation insofar as it applies to non-executive directors or to the directors of private companies may not be the same as that applicable to the senior executives of a listed company. Thus, one would expect the courts to make some adjustment in the case of non-executives who may not have ready access to relevant information. Nevertheless, in a listed company, the board as a whole is obliged to maintain a sound system of internal control and periodically review and report on its effectiveness.[268] This means that, at the very least,

[262] [1993] B.C.L.C. 1297.

[263] [1899] 1 Ch. 393 at 406.

[264] If a "sleeping" director is in receipt of remuneration this may intensify the basic obligation.

[265] *Re Majestic Recording Studios Ltd* [1989] B.C.L.C. 1; *Re Melcast (Wolverhampton) Ltd* [1991] B.C.L.C. 288; *Re City Investment Centres Ltd* [1992] B.C.L.C. 956; *Re Peppermint Park Ltd* [1998] B.C.C. 23; *Re Westmid Packing Services Ltd, Secretary of State for Trade and Industry v Griffiths* [1998] 2 All E.R. 124; *Re Park House Properties Ltd, Secretary of State for Trade and Industry v Carter* [1997] 2 B.C.L.C. 530; *Re Landhurst Leasing Plc, Secretary of State for Trade and Industry v Ball* [1999] 1 B.C.L.C. 286; *Re Interim Management.com.Ltd, Secretary of State for Trade and Industry v Thornbury* [2008] 1 B.C.L.C. 139 at [44].

[266] See [1999] 1 B.C.L.C. 433 at 499G, 517A, 540E, 544D, 547F, 550B, 554–555, 559, 561B, 565–566, 568, 571I, 584–585, 587E–H, 588F–589F, 591C, 592, 593D–E.

[267] [1999] 1 B.C.L.C. 433 at 487, B3 and see also *Re Barings Plc* [1998] B.C.C. 583 at 586.

[268] Principle D.2 of the Combined Code.

non-executive directors bear some responsibility for ensuring that internal controls are in place and operating properly.[269]

Are higher standards of conduct expected from experienced directors and directors with special expertise?

5–92 It has been seen that directors cannot escape disqualification by reason of inexperience or lack of expertise where there has been a failure to exercise proper financial responsibility. This is because the courts treat the duty to monitor the company's financial position and associated obligations as a universal minimum standard applicable to all directors. At the same time, it appears that, as now reflected in s.174(2)(b) of the Companies Act 2006, the courts do expect directors who possess particular expertise to achieve higher standards of conduct in relation to matters falling within the scope of that expertise.[270] In *Re Cladrose Ltd*,[271] the application concerned three insolvent companies of which the two defendants, JP and DP, were owner-managers. There was a total failure in all three companies to produce audited accounts and file annual returns. However, this was not a case in which the directors failed to maintain accounting records. Indeed, the evidence was that all three companies had good core accounting records and that internal management accounts were regularly produced. JP claimed that he relied on DP, a qualified chartered accountant, to take responsibility for the production of full accounts and the filing of annual returns. In his evidence, DP accepted that the default was largely his responsibility and that it was reasonable for JP to rely on him. The judge held that there was a collective failure but that the extent of JP's responsibility was insufficient to make him unfit. DP, however, was disqualified for two years for failing to perform duties falling squarely within the scope of his professional expertise. As a chartered accountant DP could:

> "properly be expected, both by his fellow directors and by the court, to have a better knowledge and understanding of company law and of the formal duties to make returns . . . than persons who do not hold that distinguished qualification . . ."[272]

[269] For discussion of the position of non-executives see also *Re TLL Realisations Ltd, Secretary of State for Trade and Industry v Collins*, November 27, 1998, Ch.D., unreported, where Lloyd V. accepted in principle that a non-executive can rely on what he is told by the executive directors but went on to say that he or she is required to consider and assess such information critically and objectively and be prepared to query it if it does not stand up to scrutiny.

[270] See factor (b) in 5–85.

[271] [1990] B.C.L.C. 204.

[272] [1990] B.C.L.C. 204 at 208. One distinguished commentator has argued that the decision in *Cladrose* was based more on punitive considerations than on a principle of public protection: see V. Finch, "Disqualification of Directors: A Plea for Competence" (1990) 53 M.L.R. 385. Finch contends that both directors would have been disqualified had a protective principle been in play as both were responsible by statute for preparing and filing accounts. Note, however, that the CDDA's concern with individual responsibility is always likely to produce this kind of result and that the approach in *Cladrose* is consistent with the position at common law: see, e.g. *Dorchester Finance Co Ltd v Stebbing* [1989] B.C.L.C. 498; *Re D'Jan of London Ltd* [1994] 1 B.C.L.C. 561. It is doubtful that JP would have escaped disqualification in the event of a collective failure to maintain core accounting records. See now Companies Act 2006 s.174.

5–93 Similarly, in the case of *Re Continental Assurance Co of London Plc*, the court appeared to demand a higher standard of conduct from the defendant based on his experience as a banker and corporate financier. His failure as a non-executive director to appreciate that the subsidiary, CAL was giving unlawful financial assistance was described by Chadwick J. in these terms:

> "Those in the position of [B], being senior employees of major banks, who accept appointment as directors of client companies of those banks, are lending their name and the status associated with their employer to the board of directors of that client company. Those dealing with the client company are entitled to expect that external directors appointed on the basis of their apparent expertise will exercise the competence required by the Companies Act . . . in relation to the affairs of the company of which they have accepted office as directors. The competence required by the [Companies] Act extends, at the least, to a requirement that a director who is a corporate financier should be prepared to read and understand . . . statutory accounts . . . and satisfy himself that transactions between holding company and subsidiary are properly reflected in the statutory accounts of the subsidiary."[273]

This suggests that a non-executive or nominee appointed to represent the interests of a bank or venture capital financier is expected to bring at least some basic knowledge of accounts and financial reporting to the task. As discussed above, *Re Barings Plc (No.5)* also suggests that the standard of competence demanded of senior executives may also be adjusted upwards to reflect their role, status, experience and level of remuneration.[274]

Is a director less exposed to disqualification if he relied on professional advice?

5–94 It has been seen in the case of *Re Cladrose Ltd* that a director may escape disqualification if it is reasonable for him to rely on the professional expertise of his co-director in relation to certain functions. Similarly, in the earlier case of *Re Douglas Construction Ltd*, the court declined to disqualify the defendant who, in trying to refinance a struggling company, relied on professional advice.[275] In marginal cases such as these, a director's reliance on a professionally qualified co-director or on independent professional advice may tip the balance in his favour. However, it is not necessarily safe for a director to rely on a decision by

[273] [1997] 1 B.C.L.C. 48 at 47–48.

[274] See further *Re CSTC Ltd, Secretary of State for Trade and Industry v Van Hengel* [1995] 1 B.C.L.C. 545 (finance director); *Re AG (Manchester) Ltd, Official Receiver v Watson* [2008] 1 B.C.L.C. 321 (finance director); *Re Queens Moathouses Plc, Secretary of State for Trade and Industry v Bairstow* [2005] 1 B.C.L.C. 136 (chairman and executive director of listed company); *Re Finelist Ltd, Secretary of State for Trade and Industry v Swan* [2005] B.C.C. 596 (chairman and chief executive of listed company) and Companies Act 2006 s.174(2)(b).

[275] [1988] B.C.L.C. 397. Even if the advice proves incorrect the director may still be exonerated provided that it is reasonable for the defendant to rely on the professional adviser: *Re McNulty's Interchange Ltd* [1989] B.C.L.C. 709. For other cases of successful reliance see *Re Moonlight Foods (UK) Ltd, Secretary of State for Trade and Industry v Hickling* [1996] B.C.C. 678; *Re Stephenson Cobbold Ltd, Secretary of State for Trade and Industry v Stephenson* [2000] 2 B.C.L.C. 614.

the company's bank to extend its overdraft facility as a justification for continuing to trade.[276] Furthermore, a director cannot absolve himself of the statutory responsibility to prepare accounts giving a true and fair view of the company's affairs by relying on an auditor's certificate where the accounts turn out to be materially misleading.[277]

5–95 Moreover, it is clear that reliance on the involvement of professionals will not be a panacea in every case. In *Re Bradcrown Ltd, Official Receiver v Ireland*,[278] the defendant, S, was one of three directors of a company that, as part of a demerger of a group of which it had originally been the parent company, disposed of assets worth more than £3.7 million for no consideration. The company was left with a lease under which substantial liabilities for rent had accrued and would continue to accrue in the future. The demerger was therefore detrimental to the interests of the company's landlord. S conceded that he had inadvertently breached his fiduciary duty in allowing the company's assets to be removed, but argued that he should not be disqualified because he had relied on, and been entitled to rely on the advice of the solicitors retained by the company in connection with the demerger and, at no point, had they questioned the propriety of the transaction. It was held that S had abdicated his responsibility and he was disqualified for two years. The following matters appear to have been significant:

(1) S was an experienced chartered accountant and the company's finance director.
(2) S admitted that he knew that the assets were being transferred for no consideration, but he never stopped to consider whether this was in the best interests of the company.
(3) S was party to a statutory declaration as to the company's solvency made in connection with the demerger and to resolutions of the board authorising the transaction. However, he did not exercise any independent judgment but "simply followed the instructions of his fellow directors and the professional advisers who were driving the transactions."[279]
(4) S knew (so the judge found) that the lease was to be left behind with the company.

In short, it was not open to an intelligent and experienced finance director simply to wait for the solicitors to advise that the demerger was improper when there was enough material available for such a person to have reached that conclusion for himself. As the judge put it:

[276] See *Re GSAR Realisations Ltd* [1993] B.C.L.C. 409. The reason for this is that the bank is acting in its own interests as a lender rather than giving advice to the company or its directors. In any event, any claim to have relied on advice will be judged against the full background of the advice, i.e. what advice was sought and what information was provided to the adviser.

[277] *Re Queens Moathouses Plc, Secretary of State for Trade and Industry v Bairstow* [2005] 1 B.C.L.C. 136 at [32].

[278] [2001] 1 B.C.L.C. 547.

[279] [2001] 1 B.C.L.C. 547 at [47].

> "... [S] cannot absolve himself from his responsibility as a director by claiming either that he simply had the title of director but was really a bookkeeper and accountant, or that he relied exclusively on the involvement of professionals in transactions which he knew were divesting the company of more than £3.7 million in assets without consideration, and where he was a party to a resolution that the transactions were in the best interests of [the company] without giving any thought as to whether they were, and executed a declaration of solvency without making the slightest investigation to determine whether it could be properly made ... He asked no questions and sought no advice. He simply did what he was told, and abdicated all responsibility. In these circumstances he cannot seek refuge in the fact that professional advisers were involved in the transactions. This is the clearest possible case of a person who was appointed to the office of director, and who accepted that office without any intention of acting otherwise as a loyal employee."[280]

Bradcrown shows that the question of whether it is reasonable for a director to rely on professional advice will depend on a variety of factors including the role, function and expertise of the particular director and the nature of the advice sought. It also makes clear that, in order to discharge the obligations of participation and supervision that flow from the *Barings* propositions discussed above, a director must be prepared to exercise independent judgment and, if necessary, voice concerns. In truth, the defendant in *Bradcrown* was trying to claim that he was entitled to ignore what he knew, or could have inferred, simply because solicitors were involved in the process.[281] It is conceivable that the outcome would be different in a case where the defendant relies on actual specialist advice (as opposed to an absence of advice) about matters that are beyond the scope of what he can reasonably be expected to know, and the advice turns out to be wrong.

Should a director who proves unable to exert appropriate influence over the board or company despite best efforts consider resigning?

5–96 A difficult issue that is not easy to resolve concerns the position of a director who is incapable of exercising appropriate influence over board or company decisions because he is in a minority on the board or unwilling to exercise any influence he may have because of the presence in the company of a dominant personality or where the board of which he is member is (inappropriately) overridden by the shareholders.[282] If, for instance, the company continues to trade while insolvent and the board makes no attempt to review its trading prospects, each director is at risk of disqualification even though for practical purposes they may have no real control over board decisions as individuals. As discussed above, every director must keep himself properly informed, especially with regard to the company's financial position, and join in the supervision of its business. Furthermore, the case of *Re Park House Properties Ltd* (considered in 5–88) suggests that there is

[280] [2001] 1 B.C.L.C. 547 at [56]–[58].
[281] See also *Re Skyward Builders Plc, Official Receiver v Broad* [2002] EWHC (Ch) 2786 at [427].
[282] As regards shareholder dominance see, e.g. *Re AG (Manchester) Ltd, Official Receiver v Watson* [2008] 1 B.C.L.C. 321.

an obligation on every director to see that the board as a whole is acting responsibly.[283] For a director who, for whatever reason, has limited influence, this is a difficult proposition. What should a director do if he is unable to persuade his co-directors to act responsibly? Is resignation the best course? This question has received differing answers, depending on the facts of the particular case.

5–97 In *Re Thorncliffe Finance Ltd, Secretary of State for Trade and Industry v Arif*, Chadwick J. suggested that a director should resign his office if he is unable to compel the board to act responsibly. In that case, D, the company's managing director, continued in office despite having identified the irregularity (namely the lack of security for inter-company indebtedness within a series of affiliated companies) that ultimately precipitated its downfall. He wrote expressing his concerns to the company's controller and made proposals for resolving the situation that were never implemented. He did resign later but the fact that he remained in office despite lacking the influence to address the problem was said to make him unfit and he was disqualified for three years. The judge's message was unequivocal:

> "In my view it should be made clear that those who assume the obligations of directors, which they know they cannot fulfil, are persons whose conduct makes them unfit to be concerned in the management of a company. It is no answer to that charge to say, 'I did what I could'. If a director finds that he is unable to do what he knows ought to be done then the only proper course is for him to resign."[284]

5–98 In the subsequent case of *Re CS Holidays Ltd, Secretary of State for Trade and Industry v Taylor*, the same judge sought to confine the scope of this apparent obligation on a director to resign to circumstances where the defendant is unable to compel the board as a whole to comply with the statutory duty to maintain proper accounting records. The relevant defendant was one of the company's three directors. He also had a minor shareholding and was employed by the company on a small salary as a bookkeeper. The company's bankers expressed concern that the company was trading to the detriment of creditors. The defendant reacted to this by producing a written report to the board recommending specific cost cutting measures. He discussed these recommendations with the company's auditor who said at trial that the company would have had a reasonable chance of trading out of its difficulties had they been implemented. The company continued trading without following the recommendations. Later the auditor wrote to the company at the defendant's instigation making further recommendations that were again not acted on. The allegation against all three directors was that they allowed the company to continue trading while insolvent to the detriment of creditors. In relation to the defendant, it was argued that, having failed to persuade the board to adopt his recommendations, he ought to

[283] See also *Re Westmid Packing Services Ltd, Secretary of State for Trade and Industry v Griffiths* [1998] 2 All E.R. 124 in which it was suggested that a board of directors should not allow one person to dominate them as to do so might amount to an abrogation of responsibility. *Re Bradcrown Ltd, Official Receiver v Ireland*, discussed in the previous paragraph, is to similar effect.

[284] [1997] 1 B.C.L.C. 34 at 46.

have resigned and that, by continuing in office, he benefited at the expense of the company's creditors because he continued to draw a salary. Significantly, the Secretary of State made no criticism of the way in which the defendant had maintained the company's financial records and statutory books. The district judge's decision to dismiss the case against the defendant was upheld by Chadwick J. on appeal. The judge distinguished his previous decision in *Arif* by saying that his remarks there were made in the context of a failure by the directors to fulfil their statutory obligations and, in particular, the obligation imposed by s.221 of the Companies Act 1985, the statutory predecessor of s.386 of the Companies Act 2006. Thus, a failure to resign should not necessarily lead to the conclusion that a director is unfit. Directors have no *statutory* obligation to ensure that their company avoids trading to the detriment of creditors or at a loss. Their obligation under the Insolvency Act 1986 is to ensure that they do not cause the company, knowing it to be insolvent, to continue trading in circumstances where there is *no reasonable prospect* of avoiding insolvent liquidation. A director who, like the defendant, fails to resign having used such influence as he possesses to persuade the board to review its policy of continuing to trade is therefore in a different category from a director who remains in office in circumstances where he knows that the company is in breach of a statutory provision such as s.221. There is therefore a clear link between the "duty" to resign and the wider duty to exercise financial responsibility.[285] Nevertheless, Chadwick J. left open the possibility that a director might be disqualified in appropriate circumstances for failing to resign in a case not involving breach of statutory accounting obligations:

> "I am not to be taken as expressing the view that there may not be circumstances in which a director who has ceased to exercise any influence in the deliberations of the board will be at risk of being held unfit if he fails to resign. The duties of a director include . . . the duty to inform himself as to the company's affairs and the duty to make his views known to the other directors. If there comes a point at which his attendance at board meetings is purposeless because he must recognise that his co-directors take no account of his views . . . it may well be appropriate to ask why he continues to remain as a director. If he continues to remain as a director in those circumstances for no purpose other than to draw his . . . fees or to preserve his status, a court might well come to the conclusion that he was so lacking in appreciation of a director's duties that he was unfit . . ."[286]

Thus a powerless director who carries on in office despite having no practical influence on managerial policy is exposed to disqualification if it can be established that in continuing to draw his remuneration he acted without regard for creditors' interests. On the facts of *Taylor* the defendant was only paid a salary equivalent to that of a junior employee and Chadwick J. refused to interfere with the district judge's finding that he had not sought to gain an advantage at the expense of creditors.[287]

[285] See also *Re Galeforce Pleating Co Ltd* [1999] 2 B.C.L.C. 704 at 716.
[286] [1997] 1 W.L.R. 407 at 414–415, [1997] 1 B.C.L.C. 341 at 349, [1997] B.C.C. 172 at 178–179.
[287] For a case arguably falling within the scope of Chadwick J.'s dictum see *Re Peppermint Park Ltd* [1998] B.C.C. 23, especially in relation to the third defendant, Mr Love.

5–99 *Arif* and *Taylor* can be contrasted with the earlier case of *Re Polly Peck International Plc, Secretary of State for Trade and Industry v Ellis (No.2)*.[288] The four defendants were at all times in a minority on the board and at the date on which the company went into administration they represented less than one-third of the serving directors. One of the defendants was the company's finance director while the others served as non-executive directors. The company's prime mover and chairman, Asil Nadir, was not among the defendants. The case against the four was based on their failure to exercise adequate control over Nadir who had systematically transferred large amounts of funds from the company to a series of foreign subsidiaries. The need of the foreign subsidiaries for such substantial funding was never seriously questioned. The Secretary of State developed the case by arguing that the four defendants ought to have threatened their resignation in the face of the board's continuing failure to exercise any sort of control over Nadir's activities and that by remaining in office they shared responsibility for the overall failure to institute proper controls. The question arising was whether the case was sufficiently strong for the court to grant the Secretary of State permission under s.7(2) to commence proceedings outside the two-year time limit.[289] Lindsay J. refused to grant permission and in so doing expressed grave reservations over whether the failure of this small minority of directors to resign could be regarded as sufficiently serious to justify a finding of unfit conduct. It is perhaps significant that there was no suggestion that the directors were in breach of basic statutory obligations such as s.221 of the Companies Act 1985. It follows that *Polly Peck* can arguably be distinguished from *Arif* on the same basis as *Taylor*.[290]

Another relevant case in which the obligations of directors in circumstances of shareholder dominance of decision making were considered is *Re AG (Manchester) Ltd, Official Receiver v Watson*.[291] In that case it was found that if the shareholders were determined to pay themselves dividends at a level which the company could not afford and were prepared to overrule any objections the board might have, then the directors had no option but to resign. Furthermore, it was a dereliction of duty to acquiesce in dividend decisions which might be

[288] [1994] 1 B.C.L.C. 574.

[289] On permission to commence proceedings for an order under s.6 out of time see generally Ch.7.

[290] Moreover there is arguably an analogy between *Polly Peck* and the common law position as advanced in *Dovey v Corey* [1901] A.C. 477. In that case the court held that the director of a bank was not liable to make good the bank's losses in circumstances where the company had paid dividends out of capital and made advances on improper security. It was accepted that it was reasonable for the director in relation to these matters to rely on the bank's chairman and general manager whose skill and competence he had no cause to doubt. The suggestion that he should have taken steps to monitor the activities of lesser bank officials or check the audit files was rejected. The case of *Re Barings Plc (No. 5)* discussed in the main text above suggests that the allegations raised in *Polly Peck* would now be couched in terms of directorial incompetence. In this respect it is noticeable that Lindsay J.'s approach demands a much higher threshold of culpability for a finding of unfit conduct than the approach in *Barings*. Indeed, as a matter of law (as opposed to policy) some aspects of the decision look distinctly shaky in the light of subsequent authority. This is particularly true of Lindsay J.'s "director-friendly" approach to the issue of present unfit conduct on which see now *Grayan* discussed above from 4–11.

[291] [2008] 1 B.C.L.C. 321.

inappropriate without actively considering the issues involved in accordance with the obligation to ensure that the company operated on a solvent basis and in accordance with the distribution requirements of the Companies Acts.

Can a director rely on an agreed division of responsibilities?

5–100 In a case where the directors have failed collectively to comply with the minimum obligation of proper financial responsibility, it is unlikely that any one of them would escape disqualification by trying to shift the blame onto the others. Although it is open to the court to find that one director is less responsible (and deserving of a lesser period of disqualification) than another, a defendant will rarely be able to shift all the responsibility for non-compliance with basic statutory obligations such as s.386 of the Companies Act 2006 onto a co-defendant. Moreover, if a defence along these lines is unsuccessful, the defendant running it risks being penalised in costs.[292] However, it is clear that the court may take account of the manner in which the company was run and, in particular, the functions and responsibilities undertaken by each individual member of the board. Thus, in circumstances where a particular task is habitually discharged by one director, the others may be able to shift responsibility onto him in the event that failure to discharge that task becomes an issue in disqualification proceedings. This is consistent with Sch.1 which, in relation to the majority of the matters listed, requires the court to consider the extent of each defendant's personal responsibility. It is also consistent with the law as stated in *Re Barings Plc (No.5)*. In *Re Cladrose Ltd*, considered above, one of the defendants escaped disqualification where it was accepted that his co-defendant, a qualified chartered accountant, had assumed particular responsibility for the preparation and filing of accounts and returns. The decision turned on the court's view that it was reasonable in the circumstances for him to expect an accountant to discharge the board's statutory obligations.[293] Thus, if there is a habitual division of roles and functions and, it is reasonable for one director to rely on the expertise of another to discharge his assigned function, then the court may decide that the former was not sufficiently responsible to justify a finding of unfitness. This is particularly so in the context of a large company where division of function and the delegation of specific tasks to individual directors and senior managers is a practical necessity. However, it will be rare for a reliance-based defence to succeed in the case of a small company where there has been a collective failure to discharge basic

[292] See *Re Sykes (Butchers) Ltd, Secretary of State for Trade and Industry v Richardson* [1998] 1 B.C.L.C. 110 at 132–133 (one defendant, R, ordered to pay 25% of his co-defendant O's costs in circumstances where proceedings against O were dismissed and the trial had been substantially lengthened by reason of R's unsuccessful attempt to shift responsibility onto O).

[293] While there are dangers for a defendant who defends himself by saying that a particular default was someone else's responsibility, it is clear that his perceptions concerning the reliability of his co-defendants can be adduced in evidence: see *Re Dawes & Henderson (Agencies) Ltd, Secretary of State for Trade and Industry v Dawes* [1997] 1 B.C.L.C. 329. All will turn on the facts however. In most properly run companies which are actively trading, the board will need to see accounts on a regular basis for financial management purposes and it may therefore be reasonable to expect a failure to prepare audited accounts on time to be picked up at an early stage.

minimum obligations such as the duty to maintain proper accounting records.[294] Furthermore, the defendant will need to show that he was justified in relying on his co-defendant to discharge the relevant task or function and that he did exercise at least some degree of supervision or monitoring of its performance in accordance with the second *Barings* proposition.

Summary

5–101 From the foregoing it appears that the CDDA, like s.214 of the Insolvency Act 1986, has been used by the courts to fashion a universal minimum standard of skill and competence.[295] The basic obligations of participation and supervision are non-delegable and an individual director will not be able to rely on ignorance or lack of relevant experience as an excuse. At the same time, a director who has special expertise or experience will be expected to achieve standards of conduct at a level above the basic minimum required of directors who are not so qualified. This shift towards an objective minimum standard capable of being adjusted upwards to take into account the skill, knowledge and experience of each director echoes judicial attempts to modernise the common law duty of care and skill before its codification as s.174 of the Companies Act 2006.[296] The focus of the CDDA on individual responsibility means that the court can take into account the particular function and responsibilities of each director and any agreed division or delegation of functions within the company in making its assessment.

PERIOD OF DISQUALIFICATION

Introduction

5–102 If a director is found to be unfit at trial the effect of s.6(4), in relation to s.6 cases, is that the court must disqualify him for the minimum period of two years. The maximum period of disqualification that the court can impose is 15 years. Otherwise, the period of disqualification is a matter within the court's discretion.[297] The Court of Appeal has provided general guidance concerning the exercise of the court's discretion in two cases: *Re Sevenoaks Stationers (Retail) Ltd*[298]

[294] Though see the generous approach in *Re Austinsuite Furniture Ltd* [1992] B.C.L.C. 1047 (director responsible for production not disqualified despite failing to monitor the company's financial position, the judge noting that he was a member of a large executive board which included a finance director and a manager both with accounting qualifications); and *Re Moonlight Foods (UK) Ltd, Secretary of State for Trade and Industry v Hickling* [1996] B.C.C. 678 (two directors exonerated where responsibility for maintenance of accounting records was said to rest with a chartered accountant).

[295] See further, A. Walters, "Directors' Duties: The Impact of the Company Directors Disqualification Act" (2000) 21 Co. Law. 110.

[296] *Norman v Theodore Goddard* [1992] B.C.L.C. 1028; *Re D'Jan of London Ltd* [1994] 1 B.C.L.C. 561. For further discussion see A. Walters, "Directors' Duties: The Impact of the Company Directors Disqualification Act" (2000) 21 Co. Law. 110.

[297] Note, however, that the period of disqualification is no longer *exclusively* a matter for the court as it is now open to the parties to settle disqualification cases by the offer and acceptance of undertakings: see further Ch.9. Before the introduction of the statutory undertakings regime, the court had the final say and was not strictly bound by any purported agreement between the parties as to period.

[298] [1991] Ch. 164.

and *Re Westmid Packing Services Ltd, Secretary of State for Trade and Industry v Griffiths*.[299] The second of these decisions explicitly acknowledges that, in fixing an appropriate period of disqualification, the court is engaged in something akin to a sentencing exercise. In contrast to s.6, there is no minimum period of disqualification under s.8. The maximum period is 15 years. It was said in *Re Samuel Sherman Plc* that the lack of a minimum period did not mean that the court should treat directors more leniently under s.8 than under s.6.[300] In s.8 cases the courts generally refer to and use the *Sevenoaks Stationers* brackets (discussed below) when assessing the appropriate period of disqualification, although it was accepted in *Re Atlantic Computers Plc*[301] that for misconduct falling within the lowest bracket the court can make an order of one year or less reflecting the fact that there is no statutory minimum period. Given that unfit conduct under s.6 has to be so serious as to justify a two-year period of disqualification, this raises the interesting question of whether unfit conduct for s.8 purposes can be less serious. In other words, can misconduct amount to unfit conduct for s.8 purposes when it would not amount to unfit conduct for s.6 purposes?

Court of Appeal "sentencing" guidelines

The Sevenoaks Stationers "brackets"

5–103 In *Sevenoaks Stationers* Dillon L.J. endorsed a division of the potential 15-year disqualification period into three brackets as follows:

(1) a top bracket of over 10 years to be reserved for "particularly serious cases". These may include cases where a director who has already had one period of disqualification imposed on him, falls to be disqualified again;
(2) a middle bracket of between six and 10 years for serious cases not meriting the top bracket;
(3) a minimum bracket of between two and five years to be applied where, though disqualification under s.6 is mandatory, the case is not, relatively speaking, very serious.

Thus, the court is required to determine the appropriate period of disqualification in each case according to a sliding scale of culpability. Somewhat surprisingly, it was not suggested specifically in *Sevenoaks Stationers* that the court should have regard to the overall purposes of the CDDA when exercising the discretion, although Dillon L.J. did make the general statement that the undisputed purpose of s.6 is to protect the public, and, in particular, potential creditors of companies, from unfit directors. *Sevenoaks Stationers* therefore gives the impression that the public's need for protection is to be measured crudely by reference to the degree of the defendant's past culpability and without any real

[299] [1998] 2 All E.R. 124.
[300] [1991] 1 W.L.R. 1070 at 1085.
[301] June 15, 1998, Ch.D., unreported.

assessment of the risk that he may pose to the public in the future. Care should be taken not to treat the brackets as if they had the force of a statute. Each bracket encompasses a broad spectrum. It is difficult to be precise about whether conduct falling, for example, in the minimum bracket merits a two-year order or a three-year order and so on. What is important is that the broad spectrum of conduct should not vary within each bracket. A further point to note is that, on a literal reading, Dillon L.J.'s judgment leaves open the question of whether a disqualification of between five and six years falls within the middle or minimum bracket. The courts tend to make orders in round years, although they can (and occasionally do) make orders that involve fractions of years (provided, in the case of s.6, that the order is for not less than two years). It is suggested that the qualitative comparative difference between conduct that will justify a six-year order rather than a five-year order is the same in degree as that between conduct justifying a four-year rather than a three-year order. The 15-year span is itself a spectrum and the *Sevenoaks Stationers* brackets should be treated as guidance and not as rigid categories.

Westmid Packing

5–104 In *Westmid Packing*, the Secretary of State failed to persuade the Court of Appeal to increase the period of disqualification imposed on two defendants by the trial judge. Lord Woolf M.R. took the opportunity to lay down some general guidance from which the following points emerge:

(1) Although disqualification is not strictly a punishment, the court is, in effect, engaged in a sentencing exercise. As such, the period of disqualification must reflect the gravity of the misconduct and (in keeping with the approach in *Grayan* discussed in Ch.4 above) it must contain deterrent elements. The Court of Appeal thus acknowledged that the purpose of disqualification is to protect the public in three senses: (a) by keeping unfit directors "off the road"; (b) by deterring the unfit director from repeating the misconduct (individual deterrence); and (c) by deterring other directors (general deterrence). It is implicit in this acknowledgment that the court should seek to advance the purpose of the CDDA in all three of these senses when fixing the period of disqualification.
(2) The court should start by arriving at the appropriate period to fit the gravity of the conduct. Allowance should then be made for any mitigating factors and the period reduced accordingly. The court should not be influenced in determining the period of disqualification by the existence of its power to grant a disqualified director permission to act. The power to grant permission is a separate question and, if (as will often be the case) the defendant has cross-applied for permission anticipating that a disqualification order will be made, that question should only be considered after the period of disqualification has been fixed.
(3) On the question of whether the director's conduct makes him unfit, the court is required to have "tunnel vision" and concentrate only on the instances of

past misconduct alleged by the claimant.[302] While the director's past misconduct is obviously relevant in determining the period of disqualification, the court is less restricted in the factors that can be taken into account. A wide variety of factors may be relevant including: the director's general reputation; his age and state of health; the length of time taken to bring the matter to trial; whether he admitted any of the allegations; his general conduct before and after the unfit conduct; and any periods of disqualification ordered by other courts on his co-directors. Some of these matters are considered further below in the discussion of mitigating factors.[303]

(4) The citation of authorities as to the period of disqualification will, in the majority of cases, be unnecessary and inappropriate as, in relation to the period of disqualification in particular, the court should adopt a broad brush approach and exercise the jurisdiction in a summary manner.

5–105 It is possible at a theoretical level to criticise the Court of Appeal's guidelines. The emphasis in both *Sevenoaks Stationers* and *Westmid Packing* on the need to tailor the period of disqualification to the gravity of the offence seems to reflect a policy of tariff-based "punishment" rather than public protection. The court is not required to evaluate the extent of the risk posed to the public by the defendant in the future.[304] Also, the point in (4) above is something of a pious hope. In practice, there is a natural tendency for lawyers advising the parties to disqualification proceedings to try to match the given case to the facts of previous cases in much the same way as personal injury lawyers resort to previous fact patterns in order to advise on the likely quantum of a claim. Despite these criticisms, it is hard to see how the courts could do much better. The current approach is pragmatic and holds out at least some hope that directors will receive fair and consistent treatment. In what follows there is an attempt to flesh out these Court of Appeal guidelines and offer some insights as to how they are applied.

The Sevenoaks Stationers "brackets" in practice

Minimum bracket cases

5–106 The majority of disqualifications in reported cases have tended to fall within the minimum bracket of two to five years. In practice, the courts tend to make an order for a period within this bracket in cases of unfit conduct where there is no evidence of dishonesty or deliberate misconduct. Conduct such as trading to the detriment of creditors, even when coupled with other allegations such as

[302] See text from 4–11.

[303] On the need to maintain the distinction between matters relevant to the assessment of whether the defendant's conduct makes him unfit and matters relevant only in mitigation of the period of disqualification see *Re The Premier Screw and Repetition Co Ltd, Paulin v Secretary of State for Trade and Industry* [2005] 2 B.C.L.C. 667 at [60]–[69].

[304] Although, in practice, the period of disqualification may be discounted because of the presence of mitigating factors that tend to reduce the risk to the public: see further from 5–110.

failure to monitor the company's financial position, filing default and excessive remuneration has rarely attracted more than a minimum bracket period of disqualification.[305] If there is an established pattern of this sort of conduct across two or three companies or a particular aggravating factor the court may be persuaded to make an order towards the top of the minimum bracket or into the middle bracket.[306] Although far from an exact science, it seems that in cases where there is no proven dishonesty, the court is likely to assess the period at between two and five years, depending on the degree of misconduct (such as how long the defendant allowed the company to continue trading to the detriment of creditors or the extent of the resulting harm) and then, in accordance with the approach in *Westmid Packing*, to apply a discount if there are any admissible mitigating factors.

Middle bracket cases

5–107 As a rule of thumb, if there is at least some evidence of deliberate, dishonest or self-serving conduct this may either of itself fall within the middle bracket or take what is otherwise a minimum bracket case up into the middle bracket. Thus, in *Re Godwin Warren Control Systems Plc* where it was found that the first defendant had deliberately failed to disclose his personal interest in a corporate transaction to the company's directors and shareholders, he was disqualified for six years.[307] Evidence of deliberate breach of fiduciary duty involving the misappropriation of corporate assets or other forms of deliberate misconduct will often take the case into the middle bracket especially when combined with more mundane

[305] See, e.g. *Re Hitco 2000 Ltd, Official Receiver v Cowan* [1995] 2 B.C.L.C. 63 (short period of trading to the detriment of creditors coupled with abdication of financial control, misuse of bank account, filing defaults: two years); *Re Grayan Building Services Ltd, Secretary of State for Trade and Industry v Gray* [1995] Ch. 241 (preference, trading to the detriment of creditors, failure to keep proper accounting records, minor filing default: two years); *Re Verby Print for Advertising Ltd* [1998] 2 B.C.L.C. 23 (policy of discrimination against Crown creditors: two years); *Re GSAR Realisations Ltd* [1993] B.C.L.C. 409 (trading to the detriment of creditors, failure to co-operate with insolvency practitioner, late preparation and filing of accounts: three years); *Re Ward Sherrard Ltd* [1996] B.C.C. 418 (trading to the detriment of creditors, excessive remuneration, late preparation and filing of accounts: three years).

[306] See, e.g. *Re Linvale Ltd* [1993] B.C.L.C. 654 (trading to the detriment of creditors in three successive companies with phoenix aspect albeit no finding of dishonesty: five years); *Re Skyward Builders Plc, Official Receiver v Broad* [2002] EWHC (Ch) 2786 (proven misconduct in relation to a series of companies but no finding of dishonesty: six years); *Re Genosyis Technology Management Ltd, Wallach v Secretary of State for Trade and Industry* [2007] 1 B.C.L.C. 208 (entering into manifest transaction at undervalue in breach of fiduciary duty: five years). Trading on customer deposits is likely to be an aggravating factor: see *Re Western Welsh International System Buildings Ltd* (1988) 4 B.C.C. 449 (five years); though note that when this case was decided the maximum period of disqualification was five years and similar conduct could conceivably now fall within the middle bracket.

[307] [1993] B.C.L.C. 80. See also *Re Austinsuite Furniture Ltd* [1992] B.C.L.C. 1047 where the first defendant was disqualified for seven years. Here the court was strongly influenced by his conduct in procuring a company to enter into a worthless acquisition which was represented in the accounts in such a way that they gave a misleading impression of the company's true financial position.

matters.[308] A similar fate may befall a director who deliberately and persistently disregards his statutory obligations or indulges in repeated misconduct in a number of companies without showing any sign that he has learned the lessons of previous insolvencies.[309] Middle bracket disqualifications have been imposed in cases where there was no allegation of dishonesty and the misconduct related to a single company or an insolvent group.[310] While rare, such cases illustrate the difficulty that practitioners face in trying to predict a possible outcome.

Top bracket cases

5–108 It is rare for a director to be disqualified for over 10 years.[311] To merit a disqualification in the top bracket it appears that the misconduct would need to be

[308] See, e.g. *Re Tansoft Ltd* [1991] B.C.L.C. 339 (repeated pattern of misconduct across three companies including misapplication of company monies: seven years); *Re Moorgate Metals Ltd, Official Receiver v Huhtala* [1995] 1 B.C.L.C. 503 (de facto director who caused company to trade while insolvent, took excessive remuneration, acted dishonestly and deceitfully and took part in the management of a company while bankrupt in breach of CDDA s.11 disqualified for 10 years); *Re Continental Assurance Co of London Plc* [1997] 1 B.C.L.C. 48 (executive director who instigated illegal financial assistance and used the assets of two companies as if they were his own disqualified for nine years); and *Secretary of State for Trade and Industry v Amiss* [2003] EWHC (Ch) 523, [2003] 2 B.C.L.C. 206 (chief executive of insurance brokerage who caused it to engage in dishonest practices disqualified for nine years). See also *Re Mayfair Interiors (Wolverhampton) Ltd, Secretary of State for Trade and Industry v Blunt* [2005] 2 B.C.L.C. 463; *Re The Premier Screw and Repetition Co Ltd, Paulin v Secretary of State for Trade and Industry* [2005] 2 B.C.L.C. 667; *Re Bunting Electric Manufacturing Co Ltd, Secretary of State for Trade and Industry v Golby* [2006] 1 B.C.L.C. 550.

[309] See, e.g. *Re Melcast (Wolverhampton) Ltd* [1991] B.C.L.C. 288 (first defendant guilty of "gross irresponsibility in his financial conduct" of two successive companies disqualified for seven years reduced from 10 years on grounds of his age); *Re Brooks Transport (Purfleet) Ltd* [1993] B.C.C. 766 (persistent conduct within two owner-managed companies described at best as "cavalier" and at worst as "a deliberate refusal to comply with legal requirements where [the defendant] considered them inconvenient or an obstacle to the conducting of the business . . .": seven years); *Re Copecrest Ltd, Secretary of State for Trade & Industry v McTighe (No.2)* [1996] 2 B.C.L.C. 477 (second defendant's period of disqualification raised from four to six years on appeal where evidence of repeated failings in a number of companies including some responsibility for misappropriation of corporate assets). See also *Re Saver Ltd* [1999] B.C.C. 221.

[310] See, e.g. *Re Synthetic Technology Ltd, Secretary of State for Trade and Industry v Joiner* [1993] B.C.C. 549 (sustained trading to the detriment of creditors in loss-making company, excessive remuneration and filing defaults: seven years); *Re Firedart Ltd, Official Receiver v Fairhall* [1994] 2 B.C.L.C. 340 (trading to the detriment of creditors coupled with excessive remuneration and failure to maintain proper accounting records in relation to a single company: six years); *Re Richborough Furniture Ltd, Secretary of State for Trade and Industry v Stokes* [1996] 1 B.C.L.C. 507 (trading to the detriment of creditors, misuse of bank account and failure to maintain proper accounting records in relation to a single company: first defendant disqualified for six years); *Re Thorncliffe Finance Ltd, Secretary of State for Trade and Industry v Arif* [1997] 1 B.C.L.C. 34 (first defendant disqualified for seven years primarily for failure to exercise proper financial responsibility within a group of companies despite no finding of dishonesty). It is perhaps significant that in *Synthetic Technology* the defendant appeared in person and that in *Firedart* the defendant made no appearance at all with the effect that the claimant's evidence was wholly unchallenged. Lesser periods might have resulted if there had been a more effective attempt to contest these proceedings or put forward mitigating factors. The use of the middle bracket in *Richborough Furniture* may reflect the lenient treatment previously given to the same defendant in *Re Austinsuite Furniture Ltd* [1992] B.C.L.C. 1047.

[311] In the five years to March 31, 2008, figures reported by the Insolvency Service suggest that, while the rate of incidence of disqualifications for 11–15 years is rising, it remains less than 10% per annum of all disqualifications: see the Insolvency Service, *Annual Report and Accounts 2007–2008* H.C. 800 (London: The Stationery Office, 2008), p.14.

very severe. Criminally culpable conduct such as persistent fraud may fit the bill.[312] A pattern of serious repeated misconduct across a number of companies consisting primarily of dishonest misappropriation of corporate assets and/or phoenix activity may also attract a period of disqualification within this bracket.[313]

Summary

5–109 Much seems to depend on the defendant's culpability, the duration of the misconduct, the extent of the resulting harm and on whether the misconduct occurred in isolation or was repeated across several companies. In *Sevenoaks Stationers*, the Court of Appeal endorsed the use of brackets in an attempt to introduce some consistency of approach. In particular, there was a perception that the High Court tended to impose lower periods of disqualification than county courts for conduct that was closely comparable. However, no rule of thumb will ever produce absolute consistency. For instance, it is difficult to predict what may tip the balance and turn minimum bracket conduct into middle bracket conduct or middle bracket conduct into top bracket conduct. The "broad brush" approach favoured in *Westmid Packing* is perhaps an acknowledgment of this difficulty. Some inconsistency is therefore inevitable and it creates problems for the practitioner faced with the task of advising on likely outcome, especially in circumstances where, as will often be the case, the ability to compromise the proceedings turns on a sensible and realistic appraisal of the appropriate period of disqualification. Moreover, as discussed below, it is not always easy to gauge what impact mitigation will have on determination of the appropriate period.[314] It is also noticeable that defendants who are not represented or who litigate in person seem to attract what appear to be relatively high periods of

[312] *Re Vintage Hallmark Plc, Secretary of State for Trade and Industry v Grove* [2007] 1 B.C.L.C. 788 (directors who had engaged in various forms of fraudulent trading disqualified for the maximum period of 15 years); *Re Plazoo Pipe Systems Ltd, Kappler v Secretary of State for Trade and Industry* [2008] 1 B.C.L.C. 120 (director who knowingly allowed false invoices to be issued in order to obtain credit on the company's invoice discounting facility disqualified for 11 years).

[313] See, e.g. *Re Defence & Microwave Devices Ltd*, October 7, 1992, Ch.D., unreported (principal defendant disqualified for 12 years in a case involving proven dishonesty); *Re Copecrest Ltd, Secretary of State for Trade & Industry v McTighe (No.2)* [1996] 2 B.C.L.C. 477 (in which the first defendant's period of disqualification was raised from 8 to 12 years on appeal); *Re Windows West Ltd, Official Receiver v Zwirn* [2002] B.C.C. 760 (defendant found to have dishonestly engineered a series of phoenix successions at the expense of Crown creditors disqualified for 11 years).

[314] It appears also that the criminal courts exercising their powers under CDDA s.2 do not necessarily act in line with the approach of the civil courts under ss.6 and 8 on the question of the period of disqualification: see discussion in Ch.10.

disqualification.[315] This is probably best explained by the failure of these defendants to mount an effective challenge to the claimant's evidence and/or to put forward any compelling mitigation.

Mitigating factors

5–110 It was suggested in *Re Dawes & Henderson (Agencies) Ltd, Secretary of State for Trade and Industry v Dawes* that the defendant can only rely in mitigation on matters which are relevant to the conduct established.[316] As discussed above, this narrow approach was rejected by the Court of Appeal in *Westmid Packing* in favour of a more flexible approach. The specific factors discussed below suggest that the court may engage in a broad enquiry and take into account matters that are personal to the defendant including the impact of the disqualification process on him. A number of factors often taken into account at this stage are not strictly mitigating factors at all but rather points of emphasis. For instance, the court may lay emphasis on the fact that the defendant was not dishonest and/or did not benefit personally from his misconduct. Strictly speaking, this amounts to an assessment of the defendant's degree of culpability for the purposes of the *Sevenoaks Stationers* approach rather than genuine mitigation.[317] Needless to say, points like these bear repetition by defendant's counsel as they tend to indicate a period of disqualification within the minimum bracket. Thus, one aspect of "mitigation" is the attempt to draw out factors which point to a lesser degree of culpability and to emphasise what the defendant got right. It is difficult to know with any certainty the level of discount that the court will apply to reflect a particular mitigating factor. The cases suggest that the specific factors discussed below may be taken into account.[318] It appears that these various mitigating factors, which

[315] The cases suggest that an unrepresented defendant or a litigant in person can be at a serious disadvantage: see, e.g. *Re T & D Services (Timber Preservation & Damp Proofing Contractors) Ltd* [1990] B.C.C. 592 (unrepresented defendant disqualified for 10 years); *Re Tansoft Ltd* [1991] B.C.L.C. 339 (litigant in person disqualified for seven years); *Re City Investment Centres Ltd* [1992] B.C.L.C. 956 (two unrepresented defendants disqualified for 10 and six years respectively, one litigant in person disqualified for six years); *Re Ask International Transport Ltd, Secretary of State for Trade and Industry v Keens*, May 5, 1992, Ch.D (two unrepresented defendants disqualified for four years where trading to the detriment of creditors had only occurred over a short period); *Re Looe Fish Ltd* [1993] B.C.L.C. 1160 (a s.8 case in which an unrepresented defendant was disqualified for a period only six months less than his represented co-defendant despite the latter's more significant involvement in the relevant misconduct); *Re Synthetic Technology Ltd* [1993] B.C.C. 549 (litigant in person disqualified for seven years); *Re Firedart Ltd* [1994] 2 B.C.L.C. 340 (unrepresented defendant disqualified for six years in a routine case of trading to the detriment of creditors and failure to maintain accounting records); *Re Copecrest Ltd, Secretary of State for Trade & Industry v McTighe (No.2)* [1996] 2 B.C.L.C. 477 (period of disqualification imposed on unrepresented defendant raised from eight to 12 years); *Re Continental Assurance Co of London Plc* [1997] 1 B.C.L.C. 48 (unrepresented defendant disqualified for nine years); *Re Skata Ltd, Secretary of State for Trade and Industry v Zevides* [2002] EWHC (Ch) 813 (litigant in person disqualified for seven years). For a more sympathetic approach, see *Re Land Travel Ltd, Secretary of State for Trade and Industry v Tjolle* [1998] 1 B.C.L.C. 333.

[316] [1997] 1 B.C.L.C. 329 at 338.

[317] See, e.g. *Re GSAR Realisations Ltd* [1993] B.C.L.C. 409.

[318] Note that in the interests of economy of court time, the judge may frown upon the citation of numerous cases as to the appropriate period of disqualification: see *Re Westmid Packing Services Ltd, Secretary of State for Trade and Industry v Griffiths* [1998] 2 All E.R. 124 at 134.

are admissible in proceedings for an order under s.6, are also relevant and admissible in s.8 proceedings.

General character and reputation

5–111 It appears that evidence relating to the defendant's general ability and conduct as a director can be adduced by way of mitigation. General evidence of good character is ordinarily inadmissible in civil proceedings because it is not probative of any issue. However, it was suggested in *Westmid Packing* that evidence relating to the defendant's conduct and track record in the discharge of the office of director may be admissible because it is relevant in determining the extent of the public's need for protection.[319] The evidence must be relevant. As Scott V.C. put it in *Re Barings Plc, Secretary of State for Trade and Industry v Baker*, "it would not be relevant in the least whether the director was a good family man or whether he was kind to animals".[320]

Impact of corporate failure

5–112 It appears that if the defendant has suffered personal financial loss in the company's collapse then this can be taken into account in mitigation. At first sight, this seems somewhat incongruous in the light of the oft-stated view that disqualification is concerned with the protection of the public. The rationale seems to be that the public needs less protection from a director who lost out along with creditors than from one who manipulated the company entirely for his own ends in circumstances where his personal fortune was not at stake. One difficulty is that in an owner-managed company, the controller's failure to monitor the running of the company and the value of his own investment may of itself indicate a lack of regard for creditors' interests.[321] Thus, in cases where an owner-manager is said to have abdicated responsibility, his personal financial loss may not be of much significance as a mitigating factor. Nevertheless, the impact of the company's failure on the defendant was taken into account in *Sevenoaks Stationers* and other cases.[322]

[319] [1998] 2 All E.R. 124 at 133, citing with approval *Re Barings Plc* [1998] B.C.C. 583 at 590 though cf. *Re Dawes & Henderson (Agencies) Ltd* [1997] 1 B.C.L.C. 329. General character evidence is admissible in criminal proceedings where there is a presumption that a person of good character would not commit a crime. The flexible approach taken in *Westmid Packing* appears to reflect the Court of Appeal's acceptance that the process of determining the appropriate period of disqualification is analogous to a criminal sentencing exercise.

[320] [1998] B.C.C. 583 at 590.

[321] See, e.g. *Re Burnham Marketing Services Ltd, Secretary of State for Trade and Industry v Harper* [1993] B.C.C. 518.

[322] See also *Re Cargo Agency Ltd* [1992] B.C.L.C. 686; *Re Pamstock Ltd* [1994] 1 B.C.L.C. 716; *Re Hitco 2000 Ltd, Official Receiver v Cowan* [1995] 2 B.C.L.C. 63 and contrast with *Re Ipcon Fashions Ltd* (1989) 5 B.C.C. 773 where a director who lost no personal capital in three successive failed companies having traded entirely at the risk of creditors was disqualified for five years. See also *Re Firedart Ltd* [1994] 2 B.C.L.C. 340 at 352 where Arden J. did not regard the defendant's guarantee of the bank overdraft and provision of personal security as a matter of mitigation. Given that the company was seriously undercapitalised from the start, the monies should, in the judge's view, have been injected in exchange for issues of share capital.

Age and/or state of health

5–113 In *Re Melcast (Wolverhampton) Ltd*, the court considered it appropriate to disqualify the first defendant for 10 years but reduced it to seven to take account of his advancing age.[323] At the time of trial he was 68 and it was felt that a seven-year disqualification would adequately protect the public because there was little risk of him wanting to take an active part in the management of a company after the age of 75. Similarly in *Official Receiver v Cummings*,[324] the defendant's age (53) was regarded as a mitigating factor. On the other hand, in *Re Moorgate Metals Ltd, Official Receiver v Huhtala*, Warner J. did not consider that the second defendant's age (he would have been 80 by the time the period of disqualification ended) was a reason for reducing the period.[325] At the opposite end of the spectrum, a young and inexperienced director may expect to receive some credit especially for a "first offence".[326] Where the defendant is in ill health, the court may be persuaded, by analogy, to apply a discount if the illness reduces the likelihood of him being able to take up directorships in the future. It is suggested that the restrictive approach in *Moorgate Metals* should apply in the case of a defendant who seeks to rely on age or ill health as a mitigating factor unless it can be shown that either factor had a direct bearing on the unfit conduct.

Reliance on professional advice

5–114 It was seen earlier that in some cases the defendant may escape a finding of unfit conduct where he has relied on professional advice or on the special expertise of a co-director. Even if he is not able to persuade the court to dismiss the application altogether, it is likely that such reliance would be treated as a mitigating factor. Thus in *Re Rolus Properties Ltd*,[327] the court assessed the appropriate period of disqualification at between four and six years but reduced it to two years to take account of the fact that the defendant had procured the services of a chartered secretary to assist in the company's administration.[328]

Conduct after the unfit conduct

5–115 Instances of positive conduct after the unfit conduct have been taken into account in some cases. It will usually go to the defendant's credit if he co-operated fully with the insolvency practitioner appointed to take charge of the company's affairs following its collapse.[329] Similarly, it was suggested in *Re Firedart Ltd* that an attempt by the defendant to improve the position of creditors by making a payment to the liquidator could be a relevant mitigating factor.[330] This presumably reflects

[323] [1991] B.C.L.C. 288.

[324] November 1, 1991, Ch.D., unreported.

[325] [1995] 1 B.C.L.C. 503 at 520.

[326] There is the hint of such an approach in the treatment of the defendant LS in *Re Austinsuite Furniture Ltd* [1992] B.C.L.C. 1047.

[327] (1988) 4 B.C.C. 446.

[328] See also *Re Keypak Homecare Ltd* [1990] B.C.L.C. 440 where the defendants received some credit for having relied on bad professional advice.

[329] See, e.g. *Re Cargo Agency Ltd* [1992] B.C.L.C. 686; *Re City Investment Centres Ltd* [1992] B.C.L.C. 956.

[330] [1994] 2 B.C.L.C. 340 at 352.

the idea that an act of contrition based on the defendant's recognition of the damage suffered by creditors is worthy of some discount. However, such an argument is unlikely to cut much ice if the payment was made in satisfaction of civil proceedings brought by the liquidator.[331] In *Re The Premier Screw and Repetition Co Ltd, Paulin v Secretary of State for Trade and Industry*, Morritt V.C. refused to disturb a registrar's decision to disqualify the defendant for seven years where, despite what was described as a "very serious and flagrant breach of fiduciary duty", he had subsequently taken steps to restore the position with the result that 91 per cent of the creditors were paid. It appears that the registrar accepted that there should be some discount but not sufficient to take the case out of the middle bracket into the minimum bracket as was contended by the defendant's counsel.[332]

Conduct during proceedings

5–116 Credit may be given if the defendant refrains from acting as director while proceedings against him are pending.[333] To what extent the defendant will receive any credit for the way in which the proceedings are conducted on his behalf remains, however, something of a moot point. It was suggested in *Re Firedart Ltd* that a discount may be available if the defendant makes admissions during proceedings.[334] In *Re Barings Plc*, Scott V.C. stated categorically that there was no scope for plea bargaining in disqualification proceedings and that directors should not be given credit for assisting the court in its disposal of their case by not disputing the indisputable.[335] However, he does seem to have accepted that credit could be given to a director who realistically accepts that his conduct makes him unfit, as this indicates a state of mind that suggests that he may pose less of a danger to the public in the future than someone who adamantly insists that he was not responsible for any misconduct. The Court of Appeal in *Westmid Packing* disagreed with Scott V.C. and the present state of the law is best reflected in the following passage from Lord Woolf M.R.'s judgment in that case:

> "In the criminal sentencing context . . . there is no room for plea bargaining if by that it is meant some form of agreement as to the sentence if a plea is entered. But there can be negotiation as to the acceptability of an admission on a certain basis of fact, and that would seem to be as sensible in this context as in the criminal context. That is indeed already recognised in the *Carecraft* procedure.[336] Furthermore in the criminal context very little discount is given if there is an admission of what is 'indisputable', but an

[331] See *Re Grayan Building Services Ltd, Secretary of State for Trade and Industry v Gray* [1995] Ch. 241 in which the Court of Appeal held that the trial judge had been wrong to give weight to the fact that the liquidator had previously achieved an advantageous settlement of proceedings brought against the defendants under s.239 of the Insolvency Act 1986.

[332] [2005] 2 B.C.L.C. 667 at [70]–[76].

[333] *Official Receiver v Cummings*, November 1, 1991, Ch.D., unreported. See also *Re Transtec Plc, Secretary of State for Trade and Industry v Carr* [2007] 2 B.C.L.C. 495 where credit appears to have been given for the fact that the defendant had not undertaken any management responsibilities since the collapse of the relevant company.

[334] [1994] 2 B.C.L.C. 340 at 352.

[335] [1998] B.C.C. 583 at 590.

[336] On *Carecraft* disposals generally see Ch.9.

admission of what might otherwise have taken a great deal of time and expense to prove surely merits some recognition, provided of course that the starting point correctly reflects the gravity of the conduct."[337]

Thus, if the defendant admits an allegation before trial that would otherwise have occupied considerable court time, a discount may be appropriate. Once again, the idea that the exercise is closely analogous to criminal sentencing is to the fore.

Delay in bringing proceedings: "de facto" disqualification[338]

5–117 In *Re Thorncliffe Finance Ltd, Secretary of State for Trade and Industry v Arif*, the first defendant argued that, in fixing the appropriate period of disqualification, the court should have regard to the fact that since the institution of the proceedings he had been prevented from taking up appointments as a director because the sort of directorship that would be attractive to him (namely, one in a company engaged in the motor trade) would not be offered to a person against whom disqualification proceedings were pending. He therefore sought credit for what was described as the period of de facto disqualification between the commencement and conclusion of proceedings. Chadwick J. held that no credit could be given because of the structure of the CDDA. If the court makes a finding of unfit conduct, the court must disqualify the defendant for a minimum of two years even if he no longer poses any threat to the public under the rule in *Re Grayan Building Services Ltd* discussed in Ch.4. In circumstances where the minimum period of disqualification is appropriate, it is not open to the court to give any credit for the period during which the proceedings were pending. The judge concluded that, if a period of so-called de facto disqualification cannot be taken into account in a case of that nature, then it cannot be taken into account either in a case where the appropriate starting point, as in *Arif*, is a period of disqualification longer than the two-year minimum.[339] However, in *Westmid Packing*, the Court of Appeal disagreed expressly with Chadwick J.'s view and said that the length of time for which a director has been in jeopardy may be a relevant factor.

5–118 There are difficulties with both of these conflicting views. Chadwick J.'s view suffers from a flaw in logic. It is clear that if the minimum period of disqualification is appropriate the court has *no scope whatsoever* for taking mitigating factors into account. The minimum period simply cannot be discounted. If *Arif* is correct in respect of de facto disqualification, it follows that mitigation of any sort can never be relevant because it is impossible for the court to rely on mitigating factors where to do so would reduce the period below two years. Equally, however, there is no clear guidance in *Westmid Packing* as to the circumstances

[337] [1998] 2 All E.R. 124 at 132. See also *Re Mayfair Interiors (Wolverhampton) Ltd, Secretary of State for Trade and Industry v Blunt* [2005] 2 B.C.L.C. 463 at [26]; *Re Transtec Plc, Secretary of State for Trade and Industry v Carr* [2007] 2 B.C.L.C. 495 at [107].

[338] The assumption here is that the delay is not such as to warrant the striking out of the proceedings on grounds of abuse of process and/or infringement of the defendant's rights under ECHR art.6. On delay as a ground for striking out, see further Ch.8.

[339] [1997] 1 B.C.L.C. 34 at 44–45.

in which a period of de facto disqualification might be taken into account. Strictly speaking, while proceedings are pending, the defendant is not *legally* restricted from taking up directorships. There is no obvious reason why the court should *automatically* conclude that the period between commencement of proceedings and trial operates as a de facto disqualification.[340] It may be different if there is cogent evidence establishing that the defendant was de facto disqualified or in cases where there has been an unreasonable delay on the part of the claimant in bringing the matter to trial. The task of determining the extent to which a defendant's right to due process can affect the substantive outcome of his case is a complex and controversial one. Once proceedings have been commenced, it is clear that any unreasonable delay in bringing the case to trial will infringe the defendant's right to a fair trial under art.6 of the ECHR.[341] At the same time, delay in the prosecution of disqualification proceedings arguably harms the public because the defendant is technically free to act as a director (and potentially free to indulge in further misconduct) until such time as a disqualification order is made. This tension between individual rights and the public interest may give rise to conflicting characterisations of the period between commencement of proceedings and trial. Thus, there is no guarantee that the court will always treat it as a period of de facto disqualification. Moreover, even if a discount is applied, it is unlikely to take the form of a "day for day" credit against the period of disqualification that the court would otherwise have ordered.[342]

5–119 There has been a tendency in appeal cases for the appellate court to give the defendant some credit in respect of the length of time for which he was "in jeopardy".[343] Defendants have also received credit at first instance.[344] However, if the

[340] See *Re Sykes (Butchers) Ltd, Secretary of State for Trade and Industry v Richardson* [1998] 1 B.C.L.C. 110.

[341] *EDC v United Kingdom* [1998] B.C.C. 370; *Davies v United Kingdom* (2002) 35 E.H.R.R. 29.

[342] See, e.g. *Re Skyward Builders Plc, Official Receiver v Broad* [2002] EWHC (Ch) 2786 at [431]–[432].

[343] See *Re Grayan Building Services Ltd, Secretary of State for Trade and Industry v Gray* [1995] Ch. 241; *Re City Pram & Toy Co Ltd* [1998] B.C.C. 537. Both cases involved successful appeals by the Secretary of State against an earlier refusal to disqualify the defendants. In *City Pram* the court expressly adopted the practice followed by the Court of Appeal (Criminal Division) on successful appeals by the Crown against sentence in criminal cases and substituted a lesser period of disqualification than it felt the registrar should have ordered to reflect the additional strain placed on the defendants by the Secretary of State's appeal.

[344] See, e.g. *Re Aldermanbury Trust Plc* [1993] B.C.C. 598; *Re A & C Group Services Ltd* [1993] B.C.L.C. 1297 (though in the latter the credit given also reflected the fact that one of the defendants had spent some of the period between commencement of proceedings and trial under automatic disqualification as an undischarged bankrupt); *Re Admiral Energy Group Ltd, Official Receiver v Jones*, August 19, 1996, Ch.D., unreported (18 month discount where proceedings had been pending for six and a half years); *Re Skyward Builders Plc, Official Receiver v Broad* [2002] EWHC (Ch) 2786 at [431]–[432]. It is interesting to reflect that substantial delay often occurs because parallel criminal or regulatory proceedings are in train. In the light of *EDC v United Kingdom* [1998] B.C.C. 370 it is likely that the courts will try to safeguard defendants against such delay (especially in cases where disqualification proceedings are stayed against the defendant pending the outcome of parallel proceedings against a co-defendant in which he is not involved). The fact that a defendant's conduct may expose him to parallel proceedings (and therefore additional "jeopardy") has not of itself attracted a discount: see, e.g. *Re Living Images Ltd* [1996] 1 B.C.L.C. 348 (existence of parallel disciplinary proceedings brought by accountancy body not taken into account).

defendant's art.6 rights are complied with and there is no specific evidence that the defendant's livelihood has been affected as a result of pending proceedings, there is no obvious reason why the courts should apply a discount as a matter of course. On a separate point, the general approach in *Westmid Packing* suggests that the court may be persuaded to give some form of discount if the defendant is already or has already been the subject of automatic disqualification on the ground of personal bankruptcy under s.11.[345]

Treatment of any co-director

5–120 Although not strictly a mitigating factor, the courts do appear to be influenced by a desire to fix periods of disqualification that reflect a fair balance in cases involving a number of unfit co-directors.[346] Thus, the way in which one director is treated may well affect the court's treatment of his co-directors. Similarly, the compromise or discontinuance of proceedings against one director may influence the court's attitude in determining the length of the period for which any co-director who has contested the proceedings to trial should be disqualified.[347]

[345] See also dicta in *Re Swift 736 Ltd, Secretary of State for Trade and Industry v Ettinger* [1993] B.C.L.C. 896 suggesting that a period of disqualification by reason of bankruptcy might be taken into account in an appropriate case.

[346] See, e.g. *Re Sevenoaks Stationers (Retail) Ltd* [1991] Ch. 164 (where Dillon L.J. expressed doubt obiter as to whether it would have been right to disqualify the appellant for more than twice as long as his co-director who was not involved in the appeal); *Re Swift 736 Ltd, Secretary of State for Trade and Industry v Ettinger* [1993] B.C.L.C. 896; *Re Skyward Builders Plc, Official Receiver v Broad* [2002] EWHC (Ch) 2786. Cf. *Re Transtec Plc, Secretary of State for Trade and Industry v Carr* [2007] 2 B.C.L.C. 495 at [106].

[347] See, e.g. *Re Continental Assurance Co of London Plc* [1997] 1 B.C.L.C. 48 (where the court was influenced in its treatment of a non-executive director by the fact that one of his fellow directors had been disqualified for four years under the *Carecraft* procedure).

CHAPTER 6

COMPETITION DISQUALIFICATION ORDERS

INTRODUCTION

6–01 The Enterprise Act 2002 introduced a statutory regime empowering the Office of Fair Trading ("OFT")[1] and other specified regulators to apply to court for a disqualification order against a director of a company where that company has committed a relevant breach of competition law.[2] As is the case with CDDA ss.6 and 8, the touchstone of a director's liability to disqualification under this new regime is whether the court considers that his conduct as a director makes him unfit to be concerned in the management of a company. Thus, the concept of unfit conduct, discussed in Ch.4 and illuminated by the specific instances of misconduct identified in Ch.5, has now been extended to embrace specifically the involvement of directors in infringements of competition law. For the sake of convenience, the competition disqualification regime is considered separately in this chapter, cross-referring where appropriate to material elsewhere in the book. It must be emphasised that this chapter is concerned only with the role of disqualification as an additional sanction for breach of UK and European Community competition law and the implications of the competition disqualification regime for the CDDA. The authors profess no expertise in competition law and readers requiring a general background to the subject should refer to specialist texts.[3]

[1] The OFT is the corporate body that was established to take over the functions of the former Director General of Fair Trading by Pt 1 of the Enterprise Act 2002. As regards the ability of the OFT to act through members or employees or committees of such members and/or employees, provided in each case that the same are duly authorised so to act see Enterprise Act 2002 Sch.1 para.12.

[2] The competition aspects of the Enterprise Act 2002 were the result of a DTI White Paper, *Productivity and Enterprise—A World Class Competition Regime* Cm.5233 (DTI, July 2001). The White Paper followed a joint Treasury and DTI investigation into the effectiveness of existing competition legislation. It acknowledged that the Competition Act 1998 had made changes that deterred anti-competitive behaviour, but argued that there was a strong case for the introduction of criminal penalties. See also PriceWaterhouseCoopers, *Peer Review of the UK Competition Policy Regime—Final Report to the DTI* (April 18, 2001) and KPMG, *Peer Review of Competition Policy—Report to the DTI* (May 17, 2004). The latter review does not mention disqualification.

[3] See, e.g. M. Coleman & M. Grenfell, *The Competition Act 1998* (Oxford: OUP, 1999); D. Goyder, *EC Competition Law*, 4th edn (Oxford: OUP, 2003); P. Freeman & R. Whish, *A Guide to the Competition Act 1998* (London: Butterworths, 1999); M. Furse, *Competition Law of the UK and EC*, 6th edn (Oxford: OUP, 2003); M. Furse, *Competition and the Enterprise Act 2002* (Bristol: Jordans, 2003); A. Jones & B. Sufrin, *EC Competition Law: Text, Cases and Materials*, 3rd edn (Oxford: OUP, 2007); V. Korah, *Cases and Materials on EC Competition Law*, 3rd edn (Oxford: Hart Publishing, 2006); V. Korah, *An Introductory Guide to EC Competition Law and Practice*, 9th edn (Oxford: Hart Publishing, 2007); P. Roth & V. Rose (eds.), *Bellamy and Child: European Community Law of Competition*, 6th edn (Oxford: OUP, 2008); P.J. Slot & A. Johnston, *An Introduction to Competition Law* (Oxford: Hart Publishing, 2006); B. Sufrin, *Principles of UK and EU Competition Law* (London: Butterworths, 2003); R. Whish, *Competition Law*, 6th edn (London: Butterworths, 2008).

SECTION 9A: MANDATORY DISQUALIFICATION FOR UNFIT CONDUCT FOLLOWING A BREACH OF COMPETITION LAW

The competition disqualification regime is contained in CDDA ss.9A to 9E. These provisions were inserted by s.204 of the Enterprise Act and came into force on June 20, 2003.[4] **6–02**

Under CDDA s.9A the court is obliged to make a disqualification order against a person on the application of the OFT or a specified regulator (a phrase hereafter abbreviated to "the regulator" for ease) if two conditions are satisfied in relation to him: **6–03**

(1) The first condition is that an undertaking which is a company of which he is a director commits a breach of competition law (CDDA s.9A(2)).
(2) The second condition is that the court considers that his conduct as a director makes him unfit to be concerned in the management of a company (CDDA s.9A(3)).

The maximum period of disqualification that can be imposed is 15 years.[5] There is no minimum.

The first condition

"Undertaking which is a company of which he is a director . . ."

The effect of CDDA s.9A(11) is that the term "undertaking" in s.9A should be construed in the same way as it is construed for the purposes of the Competition Act 1998 and arts 81 and 82 of the EC Treaty. In UK and EC competition law, the term has a broad meaning and encompasses "every entity engaged in economic activity, regardless of the legal status of the entity and the way in which it is financed".[6] This reflects the fact that competition law is concerned with the economic effects of anti-competitive practices rather than with the legal forms and structures through which economic activity may be carried out. It follows that a natural person acting as a sole trader, or a series of natural persons operating collectively as an ordinary trading partnership, can amount to an undertaking as well as a legal person such as a company. Furthermore, a group of companies may in certain circumstances be treated as a single undertaking, especially where, for example, a subsidiary has no operational independence from its parent company and therefore no real autonomy in determining its course of action in the market.[7] **6–04**

It is clear from CDDA s.9A(1)–(2), however, that a competition disqualification order can only be made against a *director* of a *company*. So even though the term "undertaking" has a broad meaning, the court's disqualification jurisdiction will only be triggered if the undertaking that committed a relevant breach of competition law **6–05**

[4] The Enterprise Act 2002 (Commencement No.3, Transitional and Transitory Provisions and Savings) Order 2003 (SI 2003/1397).

[5] CDDA s.9A(9).

[6] C-41/90 *Hofner and Elser v Macrotron GmbH* [1991] E.C.R. I-1979 at para.21.

[7] C-73/95 *Viho Europe BV v Commission of the European Communities* [1996] E.C.R. I-5457.

is a "company" for the purposes of the CDDA. By virtue of CDDA ss.22(2) and 22(9), "company" means a registered company but also includes any unregistered company that is capable of being wound up under Pt V of the Insolvency Act 1986. Moreover, CDDA ss.22A–D and the Limited Liability Partnerships Regulations 2001[8] expressly extend the definition of "company" to embrace, respectively, building societies, incorporated friendly societies, NHS foundation trusts, open-ended investment companies and limited liability partnerships.[9]

6–06 The term "director" in s.9A clearly includes de jure directors and is expressly extended to include shadow directors by s.9E(5). In guidance issued just before the competition disqualification regime came into force, the OFT expressed the view that "director" for s.9A purposes also includes a de facto director.[10] This must be right as it is well settled that "director" in CDDA s.6(1) includes a de facto director and there is nothing to suggest that "director" in s.9A should be construed any differently.[11] The term must also be read to include a director, shadow director or officer of a building society,[12] a member of the committee of management or officer of an incorporated friendly society,[13] a director or officer of an NHS foundation trust[14] and a member or shadow member of a limited liability partnership.[15]

"Breach of competition law"

6–07 Under CDDA s.9A(4), an undertaking "commits a breach of competition law" for the purposes of the first condition if it engages in conduct which infringes any of the following:

(1) The Chapter 1 prohibition in the Competition Act 1998. This prohibits agreements between undertakings, decisions by associations of undertakings or concerted practices which may affect trade within the United Kingdom, and which have as their object or effect the prevention, restriction or distortion of competition within the United Kingdom.[16]
(2) The Chapter 2 prohibition in the Competition Act 1998. This prohibits any conduct on the part of one or more undertakings which amounts to the abuse of a dominant position insofar as it may affect trade within the United Kingdom.[17]
(3) Article 81 of the EC Treaty. This prohibits agreements between undertakings, decisions by associations of undertakings or concerted practices which may affect trade between member states, and which have as their object or effect

[8] SI 2001/1090 reg.4(2).
[9] The meaning of the term "company" in the CDDA is discussed more fully from 3–73.
[10] OFT, *Competition Disqualification Orders—Guidance* (May 2003) at para.2.3.
[11] See text from 3–16.
[12] CDDA s.22A(2)–(3).
[13] CDDA s.22B(2)–(3).
[14] CDDA s.22C(2).
[15] Limited Liability Partnerships Regulations 2001 (SI 2001/1090) reg.4(2)(f)–(g).
[16] Competition Act 1998 s.2(1).
[17] Competition Act 1998 s.18(1).

the prevention, restriction or distortion of competition within the common market.

(4) Article 82 of the EC Treaty. This prohibits abuse by one or more undertakings of a dominant position within the common market or in a substantial part of it insofar as the abuse may affect trade between member states.

Thus, the Chapter 1 prohibition and Article 81 regulate anti-competitive agreements whereas the Chapter 2 prohibition and Article 82 regulate the abuse of market power.[18] In relation to conduct infringing the Chapter 1 prohibition or Article 81, CDDA s.9A(8) provides that "references to the conduct of an undertaking are references to its conduct taken with the conduct of one or more other undertakings". This simply reflects the fact that the anti-competitive conduct targeted by these provisions—agreements between competitors and other forms of concerted practice—by definition involves more than one party.

6–08 The regulator has indicated that it will only apply for a competition disqualification order where the relevant undertaking has been found to have breached competition law by a decision or judgment of any one or more of the OFT, a specified regulator, the European Commission, the Competition Appeal Tribunal or the Court of Justice of the European Communities.[19] This and other points arising from the OFT guidance are considered further below.

6–09 There is an overlap between the court's powers of disqualification in CDDA ss.2 and 9A. With effect from June 20, 2003, an individual commits an offence under s.188 of the Enterprise Act 2002 if he dishonestly agrees with one or more other persons to make or implement, or to cause to be made or implemented, certain specified anti-competitive arrangements relating to at least two undertakings.[20] This so-called "cartel" offence overlaps with the civil law prohibitions in Chapter 1 of the Competition Act 1998 and art. 81 of the EC Treaty, breach of which triggers the court's jurisdiction in CDDA s.9A. Where a company director is convicted of the cartel offence, the court's power under CDDA s.2 will be engaged. Section 2 empowers the convicting court to make a disqualification order against a person who is convicted of an indictable offence in connection with the management of a company.[21] Thus, it is conceivable that the same conduct could breach both the criminal and civil law and accordingly give rise to the possibility of criminal disqualification under CDDA s.2 and/or civil disqualification under CDDA s.9A. The OFT takes the view that the court by or before which a director is convicted

[18] The Chapter 1 and Chapter 2 prohibitions are closely modelled on arts 81–82 of the EC Treaty. This reflects a policy of deliberate alignment that was designed to improve the effectiveness of UK competition law and reduce the regulatory burden on businesses affected potentially by two different sets of rules: see further M. Coleman & M. Grenfell, *The Competition Act 1998* (Oxford: OUP, 1999) at pp.4–13.

[19] OFT, *Competition Disqualification Orders—Guidance* (May 2003) at para.4.6. The Competition Appeal Tribunal was established by Pt 2 of the Enterprise Act 2002. It should be noted that the OFT has proposed altering the guidance in this respect: see 6-34A below.

[20] The provision constituting this offence was brought into force by the Enterprise Act 2002 (Commencement No.3, Transitional and Transitory Provisions and Savings) Order 2003 (SI 2003/1397).

[21] See further Ch.10, especially text from 10–15.

of the cartel offence is the most appropriate venue for consideration of a disqualification order and has said that it would not expect to have to use its powers under s.9A in such circumstances.[22] This approach was borne out in the marine hose cartel case, the first and (as far as the authors are aware) the only case to date in which the s.188 cartel offence has been successfully prosecuted. In that case, three directors received custodial sentences and were disqualified under CDDA s.2 for periods ranging between five and seven years.[23]

The second condition

6–10 For the purpose of deciding whether a person is unfit to be concerned in the management of a company, CDDA s.9A(5) states that the court:

(1) must have regard to whether CDDA s.9A(6) applies to him;
(2) may have regard to his conduct as a director of a company in connection with any other breach of competition law;
(3) must not have regard to the matters mentioned in Sch.1 to the CDDA.

6–11 CDDA s.9A(6) applies to a person if as a director of the company:

(1) his conduct contributed to a relevant breach of competition law;
(2) his conduct did not contribute to the breach but he had reasonable grounds to suspect that the conduct of the undertaking constituted the breach and took no steps to prevent it;
(3) he did not know but ought to have known that the conduct of the undertaking constituted the breach.

For the purposes of the first alternative (direct contribution to the breach), CDDA s.9A(7) further provides that it is immaterial whether the person knew that the conduct of the undertaking constituted the breach. Section 9A(6) establishes what appears to be a sliding scale of culpability to which the court must have regard. However, it does not give the court any clear guidance as to where the line between fit conduct and unfit conduct should be drawn. The provision gives nothing more than a general indication that a person's direct participation in a relevant breach of competition law *could* make that person unfit while suggesting, at the same time, that something less than direct involvement may also be enough. Moreover, s.9E(4) provides that "conduct" includes omission. Thus, in cases where the defendant was not directly involved in the breach, there is scope for the court to fashion standards of conduct and further develop the positive, non-delegable obligation on directors to keep themselves informed of the company's affairs and to supervise its activities,[24]

[22] OFT, *Competition Disqualification Orders—Guidance* (May 2003) at paras 4.25–4.26.

[23] OFT Press Release 72/08 "Three imprisoned in first OFT criminal prosecution for bid rigging". See also *R. v Whittle* [2008] EWCA Crim 2560, especially at [14]. The custodial sentences were reduced on appeal. There was no appeal against the making of, or duration of, the disqualification orders.

[24] See, e.g. *Re Barings Plc, Secretary of State for Trade and Industry v Baker (No.5)* [1999] 1 B.C.L.C. 433.

albeit with particular reference to compliance with competition law. As with CDDA ss.6 and 8, the issue of whether or not a director's conduct makes him unfit will ultimately boil down to a question of judgment in individual cases. In practice, it is suggested that the courts are likely to refine and apply the broad test of probity and competence that has emerged in cases under CDDA ss.6 and 8.[25]

6–12 The court is permitted, but not required, by CDDA s.9A(5)(b) to consider the defendant's conduct as a director of a company in connection with any other breach of competition law (as defined in CDDA s.9A(4)). This allows the court to consider the cumulative effect of the principal conduct (falling within CDDA s.9A(2)–(3)) and similar conduct in relation to other companies. The provision is therefore analogous to s.6 under which the court can take into account the director's conduct in the lead company (being the company that has triggered the court's jurisdiction under s.6(1)(a)) together with his conduct as a director of any other company or companies.[26] However, unlike s.6 there must be a close correlation between the misconduct alleged in that in each case it must relate to one or more breaches of competition law. It seems that the court may "have regard" to such parallel conduct in at least two different ways. First, the mere fact of previous involvement may be relevant to the conduct in the company relied upon under s.9A(2)). For example, evidence of the director's previous involvement may suggest that he should have learned from that previous experience thus rendering the conduct in the s.9A(2) company more serious. In this example, the separate conduct is relied upon as throwing light upon or directly informing the nature of the main misconduct relied upon under s.9A(2) and (3). The second way in which parallel conduct may be relevant is as additional unfit conduct, just as under s.6 the court is entitled to take into account conduct in relation to companies other than the "lead" company.[27] The interesting question is the extent to which conduct as a director of a company in connection with any other breach of competition law may itself be taken into account as self-standing but additional misconduct which can merit either an overall increase in the period of disqualification or, if disqualification is not justified in relation to the main company identified in relation to s.9A(2) and (3), whether it alone can ground jurisdiction to disqualify. It is suggested that if the conduct in relation to the second or ancillary company itself falls within s.9A(2) and (3) there is no problem. In the language used in the context of s.6, that company can be treated as another "lead" company. Accordingly, disqualification will be compulsory if the court considers that the conditions of s.9A(2) and (3) are met in relation to that company. Further, such misconduct can be taken together with conduct relating to any other company that meets the conditions of s.9A(2) and (3) in fixing any overall period of disqualification. However, in the unlikely event that misconduct in such other company does not meet the s.9A(2) and (3) conditions then it is suggested that such misconduct could not of itself found an order under s.9A.

[25] See text in 4–22 to 4–28.
[26] See text from 3–106.
[27] See text from 3–106.

6–13 CDDA s.9A(5)(c) expressly states that the court must not have regard to the matters mentioned in Sch.1 when considering whether the defendant's conduct as a director makes him unfit for the purposes of s.9A(3). Thus, the factors to which the court must have particular regard in determining unfitness under CDDA ss.6 and 8 cannot be taken into account in determining unfitness under CDDA s.9A. The implication is that, under s.9A, the only conduct as a director which can be taken into account for the purposes of determining whether or not the director is unfit is conduct in relation to a relevant breach of competition law.

6–14 An interesting question is whether a court deciding an application under s.6 or 8 could take into account a director's conduct in relation to a breach of competition law in addition to the matters in Sch.1 to which the court must have regard by virtue of CDDA s.9(1). It is well settled in the jurisprudence on ss.6 and 8 that the matters in Sch.1 are not exhaustive and that other conduct not specifically mentioned in the Schedule can be considered.[28] Bearing in mind that a director's unfitness can be determined solely by reference to his conduct in relation to a breach of competition law under s.9A, it is suggested that there is no reason in principle why a finding of unfit conduct under s.6 or 8 could not be based, in part, on such conduct. Clearly, there is a potential for overlap. However, where the only complaint against the director concerns his conduct in relation to a breach of competition law, it is suggested that in most cases any disqualification proceedings should be brought under s.9A and not under s.6 or 8, even if those provisions have been triggered.

6–15 The approach of the regulator to the issue of managerial unfitness under CDDA s.9A is considered further below in the discussion concerning the OFT guidance.

PRELIMINARIES, PRACTICE AND PROCEDURE

Standing

6–16 CDDA s.9A(10) provides that an application for a disqualification order under s.9A can be made "by the OFT or by a specified regulator". According to s.9E(2), each of the following sectoral regulators is a "specified regulator" for the purposes of a breach of competition law in relation to a matter in respect of which he or it has a function:

(1) The Office of Communications.[29]
(2) The Gas and Electricity Markets Authority.
(3) The Water Services Regulation Authority.[30]

[28] See text in 4–46 to 4–48.

[29] Substituted for the former reference to the Director General of Telecommunications by the Communications Act 2003 s.406 and Sch.17 para.83 from December 29, 2003: see the Office of Communications Act 2002 (Commencement No.3) and Communications Act 2003 (Commencement No.2) Order 2003 (SI 2003/3142).

[30] Substituted for the former reference to the Director General of Water Services by the Water Act 2003 s.101(1), Sch.7 para.25 from April 1, 2006: see the Water Act 2003 (Commencement No.5, Transitional Provisions and Savings) Order 2005 (SI 2005/2714).

(4) The Office of Rail Regulation.[31]
(5) The Civil Aviation Authority.

By virtue of s.9D, the Secretary of State may make regulations for the purpose of co-ordinating the performance of functions under the competition disqualification regime where they are exercisable concurrently by two or more regulators. To date no such regulations have been made.

6–17 The effect of s.9E(3) is that an application for a competition disqualification order must be made to the High Court or (in Scotland) the Court of Session. In the light of amendments to the Disqualification Rules, the procedure is similar to that for applications under ss.6 and 8. Procedure is considered generally in Ch.7.

Competition investigations

6–18 Where the regulator has reasonable grounds for suspecting that a breach of competition law has occurred, CDDA s.9C(1) gives it power to carry out an investigation for the purpose of deciding whether to make an application for a competition disqualification order under s.9A. For the purposes of such an investigation, ss.26 to 30 of the Competition Act 1998, which confer powers on the OFT to gather information relating to suspected infringements of the Chapter 1 and Chapter 2 prohibitions, have direct application.[32]

Pre-action procedure: the section 9C(4) notice

6–19 If, as a result of an investigation under s.9C, it is decided to apply under s.9A for the making of a disqualification order then, before applying for the competition disqualification order, the regulator must give notice to the person likely to be affected by the application and give that person an opportunity to make representations (CDDA s.9C(4)). The OFT guidance states that the following information will be included in a s.9C(4) notice[33]:

(1) that the regulator proposes to apply for a competition disqualification order against the person;
(2) the consequences for that person of a competition disqualification order being made against him or her;
(3) the grounds of the proposed application;
(4) the evidence which the regulator intends to submit to the court in support of its proposed application;
(5) that the regulator will, if requested, allow the person to have access to the file relating to the proposed application (subject to any issues of confidentiality);

[31] Substituted for the Rail Regulator by the Railways and Transport Safety Act 2003 s.16 and Sch.2 para.19(j) from July 5, 2004: see the Railways and Transport Safety Act 2003 (Commencement No.2) Order 2004 (SI 2004/827).
[32] On these powers, see further OFT, *Powers of Investigation* (December 2004).
[33] OFT, *Competition Disqualification Orders—Guidance* (May 2003) at para.5.2.

(6) that the person has the right under CDDA s.9C(4)(b) to make written, and if requested, oral representations before the regulator makes the proposed application;
(7) a deadline for indicating to the regulator whether the person wishes to make written representations and the date by which oral representations must be requested;
(8) that if the regulator has not heard anything from the person by the stated deadline, an application for a competition disqualification order may be made forthwith;
(9) that any representations may be prepared or made by a legal adviser;
(10) that the person may wish to offer the regulator a competition disqualification undertaking, which if accepted, would obviate the need for proceedings[34];
(11) the length of a competition disqualification undertaking likely to be accepted by the regulator;
(12) the costs incurred by the regulator to date and an assurance that, if a competition disqualification undertaking is offered and accepted, that the regulator will not usually seek to recover any costs from the person;
(13) a statement that once an application has been made to the court, the award of costs will be at the court's discretion and that the court will usually award costs against the unsuccessful party.

The pre-action procedure described is analogous to that followed by the Secretary of State under s.16 in relation to other forms of civil disqualification proceeding.[35] However, the proposed procedure goes far wider than that required by s.9C in two respects. First, the OFT guidance suggests that the procedure will be followed in all cases where an application for a competition disqualification order has been decided on, whereas s.9C(4) strictly only applies where the decision to apply follows on from a s.9C investigation. Secondly, the procedure envisages that the recipient of the notice will be given far greater information than is provided for by s.9C(4) (and more information than is customarily provided by the Insolvency Service in cases that may lead to disqualification under s.6 or s.8).

Proving breaches of competition law

6–20 Procedure in civil disqualification proceedings (including competition disqualification under s.9A) is dealt with generally in Ch.7. One question that may yet prove a fertile source of litigation is the extent to which the applicant for a competition disqualification order will be required by the courts to prove a relevant breach of competition law. Given the OFT guidance, it may well be that a defendant will not consider it worthwhile to contest again the issue of whether his actions amounted to a relevant breach of competition law.[36] On the other hand, there is likely to be some scope for litigation on this point. Where the finding of

[34] Competition disqualification undertakings are considered briefly below in 6–35 and generally in Ch.9.
[35] See text in 7–31.
[36] However, note the proposed change to such guidance, considered further at 6–34A below.

a breach of competition law is embodied in a decision of a court or other tribunal in proceedings to which the defendant was party, it is likely that an estoppel will operate against the defendant to disqualification proceedings, based upon the role of the regulator in those proceedings and/or an argument that the applicant is "privy" to the person taking the relevant action leading to the decision. However, where the decision is that of the regulator itself or where the defendant was not party to the earlier proceedings,[37] there may be room for argument that the regulator can be required to prove the breach (or breaches) of competition law to the satisfaction of the disqualifying court and that it cannot simply rely upon the earlier decision.[38] Any terms on which any earlier proceedings, in their widest sense, were compromised or any rights of challenge, or appeal, were not pursued will clearly be of great importance in this context.

The OFT guidance

6–21 The OFT guidance on competition disqualification orders was published in May 2003 just before the relevant provisions of the Enterprise Act 2002 were brought into force. The guidance has no legal status but it gives a useful insight into the regulator's approach to the competition disqualification regime. Clearly, the guidance may be revised in future in the light of experience and, accordingly, it does not bind the various regulators. In this respect, at the time of writing, the OFT was consulting on proposed changes to the guidance with the stated aim of maximising the deterrent effect of the competition disqualification regime.[39] The effect of the proposed changes on the existing guidance is considered briefly in 6–34A below.

6–22 The guidance states that the regulator will follow a five-step process when deciding to apply for a competition disqualification order.[40] It will:

(1) consider whether an undertaking which is a company of which the person is a director has committed a breach of competition law;
(2) consider whether a financial penalty has been imposed for the breach;
(3) consider whether the company in question benefited from leniency;

[37] Although in this context, see the line taken by the courts in relation to directors being saddled with the court's findings in public interest winding up petitions to which they were not party where issues of costs have arisen: *Re Aurum Marketing Ltd (in liquidation)* [2000] 2 B.C.L.C. 645; *Re North West Holdings Plc, Secretary of State for Trade and Industry v Backhouse* [2001] EWCA Civ 67, [2001] 1 B.C.L.C. 468, *Brampton Manor (Leisure) v McLean* [2007] EWHC 3340 (Ch), [2009] B.C.C. 30 and also the line taken by the courts in relation to the defendant's ability to challenge the validity of the company's entry into a relevant insolvent regime in disqualification proceedings under CDDA s.6: see *Secretary of State for Trade and Industry v Jabble* [1998] 1 B.C.L.C. 598.

[38] *Re Queens Moathouses Plc, Secretary of State for Trade and Industry v Bairstow* [2003] EWCA Civ 321, [2004] Ch. 1. See further *Re David M Aaron (Personal Financial Planners) Ltd, Secretary of State for Business, Enterprise & Regulatory Reform v Aaron* [2009] 1 B.C.L.C. 55 and text from 7–126 and 7–137.

[39] OFT, *Competition Disqualification Orders—Proposed changes to the OFT's guidance* (OFT1111con, August 2009). The consultation was scheduled to close on November 20, 2009. It builds on a report carried out for the OFT by Deloitte concerning the deterrent effect of competition enforcement which was published in November 2007 (OFT962).

[40] OFT, *Competition Disqualification Orders—Guidance* (May 2003) at para. 4.2.

(4) consider the extent of the director's responsibility for the breach of competition law, either through action or omission;
(5) have regard to any aggravating and mitigating factors.

To assist in its deliberations, the regulator may use the information gathering powers in the Competition Act 1998.[41]

Breach of competition law

6–23 As discussed above, a competition disqualification order can only considered if the company of which the defendant is a director has committed a triggering breach of competition law.[42] In cases where the relevant undertaking is a group, or part of a group, of companies, the OFT has indicated that it will normally look first at the company or companies which directly committed the breach and apply its five stage test to the directors of that company or those companies. In the case of a parent company, the OFT will consider whether any of its directors, if not appointed directors of the relevant subsidiary which directly committed the breach, were shadow or de facto directors of that subsidiary and, if any were, then apply its five-stage test to such persons.[43]

6–24 The guidance states that the regulator will only apply for orders in respect of breaches of competition law that have been proven in decisions or judgments (as the case may be) of the OFT, a specified regulator, the European Commission, the Competition Appeal Tribunal[44] or the Court of Justice of the European Communities (including the Court of First Instance).[45] In the following cases, the regulator will not apply for an order:

(1) Where a breach of competition law proven in a decision of the European Commission or a judgment of the European Court of Justice does not or did not have an actual or potential effect on trade in the United Kingdom.[46]
(2) Where the breach or breaches of competition law ended before June 20, 2003 being the date on which CDDA ss.9A–9E came into force.[47]
(3) Where the decision or judgment relating to the breach remains subject to appeal, meaning either that the deadline for appeal against the decision or judgment has not yet passed, or that an appeal has been made, but has not yet been determined.[48]

[41] CDDA, ss.9C(1)–(2) and 6–18 above.
[42] CDDA, ss.9A(2), (4) and 6–07 above.
[43] OFT, *Competition Disqualification Orders—Guidance* (May 2003), paras 4.4–4.5.
[44] Established by Pt 2 of the Enterprise Act 2002 with effect from April 1, 2003: see the Enterprise Act 2002 (Commencement No.2, Transitional and Transitory Provisions and Savings) Order 2003 (SI 2003/766). However, note the proposed change to the guidance discussed further at 6–34A below.
[45] OFT, *Competition Disqualification Orders—Guidance* (May 2003) at para.4.6.
[46] OFT, *Competition Disqualification Orders—Guidance* (May 2003) at para.4.7.
[47] OFT, *Competition Disqualification Orders—Guidance* (May 2003) at para.4.8. However, breaches which started before June 20, 2003, but which continued on or after that date may still trigger an application.
[48] OFT, *Competition Disqualification Orders—Guidance* (May 2003) at para.4.9.

In effect, the regulator will only consider what amount to serious and proven breaches of competition law. It is, perhaps, surprising that the OFT should have decided to limit disqualification applications to cases where the breach has or had an actual or potential effect on trade in the United Kingdom.[49]

Financial penalty[50]

6–25 The regulator will not consider an application for a competition disqualification order to be appropriate unless a financial penalty has been imposed in respect of the breach and, in the event of an appeal, upheld in whole or part.[51] This presumably goes to the seriousness of the breach.

Leniency[52]

6–26 The regulator will not apply for a competition disqualification order against any current director of a company which has benefited from leniency in respect of the activities to which the grant of leniency relates.[53] "Leniency" means the immunity from, or any reduction in, financial penalty as described either in the OFT's guidance on penalties[54] or in the European Commission's fining notice.[55]

6–27 Similarly, the regulator will not apply for a competition disqualification order against any beneficiary of a no-action letter in respect of the cartel activities specified in that letter.[56] No-action letters grant the recipient immunity from prosecution for the cartel offence in s.188 of the Enterprise Act 2002 and are designed to encourage individuals who may have committed the offence to come forward with information and co-operate fully with the OFT.[57] Again, this is somewhat surprising. The grounds justifying a grant of immunity from criminal proceedings would, it seems to the authors, not automatically in all cases justify immunity from civil disqualification proceedings.

Extent of responsibility[58]

6–28 The greater the degree of the director's responsibility for, or involvement in, a breach of competition law, the greater the likelihood that the regulator will apply for a competition disqualification order against that person. The guidance states that the regulator:

[49] Suppose that the company in question which was furthering the improper purpose outside the jurisdiction is, in fact, English registered. It seems odd that the UK should, in this respect, be a safe haven for directors who breach EC law elsewhere in the Community. Consider also *Re Westminster Property Management Ltd (No.2), Official Receiver v Stern (No.2)* [2001] B.C.C. 305 (permission to appeal refused: [2001] EWCA Civ 111, [2002] B.C.C. 937).

[50] However, note the proposed change to the guidance discussed further at 6–34A below.

[51] OFT, *Competition Disqualification Orders—Guidance* (May 2003) at para.4.10.

[52] However, note the proposed change to the guidance discussed further at 6–34A below.

[53] OFT, *Competition Disqualification Orders—Guidance* (May 2003) at paras 4.11–4.14.

[54] OFT, *Guidance as to the Appropriate Amount of a Penalty* (December 2004). See further the OFT's guidance entitled *Leniency in Cartel Cases* (March 2005).

[55] *Notice on Immunity from Fines and Reduction of Fines in Cartel Cases* O.J. 2002 C45/3.

[56] OFT, *Competition Disqualification Orders—Guidance* (May 2003) at para.4.27. See also OFT, *The Cartel Offence: Guidance on the Issue of No-Action Letters for Individuals* (April 2003).

[57] The immunity is a statutory immunity: see Enterprise Act 2002 s.190(4).

[58] However, note the proposed change to the guidance discussed further at 6–34A below.

(1) is likely to apply for a competition disqualification order against a director who has been directly involved in the breach;
(2) is quite likely to apply for a competition disqualification order against a director whom it considers improperly failed to take corrective action against the breach;
(3) does not rule out applying for a competition disqualification order against a director whom it considers, taking into account that director's role and responsibilities, to have failed to keep himself or herself sufficiently informed of the company's activities which constituted the breach of competition law (though whether an application is made in these circumstances will depend on the regulator's priorities).[59]

Direct involvement

6–29 Evidence of direct involvement in a breach of competition law is, in the view of the regulator, evidence that the director, either alone or with other persons:

(1) actively took steps to carry out the infringement (for example, by drawing up a list of the company's prices and sending them to a competitor so as to enable the competitor to align its prices);
(2) planned, devised, approved or encouraged the activity of the undertaking which caused the breach;
(3) ordered or pressured those identified as having a direct or indirect role in the breach to engage in the activity causing the breach;
(4) attended meetings (internal or external) in which the activity constituting the breach either occurred or was discussed (or both);
(5) directed, ordered or pressured staff of the undertaking to attend meetings (internal or external) for the purpose of participating in or discussing the activity constituting the breach;
(6) ordered, encouraged or advocated retaliation against other undertakings who were reluctant to or refused to participate in the activity constituting the breach.[60]

The key consideration is whether the director had an active role in causing his or her company to carry out or agree to carry out the activity constituting the breach.[61]

Failure to take corrective action

6–30 Where there is no evidence that the director was directly involved in the breach, the regulator is still "quite likely" to apply for a competition disqualification order if there is evidence that:

(1) knowing or having reasonable grounds to suspect that persons within the company were directly or indirectly involved in the conduct which consti-

[59] OFT, *Competition Disqualification Orders—Guidance* (May 2003) at para.4.16.
[60] OFT, *Competition Disqualification Orders—Guidance* (May 2003) at para.4.17.
[61] OFT, *Competition Disqualification Orders—Guidance* (May 2003) at para.4.18.

tuted a breach, the director failed to take reasonable steps to halt the activity in question;

(2) the director authorised or approved expenditure of funds used to finance any activity relating to the breach, knowing or having reasonable grounds to suspect that those funds would be used for the activity and that the activity related to a breach.[62]

Failure to keep sufficiently informed

6–31 When considering whether to proceed on the basis that the director failed to keep himself or herself sufficiently informed in relation to the company's activities which constituted the breach, the guidance states that the regulator is likely, among other things, to consider the following factors:

(1) The director's role in the company;
(2) The relationship of the director's role to those directly responsible for the breach;
(3) The general knowledge, skill and experience actually possessed by the director in question and that which should have been possessed by a person in his or her position;
(4) The information relating to the breach which was available to the director prior to the breach.[63]

These factors reflect the approach taken by the courts in setting the standard of the directors' duty of care and skill at common law and in cases decided under CDDA ss.6 and 8.[64] The regulator does not expect directors to have specific expertise in competition law but does expect directors to appreciate that compliance with competition law is a crucial matter and to know, at least, that price-fixing, market sharing and bid-rigging agreements are likely to be in breach.[65]

Aggravating and mitigating factors

6–32 The guidance states that the presence of aggravating or mitigating factors may correspondingly increase or reduce the likelihood that the regulator will apply for a competition disqualification order.[66]

6–33 Aggravating factors include evidence that the director:

(1) has been directly or indirectly involved in breaches of competition law in the past;

[62] OFT, *Competition Disqualification Orders—Guidance* (May 2003) at para.4.19.
[63] OFT, *Competition Disqualification Orders—Guidance* (May 2003) at para.4.20.
[64] See, e.g. *Re Barings Plc, Secretary of State for Trade and Industry v Baker (No.5)* [1999] 1 B.C.L.C. 433. Compare also Companies Act 2006 s.174.
[65] OFT, *Competition Disqualification Orders—Guidance* (May 2003) at para.4.21.
[66] OFT, *Competition Disqualification Orders—Guidance* (May 2003) at para.4.22.

(2) destroyed or advised others to destroy any records relating to any breach of competition law with the objective of concealing the breach;
(3) obstructed or impeded any investigation by the regulator or the European Commission into any breach of competition law or attempted or advised others to do so;
(4) during any investigation of a breach of competition law, unlawfully refused or advised refusing to grant access to investigators from the regulator or the European Commission to any part of the company's premises;
(5) ordered, encouraged or advocated continued participation in the breach following commencement of an investigation into the breach by the regulator or the European Commission.[67]

6–34 Mitigating factors include evidence indicating that:

(1) the undertaking committed the breach as a result of coercion by another undertaking (for example, where the breach was committed as the only perceived way to avoid threatened retaliation by a dominant undertaking);
(2) there was genuine uncertainty prior to the breach as to whether the infringing activity constituted a breach;
(3) the director contributed to the company taking quick remedial steps when the breach was brought to his or her attention, including the implementation or revision of a competition law compliance programme;
(4) the director took disciplinary action against the employees responsible for the breach;
(5) the director was himself or herself under severe internal pressure (such as from controlling shareholders of the company or directors of a parent company) either to be involved in the breach or to allow it to occur (though this would not embrace pressure to meet sales or profitability targets).[68]

Obviously, the aggravating and mitigating factors mentioned in the guidance cannot and should not be regarded as exhaustive.

6–34A In a consultation exercise that was ongoing at the time of writing,[69] the OFT was proposing a number of changes to the guidance that, if implemented, would impact on each stage of the five-step process outlined above as follows:

(1) The regulator would be allowed to apply for competition disqualification orders in exceptional cases where the relevant breach of competition law has not been proven in a decision or judgment (as the case may be) of the OFT, a

[67] OFT, *Competition Disqualification Orders—Guidance* (May 2003) at para.4.23. It should be recalled that CDDA, s.9A(5)(b) allows the court to take into account the defendant's conduct as a director in connection with breaches of competition law other than and in addition to the breach that triggered the court's jurisdiction: see 6–12.

[68] OFT, *Competition Disqualification Orders—Guidance* (May 2003) at para.4.24.

[69] OFT, *Competition Disqualification Orders—Proposed changes to the OFT's guidance* (OFT1111con, August 2009).

specified regulator, the European Commission, the Competition Appeal Tribunal or the European Court of Justice (e.g. where a decision or judgment is subject to appeal only in relation to the quantum of a fine imposed and not to the finding of infringement).

(2) The regulator would be allowed to apply for competition disqualification orders in limited circumstances even where a financial penalty has not been (or not yet been) imposed.

(3) The regulator would be allowed to apply for competition disqualification orders against directors of companies that have benefited from so-called "Type C" leniency or a reduction in fine.

(4) The regulator would decide whether to apply for a competition disqualification order by reference to the facts and circumstances of each individual case and the evidence available, rather than being more likely to pursue cases in which the director was directly involved in the breach. The implication is that the regulator may be more likely to apply for a competition disqualification order in cases where there is evidence that the director had reasonable grounds to suspect the conduct constituted the breach but took no steps to prevent it and in cases where the director did not know, but ought to have known, that the conduct constituted the breach. This proposed change is designed to increase the regulatory focus on cases where directors could have taken corrective action and thereby encourage directors to take positive steps to uncover potentially anti-competitive behaviour or monitor their companies' competition law compliance.

COMPETITION DISQUALIFICATION UNDERTAKINGS

6–35 As long as the conditions in CDDA s.9B(1) are satisfied, the regulator may accept a competition disqualification undertaking from a person instead of applying for or proceeding with an application for a competition disqualification order. Competition disqualification undertakings are considered further in Ch.9, which considers the various ways in which court proceedings in civil disqualification cases can be compromised or avoided altogether.

CONCLUSION

6–36 Although s.9A does not expressly set out a public interest criterion to be applied by the applicant in determining whether to bring proceedings for a competition disqualification order, such a criterion will apply by virtue of the public law nature of the function in question. It is hard to avoid the conclusion that the general guidance issued by the OFT as to the circumstances in which competition disqualification applications are likely to be launched amounts, with limited exceptions,[70] to a

[70] For example, in cases where immunity from criminal proceedings has been granted: see 6–27.

general proposition that the more serious the misconduct in question then the more likely it is that proceedings will be launched. In focusing on the seriousness of the misconduct, it is unclear whether the guidance is suggesting that resources will not be expended on proceedings in cases where the misconduct is such that the period of disqualification is likely to be short. It is questionable whether any such restriction is necessarily desirable from the viewpoint of public policy. The statistics show that the vast majority of cases brought under CDDA s.6 are brought in relation to misconduct that justifies disqualification for a period within the lowest bracket of two to five years. The further point that can be made is that the guidance is silent on the wider public interest factors that will be taken into account in determining whether or not to launch proceedings. In this respect, the guidance is nothing like as comprehensive as, for example, that contained in the Code for Crown Prosecutors issued under s.10 of the Prosecution of Offences Act 1985 which requires a range of factors (not merely the seriousness of the offence) to be taken into account.[71]

[71] Crown Prosecutors must be satisfied that there is enough evidence to provide a reasonable prospect of conviction (the evidential stage) but must also consider whether a prosecution is in the public interest balancing a range of non-exhaustive factors (the public interest stage).

CHAPTER 7

PROCEDURE AND EVIDENCE IN CIVIL DISQUALIFICATION PROCEEDINGS

INTRODUCTION

7–01 This chapter covers the following subject matter:

(1) Court procedure in civil disqualification proceedings (other than in relation to reviews and appeals which are dealt with in Ch.13). In this context, civil procedure relates to any application for a disqualification order in the civil courts and so includes material that is relevant not only to CDDA ss.6–9E but also to disqualification proceedings under CDDA ss.2, 3, 4 and 10.
(2) Particular points regarding evidence in civil disqualification proceedings. However, this chapter does not purport to provide a comprehensive account of the law of evidence.

7–02 The focus by defendants on procedural rules as a means of escaping disqualification or, at the least and in some cases, an expensive contested trial[1] means that the Civil Procedure Rules ("CPR") and the Human Rights Act 1998 have proved a fruitful source for legal argument. The Civil Procedure Rules have now been in force for some years but, as in other areas, their impact is still being felt in the disqualification context.[2] While, in a general sense the CPR represented a decisive shift towards a new culture of civil litigation and a break with past practice, many of the cases decided under the old rules are good indicators of problems that are likely to arise and recur in disqualification proceedings under the present system. Furthermore, the applicable procedure whereby disqualification proceedings were brought quickly before the court for directions, coupled with judicial concerns about the delays and costs of such proceedings meant that, in practice, the exercise of case management techniques was common prior to the advent of the CPR. As regards the Human Rights Act, it has all too often been portrayed by some politicians as a licence to litigate. Unfortunately in the disqualification sphere there may be some truth in such a characterisation. Articles 6 and 8 of the European Convention on Human Rights have frequently been invoked in the disqualification arena as a ground for saying that previous decisions or legal

[1] A good illustration of the former is the many procedural battles waged by Mr Eastaway in connection with the Blackspur disqualification proceedings.

[2] See, e.g. *Re Finelist Ltd, Secretary of State for Trade and Industry v Swan* [2003] EWHC 1780 (Ch), [2004] B.C.C. 877.

principles need to be reconsidered.[3] In many, but not all, cases the court has found, perhaps not surprisingly, that a previous line of authority remained good authority after the Human Rights Act. Furthermore, even prior to the Human Rights Act, the European Convention had played a role in English law. Any idea that the pursuit of justice or the observance of human rights are objectives that were wholly foreign and novel to English justice and the English legal system prior to the adoption of the CPR (including the overriding objective) and the enactment of the Human Rights Act would be a mistaken one.

THE RELEVANT COURTS

7–03 In a number of cases the CDDA expressly identifies the civil courts in which proceedings must be commenced. They are as follows:

(1) Section 2(2)(a): any court having jurisdiction to wind up the company in relation to which the relevant offence was committed.[4]
(2) Section 3(4): any court having jurisdiction to wind up any of the companies in relation to which the relevant offence or other default has been or is alleged to have been committed.
(3) Section 4(2): any court having jurisdiction to wind up any of the companies in relation to which the relevant offence or other default has been or is alleged to have been committed.
(4) Section 6(3), as amended by the Insolvency Act 2000[5] and the Enterprise Act 2002,[6] defines "the court" for the purposes of ss.6 and 7 as follows:

    (a) where the company in question is being or has been wound up by the court, that court;
    (b) where the company in question is being or has been wound up voluntarily, any court which has or (as the case may be) had jurisdiction to wind it up;
    (c) in any case where neither (a) nor (b) above applies, but an administrator or administrative receiver has at any time been appointed in respect of the company in question, any court which has jurisdiction to wind it up.

    These provisions are supplemented by s.6(3A) and 6(3B).

[3] See, e.g. the unsuccessful attempt to rely upon arts 6 and 8 of the European Convention to reverse the decision of a Scottish court—itself following the English court in *Re Cedac Ltd, Secretary of State for Trade and Industry v Langridge* [1991] Ch. 402 which decided that CDDA s.16 is directory rather than mandatory—in *Secretary of State for Business, Enterprise and Regulatory Reform v Smith* [2009] B.C.C. 497.
[4] The jurisdiction to wind up companies is considered further at 7–05 below.
[5] Section 8 and Sch.4.
[6] Sch.17 paras 40–41.

(5) Section 8(3): the High Court or (in Scotland) the Court of Session.[7]

(6) Section 8A(3) (in relation to the variation or discharge of undertakings)[8]: in the case of an undertaking given under s.9B "the court" means the High Court or (in Scotland) the Court of Session and in any other case has the same meaning as in s.7(2) or 8 (as the case may be).

(7) Section 9E (in relation to competition disqualification): the High Court or (in Scotland) the Court of Session.

(8) Section 10: the court making the relevant declaration under s.213 or s.214 of the Insolvency Act 1986.

(9) Section 11 (in relation to an application for permission to act where the applicant is an undischarged bankrupt, a person in relation to whom a moratorium period under a debt relief order applies, or a person who is subject to bankruptcy restrictions or debt relief restrictions): the court by which the person was adjudged bankrupt.[9]

(10) Section 12: the court making the relevant order under s.429(2)(b) of the Insolvency Act 1986 revoking an administration order under Pt VI of the County Courts Act 1984.

(11) Section 17, as amended by the Insolvency Act 2000[10] and the Enterprise Act 2002,[11] defines "the court" for the purposes of an application for permission to act notwithstanding disqualification as follows:

(a) where a person is subject to a disqualification order made by a court having jurisdiction to wind up companies,[12] any application for permission for the purposes of s.1(1)(a) shall be made to that court[13];

(b) where a person is subject to a disqualification order made either under s.2 by a court other than a court with jurisdiction to wind up companies (i.e. a criminal court) or under s.5, any application for permission for the purposes of s.1(1)(a) shall be made to any court which, at the time at which the order was made, had jurisdiction to wind up the company (or companies, if more than one) in relation to which the offence (or any of the offences) related[14];

[7] This provision has been interpreted by the High Court as referring to the winding up jurisdiction of the two courts with the consequence that disqualification proceedings in relation to a company registered in England and Wales will take place in the High Court while disqualification proceedings in relation to a company registered in Scotland will take place in Scotland: see *Re Helene Plc, Secretary of State for Trade and Industry v Forsyth* [2000] 2 B.C.L.C. 249. The reasoning supporting this interpretation is strengthened further by amendments since made to CDDA s.17 dealt with in the main text below.

[8] The present s.8A(3) was inserted by the Enterprise Act 2002 s.204(5) with effect from June 20, 2003.

[9] CDDA s.11(2). There is no express provision in s.11 setting out which court has jurisdiction to consider applications for permission by persons in relation to whom a moratorium under a debt relief order applies or who are subject to debt relief restrictions. Strictly, such persons are not "adjudged bankrupt". The authors' view is that the relevant court is the court having jurisdiction to make orders in relation to debt relief orders as provided for by s.251M of the Insolvency Act 1986: see further 15–80.

[10] Section 8 and Sch.4.

[11] Section 204(8)–(10).

[12] Which would include the High Court in the case of disqualification orders made pursuant to CDDA ss.8 or 9A.

[13] Section 17(1).

[14] Section 17(2).

(c) where a person is subject to a disqualification undertaking accepted at any time under s.7 or 8, any application for permission for the purposes of s.1A(1)(a) shall be made to any court to which, if the Secretary of State had applied for a disqualification order under the relevant section in question at that time, his application could have been made[15];
(d) where a person is subject to a disqualification undertaking accepted at any time under s.9B, any application for permission for the purposes of s.9B(4) must be made to the High Court or (in Scotland) the Court of Session.

In broad terms, the main changes made by the Insolvency Act 2000 in this area have had the effect of dealing with certain unsatisfactory gaps in the previous language of CDDA s.6. In addition, the jurisdiction to grant permission to act notwithstanding disqualification is now vested in the civil court (broadly speaking) that imposed the original disqualification or (in the case of undertakings or disqualifications imposed by a criminal court) in the civil court that could have imposed the disqualification rather than, as previously, in the court having relevant jurisdiction over the company in relation to which permission is sought. The Insolvency Act 2000 also removes the anomaly that under the old dispensation, the court hearing (for example) an application for a disqualification order under CDDA s.6 would not necessarily have jurisdiction to grant permission to act notwithstanding disqualification in the same proceedings.[16] The Enterprise Act 2000 largely accommodates changes flowing from the introduction of competition disqualification, bankruptcy restrictions and the revamped administration procedure in Sch.B1 of the Insolvency Act 1986.

7–04 No express provision is made in the CDDA as regards applications under ss.7(4) or 15 of the CDDA. Jurisdiction in relation to proceedings under s.15 is not therefore subject to any special rules. However, as regards applications under s.7(4) the matter is further regulated by the relevant procedural rules and the applicable practice direction. Rule 2(5) of the Insolvent Companies (Disqualification of Unfit Directors) Proceedings Rules 1987 ("the Disqualification Rules")[17] provides that the Insolvency Rules 1986 shall apply to an application to enforce any duty arising under s.7(4) of the CDDA made against a person who at the date of the application is acting as liquidator, administrator or administrative receiver. It would seem to follow from this, taken in conjunction with para.18.1(3) of the Disqualification Practice Direction, that in such cases the court with s.7(4) jurisdiction is that with jurisdiction in relation to the relevant insolvency proceedings applicable to the

[15] Section 17(3). In the context this must refer to the Secretary of State's application.

[16] A difficulty associated in particular with the county courts: see, e.g. *Re Britannia Homes Centres Ltd, Official Receiver v McCahill* [2001] 2 B.C.L.C. 63 where the court managed to circumvent the problem but only by recourse to unsatisfactory reasoning. On the desirability of the proceedings for substantive disqualification and any application for permission to act being heard together, see *Re Dicetrade Ltd, Secretary of State for Trade and Industry v Worth* [1994] 2 B.C.L.C. 113; *Re TLL Realisations Ltd, Secretary of State for Trade and Industry v Collins* [1998] B.C.C. 998 and discussion in the text from 15–67.

[17] SI 1987/2023 as subsequently amended by the Insolvent Companies (Disqualification of Unfit Directors) Proceedings (Amendment) Rules 2007 (SI 2007/1906) with effect from August 6, 2007.

insolvent company in question. In other cases there is power to apply within any existing disqualification proceedings or by way of CPR Pt 8 claim form.[18]

Jurisdiction to wind up companies

7–05 The jurisdiction of the courts to wind up companies is established by s.117 of the Insolvency Act 1986. The position, subject to art.3 of the EC Regulation on Insolvency Proceedings,[19] is as follows:

(1) The High Court has jurisdiction to wind up any company registered in England and Wales.[20]
(2) A county court has jurisdiction to wind up a company (concurrently with the High Court) where two conditions are satisfied:
    (a) the company's paid-up share capital must not exceed £120,000[21];
    (b) the registered office of the company must have been situated within the district of the relevant county court[22] for the longest period (compared with any other place where the company may have had its registered office) within the six months immediately preceding the presentation of the winding up petition.[23]

However, in relation to applications for disqualification orders under CDDA s.6, these provisions must be read in the light of CDDA s.6(3A). By virtue of s.6(3A), ss.117 and 120 of the Insolvency Act 1986 apply as if the references in the definitions of "registered office" to the presentation of the petition for winding up were references:

(1) in cases under CDDA s.6(3)(b), to the passing of the resolution for voluntary winding up;
(2) in cases under CDDA s.6(3)(c), to the appointment of the administrator or (as the case may be) the appointment of the administrative receiver.

Proceedings under CDDA s.6

7–06 In cases where the relevant company is, or was, in compulsory liquidation, the court in which the company is being, or has been, wound up will have jurisdiction under s.6. In cases where the company is not (or was not) in compulsory

[18] Disqualification Practice Direction, para.18.1.

[19] Council Regulation (EC) No 1346/2000 of May 29, 2000 effective from May 31, 2002. See also Insolvency Act 1986 s.117(7) and the Insolvency Act 1986 (Amendment) (No.2) Regulations 2002 (SI 2002/1240).

[20] Winding up jurisdiction in Scotland is governed by Insolvency Act 1986 s.120 and is shared between the Court of Session and the sheriff courts.

[21] This sum can be increased or reduced by order made under Insolvency Act 1986 s.416: see s.117(3).

[22] For these purposes, the Lord Chancellor may by statutory instrument exclude specific county courts from having winding up jurisdiction and may attach their district (or part of their district) to another county court: Insolvency Act 1986 s.117(4).

[23] Insolvency Act 1986 s.117(6).

winding up, the High Court will always have jurisdiction, either alone, in parallel or concurrently with the county court. The county court will only have s.6 disqualification jurisdiction if the paid-up share capital of the company in question is within the statutory limit. The particular county court that will have jurisdiction is that for the district in which the company's registered office is situated. To deal with the possibility that the address of the registered office may be changed, it is by virtue of s.6(3A) deemed to be situated, for present purposes, in the place which has longest been the company's registered office during the six months immediately preceding the relevant insolvency event that founds jurisdiction under s.6(3). This means that the disqualification proceedings, if issued in the county court, should be issued in the court having the necessary jurisdictional connection with the company in the six months immediately prior to the commencement of the relevant insolvency regime and not, as often used to be the case prior to amendment of the CDDA, the court having a jurisdictional connection with the insolvency practitioner appointed to act in relation to the company and to whose offices the company's registered office is customarily transferred after commencement of the relevant insolvency regime. Even if the applicant for a disqualification order under CDDA s.6[24] applies in the incorrect court, the defendant is discouraged from taking the point by s.6(3B), a provision that like s.6(3A), was inserted by the Insolvency Act 2000. Such an error does not invalidate the proceedings and the court in which the application was commenced may retain the proceedings or, presumably, transfer them to the court in which they should have been commenced.

7–07 The difficulties that arose from the predecessor of the present CDDA s.6(3)[25] have therefore been swept away, subject to two points. As regards s.6(3)(a), it may be difficult to ascertain the applicable court in cases where the winding up proceedings have been transferred from one court to another court, the winding up has been completed and the company has been dissolved.[26] In that situation the question is: which court is the court that "wound up" the company? It is clear in this context that "winding up" does not refer simply to the making of the order but encompasses the winding up process.[27] It is suggested that the court that "wound up" the company will be the court that was winding it up immediately prior to the moment of dissolution.[28] As regards s.6(3)(c), that subsection confers

[24] Or an applicant under s.8A in relation to an undertaking accepted pursuant to s.7(2A).

[25] On which see A. Walters and M. Davis-White, *Directors' Disqualification: Law and Practice*, 1st edn (London: Sweet & Maxwell, 1999) at 6–04–6–06; *Re Working Project Ltd* [1995] 1 B.C.L.C. 226 (in relation to the former s.6(3)(a)) and *Re Lichfield Freight Terminal Ltd* [1997] 2 B.C.L.C. 109 (in relation to the former s.6(3)(b)).

[26] Under the former s.6(3), where the test was whether the company was in the course of being wound up, the High Court determined that a company ceased to be in the course of being wound up only once it was finally dissolved and this was so even if its affairs had been fully wound up prior to that date: see *Re Working Project Ltd* [1995] 1 B.C.L.C. 226.

[27] CDDA s.6(3), in referring to the company "being wound up", is clearly referring to winding up as a process.

[28] See, e.g. Insolvency Act 1986 s.205(1)(b). Presumably a company has been wound up by the court in cases of early dissolution (e.g. under Insolvency Act 1986 s.202) even though the winding up may not have been "completed" in the sense referred to in s.205(1)(b).

relevant jurisdiction on the court which "has jurisdiction to wind [the company] up". In the second edition of this book the hope was expressed that this expression would not be read too narrowly so that, in cases where a company had been dissolved without being wound up, it was suggested that the courts should view it as conferring jurisdiction on the court that would have had jurisdiction both to restore the company in question to the register and to wind it up. This problem reached the courts in *Re J & N International Ltd, Secretary of State for Trade and Industry v Arnold*.[29] In that case the relevant company had gone into administration but then been dissolved, without going into liquidation, by operation of para.84(6) of Sch.B1 to the Insolvency Act 1986. The disqualification proceedings were issued in the Crewe County Court but then transferred to the High Court. Three issues were before the court: (a) whether, in the circumstances, the court had jurisdiction to determine the disqualification proceedings; (b) if not, whether the proceedings were a nullity; and (c) if they were a nullity, whether permission to bring proceedings outside the two-year period laid down in CDDA s.7(2) should be granted. The court decided the first issue in favour of the Secretary of State, but indicated that had it decided otherwise on that issue it would have found the proceedings to be a nullity on the second issue but, on the third issue, would have granted permission to commence fresh proceedings outside the two-year period to enable an application to be made in the first instance to restore the company to the register. On the first issue, the court determined that, in s.6(3)(c), the reference to the word "has" in the phrase "any court which has jurisdiction to wind up" was a reference back to the earlier use of the word "has" in the subsection focussing on whether an administrator or administrative receiver "has at any time been appointed". Accordingly, the question under s.6(3)(c) is which court had jurisdiction to wind up the company at the time of the relevant appointment. The result is very sensible but, on one view, does some violence to ordinary words of the English language. It involves reading the words "has jurisdiction" as equivalent to "at that time had jurisdiction". It is also somewhat at odds with the approach taken by Neuberger J. in *Re Lichfield Freight Terminal Ltd*[30] (in relation to the former s.6(3)(b)).[31]

Proceedings under CDDA ss.2(2)(a), 3(4), 4(2)

7–08 In the case of CDDA ss.2(2)(a), 3(4) and 4(2) it is possible to conceive of a number of permutations that could give rise to difficulty. It would appear that jurisdiction is to be determined by reference to the date that the disqualification proceedings are commenced. It might also be thought that the approach and result in *Re Lichfield Freight Terminal Ltd*[32] is to be applied. On that footing the test is

[29] [2007] EWHC 1933 (Ch), [2008] 1 B.C.L.C 581.
[30] [1997] 2 B.C.L.C. 109.
[31] This point was recognised by HHJ Pelling Q.C. but he asserted that he was considering different wording (the current s.6(3)) compared with that considered by Neuberger J. so that the cases could be distinguished.
[32] [1997] 2 B.C.L.C. 109.

which court has jurisdiction to wind up the relevant company at the date of the disqualification application. That causes difficulties if the company is by that time dissolved.[33] If the company is not then dissolved and the financial limit on county court jurisdiction is not exceeded, the relevant county court with jurisdiction would appear to be that which would have jurisdiction based on the six month registered office rule, the six month period ending with the disqualification application. However, suppose that the company is in the course of being wound up compulsorily, say by a particular county court, at the time of inception of the disqualification application. Presumably in those circumstances that court "has jurisdiction" to wind up, because it is actually doing so. However, that court may not be the same county court that would have jurisdiction to wind up if the test applied related to the location of registered office over the six month period ending with the inception of the disqualification proceedings. It remains to be seen whether the approach taken in *Re J & N International Ltd, Secretary of State for Trade and Industry v Arnold*[34] will provide any assistance in this area.

Foreign companies

7–09 As regards foreign companies and CDDA ss.2–4, 6, 8, 9A, 10 and 17, the relevant deeming provisions for the purposes of establishing and allocating jurisdiction within the United Kingdom are set out in s.221(3) of the Insolvency Act 1986. In summary, an unregistered company (as defined by Pt V of the Insolvency Act 1986)[35] is deemed to be registered in England and Wales or Scotland according to the jurisdiction in which its principal place of business is situated. If it has a principal place of business situated in both countries, it will be deemed to be registered in both countries. The principal place of business situated in that part of Great Britain in which proceedings are being instituted is deemed to be its registered office. An unregistered company with a principal place of business situated in Northern Ireland cannot be wound up under Pt V of the Insolvency Act unless it has a principal place of business situated in England and Wales and/or Scotland.[36]

The EC Regulation on Insolvency Proceedings

7–10 The jurisdiction to entertain insolvency proceedings, in relation to both UK and overseas companies (whether or not incorporated within the EU) has been drastically affected by the EC Regulation on Insolvency Proceedings. In very broad terms, the regulation establishes a regime under which the courts of a member state may open insolvency proceedings only if the debtor's centre of main interests is situated within its territory (in the case of so-called main proceedings) or, subject to certain limitations, if the debtor possesses an establishment within that

[33] On the face of it an application to undo the dissolution would be required, as in the parallel situation under CDDA s.6(3) prior to its amendment: see *Re Working Project Ltd* [1995] 1 B.C.L.C. 226 and *Re Townreach Limited* [1995] Ch 28.
[34] [2008] 1 B.C.L.C 581.
[35] See further Chs 3, 14 and 16 on the definitions of "company" and "unregistered company".
[36] Insolvency Act 1986 s.221(2) and see *Re Normandy Marketing Limited* [1994] Ch. 198.

territory (in the case of so-called secondary or territorial proceedings). Thus, on the face of it, the courts in England and Wales could not open main winding up proceedings in relation to a domestic registered company the centre of main interests of which is situated elsewhere within the EU.[37] Further, if such a company did not have an establishment in England and Wales there would be no power to open secondary winding up proceedings. However, the EC Regulation has been interpreted as not applying to public interest winding up proceedings brought under s.124A of the Insolvency Act 1986.[38] It therefore seems to follow that, even in cases where no winding up order has been made in relation to the company in question, the court will be treated as having jurisdiction to wind up such company without reference to any provision of the EC Regulation that might otherwise prevent the court from exercising its ordinary winding up jurisdiction.[39]

Jurisdiction under ss.7(2), 7(4) and 15

It is convenient to consider the position under these provisions separately. **7–11**

(1) Applications for permission to commence proceedings under CDDA s.6 after the expiry of the two-year period from the onset of insolvency (CDDA s.7(2)) are dealt with in Ch.8. The relevant court in which the application should be launched is the court having jurisdiction over the substantive disqualification proceedings that will be commenced if permission is granted (see CDDA s.6(3) as to the meaning of "the court" in ss.6 and 7).

(2) Section 7(4) of the CDDA is dealt with in Ch.3. If the relevant insolvency is ongoing and the relevant insolvency practitioner is the officeholder, then the application against the officeholder should be brought under the Insolvency Rules 1986 and presumably within the substantive insolvency proceedings.[40] In other cases, an application may be brought by way of claim form under CPR Pt 8 or within the disqualification proceedings as provided for in para.18 of the Disqualification Practice Direction. In the former case, it is not clear to which court the application should be made and the safest course would be to make it in the High Court. However, it is possible that the court which has, or would have, jurisdiction with regard to the substantive proceedings (if brought) could entertain an application under s.7(4).

(3) Proceedings seeking to impose civil liability on a disqualified person for acting in breach of a disqualification order or undertaking can be brought either in the High Court or the appropriate county court subject to the relevant monetary limits. In this context reference should be made to the Practice Direction to Pt 7 of the CPR. Where a county court has jurisdiction, proceedings may not be commenced in the High Court unless the value of the claim

[37] Denmark is, however, outside the scope of the regulation.

[38] *Re Marann Brooks CSV Ltd* [2003] B.C.C. 239.

[39] See further discussion in the text from 16–18.

[40] Disqualification Rules, r.2(5). If court proceedings are not on foot, presumably the application should be made as if it were any other application relating to the insolvency, effectively initiating the creation of a court file, and court proceedings, in relation to that insolvency.

is more than £15,000 (Practice Direction to Pt 7, para.2.1). However, there is jurisdiction to transfer proceedings between courts (considered in more detail below). The starting point with regard to the jurisdiction to transfer is that (in general) proceedings with a value of £50,000 or less should be heard in a county court (Practice Direction to Pt 29, para.2.2). This starting point is subject to qualification. In deciding questions of transfer, the court must also have regard to the matters set out in CPR r.30.3 which are discussed further below. Within a particular court there is then the further question of allocation to the relevant "track": the small claims track (broadly, claims having a value of not more than £5,000), the fast track (broadly, claims having a value of more than £5,000 but not more than £15,000) and the multi-track. However, in deciding track allocation, the court must also have regard to a number of other specific factors under CPR r.26.8 which share some similarities with the criteria for transfer set out in CPR r.30.3.

Transfer and proceedings commenced in the wrong court

Powers of transfer

7–12 There are wide powers of transfer. As explained below, the CPR (subject to modifications) apply to disqualification proceedings in civil courts. Transfer is regulated by CPR Pt 30 and the relevant practice direction. As mentioned earlier, CDDA s.6(3B) also makes specific provision for a court to retain proceedings governed by that section even if it is the wrong court. The following should therefore be read subject to the caveat that the court in which proceedings under CDDA s.6 were commenced may retain those proceedings even though it may not be the court in which they ought to have been commenced. As regards the CPR, the position, in summary, is as follows:

(1) If proceedings are commenced in the wrong county court, that county court can transfer them to the county court in which they should have been started or strike them out (CPR r.30.2(2)). In cases where s.6(3B) applies the county court can retain the proceedings even if it otherwise would not have jurisdiction. In cases where s.6(3B) does not apply, a county court which does not have jurisdiction under the CDDA does not have the option of retaining proceedings wrongly commenced there (CPR r.30.2(2)(b) and (7)). Application for transfer should be made to the county court in which the claim is proceeding (CPR r.30.2(3)).

(2) If proceedings are wrongly commenced in a county court when they should have been commenced in the High Court, there is power in that county court either to transfer the proceedings to the High Court or, if satisfied that the person bringing the proceedings knew, or ought to have known, that they should have been brought in the High Court, to strike them out (s.42(1), (7) of the County Courts Act 1984). In cases governed by CDDA s.6(3B), the court may retain the proceedings. It is suggested that the power to strike out under the County Courts Act 1984 is not affected by s.6(3B). Where the

power to strike out is exercised, the proceedings are not "invalidated" automatically for lack of jurisdiction under CDDA s.6(3) but are struck out as a matter of discretion.

(3) If proceedings are wrongly commenced in the High Court when they should have been commenced in a county court, there is power in the High Court either to transfer the proceedings to the High Court or, if satisfied that the person bringing the proceedings knew, or ought to have known, that they should have been brought in the High Court, to strike them out (s.40(1), (8) of the County Courts Act 1984). In cases governed by CDDA s.6(3B) the court may retain the proceedings. For the reasons set out in (2) above, it is suggested that the power to strike out under the County Courts Act 1984 is not overridden by s.6(3B).

(4) If proceedings are correctly commenced in the High Court:
   (a) There is a general power in the High Court to transfer such proceedings between the Royal Courts of Justice and a district registry of the High Court (CPR r.30.2(4) and (5)). In deciding whether or not to transfer the Court must have regard to the (presumably non-exhaustive) factors set out in CPR r.30.3(2).
   (b) There is a power in the High Court under s.40 of the County Courts Act 1984 to transfer such proceedings to a relevant county court as long as that county court also has jurisdiction under the relevant provision of the CDDA. The exercise of the power is governed by s.40(2), (4) of the 1984 Act and CPR r.30.3.

(5) If proceedings are correctly commenced[41] in a particular county court, there is no power to transfer them to another county court not having jurisdiction under the CDDA (CPR r. 30.2(1) and (7)).[42] However, provided that the High Court does have jurisdiction, there is power in the High Court (s.41(1) of the County Courts Act 1984) and a county court (s.42(2) of the County Courts Act 1984), to transfer the proceedings to the High Court. The exercise of these powers is governed by CPR r.30.3. Furthermore, provided that another county court also has jurisdiction, there is power for one county court to transfer the proceedings to that other county court if the court is satisfied that the criteria in CPR r.30.3 are satisfied (CPR r.30.2(1)).

7–13 It will be noted from the above that if a county court is seised of disqualification proceedings and has jurisdiction under the CDDA then it has no power to transfer those proceedings to a county court which does not have jurisdiction. This has caused problems in cases where a transfer was thought desirable because the relevant county court lacked expertise in disqualification matters. Thus, in *Secretary of State for Trade and Industry v Shakespeare*[43] proceedings were

[41] In which case CDDA s.6(3B) cannot apply.
[42] See *Secretary of State for Trade and Industry v Shakespeare* [2005] 2 B.C.L.C. 471.
[43] [2005] 2 B.C.L.C. 471.

correctly commenced in the Dudley County Court but transferred by that court of its own motion to the Birmingham County Court, apparently on the basis that the latter court had a judicial expertise in the area that the Dudley County Court lacked. The Birmingham County Court did not have jurisdiction under s.6 of the Act but the matter was dealt with by transferring the case from the Birmingham County Court to the High Court, Birmingham District Registry. Various other options for dealing with the general problem were canvassed in the judgment.

Transfer from wrong court

7–14 In cases where proceedings are commenced in the wrong court, the court always has a discretion to transfer or strike out.[44] The mere fact that the claimant ought to have known that the proceedings should have been commenced in a different court will not automatically result in the proceedings being struck out. In *Re NP Engineering and Security Products Ltd, Official Receiver v Pafundo*[45] the court applied the principles set out in *Restick v Crickmore*[46] (a case concerned with transfer of proceedings under s.42 of the County Courts Act 1984). In that case, the established policy of the courts was described as being as follows:

> "... [P]rovided proceedings are commenced within the time permitted by the statute of limitations, are not frivolous, vexatious or an abuse of the process of the court and disclose a cause of action, they will not as a rule be struck out because of some mistake in procedure on the part of the [claimant] or his advisers. Save where there has been a contumelious disobedience of the court's order, the draconian sanction of striking out an otherwise properly constituted [claim/application], simply to punish the party who has failed to comply with the rules of court, is not part of the court's function. No injustice is involved to the defendant in transferring [a claim/application] which has been started in the wrong court to the correct court."[47]

In *NP Engineering*, with regard to the question of the "wrong" court and in deciding to transfer rather than strike out, the Court of Appeal relied on the fact that: (a) no-one had suggested that the proceedings were obviously frivolous or vexatious; (b) the proceedings (under s.6) were brought within the two-year period as required by s.7(2); (c) it made no practical difference to the defendants whether the proceedings were commenced in the county court or the High Court; (d) the proceedings were brought in the public interest; and (e) the function of the court on a transfer application was not to punish the incompetence of the claimant. Although the court may now be more willing to punish parties, it is suggested that the basic approach remains the same under the CPR.

Transfer from correct court

7–15 In cases where proceedings are commenced in the correct court, the court, in deciding whether or not to transfer the proceedings to another court under the

[44] It is suggested that this power survives the enactment of CDDA s.6(3B).
[45] [1998] 1 B.C.L.C. 208.
[46] [1994] 1 W.L.R. 420.
[47] [1994] 1 W.L.R. 420, 427.

powers set out in 7–12 above, is required to consider the factors set out in the relevant sections of the County Courts Act 1984 and CPR r.30.3:

(1) In considering transfer from the High Court to a county court under s.40(2) of the County Courts Act 1984, the High Court must have regard to the convenience of the parties and of any other persons likely to be affected and to the state of the business in the courts concerned.[48] The court must also have regard to CPR r.30.3.

(2) Under CPR r. 30.3 the court is obliged to consider:

   (a) the financial value of the claim and the amount in dispute, if different (this is not relevant in most proceedings brought under the CDDA though it will be relevant in cases under ss.10 and 15);
   (b) whether it would be more convenient or fair for hearings (including the trial) to be held in some other court;
   (c) the availability of a judge specialising in the type of claim in question;
   (d) whether the facts, legal issues, remedies or procedures involved are simple or complex[49];
   (e) the importance of the outcome of the claim to the public in general;
   (f) the facilities available at the court where the claim is being dealt with and whether they may be inadequate because of any disabilities of a party or potential witness;
   (g) whether the making of a declaration of incompatibility under s.4 of the Human Rights Act 1998 has arisen or may arise;
   (h) in the case of civil proceedings by or against the Crown, as defined in r.66.1(2), the location of the relevant government department or officers of the Crown and, where appropriate, any relevant public interest that the matter should be tried in London.

(3) The factors enumerated in CPR r.30.3 largely mirror those previously set out in art.7 of the High Court and County Courts Jurisdiction Order 1991.[50] The one major change, which will not be relevant to most disqualification proceedings, relates to financial value. The current position is that claims having a financial value of less than £50,000 will generally be heard in a county court (CPR Pt 29; Practice Direction to Pt 29, para.2.2). It is also to be noted that the previous restriction under art.7 of the 1991 Order preventing the court from making a transfer order solely on the ground that it would result in a more speedy trial of the proceedings no longer exists.

[48] For an example of this power being used in disqualification proceedings see *Re Time Utilising Business Systems Ltd* (1989) 5 B.C.C. 851 (the report in [1990] B.C.L.C. 568 does not cover this point). On the facts the case was wrongly decided in the light of subsequent decisions of the Court of Appeal (discussed below in main text) that in s.6 disqualification proceedings appeals from a district judge of a county court lie direct to a High Court judge and not to the county court judge.

[49] For an example of a pre-CPR case in which the High Court decided that this factor had been improperly invoked see *Re Time Utilising Business Systems Ltd* (1989) 5 B.C.C. 851.

[50] SI 1991/724. This article was later repealed: see art.7 of the High Court and County Courts Jurisdiction (Amendment) Order 1999 (SI 1999/1014).

Level of judge

7–16 As considered further below, the first hearing of most disqualification cases will be before a district judge or, in the case of the High Court in London, the Companies Court Registrar. There are a number of local practices and/or practice directions setting out when it is appropriate for a disqualification case to be heard before a full county court or High Court judge as opposed to a district judge or the Companies Court Registrar. Subject to any such practice or practice direction, it will be a matter for the exercise of the court's discretion as to the level of judge that will be appropriate to hear a particular disqualification case. In *Re Digital Computer Services Ltd, Lewis v Secretary of State for Trade and Industry*[51] Neuberger J. set out a non-exhaustive list of relevant factors. These include:

(1) The length of the case (a very long hearing would probably be more appropriate for a judge than a registrar or district judge).
(2) The complexity of the case (complex issues of fact or law might be a factor weighing in favour of a hearing before a judge rather than a registrar or district judge, although it should also be borne in mind that in many respects registrars and district judges may have considerably more experience in this area than many judges and certainly many deputy judges).
(3) The likely timetable and hearing date (bearing in mind the need for disqualification proceedings to be heard speedily, both in the interests of the defendant and given the public interest nature of the proceedings and the fact that witnesses' memories fade over time).
(4) The profile of the case (a high profile case might be more appropriately heard by a judge).
(5) The seriousness of the allegations made.
(6) The wishes of the parties, though these are not of paramount importance.

It is suggested that the wishes of the parties (unless they coincide), as distinct from the reasons expressed in support of such wishes, should bear little if any, weight. It is difficult to understand why the claimant's wishes should, as was suggested by Neuberger J., carry less weight than those of the defendant. On particular facts, this may well be an appropriate course. However, it is suggested that it is more likely to flow from the reasons underlying the parties' wishes and other factors.

Appeals from transfer orders

7–17 Once an order for transfer has been made there is some uncertainty as to whether or not the provisions on appeals set out in the Practice Direction to Pt 30 of the CPR apply for the purposes of the appeal or whether the matter is regulated by the provisions on appeals set out in the Insolvency Rules. This matter is considered further in the text at 13–02.

[51] [2001] 2 B.C.L.C. 597.

Overseas directors: disputing the court's jurisdiction

7–18 In cases under CDDA ss.6 and 8 where the court has granted permission to serve disqualification proceedings out of the jurisdiction under r.5.2 of the Disqualification Rules and para.7.3 of the Disqualification Practice Direction, the defendant served with the proceedings can apply to set aside service.[52] Indeed, the standard form of acknowledgment applicable to disqualification claims contains a relevant section on this topic. The practice in a case of a defendant served overseas by virtue of an order made under either para.19.2(2)[53] or 26.2[54] of the Disqualification Practice Direction remains unclear but it is presumed that the position is the same. The question of service outside the jurisdiction of disqualification proceedings under s.6 was considered in *Re Seagull Manufacturing Co Ltd (No.2)*.[55] In summary the conclusions from that case were as follows:

(1) There is no jurisdictional limitation under s.6 of the CDDA. Section 6(1) can apply to any person, whether a British subject or a foreigner, irrespective of their presence here or at the time the activities took place. The conduct need not have taken place within the jurisdiction.
(2) Nevertheless, there remains a residual discretion in the court to refuse to order service out of the jurisdiction (or to set aside any such order for service and the service effected pursuant to such order) if the court is not satisfied that there is a "good arguable case".

THE APPLICABLE RULES OF COURT

7–19 To reach an understanding of the present position regarding the applicable rules of court and the areas that remain unclear it is necessary to have some understanding of the background to the current position and the relevant history.

Applicable rules: history

7–20 Immediately prior to the Insolvency Act 1985, civil disqualification proceedings were governed either by the Companies (Winding-Up) Rules 1949[56] (in particular, r.68) or by the originating summons procedure in the High Court.[57] In 1986 new rules were introduced governing applications under ss.6 and 8 of the CDDA[58] and, in 1987 these were replaced by the Insolvent Companies (Disqualification of Unfit

[52] This also applies in cases under other provisions of the CDDA where permission has been granted to serve proceedings outside the jurisdiction under para.7.3 of the Disqualification Practice Direction.

[53] Governing applications under CDDA ss.7(2) and 7(4).

[54] Governing applications in disqualification proceedings made by way of application notice.

[55] [1994] Ch. 91.

[56] SI 1949/330. See, e.g. *Re Blackheath Heating & Consulting Engineers Ltd* (1985) 1 B.C.C. 99,383.

[57] See, e.g. discussion in *Re Rex Williams Leisure Plc, Secretary of State for Trade and Industry v Warren* [1994] Ch. 350.

[58] The Insolvent Companies (Disqualification of Unfit Directors) Proceedings Rules 1986 (SI 1986/612).

Directors) Proceedings Rules 1987 ("the Disqualification Rules").[59] The latter rules have subsequently been amended. The main amendments have been as follows. The first series of amendments took account of the adoption of the CPR in place of the Rules of the Supreme Court and the County Court Rules. These amendments were made by the Insolvent Companies (Disqualification of Unfit Directors) Amendment Rules 1999.[60] The second series of amendments took account of the introduction of the competition disqualification regime. They were introduced by the Insolvency Companies (Disqualification of Unfit Directors) Proceedings (Amendment) Rules 2003.[61] The third main series of amendments took place in 2007 and expanded the scope of the rules to cover a wider range of civil applications. They were introduced by the Insolvent Companies (Disqualification of Unfit Directors) Proceedings (Amendment) Rules 2007.[62] The current position is unfortunate in two main respects:

(1) The nomenclature of the Disqualification Rules is confusing: proceedings under each of ss.8 and 9A can be brought in relation to companies which have not become insolvent. The title to the Disqualification Rules is also something of a mouthful.[63]
(2) The jurisdiction to make rules by way of statutory instrument under s.21 of the CDDA is effected by incorporating rule-making powers contained in the Insolvency Act 1986.[64] Originally these powers were limited in their application to ss.6–10, 15, 19(c) and 20 of and Sch.1 to the CDDA (which provisions were, for the relevant purpose, deemed incorporated into the Insolvency Act 1986). However, the Insolvency Act 2000 extended the applicable sections to include ss.1A, 13 and 14.[65] Accordingly the rule-making powers now apply to ss.1A, 6–10, 13–15, 19(c) and 20 and Sch.1. The Insolvency Act 2000 also extended the powers to ss.1 and 17 as they apply for the purposes of the previous specified provisions. The upshot is that applications under other sections of the CDDA fall to be dealt with under the CPR and the jurisdiction to modify the CPR in such cases has to be found in the CPR themselves.

It is a pity that the opportunity was not taken in the Enterprise Act 2002 to amend the CDDA by extending the wide rule-making power contained in the Insolvency Act 1986 to cover all civil disqualification proceedings thereby replacing the present limited arrangements that have emerged piecemeal as a result of historical accident. This is a fortiori given that the competition disqualification

[59] SI 1987/2023.
[60] SI 1999/1023.
[61] SI 2003/1367.
[62] SI 2007/1906.
[63] "Company Directors Disqualification Rules" would be simpler, as would the consolidation of all relevant statutory instruments within one single statutory instrument.
[64] See ss.411 and 420.
[65] Even so, it is unclear what scope there is to make (civil) rules of court in relation to the criminal offences laid down in CDDA ss.13 and 14. The extension was probably directed more at ss.420 and 422 of the Insolvency Act 1986 which are also dealt with in s.21(2) of the CDDA.

provisions have been brought directly within the scope of the insolvency legislation and the rule-making powers thereunder. As such, it is difficult to understand why the civil provisions formerly contained within the Companies Acts but now contained within CDDA ss.2–4 (inclusive) have not been treated in the same way.

Tasbian, Probe Data and the applicability of the Insolvency Rules

7–21 Prior to the amendment of the Disqualification Rules in 1999,[66] there was considerable uncertainty regarding the procedural rules applicable to disqualification proceedings. This uncertainty was caused primarily by the somewhat unsatisfactory decision of the Court of Appeal in *Re Tasbian Ltd (No.2), Official Receiver v Nixon*.[67] The point before the Court of Appeal in that case was whether or not, on an application for permission to commence proceedings under s.6 outside the two-year time limit laid down by s.7(2), an appeal from the Companies Court Registrar lay to the Court of Appeal or to a High Court judge. Clearly concerned that the Court of Appeal should not be overburdened with appeals from the Companies Court Registrar, it was decided in *Tasbian* that an appeal lay to a High Court judge. The reasoning by which this result was reached was unfortunately somewhat compressed. The Disqualification Rules did not, at that point, contain any express provisions about appeals[68] and so the Court of Appeal turned to the then wording of s.6(3) of the CDDA. The analysis proceeded thus. It was noted that the court with jurisdiction under the then s.6(3)(b) (company in voluntary winding up), was the court with "jurisdiction to wind up the company". In *Tasbian*, the relevant company was in compulsory winding up and so the relevant court having jurisdiction to disqualify was, under s.6(3)(a), the court by which the company was being wound up. Indeed, in all cases under the former s.6(3)(a)–(c), the court given jurisdiction under the CDDA was a court which had winding up jurisdiction over companies. The Insolvency Rules 1986 contain provisions about appeals in insolvency proceedings. Rule 7.47 of the Insolvency Rules governs appeals from ". . . a decision made in the exercise of . . ." the jurisdiction to wind up companies. The Court of Appeal held that the jurisdiction to wind up companies was not to be narrowly construed as referring only to a court's power to make winding up orders. In the words of Dillon L.J.:

> ". . . [I]t is plain that [the jurisdiction to wind up companies] is not limited to the mere making of winding up orders. It is a conventional formula of long-standing under successive Companies Acts . . ."

Dillon L.J. concluded that in relation to r.7.47(2) of the Insolvency Rules:

> ". . . any decision made by a registrar of the High Court, in the exercise of the jurisdiction of the Chancery Division as the court having jurisdiction to wind up companies, is subject to appeal to a single judge of the High Court and not to this court."

[66] SI 1999/1023.
[67] [1991] B.C.L.C. 59.
[68] Further, although no reference was made to this in the judgments, there was also a question as to whether the Disqualification Rules applied to applications under CDDA s.7(2).

In other words, the fact that a disqualifying court was not making a winding up order or some other order in the course of a winding up did not prevent r.7.47 of the Insolvency Rules from applying.

7–22 The matter was considered further in *Re Probe Data Systems Ltd (No.3), Secretary of State for Trade and Industry v Desai.*[69] The Court of Appeal was asked to find that *Tasbian* had been wrongly decided and to overrule it, but refused to do so. In particular, the Court of Appeal was not prepared to apply the per incuriam rule to enable it to depart from the decision in *Tasbian*. The argument proceeded, in part, on the following footing:

> "[Counsel for the director] submitted that if the decision [in *Tasbian*] were allowed to stand, the ratio would require the review and appellate procedures of rule 7.47 to be applied not only to orders made under [the CDDA] but to all orders made under the Companies Act 1985. He pointed out that 'court', in the Companies Act 1985 is defined as 'the court having jurisdiction to wind up the company' (s.744), and submitted that Dillon L.J.'s reasoning would apply the Insolvency Rules to all orders made by 'the court' so defined."

The answer to this was given by counsel for the Secretary of State:

> "Mr Richards gave the answer to this hair-raising submission. Section 411 of the Insolvency Act 1986, under which the Insolvency Rules were made, gives the Secretary of State no power to make rules for the purposes of the Companies Act 1985. *Per contra*, s.21 of [the CDDA] does permit rules made under s.411 to apply to disqualification proceedings. The Insolvency Rules 1986 could not be given an *ultra vires* effect and could not possibly apply to proceedings under the Companies Act 1985. So there is nothing in the point."

7–23 These two decisions appear to have had the following consequences and to have raised the following points of difficulty:

(1) Appeals in civil cases brought under any section of the CDDA other than ss.1A, 6–10, 13–15, 19(c), 20 and Sch.1 (including, for these purposes, applications for permission to act notwithstanding a disqualification imposed under any of these sections) cannot be governed by the Insolvency Rules 1986. This is because it would be ultra vires for such rules to be construed as applying to any provision other than the provisions referred to in s.21(2) of the CDDA (which relates among other things to the rule-making power in s.411 of the Insolvency Act 1986). Accordingly, although the civil court with jurisdiction to make disqualification orders under, for example, s.2 is defined as the court "with jurisdiction to wind up companies", the relevant rules applying to such a court exercising its jurisdiction under s.2 and on any appeal, cannot be the Insolvency Rules. The relevant rules are now the CPR.

[69] [1992] B.C.L.C. 405.

(2) In certain cases under the sections of the CDDA specified in CDDA s.21, the civil court with jurisdiction is not expressly defined by reference to its winding up jurisdiction but is referred to as "the High Court"[70]: see, for example, CDDA ss.8(3), 8A(3) and 9E(3). However, in such cases, it is suggested that the courts would equate the two on the basis that the High Court is a court having jurisdiction to wind up companies.[71]

(3) No specific provision is made in the CDDA as to the court having jurisdiction under ss.10 and 15. It is suggested that the applicable rules were, and are now, to be determined in s.10 cases, by reference to the rules governing substantive proceedings under ss.213–214 of the Insolvency Act 1986 and in the case of applications under s.15, by reference to the ordinary rules of court (now the CPR).[72]

(4) In cases where (following the decisions in *Tasbian* and *Probe Data*), the Insolvency Rules govern the question of appeals, it would seem to follow that the appeal itself will be an "insolvency proceeding" governed by the Insolvency Rules (see Insolvency Rules 1986 r.13.7). However, in another context (i.e. one not involving a question of appeals), it was decided that the applicable rules to proceedings under ss.6 and 8 were not the Insolvency Rules 1986 but rather the Rules of the Supreme Court (or the County Court Rules) by reason of r.2 of the Disqualification Rules. This point (arising from *Dobson v Hastings*) is considered in the next section below.

(5) In cases where appeals in disqualification proceedings were not governed by the Insolvency Rules, the position after *Tasbian* and *Probe Data* (but before the coming into force of the CPR) was thus as follows:

    (a) Appeals from the Companies Court Registrar sitting in the High Court lay to a High Court judge (rehearing only).[73]
    (b) Appeals from a district judge in a county court lay to a county court judge under the County Court Rules.
    (c) Appeals from a county court judge exercising original jurisdiction lay to the Court of Appeal and not (as is the case under the Insolvency Rules) to a High Court judge.

These points of difficulty have subsequently been reduced as a result of the extension of CDDA s.21 by the Insolvency Act 2000. The question of appeals is addressed further in Ch.13.

[70] Or in Scotland, the Court of Session.

[71] See *Re Helene Plc, Secretary of State for Trade and Industry v Forsyth* [2000] 2 B.C.L.C. 249. See also the approach taken by the parties and acceded to by the judge under the previous statutory provisions in *Re Ambery Metal Form Components Ltd, Secretary of State for Trade & Industry v Jones* [1999] B.C.C. 336.

[72] For a case brought under s.15 in relation to alleged breaches of s.11 see *Commissioners of the Inland Revenue v McEntaggart* [2004] EWHC 3431 (Ch), [2006] 1 B.C.L.C. 476.

[73] See discussion in *Re Rolls Razor Ltd (No.2)* [1970] Ch. 576.

Developments after *Tasbian* and *Probe Data*

7–24 In *Dobson v Hastings*,[74] the question before the court concerned the right of the public to inspect the court file of a set of disqualification proceedings brought under CDDA s.6: was such a right governed by the ordinary rules of court or by the Insolvency Rules? Basing himself firmly on the wording of what was then r.2 of the Disqualification Rules, Nicholls V.C. rejected the notion that the proceedings were "insolvency proceedings" governed by the Insolvency Rules and held that (in the High Court) the Rules of the Supreme Court (which were in force at that time) applied. Rule 2 of the Disqualification Rules formerly made provision for the form of application in proceedings under ss.6 and 8 and went on to provide that "the Rules of the Supreme Court 1965 or (as the case may be) the County Court Rules 1981 apply accordingly, except where these Rules make provision to inconsistent effect". Thus r.2, in its previous incarnation, did not simply govern the form of application: it governed the proceedings as a whole.[75] Unfortunately, r.2 was not discussed by the Court of Appeal in *Tasbian*. Further, r.2 was not mentioned by Dillon L.J. when he came to set out the relevant provisions of the Disqualification Rules. It is suggested, in the light of *Dobson v Hastings* and on the true construction of the Disqualification Rules as they stood at the time, that *Tasbian* was wrongly decided and that the Insolvency Rules (which were made exclusively under s.411 of the Insolvency Act 1986) should not have been held to apply to any proceedings under the CDDA.[76]

7–25 The question of applicable rules in s.6 proceedings arose again in *Re Circle Holidays International Plc, Secretary of State for Trade and Industry v Smith*.[77] In that case, the proceedings were in a county court. The immediate question was whether or not the applicable rules concerning hearsay in affidavits were to be found in the County Court Rules or the Insolvency Rules. His Honour Judge Micklem decided that the County Court Rules applied. His reasoning is, it is suggested, compelling. Thus, it appears that the position reached prior to the adoption of the CPR and the 1999 amendments to the Disqualification Rules was that the ordinary rules of court were treated as applying to all matters other than appeals, which (at least in relation to proceedings under s.6) were governed by the Insolvency Rules.

The current position

7–26 The current position would appear to be as follows:

(1) Civil disqualification proceedings in which a disqualification order is sought under any substantive provision of the CDDA apart from ss.6 to 9 are governed by the CPR and the Practice Directions made thereunder.

[74] [1992] Ch. 394.

[75] *Contra* Hoffmann J. in *Re Langley Marketing Services Ltd* [1992] B.C.C. 585.

[76] Contrast the Disqualification Rules which were also made pursuant to s.21(2) of the CDDA. It appears that this particular consideration may have less weight than previously thought: see, by analogy, discussion of the rules made under the Civil Procedure Act 1997 in relation to pre-action disclosure in *Burrells Wharf Freeholds Ltd v Galliard Homes Ltd* [2000] C.P. Rep. 4.

[77] [1994] B.C.C. 226.

(2) Proceedings under ss.6, 8 and 9A are governed by the Disqualification Rules. The same is now true of applications under ss.7(2) and 7(4) as a result of the 2007 amendments. The provisions of the Disqualification Rules are considered further below.
(3) Proceedings seeking permission to act notwithstanding disqualification are governed by the Disqualification Rules when brought in relation to a disqualification by undertaking or by court order made under any of ss.6, 8, 9A or 10 and otherwise by the CPR.
(4) Proceedings seeing to vary or discharge disqualification undertakings under s.8A are governed by the Disqualification Rules.
(5) Proceedings under s.10 are governed by the relevant rules governing the substantive proceedings in which the claim under s.213 or s.214 of the Insolvency Act 1986 is brought.
(6) As regards proceedings seeking permission to act notwithstanding automatic disqualification under s.11 proceedings, see the text from 15–78.

The current position: CDDA ss.6, 8 and 9A

As regards proceedings under ss.6–8 and 9A of the CDDA: **7–27**

(1) The Disqualification Rules apply to applications for the making of a disqualification order under s.6 (technically the application is made under s.7(1)), s.8 and s.9A in the first instance, rather than the CPR (see CPR r.2.1(2) and Disqualification Rules r.2). Rule 2.4 of the Disqualification Rules expressly provides that the appeal and review provisions of the Insolvency Rules (i.e. rr.7.47 and 7.49) apply to proceedings under ss.6, 8 and 9A. The 1999 amendments to the Disqualification Rules expressly give effect to the result in *Tasbian* and *Probe Data*. To the extent that the Disqualification Rules do not make "provision to inconsistent effect", and subject to the application of the Insolvency Rules rr.7.47 and 7.49, the CPR and the Practice Directions apply. In other words, the position appears to reflect that which was apparently reached prior to the adoption of the CPR, namely that the Insolvency Rules apply only in relation to questions of appeal and review.
(2) The same position applies to proceedings under s.7(2). Such proceedings have now been brought within the provisions of r.2 of the Disqualification Rules by the amendments made to them in 2007.
(3) In relation to s.7(4) the position is more complex. To the extent that an application is made "against a person who at the date of the application is acting as liquidator, administrator or administrative receiver" then the application will be made within the relevant insolvency and the Insolvency Rules will apply.[78] Otherwise, the position will be as in (1) above.
(4) As regards applications under s.8A the same position applies as in (1) following the 2007 amendments.

[78] See Disqualification Rules r.2(5).

The CPR and the Disqualification Practice Direction

7–28 On April 26, 1999, the Disqualification Practice Direction (governing civil disqualification proceedings) was adopted. The broad effect of the Disqualification Practice Direction is to restate the effect of the Disqualification Rules in relation to applications under ss.6–9E and to apply the same sort of procedures envisaged in the Disqualification Rules to civil disqualification proceedings not expressly governed by the Disqualification Rules. At this stage it is worth making two points, one of a general nature and a second which relates more specifically to disqualification proceedings:

(1) Even prior to the adoption of the CPR, the judiciary was encouraged to apply the old rules in accordance with the new spirit which eventually found expression in the CPR. It is therefore wrong to assume that the adoption of the CPR represented a completely fresh start and clear break with past practice, procedures and attitudes.
(2) Civil disqualification proceedings have always, to some extent, mirrored the approach to civil litigation now enshrined in the CPR. Cases have generally been brought before a judge fairly speedily and the technique of case management is not entirely novel so far as such proceedings are concerned. Having said that, the way in which the court exercises its case management powers is likely to be subject to continual evolution.[79] The exercise of case management techniques pre-CPR did not prevent a significant number of applications to strike out for delay, nor did it prevent the Court of Appeal expressing concerns about delay, cost and over-elaboration (see the discussion of *Westmid Packing* in 7–30 below.

The Disqualification Practice Direction

7–29 In considering the effect of the Disqualification Practice Direction, it is important to bear in mind that a practice direction may serve any one or more of three different functions:

(1) A practice direction may simply recite other provisions of law or practice as an *aide memoire* rather than create any new practice and procedure. To the extent that the Disqualification Practice Direction sets out provisions of the Disqualification Rules in relation to proceedings to which those rules apply, it is not a source of law with regard to practice and procedure. The power to make practice directions of this type derives from the court's inherent jurisdiction to regulate its own practice.
(2) As was the case before the Civil Procedure Act 1997 came into force, the court may issue practice directions under its inherent jurisdiction which regulate its own practice. An example of this sort of practice direction (which to

[79] See, e.g. *Re Finelist Ltd, Secretary of State for Trade and Industry v Swan* [2004] B.C.C. 877.

an extent overlaps with (1) above) is the provision in para.13.4 of the Disqualification Practice Direction that the court will normally sit in private when hearing a summary application under the *Carecraft* procedure.[80]

(3) Under the Civil Procedure Act 1997, practice directions may, in certain circumstances, modify, vary or disapply provisions of the CPR. This is a wholly new extension to the concept of practice directions, which could not previously be used to change rules of procedure laid down by statutory instrument. Section 1 of the Civil Procedure Act 1997 sets out the relevant rule-making powers with regard to civil procedure generally. In so doing, s.1 expressly incorporates the provisions in Sch.1 to the same Act. Paragraph 6 of Sch.1 contains the most significant power. It states that the Civil Procedure Rules may, instead of providing for any matter, refer to provisions made or to be made about that matter by directions. It follows that rules of procedure, which formerly could only be made by statutory instrument, can now be made by practice direction as long as the relevant rules in the CPR, themselves made by statutory instrument, so provide. It also follows that the distinction between court practice and court procedure are now blurred. In some cases, it is therefore necessary to consider whether or not there was jurisdiction under a specific provision of the CPR (for example, CPR, r.8.1(6)) to make a relevant provision of the Disqualification Practice Direction. It should also be noted that there is a further provision relevant to practice directions in the Civil Procedure Act 1997. In combination, para.3 of Sch.1 and s.5(1) provide that practice directions may be made governing the matters relating to transfer set out in para.3 of Sch.1. It should also be noted that some provisions of the CPR themselves have been challenged as being ultra vires.[81]

The spirit of the CPR

7–30 As indicated above, the general concerns underlying the Woolf reforms and the encouragement to address public concern in relation to cost and delay in civil litigation, found judicial voice before the CPR came into force. In *Re Westmid Packing Services Ltd, Secretary of State for Trade and Industry v Griffiths*, the following observations were made by the Court of Appeal in relation to disqualification proceedings:

> "... [W]e wish to discourage the belief that there is a complicated, arcane and inflexible code of evidential rules applicable in [disqualification] cases. In most cases the essential thing will be for the court, with the assistance of the parties, to use common sense and to adopt a practical and flexible approach to case management, so as to confine the evidence to that which is probative ..."[82]

[80] On which, see generally Ch.9.

[81] See, e.g. *Burrells Wharf Freeholds Ltd v Galliard Homes Ltd* [2000] C.P. Rep. 4; *General Mediterranean Holdings SA v Patel* [2000] 1 W.L.R. 272.

[82] [1998] 2 All E.R. 124 at 132.

It was also said:

> "We are concerned at the delay in the hearing of these cases . . . We feel that over-elaboration in the preparation and hearing of these cases and a technical approach as to what evidence is and is not admissible is contributing to delay. What is required and what the court should confine the parties to, is sufficient evidence to enable the court to adopt a broad brush approach."[83]

In *Re Barings Plc (No. 5), Secretary of State for Trade and Industry v Baker*, Jonathan Parker J. relied on these passages in connection with his refusal to admit certain alleged "expert" evidence.[84] The passages set out above do have to be treated with caution however. An overly "broad brush" approach will not be tolerated by the courts and may lead to the invocation of art.6 of the European Convention on Human Rights.

CONDUCT BEFORE PROCEEDINGS ARE COMMENCED

General points

7–31 Under the CPR, considerable emphasis is placed on the behaviour of the parties to litigation before proceedings are issued and the pre-action behaviour of the parties is something which the courts are required expressly to consider and take into account. In particular, "pre-action protocols" have been produced that are intended to encourage: (a) more pre-action contact between the parties; (b) better and earlier exchange of information; (c) better pre-action investigation by both sides; (d) the parties to reach a position where they will be able to settle cases fairly and easily without recourse to litigation; and (e) efficient and expeditious conduct of proceedings in the event that litigation does become necessary. Although there is no pre-action protocol specifically applicable to disqualification proceedings, parties should have well in mind the provisions of the relevant Practice Direction: Pre-Action Conduct. The aims outlined above are ones that the courts have been pursuing for some time. Moreover, the courts have expressed concern about the cost of disqualification proceedings and the way in which such proceedings can bear heavily upon defendants. Thus, for example, in *Re Moonlight Foods (UK) Ltd, Secretary of State for Trade and Industry v Hickling*, His Honour Judge Weeks Q.C. had this to say:

> "At this stage I want to say a little about the [claimant's] duties. It is accepted that these are not ordinary adversarial proceedings but have an element of public interest and may entail penal consequences. It follows that there is a duty on the applicant to present the case against each [defendant] fairly. Many of these applications go by default or are defended by litigants in person, and the practice[85] is for an official in the Department of Trade and Industry to swear a short affidavit referring to charges, specified in a detailed affidavit sworn by the receiver or liquidator. In my judgment that second affidavit

[83] [1998] 2 All E.R. 124 at 134–135.
[84] [1999] 1 B.C.L.C. 433 at 494.
[85] Which may, of course, be subject to change.

should not omit significant available evidence in favour of any [defendant]. It should attempt to deal with any explanation already proffered by any of the [defendants]. It should endeavour to apportion responsibility as between the [defendants] and it should avoid sweeping statements for which there is no evidence. I do not know who drafted the receiver's affidavit in the present case, but it does seem to me to fall down on all four counts."[86]

7–32 In many cases, the Secretary of State depends heavily on the reporting insolvency practitioner to identify matters such as explanations of conduct which have already been offered and evidence which may favour a defendant.[87] Although there is no pre-action protocol specific to disqualification proceedings,[88] the Practice Direction on Pre-Action Conduct provides an important overall guide and provides in para.6 as follows:

"6. Overview of Principles

6.1 The principles that should govern the conduct of the parties are that, unless the circumstances make it inappropriate, before starting proceedings the parties should—

(1) exchange sufficient information about the matter to allow them to understand each other's position and make informed decisions about settlement and how to proceed;

(2) make appropriate attempts to resolve the matter without starting proceedings, and in particular consider the use of an appropriate form of ADR in order to do so.[89]

6.2 The parties should act in a reasonable and proportionate manner in all dealings with one another. In particular, the costs incurred in complying should be proportionate to the complexity of the matter and any money at stake. The parties must not use this Practice Direction as a tactical device to secure an unfair advantage for one party or to generate unnecessary costs."

In the context of disqualification proceedings, the relevant sanctions are likely to be costs-based. Even in the absence of a specific pre-action protocol, there have been significant changes in the way that disqualification proceedings are prepared and in the amount of contact between the parties before proceedings are commenced. The Insolvency Service aims to avoid sending out a "ten-day letter" under CDDA s.16 (considered immediately below) only ten days before proceedings are to be commenced even though the statute strictly only requires ten days notice. The "letter before proceedings" that is sent will usually set out in

[86] [1996] B.C.C. 678 at 690. These general propositions were cited with approval by Laddie J. in *Re Finelist Ltd, Secretary of State for Trade and Industry v Swan* [2004] B.C.C. 877.

[87] In this connection, see Statement of Insolvency Practice 4 issued by the Association of Business Recovery Professionals (R3). See also *Re Digital Computer Licenses Ltd, Secretary of State for Trade and Industry v Lewis* [2003] B.C.C. 611 at [84]–[86] and [112].

[88] Moreover, the proposal to create a "general" pre-action protocol for all proceedings was eventually dropped: see Lord Chancellor's Department Consultation Paper, *General Pre-action Protocol* (October 2001) and Responses to the Consultation Paper, *General Pre-action Protocol* (July 2002).

[89] Mediation is not usually appropriate in the context of resolving public interest regulatory proceedings raising issues such as whether a person should be disqualified or whether permission to act notwithstanding disqualification should be granted: see *Secretary of State for Trade and Industry v Goldberg*, February 2, 2004, Ch.D., unreported (Lewison J.). This does not mean that other issues (e.g. costs) may not be appropriate for ADR.

summary form the grounds of the claim, make clear that the potential defendant is able to make representations in person[90] or in writing and that draft evidence is available on request (albeit subject to terms as to confidentiality and use). Indeed, it has become quite common for potential defendants in s.6 cases to provide further information in an attempt to persuade the Secretary of State either that there is no case under s.6 and/or that there are public interest considerations that militate against the making of a disqualification order or the imposition of disqualification through an undertaking.[91] It is interesting that in the context of disqualification proceedings following an investigation under CDDA s.9C there is a requirement similar to, but more extensive than, that under s.16.

CDDA s.16(1): the "ten-day letter"

Mandatory or directory?

7–33 Section 16(1) of the CDDA[92] starts with the words:

> "A person intending to apply for the making of a disqualification order by the court having jurisdiction to wind up a company shall give not less than ten days' notice of his intention to the person against whom the order is sought . . ."

The effect of s.16(1) is that the claimant in civil disqualification proceedings brought under CDDA ss.2(2)(a), 3, 4, 6, 8 or 9A[93] is required to give the intended defendant at least ten days' notice of his intention to commence the proceedings.[94] The first point that arises in relation to s.16(1) is whether the requirement for the defendant to be served with a "ten-day letter" is mandatory or directory. In *Re Cedac Ltd, Secretary of State for Trade and Industry v Langridge*,[95] the defendant received the ten-day letter on April 11, 1989. Proceedings under s.6 were then issued on April 21, 1989. In the earlier case of *Re Jaymar Management Ltd*,[96] it was held that the period of ten days must be calculated by excluding both the day on which the notice is given and the day on which proceedings are to be

[90] On Insolvency Service guidance regarding the holding of meetings prior to the commencement of proceedings, see discussion in *Re Finelist Ltd, Secretary of State for Trade and Industry v Swan* [2004] B.C.C. 877.

[91] On disqualification undertakings see generally Ch.9.

[92] See also CDDA s.9C(4).

[93] It should be noted that a more extensive obligation arises under s.9C(4) where an application under s.9A is contemplated following an investigation under s.9C.

[94] In relation to s.8 and s.9A proceedings, this rests on the assumption that the High Court is treated as a "court having jurisdiction to wind up a company" under s.16(1). In any event, see the dicta of Balcombe L.J. in *Re Cedac Ltd, Secretary of State for Trade and Industry v Langridge* [1991] Ch. 402 to the effect that a "ten-day letter" does not have to be sent when the application for a disqualification order is made to a court other than the winding up court, "although doubtless the rules of natural justice will require that the person concerned should be given some notice that the court is contemplating making a disqualification order". In the context it appears that he was probably referring to *criminal* disqualification proceedings under ss.2 and 5 but his remark would apply more widely if s.8 cases and s.9A cases were held not to fall within s.16 on which point see also *Re Ambery Metal Form Components Ltd, Secretary of State for Trade & Industry v Jones* [1999] B.C.C. 336. It appears that Balcombe L.J.'s dicta also governs the position in s.10 cases as these are outside the scope of s.16(1).

[95] [1991] Ch. 402 (reversing *Re Cedac Ltd* [1990] B.C.C. 555).

[96] [1990] B.C.L.C. 617.

commenced. Accordingly, in *Cedac*, either notice should have been given no later than April 10, 1989 or the proceedings should have been commenced after April 21, 1989. The short question was whether or not this failure to comply strictly with s.16(1) rendered the proceedings a nullity or whether it was merely a procedural irregularity that the court, in its discretion, could excuse. On the facts, the point was extremely significant. Had the failure to comply with the letter of s.16(1) rendered the proceedings a nullity, the Secretary of State could only have commenced fresh proceedings with the permission of the court as the two-year period in s.7(2) had long since expired.[97] In *Jaymar Management*, Harman J. held that non-compliance with s.16(1) went to jurisdiction and so rendered the proceedings a nullity. However, by a majority, the Court of Appeal in *Cedac* (effectively overruling *Jaymar Management*) held that s.16(1) was directory rather than mandatory and that, as a consequence, the failure to comply was a procedural irregularity that did not affect the validity of the proceedings.

7–34 The following points were made in support of this conclusion in the majority judgments:

(1) It was noted that the language in s.16(1) (". . . shall not give less than ten days notice . . .") is mandatory but that there is no provision in the CDDA specifying what is to happen if notice is not given. It was also noted that s.16(1) could be traced back as far as s.33(3) of the Companies Act 1947[98] and that, while it appeared to be procedural rather than substantive in nature, it had always been in the primary legislation and not in rules made under the legislation.

(2) Although the language of s.16(1) is mandatory, the court should consider the whole purpose of the CDDA, the importance of the provision within the legislative scheme and the relation of that provision to the general purpose of the CDDA in determining the legal consequences of breach. It was not the correct approach to construe the provision in isolation to ascertain whether it was mandatory or directory. The court should look at the purpose of the statute as a whole and should not decide the issue simply by stating that the provision is in mandatory or imperative form.[99]

(3) In Balcombe L.J.'s words,

> ". . . the purpose of the [CDDA] is to protect the public and its scope is the prevention of persons who have previously misconducted themselves in relation to companies, or have otherwise shown themselves as unfit to be concerned in the management of a company, from being so concerned".

[97] See Ch.8.

[98] See subsequently, Companies Act 1948 s.188(3); Insolvency Act 1976 s.9(3); Companies Act 1985 Sch.12 Pt I paras 1, 7; Insolvency Act 1985 s.108(2)(b). The original provision was in fact the Companies Act 1928 s.76(2). This seems to have been overlooked.

[99] See *Howard v Boddington* (1877) 2 P.D. 203; *Montreal Street Railway Co v Normandin* [1917] A.C. 170; *London & Clydeside Estates Ltd v Aberdeen District Council* [1980] 1 W.L.R. 182 and *In re T (A Minor)* [1986] Fam. 160. For a more recent discussion see *R. v Immigration Appeal Tribunal Ex. p. Jeyeanthan* [2000] 1 W.L.R. 354 and *R. v Soneji* [2005] UKHL 49, [2006] 1 A.C. 340.

The object of the "ten-day letter" is the protection of the person against whom a disqualification application is to be made. It is necessary to conduct a balancing exercise between these two objects. In this respect, it is significant that the protection conferred by s.16(1) is limited for the following reasons: (a) notice is only required in relation to proceedings in a court having jurisdiction to wind up a company, i.e. it is not required in all proceedings brought under the CDDA; (b) the "ten-day letter" does not have to specify the grounds on which the application is to be made; (c) the period of the notice is too short for the intended defendant to be able to do much. On point (c), Legatt L.J. had this to say:

> "It does not enable [the intended defendant] to equip himself to answer the proceedings when served, nor give him much warning of them, nor enable him to do anything that without them he would be unable to do."

As such, in arriving at a proper balance, Legatt L.J. was content to characterise the "ten-day letter" as one that is "intended to inform of intentions rather than protect rights".

(4) In all the cases to which s.16(1) applies, except for applications under s.6, the CDDA imposes no time period in which proceedings are required to be commenced. Thus, if the requirement in s.16(1) was mandatory, and failure to comply rendered the subsequent proceedings a nullity, the Secretary of State (or whoever) could simply relaunch a fresh set of proceedings by serving the requisite "ten-day letter" correctly. In the words of Balcombe L.J., it is difficult to conceive that Parliament intended so pointless and wasteful a result.

7–35 It is fair to say that *Cedac* settles the point notwithstanding Nourse L.J.'s vigorous dissent.[100] However, it should be noted that Legatt L.J. accepted that if the Secretary of State refrained altogether from complying with s.16(1), the failure to give due notice would enable the director to apply for, and if the court thought fit obtain, an order striking out the proceedings even though the provision was merely directory.[101]

Contents of the "ten-day letter"

7–36 In *Cedac*, Balcombe and Legatt L.JJ. both described the "ten-day letter" as "an unparticularised letter before action". It is clear in the light of *Cedac* and on the wording of s.16(1) that the letter need do no more than indicate that proceedings are to be commenced. Accordingly, the old practice was for the letter simply to state that it was the claimant's intention to apply for a disqualification order under the relevant section of the CDDA, to name the relevant company or companies

[100] On which see discussion in Ch.2. See also, in Scotland, *Secretary of State for Business, Enterprise and Regulatory Reform v Smith* [2009] B.C.C. 497.

[101] The point was based on a concession by the Secretary of State. It was also common ground in *Surrey Leisure* (discussed below) that the court has such a discretion. The point arose again in *Re Finelist Ltd, Secretary of State for Trade and Industry v Swan* [2004] B.C.C. 877 (also discussed below).

and to recite the terms of the order sought. There is apparently no obligation on the claimant to specify the grounds or basis on which the order is to be sought.[102] In *Re Surrey Leisure Ltd, Official Receiver v Keam*,[103] the first defendant applied to strike out a set of s.6 proceedings on the ground that alleged non-compliance with s.16(1) vitiated the proceedings. The proceedings were brought in relation to the first defendant's conduct as a director of two lead companies within an insolvent group. However, the "ten-day letter", which was otherwise properly served, only made reference to one of these companies. Jonathan Parker J. dismissed the first defendant's application. He concluded that the "ten-day letter" complied with s.16(1):

> "Section 16(1) contains no specific provisions as to what the required notice is to contain, save that it is to be not less than ten days of the would be [claimant's] intention to seek a disqualification order against the recipient 'by a court having jurisdiction to wind up a company'. The expression 'a company' in this context plainly refers to the lead company or companies. In my judgment, given the absence of any further specific statutory requirements as to the content of the notice, to hold that in order to comply with s.16(1) a notice must specify which is (or are) to be the lead company (or companies) in the intended proceedings would be to write into the subsection a requirement which, for whatever reason, Parliament has not thought fit to include."[104]

7–37 As has been noted, the Insolvency Service's practice of relying on "unparticularised letters before action" has changed and developed in the modern legal culture. However, matters were taken considerably further by the decision of Laddie J. in *Re Finelist Ltd, Secretary of State for Trade and Industry v Swan*.[105] In *Swan*, the defendant sought to strike out evidence in s.6 proceedings (but, significantly, not the proceedings themselves) on the grounds that: (a) the evidence was inadequate to support the allegations made and did not comply with the obligation of fairness; (b) the procedure adopted by the Secretary of State breached s.16(1) of the CDDA in that the letter giving notice of the Secretary of State's intention to commence proceedings arrived on the Wednesday before the Saturday on which the two-year period provided for under s.7 would have expired[106] and denied the defendant the opportunity of responding to the allegations prior to the commencement of proceedings; (c) the commencement of the disqualification proceedings was unfair and had resulted in substantial damage to the defendant; (d) the evidence contained matters that were scandalous, irrelevant and/or oppressive; and (e) the evidence included expert evidence that complied

[102] See, however, *Re Finelist Ltd, Secretary of State for Trade and Industry v Swan* [2004] B.C.C. 877 (discussed below). Under the original provision in what was s.76 of the Companies Act, 1928, the conduct complained of (suspected fraud) would have been identified in the report filed with the court.

[103] [1999] 1 B.C.L.C. 731.

[104] [1999] 1 B.C.L.C. 731, 737–738. The Court of Appeal subsequently upheld the judge's decision: see [1999] 2 B.C.L.C. 457.

[105] [2004] B.C.C. 877.

[106] In fact the period would have expired on the following Monday: see *Re Philipp & Lion Ltd, Secretary of State for Trade and Industry v Lion* [1994] 1 B.C.L.C. 739.

neither with CPR r.35 nor the claimant's duty of fairness.[107] Laddie J. decided, in the circumstances, that the correct course would have been to order further particulars or to strike out identified passages in the evidence. However, he also hinted that he could have been persuaded to strike out the proceedings had such an application been before him. For present purposes the significance of the decision lies in what the judge said about CDDA s.16.

7–38 Firstly, the point made in *Cedac* to the effect that non-compliance with s.16 did not automatically invalidate the proceedings was accepted.[108] To borrow the words of Lord Woolf M.R. in *R. v Immigration Appeal Tribunal Ex. p. Jeyeanthan*,[109] the procedural requirement in s.16 was not "... so fundamental that any departure from the requirement makes everything that happens thereafter irreversibly a nullity". However, and as Laddie J. correctly pointed out, that is not the end of the matter. Non-compliance with the requirement to send a valid s.16 notice within the prescribed time period, can result in the proceedings being struck out as an abuse of process. Laddie J. also referred to non-compliance as being something that, on specific facts, could render the subsequent disqualification proceedings "a nullity". This analysis is entirely in line with the reasoning in *Jeyeanthan*[110] where, as the following extract demonstrates, the Court of Appeal stressed the need to move away from an approach focused exclusively on the question of whether the relevant statutory provision is "mandatory" or "directory":

> "The conventional approach when there has been non-compliance with a procedural requirement laid down by a statute or regulation is to consider whether the requirement which was not complied with should be categorised as directory or mandatory. If it is characterised as directory then it is usually assumed that it can be safely ignored. If it is categorised as mandatory then it is usually assumed the defect cannot be remedied and has the effect of rendering subsequent events dependent on the requirement a nullity or void as being made without jurisdiction and of no effect. The position is more complex than this and this approach detracts from the important question of what the legislator should be judged to have intended should be the consequence of the non-compliance. This has to be assessed on a consideration of the language of the legislation against the factual circumstances of the non-compliance. In the majority of cases it provides limited, if any, assistance to inquire whether the provision is directory or mandatory. The requirement is never intended to be optional if a word such as 'shall' or 'must' is used . . . In the majority of cases, whether the requirement is categorised as directory or mandatory, the tribunal before whom the defect is properly raised has the task of determining what are the consequences of failing to comply with the requirement in the context of all the facts and circumstances of the case in which the issue arises."[111]

Laddie J. also envisaged that there may be circumstances in which non-compliance with s.16 is so abusive of the court's process that a fresh set of disqualification proceedings would not be permitted (the court either refusing

[107] On the claimant's duty to deal fairly with the defendant see *Re Moonlight Foods Ltd, Secretary of State for Trade and Industry v Hickling* [1996] B.C.C. 687.
[108] [2004] B.C.C. 877 at [58].
[109] [2000] 1 W.L.R. 354.
[110] See also the analysis in *R. v Soneji* [2005] UKHL 49, [2006] 1 A.C. 340.
[111] [2000] 1 W.L.R. 354 at 358–359.

permission for fresh proceedings to be commenced out of time under CDDA s.7(2) or simply striking out such proceedings on the basis that they amount to an abuse). In theory, the authors consider that this must be correct.

7–39 It is difficult to predict what approach the courts will take on this issue. In *Finelist*, Laddie J. did not have to consider whether the failure to comply with s.16 was, on the facts, such that justice required the proceedings to be stopped in their tracks. Indeed, it is important to note that the Secretary of State had not been called on to address the issue because the court was not being invited to make a finding of "nullity", a point acknowledged by the judge.[112] Furthermore, there had been no application to strike out the proceedings (as opposed to the evidence) as being an abuse of process. Accordingly, Laddie J.'s observations on the legal consequences of non-compliance with s.16 are strictly obiter. Given that the tenor of Laddie J.'s judgment seems to reflect the approach taken by Nourse L.J. in his dissenting judgment in *Cedac* and that it is cast in terms that go wider than was necessary to decide the application before him, it is suggested that some of his remarks need to be treated with caution.

7–40 The first point concerns the requirements of CDDA s.16 itself. As noted above, the Court of Appeal in *Cedac* construed s.16 as requiring little more than an unparticularised letter before action. Laddie J. appears to have suggested that in the light of developments in civil procedure and the Secretary of State's duty "to deal fairly with the director", s.16 should now be construed as imposing a more demanding requirement.[113] It is the authors' view that such an approach would be incorrect as a matter of law. It is difficult to dispute that good practice requires the substance of the case to be put to the director prior to the commencement of proceedings to enable him to offer an explanation or to raise matters of public interest that may militate against such proceedings. The requirement for such practice is a function of (at least) the following matters: (a) the CPR; (b) public duties of good administration directed, in particular, at the prevention of unnecessary prejudice to the defendant (whether by way of adverse publicity, the need to resign from office and/or notify third parties of such proceedings); and, possibly, (c) that aspect of the Secretary of State's duty to deal fairly with the defendant that requires him to present a balanced case.[114] However, any such requirement goes well beyond CDDA s.16 both in terms of what information is statutorily required to be made available and the stage at which it should be made available. Indeed, it adds a considerable gloss to s.16 that makes the provision read as if it was drafted in terms more akin to CDDA s.9C(4) even though Parliament has not expressly so provided. The authors' view is that the majority of the Court of Appeal in *Cedac* construed s.16 correctly, and that the interpretation of what s.16 requires cannot change over time (in the absence of express statutory intervention). However, this is not to say

[112] [2004] B.C.C. 877 at [92].

[113] [2004] B.C.C. 877 at [45] and [55]. The obligation of "fair dealing" was highlighted, in particular, by the decision in *Re Moonlight Foods Ltd, Secretary of State for Trade and Industry v Hickling* [1996] B.C.C. 687.

[114] *Re Moonlight Foods Ltd, Secretary of State for Trade and Industry v Hickling* [1996] B.C.C. 687. See also *Finelist* at [19]–[21].

that the *consequences* of a breach of s.16 (on which the CDDA is silent) cannot be measured in the light of the CPR and the duties of fairness that require directors to be given prior notice of claims against them. Shortcomings in respect of these matters may well bear on whether the approach of the claimant can properly be characterised as an abuse of the court's process and on the question of the legal consequences that should flow from a breach of s.16. The authors therefore agree with Laddie J.'s view that a breach of s.16 can be taken into account with other factors in determining whether the proceedings are an abuse of process or a nullity.[115] However, it is also important to note, as Laddie J. himself pointed out, that a party's failure to pay due regard to the objectives of the CPR is normally penalised in costs.[116] The failure to serve a s.16 notice in time will usually be treated as a failure to comply with the objectives of the CPR in relation to pre-action discussions and duties of fairness that oblige the prospective claimant to give the prospective defendant sufficient details of the case in good time prior to the commencement of proceedings to enable the prospective defendant to deal with it. If a failure of the latter type will normally be penalised in costs rather than by striking out then, in the authors' view, the failure to abide by s.16 (which requires a minimal notice period and minimal information) should not normally attract any more drastic sanction unless, for example, there is evidence that the breach of s.16 was contumelious. If, in most cases, s.16 provides the defendant with only limited protection, why should a breach of the section lead to the proceedings being struck out simply because it equates to a breach of other requirements that themselves would normally attract costs sanctions rather than striking out? Given the limited protection that s.16 provides, it is suggested that failure to comply with the section will rarely be so serious as to justify either striking out or a finding of nullity.

PARTIES TO PROCEEDINGS

The general position

7–41 As regards claimants for disqualification orders, the position in the civil courts is as follows:

(1) Applications for the making of a disqualification order under CDDA ss.2–4 (inclusive) can be brought by any of the Secretary of State, the official receiver,[117] or by the liquidator or any past or present member or creditor of a company in relation to which that person has committed or is alleged to have committed an offence or other default (CDDA s.16(2)).

(2) Prior to its amendment by the Insolvency Act 2000,[118] CDDA s.16(2) appeared to envisage that an application for the making of a disqualification

[115] *Finelist*, at [54] and [58].

[116] *Finelist*, at [97].

[117] For an analysis of the position of the official receiver as litigant see *Re Minotaur Data Systems Ltd, Official Receiver v Brunt* [1999] 1 W.L.R. 1129.

[118] Insolvency Act 2000 s.8 and Sch.4, Pt 1, paras 1, 11.

order under CDDA s.5 could be made to the civil courts. This was a drafting error as it is clear from s.5(2) that the power to disqualify vests exclusively in the criminal courts. The error has now been corrected.

(3) Applications for the making of a disqualification order under CDDA ss.6 and 8 can only be made by the Secretary of State or, under s.6, if the Secretary of State so directs in the case of a person who is or has been a director of a company which is being, or has been, wound up by the court in England and Wales, by the official receiver (CDDA ss.7(1), 8(1)).

(4) Applications under CDDA s.9A may be made by the OFT or by "a specified regulator"[119] for the purposes of a breach of competition law in relation to a matter of which the relevant regulator has a function.[120] At the time of writing, the list of specified regulators included the following: the Office of Communications; the Gas and Electricity Markets Authority; the Water Services Regulation Authority; the Office of Rail Regulation and the Civil Aviation Authority.[121]

(5) The civil court can act of its own motion under CDDA s.10 but equally the claimant in relevant proceedings under ss.213 or 214 of the Insolvency Act 1986 could apply for a disqualification order.[122] This raises the question of whether it is ever proper for a liquidator to apply for a disqualification order under s.10 (and if so in what circumstances). In any event, it is suggested that the Secretary of State, as the person responsible for regulating companies, would have the ability to intervene[123] and that, when making (or being minded to make) a relevant declaration triggering jurisdiction under s.10, the court should always require notification to be given to the Secretary of State to give him an opportunity to apply and/or make representations, as happened in *Re Brian D Pierson (Contractors) Ltd.*[124]

The liquidator as claimant

7–42 It must be open to question whether there are ever any circumstances in which it would be proper for a liquidator to commence disqualification proceedings where the Secretary of State has decided not to commence proceedings.[125] In disqualification cases it is presumably for the Secretary of State to consider the public

[119] CDDA s.9A(10).

[120] CDDA s.9E(2).

[121] See further text at 6–16.

[122] In this context, see *Official Receiver v Doshi* [2001] 2 B.C.L.C. 235 where wrongful trading proceedings and s.6 disqualification proceedings were run in tandem and heard together.

[123] By analogy with *Adams v Adams* [1971] P. 188, especially at 197–198.

[124] [2001] 1 B.C.L.C. 275.

[125] However, see in relation to criminal proceedings and, by analogy, *Re London and Globe Finance Corporation Ltd* [1903] 1 Ch. 728 discussed in *Re Pantmaenog Timber Co Ltd* [2003] UKHL 49, [2004] 1 A.C. 158 at [53] and [80]. Note also the Report of the Committee on Company Law Amendment (the Cohen Committee), Cmd.6659 (1945), especially at paras 151 and 161, which drew attention to the requirement in s.277(6) of the Companies Act, 1929 for the Director of Public Prosecutions to consider not only the likelihood that the prosecution would be successful, but also whether it was in the public interest that the director should be prosecuted or whether (alternatively) the matter was best left to any private individuals who might be minded to bring a prosecution. This second requirement was later dropped.

interest as to whether proceedings should be brought. Accordingly, the issue is not whether it is in the public interest for him, rather than someone else, to bring the proceedings (as used to be the case in relation to prosecutions). If the Secretary of State decides that it is not in the public interest to bring proceedings, why should a liquidator be authorised to do so? In cases where CDDA s.10 is, or is likely to be, triggered, it is suggested that, in normal circumstances, the most appropriate course is for the liquidator to draw the attention of the court to its powers under s.10 and invite the court to direct that the Secretary of State be notified of the relevant breach of ss.213–214 of the Insolvency Act 1986. The court should also give the Secretary of State liberty to apply, thus leaving it to him to make any representations with regard to the question of disqualification and the appropriate period.

Members and creditors as claimants

7–43 In the case of corporate members or corporate creditors there may be question marks over the company's capacity to bring disqualification proceedings and, even assuming that the company has capacity, over whether the directors would be acting properly in causing the company to launch such proceedings. Apart from this point, there is a more significant question mark over the circumstances in which members or creditors can bring disqualification proceedings. This doubt follows from the decision of Jacob J. in *Re Adbury Park Estates Ltd, Juer v Lomas*.[126] In that case, a shareholder applied for a disqualification order under CDDA s.4 against two insolvency practitioners who were successively administrative receivers and then liquidators of the company in question. The basis of the application was said to be that the insolvency practitioners had been guilty of fraud and conspiracy in knowingly admitting a false claim to proof in the liquidation and in paying dividends in respect of that claim when the relevant liability was, in fact, that of the applicant shareholder and not the company in liquidation. The liquidators admitted that they had made a mistake in admitting the debt to proof. They had corrected it (by recovering the overpaid dividend with interest) as soon as the matter had been drawn to their attention. They denied any fraud or conspiracy and asserted that there was no evidence to support such a grave allegation. Jacob J. dismissed the action on two grounds. The first was based on the applicant's standing. The second was that the standard of conduct complained of came nowhere near the standard of serious delinquency required for disqualification under CDDA s.4. The decision as to standing was founded on authorities such as *Deloitte & Touche AG v Johnson*[127] and *Cavendish Bentinck v Fenn*[128] to the effect that statutory rights to make applications conferred on contributories or creditors are subject to the further requirement that the contributory or creditor concerned must show that he has a legitimate interest in the relief sought. A renewed application for permission to appeal was refused by Robert Walker L.J.[129] on the grounds that "an appeal would be hopeless" and that there were "no arguable

[126] June 28, 2003, Ch.D., unreported.
[127] [1999] 1 W.L.R. 1605.
[128] (1887) 12 A.C. 652.
[129] [2001] EWCA Civ 1568.

grounds for overturning either of the reasons for the judge's dismissal of the application". It is important to point out that for the purposes of the application for permission to appeal, it was accepted that the applicant had to show "some financial interest". However, the authors respectfully suggest that the decision on standing was incorrect. In *Deloitte & Touche* the defendants to proceedings brought by a company in liquidation were seeking to have the liquidators removed from office. The Privy Council relied on the well established rule that the proper persons to make such an application are the creditors in an insolvent liquidation or the contributories in a solvent liquidation as these are the only persons with any stake in the process and therefore any legitimate interest in the identity of the liquidators. In the CDDA context, it is difficult to see why a claimant should be denied locus standi to bring disqualification proceedings simply because he does not have an immediate financial interest in the liquidation. First of all, the misconduct in question may well have been a significant factor in the company's transition from solvency to insolvent liquidation. If so then surely the contributories will have a very real interest in bringing disqualification proceedings even though the company has gone into insolvent liquidation and they no longer have any prospect of recovering their investment. Secondly, and perhaps more persuasively, disqualification is not, in its nature, something in which claimants can be said to have a "financial interest". To draw a historical analogy, one of the liquidator's functions under the Companies Act 1862 was to bring criminal proceedings against directors and others who were alleged to have committed offences in relation to the company. In *Re London and Globe Finance Corporation Ltd*,[130] the prosecuting authorities declined to bring criminal proceedings. However, the court authorised the liquidator to bring such proceedings at the expense of the company. Buckley J. observed that s.167 of the 1862 Act was concerned with enforcing commercial morality and "was not measured or limited or even concerned with pecuniary benefit to be obtained for the shareholders or creditors". It is suggested that the same is true of disqualification and that, contrary to the view of Jacob J., there is no need for a creditor or shareholder to show that they have a financial interest before they are entitled to bring disqualification proceedings under any of CDDA ss.2–4.

The Secretary of State or official receiver as claimant

7–44 The CDDA does not itself define the meaning of "Secretary of State" where that term is employed in the Act. As such, relevant functions under the CDDA are not allocated by the Act to a specific Secretary of State. Accordingly, they may be exercised by any Secretary of State[131] although, in practice, they are administratively entrusted to a particular Secretary of State. For many years they were entrusted to the Secretary of State for Trade and Industry. On June 28, 2007 the Prime Minister announced the creation of a new department, the Department for

[130] [1903] 1 Ch. 728.

[131] The term "Secretary of State" is defined by Sch.1 to the Interpretation Act 1978 as meaning "one of Her Majesty's Principal Secretaries of State".

Business, Enterprise and Regulatory Reform. Among the functions entrusted to the new Secretary of State[132] were those under the CDDA. So far as the Secretary of State for Trade and Industry was in the course of exercising functions under the CDDA, further provision regarding these functions were made by the Secretaries of State for Children, Schools and Families, for Innovation, Universities and Skills and for Business, Enterprise and Regulatory Reform Order 2007,[133] which order also incorporated the new Secretary of State. On June 5, 2009 the government announced the creation of a new Department for Business, Innovation and Skills. Headed by Lord Mandelson, the Business Secretary and First Secretary of State, its key role was described as being "to build Britain's capabilities to compete in the global economy". The Department was created by merging BERR and DIUS (the Department for Innovation, Universities and Skills). Accordingly, in the case of new proceedings the claimant will be the Secretary of State for Business, Innovation and Skills. Existing proceedings will continue in the name of the Secretary of State for Business, Enterprise and Regulatory Reform unless and until a relevant transfer of functions order comes into force which has the effect (as they usually do) of automatically substituting the new Secretary of State for the old. In the meantime it is usual for the old and the new offices to be held by the same individual. A new transfer of functions order was understood to be imminent at the time that this edition was published.

7–45 When the Secretary of State is the claimant, he does not usually take decisions personally but acts by a relevant officer under what is often referred to as the *Carltona* principle.[134] In practice, applications under CDDA ss.6–8 are dealt with by the Insolvency Service.[135] In some s.6 cases, proceedings will be commenced in the name of the Secretary of State but the official receiver will have actual conduct of them.[136] As a general rule, the official receiver may act by deputy official receivers.[137]

7–46 Before proceedings can be commenced under s.6 or s.8 of the CDDA, it must appear to the Secretary of State that it is expedient in the public interest that a disqualification order under the relevant section should be made. It is suggested that the same test would, in practice, apply to applications made by the Secretary of State under other sections of the CDDA. The same applies to the question of the continuation of such proceedings once commenced. This question is considered further in Ch.9. In principle, the question whether or not it is expedient in

[132] Who was also appointed Secretary of State for Trade and Industry.

[133] SI 2007/3224. For discussion of the operation of this statutory instrument in the disqualification context see *Secretary of State for Business Enterprise and Regulatory Reform v Smith* [2009] B.C.C. 497.

[134] See *Carltona Ltd v Commissioner of Works* [1943] 2 All E.R. 560; *Re Golden Chemical Products Ltd* [1976] Ch. 300. This is not delegation. Delegation of the decision to commence or continue proceedings is not permitted: see *Re Pantmaenog Timber Co Ltd* [2004] 1 A.C. 158 at [68].

[135] Section 8 cases are dealt with by the Companies Investigation branch which was formerly located within the Department, but which is now located within the Insolvency Service even though its focus is frequently companies which are not insolvent.

[136] Insolvency Act 1986 s.400.

[137] The relevant statutory provisions are discussed in *Re Homes Assured Corporation Plc, Official Receiver v Dobson* [1994] 2 B.C.L.C. 71.

the public interest to commence or continue proceedings will involve a number of issues including: (a) the likelihood of the proceedings being successful; and (b) other public interest factors. These factors will include matters such as the cost effectiveness of bringing the case weighed in the balance against the protective and deterrent purposes of the legislation.[138] If the prospects of success are less than 50 per cent, it may be thought that it could still be expedient in the public interest to commence proceedings. However, it is understood that a 50 per cent chance of success is applied as a rule of thumb in practice. This is in line with the position in relation to criminal prosecutions as set out in the Code for Crown Prosecutors. Even if the prospects of success are judged to be more than 50 per cent, it may not be expedient in the public interest to commence proceedings. Where, for example, a criminal investigation or prosecution is in train with regard to the same conduct as would found the civil disqualification proceedings, the Secretary of State may consider it expedient to leave the matter, and the imposition of any disqualification, to the criminal process.[139] Other relevant factors may include the likelihood of the directors engaging in further corporate activity and the amount of time that had passed since the events in question.[140]

7–47 There is little doubt that in exercising his powers under the CDDA, the decisions of the Secretary of State are susceptible to judicial review. If the question is whether or not existing proceedings are bound to fail or are otherwise an abuse, the matter can be dealt with in the course of the proceedings rather than requiring a separate application for judicial review.[141] Where the question is whether the Secretary of State acted unreasonably in assessing the wider public interest, the courts have shown a marked reluctance to interfere with the Secretary of State's decision, be that to commence proceedings or otherwise.[142]

[138] Such factors appear to be absent from the guidance issued by the OFT in relation to competition disqualification, a point picked up in 7–49.

[139] As regards the problems of parallel proceedings generally see the Report on Parallel Proceedings by the Financial Regulation Working Group of the Society for Advanced Legal Studies (December 1999).

[140] See, e.g. "Maxwell's escape disqualification proceedings", *Financial Times*, March 16, 2003.

[141] See in this respect the concession made in *Re Blackspur Group Plc, Secretary of State for Trade and Industry v Davies* [1998] 1 W.L.R. 422 and the subsequent decision in *R. (on the application of Eastaway) v Secretary of State for Trade and Industry* [2001] B.C.C. 365 against which permission to appeal was refused: [2000] 1 W.L.R. 2222.

[142] See *R. v Secretary of State for Trade and Industry Ex. p. Lonrho Plc* [1992] B.C.C. 325 (Secretary of State's refusal to apply under for orders under s.8 in the light of damning inspectors' report not perverse); *Re Blackspur Group Plc, Secretary of State for Trade and Industry v Davies* [1998] 1 W.L.R. 422 (Secretary of State entitled to continue proceedings against defendant notwithstanding the offer of non-statutory undertakings); *Re Barings Plc, Secretary of State for Trade and Industry v Baker (No.2)* [1999] 1 W.L.R. 1985 (Secretary of State entitled to proceed against defendant although he had already been dealt with by the relevant financial services regulator in relation to similar charges); *Re Launchexcept Ltd, Secretary of State for Trade and Industry v Tillman* [2000] 1 B.C.L.C. 36 (Secretary of State entitled to proceed against defendant in relation to a lead company that had given rise to collateral allegations in earlier disqualification proceedings); *Re Blackspur Group Plc (No.3), Secretary of State for Trade and Industry v Eastaway* [2001] EWCA Civ 1595, [2002] 2 B.C.L.C. 263, Ch.D. and CA (Secretary of State entitled to refuse a statutory disqualification undertaking that did not include grounds of unfit conduct). On the decision to commence or continue proceedings notwithstanding the offer of undertakings, see further Ch.9.

The claimant in competition disqualification cases

7–48 Under CDDA ss.9A to 9C, more than one relevant regulator may have jurisdiction to bring proceedings, accept an undertaking or carry out an investigation with a view to possible disqualification. The Secretary of State may make regulations to co-ordinate the performance of functions under these provisions.[143] Section 54(5) to (7) of the Competition Act 1998 will apply to such regulations, with certain definitions being tailored to the competition disqualification provisions of the CDDA.

7–49 The relevant guidance issued by the Office of Fair Trading[144] outlines the decision making process to be followed prior to the commencement of proceedings for the making of a competition disqualification order. The guidance confirms that the OFT or the relevant specified regulator will only make an application against a person where it considers that the conduct of that person is such as to make them unfit within the meaning of CDDA s.9A(3). It then sets out a detailed five-step process that it says will be followed involving consideration of the following factors:

(1) Whether an undertaking which is a company of which the person is a director has committed a breach of competition law (that is whether the condition for the making of a competition disqualification order set out in CDDA s.9A(2) is met).
(2) Whether a financial penalty has been imposed for the breach.
(3) Whether the company in question has benefited from leniency.
(4) The extent of the director's responsibility for the breach of competition law (this is, in effect, a factor that the court must weigh under CDDA ss.9A(5)(a), (6) and (7) for the purposes of determining whether or not there has been unfit conduct).
(5) Any aggravating and mitigating factors.

Of these factors (1) and (4) may be said to go directly to the question of whether or not the conditions for the making of a competition disqualification order are met. Factors (2) and (3) go to the seriousness of the breach and suggest that, by way of self-denying ordinance, the OFT or other specified regulator will only act in cases where the breach of competition law was so serious that a financial penalty has been levied and the company in question has not benefited from "leniency" in the relevant sense.[145] It is questionable whether or not the line being drawn in the OFT guidance is necessarily co-extensive with the line between conduct that is "unfit" for the purposes of CDDA s.9A and conduct that is not. Thus, it may be that the drawing of this line in the guidance represents a policy decision that, in the public interest, only "really serious" cases will be pursued, even if less serious cases falling the other side of the line could strictly still be

[143] CDDA s.9D(1).
[144] *Competition Disqualification Orders—Guidance* (May 2003) available on the OFT website, *http://www.oft.gov.uk* [Accessed August 24, 2009]. On the specific issues raised in this paragraph and on competition disqualification generally see further Ch.6. Proposals to amend the OFT guidance were under consideration at the time of going to press: see 6–34A.
[145] See text at 6–26.

brought within s.9A. Factor (5) also appears to go to the seriousness of the misconduct. Interestingly, the factors as a whole are effectively a repetition of the statutory criteria for establishing unfit conduct coupled with a test of "seriousness". On its face, the guidance does not refer to any wider public interest considerations. As such wider considerations will almost certainly be relevant to a decision not to proceed, it seems unlikely that their omission will prevent the OFT or specified regulator from developing and applying additional criteria. Indeed, the guidance does explicitly take account of other public interest factors because it envisages that CDDA s.2 orders will be the appropriate response in certain cases, thus avoiding the need for civil proceedings under s.9A. It is unclear whether this indicates that the OFT or specified regulator may decide to delay bringing civil disqualification proceedings where a director is subject to criminal processes such as investigation or prosecution in order to see whether a conviction is obtained and, if so, what factors will be taken into account in exercising the discretion.

Duties on organs of the state when acting as claimant to act fairly

7–50 When the Secretary of State, the Official Receiver (under CDDA s.7(2)), the OFT or other specified regulator (under CDDA s.9A) commences disqualification proceedings, duties will be owed with regard to the manner in which the proceedings are brought and conducted, akin to (but not necessarily to be equated in all respects with) those resting on public prosecutors in criminal cases. In the disqualification context, such duties have been adverted to and described (although not necessarily exhaustively) in cases such as *Re Moonlight Foods (UK) Ltd, Secretary of State for Trade and Industry v Hickling*[146] and *Re Finelist Ltd, Secretary of State for Trade and Industry v Swan.*[147] The relevant passage from the judgment in the *Moonlight Foods* case is set out at 7–31 above. In that case, the judge laid emphasis on the claimant's duty to present a disqualification case fairly. The four matters to which he particularly drew attention were that: (a) the evidence should not omit significant available material going in the defendant's favour; (b) it should attempt to deal with any explanation proffered by the defendant; (c) it should endeavour to apportion responsibility as between the defendants where more than one; and (d) it should avoid sweeping statements for which there is no evidence. It will be interesting to see how the courts develop the first of these matters. So, for example, where there is no order for disclosure, will the claimant be found to owe a duty to disclose any material in its possession that may assist the defendant in exonerating himself or in obtaining a reduction in the period of disqualification? If so, to what material will this obligation extend? Will it include, for example, material that could undermine the credibility of the claimant's witnesses and/or material that is not within the claimant's control (within the meaning of CPR r.31.3)?[148] In some cases where the proceedings have been criticised as being unfair, the unfairness has stemmed from deficiencies in

[146] [1996] B.C.C. 678.
[147] [2004] B.C.C. 877.
[148] See, by analogy, in relation to art.6 of the ECHR, *Jespers v Belgium* (1983) 5 E.H.R.R. CD305; *Edwards v United Kingdom* (1992) 15 E.H.R.R. 417 especially at [50].

the evidence put forward by the relevant insolvency practitioner[149] and it is far from clear that the officials within the Insolvency Service can be fairly criticised for failures on the part of the insolvency practitioner to reveal all relevant matters to the claimant on a full and frank basis.

7–51 Matters were taken further in the *Finelist* case. One criticism made in *Finelist* was that the director had not been given a fair opportunity to explain his conduct prior to the commencement of proceedings. Laddie J. suggested that the:

> "best way of ensuring that the Secretary of State's evidence deals with any 'explanation already proffered' by the director is to offer him an opportunity to proffer explanations".[150]

Although the logic is, with respect, contorted, the overall point is clear. If operated and handled properly, the procedure adopted by the Secretary of State prior to the commencement of disqualification proceedings should itself provide such an opportunity, as well as complying with the principles underlying the pre-action protocol regime. This point is also reflected in the internal guidance of the Secretary of State as regards pre-issue meetings with prospective defendants.[151] It is suggested that there should be limits on the extent to which the Secretary of State's officers should themselves be required to conduct a primary fact-finding investigation,[152] at least in cases where the Secretary of State is acting on the basis of information provided by an investigator (such as an officeholder reporting under CDDA s.7(3) or a person who generates investigative material relevant for the purposes of proceedings under CDDA s.8).

7–52 The fourth matter identified in the *Hickling* case was that the claimant should not rely on sweeping assertions for which there is no evidence. Set in its wider context, this may simply be an aspect of the general requirement for the claimant to confine the affidavit evidence to that which is relevant and probative and to ensure that the allegations being made, and any inferences that the court is being asked to draw, are clearly stated with the evidence relied on in each respect being clearly identified. Material that is clearly irrelevant should be avoided as being distracting at best and prejudicial "mudslinging" at worst.

7–53 The requirements of best practice identified in the previous paragraph have been emphasised in a number of cases.[153] They are said to flow, in major part, from the point that, in the disqualification context, the affidavit in support acts as a vehicle both for matters that would normally be set out in a statement of case

[149] See, e.g. *Re Digital Computer Licenses Ltd, Secretary of State for Trade and Industry v Lewis* [2003] B.C.C. 611.

[150] [2004] B.C.C. 877 at [28]. See also *Re Cubelock Ltd* [2001] B.C.C. 523.

[151] Referred to in *Finelist* at [31]–[32].

[152] Equivalent to, say, an enquiry under Companies Act 1985 s.447. In this respect, note *Re Pantmaenog Timber Co Ltd* [2004] 1 A.C. 158 at [68]: "It has never been the function of the Secretary of State to conduct an investigation or to gather information. He relies on information obtained by others; hence the investigative and reporting duties imposed on the official receiver and the responsible office-holder." Of course, this does not detract from the Secretary of State's duties qua litigator.

[153] See, e.g. *Re Pinemoor* [1997] B.C.C. 708 at 710 and *Secretary of State for Trade and Industry v Gill* [2004] EWHC 175 (Ch), [2005] B.C.C. 24.

and matters that are dealt with in written evidence.[154] On occasions, judges have expressed the wish that disqualification proceedings should be conducted on the basis of statements of case, as if they were governed by CPR Pt 7. However, it is suggested that the difficulty with disqualification proceedings is not so much the absence of statements of case but rather the lack of any standard typology from one disqualification case to the next. As is typically the case when determining whether or not there is unfairly prejudicial conduct for the purposes of s.994 of the Companies Act 2006 (formerly s.459 of the Companies Act 1985), the court in disqualification proceedings will often have to consider a myriad of facts about the company's affairs. Unlike, say, a case for breach of contract, there will usually be no neat "cause of action". As such, any statement of case would be likely to replicate in large part the written evidence. As with petitions brought under s.994, any statement of case in disqualification proceedings is unlikely to be short and simple. Indeed, in Scotland, the proceedings are commenced by way of petition—a procedure similar to that used in connection with s.994 in England and Wales—and such petitions frequently set out a large amount of factual and other material of a type similar to that contained in written evidence in civil disqualification proceedings south of the border. Furthermore, it is questionable whether, in light of the need to amend the underlying petition and answers, a need that often arises as the case develops, the use of such a procedure would provide any greater clarity or save time and cost. Clearly, this issue would benefit from careful consideration but, for now, it is respectfully suggested that the introduction of a requirement for civil disqualification proceedings to be brought under CPR Pt 7 would not necessarily be a complete panacea to the perceived weaknesses of the current system as it operates in England and Wales.

7–54 In *Re Pinemoor Ltd* Chadwick J. was faced with an application by the Secretary of State to strike out an affidavit containing alleged expert evidence filed on behalf of the defendant.[155] The affidavit and exhibit included an accountant's report which concluded that the defendant was not responsible for any of the matters raised in the Secretary of State's evidence by reference to which the defendant was alleged to be unfit to be concerned in the management of a company. The purported "expert" evidence was struck out. However, the Secretary of State was required to serve notice indicating which passages (if any) in the claimant's evidence relied on expressions of expert opinion. If there were any, the defendant was to have an opportunity to adduce his own expert evidence in response. The problem in *Pinemoor* arose because the Secretary of State's evidence used phrases such as "it appears" and "in my opinion" when inviting the court to draw inferences of secondary fact from the primary facts. It was not clear from expressions of that nature whether the Secretary of State was, in fact, relying on evidence of expert opinion and, accordingly, also not clear whether the defendant needed to

[154] See, e.g. *Finelist* at [13]–[14] and *Re Circle Holidays International Plc* [1994] B.C.C. 226 where the affidavit in s.6 proceedings was described as having something of the character of a pleading (in CPR language, a statement of case).

[155] [1997] B.C.C. 708. Under the rules of court then applicable, permission was not required to adduce expert evidence in stark contrast to the position under the CPR.

adduce expert evidence in rebuttal. It was in this context that Chadwick J. made the following observation:

> "It would be preferable, for the future, if those preparing and swearing affidavits in support of applications under this Act were careful to distinguish between the facts which they are able to establish by direct evidence, the inferences which they invite the court to draw from those facts, and the matters which are said to amount to unfitness on the part of the [defendant]. If those distinctions were observed, it might lead to [defendants] concentrating more closely on those factual matters to which they actually need to respond by affidavit evidence under r.6."

The main reason that the inferences sought to be drawn should be made clear is to enable the defendant to know what evidence he has to adduce and, as in *Pinemoor*, so as not to confuse the defendant into thinking that the "inferences" that the court is invited to draw are in fact statements of expert opinion. In the light of the stricter requirements of the CPR with regard to expert evidence, the confusion that arose in *Pinemoor* should be less common.

7–55 A different complication arose in *Re Park House Properties Ltd.*[156] In that case, the liquidator disagreed with the Secretary of State as to whether certain conduct amounted to "unfit conduct". Because the liquidator had couched the matters of unfit conduct in his affidavit as if he was expressing his own opinion, a problem arose when, in cross-examination, he resiled from his stated position. Neuberger J. correctly held that the case put forward was that of the Secretary of State and that the liquidator's personal views were therefore irrelevant. He expressed disappointment that the guidance in *Pinemoor* had apparently not been taken on board.[157] However, it is important to note that the only prejudice that arose in *Park House Properties* was the time wasted by the court on the issue. Furthermore, it is suggested that care needs to be taken not to elevate Chadwick J.'s guidance into a strict rule, any departure from which automatically breaches some "fairness" duty. Thus, it may be that in *Finelist* Laddie J. went too far in saying that the claimant is under an "obligation" to distinguish "issues proved by direct evidence" from "matters of inference".[158] It is suggested that a balanced approach needs to be, and will be taken, by the courts in this respect. If the defendant faces a genuine problem in understanding the case against him, the correct course, in the first instance, is to seek clarification. Many of these problems should disappear if there is proper communication between the parties prior to the issue of proceedings.

7–56 The judgment of Mr Jules Sher Q.C. in *Re Hitco 2000 Ltd, Official Receiver v Cowan*[159] provides a helpful illustration of the distinction between primary fact, secondary fact and allegation. The immediate context was an allegation of trading without reasonable prospect of paying creditors. In the context of such an allegation, there will be a considerable amount of primary facts concerning the financial

[156] [1997] 2 B.C.L.C. 530.

[157] Though it should be noted that the evidence in *Park House Properties* had been prepared many months before Chadwick J. made his remarks in *Pinemoor*: see [1997] 2 B.C.L.C. 530 at 535–536.

[158] [2004] B.C.C. 877 at [21]. The word used by Chadwick J. in *Pinemoor* was "preferable".

[159] [1995] 2 B.C.L.C. 63.

trajectory of the company during the period under review. Such facts could include details of debts not being paid, details of debt recovery proceedings against the company, the company's immediate and prospective financing, the available accounting information and what it showed both in terms of historic accounts and forward looking budgets and forecasts, details of dealings with the bank, advice sought from accountants and so on. From those primary facts, the court will be invited to draw inferences (or, as the deputy judge in *Hitco* preferred to put it, to evaluate the primary facts) to reach a conclusion as to whether the company had been allowed to continue trading without a reasonable prospect of paying its creditors. The final stage in the process is for the court to determine, in all the circumstances, that the director's involvement (or lack of it) in such trading is such as to render him unfit within the meaning of the relevant section of the CDDA.

7–57 A further point made by Laddie J. in *Finelist* was to the effect that the claimant's evidence should not contain irrelevant and prejudicial matters. The particular problem was that certain parts of the evidence implied that the defendant's alleged unfit conduct had directly brought about the insolvency of the relevant companies when this was not the case.[160] It is suggested that care has to be taken in applying this point in future cases divorced from the context in which it was made. Insolvency (meaning a relevant insolvency procedure) is one of the statutory criteria for the making of a disqualification order under CDDA s.6 and, just as the court is commonly informed of the company's date of incorporation, it is usual to inform the court of the date of its entry into a formal insolvency proceeding. A judge will normally be well able to deal with this sort of point. In *Finelist*, it seems that the evidence provided so much detail about the growth of the Finelist group, its assets and reported profits, the directors' remuneration and benefits and the size of the insolvency that it created the impression that the defendants' alleged unfit conduct was in some way responsible for the companies' demise. It is suggested that the vice in the evidence was not that it dealt with the group's financial collapse but the manner in which it did so. A similar point can be made regarding directors' remuneration, Laddie J. having criticised the deployment of such material in *Finelist*. However, a director's remuneration (especially when compared with that of other directors and employees) may, in many if not most cases, be relevant to his role and responsibilities within the company and to the apportionment of responsibility for misconduct among the directors.[161] In *Finelist*, Laddie J. also criticised as irrelevant statements as to damage that was capable of flowing from certain misconduct. However, it may well be relevant to explain the particular propensity for damage flowing from particular misconduct, so as to be able to assess the true extent of the vice. In this respect, the problem in *Finelist* seems to have been that the claimant's evidence did not make it sufficiently clear that it was seeking to identify potential problems that could have resulted from the alleged misconduct as distinct from asserting that those problems had in fact occurred in the instant case.

[160] For the relevant passages of the judgment see [2004] B.C.C. 877 at [67]–[71].

[161] See, e.g. *Re Barings Plc (No.5), Secretary of State for Trade and Industry v Baker* [1999] 1 B.C.L.C. 433 at 488, para.B6.

The wrong claimant

7–58 On occasions, the Secretary of State directs the official receiver to commence proceedings under CDDA s.6 in circumstances where, the company not being in compulsory liquidation, such proceedings must be commenced and prosecuted in the name of the Secretary of State (CDDA s.7(1)). There have been cases where the official receiver has mistakenly commenced the proceedings in his own name. When such problems have come to light, the Secretary of State's usual response has been to apply to amend the proceedings by substituting himself for the official receiver as claimant. The first such case to be reported was *Re Probe Data Systems Ltd.*[162] In *Probe Data*, Millett J. refused to grant the Secretary of State permission to amend the proceedings under RSC Ord.20, r.3 (by correcting the name of the claimant). However, in the later case of *Re NP Engineering and Security Products Ltd, Official Receiver v Pafundo*[163] the Court of Appeal permitted substitution of the Secretary of State for the official receiver under RSC Ord.15, r.6(2), a rule not relied on in *Probe Data*. The same result as in *NP Engineering* would be likely to follow under what is now CPR Pt 19.

The number of defendants

7–59 It is well established that there may be more than one defendant in a single set of disqualification proceedings.[164] However, in appropriate circumstances, and as a matter of fairness in case management, the court may decide that the proceedings should continue against one defendant even if for some reason, such as illness or the existence of parallel criminal proceedings, the proceedings should not continue for the time being against another defendant. Thus, in *Re Land Travel Ltd, Secretary of State for Trade and Industry v Tjolle*, Chadwick J. decided, in the circumstances, that it was appropriate to split the trial so that the proceedings continued against one defendant separately from the other two.[165] Moreover, in *EDC v United Kingdom*,[166] the European Commission of Human Rights held that a defendant's right to a fair trial under art.6 of the ECHR was infringed in circumstances where disqualification proceedings had been adjourned against him and his co-defendants pending the outcome of parallel criminal proceedings to which he was not a party. The upshot is that, in similar circumstances, the court may very well decide that there is little option but to split the proceedings, with the potential for separate trials.

The number of lead companies in s.6 cases

7–60 The concepts of "lead" and "collateral" companies are discussed at length in the text from 3–106. In *Re Surrey Leisure Ltd, Official Receiver v Keam*,[167] a submission was made on behalf of the defendant to the effect that, on its proper

[162] [1989] B.C.L.C. 561.
[163] [1998] 1 B.C.L.C. 208.
[164] See now CPR r.19.1.
[165] For the background see Jacob J.'s judgment in the case at [1998] 1 B.C.L.C. 333.
[166] [1998] B.C.C. 370.
[167] [1999] 1 B.C.L.C. 731 affirmed by the Court of Appeal: see [1999] 2 B.C.L.C. 457.

construction, the CDDA does not allow a claimant to nominate more than one lead company in proceedings under s.6. The submission was roundly rejected by the judge:

> "I see no warrant for construing the [CDDA] in that restrictive manner. It has been said many times in the authorities that the purpose of the [CDDA] is to prevent persons acting as directors who are unfit to do so . . . That being so, I can see no reason in principle why [a claimant] for a disqualification order who seeks to establish unfitness in relation to more than one company should be obliged to limit himself to naming only one of those companies as the lead company, leaving the other or others to be treated as collateral companies, since by doing so he might be limiting his chances of obtaining an order. Nor can I find anything in the [CDDA], on its true construction, which justifies such an artificial, indeed arbitrary result."[168]

The effect is that the claimant may name as many lead companies in s.6 proceedings as he wishes subject only to the requirements that: (a) such companies have "become insolvent" within the meaning of s.6(2); and (b) the proceedings are brought within two years or otherwise with the permission of the court under s.7(2).

Joining disqualification proceedings with other proceedings

7–61 It used to be common for insolvency practitioners to await the outcome of disqualification proceedings before commencing their own civil recovery proceedings, often based on one or more elements of the case brought by the claimant in the disqualification proceedings. This had at least three potential advantages all of which could be obtained at little or no cost to the insolvency practitioner and/or the relevant company. First, it might give rise to findings against a director that he would be prevented from disputing in any subsequent recovery proceedings.[169] Secondly, even if the disqualification proceedings did not give rise to such findings, any findings of fact that were made might provide a useful indication of the likely findings in a second set of proceedings. Thirdly, it gave the insolvency practitioner an opportunity to gauge the director both as litigant and witness. In *Official Receiver v Doshi*,[170] civil recovery proceedings brought by the insolvency practitioner were heard at the same time as disqualification proceedings under CDDA s.6. It is important to note that the proceedings were not formally consolidated. Given the different interests of the liquidator and the official receiver, consolidation would not have been appropriate. Although hailed at the time as a great advance, the number of subsequent cases where this course has been followed appears to have been few. This probably reflects the fact that many disqualification cases are now disposed of by way of undertaking and that insolvency practitioners still perceive there to be advantages in allowing the

[168] [1999] 1 B.C.L.C. 731 at 736–737. The Court of Appeal was struck by the fact that the official receiver could, in any event, issue separate proceedings for each lead company and then consolidate the proceedings.

[169] See *Re Thomas Christy Ltd* [1994] 2 B.C.L.C. 527.

[170] [2001] 2 B.C.L.C. 235.

disqualification process to run its course before they commence their own proceedings.

APPLICATIONS FOR THE MAKING OF A DISQUALIFICATION ORDER

Overview of procedure on an application for the making of a disqualification order

7–62 The historical evolution of the procedure in civil disqualification cases was conveniently summarised by Hoffmann L.J. in *Re Rex Williams Leisure Plc, Secretary of State for Trade and Industry v Warren*[171]:

> "... [W]hen a power to disqualify directors was first introduced in s.217 of the Companies Act 1929, the procedure was assimilated to that of the misfeasance summons, a summary procedure which went back to the Companies Act 1862: see r.66 of the Companies (Winding up) Rules 1929. Misfeasance summonses had originally followed the traditional Chancery procedure of having all the evidence on affidavit, but in 1921 the Companies Court adopted a more common law approach. Astbury J. issued a Practice Note . . .:
>
> 'In a recent case tried in this court various defects in the present practice relating to the trial of misfeasance summonses . . . were made apparent. The practice of allowing witnesses to give their evidence in chief by affidavits, prepared or settled for them by others, in cases where real disputes of fact exist and/or where various charges of misfeasance or breach of trust are involved, is open to grave objection, and when numerous or complicated issues of law or fact exist, the points relied upon are under the practice at present prevailing, as and when occasion demands, amended or raised for the first time and from time to time during the progress of the trial, which causes confusion, recalling of witnesses, possible injustice, waste of time and increased costs . . . in future the practice in these cases shall be as follows: On the return of the summons the Registrar shall give direction as to whether points of claim and defence are to be delivered or not, as to the taking of evidence wholly or in part by affidavit or orally, as to cross-examination, and generally as to the procedure on the summons. No report or affidavit shall be made or filed until the Registrar shall so direct.'
>
> Rule 66 of the Companies (Winding-up) Rules 1929 reflected this Practice Note, providing that no affidavit or report was to be filed in advance of the first appointment before the registrar and giving him a wide discretion as to the taking of evidence wholly or in part by affidavit or orally."

7–63 Hoffmann L.J. was referring here to the manner in which the relevant procedural rules have changed from time to time. His conclusion was that the Disqualification Rules reflect part of a general trend towards a greater emphasis on written procedure in advance of the hearing. As he put it:

> "The advantage of allowing both sides to discover each other's cases in detail before trial and cross-examination is perceived to outweigh the loss of spontaneity and the increase in costs in the pre-trial stage."

[171] [1994] Ch. 350.

Since *Rex Williams* was decided the CPR have themselves further accentuated this trend.

Procedural timetable

7–64 The Disqualification Rules lay down a procedural timetable for applications for the making of disqualification orders under CDDA ss.6, 8 and 9A. The Disqualification Practice Direction has largely replicated this regime for other civil applications under CDDA ss.2, 3 and 4. The procedure is broadly that under CPR Pt 8 but with modifications.[172] There is no power to alter the procedure to permit proceedings to be brought or continued under CPR Pt 7.[173] The relevant timetable is as follows.

Commencement of proceedings

7–65 Except as regards s.6 proceedings, there is no statutory time limit laid down by the CDDA within which civil disqualification proceedings must be commenced. Section 7(2) provides that an application for a s.6 disqualification order cannot be made later than the end of the period of two years beginning with the day on which the relevant company became insolvent unless the permission of the court is first obtained. The operation of this section and the circumstances in which the court will grant permission to commence proceedings outside the two-year time period is considered further in Ch.8.

The claim form

7–66 A number of points arise regarding the claim form:

(1) The claim form is in a form prescribed by the Disqualification Practice Direction, para.4.2. The following matters are relevant:

  (a) The heading will be entitled in the matter of the relevant company (which in cases brought under s.6 will be the name of the lead company or companies only) and in the matter of the CDDA (Disqualification Practice Direction, para.5.1).

  (b) The claim form is required to contain certain endorsements (Disqualification Rules r.4; Disqualification Practice Direction, para.6.1). These endorsements are in the nature of notes for defendants setting out the applicable rules, the period of disqualification that can be imposed, the section of the CDDA pursuant to which the application is made and the time limits for filing evidence. Reference should also be made to r.4 of the Disqualification Rules which provides that on the first hearing of the claim in s.6, 8 and 9A proceedings, the court can impose a period of disqualification of up to five years.

[172] Disqualification Rules rr.2, 5 and 6; Disqualification Practice Direction, para.4.2. See also CPR r.8.1(6).

[173] Disqualification Practice Direction, para.4.2.

(c) The prescribed form of claim form sets out notes to assist the claimant in filling it in. These notes are not an integral part of the claim form and a defendant would have no grounds for complaint if they did not appear.

(2) In High Court cases, the claim form should be issued out of the office of the Companies Court Registrar or a Chancery District Registry. In county court cases, the claim form should be issued out of the relevant county court office (Disqualification Practice Direction, para.4.1A(2)).
(3) On issue of the claim form, the evidence relied on in support of the claim must be filed with the court.[174] The evidence will be by way of affidavit or affirmation. Any exhibits should be lodged with the court but not formally "filed"; they are returned at the conclusion of the case. In the case of proceedings brought in the name of the official receiver, the evidence may take the form of a report by him. This form of evidence is considered further below.
(4) On issue of the claim form a hearing date is given for the first hearing of the application before a district judge or the Companies Court Registrar (as appropriate). This will be not less than eight weeks from the date of issue of the claim form (Disqualification Rules r.7(1); Disqualification Practice Direction, para.4.3).

Service of claim form

7–67 A number of points also arise regarding service:

(1) The claim form, together with copies of the evidence in support and an acknowledgment of service, must be served on the defendant (Disqualification Practice Direction, paras 9.3(3), 7.2, 7.4). The acknowledgment of service is again in a specially prescribed form (Disqualification Practice Direction, para.8), which reflects the differences in procedure between disqualification proceedings and an ordinary CPR Pt 8 claim.
(2) Service of the claim form is the responsibility of the claimant. CPR Pt 6 will apply in general except that the claim form may be served by first class post to the defendant's last known address and, if it is so served, the date of service is deemed to be the seventh day following the date on which it was posted, unless the contrary is proved (Disqualification Rules r.5(1); Disqualification Practice Direction, para.7.2). Rule 5(1) of the Disqualification Rules simply provides one way for the claimant to show that service has been effected. It does not rule out proof of actual service by some other means.[175]
(3) There is provision for the court to order service out of the jurisdiction. This is a separate regime from that under CPR rr.6.17–6.31 (Disqualification Rules

[174] CPR r.8.5(1); Disqualification Rules r.3(1) and Disqualification Practice Direction, para.9.3. With the advent of the CPR, it is unlikely that the court will be sympathetic to the filing of "holding" evidence on the basis that it will be supplemented later. For examples of the judicial approach under the old rules of court see *Re Crestjoy Products Ltd* [1990] B.C.L.C. 677 and *Re Jazzgold Ltd* [1994] 1 B.C.L.C. 38.

[175] *Re Metropolitan Ltd, Official Receiver v Hodkingson*, October 13, 2000, Ch.D., unreported.

r.5(2); Disqualification Practice Direction, para.7.3). However, the court is likely to have regard to the CPR provisions in exercising its discretion under the Disqualification Rules and Disqualification Practice Direction.

Acknowledgment and defendant's evidence

7–68 The position is as follows:

(1) Within 14 days of service of the claim form, the defendant must file and serve on the other parties the acknowledgment of service (Disqualification Rules r.5(3); Disqualification Practice Direction, para.8.3). If it is not filed within the prescribed period the defendant may attend the hearing of the application but may not take part in the hearing unless the court gives permission (Disqualification Practice Direction, para.8.4).
(2) Within 28 days of service of the claim form the defendant must file in court any affidavit evidence in opposition to the application together with any exhibits and (at the same time) serve copies on the claimant (Disqualification Rules r.6(1); Disqualification Practice Direction, para.9.4).
(3) In cases where there is more than one defendant, each defendant is required to serve his evidence on the other defendants unless the court otherwise orders (Disqualification Practice Direction, para.9.5). The court might "otherwise order" in cases where a mutual exchange is more appropriate (for example, where there is a "cut throat" defence) or where one defendant is ready to serve but another is not. It is sensible practice for the defendants to agree a procedural course, or failing that, at least agree what should happen pending the first hearing with a view to saving the costs of an unnecessary application to the court. As the timetable in the rules envisages the service of evidence in reply by the claimant, it may be necessary to involve the claimant in any relevant discussions.

Further evidence of claimant

7–69 The claimant is required to serve any further evidence by way of reply within 14 days of receiving the defendant's evidence (Disqualification Rules r.6(2); Disqualification Practice Direction, para.9.6).

Extensions of time

7–70 So far as is possible, the timetable laid down by the Disqualification Rules and/or the Disqualification Practice Direction should be followed and all evidence filed before the first hearing (Disqualification Practice Direction, para.9.8). It is to be hoped that the greater encouragement to consider matters before proceedings are launched will increase the possibility of achieving this. Nevertheless, there may be circumstances in which the timetable cannot be met. In those circumstances, there are two options:

(1) The parties themselves may be able to agree extensions of time. Prior to the first hearing, extensions may be made by written agreement. After the first hearing,

extensions are governed by CPR rr.2.11 and 29.5 (see Disqualification Practice Direction, para. 9.7).

(2) The court will regulate the procedural timetable as part of its case management function (Disqualification Practice Direction, para.11).

The first hearing

7–71 The position is as follows:

(1) The date for the first hearing will have been fixed on the issue of the claim form for a date not less than eight weeks away (Disqualification Rules r.7(1); Disqualification Practice Direction, paras 4.3 and 10.1). The first hearing will be before a district judge or the Companies Court Registrar sitting in public in either case (Disqualification Rules r.7(2); Disqualification Practice Direction, paras 4.3 and 10.2). The current practice in the Royal Courts of Justice is to list such applications for a Monday morning.

(2) On the first hearing date, the court will either determine the application or adjourn it. If the hearing is adjourned, the court will give directions and the parties should seek all interim directions that they need so far as possible with a view to avoiding the need for successive hearings (Disqualification Rules r.7; Disqualification Practice Direction, para.10.4). The court's powers of case management are wide. In addition to the general powers in the CPR, the Disqualification Practice Direction highlights a number of matters that the court and the parties should consider with regard to fixing the trial date and the like. One of the usual directions is that deponents to affidavits should attend trial for cross-examination on so many days prior written notice and that, in default, their evidence should not be read.[176] However, in a complicated case it may be appropriate to delay a decision on the precise directions as to cross-examination until the evidence has closed—that is, all evidence relied on has been served and filed. Such a course enables a more focused approach to the question of who should be called to give evidence and can avoid the situation where witnesses are required to be on "stand by" until shortly before the trial, at which point a party decides that, after all, it does not wish them to be cross-examined.

(3) In proceedings under CDDA ss.6, 8 and 9A, the judge is unable to disqualify for a period of more than five years on the first hearing. Accordingly, if on a provisional consideration, the court takes the view that a period of more than five years is likely to be appropriate, it should adjourn the application, giving reasons (Disqualification Rules r.7(4)(a)). The defendant, who may have decided not to defend on the basis that he is happy to accept a disqualification of five years or less, would then have an opportunity to take steps in the proceedings. If a defendant agrees or is present and is not prejudiced, there seems no reason why the hearing could not go ahead on the same day. It is

[176] See CPR r.8.6.

suggested that failure to comply with the strict wording of the Disqualification Rules r.7(4) will not automatically prevent the hearing from going ahead if it is just for it to do so and that, in any event, the defendant can waive his rights under this rule.

(4) One matter that may need to be considered is the question of who should hear the trial (i.e. a registrar or a judge). In *Re Digital Computer Services Ltd, Lewis v Secretary of State for Trade and Industry*,[177] Neuberger J. laid down general guidelines on this subject. The court should take into account the following factors: (a) the likely length of the hearing; (b) the complexity of the issues and the amount at stake; (c) the degree of public interest and (d) the likely length of time before a hearing date. The wishes of the parties will be relevant but not on its own decisive.[178]

(5) Some of the issues raised above concerning the conduct of the trial may best be dealt with at a pre-trial review, preferably before the judge who is to conduct the actual trial.

Pleadings and core bundles

7–72 One issue that commonly arises in disqualification cases is the absence of pleaded statements of case. In fact it may be doubted whether statements of case or points of claim and defence would, in many cases, prove to be very efficacious. In the United Kingdom, unfair prejudice petitions under what is now Pt 30 of the Companies Act 2006 have frequently been conducted on the basis that points of claim and defence are ordered. Such points of claim and defence frequently set out in great detail the life history of the company mirroring what formerly used to be set out in great detail in a petition. This reflects the fact that such proceedings are often not based upon a defined narrow cause of action or breach of director's duties but on a wider history of events and course of dealings which together are said to demonstrate "unfairly prejudicial conduct". The same broad point is relevant in many disqualification cases. Indeed, in Scotland written pleadings are an established part of court procedure in disqualification cases. However, those pleadings are frequently as long and detailed as the written evidence in a case conducted south of the border. Another approach sometimes seen[179] is the ordering of schedules setting out in columns the relevant evidence—for example, columns for the allegations, the passages in the written evidence and the pages of the exhibits supporting such allegations, the passages in the written evidence and the pages of the exhibits relied upon in defending (or presumably in mitigation) of such allegations and a column for response by the claimant. With great respect such an approach, while superficially attractive, often increases costs and is of limited assistance at trial. The same is true of attempts to direct a core bundle of documents. In many cases there are no obvious "core" documents. This is not to say

[177] [2001] 2 B.C.L.C. 597.

[178] See further 7–16 above.

[179] See, e.g. the suggestion of Creswell J. in *Re Astra Holdings Plc, Secretary of State for Trade and Industry v Anderson* [1998] 2 B.C.L.C. 44.

that there are not cases where the employment of such judicial case management techniques will be helpful. However, it is respectfully suggested that it should not routinely be assumed that such techniques will in fact save time and costs.

The trial

7–73 Further procedural requirements are set out in para.12 of the Disqualification Practice Direction dealing with such matters as trial bundles, skeleton arguments and other documents to be prepared by the claimant's advocate. The court also has powers to limit evidence (see, e.g. CPR r.32.1(2)). Use of these powers is likely to raise questions of vires and compliance with the Human Rights Act 1998 especially in cases where the court declines to hear evidence on an issue that the parties wish to have decided. In the event that a party does not appear, the court has power to continue with the trial but there is scope for the absent party to apply to set aside any order made in his absence (Disqualification Rules r.8; Disqualification Practice Direction, para.14 and, by analogy, CPR r.39.3).[180] In this field too, the Human Rights Act 1998 has had a potential impact. One point of interest has been the extent to which the "equality of arms" element of art.6 of the ECHR has been interpreted. Article 6 is not infringed simply because the defendant does not have the same level of legal representation enjoyed by the claimant. Thus, even in criminal cases, where the Crown is represented by a Q.C., a fair trial does not necessarily entail that the defendant should also be represented by a Q.C.[181] Article 6 has also been raised in relation to the availability of public funding.[182]

7–74 A further requirement under art.6 is that the tribunal should be "impartial". In *Re Windows West Ltd, Official Receiver v Zwirn*,[183] the court was faced with an appeal against a 12-year disqualification order made by the registrar based on the defendant's conduct in relation to a series of phoenix companies. One of the grounds of appeal was that the registrar's decision was "tainted by an appearance of bias" in that he had failed to recuse himself after having been made aware that the defendant had entered into negotiations for and been minded to pursue a disposal of the proceedings under the summary *Carecraft* procedure.[184] Before the trial, the registrar had been made aware that a full hearing might not be needed because of the *Carecraft* negotiations.[185] The defendant argued that whilst the judge might properly learn of the possibility of settlement negotiations prior to the trial, it was objectionable for him to have prior knowledge of *Carecraft* negotiations because the *Carecraft* procedure involves the director making admissions as to the factual

[180] See also *Re Metropolitan Ltd, Official Receiver v Hodkingson*, October 13, 2000, Ch.D., unreported.

[181] *Re Attorney General's Reference (No.82a of 2000)* [2002] EWCA Crim 215, [2002] 2 Cr.App.R. 24 at [14].

[182] See *R. (on the application of Jarrett) v Legal Services Commission* [2001] EWHC Admin 389, [2002] A.C.D. 25.

[183] [2002] B.C.C. 760.

[184] On which see further Ch.9.

[185] The fact that the registrar was aware of the position is a reflection of the professional duty of lawyers to keep the court informed of the possibility that the trial may be aborted, a duty that was re-emphasised in *Tasyurdu v Immigration Appeal Tribunal* [2003] EWCA Civ 447, [2003] C.P.Rep. 61 and *Yell Ltd v Garton* [2004] EWCA Civ 87, [2004] C.P.Rep. 29.

basis of disqualification. As it happened, the deputy judge was able to dismiss the ground of appeal on the basis that the point had been waived.[186] However, he doubted that the court's prior knowledge that a director might be prepared to dispose of a case under the *Carecraft* procedure would mean that the director could not get a fair trial should the negotiations prove unsuccessful. It is respectfully suggested that his doubts were well founded.

7–75 It may be, however, that the problem should be approached on a different basis. In *R. (on the application of Mahfouz) v Professional Conduct Committee of the General Medical Council*,[187] judicial review was sought of a refusal by the Professional Conduct Committee of the General Medical Council, in the context of a case of alleged professional misconduct, to discharge members of the Committee who had read a number of prejudicial press articles about the doctor concerned. In resolving this issue, the test applied by the Committee was to ask whether, in the circumstances of the case, a fair minded and informed observer, having considered the facts, would conclude that there was a real possibility that the tribunal was biased.[188] However, the Court of Appeal suggested that the test should be whether the risk of prejudice arising from the relevant publicity was so grave that no direction, however carefully formulated, could reasonably be expected to remove it.[189] This was a more helpful starting point than the authorities on apparent bias, which ran the risk of overcomplicating what was a relatively simple issue. "Bias" or "apparent bias" was not the same as mere knowledge of inadmissible and potentially prejudicial information.

7–75A As regards adjournments, the court has applied the criteria set out in CPR r.3.9 by way of analogy.[190] When ill health is concerned, the question will be whether a fair trial is possible.[191] In some cases ill health may be such that the proceedings will be stayed or stayed on undertakings.[192] However, with the advent of statutory undertakings it is suggested that a statutory undertaking may usually be the more appropriate route to take.

Summary procedure

7–76 If at any stage the parties wish to invite the court to deal with the matter on a *Carecraft* basis, they should inform the court immediately and obtain a date for the hearing (Disqualification Practice Direction, para.13).[193] Summary hearings under the *Carecraft* procedure are dealt with in greater detail in Ch.9.

[186] See, e.g. *Re Locabail (UK) Ltd v Bayfield Properties Ltd* [2000] Q.B. 451.

[187] [2004] EWCA Civ 233, [2004] Lloyd's Rep.Med. 377.

[188] *Porter v Magill* [2001] UKHL 67, [2002] 2 A.C. 357.

[189] Following *Montgomery v HM Advocate* [2003] 1 A.C. 641.

[190] *Re Stone & Rolls Ltd, Official Receiver v Stojevic* [2007] EWHC 1186 (Ch), [2008] Bus.L.R. 641.

[191] *Re Surrey Sackholders Ltd, Official Receiver v Ohayon*, August 25, 2004, Ch.D., unreported (Mr Ian Glick Q.C. sitting as a deputy High Court judge). As regards adjournments for ill-health in the criminal sphere see *R. v Jones (Anthony William)* [2002] UKHL 5, [2003] 1 A.C. 1 and *R. v Taylor (David Jeremy)* [2008] EWCA Crim 680.

[192] *Re Homes Assured Corp Plc* [1996] B.C.C. 297; *Re Stormont Ltd, Secretary of State for Trade and Industry v Cleland* [1997] 1 B.C.L.C. 437.

[193] On the professional duty of the parties' lawyers to keep the court informed of the possibility that the trial may be aborted see *Tasyurdu v Immigration Appeal Tribunal* [2003] EWCA Civ 447, [2003] C.P.Rep. 61; *Yell Ltd v Garton* [2004] EWCA Civ 87, [2004] C.P.Rep. 29.

Other matters

Disclosure

7–77 CPR Pt 31 now governs disclosure and inspection of documents. To the extent that the parties have documents physically within their possession, pre-trial disclosure may come more to the fore in the light of the pre-action protocols discussed earlier. Furthermore, the parties may have to give consideration to the powers of pre-action disclosure contained in the Supreme Court Act 1981 (now renamed the Senior Courts Act 1981) and the County Courts Act 1984 (see CPR rr.31.16–31.17). At present, it appears that the use of these powers to order pre-action disclosure (at least against non-parties) will be the exception rather than the rule except, perhaps, in cases where an administrator or administrative receiver has sold the company's business including its records. In that case, and if voluntary co-operation is not forthcoming, the claimant may need to persuade or require the office holder to exercise his powers under s.236 of the Insolvency Act 1986 and both parties may need to invoke the statutory powers for pre-action disclosure mentioned above.

7–78 As regards disclosure once proceedings are on foot, there is no automatic disclosure as between the parties. In this respect the position under the general court rules has now been assimilated to the position that has for long applied in civil disqualification proceedings. This does not mean, however, that informal disclosure is not encouraged or that, in appropriate cases, the parties should not submit to disclosure orders.[194]

7–79 In relation to CDDA s.6 proceedings where the official receiver is not the liquidator, it is rare for the claimant to hold many, if any, documents that have not been exhibited in evidence. Such documents will usually be retained by the relevant office holder, although the claimant may have received documents from other sources as a result of his own enquiries. In circumstances where the office holder physically retains documents, the question arises as to whether the Secretary of State is in "control" of those documents for the purposes of CPR r.31.8. In most cases the defendant will simply be unaware of the actual position. In the absence of special circumstances, it seems unlikely that the existence of the power in CDDA s.7(4) will be held to confer "control" on the claimant. In *Re Lombard Shipping and Forwarding Ltd*,[195] it was ruled that documents held by joint administrative receivers were not within the possession, custody or power of the Secretary of State for the purpose of ordering disclosure under the old rules. This was because the only power of the Secretary of State to obtain the documents was by way of an order under CDDA s.7(4). However, the court merely has a discretion whether or not to order an office holder to comply with a request on an application under s.7(4) and it was held that the Secretary of State had no absolute right to insist on production.[196] It will be interesting to see whether a

[194] An order may be required to protect against risk of breaches of confidence owed to other parties and/or to ensure limited use of the documents once disclosed.

[195] [1993] B.C.L.C. 238.

[196] The remark of Lewison J. in *Re Crystal Palace Football Club (1986), Secretary of State for Trade and Industry v Goldberg* [2003] EWHC 2843 (Ch), [2004] 1 B.C.L.C. 597 to the effect that "in the normal course of events most or all of the relevant documents will be in the possession (or at least in the power) of the Secretary of State" does not deal with the *Lombard Shipping* case.

different result would follow if the defendant joined the relevant office holder so that the office holder and the claimant were both before the court. In those circumstances, the court may be prepared to consider whether, as between claimant and office holder, an order under s.7(4), is appropriate.

7–80 In practice, the office holder will usually make documents available for inspection by the defendant on a voluntary basis but without giving disclosure by list. This can give rise to practical problems. First, the documents will often be in a chaotic state. Secondly, the office holder may seek to charge the defendant for making the documents available and/or for supervising the inspection. On the first point, as a general rule, the court is unlikely to require the preparation of a list as a means of saving time in that the defendant can usually be expected to have some acquaintance with his company's documents. However, this is only a general rule. The more extensive the documents, the more likely it is that a list will be ordered. It should be possible to deal with the issue of supervision by requiring the defendant's legal representative to attend and give any undertaking as to non-alteration and non-removal. The costs of getting the documents out of storage may be more problematic. If agreement cannot be reached, the defendant may have to consider issuing a witness summons to compel the office holder to produce the documents or an order under the CPR that the claimant should bear the relevant costs, such costs then being treated as costs in the proceedings. Where the official receiver is the liquidator he is technically in a position to make disclosure by way of list. However, unless the documents are extensive, it is likely that if he makes them available for inspection, the court would hold that any requirement of disclosure by list would be disproportionate given that the defendant ought to have at least some passing acquaintance with the company's documents and should be able to identify those documents he wants to see. Disclosure orders against third parties (on terms) for the purposes of existing disqualification proceedings were made in *Re Howglen Ltd*,[197] *Re Skyward Builders Plc*[198] and *Re Fast Track Corporation Ltd, Secretary of State for Trade and Industry v Cullen-Crouch*.[199] The facts of those cases provide a useful indication of the court's approach in this area.

7–81 Of course, documents are only liable to fall within the disclosure regime if they bear sufficient relevance to the proceedings in question. In *Re Astra Holdings Plc, Secretary of State for Trade and Industry v Anderson*,[200] a case brought by the Secretary of State under CDDA s.8 following a Companies Act inspection under s.432, the court was invited to rule on disclosure of documents generated during the course of the inspection process. The documents in question included communications and notes of meetings between the inspectors (or their staff) and the DTI, communications and notes of meetings between the inspectors and their staff, and documents produced by the inspectors or their staff for internal use (for example: analysis or working papers; internal memos or file notes; notes used to produce

[197] [2001] 1 All E.R. 376. The court considered the circumstances in which disclosure would be made under both the Bankers Books (Evidence) Act 1879 and CPR r.31.17.

[198] [2002] EWHC 1788 (Ch), [2002] 2 B.C.L.C. 750.

[199] December 19, 2000, Ch.D., unreported.

[200] [1998] 2 B.C.L.C. 44.

questions and lists of questions prepared for interview; drafts of letters; drafts of the report or parts thereof or progress reports or drafts generally). The argument for the Secretary of State was that such material was inadmissible, irrelevant and unnecessary. The weight to be attached to the evidence in the report was to be judged by reference to the material on which the report was founded, not on drafts, memos or notes. The question of whether public interest immunity should be claimed was reserved. The argument for the directors was, in essence, that the documents were required to examine the inspectors' reasoning processes to see, for example, whether they had taken into account irrelevant matters, given that such processes led to conclusions that were relied on against the directors. The judge ruled that the documents were not disclosable. The directors had been given access to the material on which the report was based, namely the documents (presumably contemporaneous to the life of the company) placed before the inspectors and the transcripts of oral evidence that the inspectors had taken. It is suggested that the judge's ruling was correct. The starting point is the basis on which a trial under s.8 is conducted. If the inspectors' report is evidence that the court is not allowed to second guess, a judicial review style of approach becomes the only basis for directors to attack its findings. In effect, they would be driven to attack the process by which the conclusions were reached. If, on the other hand, the inspectors' views and opinions are evidence, but evidence that can be challenged, and the court has freedom to reach a decision itself on the materials available, the focus shifts from the process by which the inspectors reached their conclusions to the question of whether, on the material available, the material justifies their conclusions. This latter approach, both in the winding up field where the implied exception to the hearsay rule first developed, and in disqualification cases such as *Barings* and *Atlantic Computers*, is the one that the courts have followed.[201]

7–82 The other important ruling in the *Astra* case was that a side-letter from the inspectors to the Secretary of State expressing the inspectors' views as to whether disqualification was appropriate should be disclosed. Although technically the views of the inspectors were irrelevant on this point, it was suggested that their views, and any reasons given for them, might assist the defendants in formulating their defence and evidence. In this respect, the position reached by the judge was analogous to that reached by Scott V.C. in the *Barings* disqualification proceedings as regards office holder reports provided in accordance with CDDA s.7(3),[202] which for these purposes can be viewed as fulfilling the same purpose as an inspectors' report. Indeed, it may be said that the "side letter" was, on one view, something that could be viewed as part of the inspectors' report in the widest sense of the term.

Further information

7–83 The old distinction between further and better particulars of pleading (now statements of case) and interrogatories has passed into history (see now CPR Pt 18). It should be noted that while, under the old rules, interrogatories were refused in *Re Sutton Glassworks Ltd*,[203] this did not mean that further information was not

[201] See further from 7–123 below.
[202] See further text from 3–12.
[203] [1997] 1 B.C.L.C. 26.

forthcoming in that case, as the Secretary of State had volunteered it. It is likely that if such information were not produced voluntarily, the court would now be more willing to order its production in the spirit of the CPR.[204] In making or responding to requests for information under CPR Pt 18, it is essential for parties to pay attention to the accompanying Practice Direction. One trap for the unwary is the power under para.5 of the Practice Direction, which enables the maker of a request, in certain circumstances, to apply for and obtain a court order without notice to the other side. In the ordinary case, it will be premature for the defendant to request further information until the claimant has replied to the defendant's evidence.[205]

Summary judgment and/or strike out

7–84 Summary judgment was not available in originating summons procedure under the old law. However, the effect of Pt 24 of the CPR is that the procedure for summary judgment is now applicable. To date this does not seem to have been used much in the context of disqualification proceedings.[206] Doubtless this reflects the fact that most disqualification cases involve a great deal of disputed fact and require considerable analysis before a conclusion can be reached. As such they will rarely be appropriate for summary judgment.

7–85 The court also has the power under CPR r.3.4 to strike out a statement of case and it is clear that this power can be used as a disciplinary measure, for example, in cases where there has been a failure to comply with rules of court, practice directions or court orders.[207] Rule 3.4 refers expressly to statements of case but doubtless it will apply to affidavit evidence and claim forms. There are two other principal grounds on which the court can exercise the power to strike out: (a) where the statement of case discloses no reasonable grounds for bringing or defending the claim; and (b) where the statement of case is an abuse of the court's process or is otherwise likely to obstruct the just disposal of the proceedings. The categories of abuse of process are not closed. The court's jurisdiction to strike out disqualification proceedings has been exercised in the following (non-exhaustive) circumstances:

(1) On grounds of delay (see further discussion in Ch.8).
(2) On grounds of double jeopardy. This point has been taken in disqualification cases. In *Re Barings Plc, Secretary of State for Trade and Industry v Baker*

[204] See *Re Finelist Ltd, Secretary of State for Trade and Industry v Swan* [2004] B.C.C. 877. Note however, that under CPR Pt 18 there must still be an issue between the parties to which the further information sought must relate.

[205] *Secretary of State for Trade and Industry v McAvoy* [2002] EWCA Civ 861 (permission to appeal against the dismissal of an application for further information refused).

[206] For a case where the court granted summary judgment (on the issue of whether a defendant was a director) see *Secretary of State for Trade and Industry v Becker* [2002] EWHC 2200 (Ch), [2003] 1 B.C.L.C. 555.

[207] See, however, the court's refusal to use this power to strike out proceedings where a disqualification undertaking (without a schedule of unfit conduct) had been offered: *Re Blackspur Group Plc (No.3), Secretary of State for Trade and Industry v Eastaway (No.2)* [2001] EWCA Civ 1595, [2002] 2 B.C.L.C. 263.

(No.2),[208] one of the *Barings* defendants applied unsuccessfully for a stay of disqualification proceedings on the ground that the issues arising had already been determined in regulatory proceedings brought against him by the Securities and Futures Authority. Moreover, on appeal those disciplinary proceedings had been resolved in the defendant's favour. Although, in the event, the court refused to stay the disqualification proceedings, it is clear that, in an appropriate case, the court could strike proceedings out on this ground. Another closely connected scenario is where the issues raised in the disqualification proceedings have been aired in other civil or criminal proceedings. In *Re Thomas Christy Ltd*,[209] it was held to be an abuse of process for the claimant in proceedings against a liquidator to seek to re-litigate matters that had already been determined against him as the defendant in earlier disqualification proceedings. This suggests that there are circumstances where it may be an abuse of process for the claimant *or the defendant* to seek to contest points that have already been decided in other proceedings. However, since the decision in *Thomas Christy*, the courts have appeared reluctant to use this aspect of abuse of process as a means of preventing litigants from raising defences.[210] This reluctance manifested itself in the disqualification context in *Re Queens Moat Houses Plc, Secretary of State for Trade and Industry v Bairstow*,[211] which decided not only that the defendant in disqualification proceedings was not bound by findings made in other civil proceedings as between himself and the company, but also that the Secretary of State could not rely on such findings as evidence. The case is considered further below. Parallel proceedings are also considered further below.

(3) On grounds of loss of documents (for example, by an insolvency practitioner). This category of potential abuse was raised in *Re Dexmaster Ltd.*[212] Again, while on the facts of the case the loss of documents was not regarded as being sufficiently prejudicial to justify striking out, it is clear that, in an appropriate case, there is jurisdiction.

(4) On grounds of ill health. It is possible that the court might stay or strike out proceedings against a defendant who is suffering from serious ill health. This point is discussed in the context of undertakings in Ch.9.

(5) On grounds that, on the evidence, the case had no real prospects of succeeding.[213]

[208] [1999] 1 W.L.R. 1985. See also *Re Launchexcept Ltd, Secretary of State for Trade and Industry v Tillman* [2000] 1 B.C.L.C. 36. Both cases contain a useful general test for what constitutes abuse of process.

[209] [1994] 2 B.C.L.C. 527.

[210] See *Bradford & Bingley Building Society v Seddon* [1999] 1 W.L.R. 1482 indicating that an attempt to re-litigate an issue fully investigated and decided in earlier proceedings may, but will not necessarily, constitute an abuse of process. However, for a case where the court held it to be an abuse for the defendant to re-litigate in civil recovery proceedings under CDDA s.15 the issue whether he had been a director of the relevant company at the relevant time see *Commissioners of the Inland Revenue v McEntaggart* [2006] 1 B.C.L.C. 476.

[211] [2003] EWCA Civ 321, [2004] Ch. 1.

[212] [1995] 2 B.C.L.C. 430.

[213] *Re Diamond Commodities Ltd, Secretary of State for Business, Enterprise and Regulatory Reform v Farndell*, March 19, 2008, Ch.D., unreported (Registrar Derrett).

Parallel proceedings

7–86 In the context of civil disqualification, the existence of parallel proceedings can raise a number of issues. The most common ones tend to be: (a) whether the civil disqualification proceedings should be stayed or other steps taken to accommodate the parallel civil or criminal proceedings, pending or threatened; and (b) the approach that the civil court should take where faced with an application for the making of a disqualification order based on conduct that constitutes a criminal offence and where the matter has already been before a criminal court. The issue raised in (b) can take a number of forms. The defendant may have been acquitted by the criminal court. The defendant may have been convicted by the criminal court, but not disqualified. Alternatively, the claimant in the subsequent civil proceedings may consider that the convicting court imposed too short a period of disqualification.

Stays

7–87 As a general rule, the court retains a discretion to stay disqualification proceedings where the continuation of those proceedings may prejudice the fairness of the other proceedings. However, the discretion should be exercised with great care and only where there is a real risk of serious prejudice leading to injustice.[214] Although the discretion applies whether the parallel proceedings are civil, criminal or disciplinary, it is helpful to see the way in which it has been exercised in the disqualification sphere.

7–88 So far as parallel civil proceedings are concerned, the general rule is that the existence of other civil proceedings raising overlapping factual issues will not of itself be a good ground to stay disqualification proceedings. There is a public interest in disqualification proceedings being concluded speedily. In *Re Rex Williams Leisure Plc, Secretary of State for Trade and Industry v Warren*[215] an application to stay disqualification proceedings pending the determination of civil proceedings brought by the company's administrators that had been dormant for almost two years, was rejected. The protection afforded to the public by the making of a disqualification order was not to wait on the determination of other claims against the director or depend on the whim of the parties in terms of how quickly or slowly they chose to proceed with them. Having said that, there may be cases where the court may stay, or by use of its case management powers (for example, in fixing a trial date) may accommodate, another set of proceedings. One example may be where it would be unfair and unrealistic to expect the defendant to deal with both sets of proceedings at the same (or almost the same) time. Similar approaches have been taken where the parallel proceedings have been disciplinary proceedings brought by a professional body.[216]

[214] See, albeit in a different context, *R. v Institute of Chartered Accountants in England and Wales Ex.p. Brindle* [1994] B.C.C. 297 and compare *R. v Chance Ex.p. Smith* [1995] B.C.C. 1095.

[215] [1994] Ch. 1 and 350.

[216] *R. v Institute of Chartered Accountants in England and Wales Ex. p. Brindle* [1994] B.C.C. 297; *R. v Chance Ex. p. Smith* [1995] B.C.C. 1095 and see M. Andenas, "Disciplining Auditors: Problems of Parallel Disciplinary and Civil Proceedings" (1998) 9 European Business L.R 12.; M. Beloff and C. Lewis "Bringing Accountants to Book: Statutory Regulation and Civil Litigation" [1994] Public Law 164.

7–89 A slightly different point arises where the separate civil proceedings are not truly parallel but they go to the jurisdiction of the civil court to hear the disqualification proceedings in circumstances where that court cannot or should not hear the relevant matter. In CDDA s.6 cases, one matter of jurisdiction is that the court has to be satisfied that the company in question has "become insolvent". This is given a statutory meaning in CDDA s.6(2).[217] In most cases, to become insolvent involves the company having entered into one of a number of specified forms of insolvency regime. As regards the entry into liquidation there is an additional net asset test. Satisfaction of the net asset test is capable of being resolved by the court hearing the disqualification proceedings. However, as regards entry into the specified type of insolvency regime, the rule is that the disqualification court is entitled to accept evidence that this has happened.[218] It is not the correct forum to rule that the relevant form of insolvency proceedings was incorrectly or invalidly instituted. As Millett L.J. has said:

> "[u]nless or until the order or appointment is discharged in proceedings properly constituted for the purpose, the Secretary of State is entitled to rely upon it."[219]

As any additional civil proceedings are not simply parallel but go to the court's jurisdiction in the disqualification proceedings it is not surprising that the court seised of the disqualification proceedings should be slow to refuse a stay to permit the jurisdictional issue to be tried first. If that application succeeds, the wasted time and costs of the disqualification trial will have been avoided as will (on a worse case scenario from the defendant's perspective) the prejudice to the defendant in having been disqualified in the meantime. The setting aside of any order or undertaking is unlikely fully to put the defendant in the position where he has suffered no prejudice, a point reflected in the decision in *Re Brampton Manor (Leisure) Ltd, Secretary of State for Trade and Industry v Woolf*.[220] In that case the question was whether there should be a stay of s.6 disqualification proceedings to enable a challenge to be made to the appointment of administrative receivers, that forming the jurisdictional insolvency base for the disqualification proceedings. The judge was not persuaded that in order to obtain a stay of the disqualification proceedings the defendant would need to establish that the absence of a stay caused him serious prejudice: the situation is not analogous to that of parallel proceedings findings which do not affect the disqualification proceedings. In any event he found that there was such prejudice and, given that there was a genuine triable issue in the collateral proceedings, he held that a stay was appropriate. Another relevant factor in *Brampton Manor* was delay. Although there had been some delay attributable to the defendant both in making the

[217] See further text from 3–98.
[218] *Secretary of State for Trade and Industry v Jabble* [1998] 1 B.C.L.C. 598. See also *Re Kaytech International Plc, Secretary of State for Trade and Industry v Kaczer* [1999] 2 B.C.L.C. 351 at 393–396.
[219] *Secretary of State for Trade and Industry v Jabble* [1998] 1 B.C.L.C. 598.
[220] [2005] EWHC 3074 (Ch).

application in the disqualification proceedings for a stay and in the parallel proceedings challenging the validity of the appointment of the receivers, such delays were not considered sufficient so as to swing the balance against the grant of a stay. For the future the position could be dealt with by an undertaking to keep the Secretary of State informed as to the progress of the other civil proceedings. Further delays might be met by a successful application to lift the stay. Furthermore, as factors in favour of granting a stay, the court took into account the offer of an undertaking to the court broadly in the terms of a disqualification undertaking (though not formally such an undertaking) and the fact that a fair trial of the disqualification proceedings would still be possible at the anticipated date of their trial, assuming that the issue of the validity of the receivers' appointment went against the defendant in the other civil proceedings. As a factor against the order of a stay the judge also took account of the public interest in the speedy disposal of disqualification proceedings although, in the circumstances, this had to be balanced against the public interest in the court not making disqualification orders when it did not have jurisdiction to do so.

7–90 The position regarding parallel criminal proceedings (actual or threatened) has proved more difficult. The starting point is *Jefferson Ltd v Bhetcha*.[221] The mere fact that a defendant might give an indication of his likely defence to criminal charges by entering a defence in the civil proceedings was said in that case not to debar the claimant from pursuing the civil proceedings.[222] However, the civil court has a discretion to stay the civil proceedings if justice requires. The exercise of this discretion has been considered in a number of disqualification cases. Two issues commonly arise. The first issue is possible unfairness flowing from publicity that may be given to the disqualification proceedings (and the evidence and/or findings made in such proceedings) prior to the criminal trial. The court can deal with this by directing that the trial of the disqualification proceedings should take place after the criminal trial or that publicity is to be restricted.[223] It should be noted that, as the court is exercising a discretion, it will consider a number of factors including: (a) the likely period of delay to the disqualification proceedings if stayed; (b) whether any undertakings have been given to protect the public in the meantime; and (c) the possible impact of any delay on the trial of the disqualification proceedings (for example, on the recollection of witnesses). The second issue is the extent to which the defendant should be obliged to file evidence in the disqualification proceedings.[224] The question arising is whether the defendant's position in the criminal trial would be prejudiced by a requirement to file evidence in the disqualification proceedings on the

[221] [1979] 1 W.L.R. 898.

[222] See also *Versailles Trade Finance Ltd v Clough* [2001] EWCA Civ 1509.

[223] See, e.g. *Re Landhurst Leasing Plc*, July 4, 1995, Ch.D., unreported; *Re Battery Specialists (Five Star) Ltd*, February 23, 1998, Ch.D., unreported. Compare, however, *EDC v United Kingdom* [1998] B.C.C. 370. Note that in the civil recovery proceedings brought in connection with the Maxwell affair, the civil court restricted the publicity to be given to the proceedings in the light of the parallel criminal proceedings.

[224] This also raises questions as to the extent of the "right to silence".

ground that such evidence could: (a) be put before the criminal court; (b) lead the prosecution to initiate further enquiries with a view to obtaining fresh evidence; (c) reveal the likely defence to the criminal charges and so enable the prosecution to tailor its case in the criminal proceedings accordingly; or (d) lead to unfairness in either or both proceedings due to an absence of time and/or financial resources. This has given rise to a number of cases from which it is apparent that each case will turn on its own particular facts.[225] The one general principle that has always been clear is that the burden lies on the defendant to establish that a stay is appropriate and that mere generalised allegations of possible prejudice will not be persuasive. This issue, and the effect of amendments to CDDA s.20 effected by the Youth Justice and Criminal Evidence Act 1999,[226] were considered in some detail by Ferris J. in *Re Priory Stainless (UK) Ltd, Secretary of State for Trade and Industry v Crane*.[227] As a result the position is now much clearer.

7–91 In *Crane*, the company went into liquidation in August 1997 and proceedings under CDDA s.6 were commenced in July 1999. Evidence was served and filed. The case was listed for trial in November 2000. By this stage, the Hampshire Constabulary had indicated that criminal charges would be laid against the defendant. A police officer was at court when the trial commenced and it became clear (in answers given by the officer to questions from the registrar) that the police intended to prosecute the defendant for offences arising in connection with two of the allegations of unfit conduct, and that he was present in court to see whether anything emerged which might assist the police in their intended prosecution. The registrar stayed the proceedings pending the outcome of any criminal proceedings or further order. The Secretary of State appealed against the stay. The appeal was allowed. On the appeal, Ferris J. put forward a number of helpful general propositions. Some of them are covered by what has already been said above, but the following four points deserve particular emphasis:

(1) Normally, the question is whether or not any subsequent criminal proceedings will be unfair within the meaning of ECHR art.6, rather than whether the civil proceedings infringe art.6.[228]
(2) The judge in the criminal proceedings has extensive powers to control those proceedings.[229] While the court having control of the civil proceedings will be concerned that those proceedings do not lead to injustice in the concurrent criminal proceedings, the responsibility for doing justice in the criminal

[225] See, e.g. *Re Jandra Ltd*, June 19, 1995, Ch.D., unreported; *Re Landhurst Leasing Plc*, July 4, 1995, Ch.D., unreported; *Re Gemini Display Ltd*, July 19, 1996, Ch.D., unreported; *Re Parallel Computers Ltd*, October 29, 1996, Ch.D., unreported; *Secretary of State for Trade and Industry v Jebraille*, December 20, 1997, Ch.D., unreported; *Re Battery Specialists (Five Star) Ltd*, February 23, 1998, Ch.D., unreported.

[225] In force from April 14, 2000: see the Youth Justice and Criminal Evidence Act 1999 (Commencement No.2) Order (SI 2000/1034).

[227] [2001] 2 B.C.L.C. 222.

[228] See also *V v C* [2001] EWCA Civ 1509, [2002] C.P.Rep. 8.

[229] By virtue of both the "abuse of process" doctrine and s.78 of the Police and Criminal Evidence Act 1984.

proceedings lies primarily with the criminal court. The civil court will strive to avoid a manifest risk of injustice but it should not go out of its way to anticipate the existence of a mere possibility of injustice.

(3) The Secretary of State has a public duty to seek the disqualification of unfit directors. He cannot be held up indefinitely by other proceedings. The cases in which concurrent civil disqualification proceedings and criminal proceedings arising from the same misconduct are most likely to come about are cases where serious misconduct is alleged. In such cases, the public interest in an expeditious hearing of the disqualification proceedings is particularly strong. As Jacob J. observed in *Re Lighting World Ltd, Jibrail v Secretary of State for Trade and Industry*[230]:

> "Disqualification proceedings exist for the protection of the public. It can hardly be said that the more deserving an individual is of disqualification, the more he is in a position to say he is entitled to a stay or that a stay should be granted merely because he worries about his right to silence."

(4) It is necessary to distinguish the "right of silence" from the privilege against self-incrimination. In this context, it should also be noted that, for ECHR art.6 purposes, there is also a distinction between material that is used at the criminal trial and material that is used by the prosecution for investigative purposes[231] and also between evidence that is given for the first time under compulsion and evidence that has an existence independent of the will of the suspect or accused person.[232]

7–92 Ferris J. also drew attention to CDDA s.20 (as amended by the Youth Justice and Criminal Evidence Act 1999), which in criminal proceedings prevents the prosecution (but not another defendant) from using statements that were compelled by any requirement imposed by or under the CDDA. The prohibition operates to prevent the prosecution from adducing any evidence or asking any question relating to the statement, unless the person who was compelled to make the statement adduces evidence or asks a question relating to it.[233] The compelled statements to which the section relates are, in effect, any statement made pursuant to certain specified provisions of the CDDA or any rules made for the purposes of the CDDA under the Insolvency Act 1986.[234] Ferris J. regarded statements in affidavits filed in CDDA s.6 proceedings as being covered by this definition, together with evidence given by the defendant in cross-examination. Accordingly, he took the view that s.20 provided an "additional and substantial layer of protection" in almost all cases in which there are parallel disqualification and criminal proceedings. The qualification "in almost all cases" was necessary because co-defendants

[230] November 20, 1997, Ch.D., unreported.

[231] See, e.g. *Saunders v UK* (1996) 23 E.H.R.R. 313, [1998] 1 B.C.L.C. 362; *R. v Hertfordshire County Council Ex. p. Green Environmental Industries Ltd* [2000] 2 A.C. 412; *IJL,GMR and AKP v United Kingdom* (2001) 33 E.H.R.R. 11, [2002] B.C.C. 380.

[232] See, e.g. *R. v Kearns* [2002] EWCA Crim 748, [2002] 1 W.L.R. 2815.

[233] CDDA s.20(2).

[234] CDDA s.20(1).

can still rely on compelled statements. With the greatest respect, the authors consider that Ferris J.'s analysis is flawed. The defendant is not *required* to file affidavit evidence. That is his choice.[235] As Hoffmann L.J. pointed out in *Re Rex Williams Leisure Plc, Secretary of State for Trade and Industry v Warren*,[236] if the defendant does file evidence, then the CDDA and the Disqualification Rules lay down the form and time limits within which he must do so. Ferris J. relied on *Rex Williams* as demonstrating the "involuntary nature" of an affidavit in civil disqualification proceedings under ss.6 and/or 8. However, with respect, that is not what the case was saying. The relevant issue considered in *Rex Williams*, was the form required of any evidence that the defendant wished to be taken into account. Section 16(1) of the CDDA gives the defendant the *right* to give evidence or adduce the evidence of other witnesses. The manner in which that may be done is a matter for the Disqualification Rules. This does not mean that the defendant is *required* to serve evidence. As Hoffmann L.J. pointed out:

> "[the words of r.6 of the Disqualification Rules 1987] only make sense if they mean that the evidence [the defendant] *wishes* the court to take into consideration must be filed on affidavit".[237]

The distinction between evidence that is compelled and evidence that is volunteered (albeit regulated as to form and timing of presentation) is relevant to, and well recognised in, the context of implied undertakings as to the use and further dissemination of the information contained in such evidence. Thus, while affidavit evidence produced pursuant to a freezing order made by the court will be "compelled" and subject to an implied undertaking as to use by the other party, the same is not true of affidavit evidence which is volunteered, whether on a summary judgment, or other, application.[238] Similarly, it is suggested that evidence given in cross-examination is not "compelled" for the purposes of CDDA s.20 because, essentially, it is the price of the defendant having his written evidence admitted. The defendant can usually avoid cross-examination if he so wishes. This is because the usual order is not that the defendant be cross-examined but that, if he does not attend for cross-examination, his evidence is not to be read without permission of the court. Moreover, the privilege against self-incrimination survives and can be claimed in the course of cross-examination. This leaves the question of what, if anything, is covered by CDDA s.20. It is suggested that, in practice, very little is covered apart (probably) from office holder reports required pursuant to s.7(3) and further information provided pursuant to s.7(4). However, the protection afforded in relation to those provisions would be protection afforded to the office

[235] In *Official Receiver v Cooper* [1999] B.C.C. 115 Jonathan Parker J. decided that a Carecraft statement did not fall within CDDA s.20. It is respectfully suggested that this decision was correct. In any event, it is difficult to see how it is consistent with the reasoning of Ferris J. in the *Priority Stainless* case on this point.

[236] [1994] Ch. 350.

[237] [1994] Ch. 350 at 360H (emphasis supplied).

[238] See *Prudential Assurance Co Ltd v Fountain Page Ltd* [1991] 1 W.L.R. 756 and, in particular, the discussion of *Derby & Co Ltd v Weldon (No.2), The Times*, October 20, 1988.

holder and not (for example) to the director who provided information that may be contained within the report (even where he did so under compulsion pursuant to s.235 of the Insolvency Act 1986) or other material handed over by the office holder to the Secretary of State. In relation to evidence provided under compulsion by, say, a director to an office holder under ss.235 or 236 of the Insolvency Act 1986, the director is protected by s.433 of the Insolvency Act 1986 rather than s.20 of the CDDA.

7–93 It is suggested that the reasoning relating to, and the reliance on, CDDA s.20 in *Crane* should not be followed for the reasons given above. However, the reasoning in the remainder of the judgment should still have the result that in most cases civil disqualification proceedings need not be held up by parallel proceedings, whether civil or criminal.[239] The existence of parallel proceedings is likely to have the potential to affect the timetabling and conduct of civil disqualification cases in two main respects. First, the practicalities of having to deal with more than one set of proceedings at the same time may require the defendant to be given more time to deal with them so that the timetabling does not produce unfairness. Secondly, the existence of parallel criminal proceedings may give rise to a need to delay the civil trial; or to restrict reporting of it, so as to reduce the risk of prejudice to the criminal trial process. This comes close to the view advocated by the Financial Regulation Working Group of the Society for Advanced Legal Studies which recommended that:

> "the powers to stay proceedings be used sparingly and that, where possible, multiple proceedings be allowed to proceed simultaneously, but that in appropriate cases publication of proceedings and their result be withheld until the end of related proceedings."[240]

7–94 The general position has been considered more recently by David Richards J. in *Re Transtec Plc, Secretary of State for Trade and Industry v Carr*.[241] In that case the basis for a stay was not said to be an entitlement to keep silent on his defence in the disqualification proceedings until after the criminal proceedings or that an unparticularised risk of self-incrimination justified the deferral of his written evidence until after the criminal trial. As the judge pointed out, the principle that such matters do not provide grounds for a stay, established in relation to ordinary civil claims by the decisions of the Court of Appeal in *Jefferson Ltd v Bhetcha*[242] and *Versailles Trade Finance Ltd v Clough*,[243] is equally applicable to directors in disqualification proceedings.[244] Rather three grounds of prejudice

[239] See also the analysis, in relation to a summary judgment application in civil proceedings, adopted in *V v C* [2001] EWCA Civ 1509, [2002] C.P.Rep. 8.

[240] Report on Parallel Proceedings (December 1999), para.8.8. The Group was chaired by George Staple Q.C.

[241] [2005] EWHC 1723 (Ch), [2007] 1 B.C.L.C. 93.

[242] [1979] 1 W.L.R. 898.

[243] [2001] EWCA Civ 1509.

[244] *Re Priory Stainless (UK) Ltd, Secretary of State for Trade and Industry v Crane* [2001] 2 B.C.L.C. 222; *Re Lighting World Ltd, Jibrail v Secretary of State for Trade and Industry*, November 20, 1997, Ch.D., unreported (Jacob J.).

were relied upon: (a) oppression and unfairness because of the time and resources required to prepare defences in the two sets of proceedings at the same time which, it was said, would jeopardise proper preparation; (b) prejudice flowing from possible use by other defendants in the criminal proceedings of the evidence filed in the disqualification proceedings; and (c) the risk of witness contamination in the criminal proceedings were the Secretary of State to interview actual or potential witnesses in the criminal proceedings with a view to the preparation of his evidence in reply. The Secretary of State made proposals to deal with the latter two points which the judge considered satisfactory. First, any defendant's evidence in the disqualification proceedings was to be served, pending the criminal trial, on the Secretary of State but not on any other defendant. This would enable the Secretary of State to advance preparation of evidence in reply and leave it to the judge in the criminal proceedings to determine whether disclosure should properly be ordered in that context. As regards witness contamination, the Secretary of State did not propose to interview any witness, actual or potential, in the criminal proceedings. As regards the most substantial objection, on the facts, the judge decided that the objection did not carry sufficient weight when the facts were properly analysed. Leaving aside serious prejudice, it was also sought to justify the stay on case management grounds, carrying out a balancing exercise. Although these factors were of some weight the judge decided that: (a) a disqualification trial was likely to come on more quickly than otherwise if the defendants' evidence was served promptly and a stay not ordered; (b) the offer of an undertaking to the court in the terms of a disqualification order (including an obligation to be liable for debts in circumstances akin to CDDA s.15) did not carry sufficient weight; (c) the fact that, if the defendants were convicted the criminal court could disqualify under CDDA s.2, did not carry much weight.[245]

Civil disqualification proceedings following criminal proceedings

7–95 The second area of difficulty is the extent to which the Secretary of State is permitted to apply in civil proceedings for the making of a disqualification order in circumstances where a criminal court faced with the same or similar factual material did not address the question of disqualification or, having addressed the question, declined to make a disqualification order or made an order, but for a period considered by the Secretary of State to be too short. This immediately raises the need for an appreciation of the potential overlap between civil and criminal disqualification and, in particular, criminal disqualification under CDDA s.2.[246] At first sight, it appears that there is nothing in the wording of CDDA s.2 to prevent the civil court making an order in circumstances where the matter has previously been before a criminal court. This is not least because the civil court can only make an order under s.2 following a criminal conviction. Indeed, it

[245] Agreeing with *Secretary of State for Trade and Industry v Maclean*, October 29, 1996, Ch.D., unreported (Jonathan Parker J.) and *Re Battery Specialists (Five Star) Ltd*, February 23, 1998, Ch.D., unreported (Neuberger J.).

[246] See Ch.10, especially text from 10–75.

appears that it is possible within the scheme of the CDDA, for the Secretary of State to apply to a civil court under s.2, basing his application on the same material that supported the criminal conviction. Clearly, if such circumstances arose, it would remain within the discretion of the civil court under CDDA ss.2 or 4 (but not s.6) whether or not to make an order. One peculiarity of this double exposure is that the civil proceedings would amount, in effect, to an appeal against sentence. This seems somewhat anomalous given that the prosecution generally has no right of appeal against sentence in criminal proceedings.[247] However, if it were right to regard the criminal courts as performing a different function to that performed by their civil counterparts when exercising powers under the CDDA, this would be a reason for allowing the later proceedings to go ahead.[248] On the other hand, if, in keeping with the position taken by the authors, it is correct to say that the CDDA contains a set of powers that share common features, a common purpose and common consequences, it is arguable that a civil court should decline to exercise its discretion to "correct" any error by the convicting court, especially where the material before both courts is essentially the same. It is suggested, in the light of the authorities discussed below, that the courts will steer a middle course and seek to resolve such problems of double exposure by asking whether the later civil proceedings are an abuse of process.

7–96 The starting point is the decision of the Court of Appeal in *Re Barings Plc, Secretary of State for Trade and Industry v Baker (No. 2)*.[249] This case involved an unsuccessful application by one of the *Barings* defendants for a stay of disqualification proceedings under CDDA s.6 on the ground that the issues arising had already been determined (in his favour) in regulatory proceedings brought against him by the Securities and Futures Authority.[250] It was held, in principle, that the court should stay the later proceedings as an abuse of process only where to allow them to continue would bring the administration of justice into disrepute among right-thinking people.[251] However, on the facts, the Court of Appeal concluded that there was no abuse of process because the purposes of the two sets of proceedings and the questions to be determined in each were materially different.

7–97 The same principle was applied in *Re Cedarwood Productions Ltd, Secretary of State for Trade and Industry v Murfitt*.[252] In *Cedarwood*, disqualification proceedings were commenced against two individuals under CDDA s.6. A wide

[247] The only procedure currently available to the Crown where the prosecution considers a sentence too lenient is an Attorney General's reference under Pt IV of the Criminal Justice Act 1988: see 10–104.

[248] By analogy with *Re Barings Plc, Secretary of State for Trade and Industry v Baker (No.2)* [1999] 1 W.L.R. 1985 in which proceedings under CDDA s.6 were allowed to go ahead despite the fact that the Securities and Futures Authority had made a previous ruling in relation to the same subject matter.

[249] [1999] 1 W.L.R. 1985.

[250] A self regulating organisation under the Financial Services Act 1986, the relevant regulatory regime preceding that established by the Financial Services and Markets Act 2000.

[251] See further *Johnson v Gore Wood & Co* [2002] 2 A.C. 1 and, in the disqualification context, *Re Launchexcept Ltd, Secretary of State for Trade and Industry v Tillman* [2000] 1 B.C.L.C. 36.

[252] [2001] 2 B.C.L.C. 48 (permission to appeal refused: [2001] EWCA Civ 1083).

range of allegations were made about their conduct in relation to at least four companies, including trading to the detriment of creditors, operating a policy of deliberate non-payment of Crown debts and failure to maintain proper accounting records. Criminal proceedings were also brought against the defendants arising out of their conduct and, given the apparent overlap between the criminal and civil proceedings, the Secretary of State reluctantly agreed to a stay of the disqualification proceedings pending determination of the criminal proceedings. The defendants pleaded guilty to the criminal charges (which included offences of conspiracy to defraud and false accounting) and, by their counsel, invited the trial judge to impose disqualification orders on them under s.2. The judge accepted the invitation and disqualified both defendants for two years. Counsel for the defendants had apparently taken the view that the making of a disqualification order under s.2 would be a complete answer to the civil disqualification proceedings under s.6. Accordingly, when the Secretary of State applied to lift the stay and restore the civil proceedings, the defendants opposed the application on the ground of abuse of process or as breach of "the principle of former recovery" because disqualification orders had already been made in the criminal proceedings. However, the deputy judge held that there was no abuse of process, nor was the principle of former recovery breached and accordingly he lifted the stay of the civil proceedings. For there to be an abuse of process it was incumbent on the defendants to show that:

> "the issues upon which the court will need to adjudicate in the [civil] proceedings are the same, or substantially the same, as those which have already been investigated and adjudicated upon in the [criminal] proceedings".[253]

This they were unable to do. The deputy judge relied on the following principles and factors:

(1) Parliament has entrusted the task of considering whether to seek disqualification orders in the public interest under CDDA s.6 to the Secretary of State. The Secretary of State had not been a party to the criminal proceedings and had not been given an opportunity to appear. It would require a strong and clear case for the court to conclude that the Secretary of State's continuation of proceedings that he considers to be in the public interest amounts to an abuse of process on the basis of findings made in proceedings to which he was not a party.
(2) The focus of the court in the two sets of proceedings was different. The purpose of the civil proceedings was to determine whether the conduct of the defendants as directors of the various companies made them unfit. The purpose of the criminal proceedings was to determine whether the defendants were guilty of the offences charged. The issue of disqualification is only

[253] *Re Barings Plc, Secretary of State for Trade and Industry v Baker (No.2)* [1999] 1 W.L.R. 1985 at 1990.

considered in criminal proceedings at the sentencing stage by reference to the material on which the conviction rests. There is no detailed consideration of the defendant's conduct in so far as it would have any bearing on the question of his fitness to be concerned in the management of a company under s.6.

The deputy judge concluded:

"[I]n most cases it is going to be unlikely that a disqualification in criminal proceedings will make concurrent civil proceedings an abuse of process. It is likely to be only in clear cases, which can clearly be said to be on all fours with each other, that it might be said that the criminal proceedings have covered all the bases in a way which makes the civil proceedings otiose and oppressive. Of course, the Secretary of State may take the view that, while the proceedings are not sufficiently close to make the civil proceedings an abuse of process, nevertheless no useful public purpose would be served by pursuing the latter in the light of the sentence imposed in the former, but that is precisely the sort of judgment that the Secretary of State is obliged to make by virtue of his or her office and the statutory jurisdiction."[254]

7–98 The Court of Appeal refused permission to appeal the order of the deputy judge.[255] Chadwick L.J. doubted that the principle of former recovery had any "meaningful role" in this area. This echoes the point made by the deputy judge that the parties were different, the proceedings were different in nature, the "interests" of the prosecutor and the Secretary of State were different and the two statutory regimes were different. As regards the issue of abuse of process:

". . . although there were overlapping factors—in that the same individuals, the same companies and the same general conduct lay at the root of both of the criminal proceedings and the civil proceedings—it was impossible, from the material available, to tell what factors the Crown Court judge had taken into account when reaching the conclusion that it was appropriate to make a disqualification order for two years."

This was not surprising bearing in mind that the trial judge had been invited to make the order by the defendants, through their counsel, and given the limited material that would have been before the court on a guilty plea. Chadwick L.J. expressed concern that a practice might be developing whereby defendants in criminal proceedings invite the making of a disqualification order in order to forestall "the rigorous investigation" that would take place in proceedings under s.6. As the Secretary of State raised no concern on that front and took the view that Court of Appeal guidance would neither be necessary nor helpful, the matter was taken no further.

7–99 In summary, there appear to be essentially three inter-connected reasons why a defendant disqualified by a criminal court under CDDA s.2 will find it difficult to challenge later civil disqualification proceedings under CDDA ss.6 or 8:

[254] [2001] 2 B.C.L.C. 48 at 59–60.
[255] [2001] EWCA Civ 1083.

(1) The broader nature of the enquiry in the civil disqualification proceedings.
(2) The wider range of misconduct that is likely to form the subject matter of such proceedings.
(3) The position of the Secretary of State as regulator.

7–100 Further limited support for the view that civil disqualification proceedings can be legitimately pursued after a disqualification order has been imposed by a criminal court derives from the earlier case of *Re Land Travel Ltd, Secretary of State for Trade and Industry v Tjolle*.[256] In that case, the first defendant, T, pleaded guilty to an offence of fraudulent trading under s.458 of the Companies Act 1985 and was disqualified for ten years under CDDA s.2 as well as receiving a prison sentence. T's guilty plea (and consequent disqualification) related only to his conduct over a three-month period. The Secretary of State was of the opinion that T's conduct overall (including matters to which he had not pleaded guilty or been charged in the criminal proceedings) merited a maximum period of disqualification of 15 years. Separate civil proceedings were brought under CDDA s.6 and T agreed to a hearing under the summary *Carecraft* procedure[257] as a result of which he was disqualified for 15 years. For *Carecraft* purposes, T made admissions covering a two-year period. Jacob J. was clearly of the view that it was open to the Secretary of State to seek a further order against T in civil proceedings. He warned against the dangers of the criminal courts failing to apply the same approach to "sentencing" as the civil courts:

> "It may also be important for the defendant to see that he is in fact disqualified for an appropriate period. If he is under disqualified then he may find himself on the receiving end of a civil application by the Secretary of State for which, if he loses, he will have to pay the costs."

However, the court did not consider (and, as T had agreed to submit to a *Carecraft* disposal, it was presumably not argued) whether the s.6 proceedings amounted to an abuse of process. Given their wider scope it seems unlikely that an abuse argument had any realistic prospect of success.

7–101 Where the overlap between the factual basis of the criminal and civil proceedings is close, the position becomes more problematic. In *Cedarwood*, the deputy judge specifically envisaged this as being a situation in which abuse of process in the form of the principle of "autrefois convict" could well apply. A case more directly in point in this respect, and one that deals with the possibility that the Secretary of State can pursue civil proceedings against a defendant who has already been dealt with by the criminal courts, is *Re Dennis Hilton Ltd*.[258] In that case, the Secretary of State decided not to bring proceedings against the defendant under CDDA s.6 as he was to be prosecuted for an offence of fraudulent trading

[256] [1998] 1 B.C.L.C. 333. Although *Land Travel* is a s.6 case, it is suggested that the same principles should apply to any later civil disqualification proceedings, whichever section of the CDDA is relied on.
[257] On which see Ch.9.
[258] [2002] 1 B.C.L.C. 302.

contrary to s.458 of the Companies Act 1985 and it was anticipated that the question of disqualification under CDDA s.2 would be raised, and satisfactorily dealt with, at the criminal trial. The defendant pleaded guilty and was sentenced to six months' imprisonment. However, the judge's attention was not drawn specifically to the power in s.2 and no reference was made to disqualification in the course of passing sentence. As the Crown Court had not imposed a disqualification order, the Secretary of State commenced civil proceedings for a disqualification order under CDDA s.4(1)(a).[259] The defendant applied to have the proceedings struck out as an abuse of process. Ferris J. distinguished the case from *Cedarwood* insofar as the misconduct relied on in the s.4 proceedings was precisely the same conduct that had led to the conviction for fraudulent trading in the criminal proceedings. Nevertheless, he dismissed the defendant's application primarily on the basis that the criminal court had not considered whether or not to make a disqualification order under s.2 and so had not positively determined the question and the Secretary of State had not made any representations or so conducted herself as to give rise to an estoppel preventing such civil disqualification proceedings. Obviously, the position would have been more problematic if the Secretary of State had been the prosecutor and/or if the criminal court had considered disqualification and decided to make no order or made a disqualification order for a period shorter than that considered appropriate by the Secretary of State.

7–102 Following the approach in the authorities, it is suggested that later civil proceedings will not, or are unlikely to, amount to an abuse of process if: (a) additional matters grounding jurisdiction are relied on that were not before the criminal court or (given the lower standard of proof in civil proceedings) it is sought to revisit factual allegations that were not made out in the criminal proceedings; (b) the question of disqualification is neither canvassed nor determined in the criminal proceedings (as was the case in *Dennis Hilton*); (c) the sentencing power of the criminal court did not enable it to make a disqualification order of an appropriate period (that is for a period of more than five years).[260] However, it would arguably be different if the criminal court has already disqualified the defendant or positively declined to exercise its powers under s.2 and the claimant in the civil proceedings is relying solely on the material that grounded the criminal conviction or any guilty plea. In those circumstances, the civil claim might be treated as an abuse of process not least because, if permitted to continue, its effect would be to enable the claimant to circumvent the problem that the prosecution either has no right of appeal in such a criminal case or has failed to exercise any such right of appeal that it does have.[261] In such a case the interesting

[259] See Ch.10 from 10–57. Proceedings were commenced under s.4 rather than s.6 because the two-year period provided for by CDDA s.7(2) in which proceedings under s.6 can be commenced without permission of the court had expired. Civil disqualification proceedings could also have been commenced under s.2.

[260] See CDDA ss.2(3), 3(5), 5(5).

[261] For a case where the Attorney-General successfully referred a case to the Court of Appeal with the result that a disqualification order was made see *Attorney General's References Nos. 14, 15 and 16 of 1995*, The Times, April 10, 1997 subsequently considered in *R. v Ward* [2001] EWCA Crim 1648, [2002] B.C.C. 953 considered further at 12–20.

question will be whether factors such as the regulatory role of the Secretary of State and the lack of identity (if such be the case) between the Secretary of State and the prosecutor will be sufficient to defeat a claim of abuse of process. Indeed, a powerful line of argument against there being an abuse of process may be based on the analysis of disqualification as an adjunct to, rather than a true part of, the criminal process so that the prohibition on the prosecutor being able to appeal in criminal proceedings carries little weight.[262]

7–103 In the event that a disqualification order is imposed by a criminal court and a second order is made in civil proceedings (not being an abuse of process) under any of CDDA ss.2, 3, 4, 6, 8 or 9A, CDDA s.1(3) provides that the periods specified in those orders shall run concurrently. The position would be the same by virtue of CDDA s.1A(3) were the later civil proceedings to be compromised by offer and acceptance of a disqualification undertaking. Thus, s.1(3) offers some safeguard to the defendant faced with parallel criminal and civil proceedings, a point noted by the deputy judge in *Cedarwood*.[263]

Allegations of unfit conduct: CDDA ss.6 and 8

The requirement that allegations are clear

7–104 Rule 3(3) of the Disqualification Rules requires the evidence in support of an application for the making of a disqualification order under CDDA ss.6 or 8 to include "a statement of the matters by reference to which the defendant is alleged to be unfit to be concerned in the management of a company." A practice has developed whereby, a summary of the main matters said to constitute unfit conduct is included at the end of one of the affidavits sworn on behalf of the claimant.[264] It has become common parlance to talk of this summary as constituting the "charges" though r.3(3) refers neither to charges nor even to a summary of the allegations. It is important not to confuse the summary of the allegations that it has become developed practice to set out, with the requirement to set out in written evidence "matters by reference to which" the defendant is said to be unfit (i.e. the evidence and/or any inferences that the court is asked to draw from the same). The purpose of the r.3(3) requirement was adverted to in *Re Lo-Line Electric Motors Ltd*[265] and *Re Sevenoaks Stationers (Retail) Ltd*.[266] A number of points emerge from these two cases which are further illustrated by later reported cases.

7–105 The first point is that the basis of the requirement for allegations to be made clear is one of natural justice: the defendant should know the case that he has to meet. It follows that the spirit of r.3(3) will apply in all civil disqualification proceedings and not be limited to those brought under ss.6 and 8 or 9A, a point now reflected in para.9.2 of the Disqualification Practice Direction (which covers

[262] See discussion in Ch.2 and *R. (on the application of McCann) v Crown Court at Manchester* [2002] UKHL 39, [2003] 1 A.C. 787.
[263] [2001] 2 B.C.L.C. 48 at 60.
[264] A practice alluded to in *Re Lo-Line Electric Motors Ltd* [1988] Ch. 477.
[265] [1988] Ch. 477 at 486–487.
[266] [1991] Ch. 164 at 176–177.

all civil disqualification proceedings save for those under s.10). Moreover, in *Re Pinemoor Ltd*,[267] Chadwick J. said that those preparing and swearing affidavits in support of applications under the CDDA should be careful to distinguish between the facts which they were able to establish by direct evidence, the inferences which they invited the court to draw from those facts, and the matters which were said to amount to unfit conduct on the part of the defendant. These comments were directed more at practical issues. Chadwick J. went on to say that if these distinctions were observed, ". . . it might lead to [defendants] concentrating more closely on those factual matters to which they actually need to respond by affidavit evidence . . .". It follows a fortiori that where serious allegations of misconduct are being made, it is essential that they be properly spelled out. As Lewison J. pointed out in *Re Crystal Palace Football Club (1986), Secretary of State for Trade and Industry v Goldberg*[268]:

> "[i]f dishonesty is to be alleged against a director, the allegation must be fairly and squarely made in the affidavit, and must be fairly and squarely put in cross-examination."

7–106 The second point is that any summary of allegations is not to be read as if it were an indictment or as being subject, by analogy, to the inflexible rules applicable to indictments.[269] The court will look at the substance of what is being alleged. The point is illustrated by the cases discussed below:

(1) In *Re Looe Fish Ltd*,[270] Jonathan Parker J. made clear that the summary of allegations should not be read as if it were an indictment. The director should know the substance of the allegations he has to meet but the requirement to summarise the allegations should not lead to "the technicalities associated with criminal charges".[271] Once the director knows the case that he has to meet, the requirement is satisfied. Jonathan Parker J. might have gone even further. Although, it was suggested by the Court of Appeal in *Sevenoaks Stationers*[272] that a summary was necessary, this was probably not part of the ratio of the case. Indeed, as was suggested above, r.3(3) does not necessarily require a summary of the allegations. It is suggested further that natural justice does not demand a summary. This may have been what Jonathan Parker J. was hinting at when he said that there was a requirement that the defendant should know the substance of the charge which he had to meet but,

[267] [1997] B.C.C. 708.

[268] [2004] 1 B.C.L.C. 597 at [53]–[54].

[269] In *Re Crystal Palace Football Club (1986), Secretary of State for Trade and Industry v Goldberg*, Lewison J. found this guidance to be of limited assistance (see [2004] 1 B.C.L.C. 597 at [51]) but, with respect, it appears that he was not directing his attention to the "summary" of the allegations which do share the "terseness" of a criminal indictment. See also Morritt V.C. in *Re Clean and Colour Ltd*, June 7, 2001, Ch.D., unreported, cited in *Re Plazoo Pipe Systems Ltd, Kappler v Secretary of State for Trade and Industry* [2006] EWHC 3694 (Ch), [2008] 1 B.C.L.C. 120 at [81].

[270] [1993] B.C.L.C. 1160.

[271] [1993] B.C.L.C. 1160 at 1171.

[272] [1991] Ch. 164.

"... [o]nce that situation is reached, so that natural justice is satisfied, there is in my judgment no additional requirement to state, list or summarise the 'charges' against him ...". In *Looe Fish*, the "charge" which was said not to have been spelled out was one of "breach of fiduciary duty", but it was admitted that the actual case was clear at all times. The express words of the relevant affidavit summarised the transactions of which complaint was made and referred to the fact that the transactions were illegal and that the end in question was achieved in an unscrupulous and illegal manner.

(2) In considering any "summary" of the allegations, it is necessary to consider the summary against the evidence that it summarises. Thus in *Re Hitco 2000 Ltd, Official Receiver v Cowan*,[273] the substance of the allegation was that the defendant had allowed the company to "bounce" cheques. Further misconduct came to light, namely the defendant's practice of signing cheques in blank and leaving them for the bookkeeper to use. Although the wording of the summary of the allegation looked at in isolation would have been wide enough to cover the conduct in relation to blank cheques, it was not treated as such, because the summary of the allegation had to be looked at in the context of the matters it actually summarised. The claimant was not allowed to treat the wording of the summary as covering the separate allegation in relation to signing cheques in blank.[274]

(3) In *Re Continental Assurance Co of London Plc*, Chadwick J. was faced with a submission that the summary of the allegations referred to the defendant having caused or allowed something to happen whereas the case as developed was one of "incompetence". Chadwick J. endorsed the view that it was essential that a director should know the criticism that was being levelled at him, but deplored "any tendency to introduce into this jurisdiction the inflexibility of a criminal indictment".[275] The defendant was said to have been well aware of what the criticisms of his conduct were. The judge continued:

> "It would defeat the purpose of the [CDDA] if, having held that [the defendant's] failure to do anything about the inter-company loans was due to gross incompetence rather than to deliberate abstention, I was precluded from holding that he was unfit to be concerned in the management of the company on the basis that the words 'cause and allow' in ... [the claimant's] affidavit were confined to deliberate wrongdoing."

The same point was considered further by Morritt V.C. in an appeal from a registrar's decision in *Re Clean and Colour Ltd, Secretary of State for Trade and Industry v Tuck*.[276] In that case there were various allegations that referred to specific defendants as having "caused or allowed" certain states of affairs. The Vice-Chancellor made the following comments:

[273] [1995] 2 B.C.L.C. 63.

[274] The question was considered on appeal. By then it was too late to ask to "amend" the allegation and it was therefore an open question whether permission would have been granted (and on what terms) had it been sought at the trial.

[275] [1997] 1 B.C.L.C. 48 at 58.

[276] June 7, 2001, Ch.D., unreported.

> "The courts have recognised that the director is entitled to fair notice of what is alleged against him . . . But this requirement must not be taken too far. The prescription of the relevant matters in the affidavit is not an indictment for a criminal charge and should not be treated as if it was. I agree with the views of Chadwick J. (as he then was) in *Re Continental Assurance Co of London plc* . . . that the introduction into this jurisdiction of the inflexibility of a criminal indictment is to be deplored. As the former Master of the Rolls pointed out in *Re Westmid Packaging Services Ltd* . . . in exercising this jurisdiction the court should adopt a 'broad brush approach' ".

The Vice-Chancellor also expressly adopted the view of Chadwick J. regarding the scope of "allowed". Having adverted to the use of "caused or allowed" and counsel's argument that the phrase must denote "some proactive step", the Vice-Chancellor added: "[i]n my view, a person may be said to allow a state of affairs if he knows or ought to know of it, and though entitled to take some action in respect of it does nothing."

(4) In *Re Sykes (Butchers) Ltd, Secretary of State for Trade and Industry v Richardson*,[277] Ferris J. found that it was clear on reading the summary of the allegation and the way in which the supporting facts had been set out in the main part of the affidavit, that an allegation of preferring creditors had not been limited to a narrow "charge" that the defendant had caused the company to give a preference in breach of the relevant statutory provisions in the Insolvency Act 1986.

7–107 The third point is that the claimant is limited to the evidence and the case made. The court can only consider that case in determining whether unfit conduct is established. Furthermore, the court cannot take other matters into account when it gets to the stage of fixing the period of disqualification (or what is commonly referred to as "sentencing").[278] To a limited extent, this absolute rule requires some qualification. Although conduct that is not the subject of a clear allegation cannot be relied upon as a ground of unfit conduct or as a factor affecting the period of disqualification, it appears that such conduct may be taken into account, as a matter of evidence, to confirm the court's view of other evidence. It was seen above that in *Re Hitco 2000 Ltd, Official Receiver v Cowan*,[279] the deputy judge found that the claimant could not rely on a complaint that the defendant had signed blank cheques and left them for use by the bookkeeper. The complaint did not form any part of the allegations of unfit conduct and, as there had been no application for permission to amend, the basic rule applied. However, the court held that evidence of the defendant's conduct in relation to the blank cheques could be taken into account in so far as it was relevant evidence confirming any other formal allegation. On the facts, the conduct was relevant to the general underlying complaint that the defendant had abdicated responsibility in the realm of financial control and failed to inform himself properly as to the state of the company's financial position.

[277] [1998] 1 B.C.L.C. 110.
[278] See *Re Sevenoaks Stationers (Retail) Ltd* [1991] Ch. 164.
[279] [1995] 2 B.C.L.C. 63.

Amending, reformulating or adding to allegations

7–108 The court may, in appropriate cases, permit the claimant to alter or extend the allegations even after the trial has commenced. The key question is whether or not the defendant will suffer injustice as a result of the court allowing the claimant to rely on amended, reformulated or additional allegations.[280] In this context, it is the potential injustice arising if a defendant does not have a fair and adequate opportunity to deal with any altered, reformulated or additional allegation, which is of greatest relevance. In some cases the main issue will be whether the amendment, reformulation or addition is necessary (see, for example, *Hitco 2000* where the relevant allegation was raised for the first time on appeal).[281] In other cases the amended, reformulated or additional allegation may simply amount to a different analysis of existing matters that are already fairly and squarely in issue (see, for example, *Looe Fish* and *Sykes (Butchers)* discussed above). In *Sevenoaks Stationers*, the Court of Appeal adverted to the possibility that it might be necessary to add further allegations in circumstances where new matters arise from further evidence filed, or because further evidence comes to light or for some other reason. The requirements of justice would, in each case, depend upon the circumstances. In some cases, it will be necessary for the defendant to be put on notice before the hearing as the raising of fresh matters during the hearing may come too late.[282] In other cases an adjournment may be needed and it may be appropriate for one to be granted.[283] In other cases, where an experienced advocate is representing the defendant, the advocate may be able to deal with the point without any adjournment "taking it in his stride".

Is permission needed to amend allegations?

7–109 In a sense this is a slightly academic issue. The practical question that it raises relates to the burden of proof (is it on the defendant to seek to "strike out" or have any proposed amendments disallowed or is it for the claimant to establish that it should be allowed?) However, few cases turn on burden of proof. The matter was considered by His Honour Judge Rich Q.C. (sitting as a High Court judge) in *Re New Technology Systems Ltd.*[284] In summary:

[280] See *Re New Generation Engineers Ltd* [1993] B.C.L.C. 435 at 438–439. For a case in which an application by the Secretary of State to amend an allegation was refused see *Secretary of State for Trade and Industry v Gill* [2004] EWHC 175 (Ch), [2005] B.C.C. 24.

[281] [1995] 2 B.C.L.C. 63 at 69–70.

[282] See, e.g. *Re Cubelock Ltd* [2001] B.C.C. 523.

[283] There may also be cases where an adjournment is necessary to enable the defendant to deal with the point but such adjournment may not be fair to the defendant for other reasons, depending on (for example) at what stage of the proceedings the point was raised, how long the proceedings have been outstanding, how long ago the events in question arose and whether, if established, the new matters would be likely to seriously affect the end result one way or the other. The proportionality principle in Pt I of the CPR (see r.1.1(2)(c)) could be particularly important in this context. For an instructive pre-CPR case see *Re New Technology Systems Ltd* [1996] B.C.C. 694 affirmed at [1997] B.C.C. 810. In that case, the judge decided that there had been inordinate delay in the proceedings but found that the defendant's solicitor's conduct made such delay excusable. However, he did strike out certain new allegations, even though the matter was not then ready for trial, but on terms that the claimant could re-file the new evidence in a different form.

[284] [1996] B.C.C. 694.

(1) If the allegation is filed in written evidence, the question will be whether such written evidence was permitted and, put more precisely, whether the new or amended allegation was also permitted under the relevant direction of the court.

(2) In many cases (including *New Technology Systems* itself), the further allegation will be contained in written evidence "in reply" to evidence of the defendant and the court will have made a direction permitting evidence in reply without specifically considering the question of amended allegations (because the point will not have been raised at the directions stage). The question then will be whether or not the amended allegation can properly be seen as being part of the evidence in reply. In some cases it will be allowed under the direction permitting the filing of evidence in reply. Three examples of such cases are: (a) where the allegation is a reformulation of an existing allegation (perhaps meeting a particular technical objection to the charge as laid); (b) where the evidence giving rise to the allegation is contained within the defendant's evidence in answer to the claimant's original evidence; and (c) where the defendant's evidence seeks to refute a particular charge by alleging facts that give rise to another charge. In other cases, the amendment may not be treated as being allowed by the direction for evidence in reply.

(3) In practice, it may be unnecessary to consider the question of whether or not a particular allegation is or is not permitted by any existing direction of the court. It is open to the court to deal first with the next logical question, namely, assuming permission is needed, whether or not the court would be minded to give it.

7–110 It is suggested that it will not always be necessary for a new allegation to be included in written evidence and that the parties can agree, or the court can permit, an allegation to be made without the need for the claimant to waste time and costs filing further written evidence, which is not really "evidence", but rather something that would normally be found in a statement of case. His Honour Judge Rich Q.C. recognised that the question of "amending" the allegations in a civil disqualification case is not the same as amending a pleading (or now a statement of case) because the issue arises in the context of the wider question of whether further evidence should be admitted. In *Re Crystal Palace Football Club (1986), Secretary of State for Trade and Industry v Goldberg*, Lewison J. referred to the lack of need in civil disqualification proceedings for formal amendments in the following terms:

> "[T]here is no formal statement of case. Although the evidence served in support of the application must state the matters by reference to which the defendant is alleged to be unfit to be concerned in the management of a company, if the Secretary of State wishes to amend the allegation or introduce new ones, there is no master document which she must apply to amend."[285]

[285] [2004] 1 B.C.L.C. 597 at [55].

This and other factors, such as the inability to bring the case under CPR Pt 7, reinforced the conclusion that he should be cautious before allowing the Secretary of State to change the thrust of the allegations as they were originally set out.[286] It will be interesting to see to what extent the approach in this area will be coloured by experience under CPR Pt 17.

7–111 The matter has more recently been considered by HH Judge Roger Kaye Q.C. and HH Judge Hodge Q.C. respectively in two cases in the High Court, *Re Plazoo Pipe Systems Ltd, Kappler v Secretary of State for Trade and Industry*[287] and *Re Baysouth Ltd, Secretary of State for Trade and Industry v Knowles*.[288] In the former case HH Judge Roger Kaye Q.C. was faced with an appeal from the order of a district judge disqualifying him for 11 years. Two of the grounds of appeal related to the manner in which the case and the allegations against the director had been permitted to proceed. The summary of the relevant allegation was that the director had "caused" (as opposed to "allowed") the company to raise certain false invoices implying that he had dishonestly been instrumental in the company raising false invoices in order to enable the company to raise substantial finance from the bank. However, in closing it was made clear that the case put was that the defendant had "caused" the company to raise the false invoices by being aware of them, knowing they were fraudulent, and doing nothing to stop them. In the circumstances the situation was somewhat similar to the *Hitco* case where the words of the summary of the specific allegation were capable as a matter of construction of covering various factual scenarios but where the case had been conducted on the basis that a specific meaning was attributed to the words. It was then later sought to give a different interpretation to the relevant words. The two relevant grounds of appeal on this aspect were, in substance, that: (a) the defendant had not been "charged" with "allowing" the company to issue false invoices; and (b) there was a serious irregularity in the trial in that the revised closing case should not have been permitted. As the judge, it is respectfully suggested, correctly identified, the question on appeal was relatively simple: had Mr Kappler had a fair trial? The principles were as follows[289]:

(1) The court has a complete discretion to permit new, additional, extended or reformulated allegations to be put at any stage. There must be written evidence or matters by reference to which the defendant is alleged to be unfit set out in the written evidence. However, there is no formal document to amend and there is no requirement that existing allegations be "amended" or the new or changed allegation reduced to writing, though the latter course may be sensible. (It is respectfully suggested that this is correct and that it reflects the distinction between the requirement that the matters by reference to which the director is said to be unfit must be set out in the evidence and the

[286] [2004] 1 B.C.L.C. 597 at [55]–[56].
[287] [2006] EWHC 3694 (Ch), [2008] 1 B.C.L.C. 120.
[288] March 7, 2007, Ch.D., unreported (Preston District Registry).
[289] See especially at [83]–[85], [87].

summary of the allegations, which is not technically a requirement of the Disqualification Rules.)

(2) The key question is whether or not the director fairly knows and understands the substance of the allegations that he has to meet and whether or not he will suffer injustice as a result of the court allowing the defendant to rely on the amended, altered or additional allegation.

(3) The court will take a wide range of circumstances into account in deciding whether to permit new or reformulated allegations including (without limitation): the stage at which they are introduced; the circumstances in which they are introduced; whether new evidence is appropriate or necessary (and should be permitted to be adduced); whether the altered allegation is simply a new way of looking at the existing evidence or whether it is entirely new; whether an adjournment would be necessary in consequence of the proposed changes (if permitted); whether the defendant will have a fair opportunity to deal with the revised allegations; and whether the defendant is represented or not and so on.

(4) The factors that the court may take into account are not exhaustive as each case turns on its own facts and extended analysis of previous cases will not always be illuminating. The overriding principle is whether the defendant will have (or have had) a fair opportunity of dealing with the substance of the case, including those parts of it giving rise to new or modified allegations.

On the facts of the particular case, the director had had such a fair opportunity to deal with the revised case and there was no irregularity in the trial. In particular, the judge took into account the following matters: the fact that the new case was not a wholly new case so much as a revised interpretation or evaluation of the evidence; that it was foreshadowed at a hearing months in advance of the trial; that the substance had been put to the director in cross-examination and he had had every opportunity to deal with it in his evidence or by way of his own cross-examination; and finally, although acting in person, the defendant was, in the words of the district judge, "light years from being a moron."

7–112 In the *Baysouth* case, HH Judge Hodge Q.C. was faced with an argument that the judgment of HH Judge Roger Kaye QC was inconsistent with the following passage in the judgment of Laddie J. in the *Finelist* case:

> "It is not sufficient for the director to know and understand the allegations he has to meet. There is an obligation on the Secretary of State to set out in the affidavit or affirmation in support the main parts of the evidence on which she is to rely."[290]

The submission made on behalf of the Secretary of State to HH Judge Hodge Q.C. was that Laddie J. was dealing with an entirely separate point. In that case the director knew the nature of the allegations that he had to meet. The issue was whether the evidence on which the Secretary of State sought to rely was adequate.

[290] *Re Finelist Ltd, Secretary of State for Trade and Industry v Swan* [2004] B.C.C. 877 at [17].

HH Judge Hodge Q.C., having decided that there was no tension between the two judgments properly understood, therefore suggested a reformulation of part of para.[84] of the judgment of HH Judge Roger Kaye Q.C. in the *Plazoo Pipe Systems* case as set out below (insertion underlined):

> "... The key question in all cases is whether or not the defendant fairly knows and understands the substance of the allegations he has to meet (including any new or altered allegations); whether he knows and understands the essential facts which are to be relied upon in support of those allegations; and, where new or altered allegations are relied upon, whether or not he will suffer injustice as a result of the court allowing the Secretary of State to rely on such amended, altered or additional allegations."

The significance of the two-year period under s.7(2) on the question of amendment

7–113 The two-year period under s.7(2) is not strictly a limitation period.[291] As such, it is suggested that there is no presumption that because the period has expired either that: (a) permission is automatically required to amend or add to allegations; or that (b) any amended or further allegations should not be permitted. In this context, it has been said that it is unhelpful to treat the two-year period for commencing disqualification proceedings under s.6 as a limitation period.[292] It is suggested that in deciding whether to allow amended or additional allegations to be introduced, the court has an unfettered and general discretion and must consider all the circumstances. The circumstances that will usually be relevant are those referred to in the *Sevenoaks Stationers* and *Lo-Line* cases referred to above together with the issue of procedural fairness. The fact that the two-year period has expired before the claimant seeks to introduce amended or further allegations should not usually be treated as a decisive or significant factor weighing against him.[293] This is for the following reasons:

(1) The two-year period in s.7(2) has two primary functions: (a) to aid good administration by encouraging the timeous obtaining of disqualification orders in cases where the public needs to be protected against unfit directors;[294] and (b) to protect potential defendants so that they know within a reasonable period whether they will have to face proceedings.
(2) If proceedings are commenced in time, the two-year period will have served its purpose.
(3) Good administration of the CDDA (referred to in (1) above), and the due administration of justice,[295] both factors underlying s.7(2), continue to be

[291] On s.7(2) generally, see Ch.8.

[292] See *Re Blackspur Group Plc, Secretary of State for Trade and Industry v Davies (No.2)* [1996] 4 All E.R. 289 at 298–299.

[293] See *Re Jazzgold Ltd* [1994] 1 B.C.L.C. 38 at 47–48.

[294] *Re Blackspur Group Plc, Secretary of State for Trade and Industry v Davies* [1996] 4 All E.R. 289 at 298–299.

[295] Due administration of justice demands, for example, that a party is not permitted to draw out the proceedings with the result that the memories of witnesses fail and/or the proceedings become oppressive.

factors relevant to the exercise of the court's discretion in controlling proceedings generally. These factors are particularly relevant when the court is considering, for example, the exercise of the discretion to strike out for want of prosecution or whether to extend the time that a party has for the service of evidence.

(4) Good administration of the CDDA and the due administration of justice may also weigh against the granting of permission to amend. However, in circumstances where the granting of permission: (a) does not add to the overall timescale; and/or (b) does not materially affect the defendant's ability to defend himself it is suggested that any amendment should readily be allowed. The same is true where the new or amended allegations are ones that the claimant considers it proper in the public interest to pursue.

EVIDENCE

7–114 The remainder of this chapter considers various matters of law and practice that are particularly pertinent to the question of evidence in civil disqualification proceedings. It is not intended to be a comprehensive account of the law of evidence.

Written evidence

Form of written evidence: affidavits, witness statements, statements of truth

7–115 Evidence in connection with disqualification proceedings is by way of written evidence. In some cases affidavits are required. In what follows, references to affidavits should be taken as including a reference to affirmations.[296] In other circumstances, written evidence, verified by a statement of truth, can be used (in practice this would be by way of witness statement and/or an application notice; each of these must be verified by statement of truth).[297]

Affidavits

7–116 Affidavits are required in the following cases[298]:

(1) Substantive evidence (whether in support or in opposition) on an application for the making of a disqualification order. There is a specific exception in the case of the official receiver who may give evidence by way of report.[299]

[296] See, e.g. para.1.7 of Practice Direction 32 to the CPR (entitled "Written Evidence").

[297] See CPR r.32.6(2). Statements of truth are the subject of CPR Pt 22. By CPR r.32.14, a person who makes or causes to be made a false statement in a document verified by a statement of truth without an honest belief in its truth is liable to proceedings for contempt of court brought by the Attorney General or with the permission of the court. In the case of affidavits there is, in such circumstances, the possibility of proceedings for perjury.

[298] By virtue of CPR r.32.15 evidence must be given by affidavit if this is required by the court, a provision contained in any other rule, a practice direction or any other enactment.

[299] In the case of proceedings under CDDA ss.7, 8 and 9A see r.3(2) of the Disqualification Rules. In the case of other civil proceedings see para.9.1 of the Disqualification Practice Direction. The power to impose such a requirement by practice direction would appear to follow from CPR r.32.15(1).

(2) Substantive evidence (whether in support or in opposition) on an application for permission to act notwithstanding the making of a disqualification order.[300]

The requirement for affidavits in s.6, s.8 and s.9A proceedings (as set out in the Disqualification Rules) is extended to all civil disqualification proceedings governed by the Disqualification Practice Direction (namely, proceedings under ss.2(2)(a), 3, 4, 7 and 8 but not s.10). When the Disqualification Rules were amended to take account of the CPR, the opportunity was not taken to replace affidavits with written statements in proceedings under ss.6 and 8 of the CDDA. This contrasts with the position under the Insolvency Rules 1986[301] and in relation to proceedings for the making of bankruptcy restrictions and debt relief restrictions orders. The original reason for the retention of affidavits is likely to have been that both the court and the Secretary of State may have to act on written evidence without it being tested. It would appear that affidavits are recognised by the CPR as being qualitatively different from witness statements, because, for example, affidavits are required in the case of applications for the making of search orders and freezing orders and in relation to contempt proceedings.[302] In practice, the main difference appears to be that a false statement on oath will give rise to the possibility of proceedings for perjury, whereas a false statement verified by statement of truth only opens up the possibility of proceedings for contempt of court. However, the distinction between the form of written evidence that can be used in bankruptcy restrictions and debt relief restrictions proceedings as opposed to disqualification proceedings creates an unfortunate tension in the law as well as undermining the justification for the requirement for affidavits in disqualification proceedings. It is time that the two forms of proceeding were put on the same footing in this respect. It should be noted that the old distinction between affidavits and witness statements (the former could be used by other parties once filed, the latter could not) relied on unsuccessfully to challenge affidavit evidence in *Re Rex Williams Leisure Plc, Secretary of State for Trade and Industry v Warren*[303] has now disappeared under the CPR (see CPR r.32.5). Also, the old rule that a submission of "no case to answer" could only be made if the party making it elected to call no evidence seems to have been replaced by a more flexible practice.[304] It was recognised in *Rex Williams* that a witness could be

[300] para.22.1 of the Disqualification Practice Direction.

[301] As amended by the Insolvency (Amendment) (No.2) Rules 1999 (SI 1999/1022) substituting new r.7.57 (see especially r.7.57(6)). The trend in favour of witness statements verified by statement of truth as opposed to affidavits in the context of insolvency proceedings is continuing: see the Legislative Reform (Insolvency) (Miscellaneous Provisions) Order 2009 available only in draft at the time of writing and due to come into force on April 6, 2010.

[302] CPR Pt 25 and para.3.1 of the relevant Practice Direction ("Interim Injunctions"). See also para.1.4 of the Practice Direction to Pt 32 ("Written Evidence").

[303] [1994] Ch. 1 and 350.

[304] See, e.g. *Ronald Mullan v Birmingham City Council* [2000] C.P.Rep.61; *Al Malik Carpets Ltd v London Buildings (Highgate) Ltd*, August 12, 1999, Ch.D., unreported; *Landare Investments Ltd v Welsh Development Agency*, November 25, 1999, Q.B.D., unreported.

asked questions designed to supplement his affidavit evidence before being cross-examined. However, the court would not normally permit a party to call brand new evidence that would take the other party by surprise. In cases where a party is unable to obtain affidavit evidence from a hostile witness, he may need to summons the witness to give oral evidence. In these circumstances, the party will have to apply to the court for permission to lead oral evidence. The likelihood is that the court will require the party to submit a "witness summary" by analogy with CPR r.32.9.

7–117 In other types of civil disqualification proceeding, it is possible to rely on witness statements and, moreover, there is an incentive to do so. This is because, although an affidavit may be used whenever written evidence is called for, there is the potential costs sanction of CPR r.32.15 if an affidavit is used when it is not required by the CPR or any other relevant provision.

Witness statements or application notices

7–118 In practice, written evidence by way of witness statement or application notice may be used in the following situations:

(1) Any interim application in the course of proceedings in which a disqualification order is sought or in the course of proceedings in which permission is sought to act, notwithstanding the making of a disqualification order (such as an application to extend time, for disclosure, for further information, for summary judgment, to strike out and so forth).[305]
(2) An application for permission to act notwithstanding bankruptcy, a moratorium under a debt relief order or insolvency restrictions under s.11 and the Insolvency Rules 1986 rr.6.203 et seq.[306]
(3) An application under s.7(2) for permission to commence s.6 proceedings after expiry of the two-year period.
(4) An application under s.7(4).

Affidavits and witness statements: formal requirements

7–119 The formal requirements are as follows:

(1) **Headings:** The headings to affidavits and witness statements must comply with the requirements of the Disqualification Practice Direction. This means that they must be entitled in the matter of the relevant company or companies and in the matter of the CDDA (Disqualification Practice Direction, paras 5.1, 19.1, 21.1, 25.1). In the case of s.6 proceedings, it is only necessary to set out the lead companies in the heading (Disqualification Practice Direction, para.5.1). Affidavits must also comply with the relevant provisions of the

[305] Interim applications are governed primarily by CPR Pt 23 and Practice Directions made in relation to it: see para.24 of the Disqualification Practice Direction.

[306] See Insolvency Rules 1986 r.7.57(5) as amended by the Insolvency (Amendment) (No.2) Rules 1999 (SI 1999/1022).

CPR and the Practice Directions made thereunder. In relation to affidavits, the following matters should clearly be written in the top right hand corner of the first page and on the back sheet:

(a) The party on whose behalf the affidavit is made.
(b) The initials and surname of the deponent.
(c) The number of the affidavit in relation to that deponent.
(d) The identifying initials and number of each exhibit referred to.
(e) The date sworn.[307]

The title of the proceedings should be set out save that it is not necessary to set out all the claimants (or all the defendants) if there are more than two.[308] In relation to witness statements, similar provisions apply (see paras 17.1–17.2 of the Practice Direction to Pt 32 of the CPR entitled "Written Evidence" ("PD 32").

(2) **Other matters:** PD 32, also contains similar provisions regarding affidavits and witness statements on the following matters (references to PD 32 unless otherwise stated):

(a) The body of the document (para.4: affidavits; para.16: affirmations; para.18: witness statements).
(b) Exhibits (paras 4.3, 11–15: affidavits; paras 18.3–18.6: witness statements).
(c) Jurat (para.5: affidavits)[309] and statement of truth (para.20: witness statements).
(d) Format (para.6: affidavits; para.19: witness statements).
(e) Inability of person to read or sign affidavit (para.7) or witness statement (para.21).
(f) Alterations (para.8: affidavits; para.22: witness statements).
(g) Filing and written evidence in a foreign language (para.10: affidavits; para.23: witness statements). The Disqualification Practice Direction also contains provisions dealing with filing. Broadly, exhibits to affidavits are lodged with the court (rather than formally filed) and returned at the end of the relevant proceedings (Disqualification Practice Direction, paras 9.3(2), 9.4(2), 9.6(2)).
(h) Defects (para.25).

The burden and standard of proof

7–120 In civil proceedings where a disqualification order is sought, the burden of proof lies on the claimant to establish that there is jurisdiction to make a disqualification order and either that a disqualification order is required to be made (under s.6 or s.9A) or that, as a matter of discretion, one should be made. The basic standard of proof is the civil standard, i.e. the balance of probabilities. It has been argued by those who regard disqualification as a penal sanction that the stricter criminal stan-

[307] Practice Direction 32 to CPR Pt 32 ("Written Evidence"), para.3.2.
[308] Practice Direction 32, para.3.1 and see also para.4 of the Practice Direction to CPR Pt 7 and para.7 of the Practice Direction to CPR Pt 20.
[309] See also para.9 with regard to oaths and para.16 on affirmations.

dard of proof should apply.[310] However, the application of a criminal standard of proof has been rejected. The courts have nevertheless recognised that in certain factual situations the basic civil standard has to be applied with care where certain matters, such as fraud, are alleged in disqualification proceedings. In practice, the more serious the allegation, the more cogent the evidence required to establish it. As Lord Nicholls has said: "[b]uilt into the preponderance of probability standard is a generous degree of flexibility in respect of the seriousness of the allegation".[311] In *Re Living Images Ltd*, Laddie J. summarised the position thus:

> "These are civil proceedings. The appropriate standard of proof is therefore a balance of probabilities. However disqualification does involve a substantial interference with the freedom of the individual . . . Furthermore, some of the allegations . . . may involve serious charges of moral turpitude . . . In such cases the court must bear in mind the inherent unlikeliness of such serious allegations being true. The more serious the allegation, the more the court will need the assistance of cogent evidence . . . But in the end these are civil, not criminal, proceedings. [Counsel] argued that the director must be given the benefit of any reasonable doubt . . . If that is the correct approach, then the standard of proof in these applications would be the same as that used in criminal proceedings."[312]

The House of Lords have considered the point in a number of cases. Extracts from two speeches in particular provide useful illustrations. In this context, reference is frequently made to Lord Hoffmann's dictum:

> "It would need more cogent evidence to satisfy one that the creature seen walking in Regent's Park was more likely than not to have been a lioness than to be satisfied to the same standard of probability that it was an Alsatian. On this basis, cogent evidence is generally required to satisfy a civil tribunal that a person has been fraudulent or behaved in some other reprehensible manner. But the question is always whether the tribunal thinks it more probable than not."[313]

However, what matters, as always in weighing evidence, is the context, as Baroness Hale has more recently observed:

> "As to the seriousness of the allegation, there is no logical or necessary connection between seriousness and probability. Some seriously harmful behaviour, such as murder, is sufficiently rare to be inherently improbable in most circumstances. Even then there are circumstances, such as a body with its throat cut and no weapon to hand, where it is not at all improbable. Other seriously harmful behaviour, such as alcohol or drug abuse, is regrettably all too common and not at all improbable. Nor are serious allegations made in a vacuum. Consider the famous example of the animal seen in Regent's Park. If it is seen outside the zoo on a stretch of greensward regularly used for

[310] See discussion in Ch.2 and *Re Polly Peck International Plc, Secretary of State for Trade and Industry v Ellis (No.2)* [1994] 1 B.C.L.C. 574 at 581 where Lindsay J. (albeit faced with a preliminary issue under s.7(2)) said that a director should be given the benefit of any reasonable doubt because disqualification has penal consequences for the individual.

[311] *Re H (Minors) (Sexual Abuse: Standard of Proof)* [1996] A.C. 563 at 586.

[312] [1996] 1 B.C.L.C. 348 at 355.

[313] *Home Secretary v Rehman* [2001] UKHL 47, [2003] 1 A.C. 153 per Lord Hoffmann at [55].

walking dogs, then of course it is more likely to be a dog than a lion. If it is seen in the zoo next to the lions' enclosure when the door is open, then it may well be more likely to be a lion than a dog."[314]

This approach to standard of proof and evidential burden is now fairly settled.[315] It is suggested that the same approach should apply to cases brought under CDDA s.4(1), notwithstanding that the jurisdictional "gateway" to disqualification under that provision is a criminal offence.[316]

7–121 In assessing the defendant's conduct, the courts must guard against the application of hindsight. In *Re Living Images Ltd*, Laddie J. made the point in the following terms:

> "By the time the application comes before the court, the conduct of the directors has to be judged on the basis of statements given to the Official Receiver, no doubt frequently under stress, and a comparatively small collection of documents selected to support the Official Receiver's and the [defendants'] respective positions. On the basis of this the court has to pass judgment on the way in which the directors conducted the affairs of the company over a period in days, weeks or, as in this case, months. Those statements and documents are analysed in the clinical atmosphere of the courtroom. They are analysed, for example, with the benefit of knowing that the company went into liquidation. It is very easy therefore to look at the signals available to the directors at the time and to assume that they, or any competent director, would have realised that the end was coming. The court must be careful not to fall into the trap of being too wise after the event."[317]

The same point has been put even more colourfully by Professor Goode:

> "It is necessary to be particularly cautious in applying hindsight to cases involving personal liability, *e.g.* for wrongful trading, or the setting aside of a preference. Business life is neither static nor certain. Information has constantly to be updated, predictions made about a range of uncertain events, snap judgments formed, rapid decisions taken and adaptations continually made in the light of shifts in customer demand, tax changes, industrial action, political events, international relations, and the like. Just as it is all too easy for historians to pick their way leisurely across the battlefields of Waterloo identifying Napoleon's errors in the tranquillity of academic research, unhindered by all the confusions engendered by blazing guns, cavalry charges, mud, darkness, uncertainty as to the current arrivals or dispositions of troops and ignorance of the intentions of the

[314] *Re B (Children) (Care Proceedings: Standard of Proof)* [2008] UKHL 35, [2009] 1 A.C. 11 per Baroness Hale at [72]. See also, as regards penalties in the income tax area, *Revenue & Customs Commissioners v Khawaja* [2008] EWHC 1687 (Ch), [2009] 1 W.L.R. 398.

[315] See also *Re Verby Print for Advertising Ltd* [1998] 2 B.C.L.C. 23. The approach is consistent with ordinary principles: see *Bater v Bater* [1951] P. 35 at 36–37; *Hornal v Neuberger Products Ltd* [1957] 1 Q.B. 247 at 260–267; *Khawaja v Home Secretary* [1984] A.C. 74 at 113–114; *Re H (Minors) (Sexual Abuse: Standard of Proof)* [1996] A.C. 563.

[316] This is for two main reasons. First, by analogy with the reasoning in cases such as *R. (on the application of McCann) v Crown Court at Manchester* [2003] 1 A.C. 787. Secondly, because the facts founding a criminal conviction under Companies Act 2006 s.993 (formerly Companies Act 1985 s.458) are also capable of founding civil liability under Insolvency Act 1986 s.213 which is a separate (civil) gateway to disqualification under CDDA s.10.

[317] [1996] 1 B.C.L.C. 348 at 356.

enemy, so also a professional acquainted with subsequent events in a company's life is all too readily beguiled into the view that he would have done things differently, that what is now apparent was obvious from the start."[318]

7–122 Where an application is made for permission to act notwithstanding disqualification, bankruptcy, a debt relief order or insolvency restrictions, the burden of proof lies on the applicant for permission.

Hearsay and "opinion" evidence

7–123 The position with regard to hearsay evidence has changed substantially following the coming into force of the Civil Evidence Act 1995 ("CEA 1995"). Before the commencement of the CEA 1995, the general position was that the Secretary of State was entitled to adduce and rely on hearsay evidence by reason of implied statutory exemptions arising from judicial construction of the CDDA. Furthermore, where s.6 proceedings were commenced by the official receiver and he filed a written report (as he is entitled to do under the Disqualification Rules), such a report (and any exhibits) could, by virtue of r.3(2) of the Disqualification Rules, contain matters of hearsay.[319] These exceptions, which remain extremely wide ranging, are considered in more detail below. The general position for defendants prior to the CEA 1995 was less favourable. A defendant was generally only able to rely on hearsay evidence if it came within an established exception to the hearsay rule. The main established exception, deriving from the Civil Evidence Acts 1968 and 1972 and complementary rules of court, was fairly narrow. In the High Court, the notice procedure under RSC Ord.38, r.25 (and following) expressly did not apply to affidavits. Moreover, affidavits (other than those for use at interlocutory or interim hearings) could not contain hearsay by reason of RSC Ord.41, r.5. However, there was power in the court to make an order permitting hearsay evidence, but this power was rarely exercised.[320] A more relaxed approach was taken to hearsay in affidavits in the county courts under CCR Ord.20, r.10. Hearsay evidence could be used provided that the affidavit stated which of the facts deposed to were within the deponent's knowledge and which were based on information or belief and, in the former case, the deponent's means of knowledge and, in the latter case, the sources and grounds of the information and belief.[321] The CEA 1995 significantly changed the position for defendants.[322] Generally speaking, they are now entitled to rely on hearsay evidence. While the CEA 1995 also applies in favour of the Secretary of State, it appears that the Secretary of State can continue to rely on the exceptions that were available to him before that Act came into force.

[318] *Principles of Corporate Insolvency Law* 2nd edn (1997) at pp. 94–95.

[319] See *Re Moonbeam Cards Ltd* [1993] B.C.L.C. 1099.

[320] RSC Ord.38, r.3. The exact scope of this power in relation to hearsay appears to have been uncertain though see *Arab Monetary Fund v Hashim (No.7)* [1993] 1 W.L.R. 1014.

[321] See discussion in *Re Circle Holidays International Plc* [1994] B.C.C. 226.

[322] The regime in place before the coming into force of the Civil Evidence Act 1995 was challenged before the European Court of Human Rights in *DC, HS and AD v United Kingdom* [2000] B.C.C. 710. However, the European Court was able to side-step the issue. It determined that the director's evidence which was excluded was excluded not on the basis that it was hearsay but on the basis that it was irrelevant character evidence.

7–124 A separate rule to the hearsay rule is the common law rule that, other than "expert" opinion, "opinion" evidence is generally inadmissible. For these purposes "opinion" evidence means exactly that and encompasses inferences or conclusions drawn from the observance of primary facts. Thus in *Hollington v F Hewthorn & Co Ltd*[323] the principle was articulated that judicial findings made in a previous case were not admissible in later proceedings as evidence of the facts found. In that case the earlier decision was a criminal conviction. A specific statutory exemption to that particular case was later created by the Civil Evidence Act 1968 ss.11 and 13. However, in relation to findings made in civil proceedings the general principle was found still to apply by the Court of Appeal in *Re Queens Moat Houses Plc, Secretary of State for Trade and Industry v Bairstow*.[324] Of course there are exceptions to the general principle. One is where the principles of estoppel apply; another is where the principle of abuse of process applies. The key question in the disqualification sphere is the extent to which there is an implied statutory exception to this principle. The relevant authorities have hitherto suggested that there is an implied statutory exception which applies both to the common law hearsay rule and the opinion evidence rule. However, in the light of the decision of the Court of Appeal in *Re David M Aaron (Personal Financial Planners) Ltd, Secretary of State for Business, Enterprise & Regulatory Reform v Aaron*,[325] the scope of these exceptions is now different as regards the hearsay rule and the "opinion" rule.

The express exception: s.6 proceedings where the official receiver is claimant

7–125 If the relevant company is being wound up by the court, the Secretary of State may direct the official receiver to commence disqualification proceedings in the name of the official receiver (CDDA s.7(1)(b)). In other cases, the official receiver may, in practice, have conduct of the proceedings although the formal claimant is the Secretary of State. In cases where the official receiver is the formal claimant, a special rule applies. Under r.3 of the Disqualification Rules, the official receiver may give evidence by written report rather than by affidavit. The effect of r.3(2) is that such a report will be treated as if it had been verified by the official receiver on affidavit and as prima facie evidence of any matter contained in it. The courts have held that r.3(2) covers not only the body of the report itself, but also any exhibits to the report.[326] This means that the official receiver's evidence may contain and exhibit matters of hearsay. The admissibility of such evidence in no way depends on the Civil Evidence Acts. The same would appear to apply to any further report filed by the official receiver by way of reply to the defendant's filed evidence. It would appear that this rule also provides an express exception to the

[323] [1943] K.B. 587.
[324] [2003] EWCA Civ 321, [2004] Ch. 1.
[325] [2008] EWCA Civ 1146, [2009] 1 B.C.L.C. 55. The *Aaron* case is discussed further in the text from 7–129.
[326] See *Re City Investment Centres Ltd* [1992] B.C.L.C. 956; *Re Moonbeam Cards Ltd* [1993] B.C.L.C. 1099.

opinion evidence rule. Unfortunately this point was not addressed by the Court of Appeal in the *Aaron* case dealing with opinion evidence and which is considered from 7–129 below. If the official receiver files an affidavit rather than a report, the exception in r.3(2) does not apply, but the implied statutory exception discussed below may apply. Under para.9.1 of the Disqualification Practice Direction, the r.3(2) provision may be said to have been purportedly extended to cover other CDDA proceedings (e.g. for permission to act under s.17) where the official receiver is a party. While the Disqualification Practice Direction is wider in scope than r.3(2) of the Disqualification Rules (which only applies expressly to proceedings under ss.7(1), 8 and 9A), it is doubtful that it can have created a wider express exception to the hearsay or opinion rules.[327] The paragraph is best understood as: (a) setting out the position under r.3(2) where such rule applies (i.e. in cases brought under s.7(1)(b)); and (b) otherwise confirming the position under CEA 1995 (on which see further below).

Express exceptions to the hearsay and opinion evidence rules under the Companies Act 1985

7–126 The Companies Act 1985 creates specific exceptions to the hearsay and opinion rules. The most important exception in the present context is the one in s.441 (as amended by the Insolvency Acts 1985 and 1986). This provides that a copy of the report of an inspector appointed under Pt XIV of the Act which is certified by the Secretary of State:

> ". . . is admissible in any legal proceedings as evidence of the opinion of the inspectors in relation to any matter contained in the report and in proceedings under s.8 of the CDDA as evidence of any fact stated therein . . ."

The first part of this phrase deals solely with the mechanics by which an inspector's report may be proved but does not deal with the question of whether, as a matter of the law of evidence, such a report is admissible evidence.[328] However, the closing words, which refer to s.8, make plain that in proceedings under that section the report will be admissible evidence of any matter contained in it. This is likely to mean that, as well as hearsay evidence, material containing evaluation of the recited facts will also be admissible: in other words, material commonly referred to as opinion evidence otherwise inadmissible under the line of authority starting, in modern times, with *Hollington v F Hewthorn & Co Ltd.*[329]

Proceedings under ss.6 and 8: the "implied statutory exception"

7–127 In cases decided under ss.6 and 8, the courts have construed the CDDA as containing an implied statutory exception to the hearsay rule that operates in

[327] There having been no relevant statutory instrument under either the CDDA or the Civil Procedure Act 1997 conferring such a power: see discussion in the text at 7–29.

[328] See *Savings & Investment Bank Ltd v Gasco Investments (Netherlands) BV* [1984] 1 W.L.R. 271.

[329] [1943] K.B. 587.

favour of the claimant.[330] It has also been construed as containing an implied statutory exception to the opinion rule. However, very unsatisfactorily, the scope of these exceptions seems to be unclear in the light of the Court of Appeal decision in the *Aaron* case considered from 7–129.

7–128 The implied statutory exception in the context of the hearsay rule is now very wide. In practice, its width in this context is of limited importance given the width of the statutory exceptions to the rule provided for by the Civil Evidence Act 1995. In *Re Barings Plc (No. 2), Secretary of State for Trade and Industry v Baker*, Evans-Lombe J. reached a conclusion in the context of a strike out application that meant, in his own words, that, ". . . the hearsay rule does not apply to evidence sought to be adduced by the Secretary of State in support of an application under [s.6 of the CDDA] . . .".[331] The correctness of this decision is now open to doubt. It is important to understand the incremental way in which the law has developed in this area because its historical development assists in explaining the limits now placed on the application of the hearsay rule and the opinion rule. The "implied statutory exception" originates from a line of cases involving public interest winding up petitions. A summary explaining how the exception has developed is set out below:

(1) The relevant statutory scheme governing public interest winding up petitions formerly provided that the Secretary of State (originally the Board of Trade) could present a petition on the just and equitable ground if it appeared from a report of inspectors (appointed under what is now ss.431–432 of the Companies Act 1985), that it was expedient to do so. As Hoffmann L.J. explained in *Re Rex Williams Leisure Plc, Secretary of State for Trade and Industry v Warren*, it became established law that a report of inspectors could be adduced and relied on as evidence in public interest winding up cases.[332]
(2) It was established in *Re Koscot Interplanetary (UK) Ltd*[333] that the relevant reports were evidence (as opposed to "material") and further established in *Re Armvent Ltd*[334] that a challenge to such evidence did not cause it to cease to be evidence and so require the Secretary of State to prove his case *de novo* "as though the inspectors had never come on the scene at all".
(3) The relevant statutory scheme was subsequently widened to allow the Secretary of State to take into account not only inspectors' reports produced under what is now ss.431–432 of the Companies Act 1985, but also material gathered under

[330] These cases have concerned proceedings in which the claimant's evidence was required to be on affidavit rather than by way of written report. It is suggested that r.3(2) (discussed above) does not extend the favourable hearsay regime applicable to official receiver's reports to affidavits. The point was argued but not decided in the *Ashcroft* case discussed further below.

[331] [1998] 1 B.C.L.C. 590 at 596.

[332] [1994] Ch. 350 at 365–366. See also *Re Travel and Holiday Clubs Ltd* [1967] 1 W.L.R. 711; *Re SBA Properties Ltd* [1967] 1 W.L.R. 799; *Re Armvent Ltd* [1975] 1 W.L.R. 1679; *Re St Piran* [1981] 1 W.L.R. 1300.

[333] [1972] 3 All E.R. 829.

[334] [1975] 1 W.L.R. 1679.

other Companies Act powers of investigation and inspection, including a "books and paper" appointment (under what is now s.447 of the 1985 Act).

(4) Under CDDA s.8, the Secretary of State is entitled to apply for a disqualification order if it appears to him, from investigative material gathered pursuant to various statutory powers,[335] expedient in the public interest that such an order should be made. In *Re Rex Williams Leisure Plc, Secretary of State for Trade and Industry v Warren*,[336] the Court of Appeal considered that the analogy between s.8 and the power to petition for winding up on public interest grounds (under what is now s.124A of the Insolvency Act 1986) was a powerful one and that hearsay evidence arising in the course of an appointment under s.447 of the Companies Act 1985 was admissible in disqualification proceedings on the basis of the implied statutory exception to the hearsay rule. If the evidence admitted under this exception was challenged, it was said that the Secretary of State might be well advised to supplement it by direct evidence because of its relative lack of weight. Nonetheless, hearsay evidence would remain evidence in the case. At first instance in *Rex Williams*, Nicholls V.C. put forward the cogent view that it would be absurd to expect the Secretary of State to construct a case based exclusively on evidence within his personal knowledge. Moreover there were sound reasons of procedure and economy that justified the Secretary of State's reliance on hearsay evidence:

> "There is a measure of practical good sense in a procedure whereby the [claimant] has first to set out his case, with sufficient clarity and identification of the evidence being relied on for the defendant to know where he stands. Then the defendant puts in his evidence. The [claimant] can see what factual issues there are, and he can then take steps and incur expense in adducing where necessary first-hand evidence on these issues, before the hearing. In this way genuine issues can be resolved properly and fairly in the interests of the defendant and in the public interest."[337]

(5) In *Secretary of State for Trade and Industry v Ashcroft*,[338] the Court of Appeal applied the logic of *Rex Williams* to proceedings under CDDA s.6 in relation to hearsay evidence deriving from reports made to the Secretary of State by the relevant insolvency practitioner pursuant to s.7(3). Allowing the Secretary of State's appeal, Millett L.J. made the following points:

  (a) The Court of Appeal in *Rex Williams* could have drawn a line between cases where the Secretary of State was applying for a winding up order and cases where he was applying for a disqualification order, but it had declined to do so.

  (b) The Court of Appeal in *Rex Williams* could have drawn a line between evidence that was expressly admissible by statute under s.441 of the Companies Act 1985 (meaning inspectors' reports) and evidence that was not so admissible (for example, s.447 material), but it had declined to do so.

[335] See Ch.3 from 3–115.
[336] [1994] Ch. 350.
[337] [1994] Ch. 1 at 15.
[338] [1998] Ch. 71.

(c) There appeared to be no discernible distinction between material gathered by the Secretary of State's own officials and material deriving from information supplied to him by an office holder.

Having identified three safeguards—(a) that the information was obtained by a professional insolvency practitioner or department official who must have thought it worthy of credence; (b) that the Secretary of State must have thought it to have credence; and (c) that the defendant would have an opportunity to challenge it—Millett L.J. ruled that the evidence was admissible. Hutchison and Hirst L.JJ. agreed, the latter approving the cogent considerations of policy identified in *Rex Williams* by Nicholls V.C. and confirming that they applied with equal force in s.6 proceedings.

(6) In *Re Barings Plc (No.2), Secretary of State for Trade and Industry v Baker*,[339] Evans-Lombe J. was faced with an application to strike out an affidavit filed on behalf of the Secretary of State on the ground that it contained inadmissible hearsay. The material in question comprised transcripts of interviews conducted by inspectors appointed in Singapore and by representatives of the Board of Banking Supervision enquiry, with officers of the collapsed Barings group, as well as the final reports of those bodies. The judge held that all the relevant material was admissible evidence. The fact that the material in question was presented by an accountant rather than by an office holder and the fact that the material was not produced pursuant to the exercise of statutory powers did not affect its admissibility and did not amount to good grounds for distinguishing the case from *Ashcroft*. The key question was: "what was the information on which the Secretary of State took the decision to launch the proceedings?" He also held that, if necessary, the material was also admissible under the CEA 1995 on the ground that this had impliedly overruled RSC Ord.41, r.5.

(7) At the conclusion of s.6 proceedings against three of the former Barings executives, Jonathan Parker J. confirmed, in so far as he felt it was necessary in the light of Evans-Lombe J.'s earlier ruling, that the implied statutory exception went beyond "pure" hearsay to encompass the findings of fact made by relevant inspectors, i.e. evaluative judgments or opinion evidence of the sort normally inadmissible under the principle in *Hollington v F Hewthorn & Co Ltd*.[340] Although the point was not specifically challenged on appeal, Morritt L.J. made the following remark:

[339] [1998] 1 B.C.L.C. 590.

[340] [1943] K.B. 587. See *Re Barings Plc (No.5), Secretary of State for Trade and Industry v Baker* [1999] 1 B.C.L.C. 433 at 495–496. The principle in *Hollington v Hewthorn* is now confined to the use that can be made of earlier judicial findings made in civil proceedings: see Civil Evidence Act 1968 ss.11 and 13. Criminal convictions will now amount to prima facie evidence only. As to the evidence required to displace such a presumption see discussion in *Re Queens Moat Houses Plc, Secretary of State for Trade and Industry v Bairstow* [2003] EWCA Civ 321, [2004] Ch. 1 of the possible application of the principle in *Phosphate Sewage Co Ltd v Molleson* (1879) L.R. 4 App. Cas. 801. See also *Stupple v Royal Insurance Co Ltd* [1971] 1 Q.B. 50 (as to whether the fact of conviction is itself evidence); *Brinks Ltd v Abu-Saleh (No.1)* [1995] 1 W.L.R. 1478 and *J v Oyston* [1999] 1 W.L.R. 694.

"We see no reason to doubt the validity of the judge's conclusions, quite the reverse; but, as will be seen, they are important in that Mr Baker in asserting that there was no evidence on a particular point appears to have ignored the evidence given to [the Bank of England inquiry] and the [Singaporean Companies Act investigation] and their findings."[341]

(8) In *Re Queens Moat Houses Plc, Secretary of State for Trade and Industry v Bairstow*,[342] the court was faced with the issue of whether the Secretary of State, in s.8 proceedings, could rely on judicial findings in earlier civil proceedings between the company and the director, but to which the Secretary of State was not party. No relevant express or implied statutory exception applied. The Court of Appeal held not only that the earlier judicial findings did not bind the directors, i.e. that it would not be an abuse of process for them to seek to re-litigate the issues, but also that the judicial findings could not be relied on as evidence by the Secretary of State, thus restating the normal principle derived from *Hollington v Hewthorn*. As regards *Barings*, the Court of Appeal did not have to consider the decisions of Evans-Lombe J. or Jonathan Parker J. because the Secretary of State accepted in *Bairstow* that there was no relevant applicable statutory or common law exception to the usual rule.

(9) Subsequent to the *Queens Moat* decision, two first instance decisions in s.6 proceedings confirmed that the implied statutory exception applied not just to the hearsay rule but also the opinion evidence rule. They further confirmed that the width of the exception was the same as the width of the exception to the hearsay rule. In both cases, the court determined that the width of the statutory exception in s.6 cases was as wide as it had been drawn by Evans-Lombe J. in the *Barings* case and that it applied to material on which the Secretary of State had based the decision to commence the proceedings. In the first,[343] the relevant opinion evidence comprised the findings of a Commercial Court judge[344] after a contested trial between, on the one hand, a bank and, on the other hand, a director and his company. In the second, the opinion evidence comprised, in particular, "factual findings and conclusions" in a Financial Services Authority investigation and final notice.[345] It is this second case—the *Aaron* case—which subsequently went to the Court of Appeal.

The Aaron case in the Court of Appeal

7–129 The Court of Appeal upheld the decision of the judge at first instance to allow the Secretary of State to adduce in evidence a Financial Services Authority investigation

[341] [2000] 1 B.C.L.C. 523 at [41].
[342] [2003] EWCA Civ 321, [2004] Ch. 1.
[343] *Re Stone & Rolls Ltd, Official Receiver v Stojevic* [2007] EWHC 1186 (Ch), [2008] Bus.L.R. 641.
[344] *Komercni Banka AS v Stone & Rolls Ltd* [2002] EWHC 2263 (Comm), [2003] 1 Lloyd's Rep. 383.
[345] *Re David M Aaron (Personal Financial Planners) Ltd, Secretary of State for Business, Enterprise & Regulatory Reform v Aaron* [2009] 1 B.C.L.C. 55.

into the sale by the relevant company of a particular type of structured financial product. Unfortunately the basis for the Court of Appeal's decision is far from clear. Thomas L.J. gave the only reasoned judgment. He reviewed the line of authority discussed above and, at para.[29] of his judgment, set out the underlying rationale of the implied exception to the hearsay and opinion rules stating that:

> "... Parliament must have intended that a court should have regard to the materials produced under clear statutory procedures on which the Secretary of State had relied in bringing the proceedings".

He rejected the argument that the implied statutory exception was limited to providing an exception to the hearsay (as opposed to the opinion) rule and rejected the argument that it would be unfair if such evidence was admissible. The submission on behalf of the directors that "... directors would be condemned on the basis of the opinion of third parties and not of the court determining the matter" could not be accepted "as having any semblance of reality." Thomas L.J. continued:

> "A judge of the Chancery Division will receive all the evidence, including the FSA report and the evidence for the defendants. It is, with respect, absurd to suggest that a judge of the Chancery Division who tries this case will not make up his or her own mind but will meekly follow or be influenced by the views of the FSA investigators. In my view, to exclude the FSA report would be to cause injustice by bringing about further delay and expense in these proceedings."

Thus far, the decision is entirely in line with the earlier authorities considered above. However, Thomas L.J. went on to hold that the Secretary of State could not rely on decisions (and conclusions) reached by the Financial Ombudsman Service in relation to complaints that had been made against the relevant company and conclusions set out in a final notice served under the financial services regulatory regime and various other materials. For present purposes it is necessary to understand that such materials were not capable of forming the basis on which the Secretary of State could have made the decision in the public interest to initiate CDDA s.8 proceedings because they were not "investigative material" as defined by CDDA s.8(1A). On the other hand, while in the end the Secretary of State had decided to bring proceedings under CDDA s.6 after the relevant company had gone into administration, the FSA investigation report would have fallen squarely within s.8 of the CDDA as it was the report of an investigation carried out pursuant to ss.167–168 of the Financial Services and Markets Act 2000.[346] In the *Aaron* case on appeal, and in accordance with the decision of the judge at first instance, it was submitted on behalf of the Secretary of State that all the material, not merely that which was clearly investigative material for the purposes of s.8, had been relied on by the Secretary of State in

[346] See CDDA s.8(1A)(a)(ii). Thomas L.J. accepted that the Secretary of State could have legitimately proceeded either under CDDA s.6 or s.8: see [2009] 1 B.C.L.C. 55 at [6].

reaching the decision to commence proceedings under ss.7 and 6. Thus, it was further submitted, in line with Evans-Lombe J.'s decision in the *Barings* case, that all the material should accordingly be admitted as evidence. However, Thomas L.J. responded as follows:

> "[36] I am not persuaded that this is correct. I see no reason to make a distinction between s.6 and s.8. The basis of the decision in *Ashcroft* . . . was that it was not sensible to make a distinction as to the admissibility of evidence between the two different powers under the CDDA; that that is a proper and correct conclusion is underlined by the fact that in this case an application could have been made under s.8. It would make little sense if the evidence was admissible if the application was made under s.6, but not under s.8. Furthermore the whole basis for the rationalisation in the cases is the statutory scheme. I cannot see any reason to hold that anything relied on by the Secretary of State is admissible in disqualification proceedings; the rationale for relying on the reports and other material fits into the statutory scheme, but there is nothing to suggest that the Secretary of State can go outside this scheme. If he could, it would be difficult to see what limit there could be to the materials relied on. There is also good sense in restricting the material relied upon to material produced through the statutory scheme for investigation; this is understood by everyone and the procedure clear. Moreover a report or other material produced in this way can readily be distinguished from a decision in an adjudicative process (such as the decision of the [Financial Ombudsman Service] or the final notice) where the decision maker is deciding a matter between two parties."

Accordingly, the Financial Ombudsman Service decisions and other material outside the scope of CDDA s.8(1A) did not fall within the implied exception.

7–130 A number of points arise from this decision and the reasoning underpinning it. First of all, the reasoning fails to address the point that CDDA ss.6 and 8 enable the Secretary of State to decide to bring disqualification proceedings based upon different materials. Even if the implied statutory exception should not be considered to be as wide as appears from the decision of Evans-Lombe J. in *Barings*, the *Ashcroft* case did not decide that the material admissible in s.6 cases must be determined by reference to material that would be admissible in s.8 cases (or vice versa). What the *Ashcroft* case did decide is that material that flowed from the investigation and report by the office holder of the insolvent company made pursuant to CDDA s.7(3) and on which the Secretary of State relied in bringing the s.6 proceedings was admissible. It did not decide that the material also had to be admissible under s.8. The reasoning also fails to address the operation of r.3(2) of the Disqualification Rules in relation to reports of the official receiver. The reasoning is also somewhat curious in suggesting that it is preferable to rely on a statutory investigation rather than conclusions reached by (for example) a judicial tribunal which has had the benefit of having a case dissected and tested following disclosure and oral evidence. A further set of issues revolves around the scope and operation of the principle for practical purposes.

7–131 The sentence in Thomas L.J.'s judgment that "[i]t would make little sense if the evidence was admissible if the application was made under s.6, but not under s.8" might be read as meaning that only evidence admissible as an exception to the hearsay/opinion evidence rules in s.8 proceedings can be admissible by way of similar exception in s.6 proceedings. However, it is respectfully suggested that such a reading is inconsistent with the Court of Appeal's approach and decision in *Ashcroft*. Even if the implied exception only applies to material emanating from the office holder and does not extend (as the *Barings* decision held that it did) to any material coming into the hands of the Secretary of State and on which he relies in reaching a decision to initiate s.6 proceedings, the *Ashcroft* case is still binding. It is also suggested that it cannot be the case that material that comes to the Secretary of State from the office holder under s.7(3) is admissible as an exception to the hearsay/opinion evidence rules in s.8 proceedings, even if it does not form "investigative material" within the meaning of s.8(1A) and even if it was not the basis for the Secretary of State's decision to institute proceedings under s.8(1).

7–132 The next problem with *Aaron* is the basis upon which the Financial Services Authority investigative material was allowed into evidence in s.6 proceedings. There is no suggestion that that investigation was in any way a product of the office holder's investigation and conclusions. How then could it be admissible into evidence under the principle in *Ashcroft* (on the assumption that this is given a narrow reading as opposed to the wider reading in *Barings*)?

7–133 The final issue concerns the basis on which other material that is similar to "investigative material" within the meaning of CDDA s.8(1A) but is, in fact, not such material as defined, can be admitted in evidence. In the *Barings* case neither the Board of Banking Supervision report nor the material deriving from the Singaporean inspectors, including their report, fell within what was then s.8 of the CDDA. Thomas L.J., however, decided that such material might be admissible "by analogy" though it is unclear what the analogy would be[347] nor why in *Aaron* decisions of the Financial Ombudsman Service or the Financial Services Authority as set out in the final notice were not admissible "by analogy".

Other points on the implied statutory exception

7–134 Three main points are left outstanding following the discussion above:

(1) The status of hearsay/opinion evidence under the implied statutory exception, once such evidence is challenged.
(2) The interrelationship of the implied statutory exception and the CEA 1995.
(3) Whether there is an implied statutory exception to the hearsay rule in disqualification proceedings brought under other provisions of the CDDA (i.e. not restricted to proceedings under ss.6 and 8).

On the first point, it is clear from the cases in relation to both public interest winding up and disqualification, that if evidence is challenged, the Secretary of State may be well advised, as a practical or tactical matter to strengthen any

[347] At [37] reference was made to "investigative reports carried out by other regulators or under statutory authority in other states."

hearsay evidence by first-hand evidence and to strengthen any opinion evidence by further primary evidence. However, he is not bound to do this and the material remains in evidence. On the second point, it is suggested that the wording of CEA 1995 s.1 makes clear that other exceptions to the hearsay rule remain intact and that, technically speaking, the Act does not repeal the hearsay rule but simply provides a further exception (albeit one so wide that, in effect, it does abolish the rule). Although the Court of Appeal in the *Aaron* case said that the implied statutory exception as an exception to the hearsay rule was less important after the CEA 1995 it was not suggested that it had been replaced. The third point is considered in the next paragraph.

What material is covered by the implied statutory exception?

7–135 As regards CDDA s.6, the implied statutory exception was, until *Aaron* in the Court of Appeal, widely interpreted as encompassing any material that the Secretary of State takes into account in deciding to bring (or presumably continue) disqualification proceedings. It is suggested that as regards s.6 cases, the decision in the Court of Appeal in *Ashcroft* remains good law and that material derived from the office holder under ss.7(3) or (4) will be material within the exception. In relation to CDDA s.8, the exception is (as discussed above) presumably limited to the types of investigative material identified in s.8 and relied on in commencing proceedings, subject to any question as to whether other material is "analogous". As regards s.9A, the position is problematic. The first condition that has to be satisfied before a competition disqualification order can be made is that the company, of which the defendant is a director, commits a relevant breach of competition law. The OFT has indicated that it will normally bring competition disqualification proceedings only where such breaches have previously been established.[348] If the relevant breach has been established by proceedings that will give rise to an issue estoppel as against the director then the way ahead is clear. However, if this is not the case there must be a real risk that, in the absence of any available express or implied statutory exception, the OFT or relevant regulator will be forced to prove the relevant breach of competition law again. This point is also considered in the text at 6–20.

Hearsay and the Civil Evidence Act 1995 ("CEA 1995")

7–136 The position, at least for defendants, has been changed greatly by the coming into force of the CEA 1995.[349] That Act does not abolish the hearsay rule in civil

[348] A proposal by the OFT to revise this approach was under consideration at the time of writing: see 6–34A above.

[349] See earlier discussion from 7–123. In cases proceeding in a county court, either side could rely on hearsay evidence. In the High Court, the inability of a defendant to rely on hearsay as of right was, when contrasted with the position of the Secretary of State, manifestly unfair. In practice, the courts sometimes ameliorated the position by ordering under RSC Ord.38, r.3 that the defendant would be permitted to prove a fact by adducing hearsay evidence on a particular point. This was invoked in at least one case where the combined effect of the notice procedure under RSC Ord.38, r.25 and following (which did not apply to affidavits) and the Civil Evidence Acts 1968 and 1972 would have enabled hearsay evidence to be admitted. See further discussion in *Re Circle Holidays International Plc* [1994] B.C.C. 226.

proceedings as such (s.1(3), (4) preserve the existing exceptions to the rule), but it does provide that evidence is not to be excluded on the ground that it is hearsay (s.1(1)).[350] As a general matter, the fact that evidence is hearsay goes to weight only and not to admissibility. In assessing weight, the court is required by s.4(1) to have regard to ". . . any circumstances from which any inference can reasonably be drawn as to the reliability or otherwise of the evidence . . .". A non-exhaustive list of circumstances is set out in s.4(2). These are largely a matter of common sense and, to a considerable extent, reflect the sort of factors that the court would have taken into account under the old legislation in deciding whether or not a party should be allowed to adduce hearsay evidence.[351] On the question of the weight to be attached to hearsay evidence in disqualification proceedings, it is suggested that the principles set out in s.4 will, in practice, be applied, even if the evidence is admissible under some other exception outside the CEA 1995. Although CEA 1995 s.2 envisages a requirement on the party proposing to adduce hearsay evidence to give notice, this requirement is governed by rules of court that are considered below.

7–137 The most important point to note is that the effect of failure to give notice differs fundamentally under the CEA 1995 compared with the position under the Civil Evidence Acts of 1968 and 1972. Under the old provisions, the giving of a notice was a pre-requisite to hearsay evidence being adduced. The court had power to dispense with the notice requirement but exercised this power sparingly.[352] In contrast, under the CEA 1995, a failure to give notice as required by s.2(1) and/or rules of court does not affect the admissibility of the evidence, but may be taken into account by the court when considering the exercise of its powers of case management, the issue of costs and as a matter adversely affecting the weight to be given to the evidence (s.2(4)).[353] The other important difference is that under RSC Ord.38, r.26, the other party or parties were able to serve a counter-notice requiring the party giving the hearsay notice to call the maker of the relevant statements as a witness. Unless he could rely on a limited number of circumstances set out in s.8 of the Civil Evidence Act 1968,[354] the party who sought to adduce the hearsay evidence was forced to call the maker of the

[350] Note also the effect of s.14(1) which makes clear that the CEA 1995 is not to be taken as barring the exclusion of hearsay evidence on other grounds, e.g. failure to comply with rules of court.

[351] See, e.g. *Rasool v West Midlands Passenger Transport Executive* [1974] 3 All E.R. 638.

[352] See RSC Ord. 38, r. 29 and e.g. *Morris v Stratford-on-Avon Rural District Council* [1973] 1 W.L.R. 1059.

[353] At first instance in *Re Westminster Property Management Ltd (No.1), Official Receiver v Stern (No.1)* [2000] 1 W.L.R. 2230, the defendants submitted that the superior status afforded to the official receiver's evidence (see above) meant that there was a lack of "equality of arms" between the parties for the purposes of ECHR art.6. Scott V.C. rejected the argument on the ground that any difference in treatment was now slight. He said (at [44]): "It is true that the respondents may need to accompany their hearsay evidence with a hearsay notice whereas the official receiver's report need not be so accompanied. This is a mere formality. It is not a point of substance." The point was not pursued on the subsequent appeal.

[354] For example, that the maker of the relevant statements was dead or overseas.

relevant statements as a witness and was otherwise not entitled to rely on that evidence. The CEA 1995 contains no provision for the service of counter-notices requiring the maker of any hearsay statements to be called as a witness. However, the other party (or parties) does have the power to ask that the maker of the statement be called for the purposes of cross-examination.

The provisions of the CPR on hearsay evidence

7–138 There is not scope in this book for a detailed consideration of either the CPR or the CEA 1995. The provisions of the CPR likely to be of most importance in disqualification proceedings are considered below.

7–139 **The notice requirement.** As indicated above, CEA 1995 s.2 contemplates a notice requirement but provides that this requirement will be governed by rules of court. Under RSC Order 38, r.21(3)(a) (as amended to take account of the CEA 1995), there was no requirement to serve hearsay notices in relation to material contained in affidavits. This also probably applied to documents contained in exhibits to affidavits.[355] Although RSC Ord.41, r.5 did not permit affidavits (other than those prepared for use at interim or interlocutory hearings) to contain hearsay material, this rule was held to have been impliedly overruled (at least in disqualification proceedings) by the CEA 1995 in *Barings (No.2)* (discussed above). The result was, to some extent, a victory for common sense. If the relevant material is set out in an affidavit, the other side has notice of what the material is and the fact that the party intends to rely on the material as hearsay evidence. Unfortunately, the provisions in Pt 33 of the CPR do not fully reflect the position under the RSC. CPR r.33.3(aa) currently provides that the requirement to serve a notice under CEA 1995 s.2 does not apply to affidavits or witness statements for use at trial "... which [do] not contain hearsay evidence". Therefore, on the face of it, a party relying on an affidavit containing hearsay still needs to give notice under s.2. The service of a witness statement containing hearsay is deemed to comply with the s.2 notice requirement (CPR r.33.2(1)). However, the same is not true of affidavits even though, for all practical purposes, they fulfil the same function as witness statements. It seems anomalous that witness statements and affidavits are treated differently in this respect. In practice, the effect of a failure to serve a s.2 notice does not affect the admissibility of the evidence, but may be taken into account by the court when considering the exercise of its powers of case management, the issue of costs and as a matter adversely affecting the weight to be given to the evidence (CEA 1995 s.2(4)). If the relevant information is set out in the affidavit, it is hard to see how the other party could be prejudiced by non-receipt of a s.2 notice and, it is suggested, that it would be unreal for the court to impose a costs sanction as punishment for a breach of the rules in circumstances where it appears that there is no requirement

[355] On the basis that the relevant rule of court was in a different form to that considered in *Re Koscot Interplanetary (UK) Ltd* [1972] 3 All E.R. 829 and/or on the basis that that case was wrongly decided.

to serve a notice in the case of a witness statement. Furthermore, it is suggested that the weight of the evidence should not normally be affected if it is set out in proper detail in the affidavit. Section 2 only applies to hearsay evidence admissible exclusively under the exception in the CEA 1995. It does not apply to evidence that would be admissible under an exception arising outside the CEA 1995 as well as under the CEA 1995 (CEA 1995 s.1(4)).

7–140 **Power of a party not relying on hearsay to ask the maker of hearsay statements to be called as a witness.** Section 3 of the CEA 1995 stipulates that rules of court may provide that, where a party to civil proceedings adduces hearsay evidence of a statement made by some person and does not call that person as a witness, any other party to the proceedings may, with the court's permission, call that person as a witness and cross-examine him on the statement as if he had been called by the first party and as if the hearsay statement stood as evidence-in-chief. Although s.3 does not apply to hearsay evidence admissible by reason of an exception arising outside the CEA 1995 (see s.1(4)), the relevant provisions of the CPR extend this power to all hearsay statements. This means that the provision applies to hearsay evidence that is relied on under either: (a) r.3(2) of the Disqualification Rules; or (b) the implied statutory exception. CPR r.33.4 provides that the relevant application should be made not less than 14 days after the date on which notice of intention to rely on the hearsay statement was served. In the light of the discussion above, this will presumably be construed as meaning 14 days after service of any relevant affidavit. The 14-day period is likely to be extended to any later directions hearing if appropriate. The mere fact that a party can ask the court's permission to call the maker of the hearsay statement does not mean that the court will necessarily grant it. The court will probably want to be satisfied that the relevant statement is really significant and is materially challenged. Cases are likely to arise where it will be difficult to judge whether to ask for permission to cross-examine or to submit that little weight should be given to the statement on the basis that the party seeking to rely on it could and should have been expected to have called the witness (see CEA 1995 s.4(2)(a)). Before any application under CPR r.33.4 is made, it is important to discuss the position with the party relying on the hearsay statement. If that party knows that an application is to be made seeking permission to have the witness called, it is possible that the party will prefer to put in first-hand affidavit evidence from the maker of the statement and call that person to give evidence at trial.

7–141 **Attacking the credibility of the maker of hearsay statements.** If a party proposes to attack the credibility of the maker of a hearsay statement who is not to be called as a witness, he must give notice of his intention to do so not more than 14 days after service of the original notice of intention to rely on hearsay evidence (CPR r.33.5). This provision is further regulated by CEA 1995 s.5(2). As CPR r.33.5 is wider in scope than s.5(2), it is unclear to what extent s.5(2) will in fact apply. This may be a matter that requires clarification at a pre-trial or directions hearing. In any event, as evidence in disqualification proceedings is generally on affidavit, the point should become clear. In so far as a witness who is giving oral evidence may find his credibility attacked, it appears that evidence may still be "sprung" on him.

Expert evidence

7–142 Before the CPR came into force, two particular problems were common in disqualification cases. First, because the evidence in support of disqualification proceedings contained a mixture of evidence, inference and submission, confusion could arise over whether the evidence purported to be expert evidence. The problem arose in particular with affidavits sworn by professional persons such as insolvency practitioners. As a result, on occasions, defendants would file what purported to be expert evidence to answer matters in the claimant's evidence that were perceived to be "expert" or "opinion" evidence. The case of *Re Pinemoor Ltd*[356] concerned an application by the Secretary of State to strike out purported expert evidence filed on behalf of the defendant director. The "evidence" in question was not, in truth, expert evidence. Chadwick J. struck the evidence out but subject to conditions. The main condition was that the Secretary of State serve notice on the defendant flagging up any passages in the liquidator's affidavit that relied on expressions of expert opinion. If there were any, the defendant would have a further opportunity to file evidence in response. If there were none, it would be clear to the defendant that he was not facing a case based on the opinion of the Secretary of State's deponents. Chadwick J. also said that it was desirable for those who prepare and swear affidavits in support of applications under the CDDA to distinguish carefully between the facts that they were able to establish by direct evidence, the inferences that they invited the court to draw from those facts, and the matters that were said to amount to unfit conduct on the part of the defendant. If those distinctions were observed, the judge continued, it might lead defendants to concentrate more closely on those factual matters to which they actually need to respond by affidavit evidence under r.6 of the Disqualification Rules.

7–143 The second, connected problem was that, in any event, there were occasions when defendants sought to rely on purported expert evidence when the evidence in question was not really expert evidence at all. Three choices were open to the claimant. He could: (a) apply to strike out the evidence[357]; (b) reserve the right to object to the evidence but cross-examine the witness; or (c) decide not to cross-examine but await final submissions.[358] The problem was probably exacerbated by the fact that permission was not required under the Rules of the Supreme Court to serve expert evidence contained in affidavits (see RSC Ord.38, r.36(2)). The position has significantly changed and costs are likely to be saved under the CPR

[356] [1997] B.C.C. 708. See further from 7–54 above.

[357] As happened in *Pinemoor* itself and in *Oakfame* (on which see further below).

[358] For a case in which the third course was adopted in relation to purported expert evidence from a merchant banker, see *Re Barings Plc (No.5), Secretary of State for Trade and Industry v Baker* [1999] 1 B.C.L.C. 433.

as there is a requirement that the permission of the court be sought before expert evidence can be adduced.

The position under the CPR

7–144 Part 35 of the CPR lays down a detailed code in relation to experts. An expert cannot be called or expert evidence put in without the permission of the court (CPR r.35.4). In seeking the permission of the court to adduce expert evidence, the relevant party is required to identify the expert's field of expertise and, where practicable, the identity of the party's preferred expert. The court has wide powers and can, for example, impose a ceiling on the costs recoverable from the other side in relation to the expert's fees and expenses (CPR r.35.4(4)) and, in cases where each side proposes to adduce expert evidence in a given field, impose a single joint expert on the parties (CPR r.35.7). Although a number of difficult and interesting points arise both in theory and practice, these points are not peculiar to disqualification and they are accordingly beyond the scope of this book. The general point to make is that cases where expert evidence will be permitted in disqualification proceedings are likely to be quite rare.[359] Where expert evidence is given it is essential that the expert is fully aware of his overriding duty to the court under CPR Pt 35,[360] the applicable Practice Direction and the "Protocol for the Instruction of Experts to give Evidence in Civil Claims", published by the Civil Justice Council in July 2005,[361] and that the written evidence complies with the CPR requirements both in form[362] and substance.

Expert evidence: general points

7–145 Although cases that have been reported in the field of disqualification amount merely to illustrations of the applicable law of evidence, it is helpful to see how the relevant rules have been applied hitherto in the disqualification context:

(1) Any expert must be "independent".[363] Thus, it is not possible for the Secretary of State to put forward his or her principal deponent (who is setting out the case for disqualification) as an expert. The need for independence is now stressed and underpinned by Pt 35 of the CPR.

[359] See *Re Barings Plc (No.5), Secretary of State for Trade and Industry v Baker* [1999] 1 B.C.L.C. 433 at 494–495 on the need to admit evidence only where plainly relevant and helpful so as to avoid proceedings becoming "unwieldy, time-consuming and expensive". For a rare example where expert evidence was needed to buttress an allegation relating to a transaction at undervalue see *Re Fast Track Corporation Ltd, Secretary of State for Trade and Industry v Cullen-Crouch*, December 19, 2000, Ch.D., unreported.

[360] CPR r.35.3 and para.1 of the Pt 35 Practice Direction.

[361] Replacing the earlier Codes of Guidance on Expert Evidence produced by the Expert Witness Institute and the Academy of Experts.

[362] See, e.g. the requirements of CPR r.35.10 and para.2 of the Pt 35 Practice Direction.

[363] See especially *The Ikarian Reefer* [1993] 2 Lloyd's Rep. 68.

(2) The expert must be properly qualified. In *Re Oakfame Construction Ltd*,[364] doubts were raised over the qualifications of the relevant deponents, but the court struck out the evidence in question without having to determine the point.
(3) The contents of the evidence must genuinely be "expert evidence":

(a) In *Re Oakfame Construction Ltd*,[365] the court struck out purported expert evidence that was in reality a combination of hearsay, advocacy and submissions rather than expert opinion. Although the "evidence" was useful to the defendants in "... priming themselves for making submissions and for cross-examining deponents ...", it was not "material which can properly be placed before the court as expert testimony".
(b) In *Re Barings Plc (No.5)*,[366] evidence was adduced on behalf of the defendants from Sir John Craven, a distinguished former merchant banker and businessman. His affidavit was read as part of the evidence in the case but the question of its admissibility was left for closing speeches. Sir John Craven was not cross-examined so that his evidence (if admissible) remained unchallenged. The Secretary of State objected neither to Sir John's testimonial evidence nor to his factual account of the growth and development of merchant banking over time. Equally, there was no objection to evidence of Sir John's understanding of how the Barings group was organised in managerial terms and how it had developed. This evidence was simply a hearsay repetition of what had been communicated to him after the event and its purpose was to provide a factual basis for the statements of opinion that followed. The statements of opinion to which the Secretary of State took objection were those that amounted to comments and views as to the reasonableness or otherwise of the conduct of one of the defendants in his role as chairman of the bank and of its principal management committee. The following useful points emerge from the decision:

(i) Section 3 of the Civil Evidence Act 1972 does not make admissible evidence that is otherwise irrelevant.[367] That section simply makes evidence "on a relevant matter" admissible.
(ii) As a general matter, expert evidence as to what is the legal test applicable in any proceedings is, by definition, inadmissible. Expert evidence on the question whether the legal test has been satisfied in a particular case *may* be relevant, for example, if it is evidence of "some practice in a particular profession, some accepted standard of conduct which is laid down by a professional institute or sanctioned

[364] [1996] B.C.C. 67.
[365] [1996] B.C.C. 67.
[366] [1999] 1 B.C.L.C. 433 at 489–495.
[367] See discussion in *Barings (No.5)* of Jacob J.'s decision in *Routestone Ltd v Minories Finance Ltd* [1997] B.C.C. 180.

by common usage . . .".[368] However, it will not be relevant if, on analysis, it amounts to no more than an expression of opinion as to what the expert would himself have done in similar circumstances.[369]

(iii) The issue in the case was one of whether or not the particular defendant was incompetent and, if so, incompetent in a sufficient degree to "make him unfit" within the meaning of s.6. On that issue, Sir John's evidence was of no assistance.

Character evidence

7–146 In *Re Dawes & Henderson (Agencies) Ltd, Secretary of State for Trade and Industry v Dawes*,[370] Blackburne J. acceded to an application by the Secretary of State to strike out (among other things) two affidavits sworn on behalf of the defendants. The deponents were persons of responsibility within the commercial and legal world and their affidavits referred to the fitness, honesty and general good character of the defendants. The judge decided that, in so far as the affidavits expressed an opinion on each defendant's fitness to be a company director, they were inadmissible as the question of fitness or unfitness was for the trial judge to determine and that, in so far as they contained evidence of good character, they were equally inadmissible as the general character of the defendants was not in issue. The fact that the allegations involved imputations against the honesty of the defendants and that an adverse finding was likely to lead to a finding of unfit conduct and, in turn, to a disqualification order, did not justify a departure from the salutary rule that excludes evidence of general reputation. In civil proceedings, it is not possible to adduce evidence of general reputation with a view to proving that a person with an excellent reputation would not have done the things alleged against him. Blackburne J. also decided that any extenuating circumstances (of the type referred to in the *Grayan* case)[371] related to matters that might explain the conduct alleged by the Secretary of State, but did not extend to matters of the kind catalogued in the relevant affidavits that were entirely extraneous to the establishment or otherwise of the matters alleged. Moreover, the affidavits contained no material that might be relevant on the question of the appropriate period of disqualification as, again, the court was only concerned with the defendant's conduct in relation to the company named in the proceedings and any mitigation was also referable only to the conduct that had been established. The European Court of Human Rights subsequently decided that the exclusion of character evidence did not breach the defendants' rights to a fair trial under art.6 of the ECHR.[372] This was primarily on the basis that the evidence was not probative of the issues raised in the case.

[368] *Midland Bank Trust Co Ltd v Hett, Stubbs & Kemp* [1979] Ch. 384 at 402.

[369] *Midland Bank Trust Co Ltd v Hett, Stubbs & Kemp* [1979] Ch. 384; *Bown v Gould & Swayne* [1996] P.N.L.R. 130.

[370] [1997] 1 B.C.L.C. 329.

[371] On which see generally Chs 2, 4 and 5.

[372] *DC, HS and AD v United Kingdom* [2000] B.C.C. 710.

7–147 The question of character evidence was revisited by Scott V.C. in one of the *Barings* hearings.[373] Although he accepted that general evidence of character and reputation was irrelevant to the question of whether or not specific past conduct as a director was such as to make the defendant unfit, he took a different view in relation to the period of disqualification, which is a matter for the discretion of the court:

> "I do not for my part see how it can be said that the evidence relating to the general ability and conduct as a director of the individual in question is necessarily irrelevant to the exercise of this discretion. I do not believe that discretion can be put into a closet from which general evidence of the sort I have described is excluded. Of course, not all evidence of character would be relevant. It would not be relevant in the least whether the director was a good family man or whether he was kind to animals. But evidence of his general conduct in discharge of the office of director goes to the question of the extent to which the public needs protection against his acting in that office. It seems to me that evidence of that character is relevant to be taken into account by the court in exercising its discretion and cannot be excluded as being inadmissible."[374]

The matter has now been settled by the Court of Appeal in *Re Westmid Packing Services Ltd, Secretary of State for Trade and Industry v Griffiths* where the court agreed with Scott V.C.'s observations in the passage cited above.[375] General character and reputation evidence may be relevant to fixing the period of disqualification and on applications for permission to act notwithstanding disqualification, but it will not be relevant on the central issue of whether the director's conduct makes him unfit.[376] Furthermore, the court should control evidence to minimise repetition that increases costs and wastes time (see now CPR r.32.1).

Compelled evidence

7–148 An important question is the extent to which the claimant can rely in civil disqualification proceedings on evidence provided and, in particular, admissions, made by the defendant under compulsion (for example, pursuant to ss.235–236 of the Insolvency Act 1986). In *Re Westminster Property Management Ltd (No.1), Official Receiver v Stern (No.1)*,[377] the relevant company had been compulsorily wound up and the official receiver had obtained information from the defendants during interviews conducted under s.235 of the Insolvency Act. The defendants argued that the use of the compelled material in subsequent civil disqualification proceedings breached the privilege against self-incrimination and therefore

[373] *Re Barings Plc, Secretary of State for Trade and Industry v Baker* [1998] B.C.C. 583.
[374] [1998] B.C.C. 583 at 590.
[375] [1998] 2 All E.R. 124 at 133–134.
[376] Though note that testimonial evidence was not objected to and was accepted in evidence in *Barings (No.5)* discussed above.
[377] [2001] 1 W.L.R. 2230.

infringed their right to a fair trial under art.6 of the ECHR.[378] At first instance, Scott V.C. held that in regulatory civil proceedings, such as disqualification proceedings, the mere fact that the applicant's evidence included material obtained from the defendant under compulsion would not make the hearing unfair for the purposes of art.6(1). In so doing, he distinguished between a defendant's admission that his conduct as a director made him unfit (i.e. an admission of the central matter requiring proof) and the admission of facts or disclosure of documents that might be used to establish the existence of unfit conduct. He also distinguished *Saunders v United Kingdom*,[379] in which the use of investigative material obtained from the applicant by DTI inspectors pursuant to Companies Act powers as evidence in his subsequent criminal trial was held to infringe his art.6 rights, on the ground that disqualification proceedings are civil regulatory proceedings rather than criminal proceedings.[380] In response to the wide submission that reliance on the official receiver's report as a whole would be unfair simply because it contained information that had been supplied by the defendants pursuant to s.235 of the Insolvency Act, and having considered the contents of the report in detail, Scott V.C. had this to say:

> "I do not believe it could possibly be said that the inclusion in the evidence in support of the disqualification application of [various] references to information supplied by the respondents would be unfair to them. In some instances the statements are exculpatory in character. In others they are statements of the obvious. In relation to all, the respondents can, if they wish, qualify them, explain them or contradict them."[381]

He concluded that it would only be in rare cases—where, for example, a defendant was not permitted at the hearing to contradict or explain away an admission—that the use of material obtained from him by compulsion would make the hearing unfair for the purposes of art.6(1).[382]

7–149 The defendants' appeal against Scott V.C.'s decision was dismissed. Stripped to its core, the Court of Appeal's decision, which was unanimous, can be reduced to the following propositions:

[378] The defendants' case was based on European Community law in so far as it was argued that any disqualification order would unlawfully restrict their freedom of establishment and freedom to provide services within the Community. While conceding that the making of an order would affect such directly effective Treaty rights, the official receiver's case was that any restriction was justified on the grounds that it satisfied the conditions for legitimate state interference with freedom of establishment laid down in *Gebhard v Consiglio dell'Ordine degli Avvocati e Procurartori di Milano* (Case C-55/94) [1995] ECR I-4165. As state restrictions that are incompatible with human rights are unacceptable as a matter of Community law, the case ultimately turned on the question of whether the manner in which the disqualification might be imposed would infringe ECHR art.6. The reliance on Community law got around the difficulty that the Human Rights Act 1998 was not fully in force at the time of the hearing.

[379] [1998] 1 B.C.L.C. 362.

[380] A classification that has been accepted by the European Court of Human Rights: see, e.g. *EDC v United Kingdom* [1998] B.C.C. 370; *DC, HS and AD v United Kingdom* [2000] B.C.C. 710. The Court of Appeal had also previously distinguished *Saunders* on similar grounds in *R. v Secretary of State for Trade and Industry Ex p. McCormick* [1998] B.C.C. 379.

[381] [2001] 1 W.L.R. 2230 at [41].

[382] [2001] 1 W.L.R. 2230 at [36].

(1) The privilege against self-incrimination is a basic right that is safeguarded by ECHR art.6(1).[383]

(2) The question of whether the use of compelled material renders a trial unfair under art.6(1) is not exclusively confined to criminal proceedings. The fact that proceedings are classified as regulatory civil proceedings rather than criminal proceedings does not remove a person's right to a fair hearing. There is a hierarchy of types of proceedings in which civil cases concerned with the imposition of penalties by a public authority fall somewhere in between criminal cases and civil cases in the private law sector.[384]

(3) Contracting states have greater latitude when dealing with civil cases concerning civil rights and obligations than they have when dealing with criminal cases. The requirement of fairness therefore does not necessarily demand the same treatment in civil cases as in criminal.[385]

(4) In assessing fairness, the court should have some regard to the extent to which the relevant statutory power ought to be regarded as an engine for self-incrimination. In this respect, it was noteworthy that s.235 of the Insolvency Act was not directed exclusively, or even mainly, at obtaining material of a self-incriminatory nature. Its principal purpose is to furnish the office holder with such information as he may reasonably require as to the affairs of a company in compulsory liquidation.[386]

(5) The use in disqualification proceedings of statements obtained under s.235 does not necessarily violate ECHR art.6(1). The issue of fair trial is one that must be considered in the round having regard to all relevant factors. These factors include (but are not limited to): (a) that disqualification proceedings are not criminal proceedings, and are primarily for the protection of the public, but do nevertheless involve serious allegations and carry a degree of stigma for anyone who is disqualified; (b) that there are degrees of coercion involved in different investigative procedures available in corporate insolvency, and these differences may be reflected in different degrees of prejudice involved in the admission, in disqualification proceedings, of statements obtained by such procedures; and (c) that it is generally best for the issue of fairness to be decided by the trial judge, either at a pre-trial review or in the course of the trial.[387]

[383] [2001] 1 W.L.R. 2230 at 2246, relying on *Re Arrows Ltd (No.4), Hamilton v Naviede* [1995] 2 A.C. 75 at 95.

[384] [2001] 1 W.L.R. 2230 at 2250–2251, 2254–2255, relying on *Orkem v EC Commission* [1989] E.C.R. 3283; *Albert and Le Compte v Belgium* (1983) 5 E.H.R.R. 533 and *WGS and MSLS v United Kingdom* [2000] B.C.C. 719. The latter case concerned a direct application by the defendants in *Stern* to the European Court. The application was ruled inadmissible on the grounds that it was premature given that it had been made in advance of the hearing of the disqualification proceedings.

[385] [2001] 1 W.L.R. 2230 at 2250–2251, 2256.

[386] [2001] 1 W.L.R. 2230 at 2255–2257. Moreover, it is settled that the official receiver may invoke the powers in ss.235–236 of the Insolvency Act solely or mainly to enable him to carry out his investigative and reporting functions: see *Re Pantmaenog Timber Co Ltd* [2004] 1 A.C. 158.

[387] [2001] 1 W.L.R. 2230 at 2258.

7–150 Albeit outside the disqualification context, the Privy Council in *Brown v Stott*[388] has provided further guidance with regard to the use of compelled material in the light of ECHR art.6(1). Indeed, it is suggested that the speeches in *Brown v Stott* have brought the key issues into much sharper focus than did the Court of Appeal's judgment in *Stern*. In particular, it will be seen that the main question is essentially one of proportionality. In *Stott*, the defendant was suspected of having stolen a bottle of gin from a superstore. When the police arrived, as she appeared to have been drinking, they asked her how she had got to the store. She said that she had travelled by car and pointed to a car in the parking area that she claimed was hers. At the police station, she was required pursuant to s.172(2)(a) of the Road Traffic Act 1988 to say who had driven the car to the superstore. She admitted that she had been the driver and, following a positive breath test, she was charged with an offence of drink driving. The High Court of Justiciary in Scotland ruled, following *Saunders v United Kingdom*,[389] that the procurator fiscal had no power to lead and rely on evidence of the admission that the defendant had been compelled to make under s.172(2)(a) of the 1988 Act. In reaching this conclusion, the High Court of Justiciary appears to have read *Saunders* to mean, in effect, that the use of compelled material in criminal proceedings, whatever the nature and extent of that material, was absolutely barred. It seems likely that the courts in *Stern* and in the earlier *McCormick* case (which was concerned with the use of investigative material in proceedings under CDDA, s.8) took a similar view of *Saunders*. However, they were able to skirt around the point by classifying disqualification proceedings as civil regulatory proceedings rather than criminal proceedings and then distinguishing *Saunders* on the ground that it applied to the latter and not the former.[390]

7–151 The Privy Council allowed the procurator fiscal's appeal in *Stott*. The relevant points that emerge from the speeches are as follows:

(1) The right to a fair trial enshrined in ECHR art.6 is an absolute right. However, what is "fair" in a given case is not an absolute concept. As Lord Clyde put it:

> "[W]hile there can be no doubt that the right to a fair trial is an absolute right, precisely what is comprised in the concept of fairness may be open to a varied analysis. It is not to be supposed that the content of the right is necessarily composed of rigid rules which provide an absolute protection for an accused person under every circumstance."[391]

(2) The privilege against self-incrimination is not expressly safeguarded by art.6. It is an implied right. Like all constituent rights within art.6

[388] [2003] 1 A.C. 681.
[389] [1998] 1 B.C.L.C. 362.
[390] See *Stern* [2001] 1 W.L.R. 2230 especially at 2256, 2258; *R. v Secretary of State for Trade and Industry Ex p. McCormick* [1998] B.C.C. 379, Ch.D. and C.A. especially at 392H–394D.
[391] [2003] 1 A.C. 681 at 727.

(whether express or implied), the privilege against self-incrimination is not absolute.[392]

(3) The rationale of the privilege against self-incrimination lies in the protection of the accused against improper compulsion by the authorities thereby contributing to the avoidance of miscarriages of justice and to the fulfilment of the aims of art.6. In particular, it presupposes that the prosecution in a criminal case should seek to prove their case against the accused without resort to evidence obtained through methods of coercion or oppression in defiance of the will of the accused.[393]

(4) As the right is not absolute, some interference with it may be justifiable. In particular, in the words of Lord Steyn:

> "an interference with the right may be justified if the particular legislative provision was enacted in pursuance of a legitimate aim and if the scope of the legislative provision is necessary and proportionate to the achievement of the aim."[394]

Whether a particular interference can be justified is therefore a matter of proportionality and/or fair balance to be determined in the circumstances of each case.[395]

(5) The High Court of Justiciary had placed too much weight on observations in *Saunders v United Kingdom* that tended to suggest that the privilege against self-incrimination was an absolute standard. Such a reading was inconsistent with the general body of art.6 jurisprudence.[396]

(6) On the facts, there was a strong and legitimate public interest in the promotion of road safety. This legitimate concern underpinned s.172 of the 1988 Act. At the same time, the interference with the rights of the accused was relatively narrow. While the provision did require the accused to admit that she was the driver, and this did amount to an important element of the offence, it "[did] not permit open-ended questioning of the person keeping the vehicle in order to secure an admission of guilt as to the offence".[397] The limited nature of the interference was clearly proportionate to the legitimate social aim that lay behind the provision.

7–152 In the light of *Brown v Stott*, it is suggested that successful challenges on art.6 grounds to the admissibility of compelled material obtained under the Insolvency Act (of particular relevance in proceedings under CDDA s.6) or under one of the various statutory investigatory powers the exercise of which is a necessary precursor to proceedings under CDDA s.8, will be rare. Clearly, the question of

[392] [2003] 1 A.C. 681 at 704, 709, 719, 727–728, 730. In this respect, it is noteworthy that even the right to silence, which in *Saunders v United Kingdom*, was regarded as closely related to the privilege against self-incrimination, is not treated as absolute within the jurisprudence of the European Court: see, e.g. *Murray v United Kingdom* (1996) 22 E.H.R.R. 29.

[393] *Saunders v United Kingdom* [1998] 1 B.C.L.C. 362 at [68].

[394] [2003] 1 A.C. 681 at 709.

[395] [2003] 1 A.C. 681 at 704, 720–723, 728, 730, 733.

[396] [2003] 1 A.C. 681 at 711–712, 721–722, 728, 733.

[397] [2003] 1 A.C. 681 at 723 (Lord Hope).

art.6 violation must be considered in the context of each individual case and, it is suggested that the court will take into account at least the following matters: (a) the strength of the public interest in the disqualification of unfit directors; (b) the nature of the relevant statutory provision pursuant to which the material has been obtained; (c) the degree of compulsion, including the penalties for non-compliance; (d) the circumstances and manner in which information was in fact obtained; (e) the nature of compelled evidence which has been obtained and the extent of reliance on it, either alone or in conjunction with other evidence; and (f) the nature of disqualification and its potential impact on the individual. If it is accepted that there is a strong public interest in the proper regulation of those who are involved in the management of companies and that effective regulation depends to a considerable extent on the regulator being able to obtain information from those most closely involved in a corporate failure and make use of such information, there would appear to be a powerful justification for statutory powers of compulsion in this area. Moreover, while the exercise of such powers may lead to the disclosure of facts and documents that may be used by the Secretary of State to establish that a director is unfit, the information obtained will rarely, if ever, amount to a direct admission of "guilt". For these reasons, the Secretary of State should, more often than not, be able to justify the reliance on compelled evidence as being proportionate.[398] This issue is likely to come particularly to the fore in the context of investigations that precede, and provide the basis for, proceedings under CDDA s.8. In this context, consideration will also have to be given to the extent to which fairness to the defendant requires the court to be given information about the defendant's explanations for his conduct under the principles discussed earlier in connection with the decision in *Finelist*.[399]

COSTS

7–153 Particular points on costs relating to applications under the CDDA (for example, for permission to act) that do not involve substantive proceedings for a disqualification order are dealt with elsewhere in this book. The general principle is that disqualification proceedings are no different to any other civil proceedings and the "public interest" nature of the proceedings does not entitle the Secretary of State or official receiver[400] to be treated differently on questions of costs to any

[398] It should be added that in the jurisprudence of the European Court a distinction is drawn between statements and documents or other products (such as blood, breath or DNA) obtained under compulsion. The privilege against self-incrimination apparently does not extend to documents etc. as these have an existence independent of the will of the accused: see *Saunders v United Kingdom* [1998] 1 B.C.L.C. 362 at [69] but note also the obiter remarks of Lord Bingham in *Stott* [2003] 1 A.C. 681 at 705 suggesting that the distinction should not be pushed too far.

[399] See from 7–50 above.

[400] When acting, without lawyers, as the named claimant in disqualification proceedings the official receiver will be entitled to any costs awarded in the claimant's favour on the basis that he is a litigant in person: *Re Minotaur Data Systems Limited, Official Receiver v Brunt* [1999] 1 W.L.R. 1129. Query what is the position where the official receiver acts at the direction of the Secretary of State in cases where the named claimant is the Secretary of State.

other civil litigant. This is so, by way of example, whether the question concerns the basis on which costs are awarded[401] or costs payable on the withdrawal of proceedings.[402] The costs of disqualification proceedings can be high and, if a defendant is ultimately unsuccessful in resisting disqualification, he may find that the ultimate bill for costs is crippling. The judiciary has often referred to the need for costs to be controlled and for disqualification proceedings to be dealt with in a summary fashion.[403] However, in many cases, at least where the case is fought, it is unlikely that costs will be significantly reduced. For this reason, the disposal of a case by means of a disqualification undertaking or the possibility of settlement through the mechanism of a summary hearing may prove to be attractive options.[404] A number of general points can be made which arise from the CPR and the experience in disqualification proceedings to date:

(1) The question of what order as to costs should be made is a matter in the discretion of the court, taking into account all relevant factors (see generally CPR Pt 44).
(2) As a general matter, costs will follow the event, that is the court will order the unsuccessful party to pay the successful party's costs (CPR r.44.3(2)). However, the court will perhaps be more ready than in the past to consider which party has won or lost on specific issues and to divide costs accordingly.[405] The court will also have regard (among other things) to the conduct of the parties during the course of the proceedings and costs can therefore become a disciplinary matter.[406]
(3) In cases involving more than one defendant, a single costs order against all defendants will be treated as joint and several.[407] Defendants may wish to consider asking for costs to be apportioned. The court may, in appropriate circumstances: (a) make a single costs order but provide that, as between the defendants, the contribution of each defendant will be fixed in certain proportions; or (b) apportion the costs separately so that the successful claimant receives an entitlement to costs in a fixed proportion as against each defendant. In carrying out an apportionment exercise, the court should probably consider the guidance given (albeit in criminal proceedings) in the course of the *Guinness* prosecutions.[408] The starting point would be to consider what a

[401] *Re Dicetrade Ltd, Secretary of State for Trade and Industry v Worth* [1994] 2 B.C.L.C. 113.
[402] *Re Southbourne Sheet Metal Co Ltd* [1993] 1 W.L.R. 244.
[403] See, e.g. *Re Westmid Packing Services Ltd, Secretary of State for Trade and Industry v Griffiths* [1998] 2 All E.R. 124.
[404] See generally Ch.9 which also deals with the issue of Pt 36 offers and costs implications of other offers to settle.
[405] For a relevant case under the old law, see *Re Elgindata Ltd (No.2)* [1992] 1 W.L.R. 1207 and, in the disqualification context, *Re Pamstock Ltd* [1994] 1 B.C.L.C. 716 and, on the costs point [1996] B.C.C. 341.
[406] See, e.g. *Gruppo Torras SA v Al Sabah*, July 5, 1999, Commercial Court, unreported, where successful defendants were deprived of up to two-thirds of their costs.
[407] See *Mainwaring v Goldtech Investments Ltd (No.2)* [1999] 1 W.L.R. 745.
[408] *R. v Ronson* (1992) 13 Cr.App.Rep.(S.) 153.

reasonable estimate of costs would be had each defendant been tried alone. There is something to be said for the view that, in an appropriate case, the total proportion of costs ordered against the defendants as a whole could be more than 100 per cent of the starting estimate provided that the claimant was not entitled to recover more than 100 per cent in total. Otherwise, the defendant might be relieved of costs that he would otherwise have had to pay had the proceedings been conducted separately against him, and the claimant might receive much less than the costs otherwise attributable to that defendant because of the financial position of other defendants. In such circumstances, there might be room for a complicated formula requiring the claimant to exhaust his remedies against one defendant first or go up to a specific amount on top of detailed provisions for contribution as between each defendant. The courts have, on occasions, apportioned costs as between defendants on the basis of the relative seriousness of the wrongdoing established against each defendant. However, it is suggested that the correct criterion is the length of time and costs involved in establishing a particular allegation rather than the degree of seriousness of the relevant conduct. The application of the latter as a criterion amounts to a punitive use of the costs rules. Even so, in practice, the more serious the allegation, the more time and cost are likely to be expended in establishing or defending an allegation. Finally, it should be noted that, in an appropriate case, there may be scope for an order that the claimant recover some (or all) of the costs he is ordered to pay to one defendant, from another defendant.[409]

7–154 The issue of costs has surfaced in argument before the European Court of Human Rights. In *DC, HS and AD v United Kingdom*,[410] the directors complained that the requirement that they pay the Secretary of State's costs was a violation of art.8 of, and art.1 of Protocol No.1 to, the ECHR in that the liability was incurred in furtherance of a breach of art.6 of the ECHR. The European Court was not impressed. As for art.8, the court considered that any interference with the applicants' right to respect for their private and family life, their home and correspondence was justified as being in accordance with the law and as being necessary in a democratic society. Moreover, there was no lack of proportion in the results of the proceedings:

> "whether as a consequence of the application of the established principle that the unsuccessful party in civil proceedings should pay the other party's costs, or in the length of the disqualification in this case."

The point was raised again by the Sterns in *WGS and MSLS v United Kingdom*.[411] The argument, in part, was that in reliance on art.1 of Protocol No.1 to the ECHR, the disqualification proceedings, which were in themselves unfair,

[409] *Re Sykes (Butchers) Ltd, Secretary of State for Trade and Industry v Richardson* [1998] 1 B.C.L.C. 110.
[410] [2000] B.C.C. 710.
[411] [2000] B.C.C. 719.

gave rise to substantial costs that would have to be borne by the applicants if the official receiver won his case. This complaint was rejected as being premature as, at that point, the domestic proceedings had not been completed.

Public funding

7–155 The ECHR has also been invoked in relation to public funding for disqualification proceedings, or the absence thereof. A significant change to public funding of civil proceedings came about by reason of the Access to Justice Act 1999 ("AJA 1999"). Under that legislation, the Community Legal Service replaced the old civil scheme of legal aid from April 1, 2000. Under s.6 of the AJA 1999, the Legal Services Commission is not permitted to fund the services set out in Sch.2 to the AJA 1999. Included in Sch.2 are services:

> "consisting of the provision of help (beyond the provision of general information about the law and the legal system and the availability of legal services) in relation to . . . (g) matters of company or partnership law, or (h) other matters arising out of the carrying on of a business."

These matters cover disqualification proceedings.[412] However, under s.6(8), the Lord Chancellor may, in certain circumstances, authorise funding of such services. Section 6(8) envisages two sets of circumstances: (a) where, by direction, the Lord Chancellor requires the Commission to fund the provision of any of the services specified in Sch.2 in circumstances specified in the direction; and (b) where the Lord Chancellor authorises the Commission to fund the provision of any of those services in specified circumstances or, if the Commission requests him to do so, in an individual case.

7–156 The Funding Code Guidance[413] sets out the Lord Chancellor's guidance issued under AJA 1999 s.23 explaining the government's intentions regarding the excluded services set out in AJA 1999 Sch.2, paras 1(g) and (h). As regards the excluded matters set out in these sub-paragraphs, the government's position is that they are not considered to have sufficient priority to justify public funding. Although it may be appropriate for these matters to be funded by way of conditional fee or other arrangements, this is not the basis of their categorisation as excluded services. Instead, the government is of the view that public expenditure on helping business persons who fail to insure against the risk of legal costs is not justified.[414] The Funding Code Guidance confirms expressly that directors' disqualification proceedings are treated as falling within the Sch.2 excluded matters. The Lord Chancellor has issued no general directions having the effect of bringing disqualification proceedings back within the scope of public funding.

[412] In *R. (on the application of Jarrett) v Legal Services Commission* [2001] EWHC Admin 389, [2002] A.C.D. 25 the court considered that disqualification proceedings fell within both paragraphs but that, in any event, they certainly fell within one or other paragraph.

[413] Available online at *http://www.legalservices.gov.uk/civil/guidance/funding_code.asp* [Accessed August 24, 2009].

[414] It is undoubtedly the case that certain defences to disqualification proceedings have been run on the basis of conditional fee arrangements and/or insurance.

The guidance in relation to the circumstances in which the Lord Chancellor might be prepared to give an individual direction authorising funding in a particular case, makes clear that such authorisation will be exceptional. The circumstances identified cover significant wider public interest,[415] "overwhelming importance" to the client[416] and cases where:

> "there is convincing evidence that there are other exceptional circumstances such that without public funding for representation it would be practically impossible for the client to bring or defend proceedings, or the lack of public funding would lead to obvious unfairness in the proceedings."

As regards this latter head, the guidance indicates that the Lord Chancellor will follow Strasbourg jurisprudence but that such funding will be exceptional. Difficulties in language, it is pointed out, can often be accommodated by assistance from family, friends or a translator provided by the court. The mere fact that the opponent is funded will not be enough: the courts are used to assisting litigants in person. The guidance also indicates that effective preconditions to any application to the Lord Chancellor by the Legal Services Commission for individual funding would include: (a) satisfaction that the client is financially eligible for public funding; (b) that all relevant criteria in the Funding Code are satisfied; and (c) that the applicant has produced evidence to establish that no alternative method of funding is available (whether conditional fees or otherwise).

7–157 The new public funding regime for disqualification proceedings was challenged in the case of *R. (on the application of Jarrett) v Legal Services Commission.*[417] The guidance has been altered to take account of certain observations of the judge made in that case but, in broad terms, the judge confirmed that the current dispensation is compliant with the ECHR.

7–158 In the event that a party is in receipt of public funding then any costs ordered to be paid by the publicly funded client must not exceed the amount that it is reasonable for him to pay having regard to all the circumstances including the financial resources of all parties to the proceedings and their conduct in connection with the dispute to which the proceedings relate.[418] The protection afforded by AJA 1999 s.11 is often referred to as the "costs protection". This general statutory provision is subject to regulations. The current applicable regulations are the Community Legal Service (Cost Protection) Regulations 2000 (as amended)[419]

[415] That is, where the case has the potential to produce real benefits for individuals other than the applicant for funding, such as protection of life or other basic human rights, direct or potential financial benefit or intangible benefits such as health, safety and quality of life.

[416] Defined in the Funding Code as cases having exceptional importance for the applicant for funding because they concern the life, liberty or physical safety of the applicant or his family. This is regarded as an "exceptional" head.

[417] [2001] EWHC Admin 389, [2002] A.C.D. 25.

[418] AJA 1999 s.11.

[419] SI 2000/824. For amendments see the Community Legal Service (Cost Protection) (Amendment) Regulations 2001 (SI 2001/823), the Community Legal Service (Cost Protection) (Amendment No.2) Regulations 2001 (SI 2001/3812) and the Community Legal Service (Cost Protection) (Amendment) Regulations 2005 (SI 2005/2006).

and the Community Legal Service (Costs) Regulations 2000 (as amended).[420] The former regulations cover a number of matters, including: (a) the detailed application of AJA 1999 s.11(1) (for example, with regard to the type of public funding which triggers the protection, the time during which the protection applies by reference to the dates on which certificates are granted and what happens on discharge or revocation of such a certificate and so on); and (b) the circumstances in which costs may be ordered against the Legal Services Commission. The latter regulations set out, among other things, the manner of assessing the publicly funded person's resources and the procedure to be followed (and applicable forms of order to be made) when costs protection under AJA 1999 s.11 applies.

CONFIDENTIALITY AND USE OF DISQUALIFICATION MATERIAL FOR NON-DISQUALIFICATION PURPOSES

7–159 The circumstances in which information arising from the disqualification process can be made available to third parties for non-disqualification purposes is one of great importance and complexity. It is often the case that office holders of insolvent companies contemplating or conducting asset recovery proceedings, other parties contemplating litigation against a director, regulators and criminal investigators or prosecutors will have an interest, not just in the outcome of the disqualification process, but in the material which may have come into existence in the course of that process. Apart from inspecting the disqualification register and the terms of any judgment, there are a number of routes by which information can be obtained but equally, a number of difficulties face those seeking such information. Two particular problems arise in this context. The first is the increased use of the photocopier to support the court process and the increasing reliance in court procedure on written materials, with the result that much of a trial can be largely unintelligible to the outside observer. The second is the increasing complication of legislation seeking to strike a balance between human rights and the regulatory and other needs of the state to obtain information. In many cases the seeker of information will have to deploy some compulsory method to obtain information: for example, by invoking s.236 of the Insolvency Act 1986 or the court's powers to order third party disclosure.

7–160 The area of general law which is most relevant in this area is that of confidentiality. In very broad terms, this is a description of that area of the law which lays down obligations that restrict the use (including disclosure) that can be made of information. In any particular case it is necessary to identify the extent of any private and public duties of confidentiality. In general terms, and for present purposes, the most significant circumstances in which duties of confidentiality

[420] SI 2000/441. For amendments see the Community Legal Service (Costs) (Amendment) Regulations 2001 (SI 2001/822), the Community Legal Service (Costs) (Amendment) Regulations 2003 (SI 2003/649) and Community Legal Service (Costs) (Amendment) Regulations 2007 (SI 2007/2444).

will arise are where information is required to be given under pain of penalty[421] ("the compulsion principle"), and where information is imparted in circumstances where duties of confidentiality apply by reason of the particular circumstances.[422] In any particular case, it is necessary to identify the extent of the private and public duties of confidentiality. So, for example, compelled evidence can be used for the purposes for which the power was conferred.[423] As regards duties of confidentiality,[424] the following general points can be made:

(1) In general, the duty of confidentiality will cease if and to the extent that consent of the relevant person is obtained.
(2) In general, duties of confidentiality are always subject to the limitation that disclosure may be permitted, or even required, by the overall public interest. This refers to the carrying out of a balancing test, the interests in balance being the interest in confidentiality and any public interest factors in favour of disclosure, and the result being that the balance falls in favour of disclosure. (The academic debate as to whether this public interest "override" itself forms part, and defines the extent, of the duty of confidence or is a defence to a claim for breach of such duty is one that need not be considered further here). In this context, there is a strong public interest in favour of disclosure for use in criminal investigations and proceedings connected with the collection of tax and prosecution of tax evaders and disclosure to regulatory bodies.[425]
(3) Finally, duties of confidentiality usually, but not always, cease once the information has reached the public domain. An example of circumstances where duties of confidentiality may nevertheless continue after the information has entered the public domain is the court's power to impose restriction on the use of documents disclosed in civil proceedings even after they have been read at a public hearing in CPR r.31.22.

As well as the law of confidentiality, disclosure and use of information can give rise to issues in relation to the duties applying to public bodies, defamation law, public interest immunity, data protection,[426] the application of particular statutory

[421] For example, pursuant to statutory compulsion under ss.235 and 236 of the Insolvency Act 1986, pursuant to express court order (for example, a disclosure order ancillary to a freezing injunction) or pursuant to rules of court (such as the requirement to give disclosure).

[422] For example, the master/servant relationship or the litigating party/witness relationship: see *Preston Borough Council v McGrath* [2000] EWCA Civ 151.

[423] See, e.g. *Re Pantmaenog Timber Co Ltd* [2004] 1 A.C. 158; *R. v Brady* [2004] EWCA Crim 1763, [2004] 1 W.L.R. 3240.

[424] On which, see generally *Attorney General v Guardian Newspapers (No.2)* [1990] 1 A.C. 109 at 176H–178B, 214F–215G, 218H–219H, 220A–H, 268B–269E and 282E–283B; *Price Waterhouse v BCCI Holdings (Luxembourg) SA* [1992] B.C.L.C. 583 at 601F.

[425] See, e.g. family cases such as *A v A, B v B (Ancillary Relief)* [2000] 1 F.L.R. 701, cases involving children (where there is a strong presumption of confidentiality) such as *Re C (A Minor) (Care Proceedings: Disclosure)* [1997] 2 W.L.R. 322 and the public interests recognised by various specific statutory "gateways" for example under s.449 of the Companies Act 1985.

[426] See Data Protection Act 1998.

regimes regarding uses to which information can be put[427] and human rights. As regards duties applying to public authorities, the Secretary of State, as a public body, is under a duty to act reasonably and fairly with regard to the disclosure of information that it may have about a person, whether or not there are any duties of confidentiality attaching specifically to such information. Such a duty was recognised in *R. v Chief Constable of North Wales Police Ex p. AB*.[428] In that case the police revealed public information about the conviction of certain paedophiles to the caravan site owner where the convicted paedophiles were staying. There was no question of private duties of confidentiality applying. However, the court recognised that there is a fundamental rule of good public administration that prevents a recipient of information, which is a public body, from freely disseminating the information.[429]

Supply of documents from court records

7–161 The old law concerning inspection of the court's file (or as it would now be called, supply of documents from court records) in relation to disqualification proceedings can be found in *Dobson v Hastings*.[430] The position is now governed by CPR rr.5.4–5.4C (as amended). It should be noted that the documents, supply of which may be sought under these rules, are limited to documents which have been, and remain, part of the court records. Certain documents may never be filed at court or may be returned after the proceedings are completed. It should also be noted that other rules and practice directions may also impinge upon the width of these rules and limit what might otherwise be the rights to supply that they set out (see CPR r.5.4D).

7–162 CPR r.5.4B allows any party to proceedings to be supplied from the records of the court with copies of a wide range of documents relating to those proceedings, unless the court otherwise orders[431] (though not an application notice or evidence relating to an application by a solicitor for an order declaring that he has ceased to be the solicitor acting for a party or an application notice or evidence relating to an application for an order that the identity of a party or witness should not be disclosed). The documents, of which copies can be obtained include (the following list is not exhaustive): a statement of case; an acknowledgement of service; most types of certificate of service; an allocation questionnaire; a judgment or order given or made in public (whether or not at a hearing); an application notice; any filed written evidence; a notice of payment into court; an

[427] See, e.g. Companies Act 1985 s.449 (so far as it applies to information obtained under Companies Act 1985 s.447); Companies Act 1985 s.451A (dealing with information obtained under a Companies Act inspection and see *Soden v Burns* [1996] 1 W.L.R. 1512 at 1521D and *Re Atlantic Computer Systems Plc* [1998] B.C.C. 200 at 211G–212D); Financial Services and Markets Act 2000 ss.328 and 352 (and see one of its predecessor provisions: the Banking Act 1987 s.82 discussed in *BCCI v Price Waterhouse (No.2)* [1998] Ch. 84); Enterprise Act 2002 Pt 9; Criminal Justice Act 1987 ss.2 and 3; *Morris v Serious Fraud Office* [1993] Ch. 372.

[428] [1999] Q.B. 396.

[429] [1999] Q.B. 396 at 409F–410C, 414G–415G, 426G–427F.

[430] [1992] Ch. 394.

[431] As specified by Practice Direction.

appellant's notice or a respondent's notice of appeal. This is subject to any court order to contrary effect. In addition, a party to proceedings may, if the court gives permission, obtain from the court records a copy of any other document filed by a party, or of any communication between the court and a party or another person.

7–163 Unless the court otherwise orders, under CPR r.5.4C, a non-party may obtain from the records of the court a copy of a statement of case[432] or a judgment or order given in public (whether or not at a hearing), provided that certain conditions are met. Further, the defendant (or, if more than one defendant, all the defendants) must have filed an acknowledgement of service or a defence. If there is more than one defendant, but at least one has filed an acknowledgement of service, an application must be made to the court for permission.

7–164 In each case, the prescribed fee must be paid and, either a written request or, if the court's permission is required, a Pt 23 application notice, must be filed. The application may be made without notice but the court may direct notice to be given and it is to be hoped that the starting point will be that the court will usually direct notice to be given to the other party or, where the application is by a non-party, to both parties, unless persuaded that there are appropriate circumstances why notice should not be given. As explained further below, once relevant documents have been brought into the public domain, the court is likely to permit inspection under this rule.[433] Indeed, as a working guideline it can be anticipated that the jurisprudence with regard to CPR rr.31.22 and 32.12 is likely to be highly relevant by way of analogy.

Availability of court documents otherwise than through inspection of the court file

7–165 The use of the photocopier and the growing tendency of the courts to rely on written submissions means that the concept of a trial in public at which relevant information truly enters the public arena is very far from the reality. A person attending a trial will in practice be severely hampered in understanding the detail of what is going on, unless he is able to gain access to underlying documentation.

Affidavits

7–166 As mentioned above, there is a distinction in the rules between affidavits and witness statements. CPR r.32.12 prevents witness statements from being used for anything other than the purposes of the proceedings in which they have been filed, unless and to the extent that the witness gives consent in writing to some other use, the court gives permission or the witness statement has been put in evidence at a hearing held in public. Although the same rule does not apply to

[432] There are different regimes for statements of case filed before and those filed on or after October 2, 2006. The position regarding statements of case filed before October 2, 2006 is subject to further restriction.

[433] See, e.g. *Dian AO v Davis Frankel & Mead* [2004] EWHC 2662 (Comm), [2005] 1 W.L.R. 2951; *Chan U Seek v Alvis Vehicles Ltd* [2004] EWHC 3092 (Ch), [2005] 1 W.L.R. 2965 and contrast the approach in these cases with that taken in relation to applications to inspect the court file under the Insolvency Rules 1986: see, e.g. *Mansell v Acton* [2005] EWHC 3048 (Ch), [2006] B.P.I.R. 778.

affidavits, it is suggested that the position is effectively the same. This is not by reason of any rule of court but would reflect the expectations of the parties that their evidence is private and only to be used for the court proceedings, unless and until the court otherwise orders (for example, under CPR r.5.4), they expressly consent or the evidence has already become public.[434]

Skeleton arguments and other documents

7–167 The general position is that disclosure will be permitted once the skeleton argument has been relied on in the context of a public hearing. In this context, the courts have had to grapple with the concept of when documents can be said to have entered the public domain.[435] The application of the principles to particular facts can give rise to great difficulties.

[434] See *A v A, B v B (Ancillary Relief)* [2000] 1 F.L.R. 701 especially at 713B.

[435] See, e.g. *GIO Personal Investment Services Ltd v Liverpool and London Steamship Protection and Indemnity Association Ltd* [1999] 1 W.L.R. 984; *Barings Plc v Coopers & Lybrand* [2000] 1 W.L.R. 2353; *Law Debenture Trust Corporation (Channel Islands) Ltd v Lexington Insurance Co (Application for Disclosure)* [2003] EWHC 2297 (Comm).

CHAPTER 8

PERMISSION TO COMMENCE SECTION 6 PROCEEDINGS OUT OF TIME AND THE IMPACT OF DELAY IN CIVIL DISQUALIFICATION PROCEEDINGS

INTRODUCTION

8–01 The effect of s.7(2) of the CDDA is that an application for a s.6 disqualification order cannot be made later than two years after the relevant company became insolvent[1] unless, the permission[2] of the court is first obtained.[3] Section 7(2) contains no formal guidance as to the approach the court should adopt when faced with an application for permission to bring proceedings after the expiry of the two-year time limit. It has been left to the courts to develop their own approach. The factors the courts take into account in determining whether or not to grant permission under s.7(2) form the main subject matter of the first part of this chapter. The second part of this chapter deals with the closely related question of the effect of delay in disqualification proceedings and, in particular, the circumstances in which such delay may amount to a breach of art.6 of the European Convention on Human Rights and/or lead to the proceedings being struck out by the court.

8–02 In determining whether the Secretary of State or official receiver[4] should be given permission under CDDA s.7(2) to proceed out of time, the court must perform a difficult balancing act. A number of competing aspects of the public interest are in play. First, at the heart of the CDDA, there is the broad interest in the protection of the public from directors whose past conduct makes them unfit to be concerned in the management of a company. However, the public's need for protection must be weighed against the rights of the individual director. As discussed in Ch.2, the impact of disqualification on the person affected can be characterised, at different ends of the spectrum, either as an interference with a fundamental freedom or the removal of a special trading privilege. The tendency of the higher courts in England is to see disqualification more as a sanction for abuse of a privilege than an interference with a fundamental freedom.[5] Even so,

[1] Within the statutory definition set out in CDDA s.6(2). See from 3–98.

[2] The modern term "permission" is used throughout rather than the old term "leave" except in the case of direct quotes from the CDDA.

[3] There is no such time limit where civil disqualification proceedings are brought under the other substantive provisions in the CDDA.

[4] Reference hereafter to the Secretary of State should be read as including a reference to the official receiver.

[5] See, e.g. *Re Cedac Ltd, Secretary of State for Trade and Industry v Langridge* [1991] Ch. 402 discussed in Ch.2 and *R. v Secretary of State for Trade and Industry Ex p. McCormick* [1998] B.C.C. 381.

the courts recognise that the individual has procedural rights that should be respected and accorded weight. The time limit in s.7(2) is itself a form of procedural safeguard given that the Secretary of State has no automatic right to commence proceedings for disqualification under s.6 after expiry of the two-year period. As such, s.7(2) amounts to an indication from Parliament that directors are entitled to have s.6 proceedings commenced against them reasonably quickly and a requirement that, outside the two-year period, proceedings should only be started once the court has had an opportunity to balance the need for public protection against the director's rights.[6] A further related matter is the public interest in the fair and expeditious administration of justice coupled with the individual's right to a fair trial. The public interest in the fair and expeditious administration of justice is given expression in the overriding objective of the Civil Procedure Rules.[7] The right to a fair trial within a reasonable time is enshrined in art.6 of the European Convention on Human Rights which now forms part of English law following the enactment of the Human Rights Act 1998. Under art.6(1) everyone is entitled to a fair hearing within a reasonable time and this applies to proceedings which involve the determination of the individual's civil rights and obligations as well as to criminal proceedings.[8] As there are similarities in the way in which the courts approach an application for permission under s.7(2) and an application to dismiss for delay or want of prosecution, applications of the latter type are also considered in the second part of this chapter.

8–03 One of the more curious aspects of the CDDA is that only s.6 is subject to an explicit time limit (albeit one that the court can extend) on the commencement of disqualification proceedings. This is curious, not least because, as discussed elsewhere, in a given factual situation disqualification proceedings may be capable of being brought under more than one section of the CDDA. At least as regards s.8 proceedings it is, perhaps, surprising that there is no time limit for the commencement of proceedings laid down by reference to the receipt of the relevant investigatory material by the appropriate body. As discussed further below, it appears that art.6 of the European Convention can only be prayed in aid in relation to

[6] It should be stressed that the courts do not regard s.7(2) as a limitation period in the classic sense of an absolute time-bar conferring a full immunity from suit: *Re Blackspur Group Plc, Secretary of State for Trade and Industry v Davies* [1996] 4 All E.R. 289 at 298–299. Indeed, the tendency is for applications under s.7(2) to be treated as being more akin to applications for an extension of time to comply with a procedural step.

[7] CPR r.1.1.

[8] It is well settled that disqualification proceedings constitute a dispute over "civil rights and obligations" within the meaning of art.6(1) and that a director is therefore entitled to have the case against him determined within a reasonable time: see *EDC v UK* [1998] B.C.C. 370; *Wilson v United Kingdom* (1998) 26 E.H.R.R. CD195; *DC, HS and AD v United Kingdom* [2000] B.C.C. 710; *WGS and MSLS v United Kingdom* [2000] B.C.C. 719; *Eastaway v United Kingdom* (2005) 40 E.H.R.R. 17, [2006] 2 B.C.L.C. 361. It is also fairly well settled that art.6 is only triggered once proceedings commence and that it does not, of itself, provide a basis for establishing a limitation period within which proceedings must be commenced, a point picked up in the main text below.

delays in the judicial process once proceedings have commenced,[9] and is not available to establish a "limitation period" that prevents judicial process from being initiated. However, the question arises whether, as a matter of administrative law or otherwise, the courts will develop the tool of "abuse of process" so as to enable them to stay or strike out proceedings which are unreasonably begun years after the events in question. That there is no current jurisprudence on this area in the way of decided case law probably reflects the operation of overriding public interest considerations that may justify disqualification years after the relevant events.[10]

PERMISSION TO COMMENCE PROCEEDINGS OUT OF TIME UNDER SECTION 7(2)

General points

8–04 Section 7(2) provides that an application for the making of a disqualification order under CDDA s.6 shall not be made after the end of the period of two years beginning with the day on which the relevant company became insolvent. For these purposes an application for a disqualification order is made when the claim form is lodged with the court office rather than the date on which it is sealed and issued by the court.[11]

The Secretary of State will need permission under s.7(2) in two circumstances:

(1) Where proceedings for a s.6 order are to be commenced more than two years after the relevant company became insolvent within the meaning of CDDA, s.6(2).[12]
(2) Where the proceedings are commenced within the two-year period against one or more defendants but the Secretary of State later wishes to add a further defendant to proceedings after the two-year period has expired.[13]

One further situation that has arisen should not pass without comment. In *Re Blackspur Group Plc, Secretary of State for Trade and Industry v Davies*[14] proceedings for disqualification under s.6 were commenced within the two-year time limit but the evidence in support of the proceedings was not ready to be filed

[9] Criminal proceedings are regarded as having commenced with the "charge" which has an autonomous meaning in Convention jurisprudence.

[10] In relation to the Barlow Clowes debacle, for example, Mr Peter Clowes was disqualified in 1992 following his conviction in criminal proceedings but other key players were not subjected to civil disqualification proceedings until 1996 after publication of the inspectors' report under Companies Act 1985 s.432 and were only eventually disqualified in 1999 many years on from the original events: see DTI Press Release P/99/893, November 4, 1999.

[11] *Secretary of State for Trade and Industry v Vohora* [2007] EWHC 2656 (Ch).

[12] See from 3–98.

[13] *Re Westmid Packaging Services Ltd, Secretary of State for Trade and Industry v Griffiths* [1995] B.C.C. 203.

[14] [1996] 4 All E.R. 289 (affirming Carnwath J. [1995] B.C.C. 835).

and served with the originating process. The Secretary of State sought an extension of time to serve the evidence to a date long after the expiry of the two-year period.[15] Although it was accepted by both parties that, in exercising his discretion, the judge should treat the application for an extension as if it had been an application for permission to issue the originating process out of time under s.7(2), Millett L.J. disagreed. He accepted that in such circumstances a similar approach would be adopted to the approach taken on an application to commence proceedings out of time and that similar factors would be taken into account. However, he took the view that it would be easier to justify a failure to serve evidence than a failure to commence proceedings at all, especially where the proceedings were served together with a statement of the grounds on which disqualification was being sought. It is suggested that what was significant in *Blackspur* was not so much the mere commencement of the proceedings within the two-year period, but the commencement *and prior notification* of the proceedings taken together with notification of the grounds. There may well be cases where the claimant has insufficient time to go through the desirable process of notifying the prospective defendant of the allegations against him and giving him an opportunity to respond before proceedings are issued. There may even be cases where the claimant is unable to give prior notification within the time limit laid down in CDDA s.16. In such circumstances it is suggested that, the more desirable course will usually be for the claimant to go through the notification process and commence the proceedings out of time rather than to issue the proceedings within the two-year period (whether or not the evidence is in final form and ready to be served), but without prior notification. The court's decision whether, in such circumstances, to allow the proceedings to go ahead should be weighted so as to encourage compliance with a pre-commencement notification process.[16] It would be undesirable if the court exercised its discretion under s.7(2) in such a way as to encourage the commencement of proceedings within the two-year period but without the prior notification process having been followed thus making it harder for a defendant to stop such proceedings than to prevent the claimant obtaining an extension of time under s.7(2). It is suggested that, in most cases, the key factors to weigh in the balance will be whether there has been prior notification of the proceedings and, if so, how much detail the claimant has given to the prospective defendant of the underlying grounds before the two-year

[15] In *Re Jazzgold Ltd* [1994] 1 B.C.L.C. 38, it was suggested that the issue of the originating process within two years would be sufficient to comply with s.7(2) even if the evidence in support was filed and served outside the two years. However, it appears from certain observations made by Harman J. in *Re Crestjoy Products Ltd* [1990] B.C.L.C. 677 at 683 that the view taken by the Secretary of State at the time of the *Crestjoy* decision was that all the supporting evidence had to be available at the time the originating process was issued.

[16] In which case, if proceedings have not been commenced, the only question will be whether the claimant should be granted permission to commence proceedings out of time. If, alternatively, the proceedings have been commenced, the question will be one of abuse of process, breach of CDDA s.16 and/or of whether permission should be given to adduce evidence out of time.

period expired. Whether or not the proceedings are, in fact, commenced within the two-year period should not necessarily, and in all cases, carry any great significance.

8–05 It was suggested by the Court of Appeal in *Re Blackspur Group Plc, Secretary of State for Trade and Industry v Davies* that s.7(2) serves two purposes. First, it reflects the public interest in the disqualification of unfit persons. The important point here is that a person who is potentially unfit is technically free to act as a director until a disqualification order is made. As Hobhouse L.J. put it, ". . . the worse the case of unfitness, the greater need that a disqualification order be applied for and made at the earliest practicable date . . .".[17] Secondly, it gives the director a procedural right to object where proceedings are not commenced in time that he should not be subjected to a stale, oppressive or unmeritorious application. The crucial point here is that if the two-year period expires without the director hearing anything from the authorities, he should be entitled to assume that he is free to go about his business without the threat of proceedings. However, s.7(2) does not confer an immunity from suit. Its effect is that the application may only proceed if the court, in the exercise of what amounts to an unfettered discretion, considers that it should. Thus, s.7(2) is more closely analogous to a procedural rule than to an absolute limitation and an application for permission resembles an application to extend the time available under rules of court for compliance with a procedural step. The same analysis led Millett L.J. to conclude in *Davies* that the true function of the two-year period is not to provide the director with an absolute immunity but to ensure that he is aware in good time of the fact that proceedings are to be commenced and of the grounds for those proceedings:

> "One of the purposes which Parliament had in mind in enacting the two-year time limit must have been to allow directors of companies which have become insolvent a reasonable degree of security from disqualification with the passage of time. If they have been notified within the time limit, not only of the Secretary of State's decision to bring disqualification proceedings against them but also of the nature of the allegations upon which they are to be based, the statutory purpose has to this extent been fulfilled."[18]

8–06 The onus is on the Secretary of State to satisfy the court that permission to commence proceedings out of time should be granted. The Secretary of State must show that there is a good reason to justify an extension of the two-year period.[19] It appears from the authorities that the court will only be prepared to grant prospective permission and not retrospective permission

[17] [1996] 4 All E.R. 289 at 302.

[18] [1996] 4 All E.R. 289 at 299.

[19] *Re Copecrest Ltd, Secretary of State for Trade and Industry v McTighe* [1994] 2 B.C.L.C. 284 at 287; *Re Blackspur Group Plc, Secretary of State for Trade and Industry v Davies* [1996] 4 All E.R. 289 at 296.

designed to enable existing proceedings already commenced (albeit out of time) to continue.[20]

Principles on which the discretion to grant permission is exercised

8–07 In *Re Probe Data Systems Ltd (No.3), Secretary of State for Trade and Industry v Desai*, Scott L.J. said:

> "In considering an application under s.7(2) for [permission] to commence disqualification proceedings out of time the court should, in my opinion, take into account the following matters: (1) the length of the delay, (2) the reasons for the delay, (3) the strength of the case against the director and (4) the degree of prejudice caused to the director by the delay."[21]

In the subsequent case of *Re Blackspur Group Plc, Secretary of State for Trade and Industry v Davies* Millett L.J. took the view that this was not an exhaustive statement and that all relevant circumstances should be taken into account including, but not limited to, the four particular matters mentioned by Scott L.J.[22] The main factors are considered in greater detail below. The general impression is that the pivotal factors to be balanced are the strength of the Secretary of State's case and the seriousness of the misconduct alleged (meaning, in effect, the strength of the public interest in pursuing the defendant) and the countervailing effect of delay on the individual director. It cannot be emphasised enough that the court is exercising a discretion and that much will turn on the circumstances of the particular case. Moreover, there may be scope for differences in emphasis among the judges depending on their overall, but often unarticulated, view of the disqualification process.[23]

Length of delay

8–08 It is clear that the court should take into account delay in bringing proceedings which occurs *before* the initial two years has expired. The court can and should

[20] *Re Stormont Ltd, Secretary of State for Trade and Industry v Cleland* [1997] 1 B.C.L.C. 437; *Re Westmid Packaging Services Ltd, Secretary of State for Trade and Industry v Griffiths* [1995] B.C.C. 203. In such circumstances, the costs of such proceedings may not be wholly wasted. The court would likely order that the evidence in the proceedings commenced out of time should stand as evidence in any new proceedings for which permission was granted and may be prepared to adjourn issues of costs relating to the earlier proceedings to the final hearing of the new proceedings. As regards the statutory requirement on parties to obtain permission to commence proceedings in relation to persons who are subject to certain insolvency regimes, see *Re Saunders (a bankrupt)* [1997] Ch. 60; *Re Linkrealm Ltd* [1998] B.C.C. 478; *Re Taylor (a bankrupt), Davenham Trust Plc (t/a Booker Montagu Leasing) v CV Distribution (UK) Ltd* [2006] EWHC 3029 (Ch), [2007] Ch. 150; *Godfrey v Torpy* [2007] EWHC 919 (Ch), [2007] B.P.I.R. 1538. As a general matter and on the approach to be taken to the interpretation of a provision such as s.7(2), see now the guidance of the House of Lords in *Seal v Chief Constable of South Wales* [2007] UKHL 31, [2007] 1 W.L.R. 1910 and of the Court of Appeal in *Adorian v Commissioner of Police of the Metropolis* [2009] EWCA Civ 18.

[21] [1992] B.C.L.C. 405 at 416. These factors derive from *C M Van Stillevoldt v El Carriers Inc* [1983] 1 W.L.R. 207 which involved consideration of the exercise of the discretion to extend time for setting down a matter for hearing in the Court of Appeal.

[22] [1996] 4 All E.R. 289 at 296.

[23] See general discussion in Ch.2.

consider why it was that the Secretary of State was unable "to get his tackle in order" within the two-year period. In the words of Harman J. in *Probe Data*, it is not correct to assume that the two years can be taken up by "any amount of indolence" just because Parliament has seen fit to allow the Secretary of State an initial period in which proceedings can be commenced as of right.[24]

The need for a s.7(2) application often arises in circumstances where proceedings were originally commenced in time but the validity of those original proceedings is contested by the defendant. A considerable period after expiry of the initial two years may well be used up in interim proceedings to determine whether the original proceedings were properly brought or should be struck out. Delays of this nature have not generally been taken into account by the court on an application by the Secretary of State to commence a fresh set of proceedings out of time.[25] This means that in many cases it is the nature of the delay *within* the two-year period that will be critical. It should be possible in the majority of cases for the court to deal with the question of whether the proceedings were commenced out of time, and if so, whether permission to extend time should be granted, at one and the same time.

8–09 In a case where the need for permission does not depend on the validity or otherwise of an earlier set of proceedings, the Secretary of State should make the application for permission without delay. If it is anticipated that the evidence in support of the originating summons will not be ready in time, there is authority that the application for permission should be made (in that it will then have greater prospects of success) before the two-year period expires.[26] In *Re Crestjoy*

[24] [1991] B.C.L.C. 586 at 592. See also *Re Copecrest Ltd, Secretary of State for Trade and Industry v McTighe* [1994] 2 B.C.L.C. 284 at 287; *Re Stormont Ltd, Secretary of State for Trade and Industry v Cleland* [1997] 1 B.C.L.C. 437.

[25] See *Re Cedac Ltd* [1990] B.C.C. 555 (original proceedings held to be invalid by Mummery J. because of inadequate prior notification under s.16; period of delay arising while validity of original proceedings was contested not relevant; Mummery J. later reversed by the Court of Appeal on the s.16 point); *Re Probe Data Systems (No.3), Secretary of State for Trade and Industry v Desai* [1992] B.C.L.C. 405 (original proceedings commenced incorrectly in the name of the official receiver rather than in the name of the Secretary of State; period of delay during which strike-out proceedings were on foot not taken into account); *Re Tasbian Ltd (No.3), Official Receiver v Nixon* [1993] B.C.L.C. 297 (argument over whether original proceedings were commenced within time resolved in favour of defendant; court paying no attention to the period of delay occurring after the date of the original proceedings).

[26] *Re Blackspur Group Plc, Secretary of State for Trade and Industry v Davies* [1996] 4 All E.R. 289 at 299 and discussion in 8–04. If the director knows within the two years, at the very least, that the proceedings are to be brought on specified grounds, permission is likely to be granted as long as the delay is short: see *Secretary of State for Trade and Industry v Carmichael* [1995] B.C.C. 679 (noting that the court considered the scheduling and management of the case in the context of the Secretary of State's overall priorities and resources). The one situation in which failure to issue the originating summons or even to put the director on proper notice in time might be treated sympathetically is where the delay is wholly or partly attributable to the defendant's lack of co-operation with the official receiver or with the relevant office-holder: see *Re Copecrest Ltd* discussed below in main text. Even then, however, there will be little point in the court granting permission for proceedings to be commenced out of time if the claimant is not in a position to commence the proceedings and serve the relevant evidence immediately.

Products Ltd[27] the defendants were sent ten-day letters in accordance with CDDA s.16 shortly before the expiry of the two-year period. However, the application for permission was not made until some ten weeks after the end of the two years. A further delay then occurred because the application for permission was drawn in the wrong form. Harman J. was not satisfied that a good reason for an extension of time had been shown and refused to give permission. Following the approach of Lord Brandon in *Kleinwort Benson Ltd v Barbrak Ltd, The Myrto (No.3)*[28] (a case concerning an extension of time for service of a writ), the judge held that an extra hurdle must be overcome where permission is sought after expiry of the two-year period. The Secretary of State's failure to explain why an application for permission had not been made before the expiry of the two-year period when it must have been clear that the evidence required by r.3 of the Disqualification Rules would not be ready in time proved fatal. It is striking that Harman J. expressed the view earlier in his judgment that mandatory disqualification under s.6 was "more nearly penal" when compared with disqualification under the former s.300 of the Companies Act 1985:

> "where a judge could, in the exercise of his discretion, say that although the conduct had been bad yet he was now convinced that a disqualification should not be made because, for example, the defendant had learnt his lesson".[29]

Any delay by the Secretary of State in making the application for permission is likely to be compounded if the case against the defendant is not particularly strong.[30] However, even where the application for permission is made outside the two-year period, it should not be assumed that it will automatically fail. *Crestjoy* notwithstanding, it is submitted that the court should consider all relevant factors "in the round" and carry out a full balancing exercise while recognising that the Secretary of State's failure to apply for permission inside the two-year period is a factor weighing in the defendant's favour.

Reasons for delay

8–10 One important question which has arisen is whether, on an application for permission under s.7(2), the Secretary of State must provide a good explanation for the failure to commence proceedings in time. In *Re Cedar Developments Ltd*,[31] the official receiver failed to commence proceedings in time as a result of

[27] [1990] B.C.L.C. 677.

[28] [1987] A.C. 597.

[29] [1990] B.C.L.C. 677 at 681.

[30] See *Re Packaging Direct Ltd* [1994] B.C.C. 213; *Re Westmid Packing Services Ltd (No.2), Secretary of State for Trade and Industry v Morrall* [1996] B.C.C. 229. A notable feature of the *Packaging Direct* case was that the ten-day letters under s.16 were sent some nine months before the end of the two-year period indicating that the decision to proceed had actually been taken in good time. The application for permission was not made until nearly a year later, a delay described by Jacob J. as "very substantial and excessive".

[31] [1994] 2 B.C.L.C. 714.

an administrative muddle. The application for permission was made under a week after the two years had expired. Permission was refused. The judge took the view that disqualification proceedings were quasi-penal in nature with the consequence that on an application for permission there was a real onus on the applicant to show a good reason why an extension of time should be granted. This onus had not been discharged. There was no sufficient explanation as to why it had taken the official receiver two years to prepare the case and why no margin had been allowed for unforeseen problems or mistakes of the type that had actually occurred. The court could not be expected to grant permission "semi-automatically" on the basis that the time limit had been missed by the small matter of a few days because of an administrative mistake. The judge added that, in his view, "there can hardly be a good reason for permission without a good reason being shown why the time limit was missed".[32] In *Re Blackspur Group Plc, Secretary of Trade and Industry v Davies*,[33] an attempt was made on behalf of the defendants to elevate this remark to the status of a threshold test. They submitted that it was always necessary for the Secretary of State to provide a satisfactory explanation for the delay and, that if an adequate explanation were not forthcoming, the defendant should be entitled to have the application for permission dismissed without consideration of any countervailing factors such as the strength of the case or lack of prejudice. However, the Court of Appeal categorically rejected the notion of a threshold test.

8–11 The following salient points were made to support this conclusion:

(1) The Secretary of State is obliged to explain why he failed to issue the proceedings or serve the supporting evidence (as the case may be) in time. Once an explanation is given it becomes a matter to be considered along with all the other relevant circumstances. There is no justification for treating the adequacy of the explanation as a free-standing or threshold test which must be satisfied before other considerations can be taken into account.
(2) The notion of a threshold test was incorrect in principle and unworkable in practice. In the absence of a deliberate decision to disregard the rules, there is no such thing as a "good" or "bad" reason for delay or a reason which is inherently acceptable or unacceptable. The correct test is whether the reason for delay may reasonably be accepted as sufficient to justify an extension of time in all the circumstances of the particular case. The court might be satisfied with an explanation such as forgetfulness where the delay was minimal but not for a longer delay. Thus, while forgetfulness is not itself a satisfactory reason for delay, it might be accepted as sufficient to justify an extension of time where it was supported by other considerations including the fact that the delay was minimal.
(3) There was nothing in the test put forward by Scott L.J. in *Probe Data* to suggest that a "good" reason for the delay must be shown before any other

[32] [1994] 2 B.C.L.C. 714 at 719.
[33] [1996] 4 All E.R. 289.

factors are considered. The Secretary of State must show a good reason to justify an extension of time but this is not the same as having to show a good reason for the delay as a pre-condition.[34]

(4) The notion of a threshold test ran contrary to the public interest in the disqualification of unfit directors. Directors responsible for serious misconduct would escape disqualification in cases where there is no "good" explanation for the delay without any consideration being given to the strength and serious nature of the charges against them.

8–12 In *Davies*, the Secretary of State issued the originating summons within the two-year period but was unable to file the evidence in support required by r.3 of the Disqualification Rules in time. The problem had arisen because the directors of the relevant group of companies were also under investigation by the Serious Fraud Office which had taken possession of the group's books and records. The Secretary of State requested assistance from the Serious Fraud Office but this was not forthcoming until about six weeks before the two-year deadline was due to expire. Without access to the books and records it was not possible to prepare detailed evidence in support of the originating summons. By the time the Serious Fraud Office agreed to make the relevant information available there was insufficient time to finalise the evidence before the end of the two-year period. It was accepted by the court that the reasons put forward by the Secretary of State were far from satisfactory. However, this was outweighed by a number of other countervailing considerations. The most important of these was the seriousness of the case against the defendants but also relevant was the absence of any prejudice to the defendants and the fact that the timetable for the disqualification proceedings had not been affected because the hearing could not realistically have taken place until after the parallel criminal proceedings had been determined.[35]

8–13 If the delay, or any part of it, is attributable to the conduct of the defendant this will weigh in the Secretary of State's favour. In *Re Copecrest Ltd, Secretary of State for Trade and Industry v McTighe*,[36] the Insolvency Service did not receive the final D report from the liquidator of the relevant company until less than one month before the two-year period was due to expire. The application for permission was made one week after the expiry of the two-year period. Even so, the Court of Appeal allowed the Secretary of State's appeal against an earlier refusal by the judge to grant permission. The primary responsibility for the delay lay with the defendants. A statement of affairs had been sworn which suggested that the company, although unable to pay its debts as they fell due, was solvent on a

[34] In *Cedar Developments* a submission that it was unnecessary for the court to carry out a detailed balancing exercise unless a good reason were shown as to why proceedings were not commenced in time was also expressly rejected by the judge: see [1994] 2 B.C.L.C. 714 at 719.

[35] Conversely, if no satisfactory explanation is forthcoming, the court may refuse an application for permission where the case against a director is not particularly strong even though the Secretary of State erred in missing the two-year deadline by only a single day: *Re Stormont Ltd, Secretary of State for Trade and Industry v Cleland* [1997] 1 B.C.L.C. 437.

[36] [1994] 2 B.C.L.C. 284.

balance sheet basis. The company had ceased trading and sold its assets and business to a second company controlled by the defendants for the sum of £1.4 million payable over five years. The company's only asset in the liquidation was the unpaid balance of the purchase price, a sum of around £1.2 million which was said in the statement of affairs to be fully recoverable. The liquidator then spent some 18 months attempting to collect the debt on the basis that if payment was received the company would be solvent and its creditors would be paid in full. On this basis he also delayed in submitting a D report. Despite the liquidator's best efforts, the company received only a single payment of £5,000 and no concrete proposals for payment of the rest of the outstanding balance were ever forthcoming. The fact that the defendants had contributed to the delay by stringing the liquidator along with promises of payment taken together with the serious nature of the allegations made against them were critical factors weighing in the Secretary of State's favour. A summary of the Court of Appeal's conclusions can be found in the following passage from Hoffmann L.J.'s judgment:

> "[The Secretary of State] is not entitled to assume that any period of delay for which he is not responsible will automatically be added by the court on to the two-year period. He must take into account that such delays may curtail the period available to him. What, however, the learned judge does not appear to have taken into account is the directors' own responsibility for the delay on the part of the liquidator. The directors had sworn a statement of affairs showing the company to be solvent and thereafter tried . . . to string the liquidator along with promises of payment. The defendants say that the liquidator should have realised much earlier that the debt would never be paid, but in my view it does not lie in the mouths of the directors to say that the liquidator should have realised that they were only prevaricating. I regard the directors' responsibility for the curtailment of the period available to the Secretary of State from 18 months to three weeks as a very significant feature in this case . . . If, therefore, one takes into account, as the judge did not, the directors' responsibility for the earlier delay and what the judge agreed to be the serious nature of the allegations being made against these directors, the balance, in my view, clearly comes down in favour of the grant of an extension."[37]

8–14 On a similar note, the Secretary of State may receive a sympathetic hearing in circumstances where the office-holder delays in submitting a D report because his investigation into the company's affairs has been hampered by a lack of proper books and records. It is logical that the Secretary of State should not be penalised for a delay which is directly attributable to the failure of directors to maintain proper books and records in breach of Companies Act requirements, not least because such a failure may itself be indicative of unfit conduct.[38] Against this, there is some onus on the Secretary of State to monitor the position closely and, where necessary, to use the threat of sanctions under the Insolvent Companies (Reports on Conduct of Directors) Rules 1996 and the powers in s.7(4) as a

[37] [1994] 2 B.C.L.C. 284 at 287–288. Further support for the view that permission may be granted where the delay is occasioned by the conduct of the defendant can be derived from dictum of Harman J. in *Re Jaymar Management Ltd* [1990] B.C.L.C. 617 at 623–624.

[38] See generally Ch.5.

means to press matters forward.[39] A realistic timetable for each case needs to be set and periodically reviewed. The office-holder should be asked to estimate how long it will take him to submit a final report and assemble supporting evidence. If a case has been properly monitored in this way and the application for permission is made before the end of the two years, there is a fair chance that any delay which is not directly attributable to the Insolvency Service will not weigh heavily against the Secretary of State.[40]

Strength of case

8–15 In *Re Blackspur Group Plc, Secretary of State for Trade and Industry v Davies*, the "strength of case" factor was expressed in terms of the public interest. Millett L.J. stated:

> "One factor which is always present but always relevant is the nature of the proceedings. The Secretary of State is not seeking to vindicate a private right, but to protect the public from the actions of a person alleged to be unfit to be a director of a company. Scott L.J.'s reference [in *Probe Data*] to 'the strength of the case against the director' must be read in this light."[41]

In similar vein, Hobhouse L.J. said:

> "If a 'good reason' has to be looked for, it is not a reason for the delay but a reason for giving [permission] . . . that reason will normally be found in the public interest that unfit directors be disqualified unless the proposed application under s.6 lacks substance or there is some sufficient countervailing factor."[42]

Seen in these terms, a strong case for disqualification will be a powerful factor weighing in the Secretary of State's favour on an application for permission. However, it is not entirely clear what the Secretary of State is required to show in order to establish a "strong case". First, there is some debate as to whether the Secretary of State must establish a strong case by reference to *the allegations* or *the evidence*. Millett L.J. expressed the view in *Davies* that "the strength of the case" was a reference to the gravity of the charges made rather than to the strength or credibility of the supporting evidence.[43] However, in *Re Stormont Ltd, Secretary of State for Trade and Industry v Cleland*, Lloyd J. concluded that,

[39] See discussion in Ch.3 and in *Re Launchexcept Ltd, Secretary of State for Trade and Industry v Tillman* [2000] 1 B.C.L.C. 36.

[40] See dictum of Millett L.J. in *Re Blackspur Group Plc, Secretary of State for Trade and Industry v Davies* [1996] 4 All E.R. 289 at 295.

[41] [1996] 4 All E.R. 289 at 296–297.

[42] [1996] 4 All E.R. 289 at 304. Hobhouse L.J. drew an analogy with the approach taken on applications to dismiss disqualification proceedings for want of prosecution where the court rests its decision on an assessment of the public interest in allowing the proceedings to continue: see below from 8–35.

[43] [1996] 4 All E.R. 289 at 297. He expressed the same view in *Re Probe Data Systems (No.2), Secretary of State for Trade and Industry v Desai* [1990] B.C.L.C. 574 at 576.

despite the observations of Millett L.J., the court should consider not just the nature and gravity of the charges but also whether, and to what extent, those charges were fairly raised by the evidence.[44] On the latter view, the court must form a provisional opinion of the Secretary of State's case having given some consideration to the supporting evidence and the defendant's evidence in reply. Lloyd J. was reinforced in this conclusion by the approach in *Probe Data (No.3)* where Scott L.J. considered affidavits sworn by the relevant office-holder and the defendant before resolving the application in the Secretary of State's favour.[45] This appears to be the better view. However, as an application for permission is an interim proceeding designed to determine merely whether a case can go forward for trial, the court should be careful not to allow it to turn into a mini-trial.[46] In conclusion, it is suggested that the seriousness of the *allegations* made is one factor to be taken into account and weighed in the balance and that the *evidential strength* of the case is another factor. However, given the nature of the hearing, the court should avoid spending a lot of time weighing all the evidence to reach a view about the evidential strength of the case. Only in the clearest of cases should the court decide that the evidence is too weak to sustain a case.

8–16 The second (and closely related) area of debate has surrounded the applicable test for a "strong case" on the evidence. It was suggested by Balcombe L.J. in *Re Tasbian (No.3), Official Receiver v Nixon* that the case must be "fairly arguable":

> "On an application . . . for [permission] to bring proceedings . . . out of time what is the test to be applied? In my judgment, it is the same test as that which is used on any application to the court for [permission] to take some initiating procedure out of time, for example [permission] to appeal out of time. There can be no point in extending the time if the application is going to fail. If, however, the court is satisfied that the evidence shows a fairly arguable case on the applicant's part, then on this ground alone, that is leaving aside the reasons for the delay and any questions of prejudice to the other party, the court will not refuse [permission]."[47]

The implication is that the Secretary of State need only show that there is a reasonable prospect of success for this factor to count in his favour. However, in *Re Packaging Direct Ltd*, Jacob J. indicated that an "arguable case" test was inappropriate and that what had to be established was a "strong case" taking into account all the available evidence while having regard in the overall balance to

[44] [1997] 1 B.C.L.C. 437 at 447.

[45] [1992] B.C.L.C. 405 at 416–418. See also *Re Packaging Direct Ltd* [1994] B.C.C. 213 in which a "broad brush" assessment of the merits was favoured.

[46] *Re Packaging Direct Ltd* [1994] B.C.C. 213 at 215–216. There has been further debate over how the court should approach the available evidence. In *Re Polly Peck International Plc (No.2)* [1994] 1 B.C.L.C. 574 at 598 Lindsay J. suggested that the court could treat any part of the defendant's evidence not expressly countered by the Secretary of State's evidence or submissions as undisputed for the purposes of assessing the strength of the case. This approach (which was premised expressly on the view that the legislation was quasi-penal) was not followed in *Re Stormont Ltd, Secretary of State for Trade and Industry v Cleland* [1997] 1 B.C.L.C. 437 at 446–447 because of the danger that the Secretary of State would feel bound to controvert everything that might be in issue with the result that the application for permission would become weighed down with a mound of evidence.

[47] [1993] B.C.L.C. 297 at 301–302.

other factors such as the length of the delay and the explanation given for it.[48] In *Re Polly Peck International Plc (No.2)*,[49] Lindsay J. set out a two-stage approach, which amounts to a synthesis of these various competing approaches. He suggested that the court should first apply an initial threshold test to determine whether the allegations made by the Secretary of State could result in disqualification assuming those allegations to be true. Only once this threshold was crossed should the court consider the strength of the case on the evidence and balance that along with the other relevant factors. If it was not crossed then, in Lindsay J.'s view, the application should fail without any consideration of other factors, "... as it would be pointless to allow to proceed a case which could not succeed".[50] Similarly, in *Re Stormont Ltd, Secretary of State for Trade and Industry v Cleland*, Lloyd J. asked himself whether there was evidence on which the court might conclude that the conduct of the defendant as a director made him unfit to be concerned in the management of a company, describing this also as a "threshold test".[51] It is submitted that there is no necessity for this kind of threshold test. The true test is whether, on the available evidence and in the light of all the circumstances, the Secretary of State has shown a "good reason" why the court should grant permission. If the case is unlikely to succeed, the Secretary of State will find it very difficult to show a "good reason". Moreover, it is hard to imagine the Secretary of State going to the trouble of putting together a case unless it contains some allegations which are at least *indicative* of unfit conduct. It was seen in Ch.4 that it may be difficult in a marginal case to determine whether the defendant's conduct falls on the acceptable or unacceptable side of the line. In the light of this difficulty the court will usually have to move to Lindsay J.'s second stage anyway with the result that the threshold test becomes superfluous. As such, a court faced with an application for permission is likely to adopt the safest course and carry out a full balancing exercise.

8–17 A further issue concerns the treatment of allegations relating to collateral companies. In *Re Westmid Packaging Services Ltd (No.2), Secretary of State for Trade and Industry v Morrall*,[52] the court did not give any weight to collateral allegations in assessing the seriousness of the case against the defendant. The judge made the point that the Secretary of State had chosen not to bring proceedings in relation to those allegations within two years of the collateral companies becoming insolvent. The inference drawn was that the Secretary of State did not regard the collateral allegations as having sufficient weight to justify full "lead company" proceedings. That being so, the court was not prepared to give them much weight either. It is suggested that this approach to collateral allegations in the context of an application under s.7(2) should be treated cautiously. As a

[48] [1994] B.C.C. 213 at 218, 220.
[49] [1994] 1 B.C.L.C. 574.
[50] [1994] 1 B.C.L.C. 574 at 591.
[51] [1997] 1 B.C.L.C. 437 at 455.
[52] [1996] B.C.C. 229.

matter of principle, it is open to the Secretary of State to raise allegations concerning collateral companies more than two years after such companies became insolvent. The two-year rule applies only to lead companies. The justification for this is that a pattern of repeated misconduct may only emerge after a series of insolvencies. Even if the judge in *Westmid Packing (No.2)* was right on the facts to give little weight to the collateral allegations, it is suggested that it is wrong in principle to give *no* weight to collateral allegations simply because the Secretary of State has chosen not to bring "lead company" proceedings on the basis of those allegations.[53]

Degree of prejudice caused by delay

8–18 Prejudice to the defendant may arise in (at least) three possible forms. The first type of potential prejudice is the prolonged stress and worry that a director may suffer from having the threat of proceedings hang over him beyond the expiry of the two years. It was suggested in *Re Polly Peck International Plc (No.2)* that prolonged stress arising because the threat of proceedings remained a possibility for longer than two years may, on suitable facts, represent such serious prejudice that the court will refuse permission.[54] The second type of potential prejudice is that which the delay may have on the prospects for a fair trial. The strength of the director's evidence may weaken with the passage of time and the dimming of witnesses' memories. In *Polly Peck (No.2)*, Lindsay J. calculated that the full trial in that case would have been delayed by at least a year as a result of the Secretary of State's failure to launch proceedings in time. One defendant was seeking to rely on evidence from three elderly co-directors two of whom were suffering from failing health. The judge concluded that there was a real risk of prejudice to the defendant because, in the circumstances, the delay of a year was likely to result in a diminishing of the strength and availability of his evidence.[55] However, the delay in the overall timetable caused by the need for an application for permission should not be exaggerated as in preparing evidence to be adduced on the "strength of case" factor, the parties may end up saving time later should the

[53] For a full discussion of "lead" and "collateral" companies in proceedings under CDDA, s.6 see text from 3–106.

[54] [1994] 1 B.C.L.C. 574 at 602. One of the defendants was in his seventies and in poor health. In the light of the medical evidence, Lindsay J. thought that the mere prolongation of the proceedings would cause substantial prejudice to him. However, at least prior to the CPR, mere anxiety arising because of the prolongation of proceedings was not generally treated as sufficient to justify the striking out of an action for want of prosecution: see, e.g. *Department of Transport v Chris Smaller (Transport) Ltd* [1989] A.C. 1197 and, in the disqualification context, *Re Manlon Trading Ltd, Official Receiver v Aziz* [1996] Ch. 136.

[55] [1994] 1 B.C.L.C. 574 at 603. This can be contrasted with the decision in *Davies* discussed earlier where there was no prejudice because, in the light of the need to determine the parallel criminal proceedings first, the timetable for the disqualification proceedings was unaffected by the Secretary of State's failure to apply within two years. See also *Re Manlon Trading Ltd, Official Receiver v Aziz* [1996] Ch. 136. It remains to be seen whether the decision of the European Commission of Human Rights in *EDC v United Kingdom* [1998] B.C.C. 370 will lead to a treatment of delay arising as a result of parallel proceedings which is more favourable to directors.

matter proceed.[56] The third type of potential prejudice is the impact which the threat of proceedings may have on a director's job prospects and livelihood. This has been taken into account in cases involving "professional" directors who earn their living from holding directorships. For instance in *Polly Peck (No.2)*, the judge accepted the contention of one of the defendants that the continued risk of disqualification would reduce his prospects of obtaining employment at a level commensurate with his qualifications and experience. Moreover, as he had reached the age of 60, this amounted to real prejudice because he only had a few years left in which to earn a living and provide for his retirement.[57] However, it may be difficult for the owner-manager of a small private company to establish that the continued threat of proceedings is prejudicial to his livelihood as it is open to him to carry on the same business without the benefit of limited liability.[58] This third type of prejudice is controversial because the impact which disqualification or the threat of disqualification may have in an individual case will often be a matter of pure speculation. Whether evidence of such prejudice is favourably or poorly received may depend in part on the court's overall view of the disqualification process and the nature of its impact on the person.[59] If this factor is to carry much weight it will need to be established at the very least that the prejudice arose as a result of the delay in the commencement of proceedings. It is technically possible for a defendant to resist an application for permission successfully without establishing that the delay has caused actual prejudice or given rise to a substantial risk that a fair trial will no longer be possible. The onus

[56] See *Re Stormont Ltd, Secretary of State for Trade and Industry v Cleland* [1997] 1 B.C.L.C. 437 at 448. The loss by an office-holder of company documents that could potentially assist the director might not be treated as being sufficiently prejudicial to justify the refusal of permission: see *Re Dexmaster Ltd, Secretary of State for Trade and Industry v Joyce* [1995] 2 B.C.L.C. 430 though it should be noted that this case involved an application to strike out proceedings which had been commenced in time rather than an application for permission under s.7(2).

[57] [1994] 1 B.C.L.C. 574 at 603. See also *Re Westmid Packing Services Ltd (No.2), Secretary of State for Trade and Industry v Morrall* [1996] B.C.C. 229 at 244–245.

[58] See the observation of Harman J. at first instance in *Probe Data* [1991] B.C.L.C. 586 at 593 to the effect that the director could have chosen to run his current business through the form of a partnership rather than a limited company. This finding was left untouched on the subsequent appeal. Applications brought by owner-managers under s.17 for permission to act as directors while disqualified have failed on similar reasoning: see *Re Streamhaven Ltd, Secretary of State for Trade and Industry v Barnett* [1998] 2 B.C.L.C. 64; *Re Amaron Ltd, Secretary of State for Trade and Industry v Lubrani* [1998] B.C.C. 264 (the supplementary judgment on the leave application is omitted from the B.C.L.C. report of the case); *Re Universal Flooring and Driveways Ltd, Secretary of State for Trade and Industry v Woodward*, May 15, 1997, Ch.D., unreported and further discussion in Ch.15.

[59] See Ch.2, the discussion of de facto disqualification in Ch.5 and the further discussion below of "inherent" prejudice in the context of dismissal for want of prosecution. One possible solution to the problems of delay and potential prejudice which balances the protective aspect of the legislation and the rights of the individual director (giving priority to the former) is for the case to proceed and the defendant to be "compensated" for delay etc. by a reduction in any period of disqualification ordered. However, as was pointed out in *Re Manlon Trading Ltd, Official Receiver v Aziz* [1996] Ch. 136 and *Re Westmid Packing Services Ltd (No.2), Secretary of State for Trade and Industry v Morrall* [1996] B.C.C. 229 at 245, such a reduction could not be made where the defendant is liable to be disqualified on the facts for no more than the minimum period of two years.

remains with the Secretary of State to show "good reason".[60] Equally, the Secretary of State will not necessarily fail simply because the court accepts that there is prejudice. It is a question of balancing all the factors.

The balancing exercise

8–19 It was seen above how the Court of Appeal carried out the balancing exercise in *Davies*, the unsatisfactory delay in that case being outweighed by the strength of the allegations, the lack of any prejudice to the defendants and the fact that the late-filing of the applicant's evidence had not delayed the hearing which would have had to await the outcome of parallel criminal proceedings in any event. Further illustrations of how the court balances the various factors are provided below.

Successful applications

8–20 The following are examples of cases where the application for permission was successful:

8–21 ***Re Cedac Ltd, Secretary of State for Trade and Industry v Langridge.***[61] In this case, it was held at first instance that the original proceedings were invalid because the Secretary of State had failed to give at least ten days' notice of intention to proceed as required by CDDA s.16. However, the Secretary of State was given permission to commence fresh proceedings out of time. The original proceedings had been issued in time. The allegations against the defendant (which included trading to the detriment of creditors and causing the company to enter into a transaction at undervalue) were described as "grave". There was no prejudice to the defendant as all the evidence filed in relation to the original proceedings was available for use in the fresh proceedings and so the timetable for the hearing had not been affected. These matters outweighed the Secretary of State's failure to provide an adequate explanation as to why the giving of notice and commencement of proceedings had been left until the end of the period.[62]

8–22 ***Re Probe Data Systems Ltd (No.3), Secretary of State for Trade and Industry v Desai.***[63] The original proceedings were commenced in time in the name of the official receiver but were later struck out because the official receiver has no locus standi to commence proceedings in his own name where the relevant company has gone into creditors' voluntary liquidation.[64] The Court of Appeal (affirming Harman J.) gave the Secretary of State permission to commence fresh proceedings out of time. The original proceedings had been issued two weeks before the end of the two-year period. The evidence (supporting allegations of

[60] In contrast, on an application to dismiss a claim for want of prosecution, the onus is on the defendant (at least under pre-CPR law) to establish that the delay has caused actual prejudice: see, e.g. *Birkett v James* [1978] A.C. 297 and discussion below from 8–35.

[61] [1990] B.C.C. 555.

[62] The decision on the s.16 point was overturned on appeal and the original proceedings reinstated: see [1991] Ch. 402. The majority in the Court of Appeal expressed the view obiter that there would have been no ground for interfering with the judge's decision to grant permission had they upheld his conclusion on s.16.

[63] [1992] B.C.L.C. 405.

[64] See *Re Probe Data Systems Ltd (No.2)* [1990] B.C.L.C. 574. A different result was reached in *Re NP Engineering and Security Products Ltd, Official Receiver v Pafundo* [1998] 1 B.C.L.C. 208.

breach of fiduciary duty, undervalue transactions and trading to detriment of creditors) disclosed a "well arguable case" that the defendant was unfit. The delay attributable to the procedural error was reasonably explained. Any criticism which could be levelled at the authorities for failing to commence the original proceedings earlier than two weeks before expiry of the two years was outweighed by the strength of the case against the defendant.[65]

8–23 ***Re Tasbian Ltd (No.3), Official Receiver v Nixon.***[66] The original proceedings were commenced less than two years after a compulsory winding up order had been made in relation to the relevant company. However, the company had gone into administrative receivership some two months before the date of the winding up order. The defendant successfully argued that the proceedings were out of time because the two-year period ran from the date of the earlier receivership.[67] The Court of Appeal subsequently gave the official receiver permission to commence fresh proceedings out of time. The evidence disclosed an "arguable case" that the defendant, who was described as a consultant, had acted as a de facto director of the company. In particular, the evidence suggested that the defendant had exerted a considerable degree of control over the company's finances in that its bank account could not be operated without his consent. He also played an influential part in the decision to transfer all of the employees to a separate company set up for the purpose of supplying their services back to the company on a subcontracted basis. In addition to an "arguable case" for disqualification, the delay in the commencement of proceedings was, in the Court of Appeal's view, sufficiently explained by the official receiver's mistaken assumption that a fresh two years ran from the date of the winding up order.

8–24 ***Re Copecrest Ltd, Secretary of State for Trade and Industry v McTighe.***[68] The Secretary of State failed to commence proceedings in time because the final D report was only received by the Insolvency Service just under a month before the end of the two-year period. A further period of 11 weeks was allowed to pass before the Secretary of State issued the application for permission. This further period of delay attracted some criticism in the Court of Appeal. However, the overall balance favoured the Secretary of State, as much of the earlier delay had been attributable to the unco-operative attitude displayed by the defendants towards the company's liquidator and the allegations against them were serious in nature.[69]

[65] The Court of Appeal was also unimpressed by the defendant's claim that the delay between 1988 (when the original proceedings were commenced) and the end of 1991 (when the decision under discussion was made) had led to the evidence of various witnesses being lost. These matters of potential prejudice were said to carry little weight because the defendant had been aware since 1988 of the likelihood that he would be proceeded against. The implication is that he should have taken steps to obtain affidavits from relevant witnesses in 1988 on the basis that their evidence might still have been admissible if, as was claimed, they had subsequently died or lost touch.

[66] [1993] B.C.L.C. 297.

[67] See *Re Tasbian Ltd (No.1)* [1991] B.C.L.C. 54.

[68] [1994] 2 B.C.L.C. 284.

[69] See discussion in 8–13 and on the nature of the allegations see *Re Copecrest Ltd, Secretary of State for Trade and Industry v McTighe (No.2)* [1996] 2 B.C.L.C. 477.

8–25 ***Re Stormont Ltd, Secretary of State for Trade and Industry v Cleland.***[70] The original proceedings were issued one day late by mistake. Permission to commence fresh proceedings out of time was granted in respect of the first defendant. The Secretary of State and Treasury Solicitor were criticised for proceeding with "less urgency than they might have done" during the two-year period and, in allowing matters to run right up to the wire, they had risked the possibility of failing to commence proceedings in time. Against this, the judge was not satisfied that any real prejudice had been caused by the delay because much of the evidence had already been prepared and so the timetable for the proceedings would not be seriously affected. Moreover, the case against the first defendant (including allegations of excessive remuneration, misapplication of funds and misrepresentation of the company's financial position to creditors) was sufficiently strong to amount to a good reason why permission should be granted.[71]

Unsuccessful applications

8–26 By way of contrast, the following are examples of cases where the application for permission was dismissed:

8–27 ***Re Crestjoy Products Ltd.***[72] The application for permission was not made until some ten weeks after the end of the two-year period even though notice under s.16 was given in time. The Secretary of State's explanation for the delay was that by the time investigations in relation to two of the four defendants were completed only three weeks of the two-year period remained. Harman J. criticised the Secretary of State for failing to explain why it was not decided to proceed separately against the other two defendants (in relation to whom investigations were completed roughly two months before the end of the two years) and why the application for permission was not issued within the two years once it was realised that it would be impossible to prepare the evidence in support of substantive proceedings in time. The judge said that an extra hurdle must be overcome where the application to extend time is made after the relevant time limit has expired. In this instance there was no good reason to extend time principally because of the Secretary of State's failure to explain why it had taken ten weeks to issue the application for permission. The strength of the case against the defendants and the question of prejudice caused by the delay were not canvassed in the judgment. Moreover, Harman J. expressed the view that mandatory disqualification under s.6 amounts to a serious matter involving a substantial interference with the freedom of the individual and this appears to have influenced his approach. One possible justification for the decision is that once a period well in excess of two years has passed by without proceedings being commenced the individual may fairly and reasonably assume that it is safe to take up directorships with the consequence that

[70] [1997] 1 B.C.L.C. 437.

[71] Permission was refused in relation to the second defendant as the case against him was regarded as "too weak". The only matter which the judge considered would go towards justifying a finding of unfit conduct in his case was an allegation that he had received excessive bonus payments.

[72] [1990] B.C.L.C. 677.

the late commencement of proceedings could give rise to actual prejudice. In other words, there may come a point (albeit one that is difficult to identify with any precision) where prejudice becomes a very strong factor against the grant of permission to bring proceedings out of time because the delay is such that it gives the impression that no proceedings are contemplated. Thus, if the individual takes up new directorships on the reasonable assumption that he is immune from suit, it is arguably unfair for the Secretary of State to be given permission.[73]

8–28 ***Re Polly Peck International Plc (No.2).***[74] Application for permission to proceed out of time was made in relation to four defendants, two of whom were non-executive directors. Disqualification proceedings were originally commenced within time but these were later withdrawn by consent and the application for permission was eventually made just over three months after the expiry of the two-year period. The main difficulty facing the administrators and the Insolvency Service in this case was the sheer scale and complexity of the company's affairs. The company had subsidiaries in several countries including North Cyprus, Turkey, Hong Kong, the United States, Switzerland, Liberia and the Cayman Islands. The upshot was that the joint-administrators were late in submitting interim returns and by the time a final report on the company's directors was submitted less than four months of the two years was left. Further delays occurred in the preparation of affidavit evidence firstly because of a failure on the part of the Treasury Solicitor to issue formal instructions to counsel and later because a question arose as to whether the joint-administrators could properly disclose information obtained by them under ss.235–236 of the Insolvency Act 1986 to the Secretary of State for the purposes of the disqualification proceedings.[75] Lindsay J. criticised the Secretary of State's lack of urgency and, in particular, the failure either to press the joint-administrators on their reporting obligations or to make use of the information gathering powers in s.7(4).[76] Moreover, the judge found that the case against the defendants was not sufficiently serious to justify the grant of

[73] However, if the defendants receive notice of intention to proceed under s.16 within the two years the point is weakened. It is also to be noted that the exclusive concentration on the length of the delay in *Crestjoy* may have elevated this factor to a threshold test of the kind discredited in *Davies*: see 8–10 to 8–12. Nevertheless, the Secretary of State can expect a rough ride in similar circumstances if he fails either: (a) to issue the application for permission within the two years; or (b) to issue the substantive disqualification proceedings within the two years coupled with an application for permission to file and serve the evidence in support out of time.

[74] [1994] 1 B.C.L.C. 574.

[75] Directions from the court were sought on this point: see *Re Polly Peck International Plc, Ex p. the joint administrators* [1994] B.C.C. 15.

[76] Lindsay J.'s view that there had been unreasonable delay is best summed up in the following passage from his judgment ([1994] 1 B.C.L.C. 574 at 590):

> "Even in this complicated matter, given the resources of the joint administrators, the powers available to the Secretary of State, the fact that almost from the outset it had been seen as a case in which disqualification proceedings might be appropriate and the other circumstances which I have described, the . . . proceedings could have been launched within the time prescribed by Parliament had only the matter been attended with a sense of purpose and, later, of urgency with which it should have been marked."

permission. The collapse of Polly Peck was caused by the movement of substantial funds out of the company ostensibly to support several of the subsidiaries. The person directly behind this transfer of funds was the company's chairman, Asil Nadir. The case against the defendants was essentially that they had not taken proper care. It was claimed that they failed: (a) to institute adequate financial controls over the expenditure and transfer of monies from the company; (b) to ensure that adequate financial controls and reporting procedures were implemented and adhered to in respect of the subsidiaries; (c) to obtain appropriate responses to the question of the subsidiaries' need for substantial funding from the company; and (d) to monitor, or set up proper procedures for monitoring, the actual expenditure incurred by the subsidiaries, the funds which had been provided to them and their ability to repay their indebtedness to the company as and when required or at all. It was also claimed that they should have threatened to resign in the event that their attempts to rectify these matters met with resistance from Nadir. There were no allegations of fraud or dishonesty and the four defendants were at all times in a minority on the board. Lindsay J. held that the case was so weak that it could not lead to disqualification and was prepared to refuse permission on that basis alone without considering other factors.[77] On the supposition that this conclusion was wrong, the judge went on to carry out a full balancing exercise reaching the same result. The case was simply not strong enough to justify the granting of permission given the delay and (in relation to three of the defendants) the risk of prejudice.[78]

8–29 ***Re Packaging Direct Ltd, Secretary of State v Jones.***[79] The application for permission was made some nine weeks after expiry of the two-year period. The judge regarded the delay as culpable because notices of intention to proceed under s.16 had been sent to the defendants nine months before the end of the two

[77] An initial threshold test was applied. According to the judge, the Secretary of State had not crossed the initial threshold because the defendants' shortcomings did not amount to a serious and deliberate failure or a demonstrable lack of commercial probity (applying *Re Bath Glass Ltd* [1988] B.C.L.C. 329 and *Re Lo-Line Electric Motors Ltd* [1988] Ch. 477). Moreover, to the extent that they were incompetent they had not been incompetent "in a very marked degree" (applying *Re Sevenoaks Stationers (Retail) Ltd* [1991] Ch. 164).

[78] There are a number of problems with Lindsay J.'s judgment. Firstly, his views on the scope of the court's enquiry under CDDA s.6 probably do not survive the Court of Appeal decision in *Re Grayan Building Services Ltd, Secretary of State for Trade and Industry v Gray* [1995] Ch. 241 on which see Ch.4. Moreover, in the light of the *Barings* disqualifications and cases like *Re Continental Assurance Co of London Plc, Secretary of State for Trade and Industry v Burrows* [1997] 1 B.C.L.C. 48 and *Re Westmid Packing Services Ltd, Secretary of State for Trade and Industry v Griffiths* [1998] 2 All E.R. 124, the standards of competence and financial vigilance now expected from directors are arguably much higher than they were when *Polly Peck* was decided: see Chs.4 and 5. Lindsay J.'s view that the director should be given the benefit of any reasonable doubt because disqualification has penal consequences is also open to criticism. A further point (admittedly speculative) is that the judge may have been influenced by the fact that, for practical reasons, no proceedings were contemplated against Nadir. In other words, it might have seemed unfair that four directors comprising less than one-third of the company's board were left exposed to disqualification when the man primarily responsible for the company's collapse was not so exposed. For these reasons *Polly Peck* is perhaps best regarded as a unique case.

[79] [1994] B.C.C. 213.

years. This was said to indicate that a firm decision to proceed had actually been made at that point. The Secretary of State was criticised on two counts for lack of urgency. First, there was a failure to ensure that the relevant office-holder swore his affidavit in sufficient time to enable the Secretary of State to commence proceedings within the two-year period. Secondly, the further nine-week delay between the end of the two years and the issue of the application for permission was indicative of what the judge described as a "relaxed approach". It was held that the case against the defendants was not, in the circumstances, strong enough to provide a good reason why permission should be granted.[80]

8–30 ***Re Westmid Packing Services Ltd (No. 2), Secretary of State for Trade and Industry v Morrall.***[81] The application for permission concerned M, an alleged de facto director of the relevant company. Proceedings against the three de jure directors of the company were commenced in time. However, the Secretary of State did not become aware until about six months after the expiry of the two-year period that there might be a case against M. The Insolvency Service was alerted to this possibility by the contents of an affidavit sworn by M which formed part of the evidence put forward by two of the de jure directors in the main proceedings. Some three months later, on counsel's advice, the Secretary of State made an ordinary application in the existing proceedings to join M as a defendant out of time. This application was struck out on the ground that the Secretary of State had adopted an incorrect procedure and should simply have applied for permission to commence proceedings out of time by fresh originating summons under s.7(2) of the CDDA.[82] By the time the application for permission was finally made nearly a full year had elapsed since the end of the two-year period. The Secretary of State came in for criticism on a number of counts. It was said that if proceedings against the de jure directors had been commenced more expeditiously it was possible that the evidence against M would have surfaced much earlier. The judge added that there was no satisfactory explanation as to why the Secretary of State had risked further delay by deciding to adopt what turned out to be an incorrect procedure for seeking permission. Moreover, a number of other factors weighed in M's favour. First, the judge formed the view that the case against M was a weak one. It was the Secretary of State's case that M had effectively acted as the financial director of the company. He was the de jure financial

[80] The case against the first defendant (who had been responsible for the day-to-day running of the company) was a mixture of trading to detriment of creditors and related "low bracket" allegations (including failure to exercise financial responsibility, trading at the expense of Crown creditors and excessive remuneration). The evidence suggested that trading was only continued with a view to a going concern sale of the company's assets and that major creditors (including the Crown) were kept regularly informed of the position. This considerably weakened the case against him. The case against the second defendant (who was only involved with the company for around one day per week) was weakened by the fact that he had appointed, paid for and relied on a chartered accountant to oversee the company's finances and report to him.

[81] [1996] B.C.C. 229.

[82] See [1995] B.C.C. 203. It should be noted that under the Disqualification Practice Direction an application can be made in current proceedings both for permission to proceed out of time and to join additional parties. To this extent, the case no longer reflects the current procedural arrangements.

director of the company's parent and there was evidence that he was regarded as having direct responsibility for all financial matters within the group. He was a signatory to the company's bank account and was described as financial director in the mandate. Nevertheless, the judge appears to have taken the view that, on the evidence as a whole, the tasks carried out by M were consistent with those of a manager or a group accountant and did not fall within the exclusive province of a director. Furthermore, the court gave little weight to collateral allegations relating to M's conduct as a de jure director of the parent company. The Insolvency Service had known of M's involvement in the parent company within seven months of it going into administrative receivership but had not seen fit to launch proceedings against him in relation to that company as a lead company inside two years. The Secretary of State's decision not to bring substantive disqualification proceedings against M on the basis of the parent company allegations was treated as being indicative of the weakness of those allegations and of the public interest in pursuing them. Secondly, it was accepted that M would suffer prejudice if the Secretary of State was allowed to proceed given that he had taken up a number of directorships since the collapse of the company.[83]

Procedure on applications for permission under section 7(2)

Form of proceedings

8–31 An application for permission under s.7(2) should be made by Practice Form N208, that is a Part 8 Claim form as adapted by the applicable Practice Direction, under CPR Pt 8 save where it is sought to join a director or former director to existing proceedings, in which case the application must be made by application notice under CPR Pt 23.[84] In the former case, the application should be made to the court that would ordinarily have had jurisdiction had the proceedings been issued in time.[85] Under the pre-CPR procedure there was some difference of judicial opinion over the procedure to be adopted. In *Re Probe Data Systems Ltd (No.2)*,[86] Millett J. held that the proper procedure was for the Secretary of State (or, where appropriate the official receiver) to apply to the registrar without notice to the defendant, putting before the registrar the whole of his evidence both on the question of permission and on the merits. Following this procedure, if the registrar was satisfied that there was a prima facie case for granting permission he should then give directions for a full hearing. At that hearing (of which the defendant would be given notice), the defendant was entitled to oppose permission. However, according to Millett J., the defendant's evidence should do no more than challenge the reasons for granting permission and should not go to the merits, a point developed in the passage below:

[83] However, it is not clear from the facts whether M accepted these positions after expiry of the two years in the reasonable expectation that disqualification proceedings would not be commenced against him.

[84] Disqualification Practice Direction, paras 17.1 and 19.

[85] i.e. the High Court, the appropriate county court or (in Scotland) the Court of Session: see CDDA s.6(3).

[86] [1990] B.C.L.C. 574.

"Matters which will have to be considered by the registrar will include the gravity of the allegations made by the Secretary of State, the reasons for the delay and the extent, if any, to which the defendant may have contributed to the delay, and any reasons which the defendant may wish to put forward to show why he would be unfairly prejudiced as a result of the delay which has occurred. In dealing with the gravity of the allegations in my judgment the defendant ought not to controvert the soundness of the allegations or deal with their merit but ought to reserve his position. The question will be whether the allegations are sufficiently grave to require to be adjudicated on notwithstanding the expiry of the two-year period. The question will not be whether those allegations are well founded."

Millett J.'s view was that the "without notice" stage would provide a quick means of filtering out unjustified applications.

8–32 However, in *Re Crestjoy Products Ltd*,[87] it was suggested that only one hearing was appropriate and that the application should be made on notice to the defendant. Following this procedure, a separate originating process seeking a disqualification order would then be issued if permission was granted. Harman J. took the view in *Crestjoy* that the "without notice" stage proposed by Millett J. was unnecessary as it was unlikely that the Secretary of State would bring frivolous or baseless applications. The further difficulty with Millett J.'s approach is that the courts do not simply consider the gravity of the unchallenged allegations against the defendant. As was indicated above,[88] the tendency is for the courts, in evaluating "strength of case", to form a provisional view on the merits in the light of the available evidence. The current practice of the Secretary of State and the courts, now reflected in the Disqualification Practice Direction, is to follow the *Crestjoy* procedure so far as there is one hearing of which the defendant is given notice.[89]

The other question that arose previously was whether or not the ability to use an application notice was limited to those cases, such as *Re Westmid Packing Services Ltd (No.2), Secretary of State for Trade and Industry v Morrall*,[90] where proceedings were already on foot and the claimant wished to join another defendant after expiry of the two-year period. In particular, in cases where no existing proceedings were on foot there was doubt over whether it was necessary for the claimant to issue a claim form under Pt 8 seeking permission to commence proceedings out of time on the basis that an application notice under CPR Pt 23 is not strictly a form of originating process. In the second edition of this book the authors suggested that the Disqualification Practice Direction could usefully be clarified on this point. This has now been done and it is clear from para.17.1 of the Disqualification Practice Direction that applications under CDDA s.7(2) for

[87] [1990] B.C.L.C. 677.

[88] See paras 8.15–8.16.

[89] See also *Re Cedac Ltd* [1990] B.C.C. 555; *Re Westmid Packaging Services Ltd, Secretary of State for Trade and Industry v Griffiths* [1995] B.C.C. 203. Other commentators have supported Millett J.'s two-stage approach. The authors are not persuaded that there is any great merit in it because it takes time and duplicates costs.

[90] [1996] B.C.C. 229.

permission to commence s.6 proceedings out of time where there are no existing proceedings on foot are to be made by Practice Form N208 under CPR Pt 8.

Interim nature of proceedings

8–33 An application for permission under s.7(2) has always been regarded as interlocutory or interim in character.[91] This has the following consequences:

(1) The hearing will be based solely on written evidence[92] and (save in highly exceptional circumstances) without cross-examination of deponents.[93]
(2) It will not generally be appropriate for the court to order disclosure of any documents referred to in the Secretary of State's evidence in support of the application.[94]
(3) The rules in *Ladd v Marshall*[95] governing the admissibility of fresh evidence on an appeal do not apply with full rigour to an appeal against a decision to grant permission.[96]

Costs

8–34 If the defendant successfully resists an application for permission he is generally entitled to an order for his costs to be paid by the Secretary of State. The successful defendants in *Re Polly Peck International Plc (No.2)* argued that they were entitled to costs on the indemnity basis on the ground of double default in that the Secretary of State had not only failed to commence proceedings within time but had also failed to persuade the court to grant permission under s.7(2). Lindsay J. decided that this alone was insufficient to displace the ordinary disposition of the court to order costs on the standard basis.[97] If the Secretary of State is successful then the usual order is for the costs to be costs in the disqualification proceedings. Though there have been cases where the court has ordered the defendant to pay the costs. The matter is one entirely for the discretion of the court. It may well be that, in line with the general indication that costs will not necessarily follow the event and that the court may be more prepared to consider

[91] *Re Probe Data Systems Ltd (No.3), Secretary of State for Trade and Industry v Desai* [1992] B.C.L.C. 405 at 417.

[92] In contrast to substantive disqualification proceedings and applications for permission to act notwithstanding disqualification, such written evidence need not be by affidavit: contrast the Disqualification Rules with the Disqualification Practice Direction, paras. 9.1, 22.1.

[93] In *Re Manlon Trading Ltd, Official Receiver v Aziz* [1996] Ch. 136, the registrar's decision to make an order for the cross-examination of deponents on an application for dismissal for want of prosecution was criticised by the Court of Appeal. Peter Gibson L.J. said that such an order would only be justified in "highly exceptional circumstances" adding that the utility of interim proceedings as a method for bringing to an end or reducing the scope of a case would be destroyed if "they became occasions for lengthy trials within trials, extended by oral evidence".

[94] See *Re Polly Peck International Plc, Secretary of State for Trade and Industry v Ellis (No.3)* [1994] 1 B.C.L.C. 661. On disclosure (formerly discovery) generally see CPR Pt 31 and see Ch.7.

[95] [1954] 1 W.L.R. 1489.

[96] *Re Probe Data Systems Ltd (No.3), Secretary of State for Trade and Industry v Desai* [1992] B.C.L.C. 405 at 417.

[97] [1993] B.C.C. 890 at 917 (that part of the judgment relating to costs is omitted from the report of the case in B.C.L.C.).

success or failure on particular issues and make split orders for costs, more complicated costs orders will be made in future. In any event, and even before the advent of the CPR, it was not unknown for the court to order the costs of a successful application for permission under s.7(2) to be paid by the applicant on the ground that the applicant was seeking an indulgence of the court.

DISMISSAL FOR DELAY

8–35 Many of the considerations taken into account on applications for permission under CDDA s.7(2) are also relevant in the context of an application by the defendant to strike out disqualification proceedings against him for delay, or want of prosecution. It is beyond doubt that proceedings for an order under CDDA s.6 are capable of being struck out for delay. The same is also true of other forms of civil disqualification proceedings (i.e. proceedings brought under any of ss.2, 3, 4, 8 or 9A) although, to date, the reported cases have generally been concerned with applications to strike out proceedings for an order under s.6. In these cases the courts have been content to apply the usual principles applicable in ordinary civil litigation, although it has been recognised that some adjustment of approach may be required to reflect the fact that disqualification is not an ordinary form of civil proceeding. The hope is that with more rigorous case management under the CPR there should be less scope for such applications. However, it has to be borne in mind that, even prior to the CPR, disqualification proceedings under ss.6 and 8 were rigorously controlled by reason of the requirement in the Disqualification Rules that the matter come before the court within a comparatively short period after commencement, without any one party taking the initiative.[98]

The position prior to the CPR

8–36 Under the procedural law that had developed prior to the CPR, the question of whether civil proceedings should be struck out for delay depended on the defendant establishing one of two grounds. The first ground was that the plaintiff had been guilty of intentional and contumelious default. The second ground was inordinate and inexcusable delay on the part of the plaintiff or his lawyers such as to give rise to a substantial risk that a fair trial was no longer possible or of past or future substantial prejudice to the defendant. These principles were established by the Court of Appeal in *Allen v Sir Alfred McAlpine & Sons Ltd*[99] and approved by the House of Lords in *Birkett v James*.[100] In broad terms, contumelious default covered conduct which amounted to a deliberate default in compliance with a peremptory order[101] or conduct amounting to an abuse of the process of the

[98] Disqualification Rules r.7 (in the 1987 version). The extensions granted in *Manlon Trading* (main text below) illustrate the point.

[99] [1968] 2 Q.B. 229.

[100] [1978] A.C. 297.

[101] That is, an order where it is clear from the terms or the circumstances in which it was made that exact compliance is required within a certain time and that default will incur serious consequences. A typical example was an "unless" order.

court.[102] As regards inordinate and inexcusable delay, the passage of time before commencement of the proceedings was not of itself sufficient,[103] but delay prior to issue could "tip" short delay after issue into inordinate and inexcusable delay. Generally, inordinate delay meant delay that was "materially longer than the time usually regarded by the profession and the courts as an acceptable period".[104] In this context, the delay probably had to exceed "by a substantial margin" the time prescribed by rules of court for the taking of steps in the proceedings.[105] As regards prejudice, a causal connection between the relevant delay and the prejudice had to be established. Prejudice was not limited to prejudice to the trial process but could include, for example, prejudice to the defendant's business interests.[106] The defendant could not rely on prejudice flowing solely from delay prior to issue of proceedings. The prejudice had to be caused by delays occurring after issue of proceedings. However, the prejudice caused by delay after issue of proceedings had to be evaluated in context and was therefore likely to require consideration of the impact of the overall lapse of time since the events giving rise to the litigation. Where there was a long delay prior to the issue of the proceedings and that delay caused prejudice to the defendant, the defendant only had to show something more than minimal additional prejudice caused by delay after commencement to justify a striking out of the proceedings.[107]

Manlon Trading: balancing the public interest against prejudice suffered by the defendant

8–37 The leading authority on the application of pre-CPR practice in the disqualification context is the Court of Appeal decision in *Re Manlon Trading Ltd, Official Receiver v Aziz.*[108] In *Manlon Trading*, proceedings for an order under s.6 were issued in June 1990, on the last day of the two-year period. The defendant's evidence was filed in April 1991, at which point the official receiver was directed by the registrar to file and serve further evidence in reply by mid-May 1991. Between May and November 1991 the official receiver applied to the registrar for five extensions of time all of which were granted. A period of a year elapsed without any further step being taken. In November 1992 the Treasury Solicitor gave notice of intention to proceed to the defendant's solicitors. However, it was not until late-January 1994 that the evidence in reply was finally filed and served. The Court of Appeal upheld Evans-Lombe J.'s decision[109] to strike out the proceedings. The following points emerge from the judgments:

[102] Such as commencing litigation with no intention of progressing it to a conclusion see, e.g. *Grovit v Doctor* [1997] 1 W.L.R 640.

[103] Not surprisingly as the claimant is prima facie entitled to commence proceedings as long as any applicable limitation period has not expired.

[104] *Birkett v James* [1978] A.C. 297.

[105] *Trill v Sacher* [1993] 1 W.L.R. 1379.

[106] *Department of Transport v Chris Smaller (Transport) Ltd* [1989] A.C. 1197.

[107] *James Investments (IOM) Ltd v Phillips Cutler Phillips Troy, The Times*, September 16, 1987; *Department of Transport v Chris Smaller (Transport) Ltd* [1989] A.C. 1197.

[108] [1996] Ch. 136.

[109] [1995] 3 W.L.R. 271.

(1) The conventional approach to dismissal for want of prosecution in ordinary civil proceedings was applicable in disqualification proceedings. On the conventional pre-CPR approach, as noted above, the inherent jurisdiction to strike out on this ground was only to be exercised where the court was satisfied:

"... either (1) that the default [had] been intentional and contumelious, *e.g.* disobedience to a peremptory order of the court or conduct amounting to an abuse of process of the court; or (2) (a) that there [had] been inordinate and inexcusable delay on the part of the [claimant] or his lawyers, and (b) that such delay [gave] rise to a substantial risk that it [was] not possible to have a fair trial of the issues in the action or [was] such as [was] likely to cause or to have caused serious prejudice to the defendants ..."[110]

(2) The conventional approach should be modified in disqualification cases to reflect the fact that disqualification proceedings were not brought to enforce private rights but were brought in the public interest and should not therefore be struck out lightly. The "public interest" nature of the proceedings was to be balanced against any prejudice suffered by the defendant as a result of the inordinate and inexcusable delay.[111]

(3) As the question of whether the defendant was unfit was determined by reference to his past conduct,[112] the public interest in obtaining the protection of a disqualification order did not diminish with the passage of time. However, a point might be reached where the prejudice to the defendant flowing from the passage of time deserved to be accorded greater weight than the public interest.

(4) It was largely conceded by the official receiver that the period of delay between May 1991 and January 1994 was inordinate and inexcusable.[113] The question for the court on the conventional pre-CPR approach was whether the defendant was seriously prejudiced as a result. On the question of prejudice

[110] Per Lord Diplock in *Birkett v James* [1978] A.C. 297 at 318. A further effect of *Birkett v James* was that the court would not strike out proceedings for an order under CDDA s.6 before the expiry of the two-year period on the basis that it would be open to the Secretary of State to commence a fresh set of proceedings without permission. In the period immediately prior to the CPR, the courts became more willing to treat a failure to obey court orders as an abuse of process and to take into account not only the effect of delay on the parties but also its effect on the reputation of civil justice and on parties to other sets of proceedings: see *Grovit v Doctor* [1997] 1 W.L.R. 640; *Arbuthnot Latham Bank Ltd v Trafalgar Holdings Ltd* [1998] 1 W.L.R. 1426. Compare also *Shikari v Malik (No.2), The Times*, May 20, 1999.

[111] Though, in this respect, the views of Beldam L.J. should be contrasted with those of Peter Gibson and Staughton L.JJ. The majority thought that the "public interest" nature of disqualification proceedings was a factor to be taken into account. Beldam L.J., however, seems to have treated the case entirely on the conventional basis and disregarded the special nature of disqualification proceedings.

[112] *Re Grayan Building Services Ltd, Secretary of State for Trade and Industry v Gray* [1995] Ch. 241.

[113] On what constitutes "inordinate and inexcusable delay" see generally *Birkett v James* [1978] A.C. 297; *Department of Transport v Chris Smaller (Transport) Ltd* [1989] A.C. 1197. Under the old civil justice system a delay could only be treated as inordinate and inexcusable if it exceeded the period allowed by the RSC or CCR for taking a particular step. For this purpose the period allowed would include any court-sanctioned extension of time with the effect that proceedings delayed as a result of repeated extensions could not be struck out even if the delay was prejudicial to the defendant or harmful to the prospects of a fair trial: see *Re G Barraclough (Soft Drinks) Ltd, Secretary of State for Trade and Industry v Cawthray*, November 2, 1995, Ch.D., unreported.

to the defendant, the court decided that it should take into account prejudice caused by delay both before and after commencement of the proceedings. Thus, where the Secretary of State delayed the institution of proceedings for an order under CDDA s.6 right until the end of the two-year period, the court would expect the matter to be pressed forward with extra diligence thereafter.[114]

(5) It was accepted that there was an *inherent* prejudice to a director where disqualification proceedings were hanging over him. This inherent prejudice consisted of: (a) the practical disadvantage to the director of having his status and reputation called into question; (b) the loss of business opportunities arising should the allegations become known to potential business partners; and (c) the difficulty he faced in ordering his affairs with a view to the future while his status remained open to question. Such inherent prejudice could be inferred by the court without evidence of specific prejudice. However, it would rarely be sufficient on its own to justify striking out especially when taking into account the public interest in obtaining a disqualification order against the defendant and the fact that while proceedings were pending he remained free to act as a director.[115] Some additional prejudice normally had to be shown. In *Manlon Trading* additional prejudice was found in the effect of the delay on the memories of witnesses. The allegations against the defendant mostly concerned events that had taken place over six years before the official receiver's evidence in reply was finally served. Moreover, there was an allegation of fraudulent trading that related to events going back more than ten years. The Court of Appeal concluded that the inherent prejudice combined with the impact of the delay on the recollection of witnesses amounted to "serious prejudice" which outweighed the public interest in the continuation of the proceedings.[116]

[114] See generally *Department of Transport v Chris Smaller (Transport) Ltd* [1989] A.C. 1197 and, in the disqualification context, *Re Noble Trees Ltd* [1993] B.C.L.C. 1185.

[115] Some might argue that inherent prejudice is further reduced by the fact that the director is free to organise his business affairs in other ways without recourse to corporate form or limited liability. Moreover, the anxiety suffered by the defendant as a result of having the proceedings hanging over him was, under the pre-CPR approach, only sufficient to justify striking out in exceptional cases: see *Department of Transport v Chris Smaller (Transport) Ltd* [1989] A.C. 1197; *Biss v Lambeth, Southwark and Lewisham Health Authority* [1978] 1 W.L.R. 382.

[116] This at least was the conclusion of Peter Gibson and Staughton L.JJ. (although the former was more critical of the judge's approach). Beldam L.J. referred in passing to the public interest in the disqualification of unfit directors but gave greater weight to a wider public interest in the efficient administration of justice and disposed of the appeal largely on the conventional approach. It is to be noted that the reliance on the dimming of witnesses' recollections does not fit very well with the finding of Evans-Lombe J. that it was possible to have a fair trial. Also, the express finding of Evans-Lombe J. that the ground of specific prejudice to job opportunities was not established makes the Court of Appeal's reliance on general or inherent prejudice look strained. It is suggested that the Court of Appeal judgments should be treated with caution as regards the application of the law as stated to the facts of the case. This is because the Court of Appeal seems to have disagreed with the findings of fact made by the judge at first instance. However, as Evans-Lombe J. had heard oral evidence which the Court of Appeal had not heard, it was not possible for the latter (as would usually be the case on an interim application on written evidence alone) to make its own findings on the basis of being in as good a position as the judge to evaluate the evidence.

8–38 The approach in *Manlon Trading* was subsequently applied in *Secretary of State for Trade and Industry v Martin*.[117] In *Martin* the court found that the defendant had been seriously prejudiced by delay in several respects. First, it emerged during the strike-out proceedings that the thrust of the Secretary of State's case against the defendant had changed from that advanced in the affidavit evidence supporting the originating summons. It was said that the delay in raising the new allegations would inevitably have resulted in the dimming of witnesses' memories in relation to those matters. Secondly, there was specific prejudice in that the defendant had been suspended from one job on the commencement of the proceedings and rejected for others on the ground that the proceedings were pending. He had managed to obtain casual employment but the employer concerned had refused to offer him a full contract of employment until the proceedings were resolved. Thirdly, the defendant had the benefit of legal aid at the time when, in the court's view, the trial should have taken place. As he had subsequently obtained employment it was likely that he would no longer qualify for legal aid and would therefore be prejudiced in financing his defence.[118] Fourthly, he had suffered family problems which appear to have been attributable, at least in part, to the continuing proceedings. The judge held that the prejudice to the defendant outweighed the public interest in disqualifying the defendant. He agreed that the public interest was not diminished by lapse of time but added that the quantum of the public interest may be affected by factors such as the strength of the case, the seriousness of the allegations and the fairness with which the proceedings have been conducted. As there were no allegations of fraud or dishonesty, the judge formed the view that, at best, the Secretary of State would obtain a disqualification order falling within the minimum bracket between two and five years. The public interest in a "minimum bracket" disqualification was not strong enough to justify the proceedings continuing. Furthermore, it was found that the Secretary of State's case had not been presented in a proper, objective way as material favourable to the defendant had been omitted or downplayed in the office-holder's affidavit evidence. Notably, a submission on behalf of the Secretary of State that there was a heightened public interest in the defendant's disqualification because members of the investing public had lost money in his venture and wished to see justice done was categorically rejected. In the judge's words:

> "I do not accept that submission, and it seems to me that the purpose of disqualification is to protect the public for the future against directors whose past conduct shows them unfit to run a company. It is not to punish delinquent directors . . . Still less are disqualification proceedings designed to satisfy the understandable desire for revenge of creditors who blame directors for their losses. The creditors or their representatives can take other civil proceedings, if so advised, to recoup their losses."[119]

[117] [1998] B.C.C. 184.
[118] Every party to litigation is entitled under art.6 of the European Convention on Human Rights to be given a reasonable opportunity of presenting his case to the court in conditions which do not place him at a substantial disadvantage in relation to his opponent.
[119] [1998] B.C.C. 184 at 190.

Other pre-CPR cases

8–39 In two cases decided before *Manlon Trading* the courts struck out disqualification proceedings by applying the conventional approach in ordinary civil litigation without modification. In *Re Noble Trees Ltd*[120] proceedings for an order under CDDA s.6 were issued nine days before the expiry of the two-year period. Subsequently, the Secretary of State was late filing evidence in reply in breach of a court order and took only limited steps for a period of almost 20 months after that. In reaching the conclusion that there had been inordinate and inexcusable delay, Vinelott J. said that greater diligence was expected of a litigant who delays issuing proceedings right until the end of a limitation period. Moreover, it was held that the defendant was prejudiced by the delay as he had invested time and expense pursuing business opportunities which would necessitate his appointment as a director. No other specific prejudice was identified.

In *Official Receiver v B Ltd*[121] proceedings for orders under s.6 were issued against two defendants three days before expiry of the two-year period. Again, the delay in this case arose initially because of the official receiver's failure to file evidence in reply on time. Subsequently, the official receiver did very little to move matters forward (apart from giving notice of intention to proceed) between September 1991 and January 1993. The official receiver conceded that the delay could not be excused and so the court was concerned solely with the question of whether the defendants had suffered serious prejudice as a result. The judge found that serious prejudice had arisen on the basis of evidence that the defendants were forced, owing to the existence of the proceedings, to forego a number of specific opportunities to take up directorships and to pursue their existing business interests through the medium of partnership rather than a limited company. As in *Noble Trees*, no other specific prejudice was identified. It should be noted that in both cases that the specific prejudice to business interests was held sufficient to justify striking out. The following observations can be made about these cases:

(1) The approach in *Noble Trees* and *Official Receiver v B Ltd* gave no particular weight to the public interest in disqualifying directors. To this extent, an important principle was not expressly articulated. However, this does not mean that the cases would have been decided differently had the public interest specifically been identified and taken into account. Indeed, it is such an obvious point that it is difficult to believe that the judges in question did not have it in mind.[122] Furthermore, both decisions are premised on the assumption that disqualification (or the threat of disqualification) amounts to a serious interference with individual freedom and this had the effect of

[120] [1993] B.C.L.C. 1185.

[121] [1994] 2 B.C.L.C. 1.

[122] See e.g. *Noble Trees* [1993] B.C.L.C. 1185 at 1191 where Vinelott J. made reference to the public interest in disqualifying persons shown to be unfit in the context of considering evidence about lack of resources in the legal department of the DTI and the office of the Treasury Solicitor.

lowering the threshold required for the defendant to establish "serious prejudice". The passage extracted below from the judgment in *Official Receiver v B Ltd* betrays this kind of thinking:

> "Where a businessman has proceedings of this kind hanging over him, their mere existence is prejudicial in that he cannot order his affairs with any certainty. To some degree he has to accept that. If the application is prosecuted diligently . . . he cannot complain of the effect upon the ordering of his affairs. Further, if he is found unfit, he cannot complain that he cannot continue to have the benefit of trading with the benefit of a limited liability for the period of disqualification, save with the permission of the court which may be withheld or granted subject to restrictive conditions. *Nevertheless, the right to be a director of a limited liability company is an important right*. It prejudices a businessman to leave him in a state of uncertainty for an inordinate period of time in relation to a specific business opportunity or interest which involves him becoming a director of a particular company. It is no answer . . . that he can become involved in a manner short of becoming a director, *e.g.* by shareholder's agreement or a partnership . . ."[123]

(2) The Court of Appeal's view in *Manlon* that inherent prejudice to business interests was insufficient to justify striking out was confined to prejudice which was simply inferred from the nature of the proceedings. In *Noble Trees* and *Official Receiver v B Ltd* the defendants gave specific evidence showing how their business interests had been affected and so the prejudice was not simply inferred. It will be recalled that in *Secretary of State for Trade and Industry v Martin*, a case which followed the approach in *Manlon Trading*, the court also relied to an extent on specific evidence of prejudice to job prospects rather than prejudice inferred simply from the existence and nature of the proceedings.

(3) *Noble Trees* was arguably a special case as confusion had arisen over whether the proceedings had been struck out at an earlier stage because of the Secretary of State's failure to file evidence in reply in compliance with an "unless" order. It emerged some time later that the Secretary of State had not consented to an order in "unless" terms and the proceedings were restored before subsequently being dismissed for want of prosecution. The view of the judge was that the confusion would have come to light much earlier had the Secretary of State pursued the proceedings with proper diligence. The point for present purposes is that the defendant had acted for some time on the assumption that the proceedings were at an end and, in the circumstances, it is perhaps not surprising that the court concluded that the Secretary of State's delay in reviving the proceedings had caused prejudice to the defendant.

8–40 By way of contrast, in *Re New Technology Systems Ltd*,[124] aspects of the conventional pre-CPR approach were deployed to reject an application to strike

[123] [1994] 2 B.C.L.C. 1 at 15 (emphasis added) and see general discussion on the nature and impact of disqualification proceedings in Ch.2.

[124] [1996] B.C.C. 694, affirmed [1997] B.C.C. 810.

out disqualification proceedings. Again, this was a case in which proceedings for an order under CDDA s.6 were issued just before the expiry of the two-year period. The defendant was nearly two years late in filing his evidence in an appropriate form. That step was finally taken in May 1994. A further year elapsed without any response from the official receiver. In a telephone conversation which took place in early August 1995, the defendant's solicitors agreed to the official receiver being allowed an extension of time until September 1, 1995. This was despite the fact that the official receiver had not given notice of intention to proceed. Applying principles laid down in *Roebuck v Mungovin*,[125] the court exercised its discretion in the official receiver's favour on the basis that the consent given by the solicitors was an indication of the defendant's willingness to excuse the delay. It must be open to doubt whether such an approach would find favour now.

The position under the CPR and art.6 of the ECHR

8–41 Prior to the CPR, the court's power to strike out proceedings for delay was founded on the inherent jurisdiction. Under the CPR the position is regulated primarily by CPR r.3.4(2)(b) and (c) which are in the following terms:

> "(2) The court may strike out a statement of case[126] if it appears to the court—
>
> (a) . . . .
> (b) that the statement of case is an abuse of the court's process or is otherwise likely to obstruct the just disposal of the proceedings[127]; or
> (c) that there has been a failure to comply with a rule, practice direction or court order."

In practice, however, it has been for the courts to develop the principles on which, and the circumstances in which, the power will be exercised, taking into account both the overriding objective of the CPR and the European Convention on Human Rights. Insofar as is relevant for present purposes, art.6 of the European Convention provides:

> "In the determination of his civil rights and obligations . . . everyone is entitled to a fair and public hearing within a reasonable time by an independent and impartial tribunal established by law."

[125] [1994] 2 A.C. 224.

[126] Which includes a claim form: CPR, r.2.3(1).

[127] This sub-paragraph will not normally be relevant where delay is in issue. Instead, sub-para.(c) will be applicable: *Western Trust & Savings Ltd v Acland & Lenson*, May 23, 2000, Q.B.D., unreported. However, delays caused by a claimant acting in wholesale disregard of the norms of conducting civil litigation and doing so with full awareness of the consequences may lead the court to invoke sub-para.(b): see *Habib Bank Ltd v Jaffer* [2000] C.P.L.R. 438 and compare the similar approach that was evolving in the period immediately prior to the CPR as illustrated by *Grovit v Doctor* [1997] 1 W.L.R. 640.

Although, in the period leading up to the adoption of the CPR, judicial dissatisfaction was expressed with the rigidity of the principles approved in *Birkett v James*,[128] the problems facing the courts in dealing judiciously with delay have not significantly changed in nature since 1999. While the relevant principles may now be slightly different and additional matters must now be taken into account with the result that the pre-CPR cases should be treated with caution, it would probably be wrong to assume that the position under the CPR is entirely virgin territory. So far as the pre-CPR principles are concerned, the court has taken them into account in cases where periods of delay occurred prior to the CPR, that being the procedural regime under which the parties were then operating.[129] Otherwise, the court will not be interested in the citation of pre-CPR authority. The court must instead concentrate on the requirements of justice in each case in the light of the overriding objective. However, this does not mean that the thought processes manifested in the pre-CPR authorities should be completely thrown overboard.[130] Thus, factors such as prejudice to the defendant and acquiescence of the defendant will continue to be relevant. However, a much broader approach is now applied. There is, for instance, no need to engage in the mental gymnastics formerly required to identify which period of delay caused any relevant prejudice. **8–42**

Under the current approach a number of factors need to be borne in mind: **8–43**

(1) The question is what justice requires in the individual case, bearing in mind the overriding objective. This enables the court to consider not only justice to the parties but justice to other parties engaged in litigation in the courts. The technical approach under the old procedural regime has now been entirely discarded.
(2) Under the CPR, the court has several alternatives to striking out for delay, particularly where the delay involves non-compliance with a court order, rule or practice direction. These include (among others) ordering payment of a sum of money into court, repetition of the court order imposing conditions and/or specifying the consequences of further default in compliance, awarding costs on the indemnity basis payable forthwith and awarding interest on any damages at a higher or lower rate. In many cases it will be more appropriate to adopt one of these lesser sanctions.[131] However, if a fair trial is no longer possible the proceedings are almost bound to be struck out.[132]
(3) Under art.6 of the ECHR a party is entitled to have his civil rights and obligations determined within a reasonable time. However, the right to a trial

[128] [1978] A.C. 297.
[129] *Biguzzi v Rank Lesiure Plc* [1999] 1 W.L.R. 1926.
[130] Per May L.J. in *Purdy v Cambran* [2000] C.P. Rep. 67.
[131] *Biguzzi v Rank Lesiure Plc* [1999] 1 W.L.R. 1926.
[132] See discussion below of *Attorney General's Reference (No.2 of 2001)* [2003] UKHL 68, [2004] 2 A.C. 72.

without undue delay is not a right not to be tried after undue delay.[133] In ordinary civil proceedings, if a failure to comply with a rule, practice direction or court order has not rendered a fair trial impossible, an order striking out the proceedings, even for contumacious breach, is likely to be a breach of the *claimant's* art.6 rights.[134] However, this analysis is not entirely apposite to regulatory proceedings such as disqualification proceedings. The claimant, as guardian of the public interest and representative of the organs of the state, will not have "human rights" in such cases. Indeed, on the spectrum of criminal/civil proceedings identified in the *Westminster Property Management* case,[135] it is suggested that the principle that should be applied is one that is closer to that applicable in criminal cases. In *Attorney General's Reference (No.2 of 2001)* the House of Lords emphasised both the public importance of criminal proceedings and the concept that a breach of the "reasonable time" requirement of art.6 does not carry with it the necessary consequence that the proceedings should be struck out or stayed. In the words of Lord Bingham:[136]

> "The appropriate remedy will depend on the nature of the breach and all the circumstances, including particularly the stage of the proceedings at which the breach is established. If the breach is established before the hearing, the appropriate remedy may be a public acknowledgement of the breach, action to expedite the hearing to the greatest extent practicable and perhaps, if the defendant is in custody, his release on bail. It will not be appropriate to stay or dismiss the proceedings unless (a) there can no longer be a fair hearing or (b) it would otherwise be unfair to try the defendant. The public interest in the final determination of criminal charges requires that such a charge should not be stayed or dismissed if any lesser remedy will be just and proportionate in all the circumstances. The prosecutor and the court do not act incompatibly with the defendant's Convention right in continuing to prosecute or entertain proceedings after a breach is established in a case where neither of conditions (a) or (b) is met, since the breach consists in the delay which has accrued and not in the prospective hearing. If the breach of the reasonable time requirement is established retrospectively, after there has been a hearing, the appropriate remedy may be a public acknowledgement of the breach, a reduction in the penalty imposed on a convicted defendant or the payment of compensation to an acquitted defendant. Unless (a) the hearing was unfair or (b) it was unfair to try the defendant at all, it will not be appropriate to quash any conviction. Again, in any case where neither of conditions (a) or (b) applies, the prosecutor and the court do not act incompatibly with the defendant's Convention right in prosecuting or entertaining the proceedings but only in failing to procure a hearing within a reasonable time."

[133] It follows that a finding that a person's right to have his civil rights and obligations determined within a reasonable time has been violated does not mean that the proceedings will be vitiated if a fair trial is still possible notwithstanding the delay: see *Attorney General's Reference (No.2 of 2001)* [2004] 2 A.C. 72 at paras [20]–[24]; *Re Blackspur Plc (No.4), Eastaway v Secretary of State for Trade and Industry* [2007] EWCA Civ 425, [2008] 1 B.C.L.C. 153 at paras [26]–[28]. The further implication is that the fair trial guarantee and reasonable time requirement in art.6 are to be regarded as separate and distinct with the result that the consequences of their violation will not necessarily be the same: see *Attorney General's Reference (No.2 of 2001)* [2004] 2 A.C. 72 at [12].

[134] *Arrow Nominees Inc v Blackledge* [2000] 1 B.C.L.C. 709 at 724 reversed on other grounds [2000] 2 B.C.L.C. 167.

[135] *Re Westminster Property Management Ltd (No.1), Official Receiver v Stern (No.1)* [2000] 1 W.L.R. 2230 and see discussion in Ch.2.

[136] [2004] 2 A.C. 72 at [24].

This approach is consistent with *Manlon Trading* insofar as that case makes clear that the public interest in the determination of disqualification proceedings is a factor to be taken into account against striking out proceedings.

(4) The principle from the *Attorney General's Reference (No.2 of 2001)* that the proceedings must have been rendered unfair before they will be struck out was subsequently applied in the disqualification context by the Court of Appeal in *Re Blackspur Plc (No.4), Eastaway v Secretary of State for Trade and Industry*.[137] In that case, Mr Eastaway had previously succeeded in establishing before the European Court of Human Rights that the disqualification proceedings against him had breached the reasonable time requirement.[138] However, his consequential application to the English court to have the original proceedings dismissed and a disqualification undertaking given to compromise those proceedings set aside was unsuccessful. The violation of the reasonable time requirement did not of itself render the proceedings unfair.

(5) Under art.6, the period of delay is measured from the time when proceedings are treated as having commenced. One issue that it appears has not been fully discussed by the European Court is whether disqualification proceedings might be treated, for art.6 purposes, as having been commenced prior to the issue of formal proceedings (for example, from when a prospective defendant receives notification under CDDA s.16).[139]

Case law

8–44 The effects of delay have been considered in a number of cases, both by reference to the ECHR and the CPR. These cases reflect the development of an approach which is currently best represented by *Biguzzi v Rank Leisure Plc*[140] and *Attorney General's Reference (No.2 of 2001)*.[141] However, that approach is still evolving, and given the stress laid in more recent authorities on the court's ability to fashion a remedy for delay short of striking out, regardless of whether or not the delay amounts to a breach of art.6 of the ECHR, suggests that the courts may not need to strive so carefully to avoid a finding that there has been relevant unacceptable delay.

8–45 In *EDC v United Kingdom*[142] the European Commission of Human Rights reported that there had been a breach of the reasonable time requirement of art.6 of the ECHR. The company went into voluntary liquidation in August 1989. Three ex-directors were charged with criminal offences in April 1991. On August 7, 1991 the official receiver gave notice under CDDA s.16 to seven ex-directors

[137] [2008] 1 B.C.L.C. 153 especially at [26]–[28]. For the history of the litigation involving Mr Eastaway see further text from 8–48.

[138] *Eastaway v United Kingdom* (2005) 40 E.H.R.R. 17, [2006] 2 B.C.L.C. 361.

[139] Criminal proceedings are said to commence with "the charge", a concept which has an autonomous Convention meaning: see *Attorney General's Reference (No.2 of 2001)* [2004] 2 A.C. 72 at [26]–[27].

[140] [1999] 1 W.L.R. 1926.

[141] [2004] 2 A.C. 72.

[142] [1998] B.C.C. 370.

(including the three ex-directors the subject of the criminal charges and the applicant, DC) and disqualification proceedings were commenced on August 28, 1991. On November 14, 1991 the High Court refused an application for the criminal proceedings to be stayed pending the resolution of the criminal charges but ordered that the civil trial should not take place until after the criminal trial. Thereafter a number of directions hearings (and appeals) took place in relation to service of evidence in answer by the defendants. DC filed his evidence on October 15, 1992 but the position of some of the other defendants was then unresolved, as they had not all served evidence and were seeking further time. By April 2, 1993 one defendant had been given an extension of time to serve his evidence in the disqualification proceedings until after the criminal trial and his co-defendants had also been given time to file further evidence in response to a specific matter after that. Two of the defendants were convicted of the criminal charges and disqualified under CDDA s.2 on August 27, 1993. There were subsequent appeals against conviction. All the required evidence of the defendants in the disqualification proceedings was filed by December 1993. In February 1994 the official receiver was ordered to serve evidence in reply by May 17, 1994. It was eventually served on June 23, 1994. The criminal appeal process ended with the upholding of the earlier convictions on August 5, 1994. On October 12, 1994 the trial of the disqualification proceedings was fixed for January 11, 1996. On January 22, 1996 the court stayed the proceedings against DC on his (non-statutory) undertaking not to act as a director without permission of the court. The European Commission decided that the overall delay of nearly four-and-a-half years was, in the circumstances, a breach of art.6. It was also decided, albeit without any discussion, that, for art.6 purposes, the disqualification proceedings were commenced when the process was issued.[143]

8–46 A novel point arose in *Re Rocksteady Services Ltd, Secretary of State for Trade and Industry v Staton*[144] as the principal delay complained of in that case was caused by the court rather than the claimant. The proceedings had been commenced in April 1997. The claimant was slow in serving evidence in reply and time was extended on five separate occasions between June 1997 and June 1998. In January 1999 the trial was fixed for three days, commencing on May 18, 1999. Three days proved insufficient and at least three further days were estimated as necessary. Dates in August were offered but were inconvenient for the defendants' counsel. On September 16 the case was fixed for a resumed hearing in February 2000. At the end of January 2000 it was belatedly discovered by court staff that the registrar was not available to continue the hearing on the relevant dates. The resumed hearing dates were vacated. The defendants asked the Secretary of State to discontinue the proceedings. Their solicitors advised the court that they could not attend a hearing in March. At the end of February applications to strike out the proceedings were launched. In early March hearing dates

[143] Rather than, for example, when the s.16 notices were served.
[144] [2001] B.C.C. 467.

in May were offered and fixed. The Court of Appeal upheld the ruling of the judge that the proceedings could continue. A number of points emerge:

(1) The approach when considering delay caused by a party and delay caused by the court may have to be different. It was wrong to equate the Secretary of State with the court for these purposes. Talk of "abuse of process" was therefore inapposite.
(2) The judge had correctly addressed the issue of whether or not there was a "serious risk" of a fair trial and this did not state the test too highly. In any event there was little, if any, difference between "serious risk" and the test contended for as correct by the defendants, namely "real danger" of an unfair trial.
(3) As regards prejudice to the defendants, it was important to bear in mind that the relevant delay was, in reality, limited to the ten-week period between February and May 1999.
(4) The alleged prejudice relied on was very unspecific and accordingly not a significant factor. It was difficult to see how any inherent prejudice (consisting of general anxiety caused by the proceedings and disruption to the defendants' business careers) had been significantly exacerbated by the ten-week delay.
(5) Compared with the *EDC* case, which was persuasive rather than binding, the case not having gone to the European Court of Human Rights, the proceedings had been on foot for a little over three years. It was therefore open to the judge to conclude, as he had done, that there had been no breach of art.6.
(6) The real issue was whether the public interest in obtaining a disqualification order for the protection of the public was outweighed by the public interest in the due administration of justice and, in particular, the affording of a fair trial to the defendants. To dismiss the proceedings for delay would have been a disproportionate response. On the face of it, the proceedings were properly brought in the public interest, the prejudice alleged was not very serious, the delay was minimal and if the registrar on the resumed hearing felt a fair trial was not possible he could stop the trial.

8–47 In *Re Abermeadow Ltd*[145] the judge rejected an application to strike out disqualification proceedings which had been on foot for some five years. The proceedings had been commenced in June 1995. Initially the defendants were tardy in filing evidence. Subsequently, in November 1996 it was ordered that the disqualification proceedings should not be tried against the third defendant before the conclusion of parallel criminal proceedings against him. At that time, it was understood that the criminal proceedings would begin on no later than October 31, 1997. In November 1997 an application by the Secretary of State to lift the stay and an application by the second defendant to stay the disqualification proceedings against him until the criminal proceedings (also against him) were determined, were adjourned by the court pending clarification as to the date of the

[145] [2002] 2 B.C.L.C. 824.

criminal trial. In May 1998 the Secretary of State's application was dismissed and it was ordered that the disqualification proceedings should not be tried before conclusion of the criminal proceedings. The criminal trial finally concluded in August 1999. In October 1999 the civil disqualification proceedings came before the court for further directions and, in November 1999, the trial was fixed for July 2000. The first defendant, a former non-executive director of the company, issued his application to strike out for delay in April 2000. The delay complained of was primarily that from May 1998 to August 1999. It was argued that the Secretary of State should have sought a split trial. However, in the judge's view, the Secretary of State was right in the circumstances to take the position that, if at all possible, all three defendants should be tried together. The judge rejected the submission that the dimming of the first defendant's memory amounted to significant prejudice given that the case against him, based on his own evidence, was that he had no or minimal knowledge of and played no role in the company's decision-making process. So far as prejudice was concerned, although there was inevitable stress, the first defendant had been able to earn his living as managing director of another company and accordingly the prejudice did not carry great weight. The case had some similarities with *EDC v United Kingdom* in that the delay had been caused by the decision to await the outcome of parallel criminal proceedings against the other defendants in circumstances where it was sensible to have the disqualification proceedings against all defendants tried together rather than split them. However, *EDC v United Kingdom* was distinguishable as in that case: (a) there had been unwarranted delay of 14 months in fixing the date of the civil trial after the criminal proceedings had been disposed of; and (b) the civil proceedings would have had a considerable impact on the ability of the relevant defendant to practice his profession whilst those proceedings were outstanding.

8–48 In *Re Blackspur Group Plc, Secretary of State for Trade and Industry v Eastaway*,[146] the Vice-Chancellor had to consider the effect of delay in the *Blackspur* disqualification proceedings. The proceedings had a complex history, the relevant parts of which are set out below. They were issued in July 1992 against Mr Eastaway and four co-directors (including Mr Davies). It was accepted that it was reasonable to join the defendants in the same proceedings.

July 1992 to May 1996

(1) The Secretary of State's evidence was not ready when proceedings were issued and was finally served in December 1992.
(2) An application to strike out was heard in January 1994 but rejected by the registrar. The delay at that stage appeared longer than ought to have been necessary but was, in Morritt V.C.'s view, not material because of pending parallel criminal proceedings that had been commenced at the same time as the disqualification proceedings.
(3) The criminal trial commenced in March 1994 and concluded in June 1994 with Mr Eastaway's acquittal. Morritt V.C. concluded that no real progress

[146] [2003] B.C.C. 520. Judgment delivered on February 15, 2001.

could have been made with the disqualification proceedings until after the conclusion of the criminal trial.

(4) In September 1994 Mr Eastaway asked the Secretary of State to discontinue the disqualification proceedings in light of his acquittal. This request was refused.

(5) In April 1995 Mr Eastaway sought permission to appeal from the registrar's order of January 1994. That appeal (also pursued by two of his co-defendants) was dismissed on May 2, 1995 and an appeal to the Court of Appeal by Mr Davies was dismissed on May 24, 1996.[147] Although Mr Eastaway was not party to the latter appeal, he would have been able to take advantage of any decision that had gone in Mr Davies' favour and so proceedings against him could not sensibly have been pursued until the appeal had been concluded.

(6) The period July 1992 to May 1996 was, in Morritt V.C.'s view, taken up with the criminal proceedings and the defendants' various attempts to have the civil proceedings struck out.

May 1996 to November 1997

(7) In June 1996, Mr Davies invited the Secretary of State to accept (non-statutory) undertakings rather than proceeding to trial. The Secretary of State declined and Mr Davies then sought a stay of proceedings and judicial review of the Secretary of State's decision in October and November 1996. By letter of November 1996, Mr Eastaway indicated to the Secretary of State that he too would like to offer undertakings if it were decided that this were an appropriate means of resolving the disqualification proceedings. The stay and judicial review applications were finally determined by the Court of Appeal in the Secretary of State's favour in November 1997.[148] In Morritt V.C.'s view, it was unrealistic to expect the proceedings against Mr Eastaway to have continued pending determination of Mr Davies' applications and accordingly there was no unreasonable delay in the period May 1996 to November 1997.

November 1997 to October 1998

(8) During this period, evidence was outstanding from Mr Eastaway or he and the Secretary of State were actively negotiating a *Carecraft* statement as a basis for disposing of the proceedings.[149] In October 1998, those negotiations were broken off by Mr Eastaway.

October 1998 to September 1999

(9) During this period a trial date was fixed for October 1999. In June 1999 Mr Eastaway indicated that he wished to re-open the *Carecraft* negotiations.

[147] See *Re Blackspur Group Plc, Secretary of State for Trade and Industry v Davies* [1996] 4 All E.R. 289 and 8–04 to 8–05, 8–07, 8–10 to 8–12.

[148] See *Re Blackspur Group Plc, Secretary of State for Trade and Industry v Davies (No.2)* [1998] 1 W.L.R. 422 and 9–12 to 9–14.

[149] On the *Carecraft* procedure see generally Ch.9.

The Secretary of State advised Mr Eastaway that he intended to continue the disqualification proceedings. In August 1999, Mr Eastaway applied for judicial review of the Secretary of State's decision to continue the proceedings indicating that he would consent to a *Carecraft* disposal were the application to fail. On September 13, 1999 the trial date for the disqualification proceedings was vacated on Mr Eastaway's undertaking to the court to sign the *Carecraft* statement (the terms of which had been agreed in principle) and to have the proceedings determined under the *Carecraft* procedure in the event that his application for judicial review was unsuccessful. It is clear that between October 1998 and September 1999, Mr Eastaway was actively seeking to avoid a trial.

September 1999 to February 2003

(10) The application for judicial review was pursued until, in November 2000, it was finally disposed of by the House of Lords on jurisdictional grounds. Mr Eastaway lost at every stage. In the same month the Secretary of State indicated that he wished to refix the hearing of the disqualification proceedings with a view to disposing of the matter under the *Carecraft* procedure in accordance with Mr Eastaway's earlier undertaking to the court. Mr Eastaway cross-applied for a declaration that the proceedings were in breach of or incompatible with art.6 of the ECHR and for an order that they be struck out or dismissed.

8–49 Morritt V.C. reached the following conclusions on Mr Eastaway's cross-application:

(1) There was no breach of art.6. Mr Eastaway had not claimed that a fair trial was not possible and, although it was true that the proceedings had been on foot for eight-and-a-half years, most of the time that had elapsed could be attributed to the requirements of justice (the period up to the disposal of the criminal proceedings) or to the conduct of Mr Eastaway, whose various actions had been taken with a view to avoiding a fair and public hearing by an independent and impartial tribunal either within a reasonable time or at all.
(2) If, contrary to the Vice-Chancellor's view there had been a breach of art.6, Mr Eastaway had waived the breach by giving the undertaking to the court in September 1999.
(3) There were no grounds for releasing Mr Eastaway from his undertaking.

8–50 On October 23, 2001, the European Court of Human Rights considered the admissibility of an application by Mr Davies alleging that the *Blackspur* proceedings and related disqualification proceedings commenced under CDDA s.8 arising from the collapse of Atlantic Computers violated the reasonable time requirement in art.6. The complaint in relation to the s.8 proceedings was ruled inadmissible. These proceedings were treated for art.6 purposes as having commenced when the formal proceedings were issued rather than when government inspectors were appointed to produce the underlying report. The proceedings lasted two years and ten months, a period held not to be unreasonable given the admitted complexity of the case and that Mr Davies had used up the first 13 months preparing his evidence in response to that of the Secretary of State.[150] The complaint in relation to the *Blackspur* proceedings was ruled admissible.

8–51 On July 16, 2002 the European Court of Human Rights decided that the periods of delay in the *Blackspur* proceedings up to January 1998 amounted to a breach of the "reasonable time" requirement of art.6 in relation to Mr Davies.[151] The Court noted that the proceedings against Mr Davies had been on foot for approximately five-and-a-half years. It implicitly criticised the Secretary of State's initial delay in serving evidence, the time taken for the various applications and the appeal relating to this to be determined (approximately four years), the four-month delay (March-June 1994) while criminal proceedings against other defendants were running their course and the further five months taken by the Secretary of State to reach a decision whether or not to continue the disqualification proceedings after the conclusion of the criminal trial. No sums in respect of alleged pecuniary loss were awarded. Mr Davies had agreed to pay the Secretary of State's costs as part of an earlier *Carecraft* settlement but the European Court ruled that these costs were not attributable to the unreasonable length of the proceedings. Some 4,500 euros was awarded for non-pecuniary damage.

In light of this decision, it was not surprising that the European Court disagreed with the Vice-Chancellor's finding that art.6 was not breached in relation to Mr Eastaway. On July 20, 2004, it decided that the *Blackspur* proceedings against Mr Eastaway had also violated the reasonable time requirement in art.6.[152] Having pointed out that the proceedings against Mr Eastaway had lasted some three and a half years longer than those against Mr Davies, the European Court accepted that a great deal of the responsibility for that latter period of delay could be laid at the door of Mr Eastaway as it related to the pursuit of his unmeritorious application for judicial review of the Secretary of State's decision to continue the proceedings. As this application had been dealt with fairly expeditiously, no blame could be attributed to the state authorities in respect of the delay that it occasioned. However, based on the first five and a half years of the proceedings, it was difficult to distinguish the case from that of *Davies*. Accordingly, the European Court made the same award—4,500 euros compensation for non-pecuniary damage—that it had made in the *Davies* case.

8–52 Armed with the European Court's finding that the *Blackspur* proceedings had violated the reasonable time requirement, Mr Eastaway applied to the domestic courts to have the proceedings dismissed and his disqualification undertaking set

[150] European Court of Human Rights (Third Section), Final Decision as to the Admissibility of Application no. 42007/98 by Vernon John Davies against the United Kingdom, October 23, 2001.

[151] *Davies v United Kingdom* [2006] 2 B.C.L.C. 351, (2002) 35 E.H.R.R. 29. The proceedings against Mr Davies had finally been disposed of under the *Carecraft* procedure in January 1998.

[152] *Eastaway v United Kingdom* (2005) 40 E.H.R.R. 17, [2006] 2 B.C.L.C. 361.

aside.[153] His primary submission was that Morritt V.C. would (or at least should) have acceded to the original strike-out application had he not erred in ruling that there was no breach of art.6. However, the original strike-out application had proceeded on the mistaken assumption that once a breach of the reasonable time requirement had been established, the continuation of the proceedings thereafter would automatically violate the fair trial guarantee. Thus Lightman J. ruled that, whilst Morritt V.C. ought to have concluded that there had been a breach of the reasonable time requirement, it was clear in the light of the subsequent House of Lords decision in *Attorney General's Reference (No.2 of 2001)*[154] that such a breach (in the absence of additional proof that the delay had prejudiced a fair trial) did not of itself justify the striking out of the proceedings. This ruling was upheld by the Court of Appeal, Arden L.J. reasoning that it was not implicit in the European Court's finding that the proceedings had violated the reasonable time requirement that a fair trial was no longer possible.[155] The Court of Appeal also held that: (a) there was no public interest which prevented Mr Eastaway's undertaking to the court and subsequent disqualification undertaking from operating as an effective waiver of his right to a fair trial; and (b) his assertion, unsupported by detailed evidence, that the prolongation of proceedings had caused prejudice to his professional standing, was not sufficient to support the conclusion that the proceedings should be struck out.[156]

Delay by defendant in pursuing an appeal

8–53 In the unusual case of *Re Simmon Box (Diamonds) Ltd, Secretary of State for Trade and Industry v Selby*,[157] Park J. concluded that the defendant's delay in pursuing an appeal was such that the appeal process should be terminated. The judge relied essentially on six factors:

(1) The appeal was stale. It had been launched in 1998 and the disqualification order appealed against had expired in May 2001.
(2) A disqualification order is a civil matter not a criminal conviction.
(3) The appeal had been allowed to remain on foot whilst the defendant's solicitors pursued a wild goose chase for legal aid.
(4) The Treasury Solicitor had not been kept fully and fairly informed of developments.
(5) There is a public interest in appeals in disqualification proceedings being disposed of promptly.
(6) The matter itself had proceeded in an unsatisfactory fashion with new items of evidence being produced in bits and pieces.

[153] *Re Blackspur Plc (No.4), Eastaway v Secretary of State for Trade and Industry* [2006] EWHC 299 (Ch), [2006] 2 B.C.L.C. 489 affirmed [2007] EWCA Civ 425, [2008] 1 B.C.L.C. 153. The disqualification undertaking had itself been the subject of extensive proceedings: see further text from 9–27.
[154] [2004] 2 A.C. 72. See 8–43.
[155] [2004] 2 A.C. 72 at [27].
[156] [2008] 1 B.C.L.C. 153 at [46]–[47], [57].
[157] *Re Simmon Box (Diamonds) Ltd, Secretary of State for Trade and Industry v Selby*, April 15, 2002, Ch.D., unreported.

Permission to appeal against Park J.'s decision was refused by Mummery L.J. on a renewed oral application.[158]

Conclusion

8–54 For the reasons given by Morritt V.C. when dealing with Mr Eastaway in the *Blackspur* proceedings, each case is so individual that comparisons of delay (and their effect) in one case with delay in another will ultimately be of little value. Nevertheless, in terms of the arguments that are likely to be run and the likely approach of the courts, the previous cases are all that the lawyer advising his client has to go on. It seems inevitable that the courts will continue to balance the public interest in disqualification against the reasonableness or otherwise of any delays in the prosecution of proceedings and, in particular, the risk that such delays may give rise to substantial prejudice. Although failure to comply with the reasonable time requirement of art.6 amounts to a breach of the ECHR, it appears likely in the light of the recent ECHR jurisprudence that the automatic striking out of disqualification (and therefore public interest) proceedings on the basis of a breach of an art.6 right will be a wholly disproportionate response. The focus appears to be shifting to an approach premised on consideration of the appropriate remedy for the relevant breach taking into account its particular context and consequences. This may mean that, in contrast to the approach taken by Morritt V.C. in Mr Eastaway's case, the English courts will become increasingly more willing to find breaches of art.6 and to fashion a range of appropriate and proportionate procedural responses to such breaches falling short of strike out.

[158] [2002] EWCA Civ 1164.

CHAPTER 9

CIVIL DISQUALIFICATION CASES: TERMINATION WITHOUT A FULL TRIAL

INTRODUCTION

9–01 This chapter examines the principal means by which civil disqualification cases may be brought to an end without the matter proceeding to a fully contested trial. In particular, the following matters are considered:

(1) Discontinuance of disqualification proceedings by the claimant.
(2) The offer and acceptance of a disqualification undertaking under CDDA ss.7(2A) and 8(2A) either before or after the issue of proceedings for a disqualification order.
(3) The offer and acceptance of a competition disqualification undertaking under CDDA s.9B either before or after the issue of proceedings for a disqualification order under s.9A.
(4) A summary disposal of disqualification proceedings commonly referred to as a "*Carecraft*" hearing.
(5) A hearing at which the claimant's evidence is not contested.
(6) Offers to settle.

All of these matters are capable of being brought into play in the period between the issue of disqualification proceedings and trial. However, it is important to stress that undertakings (items (2) and (3) above) can also be used to dispose of cases without the need for formal court proceedings (hence the use of the term "civil disqualification cases" rather than "civil disqualification proceedings" in the chapter title). Strictly speaking, offers to settle (item (6)) do not of themselves result in the disposal of proceedings without the need for a trial. However, they are a means by which one party can attempt to agree a method of terminating or avoiding proceedings, backed up with the possibility of costs sanctions if the other party fails to react appropriately. It is accordingly convenient to deal with them in this chapter.

DISCONTINUANCE OF PROCEEDINGS

9–02 The question of the proper claimant in disqualification proceedings is considered in Chs 7 and 10. Proceedings seeking disqualification orders under CDDA ss.6 and 8 can only be brought by the Secretary of State or, in certain s.6 cases where he is so directed by the Secretary of State, by the official receiver. A pre-condition of such proceedings is that ". . . it appears to the Secretary of State . . . expedient in the public interest that a disqualification order . . . should be made" against the relevant person (CDDA ss.7(1) and 8(1)).[1] The practice of the Secretary of State is to keep the question of whether it remains expedient in the public interest to continue with such proceedings under review. Thus, if new evidence emerges relating to the defendant's conduct or there is some other change of circumstance, it is possible that the Secretary of State may form the view that it is no longer expedient in the public interest that a disqualification order should be made. In those circumstances, the Secretary of State will withdraw the proceedings. The court has confirmed that this is what the legislation requires as the following extract from Ferris J.'s judgment in *Re Carecraft Construction Co Ltd* makes clear:

> "[T]he Secretary of State can and should cause an application for a disqualification order under s.6 or s.8 to be abandoned if it ceases to appear to him that the making of a disqualification order against the [defendant] to that application is 'expedient in the public interest'. I was told that the Secretary of State does in fact act upon this principle and I have no doubt that this is so."[2]

Civil proceedings brought against a person under CDDA ss.2 to 4 may be brought by the Secretary of State, the official receiver or by the liquidator or any past or present member or creditor of the company in relation to which the person has committed or is alleged to have committed an offence or other default.[3] Although the CDDA lays down no express limitations on the power of the Secretary of State or the official receiver to commence proceedings akin to those applicable to applications under CDDA ss.6 and 8, it is suggested that in practice proceedings will only be commenced if it appears to such person expedient in the public interest that a disqualification order should be made. Equally, if it ceases to appear expedient in the public interest that such proceedings should be continued, they would doubtless be withdrawn. Subject to questions of abuse of the court's process, creditors and members can pursue what they perceive as their own interests.[4] Liquidators, who will be under costs constraints and subject to a number of duties, not least as officers of the court in the case of companies in compulsory liquidation, will not have so much freedom of action.[5]

9–03 Proceedings seeking a disqualification order under CDDA ss.6 or 8 will also need to be withdrawn where, after they have been commenced, the Secretary of State decides that it is expedient in the public interest to accept a disqualification undertaking from the defendant as a means of disposing of the case. The same

[1] See *Secretary of State for Trade and Industry v Baker (No.2)* [1999] 1 W.L.R. 1985 at 1989.

[2] [1994] 1 W.L.R. 172 at 180H–181A. To similar effect see *Re Blackspur Group Plc* [1998] 1 W.L.R. 422 at 426G–H.

[3] CDDA s.16(2).

[4] A creditor or member would have to demonstrate a legitimate interest in the relief sought: see *Re Adbury Park Estates Ltd*, June 28, 2001, Ch.D., unreported and (on the application for permission to appeal), *Re Adbury Park Estates Ltd, Juer v Lomas* [2001] EWCA Civ 1568 which follow the guidance given by the Privy Council in *Deloitte & Touche AG v Johnson* [1999] 1 W.L.R. 1605. For criticism of the *Adbury Park Estates* case see further 7–43.

[5] See further 7–42.

applies where a relevant regulator accepts a competition disqualification undertaking after proceedings have been issued under CDDA s.9A.

9–04 Under the CPR, discontinuance is dealt with in Pt 38. Under CPR r.38.2 a claimant can discontinue a claim[6] at any time and, in cases where there is more than one defendant, against all or any of the defendants. The court's permission is required in very limited circumstances, for example in the event that the court has granted an interim injunction or any party has given an undertaking to the court (CPR r.38.2(2)(a)). The procedure for discontinuing is governed by CPR r.38.3. A notice of discontinuance must be filed and a copy served on every other party to the proceedings.[7] The notice filed must state that copies have been served on every other party and, where there is more than one defendant, the notice must specify against which defendant the claim is discontinued. Discontinuance will take effect when the notice of discontinuance is served (CPR r.38.5(1)). The defendant has the right to apply within 28 days of service of the notice of discontinuance upon him to have the notice set aside (CPR r.38.4).[8] The rules do not specifically provide for circumstances in which a claimant may be able to apply to set aside a notice of discontinuance. In principle, a claimant may be able to apply to set aside such a notice[9] but the circumstances in which such an application would succeed are likely to be wholly exceptional.

9–05 Subject to the notice of discontinuance not being set aside, the proceedings will come to an end on the date of its service (CPR r.38.5(2)). This does not affect proceedings to deal with any question of costs (CPR r.38.5(3)). It should be noted that discontinuance is a voluntary act by the claimant. It is not necessary (or appropriate) for the court to "order" that the proceedings are discontinued. In theory, the court would have jurisdiction to order a claimant to discontinue or to declare that proceedings have been discontinued. It may dismiss proceedings. However, it would not itself "discontinue" them. Where, on or following discontinuance, the court makes a costs order, it is usual for the order to recite the fact of discontinuance.

9–06 Unless the court otherwise orders, a claimant who discontinues is liable for the costs incurred by a defendant on or before the date on which the notice of discontinuance was served (CPR r.38.6(1)). If a claim is discontinued after the filing of a defence by the relevant defendant, the court's permission is required before another claim can be made arising out of facts that are the same or substantially the same as those relating to the discontinued claim (CPR r.38.7). In relation to

[6] For these purposes withdrawal of an allegation is not the same as withdrawal of a claim for disqualification. There is only one claim for disqualification against each defendant however many allegations of unfit conduct there may be: *Re Mayfair Interiors (Wolverhampton) Ltd, Secretary of State for Trade and Industry v Blunt* [2005] 2 B.C.L.C. 463 at [9].

[7] As regards the need immediately to notify the listing officer where notice of discontinuance is served after the fixing of a trial date or trial window and the potential for adverse costs consequences in the event of failure so to notify, see Chancery Guide, para.6.13.

[8] On the assumption that CPR r.38.7 applies (see further text at 9–06), it may be that the most common ground for the defendant to apply prior to the CPR, namely that a discontinuance permitted an unrestricted right to commence proceedings seeking the same relief, will now be less common.

[9] See, e.g. *Sayers v Smithkline Beecham Plc* [2005] EWHC 539 (QB).

disqualification proceedings under CDDA ss.6, 8 or 9A the procedure for the commencement of new proceedings following discontinuance is governed by the Disqualification Rules and Pt 8 of the CPR, the matter proceeding by way of affidavit rather than by statement of case. By virtue of the Disqualification Practice Direction, the Pt 8 procedure also applies in relation to civil proceedings commenced under CDDA ss.2, 3 or 4. If the wording of CPR r.38.7 is taken literally, it would appear not to apply to disqualification proceedings on the basis that no statement of case called a "defence" is served. However, it seems likely that the courts would interpret the rule purposively and hold that an affidavit in answer, filed by a defendant, is a defence for the purposes of the rule. Subject to this point, there would appear to be no automatic bar to the commencement of new proceedings following discontinuance of disqualification proceedings. Assuming this to be so, in practice, a defendant would in most cases seek to raise a defence based upon the line of cases starting with *Henderson v Henderson*, and apply to strike out the new proceedings as an abuse of process.[10]

Costs on discontinuance

9–07 If disqualification proceedings are discontinued the most important question for the defendant is likely to be the incidence of costs. Except in the case of discontinuance following the acceptance of a disqualification undertaking,[11] the basic rules are the same as those applicable in ordinary civil litigation. These are as follows. If proceedings are discontinued without the court's permission and, unless an order to contrary effect is made, the claimant will have to pay the defendant's costs incurred on or before the date of service of the notice of discontinuance with the costs to be assessed on the standard basis (CPR rr.38.6(1), 44.12(1)(d)). If permission to discontinue is obtained, costs are in the discretion of the court. Equally, in cases where the court is asked to make a different costs order, it retains its general discretion as to the allocation of costs under CPR r.44.3.[12] Naturally, however, the court's discretion is to be exercised according to principle. Until recently it was fairly clear that the fact that the claimant was the Secretary of State or the official receiver would not of itself justify the discretion being exercised any differently than if the claimant was a private individual. The Secretary of State, the official receiver and a relevant regulator who commences proceedings under CDDA s.9A were treated as being in the same position as any other litigant and accordingly there were said to be no special costs rules derived from the fact that the proceedings in question are public interest proceedings. The

[10] (1843) 3 Hare 100. As regards the application of the principle in *Henderson v Henderson* in the context of disqualification proceedings see, e.g. *Re Launchexcept Ltd, Secretary of State v Tillman* [2000] 1 B.C.L.C. 36.

[11] As to which, see 9–09.

[12] See, e.g. *Re Smart-Tel (UK) Plc, Official Receiver v Doshi* [2007] B.C.C. 896 (Registrar Baister) (defendant awarded only 80% of his costs where his conduct had contributed to some extent to the official receiver's decision to pursue proceedings); *Re City Truck Group Ltd, Secretary of State for Trade and Industry v Gee* [2006] B.C.C. 384 (Registrar Baister) (costs awarded on the indemnity basis rather than the standard basis where the claimant's case had been based on unparticularised and unjustified allegations of fraud).

leading authority on the point in the disqualification context was the Court of Appeal ruling in *Re Southbourne Sheet Metal Co Ltd.*[13] However, a different line of authority was referred to more recently by the Court of Appeal in *Secretary of State For Business, Enterprise And Regulatory Reform v Amway (UK) Ltd*,[14] a public interest winding up case. The relevant line of authority consists of three cases: *R. (on the application of Gorlov) v Institute of Chartered Accountants in England and Wales*,[15] *Bradford MDC v Booth*[16] and *Baxendale-Walker v The Law Society*.[17] The Court of Appeal in *Amway (UK)* noted that these cases were cited in an editorial note in the 2008 edition of the White Book[18] in support of the following series of propositions:

> "A regulator brings proceedings in the public interest in the exercise of a public function which it is required to perform. In those circumstances the principles applicable to an award of costs differ from those in relation to private civil litigation. Absent dishonesty or a lack of good faith a costs order should not be made against such a regulator unless there is good reason to do so. The reason must be more than that the other party has succeeded."

The question of whether the practice governed by *Re Southbourne Sheet Metal Co Ltd* should be reconsidered in the light of the more recent authorities was left open, the point not having been argued. Even assuming, however, that *Southbourne Sheet Metal* remains good law, this does not mean that the claimant who discontinues will automatically have to pay the defendant's costs. If a defendant has conducted himself in such a way as to encourage the claimant to bring or continue the proceedings—for example, by withholding his true defence when he has had an opportunity to disclose it[19]—he may be deprived of the whole or part of his costs. The relevant principles have been considered by the Court of Appeal (albeit outside the disqualification context) in *RTZ Pension Property Trust Ltd v ARC Property Developments Ltd.*[20] The guidance laid down there is broadly as follows. It will be necessary to consider why the proceedings have been discontinued. If they have been discontinued in circumstances tantamount to an

[13] [1993] 1 W.L.R. 244 at 250. This accords with the position in the judicial review context where the government is usually on the receiving end of proceedings. See, e.g. *R. (on the application of Boxall) v Waltham Forest LBC* (2001) 4 C.C.L. Rep.; *R. (on the application of Scott) v Hackney LBC* [2009] EWCA Civ 217.

[14] [2009] EWCA Civ 32.

[15] [2001] EWHC 220 (Admin).

[16] (2001) 3 L.G.L.R. 8.

[17] [2007] EWCA Civ 233, [2008] 1 W.L.R. 426.

[18] Vol.I, para.44.3.8.1.

[19] The example given by Nourse L.J. in *Southbourne Sheet Metal* at 250B. See also *Re Smart-Tel (UK) Plc, Official Receiver v Doshi* [2007] B.C.C. 896 (Registrar Baister) in which the official receiver was ordered to pay 80% of the defendant's costs on discontinuance to reflect the court's finding that, while the defendant had adopted a stance that could not be described as unreasonable or unjustified, he had contributed to some degree to the official receiver's decision to pursue the proceedings.

[20] [1999] 1 All E.R. 532. See also *Re Walker Wingsail Systems Plc* [2005] EWCA Civ 247, [2006] 1 W.L.R. 2194; *RGB Resources Plc v Rastogi* [2005] EWHC 994 (Ch), [2005] 2 B.C.L.C. 592.

admission of defeat by the claimant then the normal rule as to costs will apply, unless good reason to the contrary can be shown. The normal rule is that the claimant should pay the defendant's costs. Normally, a "good reason" justifying an order that the defendant pay the claimant's costs will not be shown unless the claimant is able to demonstrate misconduct of the defence. Such misconduct will usually be some act, omission or course of conduct on the part of the defendant which is unreasonable or improper for the purposes of CPR r.44.14. To justify an order that there be "no order as to costs", depriving the defendant of his costs but without making him pay the claimant's costs, the test is less severe and is the wider one of "what is fair and just in all the circumstances". These principles apply equally in the context of civil disqualification proceedings.[21]

9–08 It is conceivable that the discontinuing claimant in disqualification proceedings could be awarded costs. A set of civil disqualification proceedings could become academic because, for example, a disqualification order which is perceived to be of no lesser period than that which would be achieved in the civil proceedings, is made against the defendant in parallel criminal proceedings under CDDA s.2. If the criminal proceedings are concerned with unrelated conduct and the claimant can show, on the basis of the filed evidence, that there is no defence to the civil proceedings, it is suggested that the court in the civil proceedings may well be prepared to order costs in favour of the discontinuing claimant, even in the absence of any misconduct on the defendant's part in the course of such proceedings. As regards applicable principles it is suggested that helpful guidance can be drawn by analogy from the cases on judicial review as well as from the *RTZ Pension Property* case considered in 9–07. Of particular relevance is the following guidance which, with appropriate modification, derives from the judgment of Scott Baker J. in *R. (on the application of Boxall) v Waltham Forest LBC*[22]:

(1) the court has power to make a costs order when the substantive proceedings have been resolved without a trial but the parties have not agreed about costs;
(2) . . . .[position where claimant legally aided];
(3) the overriding objective is to do justice between the parties without incurring unnecessary court time and consequently additional cost;
(4) at each end of the spectrum there will be cases where it is obvious which side would have won had the substantive issues been fought to a conclusion. In between, the position will, in differing degrees, be less clear. How far the court will be prepared to look into previously unresolved substantive issues will depend on the circumstances of the particular case, not least the amount of costs at stake and the conduct of the parties.
(5) in the absence of a good reason to make any other order the fall back is to make no order as to costs.[23]

[21] *Re Smart-Tel (UK) Plc, Official Receiver v Doshi* [2007] B.C.C. 896 (Registrar Baister).

[22] (2001) 4 C.C.L. Rep. at [22] subsequently approved in *R. (on the application of Scott) v Hackney LBC* [2009] EWCA Civ 217.

[23] In the discontinuance context, however, the fall back position would appear to be to order the discontinuing claimant to pay the costs.

(6) the court should take care that it does not discourage parties from settling [disqualification] proceedings for example by [the claimant] making a concession at an early stage.

9–09 The position is different where proceedings for an order under CDDA ss.6, 8 or 9A are being discontinued because the Secretary of State (or official receiver) or relevant regulator has accepted a disqualification undertaking from the defendant. In those circumstances, the general rule is that the defendant will be ordered to pay the claimant's costs (Disqualification Practice Direction, para.28.1). However, the general rule is displaced where the court considers that the circumstances are such that it should make some other order (Disqualification Practice Direction, para.28.2). The normal practice of the Secretary of State (or official receiver) is to discontinue disqualification proceedings once an undertaking has been accepted and not to tie either acceptance of the undertaking or service of a notice of discontinuance to agreement being reached on costs. If agreement as to the costs order cannot be reached, then the matter is usually placed before the appropriate judge for a determination.[24]

DISQUALIFICATION UNDERTAKINGS

9–10 Where the director consents to being disqualified under either s.6 or s.8 and the parties are able to reach agreement on the period of disqualification, it has been possible since April 2, 2001 for the director to offer, and the Secretary of State to accept, an undertaking equivalent in effect to a disqualification order as a means of disposing of the case without the involvement of the court.[25] Disqualification undertakings have become a widely used and effective method of compromising ss.6 and 8 cases as Table 1 demonstrates.[26] The law and practice in relation to disqualification undertakings under ss.6 and 8 is discussed further below. Much of that discussion is relevant to competition disqualification undertakings under s.9B, although these are addressed separately from 9–40 onwards. First it is necessary to set the scene by considering the position prior to April 2, 2001 and the forces that shaped the current regime.

[24] As regards the width of the court's discretion in relation to costs see, by analogy, *BCT Software Solutions Ltd v C Brewer & Sons Ltd* [2003] EWCA Civ 939, [2004] C.P.Rep. 2. It is suggested that it will be rare for the court to require the parties to continue disqualification litigation on the basis that they have not agreed the costs.

[25] See the Insolvency Act 2000 (Commencement No. 1 and Transitional Provisions) Order 2001 (SI 2001/766). The substantive amending provisions and other consequential amendments to the CDDA are to be found in Insolvency Act 2000 s.6 and Sch.4. The position is the same in Northern Ireland: see the Company Directors Disqualification (Northern Ireland) Order 2002 (SI 2002/3150), arts 4, 10 and 11.

[26] The data in Table 1 derives from the Insolvency Service's evaluation of the Insolvency Act 2000 available at *http://www.insolvency.gov.uk/insolvencyprofessionandlegislation/policychange/policychange.htm* [Accessed August 26, 2009] and from Insolvency Service Annual Reports available at *http://www.insolvency.gov.uk/aboutus/annualreports.htm* [Accessed August 26, 2009]. Each period (2001/02 etc) runs from April 1 to March 31 which is the Insolvency Service's financial year.

Table 1 Disqualification orders made and undertakings accepted during 2001/02 to 2007/08

Period	Orders	Undertakings	Total	%Undertakings
2001/02	548	1213	1761	68.88
2002/03	320	1274	1594	79.92
2003/04	213	1154	1367	84.42
2004/05	290	950	1240	76.61
2005/06	267	906	1173	77.24
2006/07	246	954	1200	79.50
2007/08	248	897	1145	78.34
2008/09	255	997	1252	79.63

The law prior to April 2, 2001

Carecraft disposals

9–11 Prior to April 2, 2001, the CDDA did not permit the claimant and defendant in civil disqualification proceedings to obtain a disqualification order by consent. The law as it previously stood was set out by Ferris J. in *Re Carecraft Construction Co Ltd*:

> "In disqualification proceedings . . . there is no scope for the parties to reach an agreement and then ask the court to embody their agreement in a consent order. The court itself has to be satisfied, after having regard to the prescribed matters and other facts which appear to be material, that the [director] is unfit to be concerned in the management of a company; and the court itself must decide the period of disqualification if it decides to make a disqualification order."[27]

Thus, the court was the ultimate arbiter. Before a disqualification order could be made, the court had to be satisfied that there was jurisdiction to make the order and that the period of disqualification to be imposed was appropriate on the facts of the case. The point was simply a matter of statutory interpretation of the relevant provisions in the CDDA. The lack of any mechanism for the parties to reach a settlement by consent led to the development of a procedure, sanctioned by Ferris J. in *Re Carecraft Construction Co Ltd*[28] and approved by the Court of Appeal in *Secretary of State for Trade and Industry v Rogers*,[29] whereby civil disqualification proceedings could be disposed of on a summary basis. Under the *Carecraft* procedure, the parties place a statement of agreed or non-contested facts before the court on the basis that the facts stated warrant disqualification and

[27] [1994] 1 W.L.R. 172 at 181B–D. See also *Re Blackspur Group Plc, Secretary of State for Trade and Industry v Davies* [1998] 1 W.L.R. 422 at 426H–427C; *Secretary of State for Trade and Industry v Rogers* [1996] 1 W.L.R. 1569 at 1574.

[28] [1994] 1 W.L.R. 172.

[29] [1996] 1 W.L.R. 1569.

invite the court to make a disqualification order for an agreed period or a period falling within an agreed range. The court is asked to make findings based on the agreed statement and dispose of the matter without the necessity of a full trial. The essence of the *Carecraft* procedure is that the court is not bound by the parties' agreement. Strictly speaking, the court must make its own findings based on the *Carecraft* statement. Instead of making the order as invited, the court could hold that there is no jurisdiction to make an order, or (in cases other than those brought under ss.6 or 9A) that, as a matter of discretion, it should not make a disqualification order or (in any case) that the disqualification order should be for a different period to that suggested by the parties in the *Carecraft* statement. Thus, in cases brought under s.6 or s.8, the court could hold that the conduct described in the *Carecraft* statement is of insufficient gravity to merit a finding of unfitness. Alternatively, the court might be satisfied that the agreed conduct makes the director unfit but disagree with the parties' assessment of the appropriate period of disqualification. If the court disagrees with the parties, and if the *Carecraft* statement makes no other express provision or the parties are not prepared to agree to a different course,[30] the case would have to be adjourned to a full hearing with both sides able to adduce evidence in the normal way. Before April 2, 2001 the *Carecraft* procedure was used widely in s.6 cases and had also been used to dispose of s.8 cases.[31] Although the procedure has been largely superseded by disqualification undertakings, it may still be useful, especially as a means of settling civil disqualification proceedings brought under CDDA ss.2 to 4, which in many cases[32] fall outside the scope of the statutory undertakings regime. Accordingly, it is considered further later in the chapter.

Undertakings: the old law

9–12 As long as it continued to appear expedient in the public interest that a disqualification order should be made in an individual case, the Secretary of State (or, where appropriate, the official receiver) was entitled under the old law to insist that disqualification proceedings were carried through to a full trial or a summary hearing under the *Carecraft* procedure and was not obliged to accept a defendant's undertaking (either to the Secretary of State personally or to the court) to refrain from acting in the prohibited capacities set out in CDDA s.1. In the landmark case of *Re Blackspur Group Plc, Secretary of State for Trade and Industry v Davies* ("*Blackspur-Davies*"),[33] the Court of Appeal held that the Secretary of State's decision to continue disqualification proceedings against the defendant, despite his being prepared to undertake to refrain from acting as a director or in

[30] They may, for example, have agreed to accept the disqualification period that the court was minded to impose.

[31] *Re Aldermanbury Trust Plc* [1993] B.C.C. 598 is an example of a s.8 case in which the procedure was successfully invoked.

[32] See further 9–20 below.

[33] [1998] 1 W.L.R. 422.

any other prohibited capacity, was not an abuse of the court's process.[34] The undertakings offered would have been permanent in duration. As well as encompassing the prohibitions contained in CDDA s.1 as it then stood (the primary undertaking), they also comprised the following additional undertakings: (a) to be liable for the debts and liabilities of any company incurred in the future at any time when he was acting in relation to such company in breach of the primary undertaking; (b) never to act as a trustee of a charity; (c) never to apply to vary or to be discharged from any of the other undertakings. In the court's opinion, it was not unreasonable, in the *Wednesbury* sense, for the Secretary of State to refuse this offer of undertakings on the following grounds:

(1) The function of the Secretary of State was to decide, in the public interest, whether or not disqualification proceedings should be commenced and continued. It was a decision to be made in the exercise of a wide discretion. That decision was not a decision for the court to make. It was not the court's function to determine what was or was not expedient in the public interest. The function of the court was to determine whether the conditions of s.6 were met and, if they were, to determine the appropriate period of disqualification.
(2) It had not been unfair, oppressive or an abuse of process for the proceedings to be commenced. At the time it had appeared to the Secretary of State to be expedient in the public interest to make the applications.
(3) It was not suggested that a fair trial was not possible.
(4) Notwithstanding the undertakings offered, it appeared to the Secretary of State to be expedient in the public interest to continue with the proceedings.
(5) This view was not reached on the basis that it was impossible for the Secretary of State to discontinue proceedings against a party who had offered undertakings. In other words, the Secretary of State was not acting on a mistaken view of her powers.
(6) The reason that the particular undertakings were refused on the particular facts of the case was that they did not provide the same level of protection for the public as a disqualification order made by the court. First of all, disposal in this way would not have involved any admission of facts or findings of fact by the court. The factual basis for the making of disqualification orders ensured that disqualification, premised on findings or admissions of unfitness, had a real deterrent effect, and thus protected the public in the manner

[34] The challenge was taken on private law grounds (an application for a stay of the proceedings on the grounds that continuation would be oppressive to the defendant, prejudicial to the public interest and a misuse of the court's procedure) and on public law grounds (seeking permission to proceed with judicial review on the grounds that the decision to continue with the proceedings was unreasonable in the *Wednesbury* sense: see *Associated Provincial Picture Houses Ltd v Wednesbury Corporation* [1948] 1 K.B. 223). It was effectively common ground that the outcome was the same whichever route of challenge was pursued. Normally, therefore, the correct challenge will be by way of application to stay or strike out the proceedings: see, by analogy, the later attempt by another of the *Blackspur* defendants to challenge the decision to continue disqualification proceedings against him by way of judicial review on human rights grounds: *R. (on the application of Eastaway) v Secretary of State for Trade and Industry* [2001] B.C.C. 365 (Q.B.D. and C.A.), [2000] 1 W.L.R. 2222 (H.L.).

envisaged by the CDDA. Secondly, the undertakings offered in *Blackspur-Davies* did not provide the public with the same level of protection as that afforded by a disqualification order even though they were expressed to be permanent in duration. The *Blackspur-Davies* undertakings were inferior in four respects. First, a breach of the undertaking would not trigger the criminal enforcement provisions in CDDA s.13 and contempt proceedings for breach of an undertaking were unlikely to have the same degree of deterrent effect as criminal proceedings. Secondly, there was no statutory procedure for the policing and variation of, or for the grant of permission to act under, the undertaking. Even if procedures could be devised, they would be difficult to operate in the absence of findings or admissions of fact made at the time the undertaking was given. Thirdly, the undertaking relating to debts did not provide the same degree of protection as that provided by CDDA s.15(1)(b) (it would not have operated in the same way as s.15(1)(b) so far as third parties were concerned and there were potential enforcement problems). Finally, there was no scope for the undertaking to be publicised by means of an entry in the register of disqualification orders maintained by the Secretary of State under CDDA s.18(2).

(7) The means by which protection of the public was to be achieved was embodied in a detailed legislative scheme that did not expressly provide for the disposal of proceedings on the basis of undertakings without any admission as to the factual basis of disqualification. The Secretary of State was entitled to adhere to the statutory scheme in order to promote good regulation.

9–13 As mentioned above, in *Blackspur-Davies*, the Court of Appeal did not go as far as to rule that it would never be proper for disqualification proceedings to be compromised by means of an undertaking (whether given to the court or to the Secretary of State). Thus, it was possible, in an appropriate case, for the court, with the agreement of the Secretary of State, to stay proceedings on undertakings without formally disposing of them.[35] Equally, it was open to the Secretary of State to discontinue proceedings where undertakings had been offered if he formed the view that it was no longer in the public interest to proceed to trial.[36] The sort of case where the Secretary of State was prepared to accept undertakings were those where it was no longer possible to have a fair trial (for example, because the

[35] See, e.g. *Re Homes Assured Corporation Plc* [1996] B.C.C. 297 (on which see further *EDC v United Kingdom* [1998] B.C.C. 370) and *Re Company X*, February 1, 1996, Ch.D., unreported. See also *Re Stormont Ltd, Secretary of State for Trade and Industry v Cleland* [1997] 1 B.C.L.C. 437 where the court stayed the claimant's application to commence proceedings for an order under CDDA s.6 outside the two-year period laid down by s.7(2) in the light of the defendant's undertaking. In *Cleland* Lloyd J. accepted that there were differences between the undertaking offered and the effect of a disqualification order but stated that the undertaking would achieve "the public protection aimed at by the 1986 Act". However, the decision in *Blackspur-Davies* was grounded, in part, on the holding that undertakings did not achieve the public protection that an order would achieve. Thus, while the Court of Appeal in *Blackspur-Davies* did not expressly disapprove of the actual result in *Cleland*, the two cases were not easy to reconcile.

[36] See discussion in *Re Walker Air Conditioning Ltd, Department of Economic Development v Roche*, [2000] NICh. 41 (Northern Ireland High Court).

defendant was suffering from ill health).[37] However, for the reasons given above, the Secretary of State was entitled in most cases to decline an offer of undertakings with the result that an application by the defendant for a stay on the ground that he was acting unreasonably in continuing the proceedings could easily be resisted. The prevailing view, epitomised by the decision in *Blackspur-Davies*, was that some form of legislative intervention would be required before parties could routinely dispose of civil disqualification cases by means of undertakings.

9–14 Civil disqualification proceedings brought under CDDA ss.2, 3, 4 and 10 are, on the face of it,[38] outside the scope of the statutory undertakings regime that has been in force for ss.6 and 8 cases since April 2, 2001. It is suggested that the Secretary of State or the official receiver would be entitled to refuse an offer of undertakings in such proceedings for similar reasons to those advanced in *Blackspur-Davies*. It is unclear what view the court would take in a case where the claimant is a private litigant. However, it is arguable that the same principle should apply.

The call for reform

9–15 Despite the success of the *Carecraft* procedure, support grew in the second half of the 1990s for the idea that the CDDA should be amended to enable the Secretary of State to settle disqualification cases in a way that achieved the same legal effect as a disqualification order without the court having to hear the matter at all, even on a summary basis. The first public call for reform was made by the then Vice Chancellor, Sir Richard Scott in December 1995. Introducing a Practice Direction aimed in part at streamlining the *Carecraft* procedure, he made the following recommendation:

> "Under the 1986 Act, there is no alternative but for all applications for disqualification orders, no matter what state of agreement there may be between the parties, to be processed through the court machinery and made by a judge or registrar after a court hearing. I regard this as unnecessary and avoidable. I would recommend, accordingly, that the Secretary of State give consideration to the possibility of introducing amending legislation, under which an agreement between a director and the Secretary of State, or the Official Receiver, as to the disqualification period to be applied to the director, be given the same effect as a court order imposing the disqualification period. If the director is willing to bar himself from acting as a director for a period that the Secretary of State, or Official Receiver regards as being sufficient to protect the public interest, I do not see why time and money should be expended by insistence on bringing the case before the court."[39]

[37] See *Re Homes Assured Corporation Plc* [1996] B.C.C. 297 and *Re Company X*, February 1, 1996, Ch.D., unreported. In *Homes Assured*, there was medical evidence concerning the health of the defendant, Sir Edward Du Cann, detailing both a heart condition and problems with short-term memory and powers of concentration. This evidence satisfied the judge that it would be "hazardous and difficult" to embark on a trial of several weeks' duration where the defendant would be giving evidence and acting in person.

[38] In some cases, the facts may enable a statutory disqualification undertaking to be accepted in circumstances where the statutory criteria for accepting such an undertaking are fulfilled. See further text at 9–20.

[39] *Practice Note (Chancery Division: Directors' disqualification applications)* [1996] 1 All E.R. 442 at 443.

Similar judicial recommendations were made in the course of subsequent *Carecraft* cases[40] and were echoed by the Court of Appeal in *Blackspur*.[41] There can be little doubt that this growth in judicial support for a statutory system of undertakings reflected the increasing pressure that disqualification cases were bringing to bear on court resources. In particular, there was a strong feeling that *Carecraft* was little more than a rubber-stamping exercise that did not merit the amount of court time devoted to it. Parliament responded by enacting s.6 of the Insolvency Act 2000.

The law on and after April 2, 2001

The policy behind the statutory undertakings regime

9–16 It is clear from the available parliamentary materials that, by introducing a statutory undertakings regime, the government aimed to increase the numbers of persons being disqualified but, at the same time, reduce the amount of public expenditure and court time devoted to civil disqualification proceedings. It was suggested during the parliamentary debate that undertakings would save the DTI an estimated £300,000 per annum.[42] Although there was praise for the *Carecraft* procedure, it was felt that the procedure still involved unnecessary costs such as the costs of negotiating the statement of agreed facts and attendance at court.[43] Moreover, it also necessarily involved the issue of court proceedings. The government's key objective was to reduce the time the courts spent dealing with the 90 per cent of cases in which proceedings were commenced but did not proceed to trial.[44] As discussed below, the Secretary of State is able to dispose of cases by accepting undertakings even before formal proceedings are commenced. Cases dealt with in this way are removed from the court system altogether.[45] The undertakings regime was also expected to improve regulation by enabling more directors to be processed through the system more quickly thus providing earlier

[40] See *Secretary of State for Trade and Industry v Rogers* [1996] 1 W.L.R. 1569 at 1574; *Official Receiver v Cooper* [1999] B.C.C. 115 at 119.

[41] [1998] 1 W.L.R. 422 at 429.

[42] See report of proceedings in House of Commons Standing Committee B (5th sitting, November 7, 2000). The figure of £300,000 derives from the government's regulatory impact assessment. The financial memorandum accompanying the Bill stated that there would be no net benefit to the taxpayer. This suggests that any savings would be ploughed back in with a view to achieving efficiency gains: i.e. further increases in the numbers of directors being processed on roughly the same budget.

[43] See, e.g. Trade and Industry Select Committee, Second Report, *Draft Insolvency Bill* (December 20, 1999), para.40.

[44] Parliament was told that, on the figures then available, only 10 per cent of disqualification proceedings were contested and proceeded to a full trial. Of the remainder, 30 per cent were disposed of by agreement (presumably under *Carecraft*) while 60 per cent were simply uncontested: see Hansard, H.L., text for April 4, 2000 at col. 1251; Hansard, H.C., text for October 24, 2000 at col.166.

[45] The concern for greater efficiency in the management of court resources can be seen as part of the wider attempt to streamline the administration of justice through implementation of the Woolf reforms.

protection for the public.[46] The main features of the new regime are set out below.[47]

The prohibition

9–17 A statutory undertaking is an undertaking by a person that, for the period specified in the undertaking, he or she: (a) will not be a director of a company, act as receiver of a company's property or in any way, whether directly or indirectly be concerned or take part in the promotion, formation or management of a company unless (in each case) he has the permission of the court; and (b) will not act as an insolvency practitioner (CDDA s.1A). In substance the prohibition is in the same as that under a disqualification order.[48]

Legal effect of an undertaking

9–18 An undertaking has exactly the same legal effect as a disqualification order. The scope of the prohibition, the period of disqualification that can be agreed,[49] the sanctions for breach and the provisions on registration are now the same in all respects.[50] Unlike a *Carecraft* disposal, where the *Carecraft* statement will be on the court file and, indeed in the usual course, be annexed to the disqualification order, the undertaking will not usually be filed with the court where proceedings are discontinued following the acceptance of an undertaking. Obviously, there is no room for filing an undertaking with the court where it is offered and accepted prior to the issue of proceedings. However, the Insolvency Service will normally make copies of undertakings available on request.

[46] See, e.g. "New Insolvency Act Receives Royal Assent" (DTI Press Release P/2000/808, December 1, 2000). It is as yet unclear whether these objectives have been achieved. The government's evaluation of the Insolvency Act 2000 carried out in 2005 and available at *http://www.insolvency.gov.uk/insolvencyprofessionandlegislation/policychange/policychange.htm* [Accessed on August 26, 2009] indicates: (i) a decline in the overall number of disqualifications obtained since 2001/02 (see also Table 1 in the text above); (ii) a tendency for the cost per case to rise since 2001/02 albeit that average costs over the period 2001–2004 were still lower than average costs between 1998 and 2001; and (iii) mixed results in terms of the time taken to process cases to a disqualification outcome (declining from 27.5 months in 2001/02 to 22.4 months in 2003/04 but increasing again to 25 months in 2004/05). In terms of costs and time taken the evaluation evidence does not disaggregate the cases in which undertakings were obtained from the cases in which orders were obtained. Accordingly, averages of cost and time taken to process cases will be affected in any given period by the overall length and cost of the minority of cases that resulted in an order being obtained during that period after a full trial.

[47] All statutory references hereafter are to the CDDA, as amended by the Insolvency Act 2000 (IA 2000) s.6.

[48] The contents of a disqualification undertaking are discussed further below and in Ch.12.

[49] As regards commencement of the period of disqualification see further Ch.12.

[50] The Insolvency Act 2000 made a series of amendments to the CDDA designed to meet the objections raised in the *Blackspur-Davies* case. See CDDA ss.1A(1) and 1(1) as amended by IA 2000 s.5(1) (nature of prohibition); CDDA ss.1A(1)–(2) (period of disqualification); CDDA ss.13–15, as amended by IA 2000 Sch.4 paras 8–10 (sanctions for breach of undertaking); CDDA ss.1A(1) and 17(3), as substituted by IA 2000 Sch.4 para.12 (permission to act) and CDDA s.18 as amended by IA 2000 Sch.4 para.13 (registration).

The role of the Secretary of State

9–19 The statutory undertakings regime only applies to cases where the Secretary of State considers that the conditions of CDDA ss.6 or 8 are met and that it is expedient in the public interest to accept a statutory undertaking instead of instituting or continuing with an application for a disqualification order.[51] The importance of the role of the Secretary of State was stressed both by Patten J. and Chadwick L.J. in *Re Blackspur Group Plc (No.3), Secretary of State for Trade and Industry v Eastaway ("Blackspur-Eastaway")*.[52] In that case, Patten J. rejected a submission made on behalf of Mr Eastaway that the Secretary of State's refusal to accept an undertaking without a statement of unfit conduct should result in the exercise of the court's powers under CPR r.3.1(2)(f) to stay the disqualification proceedings on the basis of the court's own view of what was unreasonable[53]:

> "It is not for the court in the exercise of some procedural discretion to dictate to the Secretary of State how he should exercise the powers conferred upon him by an Act of Parliament."[54]

Chadwick L.J. also addressed this issue in the following terms:

> "The legislation must be taken to reflect Parliament's view that the Secretary of State is in a much better position than the court to gauge what the public interest requires in relation to the regulation of directors' conduct. The courts must recognise and respect that view."[55]

9–20 Although the statutory regime does not apply in terms to civil disqualification cases under CDDA ss.2, 3, 4 and 10, in *Re Dennis Hilton Ltd*,[56] a case brought under CDDA s.4, an undertaking was offered and accepted pursuant to s.7(2A). In that case the Secretary of State considered that the conditions of s.6 were met and that it was expedient to accept the disqualification undertaking that was on offer rather than continue with the proceedings. The correctness of this approach depends on the view that the application for a disqualification order referred to in ss.7(2A) and 8(2A) encompasses any application for a disqualification order rather than being limited to an application under s.6 or 8 (as the case may be). This construction can be supported because the phrase ". . . instead of applying, or proceeding with an application, for a disqualification order" appearing in parenthesis in ss.7(2A) and 8(2A)(b) does not specifically refer to an application under ss.6 or 8. The only qualifications are that the Secretary of State must determine: (a) that the conditions in s.6(1) are satisfied and that it is expedient in the

[51] See CDDA ss.7(2A) and 8(2A).
[52] [2001] EWCA Civ 1595, [2002] 2 B.C.L.C. 263. The decision at first instance is also reported at [2002] 2 B.C.L.C. 263. Mr Eastaway was a co-defendant in the disqualification proceedings that gave rise to the *Blackspur-Davies* decision on the old law discussed above.
[53] As opposed to unreasonable in the *Wednesbury* sense.
[54] [2002] 2 B.C.L.C. 263 at 272 (para.[14] of the judgment).
[55] [2002] 2 B.C.L.C. 263 at 287 (para.[10] of the judgment). See also Chadwick L.J.'s earlier judgment in *Secretary of State for Trade and Industry v Baker (No. 2)* [1999] 1 W.L.R. 1985 at 1989.
[56] [2002] 1 B.C.L.C. 302.

public interest to accept an undertaking under s.7(2A); or (b) that a person's conduct as a director or shadow director of a company evidenced by a report, information or documents of a type specified in s.8(1A) makes him unfit and that it is expedient in the public interest to accept an undertaking under s.8(2A).

9–21 The decision to accept a statutory disqualification undertaking is exclusively a matter within the Secretary of State's administrative discretion. Hitherto, the Secretary of State's discretion had been merely prosecutorial. Civil disqualification proceedings can be commenced under ss.6 or 8 "if it appears to the Secretary of State that it is expedient in the public interest that a disqualification order should be made".[57] Under the statutory undertakings regime, the Secretary of State enjoys a similar discretion albeit, as indicated above and discussed further below, he must make an unfit conduct determination as well as applying a public interest test before a disqualification case can be disposed of exclusively by the administrative method of accepting an undertaking.

9–22 Before an undertaking can be accepted, two criteria must be satisfied. First, the Secretary of State must consider that the conditions in CDDA ss.6(1) or 8(1) (as appropriate) are satisfied. In other words, it must appear to the Secretary of State from the material available that the person giving the undertaking is or was a director and that his conduct as a director makes him unfit.[58] It follows that the question of unfit conduct is no longer exclusively a matter for the court. Secondly, the Secretary of State must consider that it is expedient in the public interest to accept an undertaking instead of applying, or proceeding with an application, for a disqualification order.[59] It is suggested that the requirement that the Secretary of State should consider it expedient in the public interest to accept a statutory disqualification undertaking rather than instituting or continuing with proceedings will not be met[60] in cases where, for example, the Secretary of State considers that proceedings would not result in a disqualification order for want of adequate evidence or because the two-year time period under s.7(2) has expired and the prospects of successfully persuading the court to grant an extension are less than 50 per cent.[61] In other words, the Secretary of State should not normally

[57] CDDA ss.7(1) and 8(1). In practice, the Secretary of State will also apply a public interest test when deciding whether or not to bring civil disqualification proceedings under CDDA ss.2–4 although not expressly enjoined to do so by the statute.

[58] In cases under CDDA s.7(2A), the relevant company must also have become insolvent.

[59] CDDA ss.7(2A) and 8(2A)(b). The fact that in an undertakings case the Secretary of State determines the question of unfit conduct and makes the public interest decision whereas in a case that proceeds to trial the court makes the former determination has led the Insolvency Service to separate the vetting and investigation of cases from the process by which cases are authorised to proceed in the public interest. Thus, there is a separate Authorisations Team within the Investigations and Enforcement Services division which makes the public interest decision on behalf of the Secretary of State before any disqualification case can proceed. See further the Insolvency Service's evaluation of the Insolvency Act 2000, *http://www.insolvency.gov.uk/insolvencyprofessionandlegislation/policychange/policychange.htm* [Accessed August 26, 2009] at para.11.

[60] For present purposes it does not matter whether this is characterised as a question of vires under the CDDA or as a question of *Wednesbury* reasonableness.

[61] The fact that the two-year period provided for under CDDA s.7(2) has expired, is not a reason of itself to prevent the Secretary of State from accepting a statutory disqualification undertaking under s.7(2A): see *Gardiner v Secretary of State for Business, Enterprise & Regulatory Reform*, February 11, 2008, Ch.D.(Birmingham District Registry), unreported (District Judge Dowling).

be able to obtain disqualification by way of statutory undertaking in circumstances where he considers that proceedings would, in fact, fail.[62]

However, the ability to accept a statutory undertaking is probably not limited to cases where the Secretary of State would, in the absence of the statutory undertakings regime, necessarily consider it expedient to issue or continue with proceedings. For example, in a case where the director is suffering from ill health,[63] the Secretary of State should be able to accept a statutory undertaking in circumstances where he would have been prepared for proceedings to be stayed on the basis of undertakings to the court. Chadwick L.J. considered this point obiter in *Blackspur-Eastaway* and took the view that it was "tolerably clear" that:

> "Parliament envisaged that cases in which the Secretary of State will decide that it is expedient in the public interest that he . . . accept a disqualification undertaking will be cases in which (absent any offer of a disqualification undertaking) he would have decided that it was expedient in the public interest that a disqualification order should be made against that person."[64]

With the exception of cases where there are special circumstances such as ill health, it is respectfully suggested that Chadwick L.J. was correct in this respect.

9–23 It should also be noted that, prior to the enactment of the Insolvency Act 2000, it was envisaged that there might be circumstances where a full hearing would be desirable even if, in theory, it were open to the Secretary of State to agree a form of undertaking and a period of disqualification. In its Second Report on the Insolvency Bill, the Select Committee on Trade and Industry observed:

> "It is also important to recognise that there will be cases where the public interest demands a public hearing, for example in the wake of some collapse where public confidence in commercial undertakings is at risk, and where justice must be seen to be done."[65]

It follows that there may be circumstances in which the Secretary of State can legitimately refuse to accept a statutory disqualification undertaking on the ground that the case is such that the issues should be ventilated in a public hearing.

9–24 It is clear that the Secretary of State's decision to refuse an undertaking and press on with proceedings is susceptible to judicial review or to an application to strike out the relevant proceedings in the normal way.[66] In cases where a statutory undertaking has been accepted, the court has power under CDDA s.8A to vary the

[62] See further the evidence given on behalf of the Insolvency Service to the Trade and Industry Select Committee: Trade and Industry Select Committee, Second Report, *Draft Insolvency Bill*, December 20, 1999, Minutes of Evidence.

[63] See, e.g. *Re Homes Assured Corporation Plc* [1996] B.C.C. 297 and discussion in 9–13.

[64] [2002] 2 B.C.L.C. 263 at [19]. Chadwick L.J. also noted that the DTI had given evidence to this effect to the Trade and Industry Select Committee.

[65] Trade and Industry Select Committee, Second Report, *Draft Insolvency Bill* (December 20, 1999), para.42.

[66] As has always been the case with the discretion to commence and/or continue proceedings: see *Blackspur-Davies* (discussed above) and *R. v Secretary of State for Trade and Industry, Ex p. Lonhro* [1992] B.C.C. 325. Given that a statutory undertaking has the same effect as a disqualification order, a decision to press ahead with proceedings where one has been offered may be more vulnerable to challenge than a similar decision made under the old law.

undertaking, by reducing the period for which it is to be in force, or to discharge the undertaking altogether.[67] By ensuring that the matter can still be reviewed by an impartial tribunal independent of the Secretary of State, s.8A serves as a guarantee of the disqualified person's due process rights under art.6 of the ECHR.

9–25 CDDA ss.7(2A) and 8(2A) are clear in providing that the Secretary of State can accept undertakings either *before* or *after* formal court proceedings have been commenced. In practice, the Secretary of State will not consider an offer of undertakings before the point at which he would ordinarily decide to bring proceedings. This is because he is required by CDDA ss.7(2A) and 8(2A) to form a view on the merits. In his evidence to the Trade and Industry Select Committee, the late Desmond Flynn, the then Inspector General and Chief Executive of the Insolvency Service, said:

> "We propose if this measure is adopted by Parliament that we will pursue our investigations in exactly the same way as we do now and take them up to the point where under our current rubric we would be issuing proceedings. At that point when we have fully worked up a case with fully displayed grounds of what we think is unfit conduct we will then do a smart side step to the right and say, 'This is our case. We think this represents a seven-year disqualification, what the court would order if we take proceedings against you. You now have the opportunity to give us an undertaking and unless that undertaking is forthcoming in more or less those terms, related to what we think is the degree of unfitness, we will proceed to court proceedings.' "[68]

Practice under the statutory undertakings regime

9–26 As the Secretary of State is required by the legislation to consider whether a director's conduct makes him unfit before accepting a statutory disqualification undertaking, the Insolvency Service continues to follow all of its usual pre-action procedures in terms of vetting and investigation and putting together its basic case. The decision is then taken whether to commence proceedings by a separate Authorisations Team which discharges the role of the Secretary of State in relation to the public interest decision under CDDA ss.7(1), 7(2A), 8(1) and 8(2A)(b). The Secretary of State is obliged by CDDA s.16(1) to give not less than ten days' notice of his intention to apply for a disqualification order.[69] His current practice is to send the director a letter before action containing a brief schedule of the unfit conduct on which he proposes to rely and an indication of the period of disqualification that he considers would be appropriate. The director is also advised in the letter before action that it is possible for him to compromise the matter by offering a disqualification undertaking, which if accepted, would have the same effect as a disqualification order. The Insolvency Service has revised its procedures to allow time between the sending out of the letter before action and the commencement of proceedings for the parties to consider a settlement. In

[67] See, e.g. *Re INS Realisations Ltd, Secretary of State for Trade and Industry v Jonkler* [2006] EWHC 135 (Ch), [2006] 1 W.L.R. 3433. Applications to vary or discharge an undertaking are discussed further in Ch.13.

[68] Trade and Industry Select Committee, Second Report, *Draft Insolvency Bill*, December 20, 1999, Minutes of Evidence, Q172.

[69] See 7–33 to 7–40.

practice, the Secretary of State will, in most cases, make available in draft or sworn form the evidence on which he intends to rely (subject to any new matters coming to light) should proceedings be commenced.[70]

The schedule of unfit conduct

9–27 In contrast to the position under the *Carecraft* procedure, it is clear that the parties are not required by the new legislation to negotiate and agree a statement of unfit conduct. Indeed, the government rejected a recommendation by the Trade and Industry Select Committee,[71] that the parties should be required to agree a statement of unfit conduct as a statutory pre-condition to the acceptance of an undertaking.[72] Thus, it is clear that the Secretary of State has the power to accept a bare undertaking simply recording, in the terms of CDDA s.1A, that for a specified period the person giving the undertaking will not act as a director etc. without the court's permission or as an insolvency practitioner. However, in practice, the Secretary of State will normally only accept an undertaking where the director is prepared to admit (or, at least, not dispute) the factual basis of the disqualification, short details of which will then be recorded in a schedule annexed to the undertaking. Within days of the statutory undertakings regime coming into force, this practice was challenged in the *Blackspur-Eastaway* case.[73]

9–28 Having previously failed in various attempts to halt the proceedings against him, including an application to have the case dismissed on human rights grounds, and having given an undertaking to the court that he would sign a *Carecraft* statement, the terms of which had already been agreed, and implement the *Carecraft* procedure,[74] Mr Eastaway indicated that he wished to take advantage of the new law by offering a statutory disqualification undertaking. Moreover, he adopted the position that his offer of a disqualification undertaking enabled him to be released from his existing undertaking to the court. However, he was not prepared to give a disqualification undertaking in the form required by the Secretary of State. In particular, he was unwilling to agree that the *Carecraft* statement[75] that he had negotiated and undertaken to sign should be annexed to or form part of the

[70] In the light of *Re Finelist Ltd, Secretary of State for Trade and Industry v Swan* [2003] EWHC 1780 (Ch), [2004] B.C.C. 877 there is now much greater emphasis on pre-action dialogue and exchange of information with a view to achieving a disposal without the need for proceedings to be issued. See further 7–31 and the Insolvency Service's evaluation of the Insolvency Act 2000, *http://www.insolvency.gov.uk/insolvencyprofessionandlegislation/policychange/policychange.htm* [Accessed August 26, 2009] at paras 10–11.

[71] Trade and Industry Select Committee, Second Report, *Draft Insolvency Bill*, December 20, 1999. Para.41 of the Second Report contained the following recommendation: "We consider that there could usefully be explicit provision for a statement of fact on which the undertaking was based to be available to the court in the event of subsequent proceedings."

[72] See the DTI's response to the Select Committee (set out in Appendix 2 to the Select Committee's Fourth Special Report). An attempt to amend the Insolvency Bill along similar lines also failed: see reference to the debate on the Insolvency Bill in the House of Commons Standing Committee referred to in *Re Blackspur Group Plc (No.3), Secretary of State for Trade and Industry v Eastaway* [2002] 2 B.C.L.C. 263 at para.[24] of Patten J.'s judgment.

[73] [2002] 2 B.C.L.C. 263.

[74] [2001] 1 B.C.L.C. 653.

[75] Subject to necessary amendments, e.g. the removal of references relevant only to a summary hearing before the court.

undertaking. This unwillingness stemmed (so it was said) from his fear of the stigma that would result from the contents of the statement and of the impact that any admissions might have on his career as an accountant. The issue before the court was whether the Secretary of State was entitled to insist on a schedule of unfit conduct containing admissions as to the factual basis of disqualification as a pre-condition to accepting an undertaking. The case proceeded on the basis that the challenge was not specific to the facts of the case in question. Accordingly, the question for the court was whether or not, as a matter of law, it was open to the Secretary of State to take the view that it was not expedient in the public interest to accept a statutory disqualification undertaking without a schedule of unfit conduct the contents of which would not thereafter be disputed for the purposes of the CDDA and other consequential purposes. Mr Eastaway's case was that CDDA s.1A only empowered the Secretary of State to accept a bare undertaking without any admission of liability, the object being to eliminate the need for, and the costs of, court proceedings. There was nothing in the CDDA (as amended) that gave the Secretary of State power to insist that a director agree to a schedule of unfit conduct before an undertaking could be accepted nor had any such requirement been imposed in regulations made under the rule-making power in CDDA s.21(2). At first instance, Patten J. rejected Mr Eastaway's application, holding that the Act confers a discretion on the Secretary of State to seek and obtain the director's agreement to a schedule of unfit conduct in an appropriate case. The judge's grounds for reaching this conclusion were as follows:

(1) To the extent that the court could take Parliamentary materials into account in construing CDDA s.7(2A),[76] they showed that the rejection of the Trade and Industry Select Committee's recommendation that the statute should require the parties to agree a statement of unfit conduct and of amendments (along similar lines) tabled during the Bill's passage, was not intended to prohibit the Secretary of State from accepting a schedule of unfit conduct as part of a statutory disqualification undertaking. Considerations of speed might make it expedient for the Secretary of State not to insist on a schedule of unfit conduct in certain cases but that did not mean that he did not have the power to agree a schedule where appropriate.[77]

[76] On which see *Pepper v Hart* [1993] A.C. 593.

[77] The Trade and Industry Select Committee had formed the view that there could usefully be express legislative provision for a statement of facts on which the undertaking was based so as to assist the court in future proceedings. It also expressed concern about lack of transparency and publicity in the absence of such a provision: Trade and Industry Select Committee, Second Report, *Draft Insolvency Bill* (December 20, 1999), para.40. In the government's view, there was a risk that the imposition of a mandatory requirement for an agreed schedule of unfit conduct could delay disqualification and increase costs in cases where the parties found difficulty in agreeing the schedule. However, the minister responsible did state that the normal practice of the Secretary of State would be to seek agreement as to the factual basis for disqualification before accepting an undertaking: Hansard, H.C., text for October 24, 2000 at cols 186–187, 192 and report of proceedings in House of Commons Standing Committee B (5th sitting, November 7, 2000). Patten J. felt able to admit the ministerial statements made in Standing Committee under *Pepper v Hart* [1993] A.C. 593 although it is clear that he would have reached the same decision without reference to that material. Thus, the parliamentary materials reveal a concern for flexibility that is consistent with the notion that the Secretary of State enjoys a discretion.

(2) In any event, the same conclusion followed from a consideration of the structure and purpose of the legislation:

(a) The Secretary of State must as a pre-condition to the acceptance of a disqualification undertaking form the view on the evidence that the conduct of the relevant director makes him unfit so as to justify disqualification. Although this is not a judicial process as such, it does require the Secretary of State to exercise a judgment and to form a conclusion on the material before him. It would be odd if Parliament, while requiring the Secretary of State to perform that exercise in order to be able to accept the undertaking, nevertheless intended that he should have no power either to agree and accept a statement of the grounds on which he concluded that unfitness had been made out or in appropriate cases to insist on such a statement before being prepared to accept an undertaking.

(b) The factual basis for the making of disqualification orders (including orders made under the *Carecraft* procedure) ensures the deterrent effect of such orders and thereby the protection of the public against those unfit to assume the role of directors. There was nothing in the CDDA (as amended) to counter the impression that Parliament had intended disqualification undertakings to have the same effect. Moreover, if the purpose of amending the CDDA was to enable directors to give disqualification undertakings without any admission of liability, it was difficult to see why, at the same time, it required the Secretary of State to be satisfied that the director's conduct made him unfit.

(c) A knowledge and understanding of the grounds on which an undertaking was accepted will be relevant on any subsequent application by the disqualified person for permission to act as a director etc. under CDDA s.17 or for the variation or discharge of the undertaking under CDDA s.8A. If the Secretary of State is able to agree a schedule of unfit conduct then this benefits both parties as the factual basis for disqualification is clearly defined and neither party will be required or allowed to contest those matters on such an application.[78] Parliament cannot have intended that, in the case of disqualification undertakings, the court could be required to decide contested issues of fitness years after the event merely for the purpose of determining whether the director in question should be allowed to return to business.

(d) The lack of any detailed regulations made under the rule-making power in CDDA s.21 prescribing the form that an undertaking should take or requiring the parties to agree a schedule of unfit conduct was also immaterial. If, as Mr Eastaway contended, the Secretary of State had no power under the primary legislation to accept undertakings coupled with an agreed schedule, it was difficult to see how such a power could be conferred by means of delegated legislation.

[78] On this point, in the context of an application for permission to act, see further *Re Morija Plc, Kluk v Secretary of State for Business, Enterprise and Regulatory Reform* [2007] EWHC 3055 (Ch), [2008] 2 B.C.L.C. 313 especially at [46].

9–29 Patten J.'s decision was upheld by the Court of Appeal. At the outset, Chadwick L.J. sought to formulate the question before the court in precise terms having regard to the wording of CDDA s.7(2A). It was clear on the statutory wording that the Secretary of State had no power to *require* a schedule of unfit conduct because he had no power to require a statutory disqualification undertaking to be offered or given. The power conferred by the Act was to *accept* an undertaking that had been offered and that power was circumscribed by the conditions in CDDA s.7(2A). It followed that the relevant question was whether it could ever be open to the Secretary of State to form the view that it would be inexpedient in the public interest to accept a bare undertaking that did not incorporate any admissions as to the factual basis of disqualification. On that question the Court of Appeal made two main points:

(1) The statute provides that the Secretary of State may accept an undertaking if it appears to him that it is expedient in the public interest that he should do so. As a matter of statutory construction, there is no fetter (other than relevance) on the matters which the Secretary of State can take into account in deciding whether to accept or refuse an undertaking. The terms of s.7(2A) could not be construed as including some qualification that prevented the Secretary of State from taking into account, when considering what is expedient in the public interest, the desirability of a schedule of unfit conduct. If Parliament had intended that the Secretary of State should not be permitted to take into account the desirability of a schedule of unfit conduct in exercising the discretion, it could have said so.
(2) The Secretary of State was not acting irrationally in agreeing a schedule of unfit conduct (or in refusing to accept an offer of an undertaking without such a schedule). It could not be shown that such a statement served no useful purpose at all. In most cases he can reasonably take the view that a schedule of unfit conduct will serve some useful purpose. A schedule containing a statement of agreed or undisputed facts will provide a useful starting point for the court on any subsequent application to vary or discharge the undertaking under s.8A or for permission to act as a director notwithstanding disqualification. Such a schedule is also likely to prove useful as the basis on which the Secretary of State can publicise the fact that a disqualification undertaking has been offered and accepted and the underlying reasons for the disqualification, thus furthering the deterrence aspects of disqualification adverted to by Lord Woolf in the *Blackspur-Davies* case.[79]

It was also submitted on Mr Eastaway's behalf that a construction of CDDA s.7(2A) which did not fetter the Secretary of State's ability to take into account the desirability of a schedule of unfit conduct was incompatible with his rights under art.6 of the ECHR. The point turned on CDDA s.20(1) which provides:

[79] [1998] 1 W.L.R. 422.

"In any proceedings (whether or not under this Act), any statement made in pursuance of a requirement imposed by or under . . . this Act, or by rules made for the purposes of this Act under the Insolvency Act may be used in evidence against any person making or concurring in making the statement."

It was argued that admissions of fact in a disqualification undertaking could be used against him by virtue of s.20(1) to his prejudice in separate proceedings brought by persons other than the Secretary of State, such as an administrator, receiver or liquidator. The Court of Appeal held that the submission was ill founded, as an admission made in a schedule of unfit conduct was not a "statement made in pursuance of any requirement imposed by or under . . ." s.7(2A) or any other provision of the CDDA. There was no *requirement* in the CDDA for a schedule of unfit conduct and it was not made under any statutory compulsion. A schedule was simply a means by which a person offering an undertaking might persuade the Secretary of State to accept it. In any event, the form of undertaking that the Secretary of State was prepared to accept did not require Mr Eastaway to make admissions. It simply required him to state that he would not dispute the matters specified in the schedule in subsequent proceedings under the CDDA and for any other purposes consequential to the giving of the undertaking. Even if such a statement was capable of falling within CDDA s.20(1), Chadwick L.J. did not see how it could infringe Mr Eastaway's art.6 rights. Laws L.J. added that for a case to be made under ECHR art.6(1) alleging inequality of arms it would be necessary to show at least that the claimant had suffered such a detriment on particular concrete facts. In other words, the claimant would need to demonstrate that the application of the relevant statute led to an actual, as opposed to a hypothetical, violation of Convention rights.

9–30 It is suggested that the reasoning in *Blackspur-Eastaway* is compelling on both philosophical and practical grounds. For reasons of efficiency, the CDDA (as amended) provides a means by which disqualification proceedings can be compromised without the need (as is the case in the *Carecraft* procedure) for the court to make findings. In this sense, it brings disqualification proceedings into line with ordinary civil litigation. However, this does not alter the fact that, in form and substance, civil disqualification proceedings under CDDA ss.6 and 8 are brought in the public interest and so raise concerns about publicity and transparent dealing. As we saw earlier, disqualification of directors is justified on a rationale of public protection (including protection through general deterrence) and, as the courts rightly emphasised, the Secretary of State is required, in deciding whether to accept an undertaking, to consider this public interest. In keeping with that rationale, there is a compelling case for saying that, in the absence of exceptional circumstances, details of the conduct forming the factual basis for disqualification should be a matter of public record. Disqualification orders and undertakings differ in terms of public accessibility. An order is made on the basis of a judgment given in open court. The reasons for the disqualification are readily accessible. Similarly, in *Carecraft* cases, a judgment is given and it is standard practice for the agreed statement of facts to be annexed to the order.[80] In the absence of an agreed schedule of unfit conduct that could be publicised by means of press release, the factual basis of a disqualification undertaking is not obviously within the public domain. If the Court of Appeal had ruled that the only course open to the Secretary of State was to accept bare undertakings without any accompanying statement of facts, the scheme of the CDDA would have been undermined. It would have been tantamount to saying that the public interest in the speedy and efficient disposal of disqualification cases outweighed the public interest in the process of disqualification itself.[81] Finally, on the philosophical point, it seems clear that the amended legislation was designed to meet the objections raised in the *Blackspur-Davies* case. It was recognised in *Blackspur-Davies* that the factual basis for making orders, whether in contested proceedings or under the *Carecraft* procedure, ensures that disqualification, based on findings or admissions of unfit conduct, protects the public through deterrence. Indeed, one of the Court of Appeal's main reasons for upholding the Secretary of State's decision to press on with the proceedings was that undertakings without some factual basis did not offer the public the same degree of protection in this respect as a disqualification order.

9–31 The decision in *Blackspur-Eastaway* also makes abundant sense on practical grounds. In any subsequent proceedings under the CDDA, the court will need to have a clear idea as to the factual basis of the original disqualification. On an application for permission to act, the critical question is whether, if permission is granted, the public will be adequately protected from the risk that the conduct that led to the applicant's disqualification could recur. In this respect, the nature and seriousness of the applicant's previous conduct is highly material.[82] The same can be said for an application under s.8A. Take, for example, a director who gives a bare undertaking for a period of eight years but without making any admissions as to the underlying conduct. What if he subsequently applies to vary the undertaking on the grounds that there are good reasons to release him from his

[80] See 9–66.

[81] The view seemingly (and dubiously) adopted by the court in *Official Receiver v Cooper* [1999] B.C.C. 115 in relation to *Carecraft* statements although it appears to be inconsistent with the reasoning in cases such as *Blackspur-Davies* and *Blackspur-Eastaway*. In *Re Tannery Developments Ltd, Official Receiver v Young*, August 2, 1999, Newcastle County Court, unreported, the court, when considering the issue of costs, held that it was not unreasonable for the Secretary of State to refuse to proceed with a proposed *Carecraft* hearing on the basis of a *Carecraft* statement that would have prevented: (a) the publicising of the factual basis of disqualification; and (b) the use of the statement for any purpose other than that of the instant hearing (so that, for example, it could not have been used in any later application for permission to act notwithstanding disqualification).

[82] See, e.g. *Re Tech Textiles Ltd, Secretary of State for Trade and Industry v Vane* [1998] 1 B.C.L.C. 259; *Re TLL Realisations Ltd* [2000] B.C.C. 998; *Re Westminster Property Management Ltd, Official Receiver v Stern (No.2)* [2001] B.C.C. 305; *Re Morija Plc, Kluk v Secretary of State for Business, Enterprise and Regulatory Reform* [2008] 2 B.C.L.C. 313 and discussion in Ch.15. Moreover, in *Blackspur-Davies*, the Court of Appeal said that even if an extra-statutory procedure for the granting of permission to act under an undertaking could be devised, it would be difficult for it to operate in the absence of findings or admissions of fact made at the time when the undertaking was given. It seems fair to assume that Parliament did not intend the operation of the statutory undertakings regime to be similarly hampered.

agreement to an eight-year disqualification and that an eight-year disqualification is excessive?[83] In formal disqualification proceedings (including those disposed of summarily under *Carecraft*) the question of the appropriate period of disqualification is a matter for the discretion of the court[84] to be determined in accordance with guidelines laid down by the Court of Appeal.[85] In exercising the discretion, the court is required to ensure that the period of disqualification reflects the gravity of the misconduct. While there are differences between this judicial discretion and the administrative discretion in CDDA ss.7(2A) and 8(2A), the court could not easily determine the appropriate period without making some reference to the original misconduct. It is therefore in the interests of efficient regulation that the parties agree and set out the factual basis of a disqualification undertaking. Otherwise, the court would be obliged to re-open the question of the director's unfitness. This would be absurd and self-defeating given that the purpose of the statutory undertakings regime is to allow the parties to settle such questions once and for all without recourse to the court. There can be little argument either with Patten J.'s conclusion on the point concerning the rule-making power in CDDA s.21(2). An alternative argument is that the CDDA (as amended) might be read as conferring a power on the Secretary of State but one that is subject to detailed rules in regulations that have not as yet been made. However, this point can be answered by reference to the *Carecraft* procedure which came about without the need for detailed rule-making in regulations.

Form of schedule of unfit conduct

9–32 In the light of the ruling in *Blackspur-Eastaway*, the Secretary of State continues to insist on a schedule of unfit conduct as a pre-condition to accepting an undertaking.[86] A copy of the draft form of undertaking currently in use is reproduced in the appendices. It is important to stress that the current practice of the Secretary of State is not to insist upon a "full-blown" *Carecraft*-style statement. In most cases the schedule will be brief and reflect some or all of the summary matters of unfit conduct set out in the Secretary of State's evidence (or draft evidence). For this reason it is unusual for matters of mitigation to be set out in the schedule unless they are of crucial importance to the specified matters of unfit conduct.[87] In *Blackspur-Eastaway*, the form of the schedule of unfit conduct was in substance a detailed *Carecraft* statement. The reason for this was that the statement had been agreed before the statutory undertakings regime came into force and, indeed, Mr Eastaway had given an undertaking to the court to sign such a statement and implement the *Carecraft* procedure based on it.

[83] On variation of undertakings generally see further *Re INS Realisations Ltd, Secretary of State for Trade and Industry v Jonkler* [2006] 1 W.L.R. 3433 and discussion in Ch.13.

[84] *Re Bradcrown Ltd, Official Receiver v Ireland* [2001] 1 B.C.L.C. 547 at 551.

[85] In *Re Sevenoaks Stationers (Retail) Ltd* [1991] Ch. 164 and *Re Westmid Packing Services Ltd* [1998] 2 All E.R. 124.

[86] *Re Morija Plc, Kluk v Secretary of State for Business, Enterprise and Regulatory Reform* [2008] 2 B.C.L.C. 313 at [8].

[87] For example, that the person was ill in hospital at the time of the relevant events. Matters of mitigation may be dealt with in a letter to the Secretary of State but will rarely be formally "accepted".

The limited nature of the schedule of unfit conduct

9–33 It is also important to note that, as was the case in *Blackspur-Eastaway*, the Secretary of State does not require the person giving the undertaking to make admissions as such, but rather to state that certain facts and matters are not disputed for certain limited purposes. The current form of wording is:

> "For the purposes solely of the CDDA and for any other purposes consequential to the giving of a disqualification undertaking, I do not dispute the following matters . . . [list]"

This should assuage the director's concerns about the use of admitted or undisputed facts in other proceedings such as civil recovery proceedings brought by an office holder under the Insolvency Act 1986. The effect of the wording in the normal case is that the matters set out in the schedule will not formally amount to "admissions" by the person giving the undertaking that can be admitted into evidence, against him, in other proceedings. Thus, matters set out in a schedule that might satisfy, say, the test for a transaction at an undervalue under s.238 of the Insolvency Act 1986 should not be capable of being relied on by a liquidator or administrator in civil recovery proceedings. First, the various matters in the schedule are expressly said to be "not disputed" (as opposed to "admitted") and secondly such matters are "not disputed" only for the limited purposes referred to in the wording: namely the CDDA and "other purposes consequential" to the giving of the undertaking. These purposes do not include civil recovery proceedings. The position is the same as regards criminal proceedings. By way of example, facts might be specified in the schedule of unfit conduct that could amount to the constituent elements of a criminal offence. However, an undertaking that follows the current wording should not be capable of being construed as a binding admission for the purposes of any subsequent criminal proceedings against the person giving it. In this respect, the intention was that a director should be no worse off than if the proceedings had been dealt with under the *Carecraft* procedure.[88] On the other hand, purposes that are consequential could include, for example, the whole gamut of "knock on" disqualifications that can flow from the making of a disqualification order[89] and subsequent applications by the disqualified person for permission to act notwithstanding disqualification[90] or for variation or discharge of an undertaking under CDDA s.8A.

9–34 In the case of a schedule of unfit conduct that discloses facts amounting to a breach of any of CDDA ss.1, 1A or 11 (i.e. acting in a prohibited capacity while disqualified), it is suggested that the current form of undertaking will not enable the contents of the schedule to be used as admissions in proceedings alleging such breach. This is on the basis that the reference to the CDDA in the phrase ". . . the CDDA or any other purposes consequential to the giving of a disqualification undertaking" is governed and informed by the words "or any other purposes

[88] Note, however, the use made of a *Carecraft* statement in the cross-examination of one defendant by a co-defendant in *R. v Hinchcliffe* [2002] EWCA Crim 837. The Court of Appeal (Criminal Division) envisaged that the director could nevertheless "explain" why he had made the "admissions".

[89] See, e.g. Charities Act 1993, s.72 and generally Ch.14.

[90] See, e.g. CDDA s.17 and Charities Act 1993 ss.72(3) (application to court), 72(4) (application to Charity Commissioners). See further *Re Morija Plc, Kluk v Secretary of State for Business, Enterprise and Regulatory Reform* [2008] 2 B.C.L.C. 313 at [10].

consequential to . . .". On this view, separate proceedings for breach of these provisions would not be "consequential" to the giving of an undertaking and hence would fall outside the purposes for which the schedule of unfit conduct might be used. In such exceptional cases, it is understood that the Insolvency Service is prepared to consider a variation to the standard wording spelling out the uses to which the schedule may be put. It is suggested that the following wording may be appropriate:

> "For the purposes solely of the CDDA and for any other purposes consequential to the giving of a disqualification undertaking, (but for the avoidance of doubt excluding any proceedings under section[s] [11][and] [13 to 15] of the CDDA based upon the matters set out in paragraph [] below), I do not dispute the following matters . . . [list]"

Period of disqualification

9–35 It is understood that the Secretary of State is prepared to consider a small discount on the period of disqualification as an incentive to early settlement. In principle, such a practice can easily be justified. The courts have accepted that a "guilty" plea may well merit a discount.[91] The same principle clearly applies to cases where an undertaking is offered at an early stage. Bearing in mind the purposes of the statutory undertakings regime, the public interest in the acceptance of undertakings may be wide enough to justify some discount in order to secure the benefits of earlier protection and the saving of cost.

Costs

9–36 Another factor that may encourage directors to agree to an undertaking is the issue of costs. The usual rule where the court makes a disqualification order in contested proceedings is that the Secretary of State is entitled to costs on the "loser pays" principle. Where proceedings have not been issued, the Secretary of State does not currently require the disqualified person to agree to pay the costs incurred in processing the case as a condition of accepting an undertaking. However, where undertakings are accepted after proceedings have been commenced, the Secretary of State will have to seek a discontinuance and as a general rule, under para.28.1 of the Disqualification Practice Direction, the disqualified person will be ordered to pay the Secretary of State's costs of the proceedings.[92] Thus, given the position on costs, directors have an incentive to settle by means of a disqualification undertaking sooner rather than later.[93]

[91] See *Re Westmid Packing Services Ltd, Secretary of State for Trade and Industry v Griffiths* [1998] 2 All E.R. 124 at 132.

[92] See 9–09.

[93] The issue of costs is controversial. One concern is that the Secretary of State can use the "loser pays" principle to browbeat a less well-resourced opponent into accepting disqualification even though there may be substantial grounds for contesting proceedings. The former Vice-Chancellor, Lord Scott, has gone so far as to suggest that the costs rules applicable in civil disqualification proceedings should be brought into line with the practice of the criminal courts: see A. Walters, "Directors' Disqualification: The Vice-Chancellor's Address to the Chancery Bar Association" (2000) 21 Co. Law. 90, a point echoed in the parliamentary debate on the Insolvency Bill: see Hansard, H.L., text for April 4, 2000 at cols 1266, 1272. It is hardly surprising that the government did not take this suggestion on board. The introduction of a "just and reasonable" test for the imposition of costs could well give directors an incentive to fight cases that would otherwise be settled, thus undermining the policy behind the statutory undertakings regime.

Commencement of undertakings

9–37 The usual practice of the Insolvency Service is to accept an offer of a disqualification undertaking if it provides that the relevant period of disqualification will begin 21 days after acceptance of the undertaking by the Secretary of State. The commencement of undertakings is considered more fully in Ch.12.

Applications to vary or discharge an undertaking

9–38 These are covered in Ch.13 which deals with procedural matters and challenges that may arise after disqualification has been imposed (whether by order or undertaking).

Applications for permission to act

9–39 Applications by a person for permission to act notwithstanding that he is subject to a disqualification undertaking are governed by CDDA s.17 (as amended). The position is the same as for disqualification orders[94] and is considered in detail in Ch.15.

COMPETITION DISQUALIFICATION UNDERTAKINGS

Law

9–40 The competition disqualification regime introduced into the CDDA by the Enterprise Act 2002 with effect from June 20, 2003[95] also creates the facility for cases to be settled by the offer and acceptance of undertakings. Section 9B(2) of the CDDA empowers the OFT or, where relevant, a specified regulator,[96] to accept a competition disqualification undertaking (as defined by s.9B(3) and (4)) from a person instead of applying for or proceeding with an application for a disqualification order against him under CDDA s.9A.[97] An undertaking can only be accepted if all of the following conditions in CDDA s.9B(1) are met:

(1) In relation to any person, the OFT or specified regulator thinks that an undertaking which is a company of which he is a director has committed or is committing a breach of competition law (as defined by CDDA s.9A(4)).
(2) The OFT or specified regulator thinks that the conduct of the person as a director makes him unfit to be concerned in the management of a company.
(3) The person offers to give the OFT or specified regulator (as the case may be) a disqualification undertaking.

[94] See, e.g. *Re Morija Plc, Kluk v Secretary of State for Business, Enterprise and Regulatory Reform* [2008] 2 B.C.L.C. 313.

[95] See the Enterprise Act 2002 (Commencement No.3, Transitional and Transitory Provisions and Savings) Order 2003 (SI 2003/1397).

[96] Meaning the Director General of Telecommunications, the Gas and Electricity Markets Authority, the Director General of Water Services, the Rail Regulator and the Civil Aviation Authority: see CDDA s.9E(2). There is a rule-making power in CDDA s.9D that enables the Secretary of State to make regulations co-ordinating the performance of functions under s.9B in the event of any overlap between these various regulators.

[97] Competition disqualification orders under CDDA s.9A are discussed generally in Ch.6.

Subject to these pre-conditions, it is clear that the OFT or specified regulator can accept a competition disqualification undertaking for up to a maximum period of 15 years either before or after the commencement of proceedings under s.9A.

9–41 The wording of CDDA s.9B(1)–(2) differs somewhat from ss.7(2A) and 8(2A), which govern acceptance of disqualification undertakings by the Secretary of State. In particular, the OFT or specified regulator is not expressly required by s.9B(2) to consider whether "it is expedient in the public interest" for it to accept a disqualification undertaking instead of applying for or proceeding with an application for a disqualification order. It is suggested, however, that the difference in wording is not material. Like the Secretary of State, the OFT or specified regulator must satisfy itself that there is a factual basis for disqualification. Furthermore, given their nature and function and having regard also to the overall purpose of the CDDA, these regulators are, in practice, bound to exercise the power in s.9B by reference to public interest criteria. As is the case with ss.7(2A) and 8(2A), the main consideration for the relevant regulator in deciding whether to accept a competition disqualification undertaking is likely to be whether the period of disqualification offered reflects the circumstances of the case and provides adequate protection for the public.[98]

9–42 A competition disqualification undertaking is defined by CDDA s.9B(3) and (4) in the following terms:

"(3) A [competition] disqualification undertaking is an undertaking by a person that for the period specified in the undertaking he will not—

(a) be a director of a company;
(b) act as a receiver of a company's property;
(c) in any way, whether directly or indirectly, be concerned or take part in the promotion, formation or management of a company;
(d) act as an insolvency practitioner.

(4) But a [competition] disqualification undertaking may provide that a prohibition falling within subsection 3(a) to (c) does not apply if the person obtains the leave of the court."

This wording (in particular, the use of the word "may" in subsection (4)) raises the issue, also considered in Ch.12, of whether the OFT or a specified regulator can accept an undertaking in a form that excludes the court's power to grant permission to act notwithstanding disqualification. The position is best described as anomalous. It is clear from CDDA s.1 that a court making a disqualification order (including a competition disqualification order under s.9A) cannot exclude the court's power to grant permission to act because a disqualification order is defined as an order that the disqualified person:

". . . shall not be a director of a company, act as a receiver of a company's property or in any way, whether directly or indirectly, be concerned or take part in the promotion,

[98] See further Office of Fair Trading, *Competition Disqualification Orders—Guidance* (May 2003) at para.3.3.

formation or management of a company unless (in each case) he has the leave of the court . . .".

CDDA s.1A defines a disqualification undertaking in identical terms. Thus, it is difficult to see why the draftsman of s.9B chose not to follow the wording of ss.1 and 1A, especially bearing in mind that the wording used creates a curious distinction between competition disqualification orders and competition disqualification undertakings. It is unlikely that it would ever be justifiable for a relevant regulator to refuse the offer of an undertaking solely on the ground that it incorporates power for the court to grant permission to act as contemplated by s.9B(4).[99]

9–43 Once the pre-conditions in CDDA s.9B(1) are met, s.9B(2) confers a broad discretion on the relevant regulator similar to that enjoyed by the Secretary of State under ss.7(2A) and 8(2A). In the light of *Blackspur-Eastaway*, it seems that it would be open to the regulator to insist on the inclusion in the undertaking of a statement of undisputed facts forming the factual basis of disqualification prior to its acceptance. The OFT guidance on the competition disqualification provisions[100] does not mention schedules of unfit conduct but, for the reasons put forward by the courts in *Blackspur-Eastaway*, it is suggested that they can and should be used.

9–44 The court has power to vary or discharge a competition disqualification undertaking under CDDA s.8A. This is dealt with further in Ch.13.

9–45 The commencement of competition disqualification undertakings and the issue of permission to act notwithstanding disqualification where the undertaking incorporates power for the court to grant permission are dealt with in Chs 12 and 15 respectively.

Practice and costs

9–46 Before proceedings for a competition disqualification order under CDDA s.9A are commenced, the relevant regulator is obliged by s.9C to give notice to the person likely to be affected by the application and give that person an opportunity to make representations.[101] The s.9C notice will contain a statement advising the recipient that it is possible for him to avoid proceedings by offering a competition disqualification undertaking.[102] Thus, practice under s.9B is broadly comparable to the Secretary of State's practice under ss.7(2A) and 8(2A) discussed at 9–26 above. The OFT has indicated that it will not usually seek to recover costs from a disqualified person where the offer of a competition disqualification undertaking is accepted prior to the commencement of proceedings. An assurance to this effect will be included in the s.9C notice.[103] As is the case with the Secretary of State, it is likely that a relevant regulator would contemplate a small reduction in the period of disqualification in the interests of an early settlement.

[99] The guidance issued by the OFT (see previous note) is silent on the point.

[100] Office of Fair Trading, *Competition Disqualification Orders—Guidance* (May 2003). See further text from 6–21.

[101] See Ch.7.

[102] Office of Fair Trading, *Competition Disqualification Orders—Guidance* (May 2003) at para.5.2.

[103] Office of Fair Trading, *Competition Disqualification Orders—Guidance* (May 2003) at para.5.2.

SUMMARY HEARINGS: THE *CARECRAFT* PROCEDURE

9–47 The summary *Carecraft* procedure was discussed earlier at 9–11 as it forms part of the background to the introduction of the statutory undertakings regime. It will be recalled that, under this procedure, a statement of agreed or undisputed facts is put before the court and the court is invited to make a disqualification order based on those facts for an agreed period or for a period falling within an agreed range. In the event that the court is not prepared to make a disqualification order as asked, and no agreement is reached that another course should be taken, the matter must proceed to a full trial. The procedure was first sanctioned by Ferris J. in *Re Carecraft Construction Co Ltd*,[104] during the course of proceedings under s.6 of the CDDA and, subject to certain modifications, was approved by the Court of Appeal in *Secretary of State for Trade and Industry v Rogers*.[105] The procedure has been adopted and utilised in proceedings under s.8 of the CDDA.[106]

9–48 As discussed above, from April 2, 2001 onwards, it has been possible for the parties to settle proceedings under CDDA ss.6 and 8 by offer and acceptance of disqualification undertakings without the need for the court to make findings and approve the settlement reached. The same is also now true of applications for the making of a competition disqualification order under CDDA s.9A. Thus, the *Carecraft* procedure, while still available, is unlikely to be much used in those forms of civil disqualification proceeding. One circumstance where it might be of utility is where it is possible to reach agreement as to the matters of unfit conduct and a band of years but not a specific period of disqualification. Another circumstance might be where the public interest requires some form of public hearing. Furthermore, there is no reason in principle why the procedure should not be adapted for use in civil disqualification proceedings under CDDA ss.2–4 and (possibly) 10 which fall outside the scope of the statutory undertakings regime. Accordingly, the law and practice that developed in *Carecraft* cases under CDDA ss.6 and 8 remains relevant and is considered below.

Carecraft statements

9–49 The practice that developed in cases under CDDA ss.6 and 8 was for an agreed document to be submitted to the court, usually referred to as "a *Carecraft* statement". This is now required by the relevant practice direction.[107] A number of points arise in relation to the contents of a *Carecraft* statement and the manner of negotiating it. The first general point is that the basis of the *Carecraft* procedure

[104] [1994] 1 W.L.R. 172.

[105] [1996] 1 W.L.R. 1569.

[106] *Re Aldermanbury Trust Ltd* [1993] B.C.C. 598.

[107] The Disqualification Practice Direction, para.13.2 requires the claimant, except where the court otherwise directs, to submit a written statement containing in respect of each defendant any material facts which are agreed or not opposed and specify in writing the period of disqualification which the parties accept is justified on the agreed or unopposed facts or the band of years or bracket (meaning the three brackets put forward by the Court of Appeal in *Re Sevenoaks Stationers (Retail) Ltd* [1991] Ch. 164)) into which they submit that the case falls.

rests on the parties having reached agreement that the matter should be put before the court on a certain basis.[108] If either party is not prepared to agree to the matter proceeding by way of the summary procedure, or to the form of the agreed document that is to be put before the court, there is little in practice that the other party can do to force the other party to accept his terms. One possibility for a defendant is to make a Pt 36 offer, or some other offer admissible into evidence, (see further below) with a view to bringing pressure to bear. It is extremely unlikely that an application for judicial review of the Secretary of State's (or official receiver's) refusal to accept an offer to deal with the proceedings on a *Carecraft* basis (or to strike out proceedings as an abuse of process in such circumstances) would succeed. Unless the parties agree jointly to ask the court to give guidance as to the terms to be included in the *Carecraft* statement, as happened exceptionally in *Official Receiver v Cooper*,[109] the court would not appear to have power at the behest of one party or of its own volition to impose "agreed" terms on the parties.

9–50 In practice, the Secretary of State and official receiver have tended to use a fairly common format for the *Carecraft* statement and have insisted on the inclusion of a number of standard clauses. The format (and the contents of the standard clauses) has changed from time to time with experience. Although a particular clause may have been referred to without disapproval by the court, or even specifically approved, it does not follow that a party could be compelled to agree to such a term in a subsequent statement.

9–51 As a starting point to negotiation, it will usually be necessary for the defendant to put forward to the claimant the allegations that he is prepared not to dispute and the period of disqualification (or band of years) that he would be prepared to accept. A defendant can offer to dispose of proceedings on a *Carecraft* basis at any time.[110] However, it is obviously in the defendant's interests to dispose of proceedings as soon as possible. Unless the offer is to dispose of the proceedings on the basis that the claimant's evidence is not contested in its entirety,[111] the Secretary of State (or official receiver) may not be prepared to agree to a *Carecraft* disposal until the defendant has filed affidavit evidence in opposition. The defendant's evidence provides a basis for the claimant to judge whether it is appropriate for certain facts not to be placed before the court on the summary

[108] In *Official Receiver v Cooper* [1999] B.C.C. 115 the court was invited to rule upon whether the *Carecraft* statement could be made expressly "without prejudice" (in other words, confidential save for the purposes of a summary disposal). However, in that case *both parties* invited the court to rule on the matter on the footing that if the qualifications proposed on behalf of the defendant were acceptable to the court, the official receiver would drop his objection to them. Conversely, if they were not acceptable to the court, it was agreed that the defendant would drop his insistence on the incorporation of a "without prejudice" term in the statement. If the parties cannot agree to submit the issue to the court in this way, it would seem that the court has no power to require the parties to include particular wording in any agreed statement, a point recognised by Jonathan Parker J. in the *Cooper* case.

[109] [1999] B.C.C. 115.

[110] In *Secretary of State for Trade and Industry v Rogers* [1996] 1 W.L.R. 1569 at 1574B, Scott V.C. may be taken as suggesting that the Secretary of State's evidence would at the least have to be disputed before the Secretary of State could "exclude" certain allegations from a *Carecraft* statement. However, on a true reading of the judgment it is submitted that this is not, in fact, what was being said.

[111] In which case, it may be more appropriate to deal with the matter on an uncontested basis, as to which see 9–68.

hearing. It also serves to focus the negotiations and reduce the risk that the parties conduct the case (by allegation and counter-allegation) in correspondence. The *Carecraft* procedure is also regulated by the Disqualification Practice Direction. In particular, the parties are required to inform the court immediately once they have decided to seek a summary disposal.

Basis of negotiations

9–52 Both parties will doubtless wish to conduct the relevant negotiations under the "without prejudice" banner. That relevant negotiations are "without prejudice" will probably be implied,[112] but it will be safer to make that basis of proceeding express. In the event that the negotiations do not mature to fruition, the relevant course of negotiations can then be kept from the court on any full trial.[113] To avoid arguments about whether and when an agreement has been reached, it may also be sensible to conduct the negotiations on the basis that a clear step needs to be taken before final agreement is reached, for example, that the negotiations are "subject to agreement of a written statement to be placed before the court, such agreement to be signified by signature of such written statement by or on behalf of both parties".

What if the court will not make the order sought?

9–53 It is clear from the authorities that, save where recourse is had to the statutory undertakings regime, *the court*, rather than the parties, is the ultimate arbiter of whether or not the pre-conditions to the making of a disqualification order are satisfied and as to the period of any disqualification order. It is therefore important that any agreed document is clear: (a) with regard to the question of precisely what the court is being invited to do and, in particular, how far the court is entitled, on the basis of the agreed or undisputed facts, to make a disqualification order for a period other than as invited by the parties; and (b) what is to happen in the event that the court is not prepared to make the disqualification order as sought. As regards the first point, it is clear that the parties; may invite the court to make a disqualification order for a specific period or for a period (to be determined by the court) within a specific band of years. The agreed statement should make clear whether, on the summary hearing, the court is restricted to making a disqualification order for the period (or within the band) as sought and, if it is not prepared to do so, that the matter must go to a full trial or whether the court is entitled to reject the period of disqualification suggested by the parties and make an order for such period as it thinks fit, based on the facts as not disputed before it. In the event that the court is constrained to refuse to make the order sought, with the result that the matter must go to a full trial, the parties will usually want

[112] See *Phipson on Evidence*, 16th edn (London: Sweet & Maxwell, 2005).

[113] The *existence* of such negotiations (as opposed to their content) might of course be a relevant factor for the court to know about, e.g. on questions of delay in prosecuting the proceedings: see, e.g. *Walker v Wilsher* (1889) L.R. 23 Q.B.D. 335.

the agreed statement to make provision for a different judge to hear the subsequent contested trial. In these circumstances, it will also be usual to provide that the statement remains confidential and that it (and its contents) cannot be used by either party at the subsequent trial or otherwise. Exceptionally, the parties might agree that, if the court is not prepared to dispose of the matter by way of a summary hearing, the same judge should go on to hear the full trial.[114] The statement might also usefully deal with what is to happen about the costs of the summary hearing (and of negotiating the *Carecraft* statement) in the event that the court refuses to make the order as sought and the matter then proceeds to a full trial.[115]

The relevant facts

9–54 In the *Carecraft* case, Ferris J. said that the court should consider not only the facts that were agreed but also the general scope of the disputed evidence.[116] The reason for this was said to be that the disputed evidence might substantially affect the seriousness of the unfit conduct if accepted. In such circumstances, Ferris J. envisaged that the court would refuse to deal with the matter as invited and would direct a full trial. Conversely, he also suggested that if, in a s.6 case, the court was not satisfied of unfitness on the basis of the agreed or unchallenged evidence, and that it considered the remaining disputed evidence would not, even if accepted, tip the scales in favour of a finding of unfit conduct it would, no doubt, dismiss the application.[117] However, this is inconsistent with the notion that the parties have complete freedom as to what facts they invite the court to act upon and that a claimant is free to conduct his case as he thinks fit and to withdraw any part of his case at any time. Accordingly, it is submitted that the court should not act as suggested by Ferris J. unless the parties have *agreed* that it is open to the court on the summary hearing to act in that way.

[114] For example, in circumstances where the *Carecraft* statement is agreed on the morning of a trial long fixed where there will, in any event, be a trial against one or more other defendants and there is no practical possibility of having the *Carecraft* hearing before a different judge and retaining the contested trial date. It may be unfair for non-Carecrafting defendants if the matter has to be adjourned to another date. Equally, it may be impracticable to "split" the trial so that there are two trials: one against the defendant who (unsuccessfully) sought a summary disposal and one against the other defendants. Although a non-Carecrafting defendant may object to the judge conducting the summary hearing first before going on to hear the full trial, in most cases it is difficult to see that the objection would have any legal merit. Any trial against more than one defendant carries with it the risk that one defendant will make admissions which are inconvenient to another defendant. It is difficult to see that it makes a difference whether the admissions in question are in the course of a full trial or at a stage immediately prior to the trial. They have even less weight if they do not bind the non-Carecrafting defendant. Moreover, the Carecrafting defendant may have agreed not to contest the facts, which is different from making formal admissions. Furthermore, if by the time of the trial an order has been made under the summary procedure against one or more defendants, that fact and the basis on which the order was made are likely to be made available to the trial judge: (a) for the purposes of explaining why a defendant is not before him; and (b) for the purposes of considering the appropriate period of disqualification if a further order is to be made as a result of the trial.

[115] The parties might, for example, agree that costs be reserved to the trial judge, or that they be costs in the disqualification proceedings.

[116] [1994] 1 W.L.R. 172 at 183G–184A.

[117] [1994] 1 W.L.R. 172 at 184A–C.

In *Secretary of State for Trade and Industry v Rogers*, the Court of Appeal held that, on a *Carecraft* hearing, the court should not consider the scope of any disputed evidence or of any matters not put forward on the summary hearing but which had formed allegations in the proceedings. It is for the Secretary of State to decide what matters to put forward or to persist in.[118] The court will not therefore be concerned with the nature and scope of any allegations or evidence not put before it as being agreed or not contested. However, it may be sensible for the *Carecraft* statement to make express provision with regard to the status of the disputed evidence in the event that a disqualification order is made (for example, should disputed matters be treated in an analogous way to criminal charges which have been left to "lie on the file" or be formally withdrawn?). If the status of the disputed facts is not expressly dealt with in the *Carecraft* statement, it is submitted that a defendant would have a strong argument that the claimant would be barred from establishing and relying on such facts in other proceedings (whether proceedings seeking permission to act notwithstanding the making of the disqualification order or later disqualification proceedings) by reason of the principle in *Henderson v Henderson*.[119] The facts in question should be set out in the *Carecraft* statement and should not incorporate evidence set out in affidavits by reference (for example, by reciting paragraph numbers in the affidavits as being not contested).[120] This minimises the risk that the judge will (incorrectly) go beyond the *Carecraft* statement[121] and also ensures that there is a single document clearly setting out the relevant facts, which the court can then append to any judgment resulting in a disqualification order (see further below) and which can be used (for example) on an application for permission to act.

9–55 It is important that the facts in question are not ambiguous. Any ambiguity will be resolved in favour of the defendant director. Thus in *Re P S Banarse & Co (Products) Ltd, Secretary of State for Trade and Industry v Banarse*,[122] the judge was faced with a statement that the defendants "knew or ought to have known" that certain accounts, circulated to third parties, were false. He was not prepared to draw the inference of secondary fact that there was dishonesty (that is, that there was actual knowledge). The *Carecraft* statement:

> ". . . should not mince its words. Either the parties are in agreement as to the facts or they are not. If not, a trial will in the long run be the appropriate course. But if they are

[118] [1996] 1 W.L.R. 1569 at 1574. It is submitted that the claimant is free to decide that certain allegations should not be put before the court on the summary hearing whether or not they are disputed and that the correct analysis is that "the Secretary of State is entitled to decide what allegations in support of the disqualification application he will put forward, or having put forward, will persist in" (at 1574D) and that he is not restricted to agreeing to a disposal only where his evidence "is disputed" (at 1574B). If this view is wrong, it would seem difficult to justify the Secretary of State ever agreeing to a *Carecraft* disposal before the defendant has filed evidence.

[119] (1843) 3 Hare 100.

[120] A course approved by Ferris J. in *Secretary of State for Trade and Industry v Shah*, April 10, 1997, Ch.D., unreported.

[121] As seems to have happened at first instance in *Re SIG Security Services Ltd, Official Receiver v Bond* [1998] B.C.C. 978.

[122] [1997] 1 B.C.L.C. 653.

in agreement, the facts should be spelled out clearly and should leave no room for need for infilling or interpretation by way of inference of secondary fact."[123]

9–56 The defendant can either admit the recited facts or admit that there is evidence supporting those facts and not contest them. To minimise the risk of admissions being used against him in other proceedings, a defendant is best advised not to contest (rather than to admit) the relevant facts. If the *Carecraft* statement is put forward on the basis that certain facts are not contested then the statement should confirm that there is evidence which supports the relevant facts asserted and, of course, this will need to be the case in fact. In the event that the parties are content to put forward further facts which are not the subject of filed affidavit evidence (for example, because further matters have come to light) then the choice is for further affidavit evidence to be filed or for express admissions to be made. If an express admission is made the defendant is best advised to make clear that the admission is for the purposes of the summary hearing only and for any purposes consequential to disqualification.[124] Indeed, even where the defendant simply does not contest the allegations, he is best advised to require wording to be inserted into the *Carecraft* statement to the effect that such course is only being followed for the purposes of disqualification.[125]

9–57 In the *Carecraft* case, Ferris J. expressly referred to the need for there to be evidence before the court which establishes unfit conduct: "a mere assertion of no evidential value, or a mere admission which is unsupported by evidence, would not by itself suffice".[126] In this context, a mere admission of unfit conduct is not enough but an admission of a primary or secondary fact or facts (such as that the company continued to trade at a time when the defendant knew that it would not avoid insolvent liquidation and that debts substantially increased during this period) would, of course, itself be evidence. Ferris J. also said that the court is not bound to accept "unchallenged or admitted facts about which it is not, in all the circumstances, satisfied".[127] It is difficult to conceive of circumstances in which the court would not be prepared to accept unchallenged or admitted facts as to what actually happened at the relevant time (as compared with, for example, an admission of mixed fact and law that the relevant conduct was such as to render the defendant unfit).

[123] [1997] 1 B.C.L.C. 653 at 658.
[124] See 9–33 in relation to disqualification undertakings.
[125] In *Secretary of State for Trade and Industry v Rogers* [1996] 1 W.L.R. 1569 the agreed statement recited that "the admissions and concessions expressly and impliedly made in this statement are made only for the purposes of facilitating a Carecraft disposal of the proceedings and are made entirely without prejudice to the defendant's rights in any other proceedings . . ." (see at 1575F–H). However, the wording that would now be used is the same as that used in disqualification undertakings where there is a schedule of unfit conduct: see 9–33.
[126] [1994] 1 W.L.R. 172 at 183F.
[127] [1994] 1 W.L.R. 172 at 183G.

Mitigation

9–58 It is usual for the claimant to insist that any mitigation is identified and set out in the *Carecraft* statement, rather than being raised at the hearing. This should avoid (or minimise) disputes as to whether certain "mitigation" raised at the summary hearing is in fact inconsistent with the agreed or non-contested facts set out in the *Carecraft* statement. An analogous situation arose in a summary hearing in the *Barings* disqualification proceedings.[128] The summary hearing was conducted on the basis that the claimant's evidence was not contested rather than under the *Carecraft* procedure. The director (Mr Broadhurst) produced a mitigation statement, passages of which were objected to on the grounds that they did not amount to mitigation but contradicted the claimant's undisputed evidence. The defendant eventually agreed that such passages should be redacted. This issue prolonged the hearing.

9–59 An important aspect of mitigation, best dealt with expressly, is that, if the facts are not "indisputable", the defendant should obtain credit for what is, in effect, a "guilty plea" and for the fact that he has recognised the error of his ways, thereby making him less of a risk to the public.[129] Thus, an agreement to the making of a disqualification order on a summary basis, may of itself be a mitigating factor on the grounds that: (a) the defendant has admitted (or not contested) that which might otherwise have taken a great deal of time and expense to prove; and (b) that it suggests that he may be less of a risk to the public than somebody who adamantly insists that any deficiencies were not his fault and that he should not be blamed for anything that went wrong.

9–60 To the extent that the claimant agrees that certain specific matters of mitigation should be put before the court, the claimant will usually be unable to agree them as facts. The formula frequently adopted is that the claimant does not accept the truth of the matters but does not object to the court having regard to such matters in disposing of the summary hearing.

The suggested period

9–61 To minimise the need for oral submission (and, in practice, to reduce the burden of preparing the agreed statement) it is preferable if a single period can be suggested to the court. The alternative is for the parties to agree that an order should be made for a period falling within a certain bracket of years. The parties then make submissions to the court as to what specific period within the suggested bracket of years is appropriate. The Disqualification Practice Direction makes clear that a period of years can be suggested which need not coincide with or even fall exclusively within one of the three brackets referred to in *Re*

[128] *Re Barings Plc, Secretary of State for Trade and Industry v Baker*, February 24, 1998, Ch.D, unreported.

[129] See *Re Westmid Packing Services Ltd, Secretary of State for Trade and Industry v Griffiths* [1998] 2 All E.R. 124 at 132 to some extent qualifying what was said by Sir Richard Scott V.C. in *Re Barings Plc, Secretary of State for Trade and Industry v Baker* [1998] B.C.C. 583 at 590.

Sevenoaks Stationers (Retail) Ltd, (that is two to five years, six to ten years and above ten years).[130]

The hearing

9–62 It is important for the judge to have an opportunity to read the papers in advance so that if he has any doubts about whether a disqualification order should be made or whether a disqualification order for the period suggested by the parties is appropriate, those doubts can be expressed as soon as possible.[131] In an extreme case he may allow the parties a brief adjournment to re-consider their positions. In the event that there remains a fundamental difference between the judge's evaluation of the statement and that of the parties, he may be obliged to adjourn the matter for a full trial.

9–63 The Disqualification Practice Direction, para.13.4 provides that, unless the court otherwise orders, a summary hearing will be held in private, although if the court is minded to make a disqualification order it will usually give judgment and make the order in public, a point reflected in para.13.5 of the Disqualification Practice Direction. The status and remaining practical significance of s.12 of the Administration of Justice Act 1960 in the light of the CPR remains unclear. However, CPR r.39.2 and the accompanying Practice Direction make clear that a private hearing is one to which the public will not be admitted without permission of the court and that the transcript of a judgment or order made in private will not be available to the public (i.e. non-parties) without permission of the court.[132] The "without prejudice" nature of the *Carecraft* process, and the fact that it is aimed at encouraging settlement by permitting "admissions" to be withdrawn if the court refuses to make the order sought by the parties, suggest strongly that summary hearings should be fully private unless and until judgment is given making the order sought by the parties.

9–64 The judge cannot be bound by any agreement of the parties as to the appropriateness of disqualification or of any suggested period and may come to the view that the relevant facts do not merit a finding of unfitness or that the conduct in question merits a different period of disqualification to that suggested by the parties.[133] However, if the parties are agreed that the facts in question justify a disqualification order, it will be unusual for the court to disagree.[134] This is no doubt in part because

[130] [1991] Ch. 164. As regards the period of disqualification and the *Sevenoaks*' brackets see further Ch.5.

[131] *Secretary of State for Trade and Industry v Rogers* [1996] 1 W.L.R. 1569 at 1575A–B.

[132] However, it appears that the proceedings can be reported in summary form unless an order is made under s.12 of the Administration of Justice Act 1960: see *Clibbery v Allan* [2002] EWCA Civ 45, [2002] Fam. 261. See also *A F Noonan (Architectural Practice) Ltd v Bournemouth and Boscombe Athletic Community Football Ltd* [2007] EWCA Civ 848, [2007] 1 W.L.R. 2614.

[133] [1996] 1 W.L.R. 1569 at 1574H–1575A: "In summary, the Carecraft procedure can effectively and without the judge's consent, limit the facts on which the judge can base his judgment as to the order that should be made; but the Carecraft procedure cannot oblige the judge to make a disqualification order and cannot bind him as to the period of disqualification to be imposed." See also at 1574E–G.

[134] [1996] 1 W.L.R. 1569 at 1574E–F.

the Secretary of State has experience in the area.[135] Equally, it will be unusual for the court to disagree with a period of disqualification agreed by the parties.[136] In considering the period of disqualification on a *Carecraft* hearing, it is suggested that the court should apply a similar practice to that of an appellate court.[137] The court should be prepared to make the order for the period sought, even if the judge would himself have imposed a slightly different period, provided that the period suggested by the parties is within the reasonable range of what a reasonable court would impose on the basis of the agreed facts. Given that the fixing of the period of disqualification is discretionary and different persons may quite legitimately consider that different periods of disqualification are appropriate on the same facts, it would be undesirable and would act as a disincentive to *Carecraft* disposals,[138] if the court was to refuse to make an order for the period sought by the parties on the basis that the judge considered that a period of say one year's difference should be imposed. The suggested approach may in fact be applied without being articulated. However, some support for it can be found, by way of analogy, in the judgment of Ferris J. in the *Carecraft* case itself. In *Carecraft*, Ferris J. suggested that the court should consider the scope of the disputed evidence to see whether or not the resolution of the dispute might substantially affect the period of disqualification. As discussed above, that approach was held to be wrong in the *Rogers* case but it is interesting to note how it was applied in *Carecraft*. On the facts in the *Carecraft* case, Ferris J. considered that a resolution of the disputed evidence might affect the period of disqualification otherwise to be imposed by a year or so.[139] Nevertheless, he did not think that this was sufficient to require him to refuse to make the order sought and direct that the matter come on for a full trial. In effect, his view was that it was not necessary for him to refuse to make an order for the period sought where the period that might have been imposed in other circumstances would have been slightly different. The suggested approach is arguably inconsistent with that adopted by Sir Richard Scott V.C. in *Re Dawes and Henderson (Agencies) Ltd, Secretary of State for Trade and Industry v Coulthard*[140] where, on a *Carecraft* hearing, he refused to make a disqualification order for a period of five years, as sought, but was prepared to make an order of four years (which course the parties eventually agreed to). Apart from the actual language of the judgment in the *Rogers* case, the facts in that case also support the suggested approach. In *Rogers*, the trial judge was found wrongly to have made a finding of dishonesty. This finding was

[135] For a fully-contested case where the court would have imposed a longer period of disqualification had it not been for the lower period suggested by the Secretary of State and in which some emphasis was placed on the Secretary of State's status as the regulator responsible for companies see *Re Continental Assurance Co of London Plc* [1997] 1 B.C.L.C. 48.

[136] *Secretary of State for Trade and Industry v Rogers* [1996] 1 W.L.R. 1569 at 1574F–G.

[137] See *Re Copecrest Ltd, Secretary of State v McTighe (No.2)* [1996] 2 B.C.L.C. 477 at 485–486 and *Re Westmid Packing Services Ltd, Secretary of State v Griffiths* [1998] 2 All E.R. 124 at 130.

[138] Or, at the least, to a disposal on the basis of putting to the court a fixed period of disqualification as opposed to a bracket of years thereby protracting the summary hearing by making it to some degree contentious as between the parties.

[139] [1994] 1 W.L.R. 172 at 185B–E.

[140] February 4, 1997, Ch.D., unreported.

overturned by the Court of Appeal. Nevertheless, the Court of Appeal imposed the same period of disqualification as the trial judge (and as that sought by the parties at first instance).

9–65 In reaching his decision the judge cannot travel outside the terms of the *Carecraft* statement. The court cannot make findings based on affidavit evidence not contained within the *Carecraft* statement or findings which go beyond those expressed in the statement. Thus, in the *Rogers* case, there was nothing in the *Carecraft* statement to say that the director in question had acted dishonestly. However, the judge conducting the summary hearing made a finding of dishonesty. The Court of Appeal found that he had not been entitled to make such a finding as dishonesty formed no part of the agreed (or non-disputed) facts.[141] In *Re P S Banarse & Co (Products) Ltd, Secretary of State for Trade and Industry v Banarse*,[142] the court reaffirmed the proposition that the court could not be asked to draw inferences of secondary fact from the primary facts agreed.

9–66 It is convenient if the judge annexes the *Carecraft* statement to his judgment, or incorporates it within his judgment.[143] This saves judicial time otherwise spent in paraphrasing the statement and avoids the risk of inaccuracies in such a précis. The Disqualification Practice Direction, para.13.5 requires the written statement to be annexed to the disqualification order, unless the court otherwise orders. It is suggested that it will be a rare case in which an order to the contrary will be made. The general public interest in the proper administration of justice, as well as the public interest in the making of disqualification orders on the basis of publicly-found facts, both point strongly to the *Carecraft* statement being publicly available once it forms the basis of a judgment disqualifying a person.[144] Although it relates to practice under the statutory undertakings regime, the Court of Appeal decision in *Blackspur-Eastaway* provides further support for the view that the factual basis of disqualification should be fully transparent.[145] In addition, if permission to act is granted subsequently on terms that the original order is publicised by service, then annexing the *Carecraft* statement to the order provides a convenient mechanism for publicising both the order and the reasons for the disqualification. If the *Carecraft* statement is incorporated in or annexed to the judgment and such statement is very substantial this may provide a reason to make an order to the contrary.

Status of the Carecraft statement after the making of an order

9–67 To the extent that the relevant judgment annexes or recites the *Carecraft* statement or the statement is annexed to the disqualification order, it will obviously be in the

[141] [1996] 1 W.L.R. 1569 at 1578E–1579A.

[142] [1997] 1 B.C.L.C. 653.

[143] A course suggested in *Re BPR Ltd* [1998] B.C.C. 259.

[144] See the following passage in *Blackspur-Davies* [1998] 1 W.L.R. 422 at 433H:

> "The factual basis for making orders . . . ensures that disqualification orders . . . have a real deterrent effect and, in that way, afford public protection against the menace of persons unfit to enjoy the privileges of limited liability".

[145] See 9–26 to 9–31.

public domain. However, in some cases only a very short judgment is given and the statement is not incorporated or annexed. Some formulations have been adopted in *Carecraft* statements which suggest that the statement can or should remain confidential and unavailable to the public, even where a disqualification order is made on the basis of the agreed (or non-disputed) facts contained in it. Where the court finds expressly that certain facts are not made out or that the conduct disclosed is beyond criticism or falls outside the factual matrix of conduct which, taken cumulatively, would justify the making of a disqualification order, there may be an argument for keeping those facts confidential. However, it seems extremely unlikely that, absent special circumstances,[146] access to the statement would not be given by the court were a third party to seek it. The court is usually obliged to give reasons for its judgments. The statement contains the relevant facts on the basis of which the court makes the disqualification order. As such, it is suggested that when a disqualification order is made following the *Carecraft* procedure, the public are entitled to be given access to the *Carecraft* statement and that the parties do not have the ability to prevent such access.[147] Accordingly, it will be rare for the court to direct that the *Carecraft* statement should not be annexed to the disqualification order.

UNCONTESTED EVIDENCE

9–68 It is always open to a defendant not to contest the evidence which is put before the court. There is no obligation on a defendant to file evidence. In those circumstances, it would remain open to the defendant to dispute jurisdiction (for example, on the basis that the evidence did not disclose conduct such as to make the defendant unfit within the meaning of s.6). Alternatively, the defendant could accept that jurisdiction to make a disqualification order was established, but dispute the relevant period for which the order should be made.

9–69 Even after evidence is filed by a defendant it is open to him to seek to withdraw it so that the case proceeds on the basis of the claimant's evidence alone. However, once filed, evidence cannot simply be withdrawn without agreement. A claimant may wish to rely upon evidence filed by a defendant as furthering the claimant's case. The filing of an affidavit by one party may entitle the other party to rely on such evidence and to cross-examine the deponent.[148] If the claimant's evidence is not contested in its entirety it may be appropriate to deal with the matter by way of a summary hearing or it may be more appropriate simply to deal with the matter at trial.

[146] For example, prejudice to a parallel criminal process might justify a statement temporarily being kept private.

[147] See, by analogy, *FAI General Insurance Co Ltd v Godfrey Merrett Robertson Ltd* [1999] C.L.C. 566.

[148] See discussion in *Re Rex Williams Leisure Plc, Secretary of State for Trade and Industry v Warren* [1994] Ch. 1 at 6G to 10E (especially at 9D) and 350 (Court of Appeal) at 360E to 364B. It is to be noted that the procedural difference between affidavits (which could not be "withdrawn" once filed), and witness statements in the High Court (which had to be served but could not be relied on by any other party until the witness was called) that existed prior to the CPR (see RSC Ord.38, r.2A(4)) has now disappeared: see CPR r.32.5(5).

9–70 There is no reason why the parties cannot agree a modification of the *Carecraft* procedure in circumstances where the defendant is not contesting the claimant's evidence. A statement could be agreed and the court invited to deal with the matter by way of a summary hearing. The statement could record that the claimant's evidence was not disputed for the purposes only of a summary disposal of the case (reserving the defendant's rights in other proceedings), and also set out agreement as to one or more matters normally covered by a *Carecraft* statement (for example, that the case be put to the court on the agreed basis that the court has jurisdiction to make and should make a disqualification order and that the court be invited to make an order of a specific period or within a specific bracket having regard to the facts and any stated matters of mitigation).

OFFERS "TO SETTLE" INCLUDING CPR PT 36 AND *CALDERBANK* OFFERS

9–71 The topic of settlement of civil proceedings is one that itself is capable of forming the contents of a book.[149] This section does not deal with the subject in detail but highlights some points that arise in the civil disqualification context. The significance and importance of offers to compromise civil proceedings has probably increased in the light of the CPR and, in particular, the provisions of CPR r.1.3 (the duty on the parties to help in furthering the overriding objective), CPR Pt 36 (offers to settle) and CPR r.44.3(4), (5) (the requirement that the court take into account the parties' conduct and any admissible offers to settle in determining what, if any, costs orders to make). In the civil disqualification sphere the introduction and operation to date of the statutory disqualification undertakings regime has also had an impact on the overall landscape. As explained earlier in this chapter, the ability of the Secretary of State to compromise civil disqualification proceedings was extremely limited prior to the introduction of the statutory undertakings regime.

9–72 The rules and practice governing offers in civil litigation are contained primarily in CPR Pt 36 and CPR Pt 44. These provisions are applicable to civil disqualification proceedings brought pursuant to CDDA ss.6 and 8 by virtue of r.2 of the Disqualification Rules. They are applicable to other civil disqualification proceedings because they apply to all civil litigation subject to any relevant provision to the contrary, and there is none. Although the application of these rules to civil disqualification proceedings may give rise to points that are particular to disqualification proceedings and may be shaped by the nature of these proceedings, there is no reason to think that the rules themselves do not apply.[150]

9–73 If a defendant wishes to dispose of actual or proposed proceedings on a certain basis, for example, by offering a disqualification undertaking for a specified period of years, but the claimant will not agree, what can he do? One possibility

[149] See D. Foskett, *The Law and Practice of Compromise*, 6th edn (Sweet & Maxwell, 2005).
[150] See, by analogy, *Re Southbourne Sheet Metal Co Ltd* [1993] 1 W.L.R. 244.

is to make what, prior to the CPR, was commonly referred to as a *Calderbank* offer[151]: i.e. an offer "without prejudice except as to costs". In broad terms, the terms of such an offer cannot be referred to at trial, other than with regard to the question of costs.[152] If, after trial, the claimant achieves less than what has been offered then, although he may have succeeded at trial, he may be deprived of all or part of the costs which would otherwise have been ordered in his favour. Similar consequences flow from an offer defined by the CPR as "a Part 36 Offer".

9–74 In the event that an offer is not accepted, there are therefore two separate matters that may be highly relevant. The first is the extent to which, and time at which (if at all), the offer will be admissible in evidence. The second is the costs consequences that may flow from an offer having been made. So long as the dispute is unresolved, the party making an offer will often wish to keep the terms of the offer out of the public domain and, more significantly, from the court conducting the trial, as knowledge of the terms could potentially affect the court's view of the merits.

Part 36 Offers

9–75 CPR Pt 36 provides a specific regime for offers to settle. Such offers, if made in accordance with the terms of Pt 36, carry certain consequences. However, there is no prohibition against making an offer to settle in any form that a party chooses.[153] The present CPR Pt 36 came into force on April 6, 2007. Formerly a Pt 36 Offer could only be made after proceedings had been issued. The upshot was that before the issue of proceedings, a potential defendant wishing to encourage settlement would have had to resort to an offer "without prejudice except as to costs" with a view to obtaining equivalent protection. The current position is that a Pt 36 Offer may be made at any time, including before the commencement of proceedings and in appeal proceedings.[154] To constitute a Pt 36 Offer the offer must be one capable of being accepted, and given effect to, by the other party. This seems to be implicit in CPR Pt 36. It would therefore appear that an offer by a defendant to agree to a disqualification order "by consent" (as opposed to the offer of a disqualification undertaking) is not itself capable of being a Pt 36 Offer. The reason for this is that there is no power to "agree" disqualification orders and for such orders to be made by consent. However, this point is a limited one for the following reasons. The Secretary of State now has power to accept disqualification undertakings. The court, in determining what costs order to make, would have to take into account the Secretary

[151] *Calderbank v Calderbank* [1976] Fam. 93.

[152] The fact, rather than the terms, of such an offer may be admissible where relevant, for example, to explain why certain procedural delays have taken place: see, e.g. *Family Housing Association (Manchester) Ltd v Michael Hyde & Partners (a firm)* [1993] 1 W.L.R. 354. In exceptional circumstances the terms of such an offer may be admissible in evidence, for example, where the "without prejudice" protection is being misused. For judicial discussion (also in the non-disqualification sphere) see, by way of example, *Unilever Plc v The Proctor and Gamble Co* [2000] 1 W.L.R. 2436; *Savings & Investment Bank Ltd (in liquidation) v Fincken* [2003] EWCA Civ 1630, [2004] 1 W.L.R. 667; *Berry Trade Ltd v Moussavi* [2003] EWCA Civ 715.

[153] CPR r.36.1(2).

[154] CPR r.36.3(2).

of State's conduct in the proceedings and would normally expect the Secretary of State to advise the defendant of the statutory undertaking route in the event that he sought to compromise by offering a "consent" order. In other words, a bare refusal of an offer of a disqualification order by consent could amount to unreasonable conduct by the claimant if the claimant did not point out, or had not already pointed out, other possibilities, such as *Carecraft* disposal, uncontested disposal or disqualification undertaking.[155]

9–76 For present purposes the key formal requirements of a Pt 36 Offer are that[156]:

(1) It must be in writing.[157]
(2) It must state on its face that it is intended to have the consequences of Pt 36.
(3) It must state whether it relates to the whole of the claim or part of it or to an issue that arises in it and if so to which part or issue.
(4) It must state the times and conditions that must be met if it is to be accepted. There are different regimes depending on whether the offer is made less than 21 days before trial or not. Normally the offer must specify a period of not less than 21 days within which the defendant will be liable for the claimant's costs in accordance with r.36.10 if the offer is accepted. This rule does not apply if the offer is made less than 21 days before the start of the trial.

CPR r.36.7 makes provision for when a Pt 36 Offer is treated as being made. Essentially the time of service is the relevant time at which an offer is treated as being made or notice of a change in the terms of an offer becomes effective. For these purposes where the other party is acting by a legal representative, service must be on the legal representative.[158] There are also rules about the circumstances in which a Pt 36 offer may be withdrawn or its terms changed to be less advantageous to the offeree. Within certain time limits these matters are regulated by the need to obtain court permission.[159] A key concept is the "relevant time" being the period within which the defendant will be liable for the claimant's costs in accordance with r.36.10 if the offer is accepted.

It should be noted that if failure to comply with a formality prevents the offer from being a Pt 36 Offer this does not necessarily mean that the offer will not provide equivalent protection to the person making it. CPR r.36.1(2) formerly provided that the court could order that an offer not made in accordance with CPR Pt 36 should nevertheless have the consequences specified in the rules.[160] The

[155] In fact, the letter normally sent out prior to the issue of disqualification proceedings in s.6 cases in order to comply with the ten day notice requirement in CDDA s.16(1) invariably draws attention to the possibilities of disposal of the matter: see 9–26.

[156] CPR r.36.2(2).

[157] Form N242A may be used: CPR Pt 36 PD 36A para.1.1.

[158] CPR Pt 36 PD 36A para.1.2.

[159] CPR r.36.3(5)–(7).

[160] See, e.g. *Mitchell v James* [2002] EWCA Civ 997, [2004] 1 W.L.R. 158. This case is an example of the court waiving a defect in an offer that purported to be a Pt 36 Offer, the defect preventing it being such. However, there is presumably the possibility that even an offer which the maker does not specify as being a Pt 36 Offer may, on the facts, result in a costs order in the terms described in CPR r.36.10.

wording of r.36.1(2) has since changed. However, so far as costs consequences are concerned, the court retains a discretion in all cases and must take into account payments into court or admissible offers to settle whether these are Pt 36 Offers or not together with the parties' conduct and the outcome of the litigation.[161]

Acceptance of a Pt 36 Offer and its effect

9–77 A Pt 36 Offer is accepted by serving written notice of the acceptance on the offeror. Broadly speaking an offer may be accepted at any time (whether or not the offeree has subsequently made a different offer). For present purposes, the main exceptions to this general rule are that an offer may not be accepted[162]:

(1) after the offeror has served notice of withdrawal on the offeree;
(2) unless the court gives permission, after the start of a trial;
(3) unless the parties agree, after the end of trial but before judgment is handed down.

Once accepted, the claim will be stayed on the terms of the offer. Such stay does not affect the power of the court to enforce the terms of the Pt 36 Offer or to deal with any question of costs.[163] Once a Pt 36 offer is accepted within the relevant period, the costs consequences are usually that the claimant is entitled to his costs of the proceedings up to the date on which notice of the acceptance was served on the offeror. Unless otherwise agreed these costs will be assessed on the standard basis.[164] However, where the offer was made less than 21 days before the start of the trial or it is accepted after expiry of the relevant period, in the absence of agreement of the parties the court will determine what order to make as to costs. Where the offer is accepted after expiry of the relevant period the general rule is that the claimant will be entitled to his costs up to the date on which the relevant period expired and the offeree will be liable for the offeror's costs for the period from the date of expiry of the relevant period to the date of acceptance.[165]

Admissibility of offers

9–78 A defined consequence of a Pt 36 Offer is that the offer is to be treated as being "without prejudice except as to costs".[166] As explained, this means that the offer will usually be admissible in evidence when issues of costs are dealt with but not otherwise. As a practical matter, it may well be worth spelling out expressly that an offer purporting to be a Pt 36 Offer is in fact made "without prejudice except as to costs". This is because of the risk that the offer is not, in fact, a Pt 36 Offer

[161] CPR r.44.3(4).
[162] CPR r.36.9.
[163] CPR r.36.11.
[164] CPR r.36.10.
[165] CPR r.36.10.
[166] CPR r.36.13(1).

with the result that, technically, CPR r.36.13 would not apply (except by inference). As we have seen, even if an offer is not a Pt 36 Offer, the court may still take it into account when considering costs questions, provided that the terms of the offer are admissible into evidence at that point.[167]

9–79 In addition to a Pt 36 Offer a party has the option of making an offer which may be "open", "without prejudice" or "without prejudice except as to costs". "Without prejudice" offers will usually not be admissible into evidence, even on costs issues. "Open offers" will be admissible at all stages of the proceedings.

Costs consequences of offers

9–80 The costs consequences of a Pt 36 Offer are similar to the costs consequences of an offer made "without prejudice except as to costs" in the days before the CPR. The position if the offer is accepted has been dealt with in 9–77 above. If the offer is not accepted, then it is necessary to compare the offer with the judgment obtained. CPR r.36.14 provides that if at trial the claimant fails to obtain a judgment which is more advantageous than the defendant's Pt 36 offer then, unless it considers it unjust to do so, the court will order the claimant to pay any costs incurred by the defendant after the relevant date. Moreover, the current default position is that the defendant is also entitled to interest on such costs.[168] However, the court must consider all the circumstances in deciding whether such a costs order would be unjust including a number of prescribed matters.[169] It is important to note that there is always an overriding discretion in the court so that the costs order prescribed in certain circumstances will not be made if it would be unjust to make the order. Thus, in many cases, the Pt 36 Offer regime is probably not so very different in its costs consequences from any other offer to compromise. It should also be noted that it is open to a claimant to make a Pt 36 offer and that if the judgment against the defendant is at least as advantageous to the claimant as the proposals contained in the Pt 36 offer, then the presumption is that an order for costs will be made, unless the court considers it unjust to do so, whereby the claimant will receive costs on the indemnity basis from the date on which the relevant period expired with interest on those costs.

Clarification of offers

9–81 CPR r.36.8 provides a mechanism for parties to clarify the terms of Pt 36 Offers and, under this rule, if the requested clarification is not forthcoming in accordance with the prescribed timetable then, unless the trial has started, the party receiving the offer can seek an order from the court that the offer be clarified. The request must be made within seven days of the offer being made and the clarification must be provided within seven days of receipt of the request for clarification. It is suggested that even if the offer is not technically a Pt 36 Offer it will be treated as a Pt 36 Offer for the purposes of this rule if that is what it purports to

[167] See CPR rr.36.1(2) and 44.3(4)(c).
[168] CPR r.36.14(2).
[169] CPR r.36.14(4).

be. The rule gives rise to an interesting possibility that a counter offer to a Pt 36 Offer, made within the context of ongoing negotiations, might itself be treated as a Pt 36 Offer. Although the court has no power to order the clarification of offers that are not Pt 36 Offers,[170] parties will be constrained in practice to clarify offers that may be admissible into evidence because of the court's duty, in determining appropriate costs orders under CPR Pt 44, to have regard to the parties' conduct.

The disqualification regime: when is a defendant's offer "beaten" by the claimant?

9–82 What if a director offers a disqualification undertaking for, say, a period of four years? In theory, if the Secretary of State refused to accept the undertaking and the court imposed a disqualification order of only two years after a contested trial, the Secretary of State would be at risk as to costs having failed to "beat" the offer. However, it is suggested that the test of whether an offer has been "beaten" or (in the language of CPR r.36.14 the claimant has obtained a judgment that is "more advantageous" than the offer) is not capable of being answered by a simple comparison of the period of disqualification offered with the period set out in any final order after trial.

Offers of disqualification without any underlying factual basis

9–83 In most cases the claimant will not agree to a disqualification (whether by order or undertaking) unless the grounds for such disqualification are determined by the court (whether on an unopposed basis, a *Carecraft* basis or following a trial) or, in the case of a disqualification undertaking, set out in a schedule to the undertaking. If an offer is one of a period of disqualification bereft of any underlying factual basis and disqualification is achieved by court order, the order will be based on findings of fact that are publicly accessible. In relation to undertakings, the courts have accepted in principle that it is important for disqualification to be based on matters of unfit conduct either determined by the court or agreed between the parties (usually on the basis that the defendant does not dispute them). Moreover, the authorities suggest that the Secretary of State will generally be acting lawfully and in a *Wednesbury* reasonable manner when he insists that the factual basis of disqualification should be clear and transparent in a given case.[171] It is suggested that the relevant judgment (given with reasons) is "more advantageous" than a "bare" disqualification that lacks any underlying factual basis. There is an alternative analysis which points towards the same conclusion. This analysis, which is developed further below, rests on the view that the courts currently take about their own role and that of the Secretary of State in the disqualification process.

[170] For example, an offer "without prejudice except as to costs" that does not purport to be a Pt 36 Offer.

[171] See *Blackspur-Davies* (undertakings to court) and *Blackspur-Eastaway* (disqualification undertakings) discussed in the main text earlier in this chapter.

Offers of disqualification where an underlying factual basis is part of the offer

9–84 Before the creation of the statutory disqualification undertaking regime, there were serious limitations on the ability of a defendant to make an offer to settle that placed pressure on the claimant in the form of a realistic costs sanction. If the defendant was prepared to submit to an order on the basis of an uncontested hearing, the court, rather than the Secretary of State, was the sole arbiter of the period of disqualification and, accordingly, it was difficult for the defendant to show that the Secretary of State had acted so unreasonably that costs should not follow the event. At that time, the most realistic approach for a defendant who wished to settle was an offer to dispose of disqualification proceedings on a *Carecraft* basis. However, it was difficult for the defendant to formulate an offer based on a draft *Carecraft* statement in such a way that the Secretary of State could be shown to have acted unreasonably in refusing to accept it. If the parties failed to reach agreement, the sticking point was usually one, or a combination of, the following: (a) the period of disqualification; (b) the factual basis of disqualification; and/or (c) a technical matter (for example, where the preamble sought to "ring fence" the *Carecraft* statement so that it could not be used in other proceedings). As regards the period agreed to be put before the court, it was comparatively rare for properly advised parties to be widely apart on period where the underlying facts were agreed. Where a precise period could not be agreed there was always the possibility of agreeing a band of years to put before the court (although this course was unattractive because it tended to lengthen the hearing and make the precise contents of the *Carecraft* statement more difficult to agree). As regards the underlying allegations of unfit conduct, it was difficult to ensure that any *Carecraft* statement offered by a defendant revealed misconduct as serious as that eventually found by the court. Finally, as regards technical matters such as "ring fencing" the *Carecraft* statement, the courts have accepted the development of standard wording over time despite attempts by defendants to "freeze" the relevant wording by reference to previous examples in earlier cases. The general principle that the factual basis of disqualification should be made public and should be capable of being used in disqualification-related contexts and not solely for the purposes of the disqualification imposed has been accepted by the courts. These difficulties of formulation probably explain why there are no reported cases of a claimant in civil disqualification proceedings being deprived of costs on the basis that he failed to "beat" an offer of a *Carecraft* disposal couched in *Calderbank* terms.

9–85 The position has altered with the creation of the statutory disqualification undertakings regime. An offer of an undertaking, coupled with a draft statement setting out the factual basis for disqualification, does not raise the same sort of difficulties for a defendant as an offer by a defendant to proceed by way of a *Carecraft* hearing. The main reason for this is that, for the purposes of a disqualification undertaking, it will usually be acceptable for the schedule of unfit conduct to be in summary form, rehearsing briefly the principal allegations disclosed by the claimant's evidence. Accordingly, there may be cases in which the defendant can offer a disqualification undertaking in such a way as to put the claimant at risk on the question of costs.

9–86 The first point that arises is that a disqualification undertaking may not always be substantially the same as or as advantageous to the public interest as a judgment following a hearing in open court. To take one example, at the time of the introduction of the undertakings regime it was envisaged that there might be high profile cases where, notwithstanding agreement in principle as to the period of disqualification, the public interest required the case to be heard in and pronounced on by the court rather than being dealt with through the undertakings procedure.[172] Such cases are likely to be very rare. However, if the Secretary of State took the view (which was reasonable in a *Wednesbury* sense) that the public interest required a particular matter to proceed to trial and, at trial, the defendant was disqualified by the court but the period and effective grounds of the disqualification were the same as (or no more serious than) the period of disqualification (and factual basis) earlier offered by way of disqualification undertaking, would the Secretary of State be penalised in costs for rejecting the offer and insisting on a full hearing? In such a situation the court may well say that the court process (and judgment) was more advantageous than the undertaking offered and/or that it was not just to order the Secretary of State to pay costs. The Secretary of State would have acted in the public interest, a matter that the courts have accepted is for the Secretary of State, and not for them, to determine.[173] Were the courts to penalise the Secretary of State in costs it would arguably be unjust because the Secretary of State would have been properly carrying out his functions.

9–87 There are other possible situations where the interaction of the public interest and the respective roles of the courts and the Secretary of State are such that costs orders adverse to the Secretary of State should not follow, despite his rejection of an earlier offer of an undertaking by a defendant. One such case might be where the parties were agreed as to period but not as to the factual basis of disqualification. At the trial the claimant might establish an additional ground but the court might decide that this did not affect the period. Even though the period ordered would therefore be the same as the period offered by way of undertaking, if such a situation arose, there may be a good argument that: (a) the establishing of the additional ground was an important matter in the public interest given that the CDDA has a deterrence function; and (b) the court's role is not to determine the question of the public interest and the offer that should be considered is the offer of the period and the underlying factual basis, such offer having been beaten because an additional ground was established. Assuming that the decision to pursue the additional ground could not be said to be *Wednesbury* unreasonable, it may well be that a submission by the defendant that the Secretary of State should pay costs from some date after the offer was made would not be accepted. The judgment finding unfit conduct on the extra ground may well be "more advantageous" than the offer of the same period of disqualification but on the basis of fewer grounds. In practice, the outcome will turn on the facts of the case. If the

[172] Trade and Industry Select Committee, Second Report, *Draft Insolvency Bill*, December 20, 1999, para.42.

[173] See *Blackspur-Davies* and discussion in 9–12, 9–19 and 9–21 to 9–24.

Secretary of State were not to be penalised in costs, the case would probably not be one where the additional ground was peripheral and the costs incurred to establish it were wholly disproportionate by any standard. In such a scenario, much might also turn on the extent to which the parties had attempted to agree that any trial be limited to the unresolved ground.

9–88 Conversely, the situation may arise where the defendant offered fewer grounds than those eventually found by the court and the court determines that additional grounds pressed by the claimant merit a longer period of disqualification. In those circumstances, it would be surprising (though not impossible) if the court took the view that the claimant's refusal of the earlier offer and decision to continue with the proceedings were oppressive or *Wednesbury* unreasonable.[174] It is suggested that this would be so whether or not the final period of disqualification was the same as that offered. If the period imposed by the court was greater than that offered then, on the face of things, the offer has been "beaten" as regards both period and grounds. If the period imposed by the court is the same as that offered then the period offered was not justified by the (lesser) grounds offered by the defendant.

9–89 The more difficult case is one where the court imposes the same period of disqualification based on the same grounds that were contained in the rejected offer and the claimant did not reject the offer on the ground that, in the public interest, the court should be involved in the process. In this situation, there is clearly more room for the court to penalise the claimant in costs for having refused the offer. The first question is whether it is appropriate and fair to compare a fully reasoned judgment of the court with the brief particulars contained in the schedule of unfit conduct that forms part of a disqualification undertaking. If the two can be equated (and this is a large "if"), the argument for the defendant is clear: the claimant has failed to beat the offer and has unnecessarily caused the proceedings to be continued. The claimant has made a litigation decision which has proved to be wrong. Unlike some of the examples above, the decision which is attacked does not relate to some specifically "public interest" element that the court is not competent to second guess or, in relation to which, it is not competent to substitute its own view. The decision simply reflects the claimant's view as to the period of disqualification that the court might be expected to impose as a matter of discretion on the facts of the case. In this sense the claimant is in the same position as any other claimant deciding whether to accept an offer to settle where the case turns on the exercise of a discretion (the discretion being as to the period of disqualification). However, if the argument succeeds, the courts will be faced with the spectre of defendants offering periods of disqualification for, say, a year less than that which the claimant is prepared to accept. The claimant, acting in the public interest, would then be placed in a dilemma that differs strikingly from that which faces the private litigant acting in and considering his own interest. As a result, defendants may be disqualified for

[174] See obiter discussion in *Re Tannery Developments Ltd, Official Receiver v Young*, August 2, 1999, Newcastle County Court, unreported.

shorter periods than is appropriate or the public purse may suffer where the claimant considers that proceedings should be brought in the public interest even though the case would otherwise be amenable to disposal by way of undertaking. The problem may be particularly acute given that the determination of the period of disqualification is hardly scientific and is, in practice, likely to be influenced by subjective factors. The interesting question is whether the court will devise a principle to avoid this result. One possibility is that the court would consider it unfair to penalise the claimant in costs unless he has acted oppressively or unfairly in refusing the offer and that this would not be the case if the period that he was holding out for was one that a competent court acting properly could have imposed.

CHAPTER 10

ALTERNATIVE GROUNDS FOR DISQUALIFICATION: SECTIONS 2 TO 5 AND 10 OF THE CDDA

INTRODUCTION

Scope of chapter

10–01 The following substantive powers of disqualification are considered in this chapter:

(1) The range of powers in CDDA ss.2 to 5 grouped under the heading "disqualification for general misconduct in connection with companies".
(2) The power in CDDA s.10 headed "participation in wrongful trading".

General introduction: ss.2–5 and 10

10–02 The majority of the present chapter is devoted to an examination of the scope and operation of ss.2 to 5. The powers of disqualification created by these provisions are directed for the most part at persons who have committed certain substantive criminal offences or other types of criminal default. As such, it may be thought appropriate to classify the powers in ss.2–5 as powers of *criminal* disqualification. However, it will be seen that these powers are not the exclusive preserve of the criminal courts. For instance, the power of disqualification in s.2 is exercisable by either the criminal or civil courts.

Confusion has arisen in the past as to whether the rationale of disqualification in a criminal court is or should be different from the rationale of disqualification in the civil courts.[1] The view maintained in this chapter and elsewhere in this book can be summarised as follows:

(1) When the court (be that a criminal or a civil court) exercises a power of disqualification under ss.2–5, it is first and foremost exercising jurisdiction under the CDDA.
(2) The CDDA is at best a coherent legislative scheme with common features and a common purpose. Jurisdiction under the CDDA is generally triggered by some past misconduct of the individual (whether that be "general misconduct" under ss.2–5, unfit conduct under ss.6–9A etc.) that raises doubts over his suitability to direct or manage companies. The effect of disqualification and the sanctions for breach of a disqualification order[2] are the same whether the individual is disqualified under ss.2–5, 6–8, 9A or s.10. This suggests that

[1] See further discussion in Ch.2 and text from 10–79.
[2] Or disqualification undertaking under CDDA ss.7(2A), 8(2A) or 9B.

the various powers in the CDDA share a common objective and, as such, the criminal and civil courts should, in general terms, adopt a common approach when exercising jurisdiction under it.[3]

10–03 Three further points can be made by way of general introduction and by way of comparison between ss.2–5 and 10 and the unfit conduct provisions in ss.6, 8 and 9A discussed in Chs 3 to 6. First, in contrast with ss.6 and 9A but in common with s.8, the four provisions in ss.2–5 and 10 confer on the relevant court a *discretionary* power of disqualification. Thus, even if the court has jurisdiction to disqualify under ss.2–5, it is not bound to make a disqualification order. Secondly, in contrast with the unfit conduct provisions, ss.2–5 and 10 do not apply exclusively to company directors. The provisions in ss.2–5 and 10 are thus broader in scope and illustrate the important point that the CDDA is not concerned exclusively with the disqualification of directors but can extend to other persons involved in the management or affairs of companies. Thirdly, and again by way of contrast with the unfit conduct provisions, locus standi to apply for a disqualification order under ss.2–5 is not restricted to relevant organs of the state (be that the Secretary of State, the official receiver or the regulators referred to in ss.9A–9B and defined in s.9E(2)). Under ss.2–5 a wider body of applicants is provided for.[4] The power of disqualification exercisable by a civil court under s.10 is triggered by a declaration of personal liability under either s.213 or s.214 of the Insolvency Act 1986: the court can act of its own motion but there is little doubt that the Secretary of State could seek to intervene.

Meaning of "company" in ss.2–5 and 10

10–04 The width of the term "company" as it is used in the CDDA is considered in Ch.3 (where the court's jurisdiction under ss.6 and 8 is explored), in Ch.14 (which considers the extent of the prohibitions in ss.1, 1A, 11, 9B(3) and 12) and in Ch.16 (which considers the territorial scope of the CDDA and cases involving foreign elements). The main points of the discussion found in those chapters are restated briefly below for the convenience of the reader making particular reference to ss.2–5 and 10.

Building societies, incorporated friendly societies, NHS foundation trusts, open-ended investment companies and charitable incorporated organisations

10–05 It appears at first sight that the powers of disqualification in ss.2–5 apply to conduct in relation to building societies,[5] incorporated friendly societies and limited liability partnerships ("LLPs") because of the effect of ss.22A and 22B of the CDDA and reg.4(2) of the Limited Liability Partnerships Regulations 2001 ("the LLP Regulations").[6] However, on closer reading, it is doubtful whether ss.3,

[3] See further 2–01 and text from 10–79 where these points are developed.
[4] CDDA s.16(2).
[5] For building society insolvency see 10–14E below.
[6] SI 2001/1090.

4(1)(a) and 5 apply to building societies and incorporated friendly societies because those sections refer to specific provisions of companies legislation that are not expressly applied by the CDDA (or any other enactment) to these entities. The point is that under ss.3, 4(1)(a) and 5, a person is only liable to disqualification if he has committed a triggering breach of certain provisions of companies legislation specified in each section. Sections 22A and 22B do modify other sections of the CDDA so that the regulatory provisions applicable to the type of body in question, which are equivalent to the Companies Act provisions specified in the CDDA, are directly applicable in determining jurisdiction to disqualify. Thus ss.22A(4) and 22B(4) expressly provide that Sch.1 of the CDDA, which sets out criteria to be used in judging whether unfit conduct is established and includes reference to breaches of various Companies Acts and Insolvency Act provisions, should be read as referring to the corresponding provisions of the Building Societies Act 1986 and the Friendly Societies Act 1992. However, those sections do not modify ss.3, 4(1)(a) and 5.[7] CDDA s.22C extends the definition of "company" to include NHS foundation trusts. The scheme of s.22C is very similar to that for ss.22A and 22B and the same observations therefore apply. With effect from October 1, 2009, CDDA s.22D[8] makes provision for the application of the CDDA to open-ended investment companies. Again, however, it appears that ss.3, 4(1)(a) and 5 do not apply in the context of open-ended investment companies as the Open-Ended Investment Companies Regulations[9] do not expressly require any references to provisions of the Companies Acts in ss.2–5 to be taken to be a reference to the corresponding provision of the 2001 Regulations or any rules made thereunder, nor is there any reference to corresponding provisions of the 2001 Regulation in ss.3–5.[10]

10–06 The position is somewhat clearer with regard to LLPs by virtue of reg.4 of the LLP Regulations.[11] Regulation 4(2)(b) modifies the term "companies legislation" as it appears in the CDDA so as to include references to the Limited Liability Partnerships Act 2000, any regulations made thereunder and any enactment applied by regulations to LLPs. In relation to accounting periods beginning before October 1, 2008, reg.3 applies the accounts and audit provisions of Pt VII of the Companies Act 1985 (including, inter alia, the obligation to file accounts)

[7] A person is only liable to disqualification if he has committed a triggering breach of a type specified in the relevant CDDA provision. Thus, for example, under s.3 the triggering event is persistent default in relation to certain specified provisions of the Companies Acts and the Insolvency Act 1986. As a building society regulated by the Building Societies Act 1986 is not, by definition, a "company" for all the purposes of companies legislation, its directors cannot commit a triggering breach. If a building society converts into a company under ss.97–102 of the Building Societies Act then the point falls away in relation to breaches of the relevant provisions occurring thereafter. The same analysis applies mutatis mutandis to incorporated friendly societies and NHS foundation trusts.

[8] Inserted by the Companies Act 2006 (Consequential Amendments, Transitional Provisions and Savings) Order 2009 (SI 2009/1941).

[9] SI 2001/1228.

[10] However, such companies may be wound up under Pt V of the Insolvency Act 1986 so that provisions of the Insolvency Act mentioned in ss.3 and 5 may become relevant. Fraudulent trading (on which see reg.64 of the 2001 Regulations) is likely to be dealt with under CDDA s.2 or, possibly, s.4(1)(b).

[11] SI 2001/1090.

to LLPs with appropriate modification. For accounting periods beginning on or after that date, the Limited Liability Partnerships (Accounts and Audit) (Application of Companies Act 2006) Regulations 2008[12] apply the corresponding provisions of the Companies Act 2006 to LLPs. Similarly, reg.4(1) of the LLP Regulations applies (with modification) certain specified provisions of the Companies Act 1985 including, inter alia, the obligation to file annual returns, to LLPs and with effect from October 1, 2009 the corresponding provisions of the Companies Act 2006 will apply to LLPs by virtue of the Limited Liability Partnerships (Application of Companies Act 2006) Regulations 2009.[13] The effect is that CDDA ss.3 and 5 are clearly capable of applying to these entities. As by virtue of reg.4(1) of the LLP Regulations and reg.47 of the Limited Liability Partnerships (Application of Companies Act 2006) Regulations 2009, s.458 of the Companies Act 1985 and its successor, s.993 of the Companies Act 2006, are applied directly to LLPs (with modification), LLPs are also squarely within the scope of CDDA s.4(1)(a). The fact that the secondary legislation dealing with LLPs has been drafted in this way reinforces the argument rehearsed above concerning the non-applicability of CDDA ss.3, 4(1)(a) and 5 to building societies, incorporated friendly societies, NHS foundation trusts and open-ended investment companies.

10–07 Section 10 sets out, as grounds for disqualification, declarations under each of ss.213 (fraudulent trading) and 214 (wrongful trading) of the Insolvency Act 1986. It appears that s.10 is capable of applying to building societies and incorporated friendly societies because these entities are capable of being wound up under the Insolvency Act. It follows that, in appropriate circumstances, wrongful or fraudulent trading proceedings will lie.[14] Regulation 5 of the LLP Regulations applies Pt IV of the Insolvency Act 1986, which includes ss.213 and 214, to LLPs. The combined effect of regs 4(2) and 5 is that: (a) ss.213–214 of the Insolvency Act are capable of applying to LLPs; and (b) a disqualification order could be made under CDDA s.10 were these provisions to be successfully invoked in relation to the winding up of an LLP.[15]

10–08 An NHS foundation trust was described by its originating legislation, the Health and Social Care (Community Health and Standards) Act 2003, as a public benefit corporation. The constitution of such an entity is now provided for by s.30 of and Sch.7 to the National Health Service Act 2006. NHS foundation trusts have their own independent regulator, the Independent Regulator of NHS Foundation

[12] SI 2008/1911.

[13] SI 2009/1804.

[14] See, e.g. the effect of the Building Societies Act 1986 ss.37, 88–90B, Sch.15 and, more generally, s.229 of the Insolvency Act 1986. See also the Friendly Societies Act 1992 ss.23, 52 and Sch.10.

[15] It should also be noted that s.214A of the Insolvency Act, inserted by reg.5(2)(f) and Sch.3 of the LLP Regulations with effect from April 6, 2001, is expressed to be "without prejudice to s.214". Section 214A enables the court in prescribed circumstances to claw back property withdrawn from an LLP by a member or shadow member within two years of the winding up. However, a person found liable under s.214A alone could not be disqualified under CDDA s.10 as the wording of s.10 has not been extended to include a reference to that provision.

Trusts.[16] Section 53 of the 2006 Act contains an order making power enabling the provisions of Pt I of the Insolvency Act 1986 on corporate voluntary arrangements (including eligible company corporate voluntary arrangements with a moratorium) to be applied with modifications to NHS foundation trusts. Section 54 of the 2006 Act contains a similar order making power enabling the regulator to apply the provisions of Pt IV of the Insolvency Act with appropriate modification. It appears that the s.54 power has not yet been exercised. Until such time as the power is exercised to apply ss.213–214 to the members of the board of an NHS foundation trust, there is no scope for such persons to be the subject of civil proceedings under those provisions and, accordingly, no scope for CDDA s.10 to apply to them.

10–09 At the time of writing the position in relation to charitable incorporated organisations had not been settled. Draft regulations had been published which suggested that the relevant provisions of the Insolvency Act and CDDA ss.1, 1A, 6, 7, 8A, 9, 10, 14, 16, 17, 20, 20A, 21, 22 and Sch.1 would be applied expressly to charitable incorporated organisations with appropriate modifications.[17] The upshot appears to be that of the provisions under consideration in this chapter only CDDA s.10 will be capable of applying in relation to these entities. It remains to be seen whether the regulations that are ultimately enacted will take the same form.

Registered companies

10–10 Before October 1, 2009, the combined effect of s.22(9) of the CDDA, ss.1(1) and 2 of the Companies Act 2006 and s.735 of the Companies Act 1985 was that ss.2–5 and 10 were to be read as applying broadly to companies formed and registered under the Companies Act 2006 and companies formed and registered under any of its statutory predecessors on or after July 14, 1856.[18] This encompassed all forms of registered company, i.e. guarantee companies and unlimited companies as well as companies limited by shares.[19] From October 1, 2009, by virtue of CDDA s.22(2)(a) as amended[20] "company" in the CDDA includes "a company registered under the Companies Act 2006 in Great Britain". This amendment, which is merely consequential on the coming into force of the Companies Act 2006, does not appear to have materially affected the position as it stood before October 1, 2009 as regards the application of ss.2–5 and 10 to companies formed and registered under the

[16] National Health Service Act 2006 s.31.

[17] See the Cabinet Office and Office of the Third Sector joint consultation document, *The Charitable Incorporated Organisation (CIO)—Consultation on the new corporate form for charities* (September 2008), Annex B available online at *http://www.cabinetoffice.gov.uk/third_sector/consultations/completed_consultations/cio.aspx* [Accessed August 26, 2009]. See further 3–91 and 14–11.

[18] Companies formed and registered under the Joint Stock Companies Act 1844 or in Ireland under companies legislation up to and including the Companies (Consolidation) Act 1908 were excluded from the definition of companies formed and registered under the Companies Act 1985 or the former Companies Acts: see Companies Act 1985 s.735(1)(a), (b), (3). The position appears to be the same from October 1, 2009: see Companies Act 2006 s.1(1)(b)(ii).

[19] However, the court may be more minded to grant permission to a person to act in relation to an unlimited company than a limited company: see Ch.15.

[20] See the Companies Act 2006 (Consequential Amendments, Transitional Provisions and Savings) Order 2009 (SI 2009/1941).

relevant Companies Acts.[21] The references to provisions of companies legislation in ss.3, 4(1)(a) and 5 should be read as including references to provisions of Pts 1–39 and 45–47 of the Companies Act 2006, Pt 2 of the Companies (Audit, Investigations and Community Enterprise) Act 2004, Companies Act 1985 and the Companies Consolidation (Consequential Provisions) Act 1985 that remain in force, the Insolvency Act 1986 and the corresponding provisions of corresponding earlier legislation.[22] Community interest companies are also registered companies falling squarely within the scope of the CDDA.[23]

Companies liable to be wound up under Pt V of the Insolvency Act 1986

10–11 The effect of CDDA s.22(2)(b) is that ss.2–5 and 10 should be read as applying to a company which may be wound up under Pt V of the Insolvency Act 1986. The view expressed in Chs 3 and 14 is that the CDDA only extends to *companies* which are capable of being wound up under Pt V and does not encompass other associations or bodies that fall within the meaning of the broader term "unregistered companies" used in Pt V. The effect of this analysis is that ss.2–5 appear capable of applying to foreign companies,[24] open-ended investment companies[25] and European Economic Interest Groupings registered in Great Britain (which appear for domestic law purposes to be treated as bodies corporate).[26] In each case, however, there will be a question as to whether the specific Companies Acts provisions listed in ss.3, 4(1) and 5 apply to such a body. Similarly, it appears that s.10 will apply to *companies* falling within Pt V of the Insolvency Act as, by virtue of s.229(1) of the Insolvency Act, the provisions of Pt IV of that Act (including the wrongful and fraudulent trading provisions) are applicable to such entities.

[21] See, in particular, Companies Act 2006 ss.1(1), 1(2)(a). A minor technical change having no practical significance is that the current definition of "company" as "a company registered under the Companies Act 2006 . . .", rather than "formed and registered" under that Act, would appear to encompass overseas companies that register in Great Britain pursuant to Pt 34 of the 2006 Act. Before October 1, 2009, these companies would have fallen within s.22(2)(b) as companies that may at that time have been wound up under Pt V of the Insolvency Act In any event, such companies clearly fall within the scope of the CDDA whether under the current s.22(2)(a) or s.22(2)(b).

[22] See now CDDA s.22(7), (8) as substituted by SI 2009/1941 with effect from October 1, 2009. The former s.22(7), (8) were to similar effect.

[23] See 3–90.

[24] See further Ch.16.

[25] The position as regards open-ended investment companies is now governed by CDDA s.22D which puts the matter beyond doubt: see 10–05.

[26] See 3–87. However, as is the case with building societies and incorporated friendly societies, it is not clear whether the provisions of companies legislation referred to expressly in ss.3, 4(1)(a) and 5 breach of which triggers jurisdiction under the CDDA are applicable to EEIGs. Reg.20 of the European Economic Interest Grouping Regulations 1989 (SI 1989/638) states that where an EEIG is wound up as an unregistered company under Pt V, the provisions of ss.1, 2, 4–11, 12(2), 15–17, 20 and 22 of, and Sch.1 to, the CDDA shall apply in relation to an EEIG as if any reference to a director or past director of a company included a reference to a manager of the EEIG and any other person who has or has had control or management of the EEIG's business and the EEIG were a company as defined by s.22(2)(b) of the CDDA. This seems to contemplate the express application of ss.2, 4, 5 and 10 (but not 3) to EEIGs. However, their application is only triggered *where an EEIG is wound up as an unregistered company*. This suggests that an application under those sections could only be made following the winding up of an EEIG.

Unincorporated friendly societies and industrial and provident societies

10–12 Sections 2–5 and 10 would appear not to apply to unincorporated friendly societies, which are not strictly *companies* within the meaning of s.22(2)(b) of the CDDA. Further, ss.2–5 would appear not to apply to industrial and provident societies as these are not "companies" which are capable of being wound up under Pt V of the Insolvency Act 1986 and therefore do not fall within the scope of s.22(2)(b) of the CDDA.[27]

Partnerships

10–13 It should be noted that s.10 (but not ss.2–5) is applied to insolvent partnerships by art.16 of the Insolvent Partnerships Order 1994.[28] The fact that such an express extension was deemed necessary reinforces the view that CDDA s.22(2)(b) applies the provisions of the CDDA to companies only and not to unincorporated entities.

European Companies and European Private Companies

10–14 Since the coming into force of Council Regulation 2157/2001 of October 8, 2001 on October 8, 2004 it has been possible for a European Company (SE) to be incorporated in the United Kingdom provided that its head office is situated there. Although a concept of Community law, an SE must be incorporated by registration in a member state and it falls to be treated as if it were a public company formed in accordance with the law of the Member State where its registered office is located.[29] It appears that the powers of disqualification in the CDDA apply in relation to an SE registered in the United Kingdom by virtue of art.9(1)(c). That article provides that matters not governed, or only partly governed, by the Regulation, are regulated by the provisions of United Kingdom law applicable to public companies (which include the CDDA). art.68 of the Regulation obliges the Member States to make such provision as is appropriate to ensure the effective application of the Regulation.[30]

10–14A A further supranational corporate form, the European Private Company (*societas privata europaea*) is to be introduced and available in Member States with effect from July 1, 2010.[31] As its name suggests, the object of this proposal is to create a standard, uniform private company vehicle for small and medium-sized enterprises

[27] For a contrary view see C. Mills, "Does the CDDA Apply to Industrial and Provident Societies?" (1997) 13 Insolv. Law & Practice 182 and further discussion in text from 3–95.

[28] SI 1994/2421 as subsequently amended by a series of Insolvent Partnerships (Amendment) Orders: SI 1996/1308 with effect from June 14, 1996; SI 2001/767 with effect from April 2, 2001; SI 2002/1308 with effect from May 31, 2002; SI 2005/1516 with effect from July 1, 2005; SI 2006/622 with effect from April 6, 2006.

[29] See Council Regulation 2157/2001, arts 3, 4(3), 9, 10, 12(1), 15, 16(1), 63.

[30] See the European Public Limited-Liability Company Regulations 2004 (SI 2004/2326) now extended to Northern Ireland by Companies Act 2006 s.1285(1).

[31] See Proposal for a Council Regulation on the Statute for a European Private Company COM (2008) 396/3. For background see R. Drury, "The European Private Company" (2008) 9(1) European Business Organization L.R. 125; B. Mackowiz and F. Saifee, "Societas Privata Europaea: the European Private Company" (2009) 30(8) Co.Law. 227.

that wish to expand their business beyond the borders of a single Member State and provide such enterprises with an alternative to incorporating subsidiaries or establishing branches in other Member States. A European Private Company will be a creature of Community Law formed by registration in the Member State in which it has its registered office. The principal effect of the proposed Regulation is that the disqualification of a person serving as a director of a European Private Company is to be governed by the applicable national law. It follows that where the company is registered in Great Britain, the powers to disqualify directors in the CDDA will apply.

Statutory extensions and modifications introduced by the Banking Act 2009

Banks

10–14B In response to the banking crisis that occurred during 2007 and 2008, Parliament introduced a statutory regime for dealing with failing banks. Initially, the Treasury was given emergency powers under the Banking (Special Provisions) Act 2008. Subsequently, a permanent statutory regime was established by the Banking Act 2009 which, inter alia, introduced a new bank insolvency procedure based on existing liquidation provisions and a new bank administration procedure. Similar regimes have also been introduced pursuant to the 2009 Act in respect of building societies.

10–14C Section 121(4) of the Banking Act 2009 introduced a new s.21A of the CDDA with effect from February 21, 2009.[32] CDDA s.21A recites that s.121 of the Banking Act applies the CDDA "in relation to bank insolvency as it applies in relation to liquidation". Section 121 provides, inter alia, that a reference in the CDDA to liquidation includes a reference to bank insolvency, a reference to winding up includes a reference to making or being subject to a bank insolvency order and a reference to "becoming insolvent" includes a reference to becoming subject to a bank insolvency order. The effect of these provisions for present purposes is that the CDDA ss.2, 4 and 10 are capable of applying in the context of banks that have entered the bank insolvency procedure.[33]

10–14D Section 155(4) of the Banking Act 2009 introduced a new s.21B of the CDDA with effect from February 21, 2009.[34] CDDA s.21B recites that s.155 of the Banking Act applies the CDDA "in relation to bank administration as it applies in relation to liquidation". Section 155 provides, inter alia, that a reference in the CDDA to liquidation includes a reference to bank administration, a reference to winding up includes a reference to making or being subject to a bank administration order and a reference to "becoming insolvent" includes a reference to

[32] Banking Act 2009 (Commencement No.1) Order 2009 (SI 2009/296).

[33] For the application in the context of bank insolvency of ss.213–214 of the Insolvency Act 1986, which are the gateway to a possible order under CDDA s.10, see Banking Act 2009 s.103(3) and the table of applied provisions referred to therein.

[34] Banking Act 2009 (Commencement No.1) Order 2009 (SI 2009/296).

becoming subject to a bank administration order. The effect of these provisions for present purposes is that the CDDA ss.2, 4 and 10 are capable of applying in the context of banks that have entered the bank administration procedure.[35]

Building societies

10–14E Pursuant to powers in the Banking Act 2009, the Treasury made the Building Societies (Insolvency and Special Administration) Order 2009 ("the 2009 Order").[36] This applies the bank insolvency and bank administration regimes to building societies by means of a series of amendments to the Building Societies Act 1986.[37] Section 90E of the Building Societies Act, inserted by the 2009 Order, provides, inter alia, that a reference in the CDDA to liquidation includes a reference to building society insolvency and to building society special administration, a reference to winding up includes a reference to making or being subject to a building society insolvency order or to a building society special administration order and a reference to "becoming insolvent" includes a reference to becoming subject to a building society insolvency order or a building society special administration order. Article 12 of the 2009 Order introduced a new s.21C of the CDDA which recites that s.90E of the Building Societies Act applies the CDDA "in relation to building society insolvency and building society special administration". The effect of these provisions for present purposes is that the CDDA ss.2, 4 and 10 are capable of applying in the context of banks that have entered these forms of insolvency procedure.[38] Section 90E(5) of the Building Societies Act makes identical provision as regards the scope of the disqualification regime in Northern Ireland.

SECTION 2: DISQUALIFICATION ON CONVICTION OF INDICTABLE OFFENCE

10–15 Under s.2 the court may make a disqualification order against a person where he is convicted of an indictable offence (whether on indictment or summarily) in connection with the promotion, formation, management, liquidation or striking off of a company, with the receivership of a company's property or with his being an

[35] For the application in the context of bank administration of ss.213–214 of the Insolvency Act 1986, which are the gateway to a possible order under CDDA s.10, see Banking Act 2009 s.145(3) and the second table of applied provisions referred to therein.

[36] SI 2009/805 with effect from March 29, 2009.

[37] For further modifications as regards the application of the building society special administration procedure in Scotland see The Building Society Special Administration (Scotland) Rules 2009 (SI 2009/806 (s.3)).

[38] For the application in the context of building society insolvency orders and building society special administration orders of ss.213–214 of the Insolvency Act 1986, which are the gateway to a possible order under CDDA s.10, see art.2 of the 2009 Order inserting s.90C of the Building Societies Act 1986. The effect of these provisions is to apply the bank insolvency and administration legislation (which expressly applies ss.213–214 to bank insolvency and administration) to building societies with appropriate modifications.

administrative receiver of a company. Section 2 is broader than ss.6 and 8 as it is not limited in application to directors, whether de jure, de facto or shadow, [39] but applies equally to employees, managers, company secretaries, insolvency practitioners or others convicted of an offence falling within its scope.[40] It is clear that the court's discretion to disqualify a person under s.2 only arises if that person has been convicted of a relevant indictable offence. In the absence of such a conviction, the court's power simply does not arise.[41] However, in contrast to s.6, it is not necessary to establish that the company is or became insolvent. The maximum period of disqualification is five years in the case of courts exercising summary criminal jurisdiction and otherwise 15 years. There is no minimum period of disqualification. The reluctance of the criminal courts to impose disqualification orders was noted in the Report on Parallel Proceedings by the Financial Regulation Working Group of the Society for Advanced Legal Studies[42] as follows:

> "Although there are exceptions, criminal courts have not always been willing to exercise their powers in the field of company director's disqualification, perhaps because it is a jurisdiction that is slightly esoteric and with which they are not familiar."[43]

Indeed, this was a major factor underlying the Report's recommendation that specialist DTI counsel should be instructed at the sentencing stage to make submissions with regard to the CDDA where the DTI (as was) thought that disqualification was suitable in the circumstances. It appears that since that time awareness of the convicting court's powers under s.2 has begun to increase especially in fields such as health and safety[44] and tax fraud.[45]

Indictable offence

10–16 In England and Wales, an indictable offence is an offence that, if committed by an adult, is triable on indictment, whether it is exclusively so triable or triable either way.[46] The position is the same in Scotland (by virtue of s.2(2) of the CDDA) and in Northern Ireland (by virtue of art.5(1) of the Company Directors Disqualification (Northern Ireland) Order 2002).[47] It is clear from the express

[39] See further text from 3–16.

[40] See, e.g. *R. v Creggy* [2008] EWCA Crim 394, [2008] 3 All E.R. 91 (solicitor convicted of laundering money on behalf of corporate client disqualified for seven years) considered further in the text at 10–23.

[41] The position differs in other jurisdictions, e.g. Australia, New Zealand, Ireland, South Africa and Singapore where the offender is *automatically* disqualified on conviction for a relevant offence without the need for a court order. For an example see Australia's Corporations Act 2001 (Cth) s.206B.

[42] December 1999, under the chairmanship of George Staple Q.C.

[43] Report on Parallel Proceedings, para.7.13.

[44] See, e.g. A. Neal and F. Wright, *A survey of the use and effectiveness of the Company Directors Disqualification Act 1986 as a legal sanction against directors convicted of health and safety offences*, Health and Safety Executive, Research Report RR597 (HSE Books, 2007), *http://www.hse.gov.uk/research/rrhtm/rr597.htm* [Accessed August 26, 2009].

[45] See further 10–36.

[46] Interpretation Act 1978 s.5, Sch.1.

[47] SI 2002/3150.

wording of s.2 that the offence need only be *capable* of prosecution on indictment and that there will be jurisdiction to disqualify on conviction following either a summary trial or trial on indictment.[48]

10–17 The provision was first enacted in s.33(1)(a) of the Companies Act 1947 (subsequently re-enacted as s.188(1)(a) of the Companies Act 1948).[49] In its original form, the provision enabled the court to disqualify a person "convicted on indictment of any offence in connection with the promotion, formation or management of a company" for up to five years. The current wording, which extends the scope of the original provision to encompass persons summarily convicted of an indictable offence and offences in connection with the liquidation, receivership (including administrative receivership) or management of a company's property, was substituted by the Companies Act 1981 s.93 and later consolidated as s.296 of the Companies Act 1985, the immediate predecessor of the present s.2. The section has also been extended to encompass striking off.[50] While some of the cases cited in this chapter were decided under the Companies Act 1948, they are still relevant given this process of consolidation and the similarity of the statutory wording.[51]

Promotion, formation and management

10–18 The terms "promotion", "formation" and "management" appear in both ss.2(1) and 1(1)(a) of the CDDA. In s.2 their function is jurisdictional: if an offender commits an offence falling within their scope he is liable to disqualification. In s.1(1)(a) they serve to delineate the boundaries of a disqualification order: a disqualified person cannot without the permission of the court be concerned or take part in company promotion, formation or management. For convenience, a full discussion of the terms is reserved to Ch.14 where the scope of the prohibition in s.1 is considered.[52] The analysis there (which addresses questions such as "what is meant by the terms 'promoter', 'management' etc?") should be treated as applying equally to the terms as they appear in s.2(1). It is important to bear in

[48] In England and Wales a prosecution on indictment must be brought before the Crown Court: Senior Courts Act 1981 s.46(1), while summary offences are usually tried by a magistrates court. Summary jurisdiction and procedure are governed principally by the Magistrates' Courts Act 1980 and by rules promulgated under s.144 of that Act although it is possible for a Crown Court to deal with a summary offence included as part of an indictment: Criminal Justice Act 1988 ss.40–41. The position in Northern Ireland in relation to the issues of procedure discussed in this chapter is similar to that in England and Wales: see generally the Judicature (Northern Ireland) Act 1978. In Scotland offences which are capable of being prosecuted on indictment are tried in either the High Court of Justiciary (which is Scotland's supreme criminal court) or in a sheriff court while summary jurisdiction is exercised by both the sheriff and district courts.

[49] On the recommendation of the Cohen Committee: see Report of the Committee on Company Law Amendment, Cmd.6659 (1945), para.150.

[50] The "liquidation or striking off" wording was substituted for the former wording "or liquidation" by the Deregulation and Contracting Out Act 1994 s.39 and Sch.11 para.6 with effect from July 1, 1995 (SI 1995/1433).

[51] See, e.g. the treatment of *R. v Corbin* (1984) 6 Cr.App.R.(S.) 17 and *R. v Austen* (1985) 7 Cr.App.R.(S.) 214 (both decided under the 1948 Act) in *R. v Goodman* [1993] 2 All E.R. 789.

[52] See text from 14–30.

mind that for s.2 purposes there is jurisdiction to disqualify if the offender is convicted of an offence "in connection with . . ." promotion, formation or management, etc. It is not clear whether there is any difference in practical effect between this wording and the "in any way, whether directly or indirectly, be concerned or take part in. . ." promotion, formation or management wording used in s.1(1)(a). It is suggested that the "in connection wording" is capable of being, and will be, construed just as widely.

Offence in connection with promotion of a company

10–19 The common law on promoters was devised principally as a means of protecting investors in the context of a public offer. As such, it is arguable that the offence of making false or misleading statements where the company's securities are offered to the public is one in connection with the promotion of a company for the purposes of s.2(1).[53] The same may also be true of the offences of offering securities to the public or requesting admission of securities to trading on a regulated market without publication of an approved prospectus.[54] The fact that "any person" convicted of an offence "in connection with the promotion of a company" is liable to disqualification begs the question whether professional advisers, such as lawyers, accountants or merchant bankers specialising in corporate finance could be treated as "promoters" for s.2 purposes. The common law does not regard a person who simply discharges his professional duties, for example, by drafting a prospectus or preparing a profit forecast on the basis of information supplied by a client, as a promoter.[55] However, the corporate financier or accountant who actively solicits potential investors for a corporate venture or in the course of a public offer could well be treated as one. In any event, the width of the "in connection with" prefix probably renders the point academic.[56]

Offence in connection with formation of a company

10–20 "Formation" is arguably narrower than "promotion" and appears to refer only to the process of incorporation encompassing the preparation and filing of the documents required by Pt 2 of the Companies Act 2006 and culminating in the issue of

[53] See, e.g. Financial Services and Markets Act 2000 s.397(1)–(2). This presupposes that any public offering amounts to "promotion", a view which does not sit entirely comfortably with the common law on promoters: see text from 14–36. In *R. v O'Hanlon* [2007] EWCA Crim 3074, [2008] 2 Cr.App.R.(S.) 16 the former CEO of an OFEX listed company was disqualified for ten years (reduced to seven on appeal) following his conviction of an offence of making a misleading, false or deceptive statement or forecast contrary to the Financial Services Act 1986 s.47(1) (the statutory predecessor of s.397(1) of the 2000 Act). On the facts, the offence appears to be best characterised as one in connection with the management rather than the promotion of a company.

[54] Financial Services and Markets Act 2000 s.85 as substituted by the Prospectus Regulations 2005 (SI 2005/1433), reg.2(1), Sch.1 para.5. One example of a case in which directors were disqualified following conviction for an equivalent offence in Singapore is the City Country Club saga chronicled in A. Hicks, "Commercial Candour and Integrity in Singapore" (1986) 28 Malaysian L.R. 288.

[55] *Re Great Wheal Polgooth Company* (1883) 53 L.J. Ch. 42.

[56] See, e.g. *R. v Irish & Dawson* [2001] EWCA Crim 1393 where a company's accountant was disqualified following his conviction for conspiring with the directors to defraud the members by dishonestly concealing the costs of the company's promotion.

a certificate of incorporation by the Registrar of Companies. It might be argued that "formation" should bear an extended meaning and also encompass other legal requirements with which a company must comply before it can commence trading. It could then be said in the case of a public company that the offence of trading or exercising borrowing powers without a certificate under the Companies Act 2006 ss.761(1) and 767 is an offence "in connection with the formation of a company". Again, the point is probably academic as such an offence almost certainly amounts to one "in connection with" the management of a company in any event.

Offence in connection with management of a company

10–21 It appears from this wording that the court's jurisdiction to disqualify will only arise if there is a demonstrable link between: (a) the *offender* and the management of a company; and/or (b) the *offence* itself and the management of a company. Thus, prima facie, it will only be possible to show that the offence is one "in connection with . . . the management of a company" if it can be established first, that the offender is someone who identifiably performs a management role or discharges or assists in the discharge of some managerial function[57] and secondly, that there is a nexus between the particular offence and the activity of management. Perhaps wisely, Parliament chose not to define "management" even though it is a term of central importance within the scheme of the CDDA. It is therefore left to the courts to determine as a matter of law and on the facts of each case whether an offender has committed an offence in connection with management for the purposes of s.2(1). The leading case is *R. v Goodman*.[58]

R. v Goodman

10–22 The question for the Court of Appeal (Criminal Division) in *R. v Goodman* was whether the Crown Court had acted within its jurisdiction when disqualifying the appellant, the former chairman of a public company, following his conviction for an offence of insider dealing under the Company Securities (Insider Dealing) Act 1985 (now repealed).[59] The principal ground of appeal was that there was no jurisdiction to make an order under s.2(1) because the offence for which the appellant had been convicted was not one "in connection with the management of a company". Staughton L.J. considered that there were three possible approaches to the construction of s.2(1):

(1) It could be said that the "indictable offence" referred to in s.2(1) is limited to offences which involve breach of some rule of law as to what must or must not be done in the management of a company. Examples would be the failure to keep proper accounts or file returns, i.e. offences involving non-compliance with companies legislation. In the light of the authorities cited in support of the test in (2) below, the court rejected this approach as too narrow.

[57] On which see further text from 14–39.
[58] [1993] 2 All E.R. 789.
[59] See now Criminal Justice Act 1993 Pt V and Financial Services and Markets Act 2000 Pt VIII.

(2) A second, wider approach would be to say that any indictable offence committed by a person *in the course of managing a company* should fall within s.2(1). In support of this wider test, Staughton L.J. cited three previous Court of Appeal decisions: *R. v Corbin*,[60] *R. v Austen*[61] and *R. v Georgiou*.[62] The appellant in *Corbin* had pleaded guilty to several counts of obtaining property by deception. The facts were that he ran a business selling yachts through the medium of three companies. To support the business, he fraudulently obtained money from a number of finance companies. He also defrauded customers, obtained yachts and other items of property from suppliers by deception and committed mortgage fraud. Corbin appealed against a five-year disqualification order on the ground that the court had lacked jurisdiction to make it. It was argued on his behalf that "the management of a company" must mean the *internal* management of a company's affairs and that Corbin's offences were not within the subsection because they related to third parties who were *outside* the company. The court rejected this argument emphasising that Parliament had chosen to enact the words, "in connection with the management of a company" rather than "in respect of the management of a company". The court in *Austen* followed *Corbin* and upheld a disqualification order that had been imposed by the trial judge following the appellant's conviction for similar offences. In the process, the court refused to differentiate between management of a company's internal and external affairs.[63] The court went a stage further in *Georgiou*. The appellant carried on an insurance business through the medium of a company without proper authorisation under the Insurance Companies Act 1982. Again, the short question was whether that offence was one "in connection with the management of a company". The court rejected the appellant's submission that s.2(1) should be construed as applying only if the company had been used as a vehicle for the commission of indictable offences and upheld a five-year disqualification order:

> "The combined effect of [the decisions in *Corbin and Austen*] is not to confine the phrase 'in connection with management' to offences involving any actual misconduct of the company's affairs, whether internal or external. In our judgment carrying on an insurance business through a limited company is a function of management and if that function is performed unlawfully in any way which makes a person guilty of an indictable offence it can properly be said that that is in connection with the management of the company."

The overall effect of *Corbin, Austen* and *Georgiou* is that an offender is liable to disqualification under s.2 if convicted of either: (a) an indictable offence committed in the course of running a company's business and/or involving actual misconduct of the company's affairs, whether internal or external; or (b) an indictable offence that involves the running of a company's business

[60] (1984) 6 Cr.App.R.(S.) 17.
[61] (1985) 7 Cr.App.R.(S.) 214.
[62] (1988) 87 Cr.App.R. 207.
[63] See also *R. v Appleyard* (1985) 81 Cr.App.R. 319 (offender disqualified following conviction for offences of conspiracy to obtain property by deception from an insurance company).

without statutory authority where such authority is required because of the special nature of the business.[64]

(3) A third possible approach would be to say that any indictable offence having *some relevant factual connection* with the management of a company should fall within s.2(1). It was this test that the Court of Appeal favoured in *Goodman*. However, the court's reasoning was only briefly expounded and the test is accordingly somewhat opaque.[65] As Nolan has pointed out, it is difficult to ascertain what is meant by a "factual connection", let alone a "*relevant* factual connection".[66] Staughton L.J. clearly regarded the relevant factual connection test as being wider than the alternative in (2) above and, yet at the same time, he seems to have accepted that Goodman's offence of insider dealing satisfied a more demanding test "because as chairman it was unquestionably his duty not to use confidential information for his own private benefit". Thus *Goodman* clearly contemplates that s.2(1) extends to: (a) self-dealing offences of a type premised on the equitable fiduciary obligations owed by directors to their companies[67]; and (b) any other offence which, in some sense, touches upon the management of the company.

10–23 While it is difficult to ascertain the ambit of the "relevant factual connection" test, the approach in *Goodman* suggests that the courts will not be unduly restrictive in construing s.2(1). This is borne out by the subsequent decision in *R. v Creggy*.[68] In *Creggy* the defendant was a solicitor who was convicted of a money laundering offence (assisting in the retention of the proceeds of criminal conduct of others, suspecting them to be such). In addition to imposing a suspended prison sentence, the Crown Court disqualified him for seven years pursuant to CDDA s.2. The defendant had acted for a number of clients who had perpetrated a world-wide share swindle in which money was dishonestly obtained from investors in return for shares in worthless companies. The money thus obtained was channelled through a company called Pentagon Securities, which did not have a bank account, and laundered through the defendant's client account. The short point that fell to be decided by the Court of Appeal was one of jurisdiction. It was argued on the defendant's behalf that there was no power to disqualify him because the offence was not an offence in connection with the management of the

[64] It might be argued that (a) and (b) are too wide because it is possible for sole traders or members of partnerships to commit these types of offence without risk of disqualification, i.e. there is nothing specifically *corporate* about the offences in *Corbin, Austin* and *Georgiou*. This argument can be raised in relation to many regulatory offences such as health and safety etc. that apply to business managers regardless of whether the business is incorporated. However, the justification for a wide approach rests on the CDDA's protective rationale including its concern with raising standards of conduct. In other jurisdictions, certain offences (generally offences of dishonesty or fraud as opposed to regulatory offences) committed *outside* the corporate context lead to automatic disqualification: see, e.g. Australia's Corporations Act 2001 (Cth.) s.206B.

[65] As in the case of the elephant, it is probably recognised more easily when present than defined.

[66] R. Nolan, "Disqualifying directors" (1994) 15 Co. Law. 278.

[67] Now codified as ss.171–177 of the Companies Act 2006. See further 10–38 for a discussion of self-dealing offences that appear to fall within the scope of CDDA s.2(1).

[68] [2008] 3 All E.R. 91.

company: the defendant had not been a manager of Pentagon Securities and he had not been convicted of operating it for the purpose of the fraud. Applying *Goodman* the Court of Appeal held that the offence had a relevant factual connection with the financial management of Pentagon Securities and so fell within CDDA s.2(1). As Pentagon Securities had no bank account, the significant point was that those who managed Pentagon Securities' assets and disbursed its funds could not do so without the defendant's participation. Thus, *Creggy* confirms that the offence need not be committed via the management of the company or by using the company as a vehicle in order to fall within s.2(1).[69] Nevertheless, it is clear from the "in connection" wording that if a director or manager of a company is convicted of offences that are wholly unrelated to the management of a company albeit that they cast doubt on his fitness for such an office or role, he is not liable to disqualification under s.2(1). Thus, for example, if a director is convicted of an isolated offence of theft in his personal capacity after having stolen a number of items from the local supermarket, the court cannot disqualify him even though the offence may raise serious questions about his honesty and overall fitness to occupy a fiduciary position. His "fitness and propriety" can only be judged by reference to his activities in relation to a specified company or companies. This contrasts with the position in other jurisdictions where a person convicted of certain types of offence faces disqualification regardless of whether that offence has any connection with a company or not. In Australia, a conviction for an offence of dishonesty punishable by imprisonment for at least three months results in automatic disqualification for five years. The position in the Republic of Ireland is similar.[70] The formal position in these jurisdictions reflects a wider attempt to prevent those whose integrity and probity has been called into question from running companies and controlling corporate assets.

Examples of offences "in connection with . . . management" falling within CDDA s.2(1)

10–24 It has been suggested that the courts are unlikely to construe s.2(1) restrictively. A liberal approach to construction is certainly consistent with the view that the CDDA as a whole is a coherent legislative scheme concerned with protecting the public from those whose misconduct has cast doubt on their ability or suitability to run companies.[71] The aim under the present heading is to identify a range of possible offences for which a conviction may trigger the jurisdiction in s.2 so as to illustrate the potential width and practical relevance of s.2. However, it is not claimed that what follows provides an exhaustive account of every indictable offence that could conceivably fall within s.2(1). The discussion is intended to be illustrative rather than exhaustive.

[69] [2008] 3 All E.R. 91 at [13], [14].

[70] The relevant provision in Australia is the Corporations Act 2001 (Cth.) s.206B, the statutory predecessor of which is discussed in J. Cassidy, "Disqualification of Directors under the Corporations Law" (1995) 13 Company and Securities L.J. 221. For Ireland, see Companies Act 1990 s.160(1). The position in New Zealand, South Africa and Singapore is similar to that in Australia and Ireland.

[71] See general discussion in Ch.2.

Corporate offences committed with the consent or connivance of, or attributable to the neglect of a director or manager

10–25 Companies are liable to prosecution for a variety of regulatory offences in the fields of environmental protection, health and safety and consumer protection. In several instances, a director or manager of a company can also be prosecuted personally if it can be proved that the offence for which the company is liable was committed with the consent or connivance of, or was attributable to any neglect on the part of that director or manager. If a director or manager is convicted of an offence of this type the court's power to disqualify him under s.2 is bound to arise, as it will be easy to show the required connection between the offence and the management of a company in the light of the authorities discussed above. The trend in recent years has been to criminalise the conduct of directors and senior managers as well as that of the company and so the opportunities for the courts to consider s.2 are likely to increase rather than diminish in the future. Having said that, it must be appreciated that while a conviction for an indictable offence is a necessary condition for the operation of s.2, it is not of itself a sufficient condition and there has, as yet, been little debate about whether disqualification is an appropriate response to offences of this nature.[72] Nevertheless, the relevant agencies that are responsible for enforcement should be aware that the court's discretion under s.2(1) is likely to arise where a director or manager is convicted of a corporate regulatory offence.

10–26 **Environmental offences.** A wide range of indictable offences can be committed under environmental legislation. These offences are directed at mischief ranging from pollution of the environment to unauthorised disposal of waste. So, for example, it is an offence to deposit controlled waste in or on land unless an environmental permit authorising the deposit is in force[73] or to cause pollution of controlled waters.[74] These offences can be committed by "a person" (which, of course, includes a company, a director or senior manager) and are triable either way. If the offences are committed by a company and it is proved that the offence was committed with the consent or connivance of, or was attributable to any neglect on the part of any director, manager, secretary or other similar officer or any person who was purporting to act in any such capacity, then he, as well as the company, is guilty of an offence and liable to prosecution.[75] Responsibility for enforcement lies with the Environment Agency in England and Wales and the Scottish Environment Protection Agency in Scotland. It appears that the power in CDDA s.2 is being exercised in this area.[76]

[72] Such offences can also be committed by sole traders or members of general partnership firms without risk of disqualification under s.2 (although the effect of the Insolvent Partnerships Order 1994 is that members of general partnership firms that become insolvent are exposed to possible disqualification under s.6 on grounds of unfitness).

[73] Environmental Protection Act 1990 s.33(1)(a).

[74] Water Resources Act 1991 s.85.

[75] Environmental Protection Act 1990 s.157; Water Resources Act 1991 s.217.

[76] For example, on October 2, 2002, two directors of a company called Ivory Plant Hire Ltd, a Mr. John Bruce and a Ms. Ann Gartlan were disqualified at Worcester Crown Court following their conviction for offences contrary to s.33 of the Environmental Protection Act 1990 for 10 years and five years respectively: see ENDS 2002, Oct, 56.

10–27 **Health and safety offences.** The Health and Safety at Work Act 1974 imposes duties on employers (including corporate employers) to take steps both to secure the health, safety and welfare of employees and to protect the public generally against risks to health and safety arising in the workplace.[77] Under s.33(1)(a) of the 1974 Act, a person who fails to discharge any of these general duties commits an offence that is triable either way.[78] Section 37 contains precisely the same "consent, connivance or neglect" wording already observed in the context of environmental legislation with the consequence that individual directors or managers of a corporate offender can be prosecuted alongside the company. Responsibility for enforcement lies with the Health and Safety Executive, an agency that was established under the 1974 Act.

10–28 It was acknowledged during parliamentary debate on the Offshore Safety Bill[79] in 1991 that s.2 is capable of applying to offences under health and safety legislation. In the course of debate, an attempt was made in the House of Lords to amend s.2(1) to make express reference to offences under Pt 1 of the 1974 Act and related legislation. Viscount Ullswater expressed the government of the day's opposition to the amendment in the following terms:

> "To return to the particular amendment, the main reason why the government oppose the amendment is that they believe it is unnecessary or perhaps even counter-productive. It is unnecessary because in our view s.2 of the Company Directors Disqualification Act 1986 is capable of applying to health and safety matters . . . We believe that the scope of s.2(1) . . . is very broad and that 'management' includes the management of health and safety . . . Finally, I mentioned our view that the amendment could be counter-productive. By that I meant that the proposed text could have the effect of narrowing the scope of s.2(1) . . . which currently we construe very broadly. There is a danger that in seeking to define the circumstances in which s.2(1) applies, the courts will interpret the section as applying only to those specified circumstances and none other."[80]

10–29 Technical considerations aside, Viscount Ullswater also doubted whether, in practice, the court's power to disqualify directors and managers under s.2 would have much effect in improving standards of health and safety. He reasoned that it will always be easier to prove a case against an employer generally than against individual directors and pointed out that even if a director is successfully prosecuted, the court may decide that disqualification would serve no useful purpose. Nevertheless, the s.2(1) power has been exercised to disqualify offenders following conviction under s.37 of the 1974 Act.[81]

[77] See, in particular, Health and Safety at Work Act 1974 ss.2–4.

[78] The mode of trial and maximum penalties for offences under s.33 (not all of which are indictable) are set out in Sch.3A to the 1974 Act which was inserted by the Health and Safety (Offences) Act 2008 with effect from January 16, 2009 except in relation to offences committed before that date.

[79] Subsequently enacted as the Offshore Safety Act 1992 which applies the 1974 Act to offshore installations.

[80] *Hansard*, H.L. Vol. 532, cols 1431–1432, (1991).

[81] See, e.g. the cases of Rodney James Chapman and William Eid. Chapman was disqualified in 1992 following his conviction for an offence under the 1974 Act at Lewes Crown Court. Chapman's case is discussed in G. Slapper, "Litigation and Corporate Crime" [1997] Journal of Personal Injury

10–30 For many years the Government contemplated the introduction of an offence of corporate manslaughter.[82] This led finally to the enactment of the Corporate Manslaughter and Corporate Homicide Act 2007 which makes it an offence if the way an organisation's activities are managed or organised: (a) causes a person's death; and (b) amounts to a gross breach of a relevant duty of care owed by the organisation to the deceased.[83] An organisation is only guilty of the offence if the way in which its activities are managed or organised by its senior management[84] is a substantial element in the breach. The critical point about this legislation is that it seeks to resolve problems associated with the common law rules for attributing the mental states of individuals to corporations and other bodies. Its purpose is therefore solely to create corporate criminal liability. A proposed draconian power under which individuals shown to have had some influence on, or responsibility for, the circumstances in which a management failure was a cause of a person's death, could be disqualified for a potentially unlimited period from acting in a management role in any undertaking (whether a corporation or otherwise) carrying on a business or activity in Great Britain did not make it onto the statute book. However, it is clear that an organisation can be charged with and convicted of the corporate manslaughter offence together with any parallel or overlapping offence under s.33 of the 1974 Act[85] in which case prosecutions against individual directors and managers could well lie under s.37 of that Act. In these circumstances, provided the relevant organisation is a company falling within the scope of the CDDA, the s.2(1) power would be available in the manner outlined above.

10–31 **Consumer protection.** The Consumer Protection from Unfair Trading Regulations 2008[86] is a good example of legislation the primary aim of which is to protect the consumer. These Regulations, which implement the Unfair Commercial

---

Litigation 220. Eid was disqualified for three years on December 1, 1995 by Leicester Crown Court after pleading guilty to various charges brought under s.37 relating to breaches of health and safety regulations (including regulations concerning the employment of child labour): see *Health and Safety Bulletin* for February 1996. It appears, however, that these cases are isolated examples. A report funded by the Health and Safety Executive concluded in 2005 that CDDA disqualification had been used too infrequently for it to have been an effective sanction in the health and safety context: see A. Neal and F. Wright, *A survey of the use and effectiveness of the Company Directors Disqualification Act 1986 as a legal sanction against directors convicted of health and safety offences*, Health and Safety Executive, Research Report RR597 (HSE Books, 2007), *http://www.hse.gov.uk/research/rrhtm/rr597.htm* [Accessed August 26, 2009]. The report went on to recommend the adoption of a more strategic approach, including the development of guidelines for prosecutors.

[82] For background see D. Ormerod and R. Taylor "Legislative Comment: The Corporate Manslaughter and Corporate Homicide Act 2007" [2008] Crim.L.R. 589.

[83] The organisations to which the Act applies are a corporation, a police force, a partnership, trade union or employers' association that is an employer and certain specified government departments or bodies. A "relevant duty of care" is further defined in s.2 of the Act. According to s.1(4)(b) a breach of a duty of care is "gross" if the conduct alleged to amount to a breach of that duty falls far below what can reasonably be expected of the organisation in the circumstances. Factors to be considered by the jury in deciding whether a breach was "gross" are set out in s.8.

[84] Defined in s.1(4)(c) as the persons who play significant roles in: (i) the making of decisions about how the whole or a substantial part of its activities are to be managed or organised; or (ii) the actual managing or organising of the whole or a substantial part of those activities.

[85] Corporate Manslaughter and Corporate Homicide Act 2007 s.19.

[86] SI 2008/1277 (in force from May 26, 2008).

Practices Directive,[87] create a series of prohibitions and offences designed to protect consumers from misleading or aggressive trading practices.[88] The offences are triable either way and, as such, are capable of falling within s.2.[89] As is the case with environmental and health and safety offences, reg.15 of the 2008 Regulations contains "consent, connivance and neglect" wording that exposes officers of a corporate offender (defined to include directors and managers) to criminal liability. Responsibility for the enforcement of this legislation lies with Local Authority Trading Standards Services.

10–32 Under the Food Safety Act 1990, there are several indictable offences affecting food suppliers and retailers that could potentially come within s.2. Again, the directors and managers of a corporate offender are exposed to personal liability and, arguably, the possibility of disqualification, by virtue of "consent, connivance and neglect" wording in s.36 of the 1990 Act.

Financial crime

10–33 Cases like *Corbin, Austen* and *Goodman* (discussed above) show that the courts are willing to disqualify persons who perpetrate offences of theft, obtaining property by deception, fraud or insider dealing in the course of running a company. Moreover, the width of the *Goodman* relevant factual connection test means that the s.2 power may arise either where the company is the vehicle for the commission of an offence[90] or simply the victim.[91] Further examples of indictable offences in the field of financial crime that could result in disqualification under CDDA s.2 are considered below.

10–34 **Fraudulent trading.** If a company's business is carried on with intent to defraud creditors or for any fraudulent purpose, then every person who was knowingly a party to the carrying on of the business in that manner commits an indictable offence under s.993 of the Companies Act 2006 (formerly s.458 of the Companies Act 1985). Section 993 applies regardless of whether the company has been, or is in the course of being wound up. Several individuals convicted of this offence or cognate offences have been disqualified under s.2 and often for periods in excess of five years.[92] The court's power to disqualify a person convicted of this offence

[87] Directive 2005/29/EC.

[88] See further Office of Fair Trading, *Consumer Protection from Unfair Trading—Guidance on the UK Regulations implementing the Unfair Commercial Practices Directive*, OFT1008 (2008), *http://www.oft.gov.uk/ advice_and_resources/small_businesses/competing/protection* [Accessed August 26, 2009].

[89] SI 2008/1277, reg.13.

[90] As in *Corbin* and *Austen*. See also *R. v Youell* [2007] EWCA Crim 225, [2007] 2 Cr.App.R.(S.) 43 (defendant disqualified for 10 years where companies of which he was a director had been used to disguise his earnings and so facilitate the commission of a fraud on the Revenue).

[91] See, e.g. *R. v Aucott & Penn* (1989) 11 Cr.App.R.(S.) 86.

[92] See, e.g. *R. v Kazmi* (1985) 7 Cr.App.R. (S.) 115 (five-year disqualification); *R. v Cobbey* (1993) 14 Cr.App.R.(S.) 82 (six-year disqualification); *R. v Millard* (1994) 15 Cr.App.R.(S.) 445 (15-year disqualification reduced to eight years on appeal); *R. v Smith* (1996) 2 Cr.App.R. 1 (12-year disqualification); *R. v Bott-Walters* [2005] EWCA Crim 243, [2005] 2 Cr.App.R.(S.) 70 (seven-year disqualification upheld on appeal); *R. v Mascarenas* [2005] EWCA Crim 1112 (eight-year disqualifications); *R. v Furr* [2007] EWCA Crim 191 (11-year disqualification); *R. v Groves* [2007] EWCA Crim 2263 (10-year disqualification); *R. v Bright* [2008] EWCA Crim 462, [2008] 2 Cr.App.R.(S.) 102 (12-year disqualification).

under s.2 overlaps to a certain extent with the powers of the civil courts to disqualify a person under s.4 (triggered where, in the course of winding up, it appears that an offence under s.993 or other fraud has been committed) and s.10 (triggered where the court makes a declaration under s.213 of the Insolvency Act). The s.4 power and the overlap between ss.2, 4 and 10 are considered further below.

10–35 Directors have also been disqualified following conviction for various related offences such as insurance fraud,[93] fraud in anticipation of, or during the course of, winding up contrary to ss.206–211 of the Insolvency Act 1986[94] and the making of false and misleading statements contrary to what is now s.397 of the Financial Services and Markets Act 2000.[95] It should be noted that the general fraud offence created by the Fraud Act 2006 is capable of being committed by a body corporate and that s.12 of that Act provides that if the offence is proved to have been committed with the consent or connivance of a director, manager, secretary or other similar officer or a person who was purporting to act in such a capacity that person is also guilty of the offence.[96] It follows that a person within the scope of s.12 who is convicted on indictment may also be disqualified under CDDA s.2.

10–36 **Tax evasion.** A director who perpetrates tax, VAT or excise fraud through the medium of a company runs the risk of disqualification if convicted. Directors convicted of offences under tax legislation have suffered disqualification, both before[97] and after conviction.[98] A cursory search of the law reports suggests that the criminal courts do actively exercise the CDDA s.2 power as an additional weapon in their sentencing armoury where persons are convicted of offences of cheating the public revenue having perpetrated scams such as VAT missing trader intra-community (or carousel) fraud and "fresh air" invoicing.[99]

10–37 **Insider dealing.** An individual currently commits an indictable offence under the Criminal Justice Act 1993 s.52 if, having information as an insider,[100] he deals in securities that are price-affected in relation to that information, or encourages others to deal, or discloses the information to others. In *R. v Goodman* discussed above, the appellant had been convicted of an offence under the Company Securities (Insider Dealing) Act 1985, now repealed. To prove an offence under

[93] *R. v Appleyard* (1985) 81 Cr.App.R. 319.

[94] *R. v Bateson & Darlington*, October 12, 2000, CCA, unreported; *R. v Bevis* [2001] EWCA Crim 9.

[95] *R. v Feld* [1999] 1 Cr.App.R.(S.) 1; *R. v Murombe* [2007] EWCA Crim 3391; *R. v O'Hanlon* [2008] 2 Cr.App.R.(S.) 16.

[96] For background and commentary see D. Ormerod, "Legislative Comment: The Fraud Act 2006—criminalising lying?" [2007] Crim.L.R. 193; G. Scanlan, "Offences concerning directors and officers of a company—fraud and corruption in the United Kingdom" (2008) 29 Co. Law. 264.

[97] Usually under CDDA s.6.

[98] See, e.g. *R. v Sivyer* (1987) 9 Cr.App.R.(S.) 428; *R. v Dealy* [1995] 1 W.L.R. 658; *R. v Stannard* [2002] EWCA Crim 458.

[99] See, e.g. *R. v Ward* [2005] EWCA Crim 1926, [2006] 1 Cr.App.R.(S.) 66; *R. v Stannard* [2005] EWCA Crim 2717, [2005] B.T.C. 558; *R. v Beardall* [2006] EWCA Crim 577; *R. v H* [2006] EWCA Crim 2385; *Attorney General's Reference Nos 88, 89, 90 & 91 of 2006* [2006] EWCA Crim 3254, (2007) 2 Cr. App. R. (S.) 28; *R. v Youell* [2007] 2 Cr.App.R.(S.) 43; *R. v Jones* [2007] EWCA Crim 1637; *R. v Hening* [2007] EWCA Crim 2024, [2008] 1 Cr.App.R.(S.) 54; *R. v Matthews* [2008] EWCA Crim 423, [2008] S.T.C. 1999; *R. v Takkar* [2008] EWCA Crim 646, [2008] 2 Cr.App.R.(S.) 92.

[100] On which, see further Criminal Justice Act 1993 ss.56, 57.

that Act, the prosecution had to establish that there was a connection between the insider and the relevant corporate issuer. This is no longer a requirement as a person will now be treated as an insider simply by virtue of his knowledge that the relevant information is unpublished and derives from an inside source.[101] This recasting of the offence has led to speculation that a court may not now be as willing as it was in *Goodman* to contemplate the use of s.2 in a case of insider dealing.[102] It seems likely, however, that a director of a company convicted of the current insider dealing offence in relation to the shares of that company is just as likely to be disqualified under s.2 as a director convicted under the previous legislation. Although decided under the previous legislation, *Goodman* suggests that an offence of insider dealing should be treated as being analogous to a breach of directors' duties and/or a misuse of confidential information.[103] An application of the relevant factual connection test would surely lead to the conclusion that a breach of duty involving dealings in the company's shares that results in a conviction is an "offence in connection with . . . management". Thus, in the *Goodman* scenario, the offence can be converted into a straightforward matter of corporate governance bringing it within the scope of s.2. On the same analysis, the director of a corporate broking business who engages in insider dealing on behalf of himself and his clients commits offences in the course of managing the company and could face disqualification. However, the scope of the insider dealing offence is wide and not every contravention will trigger the operation of s.2. So, for example, if a private investor were to be convicted of the offence in relation to his personal share portfolio, it is difficult to see how that would be an "offence in connection with . . . management . . . of a company".

10–38 **Self-dealing offences.** If a director dishonestly misappropriates the assets of his company then he commits both an offence of theft and a breach of trust. There seems little doubt that the court can disqualify a director who has been convicted of an indictable offence *against* his company.[104] Such an offence will invariably amount to a breach of trust or fiduciary duty and, as in the case of insider dealing above, it can be readily classified as an offence "in connection with the management of a company" because fiduciary-based duties and employees' duties of mutual trust and confidence form part of the legal environment in which directors and senior managers are obliged to operate when running companies. On this analysis, it would also be open to the court to disqualify a director who has been convicted of the offence of failing to disclose an interest in a transaction or arrangement that has been entered into by the company contrary to ss.182–183 of the Companies Act 2006.[105]

[101] Criminal Justice Act 1993 ss.56, 57.
[102] See R. Nolan, "Disqualifying directors" (1994) 15 Co. Law. 278.
[103] There is an analogy with *Boardman v Phipps* [1967] 2 A.C. 46.
[104] See, e.g. *R. v Aucott & Penn* (1989) 11 Cr.App.R.(S.) 86.
[105] Given the overlaps between a number of the CDDA powers of disqualification, a director who is not prosecuted for such an offence could still be found unfit on an application to disqualify him under either CDDA ss.6 or 8: see CDDA s.9, Sch.1 Pt I paras 1–2 and, e.g., *Re Godwin Warren Control Systems Plc* [1993] B.C.L.C. 80.

Financial assistance. A public company or any of its subsidiaries are generally prohibited by the Companies Act 2006 s.678 from providing financial assistance to anyone who is acquiring or proposing to acquire or who has acquired shares in that company. If s.678 is contravened, the company and every officer of it who is in default commits an indictable offence.[106] In *Re Continental Assurance Co of London Plc*,[107] a disqualification order was made under CDDA s.6, in part based on breaches of s.151 of the Companies Act 1985, the statutory predecessor of s.678. If the director in that case had been convicted of the offence it appears that an order could equally have been made under s.2.[108] **10–39**

Carrying on an unauthorised investment business through the medium of a company

There are various types of specialised business, especially in the area of financial services, which cannot be conducted without formal authorisation from an external regulator. Thus, for example, a person who carries on investment business without authorisation is guilty of an offence contrary to s.19 of the Financial Services and Markets Act 2000. Anyone wishing to carry on investment business must, generally speaking, obtain authorisation from the Financial Services Authority ("the FSA"). It is clear by analogy with *R. v Georgiou* (discussed above) that anyone convicted of conducting investment business without authorisation through the medium of a company is liable to disqualification under s.2. This appears to be the case even if the business has otherwise been carried on properly. Disqualification under the CDDA is just one of a range of possible sanctions available to deal with those who commit the offence.[109] A leading principle in the field of financial services regulation is that only those who are considered "fit and proper" should be permitted to carry on regulated activities.[110] Thus, outside the CDDA context, anyone convicted of an offence involving dishonesty or incompetence is likely to face difficulties obtaining or retaining authorisation to engage in a regulated activity.[111] Equally, it is important to note that proceedings under the CDDA are not precluded simply on the ground that the FSA has taken disciplinary action against the person in respect of the same or related matters. This is because disqualification under the CDDA **10–40**

[106] Companies Act 2006 s.680.

[107] [1997] 1 B.C.L.C. 48.

[108] The Australian case of *Re Shneider* (1997) 22 A.C.S.R. 497 which concerned an application to relax the automatic ban then imposed on those convicted of certain offences by s.229(3) of the Corporations Law—subsequently re-enacted in Corporations Act 2001 (Cth.) s.206B—provides some limited support for this view. Shneider had been convicted of charges relating to a company which was found to have provided financial assistance for the purchase of its own shares. The court does not appear to have doubted the necessity of the application which suggests that the offence is one "in connection with the management of a corporation" within what is now s.206B of the 2001 Act.

[109] As a matter of discretion the court might decide, on the particular facts of a case, that the matter has been adequately dealt with by another regulator and that a wider disqualification is not necessary.

[110] Financial Services and Markets Act 2000 s.41 and Sch.6 para.5.

[111] As well as the power to refuse authorisation in the first place, the FSA also has power to make a prohibition order where it appears that an individual is not a fit and proper person to perform functions in relation to a regulated activity carried out by an authorised person: Financial Services and Markets Act 2000 ss.56–58 and see *R. (on the application of Davies) v Financial Services Authority* [2002] EWHC 2997 (Admin), [2003] 1 W.L.R. 1284 affirmed [2003] EWCA Civ 1128, [2004] 1 W.L.R. 185.

differs in purpose and effect from regulatory proceedings and the tests applied in each case are different.[112]

Acting in contravention of a CDDA disqualification

10–41 Any person who acts in contravention of: (a) a disqualification order or undertaking; (b) the automatic ban on undischarged bankrupts, those subject to a debt relief order and those subject to bankruptcy or debt relief restrictions in CDDA s.11; (c) the ban in CDDA s.12(2); or (d) a Northern Ireland disqualification order or undertaking (CDDA ss.12A and 12B) commits an indictable offence under CDDA s.13. If convicted, it is open to the court to impose a further period of disqualification as contravention of s.13 can be regarded as an offence "in connection with the management of a company".[113] Section 1(3) of the CDDA provides that where a disqualification order is made against a person who is already subject to such an order, the periods specified in the orders are to run concurrently not consecutively. So, for example, if X is disqualified for six years and then disqualified a second time for ten years, four years into the first ban, the second ban starts to run from year four, not from the end of year six. A director or manager convicted of an offence under s.14 is similarly liable to disqualification. Section 14 imposes criminal liability on a body corporate that acts in contravention of a disqualification order and contains the "consent, connivance and neglect" form of words encountered earlier in the discussion of corporate regulatory offences and in s.12 of the Fraud Act 2006. It should be noted that breach of a disqualification order or of certain of the prohibitions in CDDA s.11 can result in personal liability for the person in breach or an accessory under s.15. Following a conviction there is also the possibility of compensation orders being made under the Proceeds of Crime Act 2002.[114]

Competition Law

10–42 Under s.188 of the Enterprise Act 2002, it is an offence for a person to engage in various specified cartel activities. It is clear from s.90 of the Enterprise Act that the offence is indictable. It is also clear that a person who causes a company to engage in the proscribed activities would be committing an offence in connection with the management of the company and would be liable to disqualification under CDDA s.2 if convicted. This is borne out by the marine hose cartel case, the first and (as far as the authors are aware) the only case to date in which the s.188 cartel offence has been successfully prosecuted and in which three directors

[112] *Secretary of State for Trade and Industry v Baker (No.2)* [1999] 1 W.L.R. 1985. This aspect of the *Barings* proceedings involved an unsuccessful attempt by one of the defendants to have disqualification proceedings against him under s.6 stayed on the ground that he had already successfully resisted disciplinary proceedings brought by the Securities and Futures Authority in which substantially the same charges were made. He was eventually disqualified under CDDA s.6 for six years.

[113] See, e.g. *R. v Thompson* (1993) 14 Cr.App.R.(S.) 89; *R. v Ashby* [1998] 2 Cr.App.R. 37; *R. v Bateson & Darlington*, October 12, 2000, Court of Appeal (Criminal Division) unreported; *R. v Randhawa* [2008] EWCA Crim 2599.

[114] *R. v Seager* [2009] EWCA Crim 1303.

received custodial sentences and were disqualified under CDDA s.2 for periods ranging between five and seven years.[115]

Summary

10–43 The examples given above illustrate the width of the relevant factual connection test in *Goodman*. The fact that some of the offences discussed could equally be committed outside the corporate law context (for example, those relating to health and safety, the environment and the carrying on of an unauthorised business) does not take them outside the jurisdiction of s.2. If the offence is committed in the course of the management of a company's business (*Corbin, Austen* and *Georgiou*) or the offence, in some sense, touches upon management (*Goodman*), the offender is liable to disqualification under the section regardless of whether the victim is the company itself or some third party. The courts therefore have considerable scope for using s.2 to further the protective policy of the CDDA as a whole. That being said, the question of whether the court will exercise this wide jurisdiction remains a matter of discretion in each case.

Offence in connection with liquidation or striking off of a company

10–44 This wording encompasses certain provisions of the Insolvency Act 1986, including, by way of example, those which impose a duty on various people such as the officers of an insolvent company, to co-operate with the liquidator or official receiver.[116] It would also expose an insolvency practitioner convicted of theft or fraud in relation to a company of which he was liquidator to possible disqualification under s.2.[117] In this respect, the powers to disqualify under s.2(1) and s.4(1)(b) overlap. The extent of this overlap is considered below. "Striking off" refers to the process by which a company is dissolved and removed from the register of companies.[118] In particular, the Registrar of Companies himself initiates a striking-off where he has reasonable cause to believe that a company is not carrying on business or is not in operation[119] and a private company may itself apply to be struck off pursuant to ss.1003–1010 of the Companies Act 2006 (formerly ss.652A–652F of the Companies Act 1985). Under the latter provisions there are a number of statutory requirements laying on the applicant private company and its directors.

[115] OFT Press Release 72/08 "Three imprisoned in first OFT criminal prosecution for bid rigging". See also *R. v Whittle* [2008] EWCA Crim 2560, especially at [14]. The custodial sentences were reduced on appeal. There was no appeal against the making of, or duration of, the disqualification orders. Civil disqualification on competition law grounds under CDDA ss.9A or 9B is considered further in Ch.6.

[116] See, e.g. Insolvency Act 1986 ss.235, 430 and Sch.10. Failure to co-operate with an office holder can also be taken into account in determining whether a defendant's conduct makes him unfit for the purposes of ss.6 to 8: see CDDA s.9 and Sch.1 Pt II para.10 and text at 5–64.

[117] Including an absolute ban on acting as an insolvency practitioner: CDDA s.1(1)(b).

[118] The reference to "striking off" was originally added by an amendment introduced by the Deregulation and Contracting Out Act 1994 s.39 and Sch.11, para.6 with effect from July 1, 1995 (SI 1995/1433).

[119] Companies Act 2006 s.1000 (formerly Companies Act 1985 s.353). In practice the initiation of this process often acts as a means of procuring that companies which are, in fact, in operation make good filing defaults.

These are designed to prevent the process of voluntary dissolution being misused and damaging creditors. Breach of certain of these provisions is a criminal offence.

Offence in connection with receivership of a company's property

10–45 The phrase, "... with the receivership of a company's property or with his being an administrative receiver of a company" was substituted for the former wording, "receiver or manager of the property of a company" by the Insolvency Act 2000 s.8 and Sch.4 para.3 with effect from April 2, 2001.[120] Conviction of offences in connection with acting as a receiver or manager of the property of companies continue to be caught by virtue of CDDA s.22(10). The current wording makes it clear that s.2 encompasses administrative receivers (as defined by the Insolvency Act 1986 s.29(2)), receivers of part of a company's property, receivers appointed subject to the Law of Property Act 1925, receivers appointed by the court and offences committed in connection with the various forms of receivership. It does not matter whether the offence was committed by the receiver or by some other person such as a company officer. Thus, an officer who fails in his duty to provide an administrative receiver with a statement of affairs as required by s.47 of the Insolvency Act 1986 would be liable to disqualification if convicted.[121] The same is true of an insolvency practitioner convicted of theft or fraud in relation to corporate assets of which he was a receiver.[122] In this respect, there is an overlap between s.2(1) and s.4(1)(b) which is considered further below.

Section 2: procedure

10–46 According to CDDA s.2(2) any of the following courts have power to make a disqualification order under s.2(1):

(1) a civil court having jurisdiction to wind up the company in relation to which the offence was committed;
(2) the convicting court;
(3) in the case of a summary conviction in England and Wales, any other magistrates' court acting for the same local justice area.[123]

If a court of summary jurisdiction makes a disqualification order under s.2, the maximum period of disqualification it can impose is five years. Otherwise, the maximum period of disqualification is 15 years.[124] The position is very similar in

[120] Insolvency Act 2000 (Commencement No.1 and Transitional Provisions) Order 2001 (SI 2001/766).

[121] The offence is indictable: see Insolvency Act 1986 s.430 and Sch.10. Although the phrase, "in connection ... with his being an administrative receiver ..." encompasses only offences committed by the office holder, it is suggested that "in connection ... with the receivership of a company's property" is wide enough to encompass offences committed by other parties in the context of any receivership, including an administrative receivership.

[122] The consequences of disqualification for such a person would be very serious because of the absolute ban on him or her acting as an insolvency practitioner: see CDDA s.1(1)(b).

[123] The reference to "local justice area" replaced the previous reference to "petty session area" with effect from April 1, 2005: see Courts Act 2003 s.109(1), Sch.8 para.300; SI 2005/910 and SI 2005/911.

[124] CDDA s.2(3).

all respects in Northern Ireland by virtue of art.5(2) of the Company Directors Disqualification (Northern Ireland) Order.[125]

Court having winding up jurisdiction (civil cases)

10–47 The High Court has jurisdiction to wind up any company which is liable to be wound up in England and Wales under the Insolvency Act 1986. In respect of a company which has a paid up (or credited as paid up) share capital of £120,000 or less, the county court for the district in which the company's registered office is situated (or deemed to be situated) has concurrent winding up jurisdiction with the High Court.[126] The position in relation to civil disqualification proceedings in a court with winding up jurisdiction is considered in more detail in Ch.7 and so what follows is a brief summary only.

10–48 Locus standi to apply is conferred on the following by CDDA s.16(2):

(1) The Secretary of State.
(2) An official receiver.
(3) The liquidator or any past or present member or creditor of any company in relation to which the offence was committed.[127]

This procedure makes it possible for the Secretary of State, for example, to apply for a disqualification order against a person who has been convicted of a relevant offence but was not disqualified by the convicting court. Anyone intending to apply to a court with winding up jurisdiction for an order under s.2 is required by s.16(1) to give at least ten days' notice to the intended defendant before issuing the application.[128] The Disqualification Practice Direction makes it clear that the application is by way of claim form under Pt 8 of the CPR. Civil proceedings for an order under s.2 are not subject to any express limitation period. Once issued, however, they will be subject to the court's powers of case management under the CPR, the Disqualification Practice Direction and, by virtue of the Human Rights Act 1998, art.6 of the European Convention on Human Rights will also apply. Any delay in the bringing of proceedings could therefore be taken into account by the court as a possible justification for refusing to exercise its discretion to make a disqualification order.

[125] SI 2002/3150.

[126] Insolvency Act 1986 s.117(2). In Scotland, the Court of Session and the sheriff courts have a similar concurrent jurisdiction: Insolvency Act 1986 s.120. In Northern Ireland winding up jurisdiction is exercised exclusively by the Northern Ireland High Court.

[127] In the event of an application by the liquidator etc., it seems likely that the Secretary of State would be entitled, or at least permitted, to intervene in the proceedings. There is authority suggesting that a creditor or member would have to demonstrate a legitimate interest in the relief sought: see *Re Adbury Park Estates Ltd*, June 28, 2001, Ch.D., unreported and (on the subsequent application for permission to appeal) *Re Adbury Park Estates Ltd, Juer v Lomas* [2001] EWCA Civ 1568 discussed further in 7–43.

[128] For further discussion of the notice requirement in s.16(1) and the implications of non-compliance, see text from 7–33. For a full account of procedure in civil disqualification proceedings encompassing CDDA ss.2–4 as well as ss.6, 8 and 9A see Ch.7.

Convicting court

10–49 This will be the Crown Court (or, in Scotland, the High Court of Justiciary) if the trial is on indictment and a magistrates' court (or, in Scotland, a sheriff court) in the case of a summary trial. The convicting court can make a disqualification order of its own motion as an adjunct to the sentencing process. In *Re Cedac Ltd, Secretary of State for Trade and Industry v Langridge*, Balcombe L.J. observed that the ten-day notice rule in s.16(1) does not apply to proceedings where the court is empowered to make a disqualification order of its own motion, although he went on to suggest obiter that:

> "doubtless the rules of natural justice will require that the person concerned should be given some notice that the court is contemplating making a disqualification order".[129]

It is difficult to know what to make of this dictum as the reference to a "court empowered to make a disqualification order of its own motion" could refer to civil disqualification under CDDA s.10 following participation in fraudulent or wrongful trading under s.10 or criminal disqualification under CDDA s.2. In any event, there is no particularly compelling justification for a special requirement that an offender be given advance notice of his exposure to disqualification under s.2. The role of the prosecution in criminal sentencing is simply to remind the court of its powers for dealing with the offender. The prosecution does not *apply* for a disqualification order in the same way that the Secretary of State might in civil proceedings. Accordingly, it is submitted that in criminal proceedings the offender is deemed to be aware of all the possible sentencing consequences (including disqualification) which may be visited on him following conviction. If so, it is questionable whether any particular significance attaches to Balcombe L.J.'s dictum in the context of criminal disqualification.

SECTION 3: DISQUALIFICATION FOR PERSISTENT BREACH OF COMPANIES LEGISLATION

10–50 Section 3(1) provides that the court may make a disqualification order against a person where it appears that he has been persistently in default in relation to provisions of the companies legislation requiring any return, account or other document to be filed with, delivered or sent, or notice of any matter given, to the Registrar of Companies. Section 3 is perhaps best seen as a "last resort" option among the range of sanctions available to deal with companies (and relevant officers) that fail to comply with the disclosure and publicity requirements of companies legislation. An individual can be disqualified under s.3 regardless of whether the company to which the default relates is insolvent or not. In the case of a director of a company which has entered a relevant insolvency regime and so "become insolvent" within the meaning of s.6, complaints of this nature are much more likely to be brought against him as evidence of unfit conduct in proceedings for an order under CDDA

[129] [1991] Ch. 402 at 414F.

s.6.[130] Like s.2, s.3 does not apply exclusively to directors and may be of concern to other officers including company secretaries. Section 3 also overlaps substantially with s.5 which is discussed further below. The power to disqualify for persistent breaches of companies legislation is a relative newcomer that was first introduced by the Companies Act 1976 s.28. It was subsequently re-enacted first as the Companies Act 1981 s.93 and later as the Companies Act 1985 s.297, the immediate predecessor of the current provision.[131] The maximum period of disqualification is five years. There is no minimum period.

Companies legislation

10–51 For the purposes of s.3, "companies legislation" means the Companies Acts (which has the meaning given by s.2 of the Companies Act 2006)[132] and specified provisions of the Insolvency Act 1986 relating to companies.[133] Thus, an insolvency practitioner who persistently fails to file returns and documents with the Registrar of Companies as required under the Insolvency Act is liable to disqualification under s.3.[134] This is borne out by the proceedings brought against an insolvency practitioner in *Re Arctic Engineering Ltd*[135] discussed further below.

Return, account etc.

10–52 Section 3(1) covers any return, form, document or notification that is required to be filed at Companies House under the specified legislation. The provision is therefore all embracing. In practice, BIS and Companies House place much regulatory emphasis on the recurring obligations relating to annual returns and accounts, which are seen as key indicators of statutory compliance. In addition to disqualification, routes to enforcement include striking off and prosecution.

Annual return and accounts

10–53 The Companies Act 2006 s.854 (formerly Companies Act 1985 s.363) requires every company to file an annual return before the end of the period of 28 days after the company's return date.[136] The company commits a summary offence if it fails to

[130] See generally Chs 4 and 5. For examples of cases in which failure to file accounts and/or returns was taken into account in disqualification proceedings under s.6 see, e.g. *Re Cladrose Ltd* [1990] B.C.L.C. 204; *Re Synthetic Technology Ltd, Secretary of State for Trade and Industry v Joiner* [1993] B.C.C. 549; *Re Swift 736 Ltd, Secretary of State v Ettinger* [1993] B.C.L.C. 896; *Re Pamstock Ltd* [1994] 1 B.C.L.C. 716. Defaults of this nature could also be taken into account in disqualification proceedings under CDDA s.8.

[131] Comparable provisions are in force in other jurisdictions: see, e.g. Corporations Act 2001 (Cth.) s.206E (Australia) and Companies Act 1990 s.160(2)(f) (Ireland).

[132] See CDDA s.22(7) as substituted by SI 2009/1941 with effect from October 1, 2009.

[133] See CDDA s.3(4A) inserted by SI 2009/1941 with effect from October 1, 2009. The definition of "companies legislation" was previously contained in CDDA s.22(7).

[134] Presumably the references to the relevant legislation will also encompass any statutory instruments made under the relevant legislation. If so, and bearing in mind CDDA s.21(2), this provision could apply to an office holder who fails to make returns for CDDA purposes under the relevant statutory instrument requiring returns to be made, currently the Insolvent Companies (Reports on Conduct of Directors) Rules 1996 (SI 1996/1909): see further text from 3–03.

[135] [1986] 1 W.L.R. 686.

[136] The return date is the date to which the annual return is made up and is fixed initially as the anniversary of the date of incorporation.

comply which is punishable by fine. Where a company is guilty of this offence, every director or secretary of the company and every other officer who is in default is similarly liable unless he shows that he took all reasonable steps to avoid the commission or continuance of the offence. The core accounts and audit provisions are contained in Pts 15–16 of the Companies Act 2006. As regards accounts and reports different rules apply to different companies, the key categories being companies that are eligible for the small companies regime, quoted companies and unquoted companies. Generally, directors of all companies are obliged to prepare individual accounts which must be approved by the board and signed on the board's behalf. They are also obliged to prepare a directors' report for each financial year of the company. Both the accounts and report must be filed at Companies House within a prescribed period of time which varies depending on whether the company is public or private.[137] A variety of penalties can be imposed on a company and its directors for non-compliance with the obligation to file accounts and reports including fines and civil penalties.[138] A further means by which Companies House promotes compliance with these obligations is by invoking the procedure in s.1000 of the Companies Act 2006 (formerly Companies Act 1985 s.652). This provision allows the Registrar to commence striking off proceedings against a company if he has reasonable cause to believe that the company is not carrying on business or is not in operation. The view taken at Companies House is that a company's repeated failure to file annual returns and accounts amounts to "reasonable cause". The problem for the company if it fails to respond once the Registrar has invoked this procedure is that it will be struck off the register. Although it would still then be possible to apply to the Registrar of Companies for administrative restoration pursuant to s.1024 of the Companies Act 2006 within six years from the date of dissolution, it is clear from s.1025(5) that the application will be refused unless, inter alia, all outstanding documents are filed and any outstanding civil penalties for failure to file accounts are paid.[139] Thus, it is important to bear in mind that disqualification for "persistent default" is merely one of a range of regulatory sanctions and techniques that are available and that the main priority of Companies House where possible is to get companies to comply with the law by submitting returns without recourse to court proceedings.[140] It should also be noted that there are a myriad of other returns which are required to be made under companies legislation. These include (and the following list gives but a few examples) returns in connection with changes in a company's directors,[141] amendment of the articles of association,[142] alterations to share capital,[143] and allotments of shares.[144]

[137] Companies Act 2006 ss.441–442 (formerly Companies Act 1985 ss.241–242, 244).

[138] Companies Act 2006 ss.451–453.

[139] Application to the court for restoration of a dissolved company can also be made at any time after dissolution under Companies Act 2006 s.1029 but only for the purpose of bringing proceedings against the company for damages for personal injury.

[140] Indeed, it appears that s.3 is rarely invoked.

[141] Companies Act 2006 s.167 (formerly Companies Act 1985 s.288).

[142] Companies Act 2006 s.21 (formerly Companies Act 1985 s.18).

[143] Companies Act 2006 s.619 (formerly Companies Act 1985 s.123).

[144] Companies Act 2006 s.555 (formerly Companies Act 1985 s.88).

Persistent default

10–54 Under s.3(2), the fact that an individual has been persistently in default may be conclusively proved by showing that in the five years ending with the date of the application for a disqualification order, he has been adjudged guilty (whether or not on the same occasion) of three or more defaults in relation to the provisions of companies legislation described in s.3(1). For the purposes of this conclusive presumption, an individual is treated as having been "adjudged guilty" if he has either been convicted of a non-filing offence (whether on indictment or summarily) or a court order has been made against him under any of the five provisions mentioned in s.3(3)(b) all of which require him to remedy some specific default.[145] Even if persistent default can be conclusively proved in this way, the court is not obliged to disqualify the defendant. The question whether or not to do so remains a matter of discretion and the onus does not shift to the defendant to show why he should not be disqualified.[146] If the individual has not been adjudged guilty of three defaults then the conclusive presumption does not apply and the onus is on the applicant to prove persistent default in some other way.

In *Re Arctic Engineering Ltd*,[147] (a case decided under the provision as it appeared in s.93 of the Companies Act 1981), the Secretary of State applied for a disqualification order against an insolvency practitioner but did not seek to rely on the conclusive presumption. The defendant, an accountant of considerable experience, had been in default in relation to 35 returns concerning the liquidation or receivership of 34 companies over a five-year period. However, he had not been convicted of an offence and no default order had been made against him although in several instances he had only complied after summonses had been issued and served. The court had to determine whether these defaults amounted to "persistent default" in circumstances where the conclusive presumption was not available. Hoffmann J. held that the term "persistently" connotes some degree of continuance or repetition and that a person may persist in the same default or may persistently commit a series of defaults. Taking the conclusive presumption provision as a guide, the judge regarded the defendant's 35 defaults as "amply sufficient to be called persistent". In reaching this conclusion, Hoffmann J. rejected counsel for the defendant's submission that the term "persistently" connoted a culpable disregard of filing obligations. Thus, it is clear from *Arctic Engineering* that the court should not take the defendant's culpability into account when determining whether there has been "persistent default". The question goes to the frequency of default and is broadly one of fact and degree. However, once the discretion to disqualify has arisen, the defendant's culpability can be taken into account in deciding

[145] The five provisions specifically mentioned in s.3(3)(b) are Companies Act 2006 s.452 (order requiring delivery of company accounts) and s.456 (order requiring preparation of revised accounts); Companies Act 2006 s.1113 (enforcement of company's filing obligations); Insolvency Act 1986 s.41 (enforcement of receiver's or manager's duty to make returns) and s.170 (corresponding provision for liquidator in winding up). The amendments consequential upon the enactment of the Companies Act 2006 were made by SI 2008/948 with effect from April 6, 2008 and SI 2009/1941 with effect from October 1, 2009.

[146] Support for this proposition can be found in *Re Arctic Engineering Ltd* [1986] 1 W.L.R. 686.

[147] [1986] 1 W.L.R. 686.

whether to disqualify and, if so, for how long. In *Arctic Engineering* Hoffmann J. declined to disqualify the defendant despite the finding of persistent default. The consequences of disqualification would have been serious for both his employees and clients. Moreover, the judge took the view that it was unnecessary to disqualify the defendant with a view to preventing similar defaults in the future and seems to have felt that the very fact that the Secretary of State had brought the disqualification proceedings would itself be corrective. He also took into account the fact that *Arctic Engineering* was the first case in which the Secretary of State had brought proceedings without relying on the conclusive presumption. It is suggested that a court is unlikely to be as lenient if a similar case were to arise again given the strong line that has been taken in relation to filing default in subsequent s.6 cases[148] and the fact that insolvency practitioners have been subject to licensing and greater regulatory requirements since the mid-1980s.

10–55 On a different point, it is clear from *Arctic Engineering* that in circumstances where a company eventually complies with its filing obligations but only in response to the commencement of criminal or default proceedings, the withdrawal of those proceedings does not amount to a representation that the default in question will be disregarded for the future so as to estop the Secretary of State from relying on it in disqualification proceedings (whether under CDDA s.3 or ss.6–8).

Section 3: procedure

10–56 The effect of s.3(4) is that an application under s.3 can only be made to a court having jurisdiction to wind up any of the companies in relation to which the offence or other default has been or is alleged to have been committed. The criminal courts have no jurisdiction under s.3 to disqualify an individual following his conviction for a filing offence (although they would appear to have jurisdiction under s.2 insofar as the relevant offence is indictable).[149] This is in contrast to the related power in s.5 (discussed below) which is exercisable only by criminal courts of summary jurisdiction. The procedure under s.3 and the range of potential claimants is the same as for an application to a court having winding up jurisdiction under s.2.[150] The maximum period of disqualification that can be imposed is five years.[151]

[148] See, e.g. *Re Swift 736 Ltd, Secretary of State for Trade and Industry v Ettinger* [1993] B.C.L.C. 896 which suggests that the courts will use their powers of disqualification for purposes of deterrence, i.e. in an attempt to improve the general standard of compliance with basic disclosure requirements mandated by companies legislation. It appears that before *Arctic Engineering*, the Secretary of State would only proceed where there had been previous convictions for non-filing offences followed by continuing default: see *Re Civica Investments Ltd* [1983] B.C.L.C. 456 and two unreported cases noted by B. Rider at (1981) 2 Co. Law. 129 and 174. It is unlikely that the Secretary of State would proceed in relation to three or less defaults where the conclusive presumption is unavailable. However, in the light of *Artic Engineering* and the *Swift* case, it is suggested that a pattern of non-compliance could be sufficiently serious on its facts to amount to "persistent default" even where the conclusive presumption is not available because there are no specific convictions or default orders.

[149] The point is somewhat academic but one might expect a court considering such offences in the context of s.2 to regard its discretion as being subject to the parameters set out in ss.3 and 5. In other words, it is highly unlikely that a court would disqualify an offender convicted of an indictable filing offence in the absence of persistent default.

[150] See 10–46 and, on procedure in civil disqualification proceedings generally, Ch.7.

[151] CDDA s.3(5).

SECTION 4: DISQUALIFICATION FOR FRAUD ETC. IN WINDING UP

Section 4(1) states: **10–57**

"The court may make a disqualification order against a person, if in the course of a winding up, it appears that he—

(a) has been guilty of an offence for which he is liable (whether he has been convicted or not) under s.993 of the Companies Act 2006[152] (fraudulent trading), or
(b) has otherwise been guilty, while an officer or liquidator of the company, receiver of the company's property or administrative receiver of the company, of any fraud in relation to the company or of any breach of his duty as such officer, liquidator, receiver or administrative receiver."

The provision's antecedents go back as far as the Companies Act 1928. Section 75(4) of the 1928 Act is the original source of the jurisdictions now set out in CDDA s.4(1)(a) and, as regards a civil finding of fraudulent trading, under what is now s.213 of the Insolvency Act 1986, CDDA s.10. The "fraud" element of the jurisdiction now contained in s.4(1)(b) traces back to s.76 of the 1928 Act. That section permitted the winding up court to impose a disqualification order in cases where the official receiver had reported that, in his opinion, a relevant fraud had been committed.[153] The provision was later consolidated in something like its present form as s.33(1)(b) of the Companies Act 1947 (itself re-enacted shortly afterwards as s.188(1)(b) of the Companies Act 1948)[154] though the scope of what became CDDA s.4(1)(b) was restricted to officers. The wording was extended to make clear that breach of duty (as distinct from fraud) sufficed to found the jurisdiction to disqualify. In this respect, the potential overlap with CDDA ss.6 and 8 is immediately apparent. The wording was further extended to cover liquidators and receivers or managers by s.93 of the Companies Act 1981 and the provision was later consolidated as s.298 of the Companies Act 1985, the immediate predecessor of CDDA s.4. The references to a receiver of the company's property or an administrative receiver were substituted for the previous reference to receivers or managers by the Insolvency Act 2000 s.8 and Sch.4, para.4 with effect from April 2, 2001.[155]

[152] The reference to the current offence in the 2006 Act was substituted for the reference to its statutory predecessor (Companies Act 1985 s.458) by SI 2007/2194 with effect from October 1, 2007.

[153] This was a "further report" pursuant to the statutory precursor to what is now Insolvency Act 1986 s.132. Such a further report of apparent fraud was then a pre-condition to an order for public examination but this requirement has since been dispensed with: see now Insolvency Act 1986 s.133.

[154] The powers now contained in CDDA ss.2 and 4 originally appeared together in s.33(1) of the Companies Act 1947 and later s.188(1) of the Companies Act 1948: see 10–17 in relation to s.2. Under s.275 of the Companies Act 1929 (first enacted as s.75 of the Companies Act 1928) a criminal court had power of its own motion to disqualify an offender convicted of fraudulent trading though note that: (a) a conviction was necessary; and (b) it appears from the wording of s.275(1) that the company had to be in winding up before the offence could be charged. Section 10 of the CDDA can also be traced back to this provision from the Companies Acts 1928–1929.

[155] Insolvency Act 2000 (Commencement No.1 and Transitional Provisions) Order 2001 (SI 2001/766). The provision continues to extend to receivership and management of company property by virtue of CDDA s.22(10).

10–58 The governing precondition for the operation of s.4 is that the relevant misconduct must be discovered during the course of a winding up. This means that the court's discretion to disqualify a person can only arise if the conduct relates to a company that is being or has been wound up.[156] Although the company itself must have ended up as the subject of some form of liquidation procedure, it appears that the section applies to fraud whether it occurred before or during the winding up (i.e. at any stage of the company's life). Like s.2, s.4 is not confined in application to directors. However, in contrast to s.2, the court has jurisdiction to make an order under s.4 if the person is "guilty" of the conduct described in the section without any requirement for a criminal conviction. Moreover, it appears from s.1(4) of the CDDA that civil disqualification proceedings could be commenced under s.4 even if a criminal prosecution based on the same subject matter is pending.[157]

Section 4(1)(a): fraudulent trading

10–59 The Companies Act 2006 s.993 provides that if any business of a company is carried on with intent to defraud creditors of the company or of any other person, or for any fraudulent purpose, every person knowingly a party to the carrying on of the business in that manner commits an offence for which he is liable to imprisonment or a fine, or both. Section 993 applies whether or not the company has been, or is in the course of being wound up. The upshot is that *anyone* knowingly a party to fraudulent trading as defined, appears liable to disqualification under s.4 regardless of whether they have been convicted or not, provided that (for s.4 purposes) the company is being wound up. However, in *R. v Miles*,[158] the Court of Appeal held that the immediate statutory predecessor of s.993 (which in all material respects was in the same terms) can only apply to those who exercise a controlling or managerial function with the result that s.4(1)(a) of the CDDA may not be as wide in scope as it first appears. If the fraudulent conduct comes to light in the course of a winding up and the offender is subsequently convicted of the offence, he is liable to disqualification under either CDDA s.4 or s.2.[159] If a person is convicted of the offence before the company goes into winding up, then at that point he could only be disqualified under s.2.

[156] As long as there is or has been a winding up, it does not appear to matter whether it is an insolvent winding up or not. Thus, it suffices if the company is in members' voluntary winding up following a declaration of solvency by its directors.

[157] Section 1(4) states: "A disqualification order may be made on grounds which are or include matters other than criminal convictions, notwithstanding that the person in respect of whom it is to be made may be criminally liable in respect of those matters". However, the civil proceedings will only be allowed to continue if they are not an abuse of process. On parallel proceedings see text from 7–86 and 10–75.

[158] Noted at [1992] Crim.L.R. 657.

[159] Where the convicting court specifically declines to make a disqualification order under s.2 (but not so that the matter can be dealt with by the civil court), there may be a strong case for saying that any subsequent civil proceedings commenced under s.4(1)(a) would be an abuse of process: see *Re Dennis Hilton Ltd* [2002] 1 B.C.L.C. 302 and discussion concerning parallel proceedings from 7–95.

Section 4(1)(b): fraud or breach of duty by an officer or liquidator or receiver of company property

10–60 Section 4(1)(b) applies to a prescribed class of persons. The term "officer" is not defined exhaustively but includes a director, manager or company secretary[160] and a shadow director.[161] The phrase, "receiver . . . or administrative receiver" embraces administrative receivers (as defined by the Insolvency Act 1986 s.29(2)), receivers of part of a company's property, receivers appointed subject to the Law of Property Act 1925 and receivers appointed by the court, as well as managers.[162]

10–61 There are doubts as to whether an auditor, a supervisor of a corporate voluntary arrangement or an administrator fall within the scope of s.4(1)(b). An auditor and an administrator have both been held to be an "officer" for the purposes of other statutory provisions.[163] A good case can be made for saying that they are both "officers" for the purposes of s.4. The same could be said of liquidators and yet they are expressly mentioned. It appears that a supervisor of a corporate voluntary arrangement falls outside the scope of s.4 in the absence of express provision. Such a person is not usually an officer of the company but an office-holder in relation to the arrangement.

10–62 Section 4(1)(b) applies to fraud and breach of duty. Thus, it is not confined to fraudulent trading and may encompass, for example, fraudulent activities of a type proscribed by s.206 of the Insolvency Act 1986 (which include concealment, destruction or falsification of company books and records) and general misfeasance. An officer or insolvency practitioner convicted of an indictable offence of fraud is potentially liable to disqualification under either s.2 or 4 though if he has not yet been convicted, s.2 would not be available. Given the width of the phrase "breach of duty", it appears that many of the substantive offences that fall within the scope of s.2 could equally support an application under s.4 provided that there is or has been a winding up.[164] Where a director has acted fraudulently or in breach of duty and this comes to light during an insolvent winding up, it may give rise to proceedings for an order under CDDA s.6 which are discussed extensively in earlier chapters. There is also an overlap between CDDA s.4 and s.10 which is considered further below.

[160] CDDA s.22(6) which provides that "officer" has the meaning given by Companies Act 1985 s.744. The scope of the terms "manager" and "management" is discussed principally in Ch.14, though see also text from 10–21.

[161] CDDA s.4(2). For discussion of the terms "director" and "shadow director" see Ch.3.

[162] CDDA s.22(10).

[163] See, e.g. *Re London & General Bank* [1895] 2 Ch. 166 (though in that case "officer" was defined expressly in the company's articles of association to include an auditor); *R. v Shacter* [1960] 2 Q.B. 252; *Re Home Treat Ltd* [1991] B.C.L.C. 705 (relieving provision in what was then Companies Act 1985 s.727 held to apply to an administrator). For more recent cases concerning whether auditors can be regarded as officers, see *Mutual Reinsurance Co Ltd v Peat Marwick Mitchell & Co* [1997] 1 Lloyd's Rep. 253; *Aquachem Ltd v Delphis Bank Ltd* [2008] UKPC 7, [2008] B.C.C. 648.

[164] See 10–15 to 10–45. Where a director commits an offence *against* the company (e.g. theft or self-dealing), the breach of duty is plain. Controlling directors, like those in *R. v Corbin* (1984) 6 Cr.App.R.(S.) 17 and *R. v Austen* (1985) 7 Cr.App.R.(S.) 214, who use companies as a vehicle for fraudulent activity also act in breach of duty because their actions expose the company to potential criminal liability.

Section 4: procedure

10–63 It is clear from CDDA s.4(2) that an application under s.4 can only be made to a court having jurisdiction to wind up any of the companies in relation to which the offence or other default has been or is alleged to have been committed. The procedure under s.4 is the same as for an application to a court having winding up jurisdiction under s.2. The maximum period of disqualification that the court can impose under s.4 is the overall statutory maximum of 15 years.[165] The fact that a criminal prosecution may be pending in relation to the matters complained of is not a bar to separate disqualification proceedings based on the same matters under s.4.[166] However, if the criminal court addresses the issue of disqualification under s.2 during sentencing, any subsequent civil proceedings may be susceptible to challenge on grounds of abuse of process.[167]

SECTION 5: DISQUALIFICATION ON SUMMARY CONVICTION

10–64 Section 5 covers much the same substantive ground as s.3. The main difference is that the power in s.5 is exercisable by the criminal courts whereas s.3 is exclusively the preserve of the civil courts that have winding up jurisdiction. Section 5(2) provides that where a person is convicted of a summary offence counting for the purposes of the section, the court by which he is convicted (or, in England and Wales, any other magistrates' court acting in the same local justice area) may make a disqualification order against him for a period up to a maximum of five years if the circumstances specified in s.5(3) are present.

10–65 The first point to note is that the court's discretion to disqualify can only be triggered by a conviction for a "summary offence" which, for the purposes of s.5, means an offence that is triable only summarily (i.e. by a magistrates' court or the Scottish equivalent).[168] According to s.5(1), an offence counting for the purposes of the provision is one of which a person is convicted (either on indictment or summarily) in consequence of a contravention of, or failure to comply with, any provision of the companies legislation[169] requiring a return, account or other document to be filed with, delivered or sent, or notice of any matter to be given, to the Registrar of Companies (whether the contravention or failure is on the person's own part or on the part of any company). Thus, like s.3, s.5 is directed at non-compliance with statutory filing obligations but, unlike s.3, it enables

[165] CDDA s.4(3).

[166] CDDA s.1(4).

[167] *Re Cedarwood Productions Ltd, Secretary of State for Trade and Industry v Murfitt* [2001] 2 B.C.L.C. 48; *Re Dennis Hilton Ltd* [2002] 1 B.C.L.C. 302. See further discussion concerning parallel proceedings in text from 7–95.

[168] Interpretation Act 1978 Sch.1. This definition applies for Scotland as well as England and Wales: CDDA s.5(4)(a). For Northern Ireland, the relevant wording is, ". . . convicted by a court of summary jurisdiction" which has the same effect: Company Directors Disqualification (Northern Ireland) Order 2002 (SI 2002/3150), art.8(2).

[169] As in s.3, "companies legislation" means the Companies Acts (defined in CDDA s.22(7) by reference to the definition in Companies Act 2006 s.2(1)) and Pts 1 to 7 of the Insolvency Act 1986: see CDDA s.5(4A) inserted by SI 2009/1941 with effect from October 1, 2009.

the convicting magistrates court to disqualify the offender subject to what follows.

10–66 The triggering circumstances specified in s.5(3) are that, during the five years ending with the date of conviction, the person has had made against him, or has been convicted of, in total, not less than three default orders[170] and offences counting for s.5 purposes (including the current conviction and any other offence of which he is convicted on the same occasion). Thus, the court's jurisdiction under s.5 arises on a "totting up" basis. There will, of course, need to be at least one conviction because the jurisdiction can only arise where a person is convicted of a relevant summary offence. Otherwise, any combination of default orders and convictions will suffice, provided that there is an aggregate of at least three in the previous five years. Furthermore, while the triggering conviction must be one for a *summary* offence, it appears from the wording of s.5(1) that previous convictions for summary *or* indictable offences can be counted.[171] There is a close analogy between s.5(3) and the conclusive presumption of "persistent default" in s.3(2) that triggers the court's discretion to disqualify under that provision.

Section 5: procedure

10–67 The main procedural difference between ss.5 and 3 is that a convicting court can exercise the power to disqualify under s.5 but not under s.3. The s.5 power was originally introduced by s.93(1A) of the Companies Act 1981. It was thought that it would make it easier to obtain a disqualification order for persistent default if the convicting court was given the power to disqualify individuals for repeated filing offences whereas previously it had only been possible to apply to a court having winding up jurisdiction for an order under what is now s.3. The convicting court for s.5 purposes must, in general, be a magistrates' court (or Scottish equivalent) although earlier convictions which may be counted can be by the magistrates or the Crown Court. The convicting court can make a disqualification order of its own motion as part of the sentencing process. The ten-day notice rule in s.16(1) does not apply to criminal proceedings.

10–68 Section 16(2) formerly proceeded on the basis that an application for an order under s.5 could lie to a court having winding up jurisdiction. This was a nonsense as it has always been clear from s.5(2) that a disqualification order under s.5 can only be made by the convicting court or, in England and Wales, by any other magistrates' court acting for the same local justice area. Accordingly, the reference to s.5 in s.16(2) has now been deleted.[172]

[170] Which bear the same meaning as in s.3(3)(b): see CDDA ss.5(4)(b) and 5(4A).

[171] Section 5(1) starts:

> "An offence counting for the purposes of this section is one of which a person is convicted (*either on indictment or summarily*) . . ." (emphasis supplied).

A disqualification order can only be made on conviction of a summary offence but the previous convictions which can be taken into account for totting-up purposes can be summary convictions or convictions on indictment.

[172] Insolvency Act 2000 s.8 and Sch.4 para.11.

SECTION 10: DISQUALIFICATION FOLLOWING PARTICIPATION IN WRONGFUL TRADING

10–69 Section 10(1) states:

> "Where the court makes a declaration under section 213 or 214 of the Insolvency Act that a person is liable to make a contribution to a company's assets, then, whether or not an application for such an order is made by any person, the court may, if it thinks fit, also make a disqualification order against the person to whom the declaration relates."

The heading for the provision, "participation in wrongful trading" is somewhat misleading as s.10 is triggered by the imposition of civil liability for fraudulent trading (s.213 of the Insolvency Act) as well as wrongful trading (s.214 of the Insolvency Act). Under CDDA s.10, the court imposing civil liability for fraudulent or wrongful trading can make a disqualification order of its own motion. A declaration of personal liability under either provision is a prerequisite. Jurisdiction under s.10 does not arise if the fraudulent or wrongful trading proceedings are dismissed.

10–70 The origins of s.10 trace back all the way to the Companies Acts 1928 and 1929. Section 75(1) of the Companies Act 1928 (consolidated as s.275(1) of the 1929 Act) was the earliest version of the civil fraudulent trading provision now found in s.213 of the Insolvency Act 1986. Section 75(4) of the 1928 Act contained an equivalent power in relation to fraudulent trading to that now found in CDDA s.10 though at that time the maximum period of disqualification was five years.[173] The power was carried over into s.188(1)(b)(i) of the Companies Act 1948. It was then carved out of what is now CDDA s.4(1) by s.16 of the Insolvency Act 1985, the immediate predecessor of the present provision, and extended to encompass wrongful trading which was itself introduced for the first time by s.15 of the same Act. The maximum period of disqualification under s.10 is 15 years.[174] There is no minimum period.

Insolvency Act 1986 s.213

10–71 If in the course of the winding up of a company it appears that any business of the company has been carried on with intent to defraud creditors of the company or creditors of any other person, or for any fraudulent purpose, any persons knowingly party to such activities may be liable to contribute personally to the company's assets under s.213 on the application of a liquidator. "Any persons who were knowingly parties to the carrying on of the business . . ."[175] are exposed to liability under s.213

[173] Section 75(3) of the 1928 Act also created an offence of fraudulent trading (the earliest version of what is now s.993 of the Companies Act 2006). An offender convicted of the offence was also liable to disqualification by the convicting court under s.75(4).

[174] CDDA s.10(2).

[175] Relevant authorities include: *Re Patrick and Lyon Ltd* [1933] Ch. 786; *Morris v State Bank of India* [1999] B.C.C. 943; *Morris v Bank of America National Trust* [2000] 1 All E.R. 954; *Banque Arabe Internationale d'Investissement SA v Morris* [2001] 1 B.C.L.C. 263; *Morphitis v Bernasconi* [2002] EWCA Civ 289, [2003] Ch. 552; *Morris v Bank of India* [2005] EWCA Civ 693, [2005] 2 B.C.L.C. 328.

and also therefore exposed to disqualification under CDDA s.10. In *Re Maidstone Building Provisions Ltd*[176] it was held that to be "knowingly party to the carrying on of the business" a person would need to have taken some active steps in the management of the business. However, it appears that the provision would also catch a creditor who accepts money knowing it was obtained by fraudulent means.[177] Thus, s.213 of the Insolvency Act is not confined, as is s.214, to company directors. The power of disqualification for fraudulent trading in s.10 overlaps with the power in s.4(1)(b) discussed earlier. Allegations of fraudulent trading could also be raised against a director in proceedings for an order under s.6. A conviction under s.993 of the Companies Act 2006 (formerly s.458 of the Companies Act 1985), the criminal equivalent of the civil remedy under s.213 of the Insolvency Act, could also result in disqualification under CDDA s.2.

Insolvency Act 1986 s.214

10–72 On the application of a liquidator under s.214, the court can declare that a director or shadow director of a company is liable to contribute personally to the company's assets provided that:

(1) the company has gone into insolvent liquidation; and
(2) at some time before the commencement of the winding up of the company, he knew or ought to have concluded that there was no reasonable prospect that the company would avoid going into insolvent liquidation.

If these elements are established, the court may make an order, but is not obliged to do so.[178] A defence is available if the defendant in s.214 proceedings establishes that having reached the state of knowledge referred to in (2), he took every step with a view to minimising the potential loss to the company's creditors as he ought to have taken. The applicable standard (for the objective test of knowledge in (2), and for determining whether the defendant took "every step") is that of a reasonably diligent person having both the general knowledge, skill and experience that may reasonably be expected of a person carrying out the same functions as are carried out by the defendant in relation to the company, and the general knowledge, skill and experience possessed by the defendant.[179] Section 214 applies only to directors, former directors and shadow directors and so is

[176] [1971] 1 W.L.R. 1085.

[177] *Re Gerald Cooper Chemicals Ltd* [1978] Ch. 262.

[178] For judicial consideration see *Re Produce Marketing Consortium Ltd (No.2)* [1989] B.C.L.C. 520; *Re DKG Contractors Ltd* [1990] B.C.C. 903; *Re Purpoint Ltd* [1991] B.C.L.C. 491; *Re Sherborne Associates Ltd* [1995] B.C.C. 40; *Re Continental Assurance Co of London Plc* [2001] B.P.I.R. 733; *Official Receiver v Doshi* [2001] 2 B.C.L.C. 235; *Liquidator of Marini Ltd v Dickenson* [2003] EWHC 334 (Ch), [2004] B.C.C. 172; *Re Rod Gunner Organisation Ltd* [2004] EWHC 316 (Ch), [2004] 2 B.C.L.C. 110; *Re Hawkes Hill Publishing Co Ltd* [2007] B.C.C. 937; *Re Bangla Television Ltd* [2009] EWHC 1632 (Ch). See also A. Walters, "Enforcing Wrongful Trading" in B. Rider (ed.), *The Corporate Dimension* (Bristol: Jordans, 1998).

[179] This is an objective minimum standard: see *Re Brian D Pierson (Contractors) Ltd* [2001] 1 B.C.L.C. 275. It is also the standard now applied by s.174 of the Companies Act 2006 in relation to a director's general duty to exercise reasonable care, skill and diligence.

more limited in scope than s.213 which applies to "any persons who were knowingly parties to the carrying on of the business . . ." However, a director who exercises no particular function or takes no active part in the carrying on or management of the company's business will not necessarily be absolved from liability under s.214.[180] Allegations of trading to the detriment of creditors and/or wrongful trading are frequently raised in proceedings for an order under CDDA s.6. Proceedings under s.6 have a number of advantages:

(1) A disqualification order can be obtained by the Secretary of State under s.6 without the need for the office holder to bring fraudulent or wrongful trading proceedings.
(2) Section 6 is much wider in scope than s.10 with the result that other types of misconduct can be taken into account as well as fraudulent or wrongful trading.
(3) Under s.6, if the court is satisfied that the defendant's conduct makes him unfit, it must disqualify him for at least two years. An order under s.10 is at the court's discretion.
(4) Proof that the defendant traded to the detriment of creditors may be sufficient to justify a finding of unfit conduct under s.6 even though the conduct would not have satisfied the statutory test for wrongful trading in s.214 of the Insolvency Act.[181]

There is therefore a greater likelihood that a director will be disqualified under s.6 than under s.10. Indeed, in one reported case, a liquidator's wrongful trading action was brought on at the same time as and heard together with a set of proceedings brought under s.6.[182] In the case of director defendants it is perhaps rare that civil proceedings will be brought under s.213 because in many cases it will be easier for the claimant to succeed in proceedings under s.214.

10–73 Nevertheless, the power in s.10 has been exercised. In *Re Brian D Pierson (Contractors) Ltd*[183] the two directors of a failed company were disqualified for five and two years respectively under s.10 following the making of contribution orders against them under s.214 of the Insolvency Act. The report of this case simply records that the judge made disqualification orders after discussion with counsel for the liquidator and the defendants, and in the light of written comments received from the Department of Trade and Industry's solicitors.[184]

Section 10: procedure

10–74 The relevant court for s.10 purposes is the court seised of the main civil proceedings under either s.213 or s.214 of the Insolvency Act. This will be a court having winding up jurisdiction over the company in relation to which complaint is

[180] *Re Brian D Pierson (Contractors) Ltd* [2001] 1 B.C.L.C. 275.
[181] See text from 5–05.
[182] *Official Receiver v Doshi* [2001] 2 B.C.L.C. 235.
[183] [2001] 1 B.C.L.C. 275.
[184] A disqualification order under s.10 was also apparently made in *Re Purpoint Ltd* [1991] B.C.L.C. 491.

made.[185] The court may make a disqualification order "whether or not an application for such an order is made by any person". This is a clear indication that the court can make an order of its own motion but also seems to imply that an application could be made by someone other than the liquidator who is bringing the main civil recovery proceedings. However, s.16 of the CDDA (which governs applications to a court of winding up jurisdiction for orders under ss.2 to 4) makes no specific provision for locus standi in relation to s.10 and so it is difficult to know what to make of this wording. It does appear that any "application" would have to be made in the main action. It would be odd, as well as inconsistent with s.16, if the word "application" in s.10 were to be read as including "originating application". It is settled that the ten-day notice provision in s.16(1) does not apply in cases where the court is empowered to make a disqualification order of its own motion. However, in *Re Cedac Ltd, Secretary of State for Trade and Industry v Langridge*, it was suggested obiter by Balcombe L.J. that:

> "doubtless the rules of natural justice will require that the person concerned should be given some notice that the court is contemplating making a disqualification order".[186]

As a matter of practice, the court should refer the matter to the Secretary of State and invite written representations on the question of disqualification.[187] Indeed, it is suggested that the Secretary of State would have locus to intervene in the proceedings and apply for a disqualification order as the person having regulatory responsibility under the CDDA.[188] One final point of some significance is that a director against whom wrongful trading proceedings are commenced faces a double exposure to disqualification under s.10 and (assuming proceedings are commenced) under s.6. For instance, a director disqualified under s.10 could subsequently face proceedings under s.6 in which the court could take into account other conduct as well as wrongful trading. If a further period of disqualification is imposed or agreed by way of undertaking, the two periods would run concurrently.[189]

PARALLEL CIVIL AND CRIMINAL PROCEEDINGS

10–75 The overlapping jurisdiction to disqualify is perhaps best illustrated where a director has completed all the elements necessary to establish the offence of fraudulent trading as defined by s.993 of the Companies Act 2006 (formerly s.458 of the Companies Act 1985).[190] In that situation he would be at risk of disqualification:

[185] See Insolvency Act 1986 ss.117–121.
[186] [1991] Ch. 402 at 414F.
[187] See *Re Brian D Pierson (Contractors) Ltd* [2001] 1 B.C.L.C. 275 at 312.
[188] By analogy with *Adams v Adams* [1971] P. 188. See also *Re TLL Realisations Ltd, Secretary of State for Trade and Industry v Collins* [2000] 2 B.C.L.C. 223.
[189] CDDA s.1(3). Given the wider focus of s.6 proceedings, it is unlikely that they would amount to an abuse of process: see *Re Cedarwood Productions Ltd, Secretary of State for Trade and Industry v Murfitt* [2001] 2 B.C.L.C. 48; permission to appeal refused: [2001] EWCA Civ 1083, [2004] B.C.C. 65.
[190] See also the circumstances that arose in *Re Dennis Hilton Ltd* [2002] 1 B.C.L.C. 302.

(1) if convicted, by the criminal court which convicts him under s.2;
(2) if convicted, by the civil court under s.2;
(3) whether or not convicted, under s.4(1)(a), by the civil court provided that the company in question is being or has been wound up;
(4) if the court has become insolvent within the meaning of CDDA s.6, by the civil court under s.6;
(5) if there has been some form of relevant investigation, by the civil court under s.8;
(6) if the company is being or has been wound up and civil recovery proceedings have been successfully brought under s.213 of the Insolvency Act, by the civil court under s.10.

10–76 In the event that a disqualification is imposed at a time when a person is already subject to disqualification, the relevant periods run concurrently. CDDA s.1(3) provides that the periods specified in any orders shall run concurrently and CDDA s.1A(3) provides that the periods specified in one or more undertakings or an undertaking and an order will also run concurrently. This offers a limited safeguard to the defendant faced with parallel criminal and civil proceedings, a point noted by the deputy judge in *Re Cedarwood Productions Ltd, Secretary of State for Trade and Industry v Murfitt*.[191]

10–77 Questions of some difficulty arise in relation to the interaction of the jurisdiction exercised by the civil courts and that exercised by the criminal courts. In the context of the civil courts the issues tend to be: (a) whether civil disqualification proceedings should be stayed or other steps taken to accommodate criminal proceedings, pending or threatened; and (b) what approach the civil court should take in circumstances where it is faced with an application for the making of a disqualification order in relation to conduct which constitutes a criminal offence and the matter has already been before a criminal court. The criminal court may have acquitted the defendant or declined to disqualify him under CDDA s.2 notwithstanding conviction or imposed a period of disqualification which the applicant to the civil court considers too short. As regards the criminal courts, the principal issue that has arisen is how they should approach disqualification bearing in mind the approach of the civil courts. In a particular case, this issue can become more acute where: (a) the criminal court is aware that there are ongoing (but perhaps stayed) civil disqualification proceedings (or the possibility of civil proceedings after the criminal proceedings); or (b) there have been civil disqualification proceedings, which were concluded prior to the criminal trial. A further issue that can arise is the extent to which earlier civil proceedings and/or the evidence obtained in such proceedings or by an office holder may be used in a criminal investigation or trial without making the trial unfair, an abuse of process or an infringement of the defendant's human rights.

10–78 Issues of this kind that may face the civil courts are considered in Ch.7. This chapter addresses the issue of parallel proceedings solely from the perspective of

[191] [2001] 2 B.C.L.C. 48 at 60.

the criminal courts. Usually, where civil and criminal proceedings are on foot at the same time, there is no question of the criminal court staying the criminal proceedings to accommodate civil proceedings. The key issues are therefore the approach to be taken by the criminal court in deciding whether, and if so on what basis, to impose disqualification. The general approach that the criminal courts have taken is considered below. It is suggested that the correct approach is for the criminal courts to treat disqualification as a discrete sentencing power and impose the same period that the civil courts would impose if faced with the relevant facts in free standing civil disqualification proceedings. In so doing, it is strongly arguable that the criminal courts should not give credit for any other sentence that may be imposed (such as fine or imprisonment). One powerful reason in favour of such a course is the potential for parallel proceedings. If civil disqualification proceedings are heard first (as they very often are) and a disqualification order is made, the civil court will not take into account the possibility of the overall sentence that might be imposed in criminal proceedings as some form of mitigating factor in fixing the period of disqualification. If this is correct, it would seem inconsistent and unfair that a defendant the subject of a criminal conviction (but at that stage no civil disqualification in respect of such conduct) should be treated differently from a defendant who is disqualified first by a civil court. Two contrary arguments are that either the criminal court should allow for the civil disqualification when imposing any criminal sanction or that the civil courts should exercise their review powers, where available, and vary a disqualification order to take into account a criminal sentence passed after the original civil disqualification. The other more specific issue that could arise is where a person is convicted of a relevant offence that triggers jurisdiction to disqualify, but he has already been disqualified by the civil courts or by undertaking. Should the criminal court ever re-visit the earlier disqualification? If the earlier disqualification was based (either alone or among other things) on the circumstances giving rise to the offence of which the defendant is now convicted, there is, it is suggested, no room for the criminal court to "disagree" with the earlier period and impose some further period of disqualification. Equally, if the earlier civil disqualification was not based on the circumstances of the offence, but on wholly different matters, again there is no difficulty: the criminal court can approach the conviction and the issue of disqualification untrammeled by the earlier disqualification (though it may be relevant as a matter of mitigation). However, there are two intermediate positions that cause difficulty. One is where the disqualification imposed by the civil court or by undertaking is based on the same factual matrix as the conviction, but the full offence is not the basis of the civil disqualification. Thus, the civil court may have disqualified the defendant for three years on the basis that he caused the company to trade improperly whilst insolvent at the risk of creditors, but in circumstances where it was not asked to determine and/or has not determined that the facts amounted to fraudulent trading under either s.993 of the Companies Act 2006 or s.213 of the Insolvency Act 1986. If the criminal court, say a year later, subsequently convicts of fraudulent trading under s.993, is it entitled to consider imposing a longer period of disqualification (say for six years) on the basis that the conviction is of a much more serious matter to those on which the civil disqualification was founded? It is suggested that in principle this is permitted and is, to some extent, the mirror image of the parallel proceedings issues raised by the judgment in *Re Land Travel Ltd, Secretary of State for Trade and Industry v Tjolle*,[192] a s.6 case discussed in Ch.7. However, it seems likely that the criminal court will feel uneasy about taking such a step. The other related scenario that raises the question of how the criminal court should act arises where the precise basis for the earlier civil disqualification is unclear (e.g. because the schedule to the disqualification undertaking setting out the factual basis of the disqualification is short and, on the relevant point, unclear).

FACTORS CONSIDERED BY THE COURT IN EXERCISING ITS DISCRETION UNDER SS.2–5 AND 10

10–79 If the preconditions of any of ss.2–5 or 10 are satisfied, the relevant court has jurisdiction to make a disqualification order. However, it remains in the court's discretion whether or not to make an order. The CDDA provides considerable guidance on the factors that the court should take into account when determining the question of unfitness under ss.6 and 8.[193] However, there is no express statutory guidance as to how the court should go about exercising its discretion under ss.2–5 or 10.

The nature of the discretion

10–80 In deciding whether to exercise its discretion the court is faced with two questions:

(1) Is it appropriate to disqualify the individual?
(2) If so, what is the appropriate period of disqualification?

A number of basic points can be made about the first stage of the discretion. First, while Parliament has decided that a power of disqualification should be available in the circumstances defined in ss.2–5 and 10, it has been left to the court to decide whether it is *appropriate* to impose an order in an individual case. Thus, for example, in the cases of ss.2 and 5, a conviction for an offence that triggers the court's discretion is not of itself regarded as a sufficient justification for the conclusion that in all cases the convicted individual should not be involved in the management of a company. This contrasts with the position in other jurisdictions where an individual convicted of a relevant offence is automatically disqualified without the need for any further order of the court.[194] Equally, once it has

[192] [1998] 1 B.C.L.C. 333. Although *Land Travel* is a s.6 case, it is suggested that the same principles should apply to any later civil disqualification proceedings, whichever section of the CDDA is relied on.

[193] CDDA s.9 directs the court to have regard in particular to the matters mentioned in CDDA Sch.1. See discussion in Ch.4.

[194] See, e.g. Corporations Act 2001 (Cth.) s.206B (Australia); Companies Act 1990 s.160(1) (Ireland).

decided to impose an order, it is also left to the court to determine the period of disqualification. The only guidance provided by the CDDA on this second question comes in the form of the statutory maxima of five or fifteen years. Parliament has thus left it almost entirely to the courts to establish the principles on which the discretion should be exercised.

10–81 It is not easy to determine how the discretion will be exercised in a given case or to point with any certainty to a set of factors and say that those factors will (or should be) taken into account. This raises the fundamental questions canvassed in Ch.2 about the nature of the court's power to disqualify an individual, the general purpose (or purposes) of the CDDA and the proper functions of the criminal and civil courts in the context of disqualification.

10–82 The first issue to consider is how civil courts should deal with cases under CDDA ss.2, 3 and 4. As with CDDA s.8, it is suggested that where a discretion is exercisable, the court should have regard to cases decided under s.6. If the case had been brought within s.6 proceedings and a mandatory period of disqualification would have been imposed then, in general, a similar approach should be taken under any of the discretionary disqualification provisions. This appears to have been the approach taken by Lloyd J. when imposing disqualification orders in the s.8 proceedings arising out of the collapse of Atlantic Computers.[195] The common sense of this approach is made manifest when considering how, for example, disqualification may follow for fraudulent trading under any of CDDA, ss.2, 4, 6, 8 or 10. In each case the misconduct is as serious. Should the question of whether a disqualification order is imposed at all or the question of the relevant period turn on what may be happen chance as to the provision under which the court is exercising its jurisdiction? If the approach in civil disqualification proceedings other than proceedings under s.6 is (broadly speaking) to follow that adopted in s.6 cases, then what of the criminal courts?

10–83 It has been seen that CDDA ss.2–5 are concerned primarily with conduct that is defined by reference to criminal offences or defaults. However, only s.5 is exclusively the preserve of the criminal courts. Indeed, the powers in ss.3 and 4 are exercisable only by a civil court having winding up jurisdiction. This begs the question whether a criminal court exercising jurisdiction under s.2 or 5 is engaging in a qualitatively different exercise from a civil court exercising jurisdiction under ss.2–4, 6–8, 9A or 10. The thesis of this book is that the various powers in the CDDA share common features and a common purpose. It follows that the criminal and civil courts should adopt a common approach when exercising jurisdiction under it. As noted above, there is considerable overlap between the various jurisdictional gateways enabling, or requiring, the court to make a disqualification order. Even an order under CDDA s.2 can be made either by the convicting criminal court of its own motion or on a later application to a civil court. In the absence of any specific guidance in the CDDA, it is difficult to argue that Parliament intended the criminal and civil courts to adopt different

[195] *Re Atlantic Computers Plc, Secretary of State for Trade and Industry v Ashman*, June 15, 1998, Ch.D., unreported.

approaches when exercising the *same* power. Moreover, it may be possible to contend that CDDA powers of disqualification are essentially *civil* powers and that the vesting of limited powers in the criminal courts under ss.2 and 5 is purely a matter of practical convenience.[196]

10–84 Similarly, when a criminal court comes to exercise discretion at the second stage (period of disqualification), it is suggested that it should follow the same approach as the civil courts in the interests of consistency. As it happens, and perhaps not surprisingly, the civil courts have tended to treat the determination of the period of disqualification as equivalent to a tariff-based sentencing exercise.[197] Accordingly, the courts should decide the period of disqualification by reference to the facts as established taking account of any mitigation. However, the power of the civil courts to grant the defendant permission to act notwithstanding disqualification should not be taken into account.[198]

10–85 Support for a common approach can be derived from *Re Land Travel Ltd, Secretary of State for Trade and Industry v Tjolle*.[199] In that case, the first defendant in s.6 proceedings was disqualified for ten years by a criminal court under s.2 following his conviction for an offence of fraudulent trading. The Secretary of State persisted with the s.6 proceedings (which arose out of similar circumstances) because it was felt that a maximum 15-year disqualification should be sought in the public interest. In a passage of his judgment apparently critical of the criminal court for "under-disqualifying" the defendant, Jacob J. stated that:

> ". . . it is self-evident that civil and criminal courts should be applying the same standards: the purpose of disqualification (to protect the public from the activities of persons unfit to be concerned in the management of a company) is the same in both kinds of court".[200]

In the circumstances, Jacob J.'s criticism seems rather harsh. The defendant had pleaded guilty in the criminal proceedings to fraudulent trading over a period of some three months whereas, for the purposes of a *Carecraft* disposal of the s.6 proceedings,[201] he had agreed to a 15-year disqualification based on admitted misconduct of a much greater magnitude. Nevertheless, it is suggested that, in principle, the judge was correct. Thus, a criminal court should have in mind the overall purposes of the CDDA and exercise its discretion under ss.2 or 5 accordingly.[202]

[196] In this connection, see the reasoning in *R. v Field & Young* [2002] EWCA Crim 2913, [2003] 1 W.L.R. 882.
[197] See *Re Civica Investments Ltd* [1983] B.C.L.C. 456; *Re Sevenoaks Stationers (Retail) Ltd* [1991] Ch. 164; *Re Westmid Packing Services Ltd, Secretary of State for Trade and Industry v Griffiths* [1998] 2 All E.R. 124.
[198] *Re Civica Investments Ltd* [1983] B.C.L.C. 456. In other words, the court should not impose the longest period of disqualification that could possibly be appropriate and treat the hearing of an application for permission to act as a forum for mitigation.
[199] [1998] 1 B.C.L.C. 333.
[200] [1998] 1 B.C.L.C. 333 at 336.
[201] On *Carecraft* disposals see further Ch.9.
[202] See also *R. v Evans* [2000] B.C.C. 901 and dicta in *R. v Cole, Lees & Birch* [1998] 2 B.C.L.C. 234.

10–86 It has been argued that CDDA powers are quasi-criminal in nature and that civil courts exercising those powers should *in all respects* (i.e. in relation to questions of procedure and evidence as well as "sentencing") behave like criminal courts.[203] This view does not command wide support in the authorities. The view of the authors is that the "sentencing" analogy[204] is appropriate but should not be taken too far. As there is no guidance in the CDDA with regard to discretion or period of disqualification it is not surprising that the civil courts have drawn such an analogy. It does not necessarily mean that a civil court should behave like a criminal court on questions of procedure and evidence. Rather than the civil courts exercising quasi-criminal powers, the converse is arguable: i.e. that a criminal court exercising jurisdiction under the CDDA is imposing a *civil law or regulatory* prohibition.[205]

Specific problems of discretion in the criminal courts

10–87 For the purposes of the present discussion, criminal courts do differ from civil courts in one obvious respect. A civil court exercising the powers in ss.2–4 and 10 of the CDDA is concerned only with the question of disqualification. Its sole function is to consider whether or not to make a disqualification order and, if so, for how long. A convicting criminal court has a wider remit. As Nourse L.J. pointed out in his dissenting judgment in *Re Cedac Ltd, Secretary of State for Trade and Industry v Langridge*,[206] a disqualification order is only one of a range of orders that a criminal court can make in dealing with a convicted offender. It follows that disqualification will rarely, if ever, be considered in isolation. This has had some impact on the use of the discretion in the criminal courts as the decisions of the Court of Appeal (Criminal Division) in *R. v Young*[207] and *R. v Holmes*[208] illustrate. These cases explore the extent to which a sentencer is able to combine a disqualification order under s.2 with other types of order from the range of possible sentences available to a criminal court.

R. v Young

10–88 In the *Young* case the appellant pleaded guilty to an offence of managing a company without the permission of the court while he was an undischarged bankrupt. The offence had been committed during 1984 and 1985 before the appellant's discharge from bankruptcy in 1986. The trial judge conditionally discharged him for three years and disqualified him for two years under CDDA

[203] See J. Dine, "Wrongful Trading—Quasi-Criminal Law" in H. Rajak (ed.), *Insolvency Law: Theory and Practice* (London: Sweet and Maxwell, 1993); "Punishing Directors" [1994] J.B.L. 325. Dine's view is discussed more fully in Ch.2.

[204] See, e.g. *Re Westmid Packing Services Ltd, Secretary of State for Trade and Industry v Griffiths* [1998] 2 All E.R. 124 at 132 per Lord Woolf: "Despite the facts that the courts have said disqualification is not a 'punishment' in truth the exercise that is being engaged in is little different from any sentencing exercise".

[205] See *Re Westminster Property Management Ltd (No.1), Official Receiver v Stern (No.1)* [2000] 1 W.L.R. 2230 and, by analogy, *R. v Field & Young* [2002] EWCA Crim 2913, [2003] 1 W.L.R. 882.

[206] [1991] Ch. 402 at 423F.

[207] (1990) 12 Cr.App.Rep.(S.) 262.

[208] (1992) 13 Cr.App.Rep(S.) 29.

s.2. He appealed against the making of the disqualification order. The Court of Appeal held that a conditional discharge and a disqualification were incompatible and, with some reluctance, quashed the disqualification order. The following extract from Brooke J.'s ex tempore judgment forms the narrow ratio of *Young*:

> "It appears to the court that as the order for disqualification under s.2 of the Act is unquestionably a punishment, it would be quite inappropriate for a punishment of this kind to be linked with a conditional discharge in a case . . . in which the sentencing court thought that a punishment was inexpedient."

Although not immediately apparent from this passage, it is clear from the grounds of appeal that the court based its decision on what was then s.7 of the Powers of Criminal Courts Act 1973 which provided that a court could not grant a conditional discharge unless satisfied that it was inexpedient to inflict punishment. In *R. v Savage*,[209] this was construed to mean that a conditional discharge could not be combined with a punitive order and although *Savage* was not considered in *Young*, the court applied exactly the same logic. Thus, the effect of *Young* was that the exercise of the discretion under s.2 was constrained by, and had to be balanced against, other aspects of the sentencing process.

10–89 On the narrow point (the incompatibility of absolute or conditional discharge and disqualification), *R. v Young* has been overruled by s.12 of the Powers of Criminal Courts (Sentencing) Act 2000. This re-enacts the power to grant a conditional or absolute discharge where, in the court's opinion, it is inexpedient to inflict punishment. However, s.12(7) goes on to provide that the power shall not be construed as "preventing a court, on discharging an offender absolutely or conditionally, from . . . imposing any disqualification on him". This does not demand that disqualification should always be regarded as non-punitive. Its effect is rather to say that even if disqualification can be classified as penal, it is not necessarily incompatible with an absolute or conditional discharge. Accordingly, *Young* remains authority for the wider proposition that disqualification is a form of punishment.

R. v Holmes

10–90 In the *Holmes* case the appellant pleaded guilty to an offence of fraudulent trading. He received a suspended prison sentence and was disqualified for 12 months under CDDA s.2. He was also ordered to pay compensation of £25,000 to the National Westminster Bank Plc, the victim of his fraudulent activities. This case differed from *Young* in that the appeal was against the criminal compensation order and not the disqualification order. However, the main question again concerned the compatibility of a disqualification order with other types of order available to the sentencer. The Court of Appeal held that a criminal compensation order was inconsistent with an order disqualifying the appellant from acting as a director. In the court's view, it was wrong in principle to disqualify an individual at the same time as imposing a compensation order on him if disqualification

[209] (1983) 5 Cr.App.R. 216(S.)

might prejudice his ability to earn the means to pay the compensation order. Accordingly, the compensation order was quashed. The Court of Appeal made clear that, if considering a compensation order, the sentencing court should not combine it with a disqualification order. However, what the court did not address was whether the sentencing court should give primacy to making a disqualification order or to making a compensation order. It also does not seem to have considered the question of whether permission to act, notwithstanding disqualification, might have been granted.

Balanced sentencing

10–91 According to Brooke J. in *R. v Young*, the criminal courts have a "completely general and unfettered power" under CDDA s.2. Given, however, that disqualification is one of a range of sentencing options, the wider implication of *Young* and *Holmes* is that the criminal courts are likely, perhaps not surprisingly, to allow themselves to be constrained in exercising the power by the need to arrive at a balanced sentence. Thus, if the court has decided to impose a custodial sentence or a heavy fine, it may be inclined to discount the period of disqualification below a level that a civil court would regard as appropriate or make no order at all. It is arguable that such an approach, while understandable, could undermine the policy behind the CDDA. In its favour, it could be argued that the approach is in line with that of the civil courts in determining the period of disqualification, which has been described by Lord Woolf, as being "little different to any sentencing exercise".[210] A continuation of the same argument would be that the civil and criminal courts are not applying different approaches to fixing the period (or even to determine whether or not to disqualify) but that the same approach leads to different answers in the civil case (where the court considers only disqualification) and the criminal case (where the court may be considering a number of other available sentencing tools and attempting to reach an overall balanced sentence). It is suggested, however, that the approach would be flawed. A major reason for this is that it would lead to unfairness depending on which court a defendant came before first. A defendant disqualified first by the civil court, considering only civil disqualification, would have the period fixed by the civil court without reference to the later overall sentence that a criminal court might impose in respect of the same matter. A defendant convicted first by the criminal court would, on the above argument, often receive a discount in the period of disqualification to reflect the other elements of the overall sentence. It is suggested by the authors that this is an inconsistent, unfair and incorrect approach. It fails to give adequate weight to the point that disqualification is not a sentencing option conferred on the criminal courts as part of an overall criminal sentencing regime, but that the jurisdiction to disqualify is conferred on them, in parallel with the civil courts, as a convenient way of avoiding multiplicity of proceedings and that disqualification is a free standing regulatory response to past misconduct generally rather than a specific penalty for criminal offences. These points are developed further below.

[210] *Re Westmid Packing Services Ltd, Secretary of State for Trade and Industry v Griffiths* [1998] 2 All E.R. 124 at 132.

Should disqualification imposed by a criminal court under the CDDA be regarded as a punishment?

10–92 Having concluded that disqualification was a "punishment", the Court of Appeal in *Young* was constrained by statute to quash the disqualification order because of its incompatibility with a non-punitive conditional discharge. This constraint apart, it is clear that Brooke J. would have regarded a disqualification order as appropriate despite the fact that the appellant had been trading successfully for three-and-a-half years since obtaining his discharge from bankruptcy and could hardly have been regarded as a present danger to the public. It is clear that a disqualification order can be imposed under CDDA s.6 in circumstances where the defendant no longer poses any risk to the public. However, Brooke J.'s view of disqualification as a form of punishment rests on the broader proposition that a criminal court exercising jurisdiction under CDDA s.2 is in a "quite different situation" from a civil court exercising jurisdiction under s.6.

10–93 The related assumptions that: (a) criminal courts exercising jurisdiction under the CDDA are doing something fundamentally different from their civil counterparts; and (b) criminal disqualification is concerned exclusively with punishment are suspect for the following reasons[211]:

(1) When a criminal court considers disqualifying a person under ss.2 or 5, it is first and foremost exercising jurisdiction *under the CDDA*. It just so happens that within the scheme of the legislation, this jurisdiction is ancillary to the court's primary criminal jurisdiction. Given the history and evolution of the CDDA and its overall focus on the regulation of misconduct in the corporate context, there seems little justification for saying that disqualification by a criminal court is somehow qualitatively different from disqualification by a civil court. A common approach to disqualification founded primarily on principles of public protection, including the need for deterrence, is more appropriate. This criticism of *Young* can be supported with reference to the unitary features of the CDDA identified at the beginning of Ch.2. Disqualification by the court under s.2 (and, for that matter, under ss.3, 4, 5, 9A and 10) has exactly the same legal consequences as disqualification by the court under s.6. The provisions should therefore be seen as operating for broadly similar ends. Moreover, the fact that the criminal courts have been given jurisdiction in s.2 (and also s.5) can be seen simply as a device designed to save the necessity of further civil proceedings. Thus, to reiterate, it may be that CDDA powers should properly be classified as civil powers that, for reasons of convenience, can be exercised by criminal courts in limited circumstances.[212]

[211] Restating points first made in Ch.2.

[212] See *Re Westminster Property Management Ltd (No.1), Official Receiver v Stern (No. 1)* [2000] 1 W.L.R. 2230 and, by analogy, *R. v Field & Young* [2002] EWCA Crim 2913, [2003] 1 W.L.R. 882.

(2) If the principle in *Young* were correct, it would follow that a criminal court exercising the power in s.2 would be doing something quite different from a civil court exercising the same power. This would be an odd result.[213]
(3) Support for the view that the s.2 power should be regarded as protective rather than punitive can be derived from Commonwealth jurisdictions. Australia, for example, has a provision under which directors are automatically disqualified on being convicted of certain criminal offences.[214] This equivalent to s.2 is regarded by the courts in that jurisdiction as being primarily concerned with protection of the public rather than the punishment of the offender.[215]

10–94 It is not absolutely clear whether Brooke J. (who did not enjoy the luxury of being able to reserve judgment) meant that disqualification under CDDA s.2 should *only* be seen as a punishment and nothing else. If the arguments of the authors are correct, it would be preferable for the criminal courts to adopt broadly the same view of the CDDA that has been adopted by the civil courts in relation to s.6 (i.e. that disqualification is concerned primarily with protection of the public, although recognising that such protection involves deterrence aspects).[216]

Period of disqualification

Section 2 cases

10–95 There are signs (*Young* notwithstanding) that the criminal courts do follow broadly the same sort of approach as their civil counterparts on the question of the appropriate period of disqualification.[217] The cases on s.2 suggest that the two main factors taken into consideration are the culpability of the offender and the public's need for protection. In *R. v Cobbey*,[218] the Court of Appeal upheld a six-year disqualification order made against the appellant who had pleaded guilty to a count of fraudulent trading. The facts were that over a period of ten months, the appellant caused a company to obtain goods, services and credit with no prospect of paying for them and accepted deposits from customers in respect of contracts that he then failed to perform. In all, the company incurred liabilities of around £68,000

[213] This criticism is echoed in more recent cases where it has been suggested that the criminal and civil courts should adopt a common approach to disqualification: see, e.g. dicta in *R. v Cole, Lees & Birch* [1998] 2 B.C.L.C. 234; *Re Land Travel Ltd, Secretary of State for Trade and Industry v Tjolle* [1998] 1 B.C.L.C. 333 and discussion in 10–80 to 10–86 above.

[214] Corporations Act 2001 (Cth.) s.206B.

[215] See J. Cassidy, "Disqualification of Directors under the Corporations Law" (1995) 13 Company and Securities L.J. 221; A. Hicks, "Disqualification of Directors—Forty Years On" [1988] J.B.L. 27 and, e.g. *Re Magna Alloys & Research Pty Ltd* (1975) 1 A.C.L.R. 203 at 205. As the offender is automatically disqualified without further order on conviction of a relevant offence, this view has been articulated by Australia's civil courts on applications for permission to act rather than by the criminal courts.

[216] It is not clear from the report of the case whether the Crown made submissions on the appeal. It also appears that the Secretary of State was not invited to make representations. Doubts have been expressed in subsequent cases as to the wider reasoning in *Young*: see *R. v Cole, Lees & Birch* [1998] 2 B.C.L.C. 234 at 239–240. See also *R. v Evans* [2000] B.C.C. 901.

[217] For the approach of the civil courts under s.6 see *Re Sevenoaks Stationers (Retail) Ltd* [1991] Ch. 164; *Re Westmid Packing Services Ltd, Secretary of State for Trade and Industry v Griffiths* [1998] 2 All E.R. 124 and discussion in Chs 4 and 5.

[218] (1993) 14 Cr.App.R.(S.) 82.

during this period that could not be met. The Court of Appeal held that a six-year disqualification order was an appropriate reflection of the appellant's culpability, the harm that he had caused to creditors and customers and the need to protect the public from him in the future. As Auld J. put it:

> "It is a case of dishonesty—dishonesty extending over several months, causing loss to many . . . The fact that he may have derived little or no personal benefit from his dishonesty has little relevance to the losses he caused and might cause again to others until he has learnt the importance of straight and careful business dealings."

In *R. v Millard*,[219] the Court of Appeal held that an eight-year disqualification was appropriate to deal with an individual described as "devious . . . manipulative, and thoroughly dishonest in the conduct of the affairs of [his] companies". In this case, the fraudulent conduct had lasted for a period of four years and resulted in a deficiency of approximately £728,000. The Court of Appeal thought that it was appropriate to disqualify Millard for two years longer than Cobbey because he had caused a greater degree of harm over a longer period.[220]

10–96 In the important case of *R. v Edwards*,[221] the Court of Appeal reduced the period of disqualification imposed at trial on the appellant from ten to three years. The appellant was a minor participant in a fraudulent scheme involving the use of companies to acquire large quantities of goods on credit that were subsequently re-sold for cash at a discount. Each company operated for only a short period of time before it ceased trading. As the following extract from Potter L.J.'s judgment illustrates, the Court of Appeal favoured a broad protective approach that is arguably of general application:

> "The rationale behind the power to disqualify is the protection of the public from the activities of persons who, whether for reasons of dishonesty, or of naivety or incompetence in conjunction with the dishonesty of others, may use or abuse their role and status as a director of a limited company to the detriment of the public. Frauds of the kind in this case archetypally give rise to a situation in which the exercise of the court's power is appropriate. In the case of this appellant, it appears that, in a period of unemployment, he was persuaded to participate in a fraudulent enterprise as a director, for which role, by reason of his inexperience, he was quite unsuited. While it is said that he did not appreciate the fraud until late on . . . it is clear that he pleaded guilty on the basis that he had at some stage towards the end of the enterprise participated knowingly in it. It seems to us that such a position might well in principle arise again, whatever his present intentions may be."

However, in comparison with his co-defendants and the defendant in *Millard*, the defendant in *Edwards* had played only a minor role in the scheme. In all the circumstances, it was felt that a three-year disqualification was appropriate.

10–97 It is possible that the court may decline to make an order in a case of less culpable wrongdoing or where it is not obvious that the public is in need of protection from the

[219] (1994) 15 Cr.App.R.(S.) 445.

[220] Nevertheless, Millard could count himself lucky. The Court of Appeal substituted an eight-year order for the maximum 15-year order originally imposed by the trial judge. A differently constituted Court of Appeal in *R. v Edwards* [1998] 2 Cr.App.R.(S.) 213 clearly felt that Millard had received light treatment.

[221] [1998] 2 Cr.App.R.(S.) 213.

particular individual. Thus, in *R. v Green and Green*,[222] the Court of Appeal quashed two-year disqualification orders made against the appellants on two grounds. First, it was held that they had not set out to use the corporate form for fraudulent purposes but had over-expanded the company's business in an unfavourable economic climate and continued to trade at the expense of creditors while taking too optimistic a view of the company's survival prospects. The court also took account of the fact that in the five years that had elapsed between the winding up of the company and the trial, the appellants had been running another company successfully and the making of disqualification orders would effectively have removed their livelihood.[223]

Should the criminal courts apply the Court of Appeal's guidelines from Re Sevenoaks Stationers (Retail) Ltd in determining the period of disqualification?

10–98 In *Re Sevenoaks Stationers (Retail) Ltd*[224] the Court of Appeal laid down guidelines with a view to establishing consistent practice in civil disqualification cases under CDDA s.6. It held that the statutory period of between two and fifteen years in CDDA s.6(4) should be divided into three brackets: a top bracket of over ten years that should be reserved for particularly serious cases, a middle bracket of six to ten years for serious cases that do not merit the top bracket and a minimum bracket of two to five years for less serious cases. One question that has arisen is whether these guidelines should be applied by the criminal courts in determining periods of disqualification. The first obvious point to make is that the guidelines of themselves provide limited assistance to magistrates' courts in determining how they should exercise their powers under ss.2 and 5 as the maximum period of disqualification that a court of summary jurisdiction can impose is limited to five years.[225] The question is therefore only of direct relevance to the Crown Court exercising its powers under s.2.

10–99 In *R. v Goodman* Staughton L.J. cast doubt on whether it was appropriate to apply the *Sevenoaks Stationers* guidelines in criminal proceedings.[226] Despite this, in both *R. v Millard* and *R. v Edwards*, the Court of Appeal expressly applied the guidelines. In *Millard* the view was that the case fell into the middle bracket; in *Edwards*, the minimum bracket.[227] There is no reason in principle why the

[222] (1981) 3 Cr.App.R.(S.) 22.

[223] The degree of the offender's culpability is also regarded by the civil courts as being relevant in determining the appropriate period of disqualification: see *Re Civica Investments Ltd* [1983] B.C.L.C. 456 at 458 and the Australian case, *Commissioner for Corporate Affairs v Ekamper* (1988) 12 A.C.L.R. 519. Although there are no reported cases, it is assumed that the approach under CDDA ss.4–5 would be similar.

[224] [1991] Ch. 164. The case is discussed more fully in Chs 4 and 5.

[225] This is equally true of a civil court exercising its powers under s.3. Nevertheless, one would expect these courts to adopt a similar approach with regard to periods of disqualification towards the top end of the five-year maximum. See e.g. *Re Civica Investments Ltd* [1983] B.C.L.C. 456 at 458 where Nourse J. said that "the longer periods of disqualification are to be reserved for cases where the defaults and conduct of the person in question have been of a serious nature, for example, where defaults have been made for some dishonest purpose, or wilfully and deliberately, or where they have been many in number and have not been substantially alleviated by remedial action . . .".

[226] [1993] 2 All E.R. 789 at 793.

[227] The Court of Appeal in *Edwards* felt that *Millard* was a "top bracket" case, a disagreement which reflects the universal difficulties experienced by courts in applying any type of general sentencing guidance.

criminal courts should not use the guidelines. Indeed, they are closely analogous to the sentencing guidelines that the Court of Appeal (Criminal Division) regularly provides and it appears that the criminal courts have continued to apply them since *Millard* and *Edwards*.[228] The only caveat is that there is no minimum period of disqualification under ss.2 and 5 with the result that the minimum bracket of two to five years for s.6 cases needs some adjustment to take account of the fact that a criminal court can impose a disqualification order of less than two years' duration. In relation to s.10, the criminal courts have no jurisdiction and it is safe to assume that the civil courts would adopt a similar approach on the question of period to that taken by their counterparts under s.6.

Assistance to the court

10–100 In general the prosecutor's duty is only to draw the court's attention to relevant sentencing powers. Given the nature of disqualification it is, perhaps, unfortunate that the Court of Appeal (Criminal Division) has not called on the Secretary of State (or a friend of the court) to assist it on the question of the correct approach of the criminal courts to disqualification. This has been so even where the court has been considering whether to exercise the s.2 power.[229] Indeed, one of the specific recommendations contained in the Report on Parallel Proceedings by the Financial Regulation Working Group of the Society for Advanced Legal Studies was that:

> "it would be useful, at the sentencing stage, for specialised counsel instructed by the [Secretary of State] to make submissions about disqualification, where the [Secretary of State] thought the case was a suitable one for disqualification."[230]

APPEALS AGAINST DISQUALIFICATION ORDERS MADE UNDER SS.2–5 AND 10[231]

Appeals

10–101 Appeals against disqualification orders made under CDDA ss.2–4 and 10 of the CDDA by a civil court having winding up jurisdiction are dealt with in Ch.13.

[228] *R. v Bott-Walters* [2005] 2 Cr.App.R.(S.) 70; *R. v Youell* [2007] 2 Cr.App.R.(S.) 43; *R. v Nevitt* [2007] EWCA Crim 1210; *R. v Creggy* [2008] 3 All E.R. 91; but compare *R. v Johnson* [2005] EWCA Crim 3074; *R. v O'Hanlon* [2008] 2 Cr.App.R.(S.) 16.

[229] See, e.g. *Attorney-General's Reference Nos.14, 15 and 16 of 1995, The Times*, April 10, 1997 where the delay in dealing with the appeal was found by the European Court to involve an infringement of art.6 rights and the matter later returned to the Court of Appeal (Criminal Division) when it became apparent that, on the earlier occasion, the court had pronounced an incomplete disqualification order: see *R. v Ward* [2001] EWCA Crim 1648, [2002] B.C.C. 953.

[230] Paragraph 7.13 of the Working Group's report which was published in December 1999. The Working Group was chaired by George Staple Q.C. See also A. Neal and F. Wright, *A survey of the use and effectiveness of the Company Directors Disqualification Act 1986 as a legal sanction against directors convicted of health and safety offences*, Health and Safety Executive, Research Report RR597 (HSE Books, 2007), *http://www.hse.gov.uk/research/rrhtm/rr597.htm* [Accessed August 26, 2009] recommending guidelines for prosecutors in the particular context of health and safety offences.

[231] The main concern in this section is procedure relevant to appeals from the criminal courts. The coverage is necessarily limited and for a fuller understanding of criminal procedure readers should refer to standard practitioner works such as *Archbold* and *Stone's Justices' Manual*.

10–102 Appeals from a magistrates' court against sentence lie generally to the Crown Court.[232] It appears that an appeal by the defendant either against the making of a disqualification order under CDDA ss.2 or 5 (magistrates' courts have no power to disqualify under ss.3–4) or against the length of disqualification imposed by the magistrates will lie as an offender has a right of appeal against "any order" made by a magistrates' court when dealing with him,[233] although this right does not extend to appeals against certain specified orders including an order for the prosecution's costs.[234] Notice of appeal must be given to the designated officer of the relevant magistrates' court not later than 21 days after the day on which the decision or sentence appealed against was given.[235] There is a risk, on appeal, that the Crown Court might increase the length of disqualification rather than reduce it or quash the order.[236] However, the Crown Court cannot increase the length of disqualification beyond the statutory maximum period of five years which the magistrates can impose. The prosecution has no right of appeal to the Crown Court. Scottish appeals from inferior courts of summary jurisdiction lie ultimately to the High Court of Justiciary, Scotland's supreme criminal court.

10–103 Under the Magistrates' Courts Act 1980 s.111:

> "any person who was party to proceedings before a magistrates' court, or is aggrieved by the conviction, order, determination or other proceeding of the court",

may appeal by way of case stated to the Divisional Court of Queen's Bench Division on the ground either that the magistrates' decision was wrong in law or in excess of jurisdiction. The significant point is that it is theoretically open to the prosecution as well as the defence to challenge an exercise of the magistrates' discretion under CDDA ss.2 or 5 using the "case stated" procedure whereas the prosecution has no right of appeal to the Crown Court. The application must be made within 21 days after the day on which the magistrates made their decision.[237] A defendant using this procedure will lose his right of appeal to the Crown Court.[238] Also, the risk for a defendant is that the Divisional Court will decline to review a sentence (including, it is submitted, a disqualification order), if the right of appeal to the Crown Court has not been exercised or exhausted.[239] Presumably, a similar fate would befall an application for judicial review.

[232] Senior Courts Act 1981 s.48; Magistrates' Courts Act 1980 s.108. Note that in relation to procedure on appeal in the criminal courts we deal exclusively with appeals against sentence which is taken to include a disqualification order under the CDDA. We do not deal with the procedure relating to appeals against *conviction* or a combined appeal against conviction and sentence.

[233] Senior Courts Act 1981 s.48(6); Magistrates' Courts Act 1980 s.108(3).

[234] Magistrates' Courts Act 1980 s.108(3).

[235] See now Criminal Procedure Rules 2005 (SI 2005/384) rr.2.1, 63.2. Under the rules, the Crown Court may extend time for giving notice of appeal either before or after expiry of the 21-day period.

[236] Senior Courts Act 1981 s.48(4).

[237] Magistrates' Courts Act 1980 s.111(2). The High Court cannot generally extend the 21-day period: *Michael v Gowland* [1977] 1 W.L.R. 296. For procedure see now Criminal Procedure Rules 2005 (SI 2005/384), r.64. The application should be sent to a court officer for the magistrates' court whose decision is questioned.

[238] Magistrates' Courts Act 1980 s.111(4).

[239] *R. v Battle Magistrates Court Ex p. Shepherd* (1983) 5 Cr.App.R.(S.) 124; *Tucker v Director of Public Prosecutions* [1992] 4 All E.R. 901.

10–104 Appeals against sentences imposed by the Crown Court are governed generally by the Criminal Appeal Act 1968 and lie to the Court of Appeal (Criminal Division). Again, it appears that the term "sentence" is sufficiently wide to include a disqualification order made under CDDA s.2.[240] Indeed, a number of appeals against s.2 orders have been heard, many of which are discussed elsewhere in this chapter.[241] Unless the trial judge certifies that the case is fit for appeal, leave to appeal must be obtained from the Court of Appeal.[242] The appellant must either serve the trial judge's certificate on the appropriate Crown Court officer together with a notice of appeal or apply to the Court of Appeal for leave to appeal within 28 days from the date of the original order.[243] On an appeal against sentence, the Court of Appeal cannot increase the sentence and thus cannot generally increase the period of disqualification.[244] The prosecution has no direct right of appeal. However, under the procedure introduced by Pt IV of the Criminal Justice Act 1988, the Attorney-General may refer certain sentences to the Court of Appeal if it appears to him that the sentencing of a person in the Crown Court has been unduly lenient. This procedure is available exclusively in respect of offences triable only on indictment and in a limited range of other instances specified by statutory instrument. On an Attorney-General's reference, the Court of Appeal can impose a heavier sentence than that previously imposed (provided it does not exceed the sentencing powers of the court below). In *Attorney General's Reference Nos. 14, 15 and 16 of 1995,* the Court of Appeal used this power to impose lengthy disqualification orders on two of three defendants who had been convicted of offences of market rigging in relation to the shares of public companies.[245] An appeal does not generally lie from a CDDA s.2 order made in Scotland's High Court of Justiciary as this is the supreme court of jurisdiction in respect of criminal matters north of the border.

[240] Criminal Appeal Act 1968 s.50 as substituted by Criminal Justice Act 1993 s.79(13), Sch.5 Pt I para.1 with effect from August 14, 1995 (SI 1995/1958) and subsequently amended thereafter.

[241] For a successful appeal based on inappropriate judicial intervention during the trial see *R. v Copsey* [2008] EWCA Crim 2043.

[242] Criminal Appeal Act 1968 ss.9(1) and 11(1), as amended by the Criminal Justice Act 1982. Procedure is governed by Pt 68 of the Criminal Procedure Rules 2005 (SI 2005/384). See also *Guide to Proceedings in the Court of Appeal (Criminal Division)* [1983] Crim. L.R. 415.

[243] Criminal Appeal Act 1968 s.18(1); Criminal Procedure Rules r.68.2. The Court of Appeal can extend the 28-day period: Criminal Appeal Act 1968 s.18(2).

[244] Criminal Appeal Act 1968 s.11(3). This contrasts with the position under CDDA s.6 where the Court of Appeal (Civil Division) can and has increased the period of disqualification on appeal by the Secretary of State: see e.g. *Re Copecrest Ltd, Secretary of State for Trade and Industry v McTighe (No.2)* [1996] 2 B.C.L.C. 477.

[245] *The Times*, April 10, 1997. The trial judge had not disqualified the defendants. The Attorney General's referral was allowed, a specific complaint being that the sentence had been too lenient because a disqualification order was not made. The appeal court decided not to disqualify the third defendant, Hendry, who was in poor health and received, per McCowan L.J., "very great credit for having established, despite his ill health, a small business on which he and his family are dependent". The disqualification orders which the court did make were incomplete. The two other defendants, Ward and Howarth, were disqualified from holding any directorship of a *public company* for periods of 7 and 5 years respectively. This led subsequently to a further hearing before the Court of Appeal: see *R. v Ward* [2001] EWCA Crim 1648, [2002] B.C.C. 953. See also *Attorney General's Reference Nos 88, 89, 90 & 91 of 2006* (2007) 2 Cr.App.R. (S.) 28 (imposition of disqualification on conviction for VAT fraud). The Attorney-General's reference procedure is available in respect of criminal sentencing in England, Wales and Northern Ireland but does not extend to Scotland: see Criminal Justice Act 1988 s.172.

Stays

10–105 A final question which is of some importance in practice is whether the court has power to suspend or stay a disqualification order pending hearing of an appeal against it. As discussed further in Ch.12, the change effected to s.1 of the CDDA by the Insolvency Act 2000 effectively gives every court imposing a disqualification order a power to stay or suspend the coming into effect of a disqualification order. For the reasons set out in that chapter, it is suggested that the power should be sparingly exercised and, if at all, for a short period only (such as 28 days). Accordingly, the need, prior to that amendment, to find some other power now no longer arises. It has been pointed out by Professor Sealy that a magistrates' court appears to have no power to suspend or stay a disqualification order[246] leaving aside the power effectively conferred by the amendment to s.1 referred to above. If so, then as Sealy indicates, the best that could have been done for the defendant prior to the amendment of s.1, was to seek an expedited hearing of his appeal. In contrast, it appears from the wording of the Powers of Criminal Courts (Sentencing) Act 2000 s.154(1) (formerly Supreme Court Act 1981 s.47(1)) that the Crown Court possesses a general power to stay its sentences or orders in addition to the power now contained in CDDA s.1.[247]

DEPARTMENT OF BUSINESS, INNOVATION AND SKILLS AS PROSECUTOR

The Criminal Investigations and Prosecution Team

10–106 It will be apparent from the above that many of the potential criminal gateways to disqualification arise from matters falling within the responsibility of BIS. BIS has provided guidance on this issue in which it is stated that one of BIS's key aims is to deliver free and fair markets with greater competition for businesses, consumers and employees.[248] The Criminal Investigations and Prosecutions team is said to contribute to this aim by taking action to deter fraud. That team investigates and prosecutes a range of offences, primarily relating to personal or company insolvencies. The offences that are prosecuted most often are apparently:

(1) Wrongdoing by a bankrupt both before and after a bankruptcy order has been made (ss.353–360 of the Insolvency Act 1986 and the Fraud Act 2006);
(2) Malpractice by company officers before and during the winding up/liquidation of a limited liability company (ss.206–211 of the Insolvency Act 1986 and the Fraud Act 2006);
(3) Offences related to the re-use of a liquidated company's name by a successor company ("phoenix companies") (s.216 of the Insolvency Act 1986);
(4) Breach of directors disqualification orders, bankruptcy orders and bankruptcy restriction orders (ss.11 and 13 of the CDDA);

[246] L.S. Sealy, "Company directors' disqualification—suspension of disqualification pending appeal" (1989) 5 Insolv. Law & Practice 102.
[247] See text at 12–32.
[248] See *http://www.berr.gov.uk/whatwedo/businesslaw/criminal-investigations/index.html* [Accessed October 17, 2009].

(5) Fraudulent trading (s.458 of the Companies Act 1985 and s.993 of the Companies Act 2006);
(6) Malpractice by company directors in relation to the keeping and preservation of company accounting records (ss.221–222 of the Companies Act 1985 and ss.387 and 389 of the Companies Act 2006).

The majority of the offences that are prosecuted are punishable by a maximum penalty of between two and ten years imprisonment and/or a fine. In addition, the team always considers making an application for ancillary orders. For example, after a conviction it will apply for confiscation and compensation wherever appropriate. The CDDA s.2 powers are specifically mentioned in the guidance issued. Most complaints about suspected criminal offences are apparently referred from the Insolvency Service, Companies House and Companies Investigation Branch. The team also prosecutes for offences referred to it by other parts of the Department such as the Employment Agency Standards Inspectorate. However complaints are not received directly from members of the public.

The investigation process

10–107 The BIS guidance also deals with the investigation process. Where appropriate, the Criminal Investigations and Prosecutions Team will conduct a criminal investigation into the allegations referred to it. In some cases, the decision is made not to investigate but to leave the matter to regulatory enforcement. However, if a criminal investigation is commenced, it will be conducted by the team's Investigation Officers. Anyone whom it is believed may assist the investigation may be approached and requested to provide a written witness statement. In many cases, the investigation will include an invitation to an "interview under caution" for the person suspected of criminality. That person cannot be compelled to attend the interview but it provides an opportunity for the person to answer the allegations.

The decision to prosecute

10–108 In each case referred to the team, one of the team's lawyers will decide whether or not to prosecute any individual or company. This decision is made by considering all of the evidence available and applying the Code for Crown Prosecutors. A prosecution will only take place where it is believed that there is sufficient evidence for there to be a realistic prospect of conviction and where it is in the public interest to prosecute. The team sometimes decide to prosecute even when there are already civil disqualification proceedings ongoing or a disqualification order has been made. This is because the purpose of the civil and the criminal proceedings are regarded as distinct. The criminal prosecution seeks to provide the court with the opportunity to punish the individual for their criminal conduct. The purpose of disqualification proceedings, however, is, according to the BIS website, "to protect the public from the abuse of the privilege of limited liability status and therefore to maintain the integrity of the business environment."[249]

[249] See *http://www.berr.gov.uk/whatwedo/businesslaw/criminal-investigations/index.html* [Accessed October 17, 2009].

CHAPTER 11

BANKRUPTCY, INSOLVENCY RESTRICTIONS AND COUNTY COURT ADMINISTRATION ORDERS

INTRODUCTION

11–01 This chapter is concerned with: (a) the substantive provisions of the CDDA that apply in the context of personal insolvency; (b) the bankruptcy restrictions regime introduced into the Insolvency Act 1986 by the Enterprise Act 2002; and (c) the debt relief restrictions regime introduced into the Insolvency Act 1986 by the Tribunals, Courts and Enforcement Act 2007. The bankruptcy restrictions regime is modelled on the directors' disqualification regime and it also provides the template for the debt relief restrictions regime which has been introduced as a parallel means of sanctioning misconduct by debtors who have obtained administrative bankruptcy relief under a debt relief order. Although strictly the debt relief restrictions regime is a separate legal regime it is best viewed as operating in parallel to the bankruptcy restrictions regime on the basis that debt relief orders are a parallel bankruptcy process for low income, low asset debtors who meet prescribed financial criteria. For clarity and ease of exposition, in this chapter the phrases "bankruptcy restrictions" and "debt relief restrictions" are used when discussing the separate legal regimes and "insolvency restrictions" is used as a blanket term encompassing both bankruptcy and debt relief restrictions. Scotland and Northern Ireland have their own devolved personal insolvency regimes. Unless otherwise stated, this chapter is concerned solely with the legal position in England and Wales.

11–02 The CDDA provisions applicable in the personal insolvency context provide for disqualification from relevant involvement in companies and take the following form:

(1) The automatic disqualification of undischarged bankrupts.[1]
(2) The automatic disqualification of persons in relation to whom a moratorium period under a debt relief order applies ("DRO debtors").[2]
(3) The disqualification of a person who has been discharged from bankruptcy but in respect of whom a bankruptcy restrictions order or bankruptcy restrictions undertaking is in force.[3]
(4) The disqualification of a person who has ceased to be subject to a debt relief order but in respect of whom a debt relief restrictions order or debt relief restrictions undertaking is in force.[4]

[1] See text from 11–18.
[2] See text from 11–18.
[3] See text from 11–43.
[4] See text from 11–92.

(5) Disqualification following revocation of a county court administration order made under Pt VI of the County Courts Act 1984.[5]

In each case the disqualification applies automatically for so long as the relevant regime is in force.

11–03 The automatic disqualification of undischarged bankrupts is one of the oldest forms of directors' disqualification on the statute book.[6] Prior to the coming into force of the relevant provisions of the Enterprise Act 2002 on April 1, 2004, a bankruptcy could usually be expected to last for three years. The current position is that bankruptcy will last, in most cases, for a maximum period of one year and, in many of those cases, the actual period of disqualification may be considerably shorter by virtue of the early discharge provision in s.279(2) of the Insolvency Act 1986. The debt relief order regime came into force from April 6, 2009.[7] It was introduced by s.108(1) of the Tribunals, Courts and Enforcement Act 2007.[8] It provides for debt relief, subject to some restrictions and is an alternative to bankruptcy. It is aimed at people who do not own their own home, have little surplus income and assets and less than £15,000 of debt. An order lasts for 12 months. In that time creditors named on the order cannot take any action to recover their money without permission from the court (the moratorium period). At the end of the period, if the debtor's circumstances have not changed, he is freed from the debts that were included in the order. During the moratorium period, as during bankruptcy, the debtor is subject to automatic disqualification. The bankruptcy restrictions regime was introduced in England and Wales with effect from April 1, 2004 by s.257 of the Enterprise Act 2002 to deal with debtors who have behaved culpably either before or during bankruptcy.[9] The debt relief restrictions regime was introduced in England and

[5] See text from 11–113.

[6] The practical impact of the provision can readily be illustrated by reference to the exponential growth in bankruptcy numbers over the last decade peaking at a rate of in excess of 67,000 per annum in the calendar year 2008. In the years April 1 to March 31, 2006–7 and 2007–8 new bankruptcies occurred at a rate of 64,610 and 62,357 respectively: see the Insolvency Service Annual Report and Accounts for those two years.

[7] Tribunals, Courts and Enforcement Act 2007 (Commencement No.7) Order 2009 (SI 2009/382).

[8] Scotland does not have a separate DRO regime but has instead provided low income, low asset debtors who fall within defined financial eligibility criteria with a special route into sequestration: see Bankruptcy (Scotland) Act 1985 ss.5(2B)(c)(ia), 5A inserted by the Bankruptcy and Diligence etc (Scotland) Act 2007 s.15(1)(b), (2); Bankruptcy (Scotland) Act 1985 (Low Income, Low Asset Debtors etc) Regulations 2008 (SSI 2008/81). As a result, these debtors are within the scope of the Scottish bankruptcy restrictions regime and there was no need for the Scottish Parliament to enact a separate DRRO regime. During 2009 the Northern Ireland Department of Enterprise, Trade and Investment consulted on a proposal to introduce an equivalent DRO scheme and DRRO regime for Northern Ireland. At the time of writing, the proposal had not been implemented but it is anticipated that legislation will be enacted for Northern Ireland aligning the position with that in England and Wales.

[9] An equivalent regime was introduced in Scotland with effect from April 1, 2008: see Bankruptcy (Scotland) Act 1985 ss.56A–56K inserted by the Bankruptcy and Diligence etc (Scotland) Act 2007 s.2(1) and Bankruptcy and Diligence etc (Scotland) Act 2007 (Commencement No.3, Savings and Transitionals) Order 2008 (SSI 2008/115). There is also an equivalent regime in Northern Ireland: see Insolvency (Northern Ireland) Order 1989 (SI 1989/2405) (N.I.19), art.255A and Sch.2A inserted by Insolvency (Northern Ireland) Order 2005 (SI 2005/1455) (N.I.10), art.13.

Wales with effect from April 6, 2009[10] by s.108(2) of the Tribunals, Courts and Enforcement Act 2007.[11] It is also directed at debtors who have behaved culpably, but in relation to debtors who have entered the debt relief order regime rather than the bankruptcy regime. The two insolvency restrictions regimes give rise under CDDA s.11(1) to automatic disqualification from involvement in companies without permission of the court. The imposition of insolvency restrictions may be by way of bankruptcy restrictions order (interim or final) ("BRO"), bankruptcy restrictions undertaking ("BRU"), debt relief restrictions order (interim or final) ("DRRO"), or debt relief restrictions undertaking ("DRRU").

11–04 Disqualification under the CDDA is but one of a number of wider restrictions and disqualifications that apply while a person is subject to insolvency restrictions. The regimes for the imposition of insolvency restrictions are closely modelled on the directors' disqualification regime under the CDDA. As such, these regimes are best viewed as a mode of extending restrictions that have historically applied to undischarged bankrupts to discharged bankrupts and persons who have been subject to debt relief orders whose conduct is materially culpable (whether through dishonesty, fraud, recklessness, negligence or a combination of some or all of these). However, as one of the policies underpinning the Enterprise Act reforms was to alleviate the stigma attaching to bankruptcy by lifting many of the restrictions that previously applied to undischarged bankrupts and reimposing them only on culpable debtors, the restrictions applicable to undischarged bankrupts and DRO debtors are no longer necessarily in alignment with the restrictions that apply to persons subject to insolvency restrictions.[12] This chapter considers not only the directors' disqualification aspects of being an undischarged bankrupt, a DRO debtor or a person subject to insolvency restrictions, but also the circumstances in which insolvency restrictions may be imposed or agreed, and some of the wider restrictions, going beyond the boundaries of the CDDA, that are imposed by law on undischarged bankrupts, DRO debtors and those subject to insolvency restrictions.

BACKGROUND TO THE CURRENT BANKRUPTCY REGIME

11–05 This section sets out the background to the reforms of the bankruptcy regime that were introduced by the Enterprise Act 2002. This background is necessary to

[10] Tribunals, Courts and Enforcement Act 2007 (Commencement No.7) Order 2009 (SI 2009/382).

[11] Scotland does not have a separate DRO regime but has instead provided low income, low asset debtors who fall within defined financial eligibility criteria with a special route into sequestration: see Bankruptcy (Scotland) Act 1985 ss.5(2B)(c)(ia), 5A inserted by the Bankruptcy and Diligence etc (Scotland) Act 2007 s.15(1)(b), (2); Bankruptcy (Scotland) Act 1985 (Low Income, Low Asset Debtors etc) Regulations 2008 (SSI 2008/81). As a result, these debtors are within the scope of the Scottish bankruptcy restrictions regime and there was no need for the Scottish Parliament to enact a separate DRRO regime. During 2009 the Northern Ireland Department of Enterprise, Trade and Investment consulted on a proposal to introduce an equivalent DRO scheme and DRRO regime for Northern Ireland. At the time of writing, the proposal had not been implemented but it is anticipated that legislation will be enacted for Northern Ireland aligning the position with that in England and Wales.

[12] See further Enterprise Act 2002 ss.266–268; Enterprise Act 2002 (Disqualification from Office: General) Order 2006 (SI 2006/1722).

arrive at an understanding of the wider policy context and the regulatory role that the disqualification and insolvency restrictions regimes are intended to play. Although debt relief orders ("DROs") and the associated debt relief restrictions regime are a more recent addition premised on somewhat different policy considerations,[13] the broad legislative technique employed—provision of access to generous debt relief coupled with sanctions in the form of legal restrictions and disqualifications to deal with "blameworthy" or "culpable" debtors—is the same in both cases. For present purposes, the key aspects of the current bankruptcy regime brought in by the Enterprise Act 2002 were as follows:

(1) A default rule that bankruptcy should not ordinarily last longer than one year.
(2) The post-discharge bankruptcy restrictions regime.
(3) The lifting of statutory restrictions and disabilities hitherto imposed on all undischarged bankrupts regardless of their conduct.

11–06 The Enterprise Act reforms of the bankruptcy regime can be traced back to a speech given to the British American Chamber of Commerce in New York in October 1998 by the then Trade Secretary, Peter (now Lord) Mandelson:

> "We need to examine all our regulatory systems to ensure they do not needlessly deter entrepreneurs such as our bankruptcy laws. Are we sure that they create confidence in enterprise and commerce? I don't think we are confident. I think we need fundamentally to re-assess our attitude in Britain to business failure. Rather than condemning it and discouraging anyone from risking failure, we need to encourage entrepreneurs to take further risks in the future. Here in the United States, I am told that some investors actually prefer to back businessmen and women with one or more failures under their belt because they appreciate the spirit of enterprise shown and recognise the experience that has been gained from it. Can you imagine that in Britain? Rather than sharing the risks with entrepreneurs in this way, most creditors are much more wary of supporting those who have experienced business failure, indeed many of them, including a lot of our high street banks, just run a mile from anyone who taken a leap [sic], taken the risk, failed but wants to try again and those people should be backed."

In Mandelson's vision, the liberalisation of personal insolvency laws was one of the steps that needed to be taken in order for Britain to emulate the United States by creating what he described as an "enterprise-oriented, risk-taking, failure-tolerant business culture".

11–07 A consultation paper was subsequently issued by the Insolvency Service in April 2000 entitled *Bankruptcy: a Fresh Start* (hereinafter "*Fresh Start*"). The foreword, by the Mandelson's successor as Trade Secretary, Stephen Byers, gives an indication of the thinking that lay behind the Enterprise Act reforms. As it is essential to an understanding of the underlying policy, the foreword is reproduced below in full:

> "Building wealth and prosperity for all citizens in the UK is a key Government objective. Entrepreneurial activity is a major determinant of growth and is in turn affected by four principal drivers: the perception of opportunities, the capacity of the population,

[13] On the policy drivers behind the introduction of DROs see text from 11–93 below.

the entrepreneurial infrastructure of the country and attitudes towards the creators of businesses. UK *cultural attitudes* are among the least supportive of entrepreneurs and respect for them is lower here than in any other comparable economy, except Japan. This is very serious, since a person is only likely to start a business if success brings social recognition and failure does not mean public humiliation. The Government must take a lead in helping to tackle the low level of motivation to start and grow new businesses because motivation correlates directly with entrepreneurial activity.

One of the reasons why people in the UK tend to be risk averse is because they see the financial and social costs of failure as outweighing the benefits of success. Bankruptcy law currently makes no distinction (and therefore third parties cannot tell the difference) between those who are honest but unlucky or undercapitalised and the reckless or fraudulent. All lose their personal wealth (with some limited exceptions), are automatically disqualified from being a director of a limited company and suffer a number of other restrictions for a period of up to three years. We believe that a distinction can and should be made between the two groups so that the vast majority of honest bankrupts do not continue to be stigmatised through association with the dishonest. This consultation document proposes a much earlier discharge from bankruptcy for the large majority whose failure is honest. For those who have invested capital in their businesses, we propose a relaxation of the rules on exemption of personal property. The small minority of those guilty of misconduct would be subject to the full rigour of a new, tougher and more restrictive regime. We are also consulting on proposals to help those who would benefit from financial counselling. These changes would both alleviate the serious social consequences of failure and allow those who have failed honestly to have a second chance to make an economic contribution.

What we are now proposing represents a radical reappraisal of the impact of financial failure on individuals. I hope that it will stimulate real debate about these issues, which are central to the development of a culture of responsible risk-taking."

11–08 The Insolvency Service consultation paper was followed in July 2001 by a White Paper, *Productivity and Enterprise—Insolvency: A Second Chance* (Cm.5234) (hereinafter "*Second Chance*"). The White Paper addressed not only proposed changes to personal insolvency law but also proposed changes to corporate insolvency law. The executive summary sets out the basic changes proposed and the underlying philosophy. The relevant part of the executive summary is as follows:

"The proposed measures will modernise the framework of the law of personal and corporate insolvency. They will encourage responsible risk taking, facilitate the rescue of viable businesses and provide certainty and fairness to creditors and other stakeholders. Our proposals will address the fear of failure and reduce the stigma of bankruptcy. This will encourage those who have failed honestly to try again while providing a robust and effective remedy against the small minority who abuse their creditors.

Personal Insolvency Reforms

We propose the following changes to the personal insolvency regime:

- a reduction in the discharge period for most bankrupts from the current three years to a maximum of 12 months. This will mean that a person is free of the restrictions imposed by the bankruptcy order at an earlier stage which will aid rehabilitation and business start-ups and re-starts . . .;
- reducing the stigma of failure by reviewing the relevance of statutory restrictions on undischarged bankrupts that appear unnecessary or outdated . . .; and

- providing for a tougher regime of restrictions on bankrupts whose conduct has been irresponsible, reckless or otherwise culpable."

The Enterprise Bill was introduced into the House of Commons in March 2002 and the resulting Act received the Royal Assent on November 7, 2002. In addition to bankruptcy law reforms, the Act contains a large number of other provisions dealing with corporate insolvency and setting out a new framework for competition law.

11–09 The main perceived advantages of the reforms to the bankruptcy regime were identified in the Regulatory Impact Assessment of the Enterprise Bill as being:

(1) Early discharge leading to the prompt rehabilitation of non-culpable bankrupts.
(2) Removal of the automatic application of unnecessary restrictions, disqualifications and prohibitions, so reducing the stigma attaching to bankruptcy and increasing both business start-ups and restarts by encouraging responsible risk takers back into business and thereby contributing to the economy.
(3) Bankruptcy restrictions imposing greater restrictions on "rogues", so protecting the public and business community.[14]

It is, perhaps, ironic that, at the time that the United Kingdom government was in the process of liberalising the bankruptcy laws in England and Wales, apparently having been impressed by the United States model, the United States was taking steps to tighten up its federal bankruptcy laws at the behest of the American credit industry.[15] Bankruptcy law was also tightened in Australia shortly after the turn of the century.[16]

11–10 Despite these signs of retrenchment elsewhere, the reform process in the United Kingdom seems to have acquired an unstoppable momentum which may, in part, be explained by policy thinking at the European level. Following the Lisbon and Feira councils in 2000, the European Commission, through its Enterprise Directorate-General, conducted its own contemporaneous assessment of the bankruptcy laws of member states[17] with a view to setting benchmarks for the implementation of policies supportive of enterprise at national level. This process culminated in the publication of a report, the executive summary of which contains the following statement:

> "[L]egal systems can be a real deterrent to a fresh start. Failed entrepreneurs usually learn from their mistakes and can be more successful in the future. The possibility of continuing or starting a new business is affected by both the general consequences of bankruptcy and on the disqualifications and restrictions imposed on those subject to bankruptcy proceedings. At present there is no distinction made between bankrupts who fail through no fault of their own and those who are culpable and little regard is given,

[14] It would appear that this point is primarily based on the fact that under the Insolvency Act 1986 the only equivalent penalty was a criminal one and that, of course, required proof to a higher standard.
[15] Steps which culminated in the enactment of the Bankruptcy Abuse Prevention and Consumer Protection Act of 2005 introducing means tested access to a Chapter 7 discharge and mandatory credit counselling.
[16] See the Bankruptcy Legislation Amendment Act 2002 (Cth.).
[17] *Second Chance*, paras 1.7–1.8.

in terms of their treatment, to the facts of the individual case. By treating each individual in a proportionate and appropriate manner, non-fraudulent debtors would not be stigmatised through association with fraudulent ones."[18]

The Enterprise Act reforms therefore anticipate wider policy initiatives at the European level that, in line with the goal set by the European Council in Lisbon in 2000, sought to make Europe "the most competitive and dynamic knowledge-based economy in the world" by 2010.[19] These European initiatives were also explicitly premised on the desire to stimulate entrepreneurial activity or, at least, to remove possible barriers to such activity. It remains an open question whether bankruptcy law is an appropriate or useful tool for facilitating enterprise and entrepreneurship. Subsequent experience in England and Wales suggests that the bankruptcy system now functions as a system for the relief of consumer debtors rather than self-employed traders.[20] However, data about bankruptcy usage tell us little about changes in perceived stigma and attitudes to business risk among would-be entrepreneurs.[21]

DURATION OF BANKRUPTCY

11–11 The duration of bankruptcy is important in the disqualification context because it determines the period for which the automatic disqualification imposed by CDDA s.11(1)(a) will last. It is also relevant for the purposes of considering the operation of the bankruptcy restrictions regime because an application to the court for a BRO must generally be made before the bankruptcy is discharged.

Commencement of bankruptcy

11–12 The bankruptcy of an individual commences with the day on which a bankruptcy order is made against him.[22] The automatic prohibition takes effect and continues

[18] *Best Project on Restructuring, Bankruptcy and a Fresh Start: Final Report of the Expert Group* (September 2003) available at *http://ec.europa.eu/enterprise/entrepreneurship/sme2chance/doc/failure_final_en.pdf* [Accessed August 27, 2009]. See, e.g. the Expert Group's recommendation at para.7.3.2 regarding the drawing of a distinction between fraudulent and non-fraudulent debtors. The Best Project Report also cites the Enterprise Act reforms as an example of good practice: see para.5.3.2.

[19] *Best Project*, para.2.1.

[20] See Insolvency Service, *Enterprise Act 2002—the Personal Insolvency Provisions: Final Evaluation Report* (November 2007), *http://www.insolvency.gov.uk/insolvencyprofessionandlegislation/legislation/evaluation/finalreport/home.htm* [Accessed August 27, 2009], at pp.27–31.

[21] Surveys carried out by the Insolvency Service in 2004 and 2006–2007 suggest that there is a continuing stigma associated with bankruptcy at least so far as sole traders are concerned. Moreover, a study of self-employed bankrupts found that the percentage of respondents who recommenced trading within one year of entering bankruptcy fell from 49% to 44% after the Enterprise Act provisions came into force. The findings of these surveys are available at *http://www.insolvency.gov.uk/insolvencyprofessionandlegislation/policychange/policychange.htm* [Accessed August 27, 2009]. Equally, there is evidence that countries with "forgiving" bankruptcy laws (using duration of bankruptcy to calibrate the extent to which the law is "forgiving" or "unforgiving") have higher rates of self-employment: see J Armour and D Cumming, "Bankruptcy Law and Entrepreneurship" (2008) 10(2) American Law and Economics Rev. 303.

[22] Insolvency Act 1986 s.278. For the circumstances in which and by whom a bankruptcy petition may be presented see Insolvency Act 1986 ss.264–277.

from that point until such time as the individual is discharged from bankruptcy or the bankruptcy order is either rescinded or annulled.

Discharge

11–13 So as to understand the significance of the bankruptcy restrictions regime and the current discharge regime, it is important to appreciate in outline the previous discharge regime that applied prior to April 1, 2004. From April 1, 2004, the current regime, introduced by the Enterprise Act 2002, which is discussed below, applies. There were transitional provisions that dealt with individuals who, as at that date, were still undischarged bankrupts. These are also discussed briefly below.

The position prior to the Enterprise Act 2002

11–14 It was not until 1705 that discharge from bankruptcy in any real sense was made possible. Under the 1883 legislation, discharge, on application to the court, was consolidated. The effect of the order of discharge was to release the bankrupt from all debts that were provable in the bankruptcy, save for a limited number of exemptions. In addition, there was immediate discharge from certain disqualifications and, after five years, the bankrupt was discharged from prohibitions against holding certain public offices. The Insolvency Act 1976 provided for an automatic discharge in the case of certain old bankruptcies. Otherwise it effectively gave the court power to grant an automatic discharge after five years coupled with provisions whereby there would be automatic court review of the question of discharge, if the bankruptcy continued beyond five years.[23] Under the Insolvency Act 1986 the position was, in broad terms, as follows. In the case of criminal bankruptcy orders and bankruptcies occurring within 15 years of the person having previously been an undischarged bankrupt, discharge was by court order only.[24] In other cases there was automatic discharge upon expiration of "the relevant period" counted from the commencement of the bankruptcy. That period was two years in the case of summary administration and otherwise three years. However, there was power for the official receiver to apply to the court for an order suspending the running of the relevant period in cases where the bankrupt was not fulfilling his obligations under the Act.[25]

The current regime

11–15 With effect from April 1, 2004, the current s.279 of the Insolvency Act 1986 was substituted by s.256 of the Enterprise Act 2002.[26] The former requirement in

[23] For the position immediately prior to the enactment of the Insolvency Act 1986, see further Report of the Review Committee, *Insolvency Law and Practice*, Cmnd.8558 (London: HMSO, 1982), paras 136–140.

[24] The application could only be made after the expiry of five years from commencement of the bankruptcy.

[25] A power still available: see Insolvency Act 1986 s.279(3).

[26] The current s.279 was brought into force by the Enterprise Act 2002 (Commencement No.4 and Transitional Provisions and Savings) Order 2003 (SI 2003/2093), art.2(2) and Sch.2. The provisions on personal insolvency introduced by the Enterprise Act do not apply in Scotland and Northern Ireland which have their own devolved regimes: see Insolvency Act 1986 ss.440(2)(b) and 441.

relation to criminal bankruptcy orders, namely that discharge is by court order and that any application can only be made after five years, was effectively retained.[27] However, in all other cases, unless the court intervenes, discharge from bankruptcy will, if it has not occurred earlier, occur automatically at the end of the one-year period beginning with the date on which the bankruptcy commenced. The one-year period is not the minimum period. If before the end of the one-year period the official receiver files a notice in court stating that investigation of the conduct and affairs of the bankrupt ordinarily required by s.289 of the Insolvency Act is unnecessary or concluded, the bankrupt will be discharged on the date the notice is filed.[28] Accordingly, there is scope for bankrupts to obtain their discharge within one year of the date of the order. Indeed, the possibility of eight-week bankruptcies was canvassed, with some dismay, in the House of Lords when the Enterprise Bill was being debated.[29] The government's evaluation evidence suggests that somewhere between 40 and 50 per cent of debtors who enter bankruptcy receive an early discharge and, of these, the average period from commencement to discharge is seven months.[30] The Insolvency Service's internal policy is that official receivers will not consider activating the early discharge provisions until three months after they have issued the report to creditors.[31] As previously, the court may extend the bankruptcy by suspending discharge where there is non-compliance with the Insolvency Act 1986. An application in this respect may now be made by the official receiver or the trustee in bankruptcy.[32]

Transitional provisions

11–16 A person who was an undischarged bankrupt immediately before April 1, 2004 ("a pre-commencement bankrupt") was subject to the transitional provisions set out in s.256(2) and Sch.19 of the Enterprise Act 2002. The general principle is

[27] Insolvency Act 1986 ss.264(1)(d), 279(6), 280.

[28] Insolvency Act 1986 s.279(2); Insolvency Rules 1986 r.6.214A.

[29] Hansard H.L. Vol.639, col.1134 (Lord Hunt).

[30] Insolvency Service, *Enterprise Act 2002—the Personal Insolvency Provisions: Final Evaluation Report* (November 2007), *http://www.insolvency.gov.uk/insolvencyprofessionandlegislation/legislation/evaluation/finalreport/home.htm* [Accessed August 27, 2009], at 57–58. In 2007–08 42% of bankrupts were granted an early discharge, with an average bankruptcy period of 7.2 months: see Insolvency Service, *Annual Report and Accounts 2007–2008* H.C. 800 (London: The Stationery Office, 2007). The same report states that "early discharge will only be considered where the official receiver is satisfied that the debtor's conduct has been satisfactory and that they (sic) have fully complied with the official receiver's enquiries. Early discharge applications are subject to the agreement of the debtor's creditors."

[31] Insolvency Service, *Enterprise Act 2002—the Personal Insolvency Provisions: Final Evaluation Report* (November 2007), 59.

[32] Insolvency Act 1986 s.279(3)–(5). For the rules relating to applications and orders suspending discharge see Insolvency Rules 1986 rr.6.215–6.216. Under the old law only the official receiver could apply for suspension of discharge. As a consequence, if the occasion arose, the trustee in bankruptcy needed to give sufficient notice to enable the official receiver to make the application before the debtor was automatically discharged. The current s.279(3) extends the power to enable a trustee in bankruptcy to apply without having to refer the matter to the official receiver. For an illustration of the problems that arose in practice see *Bagnall v Official Receiver* [2003] EWHC 1398 (Ch), [2003] 3 All E.R. 613; affirmed [2003] EWCA Civ 1925. Where the trustee makes the application, he must send copies of his evidence in support to the official receiver: Insolvency Rules 1986 r.6.215(5).

that a pre-commencement bankrupt will be discharged from bankruptcy at whichever is the earlier of:

(1) the end of the one-year period beginning on April 1, 2004 or;
(2) the end of the relevant period applicable to the bankrupt under s.279(1)(b) of the Insolvency Act 1986 as it had effect immediately before April 1, 2004 (three years beginning with the date of the bankruptcy order or two years in the case of summary administration).

So, for example, an individual made bankrupt on March 31, 2004 would have fallen within (a) and have been entitled to automatic discharge on March 31, 2005 (the end of the one-year period that commenced on April 1, 2004). However, an individual made bankrupt on September 1, 2001 would have fallen within (b) and have been entitled to automatic discharge on August 31, 2004. Schedule 19 of the Enterprise Act 2002 applied a special rule to pre-commencement bankrupts who had been undischarged bankrupts in the 15 years before the most recent adjudication (i.e. a repeat or serial bankrupt) to deal with the fact that repeat bankrupts whose most recent bankruptcy commenced on or after April 1, 2004 no longer have to apply to court for discharge and, like any bankrupt, are entitled to discharge one year after the bankruptcy order.[33] As the cases governed by the transitional provisions have diminished with the passage of time, so has their practical relevance in determining the point at which an individual ceases to be subject to the prohibition in CDDA s.11(1)(a).

Annulment or rescission of bankruptcy order

11–17 Section 282 of the Insolvency Act 1986 gives the court power to annul a bankruptcy order on the basis that: (a) there were grounds existing at the time of the order supporting the conclusion that the order ought not to have been made; or (b) the bankruptcy debts and expenses of the bankruptcy have all, since the making of the order, been either paid or secured to the satisfaction of the court. If the order is annulled, the individual is restored to his original pre-bankruptcy position, i.e. it is (broadly) as if the bankruptcy order had never been made.[34] It follows that the prohibition in CDDA s.11(1)(a) will cease on annulment. The question whether the prohibition is removed retrospectively, or only prospectively, in which latter event any breach of the prohibition between adjudication and annulment would still result in civil and/or criminal liability, was addressed in *Commissioners of Inland Revenue v McEntaggart*.[35] In that case a civil

[33] Compare the former s.279(1)(a) and the present s.279(6).

[34] *Bailey v Johnson* (1872) L.R. 7 Ex. 263. The effects of annulment on BROs and BRUs and revocation of DROs on DRROs and DRRUs are considered further below in the text at 11–89 and 11–108. In broad terms BROs and BRUs are also annulled, unless the bankruptcy order is annulled only because of financial arrangements made after the bankruptcy, such as payment of debts or following the debtor entering into a post-bankruptcy individual voluntary arrangement: see Insolvency Act 1986 Sch.4A, paras 10–11.

[35] [2004] EWHC 3431 (Ch), [2006] 1 B.C.L.C. 476.

recovery claim under CDDA s.15 had been commenced on the basis of a breach of s.11, flowing from a bankrupt having acted as a director of a company. The bankrupt's argument was that an annulment on the basis that the relevant debts and expenses had since been paid meant that the slate was wiped clean and it was as if the debtor had never been bankrupt. Therefore, it was argued, no liability could attach for breach of s.11 because the debtor was to be treated as never having fallen within s.11. Patten J. disagreed and considered that the annulment operated only prospectively for these purposes. Although he was dealing with a case of annulment on the basis of subsequent payment rather than on the basis of grounds existing at the date of the order, the reasoning in the judgment would apply the same result whichever the ground of the annulment.[36] The court also has a separate power to rescind a bankruptcy order under Insolvency Act 1986 s.375. This power is used sparingly but may be available as an alternative in circumstances where the conditions for annulment in s.282 are not made out.[37] If the order is rescinded the prohibition in CDDA s.11(1)(a) will cease.[38]

AUTOMATIC DISQUALIFICATION OF UNDISCHARGED BANKRUPTS, DRO DEBTORS AND THOSE SUBJECT TO INSOLVENCY RESTRICTIONS FROM INVOLVEMENT IN COMPANIES: CDDA S.11(1)

11–18 Section 11(1) of the CDDA insofar as it applies in England and Wales provides:

> "It is an offence for a person to act as director of a company or directly or indirectly to take part in or be concerned in the promotion, formation or management of a company, without the leave of the court, at a time when—
>
> (a) he is an undischarged bankrupt,
> (aa) a moratorium period under a debt relief order applies in relation to him, or
> (b) a bankruptcy restrictions order or a debt relief restrictions order is in force in respect of him."

[36] [2006] 1 B.C.L.C. 476 at [38]–[41]. Australian authority also suggests, by analogy, that the s.11 prohibition still applies during the period between the bankruptcy order and the annulment: see *Re Baysington Pty Ltd* (1988) 12 A.C.L.R. 412 at 418; *Salter v National Companies Securities Commission* (1988) 13 A.C.L.R. 253 at 256. Moreover, the offence in CDDA s.11 is not a "bankruptcy offence" for the purposes of the Insolvency Act 1986 s.350(2), which prevents institution of prosecutions for such offences after annulment. Whether, having regard to the public interest, the prosecuting authorities would initiate a prosecution in such circumstances is unclear and open to doubt.

[37] For the principles on which the court will exercise its discretion under s.375 see, e.g. *Fitch v Official Receiver* [1996] 1 W.L.R. 242; *Inland Revenue Commissioners v Robinson* [1999] B.P.I.R. 329. The review power in s.375 is not just confined to bankruptcy orders but extends to any order made by the court in the exercise of its bankruptcy jurisdiction. For the exercise of the power in the context of BROs see *Official Receiver v Bathurst* [2008] EWHC 2572 (Ch), [2008] B.P.I.R. 1548.

[38] The prohibition applies in the period between the making and rescission of the order. As in the case of annulment, it is suggested that rescission will not prevent any breach of s.11 that took place prior to rescission from constituting an actionable breach with the usual criminal and civil law consequences.

A provision making reference to BROs was first introduced by s.257(3) and Sch.21 para.5 of the Enterprise Act 2002 with effect from April 1, 2004.[39] The present wording of s.11(1), containing the additional references to DROs and DRROs, was substituted by s.108(3) and Sch.20 para.16 of the Tribunals, Courts and Enforcement Act 2007 with effect from April 6, 2009.[40] This version of s.11(1), substituted and amended by the 2002 and 2007 Acts, applies only in England and Wales. The original CDDA s.11(1) remains in force in Scotland. The implications of this are considered further in the text at 16–28.

11–19 The effect of CDDA s.11(1)(a) is that a bankrupt is automatically prohibited from acting as a company director etc. without the permission of the court for so long as he remains undischarged. Where the bankrupt is a director of a company or companies the articles of which provide that a director automatically vacates office if a bankruptcy order is made against him, his authority to act as agent for the company ceases on the making of the order.[41] The effect of CDDA s.11(1)(aa) is the same for a person in relation to whom a DRO has been made for so long as the DRO moratorium remains in force,[42] as s.11(1)(a) is for bankrupts during the currency of the bankruptcy. The effect of CDDA s.11(1)(b) is that a person who is subject to a BRO or a DRRO is prohibited from acting as a company director etc. without the permission of the court for the duration of the order. The same is true of persons subject to a BRU or a DRRU as reference to either form of insolvency restrictions order includes a reference to either form of insolvency restrictions undertaking.[43] The term "company" in s.11(1) includes an unregistered company and a company incorporated outside Great Britain which has an established place of business in Great Britain.[44] The court for the purpose of an application for permission to act in a prohibited capacity under s.11(1) in the form applying in England and Wales or Scotland is the court by which the person was adjudged bankrupt or, in Scotland, sequestration of his estates was awarded.[45] Section 11 only applies to individuals[46] made bankrupt in England and Wales or

[39] The Enterprise Act 2002 (Commencement No. 4 and Transitional Provisions and Savings) Order 2003 (SI 2003/2093), art.2(2) and Sch.2.

[40] Tribunals, Courts and Enforcement Act 2007 (Commencement No.7) Order 2009 (SI 2009/382), art.2.

[41] *Witherdale Ltd v Registrar of Companies* [2005] EWHC 2964 (Ch), [2008] 1 B.C.L.C. 174.

[42] The default rule is that the moratorium period lasts for one year beginning with the effective date of the DRO: see Insolvency Act 1986 s.251H introduced by Tribunals, Courts and Enforcement Act 2007 s.108(1), Sch.17 with effect from April 6, 2009.

[43] Insolvency Act 1986 Sch.4A para.8 (inserted by s.257 of the Enterprise Act 2002); Insolvency Act 1986 Sch.4ZB para.8 (inserted by s.108(2) of the Tribunals, Courts and Enforcement Act 2007).

[44] CDDA s.22(2)(a). On the territorial extent of the CDDA prohibitions see further Chs 14 and 16.

[45] CDDA s.11(2). This wording, which appears to need amendment, causes problems in relation to applications for permission to act by persons who are subject to DROs or debt relief restrictions: see further text at 15–80.

[46] As insolvent partnerships are treated as companies for CDDA purposes the applicability of the CDDA to them is considered elsewhere: see, in particular, Chs 3 and 14. It suffices to say that where an insolvent partnership is being wound up as an unregistered company under the terms of the Insolvent Partnerships Order 1994 and there are concurrent bankruptcy petitions against the individual partners then those partners will be automatically disqualified.

made the subject of sequestration in Scotland.[47] It does not extend to an individual adjudicated bankrupt by a foreign court.

11–20 A person who enters into an individual voluntary arrangement with his or her creditors pursuant to Pt VIII of the Insolvency Act 1986 clearly falls outside the scope of CDDA s.11. For this reason an individual voluntary arrangement may be a useful practical alternative for debtors who wish to avoid the impact of s.11 and the wider consequences which bankruptcy may have for those debtors whose livelihood derives from their professional status.[48] However, if the debtor fails to comply with terms of the voluntary arrangement, the supervisor or an arrangement creditor have standing to petition for a bankruptcy order which, if made, would, of course, trigger the CDDA s.11 prohibition in the usual way.[49] Also, if the debtor enters bankruptcy first and then seeks to exit bankruptcy by proposing a post-bankruptcy individual voluntary arrangement, then s.11(1)(a) will apply for so long as the debtor remains an undischarged bankrupt.[50] Although entry into an approved individual voluntary arrangement does not trigger disqualification under the CDDA it will amount to a "composition or arrangement" with the debtor's creditors that may trigger disqualifications and restrictions under other legislation.[51]

11–21 Disqualification from acting as a receiver or an insolvency practitioner, equivalent to that imposed by a disqualification order or undertaking, is imposed not by the CDDA but by various provisions of the Insolvency Act 1986 (as amended). Thus, under s.31 of the Insolvency Act 1986, it is an offence for a person to act as receiver or manager of the property of a company on behalf of debenture holders while he is an undischarged bankrupt, a moratorium period under a DRO applies in relation to him, or he is subject to insolvency restrictions.[52] The prohibition does not apply to court appointed receivers. Similarly, ss.390(4)(a), (4)(aa) and 390(4), (5) of the Insolvency Act 1986 (as amended) provide (respectively) that an undischarged bankrupt, a person in relation to whom a moratorium period under a DRO applies and a person subject to insolvency restrictions are not qualified to act as an insolvency practitioner.[53] Where the s.390 disqualification has effect, the

[47] A prohibition equivalent to that in CDDA s.11(1)(a) also applies in Northern Ireland: see now the Company Directors Disqualification (Northern Ireland) Order 2002 (SI 2002/3150), art.15 and for its commencement the Company Directors Disqualification (2002 Order) (Commencement) Order (Northern Ireland) 2003 (SI 2003/345). On the two versions of s.11(1) having separate application in England and Wales and in Scotland see further text from 16–28.

[48] See further A. Walters, "Individual Voluntary Arrangements: A 'Fresh Start' for Salaried Consumer Debtors in England and Wales?" (2009) 18(1) International Insolvency Rev. 5.

[49] Insolvency Act 1986 ss.264(1)(c), 276.

[50] The usual course for a bankrupt who has entered an approved voluntary arrangement will be to apply for the annulment of the bankruptcy order under Insolvency Act 1986 s.261 (as substituted with effect from April 1, 2004 by the Enterprise Act 2002 s.264 and Sch.22) or s.263D where the voluntary arrangement was approved under the fast-track procedure. For the effect of annulment on a bankruptcy order see 11–89.

[51] See, e.g. Charities Act 1993 s.72(1)(c).

[52] The present wording was substituted by Enterprise Act 2002 s.257(3), Sch.21, para.1 and further amended to introduce the references to a DRO and a DRRO by Tribunals, Courts and Enforcement Act 2007 s.108(3), Sch.20 paras 1–2.

[53] The present wording was substituted by Enterprise Act 2002 s.257(3), Sch.21 para.4 and further amended to introduce the references to a DRO and a DRRO by Tribunals, Courts and Enforcement Act 2007 s.108(3), Sch.20 paras 1, 6.

individual will not be able to act as a liquidator, provisional liquidator, administrator or administrative receiver of a company or as nominee or supervisor of a proposed or approved voluntary arrangement in relation to a company[54] or as insolvency practitioner, broadly covering the same activities, in relation to insolvent partnerships.[55] As discussed further below, the prohibition on acting as an insolvency practitioner also prevents the person from acting as an office holder in relation to insolvent individuals. Breach of these prohibitions constitutes an offence.[56]

11–21A The criminal consequences of a breach of CDDA s.11 are dealt with by s.13. On conviction on indictment the person is liable to imprisonment for not more than two years or a fine or both. On summary conviction the offender is liable to imprisonment for not more than six months or a fine not exceeding the statutory maximum. Section 14, dealing with offences by bodies corporate and extending the offence to various persons, broadly officers and managers of the body corporate, who may be said to be accessories, although extended to cover breaches of s.12, is not extended to breaches of s.11. In addition, offenders who act in breach of s.11 may find themselves the subject of criminal confiscation or compensation orders, as well as at risk of being made the subject of a disqualification order under CDDA s.2.

11–21B Section 15 of the CDDA provides for civil liability for the debts of a company where a person has acted in breach of a disqualification order or disqualification undertaking in relation to that company and also extends such civil liability to what might be conveniently described as "accessories". However, as regards the prohibition in s.11(1), as applicable in England and Wales, personal liability for the debts of a company under s.15 is not extended equally in respect of all types of breach. Any breach of the s.11 prohibition will result in personal liability for the debts of the company in question by the person acting in breach.[57] However, as regards accessories, liability under s.15 only extends to accessories as regards the prohibition on undischarged bankrupts and not as regards the prohibition in relation to insolvency restrictions or, even more surprisingly, debt relief orders. Under s.15(1)(b)(ii), a person who is involved in the management of a company and who acts or is willing to act on instructions given without the permission of the court by a person whom he knows at the time to be an undischarged bankrupt, will be jointly and severally liable for the relevant debts of the company. For these purposes the relevant debts are defined as being such debts and other liabilities as are incurred at a time when that person was acting or was willing to act on instructions given by the undischarged bankrupt.[58] There is also a rebuttable presumption that where a person involved in the management of a company has at any time acted on instructions given without the permission of the court by a person who at that time he knew to be an undischarged bankrupt then he will be

[54] Insolvency Act 1986 s.388(1).
[55] Insolvency Act 1986 s.388(2A).
[56] Insolvency Act 1986 s.389.
[57] CDDA s.15(1)(a).
[58] CDDA s.15(3)(b).

presumed to have been willing at any time thereafter to act on any instructions given by that person.[59] For the purposes of s.15, a person is involved in the management of a company if he is a director or concerned, whether directly or indirectly, or takes part, in the management of a company.[60]

History and rationale

11–22 A provision automatically disqualifying undischarged bankrupts from acting as a director of, or directly or indirectly taking part in the management of a company without the leave of the court was originally enacted in the Companies Act, 1928 and shortly after consolidated in the Companies Act, 1929. It was therefore one of the first directors' disqualification provisions to be introduced. Only the fraud and fraudulent trading aspects of the provisions now found in CDDA ss.4(1) and 10 have origins that can be traced back as far. The provision was extended by an amendment introduced in the Companies Act 1981 to prevent undischarged bankrupts from taking part in the promotion or formation of companies. Apart from that change, there is little substantive difference between the present s.11(1)(a) and the original provision.

11–23 Automatic disqualification of undischarged bankrupts was introduced on the recommendation of the Greene Committee.[61] The problem that the Greene Committee identified was the ease with which undischarged bankrupts were able to obtain credit through the medium of a limited company:

> "The evidence upon this subject discloses a state of affairs which is difficult to deal with but in our opinion demands a remedy. Many cases have been brought to our notice where bankrupts who have not obtained their discharge have been able, by using the machinery of the Companies Acts, to continue trading under the disguise of a limited company, with results often disastrous to those who have given credit to the company. In many cases, traders have been far too ready to give credit to private companies of which they know nothing, without making any or sufficient inquiries as to the financial standing of the company or the persons who control it, and to this extent it may fairly be said that the trouble lies at their own door. This is particularly the case where manufacturers in periods of trade depression have been eager at any risk to find a sale for their goods. But in spite of these considerations, we are of opinion that an amendment of the law so as to prohibit an undischarged bankrupt from taking part in the management of a company without the leave of the Bankruptcy Court concerned is desirable."[62]

At the time of the Greene Committee's deliberations, there was an obvious anomaly. It had long been an offence for an undischarged bankrupt to obtain credit above a prescribed amount without disclosing relevant information about his personal status.[63] However, before the enactment of what is now CDDA s.11(1)(a),

[59] CDDA s.15(5).
[60] CDDA s.15(4). On the criminal and civil consequences of breach of the CDDA prohibitions see further text from 14–86.
[61] Report of the Company Law Amendment Committee (the Greene Committee), Cmd.2657 (1926).
[62] Greene Committee, para.56.
[63] See now the Insolvency Act 1986 s.360. For the former provision see the Bankruptcy Act 1914 s.155.

a bankrupt was free to obtain credit through the medium of a company and enjoy the benefit of limited liability. Thus, the requirement for the bankrupt to disclose his personal status when seeking credit could effectively be side-stepped. Following the British example, a number of other jurisdictions have enacted similar prohibitions.[64]

11–24 The extract from the Greene Committee's report suggests that the original rationale of what is now CDDA s.11(1)(a) was quite narrow. However, it appears to have been accepted by the English courts that the provision does not serve merely to buttress the offence of obtaining credit without disclosure of bankruptcy status but has a wider purpose. In keeping with the rationale of the CDDA as a whole, it is suggested that the wider aim of s.11(1)(a) is to protect the public by prohibiting individuals whose bankruptcy suggests that they may be deficient in running their own affairs from being involved in the management of companies. Support for this view can be derived both from decisions on the original prohibition under s.11 (including equivalent prohibitions in other jurisdictions) and from the fact that the extension of the prohibition in s.11(1)(b) to cover persons who are subject to insolvency restrictions is clearly directed at this end. A good starting point is the case of *Re Altim Pty Ltd* in which the Supreme Court of New South Wales rejected the application of an undischarged bankrupt for permission to act in prohibited capacities notwithstanding disqualification. Street J. described the purpose of the equivalent applicable provision in New South Wales in the following terms:

> "The section under which this application is made proceeds upon the basis that a person who is an undischarged bankrupt is prima facie not to be permitted to act as a director or to take part in the management of a company . . . It should be borne in mind that the section is not in any sense a punishment of the bankrupt . . . The prohibition is entirely protective, and the power of the court to grant [permission] is to be exercised with this consideration in the forefront."[65]

It is striking that the applicant was refused permission in *Altim Pty* because, according to the judge, his history of failed financial ventures was ". . . such as to raise real doubts as to whether he should, whilst an undischarged bankrupt, be let loose again to take part in the commercial life of this community, in a managerial capacity in connection with a company".[66] The case suggests, by analogy, that s.11 amounts to a statutory presumption that an individual who becomes bankrupt is unfit

[64] See, e.g. Corporations Act 2001 (Cth.) s.206B(3) (Australia) and Companies Act 1963 s.183 (Ireland). Several jurisdictions have introduced automatic disqualification provisions that are much wider in scope than CDDA s.11(1)(a). For instance, under the Corporations Act 2001 in Australia, a person convicted of an offence in connection with the promotion, formation or management of a corporation is automatically prohibited from managing any other corporation without the permission of the court for a period of five years. This contrasts with the discretionary power of disqualification on conviction of a relevant indictable offence in CDDA s.2. One consequence is that Australian jurisprudence on disqualification is dominated by cases concerned with applications for permission. The potential increase in court time needed to hear applications for permission was one of the objections used to defeat the United Kingdom Government's attempt in the mid-1980s to extend automatic disqualification to the directors of any company going into compulsory liquidation: see Ch.1.

[65] [1968] 2 N.S.W.R. 762 at 764.

[66] [1968] 2 N.S.W.R. 762 at 764.

to be involved in the management of companies.[67] In England and Wales, the High Court has taken a similar view of the purposes underlying the automatic disqualification of undischarged bankrupts. In *Re Clean and Colour Ltd*[68] disqualification proceedings were brought under CDDA s.6 against a number of company directors. The Registrar disqualified the third defendant for six years. The third defendant appealed against the making of that order and against the period of disqualification imposed. One of the grounds of misconduct relied on, and found to have been made out both at first instance and on appeal, was that the defendant had allowed an undischarged bankrupt, T, to act as director of, and/or in the management of, the company. In dismissing the appeal against the period of disqualification, Morritt V.C. emphasised the gravity of the allegation regarding the bankruptcy of T:

> "There are good and obvious reasons for preventing undischarged bankrupts from acting as directors (see *Walters and Davis-White on Directors' Disqualification: Law and Practice*, paras 10–03 to 10–05), but the ban is not absolute. If there is a good reason why an undischarged bankrupt should be allowed to act as a director, then the court may give him leave to do so . . . One of the more important duties of a director is to ensure that the business and assets of the company are in the hands of persons fitted to receive them. An undischarged bankrupt, who has not been given leave to act as a director, is not such a person."

11–25 Automatic disqualification of undischarged bankrupts under CDDA s.11(1)(a) has survived the review of the prohibitions and disqualifications that flow from bankruptcy and persisted notwithstanding the policy behind the Enterprise Act reforms outlined earlier in this chapter. Moreover the provision has been extended to DROs which are best seen as a form of administrative bankruptcy for persons having limited income and assets.[69] As CDDA s.11(1)(a) applies irrespective of culpability, it is clearly arguable as a matter of policy in the light of the Enterprise Act that (subject to removal of the restriction on bankrupts from obtaining credit, which itself lies at the root of the original prohibition) this automatic disqualification is inappropriate. However, a contrary argument is that it may be unclear whether a bankrupt is culpable before he has been discharged and that the protection of the public justifies the continued existence of the automatic disqualification provided for by s.11(1)(a) especially as it will now last no more than a year in the vast majority of cases.

KNOCK ON EFFECTS OF BANKRUPTCY, DEBT RELIEF ORDERS AND INSOLVENCY RESTRICTIONS

Wider restrictions on undischarged bankrupts

11–26 As well as the prohibition in CDDA s.11(1)(a), an undischarged bankrupt was historically subject to hundreds of other disqualifications, prohibitions and

[67] *Altim Pty* has been expressly followed in a number of cases: see, e.g. *Re Ansett* (1990) 3 A.C.S.R. 357; *Re McQuillan* (1989) 5 B.C.C. 137. Furthermore, the court's approach to an application by a bankrupt for permission to act is similar to that taken on an application for permission to act by a person disqualified under CDDA s.6: see further Ch.15. This tends to reinforce the point being made in the text.

[68] June 7, 2001, Ch.D., unreported.

[69] On DROs generally see text from 11–93.

restrictions imposed by other legislation.[70] These ranged from personal and political restrictions to business and professional restrictions. While, in line with the Enterprise Act policy, some of these have been lifted or modified so that they apply only to persons who are subject to insolvency restrictions,[71] many still remain in place. So, for example:

(1) An undischarged bankrupt is automatically banned, on pain of criminal sanction, from obtaining credit to the extent of the prescribed amount[72] or more without disclosing his status as a bankrupt and from engaging in a business under a name other than that in which he was adjudged bankrupt without disclosing the name in which he was so adjudged.[73]
(2) An undischarged bankrupt is disqualified from acting as an insolvency practitioner.[74]
(3) An undischarged bankrupt is disqualified from acting as a receiver or manager of the property of a company (unless acting under an appointment made by the court).[75]
(4) An undischarged bankrupt who is chairman of a land tribunal may have his appointment revoked.[76]
(5) A person whose estate is subject to sequestration in Scotland (though not now an undischarged bankrupt in England and Wales) is disqualified from holding office, or continuing to hold office, as a school governor.[77]
(6) An undischarged bankrupt is disqualified from being or becoming a member of a regional or local flood defence committee.[78]
(7) An undischarged bankrupt is disqualified from engaging in estate agency work otherwise than as an employee of another person.[79]
(8) A practising solicitor is automatically suspended from practice on the making of bankruptcy order against him.[80]

[70] Prior to the commencement of the relevant provisions of the Enterprise Act 2002 the number of restrictions and/or disabilities was calculated as being in the region of 360: see Stephen Davies Q.C. (ed.), *Insolvency and the Enterprise Act 2002* (Bristol: Jordan, 2003), para.20.7, fn.5. For further examples of disqualifications and restrictions that affected undischarged bankrupts see Annex A of the *Second Chance* White Paper.

[71] Though note that, at the time of writing, the knock on effects of DRROs and DRRUs were limited to certain provisions of the Insolvency Act 1986 such as the prohibition on acting as an insolvency practitioner or as a receiver and manager. See text from 11–41.

[72] Currently £500, having been raised from £250 with effect from April 1, 2004 by the Insolvency Proceedings (Monetary Limits) (Amendment) Order 2004 (SI 2004/547).

[73] Insolvency Act 1986 s.360(1).

[74] Insolvency Act 1986 ss.390(4)(a), 389(1). This is an absolute ban because the prohibition flows from s.390(4)(a) of the Insolvency Act 1986 rather than from the wording of CDDA s.11 and the Insolvency Act contains no dispensing power.

[75] Insolvency Act 1986 s.31(1)(a). This is an absolute ban for the same reason given in the previous footnote.

[76] Agriculture Act 1947 Sch.9 para.13(4).

[77] School Governance (Constitution) (England) Regulations 2007 (SI 2007/957), reg.21, Sch.6 para.6(a).

[78] Environment Act 1995 Sch.5 para.3.

[79] Estate Agents Act 1979 s.23.

[80] Solicitors Act 1974 s.15(1).

(9) An undischarged bankrupt is disqualified from acting as a charity trustee unless, in the case of a charitable company, he has been granted permission to act in the management of the company under CDDA s.11 or, in the case of a charity which is an unincorporated association, the Charity Commissioners have waived the disqualification in writing.[81]

(10) An undischarged bankrupt is disqualified from acting as a pension trustee unless the Occupational Pensions Regulatory Authority has waived the disqualification in writing.[82]

(11) An undischarged bankrupt who is a member of a Housing Corporation may be removed from office.[83]

(12) The Welsh Ministers may order the removal of a director or trustee of a registered social landlord which is a registered charity or a committee member of a registered social landlord which is an industrial and provident society or a director of a registered social landlord which is a registered company if he has been made bankrupt.[84]

(13) An undischarged bankrupt who is a member of a regional development agency may be removed from office.[85]

(14) Certain licences, for example, a consumer credit licence and a public service vehicle operator's licences, are automatically terminated where the licence holder is made bankrupt.[86]

(15) An undischarged bankrupt is disqualified from being appointed commissioner in relation to several harbours.[87]

The list is illustrative rather than exhaustive.[88] The number of disqualifications, prohibitions and restrictions flowing from bankruptcy remains prodigious notwithstanding the stated policy of the Enterprise Act.

[81] Charities Act 1993 ss.72(1)(b), (3) and (4). See also s.18 of the same Act.

[82] Pensions Act 1995 ss.29(1)(b) and (5)(a).

[83] Housing Associations Act 1985 s.74, Sch.6 para.3(3)(a).

[84] Housing Act 1996 Sch.1 para.4(1), (2)(a). The registered social landlord system is now restricted to Wales by virtue of the s.61 of the Housing and Regeneration Act 2008.

[85] Regional Development Agencies Act 1998 s.2, Sch.2 para.1(3)(b).

[86] Consumer Credit Act 1974 s.37(1)(b); Public Passenger Vehicles Act 1981 s.57(2)(b). Note also the power of a traffic commissioner in respect of goods vehicle operator's licence pursuant to Goods Vehicles (Licensing of Operators) Act 1995 s.26, the impact of Licensing Act 2003 s.27 in relation to licensed premises, and the provisions relation to the fitness of a railway undertaking to hold a European licence in Sch.2 of the Railway (Licensing of Railway Undertakings) Regulations 2005 (SI 2005/3050).

[87] See, e.g. The Blyth Harbour Revision (Constitution) Order 2004 (SI 2004/148), art.9(b).

[88] Searches in relevant legal databases for the phrase "adjudged bankrupt" reveal many more extant provisions. For example, there are restrictions on the involvement of undischarged bankrupts in the governance of (inter alia) care homes, children's homes, the Council for Healthcare Regulatory Excellence, the Food Standards Agency, the General Chiropractic Council, the General Medical Council, the General Optical Council, the General Osteopathic Council and the Nursing and Midwifery Council.

The lifting of certain prohibitions and restrictions on undischarged bankrupts

11–27 The prohibition on an undischarged bankrupt being or becoming a justice of the peace formerly contained in the Justices of the Peace Act 1997 s.65 was repealed by s.265 of the Enterprise Act 2002 with effect from April 1, 2004.[89] The disqualification of a bankrupt from both Houses of Parliament was dropped by s.266(2) of the Enterprise Act 2002 and replaced by similar prohibitions applying only to persons the subject of bankruptcy restrictions[90] and now extended to persons the subject of debt relief restrictions.[91] The prohibition in s.80 of the Local Government Act 1972 on an undischarged bankrupt from being or becoming a member of a local authority was relaxed by s.267 of the Enterprise Act, also with effect from April 1, 2004, and replaced by a similar prohibition applying to persons the subject of bankruptcy restrictions. At the time of writing, this prohibition had not been extended to persons who are subject to debt relief restrictions.

The statutory power to remove and extend further prohibitions and restrictions

11–28 There have been historically, and there remain, a plethora of disqualifications, prohibitions and restrictions on undischarged bankrupts imposed by a wide variety of statutory provisions which are the responsibility of different government departments. As has been seen, one objective of the Enterprise Act 2002 was to reduce the stigma of bankruptcy. To this end s.268 of the 2002 Act confers a power on the Secretary of State to make an order repealing, revoking, amending or modifying the effect of a "disqualification provision".[92] A "disqualification provision" is one which disqualifies (permanently, temporarily, absolutely or conditionally) a bankrupt from: (a) being elected or appointed to an office or position; (b) holding an office or position; or (c) becoming or remaining a member of a body or group. A reference to a provision which disqualifies a person conditionally includes a provision that enables a bankrupt to be dismissed. This power enables the Secretary of State to lift restrictions on undischarged bankrupts without the need for primary legislation where he considers it appropriate to do so. It reflects the policy concern that restrictions based solely on the fact that a person has become bankrupt may unnecessarily stigmatise honest and responsible risk-takers whose businesses have failed through misfortune and deter such people from starting up new businesses in the future.[93]

[89] The Enterprise Act 2002 (Commencement No.4 and Transitional Provisions and Savings) Order 2003 (SI 2003/2093), art.2(2) and Sch.2. For the rationale behind the lifting of this restriction see Hansard H.C. Standing Committee B, Session 2001–2002, May 14, 2002 at cols 675–676.

[90] Amending Insolvency Act 1986 s.427 so as to omit reference to bankruptcy orders made by courts in England and Wales. The prohibition flowing from Northern Irish and Scottish bankruptcies remains. The prohibition flowing from bankruptcy restrictions is applied by s.426A of the Insolvency Act 1986.

[91] Insolvency Act 1986 s.426A as amended by the Tribunals, Courts and Enforcement Act 2007 s.108(3), Sch.20 para.12.

[92] The power vests in the National Assembly of Wales in relation to a disqualification provision made by, or relating to a function of, that Assembly: Enterprise Act 2002 s.268(14).

[93] See *Fresh Start*, especially paras 9.1–9.4; *Second Chance*, especially paras 1.21–1.24 and discussion in the text from 11–05.

11–29 The power to amend, or modify the effect of, a disqualification provision enables the Secretary of State to: (a) reduce the class of bankrupts to whom the disqualification provision applies[94]; (b) extend the disqualification to some or all individuals subject to a bankruptcy restrictions regime; (c) provide that the disqualification provision only applies to some or all individuals who are subject to a bankruptcy restrictions regime; or (d) make the application of the disqualification provision wholly or partly subject to the discretion of a specified person, body or group. For the purposes of (d), the discretion may be subject to the approval of a specified person or body or to an appeal to a specified person or body. At the time s.267 was enacted, it was anticipated that, in many cases, orders under the section would follow the pattern of s.267 of the Enterprise Act in respect of membership of a local authority by replacing prohibitions on undischarged bankrupts with equivalent prohibitions applicable to persons the subject of bankruptcy restrictions to reflect the policy that bankruptcy per se should not be stigmatised in the absence of proven misconduct. As will be seen below in 11–31, this has to some extent been borne out by the terms of the one Order that the Secretary of State has made to date under s.268.

11–30 Section 268 of the 2002 Act is expressly applied with modifications to the provision in Sch.4 para.2(1)(c) of the Local Government Act 2003 which disqualifies a Northern Irish bankrupt and a person whose estate is in sequestration in Scotland from being appointed as a member of the Valuation Tribunal Service.[95] The power is similarly applied to the provision in the Human Tissue Act 2004 which disqualifies a Northern Irish bankrupt and a person whose estate is in sequestration in Scotland from being appointed as the chairman or a member of the Human Tissue Authority.[96] However, the scope of s.268 has not been amended by the Tribunals, Courts and Enforcement Act 2007 to include express reference to debt relief restrictions. It is clear from s.268(10) that the power to extend disqualifications to the bankruptcy restrictions regime is limited to the bankruptcy restrictions regime contained in Sch.4A to the Insolvency Act 1986 (or schemes in Northern Ireland or Scotland considered by the Secretary of State to be equivalent to that regime) and that it does not extend to the debt relief restrictions regime. Such an extension was presumably thought unnecessary as there is no historic legacy of debt relief restrictions, the regime only having been brought into force in April 2009.

The Enterprise Act 2002 (Disqualification from Office: General) Order 2006

11–31 At the time of writing the Secretary of State has made one Order in exercise of the powers conferred on him by s.268 namely The Enterprise Act 2002 (Disqualification from Office: General) Order 2006.[97] An Explanatory Memorandum to the Draft

[94] It may, for example, be appropriate in some cases to retain a relevant disqualification in relation to those made the subject of a criminal bankruptcy order.
[95] Local Government Act 2003 s.105(9), Sch.4 para.25.
[96] Human Tissue Authority s.56, Sch.6 para.6.
[97] SI 2006/1722. The Order was made on June 28, 2006 and came into force on the following day.

Order set out the background to s.268 and explained the government's approach to its exercise. In order to further the Enterprise Act policy, every government department was invited to review existing bankruptcy disqualifications, prohibitions and restrictions in legislation falling within its sphere of policy responsibility. This yielded three different outcomes. First, in a handful of cases where the relevant legislation was rarely used, departments wanted the bankruptcy disqualification removing entirely.[98] Secondly, where the bankruptcy disqualification concerned a position or office to which fiduciary duties attached, departments wanted to retain the bankruptcy disqualification and extend it to persons who were subject to post-discharge bankruptcy restrictions. The most notable examples of this "retain and extend" approach relate to charity and pension fund trustees.[99] Thirdly, in some cases where no fiduciary duty attached to the post or office, departments took the view that the bankruptcy disqualification could safely be removed and replaced with an equivalent disqualification applying only to persons who were the subject to post-discharge bankruptcy restrictions.[100] Overall, while the third approach was followed in the case of fourteen disqualification provisions across a range of different legislation, the 2006 Order suggests that, in official circles, the idea that bankruptcy per se raises a presumption that debtors are unfit to hold fiduciary offices or positions has persisted notwithstanding the Enterprise Act policy which sought to ameliorate the social consequences and penal effects of bankruptcy for the non-culpable.

Wider restrictions on persons subject to DROs

11–32 As well as the prohibition in CDDA s.11(1)(aa), a person in relation to whom a moratorium period under a DRO applies is subject to the following disqualifications, prohibitions and restrictions imposed by other legislation:

(1) A DRO debtor cannot obtain credit of £500 or more without disclosing his status and is prohibited from engaging in a business under a name other than that in which the DRO was made without disclosing that name.[101]
(2) A DRO debtor is disqualified from acting as an insolvency practitioner.[102]
(3) A DRO debtor is disqualified from acting as a receiver or manager of the property of a company (unless acting under an appointment made by the court).[103]

[98] SI 2006/1722 art.2(1), Sch.1 (removal of restrictions on undischarged bankrupts relating to membership of water boards, internal drainage boards and the British Wool Marketing Board).

[99] SI 2006/1722 art.2(2), Sch.2 Pt 2 paras 4–5.

[100] SI 2006/1722 art.2(2) Sch.2 Pt 2 paras 1.

[101] Insolvency Act 1986 s.251S(1), (2)(a) inserted by the Tribunals, Courts and Enforcement Act 2007 s.108(1), Sch.17 with effect from April 6, 2009.

[102] Insolvency Act 1986 ss.390(4)(aa), 389(1). This is an absolute ban because the prohibition flows from s.390(4)(aa) of the Insolvency Act 1986 rather than from the wording of CDDA s.11 and the Insolvency Act contains no dispensing power. Section 390(4)(aa) was introduced by the Tribunals, Courts and Enforcement Act 2007 s.108(3), Sch.20 Pt 1 paras 1, 6(1), (2) with effect from April 6, 2009.

[103] Insolvency Act 1986 s.31(1)(aa). This is an absolute ban for the same reason given in the previous footnote. Section 31(1)(aa) was introduced by the Tribunals, Courts and Enforcement Act 2007 s.108(3), Sch.20 Pt 1 paras 1, 2(1)(a).

Although it does not impose a disqualification, provision has been made so that an employer who becomes a DRO debtor is treated as an insolvent employer for the purposes of Pt XII of the Employment Rights Act 1996.[104]

The effect of BROs and BRUs

11–33 As discussed above, one of the main effects of a BRO, an interim BRO[105] and a BRU[106] is to disqualify the bankrupt from acting as a director of a company etc. without the permission of the court under CDDA s.11(1)(b). There are several other disqualifications, prohibitions and restrictions imposed by various enactments (set out below). For convenience, reference is made to bankruptcy restrictions. That term encompasses BROs and the relevant prohibition is usually stated by reference to BROs. However, an interim BRO is stated to have the same effect as a BRO[107] and references in enactments to a person in respect of whom a BRO has effect (or who is "the subject of" or a BRO) include a reference to a person in respect of whom a BRU has effect.[108] At the time of writing, a person subject to bankruptcy restrictions in England and Wales is subject to various disqualifications, prohibitions, restrictions and other knock-on consequences. Several examples are provided below.[109] Judicial disquiet has been expressed at the fact that there is no clear and comprehensive statement of what a BRO (or BRU) prohibits a person from doing especially bearing in mind that failure to comply with it may expose the person to criminal sanctions.[110]

Insolvency Act restrictions

11–34
(1) A person subject to bankruptcy restrictions cannot obtain credit of £500 or more without disclosing his status and is prohibited from engaging in a business under a name other than the name in which he was adjudged bankrupt without disclosing that name.[111]
(2) A person subject to bankruptcy restrictions cannot act as an insolvency practitioner.[112]

[104] Employment Rights Act 1996 s.183(2)(a)(ai) inserted by the Tribunals, Courts and Enforcement Act 2007 s.108(3), Sch.20 Pt 2 para.17 with effect from April 6, 2009.
[105] Insolvency Act 1986 Sch.4A para.5(4).
[106] Insolvency Act 1986 Sch.4A para.8.
[107] Insolvency Act 1986 Sch.4A para.5(4).
[108] Insolvency Act 1986 Sch.4A para.8.
[109] The coverage is not exhaustive. Searches carried out for the phrase "bankruptcy restrictions order" in appropriate legal databases reveal a number of other extant provisions.
[110] *Randhawa v Official Receiver* [2006] EWHC 2946 (Ch), [2007] 1 W.L.R. 1700 at [55]; *Official Receiver v Bathurst* [2008] EWHC 1724 (Ch), [2008] B.P.I.R. 1548 at [8].
[111] Insolvency Act 1986 s.360(5) (inserted by the Enterprise Act 2002 s.257(3) and Sch.21 para.3) and the Insolvency Proceedings (Monetary Limits) (Amendment) Order 2004 (SI 2004/547).
[112] Insolvency Act 1986 ss.390(5) (added by Enterprise Act 2002 s.257(3) and Sch.21 para.4), 389(1). This is an absolute ban because the prohibition flows from s.390(5) of the Insolvency Act rather than from the wording of CDDA s.11 and the Insolvency Act contains no dispensing power.

(3) A person subject to bankruptcy restrictions cannot act as a receiver or manager of the property of a company (unless acting under an appointment made by the court).[113]

(4) A person subject to bankruptcy restrictions is barred from: (a) membership of the House of Commons; (b) sitting or voting in the House of Lords; and (c) sitting or voting in a committee of the House of Lords or a joint committee of both Houses.[114]

Fiduciary offices

11–35 (1) A person subject to bankruptcy restrictions cannot act as a charity trustee unless, in the case of a charitable company, he has been granted permission to act in the management of the company under CDDA s.11 or, in the case of a charity which is an unincorporated association, the Charity Commissioners have waived the disqualification in writing.[115]

(2) A person subject to bankruptcy restrictions cannot act as a pension trustee unless the Occupational Pensions Regulatory Authority has waived the disqualification in writing.[116]

(3) A person subject to bankruptcy restrictions is treated as having ceased to act as the fiscal representative of an aircraft operator by the Air Passenger Duty Regulations 1994.[117]

(4) A person subject to bankruptcy restrictions ceases to qualify as an account manager of an individual savings account.[118]

Public offices or appointments

11–36 (1) A person subject to bankruptcy restrictions cannot be or become a member of a local authority.[119]

(2) A person subject to bankruptcy restrictions cannot hold office as a school governor.[120]

[113] Insolvency Act 1986 s.31(1)(b) (as substituted by the Enterprise Act 2002 s.257(3) and Sch.21 para.1). This is an absolute ban for the same reason given in the previous footnote.

[114] Insolvency Act 1986 s.426A (inserted by the Enterprise Act 2002 s.266 with effect from April 1, 2004). If a member of the Scottish Parliament, the Northern Ireland Assembly or the National Assembly for Wales becomes the subject of a BRO, interim BRO or BRU, the court (or Secretary of State in the case of a BRU) is required to notify the presiding officer of the relevant body: Insolvency Act 1986 s.426B.

[115] Charities Act 1993 ss.72(1)(b), (3) and (4). See also s.18 of the same Act.

[116] Pensions Act 1995 ss.29(1)(b) and (5)(a).

[117] SI 1994/1738 reg.7(2)(d).

[118] Individual Savings Accounts Regulations 1998 (SI 1998/1870), reg.20(1)(b).

[119] Local Government Act 1972 s.80(1)(b) (as substituted by Enterprise Act 2002 s.267 with effect from April 1, 2004). The former provision also disqualified undischarged bankrupts from being or becoming a member of a local authority. The lifting of this restriction reflects the policy of the Enterprise Act, i.e. that the mere fact of bankruptcy should not attract stigma in the absence of proven misconduct.

[120] School Governance (Constitution) (England) Regulations 2007 (SI 2007/957), reg.21, Sch.6 para.6(b).

(3) A person subject to bankruptcy restrictions can be dismissed from membership of the Office of Railway Regulation.[121]

(4) A person subject to bankruptcy restrictions cannot be appointed or continue as a member of the Valuation Tribunal Service[122] or a Valuation Tribunal.[123]

(5) A person subject to bankruptcy restrictions cannot enter into a general medical services contract under Pt 4 of the National Health Service Act 2006 with a Primary Care Trust or, in Wales, a Local Health Board.[124]

(6) A person subject to bankruptcy restrictions cannot enter into a personal medical services agreement with a Primary Care Trust or a Strategic Health Authority.[125]

(7) A person subject to bankruptcy restrictions is disqualified for appointment in connection with various health bodies, including (among others) as chairman or non-officer member of the National Institute for Clinical Excellence[126] and from membership of the Health Professions Council.[127]

(8) A person subject to bankruptcy restrictions is not qualified for appointment to any registration office under the Registration of Births, Deaths and Marriages Regulations 1968.[128]

(9) The Secretary of State has power to remove the chairman or non-executive member of the Nuclear Decommissioning Authority and the chairman or a member of the Civil Nuclear Police Authority where any such person is subject to bankruptcy restrictions.[129]

(10) A person who is or has been subject to bankruptcy restrictions cannot be appointed to act as an intermediary in relation to DROs.[130]

[121] Railways and Transport Safety Act 2003 s.15 and Sch.1 para.2(c) with effect from July 5, 2004: SI 2004/827. The Act makes no provision for undischarged bankrupts in line with the Enterprise Act policy.

[122] Local Government Act 2003 s.105 and Sch.4 para.2(1)(b) brought into force by SI 2003/2938.

[123] See the Valuation and Community Charge Tribunals Regulations 1989 (SI 1989/439), reg.9(1)(a) substituted by the Valuation Tribunals (Amendment) (England) Order 2004 (SI 2004/482), art.2 with effect from April 1, 2004. It should be noted that reg.9 of the 1989 Regulations continues to apply this disqualification to persons subject to a Northern Ireland bankruptcy order or a sequestration order in Scotland. See also the Valuation Tribunal for England (Membership and Transitional Provisions) Regulations 2009 (SI 2009/2267).

[124] National Health Service (General Medical Services Contracts) Regulations 2004 (SI 2004/291) reg.5(2)(i)(ii). For Wales see the National Health Service (General Medical Services Contracts) (Wales) Regulations 2004 (SI 2004/478), reg.5(2)(i)(ii). The disqualification also applies as regards general medical services contracts with Scottish Health Boards: see National Health Service (General Medical Services Contracts) (Scotland) Regulations 2004 (SSI 2004/115), reg.5(2)(i)(ii).

[125] National Health Service (Personal Medical Services Agreements) Regulations 2004 (SI 2004/627), reg.5(3)(i)(ii).

[126] National Institute for Clinical Excellence Regulations 1999 (SI 1999/260).

[127] Health Professions Council (Constitution) Order 2009 (SI 2009/1345). See also General Optical Council (Constitution) Order 2009 (SI 2009/442); General Osteopathic Council (Constitution) Order 2009 (SI 2009/263); General Chiropractic Council (Constitution) Order 2008 (SI 2008/3047); General Medical Council (Constitution) Order 2008 (SI 2008/2554); Nursing and Midwifery Council (Constitution) Order 2008 (SI 2008/2553); Care Quality Commission (Membership) Regulations 2008 (SI 2008/2252). See also SI 2008/2927.

[128] SI 1968/2049 reg.5(a)(i).

[129] Energy Act 2004 s.2 and Sch.1 para.1(7)(b); s.51 and Sch.10 para.2(6)(b). As regards the Office of the Renewable Fuels Agency see SI 2007/3072.

[130] Debt Relief Orders (Designation of Competent Authorities) Regulations 2009 (SI 2009/457) as amended by SI 2009/1553.

Public offices or appointments—The Enterprise Act 2002 (Disqualification from Office: General) Order 2006

11–37 With effect from June 29, 2006, the 2006 Order (see 11–31 above) replaced bankruptcy disqualifications with disqualifications triggered by the making of a BRO or BRU in a number of cases. Those that remain in force are as follows:

(1) Where any member of a tribunal established under the Industry Act 1975 is the subject of bankruptcy restrictions his office automatically becomes vacant.[131]
(2) The office of director of Associated British Ports is automatically vacated if a director is the subject of bankruptcy restrictions.[132]
(3) A person subject to bankruptcy restrictions is disqualified from being elected or being Mayor of London or a member of the London Assembly.[133]
(4) A person subject to bankruptcy restrictions is disqualified for appointment as the chairman or a non-executive director of an NHS trust.[134]
(5) A person subject to bankruptcy restrictions is disqualified for appointment as the chairman or a non-officer member of the NHS Litigation Authority.[135]
(6) A person subject to bankruptcy restrictions is disqualified for appointment as the chairman or a member of a Health Authority.[136]
(7) A person subject to bankruptcy restrictions is disqualified for appointment as the chairman or a non-officer member of a Primary Care Trust.[137]
(8) A person subject to bankruptcy restrictions is disqualified for holding, or for continuing to hold, office as a member of a foundation body established under the School Standards and Framework Act 1998.[138]
(9) A person subject to bankruptcy restrictions is disqualified for appointment as the chairman or a non-officer member of the National Treatment Agency.[139]
(10) A person subject to bankruptcy restrictions is disqualified for appointment as the chairman or a non-officer member of the National Patient Safety Agency.[140]
(11) A person subject to bankruptcy restrictions is disqualified for appointment as the chairman or a member of the General Social Care Council.[141]

[131] Industry Act 1975 s.20 and Sch.6(1)(c).
[132] Transport Act 1981 s.7 and Sch.2 para.3(2)(a).
[133] Greater London Authority Act s.21(1)(c).
[134] National Health Service Trusts (Membership and Procedure) Regulations 1990 (SI 1990/2024), reg.11(1)(b).
[135] National Health Service Litigation Authority Regulations 1995 (SI 1995/2801), reg.7(1)(b).
[136] Health Authorities (Membership and Procedure) Regulations 1996 (SI 1996/707), reg.10(1)(b).
[137] Primary Care Trusts (Membership, Procedure and Administration Arrangements) Regulations 2000 (SI 2000/89), reg.5(1)(b).
[138] Education (Foundation Body) (England) Regulations 2000 (SI 2000/2872), reg.12 and Sch.4 para.2(b).
[139] National Treatment Agency Regulations 2001 (SI 2001/715), reg.3(1)(b).
[140] National Patient Safety Agency Regulations 2001 (SI 2001/1742), reg.3(1)(b).
[141] General Social Care Council (Appointments and Procedure) Regulations 2001 (SI 2001/1744), reg.4(1)(d).

Impact of BROs on lasting powers of attorney

11–38 Section 13 of the Mental Capacity Act 2005 provides that a lasting power of attorney is subject to revocation where the donor of the power becomes subject to bankruptcy restrictions. Section 64(3) of the same Act provides that if the donee of a lasting power of attorney becomes subject to bankruptcy restrictions, the appointment is terminated and the power revoked other than in relation to the patient's personal welfare.

Future prospects

11–39 Notwithstanding the policy of the Enterprise Act and the order-making power in s.268 of that Act, it has been seen that numerous disqualifications, prohibitions and restrictions continue to apply to undischarged bankrupts across a range of legislation. That said, it seems likely that where new disqualifications are contemplated (for example, arising from the establishment of new public bodies and offices in the future) the default position will be to apply the disqualification to persons the subject of insolvency restrictions and only to extend it to undischarged bankrupts in exceptional cases (for example, where the relevant appointment or office is fiduciary in nature). This default position reflects the policy that undischarged bankrupts should not generally be stigmatised unless their conduct proves to be worthy of sanction under the insolvency restrictions regimes.

Territorial extent of BROs/BRUs within the United Kingdom

11–40 Although bankruptcy restrictions regimes have been introduced in Scotland and Northern Ireland questions arise over the extent to which Scottish and Northern Ireland BROs and BRUs[142] produce knock-on consequences throughout the United Kingdom. This is because the effect of a BRO or BRU made in one part of the United Kingdom is not automatically extended to other jurisdictions in the United Kingdom. Sections 426A and 427 of the Insolvency Act 1986 provide one example of a misalignment between the consequences of BROs and BRUs made in England and Wales and those made in Scotland pursuant to the Bankruptcy (Scotland) Act 1985 (as amended) and in Northern Ireland. Whereas the effect of s.426A is that a person the subject of bankruptcy restrictions in England and Wales suffers various disqualifications in connection with membership of the Westminster Parliament, s.427 currently only applies the same disqualifications to Scottish and Northern Ireland undischarged bankrupts. It appears that s.427 needs to be aligned with s.426A so that a BRO or BRU has the same effect regardless of whether it was made in England and Wales, Scotland or Northern Ireland. There may be other cases of misalignment as regards the consequences of BROs and BRUs made in different parts of the United Kingdom and so the position will need to be checked carefully in each case. The extra

[142] Made respectively under Bankruptcy (Scotland) Act 1985 ss.56A–56K and Insolvency (Northern Ireland) Order 1989 (SI 1989/2405) (N.I.19), art.255A and Sch.2A.

territorial effect of England and Wales BROs/BRUs and Scottish BROs/BRUs is considered further in the text from 16–28 and at 16–41.

The effect of DRROs and DRRUs

11–41 The principal effect of a DRRO, an interim DRRO and a DRRU is a disqualification from acting as a director of a company, etc. without the permission of the court.[143] For convenience, DRROs etc. are referred to collectively as debt relief restrictions.[144] The other principal disqualifications, prohibitions and restrictions that flow from debt relief restrictions are set out below:

(1) A person subject to debt relief restrictions cannot obtain credit of £500 or more without disclosing his status and is prohibited from engaging in a business under a name other than the name in which he was made subject to a DRO without disclosing that name.[145]
(2) A person subject to debt relief restrictions cannot act as an insolvency practitioner.[146]
(3) A person subject to debt relief restrictions cannot act as a receiver or manager of the property of a company (unless acting under an appointment made by the court).[147]
(4) A person subject to debt relief restrictions is barred from: (a) membership of the House of Commons; (b) sitting or voting in the House of Lords; and (c) sitting or voting in a committee of the House of Lords or a joint committee of both Houses.[148]
(5) A person who is or who has been subject to debt relief restrictions cannot be appointed to act as an intermediary in relation to DROs.[149]

[143] CDDA s.11(1)(aa). See 11–18.

[144] Prohibitions are stated by reference to DRROs but interim DRROs have the same effect as DRROs and a reference in an enactment to a person in respect of whom a DRRO has effect (or who is "the subject of" a DRRO) includes a reference to a person in respect of whom a DRRU has effect: see Insolvency Act 1986 Sch.4ZB paras 5(4), 8 inserted by inserted by the Tribunals, Courts and Enforcement Act 2007 s.108(2), Sch.19 with effect from April 6, 2009. The position mirrors that in relation to BROs, interim BROs and BRUs: see 11–33.

[145] Insolvency Act 1986 s.251S(1), (2)(b), (c) inserted by the Tribunals, Courts and Enforcement Act 2007 s.108(1), Sch.17 with effect from April 6, 2009.

[146] Insolvency Act 1986 ss.390(5) (as amended by the Tribunals, Courts and Enforcement Act 2007 s.108(3), Sch.20 Pt 1 paras 1, 6(1), (3)), 389(1). This is an absolute ban because the prohibition flows from s.390(5) of the Insolvency Act rather than from the wording of CDDA s.11 and the Insolvency Act contains no dispensing power.

[147] Insolvency Act 1986 s.31(1)(b) (as amended by the Tribunals, Courts and Enforcement Act 2007 s.108(3), Sch.20 Pt 1 paras 1, 2(b)). This is an absolute ban for the same reason given in the previous footnote.

[148] Insolvency Act 1986 s.426A (as amended by the Tribunals, Courts and Enforcement Act 2007 s.108(3), Sch.20 Pt 1 paras 1, 12(1), (2), (4)). If a member of the Scottish Parliament, the Northern Ireland Assembly or the National Assembly for Wales becomes the subject of a DRRO, interim DRRO or DRRU, the court (or Secretary of State in the case of a DRRU) is required to notify the presiding officer of the relevant body: Insolvency Act 1986 s.426B (as amended by the Tribunals, Courts and Enforcement Act 2007 s.108(3), Sch.20 Pt 1 paras 1, 13).

[149] Debt Relief Orders (Designation of Competent Authorities) Regulations 2009 (SI 2009/457) as amended by SI 2009/1553.

Other potential effects of bankruptcy and insolvency restrictions

11–42 In addition to the various automatic statutory restrictions and disabilities set out above, bankruptcy and insolvency restrictions may have other legal consequences. An individual may be required to be and remain a "fit and proper person" if he is to retain his membership of a professional body or his licence to carry out a particular activity. So, for example, the bankruptcy of a person who is authorised to carry on business under the Financial Services and Markets Act 2000 could prompt the Financial Services Authority to withdraw his authorisation on the ground that he is no longer a fit and proper person.[150]

THE BANKRUPTCY RESTRICTIONS REGIME: BANKRUPTCY RESTRICTIONS ORDERS ("BROs") AND BANKRUPTCY RESTRICTIONS UNDERTAKINGS ("BRUs")

11–43 The bankruptcy restrictions regime is contained in s.281A and Sch.4A of the Insolvency Act 1986. These provisions were inserted into the Insolvency Act by s.257 and Sch.20 of the Enterprise Act 2002 with effect from April 1, 2004.[151]

Background

11–44 As discussed above, the Enterprise Act significantly liberalised bankruptcy law by reducing the period of discharge to, in most cases, a maximum of one year. The reduction in the period of discharge is particularly designed to stimulate entrepreneurial activity by providing early rehabilitation for honest but unfortunate individuals whose businesses have failed, in the hope that they will be encouraged to make a fresh start in business. The bankruptcy restrictions regime is a counterbalancing measure designed to protect the public from bankrupts who have acted recklessly, irresponsibly or dishonestly. The theory is that, while such "culpable" bankrupts will still generally be released from their debts, they should be subjected to continuing restrictions beyond discharge for between two and fifteen years in order to protect the public from any repetition of their misconduct.[152] Although disqualification from involvement in companies, as provided for by CDDA s.11(1)(b), is simply one "knock on" effect of bankruptcy restrictions, it will be seen that the regime for the imposition of bankruptcy restrictions is structurally similar to the civil disqualification regime in CDDA ss.6–9.

Prior investigation

11–45 The investigation into the conduct of bankrupts is carried out by the official receiver. Under the Insolvency Act 1986 s.289,[153] the official receiver has a

[150] See Financial Services and Markets Act 2000 ss.40–41 and Sch.6 Pt I para.5.

[151] For commencement see the Enterprise Act 2002 (Commencement No.4 and Transitional Provisions and Savings) Order 2003 (SI 2003/2093) art.2(2) and Sch.2. Scotland and Northern Ireland have their own devolved regimes for personal insolvency and have subsequently introduced BROs and BRUs.

[152] For background, see *Fresh Start* and *Second Chance*. For a useful summary of the policy background see *Randhawa v Official Receiver* [2007] 1 W.L.R. 1700 from [57].

[153] Substituted by Enterprise Act 2002 s.258 with effect from April 1, 2004.

discretion to decide that an investigation is unnecessary. Otherwise he is required to investigate the conduct and affairs of each bankrupt (including the bankrupt's conduct and affairs before the making of the bankruptcy order) and make such report to the court (if any) as he thinks fit. Many of the points considered in relation to the official receiver's duty to investigate a company's affairs under s.132 of the Insolvency Act are apposite to this duty. As in the case of directors of companies which have gone into compulsory liquidation, having carried out the initial investigation and determined that further action is required, the official receiver seeks authorisation to proceed from the Authorisations Team in the Investigations and Enforcement Services Directorate of the Insolvency Service.[154] If the Authorisations Team grants authorisation the case is referred back to the official receiver so that proceedings can be commenced.

BROs: substantive law

11–46 The court may make a BRO on the application of either the Secretary of State or the official receiver acting on a direction of the Secretary of State.[155] "The court" for these purposes is the High Court or the appropriate county court as the county courts have bankruptcy jurisdiction under the Insolvency Act 1986.[156] The application is made as an ordinary application in the bankruptcy and not in separate free standing proceedings (as is the case with an application for a civil disqualification order).[157]

11–47 Schedule 4A, para.1 of the Insolvency Act 1986 provides that a BRO may be made only on the application of the Secretary of State or the official receiver. There is no express equivalent of the public interest test set out in CDDA ss.7(1) and 8(1). In other words, the statute does not expressly require the Secretary of State to consider whether it is expedient in the public interest that a BRO should be made before making or continuing with an application. Nevertheless, as a matter of general administrative law and because the bankruptcy restrictions regime is founded on a rationale of public protection, the Secretary of State is bound to apply public interest criteria in determining whether or not to proceed.[158] Moreover, *Randhawa v Official Receiver*, the leading case to date on BROs, confirms that the bankruptcy restrictions regime was intended to be "broadly analogous" to the directors' disqualification regime in all material respects including the Secretary of State's role in deciding whether to initiate proceedings.[159] Thus, in principle, it is clear that the courts regard the Secretary of State's role under the bankruptcy restrictions regime as closely anal-

[154] This internal process is designed to separate the investigation of cases from the decision to bring proceedings in the public interest. See further a review of the Insolvency Service's investigations and enforcement functions carried out in July 2008, *http://www.insolvency.gov.uk/aboutus/reportweb.pdf* [Accessed August 27, 2009].

[155] Insolvency Act 1986 Sch.4A para.1. Hereafter references to the Secretary of State in relation to the discussion of BROs include a reference to the official receiver.

[156] Insolvency Act 1986 s.373.

[157] Practice Direction—Insolvency Proceedings, para.16A.1.

[158] See *Fresh Start* at para.7.15 and *Second Chance* at para.1.29.

[159] *Randhawa v Official Receiver* [2007] 1 W.L.R. 1700 at [60].

ogous, if not identical, to his role in directors' disqualification proceedings. It follows that courts will be equally as slow to substitute their own judgment of whether the public interest required the proceedings to be brought for that of the Secretary of State. The fact that the administrative process within the Insolvency Service is effectively the same for BROs as it is for the investigation and commencement of disqualification proceedings against the directors of companies that have gone into compulsory liquidation is further practical reinforcement of the view that the decision to initiate these forms of proceeding is subject to the application by the Secretary of State of public interest criteria.[160]

Grounds for making a BRO

11–48 Schedule 4A, para.2(1) of the Insolvency Act 1986 provides that the court "shall grant an application for a bankruptcy restrictions order if it thinks it appropriate having regard to the conduct of the bankrupt (whether before or after the making of the bankruptcy order)". Schedule 4A para.2(1) further provides that the court can take into account the bankrupt's conduct either before or after the making of the bankruptcy order. Thus, the Secretary of State could conceivably target: (a) conduct that occurred before the date of the bankruptcy petition; and/or (b) conduct that occurred in the period between the date of the petition and the date of the order[161]; and/or (c) conduct that occurred, or is occurring, after the commencement of bankruptcy. However, under transitional provisions, the court can only take into account conduct that occurred on or after April 1, 2004.[162] Paragraph 2(1) is amplified by para.2(2) which provides that the court shall, in particular, take into account any of the following kinds of behaviour on the part of the bankrupt:

(1) Failing to keep records which account for a loss of property by the bankrupt, or by a business carried on by him, where the loss occurred in the period beginning two years before the presentation of the bankruptcy petition[163] and ending with the date of the application for a BRO.
(2) Failing to produce records of the kind referred to in (1) above on demand by the official receiver or the trustee in bankruptcy.
(3) Entering into a transaction at an undervalue ("undervalue" to be construed in accordance with s.339 of the Insolvency Act 1986).[164]

[160] See 11–45.

[161] The so-called "initial period" defined in Insolvency Act 1986 s.351(b) for the purposes of the bankruptcy offences in Pt IX, Ch.VI of that Act. For cases where misconduct occurring while a bankruptcy petition was pending was taken into account by the court in making a BRO see, e.g. *Randhawa v Official Receiver* [2007] 1 W.L.R. 1700; *Official Receiver v Bathurst* [2008] B.P.I.R. 1548.

[162] The Enterprise Act 2002 (Commencement No. 4 and Transitional Provisions and Savings) Order 2003 (SI 2003/2093) art.7; Practice Direction—Insolvency Proceedings, para.16A.12; *Randhawa v Official Receiver* [2007] 1 W.L.R. 1700 at [39], [41], [54], [67].

[163] See Insolvency Act 1986 Sch.4A, para.2(2)(a), (4) and s.351(c).

[164] *Official Receiver v Tilbrook*, October 23, 2008, Ch.D., unreported (Roger Kaye Q.C.)

(4) Giving a preference ("preference" to be construed in accordance with s.340 of the Insolvency Act 1986).[165]
(5) Making an excessive pension contribution ("excessive pension contribution" to be construed in accordance with s.342A of the Insolvency Act 1986).
(6) Failing to supply goods or services which were wholly or partly paid for which gave rise to a claim provable in the bankruptcy.
(7) Trading at a time before commencement of the bankruptcy when the bankrupt knew or ought to have known that he was himself to be unable to pay his debts.
(8) Incurring, before commencement of the bankruptcy, a debt which the bankrupt had no reasonable expectation of being able to pay.[166]
(9) Failing to account satisfactorily to the court, the official receiver or the trustee for a loss of property or for an insufficiency of property to meet bankruptcy debts.
(10) Carrying on any gambling, rash and hazardous speculation or unreasonable extravagance which may have materially contributed to or increased the extent of the bankruptcy or which took place between presentation of the petition and commencement of the bankruptcy.
(11) Neglect of business affairs of a kind which may have materially contributed to or increased the extent of the bankruptcy.
(12) Fraud or fraudulent breach of trust.
(13) Failing to co-operate with the official receiver or trustee in bankruptcy.[167]

11–49 Schedule 4A para.2(3) adds that the court shall also, in particular, consider whether the bankrupt was an undischarged bankrupt at some time during the period of six years ending with the date of the bankruptcy to which the application relates. It is unclear what bearing the mere fact of a previous bankruptcy falling within para.2(3) would have on the court's consideration of the bankrupt's conduct.[168]

It is readily apparent that the legislation is structured along similar lines to CDDA s.9 and Sch.1, which deals with the matters to which the court must have particular regard in determining whether a person's conduct makes him unfit for the purposes of CDDA ss.6 and 8.[169] However, given the absence of any overriding statutory test for the making of a BRO, other than "appropriateness", these specified criteria provide a useful generic indication of the types of misconduct that are likely to form the factual basis for the making of a BRO.[170] Of course, just like Sch.1, the fact that particular conduct falls within any of the specified types will not automatically mean that a BRO is necessarily appropriate and the

[165] *Official Receiver v Bathurst* [2008] B.P.I.R. 1548; *Official Receiver v Tilbrook*, October 23, 2008, Ch.D., unreported (Roger Kaye Q.C.).
[166] For a case where this was alleged not proved see *Official Receiver v Southey* [2009] B.P.I.R. 89.
[167] *Official Receiver v Bathurst* [2008] B.P.I.R. 1548.
[168] See further text from 11–66.
[169] See text from 4–41.
[170] See further *Official Receiver v Bathurst* [2008] B.P.I.R. 1548 at paras [15]–[16] of Morritt C.'s second judgment.

fact that there was misconduct falling outside the relevant types does not mean that it could not form the basis for a BRO. On the latter point, although the court is required to take into account the matters specifically mentioned in paras 2(2) and (3), the use of the expression "in particular" makes it clear that Sch.4A, para.2 was not intended to be exhaustive.[171] This mirrors the position in relation to CDDA ss.6–9 and Sch.1.[172] Thus, for example, the court could take into account conduct that constitutes a criminal offence (e.g. obtaining credit of £500 or more without disclosure of status in contravention of Insolvency Act 1986 s.360(1)(a)) or the bankrupt's conduct during the course of an individual voluntary arrangement where the bankruptcy order was made on a supervisor's petition under Insolvency Act 1986 s.264(1)(c), even though these matters are not specifically mentioned in Sch.4A.

11–50 Taken collectively, the sheer width of the types of behaviour specified in para.2(2) range from downright dishonest conduct to conduct characterised by lesser states of culpability such as negligence, recklessness, incompetence or extravagance. They are capable of embracing misconduct by self-employed debtors in a trading context or consumer debtors who have not carried on a business and whose bankruptcy debts comprise, broadly speaking, credit card debt, personal loans and other forms of consumer credit indebtedness.[173] While the court is directed to take into account the matters specified in paras 2(2) and (3), there is no guidance in Sch.4A as to the applicable standard of conduct and/or the degree of misconduct that will make a BRO appropriate. Similarly, there is no indication of the relative weight that the court should give to the specified matters. None of this should come as any surprise given that is difficult (possibly even futile) to arrive at a comprehensive legislative definition of culpable behaviour which is sufficiently flexible and inclusive to accommodate changing patterns of behaviour over time. Accordingly, the policy behind Sch.4A rests on the view that it is safer to rely on the expertise and experience of the Secretary of State (through the official receiver) and, ultimately, the judgment of the courts on the merits of individual cases as the principal means of differentiating culpable from non-culpable

[171] *Fresh Start* at para 7.16 confirms that the list of specific matters of misconduct was intended to be "non-exhaustive". *Second Chance* at para 1.30 refers to a "statutory but non-exhaustive schedule of unfitted conduct". See also discussion at the committee stage of the parliamentary debate: Hansard H.C. Standing Committee B, Session 2001–2002, May 14, 2002 at col. 654. For case law in support of the point see *Randhawa v Official Receiver* [2007] 1 W.L.R. 1700 at [66]; *Official Receiver v Bathurst* [2008] B.P.I.R. 1548 at paras [15]–[16] of Morritt C.'s second judgment.

[172] See text from 4–46.

[173] Although the Enterprise Act reforms are motivated by a desire to encourage those whose businesses have failed through no fault of their own to try their hand in business again, the availability of bankruptcy is not limited to traders. Indeed, the bankruptcy and DRO regimes function predominantly as mechanisms for the relief of consumer debt. See further Insolvency Service, *Enterprise Act 2002—the Personal Insolvency Provisions: Final Evaluation Report* (November 2007), *http://www.insolvency.gov.uk/insolvencyprofessionandlegislation/legislation/evaluation/finalreport/home.htm* [Accessed August 27, 2009], at 27–31; D. McKenzie Skene and A. Walters, "Consumer Bankruptcy Law Reform in Great Britain" (2006) 80(4) American Bankruptcy L.J. 477; A. Walters, "Individual Voluntary Arrangements: A 'Fresh Start' for Salaried Consumer Debtors in England and Wales?" (2009) 18(1) International Insolvency Rev. 5.

bankrupts and determining which debtors will be granted a full "fresh start" free from both bankruptcy debts and post-discharge restrictions.[174]

11–51 Despite the use of the word "shall", at first blush, it might be thought that the phrase "if [the court] thinks it appropriate . . ." confers on the court a general discretion to decide whether or not a BRO is "appropriate" in the light of the bankrupt's conduct and all the relevant circumstances. Indeed, this was the view expressed by the authors in the second edition of this work. However, in the light of *Randhawa v Official Receiver* it is clear that the jurisdiction in para.2(1) should not be regarded as discretionary but should be treated instead as broadly analogous to the jurisdiction in CDDA s.6 and approached by the court in much the same way.

11–52 The *Randhawa* case turned on an allegation by the official receiver that a former bankrupt had caused a £9,500 debt to be incurred on his wife's credit card which he had no reasonable expectation would be repaid. On the premise that the court's jurisdiction was discretionary, a point that was initially conceded by the official receiver, the district judge at Worcester County Court had made a BRO for three years. Mr Randhawa appealed to the High Court against the making of the order on two grounds that: (a) the district judge had wrongly rejected his version of events, and had he accepted it he would have concluded that there was no public interest in making a BRO; or (2) an order should not have been made since there was no allegation of misconduct for the period from the date of his bankruptcy (the official receiver's allegation related exclusively to conduct in the month before the bankruptcy order was made) and accordingly there was no continuing danger from which the public needed to be protected. The official receiver having withdrawn the initial concession, the question at the heart of the appeal was whether the jurisdiction was essentially discretionary or more akin to the jurisdiction under CDDA s.6. If the jurisdiction were to amount to an "in all the circumstances" discretion this would allow the court to consider and weigh up the defendant's conduct both before and after the bankruptcy order together with the issue of whether the defendant remained a threat to the public at the time of the BRO hearing. The deputy judge dismissed the appeal and in so doing made the following points of general significance:

(1) It was apparent from the legislative background that the BRO regime was intended to be "broadly analogous" to the directors' disqualification regime in the CDDA. This intention was reflected ". . . in the proposed role of the Secretary of State in deciding whether to initiate proceedings for a BRO; in the proposed period for which BROs can be made, which is the same as under the directors' disqualification regime; and in the proposed adaptation of specific instances of misconduct from one regime to the other."[175]

[174] See, e.g. Hansard H.C. Standing Committee B, Session 2001–2002, May 14, 2002 at cols 638 and 655.

[175] *Randhawa v Official Receiver* [2007] 1 W.L.R. 1700 at [60].

(2) Paragraph 2(1) provides in mandatory terms that the court "shall" grant an application for a BRO "if it thinks it appropriate having regard to the conduct of the bankrupt". The phrase "if it thinks it appropriate" requires the court to form a judgment but the nature of the exercise is not properly characterised as the exercise of a discretion. The question whether it is appropriate to make a BRO is not at large but has to be answered "having regard to the conduct of the bankrupt". The court must therefore examine and evaluate the defendant's conduct and form a view whether that conduct merits the making of a BRO. Once the court concludes that a BRO is merited it has no choice in the matter and is obliged to make a BRO for at least the minimum period of two years.[176]

(3) The court is required to take into account any of the kinds of behaviour specified in para.2(2) (all of which involve some element of misconduct, neglect or financial irresponsibility and may include behaviour both before and after the making of the bankruptcy order) and any previous bankruptcy falling within para.2(3)[177] though these matters are not exhaustive. The court will not carry out a roving inquiry into the defendant's conduct but, pursuant to the procedural requirements in rule 6.241(1) and (2) of the Insolvency Rules 1986, will focus on the specific allegations of misconduct and decide whether they are made out on the evidence.[178]

(4) There is no express legislative guidance on the criteria or standards that the court must apply in deciding whether it is appropriate to make a BRO. However, in general terms, what is envisaged is a failure in some significant respect to live up to proper standards of competence or probity in the conduct of one's financial affairs. An element of culpability or irresponsibility will usually, if not always, need to be present.[179]

(5) The main object of making a BRO is the protection of the public and BROs are intended to have a deterrent effect. The element of deterrence was demonstrated by the imposition of the two-year minimum period. If Parliament had intended the court to have an unfettered discretion, and to consider only whether the public still needed protection from the debtor as at the date of the hearing, it was hard to see why a minimum period for a BRO had been stipulated. The minimum period suggested rather that Parliament intended to impose a substantial sanction in any case where the debtor's conduct is shown to have fallen below the appropriate standard, whether or not he still represents a danger to the public by the date of the hearing.[180] Thus, the Court of Appeal's

[176] [2007] 1 W.L.R. 1700 at [65].

[177] See 11–48.

[178] *Randhawa v Official Receiver* [2007] 1 W.L.R. 1700 at [66]–[67].

[179] [2007] 1 W.L.R. 1700 at [68].

[180] [2007] 1 W.L.R. 1700 at [69]. On the relevance of deterrence to the issue of the duration of a BRO see further *Official Receiver v Bathurst* [2008] B.P.I.R. 1548 at [30]–[31]. See also *Jenkins v Official Receiver* [2007] EWHC 1402 (Ch), [2007] B.P.I.R. 740 at [15]; *Official Receiver v Pyman* [2007] EWHC 2002 (Ch), [2007] B.P.I.R. 1150 at [24]; *Official Receiver v May* [2008] EWHC 1778 (Ch), [2008] B.P.I.R. 1562 at [24].

reasoning in *Re Grayan Building Services Ltd, Secretary of State for Trade and Industry v Gray*[181] applied with appropriate modifications to BROs.[182]

11–53 The scope of the BRO regime is clearly different from that of CDDA ss.6–8. The CDDA provisions are concerned with the defendant's conduct as a director (or shadow director) of a company or (in the case of s.8) conduct in relation to a company whereas the BRO regime is concerned with the conduct of a bankrupt which is potentially much wider. This point was acknowledged by the deputy judge in *Randhawa*:

> "... [T]he directors' disqualification regime is concerned only with conduct as a director (or shadow director) of a company which is of course a separate legal person to which directors stand in a fiduciary relationship, whereas personal bankruptcy is concerned only with the bankrupt's own financial affairs and does not usually involve a fiduciary relationship, while the types of conduct which may lead to it are of almost infinite variety. There is no single activity comparable to acting as a director of a company on which the legislation can focus, and in respect of which a specific sanction (such as disqualification from acting as a director) can be imposed. It is no doubt for this reason that Parliament has not attempted to define a BRO, but has instead provided in a piecemeal fashion for the various prohibitions, disqualifications and disabilities which flow from the making of a BRO."[183]

However, the difference between the regimes should not be exaggerated. Both are concerned with misconduct that is capable of impacting on third parties such as creditors. Accordingly, no particular significance attaches to the presence or absence of a fiduciary relationship in the context of personal debtors and it is not surprising that the courts have sought to adopt a more or less harmonised approach.[184]

11–54 The critical point emerging from *Randhawa* is that the phrase "appropriate having regard to the conduct of the bankrupt" is to be regarded as equivalent to the phrase "conduct as a director ... makes him unfit to be concerned in the management of a company" in CDDA s.6. In determining whether conduct makes a director "unfit" or a BRO "appropriate" the court must evaluate whether the conduct falls short of required standards of probity and competence, a mixed question of fact and law.[185] Although a person subject to a BRO is disqualified, among other things, from acting as a director or taking part in the management of companies, the "appropriateness" of a BRO does not depend on whether or not the person is unfit to manage companies. In effect, the question as regards a BRO is whether it is appropriate on the evidence of the individual's conduct that he be

---

[181] [1995] Ch. 241. See further text from 4–11.

[182] *Randhawa v Official Receiver* [2007] 1 W.L.R. 1700 at [72]–[74].

[183] [2007] 1 W.L.R. 1700 at [62].

[184] In *Official Receiver v May* [2008] B.P.I.R. 1562 the deputy judge did not find the analogy with CDDA s.6 compelling but nevertheless held that on the wording of Sch.4A para.2(1) *Randhawa* had been correctly decided.

[185] See further text at 4–23.

subjected to continuing restrictions (including a prohibition on acting as a director or taking part in the management of companies) in the public interest. Given the width of the prohibitions that currently flow from bankruptcy restrictions it is clearly not feasible for the court to ask whether the conduct of the debtor is such as to require him to be disqualified in the terms of each and every applicable disqualification, prohibition and restriction. It is therefore hardly surprising that the court in *Randhawa* formulated the test for "appropriateness" in terms of a failure on the debtor's part to meet proper standards of probity and competence in the conduct of his financial affairs.

11–55 The practical consequence of the approach in *Randhawa* is that the court must have "tunnel vision".[186] In other words, if the court considers that the debtor's conduct was such that a BRO is appropriate, it must impose a BRO of at least two years duration. It is not open to the court to conclude that the conduct was sufficiently culpable to merit a BRO but then decide in the light of all the circumstances (including any mitigating factors) not to make a BRO. In allowing an appeal against the refusal of a district judge to make a BRO in *Official Receiver v May*, the deputy judge expressed the point in the following way:

> "[T]he combination of the word 'shall' in para.2(1) of Sch.4, and the fact that what the court has to do is not simply consider whether it is appropriate in all the circumstances to make a BRO, but consider whether it is appropriate to do so having regard to his conduct, leads to the conclusion that the exercise the court has to carry out is to consider whether the conduct of the bankrupt is such as to make a BRO appropriate, and if it concludes that it is, the court is obliged to make one. It follows that I accept [counsel for the official receiver's] submission that the decision of the district judge cannot stand, because she plainly proceeded on the basis that she had a discretion. As . . . *Randhawa* explains, the nature of the exercise the court has to undertake is an evaluative one rather than a discretionary one. Since the district judge herself said that she had a discretion, and since it seems clear that it was this that persuaded her not to make a BRO . . . despite finding the allegations of conduct made out, and despite accepting that [the debtor's] action was a culpable one, in my judgment it follows that her decision was made on a flawed basis and must be set aside."[187]

In evaluating whether the debtor's conduct merits a BRO the court may take into account extenuating circumstances insofar as they relate directly to the allegations of misconduct put forward by the claimant.[188] There is a suggestion in *Randhawa* that mitigating circumstances can be taken into account and need not be confined either to matters directly related to the allegations of misconduct or to events after April 1, 2004.[189] In the context, it appears that the deputy judge was referring to circumstances that can be taken into account by the court in determining whether a BRO is appropriate rather than circumstances which may

[186] See, in the CDDA context, text from 4–12.

[187] [2008] B.P.I.R. 1562 at [16]–[17].

[188] *Re Grayan Building Services Ltd, Secretary of State for Trade and Industry v Gray* [1995] Ch. 241 at 253; *Official Receiver v May* [2008] B.P.I.R. 1562 at [20]–[21] (debtor suffering from depression at the time of the alleged misconduct).

[189] [2007] 1 W.L.R. 1700 at [68].

be relevant in mitigating the duration of the BRO. In the authors' view such an approach is too wide and out of line with the approach taken under the CDDA.

11–56 A number of additional points can be made by way of commentary on the kinds of behaviour specified in Sch.4A para.2(2) which the court is required to take into account.

Grounds linked to previous bankruptcy provisions

11–57 Several of the kinds of behaviour specified in the Schedule are the same as or similar to the grounds on which the court could refuse to discharge an individual from bankruptcy under the Bankruptcy Acts 1883 and 1914.[190]

Transactions detrimental to creditors

11–58 In relation to transactions detrimental to creditors, such as preferences, transactions at undervalue and excessive pension contributions, it is suggested that the court could take into account the relevant conduct and that the Secretary of State would not have to establish all the elements that a trustee in bankruptcy would be required to establish in order to claw back assets under the relevant avoidance provisions in the Insolvency Act 1986 ss.339, 340 and 342A. So, for example, if the bankrupt has given a preference as defined by s.340(3) of the Insolvency Act, the court could take this into account in deciding whether or not to make a BRO even though there was no evidence that the bankrupt was influenced by a desire to prefer, a pre-condition for claw back under s.340(4).[191] Schedule 4A para.2(4) bears this out as it provides, among other things, that the term "preference" shall be construed in accordance with s.340 which, on any sensible reading of the provision, must mean a factual preference within the meaning of s.340(3). Even so, the question of whether a BRO is appropriate and, if so, the duration of the BRO, will depend on the culpability of the conduct and, in this respect, it seems clear that a deliberate strategy of paying off debts owing to friends and relatives is likely to be regarded as more culpable than a commercial decision to pay one or two pressing creditors who were at arms' length.[192]

11–59 Another instance of a transaction detrimental to creditors that arose in *Official Receiver v May*[193] is the sale at an undervalue of assets held by the debtor on hire purchase without the authority of the owner. Although in that case it was accepted that the misconduct was a one-off incident, the product primarily of the debtor's desperate need to stave off the bailiffs, a BRO of two and a half years was

[190] See Bankruptcy Act 1883 s.28; Bankruptcy Act 1914 s.26 and for background see the Report of the Review Committee, *Insolvency Law and Practice*, Cmnd.8558 (1982) at paras 115–143.

[191] See, by analogy, *Re Sykes (Butchers) Ltd, Secretary of State for Trade and Industry v Richardson* [1998] 1 B.C.L.C. 110 and discussion in the text from 5–57.

[192] See, e.g. *Official Receiver v Pyman* [2007] B.P.I.R. 1150 (proceeds of sale of debtor's business used to repay loan from debtor's son); *Official Receiver v Bathurst* [2008] B.P.I.R. 1548 (charge securing debt owed to debtor's cousin created on debtor's property after presentation of bankruptcy petition); *Official Receiver v Tilbrook*, October 23, 2008, Ch.D., unreported (Roger Kaye Q.C.) (declaration of trust of matrimonial home in favour of debtor's wife with a view to putting it beyond the reach of creditors).

[193] [2008] B.P.I.R. 1562.

imposed because he sold the asset (a motorbike) knowing that he did not have the authority of the owner to do so and in such a way as to expose the owner to the risk that it would recover neither the debt owed nor the motorbike.

Failure to supply goods or services and trading to the detriment of creditors

11–60 Failure to supply goods or services having accepted a customer pre-payment (Sch.4A para.2(2)(f)) and continuing to trade with actual or constructive knowledge of insolvency (Sch.4A para.2(2)(g)) are kinds of behaviour that are also taken into account by the courts in determining whether a director's conduct makes him unfit to be concerned in the management of a company for the purposes of CDDA s.6.[194] It is likely that the court's approach to these types of misconduct under the CDDA will influence the court's approach to similar conduct under the bankruptcy restrictions regime (and, in time, vice versa).

Incurring debts with no reasonable expectation of being able to repay

11–61 On the face of it, continuing to trade with actual or constructive knowledge of insolvency (Sch.4A para.2(2)(g)) and incurring before commencement of bankruptcy a debt which the bankrupt had no reasonable expectation of being able to pay (Sch.4A para.2(2)(h)) appear to be similar or overlapping forms of misconduct. However, the former applies to traders whereas the latter is capable of applying to both traders and consumer debtors. Thus, for example, if an individual takes out a personal loan or a consolidation loan knowing full well that he has insufficient income to meet the monthly repayments, such conduct would apparently fall within Sch.4A para.2(2)(h)).[195] Furthermore, the incurring of a single debt (as opposed to a series of debts) would be sufficient to fall within the wording although it may not necessarily result in the imposition of a BRO. Another example of misconduct that is likely to be targeted is where a debtor borrows on credit cards on the eve of, and in anticipation of, bankruptcy.[196]

Failure to account satisfactorily for loss of property

11–62 The reference to property in Sch.4A para.2(2)(i) is general and is not limited to property belonging to the debtor.[197] Thus, an allegation of failure to account satisfactorily to the court, the official receiver or the trustee for a loss of property may relate to property held by the debtor on hire or hire purchase.

Overlap with bankruptcy offences

11–63 There is some overlap between Sch.4A para.2(2) and the bankruptcy offences in Pt IX, Chap.6 of the Insolvency Act 1986 (starting at s.350):

[194] See text from 5–05 and 5–56.
[195] See, e.g. *Official Receiver v Southey* [2009] B.P.I.R. 89 (though on the facts Registrar Baister declined to make a BRO as, in his judgment, there had been some chance of repayment, albeit this fell short of a likelihood of repayment, at the point the relevant loan was made to the debtor).
[196] See, e.g. *Randhawa v Official Receiver* [2007] 1 W.L.R. 1700.
[197] *Official Receiver v Doganci* [2007] B.P.I.R. 87 at [18].

(1) Failure to keep records which account for a loss (Sch.4A para.2(2)(a)) overlaps to some extent with the offence of failure without reasonable excuse to account for or give a satisfactory explanation of the loss of any substantial part of the bankrupt's property in s.354(3) of the Insolvency Act 1986.
(2) The term "fraud" (Sch.4A para.2(2)(l) is clearly capable of encompassing conduct of the following kind: (i) non-disclosure or concealment by the bankrupt of property comprised in his estate to the official receiver or trustee in bankruptcy (Insolvency Act 1986 ss.353–354); (ii) concealment, destruction, falsification or alteration by the bankrupt of books and records relating to his estate and affairs (Insolvency Act 1986 s.355); (iii) false statements by the bankrupt relating to his affairs (Insolvency Act 1986 s.356); (iv) the fraudulent disposal or concealment by the bankrupt of his property (Insolvency Act 1986 s.357); (v) absconding with property (Insolvency Act 1986 s.358); (vi) fraudulent dealing by the bankrupt with property that he had obtained on credit (Insolvency Act 1986 s.359). Where the conduct that could be targeted as a possible offence under these provisions occurs after the commencement of bankruptcy (for example, non-disclosure of property in contravention of Insolvency Act 1986 s.353), it could also be classified as failure to co-operate with the official receiver or trustee in bankruptcy falling within Sch.4A para.2(2)(m).[198]
(3) The former offence of gambling or rash and hazardous speculation formerly contained in Insolvency Act 1986 s.362 was repealed by the Enterprise Act 2002 but is now mirrored in Sch.4A para.2(2)(j) and also covers "unreasonable extravagance".

Where there is evidence of misconduct suggesting, prima facie, that a bankruptcy offence under the Insolvency Act 1986 has been committed, it seems highly likely that there will also be a strong prima facie case for a BRO, especially where the bankrupt has disposed of or concealed assets that form part of his estate to the detriment of his creditors. One problem for the Secretary of State is that the criminal courts have no power equivalent to CDDA s.2 to impose a BRO on conviction of a bankruptcy offence. As a result, the Secretary of State will be forced to consider applying to the civil courts for a BRO in cases where a criminal prosecution has been commenced or is being contemplated. In any event, the Secretary of State may take the view that a BRO is necessary to protect the public while the criminal trial is pending. Thus, there is clearly scope for parallel proceedings. The lower standard of proof in civil proceedings means that conduct falling within the scope of the bankruptcy offences is perhaps now more easily addressed through the BRO regime.[199]

[198] For a case where allegations that a debtor had failed to declare assets and liabilities and failed to account properly to the official receiver were made out and a seven-year BRO imposed see *Official Receiver v Pyman* [2007] B.P.I.R. 1150.

[199] This is hinted at in *Second Chance* at para.1.26 and Annex D, para.2.3 and is perhaps reflected in the abolition of the offences formerly in Insolvency Act 1986 ss.361 (failure to keep proper accounting records) and 362 (gambling and speculation) by Enterprise Act 2002 s.263.

Duties to co-operate

11–64 Schedule 4A para.2(2)(m) reinforces the bankrupt's obligations in ss.291 and 333 of the Insolvency Act 1986 to co-operate respectively with the official receiver and his trustee in bankruptcy. These obligations are central to the proper functioning of the bankruptcy system. At its core, bankruptcy involves a trade-off. In return for the fresh start provided by the bankruptcy discharge, the bankrupt must surrender his non-exempt assets[200] for distribution among his creditors and, where appropriate, his surplus income.[201] The bankrupt's co-operation is vital to the identification and collection of his assets, the determination of his liabilities and the provision of information concerning his affairs. Prior to discharge, the official receiver and the trustee in bankruptcy have a clear interest in compelling the bankrupt to co-operate for the benefit of the estate. The principal means of enforcement is an application to the court under s.279(3) of the Insolvency Act 1986 to suspend the bankrupt's discharge on the ground that the bankrupt has failed or is failing to comply with his obligations to co-operate. Suspension of discharge is a powerful sanction as, until the court lifts the suspension, it stops the one-year discharge period in s.279(1) from running. This has a number of consequences. First, the various restrictions and prohibitions on undischarged bankrupts continue to apply. Secondly, the information and asset-gathering provisions of the Insolvency Act 1986, such as the official receiver's power to apply for public examination under s.290 and the trustee in bankruptcy's power to claim after-acquired property under s.307, which only apply before discharge, also continue to apply. Thirdly, the one-year period in which the Secretary of State can apply for a BRO without the court's permission ceases to run. Accordingly, an application for suspension is likely to be the weapon of first resort. However, once the suspension has been lifted, it is conceivable that the Secretary of State could rely on the bankrupt's previous failure to co-operate as a ground for a BRO either: (a) on a cumulative basis where other kinds of misconduct have come to light in the meantime; or (b) on its own where the failure to co-operate has caused obvious harm to the debtor's creditors.[202] It is as yet unclear whether the Secretary of State would seek to rely on the debtor's failure to co-operate where such failure had not been regarded as sufficiently serious to merit an application for suspension of discharge. It seems unlikely that a lesser degree of un-co-operative behaviour would give adequate ground, by itself, for a BRO although much will depend on the circumstances of the case.

Incompetence

11–65 There is clear scope in Sch.4A para.2(2)(k) for the court to take into account incompetence on the part of a bankrupt trader. Bearing in mind that para.2(2) is

[200] The scope of the bankruptcy estate is defined by Insolvency Act 1986 ss.283, 307–308A and 436.

[201] Insolvency Act 1986 ss.310–310A as amended and inserted by the Enterprise Act 2002 ss.258–259 with effect from April 1, 2004.

[202] See, by analogy, CDDA s.9 and Sch.1 Pt II para.10 and *Re Copecrest Ltd, Secretary of State for Trade and Industry v McTighe (No.2)* [1996] 2 B.C.L.C. 477. In the BRO context see *Official Receiver v Bathurst* [2008] B.P.I.R. 1548 at paras [19], [23]–[24] of Morritt C.'s first judgment.

not exhaustive, it is clear that the court could impose a BRO on a bankrupt debtor (trader or consumer) on the basis of his demonstrable inability to manage his personal financial affairs.[203] This is especially so where the debtor's lack of expertise has caused harm to his creditors or is of such a degree that he poses a risk to the public.[204]

Serial bankruptcy

11–66 Under the law as it stood prior to April 1, 2004, a repeat or serial bankrupt, meaning a person who had been an undischarged bankrupt at any time in the period of 15 years ending with the commencement of his present bankruptcy, was not entitled to an automatic discharge. Instead, a debtor who was a repeat bankrupt had to apply to the court for discharge and could only make the application after five years in bankruptcy. Since April 1, 2004, this has no longer been the case: a repeat bankrupt is prima facie just as much entitled to automatic discharge after one year as a first-time bankrupt. However, in the BRO context, the court is directed by Sch.4A para.2(3) to "consider whether the bankrupt was an undischarged bankrupt at some time during the period of six years ending with the date of the bankruptcy to which the application [for a BRO] relates". Thus, while no longer a reason for restricting the availability of discharge, a previous bankruptcy within six (rather than 15) years is a matter that the court must, in particular, consider under the BRO regime. The wording appears to suggest that the court should take into account the mere *fact* of a previous bankruptcy. Given that the fresh start policy has been extended to include repeat bankrupts, it seems inconceivable that the Secretary of State could rely on the fact of a previous bankruptcy without more as the basis for a BRO.[205] Apart from the preservation of the court's jurisdiction to suspend discharge on grounds of the bankrupt's failure to co-operate, the reforms introduced by the Enterprise Act make it clear that discharge cannot generally be withheld because of misconduct prior to the bankruptcy and it certainly cannot be withheld simply because of a previous bankruptcy. The BRO regime addresses issues of misconduct. Moreover, the overriding requirement in Sch.4A is the requirement in para.2(1) for the court to have regard to "the conduct of the bankrupt". However, it would appear to follow that that the reference to previous bankruptcy in Sch.4A para.2(3) could be read as permitting the court to have regard to the bankrupt's *conduct* in the previous bankruptcy. Thus, the fact that certain misconduct was "serial" might be important in assessing the seriousness of the misconduct in a later bankruptcy. Similarly, the mere fact of a previous

[203] See *Randhawa v Official Receiver* [2007] 1 W.L.R. 1700 at [66], [68], [71], [79] (referring variously to acceptable standards of financial competence).

[204] It was suggested in *Fresh Start* at paras 7.19–7.21 that bankrupts could be offered financial counselling on either a mandatory or optional basis (as is the case in Canada). However, the idea was subsequently dropped: see *Second Chance* at para.1.5. Incompetence in the CDDA context is considered in Chs 4 and 5.

[205] The Under-Secretary of State for Trade and Industry said during the parliamentary debate: "We want to reduce the stigma for bankrupts, including those who may have failed before, as long as there is not misconduct." (Hansard H.C. Standing Committee B, Session 2001–2002, May 14, 2002 at col.660).

bankruptcy may throw light on the conduct connected with the later bankruptcy, on the basis that the debtor should have learned certain lessons from the first bankruptcy. So, for example, a debtor's failure to comply with his duties to the official receiver or trustee in bankruptcy may be regarded as more culpable in a later bankruptcy on the basis that he should have been well aware of his obligations given his previous experience of bankruptcy.[206]

11–67 An interesting question is whether the courts will take the matter even further, so that the earlier bankruptcy becomes relevant not just because it casts light on the misconduct in the second bankruptcy but in relation to any misconduct relevant to the earlier bankruptcy which can itself be taken into account on a cumulative basis with the misconduct relating to the second bankruptcy. In a case where there is relevant misconduct in the first bankruptcy that is perhaps insufficient of itself to justify a BRO, could the effect of para.2(3) be that the court is entitled to consider the conduct in the first bankruptcy together with conduct in the subsequent bankruptcy on a cumulative basis (and not simply consider the earlier misconduct as explaining, shedding light on or putting in context the later misconduct)? If so, it is possible that law and practice under the BRO regime in this respect could develop by analogy with law and practice under CDDA s.6 in relation to lead and collateral companies.[207] However, the authors consider that this last suggestion probably goes too far. Paragraph 2(3) is, it is suggested, directed at throwing light on identified misconduct in relation to the later bankruptcy and not as providing an additional area of potential misconduct to take into account in its own right. That said, there is, on the face of it, no time limit (other than by reference to the transitional provisions) on the conduct, prior to bankruptcy, which can be taken into account. In theory at least, there is no reason why relevant misconduct wholly unconnected with the bankruptcy and some years earlier could not be relied upon by the Secretary of State. A further point arises in connection with the transitional provisions under which conduct prior to April 1, 2004 is not permitted to be taken into account.[208] Does this provision prevent the courts taking into account the fact of a previous bankruptcy if that took place prior to April 1, 2004? It is suggested that if the relevance of the earlier bankruptcy is that the debtor should have learned something from that bankruptcy then what is being taken into account is the fact of the earlier bankruptcy and the continuing state of knowledge thereafter of the debtor and not conduct prior to April 1, 2004. However, if the relevance of the earlier bankruptcy is, for example, to show that particular misconduct (taking place prior to April 1, 2004) is serial, then that would appear to be prohibited by the relevant transitional arrangements because it would amount to taking the relevant conduct "into account".

[206] *Official Receiver v Pyman* [2007] B.P.I.R. 1150 at [31].
[207] See text from 3–106.
[208] The Enterprise Act 2002 (Commencement No. 4 and Transitional Provisions and Savings) Order 2003 (SI 2003/2093), art.7; *Randhawa v Official Receiver* [2007] 1 W.L.R. 1700 at [39], [41], [54], [67].

Conduct as a director

11–68 Given the width of Sch.4A para.2 and the fact that the matters mentioned in para.2(2) are not exhaustive, one intriguing question is whether the court could take into account the conduct of the debtor in his capacity as a director of a company for the purposes of determining an application for a BRO. The question could arise where a director of an insolvent company is subsequently bankrupted having defaulted on a personal guarantee of company indebtedness. It is suggested that the court determining the BRO application should not focus on the person's conduct as a director of the company because: (a) this is a matter for separate proceedings under CDDA s.6; and (b) read as a whole, Sch.4A para.2 is concerned with the bankrupt's conduct before the making of the bankruptcy order insofar as it relates to or affects the bankruptcy estate and/or the bankrupt's conduct during the bankruptcy. There may be hybrid cases in which it is not easy to draw the line. One example is where the director's neglect of the company's affairs was responsible for its default and, in turn, for the director's default that led to his bankruptcy. Even so, the point remains that conduct as a director is strictly a CDDA matter. As a result, the Secretary of State may be faced with a tactical decision whether to apply for a BRO or proceed under the CDDA (or both).[209]

Enforcement patterns

11–69 At the time of writing, the number of BROs and BRUs made is running at around 1,800 per year.[210] Patterns have begun to emerge in terms of the types of misconduct that the Insolvency Service targets for enforcement action. The three most prevalent allegations that supported the making of BROs and BRUs between April 1, 2006 and March 31, 2008 were: (i) incurring debt without reasonable prospect of payment; (ii) transactions to the detriment of creditors (preferences or transactions at undervalue); and (iii) gambling, rash and hazardous speculation or unreasonable extravagance.[211] However, present patterns of enforcement are merely indicative and it must be remembered that Sch.4A para.2 is broad and flexible in scope and capable of accommodating changing patterns of misconduct over time. Accordingly, it will be for the courts to determine on the facts of each case whether a BRO is appropriate having regard to the bankrupt's conduct and the public interest. The Regulatory Impact Assessment for the insolvency provisions of the

[209] See further text from 11–111.

[210] In the period April 1 to March 31, 2007–8 some 1,827 new BROs/BRUs came into force of which 1,640 (90%) were BRUs. This represented a decrease of 2% on the 1,867 BROs/BRUs secured in 2006–7: see Insolvency Service, *Annual Report and Accounts 2007–2008* H.C. 800 (London: The Stationery Office, 2008). In 2008–9 there was a further modest decrease in the number of BROs/BRUs to 1,781 of which 90% were again BRUs: see Insolvency Service, *Annual Report and Accounts 2008–2009* H.C. 623 (London: The Stationery Office, 2009).

[211] Insolvency Service, *Annual Report and Accounts 2006–2007* H.C. 752 (London: The Stationery Office, 2007), p.18, *Annual Report and Accounts 2007–2008* H.C. 800 (London: The Stationery Office, 2008) at pp.17–18; *Annual Report and Accounts 2008–2009* H.C. 623 (London: The Stationery Office, 2009) at pp.25–26. Another good source of information about current enforcement patterns is the Insolvency Service's online Bankruptcy Restrictions Bulletin: *http://www.insolvency.gov.uk/databases/ddirector/viewbrobrudetailslatest.asp* [Accessed August 27, 2009].

Enterprise Act estimated that between 7 and 12 per cent of bankruptcy cases will result in the imposition of bankruptcy restrictions. In practice, against a background of rising bankruptcy numbers, the number has been less than 5 per cent.[212]

Duration and commencement of a BRO

11–70 Schedule 4A para.4(1) provides that a BRO shall come into force when it is made and shall cease to have effect at the end of a date specified in the order. So far as commencement is concerned, there is no express power to delay the coming into force of the order comparable to that under CDDA s.1. This is presumably because it is envisaged that an interim BRO will be applied for during the bankruptcy when the individual is already subject to disabilities; he should not therefore need time to arrange his affairs. However, the premise of this presumption can be questioned bearing in mind that there is now some mismatch between the disqualifications, prohibitions and restrictions that apply to an undischarged bankrupt and that flow from a BRO. It is therefore conceivable that the extent of the court's inherent and statutory jurisdiction to stay orders will be tested in this area.[213]

11–71 By virtue of Sch.4A para.4(2), a BRO must be made for a period of at least two years but no more than 15 years. By analogy with practice under the CDDA the courts have divided the available period of two to 15 years into three brackets: a top bracket of over ten years reserved for the most serious cases; a middle bracket of six to ten years for serious cases not meriting the top bracket and a minimum bracket of two to five years for cases that are, relatively speaking, less serious although deserving of a BRO.[214] The approach the court takes to determining the duration of a BRO is well captured in the following passage from Mr Launcelot Henderson Q.C.'s judgment in *Randhawa v Official Receiver*:

> "In my judgment the appropriate period for a BRO must be fixed by reference to the gravity of the misconduct that is alleged and proved against the bankrupt, taken in conjunction with any aggravating or mitigating factors that may properly be taken into account. As in the context of directors' disqualification, the exercise should be performed with a fairly broad brush and without undue refinement or technicality."

The duration of the BRO should not only reflect the gravity of the conduct but should also contain deterrent elements.[215] Practice in relation to BROs is therefore entirely consistent with the guidance given by the Court of Appeal in *Re Sevenoaks*

[212] For further discussion see Insolvency Service, *Enterprise Act 2002—the Personal Insolvency Provisions: Final Evaluation Report* (November 2007), *http://www.insolvency.gov.uk/insolvencyprofessionandlegislation/legislation/evaluation/finalreport/home.htm* [Accessed August 27, 2009], at pp.86–89.

[213] See further text from 12–28.

[214] See *Randhawa v Official Receiver* [2007] 1 W.L.R. 1700 at [87]; *Official Receiver v Pyman* [2007] B.P.I.R. 1150 at [14]–[24]; *Official Receiver v Bathurst* [2008] B.P.I.R. 1548 at [22] of Morritt C.'s first judgment; *Official Receiver v May* [2008] B.P.I.R. 1562 at [23]; *Official Receiver v Tilbrook*, October 23, 2008, Ch.D., unreported (Roger Kaye Q.C.), paras [19]–[20], [24].

[215] *Official Receiver v Pyman* [2007] B.P.I.R 1150 at [24]; *Official Receiver v Bathurst* [2008] B.P.I.R. 1548 at paras [30]–[31] of Morritt C.'s first judgment. See also *Official Receiver v Tilbrook*, October 23, 2008, Ch.D., unreported (Roger Kaye Q.C.).

Stationers (Retail) Ltd[216] and *Re Westmid Packing Services Ltd, Secretary of State for Trade and Industry v Griffiths* as regards the period of disqualification in the CDDA context.[217]

11–72 The approach to mitigation is broadly similar to that under the CDDA in terms of the factors that can properly be taken into account by the court in reducing the duration of a BRO.[218] The Court of Appeal's guidance in *Re Westmid Packing Services Ltd, Secretary of State for Trade and Industry v Griffiths*[219] applicable in the CDDA context is equally applicable to BROs. While the past misconduct is obviously relevant in determining the duration of the BRO, the thrust of the *Westmid Packing* guidance is that the court is not restricted to considering mitigating factors that relate only to the relevant conduct. A wide variety of factors may be relevant including: the individual's general reputation; his age and state of health[220]; the length of time taken to bring the matter to a conclusion[221]; whether he acted on legal advice[222]; whether he admitted any of the allegations and his general conduct before and after the misconduct. However, credit should not be given in relation to the length of time that has elapsed since the bankruptcy or where the application for the BRO was made late in the permissible one-year time period.[223] There is nothing in the point that the bankrupt has already been subject to restrictions for the duration of the bankruptcy as these restrictions apply automatically whereas a BRO is premised on culpable misconduct and the disqualifications, prohibitions and restrictions that flow from a BRO are now more extensive in scale and scope than those that apply to undischarged bankrupts.[224] On the latter point, Parliament has allowed a period of one year in which the application for a BRO can be made without the permission of the court and, as the deputy judge in *Randhawa* pointed out, this is not a long period.[225]

[216] [1991] Ch.164.

[217] [1998] 2 All E.R. 124. See further text from 5–102.

[218] In the CDDA context see text from 5–110.

[219] [1998] 2 All E.R. 124.

[220] Though see *Official Receiver v Pyman* [2007] B.P.I.R. 1150 at [32] (the mere fact that the debtor would reach the age of 65 in a few years' time was not of itself a reason for making a BRO that would expire on his 65th birthday where the effect was to take the case out of the middle bracket into the minimum bracket) and *Official Receiver v Tilbrook*, October 23, 2008, Ch.D., unreported (Roger Kaye Q.C.), paras [16], [21], [27] (the fact that the debtor had reached the age of 60 not regarded as a significant mitigating factor bearing in mind that deterrence is an objective of the legislation).

[221] *Official Receiver v May* [2008] B.P.I.R. 1562 at [24] (duration of BRO discounted in part because BRO only imposed on appeal some seven months after the application had originally been dismissed).

[222] Though note it may be an aggravating factor to act in the light of legal advice to the effect that the proposed conduct or transaction could be susceptible to subsequent challenge: see *Official Receiver v Tilbrook*, October 23, 2008, Ch.D., unreported (Roger Kaye Q.C.), paras [15], [21], [23], [25]–[26].

[223] *Randhawa v Official Receiver* [2007] 1 W.L.R. 1700 at [88].

[224] Similarly, if an individual is already the subject of a disqualification order or undertaking under the CDDA, this of itself is not relevant as the disqualifications, prohibitions and restrictions flowing from CDDA disqualification are not co-extensive with those that flow from a BRO. For example, a CDDA disqualification order or undertaking does not prohibit the disqualified person from obtaining credit of £500 or more without disclosing his status.

[225] *Randhawa v Official Receiver* [2007] 1 W.L.R. 1700 at [88]. The permissible period is half as long as that allowed by CDDA s.7(2) for the making of an application for an order under CDDA s.6 without the court's permission.

In the BRO context, as a general rule of thumb, the court should be wary of too readily discounting the duration of a BRO in line with the following passage from Morritt C.'s judgment in *Official Receiver v Bathurst*:

> "It must be remembered that Parliament introduced [BROs] via the Enterprise Act 2002 to offset the effect of a reduction in the period of automatic discharge from bankruptcy from three years to one in cases where the bankrupt's conduct made it appropriate to impose some further restrictions on his future ability to incur liabilities or to engage in commerce . . . the protection that [BROs] afford to the public should not be underestimated, nor their deterrent effect undermined by too readily finding extenuating circumstances for conduct identified by Parliament as worthy of criticism . . ."[226]

11–73 One problem that may arise concerns the impact of mitigating factors in marginal cases. If, for example, the court thinks that a BRO for a period of two years is appropriate having regard to the bankrupt's conduct but there are mitigating factors that would ordinarily attract a discount, then presumably the court should not make a BRO because the discount would take the period below the statutory minimum.

BROs: procedure

The application

11–74 The substantive rules relating to bankruptcy restrictions are set out in Chs 28 to 30 of the Insolvency Rules 1986.[227] The relevant procedural rules that apply are the specific rules applicable to BROs, the remaining provisions of the Insolvency Rules and only then the CPR. Applications for the making of BROs are "insolvency proceedings" for the purposes of the Insolvency Rules.[228] The overall procedure for applying for a BRO is similar to that for applying for a disqualification order under CDDA s.6, although there are some significant differences. The first key difference is that an application for a BRO is an ordinary application in the bankruptcy whereas an application for a disqualification order under CDDA s.6 is free standing and not one made in the winding up of the relevant company or companies.[229] A second key difference is that the Insolvency Rules (with the CPR as a backstop) apply to BRO proceedings,[230] whereas the basic regime in connection with disqualification is the CPR (subject to the overriding nature of the Disqualification Rules and the application of the Insolvency Rules with regard to appeals and reviews). A third key difference is that witness statements may be used as an alternative to affidavits in the bankruptcy restrictions context. It is suggested that in considering the applicable procedural regime applying to BROs and BRUs it will generally be helpful for the practitioner to have in mind the applicable procedural law in the CDDA context, as considered in Ch.7.

[226] [2008] B.P.I.R. 1548 at paras [30]–[31] of Morritt C.'s first judgment.
[227] Insolvency Rules 1986 rr.6.240–6.251. These provisions were inserted by the Insolvency (Amendment) Rules 2003 (SI 2003/1730).
[228] Insolvency Rules 1986 r.13.7.
[229] Practice Direction—Insolvency Proceedings, para.16A.1.
[230] See Insolvency Rules 1986 r.7.51 and, for more specific examples, rr.7.33 and 7.57.

11–75 An application for a BRO must be made before the end of the period of one year beginning with the date on which the bankruptcy commenced unless the bankrupt's discharge is suspended under s.279(3) of the Insolvency Act 1986 in which case the one-year period will cease to run.[231] Once the one-year period has expired an application can only be made with the permission of the court.[232] The onus is on the Secretary of State to satisfy the court that permission should be granted.[233] It was anticipated that the courts would approach such an application on a similar basis to an application for permission to commence proceedings for a disqualification order under CDDA s.6 after the expiry of the two-year period in CDDA s.7(2),[234] although there might be some adjustment to reflect the purpose and spirit of the Enterprise Act. The basic policy is that an application should normally be made before the bankrupt's discharge under s.279, hence the alignment of the one-year period of bankruptcy with the one-year time limit for a BRO application without the court's permission.[235] Thus, a debtor can generally expect to be free of his debts and free from restrictions (or the threat of restrictions) after a year in accordance with the "fresh start" policy of the Enterprise Act. The primary concern of the Enterprise Act for the rehabilitation of the debtor suggests that the risk to the public will need to be considerable before the court will grant the Secretary of State permission to bring an application for a BRO out of time, although each case will turn on its own facts. The matter was considered in *Official Receiver v Barrs*[236] where the test applied in the CDDA s.7(2) context was applied in the bankruptcy restrictions context but taking account of differences in the regimes. The misconduct in question involved a failure to disclose an asset, namely an interest in a property. The court was faced with an application in March 2008 when the bankrupt had been made bankrupt in November 2004 and discharged in November 2005. As regards the four elements taken into account in CDDA cases—the length of the delay, the reasons for the delay, the strength of the case against the bankrupt and any prejudice caused—the court made findings as follows. First, the delays were neither excessive nor unreasonable. The trustee in bankruptcy had found out about the relevant non-disclosure only in February 2007 and that was the fault of the bankrupt not the trustee. The matter was

[231] Insolvency Act 1986 Sch.4A para.3(1)(a), (2).

[232] Insolvency Act 1986 Sch.4A para.3(1)(b).

[233] See, by analogy, *Re Copecrest Ltd, Secretary of State for Trade and Industry v McTighe* [1994] 2 B.C.L.C. 284 at 287; *Re Blackspur Group Plc, Secretary of State for Trade and Industry v Davies* [1996] 4 All E.R. 289 at 296.

[234] For the relevant principles see Ch.8.

[235] The court is unlikely to be sympathetic simply because the applicant has only one year to make the application compared with two years under the CDDA s.7(2). Apart from the case of companies in compulsory liquidation where the official receiver is initially involved, information gathering in CDDA s.6 cases is wholly dependent on reports from insolvency practitioners. In practice, the reporting procedures may absorb a considerable part of the two-year period in CDDA s.7(2). Information gathering for BROs is carried out by the official receiver in accordance with the Insolvency Service's usual procedures in bankruptcy cases and is not wholly dependent on insolvency practitioner reporting, although the trustee in bankruptcy is obliged to provide such information and assistance as the official receiver may reasonably require under Insolvency Act 1986 s.305(3).

[236] [2009] B.P.I.R. 524.

reported to the official receiver in May 2007. Proceedings were not issued until December 2007. Although some aspects of the case might have been dealt with a little more quickly, the court concluded that this delay was not unreasonable in all the circumstances. Beyond December 2007 any further delay was largely caused by the courts having been busy so that the application could not be listed until March 2008. As regards the strength of the case, it was by then accepted by the bankrupt that disclosure should have been made. The court treated the bankrupt's assertion that he had simply forgotten or did not believe he had a disclosable interest as not credible (although it was not tested in cross examination). As regards prejudice, the prejudice relied upon was largely the fading memory of one principal witness. However, there was another witness who was available and contemporaneous solicitors' files could also have been obtained. Moreover, any relevant evidence from the witness would only have been by way of mitigation because the bankrupt's defence was effectively one of inadvertence and lack of intention. The court stressed that any notion among bankrupts that discharge made them immune from a BRO application was misplaced. The case leaves open the question whether the court would be less willing to grant permission for an application for a BRO to be commenced after expiry of the one-year period than it would be in a comparable situation under CDDA s.7(2).

11–76 As mentioned above, an application for a BRO will be made under the Insolvency Rules and will usually be brought by ordinary application within the relevant bankruptcy proceedings. The application must be supported by a report from the applicant, be it the Secretary of State or official receiver. The report must include: (a) a statement of the conduct by reference to which it is alleged that it is appropriate for a BRO to be made; and (b) the evidence on which the applicant relies in support of the application.[237] This is similar to the requirements of the disqualification regime in CDDA ss.6–7. Where the applicant is the official receiver, the report is treated as if it were an affidavit and is prima facie evidence of any matter contained in it.[238] Any other evidence supporting the application is to be by affidavit or witness statement.[239] The date for the hearing is to be no earlier than eight weeks from the date when the court fixes the venue for the hearing. The Insolvency Rules set out a timetable for the filing of evidence and the hearing of the application.[240]

11–77 Notice of the application and the venue fixed by the court must be served not more than 14 days after the application is made at court. Service is to be accompanied by a copy of the application, copies of the applicant's report and of any other evidence filed with the court in support of the application as well as an acknowledgement of service. The Insolvency Service's current public guidance

[237] Insolvency Rules 1986 r.6.241. References to the Secretary of State include a reference to the official receiver where that person is the applicant: r.6.240. Further procedural matters are dealt with in rr.6.242–6.244.

[238] Insolvency Rules 1986 r.7.9(2), (3).

[239] Insolvency Rules 1986 rr 6.241(3), 7.57(5), (6).

[240] Insolvency Rules 1986 rr 6.241–6.244. See also Practice Direction—Insolvency Proceedings, paras 16A.1–16A.11.

indicates that the letter enclosing these documents should inform the defendant of the period that the official receiver considers would be appropriate for the BRO to run.[241] This is, no doubt, designed to enable the defendant to consider his position with regard to the possibility of offering a BRU as an alternative to proceeding to a hearing of the application.

11–78 The defendant is required to file an acknowledgement in court not more than 14 days after service on him of the application and, in default, is entitled to attend the hearing of the application but not to take part in the hearing unless the court grants permission.[242] If the defendant wishes to oppose the application, he has 28 days from service on him of the application and evidence to file written evidence in court. Copies of such evidence must be served on the applicant within three days of filing at court. The evidence may take the form of one or more witness statements or affidavits. Any evidence in reply is to be filed within 14 days from receiving the bankrupt's evidence and copies are to be served on the debtor as soon as reasonably practicable thereafter.[243]

11–79 The court retains its usual case management powers and it remains to be seen how far the timetable set out in r.6.243 is the exception rather than the norm. Hearings take place in public.[244] A BRO may be made whether the defendant appears or not and whether or not he has filed evidence.[245] Two sealed copies of a BRO must be sent by the court to the applicant who must, in turn, send a sealed copy to the bankrupt as soon as reasonably practicable after receipt.[246]

Interim BROs

11–80 According to the Explanatory Notes to the Enterprise Act 2002:

> "It is unlikely in many cases that a substantive decision will be made by the court in relation to an application for a BRO before the defendant's discharge. Thus, there is likely to be a gap in time between the discharge of the bankrupt and the making of the BRO in those cases where a BRO is being sought."

Accordingly, Sch.4A paras 5 and 6 of the Insolvency Act 1986 and Ch.29 of the Insolvency Rules 1986 make provision for the court to make an interim BRO. Any time between the institution and determination of an application for a BRO, the court may make an interim BRO if the court thinks that: (a) there are prima facie grounds to suggest that the application for the BRO will be successful; and (b) it is in the public interest to make an interim order.[247] The following points of

[241] *Bankruptcy Restriction Orders*, a leaflet distributed by the Insolvency Service and available on-line at *http://www.insolvency.gov.uk/pdfs/guidanceleafletspdf/bro.pdf* [Accessed August 27, 2009].
[242] Insolvency Rules 1986 r.6.242.
[243] Insolvency Rules 1986 r.6.243.
[244] Insolvency Rules 1986 r.6.241(5).
[245] Insolvency Rules 1986 r.6.244(1). See also Practice Direction—Insolvency Proceedings, para.16A.13.
[246] Insolvency Rules 1986 r.6.244(2), (3). See also Practice Direction—Insolvency Proceedings, para.16A.14.
[247] Insolvency Act 1986 Sch.4A para.5(1), (2).

general significance concerning interim BROs can be derived from the judgment of Chief Registrar Baister in *Official Receiver v Merchant*[248]:

(1) When considering whether to make an interim BRO, the court is exercising a discretion. In this respect, the wording of Sch.4A, para.5(2) contrasts with the mandatory wording in Sch.4A, para.2(2). Moreover, the applicant for an interim BRO must satisfy two tests: (a) that there is a prima facie case suggesting that a final order will be made; and (b) that it is in the public interest that an interim BRO be made. Accordingly, different considerations apply to the making of an interim BRO to those that apply to a BRO.
(2) The requirement to demonstrate that it is in the public interest to make an interim BRO clearly entails doing more than demonstrating a prima facie case for a BRO otherwise Parliament would not have given the court a discretion and would not have imposed an additional public interest test. An interim BRO should not automatically be imposed in the period between the institution and determination of a BRO application simply on the basis that there is a prima facie case for a BRO.
(3) The additional public interest test contemplates a requirement for the applicant to demonstrate that the public is in immediate need of protection during the gap between the institution and determination of a BRO application.
(4) There ought to be a connection between the allegations made and the need for public protection. Thus where the court is satisfied that the alleged misconduct consists, for example, of a one-off transaction where there is no prospect of a repetition or a failure to explain past conduct, the public interest test will not be made out. The applicant is required to make out and properly evidence the case for an interim BRO.

It follows from the guidance in *Merchant* that, in practice, the court will require to be satisfied that the alleged misconduct is so serious and the risk to the public so great that the overall balance of the public interest lies in favour of making an interim BRO. In the light of this approach and the points made in the next paragraph, official receivers have abandoned their previous practice of applying for an interim BRO whenever there was a gap between the first anniversary of the bankruptcy order and the hearing of the BRO application. The number of applications for interim BROs appears to have fallen as a result.[249]

11–81 As a matter of the domestic law applicable in relation to interim injunctions, it is unlikely that cross-undertakings in damages will be required from the applicant given that the applicant is acting in a law enforcement role.[250] However, the absence

[248] [2006] B.P.I.R. 1525.

[249] Insolvency Service, *Enterprise Act 2002—the Personal Insolvency Provisions: Final Evaluation Report* (November 2007), *http://www.insolvency.gov.uk/insolvencyprofessionandlegislation/legislation/evaluation/finalreport/home.htm* [Accessed August 27, 2009], at pp.89–90.

[250] *Hoffmann-La Roche & Co AG v Secretary of State for Trade and Industry* [1975] A.C. 295; *Re Highfield Commodities Limited* [1985] 1 W.L.R. 149; *Kirklees Metropolitan Borough Council v Wickes Buildings Supplies Ltd* [1993] A.C. 227; *Securities and Investments Board v Lloyd-Wright* [1993] 4 All E.R. 210.

of a cross-undertaking is likely to raise the standard of proof with regard to the need for interim protection, in the sense that the absence of such a cross-undertaking will weigh in the balance of convenience against the grant of an interim BRO because, if a final BRO is ultimately refused and the interim BRO should not have been made then the debtor will potentially have suffered great damage which is not remediable.[251] The issue of cross-undertakings in damages may give rise to a point under the Human Rights Act 1998 on the argument that it is unfair, and a breach of human rights, to impose bankruptcy restrictions on an interim basis without provision for compensation in the event that a full BRO is not subsequently made and it turns out that the interim BRO should not have been made.[252]

11–82 The following additional points should be noted:

(1) An interim BRO may only be made on the application of the Secretary of State or the official receiver acting on a direction of the Secretary of State.[253]

(2) An interim BRO comes into force when it is made and has the same effect as a BRO.[254] Thus, for example, a person who is the subject of an interim BRO at the point when he is discharged from bankruptcy will remain disqualified from acting as a director etc. under CDDA s.11(1)(b) for so long as the interim BRO continues in force.

(3) An interim BRO will cease to have effect: (a) on the determination of the application for the BRO; (b) on the acceptance by the Secretary of State of a BRU; or (c) if the court discharges the interim BRO on the application of either the applicant or the bankrupt.[255]

(4) In a case where the court makes a full BRO having previously made an interim BRO, the full BRO must be for a period of between two and fifteen years counting from the date of the interim BRO.[256] Thus, if an interim BRO has been in force for three months by the time the application for the full BRO comes on for hearing, it is open to the court to make a full BRO running for only a further one year and nine months if the case would otherwise merit a BRO of the minimum two years' duration.

[251] See, e.g. *Customs and Excise Commissioners v Anchor Foods Ltd* [1999] 1 W.L.R 1139 at 1150E–F.

[252] The restrictions may impact on the individual's right to respect for private life (ECHR art.8) and/or right to peaceful enjoyment of property (art.1 of the First Protocol). See, by analogy, *Travel Time v UK*, ECtHR, Application No.57824/00, September 18, 2003, where the point was raised in relation to the appointment of a provisional liquidator on a public interest petition presented by the Secretary of State in circumstances where (in accordance with usual practice) no cross-undertaking in damages was in place and the petition was eventually dismissed. Although in *Travel Time*, the European Court ruled the case inadmissible, it did so on the ground that the applicants had not exhausted their domestic remedies. The point therefore remains live.

[253] Insolvency Act 1986 Sch.4A, para.5(3). Procedure is governed by Insolvency Rules 1986 (as amended by the Insolvency (Amendment) Rules 2003 SI 2003/1730), rr.6.245–6.248. See also Practice Direction—Insolvency Proceedings, para.16A.16–16A.24.

[254] Insolvency Act 1986 Sch.4A para.5(4).

[255] Insolvency Act 1986 Sch.4A para.5(5). BRUs are discussed further below. Procedure on applications by a bankrupt to set aside an interim BRO is governed by Insolvency Rules 1986 (as amended by the Insolvency (Amendment) Rules 2003 SI 2003/1730), r.6.248.

[256] Insolvency Act 1986 Sch.4A para.6.

11–83 The purpose of interim BROs is to deal with the position where the Secretary of State applies for a full BRO late within the one-year period and it is not administratively possible for the application to be heard before the date on which the debtor is automatically discharged from bankruptcy.[257] In the absence of the interim BRO procedure to cover this eventuality, there would be a gap during which the individual would be free from bankruptcy restrictions. It is important to note that the Secretary of State cannot use the interim BRO procedure to buy time in which to pursue further investigations. As already explained, an interim BRO can only be made where an application for a full BRO is on foot, there is a prima facie case and the public interest test is satisfied. In practice, the application for an interim BRO will be based on the evidence filed by the Secretary of State in support of the application for the full BRO in accordance with r.6.241, together with additional evidence explaining the public interest that necessitates the making of an interim BRO. As the making of an interim BRO is a serious matter with civil and potentially criminal law consequences the court will expect the applicant to make out a case "fully and adequately by reference to the evidence and the law".[258]

11–84 The procedure for the application for an interim BRO is largely contained in the Insolvency Rules 1986 rr.6.245–6.248.[259] The court will fix a venue for the hearing.[260] Notice of the application must be given to the bankrupt at least two business days before the date set for the hearing, although the court has power to direct that the period of notice given should be longer or shorter.[261] Written evidence, by way of report, must be filed by the applicant in support of the application. Any other evidence is to be by witness statement or affidavit.[262] The evidence must include both evidence of the bankrupt's conduct which is alleged to constitute the grounds for the making of the interim BRO and evidence of matters relating to the public interest in making the order.[263] The bankrupt must file in court any evidence on which he relies and may appear at the hearing. The hearing will be in public. An interim BRO may be made whether the defendant appears or not and whether or not he has filed evidence.[264]

11–85 An interim BRO ceases to have effect: (a) on the determination of the substantive application for a BRO; (b) on the acceptance of a BRU; or (c) if discharged by the court on the application of the bankrupt or the applicant for the interim BRO.[265] Where the bankrupt applies to set aside an interim BRO, the procedure

[257] Hansard H.C. Standing Committee B, Session 2001–2002, May 14, 2002 at cols 661–662. It was suggested in *Fresh Start* at para.7.15 that discharge from bankruptcy would be suspended pending determination of a BRO. However, this approach has not been pursued presumably because it would penalise bankrupts on the basis of delays that are outside their control. The procedure adopted puts the onus firmly on the Secretary of State to make a prima facie case for a full BRO as a pre-condition for an interim BRO.

[258] *Official Receiver v Merchant* [2006] B.P.I.R. 1525 at [17].

[259] See also Practice Direction—Insolvency Proceedings, paras 16A.16–16A.24.

[260] Insolvency Rules 1986 r.6.245(1).

[261] Insolvency Rules 1986 r.6.245(2).

[262] Insolvency Rules 1986 rr.6.246, 7.57(5),(6).

[263] *Official Receiver v Merchant* [2006] B.P.I.R. 1525.

[264] Insolvency Rules 1986 rr.6.245(3), 6.247(2).

[265] Insolvency Act 1986 Sch.4A para.5(5).

is laid down by Insolvency Rules 1986 r.6.248. Written evidence by affidavit or witness statement[266] is required in support of the application. Not less than seven days before the hearing, the bankrupt must send the applicant for the interim BRO[267] notice of the application, notice of the venue, a copy of the application and a copy of the supporting written evidence. The applicant for the interim BRO may (but need not) attend the hearing and call the attention of the court to any matters which seem relevant and may give evidence or call witnesses.[268]If the court sets aside an interim BRO it must, as soon as reasonably practicable, serve the applicant for the interim BRO with two sealed copies of the order. The applicant for the interim BRO is then required, in turn, as soon as is reasonably practicable, to serve a sealed copy on the bankrupt.[269]

Costs

11–86 Civil disqualification proceedings under the CDDA are free standing proceedings and the costs will usually follow the event.[270] This means that if the Secretary of State succeeds in obtaining a disqualification order, the director will be ordered to pay costs. As the Secretary of State does not currently require the disqualified person to agree to pay the administrative costs incurred in processing his case as a condition of accepting a disqualification undertaking where the need to issue proceedings is avoided, there is a powerful costs incentive for directors to seek a compromise by means of an undertaking. It appears that the position in relation to BROs may be different. As noted above, an application for a BRO is an ordinary application in the bankruptcy rather than a free standing application. Where an application is made in bankruptcy, the usual order is that any costs will be borne by the bankruptcy estate. It is doubtful that this practice would be followed in the case of BROs as the public protection afforded by the order would effectively be purchased at the expense of the bankrupt's own creditors. In circumstances where the official receiver was the applicant, there might be grounds for saying that his costs should be recouped from the estate.[271] However, it seems likely that the costs of the proceedings will, in the first instance, be borne by the Insolvency Service rather than by the bankrupt's estate. The authors are not aware of orders for payment out of the estate having been applied for in this context. The further issue is whether, in the event a BRO is made, the bankrupt would be ordered to pay the Secretary of State's costs on the basis that it is the bankrupt's misconduct that has occasioned the application. This is clearly a possibility. However, the making of a costs order against the bankrupt is to some extent in

[266] Insolvency Rules 1986 rr.6.248(2), 7.57(5),(6).
[267] This time period can be abridged: see Insolvency Rules 1986 r.12.9(2).
[268] Insolvency Rules 1986 r.6.248(4).
[269] Insolvency Rules 1986 r.6.248(5),(6).
[270] See text from 7–153.
[271] By analogy with the old position in liquidation where criminal proceedings were brought by the liquidator at the expense of the insolvent estate: see *in Re London Globe Finance Corporation Ltd* [1903] 1 Ch. 728 and discussion in *Re Pantmaenog Timber Co Ltd* [2004] 1 A.C. 158 at [53]–[54].

tension with the policy of relieving indebtedness regardless of conduct[272] and, it is at least arguable that if the bankrupt has available income, this should be captured for the estate through an income payments order or agreement[273] rather than being absorbed by costs. Given the implications for the Insolvency Service's budget and the need for there to be clear incentives for bankrupts to make maximum use of BRUs, there are practical arguments in favour of the Secretary of State seeking, and obtaining, an order for costs in the event that a BRO is made.[274] However, indications were given at the outset that the Secretary of State would not seek costs in the event of a BRO being made[275] and to date this seems to have been the usual practice. Of course, both the Insolvency Service and the Secretary of State effectively receive funding from insolvent estates by way of case administration and the Secretary of State's fees.

BRUs

11–87 A bankrupt may offer and the Secretary of State may accept a BRU for a period of between two and fifteen years.[276] The BRU system is directly analogous to the system of disqualification and competition disqualification undertakings, which operates under the CDDA, and it serves similar ends.[277] In determining whether to accept a BRU, the Secretary of State must have regard to the matters specified in Sch.4A para.2(2) and (3).[278] While, in contrast to CDDA ss.7(2A) and 8(2A), the Secretary of State is not by the terms of the specific statutory provisions strictly required to consider the public interest in deciding whether to accept a BRU, it is suggested that as a matter of law he is required to do so. The Secretary of State will usually only accept a BRU where the bankrupt is prepared to admit (or, at least, not dispute) the factual basis of the BRU and agree to having a brief schedule containing particulars of the underlying facts annexed to the

[272] There is no general restriction on discharge based on misconduct, although the court does have a limited power to suspend discharge where the bankrupt has failed to co-operate with the official receiver or trustee in bankruptcy under Insolvency Act 1986 s.279(3),(4).

[273] Insolvency Act 1986 ss.310–310A.

[274] The Regulatory Impact Assessment for the insolvency provisions of the Enterprise Act anticipated that the cost to the Insolvency Service of the new procedures would "be met in part by refocusing investigative resources" but conceded that more specialist examining staff were needed (para.6.22). It also anticipated that through increased numbers of cases, including prosecutions for breach of BROs and BRUs, the bankruptcy restrictions regime would impact on the court system (paras 6.24–6.25). However, on the assumption that only 50 per cent of cases would require a hearing (the rest being settled by BRUs), and taking into account possible savings elsewhere (e.g. by reason of the introduction of income payment agreements in bankruptcy and out-of-court administration procedures in corporate insolvency), the overall impact on the courts was expected to be marginal. See further Insolvency Service, *Enterprise Act 2002—the Personal Insolvency Provisions: Final Evaluation Report* (November 2007), *http://www.insolvency.gov.uk/insolvencyprofessionandlegislation/legislation/evaluationfinalreport/home.htm* [Accessed August 27, 2009], at pp.84–104.

[275] In a presentation to the South West and Wales Region of R3 by a representative of the Insolvency Service: see Stephen Davies Q.C. (ed.), *Insolvency and the Enterprise Act 2002* (Bristol: Jordans, 2003), para.19.23, fn.28. See also *Official Receiver v May* [2008] B.P.I.R. 1562 at [25].

[276] Insolvency Act 1986 Sch.4A paras 7–9.

[277] See Ch.9.

[278] On which see text from 11–48.

undertaking by analogy with practice under the CDDA.[279] The Secretary of State may accept a BRU either before or after an application for a BRO has been made.

11–88 A BRU comes into force on being accepted by the Secretary of State. The BRU is deemed to have been accepted for this purpose when the Secretary of State signs it.[280] The BRU ceases to have effect at the end of the date specified in it (which must be at least two years but not more than 15 years from the date of acceptance). After the BRU has been accepted, the bankrupt may apply to have it varied or annulled under Sch.4A para.9(3).[281] This is analogous to an application to vary or discharge a disqualification undertaking or competition disqualification undertaking under CDDA s.8A.[282] As the provisions for BROs and BRUs were brought into force together at a time when the Secretary of State and the courts had no experience of operating the regimes, and since then, because of the availability of BRUs, there have been only a relatively limited number of reported BRO cases, it is conceivable that the Secretary of State will accept BRUs that subsequently become susceptible to challenge under Sch.4A para.9(3) because a pattern emerges in which the courts impose BROs for shorter periods in respect of the same or very similar conduct.[283] The opposite is also possible.

The effect of annulment on BROs, interim BROs and BRUs

11–89 Where a bankruptcy order is annulled under s.282(1)(a) of the Insolvency Act 1986 on the ground that the order ought not to have been made, any BRO, interim BRO or BRU then in force must also be annulled and from that point the former bankrupt cannot be made the subject of a new BRO, interim BRO or BRU.[284] However, where a bankruptcy order is annulled following either the approval of a voluntary arrangement[285] or the paying of all the bankruptcy debts and expenses,[286] the annulment has no effect on any BRO, interim BRO or undertaking already in force.[287] Moreover, the court may make a BRO in relation to the bankrupt on an application instituted before the annulment and the Secretary of State may accept a BRU offered before the annulment.[288] The underlying policy

[279] See *Re Blackspur Group Plc, Secretary of State for Trade and Industry v Eastaway* [2001] EWCA Civ 1595, [2002] 2 B.C.L.C. 263 and discussion in text from 9–27.

[280] Insolvency Rules 1986 (as amended by the Insolvency (Amendment) Rules 2003 (SI 2003/1730)), r.6.249.

[281] Procedure for such applications is governed by Insolvency Rules 1986 r.6.251.

[282] See Ch.13.

[283] Contrast the position under the CDDA where disqualification undertakings were not introduced until some 15 years after the substantive powers of disqualification in CDDA ss.6 and 8 with the consequence that an extensive body of case law giving guidance on matters of unfit conduct had already built up.

[284] Insolvency Act 1986 Sch.4A para.10. The same applies to a bankruptcy order annulled under s.282(2) of the 1986 Act.

[285] Insolvency Act 1986 ss.261, 263D.

[286] Insolvency Act 1986 s.282(1)(b).

[287] Insolvency Act 1986 Sch.4A para.11(a).

[288] Insolvency Act 1986 Sch.4A para.11(b),(c); *Jenkins v Official Receiver* [2007] B.P.I.R. 740 (BRO imposed for four years at the annulment hearing).

is that a bankrupt should not be able to buy his way out of a BRO. Even so, an application for a BRO or an interim BRO cannot be made after the annulment.[289]

Publicity for bankruptcy orders, BROs and BRUs

11–90 In relation to undischarged bankrupts, there is no disqualification order or disqualification undertaking to be registered as the prohibition in CDDA s.11(1)(a) flows automatically from the making of the bankruptcy order. However, the Secretary of State is required to maintain a register of matters relating to bankruptcies, DROs and individual voluntary arrangements (the Individual Insolvency Register) under Pt 6A of the Insolvency Rules 1986 which is open to public inspection on any business day between 9am and 5pm.[290] Rule 6A.4 requires the official receiver to enter on the register specified bankruptcy information received by him in relation to any bankruptcy order.[291] Provision is also made for the deletion of information from the register following discharge or annulment. To this extent, the Individual Insolvency Register serves a similar purpose to the register of disqualification orders maintained under s.18 of the CDDA and should go some way towards assisting Companies House to identify whether persons seeking to incorporate companies are disqualified by reason of bankruptcy.[292]

11–91 Schedule 4A para.12 of the Insolvency Act 1986[293] provides for the Secretary of State to maintain a register of BROs, interim BROs and BRUs. The Enterprise Act 2002[294] also amended Sch.9 to the Insolvency Rules 1986 introducing para.29A which makes it clear that rules made under s.412 of the Insolvency Act 1986 may (among other provisions relating to BROs) contain provisions enabling the register to be amalgamated with another register and the inspection of that register by the public. The relevant rules are also to be found in Pt 6A of the Insolvency Rules 1986. The Bankruptcy Restrictions Register is open to the public on business days from 9am to 5pm. Certain prescribed information is to be entered onto the register by the Secretary of State whenever a BRO or interim BRO is made or a BRU is accepted by the Secretary of State. Again, there is provision for deletion of information from this register on expiry of BROs or BRUs or where they otherwise cease to have effect. There is also provision dealing with the Secretary of State's obligations to rectify the two registers.[295]

[289] Insolvency Act 1986 Sch.4A para.11(d).

[290] This major insertion into the Insolvency Rules was brought about by the Insolvency (Amendment) Rules 2003 (SI 2003/1730). It brings together a number of provisions formally scattered around the Rules, including those formerly contained in Pt 22A of the Rules.

[291] "Specified bankruptcy information" is defined in r.6.233(B)(5). The definition is wide ranging and includes, among other things, the date of the bankruptcy order, the bankrupt's name, gender, date of birth and last known address and, significantly, full details concerning the bankrupt's discharge.

[292] On the problems of cross-checking and enforcement which arose before the introduction of the register see A. Hicks, *Disqualification of Directors: No Hiding Place for the Unfit* (A.C.C.A Research Report No.59, 1998).

[293] Inserted by Enterprise Act 2002 s.257 and Sch.20 with effect from April 1, 2004.

[294] Section 269 and Sch.23 para.16(3).

[295] Insolvency Rules 1986 r.6A.8.

The information on the BRO register should also assist Companies House. No doubt, credit reference agencies and credit providers also make use of the information on the register of bankruptcy orders and the BRO register.[296]

THE DEBT RELIEF RESTRICTIONS REGIME: DEBT RELIEF RESTRICTIONS ORDERS ("DRROs") AND DEBT RELIEF RESTRICTIONS UNDERTAKINGS ("DRRUs")

11–92 The debt relief restrictions regime is contained in s.251V and Sch.4ZB of the Insolvency Act 1986. These provisions were inserted into the Insolvency Act by s.108(1), (2), Sch.17 and Sch.19 of the Tribunals, Courts and Enforcement Act 2007 with effect from April 6, 2009.[297] The regime is modelled on the bankruptcy restrictions regime and sets out to make separate, albeit parallel, provision for DRO debtors. As DROs were introduced with the aim of providing what amounts to a form of bankruptcy relief for the financially excluded, law and practice under the bankruptcy restrictions regime will inform law and practice under the debt relief restrictions regime.

Background

11–93 In order to understand debt relief restrictions, it is essential to have some grasp of the wider context and, in particular, the legislative background to the enactment of the DRO procedure now to be found in Pt 5 of the Tribunals, Courts and Enforcement Act 2007.[298] DROs were introduced following two consultation exercises. An initial consultation paper entitled *A Choice of Paths—Better options to manage over-indebtedness and multiple debt* was issued by what was then the Department of Constitutional Affairs in 2004. This was followed by an Insolvency Service consultation paper entitled *Relief for the indebted—An alternative to bankruptcy* published in March 2005. These consultation papers identified a category of so-called NINA ("no income, no asset") debtors who cannot afford to make sustainable contributions to creditors through an individual voluntary arrangement, a county court administration order or a non-statutory debt management

[296] See, e.g. Hansard H.C. Standing Committee B, Session 2001–2002, May 14, 2002 at col.655.

[297] For commencement see the Tribunals, Courts and Enforcement Act 2007 (Commencement No.7) Order 2009 (SI 2009/382), art.2. Scotland does not have a separate DRO regime but has instead provided low income, low asset debtors who fall within defined financial eligibility criteria with a special route into sequestration: see Bankruptcy (Scotland) Act 1985 ss.5(2B)(c)(ia), 5A inserted by the Bankruptcy and Diligence etc (Scotland) Act 2007 s.15(1)(b), (2); Bankruptcy (Scotland) Act 1985 (Low Income, Low Asset Debtors etc) Regulations 2008 (SSI 2008/81). As a result, these debtors are within the scope of the Scottish bankruptcy restrictions regime and there was no need for the Scottish Parliament to enact a separate DRRO regime. During 2009 the Northern Ireland Department of Enterprise, Trade and Investment consulted on a proposal to introduce an equivalent DRO scheme and DRRO regime for Northern Ireland. At the time of writing, the proposal had not been implemented but it is anticipated that legislation will be enacted for Northern Ireland aligning the position with that in England and Wales.

[298] For a further account of the legislative background to DROs see D. McKenzie Skene and A. Walters, "Consumer Bankruptcy Law Reform in Great Britain" (2006) 80(4) American Bankruptcy L.J. 477.

plan and who are denied access to ordinary bankruptcy relief because they have insufficient means to pay the official receiver's deposit.[299] The Insolvency Service paper outlined a proposed debt relief scheme for NINAs designed to plug this perceived gap in legislative provision affecting financially excluded debtors:

"The proposed . . . scheme is aimed at people who have no assets, very little income and a relatively low level of liabilities—that is those people who, because of their financial position, cannot access any of the debt solutions that are currently available (i.e. bankruptcy, individual voluntary arrangement, county court administration order or debt management plan). Some of these people manage to apply for a bankruptcy order, and thus obtain debt relief, by obtaining a grant from a charity or by getting the money from friends or family."[300]

In the form proposed, the scheme was designed to enable debtors who satisfy certain threshold criteria, including financial eligibility criteria, low-cost access via an approved intermediary acting as gate-keeper to a DRO made administratively by the official receiver, rather than by the court, which would result in a discharge of debts after one year. A range of safeguards for creditors and the public were also proposed including a restrictions regime to deal with culpable debtors similar to the bankruptcy restrictions regime.[301]

11–94 The DRO scheme, as it became, was included in Pt 5 of the Draft Tribunals, Courts and Enforcement Bill on its publication in July 2006. The explanatory note to the Bill contained the following by way of further background:

"At present if an individual encounters difficulty paying his debts, the remedies that are available to him either require him to have assets or funds available to distribute to his creditors on a regular basis (for example IVA, county court administration order or a non-statutory debt management plan) or, as with bankruptcy, there is a fee to access the remedy. This means that the procedures that are currently available are inaccessible to some people, since they do not have the financial means to use them.

Such people often have relatively low levels of liabilities, no assets over and above a nominal amount and no surplus income with which to come to an arrangement with their creditors.

The DRO has been devised following the *Choice of Paths* consultation, which determined that there was a perceived need for a remedy for people who are financially excluded from the current debt solution procedures and a further consultation by the Insolvency Service in 2005 . . . on the detail of how it might operate. It is a procedure that will enable some individuals who meet specified criteria as regards liabilities, assets and income, to seek relief from certain debts."

Following the enactment of the Tribunals, Courts and Enforcement Act 2007, the DRO scheme together with the DRRO regime to deal with culpable DRO debtors was brought into operation on April 6, 2009.[302]

[299] A fee of £510 must currently be paid by a debtor petitioning for his own bankruptcy including £360 for the official receiver's deposit: see Insolvency Proceedings (Fees) Order 2004 (SI 2004/593), art.6(1)(b) as substituted by SI 2009/645.

[300] *Relief for the indebted*, p.18.

[301] *Relief for the indebted*, p.33.

[302] Tribunals, Courts and Enforcement Act 2007 (Commencement No.7) Order 2009 (SI 2009/382), art.2.

11–95 The legislative framework of the DRO scheme is contained in Pt 7A (ss.251A–251X) of and Sch.4ZA to the Insolvency Act 1986. These provisions were inserted in the 1986 Act by the Tribunals, Courts and Enforcement Act 2007 s.108(1),(2) and Schs.17–18 with effect from April 6, 2009. Further rules concerning DROs were introduced as Pt 5A of the Insolvency Rules 1986 by the Insolvency (Amendment) Rules 2009[303] also effective from April 6, 2009. The essential features of the scheme are broadly the same as were envisaged in the Insolvency Service's *Relief for the indebted* consultation paper. They are as follows:

(1) An application for a DRO must be made to the official receiver via an approved intermediary.[304] Approved intermediaries are individuals for the time being approved by a competent authority to act as an intermediary between a person wishing to make an application for a DRO and the official receiver. A competent authority is a person or body for the time being designated by the Secretary of State pursuant to s.251U of the Insolvency Act to approve intermediaries.[305] At the time of writing there were six organisations that had been designated as competent authorities: the National Association of Citizens Advice Bureaux; the Institution of Money Advisers; the Foundation of Credit Counselling (Consumer Credit Counselling Service); National Debtline; Baines & Ernst Ltd; and Payplan Ltd. DROs are therefore delivered through a partnership between the Insolvency Service and the debt advice sector in which reputable debt advice providers designated by the Secretary of State act as gatekeepers of the process.
(2) A person is only eligible for a DRO if he meets a number of conditions on the date of the application and as at the date the application is determined by the official receiver.[306] In particular, the debtor's overall indebtedness, monthly surplus income and the value of the debtor's property must not exceed prescribed amounts. These amounts are currently: (i) a maximum indebtedness of £15,000; (ii) monthly surplus income not exceeding £50 per month; and (iii) total gross assets not exceeding £300.[307] Furthermore, a debtor is ineligible if he is an undischarged bankrupt, subject to an individual voluntary arrangement, has had a bankruptcy petition presented against him or presented

[303] SI 2009/642.

[304] Insolvency Act 1986 s.251B. For the form of application and the information that must be included see Insolvency Act 1986 s.251B(2), (3); Insolvency Rules 1986 rr.5A.3–5A.4.

[305] The procedures for the designating of competent authorities and the granting and withdrawing of approved intermediary status are set out in the Debt Relief Orders (Designation of Competent Authorities) Regulations 2009 (SI 2009/457), as amended by SI 2009/1553, made pursuant to Insolvency Act 1986 s.251U(4).

[306] Insolvency Act 1986 s.251B, Sch.4ZA.

[307] Insolvency Act 1986 Sch.4ZA paras 6–8; Insolvency Proceedings (Monetary Limits) Order 1986 (SI 1986/1996), Sch.2 as amended by the Insolvency Proceedings (Monetary Limits)(Amendment) Order 2009 (SI 2009/465). Certain debts are excluded and certain property, including a domestic motor vehicle worth less than £1,000, is exempt: see Insolvency Act 1986 ss.251A, 251C; Insolvency Rules 1986 rr.5A.2, 5A.8–5A.10. For other barriers to entry, e.g. a DRO cannot be made in favour of a debtor who is already an undischarged bankrupt, see Insolvency Act 1986 Sch.4ZA paras 1–4, 9–10.

his own bankruptcy petition, or has had a DRO made in relation to him in the six years ending with the date of determination of his application.[308]

(3) The application is made electronically through an approved intermediary and, after the official receiver has verified whether or not the applicant satisfies the eligibility criteria, he may make a DRO.[309] There is an application fee of £90.[310] A specialist Debt Relief Order Unit has been established in Plymouth to process applications.

(4) By virtue of s.251G of the Insolvency Act 1986, a DRO becomes effective when details of it are entered on the register of prescribed matters relating to DROs that the Secretary of State is required to maintain pursuant to s.251W[311] subject to a right for creditors in s.251K to object to the making of the DRO or the inclusion of their debt within its scope.

(5) A DRO gives rise to a moratorium which prohibits unsecured creditors from taking enforcement action in relation to their debts. The moratorium generally lasts one year unless the DRO is revoked earlier.[312] The one year period can also be extended by the court in prescribed circumstances.[313] During the moratorium period a DRO debtor is subject to the prohibition on acting as a director etc. now to be found in CDDA s.11(1)(aa) and the various wider restrictions set out in the text at 11–32 above.

(6) At the end of the moratorium period the debtor is discharged from all of the qualifying debts specified in the DRO.[314] As is the case with bankruptcy some debts, such as a debt incurred in respect of any fraud or fraudulent breach of trust to which the debtor was a party, are non-dischargeable.[315]

(7) The debtor is under a duty to provide assistance to the official receiver and, during the moratorium period, to notify the official receiver of any increase in his income of if he acquires any property.[316] There are various safeguards against abuse. The official receiver can revoke a DRO during the moratorium in prescribed circumstances, such as where it transpires that the debtor has provided incomplete, incorrect or otherwise misleading information in support of the application or subsequently.[317] The official receiver has extensive powers of inquiry into the debtor's dealings and property. There are also a series of offences in ss.251O–S dealing with such matters as: making false

[308] Insolvency Act 1986 Sch.4ZA paras 2–5.

[309] Insolvency Act 1986 ss.251B–D; Insolvency Rules 1986 rr.5A.3–5A.7.

[310] Insolvency Proceedings (Fees) Order 2004 (SI 2004/593), art.4, Sch.2 as amended by SI 2009/645.

[311] See further Insolvency Rules 1986 r.6A.5A.

[312] Insolvency Act 1986 ss.251H, 251L.

[313] Insolvency Act 1986 s.251M.

[314] Insolvency Act 1986 s.251I(1).

[315] Insolvency Act 1986 s.251I(3); Insolvency Rules 1986 r.5A.2.

[316] Insolvency Act 1986 s.251J.

[317] Insolvency Act 1986 s.251L. For the purposes of the automatic disqualifications, prohibitions and restrictions that apply to DRO debtors, revocation will take effect prospectively rather than retrospectively as is the case with annulment of a bankruptcy order: see, by analogy, *Commissioners for Inland Revenue v McEntaggart* [2006] 1 B.C.L.C. 476 and text at 11–17. For the effect of revocation on DRROs see 11–108.

representations or omissions in connection with a DRO application; concealment or falsification of documents; fraudulent disposal of property in the two years ending with the DRO application date and during the moratorium; and fraudulent dealing with property obtained on credit in the period between the two years ending with the DRO application date and the date on which the application is determined by the official receiver. These are analogous to a number of the bankruptcy offences in ss.350–362 of the Insolvency Act.

(8) In addition to these safeguards, and in order to align DROs, which are, in effect, a form of administrative bankruptcy for the financially excluded, with the ordinary bankruptcy regime, s.251V and Sch.4ZB of the Insolvency Act 1986 makes provision for a debt relief restriction regime modelled closely on the bankruptcy restrictions regime. The purpose of this regime is to impose continuing restrictions on culpable debtors after the expiry of the DRO and the moratorium period.

Prior investigations

11–96 The investigation into the conduct of bankrupts is carried out by the official receiver. Under the Insolvency Act 1986 s.251K the official receiver may, as part of his consideration of a creditor's objection to a DRO or on his own investigation carry out an investigation for various prescribed purposes. It is anticipated that investigations with a view to proceedings for a DRRO will follow the same pattern as that for BROs outlined in the text at 11–45 above.

DRROs: substantive law

11–97 The court may make a DRRO on the application of either the Secretary of State or the official receiver acting on a direction of the Secretary of State.[318] "The court" for these purposes is the High Court or the appropriate county court having bankruptcy jurisdiction under the Insolvency Act 1986.[319] In these respects the position is exactly the same as it is for BROs. As the DRO is an administrative proceeding and there is no bankruptcy proceeding on foot in which an ordinary application can be made, an application for a DRRO is a separate free standing proceeding analogous to an application for a civil disqualification order.

11–98 Schedule 4ZB para.2 of the Insolvency Act 1986 provides that a DRRO may be made only on the application of the Secretary of State or the official receiver. There is no express equivalent of the public interest test set out in CDDA ss.7(1) and 8(1). Nevertheless, the position is the same as it is as regards BROs in that the Secretary of State is bound to apply public interest criteria in determining whether or not to proceed bearing in mind that the rationale of the DRRO regime is the protection of the public from culpable DRO debtors.[320]

[318] Insolvency Act 1986 Sch.4ZB para.1. Hereafter references to the Secretary of State in relation to the discussion of DRROs include a reference to the official receiver.

[319] Insolvency Act 1986 s.373.

[320] See 11–47.

Grounds for making a DRRO

11–99 Schedule 4ZB para.2(1) of the Insolvency Act 1986 provides that the court "shall grant an application for a debt relief restrictions order if it thinks it appropriate to do so having regard to the conduct of the debtor (whether before or after the making of the debt relief order)". This wording is virtually identical to the wording in Sch.4A para.2(1) referable to BROs. The court can only take into account conduct that occurred after April 6, 2009.[321] Schedule 4ZB, para.2(2) provides further that the court shall, in particular, take into account any of the following kinds of behaviour on the part of the debtor:

(1) Failing to keep records which account for a loss of property by the debtor, or by a business carried on by him, where the loss occurred in the period beginning two years before the application date for the DRO and ending with the date of the application for a DRRO.

(2) Failing to produce records of the kind referred to in (1) above on demand by the official receiver or the trustee in bankruptcy.

(3) Entering into a transaction at an undervalue ("undervalue" to be construed in accordance with para.9(2) of Sch.4ZA) in the period beginning two years before the application date for the DRO and ending with the date of the determination of that application.

(4) Giving a preference ("preference" to be construed in accordance with para.10(2) of Sch.4ZA) in the period beginning two years before the application date for the DRO and ending with the date of the determination of that application.

(5) Making an excessive pension contribution ("excessive pension contribution" to be construed in accordance with s.342A of the Insolvency Act 1986).

(6) Failing to supply goods or services that were wholly or partly paid.

(7) Trading at a time, before the date of the determination of the application for the DRO, when the debtor knew or ought to have known that he was himself to be unable to pay his debts.

(8) Incurring, before the date of the determination of the application for the DRO, a debt which the debtor had no reasonable expectation of being able to pay.

(9) Failing to account satisfactorily to the court or the official receiver for a loss of property or for an insufficiency of property to meet his debts.

(10) Carrying on any gambling, rash and hazardous speculation or unreasonable extravagance which may have materially contributed to or increased the extent of his inability to pay his debts before the application date for the DRO or which took place between that date and the date of the determination of the application for the DRO.

(11) Neglect of business affairs of a kind which may have materially contributed to or increased the extent of his inability to pay his debts.

[321] The Tribunals, Courts and Enforcement Act 2007 (Transitional Provision) Order 2009 (SI 2009/450).

(12) Fraud or fraudulent breach of trust.
(13) Failing to cooperate with the official receiver.

Schedule 4ZB para.2(3) adds that the court shall also, in particular, consider whether the debtor was an undischarged bankrupt at some time during the period of six years ending with the date of the application for the DRO. Thus, in all material respects the wording of Sch.4ZB para.2 mirrors that of Sch.4A, para.2 relating to BROs. As is the case with BROs and Sch.1 of the CDDA, the kinds of behaviour listed in para.2 of Sch.4ZB are non-exhaustive. So, for example, the court could also take into account conduct amounting to an offence pursuant to the specific provisions applicable to DRO debtors in the Insolvency Act 1986 ss.251O–251S. The general approach of the court to the determining of whether or not a DRRO is appropriate having regard to the debtor's conduct will be informed by practice under the BRO regime.[322]

Duration and commencement of a DRRO

11–100 Schedule 4ZB para.4(1) provides that a DRRO shall come into force when it is made and shall cease to have effect at the end of a date specified in the order. The effect of para.4(2) is that a DRRO must be made for a period of at least two years but no more than 15 years. The position is the same as that set out in the text at 11–70 and 11–71 above in relation to BROs.

DRROs: procedure

The application

11–101 The substantive rules relating to debt relief restrictions are set out in Chs 31 to 33 of the Insolvency Rules 1986.[323] Applications for DRROs are "insolvency proceedings" for the purposes of the Insolvency Rules.[324] The procedure for applying for a DRRO is similar to that for applying for a BRO or a disqualification order under CDDA s.6.[325] Whereas an application for a BRO is an ordinary application in the relevant bankruptcy, the application for a DRRO is free standing as DROs are an administrative rather than a court process.

11–102 An application for a DRRO must be made before the end of the moratorium period relating to the relevant DRO.[326] Once the moratorium period has ended an application for a DRRO can only be made with the permission of the court.[327] The period in which the application for a DRRO can be made without the court's permission is aligned with the one-year period of the DRO moratorium. The position is broadly similar to that in relation to BROs set out in 11–75 above.

[322] See text from 11–46.
[323] Insolvency Rules 1986 rr.6.252–6.263. These provisions were inserted by the Insolvency (Amendment) Rules 2009 (SI 2009/642).
[324] Insolvency Rules 1986 r.13.7.
[325] See, in particular, text from 11–74 in relation to BROs.
[326] Insolvency Act 1986 Sch.4ZB para.3(a).
[327] Insolvency Act 1986 Sch.4ZB para.3(b).

11–103 The application must be supported by a report from the applicant, be it the Secretary of State or the official receiver. The report must include: (a) a statement of the conduct by reference to which it is alleged that it is appropriate for a DRRO to be made; and (b) the evidence on which the applicant relies in support of the application.[328] Otherwise, the position as regards the application and supporting evidence is in all material respects the same as it is for BROs and there is a detailed timetable governing the filing of evidence and the hearing of the application set out in the Insolvency Rules 1986 rr.6.253–6.256. These provisions mirror rr.6.241–6.244 which govern the procedure relating to BROs.[329]

Interim DRROs

11–104 Schedule 4ZB paras 5 and 6 of the Insolvency Act 1986 and Ch.32 of the Insolvency Rules 1986 make provision for the court to make an interim DRRO. Any time between the institution and determination of an application for a DRRO, the court may make an interim DRRO if the court thinks that (a) there are prima facie grounds to suggest that the application for the DRRO will be successful; and (b) it is in the public interest to make an interim DRRO. Practice in relation to interim DRROs can be expected to be the same as practice in relation to interim BROs.[330] The procedure for the application for an interim DRRO, which again mirrors the procedure for interim BROs, is found in the Insolvency Rules 1986 rr.6.257–6.260. An interim DRRO ceases to have effect: (a) on the determination of the substantive application for a DRRO; (b) on the acceptance of a DRRU; or (c) if discharged by the court on the application of the debtor or the applicant for the interim DRRO.[331] The procedure for an application by the debtor to set aside an interim DRRO is set out in r.6.260 of the Insolvency Rules 1986.

Costs

11–105 The position as regards costs in the context of BROs is set out in 11–86 above. Although there are clearly arguments in favour of the applicant being awarded his costs where a DRRO is made, it is expected that the Secretary of State will not as a general rule seek costs having regard to the fact that debtors eligible for a DRO are very often unlikely to have the ability to pay.

DRRUs

11–106 A debtor may offer and the Secretary of State may accept a DRRU for a period of between two and fifteen years.[332] The provisions relating to DRRUs are identical in all material respects to those considered in the text from 11–87 above in relation to BRUs. Accordingly, practice can be expected to be the same as it is for DRRUs. It follows that the Secretary of State will usually only accept a DRRU

[328] Insolvency Rules 1986 r.6.253.
[329] See text from 11–74.
[330] See text from 11–80.
[331] Insolvency Act 1986 Sch.4ZB para.5(5).
[332] Insolvency Act 1986 Sch.4ZB paras 7–9.

where the debtors is prepared to admit (or, at least, not dispute) the factual basis of the DRRU and agree to having a brief schedule containing particulars of the underlying facts annexed to the undertaking by analogy with practice under the CDDA.[333] The Secretary of State may accept a DRRU either before or after an application for a DRRO has been made.

11–107 A DRRU comes into force on being accepted by the Secretary of State. The DRRU is deemed to have been accepted for this purpose when the Secretary of State signs it.[334] The DRRU ceases to have effect at the end of the date specified in it (which must be at least two years but not more than fifteen years from the date of acceptance). After the DRRU has been accepted, the debtor may apply to have it varied or annulled under Sch.4ZB para.9(3).[335] This is analogous to an application to vary or discharge a disqualification undertaking or competition disqualification undertaking under CDDA s.8A.[336]

The effect of revocation of a DRO on DRROs, interim DRROs and DRRUs

11–108 Where a DRO is revoked by the official receiver under s.251L of the Insolvency Act 1986, the revocation does not affect the validity of any DRRO, interim DRRO or DRRU which is in force in respect of the debtor. Moreover, the court may make a DRRO or an interim DRRO in relation to the debtor on an application instituted before the revocation and the Secretary of State may accept a DRRU offered before the revocation.[337] Similarly (and in contrast to the position in relation to BROs where the bankruptcy is annulled) the revocation of a DRO does not prevent the institution of an application for a DRRO or interim DRRO, or the offer or acceptance of a DRRU by the debtor, after that time unless the court directs otherwise.[338] Where the official receiver decides to revoke a DRO, he may revoke it either with immediate effect, or with effect from such date (not more than three months after the date of the decision) as he may specify.[339] If the official receiver is contemplating making an application for DRRO it may be wise for him to delay the effect of the revocation for sufficient time to enable proceedings to be commenced. Otherwise, if the DRO (and the associated moratorium period) are brought to an end, he will need the permission of the court to apply for a DRRO under Sch.4ZB para.3(b) of the Insolvency Act 1986.

Publicity for DROs, DRROs and DRRUs

11–109 Prescribed information relating to DROs must be entered on the Individual Insolvency Register maintained by the Secretary of State under Pt 6A of the

[333] See *Re Blackspur Group Plc, Secretary of State for Trade and Industry v Eastaway* [2001] EWCA Civ 1595, [2002] 2 B.C.L.C. 263 and discussion in text from 9–27.

[334] Insolvency Rules 1986 r.6.261.

[335] Procedure for such applications is governed by Insolvency Rules 1986 r.6.263.

[336] See Ch.13.

[337] Insolvency Act 1986 Sch.4ZB para.10. See, by analogy, *Jenkins v Official Receiver* [2007] B.P.I.R. 740.

[338] Insolvency Act 1986 Sch.4A para.10(d).

[339] Insolvency Act 1986 s.251L(5).

Insolvency Rules 1986. Provision is also made for the deletion of information from the register following revocation or discharge.[340] To this extent, the Individual Insolvency Register serves a similar purpose to the register of disqualification orders maintained under s.18 of the CDDA and should assist Companies House in identifying whether persons seeking to incorporate companies are disqualified by reason of a DRO.

11–110 Section 251W of the Insolvency Act 1986 provides for the Secretary of State to maintain a register of DRROs, interim DRROs and DRRUs, the relevant rules for which are found in rr.6A.7A–6A.7B.[341] The Debt Relief Restrictions Register is open to the public on business days from 9am to 5pm. Certain prescribed information is to be entered onto the register by the Secretary of State whenever a DRRO or interim DRRO is made or a DRRU is accepted by the Secretary of State. Again, there is provision for deletion of information from this register on expiry of DRROs or DRRUs or where they otherwise cease to have effect. The Debt Relief Restrictions Register and the Bankruptcy Restrictions Register for which provision is also made in Part 6A of the Insolvency Rules 1986 are broadly identical in terms of scope and function.[342]

OVERLAP BETWEEN S.11 AND OTHER PROVISIONS IN THE CDDA

11–111 In practice, it is not uncommon for a disqualification under CDDA s.6 to overlap with the automatic prohibition on undischarged bankrupts in s.11(1)(a). The failure of a company may well lead to the bankruptcy of its directors, more often than not because they have personally guaranteed the company's indebtedness to certain creditors (in particular, the bank). The automatic disqualification of a director in this situation is no bar to proceedings being brought against him under s.6. The Insolvency Service may decide that it would be expedient to proceed against the director with a view to securing a disqualification order based on his conduct as a director for a longer period than the one year during which he can normally expect to remain an undischarged bankrupt. Thus, to an extent, the individual cannot really complain if, having suffered automatic disqualification, he is later re-disqualified by an order under s.6. However, it appears that, in determining the appropriate period of disqualification in any subsequent s.6 proceedings, the court may be prepared to give the defendant a discount to reflect his automatic disqualification under s.11.[343]

[340] Insolvency Act 1986 s.251W(a); Insolvency Rules 1986 rr.6A.5A–6A.5B (inserted by the Insolvency (Amendment) Rules 2009 (SI 2009/642)).

[341] Inserted by the Insolvency (Amendment) Rules 2009 (SI 2009/642).

[342] For the position as regards BROs etc see 11–91.

[343] In *Re Tansoft Ltd* [1991] B.C.L.C. 339 the defendant was bankrupt at the date of trial and the earliest date on which he would be likely to obtain his discharge from bankruptcy was still some two years off. As a result, any period of disqualification imposed under s.6 would have overlapped with that resulting from the defendant's bankruptcy. Warner J. regarded this as a neutral factor that carried no weight for the purposes of determining the appropriate period of disqualification. However, dicta in *Re Swift 736 Ltd, Secretary of State for Trade and Industry v Ettinger* [1993] B.C.L.C. 896 and *Re Westmid Packing Services Ltd, Secretary of State for Trade and Industry v Griffiths* [1998] 2 All E.R. 124 suggest that a previous disqualification under s.11 is a matter that may be taken into account in determining the period of disqualification.

In this context, it may be questioned whether there would be any point in pursuing, in the public interest, a "minimum bracket" case against a director who is already or has already been disqualified automatically under s.11.[344]

11–112 The situation is particularly interesting where there is evidence of conduct in the bankruptcy that is capable of supporting an application for a BRO as well as evidence of unfit conduct in relation to the company. It is important to bear in mind that, on the face of it, the BRO and CDDA regimes are addressing two different issues. The focus under the BRO regime is on the conduct of the bankrupt whereas the focus under the CDDA regime is on the defendant's conduct qua director of the insolvent company. However, in the situation described, the Secretary of State will have a choice whether to apply to have the person disqualified from acting as a director etc. by means of a BRO or to commence proceedings under the CDDA based on the person's conduct as a director or both. Much will depend on the circumstances and the relative seriousness of the misconduct that could be taken into account in each of the regimes. In cases where the bankruptcy of the individual is reasonably contemporaneous with the company becoming insolvent for the purposes of CDDA s.6, it is conceivable that the Secretary of State would apply in the first instance for a BRO bearing in mind that the application must be brought within one year. If it transpired that the person's conduct as a director would be likely to attract a longer period of disqualification than the period of the BRO, it appears that there would be nothing to stop the Secretary of State from subsequently seeking a disqualification undertaking or commencing disqualification proceedings under CDDA s.6 given that the focus of such proceedings is different from the focus of the BRO regime. Similarly, there is no reason in principle why BRO proceedings may not be brought against a person who is already the subject of a CDDA disqualification.

DISQUALIFICATION FOLLOWING REVOCATION OF AN ADMINISTRATION ORDER MADE UNDER PART VI OF THE COUNTY COURTS ACT 1984

11–113 Under Pt VI of the County Courts Act 1984, a county court has power in prescribed circumstances to make an order providing for the administration of his estate against a judgment debtor who is unable to pay forthwith the amount of a judgment against him.[345] The effect of such an order is that no creditor of the individual whose name

[344] See further, A. Hicks, *Disqualification of Directors: No Hiding Place for the Unfit* (A.C.C.A. Research Report No. 59, 1998), p.36.

[345] An order can only be made where the debtor's whole indebtedness does not exceed the County Court limit, currently £5,000, although this will be raised to £15,000 if the provisions of Pt V of the Tribunals, Courts and Enforcement Act 2007 relating to county court administration orders are brought into force. The procedure, originally introduced in the Bankruptcy Act 1883, was designed with the small debtor in mind. For history, background and criticism, see Report of the Review Committee, *Insolvency Law and Practice*, Cmnd.8558 (London: HMSO, 1982) at paras 68–73, 151–165, 272–280; Department for Constitutional Affairs, *A Choice of Paths—better options to manage over-indebtedness and multiple debt*, CP 23/04 (2004). For procedure, see CPR Sch.2 and CCR Ord.39.

is scheduled to the order[346] may proceed unilaterally against the individual or his property without the court's permission.[347] The order may provide for the payment of the individual's debts by instalments and either in full or in part.[348] Section 429 of the Insolvency Act 1986 provides that, where an individual fails to make any payment which he is required to make by virtue of the administration order, the relevant county court may, in its discretion, revoke the order[349] and direct that that section[350] and s.12 of the CDDA shall apply to him for a period not exceeding one year.[351] Section 12 of the CDDA simply provides that where the court has revoked an administration order and made such a direction, the individual affected shall not, without the permission of the relevant county court that made the order, act as a company director or liquidator or directly or indirectly take part or be concerned in the promotion, formation or management of a company. The effect of s.429(2)(b) of the Insolvency Act 1986 is that a disqualification under s.12 cannot exceed one year. Section 429 does not apply in Scotland or Northern Ireland.[352]

11–114 Under s.429(2) of the Insolvency Act, the court clearly has a discretion whether or not to revoke an administration order. However, there has been some debate as to whether, having decided to revoke the order, the court is bound to impose a disqualification in the terms of s.12 of the CDDA. It is suggested that the word "and" between "revoke the administration order" and "make an order directing that this section and s.12 of the CDDA shall apply" in s.429(2) should be treated as conjunctive. In other words, it is suggested that when the court revokes an administration order, it must apply the disqualification under s.12 of the CDDA as well and accordingly has no choice in the matter. The position will change if the reforms to the county court administration order contained in Pt. V of the Tribunals, Courts and Enforcement Act 2007 are brought into force. This Act amends s.429(2) to make it clear that if the court revokes an administration order, it is a matter of the court's discretion whether it makes an order directing that s.429 and s.12 of the CDDA shall apply.[353] At the time of writing the 2007 Act provisions had been the subject of further consultation but had not been brought into force.[354]

[346] Before the order is made the court is required to send notice to all the creditors that have been identified by the debtor and notified to the court.

[347] County Courts Act 1984 s.114. The effect is similar albeit not as wide as that of an interim order under Pt. VIII of the Insolvency Act 1986 (which a debtor applies for in contemplation of an individual voluntary arrangement). There are also restrictions regarding the presentation of bankruptcy petitions: County Courts Act 1984 s.112(4).

[348] County Courts Act 1984 s.112(6). It may also be subject to conditions as to future earnings or income of the debtor.

[349] See especially CPR Sch.2; CCR Ord.39 rr.13A 14.

[350] Section 429 imposes a prohibition on the individual from obtaining credit or entering into certain business transactions without disclosing that the section applies to him. Breach of these prohibitions is a criminal offence.

[351] It should be noted that the making of an order under s.429(2)(b) triggers several other disqualifications and prohibitions under a variety of statutory provisions: see further Ch.14.

[352] An analogous provision is in force in Northern Ireland: see Company Directors Disqualification (Northern Ireland) Order 2002 (SI 2002/3150), art.16; Company Directors Disqualification (2002 Order) (Commencement) Order (Northern Ireland) 2003 (SI 2003/345).

[353] See Tribunals, Courts and Enforcement Act 2007 s.106, Sch.16, para.3.

[354] Ministry of Justice, *Administration and Enforcement Restrictions Orders—setting the parameters*, CP 01/08 (2008).

11–115 A breach of the s.12 prohibition is a criminal offence.[355] The penalties are the same as in the case of breach of the s.11 prohibition.[356] There is no extension of criminal liability under s.14 regarding breach of the s.12 prohibition, nor is there any personal liability for the debts of the relevant company, whether on the person in breach or by an accessory, under s.15 of the CDDA.

[355] CDDA s.13(1).
[356] See 11–21A.

CHAPTER 12

DISQUALIFICATION ORDERS AND UNDERTAKINGS

INTRODUCTION

The following matters are considered in this chapter: **12–01**

(1) The form of disqualification orders and disqualification undertakings.
(2) The commencement of disqualification orders and disqualification undertakings.
(3) Registration of disqualification orders and disqualification undertakings.

FORM OF ORDERS AND UNDERTAKINGS

Disqualification orders made on and after April 2, 2001

When a person is disqualified under any of CDDA ss.2 to 5, 6, 8, 9A or 10, the form of order that the court is required to make is that set out in CDDA s.1. The current s.1 was inserted by s.5 of the Insolvency Act 2000 and applies to all disqualification orders made on or after April 2, 2001.[1] A disqualification order is currently defined in ss.1(1) and (2) as: **12–02**

> "(1) . . . .an order that for a period specified in the order—
>
> (a) he [the disqualified person] shall not be a director of a company, act as a receiver of a company's property or in any way, whether directly or indirectly, be concerned or take part in the promotion, formation or management of a company unless (in each case) he has the leave of the court, and
> (b) he shall not act as an insolvency practitioner.
>
> (2) . . . unless the court otherwise orders, the period of disqualification . . . shall begin at the end of the period of 21 days beginning with the date of the order."

The current s.1 makes it clear that there is an absolute ban on a disqualified person acting as an insolvency practitioner and tidies up uncertainties that had arisen regarding the commencement of disqualification orders. It was suggested in the first edition of this work[2] that the previous statutory provisions did in fact impose an absolute ban on acting as an insolvency practitioner and that the court could not relieve the disqualified person from this disability by the grant of permission to act notwithstanding disqualification. Uncertainty in this respect **12–03**

[1] The Insolvency Act 2000 (Commencement No.1 and Transitional Provisions) Order 2001 (SI 2001/766).

[2] A. Walters & M. Davis-White, *Directors Disqualification: Law and Practice* (London: Sweet & Maxwell, 1999) at pp.357–358 and 397–398.

was caused by the wording of the original s.1. The old wording seemed to suggest that the court might be able to grant permission, notwithstanding disqualification, to act as an insolvency practitioner.[3] The current s.1 removes this doubt. The other main change brought about by the enactment of the current s.1 is to make clear that the period of the disqualification imposed by the order commences at the time specified by the court, and, in default of a specific court order, at the end of the 21-day period specified in s.1(2).[4]

Disqualification orders made prior to April 2, 2001

12–04 The current s.1, inserted by the Insolvency Act 2000 as from April 2, 2001, has no impact on disqualification orders still in force that were made before April 2, 2001. So, for example, the current s.1 does not apply to a disqualification order made for a period of 15 years on March 1, 2001. As a handful of orders made before April 2, 2001 for periods at the upper end of the middle bracket (6 to 10 years) or in the top bracket (over 10 years up to the statutory maximum)[5] may continue to be in force at the time of writing, it is relevant to consider them. Such orders are governed by the terms of the original s.1 which defined a disqualification order as:

> "(1) . . . . an order that [the disqualified person] shall not, without the leave of the court:
>
> (a) be a director of a company, or
> (b) be a liquidator or administrator of a company, or
> (c) be a receiver or manager of a company's property, or
> (d) in any way, whether directly or indirectly, be concerned or take part in the promotion, formation or management of a company
>
> for a specified period beginning with the date of the order."

Rule 9 of the Disqualification Rules (now repealed) contained further provisions regarding the commencement of a disqualification order.

Disqualification undertakings

12–05 It has been possible since April 2, 2001 for a person to offer and the Secretary of State to accept a disqualification undertaking by virtue of CDDA ss.7(2A) and 8(2A).[6] Since June 20, 2003,[7] the Office of Fair Trading or other specified regulator[8] has had power under CDDA s.9B to accept offers of disqualification undertakings

[3] The form of order prescribed by the original s.1 is set out in 12–04.

[4] A point discussed further in the text from 12–35.

[5] See *Re Sevenoaks Stationers (Retail) Ltd* [1991] Ch. 164 and text from 5–102.

[6] Inserted by Insolvency Act 2000 ss.6(3) and (4). The law relating to disqualification undertakings is discussed more fully in Ch.9. For Northern Ireland disqualification undertakings see the Company Directors Disqualification (Northern Ireland) Order 2002 (SI 2002/3150 (NI 4)) and CDDA s.12B (inserted by SI 2004/1941).

[7] Enterprise Act 2002 s.204; the Enterprise Act 2002 (Commencement No.3, Transitional and Transitory Provisions and Savings) Order 2003 (SI 2003/1397).

[8] Defined by CDDA s.9E(2) as the Office of Communications; the Gas and Electricity Markets Authority; the Water Services Regulation Authority; the Office of Rail Regulation; and the Civil Aviation Authority.

from persons who have infringed competition law. The provisions relating to competition disqualification undertakings are curiously drafted. It is clear from CDDA s.9A that the court must make a "disqualification order", meaning an order as defined by s.1, against a person where the conditions described in s.9A are satisfied. Thus, disqualification by the court for competition infringements under s.9A will have exactly the same consequences as disqualification by the court under CDDA ss.2–5, 6–8 and 10. However, the position in relation to undertakings is not as straightforward. Rather than adopting the definition of a disqualification undertaking in s.1A, CDDA s.9B(3) defines a competition disqualification undertaking separately, albeit in very similar language. The crucial difference is that s.9B appears to contemplate that a competition disqualification undertaking may be agreed in terms that prevent the disqualified person seeking permission from the court to act notwithstanding disqualification. This seems an unnecessary complication, as does the slightly different wording of s.9B(3) when compared with s.1A.

12–06 A disqualification undertaking is defined by s.1A as:

> ". . . an undertaking by any person that, for a period specified in the undertaking, the person—
>
> (a) will not be a director of a company, act as a receiver of a company's property or in any way, whether directly or indirectly, be concerned or take part in the promotion, formation or management of a company unless (in each case) he has the leave of a court, and
>
> (b) will not act as an insolvency practitioner."

12–07 A competition disqualification undertaking is defined slightly differently. Section 9B(3) and (4) provide as follows:

> "(3) A [competition] disqualification undertaking is an undertaking by a person that for the period specified in the undertaking he will not—
>
> (a) be a director of a company;
> (b) act as a receiver of a company's property;
> (c) in any way, whether directly or indirectly, be concerned or take part in the promotion, formation or management of a company;
> (d) act as an insolvency practitioner.
>
> (4) But a [competition] disqualification undertaking may provide that a prohibition falling within subs.3(a) to (c) does not apply if the person obtains leave of the court."

12–08 Subject to the possibility that a disqualification undertaking under s.9B may be agreed in a form that does not give the court any power to grant permission to act notwithstanding disqualification, a competition disqualification undertaking largely has the same effect and form as a disqualification order and a disqualification undertaking as defined by s.1A. It is currently unclear whether any relevant regulator will refuse an offer of an undertaking on the ground that the undertaking offered incorporates power for the court to grant permission to act notwithstanding disqualification as seemingly envisaged by s.9B(4). The authors are not aware of any case to date in which a relevant regulator has sought to rely on s.9B(4) in such a fashion.

12–09 It is clear from the terms of ss.1 and, 1A (and, where agreed, under s.9B) that a disqualified person may make a separate application for permission to act in specific respects (although not as an insolvency practitioner) notwithstanding disqualification.[9] The Court of Appeal has encouraged such applications to be heard immediately after a disqualification order has been made if at all possible.[10] This step serves to protect the defendant's position especially where he holds directorships or managerial positions in companies other than those which are the subject of the proceedings.

The scope of the prohibition under a disqualification order

12–10 A question which frequently taxed the courts prior to April 2, 2001 was whether the court was bound by the original s.1 to impose an absolute ban prohibiting the disqualified person from engaging in *all* of the activities mentioned in the original s.1(1)(a) to (d) (set out in 12–04) or whether, alternatively, the court could pick and choose as if the section were a menu and, in the absence of a formal application for permission to act in a particular capacity, make a selective disqualification order or a disqualification order that, for example, permitted the disqualified person to participate in the management of a specified company or companies. A closely related procedural question was whether the form or minute of order should recite the words of s.1 in full. Both questions are considered below.[11]

Picking and choosing

12–11 It is clear from both the original and the current s.1 that the court cannot make a disqualification order that is restricted to only certain of the types of company that can be incorporated under the Companies Act 1985. Strictly, the ban applies in relation to all companies whether limited by shares, limited by guarantee or unlimited or whether public or private.[12] Thus, for example, the court has no jurisdiction to disqualify a person in relation only to public companies and leave him free to act as a director or manager of any private company.[13] Such an effect could be achieved, in theory, if the court making the disqualification order, assuming it

[9] See generally Ch.15.

[10] *Re Dicetrade Ltd, Secretary of State for Trade and Industry v Worth* [1994] 2 B.C.L.C. 113 at 116. See also *Re TLL Realisations Ltd, Secretary of State for Trade and Industry v Collins* [2000] B.C.C. 998 (Park J.) at 1003, 1007. It is clear that there is power in the terms of CDDA s.1(1)(a) to grant permission to act in prohibited capacities. Procedure is governed by s.17. The position was the same under former provisions namely the Companies Act 1985 ss.295, Sch.12 paras.4, 5; Insolvency Act 1985 s.108(2), Sch.6 para.1(1)–(4), (14).

[11] Note that this discussion has no application to the automatic disqualification of undischarged bankrupts under s.11 or a disqualification in the terms of s.12. It applies only to disqualifications imposed by the court under ss.2–5, 6, 8 or 10 where the order was made prior to April 2, 2001.

[12] The court may look more favourably on an application by a disqualified person for permission to act in relation to an unlimited company: see *Re DJ Matthews (Joinery Design) Ltd* (1988) 4 B.C.C. 513; *Re Dawes & Henderson (Agencies) Ltd, Secretary of State for Trade and Industry v Shuttleworth (No.2)* [1999] 2 B.C.L.C. 317.

[13] *R. v Goodman* [1993] 2 All E.R. 789. See also *Attorney General's References Nos. 14, 15 and 16 of 1995, The Times*, April 10, 1997; *R. v Ward* [2001] EWCA Crim 1648, [2002] B.C.C. 953 discussed further in 12–20.

had jurisdiction to do so under s.17 of the CDDA, immediately granted the disqualified person general permission to act in the prohibited capacities in relation to all private companies. It is important to note in this context that such a result could not be achieved by a criminal court (which has no power to grant permission under the CDDA). Moreover, it is difficult to conceive of circumstances in which the court would be prepared to grant such a wide, general permission. Historically, there have been several cases in which the court has been prepared to qualify a disqualification order in some way without the defendant having made a formal application for permission to act. So far as these cases proceed on the assumption that the court is making a *qualified* order rather than a disqualification order coupled with the grant of permission to act within strictly defined parameters, they can no longer be regarded as good law. These cases fall into two broad categories as follows.

Selective orders

12–12 Before the decision in *Re Gower Enterprises Ltd (No.2)*[14] it was an established practice of the Companies Court in s.6 cases to draw up disqualification orders that only made express reference to paras (a) and (d) of the original s.1(1).[15] No mention was made in these orders of paras (b) and (c). The consequence of such an order (on its face, at least) was that the defendant was not formally disqualified from acting as a liquidator or administrator of a company or as a receiver or manager of a company's property. The practice first surfaced in two cases decided by Harman J.[16] and there was some logical justification for it. Since the enactment of the Insolvency Act 1985, a person has only been permitted to carry out the activities in paras (b) and (c) of the original s.1 where he holds a professional qualification enabling him to act as an insolvency practitioner. A person upon whom a disqualification order is imposed under the CDDA is automatically disqualified from acting as an insolvency practitioner by s.390(4) of the Insolvency Act 1986. In the *Rolus Properties* case, Harman J.'s view was that there was little to be gained from formally disqualifying a person under paras (b) and (c) where that person was disqualified from acting as an insolvency practitioner under s.390(4) of the Insolvency Act.[17] In other cases, the view was taken that an order in the terms of paras (a) and (d) would adequately protect the public and s.390 of the Insolvency Act does not seem to have been in mind. The practice of omitting paras (b) and (c) from the court's order was rejected in *Re Gower Enterprises (No.2)*, a case which was to have considerable repercussions.

[14] [1995] 2 B.C.L.C. 201.

[15] Thus following the old form of originating process issued by the Secretary of State or official receiver which usually sought a disqualification order under s.6 but then went on to particularise the order by setting out the prohibitions in s.1(1)(a) and (d) only.

[16] *Re Flatbolt Ltd*, February 21, 1986, Ch.D., unreported; *Re Rolus Properties Ltd* (1988) 4 B.C.C. 446. These cases were both decided prior to the enactment of the CDDA although nothing turns on this.

[17] However, this did not deal with the point that the prohibition on acting as a receiver and manager under the original CDDA s.1(1)(c) was in fact wider than the prohibition on acting as an administrative receiver flowing from ss.388(1)(a) and 390(4)(b) of the Insolvency Act.

12–13 In *Gower Enterprises (No.2)*, the point arose in relation to the form of the originating summons which, in line with the then established practice, sought an order under CDDA s.6 but then went on to set out the form of order sought in the terms of paras (a) and (d) only. Counsel for the official receiver advanced the view that the word "or" between each of paras (a), (b), (c) and (d) in the original s.1(1) should be read as "and/or" thus enabling the court to "pick and choose". Mr Robert Reid Q.C., sitting as a deputy High Court judge, rejected this construction, preferring instead the view expressed by Lindsay J. in *Re Polly Peck International Plc (No.2), Secretary of State for Trade and Industry v Ellis*[18] that the provisions of s.1(1)(a) to (d) were cumulative on the basis that the word "or" was intended to be conjunctive. As a result, the deputy judge concluded that an order which did not formally prohibit the disqualified person from engaging in *all* the activities described in the original s.1(1) was not a disqualification order for the purposes of the CDDA. Conversely, the court had no jurisdiction to limit the scope of a disqualification order to some but not all of the four paragraphs in the subsection. On the facts, it was held that the originating summons was not defective and that a full disqualification order could be granted either under the standard claim in the originating process for "further or other relief" or, if necessary, as a result of an amendment to the summons.[19]

12–14 At the time, the decision in *Gower Enterprises (No.2)* raised two immediate problems. First, it was unclear what impact it would have on all the other current s.6 proceedings that had been brought in line with the established practice. An obvious solution was for the court to allow the amendment of any originating summons so affected. However, if following *Gower Enterprises (No.2)*, a selective order was not a disqualification order, it was arguable that a selective originating summons was liable to be struck out as disclosing no cause of action. If this had been right, then the Secretary of State or official receiver would be forced to commence fresh proceedings. As in the majority of the affected cases the two-year time limit for commencing proceedings had already expired, it would then have been necessary for the Secretary of State to apply for permission under s.7(2) to commence a new set of proceedings out of time.[20] This particular point was taken by counsel for the defendant in *Re Seagull Manufacturing Co Ltd, Official Receiver v Slinn*,[21] a case decided a fortnight after *Gower Enterprises (No.2)*. No doubt fully appreciating its ramifications, Blackburne J. simply turned the argument on its head and refused to dismiss the official receiver's originating summons. On the assumption, following *Gower Enterprises (No.2)*, that there was no jurisdiction to make a selective order, he reasoned that the court would be bound, as a matter of course, to make a blanket order in the terms of the original s.1(1) once the official receiver had established the conditions for disqualification set out in s.6(1). The fact that the order sought in the originating summons

[18] [1994] 1 B.C.L.C. 574 at 581–582.

[19] An amendment that the judge would have been minded to permit notwithstanding that the two–year time limit under s.7(2) had expired.

[20] On applications for permission under s.7(2) generally, see Ch.8.

[21] [1996] 1 B.C.L.C. 51.

omitted any reference to paras (b) and (c) was of no consequence, as the court would be obliged to make a blanket order if the case against the defendant was made out. Blackburne J. went further, suggesting that it would be sufficient for the originating summons simply to ask for "an order under s.6 of the CDDA, full stop, without condescending to set out . . . what that order should contain". If the summons, having asked for such an order, then went on to describe such order inaccurately, this would not affect the relief that was in fact being sought. Blackburne J.'s ruling in *Seagull Manufacturing* quickly cleared away any of the difficulties that *Gower Enterprises (No.2)* appeared to have raised in relation to the form and contents of originating process in other s.6 proceedings then pending. Nevertheless, the practice adopted thereafter in the civil courts was for the claimant to seek an order under the relevant section (usually ss.6 or 8) and then to set out the full terms of the original s.1. This remains the practice with regard to the current s.1.

12–15 The second and more pressing problem concerned all the existing disqualification orders, still in force when *Gower Enterprises (No.2)* was decided, that had been drawn up according to the old practice. The apparent effect of the decision was that these orders were not strictly disqualification orders at all! This presented the authorities with a difficulty where they were seeking to prosecute a person for breach of the order under s.13 of the CDDA. Could breach of a selective order found criminal and/or civil proceedings under ss.13–15 of the CDDA? The Secretary of State's response was to apply in several of these cases for the original order to be corrected using the so-called "slip rule" so as to include reference to all four paragraphs of the original s.1(1).

Once an order has been drawn up and entered, the court has power both under its inherent jurisdiction and pursuant to CPR r.40.12 (formerly RSC Ord.20, r.11, and, in the County Court, CCR Ord.15, r.5) to correct accidental errors in its order and/or to ensure that its order reflects the intention of the court.[22] This power is discretionary and will not be exercised if injustice would be caused as a result. The first reported case in which the court used the slip rule to correct a selective disqualification order was *Re Brian Sheridan Cars Ltd, Official Receiver v Sheridan*.[23] In this case, the deputy judge held that it was appropriate to use the slip rule in RSC Ord.20, r.11 to correct a disqualification order previously made under CDDA s.6. The defendant was not prejudiced by the correction because he had clearly assumed that the original order was valid (he had made an application for permission to act as a director of certain specified companies) and the addition of a reference to paras (b) and (c) made no odds because he had not acted as a liquidator, administrator or receiver etc. since the date of the original order.[24] In

[22] For the position pre-CPR see e.g. *Thynne v Thynne* [1955] P. 272.

[23] [1996] 1 B.C.L.C. 327. See also *Secretary of State for Trade and Industry v Edwards* [1997] B.C.C. 222.

[24] Correcting the order would be prejudicial if since the date of the original order the person has engaged in activities covered by s.1(1) but not by the order itself. Even then, it is arguable that the prejudice could be avoided by the grant of retrospective and prospective permission to engage in those activities at the time of the correction.

granting the application, the court backdated the correction to the date of the original order.[25] A question having been raised as to whether r.7.47 of the Insolvency Rules applied, the deputy judge added that he would have been prepared to correct the order under r.7.47 and the court's inherent jurisdiction as well.[26]

12–16 In upholding Harman J.'s decision at first instance in *Re Cannonquest Ltd, Official Receiver v Hannan*,[27] the Court of Appeal appears to have resolved most of the remaining problems that arose in the wake of *Gower Enterprises (No.2)*. This case again involved an application to correct a selective order using the slip rule. The defendant was disqualified under s.6 for a period of six years in 1991. It was subsequently alleged that he had acted in breach of the order and criminal proceedings had been commenced against him under s.13. The immediate result was the same as that in the *Brian Sheridan* case. Harman J. corrected the order and ruled that it should be treated as having effect from the date of its original pronouncement in its corrected form. In the judge's view, this in no way prejudiced the defendant. It was not a case of the court retrospectively rendering him criminally liable by correcting the original order. It was simply that the order failed to express the court's true intention, which was to make a disqualification order pursuant to the CDDA. Developing the point taken by Blackburne J. in *Seagull Manufacturing*, Harman J. added that the court could make an order expressed simply to be a disqualification order without the need to recite in full the words in s.1(1)(a)–(d). This is because the scope of the ban is defined by the *statute* rather than by the order. The Court of Appeal also decided that, while the order in *Cannonquest* was imperfect and incomplete, it was nonetheless a disqualification order, which was effective to disqualify the defendant from doing what was set out in the imperfect order. This conclusion was based on two foundations. The first was that the judge's power to disqualify and the extent of the prohibition rested on the statute. The judge had intended to pronounce and had pronounced a period of disqualification. The second was the well-established principle that orders of a court of unlimited jurisdiction should be obeyed unless and until they are set aside. The same principle applied to require obedience to an order that said it was a disqualification order, even if on paper, the full terms of

[25] While the deputy judge took the view that a correction under the slip rule must logically be backdated to the date of the original order, he added obiter that he would otherwise have been prepared to backdate the alteration using the power in RSC Ord.42, r.3, on which see *Kuwait Airways Corp v Iraqi Airways Co (No.2)* [1994] 1 W.L.R. 985. Note however that there is no CPR equivalent to RSC Ord.42, r.3 permitting the backdating of orders. If corrected disqualification orders had been made to run from a later date (e.g. the actual date on which the court sanctioned the alteration), this would have given rise to the problem of prior breach (i.e. a breach of the corrected order falling within the terms added by the court under the slip rule occurring before the date of the correction). Furthermore, without some downward variation of the period of disqualification, the court would inadvertently have been increasing its length. Fortunately, the Court of Appeal decision in *Re Cannonquest Ltd, Official Receiver v Hannan* (see text) arguably removed the need for the court to vary selective orders using the slip rule.

[26] The precise applicability and interrelationship of the rules of court, the Insolvency Rules and the Disqualification Rules in disqualification proceedings has been something of a vexed question: see Ch.7 for a full discussion.

[27] [1997] B.C.C. 644.

the order were not fully and accurately set out.[28] As such, it was inconceivable that an application to set aside a selective order on a technicality could ever succeed if the defendant would be left undisqualified as a result. Morritt L.J. added that, even if he was wrong on the first point, namely that the order as orally pronounced was a disqualification order, there would still be power to correct the order under the slip rule. Waller L.J. did not deal with this further point and Simon Brown L.J. expressly reserved his position.

12–17 In *Cannonquest*, the Court of Appeal was not dealing with the position in respect of conduct that contravened *part* of the prohibition in s.1(1) but where the relevant part (typically paras (b)–(c)) was not included in the terms of the imperfect order. Thus, the case is only direct authority for the proposition that an imperfect disqualification order is effective to prohibit the person from engaging in activities *described in the terms of the order* (typically activities proscribed by original s.1(1)(a) and (d)). However, the reasoning goes further and supports the proposition that a selective order is an effective, albeit imperfect, disqualification order that disqualifies the relevant person from acting in all the ways described in s.1(1). The logic of the decision is that if an order is expressed to be made under any of the various powers in the CDDA, then it will be treated as a blanket order in the terms of s.1(1) whether it expressly recites the contents of paras (a) to (d) in full or not. In the light of this, there is no necessity for the court to correct any remaining selective orders under the slip rule.[29] After *Cannonquest*, it makes little sense for the persons concerned to incur the cost of contesting any further slip rule motions pursued by the Secretary of State. Although the position is now fairly settled it is still advisable when drawing up a disqualification order to take a "belt and braces" approach and recite the prohibition in s.1 in full.

12–18 The cases discussed so far in connection with the slip rule were s.6 cases brought in the High Court. An important question is whether or not the criminal courts have a similar power to correct selective disqualification orders previously made under either ss.2 or 5. In *R. v Cole, Lees and Birch*,[30] the defendants were convicted in the Liverpool Crown Court of acting as directors of a company which was known by a prohibited name contrary to s.216 of the Insolvency Act 1986. Exercising the court's power under CDDA s.2, the trial judge made disqualification orders against all three defendants. However, the orders as orally pronounced were selective. Two of the defendants were only disqualified from acting as directors. In other words, the orders pronounced in their cases made no

[28] See *Isaacs v Robertson* [1985] A.C. 97 at 101E–103F; *M v Home Office* [1994] 1 A.C. 377 at 423G–424D; *Credit Suisse v Allerdale Borough Council* [1996] 3 W.L.R. 894 at 919B–926H, 932E–939B. The High Court (which made the order in *Cannonquest*) and the Crown Court are both part of the Senior Courts and are generally regarded as courts of unlimited jurisdiction for this purpose.

[29] This was certainly the view of Simon Brown L.J. in *Cannonquest*. Given the passage of time, the issue is unlikely to arise much, if at all, in the civil courts. It is just conceivable that there could still be the odd order made during the 1990s for the maximum period of 15 years (or at least for a period towards the top end of the upper bracket) which might need to be cured by reference to the reasoning in *Cannonquest*.

[30] [1998] 2 B.C.L.C. 234.

express reference to any of the activities described in the original s.1(1)(b)–(d). The third defendant was disqualified from being a director, liquidator or administrator or a receiver or manager of a company's property but there was no reference in the order pronounced to the prohibition from being concerned or taking part in the promotion, formation or management of a company set out in the original s.1(1)(d). On their appeal against conviction and disqualification, the Court of Appeal (Criminal Division) decided that the orders could be made valid by each appellant being generally disqualified in the full terms of s.1(1) from the date of sentence and for the periods stated by the judge. Thus, the actual result was the same as that in *Cannonquest*. What the Court of Appeal appears to have done was to accept that the sentence as passed was a disqualification order (albeit one imperfectly pronounced) and, as in *Cannonquest*, to regularise the position by making it absolutely clear that the order was what it had always been. However, it is not entirely clear from the judgments on what basis the Court of Appeal achieved this result particularly when one bears in mind that, unlike Harman J. in *Cannonquest*, it was not exercising an original jurisdiction. The following explanation is suggested.

12–19 The Court of Appeal (Criminal Division) unquestionably has power under the Criminal Appeals Act 1968 s.11(3) to quash an imperfect disqualification order and replace it with any order that the Crown Court could have made when it originally dealt with the matter. The Crown Court has an inherent power analogous to the slip rule enabling it to cure irregularities in its own orders.[31] As such, it was open to the Court of Appeal to make the order that the Crown Court could have made. The argument that s.11(3) of the Criminal Appeals Act 1968 does not permit the Court of Appeal (Criminal Division) to make an order if its effect would be to increase the appellant's original sentence was considered and rejected by the Court of Appeal. It is suggested that the answer to that argument is the same answer as the one given in the civil context by the Court of Appeal (Civil Division) in *Cannonquest*. The original order having been, and having always been a disqualification order, the use of the slip rule to "perfect" the imperfections in the order as pronounced (and/or, in the civil courts, as drawn up on paper) does not retrospectively increase the sentence or impose a new penalty or disqualification. It remains to be seen what is the effect of purported "leave to act" orders made by the criminal courts at the same time as they impose disqualification orders, apparently on the basis that their attention is not drawn to their lack of jurisdiction in this respect under CDDA ss.1 and 17.

[31] *R. v Michael* [1976] Q.B. 414; *R. v Saville* [1981] Q.B. 12. In the case of a formal variation of the original order which alters the substance of the penalty, the Crown Court can only vary the order within 56 days (previously 28 days) beginning with the day on which it was imposed: see Powers of Criminal Courts (Sentencing) Act 2000 s.155(1) as amended by the Criminal Justice and Immigration Act 2008 Sch.8(3) para.28(2)(a) with effect from July 14, 2008 (formerly the Supreme Court Act 1981 s.47(2) now renamed the "Senior Courts Act 1981"; *R. v Menocal* [1980] A.C. 598 (a case on an earlier incarnation of the Crown Court's statutory power then to be found in the Courts Act 1971 s.11(2); *R. v Bukhari* [2008] EWCA Crim 2915. A magistrates' court can only correct orders made in criminal proceedings under the Magistrates' Courts Act 1980 s.142(1). This power is analogous to the Crown Court's power of review under Powers of Criminal Courts (Sentencing) Act 2000 s.155(1).

12–20 In *R. v Ward*[32] the two defendants applied to the Court of Appeal (Criminal Division) to amend an earlier order of the same court. The sentence pronounced orally by the Court of Appeal on a reference by the Attorney General[33] had been that the defendants were disqualified from being directors of public companies. As drawn up, the orders stated simply that each defendant was "disqualified from being a director of a company" for a period of seven years. The orders contained no reference to the other prohibitions contained in the original s.1(1)(a)–(d). The court decided that the orders could not be amended by restricting the prohibition to "public" companies (as orally pronounced) because this would produce a result that the court had no jurisdiction to reach. Equally, however, it decided that it should not amend the order to set out the prohibitions contained in the original s.1(1)(a)–(d) in full. In the light of the all the circumstances and the fact that there had already been criticism by the European Court of Human Rights of delay on art.6 grounds in relation to one of the defendants,[34] the decision not to amend the order to impose the full prohibitions in the original s.1(1)(a)–(d) was, perhaps, understandable. However, this left the status of the order in doubt. Presumably the prohibition expressly stated in the order (at least) was valid.

12–21 Although the decision in *Gower Enterprises (No.2)* potentially created a number of problems, these have been resolved. The basic premise that the court lacked jurisdiction to "pick and choose" and was required to pronounce a disqualification order in the comprehensive terms of the original s.1(1) is now reflected in the wording of the current s.1.

12–22 Despite the problems raised by the *Gower Enterprises* decision, the DTI decided not to appeal it and a number of compelling reasons can be found within the overall scheme of the CDDA to support the conclusion that the court reached:

(1) The focus in s.6 is on the previous conduct of the defendant *as a director*. If the court finds that the defendant's past conduct as a director is such as to make him unfit to be concerned in the management of a company it is obliged to make a disqualification order even if, for example, it considers that the defendant has since learned his lesson and is not now unfit. It is difficult to see how the court could have been left with no discretion as to the making of a disqualification order under s.6 and yet, at the same time, a discretion as to which activities could be prohibited within the terms of the order.
(2) As the focus in s.6 is on the defendant's conduct as a director, it is difficult to imagine circumstances in which the conduct, for example, of a liquidator acting as such, could ever be taken into account as a ground of unfitness on an application under that section. If conduct in other capacities is likely to be irrelevant, it is difficult to see when in a s.6 case the court would ever be able to disqualify a defendant from engaging in the activities described in the original s.1(1)(b) and (c). Moreover, if there were a discretion as to the scope of

[32] [2001] EWCA Crim 1648, [2002] B.C.C. 953.
[33] *Attorney General's References Nos.14, 15 and 16 of 1995, The Times*, April 10, 1997.
[34] *Howarth v United Kingdom* (2001) 31 E.H.R.R. 37.

the order then the court would first have to be satisfied that there was evidence of unfitness in relation to *each* of the four capacities set out in s.1(1) before making an order in relation to that capacity. The notion of a discretion sits uncomfortably alongside the wording of s.6 where only conduct qua director is relevant. The same considerations apply mutatis mutandis to CDDA ss.2–5 but on the assumption that the focus in cases under those provisions will be on a particular offence or default committed by a person acting in a particular capacity (e.g. as a director or manager).

(3) In conferring various powers (and in ss.6 and 9A, a duty) to make a disqualification order, the CDDA focuses exclusively on particular types of conduct, for example, conduct qua director (ss.6 and 9A), an offence (ss.2, 4(1)(a) and 5), persistent default (s.3) and other specified conduct (s.4(1)(b)). However, it draws no express connection between the conduct triggering the power or duty to make a disqualification order and specific paragraphs of s.1(1). Thus, for example, in a case where the conduct triggering the making of an order is conduct as a liquidator (e.g. under s.4(1)(b)), the CDDA does not expressly limit the form of order to a prohibition under s.1(1)(b) alone. On the contrary, once the relevant power or duty is triggered, the CDDA provides that the court may, or shall, make a disqualification order as defined. These wider schematic factors support the reasoning in *Gower Enterprises (No.2)*.

(4) The construction of the original s.1(1) favoured in *Gower Enterprises (No.2)* sits more naturally alongside the court's power to grant permission to act conferred by s.17. Section 6 of the CDDA, which obliges the court to make a disqualification order, allows no scope for consideration of the defendant's *present* activities. The legislative scheme is such that evidence of that nature can only be put before the court on an application for permission to act. The overall rationale of the regulatory regime established by the CDDA is that the court is empowered or obliged to make a full disqualification order based on the defendant's *past* conduct and the width of the overall prohibition is tempered by the court's ability to grant permission. The idea of a blanket prohibition is also consistent with the historical evolution of s.1(1).[35]

(5) The making of a disqualification order has wider effects under other legislation.[36] The existence of these "knock-on" provisions gives considerable credence to the theory that parliament intended the prohibition to be comprehensive and wide-ranging.

12–23 The comprehensive nature of the prohibition coupled with the lack of jurisdiction to make selective orders has serious consequences for a person who holds directorships in several companies and is found to be unfit in relation to just one

[35] Note, in particular, the amendments to the former disqualification provisions introduced by the Companies Act 1981 ss.93(1B) and 94(1) the purpose of which was to extend the scope of the prohibition to include reference to liquidators and receivers. The incremental way in which the prohibition has developed tends to support the view that it is a blanket ban which has gradually expanded in scope from the time when the Companies Act 1929 was enacted down to the present.

[36] See further Ch.14.

or two of them. He will find himself unable to continue as a director or manager of companies in relation to which there has been no complaint about his conduct. The only course of action available to a person faced with this situation is to make an application for permission to act notwithstanding disqualification.

"Specific excepted company" orders

12–24 The effect of s.1 is that the disqualified person can no longer act as a director or participate in the management of *any* company.[37] This does not just apply to the person's position in the company or companies with which the proceedings were directly concerned. It means that he will be forced to resign any other directorships or managerial positions which he holds. This is so even where there is no complaint about his conduct in relation to those other companies. The blanket nature of the ban can be justified with reference to the areas of policy discussed in Ch.2 and the schematic factors discussed above in 12–22. Even so, certain courts (but not all courts) have the power to waive the full effect of an order by granting the disqualified person permission to take part in the management of a specified company or companies. The availability of this power means that the court can take into account whether the activities contemplated by the disqualified person pose any risk to the public. The law and practice relating to applications for permission to act is considered generally in Ch.15. Suffice it to say for now that the procedure on applications for permission is governed by s.17 of the CDDA. If the disqualified person wishes to participate in the management of a specified company, the basic position is that he should make a formal application for permission to act notwithstanding disqualification. It is common practice in s.6 proceedings for the defendant to make an application to be heard immediately after the making of a disqualification order.[38] However, there have been cases in which the court was prepared to exclude specified companies from the scope of the order even in the absence of a formal application for permission. These cases suggest that the court may be able to make what can be described as a "specific excepted company" order under s.1 without the need for an application for permission. As explained below, the manner in which the law has developed suggests that, in truth, the courts do not have this power.

12–25 The approach of making a "specific excepted company" order was first taken by Mervyn Davies J. in *Re Majestic Recording Studios Ltd*,[39] a case decided under the former unfit conduct provisions in ss.295–301 of the Companies Act 1985. The judge disqualified the defendant for a five-year period on the ground that his conduct in relation to five specified companies made him unfit. However, he included a proviso in the order to the effect that he would be allowed to act as a director of a sixth company, Morton Music Ltd (which had not featured in the proceedings) during the five-year period provided that: (a) an independent

[37] For the definition of company in this context and territorial limitations see Ch.14.

[38] A practice encouraged by the Court of Appeal in *Re Dicetrade Ltd, Secretary of State for Trade and Industry v Worth* [1994] 2 B.C.L.C. 113 at 116. See also *TLL Realisations Ltd, Secretary of State for Trade and Industry v Collins* [2000] B.C.C. 998 (Park J.) at 1003, 1007.

[39] [1989] B.C.L.C. 1.

accountant approved by the court acted as his co-director throughout; and that (b) three years' worth of outstanding accounts were filed by a specified date. The defendant indicated through counsel that he would not oppose disqualification as long as he was allowed to continue as a director of Morton Music Ltd. Affidavit evidence concerning Morton Music Ltd had been filed at a late stage in the proceedings. It appears that the judge was content to dispense with the requirement for a formal application for permission although he did express some doubt as to whether there was jurisdiction to make a "specific excepted company" order under ss.295–301 of the Companies Act 1985.[40]

Shortly afterwards, Browne-Wilkinson V.C. achieved a similar result in *Re Lo-Line Electric Motors Ltd*.[41] In that case, the court disqualified the defendant for three years but allowed him to remain as a director of two family companies subject to a number of conditions. Browne-Wilkinson V.C. appears to have assumed that the Companies Act 1985 s.295 gave him the power to make a "specific excepted company" order without the need for a formal application under s.295(6), the then equivalent of CDDA s.17. Again, affidavit evidence from the defendant and the auditors concerning the two family companies was before the court. This approach appears to have been followed in a number of s.6 cases although it is not clear from the reports whether the court was simply dispensing with the requirement for a formal application under s.17.[42] The entire phenomenon can probably be attributed to the pragmatism of both the judiciary and the DTI. It should not be seen as the court assuming a general jurisdiction to grant a partial disqualification order. The cases referred to were decided almost exclusively in the Chancery Division of the High Court. This court has the power to wind up any company in England and Wales and, at that time, had jurisdiction under s.17(1) to hear applications for permission brought in any disqualification case proceeding before it.[43] If affidavit evidence concerning the companies in respect of which permission is sought is before the court (as was the case in *Majestic Recording*) and the Secretary of State adopts a neutral position, it makes sense for the disqualifying court to assume jurisdiction under s.17(1) and dispense with the need for a formal notice of application so that costs can be saved.[44] Thus, strictly speaking, the "specific excepted company" order is a full disqualification order coupled with a further order for permission notwithstanding the disqualification order.[45]

12–26 Unfortunately, it is not open to the criminal courts to adopt this convenient practice when exercising their powers to disqualify under CDDA ss.2 and 5. This is

[40] The applicable provisions regarding the scope of disqualification orders and applications for permission in *Majestic Recording* were Companies Act 1985 s.295 and Sch.12 Pt I para.4. The current provisions in CDDA ss.1 and 17 are identical in all material respects.

[41] [1988] Ch. 477. This case was also decided under the old Companies Act provisions.

[42] See, e.g. *Re Chartmore Ltd* [1990] B.C.L.C. 673; *Re Godwin Warren Control Systems Plc* [1993] B.C.L.C. 80; *Secretary of State for Trade and Industry v Palfreman* [1995] 2 B.C.L.C. 301. See also D. Milman, "Partial Disqualification Orders" (1991) 12 Co. Law. 224.

[43] As to the current jurisdictional position regarding the grant of permission see further Ch.15.

[44] This is the basis on which the Court of Session proceeded in *Secretary of State for Trade and Industry v Palfreman* [1995] 2 B.C.L.C. 301 at 302.

[45] Any other explanation falls foul of *Gower Enterprises (No.2)*: see from 12–13.

because s.17 does not confer jurisdiction on the criminal courts to hear applications for permission. The only course for a person disqualified in a criminal court is to make a free standing application for permission to a civil court having jurisdiction under s.17. It should be possible to mount an urgent application for interim permission. The ability of the courts to suspend the effect of an order so as to give a disqualified person time to apply elsewhere for permission is discussed further below.

12–27 In the case of disqualification undertakings, the current practice of the Insolvency Service in cases under CDDA s.7(2A) is to require certain parts of disqualification undertakings to be in standard form.[46] This form sets out the terms of CDDA s.1A in full. However, it must follow from the law in relation to disqualification orders that the Secretary of State has no power to agree an undertaking in anything other than the full terms of s.1A. The same is true of a relevant regulator in relation to competition disqualification undertakings under s.9B. In the event that the undertaking did not set out the full terms of the relevant prohibition, it would be a matter of contract law as to whether there had, in fact, been offer and acceptance of a disqualification undertaking (in the relevant form under ss.1A or 9B) and, in an appropriate case, declaratory relief could no doubt be sought.[47]

COMMENCEMENT AND COMING INTO EFFECT OF DISQUALIFICATION ORDERS AND UNDERTAKINGS

Orders made prior to April 2, 2001

12–28 The former s.1 provided that the period of disqualification ran from the date on which the court made the order. In other words, if X was disqualified by the court for six years on April 1, 1999 the six-year period ran from that date and would have expired on March 31, 2005. This rule applied to all disqualification orders made by a court pursuant to a substantive power contained in the CDDA (i.e. CDDA ss.2–5, 6, 8 and 10). To modify the above example, this meant that if X was disqualified by a criminal court under s.2 following his conviction of a relevant offence and he also received a custodial sentence, the disqualification ran from the date of pronouncement of sentence not the date of X's release from prison.[48] One question, discussed further below, that was of considerable practical importance, concerned the extent to which the court had any power to direct that a disqualification order would not come into effect until some time after it was pronounced (e.g. pending either the hearing of an appeal against the order or the determination of an application for permission to act).

[46] For an example see the appendices.

[47] On the extent to which disqualification undertakings can be treated as private law contracts see *Re INS Realisations Ltd, Secretary of State for Trade and Industry v Jonkler* [2006] EWHC 135 (Ch), [2006] 1 W.L.R. 3433 especially at [31].

[48] *R. v Bradley* [1961] 1 W.L.R. 398. The provision considered in that case was the Companies Act 1948 s.188. Even so, the fact that the period of disqualification runs concurrently with any period of imprisonment imposed on the disqualified person has been the subject of criticism in the past: see the Report of the Jenkins Committee, Cmnd.1749 (1962), para.81. The position under the CDDA can be contrasted with that in Australia under s.206B(2)(b) of the Corporations Act 2001 (Cth) where, if the person is sentenced to imprisonment, the period of disqualification only starts to run on his release.

Civil proceedings under CDDA ss.7, 8 and 9A

12–29 Proceedings under s.7(1) (in the High Court or a county court having winding up jurisdiction), and ss.8 or 9A (in the High Court) are governed by the Disqualification Rules. The former r.9, which was revoked with effect from April 2, 2001,[49] provided that a disqualification order in s.7(1) or s.8 proceedings took effect at the beginning of the 21st day after the day on which the order was made unless the court ordered otherwise. The implication was that the period of disqualification ordered in these proceedings should generally run from the 21st day after the date of order and not from the date of the order itself. Thus, at first sight, r.9 appeared to conflict with the mandatory terms of the original s.1(1) which defined a disqualification order as an order that the defendant shall not, without permission of the court, be a director etc. "for a specified period beginning with the date of the order".[50] This apparent conflict between r.9 and s.1 was considered and resolved by Evans-Lombe J. in *Secretary of State for Trade and Industry v Edwards*.[51] This case involved an application to amend a disqualification order. One amendment sought was to make the order reflect the entirety of the prohibitions contained in the original s.1(1)(a)–(d). The other amendment sought was to make the period of disqualification run from the date of the order rather than from 21 days after the order. This raised an issue as to the interaction of s.1 and r.9. The judge held that the two provisions did not conflict and that the effect of r.9 was merely to *suspend* the operation of the order for 21 days. The period of disqualification still ran from the date on which the court made the order even though, in relation to the first 21 days of the period, the disqualification was unenforceable. Thus, a suspension of the order's effect under r.9 was akin to a temporary stay. The relevant person was still treated as being disqualified while the stay remained in operation but the prohibition had no bite during that period. The court could abridge or extend the 21-day period.[52] Rule 9 served a useful purpose. The 21-day stay gave the disqualified person a short period of breathing space during which he could rearrange his affairs without being in breach of the disqualification order while he did so. In the absence of r.9, a person who was the subject of a disqualification order would have been faced with considerable practical difficulties in respect of any current directorships. By suspending the full operation of the order using r.9, the court could at least give the disqualified person time to resign those positions and, where necessary, to take steps in conjunction with the relevant company or companies to appoint a replacement.

[49] Insolvent Companies (Disqualification of Unfit Directors) Proceedings (Amendment) Rules 2001 (SI 2001/765) r.2.

[50] A view expressed by Chadwick J. in *Re Auto Electro and Powder Finishers*, April 5, 1995, Ch.D., unreported and echoed by Morritt L.J. in *Secretary of State for Trade and Industry v Bannister* [1996] 1 W.L.R. 118.

[51] [1997] B.C.C. 222.

[52] In *Re Travel Mondial (UK) Ltd* [1991] B.C.L.C. 120, Browne-Wilkinson V.C. extended the r.9 period so that the order took effect 21 days after personal service of the order on the director. In *Re T & D Services (Timber Preservation & Damp Proofing Contractors) Ltd* [1990] B.C.C. 592, Vinelott J. disqualified the defendant for ten years but deferred the operation of the order for two weeks to give him time to sort out the affairs of a company which had not featured in the proceedings. In *Re Ipcon Fashions Ltd* (1989) 5 B.C.C. 773, Hoffmann J. gave permission to a disqualified person to continue to act as a director for eight weeks to enable him to make alternative arrangements for the management of a company of which he remained director and manager at the date of trial.

12–30 Evans-Lombe J.'s view received support from the judgment of Harman J. in *Re Cannonquest Ltd, Official Receiver v Hannan*, another case in which rectification was sought with regard to the stated commencement of the order. The following explanation of r.9 was given by the judge:

> "The rule provides a perfectly sensible and practical provision that the man is to have a few days to put his house in order and be in a position to comply with the disqualification order pronounced against him, but that disqualification order shall run from the date of its pronouncement."[53]

It is important to realise that the suspended effect of the order under r.9 did not affect the time at which the order would expire. Thus, the shortening of the 21-day period did not bring forward the date on which the order would expire. The date of expiry of the disqualification was, as required by the then s.1, calculated from the date of the order.

Civil proceedings under CDDA ss.2(2)(a), 3, 4, 10

12–31 In cases brought in the civil courts seeking a disqualification order under any of CDDA ss.2(2)(a), 3 or 4, para.16.1 of the Disqualification Practice Direction brought the position into line with that under CDDA ss.7–8 by applying the wording used in r.9 to such proceedings. So far as orders under s.10 were concerned, the High Court would have had power to stay or suspend such an order under the Senior Courts Act 1981.[54] The position in the county courts in relation to s.10 was more problematic. The county courts are entirely creatures of statute and have no inherent jurisdiction as such. It is open to doubt whether a county court had any jurisdiction to stay an order other than that conferred by r.9 and the Disqualification Practice Direction.

Criminal proceedings

12–32 The Disqualification Rules do not apply to cases involving disqualification in the criminal courts. Even so, it appears that the Senior Courts Act 1981 s.47(1) conferred a power on the Crown Court to suspend the operation of a disqualification order similar to the power formerly contained in r.9. That provision has since been re-enacted in the Powers of Criminal Courts (Sentencing) Act 2000 s.154(1) which provides (as did its predecessor) that a sentence imposed, or other order made, by the Crown Court when dealing with an offender shall take effect from the beginning of the day on which it was imposed, unless the court otherwise directs. The similarity between this and the wording in r.9 is striking and it appears that it would have allowed the Crown Court, in much the same way, to suspend the operation of an order for a short period to enable the disqualified

[53] [1997] B.C.C. 644 at 649. While reaching no decision on the point, Morritt L.J. indicated in *Secretary of State for Trade and Industry v Bannister* [1996] 1 W.L.R. 118 that the rule-making authorities should direct attention to the question of whether or not r.9 was ultra vires the CDDA. The solution adopted by Evans-Lombe and Harman JJ. appears to have confounded any fears in this regard.

[54] *Secretary of State for Trade and Industry v Bannister* [1996] 1 W.L.R. 118. The Supreme Court Act 1981 was renamed the "Senior Courts Act 1981" by the Constitutional Reform Act 2005.

person to reorganise his affairs. It is conceivable that the Crown Court could also have exercised the power of suspension in what is now s.154(1) of the 2000 Act to enable a disqualified person to bring an application for permission to act before a civil court. This is a point of considerable importance bearing in mind that the criminal courts have no jurisdiction to hear applications for permission and are therefore unable to deal with the question of permission in the course of the main proceedings. In relation to CDDA ss.2 and 5, the magistrates' courts appear to have had no power which would have enabled them to postpone the full effect of a disqualification order until some time after the date of sentence.[55]

Was there a general power to stay or suspend a disqualification order under the inherent jurisdiction?

12–33 It should be apparent from the foregoing discussion that, prior to April 2, 2001, there was jurisdiction in the High Court, the county courts and the Crown Court to stay or suspend the operation of a disqualification order. In *Secretary of State for Trade and Industry v Bannister*[56] it was held that both the High Court and the Court of Appeal had power under their inherent jurisdiction to stay or suspend a disqualification order made in proceedings under ss.6 to 8 pending an appeal by the defendant.[57] However, in refusing the defendant's application for a stay, the Court of Appeal made it very clear that this inherent power was only to be exercised in exceptional circumstances. The following reasons were advanced in support of this conclusion:

(1) The whole purpose of the CDDA is to protect the public from those who by reason of their past conduct have shown themselves to be unfit to act as a director or in the management of a company. A relevant factor weighing against the exercise of the inherent power was that it would leave the public effectively unprotected. The Court of Appeal's approach in *Bannister* suggests that the paramount need to protect the public should generally outweigh any personal hardship that might be suffered by the defendant were a stay to be refused.[58]
(2) It is open to the civil courts having jurisdiction under s.17 to grant the defendant permission to act as a director etc. On an application for permission, the

[55] L.S. Sealy, "Company directors' disqualification—suspension of disqualification pending appeal" (1989) 5 Insolvency Law & Practice 102. A perusal of the Magistrates' Courts Rules 1981 and *Stone's Justices' Manual* confirms the view that there is no express power to stay the effect of an order although magistrates' courts can defer sentence or pass a suspended sentence. There appears to be no reason in principle why magistrates' courts should not have been able to stay a disqualification order albeit that they are creatures of statute and there is apparently no express power comparable to that available in the Crown Court under what is now the Powers of Criminal Courts (Sentencing) Act 2000.

[56] [1996] 1 W.L.R. 118.

[57] There being nothing in the CDDA to exclude the jurisdiction as statutorily recognised and preserved by the Senior Courts Act 1981 s.49(3).

[58] Those who regard the legislation as having primarily a penal objective would no doubt wish to give greater weight to the evidence of financial and personal hardship put forward by the defendant in this case. While the decision in *Bannister* can be criticised because it proceeds on the false assumption that there was a conflict between r.9 and s.1(1), the Court of Appeal's general approach, placing emphasis on the overall scheme and structure of the CDDA, is preferable to one that takes the personal consequences of disqualification as its starting point.

practice is to require the applicant to provide evidence in relation to his current activities and, in particular, the financial standing and management structure of any company with which he wishes to become or remain involved. The court can also grant permission subject to conditions. As such, an application for permission provides the court with a more appropriate means of balancing the personal interests of the disqualified person over against the overriding need to protect the public than an application for a stay. Thus, the discretion to stay or suspend a disqualification order pursuant to the inherent power was, in practice, only to be exercised in exceptional circumstances where the alternative remedy provided by s.17 would be inadequate.[59]

12–34 It is important to add that in *Bannister* the Court of Appeal assumed that there was a conflict between the requirement in the original s.1(1) that the period of disqualification commenced on the date that the order was pronounced and the operation of r.9. Ultimately the point was left open by Morritt L.J. in the leading judgments in both *Bannister* and *Cannonquest*. However, the approach taken by Harman J. at first instance in *Cannonquest* and Evans-Lombe J. in *Secretary of State for Trade and Industry v Edwards* suggests that it was open to the High Court (and a county court), as a matter of jurisdiction, to stay the effect of a disqualification order made under CDDA ss.6 or 8 by virtue of r.9. The same power was conferred on the courts in civil proceedings under ss.2, 3 and 4 by reason of para.16.1 of the Disqualification Practice Direction. The same could also be said of the Crown Court's power to stay orders under s.154(1) of the Powers of Criminal Courts (Sentencing) Act 2000 (formerly s.47(1) of the Senior Courts Act 1981).

Orders made on and after April 2, 2001

12–35 As a result of changes flowing from the current s.1, the position regarding disqualification orders made on and after April 2, 2001 is much more straightforward. The power of the court, in effect, to stay a disqualification order, is now expressly set out in s.1(2) (as amended). This states that, unless the court otherwise orders, the period of disqualification imposed by the order, shall begin at the end of the period of 21 days beginning with the date of the order. Rule 9 of the Disqualification Rules was repealed with effect from the same date. Accordingly:

(1) The power to stay the order in s.1(2) means that there is now no need to consider alternative powers to stay orders. Every court making a disqualification order has power to direct when the period of disqualification will come into force and start to run.

[59] Morritt L.J. described as exceptional circumstances, "... the extreme case in which the court below went badly wrong and the very existence of the disqualification order causes irreparable harm to the person apparently disqualified". This meant that in practical terms the question of a stay under the inherent jurisdiction invariably had to be taken to the Court of Appeal, a point well-illustrated by *Re Continental Assurance Co of London Plc* [1997] 1 B.C.L.C. 48 affirmed sub nom. *Secretary of State for Trade and Industry v Burrows*, July 4, 1996, CA, unreported.

(2) The apparent tension between the original s.1 and r.9 has been swept away.
(3) In the event that the court delays the time at which the disqualification will come into force this will not result in the period of actual disqualification being cut down. This contrasts with the position under the old provisions. Prior to April 2, 2001, the practical operation of r.9 of the Disqualification Rules and the original s.1 was that a person disqualified by the court for a three-year period would be disqualified, in most cases, and assuming the 21-day period set out in r.9 was not altered by the court, for a period of three years less 21 days.

12–36 It is suggested that the approach in *Bannister* should still be used as a guide to how the power in the current s.1(2) should be exercised. Thus, it is generally more appropriate for the court to grant interim permission to act rather than stay the order. The advantage of using s.17 from a schematic perspective is that the disqualification can take full effect on the date of the order, which gives priority to the protective aspect of the CDDA.[60] If a director needs permission to act for specific companies only, a general suspension of the disqualification order, even for a short period of time, seems to go too far. This approach also fits better with the obligation to file particulars of the disqualification order for registration, a requirement (discussed below) that is not affected by suspension of the order's effect. It is arguable that the criminal courts should be prepared to exercise their power to stay more liberally than the civil courts given that the criminal courts have no power to grant permission to act. However, the answer to this point is that it is possible to get before the civil courts very quickly on an emergency basis and, if necessary, seek an order for interim permission. This leaves the issue of "knock on" disqualifications that flow from the fact of disqualification under the CDDA. In some cases, there is no power in the relevant legislation to relieve from the "knock on" disqualification. Where this is so, it is necessary to consider carefully whether or not the postponement of the coming into effect of the disqualification order will also postpone the coming into effect of the "knock on" disqualification.

Interim permission

12–37 The upshot of *Secretary of State for Trade and Industry v Bannister* is that while the High Court and Court of Appeal retain a residual power to stay the full effect of a disqualification order, the courts should generally fall back on the scheme of the CDDA and, where appropriate, grant interim permission rather than a stay. As a means of dealing with the situation pending: (a) an appeal against the disqualification order; or (b) the hearing of an application for permission to act, this

[60] The approach taken on this question in Australian disqualification cases has been similar to that in *Bannister*: see e.g. *Tolj v O'Connor* (1988) 13 A.C.L.R. 653; *Hunter v Corporate Affairs Commission (NSW)* (1988) 13 A.C.L.R. 250; *Gray v Commissioner for Corporate Affairs (Vic)* (1988) 13 A.C.L.R. 516; *Dwyer v NCSC (No.2)* (1989) 14 A.C.L.R. 595 although some doubts were expressed by Young J. about the appropriateness of granting interim permission as opposed to a stay in *Blunt v Corporate Affairs Commission (NSW)* (1988) 13 A.C.L.R. 648 at 652.

approach has much to commend it. The question of interim permission is considered further in Ch.15.

Undertakings

12–38 In the case of disqualification undertakings falling within CDDA s.7(2A), the usual practice of the Insolvency Service is to accept an offer of a disqualification undertaking if it provides that the relevant period of disqualification will begin 21 days after acceptance of the undertaking by the Secretary of State. This is by analogy with the position regarding disqualification orders under s.1(2). The 21-day period should be sufficient to enable the disqualified person to make any required application to the court for permission to act and the Insolvency Service will not usually agree to a longer period giving the disqualified person more time to prepare the application. Of course, this system depends on the fact of acceptance being communicated to the person offering the undertaking as soon as possible after the Secretary of State has formally accepted it. There seems no reason to suppose that practice under s.8(2A) or s.9B would be any different.

12–39 It is suggested that the court has no general power to "stay" an undertaking once it has come into force. Any jurisdiction to stay an undertaking has to be sought in CDDA s.8A. Section 8A(1)(a) confers power on the court to reduce the period for which an undertaking is to be in force. Section 8A(1)(b) confers power on the court to order that an undertaking (not the period of disqualification) is to cease to be in force. In effect, this is a power to discharge an undertaking in its entirety. The following points can be made about the jurisdiction in s.8A:

(1) A reduction in the period of disqualification, as provided for by s.8A(1)(a), is not the same as a stay. The period specified in a disqualification undertaking equates to the period specified in a disqualification order, referred to in s.1(1). The court may reduce this period (e.g. from six years to five years), but it is not empowered to change the date from which the period of disqualification specified in the undertaking begins. However, against this, and as a matter of literal wording, it might be said that a stay would have the effect of reducing the period for which the undertaking is in force.
(2) An order made under s.8A(1)(b), providing for the undertaking to cease to be in force, is a final act of a "once and for all" nature. Again, it is difficult to treat this provision as conferring jurisdiction to stay.
(3) Moreover, there is no need for a stay mechanism. The availability of interim permission and the individual's freedom to choose the point at which the undertaking is offered are themselves adequate tools for avoiding injustice. As mentioned above, the current practice of the Secretary of State in cases brought under CDDA ss.6 or 8 cases is to agree undertakings which are expressed not to come into force until 21 days after the offer of the undertaking is accepted by the Secretary of State.

12–40 Whether or not, as a matter of jurisdiction, there is power in the court to stay an undertaking, it will rarely be appropriate in any event, as a matter of discretion, to stay an undertaking:

(1) In the case of an appeal from a disqualification order the more appropriate course will usually be to seek permission to act pending the hearing of the appeal.[61] The same should apply by analogy to cases where there is an application to the court, in effect, to review an undertaking.
(2) In cases where permission to act notwithstanding disqualification is to be sought and there are concerns about time, the director may seek interim permission (in cases brought under s.17), although this should be in exceptional circumstances only, for example, where the difficulty in bringing on a s.17 application lies with the court but the application is otherwise ready for hearing. There is no reason to think that (for example) the Charity Commissioners would not grant interim permission for a fixed period in an appropriate case.[62]
(3) Finally, it should be noted that an offer of an undertaking is a voluntary act by the director. If he does not wish to make such an offer or if he does not wish to make an offer under which the undertaking comes into force at a specific time he does not have to do so.

12–41 **Parties subject to more than one period of disqualification**

Where a disqualification order is made against a person who is already subject to such an order or to a disqualification undertaking, CDDA s.1(3) provides that the respective periods shall run concurrently. Where a disqualification undertaking is accepted by a person who is already subject to such an undertaking or to a disqualification order, CDDA s.1A(3) provides that the respective periods shall also run concurrently. Modified provisions are applied to insolvent partnerships by the Insolvent Partnerships Order 1994[63] art.16 and Sch.8 with similar effect.

REGISTRATION OF ORDERS AND UNDERTAKINGS

12–42 Section 18(1) of the CDDA[64] empowers the Secretary of State to make regulations requiring officers of courts to furnish him with particulars of: (a) all disqualification orders made; (b) any action taken by a court in consequence of which such an order or a disqualification undertaking is varied or ceases to be in force; or (c) any permission granted by a court for a disqualified person to act in a prohibited way notwithstanding the order. The current regulations, which came into effect on October 1, 2009, are the Companies (Disqualification Orders) Regulations 2009.[65] The effect of these regulations is that particulars of the matters referred to above must be

[61] See, e.g. *Secretary of State for Trade and Industry v Bannister* [1996] 1 W.L.R. 118; *Re Continental Assurance Co of London Plc* [1997] 1 B.C.L.C. 48. It should be noted however that some "knock on" prohibitions are absolute and not subject to any relieving power. See further Ch.14.
[62] Under Charities Act 1993 s.72(4).
[63] SI 1994/2421 as subsequently amended.
[64] As amended by Insolvency Act 2000 s.4 and Sch.4 para.13.
[65] SI 2009/2471 revoking, replacing and consolidating SI 2001/967 as amended by SI 2002/1834 and 2004/1940.

notified to Companies House on the appropriate prescribed form by the relevant officer as designated by reg.6 of the 2009 Regulations. This must be done within 14 days of the order being made or permission being granted or an order or undertaking being varied or ceasing to be in force.[66] By CDDA s.18(2), the Secretary of State (acting by the Registrar of Companies) is required to maintain a register of disqualification orders and of cases in which permission to act has been granted. The register, which was first established under s.29 of the Companies Act 1976, is open to public inspection.[67] There is no provision for registration of a disqualification order made under s.12. As regards Northern Ireland disqualification orders made under Pt II of the Companies (Northern Ireland) Order 1989,[68] an obligation to register such orders, and any grant of permission to act in relation to any such order, applies to the extent that particulars of the order made and permission to act granted were received by the Secretary of State on or after April 2, 2001.[69] There is a permissive power in relation to registration of Northern Ireland disqualification undertakings, which is considered in the next paragraph.

12–43 There is no statutory provision requiring disqualification undertakings (as opposed to any court order relaxing the effect of an undertaking) to be notified to the Secretary of State. In the case of an undertaking accepted under ss.7(2A) or 8(2A), this is perhaps not surprising. In law, at least, it might be thought strange for the Secretary of State to be required to report his own actions to himself. The absence of a mandatory reporting requirement in relation to the acceptance of competition disqualification undertakings under s.9B, is, perhaps, more surprising. However, the Secretary of State is required by s.18(2A)[70] to register such particulars as he considers appropriate of disqualification undertakings accepted by him, under ss.7 or 8, or by the OFT or a specified regulator, under s.9B and of orders granting permission to act notwithstanding disqualification by means of an undertaking. This provision has been extended to encompass Northern Ireland disqualification undertakings (or the grant of permission to act notwithstanding disqualification by such an undertaking or any order to vary or discharge such an undertaking) to the extent

[66] SI 2009/2471 reg.8. It is not clear whether the court can direct that a disqualification order need not be registered within the 14-day period if the operation of the order is stayed or suspended using the powers discussed in the text from 12–28. It has been held that the courts of New South Wales do have power to make such a direction and override a similar requirement in the Companies (NSW) Code: see *Hunter v Corporate Affairs Commission* (1988) 13 A.C.L.R. 250.

[67] A simple name search of the register can now be carried out by accessing the Companies House website at *http://www.companieshouse.gov.uk/ddir/* [Accessed August 27, 2009]. It is clear that the maintenance of a complete and accurate register is essential to the publicising and enforcement of disqualification. However, levels of notification have not always been as they might: see Public Accounts Committee, *The Insolvency Service Executive Agency: Company Director Disqualification* (London: HMSO, 1993) and A. Hicks, *Disqualification of Directors: No Hiding Place for the Unfit* (A.C.C.A Research Report No.59, 1998), Ch.11.

[68] SI 1989/2404 (NI 19).

[69] CDDA s.18(4A); Companies (Disqualification Orders) Regulations 2001 (SI 2001/967) regs 5 and 9; Companies (Disqualification Order) Regulations 2009 (SI 2009/2471) regs 5 and 9. However, the obligation to register does not extend to disqualification orders made and permission to act granted under the 1989 Order where such permission relates to disqualification orders made by the Northern Ireland courts before April 2, 2001.

[70] Originally a new s.18(2A) was inserted by the Insolvency Act 2000 but the current s.18(2A) was substituted by the Enterprise Act 2002 s.204(11) with effect from June 20, 2003: SI 2003/1397.

that the disqualification undertaking was accepted under the Company Directors Disqualification (Northern Ireland) Order 2002[71] on or after September 1, 2004.[72] On searching the relevant particulars on the Companies House website it is apparent that undertakings are, unfortunately, described as "orders". In the case of undertakings accepted under s.7(2A) it is possible to identify that an undertaking is involved, rather than an order, because the relevant statutory provision under which the "order" is described as having been made is specified as s.7(2A). However, in the case of undertakings accepted under s.8(2A) it is not possible to identify whether the disqualification flows from an undertaking or an order. The particulars simply reveal that an "order" was made and specify the relevant statutory provision as s.8. It is unfortunate that the published particulars on the Register should be misleading in this way. It is also unfortunate that the Register does not reveal whether a court order granting permission to act does so subject to conditions and, if so, what those conditions are.

12–44 Under CDDA s.18(3), when a disqualification order or undertaking of which entry is made in the Register ceases to be in force, the entry, and all particulars relating to it, should be deleted. This applies also to entries in relation to Northern Ireland disqualifications.[73]

Press releases

12–45 It is common for the Secretary of State to publish a press release when a person is disqualified, be it by undertaking or order. Such press releases usually contain a brief summary of the relevant court judgment, undertaking or *Carecraft* statement. The publication of press releases appears to be consistent with the underlying objectives of the CDDA, namely the protection of the public from the disqualified director and, through general deterrence, the raising of standards in the management of companies. There may be cases—for example, if there are parallel criminal proceedings on foot—where a more cautious approach is necessary and the details of the factual basis of disqualification in the press release may need to be reduced.[74] The mere reporting of the fact that disqualification proceedings are being pursued against an individual does not infringe his right to respect for private life under art.8 of the ECHR. In *WGS and MSLS v United Kingdom*[75]

[71] SI 2002/3150 (NI 4).

[72] See CDDA s.18(4A) (as amended by the Insolvency Act 2000 (Company Directors Disqualification Undertakings) Order 2004 (SI 2004/1941) art.2(6) and the Companies (Disqualification Orders) Regulations 2001 (SI 2001/967) reg.9(1A) (as inserted by the Companies (Disqualification Orders) (Amendment) Regulations 2004 (SI 2004/1940) reg.3(a)) as regards disqualification undertakings accepted on or before September 30, 2009. See CDDA s.18(2A) and Companies (Disqualification Orders) Regulations 2009 (SI 2009/2471) reg.9(2) as regards disqualification undertakings accepted on or after October 1, 2009.

[73] Companies (Disqualification Orders) Regulations 2001 (SI 2001/967) reg.9(2) (as amended by the Companies (Disqualification Orders) (Amendment) Regulations 2004 (SI 2004/1940) reg.3(b)) as regards orders or undertakings made or accepted on or before September 30, 2009. See CDDA s.18(3) and SI 2009/2471 reg.9(3) as regards orders or undertakings made or accepted on or after October 1, 2009.

[74] On the issues of press notices in the context of winding up see *Secretary of State for Trade and Industry v North West Holdings Plc* [1999] 1 B.C.L.C. 425.

[75] [2000] B.C.C. 719.

the applicants claimed that the damage to their reputations flowing from publication in a national newspaper of a reference to proceedings being taken against one of them before he had been formally notified of such, infringed their art.8 rights. Declaring the application inadmissible, the European Court laid emphasis on the importance of public confidence in companies, the role of regulatory mechanisms in maintaining such confidence and the public nature of disqualification proceedings. To the extent that press reporting might damage their reputations, the Court concluded that it was open to the applicants to invoke the law of defamation. In the light of this ruling, it is suggested that the publication of press reports based on DTI press releases to publicise disqualification proceedings or their outcome will not, of itself, infringe art.8 rights because any such rights will usually be outweighed by the public interest in the disqualification of unfit directors. However, any press release should be accurate and, where the proceedings have not been concluded, should not pre-judge the issues.[76]

[76] For judicial criticism of a DTI press release on grounds that it was misleading and inappropriate see *Re World of Leather Plc, Secretary of State for Trade and Industry v Gill* [2004] EWHC 933 (Ch), especially at [172]–[174].

Chapter 13

PROCEDURE IN CIVIL DISQUALIFICATION PROCEEDINGS AFTER JUDGMENT OR ENTRY INTO A DISQUALIFICATION UNDERTAKING: REVIEWS, VARIATIONS AND APPEALS

INTRODUCTION

13–01 This chapter deals with the court procedures applicable in civil disqualification proceedings after first instance judgment or after entry into a disqualification undertaking. These are: (a) reviews and variations of orders and undertakings; and (b) appeals against orders. The basis on which the court exercises its discretion in circumstances where the procedures are engaged is also addressed. So far as appeals are concerned, the chapter only covers matters specific to disqualification and, save where it is necessary for an understanding of the disqualification context, does not provide an exhaustive analysis of general practice and procedure applicable to civil appeals. Final appeals to the Supreme Court, raise no specific issues in the disqualification context and accordingly are mentioned only in passing.

THE APPLICABLE RULES

13–02 The question of which procedural rules govern appeals and reviews is considered (in the context of applicable rules generally) in some detail in Ch.7. In summary, it is suggested that the current position is as follows:

(1) Appeals and reviews in proceedings under CDDA ss.2(2)(a), 3 and 4 are governed by the provisions applicable to civil proceedings generally. The provisions in the Insolvency Rules 1986 regarding appeals have no application.[1]
(2) Appeals and reviews in connection with proceedings under CDDA ss.6, 8 and 9A are governed by the relevant provisions of the Insolvency Rules 1986 (as amended).[2]
(3) Appeals and reviews in connection with applications under CDDA s.7(2) for permission to bring s.6 proceedings after the expiry of the relevant two-year period are governed by the relevant provisions of the Insolvency Rules 1986 (as amended).[3]

[1] The rule-making power in Insolvency Act 1986 s.411 is not extended to these provisions of the CDDA: see CDDA s.21(2) and discussion in the text from 7–21 on the analogous position under the Companies Act 1985 considered in *Re Probe Data Systems Ltd (No.3), Secretary of State for Trade and Industry v Desai* [1992] B.C.L.C. 405.
[2] See Disqualification Rules rr.1(3)(c) and 2(4).
[3] See Disqualification Rules rr1.3(a) and 2(4).

(4) Appeals and reviews in connection with applications under CDDA s.7(4) are governed by the relevant provisions of the Insolvency Rules 1986 (as amended).[4]

(5) Appeals and reviews in connection with orders made under CDDA ss.10 and 15 are governed by the relevant provisions on appeals applying to the substantive proceedings in which the order was made. As regards CDDA s.10 proceedings, the Insolvency Rules 1986 would appear to apply. The position regarding s.15 proceedings is less clear. It is suggested that the substantive proceedings will be covered by the CPR as will any appeal.

(6) Appeals and reviews in connection with applications to vary or discharge disqualification undertakings under CDDA s.8A are governed by the relevant provisions of the Insolvency Rules 1986 (as amended).[5]

(7) Appeals and reviews in connection with applications for permission to act notwithstanding disqualification are governed by:

(a) the CPR in cases where the disqualification order was made under any of CDDA ss.2(2)(a), 3 or 4 (see (1) above);

(b) the relevant provisions of the Insolvency Rules 1986 in cases where the disqualification order was made, or disqualification undertaking accepted, under any of CDDA ss.6, 7, 8, 9A, 9B or 10.[6]

(8) Appeals and reviews under CDDA s.11 in connection with applications for permission to act notwithstanding bankruptcy or bankruptcy restrictions, are (apparently) governed by the Insolvency Rules 1986.

(9) Appeals in the case of orders for transfer to another court raise two questions: first, the court in which the appeal should be launched and second, the rules which should apply substantively to such appeals.

(a) As regards the court to which the appeal should be made, it is suggested that: (i) if the applicable rules are the ordinary rules of civil procedure, then para.5 of the Practice Direction to CPR Pt 30 will apply to determine the court to which the appeal should be made; and (ii) if the applicable rules are the Insolvency Rules 1986, then the only possible conflict between those rules and the Practice Direction to Pt 30 would be in cases where the order for transfer is between county courts or is an order made in county court proceedings by a judge of the county court. In the cases referred to in (ii) the question would be whether or not the provisions of the Practice Direction are inconsistent with the appeal provisions of the Insolvency Rules.[7] This would, in turn, depend on whether or not the order is regarded as one being made "in the exercise of" the winding up jurisdiction. It is suggested that, where the appeals provisions of the Insolvency Rules apply generally, then: (i) they apply to orders for transfer as much

[4] See Disqualification Rules rr1.3(b) and 2(4), (5).

[5] See Disqualification Rules rr1.3(d) and 2(4).

[6] See Disqualification Rules rr1.3(e) and 2(4).

[7] See Insolvency Rules 1986 (as amended) r.7.51, which provides that the CPR and practice and procedure in the High Court or county courts applies "except so far as inconsistent" with the Insolvency Rules.

as to any other interim order in the relevant proceedings; and (ii) they will take effect in priority to the Practice Direction to CPR Pt 30.

(b) As regards the nature of the appeal and the relevant procedure, it is suggested that if the reasoning in (a) above is correct, then the relevant provisions of the Insolvency Rules or of the CPR will apply accordingly.

REVIEWS

Review powers in insolvency proceedings

13–03 In insolvency proceedings, the court has a general power to review orders conferred by r.7.47 of the Insolvency Rules 1986.[8] The r.7.47 power is very wide. It extends to the review, rescission or variation by one judge of an order of another judge of the same court, as well as review, rescission or variation by a judge of his or her own previous orders.[9] In appropriate (but very rare) circumstances, an appeal court can consider both an appeal against an order of a lower court and an application to review the decision comprised in such order.[10] It may also entertain an appeal against a refusal of the court below to review its own decision. Nevertheless, the review jurisdiction in r.7.47 is to be exercised extremely cautiously. Save in exceptional cases where it might be necessary to correct an obvious injustice, it will generally be invoked successfully only where there is a change of relevant circumstances[11] or, more rarely, where new evidence has come to light which could not be adduced on appeal.[12] The jurisdiction should not be exercised so as to permit it to become a gateway for late appeals or to undermine the principle of res judicata or to avoid limitations on other forms of application to the court.[13] When conducting a review, the court normally proceeds by way of a true review or re-hearing of the original application with the benefit of further available evidence or submissions rather than by way of appeal. It does not ask itself the question whether the original order ought to have been made at all but

[8] In the case of personal insolvency see also the power in Insolvency Act 1986 s.375(1). Broadly speaking a similar approach should be followed to applications under s.375(1) and r.7.47: see *Midrome Ltd v Shaw* [1993] B.C.C. 659. As to the use of s.375(1) in the context of bankruptcy restrictions orders see *Official Receiver v Bathurst* [2008] B.P.I.R. 1548.

[9] *Re W & A Glaser Ltd* [1994] B.C.C. 199 at 208; *Re Thirty Eight Building Ltd (No.2)* [2000] B.C.C. 402.

[10] *Re Piccadilly Property Management Ltd* [2000] B.C.C. 44. The circumstances in which such a dual application will be appropriate are rare: see, e.g. the course taken by the Court of Appeal in *Re Casterbridge Properties Ltd (No.2), Jeeves v Official Receiver* [2003] EWCA Civ 1246; [2004] 1 W.L.R. 602 where an appeal was adjourned to allow a review application to be made to the court below. In due course the Court of Appeal heard the original appeal and a further appeal against the decision below on the review application.

[11] See, e.g. *Re Casterbridge Properties Ltd (No.2), Jeeves v Official Receiver* [2004] 1 W.L.R. 602.

[12] See, e.g. *Re A Debtor (No.32/SD of 1991)* [1993] 1 W.L.R. 314; *Fitch v Official Receiver* [1996] 1 W.L.R. 242; *Re RS & M Engineering Co Ltd, Mond v Hammond Suddards (No.2)* [2000] Ch. 40; *Re Thirty Eight Building Ltd (No.2)* [2000] B.C.C. 402; *Egleton v IRC* [2003] EWHC 3226 (Ch), [2004] B.P.I.R. 476.

[13] *Re Debtors (Nos. VA7 and VA8) Ex p. Stevens* [1996] B.P.I.R. 101; *Brillouet v Hachette Magazines* [1996] B.P.I.R. 522; *Egleton v IRC* [2004] B.P.I.R. 476.

instead considers whether the order ought to remain in force in the light of the evidence presented and submissions made.[14] In the disqualification context, the jurisdiction was invoked successfully by the official receiver to correct an order under the slip rule, the court holding that it would have prepared to use r.7.47 had it been necessary. In the same case, the rule was invoked unsuccessfully by a director seeking to avoid the legal consequences (in CDDA ss.13–15) flowing from his breach of the conditions imposed by an order granting him permission to act notwithstanding disqualification.[15] Finally, in this context, it should be noted that, even where r.7.47 of the Insolvency Rules applies, a number of provisions in the CPR are also highly relevant because r.2(1) of the Disqualification Rules provides that the CPR and any relevant practice direction apply to applications to extend the time for commencing s.6 proceedings, to enforce any duty arising under CDDA s.7(4), for orders under CDDA ss.6, 8 and 9A, to vary or discharge an undertaking under CDDA s.8A or for permission to act notwithstanding disqualification where that disqualification arises from an undertaking or an order made under CDDA ss.6, 8, 9A or 10. Moreover, the Insolvency Rules themselves (r.7.51) apply the ordinary rules of civil procedure (including practice directions) to the extent that such rules are not inconsistent with the Insolvency Rules.

Review powers under the CPR

13–04 Under the CPR there is no general power to review orders akin to that under r.7.47 of the Insolvency Rules. However, there are a number of situations in which the court has effective power under the CPR to review or vary earlier orders. The following should not be treated as an exhaustive list:

(1) With certain very important exceptions, time limits are generally capable of being varied by agreement between the parties (CPR r.2.11). In any event, the court retains general case management powers enabling it to control the time (and vary the time) at which steps within the proceedings are to take place (CPR r.3.1).
(2) Before an order is perfected (that is, drawn up and sealed) the judge retains power to alter his judgment.[16] However, as noted by May L.J.:

> "Once a judgment has been handed down or given, there are obvious reasons why the court should hesitate long and hard before making a material alteration to it. These reasons have been rehearsed in the cases to which I have referred and I need not elaborate them further. The cases also acknowledge that there may very occasionally be circumstances in which a judge not only can, but should make a material alteration in the interests of justice. There may for instance be a palpable error in the judgment and an alteration would save the parties the expense of an appeal. On the other hand, reopening contentious matters or permitting one or more of the parties to add to their case or make a new case should rarely be allowed. Any attempt to do this is likely to

[14] *Re A Debtor (No. 32/SD of 1991)* [1993] 1 W.L.R. 314 at 319; *Customs & Excise Commissioners v Allen* [2003] B.P.I.R. 830.

[15] *Re Brian Sheridan Cars Ltd* [1996] 1 B.C.L.C. 327.

[16] *Re Barrell Enterprises* [1973] 1 W.L.R. 19; *Pittalis v Sherefettin* [1986] 1 Q.B. 868; *Stewart v Engel* [2000] 1 W.L.R. 2268; *Robinson v Fernsby* [2003] EWCA Civ 1820; *Crestfort Ltd v Tesco Stores Ltd* [2005] EWHC 805 (Ch), [2005] L. & T.R. 20.

receive summary rejection in most cases. It will only very rarely be appropriate for parties to attempt to do so. This necessarily means that the court would only be persuaded to do so in exceptional circumstances, but that expression by itself is no more than a relatively uninformative label. It is not profitable to debate what it means in isolation from the facts of a particular case."[17]

(3) The court retains an inherent jurisdiction to vary its own orders to make its meaning and intention clear.[18]
(4) The court has power under "the slip rule", CPR r.40.12, to amend an order as drawn up and embodied in paper to reflect the order that was made.
(5) There is power to set aside or vary an order made on an interim application without notice (CPR r.23.10(1)). Such an application must be made within seven days of service of the order on the person making the application. Similarly, it would appear that a final order can be set aside as a matter of right, if the proceedings are effectively a nullity because they have never been served.[19]
(6) There is power to re-list an interim application for further consideration where the court has made an order but the applicant or respondent has failed to attend and (presumably) to set aside, vary, discharge or suspend the original order (CPR r.23.11(2); para.12.2 to the Pt 23 Practice Direction).[20]
(7) There appears to be power to vary case management directions by virtue of CPR r.29.5, as supplemented by the Pt 29 Practice Direction, paras 3.4, and 6.1–6.5.
(8) Rule 8(2) of the Disqualification Rules, which applies to cases where disqualification orders are made under CDDA ss.6, 8 and 9A, confers a power to set aside or vary a disqualification order made in the absence of the defendant. This is similar to the power conferred on the court by CPR r.39.3(3) to set aside a judgment or order made against a party who failed to attend the trial.[21]
(9) CPR r.3.1(7) confers power on the court to vary or revoke an order made under the CPR. The exact scope of this power is unclear, as is the extent to which it will apply in the disqualification context to orders provided for by the Disqualification Rules. It seems unlikely that this rule permits the court simply to change its mind and reverse itself when it feels like it. In *Lloyds Investment (Scandinavia) Ltd v Ager-Hanssen*[22] Patten J. suggested that the jurisdiction would be exercised where there is a material change of circumstance or where it can be shown that the judge who made the order was misled in some way.
(10) In the case of the Court of Appeal or the High Court sitting as an appeal court, there is a power, only to be exercised in exceptional circumstances,

[17] *Robinson v Fernsby* [2003] EWCA Civ 1820 at [94].
[18] Practice Direction (Judgments and Orders) to CPR Pt 40, para.4.5.
[19] See, e.g. *White v Weston* [1968] 2 Q.B. 647.
[20] See further text from 13–06.
[21] See further text from 13–06.
[22] [2003] EWHC 1740 (Ch).

enabling an appeal court to re-open an appeal after an order carrying its judgment into effect has been perfected. This power will only be exercised where there is no alternative effective remedy and where it is necessary to re-open the matter in order to avoid real injustice, permission first being required.[23]

Review powers under the Disqualification Practice Direction

13–05 Paragraph 10.6(1) of the Disqualification Practice Direction refers to the court's power to vary a direction concerning whether a trial should be heard by a judge or a registrar/district judge.[24]

Orders made in the absence of a party

13–06 It was noted above that the CPR provides for a specific review power in circumstances where an order is made in the absence of a party on an interim application and that the CPR and the Disqualification Rules also make provision for such a review power in cases where a party has not attended the trial. Of course, the power of the court to proceed in the absence of a party should be exercised with caution, especially where a litigant in person is concerned and where that litigant has asked for, but been refused, an adjournment. Normally, the court would want to be satisfied that proper notice of the hearing date had been given to the absent party before proceeding and might direct that any order should not be perfected until the position as regards notification has first been confirmed by written evidence.

13–07 As regards non-attendance at trial, the relevant provisions are CPR r.39.3(3) and Disqualification Rules r.8(2). The jurisdiction is likely to be exercised similarly under the two provisions though it is important to note that r.8(2) of the Disqualification Rules is not as restrictive as the CPR provision. Prior to the CPR, the courts exercised the r.8(2) jurisdiction by analogy with the approach under the pre-CPR equivalent of CPR r.39.3(3). That provision, RSC Ord.35, r.2(1), was considered in *Shocked v Goldschmidt*.[25] The principal matters that fell to be taken into account related to the public interest in finality of proceedings and the need to avoid court time being wasted by re-trials (the scope of any re-hearing being sought was therefore important). Other relevant factors included: the reason that the party failed to attend the hearing (unless by accident or mistake, the court was unlikely to order a re-hearing); any delay in making the application (and whether rights had been acquired or steps taken in reliance on the original order in the meantime); the prospects of success of the party seeking a re-hearing; the conduct of the party seeking a re-hearing; the conduct of the party seeking the re-hearing; and any prejudice that would flow from the setting aside of the original order. Some of the guidelines from the *Shocked* case are now expressly incorporated in CPR r.39.3(5) which provides that an application may only be granted if the

[23] *Taylor v Lawrence* [2002] EWCA Civ 90, [2003] Q.B. 528; *Seray-Wurie v Hackney London Borough Council* [2002] EWCA Civ 909, [2003] 1 W.L.R. 257 and see now CPR r.52.17 and Practice Direction (Appeals) to CPR Pt 52, para.25.

[24] Considered in *Lewis v Secretary of State for Trade and Industry* [2003] B.C.C 567.

[25] [1998] 1 All E.R. 372.

applicant acted promptly, had a good reason for non-attendance and has reasonable prospects of success at trial. This has elevated those guidelines to the status of jurisdictional pre-requisites. However, in assessing, for example, whether there was a "good" reason for non-attendance, the court has to consider the position in the round to see whether the reason given is sufficient for the court to exercise its discretion in favour of the applicant. Thus, while it appears that a reason must be given, the quality of the reason does not have to meet some free standing jurisdictional hurdle divorced from all the other circumstances of the case.[26] Prima facie, there is a formal difference in the requirements for applications under CPR r.39.3(3) and Disqualification Rules r.8(2) because, in the latter case, the court considers the matter in the round and there are no jurisdictional pre-conditions that have to be met. Having said that, it seems likely that, in most cases, the result will be the same whichever provision is applied.

13–08 In the case of non-attendance at interim applications, CPR r.23.11(2) has changed the position from that which used to apply under RSC Ord.32, r.5(3),(4).[27] The old rule was that where a party failed to attend and a substantive order was made, the court could re-hear the application (then a summons), if the order had not been perfected. After the order had been perfected a re-hearing was only possible in certain circumstances and if the parties consented. Where there was no substantive hearing because the application had been dismissed or struck out for non-attendance of the applicant, then the matter could be re-listed for hearing. These complications have all been swept away. The matter is now entirely at the discretion of the court (subject to the application of the overriding objective). Doubtless the sort of factors taken into account under CPR r.39.3 will also be relevant though their application in the case of interim applications is likely to operate less strongly against the order on the application being set aside.

SECTION 8A: THE COURT'S POWER TO VARY OR DISCHARGE DISQUALIFICATION UNDERTAKINGS

13–09 A disqualification undertaking is similar in effect to a disqualification order. An offer of a disqualification undertaking may be made before or after substantive disqualification proceedings have been commenced and may be accepted, in cases under CDDA s.7(2A) or 8(2A) by the Secretary of State or, in the competition context, by the OFT or a relevant regulator.[28] The court is not involved in this process. However, once a disqualification undertaking has come into force, the court has power under CDDA s.8A, on application of the person who gave the undertaking, to reduce the period for which it is in force or to provide for it to

[26] See, e.g. *Brazil v Brazil* [2002] EWCA Civ 1135; *Hackney London Borough Council v Driscoll* [2003] EWCA Civ 1037, [2003] 1 W.L.R. 2602.

[27] The old rule applied to applications in chambers which was where most interim applications, other than those for injunctions, were made.

[28] See generally Ch.9.

cease to be in force. There is no power to annul the undertaking from the start.[29] As the offer of an undertaking is strictly a voluntary act, the starting point is that the court will only rarely be prepared to intervene to allow a person to escape from what is, in effect, a contract that he has entered into.[30] The court has no jurisdiction under r.7.47 of the Insolvency Rules 1986 to vary or discharge statutory disqualification undertakings: r.7.47 applies only to court orders.[31]

Power of the party accepting a disqualification undertaking to vary or discharge it

13–10 It is suggested that once a disqualification undertaking has been accepted by the Secretary of State (or the OFT or a relevant regulator in the competition context), it has the relevant statutory consequences spelled out in the CDDA[32] and it is not open to him to vary it or to agree to it being discharged. The power to vary or discharge the undertaking is reserved to the courts under CDDA s.8A. There are two main justifications for this view. First, it would be odd if the person accepting the undertaking could affect third party rights (which might have accrued in the meantime) by agreeing to vary or discharge the undertaking. A disqualification undertaking is not simply a bilateral contract. It has force by virtue of statute and gives rise to third party rights and obligations as well as potential criminal liability.[33] Secondly, it is suggested that the availability of such a power would be inconsistent with the fact that the power to grant permission to act in a prohibited capacity notwithstanding a disqualification undertaking is reserved to the court. As the court and the court alone can grant permission to act and the relief given will not be general but will relate to specific companies the affairs of which have been considered in evidence,[34] it is difficult to see how the person accepting the undertaking could have power to relieve the disqualified person by varying or discharging the undertaking in its entirety. Indeed, this analysis is consistent with the background against which disqualification undertakings were originally introduced. As discussed more fully in Ch.9, undertakings were introduced so as to remove the need for court intervention in the disqualification process. Prior to the introduction of undertakings, the closest approximation to a consensual means of disposing of disqualification proceedings was the *Carecraft* procedure. However, while a *Carecraft* disqualification was premised on a statement of facts agreed between the parties, the court was still required to consider the statement and exercise its jurisdiction under the CDDA.[35] Under the statutory undertakings

[29] *Re INS Realisations Ltd, Jonkler v Secretary of State for Trade and Industry* [2006] EWHC 135 (Ch), [2006] 1 W.L.R. 3433 at [35].

[30] See *Re INS Realisations Ltd, Jonkler v Secretary of State for Trade and Industry* [2006] 1 W.L.R. 3433 and the cases considered therein including, in the disqualification context, *Re Blackspur Group Plc, Secretary of State for Trade and Industry v Eastaway* [2001] 1 B.C.L.C. 653.

[31] *Re Blackspur Group Plc, Eastaway v Secretary of State for Trade and Industry* [2007] EWCA Civ 425, [2008] 1 B.C.L.C. 153.

[32] And indeed in a range of other statutory provisions: see further Ch.14.

[33] See CDDA ss.13–15.

[34] See generally Ch.15.

[35] See generally Ch.9.

regime, a person can be disqualified without the court needing to be involved. When the undertakings regime was first introduced, it was not suggested that relief from disqualification (whether on appeal or under s.8A or by the grant of permission to act notwithstanding disqualification) would be taken out of the hands of the court. It is clear that the court is required to be involved in relation to appeals and permission to act notwithstanding disqualification. Consistent with this general position, it is suggested that s.8A provides the only route by which disqualification undertakings can be varied or discharged and that the Secretary of State (or the OFT or another relevant regulator) has no residual power to vary or discharge an undertaking once one has been accepted.

Jurisdiction under s.8A

13–11 Under CDDA s.8A(1)(a), the court may reduce the period for which a disqualification undertaking is to be in force. Under CDDA ss.1A and 9B(3) the "period" of disqualification must be specified in a disqualification undertaking. For undertakings accepted under s.7(2A), the period must be for a minimum of two years and a maximum of 15 years. It follows that, in cases where an undertaking was accepted under s.7(2A), the court under s.8A may not reduce the period of disqualification so that it is to run for less than two years from the date when the undertaking originally came into force. Under s.8A(1)(b), the court may provide that an undertaking is to cease to be in force. In effect, this is a power to discharge an undertaking in its entirety. It is important to note that under this sub-section the court may provide that the *undertaking* (rather than the period) is to cease to be in force. This is to be contrasted with s.8A(1)(a) which gives the court power to reduce the period for which the undertaking is in force.

The basis on which the court will reduce the period of an undertaking or provide for it to cease to be in force

13–12 The court's approach under CDDA s.8A was considered in some detail in the case of *INS Realisations*.[36] In that case the applicant, Mrs Jonkler, had made an offer of an undertaking for five years, with a schedule of agreed facts. That offer was accepted. Subsequently, after having received representations, the Secretary of State decided not to proceed against Mrs Jonkler's co-director and (by then, former) husband Mr Jonkler and disqualification proceedings under CDDA s.6 were discontinued against him. The judge rejected an argument that an applicant under CDDA s.8A had complete freedom to challenge the agreed factual basis set out in the schedule to the undertaking.[37] There was an interest in encouraging finality where disputes are resolved. The agreement not to dispute certain facts

[36] *Re INS Realisations Ltd, Jonkler v Secretary of State for Trade and Industry* [2006] 1 W.L.R. 3433.

[37] The importance of keeping a party to his bargain in this context is also stressed by cases that have arisen out of applications for permission to act, where a person who gave an undertaking is not allowed to resile from the factual basis set out in the written form of undertaking: see *Re TLL Realisations Limited, Secretary of State for Trade and Industry v Collins* [2000] B.C.C. 998 at 1010 (Peter Gibson L.J.); *Re Morija Plc, Kluk v Secretary of State for Business, Enterprise and Regulatory Reform* [2007] EWHC 3055 (Ch), [2008] 2 B.C.L.C. 313.

for purposes consequential to the giving of an undertaking applied in the circumstances. By analogy with the cases where the court has had to consider whether to permit a company to resile from an undertaking to the court, especially where that undertaking embodied an agreement between the parties,[38] the appropriate approach is to treat the relevant factual basis of the disqualification undertaking as binding on the applicant unless either some ground is shown which would be sufficient to discharge a private law contract or some ground of public interest is shown which outweighs the importance of holding a party to his agreement. On the facts the most that could be shown was that the facts set out in the schedule to the undertaking might be susceptible to challenge in whole or part. She was unable to show that any facts there set out were in fact wrong. Furthermore, the possibility of challenge did not arise from the emergence of some new information not available at the date of the original undertaking. As regards the overall position, however, the court did discharge the undertaking by declaring that it should cease to be in force. This was on the basis of the very special facts of the case. No public interest in the applicant remaining subject to the undertaking was identified by the Secretary of State,[39] acceptance of a shorter period of disqualification could have been justified and the one director remaining subject to disqualification was the one who had not been active in the company whereas the Secretary of State had formed the view that it was not in the public interest to pursue the active director. However, the court agreed with the Secretary of State that the jurisdiction would be sparingly exercised in circumstances where the director pleads that he only gave the undertaking because he could not afford legal advice and assistance or where the undertaking is given for a period in excess of that subsequently found appropriate by the court in relation to other directors involved in the same misconduct and the same insolvency.

13–13 The authors remain of the view that the two main sets of circumstances where s.8A may be invoked are likely to be:

(1) *Where there might have been a successful appeal had the disqualification undertaking in fact been dealt with under the Carecraft procedure.*[40] Such cases are likely to be rare. A possible example is where facts or evidence subsequently come to light, which the director could not reasonably have been expected to have identified prior to offering the undertaking such as where an undertaking is offered at a very early stage by one of a number of co-directors. In the light of subsequent evidence later received from other co-directors, the Secretary of State might withdraw certain allegations against them which would, if removed from the schedule to the undertaking, reduce the period of

[38] See, e.g. *Re Blackspur Group Plc, Secretary of State for Trade and Industry v Eastaway* [2001] 1 B.C.L.C. 653 and *Di Placito v Slater* [2003] EWCA Civ 1863, [2004] 1 W.L.R. 1605.

[39] Other than the mere undesirability of releasing from their undertaking persons whose offer of an undertaking has been accepted.

[40] See *Re INS Realisations Ltd, Jonkler v Secretary of State for Trade and Industry* [2006] 1 W.L.R. 3433 at [29] where the judge said that to the extent that the *Carecraft* analogy was helpful at all, the s.8A hearing was more akin to an appeal from an order made under the *Carecraft* procedure rather than the *Carecraft* hearing itself.

disqualification provided for by it and that would, in the circumstances, have been withdrawn and not included in the schedule to the undertaking had the true facts been known prior to its acceptance. However, the *Carecraft* procedure itself was always pregnant with the possibility that the facts included in a *Carecraft* statement would differ from those found by the court at the trial of any co-defendants who chose to fight the proceedings rather than opt for a *Carecraft* disposal. The court should be slow to decide that evidence was not reasonably available to a person offering an undertaking as otherwise the efficacy of the statutory undertaking regime could be seriously undermined. Another possible example is where there is a subsequent case that results in a relevant change in the law as it was previously understood to be.

(2) *In circumstances where the director can demonstrate that his offer of the undertaking was in fact vitiated (e.g. by lack of capacity).* Again, it is thought that such cases are likely to be rare. It is suggested that, at least in the majority of cases, any absence of funding (and the subsequent ability to fund proceedings) will not normally be an adequate reason to exercise the s.8A power in favour of the director.[41]

APPEALS

13–14 The majority of appeals in the disqualification context will be made in relation to orders made under CDDA ss.6, 8 and 9A. In those cases, the appeal provisions that apply to insolvency proceedings will be in point. In a small minority of cases, the general appeal provisions applicable to civil proceedings (other than insolvency proceedings) will be in point. However, in what follows, the appeal provisions applicable to civil proceedings are considered first because a number of aspects of such provisions are also common to insolvency appeals.

Appeal provisions applicable to civil proceedings (other than insolvency proceedings) generally

Destination

13–15 In cases where the appeals provisions applicable to ordinary civil proceedings apply, the position is governed by the Senior Courts Act 1981 s.16,[42] the County Courts Act 1984 s.77,[43] the Access to Justice Act 1999 and the Access to Justice Act 1999 (Destination of Appeals) Order 2000[44] ("the Destinations Order"). The Destinations Order changes the starting position provided for by the other statutes mentioned in a number of important respects. The general principle which now

[41] As the judge in the *INS Realisations* case also suggested. For a case where there was alleged duress in the procuring of the undertaking and a separate allegation of mistake see *Gardiner v Secretary of State for Business, Enterprise & Regulatory Reform*, February 11, 2008, Ch.D. (Birmingham District Registry), unreported (District Judge Dowling).

[42] Providing, subject to exceptions, for appeals from the High Court to go to the Court of Appeal.

[43] Providing, subject to exceptions, for appeals from any county court to go to the Court of Appeal.

[44] SI 2000/1071 made pursuant to the Access to Justice Act 1999 s.56 and as further amended by the Civil Procedure (Modification of Enactments) Order 2002 (SI 2002/439) and the Civil Procedure (Modification of Enactments) Order 2003 (SI 2003/490).

applies is that an appeal lies to the next level of judge in the court hierarchy.[45] Permission to appeal will usually be required (see further below). As regards the court to which an appeal should be made the position can be summarised as follows[46]:

(1) Appeals from a district judge sitting in a county court are to the county court (circuit) judge.[47]
(2) Appeals from the county court (circuit) judge sitting on appeal are to the Court of Appeal.[48]
(3) Appeals from the county court (circuit) judge sitting at first instance are to a High Court judge.[49]
(4) Appeals from a district judge sitting in the High Court or from the Companies Court registrar are to a High Court judge.[50]
(5) Appeals from a High Court judge, sitting at first instance[51] or on appeal,[52] are to the Court of Appeal.
(6) Appeals from the Court of Appeal are, from October 1, 2009, to the new Supreme Court.[53]
(7) There is provision for "leapfrog" appeals in exceptional cases, both direct to the Court of Appeal and direct to the Supreme Court. Such cases are so described because they involve "leaping over" and missing out a normal stage of appeal. As regards "leapfrog" appeals to the Court of Appeal, the essential requirement is that the case raises an important point of principle or practice or there is some other compelling reason for the Court of Appeal to hear it.[54] The requirements for "leapfrog" appeals to the Supreme Court are dealt with by the Administration of Justice Act 1969 ss.12–15 (as amended).

It should be noted that most disqualification proceedings are allocated to CPR Pt 8 and do not fall within a relevant specified type. Accordingly, there is no room for the operation of the rule that appeals from decisions in cases allocated to CPR Pt 7 or in cases of a relevant specified type of proceedings should be heard by the Court of Appeal.[55] The specific geographical location for appeals to a High Court judge from a county court or a district judge sitting in the High Court can be determined by reference to the Practice Direction (Appeals) to CPR Pt 52, paras 8.1–8.14.

[45] See generally *Tanfern Ltd v Cameron-MacDonald* [2000] 1 W.L.R. 1311 at [15].
[46] Summarised in Practice Direction (Appeals) to CPR Pt 52, para.2A.1.
[47] Destinations Order, para.3(2).
[48] Destinations Order, para.5.
[49] Destinations Order, para.3(1).
[50] Destinations Order, para.2.
[51] Senior Courts Act 1981 s.16.
[52] Destinations Order, para.5(a).
[53] Appellate Jurisdiction Act 1876 s.3(1).
[54] Access to Justice Act 1999 s.57 and CPR r.52.14.
[55] Destinations Order, para.4.

Permission to appeal

13–16 Permission to appeal (and cross-appeal) is needed in all cases (except, for present purposes, in contempt proceedings).[56] In cases where the decision of the High Court (or county court) that is being appealed was itself an appellate decision, permission to appeal must be obtained from the Court of Appeal.[57] In other cases, permission may be obtained from the lower court or, whether or not there has been an unsuccessful application to the lower court, the appeal court. However, in such cases, the sensible course is to apply initially to the court that made the decision in respect of which the appeal is contemplated.[58] If application for permission is made to the lower court, it should be made orally at the hearing at which the decision to be appealed against was made.[59] If permission is refused by the lower court or no application for permission is made to the lower court, then an application for permission may be made to the appeal court. Such an application should be made, in the case of the appellant, in the appellant's notice or, in the case of the respondent, in the respondent's notice.[60] An appellant's notice must be filed at the appeal court within such period as the court below directs or, if it makes no direction, within 14 days after the decision of the lower court that is sought to be appealed.[61] For these purposes, the 14 days runs from the date that the decision was reached and pronounced in court rather than the day on which the order was drawn up and perfected (or finally determined if the decision was given earlier than the date on which the form of order was finalised).[62] A respondent's notice must be filed within the time period laid down by the lower court or within 14 days after certain specified dates. The date that is most likely to apply is the date when the respondent is served with the appropriate document informing him that permission to appeal has been given.[63] Where the appeal court hears an application for permission to appeal, it will usually dispose of the application on paper. If permission is refused by the appeal court without a hearing, the applicant has the right to ask for the matter to be reconsidered at a hearing.[64] Such an application should be made within seven days after service of the notice that permission has been refused. There is then no further right of review or appeal against refusal of permission at such a hearing.[65] Permission is required for final appeals to the Supreme Court.[66]

[56] CPR rr.52.3, 52.13.

[57] Access to Justice Act 1999 s.55(1); CPR r.52.13.

[58] *Re T (A Child)* [2002] EWCA Civ 1736, [2003] 1 F.L.R. 531.

[59] CPR r.52.3(2)(a); Practice Direction (Appeals) to CPR Pt 52, para.4.6.

[60] CPR rr.52.4(1), 52.5(3).

[61] CPR r.52.4(2).

[62] *Sayers v Clarke Walker* [2002] EWCA Civ 645, [2002] 1 W.L.R. 3095; *Aujla v Sanghera* [2004] EWCA Civ 121 and regarding the requirement of the court to hand down a judgment see *Owusu v Jackson* [2002] EWCA Civ 877, [2003] 1 C.L.C. 246.

[63] For detail see CPR r.52.5.

[64] CPR r.52.3(4), (5).

[65] Access to Justice Act 1999 s.54(4); Practice Direction (Appeals) to CPR Pt 52, para.4.8.

[66] Administration of Justice (Appeals) Act 1934 s.1(1) and, as regards "leapfrog appeals", Administration of Justice Act 1969 ss.12–16 (as amended).

13–17 Where the Court of Appeal is considering an application for permission to appeal against an appellate decision (e.g. a decision of a High Court judge on an appeal from a registrar of the Companies Court), permission will not be granted unless the Court of Appeal considers that the appeal would raise an important point of principle or practice or there is some other compelling reason for the Court of Appeal to hear it.[67] In other cases, the test for permission is whether the court considers that the appeal would have a real prospect of success or there is some other compelling reason why the appeal should be heard.[68] Permission to appeal against case management decisions is granted more sparingly than in other "first appeal" cases.[69] Indeed, permission is difficult to obtain in such cases because it is difficult for the appellant to demonstrate conclusively that the court exercised its discretion wrongly. Permission may be granted subject to conditions and may also limit the issues to be heard.[70]

Procedure on appeals

13–18 The procedure under CPR Pt 52 is complex and prescriptive. Much paperwork has to be generated within prescribed time-limits. It is essential to move quickly. As regards appeals to the Court of Appeal, the need to comply with CPR Pt 52 and the relevant practice direction has been repeatedly emphasised.[71] The Court of Appeal has its own website.[72] Various helpful guidance leaflets are to be found on that website (at the time of writing these included: *Applying for Permission to Appeal to the Court of Appeal (Civil Division) (Form 206); Fees (Form 200); Form N161—Appellant's Notice; How to Appeal to the Court of Appeal (Form 202); How to Complete an Appellant's Notice (Form 203); How to Prepare an Appeal Bundle for the Court of Appeal (Form 204); Routes of Appeal (Form 201); Sources of Help for Unrepresented Appellants (Form 205)* and *Telephone Numbers*). In very broad terms, the key procedural stages to an appeal in the Court of Appeal are as follows (the stages do not necessarily occur in the order set out below):

(1) Filing and service of appellant's notice, the specified accompanying documents, appeal bundle and, in some cases, a core bundle.[73]
(2) Filing and service of any respondent's notice and skeleton argument.[74]
(3) Notification by the court in relation to hearing dates and directions made.[75]

[67] Access to Justice Act 1999 s.55(1) and CPR r.52.13.
[68] CPR r.52.3(6).
[69] Practice Direction (Appeals) to CPR Pt 52, paras 4.4 and 4.5; *Royal & Sun Alliance v T & N Ltd* [2002] EWCA Civ 1964.
[70] CPR rr.52.3(7), 52.15.
[71] See, e.g. *Harvey Shopfitters Ltd v ADI Ltd* [2003] EWCA Civ 1757, [2004] 2 All E.R. 982; *Scribes West Limited v Anstalt (No.1)* [2004] EWCA Civ 835, [2005] C.P.Rep. 2.
[72] Currently *http://www.hmcourts-service.gov.uk/cms/civilappeals.htm* [Accessed August 27, 2009].
[73] CPR r.52.4; Practice Direction (Appeals) to Pt 52, paras 5.1, 5.6, 5.6A, 5.9, 15.2, 15.11A.
[74] CPR r.52.5; Practice Direction (Appeals) to Pt 52, paras 7.1–7.13.
[75] Practice Direction (Appeals) to CPR Pt 52, paras 6.1–6.3.

(4) Lodging of Appeal Questionnaire.[76]
(5) Lodging of bundle of authorities.[77]

Appeal provisions of the Insolvency Rules 1986

13–19 The Insolvency Rules 1986 rr.7.47 and 7.49 are supplemented by the Practice Direction—Insolvency Proceedings ("the Insolvency Practice Direction"). Most disqualification cases will be within these rules.

Destination

13–20 The Destinations Order does not apply to Insolvency Rules 1986 rr.7.47 and 7.49. However, the destination of appeals in insolvency proceedings is now very similar to that applying to civil proceedings generally. The main difference is that appeals from a district judge sitting in a county court go to a High Court judge and not the county court (circuit) judge. The combined effect of s.16 of the Senior Courts Act 1981; rr.7.47 and 7.49 of the Insolvency Rules and the Insolvency Practice Direction is as follows:

(1) Appeals from a district judge sitting in a county court are to a High Court judge.[78]
(2) Appeals from a county court (circuit) judge are to a High Court judge.[79]
(3) Appeals from a district judge sitting in the High Court or from the Companies Court registrar are to a High Court judge.[80]
(4) Appeals from a High Court judge, sitting at first instance[81] or on appeal,[82] are to the Court of Appeal.
(5) Appeals from the Court of Appeal are to the Supreme Court.[83]
(6) There is provision for "leapfrog" appeals in exceptional cases, both direct to the Court of Appeal and direct to the Supreme Court. Such cases are so described because they involve "leaping over" and missing out a normal stage of appeal. As regards "leapfrog" appeals to the Court of Appeal, the essential requirement is that the case raises an important point of principle or practice or there is some other compelling reason for the Court of Appeal to hear it.[84] The requirements for leapfrog appeals to the Supreme Court are dealt with by the Administration of Justice Act 1969 ss.12–15 (as amended).

13–21 As regards appeals to the High Court judge, these are described by the Insolvency Practice Direction as "first appeals". It should be noted that for these

[76] Practice Direction (Appeals) to CPR Pt 52, paras 6.4–6.6.
[77] Practice Direction (Appeals) to CPR Pt 52, para.15.11.
[78] Destinations Order, para.3(2). As regards geography, see below.
[79] Insolvency Rules 1986 r.7.47(2). As regards geography, see below.
[80] Insolvency Rules 1986 r.7.47(2).
[81] Senior Courts Act 1981 s.16.
[82] Insolvency Rules 1986 r.7.47(2) but as regards permission note the Access to Justice Act 1999 s.55.
[83] Appellate Jurisdiction Act 1876 s.3(1).
[84] Access to Justice Act 1999 s.57; CPR r.52.14.

purposes an appeal from a High Court judge (whether sitting at first instance or on appeal) is not a "first appeal" within this defined term. As regards first appeals, para.17.10 of the Insolvency Practice Direction sets out where the relevant appeal should be lodged as follows:

> "(1) An appeal from a decision of a registrar in bankruptcy must be filed at the Royal Courts of Justice in London.
>
> (2) An appeal from a decision of a district judge sitting in a district registry may be filed—
>
> (a) at the Royal Courts of Justice in London; or
> (b) in that district registry.
>
> (3) An appeal from a decision made in a county court may be filed—
>
> (a) at the Royal Courts of Justice in London; or
> (b) in the Chancery district registry for the area within which the county court exercises jurisdiction.
>
> (There are Chancery district registries of the High Court at Birmingham, Bristol, Caernarfon, Cardiff, Leeds, Liverpool, Manchester, Mold, Newcastle upon Tyne and Preston. The county court districts that each district registry covers are set out in Schedule 1 to the Civil Courts Order 1983)."

Is permission to appeal needed in cases covered by Insolvency Rules 1986 rr.7.47 and 7.49?

13–22 In cases governed by the Insolvency Rules, it is clear that permission to appeal to a High Court judge from the decision of a district judge sitting in a county court or a county court (circuit) judge or from a district judge sitting in the High Court or a registrar of the Companies Court is needed.[85] This follows from the Insolvency Practice Direction rather than from any application of the CPR provisions. The Insolvency Practice Direction applies to "insolvency proceedings" which includes proceedings under the Insolvency Rules themselves. The irrelevancy of the CPR provisions in this context is demonstrated in part from the reasoning in *Re Busytoday Ltd*[86] and (to a limited extent) in *Re Langley Marketing Services Ltd*[87] and the later case of *Re The Premier Screw and Repetition Company Limited, Paulin v Secretary of State for Trade and Industry*[88]:

(1) In *Langley Marketing*, Hoffmann J. confirmed that in the case of an appeal governed by the Insolvency Rules from the decision of a district judge sitting in a county court to a High Court judge, permission was not needed (whereas permission was then needed for an appeal from such a district judge to a

[85] A change in the Insolvency Practice Direction means that there has been a change in the position since *Re The Premier Screw and Repetition Co Ltd, Paulin v Secretary of State for Trade and Industry* [2005] EWHC 888 (Ch), [2005] 2 B.C.L.C. 667 but that case contains a useful description of how the relevant Rules and Practice Directions interact. In *Paulin* the Vice-Chancellor expressed dismay at the obscurity of the position as it then stood.

[86] [1992] 1 W.L.R. 683.

[87] [1992] B.C.C. 585.

[88] [2005] 2 B.C.L.C. 667.

county court judge under the CCR). The decision suggests that the Insolvency Rules (in their then form) did not impose a condition that permission to appeal be obtained and the CCR provisions were not relevant.

(2) In *Busytoday*, the question arising was whether permission to appeal to a single High Court judge was needed under r.7.47 in relation to interim (or interlocutory) orders made by a registrar of the Companies Court. At that time, permission to appeal was required for appeals to the Court of Appeal from interim decisions of a High Court judge. It was submitted that this requirement was part of the "procedure and practice" of the Supreme Court (now "the Senior Courts") and that it was equally applicable to appeals under r.7.47 by virtue of r.7.49. Mummery J. rejected this submission on the basis that the requirement for permission was a matter of jurisdiction provided for by s.18(1)(h) of the Supreme Court Act 1981 (and reflected in RSC Ord. 59, r. 1A).

(3) In *Paulin*, the Vice-Chancellor considered the interface between the Disqualification Rules, the Insolvency Rules, and the Insolvency Practice Direction. On their then wording the Disqualification Rules provided that the Insolvency Rules rr.7.47 and 7.49 applied as regards disqualification proceedings under CDDA s.6, they being the proceedings before the Vice-Chancellor in the case in question. As already indicated, the Disqualification Rules now apply the appeal provisions of the Insolvency Rules to a much wider set of disqualification proceedings. Rule 7.49(1) of the Insolvency Rules provides that the procedure and practice of the Supreme Court (now "the Senior Courts") apply to appeals in insolvency proceedings (subject as thereafter provided). However, relevant provisions of the Insolvency Practice Direction dealing with appeals applied to "insolvency proceedings". Although disqualification proceedings were not specifically referred to in that definition, the definition did encompass proceedings under the Insolvency Rules. The Insolvency Practice Direction therefore applied, as did the (then) provision (since altered) that no permission was required for first appeals, i.e. for appeals to a High Court judge.

13–23 However, since *Busytoday* and *Paulin* the position has changed as a result of the changed requirements for permission to appeal now provided for by the Access to Justice Act 1999 and the provisions of the Insolvency Practice Direction, revised as from May 2, 2000 and subsequently further revised from October 1, 2007. Section 55 of the Access to Justice Act 1999 provides the jurisdictional basis for the making of rules of court governing permission to appeal. CPR Pt 52 provides for the circumstances in which permission to appeal is required (see above) but is itself subject to any other practice direction that deals with the subject of appeals.[89]

The Insolvency Practice Direction, para.17.6 provides that "first appeals"[90] are subject to the permission requirement under CPR r.52.3. As regards appeals from

[89] CPR r.52.1(4). The ability of rules of court to allow for further provision to be made by practice direction is contained in the Civil Procedure Act 1997 s.1 and Sch.1 para.6.

[90] See text at 13–20 above.

the High Court judge, sitting either at first instance or on an appeal, permission is required. In cases where the High Court judge sits at first instance, permission to appeal may be obtained either from that judge or the Court of Appeal. In this respect the Insolvency Practice Direction makes no specific provision that differs from the provisions in CPR Pt 52.[91] Where the High Court judge has sat as an appeal judge, then only the Court of Appeal can grant permission and the more restrictive terms applicable to granting permission for a second appeal apply.[92] Although r.7.47 of the Insolvency Rules suggests that, in such circumstances, permission may be obtained from the High Court or the Court of Appeal, it is clear from s.55 of the Access to Justice Act 1999 that only the Court of Appeal can give permission for second appeals. However, the High Court may give an indication of its opinion as to whether permission should be given by the Court of Appeal for a second appeal.[93] Any appeal from the Court of Appeal to the House of Lords also requires permission.[94]

Procedure on appeal

13–24 First appeals to a High Court judge are subject to the provisions of paras 17.8–17.23 of the Insolvency Practice Direction and, except as provided by that Practice Direction, CPR Pt 52 does not apply. A Companies Court registrar or, in a district registry, a district judge, will fulfil the role of the Registrar of Appeals.[95] Particular forms of appellant's and respondent's notice are specified by the Practice Direction.[96] The appellant's notice must be filed within the period specified by the lower court or, if no period is specified, within 21 days of the decision appealed against. Unless the court otherwise orders, the notice must be served on each respondent as soon as possible and in any event not later than seven days after it is filed. If an extension of time to file the notice is required, it should be sought in the appeal notice which should also set out the reasons for the delay and the steps taken prior to the making of the application. At the same time as filing an appellant's notice, the appellant must file a number of other documents including two copies of the appeal notice, an approved transcript of the judgment below (or an equivalent as referred to in para.5.12 of the Practice Direction accompanying CPR Pt 52), a copy of the order under appeal and a time estimate for the hearing. Applications to extend time for appealing must be made to the appeal court.[97] Any respondent's notice must be filed within the period specified by the lower court or, if no direction is made, within 14 days after the date on which the respondent is served with the appellant's notice. Unless the court otherwise orders, a respondent's notice must be served as soon as is practicable and, in any event, within seven days after it is

[91] Indeed, it sets out the basis upon which CPR Pt 52 and Access to Justice Act 1999 s.55 apply.
[92] Insolvency Rules 1986 r.7.47. CPR r.52.1 makes Pt 52 subject to any enactments (including statutory instruments) that make special provision in relation to any particular category of appeal.
[93] Practice Direction (Appeals) to CPR Pt 52, para.4.3.
[94] Administration of Justice (Appeals) Act 1934 s.1(1).
[95] Practice Direction—Insolvency Proceedings, para.17.8(b).
[96] Practice Direction—Insolvency Proceedings, para.17.9 and the Schedule thereto.
[97] Practice Direction—Insolvency Proceedings, para.17.13.

filed. As regards the admission of new evidence on appeal, the powers of the appellate court and other related matters, the Insolvency Practice Direction replicates for first appeals much of what is contained in CPR Pt 52.

13–25 The procedure for appeals from the High Court to the Court of Appeal is set out in CPR Pt 52. This is discussed briefly in 13–18 above. As appeals to the Supreme Court raise no issues that are particular to disqualification proceedings they are not dealt with further.

Conduct of the appeal

Admissibility of new evidence on appeal

13–26 New evidence will not be admitted on an appeal unless the appeal court so orders.[98] Under the pre-CPR law, the Court of Appeal would only admit new evidence after a trial on the merits "on special grounds".[99] In practice, the court exercised its discretion in accordance with the principles set out in *Ladd v Marshall*.[100] New evidence was only admitted if: (a) it could not have been obtained with reasonable diligence for use at the trial; (b) if admitted, it would probably have an important bearing on the result of the case, though it need not be decisive; and (c) it was credible without necessarily being incontrovertible. After the coming into force of the CPR, "special grounds" are not formally a jurisdictional requirement of the rules on admissibility of new evidence. Nevertheless, the courts have indicated that they will exercise their discretion to admit new evidence very much in line with previous authority, subject always to the overriding objective and the recognition that the courts are not subject to any straitjacket.[101] As Lord Phillips M.R. has said:

> ". . . We consider that under the new, as under the old procedure, special grounds must be shown to justify the introduction of fresh evidence on appeal . . . We do not consider that we are placed in the straitjacket of previous authority when considering whether special grounds have been demonstrated. That question must be considered in the light of the overriding objective of the new CPR. The old cases will, nonetheless remain powerful persuasive authority, for they illustrate the attempts of the courts to strike a fair balance between the need for the concluded litigation to be determinative of disputes and the desirability that the judicial process should achieve the right result. That task is one which accords with the overriding objective."[102]

The exercise of appellate jurisdiction

13–27 Under CPR Pt 52, the appeal court will only allow an appeal if it is established that the decision of the lower court was wrong or that the decision of the lower court

[98] CPR r.52.11(2). As regards "first appeals" in insolvency proceedings see Practice Direction—Insolvency Proceedings, para.17.18(2).

[99] RSC Ord.59, r.10.

[100] [1954] 1 W.L.R. 1489.

[101] *Hertfordshire Investments Ltd v Bubb* [2000] 1 W.L.R. 2318; *Hamilton v Al Fayed* [2001] E.M.L.R. 15; *Aylwen v Taylor Joynson Garrett* [2001] EWCA Civ 1171, [2002] P.N.L.R. 1; *Bentley & Skinner (Bond Street Jewellers) Ltd v Searchmap Ltd* [2003] EWHC 1621 (Ch).

[102] *Hamilton v Al Fayed* [2001] E.M.L.R. 15. In the *Barings* litigation, Mr Baker was refused permission to adduce fresh evidence on his appeal against the making of a disqualification order: see *Re Barings Plc (No.5), Secretary of State for Trade and Industry v Baker* [2001] B.C.C. 273 at [31]–[32].

was unjust because of procedural irregularity.[103] In this respect, it is important to note that, under both the CPR and the Insolvency Rules, an appeal will usually involve a review of the decision below rather than a complete re-hearing.[104] A re-hearing will take place if the appeal court considers that "in the circumstances of an individual appeal it would be in the interests of justice to hold a re-hearing".[105] However, a re-hearing will be exceptional.[106] The fact that the court below has not given reasons will not, of itself and in all circumstances, automatically justify a re-hearing although the position will be otherwise where the court refused to give reasons, or where there was some good reason why the lower court had not been asked to explain its decision,[107] or where the point is one of some complexity. If the first instance judge's reasoning is so inadequate that the losing party does not know why he lost, a re-hearing may be appropriate.[108] Failure to give reasons may result in a successful appeal. At the permission stage the trial judge may take the opportunity to provide additional reasons for his decision which may well save time and costs. However, the judge should usually abstain from providing additional reasons at a later stage, e.g. where several months have elapsed since the judgment was given.[109]

13–28 In deciding whether a decision was "wrong", the appeal court does not approach all decisions in the same way. There is a spectrum of types of decision and the appellate court's approach to the various types. At one end of the spectrum, there is the situation where the appeal court disagrees with the lower court's statement of the applicable law. In that event, the appeal court will substitute its own view of the law. At the other end of the spectrum are decisions that were in the lower court's discretion. Such decisions tend to be case management or costs decisions or, in the disqualification context, decisions whether to grant permission to commence proceedings under CDDA s.6 outside the two-year period, decisions as to the period of disqualification[110] or decisions whether to grant permission to act notwithstanding disqualification.[111] In such cases, the appeal court does not

[103] CPR r.52.11(3).

[104] CPR r.52.11(1) and, for "first appeals" to the High Court, Practice Direction—Insolvency Proceedings, para.17.18(1). For other appeals, CPR r.52.11 applies by virtue of Insolvency Rules 1986 r.7.49. It was also the position under the old law that appeals in insolvency proceedings were by way of review rather than re-hearing: see *Re Hitco 2000 Ltd, Official Receiver v Cowan* [1995] 2 B.C.L.C. 63. On the difference between review and re-hearing see *Assicurazioni Generali SpA v Arab Insurance Group* [2002] EWCA Civ 1642, [2003] 1 W.L.R. 577.

[105] CPR r.52.11(1)(b).

[106] *Asiansky Television Plc v Bayer Rosin* [2001] EWCA Civ 1792; *Audergon v La Baguette Ltd* [2002] EWCA Civ 10, [2002] C.P.Rep 27.

[107] *Lewis v Secretary of State for Trade and Industry* [2003] B.C.C 567.

[108] *Robert v Momentum Services Ltd* [2003] EWCA Civ 299, [2003] 1 W.L.R. 1577.

[109] *Flannery v Halifax Estate Agencies Ltd* [2000] 1 W.L.R. 377; *English v Emery Reimbold & Strick Ltd* [2002] EWCA Civ 605, [2002] 1 W.L.R. 2409; *Michael Hyde Associates Ltd v JD Williams & Co Ltd* [2001] P.N.L.R. 8.

[110] See, e.g. *Re Swift 736 Ltd, Secretary of State for Trade and Industry v Ettinger* [1993] B.C.L.C. 896; *Re Copecrest Ltd, Secretary of State for Trade and Industry v McTighe* [1996] 2 B.C.L.C. 477; *Re Westmid Packing Services Ltd, Secretary of State for Trade and Industry v Griffiths* [1998] 2 All E.R. 124.

[111] *Re TLL Realisations Ltd, Secretary of State for Trade and Industry v Collins* [2000] B.C.C. 998.

generally substitute its own view and will only interfere with the decision below and substitute its own view (or, as it is said, exercise the discretion afresh) in limited circumstances. The matter has been expressed differently in different cases but, broadly speaking, the appeal court will only interfere with the decision of the lower court where: (a) the lower court has erred in principle[112]; (b) the lower court has left out of account or taken into account some factor that it should, or should not, have relied on; (c) the lower court's decision is outside the generous ambit within which reasonable disagreement is possible; or (d) the lower court's decision is wrong because the court has failed to balance the relevant factors fairly in the balance.[113] Accordingly, there is much less scope for interference by an appeal court in such cases and the appeal court cannot simply substitute its own view of the "correct" answer wherever that view differs from the view of the court below.

13–29 Somewhere between decisions on applicable law and pure exercises of discretion lie decisions of "fact" and "mixed fact and law". The "labelling" of certain decisions as decisions of "fact" or "mixed law and fact" may be convenient shorthand but it does not of itself provide a useful guide to the appeal process. Thus, in *Re Sevenoaks Stationers (Retail) Ltd*,[114] the decision of the court as to whether a person's conduct was such as to make him unfit within the meaning of CDDA s.6 was described as a decision of fact whereas, as pointed out by Hoffmann L.J. in *Re Grayan Building Services Ltd, Secretary of State for Trade and Industry v Gray*[115] the decision is rather one of mixed law and fact. Even decisions of fact are not all of the same quality. Thus, findings that specific writs and demands were served on a company at certain dates and that the company had a certain level of resources to meet those demands are findings of primary fact that are quite different from findings of secondary fact, arrived at by process of inference from primary facts, concerning such matters as whether the company was factually insolvent or had some realistic prospect of avoiding an insolvency regime.[116] An appeal court will be very slow to interfere with decisions of the lower court on matters of primary fact given that the lower court will have heard oral evidence from witnesses on the issues in question. With regard to secondary facts or the evaluation of primary facts, an appeal court may be more prepared to intervene and substitute its own

[112] See the unusual case of *Secretary of State for Trade and Industry v Rogers* [1996] 1 W.L.R. 1569 where the Court of Appeal allowed an appeal against an eight-year disqualification imposed by Harman J. under the *Carecraft* procedure. The Court of Appeal exercised its discretion afresh and made a disqualification order for the same period. However, in so doing it effectively overturned findings of fact made by Harman J. in making the original order which were outside the agreed facts recorded in the *Carecraft* statement and which, under the *Carecraft* procedure, it was not open to him to make. Considered from the viewpoint of the CPR regime, this may be an example of a case where the decision was not wrong but was unjust because of a serious irregularity in the proceedings in the lower court within CPR r.52.11(3)(b).

[113] *G v G (Minors: Custody Appeal)* [1985] 1 W.L.R. 647 at 652; *AEI Rediffusion Music Ltd v Phonographic Performance Ltd* [1999] 1 W.L.R. 1507 at 1523; *Tanfern Ltd v Cameron-MacDonald* [2000] 1 W.L.R. 1311 at [32]; *Price v Price (t/a Poppyland Headware)* [2003] EWCA Civ 888, [2003] 3 All E.R. 911 at [26]–[27].

[114] [1991] Ch. 164.

[115] [1995] Ch. 241.

[116] See discussion in *Re Hitco 2000 Ltd, Official Receiver v Cowan* [1995] 2 B.C.L.C. 63.

view. However, it will do so with reluctance and the approach will be more akin to that of a review rather than the exercise of a discretion.[117] In cases under CDDA ss.6, 8 and 9A, the court must go one stage further and determine whether or not the person's conduct as a director makes him "unfit". The application of a particular standard to a given set of facts is often highly context-specific. Thus, differences in circumstances may affect the extent to which the appeal court is prepared to interfere with the decision of the lower court. Put another way, the boundaries of what is within the reasonable range of decisions a reasonable judge, properly applying the relevant law, could reach for his decision to survive an appeal may differ depending on the context. As was said in the *Grayan* case:

> "[T]he standards applied by the law in different contexts vary a great deal in precision and generally speaking, the vaguer the standard and the greater the number of factors which the court has to weigh up in deciding whether or not the standards have been met, the more reluctant an appellate court will be to interfere with the trial judge's decision."[118]

Thus, the willingness of the appeal court to interfere with decisions of mixed fact and law will vary depending on the nature of the particular decision-making process that the trial judge has had to go through and the context in which the decision was reached. In *Grayan*, Hoffmann L.J. approved of the way in which the deputy judge had expressed the matter in the *Re Hitco 2000 Ltd*[119]:

> "Plainly the appellate court would be very slow indeed to disturb such a conclusion as to fitness or unfitness. In many, perhaps most, cases, the conclusion will have been so very much assisted and influenced by the oral evidence and demeanour of the director and other witnesses that the appellate court would be in nowhere near as good a position to form a judgment as to fitness or unfitness than was the trial judge. But there may be cases where there is little or no dispute as to the primary facts and the appellate court is in as good a position as the trial judge to form a judgment as to fitness. In such cases the appellate court should not shrink from its responsibility to do so and, if satisfied that the trial judge was wrong, to say so."

[117] *Assicurazioni Generali SpA v Arab Insurance Group* [2002] EWCA Civ 1642, [2003] 1 W.L.R. 577.
[118] *Re Grayan Building Services Ltd, Secretary of State for Trade and Industry v Gray* [1995] Ch. 241.
[119] [1995] 2 B.C.L.C. 63.

CHAPTER 14

THE LEGAL EFFECT OF DISQUALIFICATION

INTRODUCTION

14–01 Like disqualification from driving a motor vehicle, disqualification under the CDDA is, in the broadest sense, a form of legal incapacitation. However, the prohibitions imposed by ss.1, 1A, 9B(3), 11 and 12 of the CDDA are considerably more open-textured than a straightforward ban from driving a motor vehicle. In addition, CDDA disqualification has wider legal effects, both under statutory provisions and professional rules and regulations, which extend the effect of disqualification beyond the scope of the disqualifications, prohibitions and restrictions in the CDDA itself. This chapter explores the legal scope of these disqualifications, prohibitions and restrictions and their wider consequences for the disqualified person. It also considers the legal consequences for persons who are acting or have acted in breach of the prohibitions. Disqualification under s.11 of the CDDA is an automatic consequence of bankruptcy, a debt relief order ("DRO"), a bankruptcy restrictions order ("BRO"), a bankruptcy restrictions undertaking ("BRU"), a debt relief restrictions order ("DRRO") or a debt relief restrictions undertaking ("DRRU").[1] Other consequences of bankruptcy restrictions and debt relief restrictions are considered in Ch.11.[2] The consideration of the consequences of disqualification in this chapter is limited to consideration of the position in England and Wales. It should be noted that there are a number of statutory provisions providing for similar consequences to those in England and Wales in the other jurisdictions in the United Kingdom. As regards Northern Ireland disqualifications, it should be noted that, subject to transitional provisions, they are brought within the scope of the CDDA, and given effect to within England, Wales and Scotland by CDDA ss.12A and 12B.

SCOPE OF DISQUALIFICATION

The prohibitions

14–02 The relevant provisions of the CDDA are ss.1, 1A, 9B(3), 11 and 12. Section 1(1) defines the parameters of a disqualification order imposed by the court under any of CDDA ss.2–5, 6, 8, 9A and 10. A disqualification order is described in s.1(1) as:

[1] In this chapter, as in Ch.11, reference to a person being subject to insolvency restrictions is a reference to a person who is subject to a BRO, BRU, DRRO or DRRU.

[2] See further text from 11–33 and 11–41.

"... an order that for a period specified in the order [the disqualified person]—

(a) ... shall not be a director of a company, act as a receiver of a company's property or in any way, whether directly or indirectly, be concerned or take part in the promotion, formation or management of a company unless (in each case) he has the leave of the court, and
(b) ... shall not act as an insolvency practitioner."

14-03 The present s.1 was inserted by s.5 of the Insolvency Act 2000 and applies to all disqualification orders made on or after April 2, 2001.[3] The scope of disqualification orders made before that date is defined by the former s.1.[4] Section 1A defines the scope of a disqualification undertaking accepted by the Secretary of State under either s.7(2A) or 8(2A) in terms that are virtually identical to s.1. The scope of a competition disqualification undertaking is separately defined in CDDA ss.9B(3)–(4) in terms that are similar, although not identical, to ss.1 and 1A.[5]

CDDA s.11(1) insofar as it applies in England and Wales[6] imposes a ban that is closely analogous to that set out in s.1(1)(a). It prohibits an undischarged bankrupt, a person to whom a moratorium period under a DRO applies (a "DRO debtor") and a person who is the subject of insolvency restrictions (a BRO, BRU, DRRO, DRRU) from acting as a director of, or directly or indirectly taking part in or being concerned in the promotion, formation or management of a company, except with the permission of the court.[7] The s.11 ban is automatic and takes effect without the need for a court order. Although, in contrast to ss.1 and 1A, s.11 does not expressly ban the disqualified person from acting as a receiver of a company's property and as an insolvency practitioner, an undischarged bankrupt, a DRO debtor and a person the subject of insolvency restrictions are disqualified from acting in either capacity by virtue of the Insolvency Act 1986 ss.31, 390(4)(a), (aa) and (5).[8] One minor point should be noted concerning the position in Scotland. It is clear from Insolvency Act 1986 ss.388(1)(a), 390(4)(a) and 390(5) that an undischarged bankrupt, a DRO debtor and a person subject in England and Wales to insolvency restrictions cannot be appointed as an administrative receiver under a Scots law floating charge. This is because the effect of

[3] The Insolvency Act 2000 (Commencement No.1 and Transitional Provisions) Order 2001 (SI 2001/766).

[4] See further text at 12–04. As it is conceivable that there may still be some orders made before April 2, 2001 in force, it will be appropriate to deal with the former s.1 at certain points during the chapter.

[5] See further text at 9–42 and from 12–05.

[6] See text from 11–18. On the effect of CDDA s.11(1) within Great Britain see text from 16–28.

[7] The CDDA and cases decided before the reform of the civil justice system use the phrases "leave of the court" and "leave to act". In the light of the CPR, the Disqualification Rules and the Disqualification Practice Direction, the term "permission" is used throughout rather than the old term "leave" except in the case of direct quotes from the CDDA.

[8] Sections 31 and 390(5) were inserted by the Enterprise Act 2002 s.257(3) and Sch.21 with effect from April 1, 2004 (for commencement see SI 2003/2093). Section 390(4)(aa) was inserted and s.390(5) amended to add reference to debt relief restrictions by the Tribunals, Courts and Enforcement Act 2007 s.108(3), Sch.20 Pt 1 paras 1, 6(1), (2), (3) with effect from April 6, 2009 (for commencement see SI 2009/382). It should be noted that the Insolvency Act ban on acting as a receiver does not extend to receivers appointed by the court: see s.31(3).

s.440 of the Insolvency Act 1986 is that ss.388–390 apply to Scotland. As a consequence, a person who is not qualified to act as an insolvency practitioner by virtue of bankruptcy, a DRO or insolvency restrictions arising in England and Wales cannot act as an administrative receiver in Scotland. Similarly, an undischarged bankrupt and a person subject to a BRO or a BRU arising in England and Wales as well as in Scotland are automatically disqualified from acting as a receiver of part only of the company's property under a Scots law floating charge[9] by s.51(3)(b), (ba) of the Insolvency Act 1986. However, the prohibition in s.51(3) does not currently extend to DRO debtors and persons the subject of debt relief restrictions arising in England and Wales.[10] The effect of these provisions within Great Britain is considered further in Ch.16.

14–04 Section 12 of the CDDA prohibits a person who is subject to it from acting as a director or liquidator of, or from directly or indirectly taking part or being concerned in the promotion, formation or management of a company without the permission of the court. This prohibition comes about as a result of a court order made under s.429 of the Insolvency Act 1986. If a person fails to make a payment which he is required to make under an administration order under Pt VI of the County Courts Act 1984, the court may revoke the administration order, apply the disqualification in CDDA s.12 and apply various other disabilities set out in s.429 of the Insolvency Act (for example, a restriction on obtaining credit without disclosing the fact that the section applies to him).[11] Although the consequence of the application of CDDA s.12 is that the person cannot act as a liquidator, there is no general automatic disqualification from acting as an insolvency practitioner under s.390 of the Insolvency Act, as there is in cases where a disqualification order is made or the person is an undischarged bankrupt, a DRO debtor, or is subject to insolvency restrictions. This is because the disqualification flows from s.429(2)(b) of the Insolvency Act and is not therefore a "disqualification order" or "disqualification undertaking" under the CDDA for the purposes of s.390(4)(b) of the Insolvency Act.

14–05 It is unfortunate that the relevant prohibitions are similar and yet differently worded and defined. As a matter of general policy it is extremely difficult to see why different prohibitions should apply in each of the cases in question. This inconsistency reflects the way that the various provisions, which came into being at different times and for different reasons, have been consolidated within a single Act of Parliament without proper consideration of how they should function as part of one effective code.

14–06 Although differently worded, the prohibitions in CDDA ss.1, 1A, 9B(3), 11(1) and 12 are comprehensive in scope and, given the protective rationale of the

[9] Not being an administrative receiver within the meaning of Insolvency Act 1986 s.29(2).

[10] The provision was extended to encompass BROs and BRUs whether imposed in England and Wales or under the parallel Scots law bankruptcy restrictions regime by the Bankruptcy and Diligence etc (Scotland) Act 2007 s.3(1)–(4) with effect from April 1, 2008.

[11] Section 429 is prospectively amended by the Tribunals, Courts and Enforcement Act 2007 s.106, Sch.16 para.3. At the time of writing the amendments had not been brought into force. See further text from 11–113.

CDDA, should be broadly construed. A person prohibited from acting as a director etc. under any of CDDA ss.1(1)(a), 1A(1)(a), 9B(3)(a)–(c), 11(1) or 12 can only act in a prohibited capacity with the express permission of the court.[12] The immediate consequence of disqualification for anyone who holds directorships or managerial positions in any company is that he will have to resign from them or obtain permission of the court to remain in such positions. The consequences for a licensed insolvency practitioner of a disqualification order, disqualification undertaking or competition disqualification undertaking are particularly serious as the prohibition on acting as an insolvency practitioner in CDDA ss.1(1)(b), 1A(1)(b) and 9B(3)(d) is absolute and cannot be waived by the court during the currency of the order or undertaking.[13]

Territorial effects of disqualification within the United Kingdom

14–07 CDDA s.24(1) provides that the CDDA extends to England, Wales and Scotland. Thus, a person the subject of a disqualification order made by the courts in England and Wales is prima facie barred from acting in a prohibited capacity in relation to a Scottish-registered company (and vice versa). Moreover, there is provision for mutual recognition and enforcement of disqualification orders as between the courts in England and Wales and the Scottish courts.[14] The position in relation to disqualification undertakings appears to be similar.

14–08 The CDDA did not originally extend to Northern Ireland,[15] which has its own separate (albeit virtually identical) disqualification regime. However, with effect from April 2, 2001 s.12A was inserted into the CDDA by s.7(1) of the Insolvency Act 2000.[16] This provides that a disqualification order made under the Northern Ireland legislation in force at that date has the same scope as a disqualification order under CDDA s.1 and would therefore have effect in England, Wales and Scotland.[17] A provision having identical effect as regards Northern Ireland disqualification undertakings was inserted as CDDA s.12B pursuant to powers in s.7(2) of the Insolvency Act 2000 with effect from September 1, 2004.[18] The

[12] The question of whether the court can make partial or selective orders under ss.1(1)(a), e.g. an order disqualifying a person from acting as a company director but allowing him to take part in the management of companies is discussed in Ch.12. A further point to note is the curious wording of CDDA ss.9B(3)–(4) which appears to suggest that a relevant regulator has the power to accept a competition disqualification undertaking in a form that excludes the court's power to grant permission to act: see further text at 9–42 and from 12–05. Applications for permission to act are considered generally in Ch.15.

[13] The introduction of this ban removed the previous uncertainty as to how Insolvency Act 1986 s.390 and the former CDDA s.1 were to be reconciled: see text at 12–03.

[14] Insolvency Act 1986 ss.426(1), (10).

[15] CDDA s.24(2).

[16] Insolvency Act 2000 (Commencement No.1 and Transitional Provisions) Order 2001 (SI 2001/766). See also the effect of SI 2009/1941, art.2(1) Sch.1, para.85.

[17] See also the Company Directors Disqualification (Northern Ireland) Order 2002 (SI 2002/3150), arts 2(2), 3 and, in relation to undertakings, arts 4, 10 and 11 brought into force by the Company Directors Disqualification (2002 Order) (Commencement) Order (Northern Ireland) 2003 (SI 2003/345) with effect from July 22, 2003. For transitional provisions see the Company Directors Disqualification (2002 Order) (Transitional Provisions) Order (Northern Ireland) 2003 (SI 2003/346).

[18] See the Insolvency Act 2000 (Company Directors Disqualification Undertakings) Order 2004 (SI 2004/1941).

effect of both ss.12A and 12B is that a person who is subject to a Northern Ireland disqualification is also made subject to a ban in terms that are very similar to ss.1 and 1A. The mechanism is closely analogous to that under CDDA ss.11 and 12 in that a qualifying condition (Northern Ireland disqualification) automatically triggers a specific ban under the CDDA in England, Wales and Scotland. It is, however, important to note that the power to relieve from a Northern Ireland disqualification by granting permission to act remains with the Northern Ireland High Court, even in relation to the extended ban imposed by ss.12A and 12B. Conversely, a disqualification order or disqualification undertaking made or accepted under the CDDA also has effect in Northern Ireland by virtue of art.17 of the Company Directors Disqualification (Northern Ireland) Order 2002.[19] Insofar as a CDDA disqualification imposed in Great Britain takes effect in Northern Ireland, art.17 confers jurisdiction on the Northern Ireland High Court (and not the relevant court in Great Britain) to grant permission to act notwithstanding disqualification.

14–09 The prohibitions in CDDA s.11(1) so far as it applies to England and Wales on a person made bankrupt, a DRO debtor or a person made the subject of insolvency restrictions in England and Wales and the prohibitions in CDDA s.12 also extend to Scottish-registered companies. Similarly, it seems that a Scottish bankrupt is barred in England and Wales from acting in a prohibited capacity in relation to a company registered in England and Wales.[20] The County Courts Act and the DRO and debt relief restrictions regimes do not extend to Scotland and so within England and Wales disqualification under CDDA ss.12, 11(1)(a) and 11(1)(b) cannot arise from any conduct in Scotland. With effect from April 1, 2008 Scotland has had its own bankruptcy restrictions regime and BROs and BRUs can be made pursuant to ss.56A and ss.56G (respectively) of the Bankruptcy (Scotland) Act 1985.[21] The question that therefore now arises is whether the prohibition in s.11(1)(b) applies to persons who are subject to Scottish BROs and BRUs as well as BROs and BRUs made in England and Wales. The government's view appears to be that a reference in primary legislation to a BRO or BRU being in force is capable of encompassing Scottish BROs and BRUs as exactly the same terminology is used in the Bankruptcy (Scotland) Act 1985.[22] BROs and BRUs can also now be imposed under Northern Ireland legislation.[23] However, s.11 cannot apply within Great Britain to Northern Ireland bankrupts or persons subject to Northern Ireland bankruptcy restrictions without

[19] SI 2002/3150 (NI 4).

[20] Doubts arise because of the enactment of a separate s.11(1) applying only in England and Wales: see text from 16–28.

[21] These provisions were inserted by the Bankruptcy and Diligence etc (Scotland) Act 2007 s.2(1). For commencement see the Bankruptcy and Diligence etc (Scotland) Act 2007 (Commencement No.3, Savings and Transitionals) Order 2008 (SSI 2008/115).

[22] The authors doubt this view: see text from 16–28.

[23] Insolvency (Northern Ireland) Order 1989 (SI 1989/2405 (N.I.19)) art.255A and Sch.2A inserted by Insolvency (Northern Ireland) Order 2005 (SI 2005/1455 (N.I.10)) art.13.

an amendment to the CDDA along the lines of ss.12A and 12B because the CDDA does not extend to Northern Ireland.

COMPANY

14–10 The prohibitions restrict the disqualified person from acting in various capacities in relation to *companies*. The meaning of "company" was considered earlier in Ch.3. However, the discussion there was confined to the question of jurisdiction. In some cases the meaning of "company" is the same whether one is considering the scope of a power to disqualify or the extent of the prohibitions. For example, by virtue of CDDA s.22A, it is clear that the court's power of disqualification in CDDA s.6 could be exercised in relation to building societies and that the prohibitions in ss.1, 1A, 9B(3), 11, 12, 12A and 12B also extend to building societies. However, the position is not always straightforward and should be checked in each case. It is not safe to assume that a disqualified person is necessarily prevented from acting as a director etc. of a particular type of body simply because the court is able in certain situations to exercise powers of disqualification in relation to that type of body.[24]

Extension to building societies, incorporated friendly societies, NHS foundation trusts, open-ended investment companies, limited liability partnerships and charitable incorporated organisations

14–11 Section 22A of the CDDA provides that the Act applies to building societies as it applies to companies. Thus references in the CDDA to "company" are treated as including references to a building society. Section 22B of the CDDA provides that the Act applies to incorporated friendly societies as it applies to companies and references to "company" shall include references to an incorporated friendly society. Similarly, s.22C of the CDDA provides that the Act applies to NHS foundation trusts as it applies to companies.[25] As a result of these provisions, the prohibitions in CDDA ss.1, 1A, 9B(3), 11, 12, 12A and 12B clearly apply to such bodies with the result that the disqualified person cannot, without the court's permission, be a director or officer of a building society (within the meaning of the Building Societies Act 1986), or a member of the committee of management or officer of an incorporated friendly society (within the meaning of the Friendly Societies Act 1992), or a director or officer of an NHS foundation trust, nor in any way, whether directly or indirectly, be concerned or take part in the promotion, formation or management of

[24] The point is particularly pertinent in the context of insolvent partnerships which are discussed in the text from 14–18.

[25] Section 22C was inserted into the CDDA by the Health and Social Care (Community Health and Standards) Act 2003 s.34 and Sch.4 paras 67–68 with effect in England and Wales from April 1, 2004: SI 2004/759.

such bodies.[26] With effect from October 1, 2009, CDDA s.22D also applies the provisions of the CDDA to open-ended investment companies.[27] The position is therefore now the same in relation to these entities as it is for building societies, incorporated friendly societies and NHS foundation trusts. The position in relation to limited liability partnerships is the same as that for building societies, incorporated friendly societies, NHS foundation trusts and open-ended investment companies by virtue of the Limited Liability Partnerships Regulations 2001.[28] It is clear from reg.4(2)(a) of these regulations that "company" in CDDA ss.1, 1A, 9B(3), 11, 12, 12A and 12B includes a limited liability partnership. It follows that any person the subject of the CDDA prohibitions is barred from acting in a prohibited capacity in relation to a limited liability partnership.[29] At the time of writing the position in relation to charitable incorporated organisations[30] had not been settled. Draft regulations relating to the insolvency and dissolution of charitable incorporated organisations had been published which suggested that the relevant provisions of the Insolvency Act 1986 and CDDA ss.1, 1A, 6, 7, 8A, 9, 10, 14, 16, 17, 20, 20A, 21, 22 and Sch.1 would be applied expressly to these bodies with appropriate modifications.[31] If enacted in this form then the prohibitions in CDDA ss.1 and 1A would extend expressly to charitable incorporated organisations. Draft general regulations had also been issued including a provision which, if enacted, would expressly extend the prohibitions in ss.11 and 12 to charitable incorporated organisations.[32]

CDDA s.22: general definitions

14–12 Section 22 sets out the general definition of "company" in the CDDA. Before October 1, 2009 the effect of s.22 was that in s.11 the expression "company"

[26] Note also the effect of Building Societies Act 1986 s.90E and CDDA s.21C inserted with effect from March 29, 2009 by arts 6 and 12 of the Building Societies (Insolvency and Special Administration) Order 2009 (SI 2009/805). In effect, these tailor the application of CDDA ss.6–7 to building societies that enter the special insolvency and administration regimes for which provision is made by the Banking Act 2009. Accordingly, these provisions do not affect the basic proposition in the text that the various prohibitions in the CDDA encompass building societies as well as registered companies. The same point can be made about the provisions in CDDA ss.21A and 21B in relation to banks that enter the Banking Act 2009 insolvency regimes. Insofar as a bank is a registered company or a banking group consists of registered companies, a person disqualified under the CDDA is prohibited from acting in a relevant capacity in relation to such bank or banking group without the permission of the court.

[27] CDDA s.22D was inserted by SI 2009/1941 on which see further text from 14–12.

[28] SI 2001/1090.

[29] The references to "director" in the CDDA are modified to include references to a member of a limited liability partnership: see regs 4(2)(f)–(g).

[30] This is a proposed form of charitable organisation which differs from a company registered under the Companies Acts. The CDDA applies to charitable companies in the same way as it does in relation to other companies.

[31] See the Cabinet Office and Office of the Third Sector joint consultation document, *The Charitable Incorporated Organisation (CIO)—Consultation on the new corporate form for charities* (September 2008), Annex B available online at *http://www.cabinetoffice.gov.uk/third_sector/consultations/completed_consultations/cio.aspx* [Accessed August 28, 2009]. See further text at 3–91.

[32] See Annex B of the consultation document referred to in the previous footnote.

included an unregistered company and a company incorporated outside Great Britain which had an established place of business in Great Britain. Elsewhere in the CDDA "company" included any company which, at that time, might have been wound up under Pt V of the Insolvency Act 1986. From October 1, 2009 the Companies Act 2006 (Consequential Amendments, Transitional Provisions and Savings) Order 2009 ("the 2009 Order")[33] substituted the present wording of CDDA s.22(2) which reads as follows:

> " 'Company' means—
>
> (a) a company registered under the Companies Act 2006 in Great Britain, or
> (b) a company that may be wound up under Part 5 of the Insolvency Act 1986 (unregistered companies)."[34]

In addition, CDDA s.22(9) provides that:

> "subject to the provisions of this section, expressions that are defined for the purposes of the Companies Acts (see section 1174 of, and Schedule 8 to, the Companies Act 2006)[35] have the same meaning in this Act."

The 2009 Order also inserted a new s.11(4) from October 1, 2009 which states that "company" for the purposes of s.11:

> ". . . includes a company incorporated outside Great Britain that has an established place of business in Great Britain."

This wording reproduces the old wording of s.22(2)(a) omitting the reference to unregistered companies. The effect of these various definitions is considered in more detail below.

Registered companies

14–13 Before October 1, 2009, the combined effect of s.22(9) of the CDDA, ss.1(1) and 2 of the Companies Act 2006 and s.735 of the Companies Act 1985 was that the prohibitions in CDDA ss.1, 1A, 9B(3), 11, 12, 12A and 12B were to be read as including relevant prohibitions in relation to companies formed and registered under the Companies Act 2006 and companies formed and registered under any of its statutory predecessors on or after July 14, 1856.[36] Accordingly, the

[33] SI 2009/1941.

[34] Part V of the Insolvency Act 1986 now seems to be referred to as Pt 5 (i.e. arabic rather than roman numeral). For convenience, throughout this chapter and throughout the book as a whole reference is made to Pt V as per the statutory predecessor of the present s.22(2)(b).

[35] The words in parenthesis were inserted by the 2009 Order with effect from October 1, 2009.

[36] Companies formed and registered under the Joint Stock Companies Act 1844 or in Ireland under companies legislation up to and including the Companies (Consolidation) Act 1908 were excluded from the definition of companies formed and registered under the Companies Act 1985 or the former Companies Acts: see Companies Act 1985 s.735(1)(a), (b), (3). The position appears to be the same from October 1, 2009: see Companies Act 2006 s.1(1)(b)(ii).

prohibitions clearly encompassed all forms of registered company, i.e. guarantee companies and unlimited companies as well as companies limited by shares.[37] From October 1, 2009, by virtue of CDDA s.22(2)(a) as amended, "company" in CDDA ss.1, 1A, 9B(3), 11, 12, 12A and 12B includes "a company registered under the Companies Act 2006 in Great Britain". This amendment, which is merely consequential on the coming into force of the Companies Act 2006, does not appear to have materially affected the position as it stood before October 1, 2009 as regards the application of the prohibitions to companies formed and registered under the relevant Companies Acts.[38]

14–14 With the coming into force of Council Regulation 2157/2001 of October 8, 2001 on October 8, 2004, it is possible to incorporate a European Company (*societas europaea*) by registration in the United Kingdom.[39] Although strictly a creature of Community Law, it is clear from arts 9, 10 and 15 of the Regulation that such a company will be treated as if it were a registered public limited company and that, accordingly, it will be a "company" falling within the scope of the CDDA prohibitions. In any event, art.47 of the Regulation provides that, as a matter of Community law, a person is prohibited from acting as a member of the management or supervisory organ of a European Company if: (a) he is disqualified under the law of the Member State in which the company's registered office is situated from serving on the corresponding organ of a public limited company governed by the law of that Member State; or (b) he is disqualified from serving on the corresponding organ of a public limited company governed by the law of a member state owing to a judicial or administrative decision in a Member State. It follows that a person disqualified under CDDA ss.1, 1A, 9B(3), 11, 12, 12A and 12B, which encompass all types of registered companies, including public companies, will be prohibited from being a member of the organs of a European Company whether registered in the United Kingdom or in any other Member State.[40] This appears to be the first example of provision being made in directly

[37] However, the court may be more minded to grant permission to a person to act in relation to an unlimited company than a limited company: see Ch.15.

[38] See, in particular, Companies Act 2006 ss.1(1), 1(2)(a). A minor technical change having no practical significance is that the current definition of "company" as "a company registered under the Companies Act 2006 . . .", rather than "formed and registered" under that Act, would appear to encompass overseas companies that register in Great Britain pursuant to Pt 34 of the 2006 Act. Before October 1, 2009, these companies would have fallen within s.22(2)(b) as companies that may at that time have been wound up under Pt V of the Insolvency Act In any event, such companies clearly fall within the scope of the CDDA whether under the current s.22(2)(a) or s.22(2)(b).

[39] For background see DTI, *Implementation of the European Company Statute: The European Public Limited-Liability Company Regulations—A Consultative Document* (2003) and *Implementation of the European Company Statute: The European Public Limited-Liability Company Regulations—Results of Consultation* (2004).

[40] One slight doubt that arises is whether a person banned under the CDDA from acting as a director of a company would be prohibited from acting as a member of the supervisory organ of a European Company where, as is contemplated by art.8 of the Regulation, a two-tier board structure is adopted. art.47(2) refers to "the corresponding organ" but in the United Kingdom, there is no requirement for public companies to have a supervisory as well as a management board. It is suggested that art.47 will be given a generous reading in line with its obvious purpose. See now also the European Public Limited-Liability Company Regulations 2004 (SI 2004/2326), especially reg.78.

applicable EC law that gives disqualification provisions in the domestic law of member states an EU-wide effect.

14–14A A further supranational corporate form, the European Private Company (*societas privata europaea*) is to be introduced and available in Member States with effect from July 1, 2010.[41] As its name suggests, the object of this proposal is to create a standard, uniform private company vehicle for small and medium-sized enterprises that wish to expand their business beyond the borders of a single Member State and provide such enterprises with an alternative to incorporating subsidiaries or establishing branches in other Member States. A European Private Company will be a creature of Community Law formed by registration in the Member State in which it has its registered office. For the purposes of domestic law, such a company will be a registered company. The winding up of such a company will also be governed by domestic law and Council Regulation (EC) 1346/2000. It follows that the prohibitions in CDDA ss.1, 1A, 9B(3), 11, 12, 12A and 12B will certainly encompass European Private Companies that are registered in Great Britain or that are registered in another Member State but have their centre of main interests in Great Britain.[42]

CDDA s.11: unregistered companies

14–15 Before October 1, 2009, by virtue of what was then CDDA s.22(2)(a), the prohibition imposed by CDDA s.11 applied in relation to "unregistered companies" which, in the context, meant unregistered companies as defined for the purposes of the Companies Acts. The then CDDA s.22(9) and Companies Act 2006 s.1043 (formerly Companies Act 1985 s.718), defined unregistered companies as including bodies corporate incorporated in and having a principal place of business in Great Britain[43] other than: (a) any body incorporated by, or registered under, any public act of Parliament (which includes registered companies); (b) any body not formed for the purpose of carrying on a business which has for its object the acquisition of gain by the body or its individual members; (c) any body for the time being exempted by direction of the Secretary of State; and (d) open-ended investment companies.[44] From October 1, 2009, the definition of company for the purposes of s.11[45] no longer makes reference to these forms of unregistered

[41] See Proposal for a Council Regulation on the Statute for a European Private Company COM (2008) 396/3. For background see R. Drury, "The European Private Company" (2008) 9(1) European Business Organization L.R. 125; B. Mackowiz and F. Saifee, "Societas Privata Europaea: the European Private Company" (2009) 30(8) Co.Law. 227.

[42] It is clear from the proposed Regulation that a European Private Company shall not be under any obligation to have its central administration or principal place of business in the Member State in which it has its registered office.

[43] Companies Act 2006 s.1043 refers to unregistered companies incorporated in and having a principal place of business in the United Kingdom because s.1299 of the 2006 Act makes it clear that, in general, it has effect throughout the United Kingdom. However, as the CDDA does not extend to Northern Ireland, its prohibitions cannot encompass unregistered companies in Northern Ireland.

[44] A "body corporate" for these purposes is defined by CDDA s.22(6) by reference to s.1173(1) of the Companies Act 2006 and therefore does not include a corporation sole or a partnership that is not regarded as a body corporate under its governing law.

[45] Now contained in CDDA ss.22(2) and 11(4).

company. However, such companies clearly remain within the scope of all the CDDA prohibitions, including the prohibitions in s.11, because they may be wound up under Pt V of the Insolvency Act and are therefore companies within the meaning of what is now CDDA s.22(2)(b).[46] This definition of unregistered company is, of course, tied to the Insolvency Act meaning rather than the Companies Act meaning.

CDDA s.11: foreign corporations with an established place of business in Great Britain

14–16 The prohibition on bankrupts, DRO debtors and those subject to insolvency restrictions having a relevant involvement in companies was extended by the then CDDA s.22(2)(a) before October 1, 2009 and is now extended by CDDA s.11(4) on or after that date to what are, in effect, overseas companies falling within the scope of Pt 34 of the Companies Act 2006. Essentially this part of the definition bites on companies incorporated overseas but with an established place of business in Great Britain. As regards the position on or after October 1, 2009 it appears that the scope of the s.11 prohibitions has been widened as, under CDDA s.22(2)(b), it now extends to companies that may be wound up under Pt V of the Insolvency Act and not merely companies incorporated outside Great Britain that have an established place of business in Great Britain. Indeed, in the light of the general application of CDDA s.22(2)(b), s.11(4) appears to be superfluous. The application of the CDDA to foreign incorporated companies and the extent to which the CDDA prohibitions encompass relevant involvement in such companies is considered further in Ch.16.

Companies which may be wound up under Pt V of the Insolvency Act 1986

14–17 Before October 1, 2009, by virtue of what was then CDDA s.22(2)(b), a "company" within CDDA ss.1, 1A, 9B(3), 12, 12A and 12B included a company which, at that time, might have been wound up under Pt V of the Insolvency Act 1986. From October 1, 2009, the effect of CDDA s.22(2)(b) (as substituted) is that "company" for the purposes of the CDDA as a whole includes a company that may be wound up under Pt V of the Insolvency Act 1986. The power to wind up companies under Pt V of the Insolvency Act 1986 identifies such companies by the expression "unregistered company". This may cause confusion with the concept of an unregistered company as defined by reference to Companies Act 2006 s.1043. Accordingly, and for present purposes, a company liable to be wound up under Pt V of the Insolvency Act 1986 is referred to as a "Pt V company". Before October 1, 2009, the effect of s.220 of the Insolvency Act 1986 was that "any association and company" was capable of being wound up under Pt V with limited exceptions. Those exceptions were: (a) a company registered in any part of the United Kingdom under the Joint Stock Companies Acts or under the legislation (past or present)

[46] For the purposes of Pt V, an unregistered company includes any association and any company, with the exception of a company registered under the Companies Act 2006 in any part of the United Kingdom: see Insolvency Act 1986 s.220 (as substituted by SI 2009/1941 with effect from October 1, 2009) and 14–17 below.

relating to companies in Great Britain; and (b) an association or company with a principal place of business situated in Northern Ireland (unless it also had a principal place of business situated in England and Wales and/or Scotland). From October 1, 2009 a Pt V company includes any association and any company, with the exception of a company registered under the Companies Act 2006 in any part of the United Kingdom. The exception for associations or companies having a principal place of business in Northern Ireland also continues to apply.[47] The main examples of Pt V companies are companies formed under private act of Parliament, foreign companies (considered further in Ch.16), companies incorporated by private (or special) Act of Parliament, companies incorporated by royal charter and companies incorporated by order in council. Although the words "any association" appear to be very wide the courts have not so construed them.[48] Moreover, it is suggested that although Pt V of the Insolvency Act 1986 is headed "winding up of unregistered companies", the use in s.22(2)(b) of the CDDA (whether before or, on or after, October 1, 2009) of the expression "*a company* which may be wound up" is significant. Section 22(2) of the CDDA (in its forms both pre- and post- October 1, 2009) neither uses the expression "any association or company which may be wound up under Pt V . . ." nor "any unregistered company which may be wound up under Pt V . . ." nor "any body which may be wound up under Pt V . .". On this basis it is submitted that the prohibitions in the CDDA relate only to *companies* which may be wound up under Pt V of the Insolvency Act 1986 and not to associations or other bodies liable to be wound up under that Part such as certain types of unincorporated association which are not partnerships. It follows that an unincorporated friendly society, which is not a body corporate, is not a Pt V company for present purposes. This view is reinforced by the fact that Parliament has seen fit to extend the application of the CDDA to building societies, incorporated friendly societies, NHS foundation trusts, open-ended investment companies, limited liability partnerships and (prospectively) charitable incorporated organisations[49] but not to unincorporated friendly societies. As discussed in Ch.3, the authors also consider that the CDDA does not extend to industrial and provident societies.[50]

Partnerships

14–18 In the authors' view, the prohibitions in CDDA ss.1, 1A, 9B(3), 11, 12, 12A and 12B do not extend to partnerships. This was the assumption of Harman J. in *Re Probe Data Systems (No.3) Ltd*[51] and it is an assumption that is widely made on

[47] Insolvency Act 1986 s.221(2). See also *Re Normandy Marketing Limited* [1994] Ch. 198, holding that a company incorporated in Northern Ireland can be wound up as an unregistered company under s.220 of the Insolvency Act 1986, provided that it had a principal place of business in England and Wales. The point may be of limited importance as the Company Directors Disqualification (Northern Ireland) Order 2002 (SI 2002/3150), art.17 extends the effect of a disqualification order or undertaking made or accepted under the CDDA to Northern Ireland in any event: see text at 14–08.

[48] See, e.g. *Re St James Club* (1852) 2 De G M & G 383, 42 ER 920; *Re International Tin Council* [1989] Ch. 309; *Re Witney Town Football and Social Club* [1994] 2 B.C.L.C. 487.

[49] See text at 14–11.

[50] See text from 3–95.

[51] [1991] B.C.L.C. 586 at 593.

applications by disqualified persons subject to the prohibitions in ss.1 and 1A for permission to act.[52] The arguments supporting the soundness of this assumption are set out below.

14–19 The critical question is whether or not partnerships are companies liable to be wound up under Pt V of the Insolvency Act 1986 within CDDA s.22(2)(b) (whether before or, on or after, October 1, 2009). Although, under art.7 of the Insolvent Partnerships Order 1994 ("the 1994 Order"),[53] the provisions of Pt V of the Insolvency Act 1986 (as modified by the 1994 Order) are applied to insolvent partnerships and the court is thereby empowered to wind up insolvent partnerships, it is submitted that a partnership is not a "*company* which may be wound up under Pt V of the Insolvency Act" falling within the scope of CDDA s.22(2)(b) for the following reasons:

(1) Partnerships are not wound up under Pt V but under the 1994 Order which applies the provisions of Pt V to partnerships in modified form.
(2) A partnership is not a "company" and s.22(2)(b) refers to "companies" liable to be wound up not "bodies" liable to be wound up.
(3) The CDDA was enacted on July 25, 1986. At that stage partnerships were not capable of being wound up under Pt V of the Insolvency Act 1986. (The reference to "any partnership", formerly contained in s.665 of the Companies Act 1985, was removed by Pt IV of Sch.10 to the Insolvency Act 1985). The power to wind up partnerships under Pt V of the Insolvency Act 1986 was conferred by the predecessor of the 1994 Order, the Insolvent Partnerships Order 1986. That Order was made on December 8, 1986. It was made under powers conferred by s.420 of the Insolvency Act 1986 and s.21(2) of the CDDA. Neither of those provisions at that time conferred authority on the rule-maker to alter the meaning or width of the prohibitions contained in CDDA ss.1 and 1A. Moreover, the scope of the rule-making powers is expressly limited to *insolvent* partnerships and does not extend to partnerships generally.
(4) Article 16 of the 1994 Order extends ss.6–10 of the CDDA (amongst other sections) to insolvent partnerships with modifications (in particular, to deal with the fact that partnerships do not have "directors"). Its predecessor was to similar effect. The fact that such modification was necessary (not least to deal with the fact that there are no "directors" of a partnership) suggests that "company" in ss.6–10 does not itself include a partnership. It would be strange if "company" had a different meaning in CDDA ss.1, 1A, 9B(3), 12, 12A, 12B and, from October 1, 2009, s.11.
(5) While CDDA ss.1(1) and 1A(1) are expressly applied to insolvent partnerships by art.16 of the 1994 Order (as amended), ss.9B(3), 12, 12A and 12B clearly do

[52] See, e.g. *Secretary of State for Trade and Industry v Barnett* [1998] 2 B.C.L.C. 64; *Re Amaron Ltd* [1998] B.C.C. 264 at 276–281.

[53] SI 1994/2421 as amended by as amended by a series of Insolvent Partnerships (Amendment) Orders: SI 1996/1308 with effect from June 14, 1996; SI 2001/767 with effect from April 2, 2001; SI 2002/1308 with effect from May 31, 2002; SI 2005/1516 with effect from July 1, 2005; SI 2006/622 with effect from April 6, 2006.

not apply. A modification akin to that effected by the 1994 Order in relation to ss.6–10 would be necessary for ss.9B(3), 12, 12A and 12B to apply. Even though ss.1(1) and 1A(1) expressly apply, it is suggested that this merely confirms that there is jurisdiction to disqualify the officers of insolvent partnerships. It does not alter the meaning or width of the prohibitions: see point (3) above.

(6) It is arguable on policy grounds that the prohibitions should not extend to partnerships. There are strong indications that the CDDA is directed primarily at those who abuse the privilege of limited liability (albeit not exclusively so).[54] However, given the difficulty of formulating a consistent policy other than in general terms such as "protection of the public", the argument that the policy of the CDDA is not to disqualify persons from acting in partnership without permission, while sustainable, is not of itself especially compelling. On the plain words of the statute, it is clear that a disqualified person cannot be a director or take part in the management of an unlimited company.

The cumulative effect of these arguments is that a person disqualified in the terms of CDDA ss.1, 1A, 9B(3), 11, 12, 12A, 12B can act in relation to an unincorporated partnership including, on the face of it, a limited partnership under the Limited Partnership Act 1907,[55] without the court's permission.

14–20 There seems to be no reason why the prohibitions imposed on undischarged bankrupts, DRO debtors and persons subject to insolvency restrictions by s.11, either before October 1, 2009[56] or on or after October 1, 2009,[57] should be read as encompassing partnerships. This is because ordinary and limited partnerships are not "companies" for the reasons set out above.

Open-ended investment companies

14–21 Before October 1, 2009, as under the Open-Ended Investment Companies Regulations 2001,[58] an open-ended investment company is wound up under Pt V of the Insolvency Act 1986, these companies fell within the previous wording of CDDA s.22(2)(b) with the effect that a person disqualified in the terms of CDDA ss.1, 1A, 9B(3), 12, 12A and 12B was disqualified from acting in the prohibited capacities in relation to such an entity. From October 1, 2009, s.22D of the CDDA applies the Act directly to open-ended investment companies with the result that the prohibitions in CDDA ss.1, 1A, 9B(3), 11, 12, 12A and 12B clearly apply.[59]

European Economic Interest Groupings

14–22 The European Economic Interest Grouping Regulations 1989[60] expressly assume that an EEIG may be wound up as an unregistered company under Pt V of the

[54] See generally Ch.2.
[55] As amended by the Legislative Reform (Limited Partnerships) Order 2009 (SI 2009/1940).
[56] The relevant definition for these purposes being the former CDDA s.22(2)(a).
[57] The relevant definition for these purposes being the current CDDA s.11(4).
[58] SI 2001/1228.
[59] See 14–11.
[60] SI 1989/638.

Insolvency Act 1986. On such winding up, the effect of reg.20[61] is that CDDA ss.1, 2, 4–11, 12(2), 15–17, 20, 22 and Sch.1 expressly apply to an EEIG. However, the effect of reg.20 appears to be circumscribed by the fact that the provisions of the CDDA mentioned only apply *where an EEIG is wound up as an unregistered company under Pt V*. In other words, it does not expressly extend ss.1, 1A, 9B(3) and 12 *for all purposes*. As such, it is far from clear that a person disqualified either on the basis of his conduct in relation to a registered company or under s.12 would be disqualified from acting in relation to an EEIG. Having said that, the regulations clearly contemplate that an EEIG registered in Great Britain is a body corporate with its own legal personality for domestic law purposes.[62] On this basis, it is arguable that an EEIG is a "*company* which may be wound up under Pt V . . ." for the purposes of CDDA s.22(2)(b). As a result, it is suggested on balance that a person disqualified in the terms of CDDA ss.1, 1A, 9B(3), 12, 12A or 12B is disqualified from acting in the prohibited capacities in relation to an EEIG.

14–23 The position in relation to CDDA s.11 is historically even more complex. Regulation 20 refers expressly to s.11 and might be read as suggesting that an undischarged bankrupt, a DRO debtor and a person the subject of insolvency restrictions cannot act in the management of an EEIG. However, the regulation appears only to apply *where an EEIG is wound up*. The only literal sense that could be made of this was that an undischarged bankrupt, a DRO debtor and a person the subject of insolvency restrictions were barred from acting in a prohibited capacity in relation to an EEIG which is wound up. The question that arose before October 1, 2009 was whether an EEIG could amount to either an "unregistered company" or "a company incorporated outside Great Britain which has an established place of business in Great Britain" within what was then CDDA ss.22(2)(a).[63] It was not clear that an EEIG could be classified as an "unregistered company" for the purposes of CDDA s.22(9) and Companies Act 2006 s.1043.[64] Moreover, an EEIG registered in Great Britain under the 1989 Regulations was clearly not "a company incorporated outside Great Britain . . .". However, it appeared that the prohibition in s.11 may have encompassed EEIGs registered in other Member States of the European Community that had an established place of business in Great Britain to the extent that the applicable national law required the EEIG to be registered as a body corporate.[65] On the assumption that the authors' conclusion in 14–22 is right, the position from October 1, 2009 is that EEIGs fall within the scope of the s.11 prohibitions because, notwithstanding the remaining difficulties with the wording in what is now s.11(4), the effect of the current s.22(2)(b) is that s.11 encompasses companies that may be wound up under Pt V.

[61] As amended and extended to encompass Northern Ireland disqualifications by SI 2009/2399 with effect from October 1, 2009.

[62] SI 1989/638, reg.3.

[63] See 14–15 and 14–16.

[64] It should be noted that EEIGs were brought within the scope of the exceptions in Companies Act 1985 s.718, the statutory predecessor of Companies Act 2006 s.1043, by virtue of Sch.4, para.20 of the 1989 Regulations.

[65] Council Regulation 2137/85 of July 25, 1985 on the EEIG leaves it to Member States to determine whether or not groupings registered at their registries have legal personality: see art.1(3).

Foreign incorporated companies

14–24 A company incorporated outside Great Britain can be wound up by the court under Pt V of the Insolvency Act 1986[66] and prima facie the CDDA prohibitions are capable of encompassing such companies. The extent of the extraterritorial reach of the CDDA prohibitions, and the CDDA generally, is considered further in Ch.16.

DIRECTOR

14–25 The prohibitions in CDDA ss.1, 1A, 9B(3), 11, 12, 12A and 12B of the CDDA each encompass acting as a "director" without the permission of the court.[67] There is no doubt that the prohibitions encompass acting as a properly and legally appointed de jure director. The need for a separate prohibition distinct from the prohibition on being involved or taking part in management is to protect the public as much from the supine director who fails to involve himself in management when he ought to have done so as from the active director. A shadow director, namely a person in accordance with whose directions or instructions the directors of a company are accustomed to act,[68] is not encompassed within the term "director" in CDDA ss.1, 1A, 11, 12, 12A or 12B[69] but a ban on acting in such a capacity is, in practice, applied by the prohibition on being involved or taking part in management. A de facto director—that is a person who acts as a director although not duly appointed as such—is also caught by the relevant bans. The concepts of shadow and de facto directors are considered at length in Ch 3. For present purposes it suffices to say that under CDDA ss.1, 1A, 9B(3), 11, 12, 12A and 12B, the prohibition on being a de facto director results from one or more of the following matters: (a) s.22(4) of the CDDA; (b) the true construction of "director" within the relevant prohibitions given the policy of the CDDA[70]; and/or (c) the prohibition on being concerned or taking part in management.

Does CDDA disqualification result in formal removal from office?

14–26 The question of whether a person the subject of a CDDA disqualification is required to vacate office as a director depends on the relevant company's articles

[66] Subject to the jurisdictional caveat relating to unregistered companies having a principal place of business in Northern Ireland: see Insolvency Act 1986 s.221(2). Although companies formed and registered under the Companies (Northern Ireland) Order 1986 are now treated as if formed and registered under Companies Act 2006, they remain unregistered companies for the purposes of the Insolvency Act as the winding up provisions in Pt IV of that Act applicable to registered companies do not extend to companies registered or incorporated in Northern Ireland: see Insolvency Act 1986 s.441(2); SI 2009/1941, Sch.1, para.84.

[67] In CDDA ss.1, 1A, 9B(3), 12A and 12B the disqualified person is banned from *being* a director. In ss.11 and 12, the ban is on *acting* as a director. It might be argued that there is nothing to stop a person disqualified under ss.11 or 12 being *appointed* as a director provided that he does not *act* as such. However, the point has very little to commend it in practical terms.

[68] CDDA s.22(5).

[69] In contrast to the position under CDDA s.9B(3): see s.9E(5).

[70] See the approach of Browne-Wilkinson V.C. in relation to s.300 of the Companies Act 1985 (the predecessor of CDDA s.6) and de facto directors in *Re Lo-Line Electric Motors Ltd* [1988] Ch. 477 at 488D–490F.

of association.[71] The model articles for private companies limited by shares, private companies limited by guarantee and public companies contained in the Companies (Model Articles) Regulations 2008[72] all provide that a person ceases to be a director if, among other things: (a) he ceases to be a director by virtue of any provision of the Companies Act 2006 or is prohibited from being a director by law; (b) a bankruptcy order is made against him; or (c) a composition is made with his creditors generally in satisfaction of his debts. This is similar to the provision in art.81 of Table A in relation to existing companies incorporated under the Companies Act 1985 with articles in that form.[73] While a disqualified person who continues in office would obviously be in breach of the relevant CDDA prohibition, the point is not entirely academic. If no provision is made in the articles, it is arguable that the disqualified person would still retain authority to act on the company's behalf at least within the terms of the company's constitution. Conversely, it is clear that where a person is a director of a company or companies the articles of which provide that his appointment terminates in defined circumstances, his authority to act as agent for the company ceases on the happening of a defined event.[74]

RECEIVER OF A COMPANY'S PROPERTY

14–27 CDDA ss.1, 1A, 9B(3), 12A and 12B all expressly prohibit the disqualified person from acting as a receiver of a company's property without the permission of the court. In this context, CDDA s.22(10)[75] provides that any reference to "acting as a receiver" includes acting as a manager or as both receiver and manager but does not include acting as an administrative receiver. The bans imposed by these provisions also prohibit the disqualified person from acting as an insolvency practitioner.[76] As a result of the ban on acting as an insolvency practitioner, the disqualified person is prohibited from acting as an administrative receiver.[77] The question that arises is how far the ban in CDDA ss.1(1)(a), 1A(1)(a), 9B(3)(b), 12A(a) and 12B(a) on acting as a receiver extends. The phrase, "receiver or manager of the property of a company" is defined in s.29 of the Insolvency Act 1986 in such a way as to include administrative receivers, receivers of part only of a company's property and receivers of income arising from that property. Strictly, this definition only applies to the phrase "receiver or manager . . ." as it appears in the Companies Act and the Insolvency Act 1986 and not to the phrase "receiver of a company's property" in the CDDA. Nevertheless, it is suggested that CDDA

[71] By contrast, where a person is a director at the time of his disqualification under Australia's Corporations Act 2001 (Cth.) s.203B, his office automatically ceases by operation of the statute and so the issue does not turn on whether there is provision in the relevant company's articles of association.
[72] SI 2008/3229 (in force from October 1, 2009).
[73] Companies Act 1985 (Tables A to F) Regulations (SI 1985/805) as subsequently amended by SI 2007/2541, SI 2007/2826, SI 2008/739.
[74] *Witherdale Ltd v Registrar of Companies* [2005] EWHC 2964 (Ch), [2008] 1 B.C.L.C. 174.
[75] As inserted by the Insolvency Act 2000.
[76] See further text from 14–56.
[77] Insolvency Act 1986 ss.230(2), 388–389.

ss.1(1)(a), 1A(1)(a), 9B(3)(b), 12A and 12B should be read in the same way (though excluding that part of the definition which includes the term "administrative receiver). Even if the definition of s.29 of the Insolvency Act does not strictly apply, the words "receiver of a company's property" are very wide and, it is suggested, as a matter of construction, apply to receivers of part of a company's property and receivers of income arising from that property. It should be noted that the court has power to grant a disqualified person permission to act as a receiver of part of the property of a company or as a receiver of income under CDDA ss.1(1)(a), 1A(1)(a), 9B(3)(b), 12A and 12B[78] but no power to grant a disqualified person permission to act as an insolvency practitioner, and therefore as an administrative receiver, under CDDA, ss 1(1)(b), 1A(1)(b), 9B(3)(d), 12A(b) and 12B(b).

14–28 CDDA s.11 as it applies in England and Wales contains no express prohibition against acting as an insolvency practitioner or as a receiver of a company's property. However, by virtue of ss.230(2), 388(1)(a), 389, 390(4)(a), (aa) and 390(5)[79] of the Insolvency Act 1986, an undischarged bankrupt, a DRO debtor and a person subject to insolvency restrictions are disqualified automatically from acting as an administrative receiver of a company. There is no power in the court to relax this ban. Such persons are also disqualified from acting as a receiver or manager of the property of a company on behalf of debenture holders, though not as a receiver or manager acting under an appointment made by the court, by virtue of the Insolvency Act 1986 s.31.[80]

14–29 CDDA s.12 expressly prohibits the disqualified person from acting as a liquidator without the permission of the court but contains no prohibition on acting as an insolvency practitioner or as a receiver of a company's property. Disqualification in the terms of CDDA s.12(2) does not trigger the automatic ban on acting as an insolvency practitioner in s.390(4)(b) of the Insolvency Act 1986 because the disqualification flows from s.429(2)(b) of the 1986 Act and is not therefore a "disqualification order" or "disqualification undertaking" under the CDDA for the purposes of the provision. It follows that a person subject to disqualification under CDDA s.12 is not prohibited by the terms of that provision from acting as an administrative receiver.

DIRECTLY OR INDIRECTLY BE CONCERNED OR TAKE PART IN THE PROMOTION, FORMATION OR MANAGEMENT OF A COMPANY

14–30 The prohibition on the disqualified person being concerned or taking part (whether directly or indirectly) in the promotion, formation or management of a company

[78] Though in relation to competition disqualification undertakings, see text at 9–42 and from 12–05. Note also that power to grant permission to act in relation to a Northern Ireland disqualification notwithstanding the effect of CDDA s.12A or 12B remains with the Northern Ireland High Court.

[79] Section 390(5) was inserted by the Enterprise Act 2002 s.257(3), Sch.21 with effect from April 1, 2004 (for commencement see SI 2003/2093). Section 390(4)(aa) was inserted and s.390(5) amended to add reference to debt relief restrictions by the Tribunals, Courts and Enforcement Act 2007 s.108(3), Sch.20 Pt 1 paras 1, 6(1), (2), (3) with effect from April 6, 2009 (for commencement see SI 2009/382).

[80] The present wording was substituted by Enterprise Act 2002 s.257(3), Sch.21 and further amended to introduce the references to a DRO and a DRRO by Tribunals, Courts and Enforcement Act 2007 s.108(3), Sch.20 paras 1–2. See further text at 14–03 which also deals with the position in Scotland.

without the permission of the court, applies under each of CDDA ss.1, 1A, 9B(3)(c), 11, 12, 12A and 12B. In terms of the scope of disqualification, this is the most difficult aspect of the prohibitions to pin down. The use of the phrase "directly or indirectly" suggests that a disqualified person would be in breach of the prohibition were he to appoint a nominee to act in the promotion, formation or management of a company on his behalf. However, "indirect" involvement is not limited to such cases and is potentially quite wide. None of the terms "promotion", "formation" or "management" is statutorily defined and so the scope of the prohibition has a fluid quality. Given the wide variation in possible forms of involvement and the wide range of potential companies and corporate structures that arise, such fluidity is probably inevitable. In the words of Ormiston J. in *Commissioner for Corporate Affairs (Vic) v Bracht*, ". . . [c]ircumstances and procedures may vary widely from company to company".[81] This makes it difficult to do anything more than offer a broad description of the prohibitions and suggests that it would be unwise for Parliament to attempt any more precise definitions. The issue of whether a disqualified person has acted in breach of the prohibition will therefore depend on all the facts of the case and, faced with the question, "do these particular activities amount to management?", the court must take a contextual approach, construing the term "management" in the light of both the overall scheme and purpose of the CDDA and the specific corporate context in which the disqualified person was operating.

14–31 Andrew Hicks has criticised the width and indeterminacy of this approach. His criticism is premised on the view that disqualification is penal in character and that, accordingly, terms such as "promotion", "formation" and "management" should be construed restrictively so that the disqualified person can be in no doubt about what he can and cannot do.[82] The argument that disqualification has at least some penal element cannot seriously be contested.[83] Nevertheless, the contrary argument is that the terms of the prohibition should be construed broadly to reflect the width of the statutory language, the protective purposes of the CDDA and the fact that it is open to the disqualified person to apply to the court for permission to act if he is any doubt as to whether he would be in breach of the prohibition by engaging in a particular activity. As Beldam J. put it, dealing with precisely this issue in *R. v Campbell*:

> "In the opinion of the court that criticism is amply met . . . by the fact that there is provision . . . for such a person, in the case of doubt, to apply to the court for [permission] to do that which he seeks to do. If he applies to the court then any question of ambiguity would be resolved because the court would either say that he could or could not do that which he proposed to do."[84]

[81] [1989] V.R. 821.

[82] A. Hicks, "Taking part in management—the disqualified director's dilemma" [1987] 1 Malaysian L.J. lxxiv. On the restrictive construction of penal statutes see, e.g. *Dickenson v Fletcher* (1873) L.R. 9 C.P. 1 at 7; *Methuen-Campbell v Walters* [1979] Q.B. 525 at 542.

[83] See discussion of the nature and purpose of disqualification (including the "quasi-criminal" view) in Ch.2.

[84] (1984) 78 Cr.App.R. 95 at 101. It should be noted, however, that Beldam J.'s view has not been universally accepted: see, e.g. *Commissioner for Corporate Affairs (Vic) v Bracht* [1989] V.R. 821. See also *Re Westminster Property Management Limited (No.2), Official Receiver v Stern (No.2)* [2001] B.C.C. 305 at 355 et seq. and the discussion concerning declaratory relief immediately below.

The prevailing judicial consensus, discussed earlier in Ch.2, is that the primary purpose of the CDDA is protective rather than penal and, as such, the courts have tended to take a broad view when construing the terms of the prohibition.

14–32 The question of whether a person is acting in a prohibited capacity or fashion is an issue of mixed law and fact. The legal meaning of the prohibition must be derived from the terms of the CDDA and the evidence then tested to determine whether, on the facts, the prohibition has been infringed. Thus, where a person is prosecuted for acting in breach of the prohibition, it is for the trial judge to direct the jury as to the legal meaning of the prohibition and for the jury to decide in the light of the evidence whether the person has, in fact, breached the prohibition.

Declaratory relief?

14–33 In at least one case following the making of a disqualification order, a party wishing to take up employment with a company sought permission under CDDA ss.1 and 17 to act notwithstanding the disqualification or, in the alternative, a declaration that the activities that he wished to pursue would not involve a breach of the s.1 prohibition.[85] The declaratory relief was not pursued but there are serious obstacles in the way of seeking such relief in this context. First, the question of whether certain activities fall within the wide wording of CDDA ss.1(1)(a), 1A(1)(a), 9B(3)(c), 12A(a) and 12B(a) will depend on all the circumstances of the case and detailed evidence as to those circumstances. It is meaningless to list a number of activities in the abstract. In most cases, to provide an answer by way of declaration, the court would have to investigate in detail the entire factual context and circumstances and this exercise would probably necessitate disclosure. Secondly, and as a matter of discretion, it is doubtful that the court should grant declaratory relief. This is because the court can only deal with the facts as found by it at the time it makes its investigation. Those facts may change in the future, rendering the declaration not only academic but also misleading.[86] The issue was touched upon in connection with an application by Mr William Stern for permission to act as a director of a number of companies following his disqualification.[87] Among other matters, a question arose as to whether or not the 12-year disqualification order made against him prevented him from acting as a director of two groups of companies. The first group comprised three companies incorporated in the United States: two in Texas and one in California. Those companies, as Mr Stern affirmed, had no nexus whatsoever with the United Kingdom, save that he conducted correspondence in relation to their affairs from his address here. Mr Stern was sole director of the Californian company and one of three directors of the Texan companies. The second group comprised a Belgian company, a Netherlands company and a New York company.

[85] *Re TLL Realisations Ltd* [2000] B.C.C. 998. The case was decided before the introduction of the current ss.1 and 1A by the Insolvency Act 2000. Nevertheless, the material wording in the former s.1(1)(d) and the current provisions is identical.

[86] See, e.g. *Amstrad Consumer Electronics Plc v British Phonographic Industry Ltd* [1986] F.S.R. 159; *R. v Medicines Control Agency Ex p. Pharma Nord (UK) Ltd* [1998] 3 C.M.L.R. 109, CA.

[87] For the judgments resulting in disqualification and relating to permission to act notwithstanding disqualification see *Re Westminster Property Management Limited (No.2), Official Receiver v Stern (No.2)* [2001] B.C.C. 305.

The first two were subsidiaries of an English registered company and the third owed a debt to that company but was not owned by it. It was said that the activities of these companies were carried out exclusively in Belgium and Holland. The judge refused permission to act. As regards the Californian and Texan companies, he was not persuaded that the receipt of communications in the jurisdiction by Mr Stern, and the communication of his management decisions from the jurisdiction, provided a strong enough nexus to satisfy the requirement of a sufficient connection with the jurisdiction to establish winding up jurisdiction and, accordingly, that the disqualification prevented Mr Stern acting in relation to those companies. Fuller evidence was needed to determine the point. As regards the second group, where there was a connection through a debt or shareholding or both to a UK company, the court reached the same conclusion. The judge made no decision on the issue of whether the CDDA and the disqualification order applied to the companies. As the burden lay on the applicant for permission to establish that the CDDA and order did apply and that permission to act was therefore needed, he refused the application. He added that even if he had been satisfied on the jurisdictional question, he very much doubted whether, as a matter of discretion, he would have granted permission and indeed he refused permission to act in relation to a number of other companies where there clearly was jurisdiction to grant it.

14–34 Permission to appeal having been refused by the judge, an application for permission to appeal came before the Court of Appeal.[88] Chadwick L.J. gave the following summary of the issue:

> "The problem for Mr Stern, of course, is that he does not know whether, if he continues to act as a director of any of the six overseas companies, he will be acting in breach of the disqualification order and so committing a criminal offence. He asks the court to resolve that problem for him."

However leading counsel for Mr Stern did not seek an order that the matter be remitted to the judge so that he could decide, with the benefit of fuller evidence, whether the companies were within the scope of the CDDA prohibition. His position was described by Chadwick L.J. as follows:

> "He says, in effect, that there is already ample evidence for that decision to be made. Further, he does not suggest that there is any useful purpose in sending the matter back to the judge to consider whether leave to act should be granted. He is mindful, perhaps, of the strong indication at the end of the judgment that leave to act would be unlikely to be granted. [Counsel for Mr Stern] says that, as a matter of principle, the judge should have resolved on the evidence before him the question whether or not the foreign incorporated companies were companies to which the order applied; and that, the judge not having decided the point, permission to appeal to this court should be granted so that this court can make an appropriate declaration. In support of that submission he has referred to *R. v Campbell* [1984] B.C.L.C. at p.83; and in particular to a passage at p.88 in the judgment of Beldam J. . . ."

[88] *Re Westminster Property Management Ltd, Official Receiver v Stern* [2001] EWCA Civ 111, [2002] B.C.C. 937.

This was a reference to the Beldam J.'s point that:

> "if a person was concerned as to whether or not he could continue to act in relation to a company, he could ask the court for permission and, if the court gave him leave, then there would be no question of any breach of the provision."

Chadwick L.J. considered that the judge had been:

> "plainly right to treat the application before him as an application for leave to act under the [CDDA] and not as an application for a declaration whether or not particular companies were companies within the jurisdiction for the purposes of Pt V of the Insolvency Act 1986 and s. 2(2)(b) of the CDDA."

If Mr Stern had wished the court to make a declaration, then it was important that this was made clear both to the court and to anybody else who would be affected by the declaration, and that the terms of the declaration were spelt out clearly and precisely so the court knew what it was being asked to do. Having decided that there was "no basis upon which this court would consider it appropriate to make a declaration on the material which is at present available" and that there were no grounds for interfering with the judge's conclusion to similar effect, Chadwick L.J. went on to give the following warning which, it is respectfully suggested, echoes the approach suggested above:

> "[F]or my part, [I would not] . . . encourage courts to take the view that it was a sensible or appropriate course to make such declarations in this kind of case. The problem is that the court can only make a declaration as to an existing state of affairs on the basis of the material which is put before it. If, relying on that declaration, a party continues as a director of a company and is then prosecuted, the question for the criminal court will be whether on the material which is put before it—which is likely to include material which has come into existence since the matter was before the civil court and may include material which, although then available, was not before the civil court—the company concerned was a company within the winding up jurisdiction at the time when the offence is said to have been committed. It is because the question in criminal proceedings is likely to be different from the question which would be before the civil court when asked to make such a declaration that the utility of any such declaration seems to me extremely doubtful."

Does this leave the disqualified person in an unacceptable position? It is suggested that the declaratory route is unattractive for all the reasons given above. However, in an appropriate case where the disqualified applicant can demonstrate, on full and proper evidence, that there is a real question as to the whether a disqualification bites then the court should be prepared to consider the grant of permission, on the basis that if there is a serious question as to whether permission is required the court should be prepared to assume that there is jurisdiction to grant it. On this basis, the *Stern* case is probably best seen as an oddity as the court was provided with only limited information and, in substance, the applicant asserted that permission was not required. In the light of that approach it is perhaps not surprising that the court was not satisfied that there was sufficient evidence of jurisdiction to enable it to grant permission.

In any way, whether directly or indirectly, be concerned or take part in . . .

14–35 The degree of involvement in prohibited activities is very widely expressed in each of CDDA ss.1, 1A, 9B(3), 11, 12, 12A and 12B. There are slight differences in wording in each case. Again, it is difficult as a matter of policy to see why there should be variations in terminology given that these tend to produce uncertainty and invite litigation over nuances of language. It is clear, in each case, that the words "directly or indirectly" govern both "take part in" and "be concerned in". In *Commissioner for Corporate Affairs (Vic) v Bracht*,[89] the Supreme Court of Victoria had to consider whether a disqualified person had acted in breach of an equivalent legislative prohibition on being involved in management. Ormiston J. considered that the simple words "take part in" connoted and proscribed the active participation of a disqualified person in the prohibited activity. Such participation would have to be "real". Having referred to English and New Zealand authority,[90] the judge considered the concept of "being concerned in" a particular activity and decided that it connoted participation at a variety of levels and at differing intensities with the effect that it is much wider in scope than the concept of "taking part in". To demonstrate that the disqualified person had "been concerned in" the particular activity, the level of participation could be relatively modest and would not require the participant to have a financial interest in, or to derive any material benefit from, the relevant activity. In practice, these descriptions of participation have to be construed together with, and as part of, the prohibited activity to which they relate.

Promotion

14–36 The terms "promotion" and "promoter" have no statutory definition. For guidance as to the meaning of the phrase "promotion of a company" it is necessary to look to the common law, that being the background against which the prohibition must be construed. A considerable body of case law was generated in the nineteenth and early-twentieth centuries with regard to so-called company promoters. The courts developed the law of promoters to tackle various abuses, principally the use of corporate form to perpetrate fraud on unsuspecting members of the investing public. The classic *modus operandi* involved an unscrupulous individual or individuals incorporating a company and selling personal assets, such as land or an existing business, to the newly incorporated company at an inflated price. The public would then be invited by advertisement or prospectus to invest in the company and, having subscribed, would lose money once the value of the shares dropped to reflect the real value of the company's assets. Public offers in those days were nothing like as heavily regulated as they are now[91] and the courts

[89] [1989] V.R. 821.

[90] *R. v Campbell* (1984) 78 Cr.App.R. 95; *R. v Newth* [1974] N.Z.L.R. 760.

[91] See, e.g. the Financial Services and Markets Act 2000 Pt VI and the Listing Rules governing admission of securities to the Official List of the London Stock Exchange promulgated by the Financial Services Authority in its capacity as the United Kingdom Listing Authority. For background, see P.L. Davies, *Gower and Davies: Principles of Modern Company Law*, 8th edn (London: Sweet & Maxwell, 2008), Ch.25.

therefore played a considerable role. One means by which the courts sought to protect investors was by imposing fiduciary obligations on company promoters.[92]

14–37 In *Twycross v Grant*,[93] Cockburn C.J. defined a company promoter as a person:

> "who undertakes to form a company with reference to a given project and to set it going, and who takes the necessary steps to accomplish that purpose".[94]

This would encompass any person who incorporates a company (or acquires one "off the shelf" from a company formation agent), raises its initial finance, acquires its initial assets and engages on its behalf in other related activities generally associated with a business "start-up". It is important to note that "promotion" is a very wide concept and can include activities carried out by a person somewhat removed from the group of persons primarily motivated in forming and promoting the company. Thus, an individual who arranges for a person to become a director or who places shares or negotiates arrangements on behalf of the company or who puts a supplier in touch with persons who may form a company to exploit, purchase or distribute the supplier's goods may be a promoter. Cockburn C.J.'s definition suggests that promotion can only encompass activities carried out during a company's formation and the early stages of its life. However, it is clear that the term "promoter" extends beyond this and will cover a person who, subsequent to the formation of a company, agrees to float off its capital in keeping with the intentions of those who came together to form the company.[95] It is tempting to read "promotion" as being even wider still so as to extend to activities that involve the use of a company to raise capital from the investing public at any stage of the company's life. Such a reading is consistent with modern usage of the term "promotion" to denote a marketing or publicity campaign designed to generate sales of a particular product or service. Furthermore, the abuse with which the judges were grappling in the old cases was not the formation of the company per se, but the use of the company, through the mechanism of a public offer, as a vehicle for defrauding investors. Such a wide construction may thus arguably reflect the true spirit of the old case law. However, it does seem to go beyond the types of mischief that arose in the old cases and that provide the background against which the CDDA was enacted. Moreover, a wide construction is probably not necessary as many of the acts that may be capable of falling within the prohibition relating to promotion are likely to be caught by the prohibition relating to management. A person subject to the relevant prohibitions under the CDDA puts himself at risk if he takes up employment with, for instance, an investment bank where he is expected to arrange underwriting or provide advice to corporate clients who are seeking to launch a public offer. The same may be true of a disqualified

[92] See, e.g. *Erlanger v New Sombrero Phosphate Company* (1878) L.R. 3 App. Cas. 1218; *Gluckstein v Barnes* [1900] A.C. 240; and, for background, see P.L. Davies, *Gower and Davies: Principles of Modern Company Law*, 8th edn (London: Sweet & Maxwell, 2008), Ch.5.

[93] (1877) L.R. 2 C.P.D. 469.

[94] See also *Whaley Bridge Calico Printing Co v Green* (1880) L.R. 5 Q.B.D. 109 at 111.

[95] *Lagunas Nitrate Co v Lagunas Syndicate* [1899] 2 Ch. 392 at 428.

person who, acting in the capacity of a financial adviser, prepares business plans for new companies which he then markets to banks or other financial institutions with a view to raising capital for his clients.[96] At common law, a person who merely discharges professional duties in connection with a public offer, for example, by drafting a prospectus or preparing a profit forecast on the basis of information supplied by the client, is not regarded as a promoter.[97] However, there is a real risk that such a person could be treated as "directly or indirectly" being concerned or taking part in the promotion of a company. It is important to keep in mind that the prohibition in the CDDA is not a prohibition on being a promoter but a prohibition on being concerned or taking part in promotion.

Formation

14–38 "Formation" is arguably narrower than "promotion" and appears to refer only to the process of incorporation encompassing the preparation and filing of the documents required by Pt 2 of the Companies Act 2006 and culminating in the issue of a certificate of incorporation by the Registrar of Companies. It is arguable that "formation" should bear an extended meaning and also encompass other legal requirements with which a company must comply before it can commence trading (such as the requirement to obtain a certificate for the purposes of Companies Act 2006 ss.761(1) and 767 before a newly incorporated public company can commence trading). The point is probably academic as the endeavour of complying with such requirements is very likely to amount to being concerned or taking part in the management of a company within the meaning of the relevant prohibitions. It is clear that a disqualified person would not be allowed to carry on in business as a company formation agent without the court's permission.

Management

14–39 "Management" of companies is a key concept within the CDDA generally. It is an activity the involvement in which is prohibited by each of CDDA ss.1, 1A, 9B(3), 11 and 12. Furthermore, under CDDA s.2, a person may be disqualified following his conviction for an indictable offence in connection with, among other things, the "management . . . of a company" and under CDDA ss.6 and 8, the court is required to consider whether or not the defendant's conduct is such as to make the person "unfit to be concerned in . . . management . . .". As suggested earlier, the fluidity of the concept of "management" is such that the court must inevitably take a contextual approach and construe it in the light of both the overall purpose of the CDDA and the specific corporate context in which the disqualified person was operating.

[96] Some, if not all of the activities mentioned may amount to regulated activities requiring the person to be authorised under the Financial Services and Markets Act 2000. A person disqualified under the CDDA would not automatically have any existing authorisation revoked but the Financial Services Authority may withdraw or suspend the authorisation if it considers that the disqualified person is no longer fit and proper to engage in regulated activities: Financial Services and Markets Act 2000 ss.40–41 and Sch.6 Pt I para.5. Equally, if a disqualified person applies for authorisation, it is open to the Financial Services Authority to refuse the application if it does not consider the applicant to be fit and proper.

[97] *Re Great Wheal Polgooth Company* (1883) 53 L.J. Ch. 42.

The court must therefore form a view of the purpose or purposes of the legislation. This will determine whether it adopts a broad or restrictive approach when construing the term "management".[98] At the same time, the court will need to take into account factors such as the size of the company, how it is organised and so on, in determining whether or not the disqualified person has directly or indirectly been concerned or taken part in the management of the relevant company in relation to which such an allegation is made. If the disqualified person assumes sole responsibility for the running of a small private company, it should not be difficult to prove that he has breached the prohibition. Indeed, it may be possible to argue that he was acting as a de facto director as well as being concerned in the management of such a company.[99] In other cases, it may be difficult to distinguish between those who are merely employees of the given company and those who are concerned or taking part in its management.[100] The larger and more complex the organisation in question, the more difficult it may be for the court to determine whether or not a given person is discharging a "management" function.

14–40 As yet, only limited assistance can be derived from ordinary principles of company law on this issue. Company law is predicated essentially on a theory of division of powers that lends itself to a crude, hierarchical view of the company in which the board of directors is viewed as the principal locus of managerial power. This reflects a basic concern within company law to offer an account of the internal constitution of the company and of the roles played by its two principal organs, the board of directors and the members, and an explanation of how these organs interrelate.[101] The doctrine of identification (also known as *alter ego* theory), which has been used as a means of determining whether a company can be criminally liable for offences with a mens rea element, has tended to reinforce the view of the company as a narrow hierarchy because of the emphasis that it places on the company's "directing mind and will".[102] Although the doctrine of identification has been subjected to vigorous criticism and some judicial revision,[103] the concept of

[98] See earlier discussion in Ch.2.

[99] See discussion on de facto directors in Ch.3 and 14–25. For an example of a case illustrating the point that it is relatively easy to prove breach of the prohibition in the context of a small private company, see *Drew v H.M. Advocate* 1996 S.L.T. 1062. In this case, an undischarged bankrupt purchased a company off the shelf and used it to obtain goods and services on credit without intending to pay for them. His appeal against conviction, on the ground that he was merely an employee of the company, was flatly rejected by the Scottish High Court of Justiciary.

[100] See, e.g. *Re Clasper Group Services Ltd* [1989] B.C.L.C. 143, a decision on the scope of similar wording in Insolvency Act 1986 s.212(1)(c). While Parliament did not attempt a comprehensive definition, it was suggested in the Cork Report—Report of the Review Committee, *Insolvency Law and Practice*, Cmnd.8558 (London: HMSO, 1982), para.1811—that the phrase "being concerned in management" would only embrace ". . . those responsible for the general management and policy of the company . . ."

[101] See, e.g. *Automatic Self-Cleansing Syndicate Co v Cuninghame* [1906] 2 Ch. 34; *John Shaw & Sons (Salford) Ltd v Shaw* [1935] 2 K.B. 113.

[102] See, e.g. *Tesco Supermarkets Ltd v Nattrass* [1972] A.C. 153.

[103] *Meridian Global Funds Management Asia Ltd v Securities Commission* [1995] 2 A.C. 500. The thrust of much of the criticism is that the scope of corporate criminal liability in the context of large and complex organisations is unrealistically constrained by the requirement to find a culpable individual within the company's high-ranking officials.

the "directing mind" has tended to encourage a view that equates the company's management with the board of directors. This view may not always capture the organisational and structural diversity of modern companies and of large companies in particular. To develop the same point, it may also fail to reflect the fact that in a complex organisation, managerial power may be wielded as much by senior employees as by the board of directors.[104] The tension between the formal view of corporate structures and commercial reality has surfaced only rarely in the context of disqualification. This may be because the courts are encouraged by the CDDA's protective rationale to adopt a "broad brush" approach rather than the narrow approach that they are more naturally inclined to follow when dealing with crimes of specific intent.

Disqualification cases on the meaning of "management"?

14–41 The two leading disqualification cases that explore the boundaries of the prohibition are *R. v Campbell*[105] and the important Australian case, *Commissioner for Corporate Affairs (Vic) v Bracht*.[106] The main issue before the appellate court in both cases was whether a person had breached the prohibition on being concerned or taking part in the management of a company while disqualified and thereby committed an offence. The appellant in *Campbell* was the subject of a five-year disqualification order. The Crown's case was that he had breached the prohibition over a five-month period by giving advice and practical support to a company in financial difficulties. It emerged from the evidence that his remit had been to make proposals with a view to turning the company's fortunes around. In carrying out this remit, he had engaged in the following activities:

(1) Advising the chairman extensively with regard to the overall structure and financing of the company.
(2) Taking part in negotiations leading to the resignation of one of the directors.
(3) Placing advertisements for the sale of part of the company's business and dealing with all responses to the advertisements.
(4) Negotiating directly with the company's bankers, the Inland Revenue and other unpaid creditors.
(5) Conducting meetings with the company's employees.
(6) Taking steps to raise additional finance for the company.

14–42 The appellant's case was that he had acted as an independent management consultant[107] and could not be said to have been concerned or have taken part in management because he had never controlled the company's decision-making process. The Court of Appeal upheld his conviction and, in so doing, endorsed a

[104] The Corporate Manslaughter and Corporate Homicide Act 2007 is intended to resolve some of these problems in the context of corporate liability for manslaughter: see text at 10–30.
[105] (1984) 78 Cr.App.R. 95.
[106] [1989] V.R. 821.
[107] He would probably now be called a turnaround advisor or manager.

distinction that the trial judge had drawn between the management of certain *specific aspects* of a company's activities (such as production, sales and trading) and the *central management* of a company, said to comprise the matters normally undertaken by its directors or officers. Having drawn this distinction, the trial judge had then directed the jury to look at the overall picture and say, in the light of the evidence as a whole, whether the appellant had taken part in management and not simply consider the isolated tasks which he had undertaken. What is not absolutely clear from the report of the Court of Appeal's decision is how the distinction between "specific aspects of a company's activities" and "central management" is to be applied to answer the basic question, "was the defendant being concerned or taking part in 'management' or not?" One possible view of *Campbell* is that the distinction simply illustrates the variety of activities capable of being classified as "management" functions, in which case the Court of Appeal was not confining the scope of "management" to the central direction of a company's affairs.[108] An alternative view is that, in endorsing the distinction drawn by the trial judge, the Court of Appeal was saying that the management of isolated aspects of a company's business does *not* of itself amount to "management" for the purposes of the CDDA, with the result that the scope of the term *is* confined to the central management and direction of the company, a view consistent with the narrow hierarchical model of the company discussed above.[109] *Campbell* is generally regarded as supporting a wide, flexible construction of the term "management". Much, in particular, is made of the following passage from Beldam J.'s judgment:

> ". . . [T]he wording is so widely cast that it is the opinion of this court that it is intended to insulate persons, against whom an order of disqualification has been made, from taking part in the management of company affairs generally. It is cast in the widest of terms . . . It would be difficult to imagine a more comprehensive phraseology designed to make it impossible for persons to be part of the management and central direction of company affairs."[110]

14–43 However, this is merely a comment on the width of the prefix "whether directly or indirectly be concerned or take part in . . ." and there is nothing in it to suggest that the term "management" embraces activities undertaken by individuals who are neither directors nor officers.[111] In any event, a case can be made on the evidence for saying that Campbell had been "directly or indirectly" involved in *central management* and, at a stretch, it is even arguable that he may have acted

[108] Hicks, "Taking part in management—the disqualified director's dilemma" [1987] 1 Malaysian L.J. lxxiv.

[109] This was the understanding of *Campbell* expressed by Ormiston J. in *Commissioner for Corporate Affairs (Vic) v Bracht*.

[110] (1984) 78 Cr.App.R. 95 at 100.

[111] It is interesting to reflect on the fact that CDDA s.2 contemplates the possibility that individuals below board level might be involved in management. It empowers the court to disqualify *any person* convicted of an indictable offence in connection with the management of a company. This suggests that "management" as that term is to be understood in the CDDA is not necessarily an activity which is reserved to directors and officers alone. On s.2 generally, see Ch.10.

as either a de facto or shadow director.[112] Not only had he advised the chairman closely on the steps that the company might take to escape its financial difficulties, he also appears to have played some significant part in implementing his own advice. The appellant's contention that he had merely acted as a consultant was thus always somewhat strained. However, it is misleadingly simplistic to regard *Campbell* as strong authority for a wide, flexible construction of the legal concept of "management" because the Court of Appeal did not conclusively determine whether the term is ever capable of encompassing activities that fall outside the scope of "central management".

14–44 In *Bracht*, the Commissioner of Corporate Affairs for the State of Victoria laid an information against the defendant alleging that over a two-year period he had been concerned in or had taken part in the management of a company while bankrupt in contravention of the Victorian equivalent of CDDA s.11. After a magistrate had dismissed the information, the matter came before the Supreme Court of Victoria by way of a review of the magistrate's decision. The company concerned was a small family company of which the defendant's parents-in-law were the only directors. It appears from the evidence that Bracht had negotiated credit facilities backed by bank guarantees on the company's behalf and had handled a rent review relating to the company's leasehold factory premises. The magistrate found that the final say in all financial decisions rested with one of the directors who had retained effective control of the company's affairs throughout. Based on this finding, she was not satisfied beyond reasonable doubt that Bracht had undertaken a managerial function or held a managerial position within the company. The principal ground for review put forward by the Commissioner was that the magistrate had been wrong to hold that the director's final say in relation to all decisions affecting the company precluded her from finding that Bracht had been concerned in management. The Supreme Court of Victoria ruled that the magistrate had misdirected herself as to the meaning of the provision, set aside the order dismissing the information and remitted the case to the magistrates for rehearing. In a lucid reserved judgment, Ormiston J. held that the term "management" embraces activities which involve policy and decision-making relating to a company's business affairs and which affect the whole or a substantial part of the company to the extent that the consequences of the formation of those policies or the making of those decisions may have some significant bearing on the financial standing of the company or the conduct of its affairs. On this view, if a person is in a position of authority which enables him to influence the affairs of a company and to implement policies or decisions which have a wide-ranging effect on the company, then he occupies a position of management whatever his official job title and whether or not he serves on the board of directors. Thus, Ormiston J. moved decisively away from a construction that restricted the activity of "management" to functions carried out by the board of directors:

[112] See Ch.3 for a full discussion of these concepts. The decision in *Campbell* can certainly be justified if it is accepted that the primary purpose of the legislation is to protect the public, especially given that the appellant was extensively involved in negotiating on the company's behalf with existing and potential creditors. It is the case's value as a workable precedent that is questioned.

"There seems little doubt that the concern of the legislatures has been with the exercise of managerial control, not confined to the level of the board of directors but extending to all who perform management functions . . . Whilst it is easy to exclude from the concept of management those activities of a corporation which consist in the carrying out of day to day routine functions in accordance with pre-determined policies, whether they be clerical or involve the ordering or supplying of goods or services on its behalf, it is harder to fix on those elements which are critical to management. It cannot be confined to those matters performed by the board of directors or a managing director, for those are already the subject of the prohibition against acting as a director."[113]

It is clear from *Bracht* that there must be an element of decision-making which affects the company as a whole, but "management" decisions need not necessarily be board-level decisions. Thus, in a closely controlled company, it is possible that a disqualified person who owns a majority of the shares could use his voting power in such a way as to breach the management prohibition even where he has not taken up a position on the board.[114] Equally, a person may be engaged in "management" where powers and functions are delegated to him which are likely, if exercised, to have a significant effect on the business and financial standing of the company. The *Bracht* test is wider and more commercially realistic than that in *Campbell* and should arguably be adopted by the courts in our jurisdiction.[115] The width of the test reflects both Ormiston J.'s view that disqualification legislation is primarily protective and the fact that significant responsibilities can be delegated widely within large companies with the result that managerial power in those companies is often diffuse. To quote him again:

". . . [T]here are those involved in large, discrete parts of a corporation's business, who, although not participating in the central administration of that corporation, nevertheless are involved in its management to the extent that their policies and decisions have a significant bearing on its business and its overall financial health. One has only to look at the published annual reports of public companies to realise that the results of one or more 'divisions' of a company can affect in large measure its general performance . . ."[116]

As to the *degree* of participation prohibited by the provision, Ormiston J. construed the phrase "being concerned in" as meaning that the involvement must be more than passing and must involve some measure of responsibility.[117] Overall, the judge was satisfied that a disqualified person may breach the prohibition even

[113] [1989] V.R. 821 at 828–829.

[114] *Re Magna Alloys & Research Pty Ltd* (1975) 1 A.C.L.R. 203 at 207.

[115] The case has not been without influence in England and Wales: see, e.g. *Re Market Wizard Systems (UK) Ltd* [1998] 2 B.C.L.C. 282.

[116] [1989] V.R. 821 at 830–831. Thus, Ormiston J. clearly rejected a hierarchical view of corporate structures. Nevertheless, he did betray some signs of discomfort over the notion that the purpose of disqualification is primarily protective. In particular, he was critical of Beldam J.'s observation in *Campbell* to the effect that it is always open to a disqualified person to apply for permission to act: see [1989] V.R. 821 at 832.

[117] See text at 14–35 and, for an application of this approach, *Re Market Wizard Systems (UK) Ltd* [1998] 2 B.C.L.C. 282.

though ultimate responsibility for his decisions lies elsewhere.[118] This may be so in a small company or a large company, though Ormiston J. was careful to emphasise that circumstances and procedures from company to company may vary widely.

14–45 The main significance of *Bracht*, when compared with *Campbell*, lies in the court's decisive conclusion that "management" extends beyond "central management" and its rejection of a rigid, hierarchical view of corporate structures. Ormiston J.'s more open-textured formulation, which emphasises the protective aspect of the prohibition, has the potential to produce some interesting results. If the argument that the purpose of disqualification is primarily protective is accepted, then there should be no objection to a disqualified person holding a position in management where his activities are subject to close supervision by some other person or persons such as the board of directors or a director nominated specifically for the task or an individual who reports regularly to the board.[119] This kind of purposive flexibility would go some way towards meeting the arguments of critics, like Hicks, who favour an approach that is more restrictive than that in *Bracht*. Even so, the best advice for a disqualified person in a comparable position remains for him to apply for permission so that the court can formally approve any supervisory arrangements.

Non-disqualification cases on the meaning of "management"

14–46 It is not only in the context of disqualification legislation that the courts have been slow to put forward comprehensive definitions of the terms "manager" and "management". While there is some guidance (especially as to the scope of "manager") to be found in non-disqualification cases, these authorities should be handled cautiously. Relevant terms have to be construed against their statutory background. In relation to disqualification itself, it can be argued with reference to the general objectives and scheme of the CDDA that a wide reading of these terms is justifiable because the disqualified person is afforded the opportunity to apply for permission to act. The views advanced in the cases discussed below turn ultimately on the nature and purpose of the legislative provisions under immediate

[118] Endorsing a similar view expressed ex tempore by Quilliam J. in *R. v Newth* [1974] 2 N.Z.L.R. 760. *Newth* was also a case in which a bankrupt was prosecuted on the ground that he had been concerned or taken part in management. Quilliam J. held that it is sufficient to show that the disqualified person took a hand in the real business of the company and it is irrelevant whether any action he took was given the approval of someone else or not. The decision in *Bracht* receives further support from *Cullen v Corporate Affairs Commission (NSW)* (1989) 14 A.C.L.R. 789. It was also applied in *Re Market Wizard Systems (UK) Ltd* [1998] 2 B.C.L.C. 282; *Griggs v Australian Securities Commission* (1999) 75 S.A.S.R. 307; *Byrnes v Australian Securities and Investments Commission* [2000] A.A.T.A. 333; *Nilant v Shenton* [2001] W.A.S.C.A. 421; and *Platcher v Australian Securities and Investments Commission* [2003] F.C.A. 9. See also Australia's Corporations Act 2001(Cth.) s.206A, which now defines "management" for the purposes of the prohibition on managing a corporation in *Bracht*-like terms.

[119] Reflecting this view, the courts in England and Wales have been prepared to give disqualified persons permission to act subject to the implementation of some form of supervisory regime by the companies concerned: see discussion in Ch.15.

consideration and it is important to keep in mind that the overall context may differ considerably from the disqualification context.

14–47 On balance, the courts have tended to adopt a restrictive view in non-disqualification cases. In *Registrar of Restrictive Trading Agreements v W.H. Smith & Son Ltd*[120] the Court of Appeal held that the local branch managers of two large companies that both operated a nationwide business were not managers of the companies for the purposes of s.15 of the (now repealed) Restrictive Trade Practices Act 1956. Consequently, the court had no jurisdiction to summon them for formal examination by the Registrar who was seeking to ascertain whether they had entered into an illegal price-fixing arrangement. Lord Denning M.R. followed *Gibson v Barton*,[121] a case decided under nineteenth century companies' legislation, and defined "manager" as a person, "who is managing in a governing role the affairs of the company itself".[122] A similar conclusion was reached in two criminal appeal cases, *R. v Boal*[123] and *Woodhouse v Walsall Metropolitan Borough Council*.[124] In both cases the main issue was the extent to which a director, manager, secretary or other company officer can be held co-extensively liable for a corporate regulatory offence. In *Boal*, the appellant was employed by a company as assistant general manager of its bookshop. On a day when he had been left in charge of the shop to cover the general manager's absence on holiday, local fire inspectors carried out an inspection of the company's premises and found a number of serious breaches of the fire certificate. Both the appellant and the company were indicted on charges under the Fire Precautions Act 1971. At trial, the appellant pleaded guilty having been advised that he was clearly a manager within the meaning of the relevant provision. He received a suspended prison sentence but his conviction was quashed on appeal. The Court of Appeal applied *Gibson v Barton* and *Registrar of Restrictive Trading Agreements v W.H. Smith & Son Ltd* to reach the conclusion that the appellant had not been engaged in managing the whole affairs of the company. As Simon Brown J. put it in his leading judgment:

> "The intended scope of [the provision] is, we accept, to fix with criminal liability only those who are in a position of real authority, the decision-makers within the company who have both the power and responsibility to decide corporate policy and strategy."[125]

14–48 An identical approach was taken by the Divisional Court in *Woodhouse v Walsall Metropolitan Borough Council* when quashing the appellant's conviction for an offence under the Control of Pollution Act 1974. The appellant was described as the general manager of a company's waste disposal site. He reported to the director with responsibility for special waste who, in turn, made a monthly

[120] [1969] 1 W.L.R. 1460.
[121] (1875) L.R. 10 Q.B. 329.
[122] [1969] 1 W.L.R. 1460 at 1468A.
[123] [1992] 1 Q.B. 591.
[124] [1994] 1 B.C.L.C. 435.
[125] [1992] 1 Q.B. 591, 597H–598A.

report concerning the site to the company's board. On the evidence, the appellant was in a position to issue instructions concerning the running of the site to a site manager and two supervisors. He also had the authority to expend company money subject to clearance from the director with responsibility for special waste. However, he had no authority to hire employees and the site manager apparently had a right to query the appellant's decisions on commercial or legal matters arising from the running of the site. Applying Simon Brown J.'s test from *Boal*, the Divisional Court concluded that the appellant was not in a "position of real authority" in the sense of being a decision-maker within the company possessing the power and responsibility to decide corporate policy and strategy.[126]

14–49 The restrictive approach in these cases can be explained by the fact that they were either criminal cases or cases from which criminal proceedings could have flowed. It is clear from the extract from Lord Denning's judgment in *Registrar of Restrictive Trading Agreements v W.H. Smith & Son Ltd* which follows that his objection to a broad construction of the term "manager" stemmed from the penal implications of the provision under consideration:

> "It is not right in this section to give the word 'manager' . . . an extended meaning. It is contrary to the spirit of our law. The law of England abhors inquisitorial powers. It does not like to compel a man to testify against himself. It never wants him to incriminate himself or to be faced with interrogation against his will. It prefers the case to be proved against him rather than that he should be condemned out of his own mouth. When Parliament thinks it right to give the power to administer questions, it should do so in clear terms, specifying who is the person to be made guilty of a criminal offence."[127]

14–50 The Federal Court of Australia took a similarly narrow view when construing the insolvent trading provisions of the New South Wales Companies Code in *Holpitt Pty Ltd v Swaab*.[128] The relevant provision imposed both criminal and civil liability for a company's insolvent trading on, "any person who was a director of the company, or took part in the management of the company . . .". The court held that it would be inappropriate to give the phrase "took part in . . . management" a loose meaning and thus create a vague, pervasive criminal liability. Applying the *noscitur a sociis* rule of construction,[129] the judge ruled that the use of the word "director" suggested that those embraced by the provision were restricted to people whose management role could be likened to that of a director. On this view, if the board delegates some part of its functions and gives the delegate full discretion to act independently of its instructions, then he can be said to be taking part in management. However, the same conclusion will not

[126] In the Scottish case of *Armour v Skeen* 1976 S.L.T. 71, the appellant's conviction under Health and Safety Act 1974 s.37, a similar provision to those under consideration in *Boal* and *Woodhouse*, was upheld. The difference there was that the court found as a fact that the appellant had responsibility for the formulation of the relevant company's safety policy.

[127] [1969] 1 W.L.R. 1460 at 1467E.

[128] (1992) 33 F.C.R. 474.

[129] A rule of language which holds that words "derive colour from those which surround them": per Stamp J. in *Bourne v Norwich Crematorium Ltd* [1967] 1 W.L.R. 691.

necessarily follow just because a subordinate is given some measure of discretion in carrying out a delegated task (as was the case in *Boal* and *Woodhouse*).[130]

14–51 *Re Racal Communications Ltd*[131] is a non-disqualification case in which the court favoured a broader view. The case concerned an application by the Director of Public Prosecutions for an order under s.441 of the Companies Act 1948 authorising an inspection of a company's books and records. The court was empowered by that section to order an inspection if the DPP could demonstrate that there was reasonable cause to believe that a person had, "while an officer of a company, committed an offence in connection with the management of the company's affairs" and that evidence of its commission was to be found in the company's books and records. The application came about because there was reason to believe that a departmental manager had been issuing fraudulent statements to customers demanding greater sums from them than the company was actually owed. Reversing the decision at first instance and ordering the inspection, the Court of Appeal held that the phrase "officer of a company" (which included "a director, manager or secretary")[132] should not be narrowly construed and included anyone who exercises some form of supervisory control which reflects the company's general policies or is related to its general administration.[133] This was in keeping with the overall object of the provision which was to enable the state to investigate criminal activities that might otherwise remain hidden behind the corporate veil. The Court of Appeal also rejected Vinelott J.'s view at first instance that "an offence in connection with the management of the company's affairs" was limited to offences within the framework of companies legislation that involve some internal misconduct by an officer of which the company itself is a victim.[134]

Summary

14–52 The case of *Commissioner for Corporate Affairs (Vic) v Bracht* suggests that a broader view than that put forward in cases such as *Boal* is likely to be favoured in the disqualification context. A broad approach to construction is justifiable for the following reasons:

(1) If the paramount consideration under the CDDA is protection of the public, a narrow view in which those said to be engaged in management are closely identified with the board of directors is inappropriate. Furthermore, such a narrow view fails to reflect the fact that in many companies a significant measure of control may vest in the senior management rather than in the board of directors.

[130] See dicta of Lord Reid in *Tesco Supermarkets Ltd v Nattrass* [1972] A.C. 153 at 171.
[131] [1980] 1 Ch. 138.
[132] "Officer" is defined identically in Companies Act 2006 s.1261. For a discussion of the term stressing, as we do here, a contextual approach to its construction see A. Hofler, "Elephants and Officers: Problems of Definition" (1996) 17 Co Law. 258.
[133] See, in particular, the judgment of Shaw L.J. at [1980] 1 Ch. 138, 144.
[134] The Court of Appeal's approach on this point is echoed in disqualification cases decided under CDDA s.2 which tend to favour a broad view of the words, "an . . . offence . . . in connection with the . . . management . . . of a company . . ." in s.2(1): see Ch.10.

(2) Taken as a whole, the CDDA reflects a general concern that the public should be protected from those whose past conduct raises doubts about whether they should be allowed to act in the *management* of companies. If the only concern of the CDDA was to prevent undesirable individuals from serving as company directors then there would be no need for the more extensive prohibitions on management activity in CDDA ss.1(1), 1A(1), 9B(3), 11, 12, 12A and 12B. To put the point another way, the fact that Parliament has seen fit to add a prohibition preventing disqualified persons from being concerned or taking part in the management of companies generally, reflects a wider attempt to exclude those people from being involved in running companies whether as directors or otherwise. Furthermore, in exercising a number of the CDDA powers, the court is not required to focus exclusively on the defendant's conduct *as a director*. This is particularly true of s.2 and, again, reflects the wider concerns of the legislation.

(3) Disqualification is not an absolute prohibition in two senses. First, it is open to the disqualified person to apply for permission to act. Secondly, the person is disqualified from acting in various capacities *in relation to companies*. He is not strictly prevented from earning a living. These factors tend to support the broad view.

(4) Finally, the prohibitions are not simply against being a "manager". The disqualified person is prohibited "in any way, whether directly or indirectly . . ." from being concerned or taking part in the management of a company. It is important to keep in mind that the prohibitions in the CDDA are not prohibitions on being a manager but amount to a wide ban on being involved or taking part in management.

Do common law rules of agency provide any guidance as to the scope of "management"?

14–53 It is trite law that a registered company is a fictional legal entity that can only act and transact through human agents. As graphically expressed by Peter Gibson L.J., "[i]t does not have a soul to be damned or a body to be kicked."[135] To determine whether the act of an individual human being can be attributed to a company, what Lord Hoffmann has described as "the rules of attribution" must be applied.[136] The law of agency is a major source of such rules. Agency rules are applied to determine, in a transactional context, whether the acts of a particular individual, the agent, can bind his principal, the company, for some legal purpose, such as entry into a contract.[137] The basic rule is that the company, as principal, is bound by transactions entered into by any of its agents, provided that they were acting within the scope of their authority which can be actual, usual or ostensible

[135] *Jonathan Alexander Ltd v Proctor* [1996] 1 W.L.R. 518 at 525.

[136] *Meridian Global Funds Management Asia Ltd v Securities Commission* [1995] 2 A.C. 500.

[137] For a general introduction concerning the application of agency rules to companies see P.L. Davies, *Gower and Davies: Principles of Modern Company Law*, 8th edn (London: Sweet & Maxwell, 2008), Ch.7. The law on the criminal liability of corporations discussed above in 14–40 is a further source of rules of attribution, this time in a non-transactional context.

authority. In keeping with the hierarchical view of corporate structures explained above, the board of directors has been regarded in law as the primary agent or organ of the company. However, it can be difficult to determine whether the company, as principal, is bound in circumstances where the third party has dealt not with the board or an individual director, but with an employee or manager who is not a director. In the absence of formal authorisation (actual authority), the answer will depend on whether that individual acted with usual authority (the authority which a person in his position and in the type of business concerned can reasonably be expected to have) or with ostensible authority (the authority which he has been held out by the company as having and which the company is therefore estopped from denying). Older cases suggest that the ostensible authority of an individual who manages a branch or area of a company's business is limited in scope.[138] However, it appears now that a manager will often have ostensible authority to undertake everyday transactions relating to the area of business for which he is responsible. Thus, in *First Energy (UK) Ltd v Hungarian International Bank Ltd*[139] it was held that a senior manager in charge of a branch office had ostensible authority to make offers of loan facilities in the bank's name which, if accepted by customers would bind the bank in contract, even though he lacked actual authority in this respect.

14–54 The question which the agency rules raise for present purposes is whether an agent who has actual, usual, or ostensible authority to bind the company can be equated with a "manager" or with a person who is concerned or taking part in its management. A similar question arose in a Canadian case, *Shou Yin Mar v Royal Bank*.[140] This case has parallels with *Registrar of Restrictive Trading Agreements v W.H. Smith & Son Ltd* discussed above, in that it concerned an application for an order that an individual be summoned to court for formal examination. The individual concerned was a former employee whose job description had been the "Chinese Manager" of a branch of the bank because of his responsibility for the branch's Chinese business. Under the applicable rule, the court only had jurisdiction to order his examination if he could be shown to have been a former "officer" of the bank. Dismissing the former employee's appeal against an order for examination, the British Columbian Court of Appeal held that the description "Chinese Manager" implied that the individual had some control and authority in relation to Chinese business sufficient to constitute him an "officer" even though he had no subordinates and had himself been subordinate to the branch manager and branch accountant. O'Halloran J.A. referred to his "apparent authority" (deriving, it seems, from his job title) and held that this should be regarded as his real authority, at least for the purpose of determining whether he could be examined as a former officer. The possible use of agency rules as a means of mapping the scope of the CDDA prohibitions is problematic however. It is clear from cases like *Woodhouse v Walsall Metropolitan Council* discussed above that the board may confer *actual*

[138] See, e.g. *Kreditbank Cassel GmbH v Schenkers Ltd* [1927] 1 K.B. 826.
[139] [1993] 2 Lloyd's Rep. 194.
[140] (1940) 3 D.L.R. 331.

authority on an agent in relation to defined tasks without necessarily constituting that agent a manager in law. Thus, much depends on the *width* of the agent's authority. The agent's actual, usual or ostensible authority may be quite limited in scope. Even the lowliest employee may have ostensible authority to bind the company for certain narrow purposes. Thus, agency rules can only serve as a useful guide if it can be said that the disqualified person has usual or ostensible authority to bind the company in relation to major transactions that affect the whole or a substantial part of the company.[141] This is not surprising given that agency rules serve transactional purposes, their main objective being to ensure that those who deal with companies enjoy security of transaction. Cases may arise in which agency rules are applied liberally to promote this objective. Even if a strong emphasis is placed on the protective aspect of disqualification, it would be going too far to say that every individual who has ostensible authority to bind the company in some particular respect should necessarily be treated as a "manager".

Do "permission to act" cases provide any guidance as to the scope of "management"?

14–55 A significant schematic feature of the CDDA is that a disqualified person may apply to the court for permission to act in capacities and engage in activities that fall within the scope of the prohibitions. The law and practice relating to applications for permission is considered at length in Ch.15. It might be expected that the authorities that deal with the question of whether a disqualified person should be given permission to act during the currency of a CDDA prohibition would shed some light on the scope of the prohibition itself. In *Re Cargo Agency Ltd*,[142] having disqualified the defendant for two years under CDDA s.6, Harman J. gave permission for him to be "engaged as a general manager" of a subsidiary of his then current employer. Unfortunately, the report is silent as to what precisely his activities as a general manager entailed. It is clear from Harman J.'s simultaneous refusal to allow the defendant in *Cargo Agency* to become a *director* of the subsidiary that a person can be a manager without necessarily being a director. This takes the matter little further forward.[143] Similarly, in *Re TLL Realisations Ltd*,[144] Park J. was faced with an application by a disqualified person for permission to act as a manager. In the end, he gave the applicant permission to act as a manager with joint responsibility for the internal accounting and financial function of a group of private companies but recorded his view as to the correctness of a concession by the applicant's counsel to the effect that the activities in question would, without permission, have involved a breach of the prohibition in CDDA s.1.[145] In general, permission to act

[141] Applying *Commissioner for Corporate Affairs (Vic) v Bracht*: see text from 14–44.

[142] [1992] B.C.L.C. 686.

[143] The same conclusion can be drawn from the fact that the prohibitions in the CDDA do not merely prevent the disqualified person from being or acting as a director.

[144] [2000] B.C.C. 998.

[145] It is clear that Park J. regarded the applicant, whose activities were said to be more significant than mere book-keeping while falling short of the role of a full finance director, as being at the very least "concerned" in management.

cases provide little firm guidance. The current practice of the court is either to grant or refuse the application without really analysing whether what is proposed amounts to being concerned or taking part in management or not. There has not been a reported case where the court refused to make an order on an application for permission on the ground the activities forming the subject matter of the application fell outside the terms of the prohibition (other than the *Stern* case, considered above in which the court was not satisfied that the prohibition applied to the companies in question). If there is any doubt as to the necessity of the application, the applicant is entitled to the benefit of it and to the certainty of the protection that is enshrined in an order granting permission to act.

INSOLVENCY PRACTITIONER

14–56 A disqualification order under CDDA s.1(1)(b), a disqualification undertaking under CDDA s.1A(1)(b), a competition disqualification undertaking under CDDA s.9B(3)(d) and the automatic bans under CDDA ss.12A(b) and 12B(b) prohibit the disqualified person from acting as an insolvency practitioner. In contrast to the position with regard to the prohibitions on acting as a director etc. in CDDA ss.1(1)(a), 1A(1)(a), 12A(a), 12B(a) and, subject to s.9B(4), s.9B(3)(a)–(c), the court has no power under ss.1(1)(b), 1A(1)(b), 9B(3)(d), 12A(b) and 12B(b) to grant the disqualified person permission to act as an insolvency practitioner. For the period of disqualification, the ban on acting as an insolvency practitioner is therefore absolute.[146] The combined effect of CDDA ss.1(1)(b), 1A(1)(b), 9B(3)(d), 12A(b) and 12B(b) read together with ss.230, 292(2) and 388–390 of the Insolvency Act 1986, is that the disqualified person is prohibited from acting in any of the following capacities:

(1) Liquidator,[147] provisional liquidator, administrator[148] or administrative receiver in relation to a company.
(2) Supervisor of a corporate voluntary arrangement.
(3) Trustee in bankruptcy or interim receiver in relation to an individual.
(4) Permanent or interim trustee in the sequestration of an individual's estate in Scotland.
(5) Trustee under a deed of arrangement for the benefit of an individual's creditors, or, in Scotland, a trust deed for creditors.
(6) Administrator of the insolvent estate of a deceased person.

[146] The current provisions were introduced by the Insolvency Act 2000 to address the point that, under the old law, there was an apparent discrepancy between the absolute disqualification imposed by s.390(4)(b) of the Insolvency Act 1986 and the wording of the former CDDA s.1 which suggested that the court had power to grant the disqualified person permission to act as a liquidator, administrator and/or administrative receiver: see further text at 12–03.

[147] The requirement applies equally whether the company is in solvent liquidation (members' voluntary) or insolvent liquidation (creditors' voluntary or compulsory).

[148] The requirement for a person acting as an administrator to be a licensed insolvency practitioner is reiterated further in Sch.B1 para.6 of the Insolvency Act 1986.

(7) Liquidator, provisional liquidator, administrator or trustee in relation to an insolvent partnership.
(8) Supervisor of a partnership voluntary arrangement.[149]

A person can act as a receiver of part of a company's property or as an income receiver without being qualified to act as an insolvency practitioner. However, if he is subject to a disqualification order, a disqualification undertaking, a competition disqualification undertaking or the automatic prohibitions in CDDA ss.12A or 12B, he will be disqualified from acting in these capacities without the permission of the court by virtue of CDDA ss.1(1)(a), 1A(1)(a), 9B(3)(b), 12A(a) and 12B(a).[150]

14–57 The prohibition in CDDA s.11 as it applies in England and Wales does not expressly prohibit an undischarged bankrupt, a DRO debtor and a person who is the subject of insolvency restrictions from acting as an insolvency practitioner. However, an absolute prohibition is imposed by ss.390(4)(a), (aa) and 390(5) of the Insolvency Act 1986. Such persons are also disqualified from acting as a receiver or manager of the property of a company on behalf of debenture holders, though not as a receiver or manager acting under an appointment made by the court, by virtue of the Insolvency Act 1986 s.31.[151] Accordingly, they cannot act as a receiver of part of a company's property or as an income receiver where (in either case) the appointment is made out of court by a debenture holder.

14–58 CDDA s.12 expressly prohibits the disqualified person from acting as a liquidator without the permission of the court but contains no prohibition on acting as an insolvency practitioner or as a receiver of a company's property. Disqualification in the terms of CDDA s.12(2) does not trigger the automatic ban on acting as an insolvency practitioner in s.390(4)(b) of the Insolvency Act 1986 because the disqualification flows from s.429(2)(b) of the Insolvency Act and is not therefore a "disqualification order" or "disqualification undertaking" under the CDDA for the purposes of s.390(4)(b). It follows that the disqualified person is not automatically prohibited by CDDA s.12 from acting as an administrator, administrative receiver, supervisor of a corporate voluntary arrangement or in the various capacities set out in 14–56 above that relate to insolvent individuals and partnerships. The fact that s.388(1)(a) of the Insolvency Act 1986 specifically refers to a provisional liquidator, as distinct from a liquidator, may also suggest that the s.12 ban, which refers only to a liquidator, does not extend to a provisional liquidator. However, in the context, it may equally be thought that "liquidator" in CDDA s.12(2) should also include "provisional liquidator". The failure of CDDA s.12 and the Insolvency Act 1986 s.390 to provide a clear and comprehensive ban is best described as anomalous.

14–59 To the average disqualified person, the absolute prohibition on acting as an insolvency practitioner is no hardship. However, the consequences for a licensed

[149] The requirement for a person acting as an office holder in relation to an insolvent partnership is reiterated further in the Insolvent Partnerships Order 1994 (SI 1994/2421) art.15.
[150] See also 14–27.
[151] See also text at 14–28.

insolvency practitioner disqualified under the CDDA are obviously very serious indeed.[152] The effect of s.390(4)(b) of the Insolvency Act 1986 is that a person made subject to a disqualification order, disqualification undertaking, competition disqualification undertaking or the automatic prohibitions in CDDA ss.12A or 12B automatically ceases to be qualified to act as an insolvency practitioner. In other words, his disqualification under the Insolvency Act 1986 does not depend on the formal withdrawal of his authorisation by the relevant licensing body.[153] The effect is that he can no longer accept an appointment to act in any of the capacities set out above in 14–56. Any current appointments to these offices or positions should be relinquished immediately.[154] Section 389 of the Insolvency Act makes it an offence for a person to act as an insolvency practitioner in relation to a company or an individual without being qualified. So, for example, an insolvency practitioner who, while the subject of the prohibition in CDDA ss.1, 1A, 9B(3), 12A and 12B, continues to act as, say, a liquidator or an administrator of a company commits an offence under both the Insolvency Act 1986 and the CDDA.

WIDER LEGAL EFFECTS OF CDDA DISQUALIFICATION

14–60 There are wider consequences for the disqualified person under a range of statutes and statutory instruments relating to various aspects of social, economic and public life. In some cases disqualification under the CDDA may be ground for removal from certain public and private offices; in other cases it may trigger the automatic removal of the disqualified person from such offices. It is necessary to consider carefully the precise terms of the provision imposing the "knock on" disqualification. A further point that should be mentioned is the unsatisfactory

[152] It is conceivable that a licensed insolvency practitioner could be the subject of disqualification proceedings arising directly from his conduct as an insolvency practitioner under CDDA ss.2, 3 or 4: see, e.g. *Re Arctic Engineering Ltd* [1986] 1 W.L.R. 686.

[153] Insolvency practitioners can be licensed to act either by a professional body recognised under Insolvency Act 1986 s.391 or by a competent authority as defined in Insolvency Act 1986 s.392. Recognised professional bodies include the Institute of Chartered Accountants in England and Wales, the Association of Chartered Certified Accountants and the Insolvency Practitioners Association. For the full list see the Insolvency Practitioners (Recognised Professional Bodies) Order 1986 (SI 1986/1764). The recognised professional bodies are required by Insolvency Act 1986 s.391(2) to maintain and enforce rules for securing that their members are fit and proper persons to act as insolvency practitioners. An insolvency practitioner who is authorised to act directly by the Secretary of State (at present the only "competent authority") is liable to have his authorisation withdrawn if he ceases to be "a fit and proper person" under Insolvency Act 1986 s.393(4)(a).

[154] This would give rise to a vacancy in relation to all companies and individuals with respect to which the disqualified person had been acting as office holder: Insolvency Act 1986 s.171(4) (voluntary liquidation); s.172(5) (compulsory liquidation); s.19(2)(a) (pre-Enterprise Act administration); s.45(2) (administrative receivership); Sch.B1 para.89 (post-Enterprise Act administration); s.298(6) (bankruptcy). Where such a vacancy occurs it may be filled by the company's creditors or the court (unless it is an administrative receiver who is required to vacate office in which case the relevant floating charge holder alone may appoint a replacement). For specific provisions, see Insolvency Act 1986 ss.92, 104 and 108 (liquidation); s.13(2) (pre-Enterprise Act administration); Sch.B1 paras 90–95 (post-Enterprise Act administration); s.7(5) (corporate voluntary arrangements); s.300 (bankruptcy); s.263(5) (individual voluntary arrangements).

manner in which the legislation relating to disqualification undertakings has been enacted when contrasted with the position in relation to insolvency restrictions. For the purposes of any enactment, which includes statutory instruments, a reference to a person in respect of whom a BRO or a DRRO has effect or who is "the subject of" a BRO or a DRRO includes, respectively, a reference to a person in respect of whom a BRU or a DRRU has effect.[155] When disqualification undertakings were introduced by the Insolvency Act 2000, the opportunity was not taken to include a similar provision. Instead specific statutes then containing references to disqualification orders under the CDDA were amended to refer also to undertakings. However, various statutory instruments were left unchanged.

14–61 Different statutory instruments have imposed "knock on" disqualifications flowing from disqualification under the CDDA. However, presumably because different statutory instruments are the responsibility of different government departments, there has been some considerable inconsistency between the circumstances in which the automatic "knock on" disqualifications will take effect.[156] In some cases they are triggered solely by disqualification orders. In other cases they are triggered by disqualification orders and by orders under s.429(2)(b) of the Insolvency Act 1986. In yet other cases they are triggered by disqualification orders, orders under s.429(2)(b) of the Insolvency Act and disqualification undertakings (though even then there may be uncertainty as to whether competition disqualification undertakings are also caught). A similar picture emerges with regard to the "knock on" effect of Northern Ireland disqualifications. All this appears to flow from the inherent complication of the CDDA as it now stands and an absence of knowledge and understanding across Government of its full workings and ramifications. It is to be hoped that some rationalisation of the position will be undertaken at some point. The exposition below attempts to set out some of the main consequences but, given the fast pace of legislative change and the constant stream of statutory instruments (and amending statutory instruments), the following should be taken as an overall snapshot at the date of preparation of this book and should not necessarily be relied on as an exhaustive and precise account of the wider consequences of disqualification under the CDDA.[157]

14–62 It will be noted that the "knock on" disqualifications are such that it may make a real difference to a disqualified person whether a disqualification is stayed or he is instead given permission to act notwithstanding disqualification. In some cases "knock on" disqualifications cannot be relieved against at all but are, like the disqualification from acting as an insolvency practitioner, absolute. In other cases dispensation from the "knock on" disqualification can be given, but by a body other than the court. It should also be noted that disqualification under the CDDA may have an

[155] Insolvency Act 1986 Sch.4A para.8 and Sch.4ZB para.8.

[156] Although the position does appear to have improved in some respects: see, e.g. the effect of the Education (Company Directors Disqualification Act 1986: Amendment to Disqualification Provisions)(England) Regulations 2004 (SI 2004/3264).

[157] Searches carried out by the authors for the phrase "Company Directors Disqualification Act 1986" in the legislation sections of the legal databases Westlaw and LexisNexis reveal many more extant provisions than there is space to cover in the text.

indirect effect on a person's ability to be appointed or retain appointment to various positions. This is because, under various statutory provisions, there is a "catch all" provision applying a "fit and proper" test to appointment to and/or removal from the position. Set out below are some examples of "knock on" disqualifications.

Charities Act 1993

14–63 A person who is disqualified by disqualification order or undertaking under the CDDA, by means of a Northern Ireland disqualification order or undertaking or by virtue of s.429(2)(b) of the Insolvency Act 1986 is automatically disqualified by s.72(1)(f)[158] of the Charities Act 1993 from acting as a charity trustee. Under s.72(4) of the same Act, the Charity Commissioners have the power to waive this automatic disqualification in the case of charitable trusts. In the case of any charity which is a company the dispensing power remains with the court and the Charity Commissioners have no relevant jurisdiction to grant permission to act notwithstanding disqualification.[159] It is clear that s.72(1)(f) does not apply where the court has granted the disqualified person permission to act under the disqualification order or undertaking or when granting an order under s.429(2)(b) of the Insolvency Act 1986 in relation to a charitable company.[160] Section 73(1) of the Charities Act 1993 makes it an offence for a person to act as a charity trustee while disqualified under s.72. However, the effect of s.73(2) is that a person who continues to act as a director of a charitable company in breach of the CDDA s.1 prohibition only commits an offence under the CDDA.[161] The Charities Act 2006 introduced as Pt VIIIA of the Charities Act 1993 the statutory framework for a new legal form of incorporation, the charitable incorporated organisation. At the time of writing, the relevant secondary legislation needed to implement this framework and make this legal form generally available had not been enacted.[162] Although a charitable incorporated organisation is a body corporate,[163] it is incorporated under the Charities Act 1993 and it is not clear that such a body is a charitable company for the purposes of s.72 of that Act. However, on the evidence of the relevant draft regulations, it appears that the intention is for charitable incorporated organisations to be treated as companies falling squarely within the prohibitions in CDDA ss.1, 1A, 11 and 12.[164] Accordingly, it is arguable that the power to grant permission to act in relation to a charitable incorporated organisation will remain exclusively with the court.

[158] As amended by the Insolvency Act 2000 Sch.4, Pt II, para.18 to include references to disqualification undertakings and Northern Ireland disqualifications.

[159] Charities Act 1993 s.72(4). In the case of Northern Ireland disqualifications, the Northern Ireland High Court retains power to grant permission to act in relation to charitable companies: Charities Act 1993 s.72(3)(aa).

[160] Charities Act 1993 s.72(3)(a).

[161] Note that Charities Act 1993 ss.72–73, are re-enactments of the Charities Act 1992 ss.45–46 which originally came into force on January 1, 1993.

[162] See text towards the end of 14–11.

[163] Charities Act 1993 s.69A(2).

[164] See text towards the end of 14–11.

Pensions Act 1995

14–64 This legislation was introduced in the wake of the Maxwell scandal to tighten regulation of occupational pension schemes. A person who is disqualified by disqualification order or undertaking under the CDDA or by means of a Northern Ireland disqualification order or undertaking is automatically disqualified by s.29(1)(f) of the Pensions Act 1995[165] from acting as a trustee of an occupational pension scheme established under a trust. A corporate trustee is similarly disqualified by s.29(1)(c) from so acting where any of its directors is the subject of a disqualification falling within s.29. The Occupational Pensions Regulatory Authority established by the Act has the power to waive this automatic disqualification.[166] Section 30 of the Pensions Act 1995 makes it an offence for a person to act as a trustee while disqualified. The Authority also has the power to suspend a trustee where CDDA proceedings against him are pending.[167] A person the subject of an order under s.429(2)(b) of the Insolvency Act 1986 (which would encompass a person disqualified in the terms of CDDA s.12) is also disqualified by s.29(1)(f) of the Pensions Act.

Police bodies

Police authorities

14–65 By reg.14 of the Police Authority Regulations 2008,[168] a person who is disqualified by disqualification order or disqualification undertaking under the CDDA is automatically disqualified from being appointed as or being a member of a police authority. The same provision formerly appeared in the Sch.2 para.11(1)(c) of the Police Act 1996. The position is the same in respect of persons who are the subject of an order under s.429(2)(b) of the Insolvency Act 1986 and therefore disqualified in the terms of CDDA, s.12 or persons who are the subject of a Northern Ireland disqualification.

The British Transport Police Authority

14–66 By s.18 and Sch.4 paras 7(3) and 8 of the Railways and Transport Safety Act 2003, a person who is the subject of disqualification order under the CDDA or a disqualification order under the equivalent Northern Ireland legislation is automatically ineligible for appointment as a member of the British Transport Police Authority. The position is the same in respect of persons who are the subject of an order under s.429(2)(b) of the Insolvency Act 1986 and therefore disqualified in the terms of CDDA s.12. However the prohibition does not appear to be triggered by a disqualification undertaking.

[165] As amended by the Insolvency Act 2000 Sch.4 Pt II para.19 to include references to disqualification undertakings and Northern Ireland disqualifications.

[166] Pensions Act 1995 s.29(5). This power is identical to that of the Charity Commissioners under the Charities Act 1993.

[167] Pensions Act 1995 s.4(1)(e). The Authority is also empowered to issue an order prohibiting a person from continuing as trustee of a scheme in prescribed circumstances: Pensions Act 1995 s.3. Penalties for breach of either a prohibition or suspension order are set out in Pensions Act 1995 s.6.

[168] SI 2008/630.

Commissioners under Part III of the Police Act 1997

14–67 Section 91 of the Police Act 1997[169] regulates the appointment and office of Commissioners. Commissioners, broadly, have an overview function in relation to authorisations to take action in respect of property under Part III of the Police Act 1997. One ground on which a Commissioner can be removed from office by the Prime Minister is if, after his appointment, such a person is disqualified by disqualification order or his disqualification undertaking is accepted under CDDA ss.7 or 8, or he is disqualified by means of a Northern Ireland disqualification order or undertaking, or an order under s.429(2)(b) of the Insolvency Act 1986 is made against him.

The Independent Police Complaints Commission

14–68 Under the Police Reform Act 2002 s.9 and Sch.2 para.1(5)(e) the Chairman of the Independent Police Complaints Commission may be removed by Her Majesty on being advised by the Secretary of State that there are relevant grounds for his removal. Included among these grounds are that he is subject to a disqualification order under the CDDA or the equivalent Northern Ireland legislation or an order made under s.429(2)(b) of the Insolvency Act 1986. This provision apparently does not encompass disqualification undertakings.

Education bodies: school companies and school governors

School companies

14–69 Under the School Companies Regulations 2002,[170] a person who is disqualified by disqualification order or disqualification undertaking under the CDDA or the equivalent Northern Ireland legislation cannot be admitted or be permitted to remain as a member of a "school company". However, the prohibition does not apply to a person who is disqualified following the making of an order under s.429(2)(b) of the Insolvency Act 1986. For these purposes, a "school company" is a company formed or joined by governing bodies of maintained schools using their powers under s.11 of the Education Act 2002. School companies which are formed with the purpose of facilitating or entering into agreements under the private finance initiative are excluded from the ambit of these regulations but are governed by the regulations referred to next.

14–70 The School Companies (Private Finance Initiative Companies) Regulations 2002[171] govern the operation of companies whose members include governing bodies of maintained schools, where the main purpose of forming the company is for it to enter into or facilitate agreements made under the private finance initiative. Persons who are disqualified from membership of such a "school PFI company" include persons who are disqualified by disqualification order or disqualification undertaking under the CDDA or the equivalent Northern Ireland

[169] As amended by the Insolvency Act 2000, Sch.4 Pt II para.22 to include references to disqualification undertakings and Northern Ireland disqualifications. See also the Insolvency Act 2000 (Company Directors Undertakings) Order 2004 (SI 2004/1941).

[170] SI 2002/2978 as amended by SI 2004/3264.

[171] SI 2002/3177 as amended by SI 2004/3264.

legislation. Again, the prohibition does not apply to a person who is disqualified following the making of an order under s.429(2)(b) of the Insolvency Act 1986.

Foundation bodies

14–71 A person who is disqualified by disqualification order or disqualification undertaking under the CDDA or the equivalent Northern Ireland legislation or following the making of an order under s.429(2)(b) of the Insolvency Act 1986 is disqualified in England from holding, or for continuing to hold, office as a member of a foundation body by virtue of reg.12 of, and Sch.4 to, the Education (Foundation Body) (England) Regulations 2000.[172] In broad terms, a foundation body is a body corporate established under s.21 of the School Standards and Framework Act 1998 to perform in relation to three or more schools ("the group") each of which is either a foundation or a voluntary school, the following functions, namely: (a) to hold property for those schools for the purposes of the schools; (b) to appoint foundation governors for those schools; and (c) to promote co-operation between schools in the group.

School governors and temporary governors of maintained schools

14–72 A person who is disqualified by disqualification order or disqualification undertaking under the CDDA or the equivalent Northern Ireland legislation or following the making of an order under s.429(2)(b) of the Insolvency Act 1986 is disqualified from holding, or continuing to hold, office as a governor of a maintained school in England by virtue of reg.22 of, and Sch.6 to, the School Governance (Constitution)(England) Regulations 2007.[173] There are a myriad of maintained schools to which the regulations apply, including community schools, maintained nursery schools, community special schools foundation schools, foundation special schools, voluntary controlled schools, and voluntary aided schools. This disqualification has been extended to regulate the circumstances in which, in England, a person can hold or continue in office, or be appointed or nominated as a temporary governor of a "new school" (as defined by s.72(3) of the School Standards and Framework Act 1998). The relevant provisions are to be found in reg.25 of, and Sch.2 to, the School Governance (New Schools) (England) Regulations 2007.[174]

Social housing

14–73 By Sch.1 Pt II para.4(2)(b)[175] of the Housing Act 1996 the Welsh Ministers may make an order removing a director, trustee or committee member of a housing

[172] SI 2000/2872 as amended by SI 2004/3264. For the equivalent provisions applicable in Wales see the Education (Foundation Body) (Wales) Regulations 2001 (SI 2001/2709 (W.228)). The Welsh provisions do not encompass Northern Ireland disqualifications.

[173] SI 2007/957. For the equivalent provisions applicable in Wales see the Government of Maintained Schools (Wales) Regulations 2005 (SI 2005/2914 (W.211)).

[174] SI 2007/958. For the equivalent provisions applicable in Wales see the New Maintained Schools (Wales) Regulations 2005 (SI 2005/2912 (W.209)), reg.25 which applies Sch.5 of the Government of Maintained Schools (Wales) Regulations 2005 (SI 2005/2914 (W.211)).

[175] As amended by the Insolvency Act 2000, Sch.4 Pt II para.21 to include references to disqualification undertakings and Northern Ireland disqualifications.

association, now termed a registered social landlord, where he is the subject of disqualification, by order or undertaking, under the CDDA or under the equivalent Northern Ireland legislation.[176] The registered social landlord system is now restricted to Wales by virtue of the s.61 of the Housing and Regeneration Act 2008. A person disqualified under CDDA who is a director of a registered social landlord constituted as a company limited by guarantee would have to resign anyway, unless the court gives him permission to act. This is also true of a trustee of a housing association constituted as a registered charitable trust by virtue of the automatic disqualification provisions in the Charities Act 1993 (see above). Otherwise, a disqualification order under the CDDA does not automatically trigger disqualification under the Housing Act 1996. The onus is on the appropriate authority to take steps to remove the person. The position is the same in relation to persons who are the subject of an order under s.429(2)(b) of the Insolvency Act 1986.

14–74 The position in England as regards social housing is currently governed by the Housing and Regeneration Act 2008. Section 266 of the 2008 Act provides that the Regulator of Social Housing may by order remove an officer of a non-profit registered provider in any of the following cases: (a) where he is subject to a disqualification order or undertaking under the CDDA or the equivalent Northern Ireland legislation; (b) where he is subject to an order under s.429(2)(b) of the Insolvency Act 1986; (c) where he is disqualified from being a charity trustee under s.72 of the Charities Act 1993.

Health and social care bodies

The Council for Healthcare Regulatory Excellence

14–75 Persons are disqualified for appointment as the chair or a non-executive member of the Council for Healthcare Regulatory Excellence, if, among other grounds, they are subject to a disqualification order or undertaking under the CDDA or the equivalent Northern Ireland legislation or to an order made under s.429(2)(b) of the Insolvency Act 1986. The relevant provisions are to be found in the Council for Healthcare Regulatory Excellence (Appointment, Procedure etc.) Regulations 2008.[177]

The Care Quality Commission

14–76 Persons are disqualified for appointment or from holding office as a member of the Care Quality Commission, a body established by s.1(1) of the Health and Social Care Act 2008, if, among other grounds, they are subject to a disqualification order or undertaking under the CDDA or the equivalent Northern Ireland legislation or to an order made under s.429(2) of the Insolvency Act 1986. The relevant provisions are to be found in the Care Quality Commission (Membership) Regulations 2008.[178]

[176] This provision came into force on October 1, 1996. The Housing Corporation previously had power under the Housing Associations Act 1985 to remove a housing association committee member in certain circumstances (e.g. bankruptcy or mental disorder). The 1996 Act extended these powers to encompass persons disqualified under CDDA.

[177] SI 2008/2927.

[178] SI 2008/2252.

The Commission for Healthcare Audit and Inspection and the Commission for Social Care Inspection

14–77 Persons are disqualified for appointment or from holding office as a member of the Commission for Healthcare Audit and Inspection, a body established by s.41(1) of the Health and Social Care (Community Health and Standards) Act 2003, if, among other grounds, they are subject to a disqualification order under the CDDA or the equivalent Northern Ireland legislation or to an order made under s.429(2) of the Insolvency Act 1986. The relevant provisions are to be found in the Commission for Healthcare Audit and Inspection (Membership) Regulations 2003.[179] They apparently do not encompass disqualification undertakings. The position is the same as regards membership of the Commission for Social Care Inspection under the Commission for Social Care Inspection (Membership) Regulations 2003.[180]

The Health Protection Agency

14–78 Persons are disqualified for appointment as the chair or a non-executive member of the Health Protection Agency, if, among other grounds, they are subject to a disqualification order or undertaking under the CDDA or the equivalent Northern Ireland legislation or to an order made under s.429(2)(b) of the Insolvency Act 1986. The relevant provisions are to be found in the Health Protection Agency Regulations 2005.[181]

The NHS Professionals Special Health Authority

14–79 The NHS Professionals Special Health Authority is established under the National Health Service Act 1977 by the NHS Professionals Special Health Authority (Establishment and Constitution) Order 2003.[182] The NHS Professionals Special Health Authority Regulations 2003[183] provide for the disqualification of a person for appointment as chairman or as a non-officer member of this authority in certain circumstances. These include the situation where the person concerned is subject to a disqualification order under the CDDA or the equivalent Northern Ireland legislation or to an order made under s.429(2)(b) of the Insolvency Act 1986. The 2003 Regulations apparently do not encompass disqualification undertakings.

The General Medical Council

14–80 Persons are disqualified from appointment as a member of the General Medical Council if, among other grounds, they are subject to a disqualification order or undertaking under the CDDA or the equivalent Northern Ireland legislation or to an order made under s.429(2)(b) of the Insolvency Act 1986. The relevant provisions are to be found in the General Medical Council (Constitution) Order 2008.[184]

[179] SI 2003/3279.
[180] SI 2003/3190.
[181] SI 2005/408.
[182] SI 2003/3059.
[183] SI 2003/3060.
[184] SI 2008/2554.

There are similar restrictions on the involvement of persons who are subject to any of these disqualifications in the governance of (inter alia) the Nursing and Midwifery Council, the General Chiropractic Council, the General Osteopathic Council and the General Optical Council.[185]

General Medical Services Contractors

14–81 The National Health Service (General Medical Services Contracts) Regulations 2004[186] ("the 2004 Regulations") set out, for England, the framework for general medical services contracts under s.28Q of the National Health Service Act 1977 (as amended). Part 2 of the 2004 Regulations prescribes the conditions which, in accordance with s.28S of the Act, must be met by a contractor before the Primary Care Trust may enter into a general medical services contract with it. Under the 2004 Regulations a Primary Care Trust may only enter into such a contract if certain conditions are met.[187] Under reg.5, contracts to be entered into with a medical practitioner, with two or more individuals practising in partnership or a company limited by shares can only be entered into if (as relevant) the medical practitioner, each such individual and the partnership and, in the case of a company, the company, any person legally or beneficially owning a share in the company and any director or secretary of the company, is not subject to certain prohibitions and provisions. One such group of prohibitions and provisions comprise persons subject to a disqualification order under the CDDA or the equivalent Northern Ireland legislation or to an order made under s.429(2)(b) of the Insolvency Act 1986. Disqualification by undertaking appears to fall outside the scope of the 2004 Regulations. As a matter of interest, a further group of relevant provisions relate to bankruptcy and take into account the bankruptcy restrictions regime but not, as yet, the debt relief restrictions regime. Under Reg.113 of the 2004 Regulations, the coming into existence of any of these prohibitions, in relation to an existing contractor also gives rise to a discretion in the Primary Care Trust to terminate the contract by notice in writing, either forthwith or on the date specified in the notice.

Regulatory and other consequences

14–82 CDDA disqualification may have regulatory consequences for a disqualified person who is a member of a professional body. It is beyond the scope of this book to examine all relevant professional rules and obligations. Two questions commonly arise. The first is whether (and, if so, at what stage) disqualification proceedings or disqualification triggers an obligation to report to the professional body.[188] The second is whether disqualification, expressly or, more usually,

[185] See SI 2008/2553, SI 2008/3047, SI 2009/263, SI 2009/442.

[186] SI 2004/291.

[187] For the position relating to Scotland and Wales see SSI 2004/115 and SI 2004/478 (W.48).

[188] See, e.g. para.905 of the Code of Conduct of the Bar of England and Wales (8th edn) applicable to barristers in this jurisdiction, where a reporting duty arises on the initiation of disqualification proceedings, or where a disqualification order is made, against an individual barrister.

impliedly,[189] is a matter that can give rise to disciplinary action. Among the most developed regimes in this context is that laid down by the relevant rules and guidance of the Institute of Chartered Accountants in England and Wales ("ICAEW") and, in particular, its disciplinary bye-laws. Under Disciplinary bye-law 4(1)(a), a member or provisional member of ICAEW is liable to disciplinary action, whether or not he was a member or provisional member at the time of the relevant triggering event, "if in the course of carrying out professional work or otherwise he has committed any act or default likely to bring discredit on himself, the Institute or the profession of accountancy". A similar liability arises in relation to firms under bye-law 5(1)(a). Under bye-law 7(2)(b), the fact that a member, member firm or provisional member has had a disqualification order made against him or has given a disqualification undertaking which has been accepted by the Secretary of State under the CDDA, is, for the purposes of the bye-laws treated as "conclusive evidence of the commission by him of such an act or default as is mentioned in bye-law 4(1)(a) or 5(1)(a), as the case may be" (emphasis supplied). Also of interest in this context is the scheme established by the Accountancy and Actuarial Discipline Board Ltd. Under para.14(3) of that scheme the fact that a Member or Member Firm has had a disqualification order made against him under the Company Directors Disqualification Act 1986, shall, for the purposes of the Scheme:

> "be conclusive evidence of an act of misconduct by the Member or Member Firm, whether or not he or it was a Member or Member Firm at the time of the conduct resulting in, or at the time of, the disciplinary proceedings or disqualification order".

14–83 Similarly, where a person carries on a regulated activity for the purposes of the Financial Services and Markets Act 2000 or authorised business under financial services or related legislation, the disqualification could prompt the Financial Services Authority to withdraw his authorisation on the ground that he is no longer a fit and proper person.[190] These are both matters of discretion for the appropriate professional body or regulator.

14–84 In the context of securities regulation, it is a requirement of the United Kingdom Listing Authority's Listing Rules that the directors of an issuer disclose in the prospectus (inter alia) details of: (a) any bankruptcies, receiverships or liquidations with which they were associated for at least the previous five years; and (b) details of any official public incrimination and/or sanctions imposed on them by statutory

[189] In many cases the relevant provision is one relating to acts or omissions in the pursuit of the profession or otherwise, which is likely to bring discredit on himself or the profession. In the case of the Code of Conduct of the Bar of England and Wales (8th edn), see para.301 prohibiting a barrister (among other things) from engaging in conduct, whether in pursuit of his profession or otherwise, which is (among other things) dishonest or otherwise discreditable to a barrister or likely to diminish public confidence in the legal profession or the administration of justice or otherwise bring the legal profession into disrepute.

[190] Financial Services and Markets Act 2000 ss.40–41, Sch.6 Pt I para.5. Equally, if a disqualified person applies for authorisation it is open to the Financial Services Authority to refuse the application if it does not consider the applicant to be fit and proper.

or regulatory authorities (including designated professional bodies) and whether they have ever been disqualified by a court from acting as a member of the administrative, management or supervisory bodies of an issuer or from acting in the management or conduct of the affairs of any issuer for at least the previous five years.[191] The requirement appears to apply only to disqualification orders and not to disqualification and competition disqualification undertakings. However, although they are not covered by the literal wording, disqualification undertakings should still be disclosed not least because of the wide general duty of disclosure imposed by s.80 of the Financial Services and Markets Act 2000.

14–85 As a CDDA disqualification is a matter of public record,[192] it is likely that it will have an adverse effect on the disqualified person's individual credit rating.

BREACH OF THE CDDA PROHIBITIONS

14–86 If a disqualified person acts in breach of the prohibitions in CDDA ss.1, 1A, 9B(3), 11, 12, 12A or 12B he is liable to criminal prosecution and possible civil sanctions under CDDA ss.13–15.[193] CDDA ss.13–15 were amended by the Insolvency Act 2000 s.8 and Sch.4 with effect from April 2, 2001[194] to extend the criminal and civil penalties for breach to persons disqualified by means of a disqualification undertaking. It is clear that the phrase "disqualification undertaking" as it appears in CDDA ss.13–15 includes what in this book is termed a competition disqualification undertaking. By virtue of CDDA ss.12A and 12B and consequential amendments to ss.13–15, a person who contravenes a disqualification order or undertaking made under the equivalent Northern Ireland legislation is also susceptible to criminal or civil proceedings in the courts in Great Britain.

Criminal liability and further disqualification

14–87 A person who acts in breach of the prohibitions in CDDA ss.1, 1A, 9B(3), 12, 12A or 12B commits an "either way" offence under CDDA s.13. A person who acts in breach of the prohibitions in CDDA s.11 commits an offence under that section. If convicted on indictment of a s.11 or s.13 offence, a person is liable to imprisonment for not more than two years or a fine or both.[195] If convicted summarily, he is liable to imprisonment for not more than six months or a fine not

[191] See Listing Rules at 2.2.10; Prospectus Rules App.3.1 at 14–1(d).

[192] For the registration requirements, see Ch.12.

[193] A hotline was launched in January 1998 which aims to encourage members of the public to report anyone suspected of acting as a director etc. while bankrupt or subject to disqualification. The 24-hour telephone number is 0845 6013546. Further details can be found on the Insolvency Service website at *http://www.insolvency.gov.uk/doitonline/ddbase.htm* [Accessed August 28, 2009]. For a critical appraisal of the enforcement process see A. Hicks, *Disqualification of Directors: No Hiding Place for the Unfit* (A.C.C.A Research Report No.59, 1998), pp.51–57.

[194] See the Insolvency Act 2000 (Commencement No.1 and Transitional Provisions) Order 2001 (SI 2001/766). CDDA s.15 was further amended by SI 2009/1941 with effect from October 1, 2009. The 2009 amendments were merely consequential on the coming into force of the Companies Act 2006.

[195] As regards the appropriateness of custodial sentences see, e.g. *R. v Atterbury* (1996) 2 Cr.App.Rep. (S.) 151; *R. v Johnson* (1996) 2 Cr.App.Rep. (S.) 228.

exceeding the statutory maximum, or both. A disqualified body corporate which acts in breach of the prohibition in CDDA ss.1, 1A, 9B(3), 12A or 12B is also guilty of an offence. By virtue of s.14, where a body corporate is guilty of the offence and it is proved that the offence occurred with the consent or connivance of, or was attributable to any neglect on the part of any director, manager, secretary or other similar officer[196] of the body corporate, or any person who was purporting to act in any such capacity then that person also commits an offence. The offences in ss.11 and 13 are offences of strict liability. Where the disqualified person breaches the prohibition as a matter of fact, the offence is committed even if he genuinely believes that his actions do not amount to a breach. In *R. v Brockley*[197] a person who had carried on the business of a hotel company was convicted of the s.11 offence. His defence rested on the belief, based on legal advice, that he had been automatically discharged from bankruptcy under the provisions of the Insolvency Act 1986 before starting up the company's business. An appeal against conviction was unsuccessful. The Court of Appeal held that as the offence was one of strict liability, it was incumbent on the bankrupt to ensure that his bankruptcy had in fact been discharged before engaging in a prohibited activity.[198] A person convicted of any of these offences is liable to further disqualification under s.2 of the CDDA as each offence is an "indictable offence . . . in connection with the . . . management . . . of a company" within that section.[199] It is also open to the sentencing court to make a confiscation order pursuant to the Proceeds of Crime Act 2002 in respect of any benefits that the convicted person received as a result of committing the offence.[200] Conviction for the offence[201] may have wider consequences, as can any conviction. One such consequence specifically provided for is that the Office of Fair Trading may make an order prohibiting the person from doing estate agency work.[202] However, the enforceability of contracts entered into by a company where a disqualified person is unlawfully participating in its management will not be affected.[203]

Civil liability

14–88 By virtue of CDDA s.15(1)(a), a person is personally responsible for all the relevant debts of a company if at any time he is involved in the management of the company in contravention of a disqualification order, a disqualification undertaking

[196] Including members where the affairs of the body corporate are managed by its members: CDDA s.14(2).

[197] [1994] 1 B.C.L.C. 606.

[198] See further *R. v Doring* [2002] EWCA Crim 1695, [2003] 1 Cr.App.R. 9.

[199] See, e.g. *R v Theivendran* (1992) 13 Cr.App.R. (S.) 601; *R. v Thompson* (1993) 14 Cr.App.R. (S.) 89; *R. v Teece* (1994) 15 Cr.App.R. (S.) 302; *R. v Atterbury* (1996) 2 Cr.App.R. (S.) 151; *R. v Randhawa* [2008] EWCA Crim 2599.

[200] *R v Seager* [2009] EWCA Crim 1303.

[201] Or indeed conviction for an offence under CDDA ss.11(1) or 12(1).

[202] See Estates Agents Act 1979 s.3 and the Estate Agents (Specified Offences) (No.2) Order 1991 (SI 1991/1091).

[203] *Hill v Secretary of State for the Environment, Food and Rural Affairs* [2005] EWHC 696 (Ch), [2006] 1 B.C.L.C. 601.

(including a competition disqualification undertaking) or any of CDDA ss.11, 12A or 12B. "Relevant debts" for this purpose are such debts and other liabilities of the company as are incurred at a time when that person was involved in the management of the company (CDDA s.15(3)(a)). Liability is joint and several with the company and any other person who may be personally liable for the debts whether under s.15 or otherwise (CDDA s.15(2)). The upshot is that a creditor owed a relevant debt could proceed against either the company or the disqualified person for the whole amount. The provision therefore confers on the creditor a separate statutory right of action against the disqualified person which supplements his contractual right against the company and on the company a right of contribution against the disqualified person who, by operation of the statute, has become the company's co-debtor.[204] A person is "involved in management" if he is a director of the company or if he is concerned, whether directly or indirectly, or takes part, in the management of the company (CDDA s.15(4)). Strictly, this means that a disqualified person who acts in breach of the prohibitions on being a receiver of a company's property or on acting as an insolvency practitioner can only be personally liable for any relevant debts to the extent that his activities amount to involvement in management. The test appears to be stricter than the test for determining whether a disqualified person has acted in breach of the prohibition on being concerned or taking part (whether directly or indirectly) in the management of a company.[205] Civil liability under s.15(1)(a) is free standing. In other words, a disqualified person risks personal liability whether or not he is prosecuted for the criminal offence under CDDA s.13. One oddity of s.15(1)(a) is that it does not appear to impose personal liability on a person who acts in breach of the prohibition in s.12(2).[206]

14–89 It is not only a disqualified person who can incur civil liability. By virtue of CDDA s.15(1)(b), a person is also personally responsible for all the relevant debts of a company if, at any time, as a person who is involved in the management of the company, he acts or is willing to act on instructions given without the permission of the court by a person whom he knows at that time to be the subject of a disqualification order or undertaking made or accepted under the CDDA or the equivalent Northern Ireland legislation or to be an undischarged bankrupt.[207] This provision is directed primarily at those who may be prepared to act as nominees or "front men" in a company run by a disqualified person. "Relevant debts" for this purpose are such debts and other liabilities of the company as are incurred at a time when that person was acting or willing to act on the instructions of the disqualified person (CDDA s.15(3)(b)). Liability is again joint and several while "involved in management" bears the same meaning as it does in s.15(1)(a). A person who has

[204] *Re Prestige Grindings Ltd, Sharma v Yardley* [2005] EWHC 3076 (Ch), [2006] 1 B.C.L.C. 440 at [11].

[205] See text from 14–30.

[206] No reference is made to s.12 in contrast to the criminal provision in s.13 which specifically refers to contravention of s.12(2).

[207] At the time of writing s.15(1)(b) had not been amended to include reference to debt relief orders or insolvency restrictions.

acted at any time on the instructions of a disqualified person is rebuttably presumed to have been willing at any time thereafter to act on any instructions given by that person (CDDA s.15(5)).[208] The defence in Companies Act 2006 s.1157 (formerly Companies Act 1985 s.727) cannot be raised to meet a claim made against a party under CDDA s.15(1)(b).[209] It appears that a person who acts on the instructions of someone disqualified in the terms of CDDA s.12 is not within the scope of s.15(1)(b).

14–90 For the purposes of CDDA s.15, liability flowing from a breach of s.11 will not be affected by the subsequent annulment of the bankruptcy order. The CDDA has no express provision removing the criminal and civil liabilities arising from CDDA ss.11 and 15 in the event of the bankruptcy order being annulled and, accordingly, if the defendant was an undischarged bankrupt at the relevant time, the subsequent annulment of the bankruptcy order will not afford him a defence to criminal or civil proceedings under these provisions.[210]

14–91 It is clear as a matter of authority that a liquidator of a company in respect of which the disqualified person has acted in breach of a disqualification order or undertaking or of the prohibitions in CDDA ss.11, 12A or 12B may not pursue an action against that person in a representative capacity on behalf of creditors. The only circumstances in which the liquidator could proceed on behalf of the liquidation estate is where the company has paid "relevant debts" before the commencement of liquidation and has a right of action for contribution against the disqualified person as a co-debtor.[211] Moreover, it appears that s.15 confers on each creditor a direct right of action to recover a relevant debt or debts owing to him or her. Accordingly, the court will not generally make an order whereby one creditor is appointed to act in a representative capacity for all creditors in s.15 proceedings.[212]

[208] Civil liability along these lines was first introduced in s.18 of the Insolvency Act 1985. There is an analogous provision in Insolvency Act 1986 s.217 imposing similar liabilities where there is contravention of the restriction on re-use of company names in s.216 of the same Act. This also derives from s.18 of the 1985 Act. For cases where creditors have had recourse to s.217 see *Thorne v Silverleaf* [1994] 2 B.C.L.C. 637; *Inland Revenue Commissioners v Nash* [2003] EWHC 686 (Ch), [2004] B.C.C. 150; *Archer Structures Ltd v Griffiths* [2003] EWHC 957 (Ch), [2004] 1 B.C.L.C. 201; *Ricketts v Ad Valorem Factors Ltd* [2003] EWCA Civ 1706, [2004] 1 All E.R. 894; *Revenue and Customs Commissioners v Walsh* [2005] EWHC 1304 (Ch), [2005] 2 B.C.L.C. 455 (application for permission to appeal refused: [2005] EWCA Civ 1291, [2006] B.C.C. 431); *Revenue and Customs Commissioners v Benton-Diggins* [2006] EWHC 793 (Ch), [2006] 2 B.C.L.C. 255; *First Independence Factors and Finance Ltd v Mountford* [2008] EWHC 835 (Ch), [2008] 2 B.C.L.C. 297.

[209] *Commissioners for Inland Revenue v McEntaggart* [2004] EWHC 3431 (Ch), [2006] 1 B.C.L.C. 476 at [45]–[47].

[210] *Commissioners for Inland Revenue v McEntaggart* [2006] 1 B.C.L.C. 476 at [38]–[41].

[211] *Re Prestige Grindings Ltd, Sharma v Yardley* [2006] 1 B.C.L.C. 440 at [11]–[15].

[212] *Re Prestige Grindings Ltd, Sharma v Yardley* [2006] 1 B.C.L.C. 440 at [22]–[25].

CHAPTER 15

PERMISSION TO ACT NOTWITHSTANDING DISQUALIFICATION

INTRODUCTION

15–01 The power of the courts to grant a disqualified person permission to act[1] as a director or take part in the management of specified companies is an important schematic feature of the CDDA. It has been emphasised throughout this book that it is not possible to arrive at a complete understanding of the purpose and operation of the legislation unless the court's power to grant permission is taken fully into account. It has been seen that ss.2–6, 8, 9A and 10 of the CDDA confer various powers on the courts (and in the case of ss.6 and 9A, a duty) to make a disqualification order, each of which focuses on particular types of past misconduct. A disqualification order made pursuant to these various powers is a blanket prohibition. The same is also true of the prohibition that flows from a disqualification undertaking and a competition disqualification undertaking.[2] As was seen earlier in Ch.12, once the court has decided or become obliged to make a disqualification order, it is bound to impose a blanket ban prohibiting the disqualified person from engaging in any of the activities covered by CDDA s.1.[3] Thus, a person who is the subject of a disqualification order is prohibited from being a director of a company, from acting as a receiver of a company's property and from in any way, whether directly or indirectly, being concerned in or taking part in the promotion, formation or management of a company.[4] An undischarged bankrupt, a person to whom a moratorium period under a debt relief order applies or a person subject to insolvency restrictions (whether by order or undertaking) is automatically prohibited by CDDA s.11 from acting as a director of, or directly or indirectly taking part in or being concerned in the promotion, formation or management of a company. A person disqualified in the terms of CDDA s.12 is prohibited from acting as a director or liquidator of, or directly or indirectly taking part or being concerned in the promotion, formation or management of, a company. As was seen in Ch.14, the scope of these various prohibitions is extensive. However, apart from the absolute ban in CDDA ss.1(1)(b), 1A(1)(b), 9B(3)(d),

[1] The CDDA and cases decided before the reform of the civil justice system use the phrases "leave of the court" and "leave to act". In the light of the CPR, the Disqualification Rules and the Disqualification Practice Direction, the term "permission" is used throughout rather than the old term "leave" except in the case of direct quotes from the CDDA. Under the CPR, the parties on an application for permission to act brought on application notice within substantive disqualification proceedings are still referred to as "applicant" and "respondent": see generally below on procedure.

[2] CDDA ss.1A, 9B.

[3] *Re Gower Enterprises Ltd (No.2)* [1995] 2 B.C.L.C. 201 and see text from 12–11.

[4] The point applies equally to disqualification undertakings and competition disqualification undertakings and to the automatic disqualifications under CDDA ss.12A and 12B triggered by disqualification under the Northern Ireland legislation.

12A(b) and 12B(b) on acting as an insolvency practitioner, none of the prohibitions is absolute because ss.1(1)(a), 1A(1)(a), 11(1), 12(1), 12A(a) and 12B(a) all provide that the disqualified person is disqualified from engaging in a prohibited activity or acting in a prohibited capacity without the permission of the court.[5] Thus, a central unifying feature of the CDDA is that a person disqualified in the terms of any of ss.1, 1A, 9B, 11, 12, 12A or 12B may apply for permission to act in certain capacities notwithstanding disqualification. It has been seen that the power of the court to grant permission has significant implications for law and practice in relation to the CDDA generally. The following points can be made:

(1) The rationale of the CDDA is that the court is empowered or obliged to make a full disqualification order based on the defendant's *previous* conduct and the width of the overall prohibition is tempered by the court's power to grant permission in relation to certain of the prohibitions. The same point can be made in relation to ss.11 and 12 (although in the case of undischarged bankrupts and debtors who are subject to debt relief orders disqualification is automatic and an order of the court is not required). This suggests that, in exercising their substantive powers to disqualify, the courts should be concerned first and foremost to protect the public and promote high standards of conduct and that, generally, any other factors (such as the defendant's *present* conduct or circumstances) should be taken into account either by way of mitigation or in the context of an application for permission to act notwithstanding disqualification.[6]
(2) The courts should take a wide, flexible view when construing the terms of the prohibition in CDDA ss.1(1)(a), 1A(1)(a), 9B, 11(1), 12(2), 12A(a) or 12B(a) taking into account the fact that there is power under the CDDA to grant permission.[7]
(3) The courts should be careful in exercising any power to stay or postpone the coming into force of a disqualification order.[8] It is generally more appropriate, having regard to the overall scheme of the Act, to consider the grant of *interim permission* under the disqualification order in relation to specific companies rather than to direct that the order is not to come into full effect until some time after it is pronounced.[9]

[5] A competition disqualification undertaking may also provide that the court's relieving power to grant permission to act notwithstanding disqualification should be available. Note, however, the curious wording of CDDA ss.9B(3)–(4) which appears to suggest that a relevant regulator has the power to accept a competition disqualification undertaking in a form that excludes the court's power to grant permission to act: see further text at 9–42 and from 12–05.

[6] *Re Westmid Packing Services Ltd, Secretary of State for Trade and Industry v Griffiths* [1998] 2 All E.R. 124.

[7] See Ch.14. The ability to grant permission has been relied on as mitigating the fact that the prohibition is wide and, to some extent, uncertain.

[8] See Ch.12 which also deals with the commencement of undertakings.

[9] *Secretary of State for Trade and Industry v Bannister* [1996] 1 W.L.R. 118; *Re Thorncliffe Finance Ltd, Secretary of State for Trade and Industry v Arif* [1997] 1 B.C.L.C. 34 at 46; *Re Continental Assurance Co of London Plc* [1997] 1 B.C.L.C. 48 at 61–62 affirmed sub nom. *Secretary of State for Trade and Industry v Burrows*, July 4, 1996, C.A., unreported; *Re Amaron Ltd, Secretary of State for Trade and Industry v Lubrani* [1998] B.C.C. 264 (supplementary judgment of Neuberger J. from p.274); *Hease v Secretary of State for Trade and Industry* [2005] EWHC 2909 (Ch), [2006] B.P.I.R. 425 and text from 15–59.

15–02 This chapter examines the principles on which the court exercises the power to grant permission to act notwithstanding disqualification, the factors that are taken into account and relevant procedural issues.

THE APPROACH OF THE COURT IN EXERCISING THE POWER TO GRANT PERMISSION

Scope of power

15–03 The courts in England and Wales will generally only grant an application by a disqualified person for permission where it relates to a specific company or companies, a point borne out by the authorities that are discussed in greater detail below. This practice suggests that the courts take the view that an application for a general relaxation of the prohibition (e.g. permission to act generally as a director of any company) should not be countenanced during the currency of a disqualification order. Apart from the obvious policy justification, support for this view can be derived from the result in *Re Shneider*[10] In that case it was held that an equivalent provision of the Australian Corporations Law did not empower the court to go beyond a limited relaxation of the ban in respect of a specific company and lift the ban to permit a disqualified person to participate in the management of companies generally. However, in *Re Harrison*[11] the Federal Court of Australia considered the matter further. The question there arose in connection with what is now s.206B of the Corporations Act 2001, which automatically prohibits a person from acting in certain capacities for five years following a relevant conviction. The court considered the purpose of such a prohibition and, interestingly, confirmed the view (often expressed in the English courts) that the purpose of such prohibition was not punitive but rather, was designed:

> "to protect the public and to prevent the corporate structure from being used to the financial detriment of investors, shareholders, creditors and persons dealing with the company"

and was:

> "calculated to act as a safeguard against the corporate structure being used by individuals in a manner which is contrary to proper commercial standards".[12]

In reasoning that is extremely persuasive, Van Doussa J. rejected the view that, as a matter of jurisdiction, the court could not grant a general permission or a permission covering a series of companies that are not described individually but share certain defined characteristics (e.g. private companies). However, he accepted that the circumstances in which the court would think it appropriate to

[10] (1997) 22 A.C.S.R. 497.

[11] (1998) 153 A.L.R. 369.

[12] Citing Bowen C.J. in *Magna Alloys & Research Pty Ltd* (1975) 1 A.C.L.R. 203 at 205.

grant such a permission would be very rare for the reasons set out in *Re Shneider* and having regard to the policy considerations underlying the provision:

> "This is particularly so in the case of trading companies. Without knowing the particulars of the type of companies, the nature of their business, the nature of their management structure, and the intended involvement of the applicant in their management, it would be impossible to know whether it was appropriate to make an order in general terms that did not specify particular corporations by name."[13]

On the facts of that case and subject to certain conditions, the court was prepared to give a general permission to act in relation to one defined category of companies, identified by their characteristics rather than by specific company names, but not in relation to a second category.[14]

15–04 Applications tend to be granted more readily in relation to companies with which the disqualified person was involved at the time of his disqualification and which had not featured in the main disqualification proceedings.[15] A second common feature of English practice is that permission to act, when given, is invariably only given subject to detailed conditions and safeguards. Doubt has been expressed in some quarters as to whether the courts have the power to impose conditions on the grant of permission. Nevertheless, the practice is now well established and unlikely to be successfully challenged.[16] The sorts of conditions and safeguards that the courts commonly impose are discussed further below.

[13] This echoes dicta of Neuberger J. in *Re Amaron Ltd, Secretary of State for Trade and Industry v Lubrani* [1998] B.C.C. 264 at 278 on the need for the court to be given up to date information about the company or companies in relation to which permission is sought.

[14] Permission was granted to be a director of "not for profit" organisations of a community service kind on condition that the relevant board retained four or more members in addition to the applicant. The court was not prepared to make a blanket order in relation to companies that consulted the applicant for sales and marketing advice. A similar "general" permission was granted in relation to one of the disqualified Barings' directors, Mr Tuckey. In his capacity as a corporate banker, there was a concern that he might be involved, in a degree otherwise prohibited, in the promotion or formation of companies that would be undertaken by clients in the course of (for example) a restructuring. Permission to be so involved was granted. See also *Re TLL Realisations Ltd, Secretary of State for Trade and Industry v Collins* [2000] B.C.C. 998. In that case, the court gave a disqualified person permission to carry out specific functions within a specified company and its existing subsidiaries. An extension of the permission was requested to cover subsidiaries that might be acquired in the future in the course of the group's expansion. The jurisdiction of the court to make such an order was not disputed but Park J., in his discretion, reluctantly refused to accede to this request.

[15] See *Re TLL Realisations Ltd, Secretary of State for Trade and Industry v Collins* [1998] B.C.C. 998, where Park J. suggested that the case for permission is stronger if the disqualified person is already involved in the company and has discharged his duties without complaint than a case in which the disqualified person wants to take on a new employment which he did not have before.

[16] For hesitancy on whether the phrase "permission of the court" can properly be construed as meaning "on such terms and conditions as the court thinks fit" see, *Re Majestic Recording Studios Ltd* [1989] B.C.L.C. 1 and the Scottish case of *Secretary of State for Trade and Industry v Palfreman* [1995] 2 B.C.L.C. 301 though see the practice of the courts discussed in the text from 15–35 and dictum of Arden J. in *Re Tech Textiles Ltd, Secretary of State for Trade and Industry v Vane* [1998] 1 B.C.L.C. 259 at 267. The question does not always arise in other jurisdictions, for example, in Australia, where the Corporations Law 2001 (Cth.) s.206G confers express power on the courts to grant permission subject to conditions.

Discretion

15–05 While the CDDA contains detailed guidance in Sch.1 on the factors to be taken into account in determining whether a person's conduct makes him unfit for the purposes of ss.6 and 8, there is, by contrast, no express statutory guidance as to how the courts should go about exercising their discretion when faced with an application for permission to act notwithstanding disqualification.[17] The factors that the courts should (or may) take into account are left to be judicially determined in the light of the overall objectives of the legislative scheme. The courts in England and Wales have generally taken the view that the CDDA is concerned primarily with protecting the public from those whose past conduct makes them unfit to act as directors or managers of companies.[18] However, the application of that rationale in the context of applications for permission to act has not always been consistent although a relatively settled approach to the discretion does now seem to have emerged.[19] The four points that can be made with confidence, judging from the case law, are that: (a) the onus lies firmly with the applicant seeking permission to establish that it should be granted (the standard of proof being the balance of probabilities)[20]; (b) there is no difference between applications for permission in cases where a disqualification order has been made under CDDA s.1 and applications in cases where a disqualification undertaking has been given under CDDA s.1A[21]; (c) the application will usually have to relate to a specified company or companies; and (d) in cases where permission is granted, it is frequently granted only subject to conditions and safeguards. In determining whether or not to grant permission to act, one approach favoured initially by the courts was to apply a two-stage test. On this approach the applicant was required to show that:

(1) There was a *need* for the applicant to act as a director or take part in the management of the company or companies specified in the application; and
(2) If an order giving permission to act were made, the public would be adequately protected.

15–06 The two-stage test originated from some dicta of Harman J. in *Re Cargo Agency Ltd*[22] that were later adopted by Sir Mervyn Davies in *Re Gibson Davies Ltd.*[23]

[17] Contrast the precise substantive and procedural guidelines in the Insolvency Rules 1986 which pertain to an application for permission to act notwithstanding disqualification under CDDA s.11: see further text at 15–78.

[18] See Ch.2.

[19] See, e.g. the observations of Park J. in *Re Morija Plc, Kluk v Secretary of State for Business, Enterprise and Regulatory Reform* [2007] EWHC 3055 (Ch), [2008] 2 B.C.L.C. 313 at [32]–[35].

[20] On standard of proof see *Re Amaron Ltd, Secretary of State for Trade and Industry v Lubrani* [1998] B.C.C. 264.

[21] *Re Morija Plc, Kluk v Secretary of State for Business, Enterprise and Regulatory Reform* [2008] 2 B.C.L.C. 313 at [32].

[22] [1992] B.C.L.C. 686 at 692:

> "It seems to me that Mr Newey must be right that applications for [permission] pursuant to s.1 should only be [granted] where there is a need for them to be granted, and should only be granted upon evidence of adequate protection from danger."

[23] [1995] B.C.C. 11.

For the purposes of a complete exposition, the two limbs of this test are analysed in detail below. However, as will become clear, the courts do not apply the so-called "need" requirement rigorously in every case and there is now considerable doubt as to whether the two-stage test (incorporating the "need" requirement) truly represents (or should represent) the present state of the law.[24] It is suggested that the test is better seen as one of whether or not, in all the circumstances, permission to act notwithstanding disqualification should be granted. The "circumstances" that will be relevant are those traditionally considered under the headings of "need" and "protection of the public" but under the suggested test no single factor is necessarily decisive. Thus, for example, the question of "need" should be regarded as a flexible matter encompassing a spectrum of possibilities. Support for this approach can be derived from the following passage of Scott V.C.'s judgment in *Re Dawes & Henderson Ltd, Secretary of State for Trade and Industry v Shuttleworth*:

> "The discretion given to the court under the 1986 Act to grant [permission] to an individual against whom a disqualification order has been made, enabling him during the currency of the disqualification order to act as a director of a particular company, is a discretion unfettered by any statutory condition or criterion. It would in my view be wrong for the court to create any such fetters or conditions. The reason why it would be wrong is that no one, when sitting in any particular case to give judgment, can foresee the infinite variety of circumstances that might apply in future cases before the court. When Parliament has given the courts an unfettered discretion I do not think it is for the courts to reduce the ambit of that discretion. But in exercising the statutory discretion courts must, of course, not take into account any irrelevant factors. The emphasis given in a judgment on a particular case on particular circumstances in that case is not necessarily a guide to the weight to be attributed to similar circumstances in a different case."[25]

It is likely that these observations will be treated as extending to applications for permission to act in other prohibited capacities (i.e. not just as director) and applications by persons disqualified under CDDA ss.11 and 12.

The proper starting point

15–07 It is suggested that the starting point should be that a person who has been disqualified is, on the face of it, unfit to act as a director or otherwise take part in the management of companies. As such, there should be a firm onus on the applicant to demonstrate why it is appropriate to grant him permission. As Van Doussa J. put it in *Re Harrison*[26]:

> "It must be a clear and appropriate case before the court gives [permission] so as to remove what Parliament *prima facie* thought was a necessary restriction."

[24] See, e.g. *Re Morija Plc, Kluk v Secretary of State for Business, Enterprise and Regulatory Reform* [2008] 2 B.C.L.C. 313 at [36].

[25] [1999] 2 B.C.L.C. 317 at 326. See also *Re Aitch Holdings Ltd, Smith v Secretary of State for Trade and Industry* [2002] EWHC 2866 (Ch).

[26] (1998) 153 A.L.R. 369.

The standard of proof is the civil standard on the balance of probabilities.[27] Nevertheless, for reasons considered further below, it is suggested that the courts need to apply a critical approach when considering an applicant's evidence and that they should not be overly-impressed by the mere fact that evidence may not have been challenged.[28] As discussed below, the Secretary of State will often have no basis on which to challenge the applicant's evidence. Moreover, the courts should be careful to avoid granting permission too readily as to do so might undermine the purposes for which the person was disqualified in the first place. It will be recalled that the purposes of disqualification include deterrence and the raising of standards of conduct among directors generally.[29] The value of disqualification as a form of protection (especially as a deterrent) would be undermined if a disqualified person were promptly given permission to act in a prohibited capacity or capacities. This general point was well made by Arden J. in *Re Tech Textiles Ltd, Secretary of State for Trade and Industry v Vane*:

> "As respects the exercise of the discretion to grant leave there is no express guidance in the statute. It is clearly relevant to the exercise of this discretion to consider the end which disqualification seeks to achieve and the reasons why that end is thought desirable. It is clear . . . that the purpose . . . of the 1986 Act is protective rather than penal, and this is the starting point. In practice . . . [it] . . . also has a deterrent function since honest directors will not wish their conduct to result in disqualification proceedings. Advisers can perform the valuable function of drawing client directors' attention to these provisions and no doubt should often do so in the best interests of their clients. [Permission] . . . is not to be too freely given. Legislative policy requires the disqualification of unfit directors to minimise the risk of harm to the public, and the court must not by granting [permission] prevent the achievement of this policy objective. Nor would the court wish anyone dealing with the director to be misled as to the gravity with which it views the order that has been made."[30]

15–08 In *Re TLL Realisations Ltd, Secretary of State for Trade and Industry v Collins*[31] the court considered the question of whether too ready a grant of permission might not bring the CDDA into disrepute. The main problem with too generous an approach is that it tends to undermine the deterrent function of disqualification but the concern may go wider than that. In *Re Barings Plc (No.3),*

[27] See *Re Amaron Ltd, Secretary of State for Trade and Industry v Lubrani* [1998] B.C.C. 264.

[28] In this sense, it is suggested that the court should approach the matter as it would an application for the making of an administration order under Sch.B1 paras 11–13 of the Insolvency Act 1986 or an application for relief under s.127 of the same Act: mere assertions without supporting evidence should not be enough. See further text at 15–11.

[29] See Ch.2 noting in particular *Re Grayan Building Services Ltd, Secretary of State for Trade and Industry v Gray* [1995] Ch. 241; *Re Westmid Packing Services Ltd, Secretary of State for Trade and Industry v Griffiths* [1998] 2 All E.R. 124.

[30] [1998] 1 B.C.L.C. 259 at 267. See also *Re Westminster Property Management Ltd (No.2), Official Receiver v Stern (No.2)* [2001] B.C.C. 305 at 361 where Lloyd J. opined that the burden of showing that permission is justified is only likely to be satisfied if (among other matters), "to allow the person in question to act . . . would not subvert or reduce the effect of the disqualification order, even if only its deterrent effect". A similar point is made by Park J. in *Re Morija Plc, Kluk v Secretary of State for Business, Enterprise and Regulatory Reform* [2008] 2 B.C.L.C. 313 at [35] and [54].

[31] [2000] B.C.C. 998.

Secretary of State for Trade and Industry v Baker, Scott V.C. accepted the general proposition that the question of permission involves a consideration of the purposes for which the original disqualification, against which partial relief is sought, was imposed:

> "The reasons for granting [permission], if [permission] is granted, must be consistent with the reasons why the disqualification was imposed in the first place."[32]

In that case, however, the Vice-Chancellor tended to dwell on protection of the public in the sense that the disqualified person is kept "off the road", rather than the deterrent function of a disqualification order. It is suggested, in the light of these general points, that the court should only exercise the discretion to grant permission if satisfied on cogent evidence that it is appropriate to do so bearing in mind all the purposes of disqualification (including deterrence).[33]

Need

15–09 As indicated above, it has become commonplace for the courts to talk in terms of a two-stage requirement for the applicant to establish that: (a) he "needs" to be a director and; (b) if permission is given, the public will continue to be adequately protected. It is suggested that the use of this language of "need" is unfortunate, as it has tended to obscure the basis for granting permission and the circumstances in which permission will be granted. Thus, as has become clear in more recent cases, "need" is better seen as a flexible concept having a spectrum of meanings. Furthermore, "need" is not a gateway or threshold condition that must be satisfied before the court will consider other factors (as some of the earlier authorities imply), but is simply one of a number of factors that the court will consider in deciding whether permission will be given. Before the current position is explained, it is necessary to consider the authorities to see how the concept of "need" has developed.

The court will not act in vain

15–10 The concept of "need" first arose in *Re Cargo Agency Ltd*.[34] Having disqualified a Mr Keeling for the minimum period of two years, Harman J. was faced with an application by him for permission to be engaged as a general manager and/or as a director or otherwise to be involved in the management of a named company, a wholly-owned subsidiary of Rolls Royce Plc. Mr Keeling had been carrying out this role for 18 months or so and the Secretary of State offered no opposition to his continuing in that occupation. Harman J. was prepared to give him permission to be engaged as a general manager but not permission to act as a director or otherwise to

[32] [2000] 1 W.L.R. 634 at 640. See also *Re Britannia Homes Centre Ltd, Official Receiver v McCahill* [2001] 2 B.C.L.C. 63.

[33] See also *Re McQuillan* (1989) 5 B.C.C. 137 at 140 (citing *Re Altim Pty Ltd* [1968] 2 N.S.W.R. 762; *Re Amaron Ltd, Secretary of State for Trade and Industry v Lubrani* [1998] B.C.C. 264 at 277; *Re Morija Plc, Kluk v Secretary of State for Business, Enterprise and Regulatory Reform* [2008] 2 B.C.L.C. 313 at [35].

[34] [1992] B.C.L.C. 686.

be involved in management. At that time, his being a director was not "an immediate issue" and so there was no "need" for a wider permission. This was because there were other directors in place who were capable of ensuring that the company continued to trade and flourish. In this context, the requirement to show "need" was little more than a requirement to show that there was some purpose to the court giving permission. As at the time there was no issue or question of the applicant being a director from the relevant company's perspective, it was inappropriate for the court to give permission. Narrow permission, analogous to the permission granted in *Cargo Agency*, has also been granted in a number of Australian cases.[35]

The concept of "need" in the *Cargo Agency* sense arose again in *Re McQuillan*,[36] a case in which the Northern Ireland High Court was faced with an application by an undischarged bankrupt for permission to act as a director. The bankrupt did not wish to resume acting as a working director but wished to return to the board of a company of which he was a director and shareholder prior to his bankruptcy with a view to causing that company to bring proceedings against certain persons (including a receiver and manager appointed by a secured creditor). The court refused permission on two connected grounds. The first was that there was no "need" for the bankrupt to become a director. He could achieve his objective by a derivative action if the shares formerly owned by him were re-assigned by his trustee. The second ground was akin to that in *Cargo Agency*. In order to become a director the bankrupt would need not only the permission of the court, but would also need to be re-appointed by the company in general meeting. This was not a practical possibility because the company's sole shareholder was not prepared to co-operate in the calling of a general meeting and in voting for the bankrupt's re-appointment. The court would not give permission where in so doing it would be giving permission in vain because of the opposition of the shareholder. It is suggested that this sense of "need" as a requirement to show that the court will not be acting in vain if an order is made is one which remains. In other words, there must be a good reason why permission should be given.

Desire or need of the applicant and of the company

15–11 In considering "need", the courts have gone further than a requirement to show that the court is not acting in vain. In *Re Gibson Davies Ltd*[37] Sir Mervyn Davies

[35] *Re Magna Alloys & Research Pty Ltd* (1975) 1 A.C.L.R. 203; *Re Zim Metal Products Pty Ltd* (1977) 2 A.C.L.R. 553 although the decision in the former case did not turn on the question of need. This approach is not beyond criticism. An order granting the applicant a narrow permission to take part in management will need to be tightly drawn so that it is quite clear what the applicant can and cannot do. Otherwise, there is a risk that his activities may amount to de facto or shadow directorship which would put him in breach of the prohibitions in ss.1(1)(a), 1A(1)(a), 9B(3)(a)–(c), 11, 12, 12A(a) or 12B(a) of the CDDA (as appropriate): see further text at 15–57. For judicial criticism of the approach in *Magna Alloys* and *Zim Metal*, see *Re Marsden* (1980) 5 A.C.L.R. 694, 702 per Legoe J.

[36] (1989) 5 B.C.C. 137.

[37] [1995] B.C.C. 11. For substantive disqualification proceedings arising out of the subsequent collapse of the company in relation to which permission was given see *Re Congratulations Franchising Ltd, Secretary of State for Trade and Industry v Davies*, March 6, 1998, Ch.D., unreported and discussion in the text from 15–38.

(sitting as a judge of the Chancery Division on an appeal from a district judge) approached the matter by considering whether there was a "need" and then whether or not, if an order was made, the public would be adequately protected. The circumstances were that the applicant had been disqualified for five years and he was seeking permission to be a director of a company called Congratulations Franchising Ltd. Interim permission was apparently in place between September 1993 and the date of the judgment on appeal in July 1994.[38] Sir Mervyn Davies discounted the desire of the applicant to be a director. However, he gave greater weight to evidence of the applicant and two others suggesting that the company was "much in need" of the applicant's services as the guiding light of the company. The district judge had considered evidence to the effect that if the applicant could not act as a director, the company would fail and jobs would be lost. Although such a consequence would be unfortunate, he considered that this danger was overstated and that the company could prosper equally well if the applicant was employed as chief salesman. Sir Mervyn Davies disagreed with this conclusion. He referred on a number of occasions to the "uncontradicted" evidence put forward by the applicant. In relation to this aspect of the judgment, it is suggested that the court should not rely so readily on the mere fact that evidence put forward is uncontradicted. Unless the Secretary of State has relevant information to the contrary or is to be expected to seek and obtain disclosure and to cross-examine witnesses,[39] the court should be slow to take the fact that evidence is uncontradicted as a positive factor adding weight to the applicant's evidence. Secondly, the judge held that the district judge had reached a conclusion that was not "justified" on the evidence. Finally, he made the point that if, as suggested by the district judge, the applicant was employed as a chief salesman he would inevitably be concerned in management (and therefore in breach of the disqualification order). It is suggested that this last point raises the question whether in *Gibson Davies* the proper course would have been to give the applicant permission to act in a reduced capacity. However, this question was not explored further. The apparent elevation of the concept of "need" to the status of a pre-condition or threshold test in some of the later authorities stems therefore from *Gibson Davies*.

15–12 As a general matter, it is suggested that the authorities as a whole can be relied upon to support the following propositions that mark a shift away from the apparent rigidity of the two-stage approach seemingly taken in *Gibson Davies*:

(1) The word "need" is misleading and too narrow. Even given the width of the prohibitions under the CDDA, cases where "necessity" can be established in the sense that the applicant will not be able to earn a livelihood or the company

[38] A protracted period now likely to attract criticism: see e.g. comments of Chadwick J. in *Secretary of State for Trade and Industry v Renwick*, July 1997, Ch.D., unreported, criticising the effective grant of interim permission for nine months.

[39] Which would greatly lengthen hearings for permission apparently against the general guidance given by the Court of Appeal in *Re Dicetrade Ltd, Secretary of State for Trade and Industry v Worth* [1994] 2 B.C.L.C. 113.

will collapse unless he is granted permission to be (say) a director are probably going to be rare. It is suggested that the function of the court is to weigh any "need", "desire" or "legitimate interest"[40] established by the applicant with other factors pointing in favour of or against the grant of permission.

(2) Any "desire" of the applicant to act in a prohibited capacity will carry much less weight than a "desire" or "need" of the company concerned ("desire" also carrying less weight than "need"). The "desire" or "need" of the relevant company may itself range in degree from a straightforward "desire" to have the applicant "on board",[41] to a "need" to have a person with the skills and experience of the applicant or to a "need" to have the applicant fulfilling a specific role or capacity for which permission is sought.

(3) In considering the "need" or "legitimate interests" of the company (to use parlance from some of the cases), there will be cases where the interests of the company cannot or should not be distinguished from those of the applicant.

These propositions and the shift away from a two-stage test towards a more nuanced "in all the circumstances" test are discussed further below.

The retreat from Gibson Davies

15–13 Although there are cases that suggest that the "desire" of the applicant for permission is irrelevant, such cases probably go too far. In *Re Gibson Davies Ltd* Sir Mervyn Davies discounted the desire of the applicant to be a director on the basis that ". . . such desire is, to my mind, not a need for present purposes".[42] In *Re Lo-Line Electric Motors Ltd*,[43] the court made reference to the "need" of the applicant to be a director, although it is not clear from the judgment what this "need" was based on. Similarly, in *Re Cargo Agency Ltd*,[44] Harman J. gave permission for a person to act as a general manager but it was not suggested in the judgment that the applicant had established, for example, that he could not have obtained employment elsewhere without breaching the terms of the disqualification order. Subsequent cases have confirmed that "need" is not a threshold requirement and that the "desire" or "need" of the applicant to obtain permission can be taken into account. In *Re Barings Plc (No.3), Secretary of State for Trade and Industry v Baker*,[45] Scott V.C. considered an application for permission made by Mr Norris, the former Chief Executive Officer of Barings who was disqualified for four years on grounds of unfit conduct under the summary *Carecraft* procedure.[46] In anticipation that a

[40] All of which are terms that have been used by the courts in this context.

[41] See *Re Barings Plc (No.3), Secretary of State for Trade and Industry v Baker* [2000] 1 W.L.R. 634.

[42] [1995] B.C.C. 11 at 15. In *Re Dawes & Henderson Ltd, Secretary of State for Trade and Industry v Shuttleworth* [1999] 2 B.C.L.C. 317 Scott V.C. suggested that the relevant passage from the judgment of Sir Mervyn Davies appeared to elevate the requirement of need into something like a sine qua non for the making of an order, an approach which he criticised.

[43] [1988] Ch. 477.

[44] [1992] B.C.L.C. 686.

[45] [2000] 1 W.L.R. 634.

[46] On *Carecraft*, see generally Ch.9.

disqualification order would be made against him, Mr Norris made an application for permission to remain as a non-executive director of three named private companies. In each case, he did not "need" to act as a director because he was able to provide the same services and be remunerated as a consultant. Equally, the three companies did not "need" him to act as a director for the same reason. Nevertheless, on the facts of the case, permission to act as a director was given on terms.[47] Having decided that no relevant "need" (of company or applicant) had been established, Scott V.C. said that the court should keep in balance the importance of protecting the public from the conduct that led to the disqualification order and the need for the applicant to act as a director.[48] This raises a conundrum: if no "need" was established, what was there to balance? There are two possible answers that may overlap. The first is to say that "need" does not have to be established. The reference to a requirement to keep "need" and "protection of the public" in balance could simply be read as a suggestion that, in a case where the grant of permission poses no great danger to the public, it would be "out of balance" to require the applicant to establish "need". The second (and arguably more satisfactory) answer is to say that "need" does not have to be established as a pre-condition, but that the "needs" or "interests" of the relevant company and the applicant (which may vary in degree from "desire" to absolute "need") are relevant factors to be taken into account in determining whether, in all the circumstances, permission should be granted. On this view, it may be that in some cases these factors will not be strong enough to outweigh other factors (principally, the public's need for protection, including protection through deterrence) that weigh against the grant of permission.[49] Scott V.C. returned to this question in *Re Dawes & Henderson Ltd, Secretary of State for Trade and Industry v Shuttleworth*.[50] In that case, he referred, with approval, to the following words of Rattee J. in *Re Streamhaven Ltd, Secretary of State for Trade and Industry v Barnett*:

> "In my judgment, the question I should ask myself is whether it is necessary for [the applicant] to be a director of a company in order to protect some legitimate interest of [the applicant] himself, or of any third party, which it is in all the circumstances of the case reasonable that the court should seek to protect . . . The extent to which it may be reasonable for the court to seek to protect the interests of the applicant himself in such a case must depend on all the circumstances giving rise to his disqualification."[51]

15–14 This move from "need" to "legitimate interest" and from a two-stage test to an "in all the circumstances" test, suggests further that "need" (beyond a narrow requirement to show that the court would not be acting in vain) is not a pre-condition to the

[47] To ensure that Norris would not assume any executive responsibilities in relation to the three companies, permission was granted in each case on condition that he remained an unpaid non-executive and be barred from entering into a director's service contract.

[48] [2000] 1 W.L.R. 634 at 641.

[49] In *Barings* itself, the court perceived that there was little risk that Norris's failings as a senior executive of a multi-national bank would recur and so allowed him to take up a non-executive position in the three private companies which formed the subject matter of his application.

[50] [1999] 2 B.C.L.C. 317.

[51] [1998] 2 B.C.L.C. 64 at 72.

grant of permission. In *Dawes & Henderson*, Scott V.C. stressed that the court should only take into account relevant factors but firmly rejected any notion that the court should fetter its discretion in deciding whether or not to grant permission by any pre-conditions or criteria.[52] Thus, he held that it would not be right to ignore any "personal, non-commercial purposes" of the applicant. On the facts of the case, the relevant "interest" lay in the ability of the applicant's business to defer tax, which was apparently only possible by running the business through the medium of a company. However, it is important to recognise that Scott V.C. did not say in *Dawes & Henderson* that "need" was an irrelevant factor. The mere fact that "need" is not a condition of obtaining permission did not mean that it would cease to be a relevant factor. In many cases its absence would be fatal:

> "In a case where no need has been demonstrated on the company's part to have the applicant as director or, from a business point of view, on the applicant's part to be a director, there would need, I think, to be only a very small risk to the public which the granting of [permission] might produce to justify the refusal of the application. *Per contra*, if a substantial and pressing need on the part of the company, or on the part of the individual in order to be able to earn his living, could be shown in favour of the grant of [permission] then it might be right to accept some slight risk to the public if the [permission] sought were granted."[53]

15–15 On the facts of the case, permission was granted to the applicant to act as a director of an *unlimited* company.[54] However, the Vice-Chancellor expressed the view that had the application been one to act as a director of a *limited* company, it would have been "a very difficult one indeed" to advance, even bearing in mind the other positive factors which were relied upon as justifying the grant of permission. The mere fact that the company in question is *unlimited* and that there may be little practical difference between the applicant carrying on business as a sole trader or through an unlimited company[55] may not be decisive in all cases. In some cases, the previous misconduct (for example, misconduct involving dishonesty or want of probity) may not justify the court in allowing the person to act in a prohibited capacity, even in relation to an unlimited company. In summary, it is suggested that the position on "need" is currently as follows:

(1) There is no threshold requirement but the court must take into account and consider the "need" or "legitimate interests" of the applicant and the relevant company as part of all the circumstances of the case.
(2) The "legitimate interests" of the applicant and the company may go beyond mere commercial interests.

[52] See the passage cited in 15–06.
[53] [1999] 2 B.C.L.C. 317 at 325.
[54] See also further discussion of *Streamhaven* in the text at 15–21 and *Re D.J. Matthews (Joinery Design) Ltd* (1988) 4 B.C.C. 513.
[55] The identifiable difference is that creditors need to wind up an unlimited company first before they can "get into [the applicant's] wallet".

(3) Such "legitimate interests" as are established have to be weighed with the other factors (particularly, the question of public protection) pointing for and against the grant of permission.
(4) The strength of the "legitimate interests" which are required in any one case to tip the scales in favour of the grant of permission will depend on all the circumstances: there is no one standard or strength of "interest" or "need" the presence of which will automatically justify the grant (or the absence of which will automatically justify the refusal) of permission.
(5) In many cases, the absence of a strong "need" for permission will result in permission being refused. As a general rule, it will be a rare case where permission will be given in the absence of some need of the company for the services of the applicant in a prohibited capacity.
(6) Equally, however, a strong case of need will not necessarily be sufficient to justify the grant of permission and may be outweighed by other factors, notably the protection of the public and the maintenance of disqualification as an effective general deterrent.[56]

Legitimate interests of the applicant of less weight than the legitimate interests of the company

15–16 The general proposition that the "interests" of the applicant weigh less heavily than the "interests" of an outside third party is borne out by authority. *Re Gibson Davies Ltd* itself is best seen as a case where the "interests" of the applicant in obtaining permission were not strong enough on its own to overcome the factors pointing against the grant of permission, but the weight given to the "interests" of the company and its employees was enough to tip the balance. The Australian courts have likewise accorded lesser weight to the applicant's personal needs as the following dictum of Zelling J. in *Re Maelor Pty Jones Ltd* illustrates:

> "Every disqualification under any Act involves in some way a hardship to an applicant and in some cases it may even threaten his livelihood and, it may be, his only source of livelihood, but when Parliament enacts disqualification sections such as these, it must be taken to know that that is their effect. Clearly in the opinion of Parliament the protection of the public outweighs the punitive effect the section may have on a person to whom it applies."[57]

15–17 This approach was also followed in *Re TLL Realisations Ltd, Secretary of State for Trade and Industry v Collins*[58] where Park J. considered that the need for the disqualified person to earn a living, while relevant, would be less influential than

[56] On this point see *Re Morija Plc, Kluk v Secretary of State for Business, Enterprise and Regulatory Reform* [2008] 2 B.C.L.C. 313 at [34], [35], [37], [54].

[57] (1975) 1 A.C.L.R. 4, 13–14. Also reported as *Re Van Reesma* (1975) 11 S.A.S.R. 322. Accordingly, hardship to the applicant alone is not a persuasive ground for the granting of permission: see further *Adams v Australian Securities & Investment Commission* (2003) 46 A.C.S.R. 68 at [5] and authorities therein cited.

[58] [2000] B.C.C. 998.

the need of the company to have the work done by that person for the purposes of its business. This general point is considered further below in connection with other cases. In *Barings*[59] and *Dawes & Henderson*,[60] permission was given although no "need", either of the company or of the applicant was made out. While the general approach in these cases to the question of need should now be followed (see discussion from 15–13 above), their outcomes are best regarded as exceptional. This is borne out further by the following passage from Scott V.C.'s judgment in *Barings*:

> "In *Re Amaron Ltd* [1998] B.C.C. 264 . . . the judge addressed the question whether the applicant had established 'need' and held that he had not. But this was a case in which the applicant had allowed the company to trade while insolvent and to retain money owed to creditors in order to fund continued trading. The need to ensure protection of the public from management techniques of that character would, in my view, have made it virtually impossible for a s.17 application to have succeeded."[61]

15–18 The same judge returned to this theme in *Dawes & Henderson* where he laid stress on the fact that the grounds on which the applicant had been disqualified did not involve any dishonesty, want of probity, deliberate breaches of the Companies Act or circumstances where any preferences or imprudent loans had been granted out of a desire for personal gain: ". . . in short, the improprieties alleged were of inadequate management and not of any dishonesty or want of probity". However, it is suggested that it would be wrong to assume that the fact that a director was disqualified for incompetence is going to be enough, in itself, to satisfy the court that permission is appropriate where there is only a weak "legitimate interest" in the application being granted. The relative weight to be given to the interests of the applicant and the interest of the company is perhaps best reflected in the following extract from the judgment of His Honour Judge Cooke in *Secretary of State for Trade and Industry v Rosenfield*:

> "I think that the question of need is best approached by saying simply does this order need to be made, and in whose interests does it need to be made? Now, so far as the director himself is concerned, I would take a good deal of persuasion that there were many, if any, cases where one can say properly the order needs to be made because the director would like it for his own purposes. The answer to that may very well be that if the director had landed himself in this position he must suffer a certain amount of inconvenience, but it does not follow that 'need' is to be construed restrictively so far as the needs of others are concerned."[62]

15–19 In *Dawes & Henderson*, Scott V.C. observed that the policy behind the CDDA is that:

> ". . . individuals against whom disqualification orders are made should nonetheless be able to earn their living in whatever business they may choose to turn their hand to".

[59] [2000] 1 W.L.R. 634.
[60] [1999] 2 B.C.L.C. 317.
[61] [2000] 1 W.L.R. 634 at 641.
[62] [1999] B.C.C. 413 at 416.

At first sight, this appears to imply that the "needs" of an applicant should be given considerable weight (*contra* the dictum of H H Judge Cooke). However, it is suggested that the Vice-Chancellor's observation should be read as a reference to carrying on a business as a sole trader or in partnership. This is because in the passage of the judgment which follows, the Vice-Chancellor referred to the applicant having "identified a business that he wants to carry on" and stated that it was consistent with the policy of the CDDA that he should carry it on in his own name and at his own risk, he being personally liable for its debts in the event of failure. It is suggested that this interpretation is consistent with the fact that the CDDA does not prohibit disqualified persons from carrying on in business as such. It only prohibits them from acting in certain capacities or carrying on certain functions in connection with companies. Thus, it is not the policy of the CDDA that disqualified persons should be able to carry on in business through the medium of a company. The policy is that they should only be able to do so with the permission of the court. As is stressed throughout this chapter, such permission should only be granted if it is consistent with the purposes for which the original disqualification was imposed and the CDDA generally.

15–20 A similar approach was taken by Lloyd J. in *Re Westminster Property Management Ltd (No.2), Official Receiver v Stern (No.2).*[63] In that case the applicant for permission to act, Mr Stern, had been disqualified for 12 years. Relying on the passage of the Vice-Chancellor's judgment in *Dawes v Henderson* set out above, the applicant submitted that the policy of the CDDA is to allow individuals who are subject to disqualification orders to earn their living in whatever business they may choose to turn their hand to, albeit that the court needs to be satisfied that the public is not at risk. This submission was rejected. Referring to the judgment of Peter Gibson L.J. in *Re TLL Realisations Ltd, Secretary of State for Trade & Industry v Collins*,[64] Lloyd J. observed that:

> "It seems to me that the Court of Appeal was endorsing the position under which, while of course the Act does not prohibit and therefore allows the disqualified person to carry on business as a sole trader, or in partnership for that matter, without the protection of limited liability, where the question is whether an individual who has been disqualified should be allowed to act as a director of a company or be concerned in the conduct and management of a company, it seems to me that there is a burden on an applicant to show that that is justified. It seems to me to emerge from the judgment of the Court of Appeal in *Secretary of State v Collins* and also from the judgment of Sir Richard Scott in *Re Barings (No.3)* that that is likely only to be satisfied if it can be shown that the corporate body in question has a need for the services of the person in question, that there is no risk to the public from the person in question acting as a director, and further that to allow the person in question to act as a director would not subvert or reduce the effect of the disqualification order, even if only in its deterrent effect. That seems to me to be a matter which the court must take into account even if it is satisfied as to the protective effect of the order, as it may be sometimes, where the order is made subject to conditions and the conditions satisfy the court that, for example, someone who has not been

[63] [2001] B.C.C. 305.
[64] [2000] B.C.C. 998 at 1013H.

suitably diligent in discharging duties is allowed to act as a director, but only as one of a board of perhaps a minimum size."

Separate third party legitimate interests

15–21 In considering the "legitimate interests" of the company (or another third party), it is important to identify those cases where the company has no separate interest from that of the applicant and, where it does have a separate interest, what that interest is and how heavily it weighs in the balance. It is clear that there may be cases where the "interests" of the applicant and the company are indistinguishable. In *Re Streamhaven Ltd, Secretary of State for Trade and Industry v Barnett*,[65] Rattee J. considered whether or not it was necessary for the applicant to be a director of the relevant company in order to protect some legitimate interest of the applicant or of a third party, which it was, in all the circumstances of the case, reasonable that the court should protect. In some cases it may be legitimate for the company to be regarded as having an interest separate from that of the applicant. For example, the relevant company may be long established and have outside investors and several employees. In such a case, it will be possible to say that the interests of the company are separate from those of the applicant as a matter of substance as well as form. In other cases, especially where the applicant is, in effect, seeking permission to act as an owner-manager, it may be artificial to distinguish the "interests" of the company from those of the applicant. *Streamhaven* falls into the latter category. The applicant and his wife were disqualified for four and two years respectively under the *Carecraft* procedure on the grounds that their conduct in relation to the relevant company, Streamhaven Ltd, which had traded in the restaurant business, made them unfit. Both parties accepted in their *Carecraft* statement that they had permitted the company to trade while insolvent, had failed to keep proper accounting records under s.221 of the Companies Act 1985 and had acted in breach of s.216 of the Insolvency Act 1986 by permitting the company to carry on its restaurant business under the same trade name that had been used when it was being run by a previous company which itself had gone into insolvent liquidation. The application for permission concerned a phoenix company controlled by the applicant and his wife that had acquired the restaurant business from Streamhaven through its liquidator. The applicant's evidence was that the restaurant business was identified with the applicant himself. He had devised the style of food for which the restaurant was known. He alone had dealt with the restaurant's suppliers. He claimed that, if he were not granted permission to act as a director, there would be no one who could run the company's business with the result that it would have to cease to trade. This would mean that bank loans would be called in and that 14 employees would lose their jobs. On the basis of this evidence, it was argued that the company needed the applicant as a director. Rattee J. refused to grant permission. His first point, as intimated above, was that it was unreal to distinguish the

[65] [1998] 2 B.C.L.C. 64.

company's needs from the needs of the applicant in a case where the relevant company was owned and run entirely by the applicant and his wife. The question of whether the court should protect the interests of the applicant in such a case must, according to Rattee J., depend on all the circumstances that gave rise to his disqualification. On the facts, the judge was not satisfied that it was appropriate for the court "to protect [the applicant's] ability to run the business under the existing name, with the advantages to him of limited liability . . ." in circumstances where the relevant company was the third incorporated incarnation of the same business in the same hands and its previous incarnations had collapsed at the expense of creditors. It follows that Rattee J. was not satisfied that the "interest" of the applicant in being a director was strong enough in all the circumstances as to require or justify the grant of permission. In this respect, the judge accepted the suggestion made on behalf of the Secretary of State that if the company could not continue in business without the applicant as a director, steps should be taken to enable the applicant to continue as a sole trader or in partnership with his wife without the benefit of limited liability.[66] This suggests that an applicant who was disqualified essentially on the ground of abuse of limited liability will find it difficult to satisfy the court that it is appropriate for him to be given permission to act, in substance, as an owner-manager of a limited company in the absence of any other compelling third party interest. The court may be prepared to grant permission in such a case if the applicant is seeking to trade through the medium of an unlimited company.[67] However, it is suggested in the light of *Dawes & Henderson* (discussed from 15–14 above) that there could still be difficulties in obtaining permission in such circumstances. *Streamhaven* appears to confirm the point that the applicant will have a stronger case for permission if the legitimate interest of the company or some other third party can be identified as being separate from the interests of the applicant.

15–22 The existence of a separate legitimate interest has been recognised in a number of cases. In *Re Tech Textiles Ltd, Secretary of State for Trade and Industry v Vane*, Arden J. made the point that there will be companies where the involvement of the applicant in the capacity sought is vital to customer or investor confidence.[68] In that case, the applicant was given permission to act as a director of a single company as the evidence showed that, in practice, it was important to the

[66] A similar conclusion was reached in *Re Universal Flooring and Driveways Ltd, Secretary of State for Trade and Industry v Woodward*, May 15, 1997, Ch.D., unreported and *Re Britannia Homes Centre Ltd, Official Receiver v McCahill* [2001] 2 B.C.L.C. 63.

[67] See, e.g. *Re D.J. Matthews (Joinery Design) Ltd* (1988) 4 B.C.C. 513 at 518. In that case which was decided under the old Companies Act provisions, the judge suggested that the defendant's application for permission might be looked upon favourably if he re-registered the relevant company as an unlimited company. There appears to be a flaw in the approach suggested in *D.J. Matthews* in that an applicant required to re-register his company as an unlimited company for the purposes of obtaining permission will be unable to convert it back into a limited company once his period of disqualification has expired: Companies Act 2006 s.105(2).

[68] [1998] 1 B.C.L.C. 259 at 269. The existence of a separate legitimate interest may provide a possible rationale for the decisions in *Gibson Davies* (discussed above in 15–11) and *Palfreman* (discussed below in 15–23). Such an interest will still need to be evidenced: see *Adams v Australian Securities & Investment Commission* (2003) 46 A.C.S.R. 68.

company and others that the applicant remained as a director. The applicant was said to be particularly important to the company because of his expertise and contacts in the specialist industry in which the company was engaged. The court accepted that in the circumstances it was important to customers and suppliers that he remained on the board.

Similarly, in *Re TLL Realisations, Re TLL Realisations Ltd, Secretary of State for Trade and Industry v Collins*[69] some weight was given to the company's need for the applicant's specialist expertise.[70] In that case, Park J. said that the court could take into account two distinct "needs" or "interests": (a) the need of the disqualified person to earn a living; and (b) the need of the company to have work done by the applicant for the purpose of its business. The judge stated that each factor carries some weight, although he would expect (b) to be more influential.[71] Within (b) he identified two different "needs": (i) a need for the company to have some person filling the particular office or capacity in question and (ii) a need for the services of the particular applicant. Park J. went on to say that while there may be gradations between these types of case, the argument for permission will generally be more cogent in case (ii). It is suggested that this helpful characterisation should not be applied too rigidly. In practice, the two "needs" identified in (b) are but two particular points on a wide spectrum of "legitimate interest" or "need". It is possible to conceive of circumstances where it is highly desirable that a particular person carry out a particular function within a company (which would be a stronger legitimate interest than simply a requirement that somebody fill the position in question) but where it cannot be said that the applicant is the only possible person who could fulfil the role in question.

15–23 An earlier case that arguably reflects a similar approach is the decision of the Court of Session in *Secretary of State for Trade and Industry v Palfreman*. In that case, permission was granted in the light of evidence tending to show that:

> ". . . the [applicant] held a position of considerable responsibility in the companies which relied upon his goodwill for their successful trading and to remove him from management of the companies could have serious effects for a number of people, not least the employees . . .".[72]

The attitude of the company's financiers towards the applicant may also be relevant.[73] The company's dependence (and, by extension, that of innocent parties such as employees) on the applicant has also been treated as an important factor

[69] [2000] B.C.C. 998.

[70] On appeal, Peter Gibson L.J. suggested that too much weight was given to this factor. For another case where emphasis was laid on the company's need for the services of the applicant as managing director in the context of a specialist industry in which he was well known see *Re Servaccomm Redhall Ltd, Cunningham v Secretary of State for Trade and Industry* [2004] EWHC 760 (Ch), [2006] 1 B.C.L.C. 1.

[71] See also *Re Morija Plc, Kluk v Secretary of State for Business, Enterprise and Regulatory Reform* [2008] 2 B.C.L.C. 313 at [34].

[72] [1995] 2 B.C.L.C. 301 at 303–304. The employees in this case numbered some 350.

[73] See, e.g. *Re Aitch Holdings Ltd, Smith v Secretary of State for Trade and Industry* [2002] EWHC 2866 (Ch).

in several cases decided by the Australian and New Zealand courts.[74] Equally, however, there are cases where the court has not been persuaded that there is a sufficiently strong "legitimate interest" to justify the grant of permission for a disqualified person to act as a director, especially where the relevant company is dormant or semi-dormant.[75]

15–24 Even if some separate interest can be identified, the court may still take the view that it is not sufficiently worthy of protection to justify any relaxation of the prohibition. In *Re Amaron Ltd, Secretary of State for Trade and Industry v Lubrani*,[76] an investor owned 25 per cent of the share capital and was a director of the company in relation to which permission was sought. The evidence showed that the applicant was the "guiding force" behind this company and that the investor did not take any direct responsibility for running the company. It was held that any alleged detrimental effects on the company (which can be taken to include any prejudice to the investor) could be met by the applicant and the investor continuing to trade through the medium of a partnership: a similar solution to that adopted in *Streamhaven*.[77] The facts of the case are of interest because the general approach of the judge to the question of "need" (even taking into account that he was applying the law as it stood before *Barings* and *Dawes & Henderson*) demonstrates the level of detailed evidence that an applicant is required to produce. As indicated above, the judge took the view that much of the impact on the company's business that it was alleged would follow if permission was not granted, could be alleviated if the applicant and the investor set up in partnership and continued to trade from the same premises. Any unfortunate tax consequences flowing from the transfer of the premises from the company to the partners could be avoided by the company retaining ownership of them. Any disadvantage flowing from the applicant not having the status of director would be avoided given that, if the business were run as a partnership, there would be no directors and no expectation that the applicant should be a director. The suggestion that the investor might be prejudiced

[74] See, e.g. *Re Zim Metal Products Pty Ltd* (1977) 2 A.C.L.R. 553; *Re Hamilton-Irvine* (1990) 8 A.C.L.C. 1057, *Murray v Australian Securities Commission* (1994) 12 A.C.L.C. 1; *Re Wallace* (1983) 8 A.C.L.R. 311; *Re Minimix Industries Ltd* (1982) 1 A.C.L.C. 511; *Re Focas* [1992] M.C.L.R. 515. In England and Wales see also *Secretary of State for Trade and Industry v Rosenfield* [1999] B.C.C. 413; *Re Servaccomm Redhall Ltd, Cunningham v Secretary of State for Trade and Industry* [2006] 1 B.C.L.C. 1.

[75] See e.g. *Re Brian Sheridan Cars Ltd* [1996] 1 B.C.L.C. 327 at 342; *Re Tech Textiles Ltd, Secretary of State for Trade and Industry v Vane* [1998] 1 B.C.L.C. 259 at 271; *Re Hennelly's Utilities Ltd, Hennelly v Secretary of State for Trade and Industry* [2004] EWHC 34 (Ch), [2005] B.C.C. 542 at [54]–[55] and [82]. In *Tech Textiles* permission was refused in relation to an investment holding company that did nothing more than hold shares in the main trading company but which was said (by the applicant) to need his services as a director (and, in particular, his knowledge and experience of the relevant industry) in relation to pursuing investment opportunities. It was said also that his position in negotiations would lack status and credibility if he were not a director. It was held that no strong interest had been shown as the evidence did not explain how the company could pursue any acquisitions or investment opportunities in the light of its stated financial position.

[76] [1998] B.C.C. 264.

[77] It is striking that in *Amaron* there was no offer from the applicant to ensure, by way of safeguard, that a professionally qualified director (such as an accountant) was appointed to the board. As a consequence, Neuberger J. was not satisfied that the public would be adequately protected in any event.

was not made out on the evidence and, having heard from the gentleman in question, it appeared to the judge that "... he had not considered the matter and was in any event far from suggesting that he would not be prepared to carry on the business in partnership ... [t]he possibility certainly did not seem to worry him when it was raised with him."[78] A question also arose in *Amaron* concerning a non-transferable waste transfer station licence that was vested in the company. The licence was not produced in court and, on the evidence, it appeared likely that if the premises remained vested in the company, the licence would not have to be transferred or renewed because ownership of the premises to which it attached was not changing. However, the judge did give interim permission for a transitional period of six weeks to enable matters to be resolved, but subject to specific measures designed to protect the public.

15–25 In *Re Hennelly's Utilities Ltd, Hennelly v Secretary of State for Trade and Industry*[79] permission to act was given in somewhat surprising circumstances. The applicant for permission to act had been disqualified for eight years in December 1998. The disqualification related to his conduct as a director of five companies that had each gone into insolvent liquidation with large debts. Together the estimated deficiency as regards creditors was nearly £10 million, the sums owed to the Crown amounting to nearly £5 million. In broad terms, the matters of unfit conduct on which the disqualification was based related to failures to submit returns to the revenue authorities, the financing of continued operations with retained Crown monies and the financing of associated companies to the detriment of the creditors of the finance provider.

The first company, in relation to which permission was sought, ("Utilities") had taken over and carried on the same business as one of the companies in relation to which the applicant was disqualified. The applicant had apparently remained involved in its management, although not formally as a director and the deputy judge considered that there was inadequate evidence to determine whether or not the applicant was a shadow director.[80] During its lifetime, Utilities had operated on the borders of cash flow solvency. Crown debts had mounted. By December 31, 2004 some £271,000 was owing to HM Customs and Excise and some £586,280 was owing to the Inland Revenue. In October 2003 instalment agreements had been agreed with these Crown departments.[81] The debts in question appeared to go back to at least the early part of 2002 and previous instalment agreements had not been observed. Interest free financing had been provided by Utilities to other companies owned by the applicant. By 2003 indebtedness in this respect was in excess of £811,000.

The deputy judge nevertheless gave the applicant permission to act as a director of Utilities, albeit subject to a number of conditions. It is questionable whether the learned deputy judge gave any, or any sufficient, weight to the deterrence aspect of

[78] [1998] B.C.C. 264 at 279–280.
[79] [2005] B.C.C. 542.
[80] [2005] B.C.C. 542 at [44].
[81] The case predates the establishment of Her Majesty's Revenue and Customs which amalgamated HM Customs and Excise and the Inland Revenue.

disqualification or to the length of the period of disqualification that had been imposed. However, of perhaps more interest is his apparent view that Utilities would have better prospects of being run properly, and of surviving, if permission were granted and that this was a strong reason for granting such permission. However, this analysis seems to have flowed not so much from the advantages to Utilities of having the applicant appointed as a director but from the associated conditions subject to which that appointment would be made. In particular, the deputy judge compared the position if an order, subject to conditions, were made with that if no such order were made. In this respect, he placed particular reliance on conditions (as part of the order for permission) that interest free loans to the associated companies be repaid, that an independent chartered management accountant be appointed to the board as finance director and that the applicant subordinate debts owed to him (or to any entity owned or controlled by him) by the company to all other creditors. These steps, it was said, would not be taken if permission were not granted.

It is respectfully suggested that this approach is flawed and, in principle, wrong. There was nothing to stop these steps being taken whether or not the order for permission was made. Furthermore, these benefits, on their face, did not flow from the appointment of the applicant as director. In respect of these matters the "need" of the company was not the need for the appointment of the applicant as director but for the regulation of its affairs, which regulation the court could only impose in connection with an order granting permission. The objection in principle to this approach is that the court apparently granted permission on the basis that the conditions that could be attached to such permission would be advantageous to the company rather than on the basis that there were positive advantages to the company from having the applicant appointed as a director in the first place. Instead of considering the risks to the public from having the applicant appointed as a director and considering whether the conditions sufficiently reduced the relevant risks, the deputy judge, in effect, considered whether the company would be better off if an order subject to stringent conditions were made. In so doing the deputy judge was not directing his mind to the correct issue, which was the need for the applicant to be appointed and the potential risks flowing from such appointment. Instead, he considered whether the conditions would improve the lot of the company compared with its position if the conditions were not required. However, he had no power to make an order imposing such conditions in the abstract, as the imposition of conditions is ancillary to, and designed to lessen the risks arising from the grant of permission to act. It is true that the deputy judge did also consider the benefits to Utilities of the applicant's appointment in terms of greater anticipated turnover. However, it is respectfully suggested that, insofar as the reasoning was based on the benefits flowing from the conditions (compared with the position were no order to be made), then it was flawed. As the result appears to rest to a significant degree on this flawed reasoning, it too can be called into question. Ironically, one consequence of the deputy judge's reasoning is that an applicant may have a stronger case for permission the more badly run the company in question is and the more it can be said that the grant of permission on conditions would (or may) improve the company's position. The conditions would not be directed so much at lessening the risks flowing from the applicant's appointment but at reducing the risks to the public inherent in the company's current position. The decision seems therefore to encourage the court to act as a form of judicial company doctor under the guise of exercising its jurisdiction to grant permission.

The postscript to this case is that Utilities entered administration in January 2006 and then creditors' voluntary liquidation in January 2007. The estimated deficiency was £2.9 million, including in excess of £2.6 million due in respect of tax and VAT. Disqualification proceedings were brought against Mr Hennelly (again). He had apparently not been formally appointed a director of Utilities following the grant of permission in 1994 on the basis (so he said) that the conditions on which permission had been granted could not be met. It was alleged first that, notwithstanding his formal resignation as a director in October 1998, he had continued to act as a director of Utilities between December 1998 and January 2006, in breach of the eight-year disqualification order made in 1998. It was further alleged that, during the period from June 2005 to January 2006, at a time when the company was insolvent by reason of being unable to pay its debts when they fell due, he caused or allowed Utilities to effect transactions to the detriment of HMRC in particular and to creditors generally. These transactions comprised various payments to and set offs of debts owing by another company of which he was beneficial owner. Both allegations were found to be made out and a disqualification order imposed for a period of 12 years.

15–26 In arriving at an overall assessment of the company's needs or legitimate interests the court may find it useful if evidence is adduced from an independent third party such as a firm of chartered accountants.[82] However, the evidence will need to be up to date and reflect the current position of the company.[83] It is clear from authorities that follow the old two-stage approach that *some* evidence as to the company's needs should be put before the court. It is suggested that this remains the position even if (as is indicated above) the court's function on an application for permission cannot properly be understood without reference to *Barings* and *Dawes & Henderson*. In *Re Lombard Shipping & Forwarding Ltd*,[84] an application for permission to continue as director of a corporate residents association was refused even though it was not a normal trading company and, it appeared that there was no great risk to the public in allowing the applicant (who had been disqualified for the minimum period of two years under s.6) to remain on the board. The deputy judge summed up the position as follows:

[82] See, e.g. *Secretary of State for Trade and Industry v Brown* 1995 S.L.T. 550 at 552 I–J, 553C–D; *Re Gibson Davies Ltd* [1995] B.C.C. 11 at 14B. This evidence will also be useful in relation to the issue of public protection particularly, where relevant, on such matters as the state of the company's internal financial controls.

[83] *Re Amaron Ltd, Secretary of State for Trade and Industry v Lubrani* [1998] B.C.C. 264 at 278; *Adams v Australian Securities & Investment Commission* (2003) 46 A.C.S.R. 68. For a case where strong evidence of need was adduced that suggested that the relevant companies would not be able to continue without the applicant's participation in management see *Re Morija Plc, Kluk v Secretary of State for Business, Enterprise and Regulatory Reform* [2008] 2 B.C.L.C. 313 at [36].

[84] March 22, 1993, Ch.D, unreported.

> "The difficulty here is that I have got no evidence at all about the operation of that company apart from the fact that [the applicant] has been a director for 12 years. I have no evidence as to whether any other director is available to do the work or whether it is essential for [the applicant] to carry on because there is no other available person."

This point is arguably of general relevance. The implication is that it will always be sensible for the applicant to adduce up to date evidence to assist the court on both the question of "legitimate interest" and the question of public protection. Only this will satisfy the broad requirement for cogent evidence discussed right at the outset by reference to *Tech Textiles*. As Neuberger J. put it in *Re Amaron Ltd, Secretary of State for Trade and Industry v Lubrani*:

> "At least in the absence of special factors, the court must have an up to date (and substantial) account of the position of a company in respect of which a s.17 application is made. Otherwise, it is difficult for an applicant to establish that the public can be protected if he is permitted to act as a director (or indeed that there is a need that he be a director)."[85]

The point was restated unequivocally by Peter Gibson L.J. in *Re TLL Realisations Ltd, Secretary of State for Trade and Industry v Collins*:

> "The application for leave should be supported by clear evidence as to the precise role which the applicant would play in the company or companies in question and up-to-date and adequate information about that company or those companies."[86]

Summary

15–27 In the light of *Barings* and *Dawes & Henderson* it is doubtful whether the old two-stage test should now be followed. The critical question is whether, if permission is granted, the public will be adequately protected from the risk that misconduct may recur. The notion that the concept of "need" amounts to a threshold test applicable in every case should, it is suggested, be discarded if it has not been already. However, this is not to say that "need" (understood as encompassing a range or spectrum of "needs/interests" including the "needs" of the applicant and of the entity in relation to which he seeks permission) cannot be taken into account in an appropriate case. For example, in the context of owner-managed companies, it may well be that variants of the approach in *Streamhaven* will continue to be used as a means of balancing the protection of the public against other interests such as the interests of investors and employees. As such, there is clearly room for the court to weigh the "needs" of such constituencies in the exercise of the discretion. However, in a case like *Streamhaven* where the only identifiable "need" is that of the applicant, the likelihood is that primacy will be given to the protection of the public. A further point flowing from this is that cases like *Streamhaven* would probably have been decided in the same way in any event. Thus, on the *Barings*

[85] [1998] B.C.C. 264 at 278.
[86] [2000] B.C.C. 998 at 1010E.

approach, the court may well have concluded that the risk of further abuses of limited liability were too great to justify the granting of permission, a point reflected in the extract from Scott V.C.'s judgment cited in 15–17 above.[87]

Protection of the public

15–28 It is suggested that in the light of *Barings* and the discussion of the concept of "need" above, that the rigid two-stage test posited in *Cargo Agency* and *Gibson Davies* should not be followed. The better view is that the court should simply ask whether, in all the circumstances of the case, permission should be granted. In considering whether permission should be granted, the court should bear in mind the reasons for the original disqualification and the purposes that disqualification is designed to serve. Key among these is the protection of the public achieved through: (a) keeping the disqualified person "off the road"; (b) deterring the disqualified person; and (c) deterring others from failing to meet the proper standards required of company directors by the courts.[88] For these purposes (as was argued in Ch.2), the "public" should be given the widest possible meaning and be taken to include investors, creditors, employees, customers and so on. It may also include relevant persons outside the jurisdiction and outside the United Kingdom.[89]

15–29 In this respect, while each case will turn on its own particular facts, it is suggested that the applicant will have to provide satisfaction on some or all of the points touched on below if he is to convince the court that the public will be adequately protected in the event that permission is granted. Typically, the court will only be satisfied that the public is adequately protected through the inclusion of detailed conditions and safeguards in the order. The court's main concern, as discerned from the authorities, is to ensure, as far as possible, that there is no repetition of the misconduct that led to the applicant's disqualification in the first place. In considering this issue, it is suggested that the court should not be concerned solely to prevent a repetition of the precise conduct or failings that led to the disqualification but to protect the public against the fault that underlies the relevant conduct in question, be that dishonesty, want of probity or incompetence. An incompetent director is as capable of causing loss and damage to the public as is a dishonest director.[90] Thus in *Re Westminster Property Management Ltd (No.2), Official Receiver v Stern (No.2)* Lloyd J. rejected the notion that the public is only to be protected against the consequences or risks of the repetition of the actual misconduct which has been made out in a particular case:

[87] The decision in *Re Amaron Ltd, Secretary of State for Trade and Industry v Lubrani* [1998] B.C.C. 264 is open to a similar interpretation.

[88] See *Re Westmid Packing Services Ltd, Secretary of State for Trade and Industry v Griffiths* [1998] 2 All E.R. 124. This was accepted by Lloyd J. in *Re Westminster Property Management Ltd (No.2), Official Receiver v Stern (No.2)* [2001] B.C.C. 305. For similar sentiments see also *Re Morija Plc, Kluk v Secretary of State for Business, Enterprise and Regulatory Reform* [2008] 2 B.C.L.C. 313 at [34].

[89] *Re Westminster Property Management Ltd (No.2), Official Receiver v Stern (No.2)* [2001] B.C.C. 305 at 358H–359C.

[90] On the range of meanings encompassed by the term "incompetence" see Ch.5.

> "Having regard to the particular findings of the court that the court has made in the particular circumstances, it seems to me that the court does need to take a view as to what risks the public may face. In a case where the established misconduct is as serious as it has been in the present case, it seems to me that it would be wrong for the court to be too precise about the particular forms of misconduct against which the public needs to be protected if the particular person is to be allowed to act as a director in the future.[91]

Factors taken into account

15–30 Most of the authorities to date have concerned applications for permission made by persons who were disqualified on grounds of unfit conduct under s.6. Applications have been successful in those cases where the applicant has convinced the courts that, on balance, there is unlikely to be any repetition of his previous unfit conduct. The court will pay close attention to the specific findings of unfit conduct that were made against the applicant or, in a case not directly involving the unfit conduct provisions, the specific conduct that triggered the disqualification, and also to conditions within the company the subject of the application so as to be satisfied that the company is not a breeding ground for further misconduct. Where the applicant is subject to a disqualification undertaking or competition disqualification undertaking, the court will similarly take note of the factual basis of disqualification set out in the schedule to the undertaking.

15–31 It is suggested that the court is not restricted, and should not restrict itself, to a consideration of whether or not the specific past failings of the applicant that led to his disqualification are likely to be repeated.[92] Thus, in a case such as *Re TLL Realisations Ltd, Secretary of State for Trade and Industry v Collins*[93] where the applicant was disqualified for his failings as a finance director, but sought permission to act as a manager and not as a director, the mere fact that the applicant may be supervised in his new position as manager is not, it is suggested, a reason for the court to refuse to consider matters such as the financial position of the relevant company, its current standard of bookkeeping and the like. There are a number of reasons why this should be so. The first arises from the general point that, once disqualified, a person has to ask the permission of the court to act in a certain capacity. The indulgence sought is an indulgence both to him and the company in question. The court should be satisfied that it is right to grant such an indulgence. It would seem strange to a member of the public if the court was aware that the company was, for example, teetering on the edge of insolvency, failing to file accounts and returns and the like and yet gave permission for the applicant to take part in such a company on the ground that he would not be directly involved in the "problem" matters. Equally, it would be odd if the court did not enquire or require evidence about such matters. In this respect, it is suggested that the position is different to that under s.216 of the Insolvency Act

[91] [2001] B.C.C. 305 at 359.
[92] [2001] B.C.C. 305.
[93] [2000] B.C.C. 998.

1986, where the courts have said that permission to use a prohibited name will be given if the vice targeted by the provision (broadly arising in connection with phoenix operations) is not present, irrespective of whether the director in question may otherwise be unfit or the new company might otherwise be in financial difficulties.[94] Other powers are available to the Secretary of State (such as powers to initiate company investigations, winding up proceedings or further disqualification proceedings) to deal with any future problems that may arise in the company in relation to which permission is sought. However, the mere existence of such powers and mere absence of the particular vice that led to the original disqualification should not, it is suggested, prevent the court from refusing permission if there is concern that the company may be about to collapse or that it is not being run according to proper standards. A second reason is that if the company in relation to which permission is sought is itself not being properly run, this must raise doubts about the extent to which the applicant can or will be properly supervised and prevented from repeating the failings that led to his disqualification. A third reason is that if a person is required to exercise some management function, the likelihood is that he will have some autonomy. Otherwise there may be no point in appointing him. As such, he represents a potential weak link in the management structure. The weakness of that link can only be considered in the context of the overall management structure and health (financial or otherwise) of the company. The authorities suggest that the following (non-exclusive) factors are likely to be taken into account in considering the question of "public protection".

Seriousness and type of conduct. Most of the applicants granted some form of permission by the courts in England and Wales have been persons disqualified for periods of five years or less and whose conduct was therefore considered by the disqualifying court to fall within the lowest bracket of seriousness on the *Sevenoaks Stationers* guidelines.[95] The fact that even in these cases the court considered it necessary to impose conditions (see further below) suggests that a disqualified person whose previous conduct was held to fall within the middle or highest brackets of seriousness will find it correspondingly more difficult to persuade the court to grant his application.[96] The nature and seriousness of the applicant's previous conduct is a factor that is also weighed in the balance in **15–32**

[94] Contrast the approach in *Re Bonus Breaks Ltd* [1991] B.C.C. 546 with that in *Penrose v Official Receiver* [1996] 1 W.L.R. 482 and *Re Lightning Electrical Contractors Ltd* [1996] 2 B.C.L.C. 302. See also discussion in G. Wilson, "Delinquent Directors and Company Names" (1996) 47 N.I.L.Q. 345.

[95] *Re Sevenoaks Stationers (Retail) Ltd* [1991] Ch. 164 and see Ch. 5. Very few successful applicants for permission to act in reported cases have been the subject of disqualification for periods of five years or more. For exceptions see: *Re Majestic Recording Studios* [1989] B.C.L.C. 1; *Re Gibson Davies Ltd* [1995] B.C.C 11; *Re TLL Realisastions, Secretary of State for Trade and Industry v Collins* [2000] B.C.C. 998; *Re Hennelly's Utilities, Hennelly v Secretary of State for Trade and Industry* [2005] B.C.C. 542.

[96] For a case in point see *Re Morija Plc, Kluk v Secretary of State for Business, Enterprise and Regulatory Reform* [2008] 2 B.C.L.C. 313 where the applicant had been disqualified for ten years for his failure to disclose fraudulent activity.

Commonwealth jurisdictions.[97] In the light of *Barings, Tech Textiles* and *Dawes & Henderson* (discussed above), it is clear that the court will also look carefully at the type of conduct that led to the applicant's disqualification and the nature of the company in relation to which permission is sought.

Re Barings Plc (No.3), Secretary of State for Trade and Industry v Baker)[98] concerned Mr Norris, the former Chief Executive Officer of Barings. Mr Norris was disqualified for four years on grounds of unfit conduct under the summary *Carecraft* procedure. The case against him did not involve any imputation of dishonesty nor was it alleged that he had abused the privilege of limited liability. It was based exclusively on Mr Norris's incompetence. Particular emphasis was placed on Mr Norris's failure, despite his senior position, to monitor the activities of the rogue trader, Nick Leeson and the demand for funds that those activities had generated. Thus, Mr Norris had to accept his share of the responsibility for the board allowing to go unquestioned the huge outflow of funds from Barings Plc into its Singaporean subsidiary which ultimately precipitated the bank's collapse.[99] Anticipating that a disqualification order would be made against him, Mr Norris made an application for permission to remain as a non-executive director of three specified private companies. He had been invited to join the boards of these companies having previously advised them in a consultancy capacity. The companies were involved in various businesses ranging from publishing to film and video production. Despite Mr Norris's failure to demonstrate any strong need for permission, his application was granted. The Vice-Chancellor approached the application by asking whether, on the facts, the public interest required that permission be refused and dispensed with the question of need. He stated:

> "The court in considering whether or not to grant [permission] should, in particular, pay attention to the nature of the defects in company management that led to the disqualification order and ask itself whether, if [permission] were granted, a situation might arise

[97] See, e.g. *Re Magna Alloys & Research Pty Ltd* (1975) 1 A.C.L.R. 203; *Re Zim Metal Products Pty Ltd* (1977) 2 A.C.L.R. 553; *Zuker v Commissioner for Corporate Affairs* [1981] V.R. 72 also reported as *Re Record Leather Manufacturers (Aust.) Pty Ltd* (1980) 5 A.C.L.R. 19; *Re Marsden* (1980) 5 A.C.L.R. 694, 702 (Australia). Note that the overall approach taken in Australia on the issue of permission has been followed in New Zealand and Singapore: see, e.g. *Re Focas* [1992] M.C.L.R. 515 (New Zealand); *A.G. v Derrick Chong Soon Choy, Quek Leng Chye v A.G.* [1985] 1 Malaysian L.J. 97, *Quek Leng Chye v A.G.* [1985] 2 M.L.J. 270, P.C. (Singapore). The Singapore cases cited arose in the wake of the City Country Club scandal which is chronicled and widely discussed in A. Hicks, "Commercial Candour and Integrity in Singapore" (1986) 28 Malaysian L.R. 288. Note further that the applicants in these Commonwealth cases had all suffered automatic disqualification without court order under a series of closely comparable statutory provisions following their conviction for various criminal offences. There is no direct equivalent in England and Wales. Nevertheless, useful guidance can still be derived from these cases because the courts in all of these jurisdictions share the broad view of our courts that the primary purpose of disqualification legislation is the protection of the public.

[98] [2000] 1 W.L.R. 634.

[99] The former chairman of the bank's asset and liability committee consented to a disqualification order on similar grounds: see *Re Barings Plc* [1998] B.C.C. 583. For the fate of three other senior executives see *Re Barings Plc (No.5), Secretary of State for Trade and Industry v Baker* [1999] 1 B.C.L.C. 433 and discussion in Ch.5.

> in which there would be a risk of recurrence of those defects. In a case like the present there seems to me to be virtually no risk at all of such a recurrence. [N will not be placed] . . . in a position in which an inadequate discharge of executive responsibilities of the sort that justified the disqualification order . . . will have any possibility of occurring. In [no] case does his directorship carry with it any executive responsibilities at all. Accordingly, the fact that a need for [N] to be given the . . . [permission] that he seeks and that companies want him to be given has not been established is not, in my judgment, a sufficient reason for withholding [permission]."

To ensure that Mr Norris would not assume any executive responsibilities in relation to the three companies, permission was granted in each case on condition that he remain an unpaid non-executive and that he be barred from entering into a director's service contract.[100] It is clear from *Barings* that the court is required to consider the question of recurrence with reference to the applicant's previous conduct and the nature of the company in relation to which permission is sought.[101]

Trading prospects of company. The fact that the company the subject of the application is trading successfully has tended to weigh in the applicant's favour. The applicant will need to show that trading conditions in the company are such that any specific misconduct highlighted by the original disqualification proceedings is unlikely to be repeated. For example, a person disqualified for allowing an insolvent company to continue trading at the expense of its creditors will need to demonstrate that the company is solvent and paying its debts as they fall due.[102] In *Secretary of State for Trade and Industry v Palfreman*,[103] the principal reason for the applicant's disqualification was that a company of which he was a non-executive director had traded while insolvent mainly at the expense of preferential creditors. A factor that contributed to the success of his application for permission to continue as a director of two other companies was evidence indicating that those companies were currently meeting their tax and VAT liabilities. It was also noted that the turnover of both companies was substantial. By way of contrast, in *Re Lombard Shipping & Forwarding Ltd*[104] the application failed because, among other reasons, one of the companies was encountering difficulty in paying its rates, a recurrence of a specific problem that had come to light in the original disqualification proceedings. Similarly, where lack of working capital is

15–33

[100] It may be questioned whether such conditions in fact provide any protection: see text at 15–53.

[101] For a further illustration see *Re Servaccomm Redhall Ltd, Cunningham v Secretary of State for Trade and Industry* [2006] 1 B.C.L.C. 1. In that case, the applicant was disqualified for two years for abrogating his responsibilities in relation to two companies which he described in evidence as "hobbies" whereas the companies to which the application for permission related were his main business and employment and he was active in their affairs. In the circumstances, the court concluded that there was little risk of the particular misconduct on which the disqualification was based being repeated in companies in which he had taken an active role as managing director.

[102] Conversely, an applicant may be given permission to act in relation to a company in financial difficulties where there is a need for his expertise and the unfit conduct on which the disqualification was based does not include anything of the nature of trading while insolvent: see *Re Servaccomm Redhall Ltd, Cunningham v Secretary of State for Trade and Industry* [2006] 1 B.C.L.C. 1.

[103] [1995] 2 B.C.L.C. 301.

[104] March 22, 1993, Ch.D., unreported.

identified as a problem during the course of the disqualification proceedings, it is likely that, on an application for permission, the court will require some evidence to suggest that the company is adequately capitalised.[105] The court will also want to be satisfied that directors' remuneration is paid at a level that the company can properly sustain.[106]

15–34 **Financial controls.** The applicant will need to adduce some evidence showing that the company the subject of the application has adequate financial controls and is complying with the statutory obligations in companies legislation as to the keeping of proper books of account and the filing of accounts and returns with the Registrar of Companies. Again, this will be especially important where complaints over lack of financial controls and/or filing defaults were upheld in the original disqualification proceedings.[107] A lack of up-to-date, reliable financial information about the company may well prove fatal to the application. If the evidence is inadequate or incomplete the court will usually dismiss the application rather than give the applicant time to adduce further evidence although this would not preclude a fresh application at a later date.[108] Even if the evidence produced is satisfactory, the court will usually require safeguards (e.g. the appointment of independent directors or regular attendance by the auditors at board meetings) with the aim of ensuring that the company's internal controls are the subject of continuous review.

Conditional permission

15–35 Even if the court is minded to grant the application, it is unlikely to give unconditional permission. The prevailing view is that the court may grant permission "on such terms and conditions as it thinks fit" despite the lack of express words in the

[105] See *Re Chartmore Ltd* [1990] B.C.L.C. 673 where Harman J. decided that his concerns about the company's lack of capitalisation could be assuaged by granting the applicant permission to act as its director for one year only with liberty to apply under the order for permission to be extended, ". . . it being understood that, if it turns out that the responsible and careful manner heretofore adopted has not been continued, there may well be no extension of that permission . . ." (676G–H).

[106] *Secretary of State for Trade and Industry v Brown* 1995 S.L.T. 550 at 552L; *Re Amaron Ltd, Secretary of State for Trade and Industry v Lubrani* [1998] B.C.C. 264. The general points made in the cases referred to in this paragraph of the text make the decision in *Re Henelly's Utilities Ltd, Henelly v Secretary of State for Trade & Industry* [2005] B.C.C. 542 all the more surprising.

[107] See, e.g. *Re Chartmore* [1990] B.C.L.C. 673 at 676A; *Re Gibson Davies Ltd* [1995] B.C.C. 11 at 14B; *Secretary of State for Trade and Industry v Brown* 1995 S.L.T. 550.

[108] *Re Lombard Shipping & Forwarding Ltd*, March 22, 1993, Ch.D., unreported. Per the deputy judge:

> "I find that on the evidence put before me I am unable to give [permission] for Mr Woollen to continue. [Counsel] said there may be an inadequacy in the evidence but it could be put right. It is not for the court to negotiate in that sort of way and say what will be satisfactory and what not."

For a similar approach in Australia see *Adams v Australian Securities & Investment Commission* (2003) 46 A.C.S.R. 68 at [32]–[33]. See also *Re Amaron Ltd, Secretary of State for Trade and Industry v Lubrani* [1998] B.C.C. 264 on the importance of current evidence of the relevant company's financial position.

statute to that effect.[109] The current practice of the courts in England and Wales, where permission is granted, is to insist either that the applicant offers certain safeguards which are then built into the order or to make an order which is limited in time and does not cover the full period of the disqualification (or some combination of the two approaches). This suggests that the court will not derogate lightly from the terms of the disqualification and reflects the view expressed in *Re Brian Sheridan Cars Ltd*[110] that a person granted permission to act as a director of a specified company is being accorded a privilege or indulgence.[111] In this respect it is interesting to note that most of the reported cases where the court has granted conditional permission concerned persons who had been disqualified for five years or less and typically no more than three years.[112] A secondary issue concerning the technical difference between a fully conditional order and an order for permission granted subject to undertakings to the court is considered below.

Permission: a derogation from protection of the public

15–36 It is important to recognise that any grant of permission is an erosion of the protection of the public otherwise afforded by a CDDA disqualification.[113] In *Re Gibson Davies Ltd*,[114] the applicant had been disqualified for five years. The findings of unfit conduct related to a small company of which the applicant had been a director. It was established that the applicant had caused that company to trade while insolvent and enter into a transaction that amounted to a preference. It was also established that misleading invoices had been raised, excessive remuneration had been paid to the directors and accounts had not been filed. The case was somewhat unusual in that the applicant made no attempt to defend the disqualification proceedings but did apply later to set aside the disqualification order[115] or, failing that, for permission to act as a director of the English subsidiary of an Irish company. The application for permission was initially refused but was granted by the Companies Court on appeal. The applicant originally offered the following specific safeguards:

[109] See, e.g. *Re Tech Textiles Ltd, Secretary of State for Trade and Industry v Vane* [1998] 1 B.C.L.C. 259 at 267. The Scottish courts have followed the English lead on grounds of comity while expressing doubt as to whether there is power to impose conditions: see *Secretary of State for Trade and Industry v Palfreman* [1995] 2 B.C.L.C. 301.

[110] [1996] 1 B.C.L.C. 327.

[111] See also the view in *Tech Textiles* cited above in 15–07.

[112] For exceptions, see *Re TLL Realisations Ltd, Secretary of State for Trade and Industry v Collins* [2000] B.C.C. 998 (eight years); *Re Hennelly's Utilities Ltd, Hennelly v Secretary of State for Trade and Industry* [2005] B.C.C. 542 (eight years). Note, however, Park J.'s remarks in *Re Morija Plc, Kluk v Secretary of State for Business, Enterprise and Regulatory Reform* [2008] 2 B.C.L.C. 313 at [38] on his earlier decision in the *TLL Realisations* case.

[113] This is especially so as regards the effectiveness of disqualification as a general deterrent, a point that has influenced judicial thinking in cases where the applicant had been disqualified for a substantial period: see, e.g. *Re Westminster Property Management Ltd (No.2), Official Receiver v Stern (No.2)* [2001] B.C.C. 305 at 363; *Re Morija Plc, Kluk v Secretary of State for Business, Enterprise and Regulatory Reform* [2008] 2 B.C.L.C. 313 at [35], [54].

[114] [1995] B.C.C. 11.

[115] Disqualification Rules r.8(2) enables the court to set aside or vary any disqualification order made in the defendant's absence under CDDA ss.6–7 or s.8.

(1) No cheque or financial agreement to be signed or executed on the company's behalf by the applicant alone.
(2) Any director's loans owed by the company to the applicant not to be repaid unless all creditors of the company were paid first.
(3) The applicant not to be granted or to accept any security over the company's assets.
(4) The applicant's total emoluments not to exceed £380 per week or such greater sum thereafter to be agreed in writing by the Secretary of State, such consent not to be unreasonably withheld.
(5) The applicant to procure the company to file annual returns and accounts at Companies House within the time limits set out in the Companies Act.
(6) The applicant to procure the company to complete the implementation of accounting controls as set out in an affidavit sworn by a representative of Messrs Robson Rhodes.
(7) The applicant to procure that the company prepare monthly management accounts and submit the same to Robson Rhodes or to the company's auditors for the time being.
(8) Robson Rhodes or the company's auditors for the time being to be instructed to report to the board of directors in writing any matters of concern related to the management or financial control of the company and, in default of prompt and appropriate action by the directors of the company, to bring these matters to the attention of the Secretary of State's solicitors.
(9) In the event that the company were to seek to change the identity of its auditors, the applicant to procure the company only to instruct auditors willing to accept and act on the obligations set out above.
(10) The applicant to take no step as a shareholder or director of the Irish parent[116] which would in any way impede, direct or control the activities of the English subsidiary.

15–37 The accounting controls referred to in (6) above were:

(a) All cheques over £2,500 to be signed by more than one director.
(b) All cheques below £2,500 to be signed both by the applicant and the company's financial controller.
(c) Monthly management accounts to be reviewed by Robson Rhodes.
(d) The company to complete the implementation of the internal accounting controls recommended by Robson Rhodes.
(e) Robson Rhodes to accept the obligation in (8) above.

After the hearing some alterations were made to these conditions by consent. Those alterations were all in the applicant's favour. First, the requirement in (4) for increases in emoluments to be approved by the Secretary of State in writing

[116] The applicant owned 50 per cent of the issued shares in the Irish company and was a director. The company's two other directors held the balance of the shares.

was replaced by a provision under which upwards variations would be allowed subject only to the unanimous consent of the board of directors. Secondly, the various accounting controls were set out individually as a separate condition in the order. The two main purposes of all these conditions was to ensure that control of the company (and, indirectly, the Irish parent) remained vested at all times in the board as a whole (as opposed to the applicant alone who was merely one of three directors)[117] and that its business would be the subject of close and continuous scrutiny by the auditors. The conditions were also designed to meet any fears of possible future repetition of the applicant's previous misconduct.[118] In terms of safeguards, the conditional order made in *Gibson Davies* is perhaps the most detailed example to date.[119]

15–38 The subsequent events that followed the granting of permission in *Gibson Davies* are instructive.[120] The original disqualification order was made in February 1993. The order granting permission for the applicant, Mr Davies, to act as a director of Congratulations Franchising Ltd ("Congratulations") was made in July 1994. In January 1995, Congratulations went into creditors' voluntary liquidation with a deficit of over £400,000. Disqualification proceedings were subsequently commenced in relation to the conduct of a number of the directors of Congratulations including Mr Davies. One main ground of complaint in these proceedings was that there had been non-compliance with the conditions in the order granting Mr Davies permission to act. Two aspects of this complaint amounted to a re-run of the position that was reached in *Re Brian Sheridan Cars Ltd*.[121] First, the applicant for permission had failed to abide by the conditions that he had offered. Secondly, the other members of the board, on whom the court was relying to protect the public, had also failed to ensure that the conditions were met.[122] Breaches of four of the various conditions in the order were found to have occurred. The following further allegations of misconduct were raised against Mr Davies:

(1) That he had hampered the realisation by the liquidator of an asset of the company by asserting that it belonged to the Irish company. This allegation was found to be made out.

[117] See further, *Re Lombard Shipping & Forwarding Ltd*, March 22, 1993, Ch.D., unreported, where the court was even more explicit in expressing the view that an applicant should not be allowed to occupy a position of unbridled control.

[118] The conditions concerned with financial controls were clearly designed with the previous insolvent trading complaint in mind. Conditions (2) and (3) appear to have been offered to allay fears over possible preferences while conditions (4) and (5) also addressed issues which had come to light in the original disqualification proceedings.

[119] For another case where several detailed conditions were imposed see *Re Hennelly's Utilities Ltd, Hennelly v Secretary of State for Trade and Industry* [2005] B.C.C. 542 especially at [85].

[120] See the judgment of His Honour Judge Boggis Q.C. (sitting as a judge of the Chancery Division) in *Re Congratulations Franchising Ltd, Secretary of State for Trade and Industry v Davies*, March 6, 1998, Ch.D., unreported.

[121] [1996] 1 B.C.L.C. 327.

[122] On this point, the position in *Brian Sheridan* was arguably worse as two professionally qualified individuals, one of whom was a solicitor, had been appointed to the relevant boards.

(2) That he had accepted advance payments from intending advertisers for a directory which was not published in circumstances where the money was mixed with the general funds of the company, that the company was undercapitalised and that these monies were used to finance the company. These allegations were found to be made out.

(3) That he had deliberately prevented access to the company's records by interfering with the relevant computer programme. This allegation was found not proven.

(4) That there had been a technical breach of s.349 of the Companies Act 1985 by reason of the company using a shortened version of its name in gift albums. This allegation was admitted.

(5) That he had caused the company to withhold payment of Crown monies (approximately £64,000) and used them to finance the company's business. This allegation was admitted.

(6) That he had failed to ensure that the company's accounts were audited and filed by the due date. This allegation was found to be made out.

15–39 In the result, Mr Davies was found to be unfit and disqualified for 12 years. If there were any doubt about the matter, what this case demonstrates, along with cases such as *Brian Sheridan* and *Hennelly's Utilities*, is that however widely conditions are framed, the protection of the public is inevitably eroded by the grant of permission. Indeed, it may be that if the approach put forward by Scott V.C. in the *Barings* and *Dawes & Henderson* cases were to be followed, the court would be much more wary of granting permission in a similar case in the future. In the original case, Mr Davies was disqualified for five years apparently[123] for: (a) causing the company to enter into a transaction affording a preference to himself and another director; (b) allowing the company to continue trading thereby allowing the position of creditors to be eroded after distress had been levied by the Inland Revenue; (c) raising misleading invoices; (d) paying undue remuneration when trading losses were increasing; and (e) failing to file audited accounts. The following extract from the Vice-Chancellor's judgment in *Barings* bears repetition here:

> "In *Re Amaron Ltd* [1998] B.C.C. 264 . . . the judge addressed the question whether the applicant had established 'need' and held that he had not. But this was a case in which the applicant had allowed the company to trade while insolvent and to retain money owed to creditors in order to fund continued trading. The need to ensure protection of the public from management techniques of that character would, in my view, have made it virtually impossible for a s.17 application to have succeeded."[124]

As has been pointed out judicially, an incompetent person can be more of a risk than a dishonest person. A dishonest person may reform. An incompetent person

[123] A note of the district judge's judgment was not available to Sir Mervyn Davies: see [1995] B.C.C. 11 at 12.

[124] [2000] 1 W.L.R. 634 at 641.

is unlikely to become competent. Of course a slipshod and careless person may take more care in the future but, it is suggested, the court should be slow to be impressed by professions of contrition and having learned lessons made in the witness box. Deeds rather than attractiveness as a witness should be the key evidential basis.[125]

It is suggested that the approach outlined in the *Barings* case by reference to *Amaron* ought to be followed in cases like *Gibson Davies*.[126] Ironically, the greater the number of conditions that are placed on the grant of permission, the greater the indication that there is a potential risk to the public in granting it. It is suggested that the court in *Gibson Davies* was attempting to regulate the management of the company in a way which manifestly demonstrated that permission should not have been given in the first place. It is also suggested that the decision to grant permission in *Gibson Davies* was made without sufficient emphasis being given to the deterrence aspect of disqualification.[127] As regards the imposition of conditions the salutary words of Ferris J. in *Re TLL Realisations Ltd, Secretary of State for Trade and Industry v Collins* should also be borne in mind:

> "... I consider that very great caution needs to be exercised in granting conditional leave. If it is felt that leave should not be unconditional this may suggest that the better view is that it should not be granted at all. Apart from this, conditions, if imposed, may be of such a nature that they are all too easily disregarded and almost impossible to police. The sanction for breach of a condition is a severe one, for the person in breach would commit a criminal offence under s.13. But a breach might well not come to light unless and until a second company managed by the disqualified director has come to grief and by then it will be too late to secure the intended protection for the public."[128]

Conditions or undertakings?

15–40 In *Gibson Davies* the applicant was granted permission to be and remain a director of the English subsidiary "upon condition that [he] do abide by the conditions set out in the schedule hereto".[129] The safeguards referred to above were then incorporated in the schedule. Similarly, the disqualified person in *Re Brian Sheridan Cars Ltd* was originally given permission ". . . subject to and so long as . . ." he complied with various conditions set out in the order.[130] The effect of drawing the order in these terms is that if the applicant fails to comply with any

[125] See, by analogy, the comments of Henry L.J. in *Re Grayan Building Services Ltd, Secretary of State for Trade and Industry v Gray* [1995] Ch. 241 regarding conduct as a witness.

[126] See the approach of the Court of Appeal in *Re TLL Realisations Ltd, Secretary of State for Trade and Industry v Collins* [2000] B.C.C. 998. Although declining to interfere with the judgment below, their lordships gave firm indications that they disagreed with the grant of permission in that case.

[127] Similar criticisms can be levelled at the deputy judge's decision in *Re Hennelly's Utilities Ltd, Hennelly v Secretary of State for Trade and Industry* [2005] B.C.C. 542. See discussion in the text at 15–25 and, on the point of principle, *Re Westminster Property Management Ltd (No.2), Official Receiver v Stern (No.2)* [2001] B.C.C. 305 at 363; *Re Morija Plc, Kluk v Secretary of State for Business, Enterprise and Regulatory Reform* [2008] 2 B.C.L.C. 313 at [35], [54].

[128] [2000] B.C.C. 998 at 1018H–1019A.

[129] [1995] B.C.C. 11 at 17C.

[130] [1996] 1 B.C.L.C. 327 at 337.

of the safeguards, he puts himself automatically in breach of the prohibitions contained in the original disqualification order. This is because the continuance of permission is expressed to depend on full and continuing compliance with the safeguards. A conditional order of this nature must therefore be observed to the letter, failing which the applicant exposes himself (and, given the scope of the civil sanction in s.15, possibly others) to the full range of criminal and civil sanctions for which provision is made in the CDDA.[131] *Re Brian Sheridan Cars Ltd* is a case that illustrates the point well. There, the defendant, who was the subject of a three-year disqualification order, had originally been granted permission to act as a director of three companies, subject to a number of conditions, for one year only with effect from July 4, 1994. He failed to comply with all of the conditions, in particular, those requiring the relevant companies to appoint a specified firm of auditors and an independent director. The court acceded to his later application for renewal of the order, giving him permission for a second year. There was a further application before the court to vary the order of July 4, 1994 with retrospective effect. The deputy judge explained the thinking behind this further application:

> "The reason why the [defendant] is anxious that I should not merely amend the s.17 order, but also backdate it, is that it would thereby validate the defendant's directorship of the companies, whereas, if I did not backdate any amending order, the defendant would have been acting as a director of the companies contrary to the provisions of the Act, because he would not have complied with the terms on which the court had given him permission to act as director of the companies."[132]

15–41 The defendant's advisers appreciated that if the amendments were not backdated he would be exposed to criminal and civil liability under the CDDA because of his failure to comply with the conditions as originally drawn and that this would still be the case even if the order for permission was renewed for a further year on fresh conditions. While acknowledging that the court has power to backdate its orders,[133] the deputy judge refused to backdate the order in this case and thus left the defendant exposed, at least in theory, to the possibility of enforcement proceedings under the CDDA. To grant the application, he observed, would be to send out the message:

> ". . . that the court does not really expect directors granted the indulgence contemplated by a s.17 order to take their responsibilities seriously [and] [n]othing would be more regrettable or inappropriate, or, indeed, inconsistent with the clear purpose of the Act".[134]

As such, the Secretary of State will usually favour a conditional order in the form adopted in *Gibson Davies* and *Brian Sheridan* so that the applicant is exposed to prosecution under s.13 the moment he breaks any of the conditions.

[131] See text from 14–86.
[132] [1996] 1 B.C.L.C. 327 at 344.
[133] See *Kuwait Airways Corp v Iraqi Airways Co (No.2)* [1994] 1 W.L.R. 985 and text at 12–15.
[134] [1996] 1 B.C.L.C. 327 at 344.

However, the applicant will prefer the order to state that he is given permission absolutely with any safeguards expressed as undertakings offered by the applicant to the court.[135] The advantage for the applicant is that while breach of undertaking would put him in contempt of court, this form of order is worded in such a way that breach does not result in the automatic cessation of permission and, thus, does not trigger the criminal and civil sanctions in the CDDA. Those favouring this alternative approach would argue that the public is protected as any breach of undertaking can be enforced in contempt proceedings which may themselves lead to criminal penalties. Moreover, it has been argued that it is inappropriate for the applicant to be exposed to criminal prosecution and civil liability under the CDDA for failure to comply with conditions of an ongoing nature especially where there are doubts as to how those conditions should be construed.[136] The problem with undertakings from the point of view of the Secretary of State is that in contempt proceedings there is a higher burden of proof than in criminal proceedings for breach of the CDDA prohibitions as the offences in CDDA ss.11 and 13 are offences of strict liability.[137] Furthermore, the Secretary of State would have to police the undertakings.[138]

15–42 In theory, as well as in practice, for the reasons considered above, it would seem right that any terms on which permission is granted should be drafted as conditions. If the applicant fails to comply with the terms on which permission is granted, why should he not be treated as being without permission and disqualified, especially bearing in mind that the grant of permission is a derogation from the terms of the disqualification? If the purpose of the conditions is to protect the public, it would be strange if the direct civil protection afforded by s.15 of the CDDA were not available to those directly affected by a breach of such conditions. The point was considered by His Honour Judge Cooke (sitting as a High Court judge) in *Secretary of State for Trade and Industry v Rosenfield*.[139] The judge concluded that it was better that the relevant terms be framed as conditions to the order rather than as undertakings, for the sort of reasons rehearsed above. He considered that any difficulties arising because of delays in compliance or mischance could be dealt with by drafting. It is worth noting in this respect that

[135] The order appears to have been drawn in this form in *Re Chartmore Ltd* [1990] B.C.L.C. 673.

[136] See A. Mithani & S. Wheeler, *The Disqualification of Company Directors* (London: Butterworths, 1996), p.230. Arguably, the applicant should be given at least a short period of time to comply with any conditions requiring, for example, the appointment of new directors or auditors. Otherwise, he would be in breach immediately the order is pronounced unless the new appointments have already been made. It was suggested, obiter, in *Brian Sheridan* [1996] 1 B.C.L.C. 327 at 346 that if the court, adopting such an approach, makes an order on terms which have to be complied with by a certain time, it would be a desirable practice for the court to require the applicant to file an affidavit (with a copy to be served on the Secretary of State or the Official Receiver) within a specified time confirming compliance.

[137] *R. v Brockley* [1994] 1 B.C.L.C. 606; *R. v Doring* [2002] EWCA Crim 1695, [2003] 1 Cr.App.R. 9 and text from 14–86.

[138] See generally on this point discussion in *Secretary of State for Trade and Industry v Rosenfield* [1999] B.C.C. 413 at 419 and *Re TLL Realisations Ltd, Secretary of State for Trade and Industry v Collins* [2000] B.C.C. 998 at 1018H.

[139] [1999] B.C.C. 413 at 419.

particular conditions can cause problems. One example is a condition requiring joint signatures on cheques. If it is not obeyed on one occasion, will permission cease forever after or just in respect of that individual cheque? Each case will turn on its own facts and careful consideration will have to be given to the terms of any draft order granting permission on, and subject to, the continued observance of conditions. There is always the possibility that permission could be given retrospectively in an appropriate case where, for example, there was a minor infraction of a condition on one occasion only or for a short period by mistake.[140]

Types of condition

15–43 In considering what conditions are appropriate in a particular case, it is important that conditions previously imposed in a different case are not unthinkingly adopted. Those conditions may not be appropriate in that they might not go far enough in meeting the particular respects in which the public requires protection.[141] It is also important to consider whether a particular condition is required and/or designed to make the order easier to police, whether as its sole or as an ancillary object. What follows is an account drawn from the authorities of the types of conditions that have been imposed.

Publicity

15–44 It is frequently the case that the court requires publicity to be given to the order (and its conditions) so that: (a) people can be warned that they are dealing with a disqualified person; and/or (b) any persons entrusted with the task of monitoring and controlling the applicant and/or ensuring that he abides by any conditions are aware of the terms on which permission is granted. Although the terms of a disqualification order (and the grant of any permission) must be entered on the register of disqualification orders (see text from 12–42), the courts do not seem to have taken the drastic step of requiring publicity to be given to the world of the fact of disqualification (for example, by requiring the person to describe himself as "... disqualified, but acting with the permission of the court ...").[142] A requirement for publicity will usually consist of two further elements: (a) notification of the fact that the person is disqualified and has been given permission;

[140] A possibility recognised, albeit not adopted, in *Re Brian Sheridan Cars Ltd* [1996] 1 B.C.L.C. 327. The relevant jurisdiction considered in that case was RSC Ord. 42, r.3. That rule gave specific power to backdate orders. The only equivalent power would now appear to be contained in CPR r.40.7 but that rule provides that an order takes effect from its pronouncement or later: it does not deal with the question of whether the order can have retrospective effect. It is suggested that the question of backdating an order is one of mechanism. The real issue is whether or not permission can be granted retrospectively (whether or not the order in question is backdated or not). Common sense would suggest that, as a matter of jurisdiction, the court should be able to grant permission retrospectively. The question is ultimately one of statutory construction: see, by analogy, *Bristol & West Building Society v Saunders* [1997] Ch. 60.

[141] See, e.g. *Secretary of State for Trade and Industry v Rosenfield* [1999] B.C.C. 413 at 417 where the conditions initially offered by the applicant were said not to address the concerns at "the heart of the case".

[142] Along the lines of the old practice which required companies to add to their names "(and reduced)" following a reduction of capital under the Companies Acts.

and (b) the reasons for the original disqualification. So, for example, in *Re Brian Sheridan Cars Ltd*,[143] notification had to be given to:

(1) General Accident Fire & Life Assurance Company (in effect, the financier of the schemes which the relevant company was seeking to implement).
(2) The proposed independent directors to be appointed to the board (being a solicitor and an accountant).[144]
(3) The proposed nominated auditors.

Notification was to be achieved by service on the above of copies of the judgments and orders relating to the disqualification and the grant of permission. As on the facts of the case, this condition had been breached, it was suggested that an affidavit of service should also have been required as a policing mechanism. Similarly, in *Re Godwin Warren Control Systems Plc*,[145] permission was granted to one of the disqualified persons to remain in a management role as chief executive provided that the order and a note of the reasons set out in the judgment were brought to the attention of the boards of directors of the two relevant companies. Permission to act as a director in relation to two other companies was envisaged in the event that further directors (other than the disqualified person's wife) were appointed to the board provided that, in considering any application in relation to these companies, the judge was satisfied that their other shareholders were aware that the court had made a disqualification order and the reasons for it.

Independent controls at board or other level

15–45 As a condition of permission, the court frequently requires that an independent person is appointed to the board and/or that such a person has primary day-to-day responsibility for any area in which the applicant's previous conduct suggests particular failings, thereby insulating the applicant, to some extent, from that area. In such cases, the court needs to be satisfied that the person so appointed is fully aware of all the facts relating to the original disqualification and the grant of permission (hence the requirement for publicity considered in the previous paragraph). There will also need to be a mechanism governing what is to happen in the event that the person appointed ceases to hold the relevant position (for example, by making provision for a short period of interim permission to allow time for a further application to the court). The company will need to demonstrate that it can afford the services of such a person.[146] In *Re Lo-Line Electric Motors Ltd*,[147] the then Vice-Chancellor made it a condition of granting permission that a named individual remained a director of the relevant companies. The individual was described as being "primarily responsible for the financial management of

[143] [1996] 1 B.C.L.C. 327.
[144] As noted earlier, this did not apparently guarantee the applicant's compliance with the conditions for permission.
[145] [1993] B.C.L.C. 80.
[146] See *Re Amaron Ltd, Secretary of State for Trade and Industry v Lubrani* [1998] B.C.C. 264.
[147] [1988] Ch. 477.

the business and [having] shown himself to be capable and responsible". In *Re Brian Sheridan Cars Ltd*,[148] a solicitor and an accountant were required to be appointed to each of the relevant boards to ensure that legal, accounting and financial standards were properly observed. The accountant was expressly required to be the finance director.

15–46 In *Re Amaron Ltd, Secretary of State for Trade and Industry v Lubrani*, Neuberger J. said that the normal course followed by the courts is:

> "... [T]o ensure that one or more professional persons, such as an accountant, is appointed to the board. This enables the order to have effective teeth: (a) if the company becomes insolvent then the accountant director may be liable himself to be disqualified under the 1986 Act; (b) the accountant director has the powers of a director ..."[149]

In that case, the condition offered was that a chartered accountant would monitor the activities of the company and report back to the court in the event of any dissatisfaction. It was not proposed that the accountant would join the board. Neuberger J. took the view that there was no good reason why the more usual proposal of an accountant-director could not have been made. He explained himself thus:

> "... [A]lthough [the accountant] is prepared to have a monitoring obligation, it is something of an imposition on him to require him to give undertakings to come back to the court in certain circumstances. If he gives no such undertakings then the situation is of doubtful value. Thus, if he performs his tasks unsatisfactorily it is pretty unclear whether anyone who suffers has a cause of action against him or whether the court has any sanction against him."[150]

This latter point does not seem to have been given sufficient weight in *Re Hennelly's Utilities Ltd, Hennelly v Official Receiver*.[151] In that case a condition of permission was that there was to be quarterly reporting to the Department of Trade and Industry by a named individual confirming that the other conditions of permission had been met. The individual was an independent chartered management accountant who was to be appointed finance director as a further condition of the permission.

15–47 In *Secretary of State for Trade and Industry v Renwick*,[152] Chadwick J. said:

> "It must be only in exceptional circumstances that a court—which has been satisfied of unfitness and has made an order disqualifying the director for four years—can take the view that, nevertheless, the person disqualified should continue to have what was, in effect, uncontrolled direction and management of another company."

[148] [1996] 1 B.C.L.C. 327.
[149] [1998] B.C.C. 264 at 278.
[150] [1998] B.C.C. 264 at 278–279. Furthermore, it is difficult to see how such a monitoring obligation could be drafted as a condition other than on the basis that the accountant be employed by the company on such and such (non-revocable) terms.
[151] [2005] B.C.C. 542.
[152] July 1997, Ch.D., unreported.

15–48 In *Re Tech Textiles Ltd, Secretary of State for Trade and Industry v Vane*,[153] there was a requirement (in relation to one company) that another person hold the position of finance director and a requirement (in relation to a second company) that another person hold the position of managing director or finance director. In *Secretary of State for Trade and Industry v Rosenfield*, His Honour Judge Cooke emphasised the need for appropriate expertise:

> "... [S]omething which I indicated would concern me in my main judgment, is the need to have on the board somebody of financial expertise. The companies in the past had nobody of any financial expertise on the board. They had expert traders, but they had people who had no real idea of how the figures were going. It seems to me to be absolutely essential that there is somebody with the appropriate degree of expertise on the board."[154]

In that case, the condition was expressed in terms that if the nominated person ceased to be a director, the permission would continue for two months after his departure so that a replacement could be found and a further application made to the court to vary the order.

15–49 In *Re TLL Realisations Ltd*,[155] permission was granted for the applicant to be engaged in management. Although, the applicant had been disqualified for his failings as a finance director, the only relevant condition imposed was that the applicant be supervised by a named individual who acted as company secretary to a number of the companies in question and who was "knowledgeable and experienced in the internal financial administration" of companies. However, on appeal, a further condition was offered and accepted, namely that a named individual remain as a director of the companies in question.

Control of the company in general meeting

15–50 In *Re Lo-Line Electric Motors Ltd*,[156] the order was conditional on a named individual and his family retaining voting control of one company and that company retaining voting control of a second company. In *Gibson Davies* (see text from 15–36 above), one of the conditions was that the applicant should take no steps in his capacity as 50 per cent shareholder and director of the company's parent, to impede, direct or control the activities of the company's directors. In *Tech Textiles*, a condition was imposed to the effect that the relevant company should remain a subsidiary of another named company.

Other outside assistance

15–51 In *Tech Textiles* the order was made subject to conditions that a consultant be appointed to ensure that accounts were properly filed, monies owed to the government paid and that no risks were taken with creditors' funds. Further conditions

[153] [1998] 1 B.C.L.C. 259.
[154] [1999] B.C.C. 413 at 418.
[155] [2000] B.C.C. 998.
[156] [1988] Ch. 477.

were that a named firm (or some other comparable firm of chartered accountants) be appointed to act as auditors and provide company secretarial services. A condition regulating the identity of the auditors was also imposed in *Brian Sheridan*.

Financial controls

15–52 In the nature of things, it is frequently the inadequacy or absence of financial management that is at the heart of many disqualification cases, especially those brought under CDDA s.6.[157] If permission is granted in such cases, financial controls of two particular types will usually be required: (a) general financial management controls; and (b) specific controls designed to prevent the recurrence of previous misconduct on the applicant's part. In addition to the appointment of named directors and auditors, further conditions are frequently imposed in relation to such persons. For example, in *Gibson Davies*, the company was required to implement the controls recommended by the accountants and the auditors were required to report on any matters of concern to the board. In *Tech Textiles, Re Chartmore Ltd*[158] and *Re Hennelly's Utilities Ltd, Hennelly v Official Receiver*,[159] there was a requirement for monthly board meetings (in *Chartmore* to be attended by the auditors). In *Tech Textiles, Gibson Davies, Rosenfield* and *Hennelly's Utilities*, conditions were imposed requiring the provision of regular (monthly or quarterly) management accounts. In *Gibson Davies* these accounts were to be submitted to the auditors. Controls in relation to the signing of cheques were also imposed in *Tech Textiles* and *Gibson Davies*.

15–53 Limits have also been placed on the amount of remuneration that the applicant can receive and conditions imposed requiring the applicant (in certain circumstances) to subordinate any investment or loan and to take no security (see *Gibson Davies, Rosenfield* and *Hennelly's Utilities*).[160] In *Barings (No.3)*, the conditions imposed were that the applicant was to remain an unpaid non-executive director of the relevant companies and was not to enter into a service contract with any of them. The purpose of these conditions is not entirely clear. Mr Norris's remuneration from the company as a consultant was unregulated and the absence of paid terms of employment as a director would not necessarily restrict the role and duties that he might undertake. In *Rosenfield*, inter-company loans were regulated by a condition as this was an area that had caused particular problems in the past.

Permission for a limited period

15–54 The question of interim permission is considered below in 15–59. On occasions, the court has granted permission limited to a year or so with the idea that the matter should then come back before the court. In cases of doubt or where, say, the

[157] See text from 5–36.
[158] [1990] B.C.L.C. 673.
[159] [2005] B.C.C. 542.
[160] In *Hennelly's Utilities* the court required certain interest free loans made by the company to other companies connected with the applicant to be repaid and the applicant to subordinate loans made by him to the company to all other creditors.

company is new and its financial position is uncertain, there are strong grounds for granting such a limited permission. The further advantage of limited permission is that it enables the court to check that any conditions are being complied with and evaluate whether it is appropriate for permission to continue. In cases where conditions are imposed to minimise risks to the public, there is something to be said for the view that the court should keep the position under review.

15–55 In *Re Chartmore Ltd*,[161] Harman J. disqualified the defendant for two years under CDDA s.6. The judge found that the defendant's company had been inadequately capitalised and had lacked proper financial controls. Consequently, the company had continued to trade at the expense of its creditors despite being insolvent. The defendant's application for permission to act as a director of another company was granted on his undertaking that the existing system of monitoring the business by a full monthly board meeting attended by the auditors would continue. The official receiver expressed some concern over how the undertaking would be policed and the judge was hesitant because the company was uncomfortably similar to the one that had featured in the main proceedings in that it too appeared to be inadequately capitalised. The solution arrived at by the court was to give permission for one year of the two-year period only, with the defendant to have liberty to apply to the registrar for further permission at his own cost before the expiry of the order. It was made clear that on any application for renewed permission the defendant would need to adduce evidence showing that the company continued to be properly run along the lines of the undertaking. Permission for a limited period was also granted at an earlier stage in the proceedings that ultimately came before the court in *Re Brian Sheridan Cars Ltd*.[162]

Conditions: the role of the court and the Secretary of State

15–56 Under ss.1 and 17 and s.11 of the CDDA, it is for the court (not the Secretary of State, official receiver or some other person) to be satisfied that permission should be granted. For the same reason, it will not usually be appropriate for a condition to be imposed that something should be done to the satisfaction of, say, the Secretary of State or for the Secretary of State to be required generally to police the management of a company in relation to which permission has been granted.[163] This principle was acknowledged explicitly in *Re Hennelly's Utilities Ltd, Secretary of State for Trade and Industry v Hennelly*.[164] In that case the deputy judge considered that the conditions could be policed in two ways without infringing the principle. First, certain of them could be made conditions precedent to the grant of permission. Secondly, the remaining conditions could be made the subject of a monthly report by an independent board member to the Department of Trade and Industry:

[161] [1990] B.C.L.C. 673.

[162] [1996] 1 B.C.L.C. 327. See also *Re Tech Textiles Ltd, Secretary of State for Trade and Industry v Vane* [1998] 1 B.C.L.C. 259.

[163] See further *Re Brian Sheridan Cars Ltd* [1996] 1 B.C.L.C. 327 at 346–347 and, by analogy, *Re Supporting Link Alliance Ltd* [2004] EWHC 523 (Ch), [2004] 1 W.L.R. 1549 at [66].

[164] [2005] B.C.C. 542.

> "The Secretary of State will not have to find out whether the conditions are complied with. He will know if they have not, either by reading the report submitted, or by the simple fact of not having received the required report at all . . ."[165]

Applications for permission to be involved in management

15–57 Applications for permission to be involved in management (rather than to act as a director) cause difficulties. The danger is that if the permission is too widely couched, the court will, in effect, be granting the applicant permission to act as a de facto or shadow director without the sorts of safeguards that could have been imposed had he asked for permission to act as a director. In two cases, the court has dealt with this difficulty by describing very precisely what the permission has been given for in the order. In *Re Lichfield Freight Terminal Ltd, Secretary of State for Trade and Industry v Rowe*,[166] Her Honour Judge Alton refused the applicant permission to act as a director but did give him permission to do the following:

(1) Make arrangements on behalf of the company for the collection and delivery of goods.
(2) Give quotations for pricing of deliveries in accordance with a preset formula determined by the board.
(3) Negotiate the pricing and storage by the company of goods for third parties in accordance with a preset formula determined by the board.
(4) Price opportunities for the company's business for the consideration of the board.
(5) Interview prospective employees with a view to recommending their engagement to the board.
(6) Act as a transport manager with responsibility for purchases of day-to-day consumables, making arrangements for maintenance of vehicles and tachographs (any purchase in excess of £250 to be approved by the board) and negotiate for the consideration of the board terms for the purchase and sale of vehicles and equipment.
(7) Check proof of delivery forms and invoices.

15–58 In *Re TLL Realisations Ltd, Secretary of State for Trade and Industry v Collins*[167] there was a similar attempt to specify in detail the activities in which the applicant was permitted to engage. The order expressly permitted him to do the following:

(1) Review a business and assemble reports for the company into the past, present and future operation of such business.
(2) Assist in the acquisition of a business by the company to the extent of carrying out research into its accounting position and liaising with the

[165] [2005] B.C.C. 542 at [72]. It is not clear that this deals with the concern raised by Neuberger J. in the *Amaron* case referred to in 15–46 above.
[166] November 19, 1997, Birmingham County Court, unreported.
[167] [2000] B.C.C. 998.

company's solicitors in the preparation of draft contracts for the purchase and establishment of a business.

(3) Act as a joint cheque signatory or counter signatory, in every case signing with one other.

(4) Recommend and set up accounting books, systems and procedures appropriate to the trading activities of the company and maintain, expand and amend such systems as necessary to meet statutory requirements.

(5) Produce on request financial forecasts, including profit and loss and cash flow figures.

(6) Produce management accounts as required, including explanations of all items which varied from forecast.

(7) Produce annual accounts and submit them for approval by the board of directors and/or audit.

(8) Produce draft agreements, reports and documentation in respect of the trading activities of group companies and provide advice and accounting matters as and when requested.

(9) Subject to and in accordance with express prior instructions from the directors of any group company: (a) without power to bind any such company, carry out negotiations with any customer; (b) place orders with any supplier of any such company, provided that each such order was specifically authorised by the company's board of directors; (c) dispose of property of any such company, provided that each such disposal was specifically and separately authorised by the said board of directors.

(10) Monitor and report on the accounts of any group company.

(11) Report to the board of directors of any group company in relation to financial and commercial issues.

Interim permission

15–59 It is conceivable that a disqualified person may wish to seek a stay of a disqualification order for a short period either: (a) to allow him to prepare evidence in support of an application for permission; or (b) pending appeal; or (c) to enable him to make arrangements for the running of companies of which he is, for example, a director at the time of his disqualification. It was seen in Ch.12 that there is jurisdiction in the civil courts to stay or suspend the operation of a disqualification order either under the CDDA and/or (in the case of the High Court and the Court of Appeal) under the inherent jurisdiction. There is similar jurisdiction in the Crown Court. However, in the light of *Secretary of State for Trade and Industry v Bannister*, the preferred approach is for the disqualified person to seek interim permission to act rather than a stay of the disqualification order.[168] The courts have followed the practice of granting interim permission in a number of

[168] [1996] 1 W.L.R. 118. See further text from 12–33. Even before the decision in *Bannister* there are cases where interim permission was granted rather than a stay: see *Re Wedgecraft Ltd*, March 7, 1986, Ch.D., unreported; *Re Ipcon Fashions Ltd* (1989) 5 B.C.C. 773.

cases since *Bannister*.[169] It is clear from these cases that interim permission should be granted for a short time only.[170] Moreover, it appears from *Re Amaron Ltd, Secretary of State for Trade and Industry v Lubrani*[171] that in a case where interim permission is sought pending the hearing of an appeal or an application for full permission, the court will apply the guidelines laid down by the House of Lords in *American Cyanamid Co v Ethicon Ltd*[172] as regards the granting of an interim injunctions. This involves the application of a balance of convenience test, with the balance to be struck between the public interest and the interests of the applicant and/or the relevant company.[173] A further point which emerges from Park J.'s judgment in *Re TLL Realisations*[174] is that the court is unlikely to tolerate a situation in which the applicant repeatedly seeks to extend an interim permission or the making of an application for interim permission without notice to the Secretary of State.

Applications for permission under ss.11 and 12

15–60 The original purpose of automatic disqualification under CDDA s.11 was to prevent undischarged bankrupts from using the medium of a company to obtain credit and so circumvent the restriction on bankrupts obtaining credit without disclosing their personal status.[175] Equally, there is support for the view that s.11 serves the wider aim of protecting the public by prohibiting individuals who are bankrupt, subject to a moratorium period under a debt relief order or subject to

[169] See *Re Thorncliffe Finance Ltd, Secretary of State for Trade and Industry v Arif* [1997] 1 B.C.L.C. 34 at 46; *Re Continental Assurance Co of London Plc* [1997] 1 B.C.L.C. 48 at 61–62 affirmed sub nom. *Secretary of State for Trade and Industry v Burrows*, July 4, 1996, C.A., unreported; *Re Amaron Ltd, Secretary of State for Trade and Industry v Lubrani* [1998] B.C.C. 264 (supplementary judgment of Neuberger J. from p.274).

[170] In *Secretary of State for Trade and Industry v Renwick*, July 1997, Ch.D., unreported Chadwick J. criticised a district judge who had purportedly relied on his earlier decision in *Re Thorncliffe Finance Ltd, Secretary of State for Trade and Industry v Arif* [1997] 1 B.C.L.C. 34. In *Renwick*, the district judge had adjourned the question of permission to a High Court judge. However, the adjournment was on terms that the matter did not come on before the judge for around nine months with interim permission in the meantime and six months to file further evidence in support of the application. The main reason for such a lengthy adjournment seems to have been the prospect that recoveries might be made in a claim being pursued against pension advisers, thereby improving the financial position of the relevant company. This was an entirely different situation from *Arif* in which a two month adjournment was allowed to enable the latest year end accounts to be made up in circumstances where there were interests other than those of the applicant at stake, evidence from professional advisers that both companies were properly managed and run and further evidence that the applicant would be deprived of any source of income unless interim permission was granted. There was no such evidence in *Renwick* and, on the facts of that case, Chadwick J. doubted whether it was appropriate to grant interim permission at all, let alone for nine months.

[171] [1998] B.C.C. 264 at 275.

[172] [1975] A.C. 396.

[173] In *Hease v Secretary of State for Trade and Industry* [2006] B.P.I.R. 425 Etherton J. refused to grant interim permission to cover a seven-day adjournment of the application for permission granted to the Secretary of State to facilitate performance of his obligations under CDDA s.17(5). The main factors that weighed against the grant of interim permission were the seriousness of the applicant's previous misconduct (he had been disqualified for six years) and the fact that the four companies in question had a finance director (albeit he was on holiday). The court was also struck by the applicant's delay in making the application for permission following acceptance of his disqualification undertaking and his failure to explain this delay.

[174] [2000] B.C.C. 998.

[175] See text from 11–22.

insolvency restrictions from being involved in the management of companies. The prevalence of such a view suggests that the courts will adopt much the same approach on an application for permission by a person disqualified under s.11 as is adopted on an application for permission to act notwithstanding a disqualification order or undertaking.[176] For similar reasons, it is unlikely that the courts would adopt a radically different approach to an application for permission made by a person disqualified in the terms of CDDA s.12.

Cases where the court cannot grant permission

15–61 There are a number of limitations on the powers of the courts to relieve from the consequences of disqualification. Thus, it is clear that a person disqualified in the terms of CDDA ss.1, 1A, 9B, 12A and 12B is prohibited from being an insolvency practitioner and cannot be relieved from this disability by the court. However the position under CDDA s.12 may be different in this respect. A person disqualified in the terms of s.12 is prohibited from acting as a liquidator without the permission of the court. One point of some difficulty is whether an insolvency practitioner disqualified in the terms of this provision could seek permission to act as a liquidator under the CDDA. Section 390(4) of the Insolvency Act 1986 provides that a person is not qualified to act as an insolvency practitioner (and therefore as a provisional liquidator, liquidator, administrator, administrative receiver or supervisor of a corporate voluntary arrangement) if, among other things, he has been adjudged bankrupt or is subject to a disqualification order made under the CDDA or the equivalent Northern Ireland legislation. Moreover, there is no power in the court under the Insolvency Act to grant dispensation from this prohibition in the form of permission to act. It seems that in the case of an insolvency practitioner the subject of a disqualification in the terms of s.12, the court strictly has jurisdiction to grant him permission to act as a liquidator. Somewhat anomalously the absolute prohibition in s.390(4)(b) of the Insolvency Act 1986 does not appear to bite as it applies only to a person who is "subject to a disqualification order made or a disqualification undertaking accepted under the CDDA". Strictly, a disqualification order in the terms of s.12 is not a disqualification order "made under the CDDA" but one made under s.429 of the Insolvency Act 1986, the scope of which is defined in the CDDA. As such it appears that the court would have jurisdiction under CDDA s.12 to grant an insolvency practitioner permission to act as a liquidator notwithstanding the prohibition imposed by that provision.[177]

15–62 The position as regards an insolvency practitioner who is bankrupt, subject to a debt relief order or subject to insolvency restrictions is more straightforward. The relevant prohibition flows from s.390(4)(a), (aa) and (5) of the Insolvency Act 1986 (which is absolute), and not from the wording of CDDA s.11 of the CDDA, with the effect that the court has no jurisdiction to grant any such person permission to act in any capacity which requires him to be qualified as an insolvency practitioner.

[176] See *Re Altim Pty Ltd* [1968] 2 N.S.W.R. 762; *Re Ansett* (1990) 3 A.C.S.R. 357; *Re McQuillan* (1989) 5 B.C.C. 137.

[177] See also text at 14–58.

15–63 Only the High Court of Northern Ireland can grant permission to act notwithstanding disqualification in circumstances where a Northern Ireland disqualification, by order or undertaking, is given effect in Great Britain by virtue of CDDA ss.12A and 12B.

15–64 Certain "knock on" disqualifications, prohibitions and restrictions which flow from the status of a person as a disqualified person under the CDDA, cannot be relieved against either at all[178] or only by some other body.[179]

Future direction

15–65 The future direction of this particular aspect of disqualification jurisprudence is likely to be affected by many of the issues discussed in Ch.2 concerning the broad rationale of the CDDA and the difficult balance to be struck between the public interest and the interests of the disqualified person. There is a strong argument for saying that even greater primacy should be given to the protection of the public than is currently the case.[180] As was pointed out in *Brian Sheridan*, the disqualified person is seeking a dispensation or indulgence in circumstances where his previous misconduct has resulted in disqualification. This suggests that the courts should exercise their power to grant permission sparingly. A further point that has been taken on board by the courts, but has perhaps not always been given sufficient weight, is that too great a willingness to grant permission may undermine the wider purposes of the CDDA, such as deterrence and the raising of standards among directors generally.[181] If a person is found to be unfit and disqualified, in part, to deter others, deterrence may be said to be significantly undermined if, on an application for permission to act, the disqualified person is promptly given permission to act in relation to those companies in respect of which he has sought permission. On the other hand, the influence of the quasi-criminal view of disqualification considered in Ch.2 may yet become more pervasive in the light of the shift in the decade after the enactment of the Human Rights Act 1998 towards a more rights-based legal culture. One possible consequence of this is that the courts may seek to use the power to grant permission as a means of tailoring a proportionate response to individual cases.[182]

[178] For example, the prohibition on acting as a school governor: see text at 14–72.

[179] For example, the Charity Commission in relation to trusteeship of a charitable trust: see 14–63. Note, however, that the court can grant permission to act in relation to a charitable company.

[180] Indeed, the dicta cited earlier from *Barings* and *Dawes & Henderson*, might suggest that the rigorous approach taken to substantive disqualification (see, e.g. the *Grayan* case discussed in Chs 2 and 4) is beginning to seep through into the area of permission to act.

[181] An emphasis on deterrence can be detected in cases where the applicant for permission has been disqualified for a substantial period: see, e.g. *Re Westminster Property Management Ltd (No.2), Official Receiver v Stern (No.2)* [2001] B.C.C. 305 at 363; *Re Morija Plc, Kluk v Secretary of State for Business, Enterprise and Regulatory Reform* [2008] 2 B.C.L.C. 313 at [35], [54].

[182] On the question of proportionality see A. von Hirsch and M. Wasik, "Civil Disqualifications Attending Conviction: A Suggested Conceptual Framework" [1997] Cambridge L.J. 599. These writers argue that disqualifications should ordinarily be seen as civil risk-prevention measures and that, as such, the imposition of a wide constraint (like the one imposed in the terms of CDDA ss.1 and 1A) is only legitimate if it amounts to an appropriate and proportionate response reflecting the magnitude of any future risk. Furthermore, if this approach is followed, there is no reason why the court should not take personal factors (such as the impact of the prohibition on the disqualified person) into account when considering applications for permission.

PROCEDURE ON APPLICATIONS FOR PERMISSION

CDDA ss.17 and 12: Procedure on an application for permission to act notwithstanding disqualification

Which court?

15–66 The substantive power to grant permission to act notwithstanding disqualification is conferred by CDDA ss.1(1), 1A(1), 9B and 12. However, it is not open to every court to exercise this power. The basic procedure governing applications for permission in such cases is contained in s.17(1).[183] This identifies the courts to which an application for permission can be brought. In summary, s.17(1) provides as follows:

(1) Where a person is subject to a disqualification order made by a court having jurisdiction to wind up companies,[184] any application for permission for the purposes of CDDA s.1(1)(a) shall be made to that court.[185]
(2) Where a person is subject to a disqualification order made either under CDDA s.2 by a court other than a court with jurisdiction to wind up companies or under s.5, any application for permission for the purposes of s.1(1)(a) shall be made to any court which, when the disqualification order was made, had jurisdiction to wind up the company (or, if there is more than one such company, any of the companies) to which the offence (or any of the offences) in question related.[186]
(3) Where a person is subject to a disqualification undertaking accepted at any time under CDDA s.7 or 8, any application for permission for the purposes of CDDA s.1A(1)(a) shall be made to any court to which, if the Secretary of State had applied for a disqualification order under the relevant section in question at that time, his[187] application could have been made.[188]
(4) Where a person is subject to a disqualification undertaking accepted at any time under s.9B any application for permission for the purposes of s.9B(4) must be made to the High Court or (in Scotland) the Court of Session.[189]
(5) Where a person is subject to two or more disqualification orders or undertakings (or to a combination of the same) any application for permission should be made to the appropriate court which would have jurisdiction to grant permission in relation to the most recent disqualification.[190]

[183] Strictly, s.17 governs the mechanics of the process when a court is asked to grant permission whereas the substantive power to grant permission is given, not under s.17, but under ss.1(1)(a), 1A(1)(a) etc. as appropriate: see *Re Morija Plc, Kluk v Secretary of State for Business, Enterprise and Regulatory Reform* [2008] 2 B.C.L.C. 313 at [41].
[184] Which would include the High Court in the case of disqualification orders made pursuant to CDDA ss.8 or 9A.
[185] CDDA s.17(1).
[186] CDDA s.17(2).
[187] In the context this must mean the Secretary of State's application.
[188] CDDA s.17(3).
[189] CDDA ss.9B(4) and 9E(3).
[190] CDDA s.17(4).

In broad terms, the effect of the amendments to CDDA s.17 effected by the Insolvency Act 2000, has been to move the jurisdiction to grant permission to act notwithstanding disqualification from the civil court with winding up jurisdiction over the company in relation to which permission is sought to the civil court that did or, in the case of disqualifications imposed by a criminal court or by undertaking, could have disqualified the person. The jurisdiction of the courts to wind up companies is established by s.117 of the Insolvency Act 1986 and is discussed fully in Ch.7.

15–67 Where the disqualification proceedings are brought in the High Court, it is possible for the defendant to make the application for permission in the original proceedings. The application for permission will only then be determined if the court makes a disqualification order. By making such an application the defendant can avoid having to expend the further time and cost of bringing a free standing application for permission after the court has disposed of the original proceedings. It is no surprise that the practice of dealing with both the disqualification and the question of permission at the same hearing is one that the civil courts have not only encouraged,[191] but have insisted should happen wherever possible. In *Re TLL Realisations, Secretary of State for Trade and Industry v Collins*, Peter Gibson L.J. commented as follows:

> "In my opinion it is highly desirable that a person who faces the possibility of a disqualification order but who in the event of such an order wishes to seek leave should both make that application early enough so that the same judge should consider both the application for disqualification and the application for leave. Of course there will be cases where it is not envisaged at the time of the hearing of the application for disqualification that an application for leave need be made. For example, a new opportunity may have arisen after the disqualification order."[192]

The general point is one that raises wider issues than those of saving costs and court time. In the same case Judge L.J. made the following observation:

> "Although some applicants may hope to derive a tactical advantage from isolating the case for disqualification (which will inevitably highlight their misconduct) from their application for leave (which will tend to focus on the mitigation) the interests of justice overall are more likely to be served if both aspects of the case are investigated together. In any event separate proceedings also involve duplication and wasted resources. In future, faced with an application for leave which was plainly in contemplation at the time of the disqualification proceedings, the judge should closely examine the explanations which purport to justify a second hearing. Quite apart from any consequential order for costs, unless satisfied that the delay arose for genuine reasons, and that a single hearing was truly impracticable, he would be entitled to approach the evidence in support of the application for leave with a proper degree of healthy scepticism."[193]

[191] *Re Dicetrade Ltd, Secretary of State for Trade and Industry v Worth* [1994] 2 B.C.L.C. 113 at 116. The court cannot make a partial or qualified disqualification order. It is obliged to make an order in the full terms of CDDA s.1: see Ch.12. As such, it may be sensible for a defendant who holds directorships and/or managerial positions within other companies not directly in issue in the disqualification proceedings to consider making an application within the main proceedings.

[192] [2000] B.C.C. 998 at 1010E–F.

[193] [2000] B.C.C. 998 at 1015C–E.

15–68 One difficulty with the legislation is that this sensible practice cannot be adopted in the criminal courts in CDDA s.2 or s.5 cases.[194] This is because the power to grant permission is restricted by s.17 to the civil courts. Thus, if a person is disqualified by the Crown Court under s.2, he will have to make a free standing application for permission to the High Court (or relevant county court) under s.17. As such, the legislation envisages that cases will arise in which the person is disqualified by a criminal court and yet granted permission by a civil court.[195] However, one difficulty was overcome by the Insolvency Act 2000. This difficulty arose where there was a divergence between the court having jurisdiction to disqualify and the court having jurisdiction to grant permission, as was the case where a person was disqualified in a county court but was seeking permission to act in respect of a company the registered office of which was situated outside that county court's jurisdiction.

15–69 Applications for permission to act notwithstanding disqualification in the terms of CDDA s.12 should be made to the relevant county court which made the order pursuant to s.429 of the Insolvency Act 1986. CDDA s.17 has no application in such a case.

Form of application and applicable rules of court

15–70 Applications for permission made under CDDA s.17 for the purposes of any of ss.1(1)(a), 1A(1)(a) or 9B(4) or under s.12(2) are governed by para.20 of the Disqualification Practice Direction. This provides that the application should be made either by Practice Form N208 under Pt 8 of the CPR or by application notice in existing disqualification proceedings. Paragraph 21 of the Disqualification Practice Direction provides that every claim form or application notice by which an application for permission to act is begun, and all affidavits, notices and other documents in the application must be entitled in the matter of the company or companies in question and in the matter of the Company Directors Disqualification Act 1986.

Section 17(5): Defendant to application for permission

15–71 It appears from s.17(5) that the defendant to the application for permission should ordinarily be the Secretary of State (or, in the case of competition disqualifications, the relevant regulator). This is a great improvement on and simplification of the position prior to the Insolvency Act 2000 when the relevant defendant would appear to have been the party who applied originally for the disqualification order. Strictly, s.17(5) imposes a mandatory duty on the Secretary of State to appear and call the attention of the court to relevant matters rather than specifying

[194] Though in any event it is questionable whether or not the criminal courts (let alone all prosecutors) have the expertise to consider the question of permission.

[195] The existence of this anomaly provides further support for the view expressed elsewhere by the authors that the civil and criminal courts should adopt a single, composite approach to the application of the CDDA. It makes no sense whatsoever for the criminal courts to work with one set of assumptions concerning the raison d'être of disqualification if the civil courts administering the provision for permission are working with a different set of assumptions.

that such person should be joined, but it is suggested that the formal joinder of the Secretary of State (or relevant regulator) is sensible.

15–72 The use of the words "shall appear" in s.17(5) indicate that the Secretary of State is under a mandatory obligation to attend the hearing and draw the court's attention to any matters which might assist the court in determining the application.[196] The court is not, of course, restricted to considering matters raised by the Secretary of State.[197] Where the Secretary of State does not oppose the application it appears that he can discharge this obligation by writing a letter to the court drawing any particular points to its attention and indicating his intention not to attend the hearing.[198] In relation to an application for permission under CDDA s.11(1), s.11(3) provides that the official receiver is under a duty to oppose the application if he is of the opinion that it is contrary to the public interest that the application should be granted. This wording differs from the more neutral wording in s.17(5) which provides only that the Secretary of State "shall appear and call the attention of the court to any matters which seem to him to be relevant, and may himself give evidence or call witnesses". Despite the more neutral wording in s.17(5), it is suggested that the Secretary of State should, in an appropriate case, oppose the application and, in the event that the application is successful in such a case, it would be open to the Secretary of State to appeal.[199]

Evidence

15–73 Paragraph 22.1 of the Disqualification Practice Direction provides that evidence in support of an application for permission to act shall be by affidavit. The question of what matters should be covered by such evidence follows from the discussion above. Current practice is for the Secretary of State or official receiver to request that evidence deals with the points set out in an annexed schedule (a copy of the current version is in the appendices). It is obviously sensible that the evidence should include the matters that a person is required to put in evidence when seeking permission to act notwithstanding his automatic disqualification under CDDA s.11.[200] In addition, the question of relevant evidence on such hearings was considered by the Court of Appeal in *Re Westmid Packing Services Ltd,*

[196] *Re Dicetrade Ltd, Secretary of State for Trade and Industry v Worth* [1994] 2 B.C.L.C. 113 at 116–117.

[197] See the following comment of Chadwick J. in *Secretary of State for Trade and Industry v Renwick*, July 1997, unreported:

> ". . . I do not myself take the view that [on an application for permission] the court is circumscribed by those matters to which the Secretary of State draws attention. The purpose of s.17(2) . . . is to provide assistance to the court by giving it the benefit of the Secretary of State's observations. It is not the purpose of s.17(2) to limit the court's own discretion whether or not to grant [permission] in respect of a person . . ."

[198] *Re Dicetrade Ltd, Secretary of State for Trade and Industry v Worth* [1994] 2 B.C.L.C. 113 at 117. Indeed, it appears from this passage that a letter in such terms to the applicant or the solicitors on record for the applicant will suffice.

[199] As effectively confirmed by the Court of Appeal in *Re TLL Realisations Ltd, Secretary of State for Trade and Industry v Collins* [2000] B.C.C. 998 at 1008C–D.

[200] See Insolvency Rules 1986 rr. 5A.24 and 6.203. See further 15–78 below.

Secretary of State for Trade and Industry v Griffiths.[201] Although the applicant's general reputation may be relevant, "detailed or repetitive evidence" should not be allowed. On this authority, it also appears that evidence of the applicant's:

> "age and state of health, the length of time he has been in jeopardy, whether he has admitted the offence, his conduct before and after the offence . . ."

are also relevant.[202] One very important aspect is that the evidence (filed by either party) should not seek to explain or gloss the original basis of the disqualification, be it judgment, sentence, *Carecraft* statement or disqualification undertaking.[203]

Costs

15–74 In *Re Dicetrade Ltd, Secretary of State for Trade and Industry v Worth*[204] the Court of Appeal made the following points as regards the costs of applications for permission:

(1) If the application for permission can be dealt with within the original disqualification proceedings and the Secretary of State merely puts forward matters which the court ought to consider, but does not oppose the application, the question of permission is unlikely to take up much time in the context of the overall hearing. In such circumstances, the appropriate order may well be "no order for costs".
(2) On a free standing application for permission, there is no general principle which entitles the Secretary of State to be paid his costs of attending on the application automatically even if the Secretary of State, on consideration, does not oppose the application.

The first point is questionable. The costs of the application may well encompass the additional cost of preparing for the hearing as well as the costs of attendance. The Secretary of State may have carried out investigations and entered into correspondence clarifying matters and/or pointing out gaps in the applicant's evidence. It is not clear how far the second point goes. Certainly, if the Secretary of State needlessly appears, he could not expect to obtain an order for costs. Similarly, if the Secretary of State needlessly prolongs any application, he might expect to have an order for costs made against him. What happens if: (a) the application is dismissed; or (b) the application is granted but the Secretary of State has played a useful role in bringing relevant matters to the court's attention is unclear.

[201] [1998] 2 All E.R. 124.
[202] See discussion of mitigating factors in the text from 5–110.
[203] *Re TLL Realisations Ltd, Secretary of State for Trade and Industry v Collins* [2000] B.C.C. 998 at 1010A–C, 1015F–H, 1016D–E. See also *Re Morija Plc, Kluk v Secretary of State for Business, Enterprise and Regulatory Reform* [2008] 2 B.C.L.C. 313 a case in which an ill-advised attempt by the applicant for permission to challenge the factual basis of a disqualification undertaking appears to have backfired.
[204] [1994] 2 B.C.L.C. 113.

15–75 If *Dicetrade* is applied, it appears that the starting assumption is that the Secretary of State is merely there to assist the court and that both sides should generally bear their own costs. However, it is suggested that such a starting assumption does not adequately reflect the position. The significant point is that the applicant is asking the court for an indulgence and the need for the application has been brought on the applicant by his own misconduct. The crux of the application is that the applicant is seeking to rid himself of a legal disability. Moreover, the Secretary of State is required to appear by s.17(5) and a similar obligation applies to the relevant regulator in competition disqualification cases by virtue of s.17(7). In such circumstances, costs will have to be incurred by him in deciding whether or not to oppose the application even if ultimately the decision is taken not to oppose. As such, it is suggested that the Secretary of State (or relevant regulator) should generally be entitled to an order for costs whatever the outcome unless his opposition to an application is found to be unreasonable (in which case the applicant might arguably be entitled to at least some of his costs). Costs in disqualification proceedings are discussed more fully in Ch.7. It is suggested that the correct approach is as follows:

(1) If the application is dismissed, it will be usual for the applicant to be ordered to pay the Secretary of State's costs on the standard basis. Although the Court of Appeal in *Dicetrade* cited a comment of Chadwick J. to the effect that there was no "lis" between the parties, it is hard to see how this fits in with other remarks of the Court of Appeal to the effect that such proceedings are "no different to other civil proceedings" and that "the Secretary of State must take his chance in such litigation, just like any other litigant . . .".
(2) If the application is granted, an order that the applicant pay the Secretary of State's costs will generally be made if the Secretary of State has been of assistance to the court and has not acted improperly or wasted time arguing issues which were ultimately decided in the applicant's favour, or turned up unnecessarily when a letter drawing relevant points to the court's attention would have sufficed. To some extent this approach follows from the actual result in *Dicetrade*. The application for permission in that case was granted. At first instance, there was no order for costs at all. On appeal, the Court of Appeal ordered the applicant for permission to pay the Secretary of State's costs. This was on the basis that a separate hearing had been necessary because the applicant had not been ready to proceed at an earlier stage. Had the applicant been ready earlier, the hearing might not have led to further costs being incurred over and above the costs in the original disqualification proceedings (though see comment above). This result (which reflects current practice) can be further justified on the following ground. The applicant for permission is under a disability and has been disqualified on the basis of his own misconduct. As a price of obtaining permission and relief from such disability, he should expect to have to pay the reasonable costs of the regulator who is required to consider his application and bring relevant matters to the court's attention. The position is analogous to that of a tenant seeking relief from forfeiture.

This approach derives some support from the *TLL Realisations* case.[205] Although it is true that, in requiring the applicant to pay the Secretary of State's costs of the application before the judge, the Court of Appeal focused on the fact that the applicant had unnecessarily caused there to be two hearings, Peter Gibson L.J. (with whom Ferris J. agreed) framed the issue of principle more widely:

> ". . . [Counsel for the applicant for permission] submitted that this court has made clear that the Secretary of State was to be treated in the same way as any other litigant. I cannot accept that. Indeed, with all respect to Dillon L.J., I have difficulty with his obiter comment, 'There is no special position of the Secretary of State.' To my mind s.17(2)[206] shows that the Secretary of State is indeed placed in a special position where he has duties to perform on the application. He is not a party to the litigation in the ordinary sense and he is not like any other litigant. The costs incurred by him are a direct consequence of the misconduct of the applicant leading to a disqualification order and of the application for leave which the applicant has chosen to make. I cannot see why it should not be the ordinary consequence that the applicant pays the costs of the Secretary of State on the application."

Registration of order granting permission

15–76 Where permission is granted by a court for a person the subject of a disqualification order or undertaking to do any thing which he is otherwise prohibited from doing, details of the order granting permission must be notified by the relevant court officer to the Secretary of State for entry on the registration of disqualification orders.[207]

Appeals

15–77 Appeals from orders granting permission to act notwithstanding disqualification imposed by virtue of CDDA ss.6–10 would appear to be governed by the Insolvency Rules 1986. This conclusion flows from the discussion in Ch.7 and the fact that s.21(2) of the CDDA (as amended) applies the rule-making power under the Insolvency Act 1986 to CDDA ss.1, 1A and 17. Applying the same reasoning, appeals in relation to the grant or refusal of permission in relation to a disqualification flowing from s.12 and ss.2–5 would appear to be governed by the ordinary rules applicable under the CPR rather than by the Insolvency Rules 1986. The subject of appeals is considered at greater length in Ch.13.

Procedure on an application for permission to act notwithstanding automatic disqualification under CDDA s.11

15–78 Applications for permission to act under CDDA s.11 made by undischarged bankrupts or persons who are subject to bankruptcy restrictions are apparently governed by rr.6.203–6.205 of the Insolvency Rules 1986. Applications for permission to act

[205] [2000] B.C.C. 998.

[206] Now s.17(5) as amended.

[207] See generally the Companies (Disqualification Orders) Regulations 2009 (SI 2009/2471).

under CDDA s.11 made by persons in relation to whom a moratorium period under a debt relief order applies or are subject to debt relief restrictions are apparently governed by rr.5A.24–5A.26 of the Insolvency Rules 1986.[208] The reason for doubt is that s.21 of the CDDA does not expressly apply the relevant rule-making power under s.411 of the Insolvency Act 1986 to s.11. In what follows, it is assumed that the relevant provisions of the Insolvency Rules do apply. The present rules provide that evidence may be given by way of affidavit, which is in keeping with the position under CDDA ss.1, 1A, 17 and 12 (see para.22.1 of the Disqualification Practice Direction). However, in the light of r.7.57(6) of the Insolvency Rules, it would appear that witness statements are a permitted alternative.

Undischarged bankrupts and those subject to bankruptcy restrictions

15–79 In the case of an undischarged bankrupt or a person subject to bankruptcy restrictions, s.11(2) of the CDDA provides that the application should be made to the court by which the person was adjudged bankrupt. If the bankruptcy proceedings have been transferred to another court, there is a practical argument for saying that the application should be made to the court in which the bankruptcy proceedings are continuing, but the CDDA does not seem to allow for this possibility. The evidence in support should contain (at the very least) the specific matters set out in Insolvency Rules 1986 r.6.203(2). These matters include details of the business of the company, where such business is to be carried on, the persons primarily responsible for running the company (and presumably their positions), the manner in which the applicant proposes to take part or be concerned in the promotion, formation or management of the company, any emoluments and benefits to be obtained from the position[209] if permission is granted, the date of incorporation and the amount of the company's nominal and issued share capital. These matters are modified to some extent in the event that the company does not exist at the time of the application. As the test of whether permission should be granted is an "in all the circumstances" test, the sort of matters considered in relation to permission to act notwithstanding a disqualification order or undertaking will also be relevant. The official receiver and the bankrupt's trustee must be notified of the venue and served with copies of the application and supporting affidavit or written statement (Insolvency Rules 1986 r.6.204(1)). The official receiver then has the right to file a report of any matters which he considers ought to be drawn to the court's attention. Any report so filed must be copied forthwith to the bankrupt and his trustee (Insolvency Rules 1986 r.6.204(2)). The applicant then has an opportunity to file in court a notice specifying any statements in the official receiver's report which he intends to deny or dispute and he must send copies of it to his trustee and the official receiver (Insolvency Rules 1986 r.6.203(4)). Insolvency Rules 1986 r.6.204(4) provides that the official receiver and the bankrupt's trustee may appear

[208] Inserted by the Insolvency (Amendment) Rules 2009 (SI 2009/642) with effect from April 6, 2009. These rules are the same in all material respects to those in rr.6.203–6.205.

[209] Insolvency Rules 1986 r.6.203(2)(d) refers to emoluments and benefits from the directorship but this is presumably too narrow.

on the hearing of the application, and may make representations and put to the bankrupt such questions as the court may allow. Section 11(3) of the CDDA requires the official receiver to be served with notice of intention to apply for permission to act and further provides that it is his duty, if he is of the opinion that it is contrary to the public interest that the application should be granted, to attend on the hearing of the application and oppose it. One difficulty which a bankrupt faces given the requirement under the Insolvency Rules 1986 to notify his trustee is that a successful application for permission to act may well trigger an application for income payments. Indeed, provision for income payments when permission is granted is specifically contemplated by Insolvency Rules 1986 r.6.205.[210] It is suggested that the position on costs should be the same as that outlined above in relation to permission to act under a disqualification order or undertaking. Appeals are presumably governed by r.7.48(2) of the Insolvency Rules, which governs appeals in bankruptcy.

Debt relief orders and debt relief restrictions

15–80 In the case of a person in relation to whom a moratorium period under a debt relief order applies or a person who is subject to debt relief restrictions, it is not immediately clear which court has jurisdiction to consider an application for permission under CDDA s.11. Although s.11(1) has been extended to cover debt relief orders and the debt relief restrictions regime introduced by the Tribunals, Courts and Enforcement Act 2007, s.11(2) still defines the court for the purposes of s.11 as "the court by which the person was adjudged bankrupt or, in Scotland, sequestration of his estates was awarded". Debt relief orders are made by the official receiver, i.e. the process is wholly administrative and the whole point of the regime is that there is no bankruptcy. Notwithstanding the words of s.11 it is suggested that the court with jurisdiction to grant permission in cases where the need for permission arises from a debt relief order is, in fact, the court identified as the court with jurisdiction to make orders in relation to debt relief orders as set out in s.251M of the Insolvency Act 1986.[211] The reason underlying this suggestion is as follows. Rule 5A.26 of the Insolvency Rules 1986[212] dealing with applications for permission under the CDDA in relation to debt relief orders, provides by para.(2) that, at the same time as granting an application for permission under s.11 of the CDDA, the court may:

> "exercise in relation to the moratorium period or the debt relief order to which the applicant for leave is subject, any power which it has under s.251M [of the Insolvency Act 1986]."

To make sense of this provision the court granting permission must be the court with jurisdiction under s.251M. That court is identified by r.5A.21 of the Insolvency Rules 1986. Not surprisingly, that rule broadly mirrors the definition

[210] As amended by SI 2003/1730.
[211] As inserted by the Tribunals, Courts and Enforcement Act 2007 s.108(1), Sch.17.
[212] Inserted by the Insolvency (Amendment) Rules 2009 SI 2009/642 with effect from April 6, 2009.

of the court that would be in a position to exercise bankruptcy jurisdiction on a debtor's own bankruptcy petition.[213] So far as debt relief restrictions are concerned, it is suggested that the court with jurisdiction in relation to s.251M of the Insolvency Act 1986 is, again, the relevant court for these purposes. The alternative, which may in many cases have the same result, is to say that the relevant court is the court that could make the person bankrupt. The difficulty with this latter approach is that the relevant court for these purposes differs depending on who presents the petition and may change over time if residence conditions change. In all other respects the procedure under Insolvency Rules 1986 rr.5A.24–5A.26 is similar to that under rr.6.203–6.205 outlined in the previous paragraph.

[213] Insolvency Rules 1986 r.6.40.

CHAPTER 16

THE INTERNATIONAL DIMENSION

INTRODUCTION

16–01 In the modern global economy, an increasing number of disqualification cases contain an international element. This chapter considers the following four areas which give rise to legal questions that are not purely domestic in nature:

(1) The extraterritorial reach of the substantive powers of disqualification in CDDA ss.2–6, 8, 9A and 10 and of the disqualification prohibitions in CDDA ss.1, 1A, 9B(3), 12, 12A and 12B.
(2) The extraterritorial reach of the substantive powers to impose insolvency restrictions.
(3) The extraterritorial reach of the prohibition on undischarged bankrupts, persons subject to debt relief orders and persons subject to insolvency restrictions contained in CDDA s.11.
(4) The extent to which, pursuant to Pt 40 of the Companies Act 2006, the courts can recognise and give effect in the United Kingdom to disqualifications equivalent or analogous to CDDA disqualifications imposed under foreign laws.

The final, fifth, section of the chapter deals in outline with disqualification law in the Crown Dependencies within the Channel Islands (Alderney, Jersey and Guernsey) and the Isle of Man. These are jurisdictions in relation to which it might be expected that the provisions of Pt 40 of the Companies Act 2006 would be applied to produce a similar result to that produced by CDDA ss.12A and 12B which automatically extend the effect of Northern Ireland disqualifications to Great Britain.

16–02 The first three areas of coverage are concerned with what may be referred to in shorthand as "outbound" issues whereas the fourth area is concerned with "inbound" issues involving the recognition and extension to the UK of foreign disqualifications. The final, fifth, area is considered here, in brief, because of the constitutional relationship between the United Kingdom and the Crown Dependencies.

OUTBOUND ISSUES

The territorial extent of CDDA powers of disqualification and the CDDA disqualification prohibitions

Great Britain

16–03 CDDA s.24 provides that the CDDA extends to England and Wales and to Scotland (i.e. the two jurisdictions that together comprise Great Britain). It does not extend to Northern Ireland. As between Scotland and England and Wales, the general rule where civil disqualification proceedings are to be issued is that a company registered in Scotland will give rise to disqualification proceedings in Scotland and a company registered in England and Wales will give rise to disqualification proceedings in England and Wales. The reason for this is that, depending on the particular provision under which jurisdiction is to be exercised, civil disqualification proceedings under the CDDA have to be issued either in the court with jurisdiction to wind up companies or (in England and Wales) the High Court or (in Scotland) the Court of Session. In the case of these latter two specifically identified courts, the English courts have, at High Court level, decided that the reference to those courts is on the basis of the insolvency jurisdiction of those courts such that, for example, proceedings under CDDA s.8 relating to a Scottish company have to be commenced in Scotland.[1]

16–04 As, by virtue of CDDA s.24, the Act extends to England and Wales and to Scotland, and given the definition of "company", a person subject to a disqualification order made by the courts in England and Wales is prima facie barred from acting in a prohibited capacity in relation to a Scottish-registered company (and vice versa). The position in relation to disqualification undertakings appears to be similar.

Company incorporated in England and Wales or in Scotland

16–05 Where the relevant company in relation to which misconduct has occurred is incorporated in England and Wales, there is no territorial restriction on the extent of the powers of the courts in England and Wales to disqualify "directors" or "persons" in CDDA ss.2–6, 8, 9A and 10 where those powers have been triggered. In other words, the court has the power to disqualify a "director" or "person" under the CDDA whether or not he resides outside, or is not present within, the normal jurisdiction of the courts in England and Wales, whether at the time of the proceedings or the time of the misconduct, provided that the relevant provision of the CDDA is otherwise applicable. This is the case regardless of the director's nationality. Moreover, there is also no requirement that the conduct complained of must have occurred within the jurisdiction or be directed from abroad but have some effect within the jurisdiction.[2] The position is the same with regard to disqualification in Scotland relating to conduct regarding a company incorporated there.

16–06 One effect of this is that a "sleeping" or nominee director who resides abroad and takes no active part in the company's affairs is, for example, exposed to the possibility of an application for disqualification under CDDA s.6 if the company becomes insolvent. The point is of particular relevance to certain residents of offshore jurisdictions whose practice is to accept nominee directorships in return

[1] *Re Helene Plc, Secretary of State for Trade and Industry v Forsyth* [2000] 2 B.C.L.C. 249.
[2] See generally *Re Seagull Manufacturing Co Ltd (No.2)* [1994] Ch. 91, considering what has been called the "territorial principle" set out in *Ex. p. Blain; In re Sawers* (1879) 12 Ch.D. 522 and considered by the House of Lords in *Clark v Oceanic Contractors Inc* [1983] 2 A.C. 130.

for a fee although they subsequently play no active part whatsoever in the running of the companies concerned.[3]

Service of proceedings abroad

16–07 However, as regards civil disqualification powers, the court may in its discretion refuse to allow disqualification proceedings to be served on a party outside the jurisdiction where it is not satisfied that there is a good arguable case against that party under the CDDA.[4] The provisions on service are set out in r.5(2) of the Disqualification Rules in relation to the powers of disqualification in CDDA ss.6, 8 and 9A and replicated for other civil disqualification proceedings by the Disqualification Practice Direction, paras 1.3 and 7.3.[5] Essentially the matter is left to the court's discretion and Section III of CPR Pt 6 does not apply.

Prohibitions

16–08 The prohibitions on acting in certain offices or capacities relating to a company incorporated in England and Wales or in Scotland also apply on a "worldwide" basis, irrespective of the nationality or location of the disqualified person concerned.

Northern Ireland and Great Britain

16–09 An equivalent regime to the CDDA was introduced in Northern Ireland by the Companies (Northern Ireland) Order 1989[6] and subsequently amended and consolidated by the Company Directors Disqualification (Northern Ireland) Order 2002.[7] The Northern Ireland regime is very similar to that under the CDDA.

Northern Ireland and Great Britain: effect of disqualification

16–10 As regards the position within Great Britain, in broad terms a disqualification imposed under the Northern Ireland disqualification regime is given effect in England and Scotland by the imposition of a Great Britain prohibition, similar to the prohibitions in CDDA ss.1 and 1A, in relation to a person disqualified in Northern Ireland. This is subject to one point, which is that in relation to a disqualification imposed under the legislation of Northern Ireland, the High Court in Northern Ireland retains jurisdiction to grant permission to act notwithstanding disqualification and there is no jurisdiction in the courts in Great Britain to grant such permission. With effect from April 2, 2001 s.12A was inserted into the CDDA by s.7(1) of the Insolvency Act 2000.[8] This provides that a disqualification order made under the Northern Ireland legislation in force at that date has the same scope

[3] See, e.g. *Re Kaytech International Plc, Secretary of State for Trade and Industry v Kaczer* [1999] 2 B.C.L.C. 351 and 16–79 below.

[4] See generally *Re Seagull Manufacturing Co Ltd (No.2)* [1994] Ch. 91. This practice is likely to be followed in Scotland and Northern Ireland.

[5] See also the Insolvency Rules 1986 r.12.12 and discussion in D. Griffiths (2005) 18(4) Insolv. Int. 54; A. Walters, I. Williams and H. Marsh (2006) 19(4) Insolv. Int. 58. See also *Re Busytoday Limited* [1992] 1 W.L.R. 683.

[6] SI 1989/2404 (NI 18).

[7] SI 2002/3150 (NI 4).

[8] Insolvency Act 2000 (Commencement No.1 and Transitional Provisions) Order 2001 (SI 2001/766).

as a disqualification order under CDDA s.1 and therefore has effect in England, Wales and Scotland.[9] A provision having identical effect as regards Northern Ireland disqualification undertakings was inserted as CDDA s.12B pursuant to powers in s.7(2) of the Insolvency Act 2000 with effect from September 1, 2004.[10] The effect of both ss.12A and 12B is that a person who is subject to a Northern Ireland disqualification is also made subject to a ban in terms that are very similar to CDDA ss.1 and 1A. Moreover, the criminal and civil liabilities for breach of disqualification orders or undertakings in CDDA ss.13–15 are expressly extended to cover breaches of the ss.12A and 12B prohibitions. The mechanism is closely analogous to that under CDDA ss.11 and 12 in that a qualifying condition (Northern Ireland disqualification) automatically triggers a specific ban under the CDDA in England, Wales and Scotland. It is, however, important to reiterate that the power to relieve from a Northern Ireland disqualification by granting permission to act remains with the Northern Ireland High Court, even in relation to the extended ban imposed by ss.12A and 12B. By art.17 of the Company Directors Disqualification (Northern Ireland) Order 2002, a person disqualified in Great Britain by order or undertaking, made or given, pursuant to the CDDA is disqualified to the same extent in Northern Ireland. Insofar as a CDDA disqualification imposed in Great Britain takes effect in Northern Ireland, art.17 of the 2002 Order confers jurisdiction on the Northern Ireland High Court (and not the relevant court in Great Britain) to grant permission to act notwithstanding disqualification.

Northern Ireland and Great Britain: power to disqualify in Great Britain

16–11 However, the power under the CDDA to disqualify regarding conduct in relation to a company incorporated in Northern Ireland is restricted. The relevant jurisdictional gateways to disqualification in the CDDA focus primarily on whether the person has held a relevant position or role with a "company". Furthermore, the court with civil jurisdiction to disqualify is usually the court with winding up jurisdiction in relation to such company. "Company" for these purposes includes a company liable to be wound up under Pt V of the Insolvency Act 1986. A company incorporated in Northern Ireland or a company incorporated outside the United Kingdom having a principal place of business situated in Northern Ireland cannot be wound up under Pt V of the Insolvency Act unless it also has a principal place of business situated in England and Wales and/or Scotland.[11] Insofar as disqualification proceedings are pursued successfully in Northern Ireland as

[9] See also the Company Directors Disqualification (Northern Ireland) Order 2002 (SI 2002/3150), arts 2(2), 3 and, in relation to undertakings, arts 4, 10 and 11 brought into force by the Company Directors Disqualification (2002 Order) (Commencement) Order (Northern Ireland) 2003 (SI 2003/345) with effect from July 22, 2003. For transitional provisions see the Company Directors Disqualification (2002 Order) (Transitional Provisions) Order (Northern Ireland) 2003 (SI 2003/346).

[10] See the Insolvency Act 2000 (Company Directors Disqualification Undertakings) Order 2004 (SI 2004/1941).

[11] Insolvency Act 1986 s.221(2) and see *Re Normandy Marketing Ltd* [1994] Ch. 198. Part V of the Insolvency Act 1986 now seems to be referred to as Pt 5 (i.e. arabic rather than roman numeral): see CDDA s.22(2)(b) as substituted by SI 2009/1941 with effect from October 1, 2009. For convenience, throughout this chapter and throughout the book as a whole reference is made to Pt V as per the statutory predecessor of the present s.22(2)(b).

regards misconduct relating to Northern Ireland companies, the point is of limited practical importance given that CDDA ss.12A–12B extend the effect of Northern Ireland disqualifications to Great Britain.

Crown Dependencies

16–12 The position regarding the law in the Crown Dependencies is dealt with below. For present purposes it is sufficient to note that, at the time of writing, there is no automatic carry over of a disqualification in one regime so that it has automatic effect in another. The position is therefore to be contrasted with that in Northern Ireland and under the CDDA. However, given the width of the effect of disqualification under the relevant legislation (both the CDDA and that of the Crown Dependencies), it will often be the case that a disqualification under one regime will have a practical effect on the ability of the disqualified person to act in relation to companies incorporated in the others. Further, the wide jurisdiction to disqualify under each regime will often mean that, as a matter of fact, the same misconduct may be open to action both in Great Britain and in any relevant connected Crown dependency. For example, a number of persons have been separately disqualified both under the CDDA and then, following separate proceedings, in the Isle of Man, on the basis of the same misconduct.

The definition of "company" in CDDA s.22(2)(b) and its effect regarding overseas companies

16–13 The various substantive powers of disqualification in the CDDA extend to the conduct of a "director" or, where relevant, a "person", relating to a "company". Further, in civil cases, the power to disqualify is vested in the court with jurisdiction to wind up that "company". Similarly, the primary prohibitions flowing from disqualification under the CDDA relate to disqualification from certain offices with, or conduct relating to, a "company". The meaning of "company" therefore becomes key. Before October 1, 2009, CDDA s.22(2)(b) provided that in all provisions of the CDDA except for s.11, the term "company" included "any company which may be wound up under Pt.V of the Insolvency Act". With effect from October 1, 2009, the current s.22(2)(b) was substituted by the Companies Act 2006 (Consequential Amendments, Transitional Provisions and Savings) Order 2009[12] with the result that "company" in the CDDA as a whole includes a company that may be wound up under Pt V. A company incorporated outside Great Britain may, in certain circumstances, be wound up by the court under Pt V and so, accordingly, conduct in relation to foreign companies is capable of falling within the scope of the CDDA disqualification powers and companies incorporated overseas may fall within the scope of all the disqualification prohibitions in the CDDA.

16–14 Under English rules of private international law, the courts have historically exercised an expansive winding up jurisdiction based on a test of sufficient connection between the foreign company and England and Wales. Sufficient connection is capable of being established, for example, where the company has carried on

[12] SI 2009/1941.

business and/or has assets in England and Wales and/or there are creditors within the jurisdiction who have an interest in the distribution of those assets.[13] However, the presence of assets within the jurisdiction should not be regarded as a pre-condition to the winding up of a foreign company. Thus, the availability of claims against the company's directors (for example, for misfeasance or wrongful trading) that would benefit creditors may justify the making of a winding up order.[14] In the normal run of cases an overseas company will be wound up only where there is a sufficient connection with the jurisdiction, there is a reasonable prospect of the winding up benefiting those applying for a winding up and the court has jurisdiction over one or more persons interested in the distribution of assets (the so-called *Latreefers* test).[15]

16–15 The first question is whether the definition in s.22(2)(b) requires the particular company to be one with a sufficient connection to the jurisdiction such that, as a matter of judicial discretion, it would, on the facts, be one that would be wound up or whether, in effect, it covers all foreign companies (subject to any bar created by the EC Insolvency Regulation or any other legislation, domestic or European) on the grounds that all foreign companies are capable of being wound up under Pt V of the Insolvency Act 1986, but irrespective of whether, on the facts of the particular case, the jurisdiction would be exercised. A similar issue has been raised in relation to the court's jurisdiction to sanction schemes of arrangement under what is now Pt 26 of the Companies Act 2006.[16]

16–16 In the context of schemes of arrangement, the issue has been whether or not a company is "liable to be wound up" under the Insolvency Act 1986. By reference to that wording, the English High Court has come to the conclusion, in *Re Drax Holdings Ltd*,[17] that the conditions which have to be satisfied under s.221(1) of the 1986 Act before the court will wind up a foreign company are matters of discretion rather than jurisdiction and that they do not have to be satisfied for the purposes of (what is now) s.895(2(b) of the Companies Act 2006. Companies are "liable" to be wound up within s.895(2)(b) even if those conditions are not satisfied. It is not necessary for the purposes of s.895(2)(b) that the grounds for winding up in s.221(5) exist on the facts of the particular case. However, the court still requires there to be a "sufficient connection" between the company and the jurisdiction, before the court will exercise its discretion to sanction a scheme.

[13] *Banque des Marchands de Moscou (Koupetschesky) v Kindersley* [1951] Ch. 112; *Re Compania Merobello San Nicholas SA* [1973] Ch. 75; *Re Eloc Elektro-Optieck and Comunicatie B.V.* [1982] Ch. 43; *International Westminster Bank Plc v Okeanos Maritime, Re a Company No.00359 of 1987* [1988] 1 Ch. 210.

[14] *Re Real Estate Development Co Ltd* [1991] B.C.L.C. 210; *Stocznia Gdanska SA v Latreefers Inc* [1999] 1 B.C.L.C. 271 affirmed [2001] 2 B.C.L.C. 116; *Re OJSC Ank Yugraneft* [2008] EWHC 2614 (Ch), [2009] 1 B.C.L.C. 298. It was also significant in *Stocznia Gdanska* that the contract debt on which the petition was based was expressly governed by English law. For a comprehensive account of the traditional jurisdiction of the English courts to wind up foreign companies see I. Fletcher, *Insolvency in Private International Law*, 2nd edn (Oxford: OUP, 2003) from p.153.

[15] See *Stocznia Gdanska SA v Latreefers Inc* [2001] 2 B.C.L.C. 116 in the context of a creditor petition. As regards public interest petitions see the slightly different formulation of the criteria in *Re Titan International Inc* [1998] 1 B.C.L.C. 102.

[16] Companies Act 2006 ss.895–901.

[17] [2003] EWHC 2743 (Ch), [2004] 1 W.L.R. 1049.

16–17 It is suggested that the words in the CDDA are to be interpreted differently to those in s.895 of the Companies Act 2006. The test of whether a company "may" be wound up looks not just to jurisdiction but also to the discretion to wind up; otherwise there is no natural limit to the mandatory requirement to disqualify in CDDA s.6 cases, nor to the prohibition on acting in relation to companies once a disqualification order is made. In such cases there is no residual discretion to be exercised, as there is in what is now s.899 of the Companies Act 2006, which enables the court to require there to be a sufficient connection with the jurisdiction. This has been the approach where the court has considered the extent of the prohibition on acting in relation to companies which flows from disqualification. Thus, in *Re Westminster Property Group Ltd (No.2), Official Receiver v Stern (No.2)*,[18] Mr William Stern had been disqualified for a period of 12 years. He sought permission to act notwithstanding disqualification in relation to 11 companies, some of which were not registered in Great Britain under the Companies Acts. The court declined to grant permission in relation to certain of the companies on the basis that it was unclear that those companies were sufficiently connected with the jurisdiction to engage the prohibition on acting. In considering the test for sufficient connection the court applied the *Latreefers* test, though it is at least arguable that the public interest discretionary test (being the *Latreefers* test adapted for those circumstances) is equally valid, in its place, or in the alternative.[19]

16–18 The second question is whether there are any limitations on the court's winding up jurisdiction flowing from more recent law and, in particular, EU law. As regards this there are at least three possible limitations which have to be considered:

(1) Council Regulation (EC) 44/2001 on jurisdiction and the recognition and enforcement of judgments in civil and commercial matters (the "2001 Judgments Regulation").
(2) EC Regulation on Insolvency Proceedings (the "EC Insolvency Regulation").[20]
(3) Other provisions of EC law, specific to certain types of company, for example: Directive 2001/17/EC of the European Parliament and of the Council of March 19, 2001 on the reorganisation and winding up of insurance undertakings as given effect to by the Insurers (Reorganisation and Winding Up) Regulations 2004 (the "2004 Insurance Regulations")[21] and Directive (2001/24/EC) of the European Parliament and of the Council of April 4, 2001 on the reorganisation and winding up of credit institutions as given effect to by the Credit Institutions (Reorganisation and Winding up) Regulations 2004 (the "2004 Credit Institutions Regulations").[22]

Leaving aside particular regimes applicable to certain types of specific company, the general position is as follows.

[18] [2001] B.C.C. 305.
[19] See, e.g. *Re Titan International Inc* [1998] 1 B.C.L.C. 102.
[20] Council Regulation 1346/2000.
[21] SI 2004/353 (as amended).
[22] SI 2004/1045 (as amended).

16–19 Under the 2001 Judgments Regulation, solvent companies will be capable of being wound up as such exclusively by the jurisdiction of their "seat". Paragraph 10 of Sch.1 of the Civil Jurisdiction and Judgments Order 2001[23] deals with the location of "seat" for the purposes of art.22 of the 2001 Judgments Regulation. Under that provision the "seat" of a company will be in the state under the laws of which it was incorporated or formed or where its central management and control is exercised. However, where the seat is in the UK because the company was incorporated or formed under the law of a part of the UK then it is not treated as having its seat in another EU state, even if its central management and control is in that state (see para.10(4) of the 2001 Order).

16–20 In the case of a company with its "centre of main interests" or an "establishment" in another Member State (with the exception of Denmark), the international jurisdiction of the English courts to wind up the company on insolvency grounds, involving collective creditor proceedings, is circumscribed by art.3 of the EC Insolvency Regulation. In this context it is immaterial whether or not the company is incorporated in an EC Member State as the EC Insolvency Regulation is engaged if the company (even if incorporated outside the EC) carries on business in a number of Member States so that an issue arises concerning how jurisdiction is to be allocated within the EC.[24] Article 3 has the following effect. Companies will normally be capable of being wound up in England and Wales on insolvency grounds in two circumstances only[25]:

(1) The English courts only have jurisdiction to open main winding up proceedings in relation to a company, wherever its place of incorporation is situated, if the company's centre of main interests is situated in England and Wales as opposed to anywhere else within the EU (apart from Denmark). There is a rebuttable presumption that the company's centre of main interests is situated in the place of its registered office. The significant point is that the test appears to be considerably stricter than the "sufficient connection" test applicable under English domestic rules of private international law.[26]
(2) The English courts may also open secondary or territorial winding up proceedings (confined to the local assets of the company) where the company has an establishment—defined in art.2(h) of the EC Insolvency Regulation as "any place of operations where the [company] carries out a non-transitory economic activity with human means and goods"—in England and Wales.

[23] SI 2001/3929 as amended by SI 2007/1655.

[24] The point derives support from *Re BRAC Rent-A-Car International Inc* [2003] EWHC 128 (Ch), [2003] 1 W.L.R. 1421.

[25] On the EC Regulation generally see I Fletcher, *Insolvency in Private International Law*, 2nd edn (Oxford: OUP, 2003), Ch.7; G Moss, I Fletcher and S Isaacs (eds), 2nd edn *The EC Regulation on Insolvency Proceedings: A Commentary and Annotated Guide* (Oxford: OUP, 2009).

[26] For the application of the centre of main interests test see, e.g. *Re Eurofood IFSC Ltd (C-341/04)* [2006] E.C.R. I-3813; *Re Daisytek-ISA* [2003] B.C.C. 562; *Re Sendo Ltd* [2005] EWHC 1604 (Ch), [2006] 1 B.C.L.C. 395; *MPOTEC GmbH* [2006] B.C.C. 681; *Hans Brochier Holdings Ltd v Exner* [2006] EWHC 2594 (Ch), [2007] B.C.C. 127; *Re Lennox Holdings Plc* [2009] B.C.C. 155; *Re Standford International Bank Ltd* [2009] EWHC 1441 (Ch).

16–21 Finally, if neither of these bases for jurisdiction are made out, there is a residual power in the English court to wind up on the just and equitable ground, essentially where the proceedings are being brought in the public interest under s.124A of the Insolvency Act 1986. This follows from the reasoning of Patten J. in *Re Marann Brooks CSV Ltd*.[27] In that case, although the point was not contested and did not arise on the facts, the court, in response to a request from the Secretary of State, ruled that public interest winding up proceedings under s.124A of the Insolvency Act 1986 fall outside the scope of the EC Insolvency Regulation. They had already been found to fall outside the scope of the 2001 Judgments Regulation.[28] This leaves open the argument that for CDDA purposes the English courts retain some winding up jurisdiction over most companies incorporated abroad based on sufficient connection, whether or not their centre of main interests is situated, or they have an establishment, in England and Wales and whether or not they are solvent with a seat in England and Wales.[29] However, even assuming that the argument that the court's winding up jurisdiction is not exhaustively regulated by the EC Regulation is correct, there remains the question of what would amount to a sufficient connection in the disqualification context. It seems unlikely that jurisdiction under the CDDA could be claimed unless the relevant conduct has affected creditors, or other stakeholders, situated in England and Wales and the need to protect the public within the jurisdiction has therefore arisen. In other words, it is suggested that the exercise of jurisdiction would be exorbitant and unjustified unless it can be demonstrated that the public here is in need of protection.[30]

16–22 The 2004 Insurance Regulations apply only to companies regulated as carrying on direct insurance business. The 2004 Credit Institution Regulations apply only to companies comprising an undertaking whose head office is in the United Kingdom with permission under Pt 4 of the Financial Services and Markets Act 2000 to accept deposits or to issue electronic money as the case may be, but does not include: (a) an undertaking which also has permission under Pt 4 of the 2000 Act to effect or carry out contracts of insurance; or (b) a credit union within the meaning of s.1 of the Credit Unions Act 1979. Various other entities (e.g. banks) are also excluded. In each case the relevant regimes cover both solvent and insolvent winding up and also appear to cover regulatory winding up proceedings. In each case the provisions limit, within the EU, the power to open winding up proceedings, broadly to the home state from where regulation takes place.[31]

[27] [2003] B.C.C. 239.

[28] *Re Senator Hanseatische Verwaltungsgesellschaft mbH* [1996] 2 B.C.L.C. 562 (Ch.D. and C.A.), [1997] 1 W.L.R. 515 (C.A.).

[29] See *Re Senator Hanseatische Verwaltungsgesellschaft mbH* [1996] 2 B.C.L.C. 562 (Ch.D. and C.A.), [1997] 1 W.L.R. 515 (C.A.); *Re Titan International Inc* [1998] 1 B.C.L.C. 102 (in which Knox J.'s test in *Re Real Estate Development Co Ltd* [1991] B.C.L.C. 210 was applied and refined in the case of a public interest winding-up petition).

[30] See, by analogy, *Re Titan International Inc* [1998] 1 B.C.L.C. 102.

[31] See generally G. Moss and B. Wessels, *EU Banking and Insurance Insolvency* (Oxford: OUP, 2006).

Allocation of jurisdiction within Great Britain

16–23 As regards foreign companies and CDDA powers that are capable of being exercised by a court having winding up jurisdiction (CDDA ss.2–4, 6 and 8),[32] the relevant deeming provisions for the purposes of establishing and allocating jurisdiction within Great Britain are set out in s.221(3) of the Insolvency Act 1986. In summary, an unregistered company (as defined by Pt V of the Insolvency Act 1986)[33] is deemed to be registered in England and Wales or Scotland according to the jurisdiction in which its principal place of business is situated. If it has a principal place of business situated in both countries, it will be deemed to be registered in both countries. The principal place of business situated in that part of Great Britain in which proceedings are being instituted is deemed to be its registered office. A company incorporated in Northern Ireland or a company incorporated outside the United Kingdom having a principal place of business situated in Northern Ireland cannot be wound up under Pt V of the Insolvency Act unless it also has a principal place of business situated in England and Wales and/or Scotland.[34]

Jurisdiction to disqualify: conclusions

16–24 In many cases, the question of whether the English or Welsh court has jurisdiction to disqualify where international elements are involved will not form the focus of any prolonged enquiry. That is usually because of other relevant jurisdictional requirements of the relevant section of the CDDA which sets out the power to disqualify. The international element will usually have to have been dealt with at the earlier stage of satisfying those jurisdictional requirements, and if those jurisdictional requirements are met then there will usually be a sufficient connection with the jurisdiction that the "company" in relation to which the misconduct has occurred will meet the statutory requirement that it is capable of being wound up within the jurisdiction. The point can be illustrated as follows.

(1) Under CDDA s.2, there first has to be a conviction of an indictable offence with a relevant connection to the company in question. Once it is established that there is jurisdiction to convict, notwithstanding relevant international elements, and once there has been a conviction then there are two possible venues for disqualification. If the convicting court is minded to exercise the power to disqualify, no further international question will arise. If the winding up court's jurisdiction to disqualify is invoked, then in most, if not all, cases it is unlikely that any international element will prevent disqualification. The conviction is likely to have taken place only if there was already sufficient connection between the misconduct and the jurisdiction. In those circumstances, there is likely to have been sufficient connection with the relevant company and the jurisdiction to found winding up jurisdiction such that the

[32] See *Re Helene Plc, Secretary of State for Trade and Industry v Forsyth* [2000] 2 B.C.L.C. 249 and 16–03 above.

[33] See further Chs 3 and 14 on the definitions of "company" and "unregistered company".

[34] See further 16–11 above.

company in question would fall within the relevant definition in CDDA s.22(2)(b). If nothing else, a public interest petition would be likely to have been well founded if based upon the matters underlying the conviction.

(2) In CDDA s.3 cases, there is a jurisdictional requirement of persistent default in relation to requirements, under provisions of companies legislation,[35] to make filings with the Registrar of Companies. In such cases, the winding up jurisdiction in relation to the company in question is likely to be self evidently applicable.

(3) In CDDA s.4 cases, the relevant misconduct has to have come to light in the context of a winding up within the jurisdiction, so that no further jurisdictional issue arising from any international element will arise.

(4) In CDDA s.5 cases, the convicting court will disqualify where there have been relevant convictions of breaches of companies legislation[36] requiring filings with the Registrar of Companies. The same comments made in relation to s.3 above apply.

(5) In CDDA s.6 cases, the lead company must first have entered a form of insolvency proceeding of a type specified by the Insolvency Act 1986. This will itself usually mean that it is obvious that the company could have been wound up under Pt V of the Insolvency Act 1986. However, as regards alleged collateral companies which are incorporated overseas there may be a very real issue on the facts as to whether such a company is capable of being wound up under Pt V of the Insolvency Act and accordingly whether it is a "company" within the meaning of s.6 of the CDDA.[37]

(6) In CDDA s.8 cases, the investigation that will first have to have been carried out will almost certainly require that a sufficient connection for jurisdiction under s.8 has been made out.

(7) Section 9A and s.10 cases may be more problematic. As regards s.10 interesting questions may arise in cases where the declaration under Insolvency Act 1986 ss.213 or 214 is made in proceedings where the court's jurisdiction has been invoked under appropriate international co-operation provisions.[38]

Disqualification prohibitions: conclusions

16–25 From October 1, 2009, "company" for the purposes of CDDA ss.1, 1A, 9B(3), 11, 12, 12A and 12B includes "a company that may be wound up under Pt 5 of the

[35] Namely the Companies Acts as defined by the Companies Act 2006 s.2(1): see CDDA s.22(7).

[36] This encompasses the same enactments for the purposes of ss.3 and.5: see CDDA s.22(7) and previous footnote.

[37] *Re Eurostem Maritime Ltd* [1987] P.C.C. 190. For these purposes, conduct in relation to a Scottish incorporated collateral company may be taken into account in English proceedings even though the Scottish court would have exclusive jurisdiction in relation to a Scottish incorporated lead company: see *Re Helene Plc, Secretary of State for Trade and Industry v Forsyth* [2000] 2 B.C.L.C. 249. On the distinction between lead and collateral companies, see text from 3–106.

[38] Such as Insolvency Act 1986 s.426.

Insolvency Act 1986."[39] It has been suggested that this formulation requires consideration to be given to whether the company in question has sufficient links to the jurisdiction to be wound up rather than that the prohibition extends to all foreign companies on the basis that they are capable of being wound up by the courts in England and Wales simply because such a connection might be established at some time in the future. The effect otherwise would be that the prohibitions in the CDDA would relate to any foreign company, even if it did not in fact have any connection with the jurisdiction. Even on this basis, the prohibitions still appear to apply very widely to foreign companies. This is clearly necessary as otherwise a disqualified person could evade the legal consequences of disqualification by the device of incorporating a company in an offshore jurisdiction.[40] It may be questioned whether the ability to wind up companies as unregistered companies is a sufficiently certain or satisfactory test for determining the scope of the prohibitions in these provisions of the CDDA. There may be something to be said for the link to be made clearer to understand as has been done in the case of some of the legislation adopted in the Crown Dependencies.[41] The question whether the court will grant permission to act in relation to foreign companies and/or declaratory relief to the effect that specified foreign companies are outside the scope of the prohibitions where there is uncertainty is considered further in the text at 14–33. As there noted, the court is unlikely to be enthusiastic about requests to clarify any difficulties flowing from factual, as opposed to legal, difficulties. This is borne out by the following passage from the judgment of Chadwick L.J., determining an application for permission to appeal in the *Stern* case, where the availability of declaratory relief to clarify whether or not on particular facts acting in respect of various overseas companies would fall within the disqualification prohibition was a live issue:

> "Nor, for my part, would I encourage courts to take the view that it was a sensible or appropriate course to make such declarations in this kind of case. The problem is that the court can only make a declaration as to an existing state of affairs on the basis of the material which is put before it. If, relying on that declaration, a party continues as a director of a company and is then prosecuted, the question for the criminal court will be whether on the material which is put before it—which is likely to include material which has come into existence since the matter was before the civil court and may include material which, although then available, was not before the civil court—the company concerned was a company within the winding up jurisdiction at the time when the offence is said to have been committed. It is because the question in criminal proceedings is likely to be different from the question which would be before the civil court when asked to make such a declaration that the utility of any such declaration seems to me extremely doubtful."[42]

[39] CDDA s.22(2)(b). Before October 1, 2009, "company" for the purposes of s.11 was separately defined in terms that were narrower in scope than the current wording of s.22(2)(b): see further 16–37.

[40] In the House of Lords debate which preceded the enactment of what became CDDA s.6, concern was expressed that: ". . . Rogues may well use Jersey or other overseas companies to avoid risk of disqualification" and that "the sanction of disqualification ought to extend to all companies which trade in the United Kingdom and are therefore likely to be compulsorily wound up there." (Lord Bruce of Donington, Hansard H.L. Vol.459, cols 571–572).

[41] See below from 16–55.

[42] *Re Westminster Property Group Ltd (No.2), Official Receiver v Stern (No.2)* [2001] EWCA Civ 111, [2002] B.C.C. 937 at [22].

The extraterritorial reach of the substantive powers to impose or agree to insolvency restrictions

Bankruptcy restrictions

16–26 The starting point as regards the power of the court to impose a bankruptcy restrictions order (or for a bankruptcy restrictions order to be agreed) is the extent of the court's bankruptcy jurisdiction in s.265 of the Insolvency Act 1986. Bankruptcy restrictions can only arise in relation to an individual where that individual has already become bankrupt.[43] The effect of s.265 is that a bankruptcy petition cannot be presented by one or more creditors or by the debtor himself (and, by extension, in such cases a bankruptcy order cannot be made) unless the debtor is: (a) domiciled in England and Wales; (b) personally present in England and Wales on the day on which the petition is presented; or (c) at any time in the period of three years ending with that day—(i) has been ordinarily resident, or has had a place of residence, in England and Wales, or (ii) has carried on business in England and Wales. For these purposes "the debtor carrying on business" includes the carrying on of business by a firm or partnership of which he is a member or the carrying on of business by an agent or manager for him or for such a firm or partnership. Section 265 is expressly subject to art.3 of the EC Regulation on Insolvency Proceedings with the consequence that in cases where the Regulation is engaged the court can only exercise bankruptcy jurisdiction where the debtor has his or her centre of main interests or an establishment in England and Wales.[44] It follows that a bankruptcy restrictions order could be made against a foreign debtor, or a bankruptcy restrictions undertaking accepted from a foreign debtor, insofar as the debtor falls within the court's bankruptcy jurisdiction. However, in addition to these main types of bankruptcy proceeding, bankruptcy may be initiated by petition by a temporary administrator (within the meaning of art.38 of the EC Insolvency Regulation), by a liquidator (within the meaning of art.2(b) of the EC Insolvency Regulation) appointed in proceedings by virtue of art.3(1) of that Regulation, by a supervisor of, or a person bound by, a voluntary arrangement proposed or approved under Pt VIII of the Insolvency Act 1986, by the Financial Services Authority under s.372 of the Financial Services and Markets Act 2000 or, following the making of a criminal bankruptcy order,[45] by the Official Petitioner or by any person specified in the order pursuant to s.39(3)(b) of the Powers of Criminal Courts Act 1973.

[43] Although not spelled out very clearly, this is inherent in the wording of Sch.4A of the Insolvency Act 1986, various paragraphs of which presuppose that the jurisdiction only arises in relation to bankrupts.

[44] For a detailed account of English bankruptcy jurisdiction see I. Fletcher, *Insolvency in Private International Law*, 2nd edn (Oxford: OUP, 2003), Ch.2. For the impact of the EC Insolvency Regulation see, e.g. *Shierson v Vlieland-Boddy* [2005] EWCA Civ 974, [2005] 1 W.L.R. 3966; *Skjevesland v Geveran Trading Co Ltd* [2002] EWHC 2898 (Ch), [2003] B.C.C. 391; *Stojevic v Komercni Banka AS* [2006] EWHC 3447 (Ch), [2007] B.P.I.R. 141; *Official Receiver v Eichler* [2007] B.P.I.R. 1636 (German national whose debts were incurred in Germany held to have moved his centre of main interests to England and Wales by the time the bankruptcy petition was presented).

[45] The power to make criminal bankruptcy orders was abolished by Criminal Justice Act 1988 s.101 with effect from April 3, 1989: see SI 1989/264.

Debt relief restrictions

16–27 The position regarding debt relief restrictions is similar to that applying to bankruptcy restrictions. Eligibility for a debt relief order is conditioned by broadly the same connecting factors that apply to bankruptcy.[46] The debtor has: (a) to have been domiciled in England and Wales on the application date; or (b) at any time during the period of three years ending with that date have been ordinarily resident, or had a place of residence, in England and Wales; or carried on business in England and Wales. For these purposes "the debtor carrying on business" includes the carrying on of business by a firm or partnership of which he is a member or the carrying on of business by an agent or manager for him or for such a firm or partnership. A debt relief restrictions order can only be made "in relation to a person in respect of whom a debt relief order has been made".[47] Although not as clear as might be expected, it would appear that a debt relief restrictions undertaking can only be accepted where a debt relief order has been made.

The extraterritorial reach of the prohibition in CDDA s.11 arising from personal insolvency and insolvency restrictions

Effect within Great Britain

16–28 In order to understand the effect of the CDDA s.11 prohibition within Great Britain it is necessary to consider in detail the legislative history of s.11 and, in particular, the impact of the Enterprise Act 2002 on its wording and overall scope. As originally enacted, s.11(1) was worded as follows:

> "It is an offence for a person who is an undischarged bankrupt to act as director of, or directly or indirectly to take part in or be concerned in the promotion, formation or management of, a company, except with the leave of the court."

It was beyond doubt that "undischarged bankrupt" in this provision included Scottish bankrupts as provision was made in s.11(2) for a Scottish bankrupt to apply for permission to act notwithstanding the s.11(1) prohibition to the court in Scotland by which sequestration was awarded. Moreover, by virtue of CDDA s.24, it was clear that the s.11(1) prohibition as originally enacted applied within Great Britain as a whole with the result that a person who was bankrupt in England and Wales was prohibited from acting in a relevant capacity in Scotland and vice versa.

The two versions of CDDA s.11(1)

16–29 By virtue of s.257(3) and Sch.21, para.5 of the Enterprise Act 2002, the original s.11(1) was substituted with effect from April 1, 2004[48] by a new s.11(1) which restated the prohibition on undischarged bankrupts and extended it to cover

[46] See Insolvency Act 1986 Sch.4ZA para.1. Debt relief orders are currently outside the scope of the EC Insolvency Regulation.

[47] Insolvency Act 1986 Sch.4ZB para.1.

[48] Enterprise Act 2002 (Commencement No. 4 and Transitional Provisions and Savings) Order 2003 (SI 2003/2093), art.2(2) and Sch.2.

persons in respect of whom a bankruptcy restrictions order is in force. However, it is clear from s.280(1) of the Enterprise Act that s.257(3) and, by extension, those amendments to other primary legislation referred to in Sch.21 to which it gives effect, extend only to England and Wales. It follows that the Enterprise Act had no effect on the original s.11(1) so far as it applied in Scotland. From April 1, 2004, the result was that the new s.11(1) applied in England and Wales while the original s.11(1) remained in force in Scotland. It is assumed that the reason for this divergence of treatment stems from devolution as, under the terms of the Scotland Act 1998, bankruptcy law provision for Scotland is, for the most part, devolved to the Scottish Parliament with the consequence that, as a general rule, the UK Parliament does not legislate on bankruptcy law in Scotland.[49]

16–30 The present wording of the version of s.11(1) introduced by the Enterprise Act 2002 was further substituted by s.108(3) and Sch.20, para.16 of the Tribunals, Courts and Enforcement Act 2007 with effect from April 6, 2009.[50] This wording extends the prohibition to persons in relation to whom a moratorium under a debt relief order applies and persons in respect of whom a debt relief restrictions order is in force. Schedule 20, para.16(1) expressly refers to "[s]ection 11(1) . . . as substituted in relation to England and Wales by the Enterprise Act 2002 . . ." thus making it clear that the 2007 Act, like the Enterprise Act, had no effect on the original s.11(1) insofar as it continues to apply in Scotland. In any event, it is clear from s.147 of the 2007 Act that s.108(3) of that Act itself extends only to England and Wales.

16–31 The bankruptcy restrictions regime was introduced in England and Wales by the Enterprise Act with effect from April 1, 2004. Since April 1, 2008 Scotland has had its own bankruptcy restrictions regime. Bankruptcy restrictions orders ("BROs") and bankruptcy restrictions undertakings ("BRUs") can be made or accepted pursuant to ss.56A and ss.56G (respectively) of the Bankruptcy (Scotland) Act 1985 which provisions were inserted in the 1985 Act by the Bankruptcy and Diligence etc (Scotland) Act 2007.[51] There is currently no debt relief order and debt relief restrictions regime in Scotland. Rather, the sequestration regime has been amended to introduce a route into bankruptcy for people on low income who do not own property and have very little in savings or other assets. This route is known as Low Income Low Assets (LILA). The policy behind LILA is much the same as the policy in England and Wales which lay behind the introduction of debt relief orders. However, the mode of implementation in Scotland has been to expand access to the Scottish bankruptcy regime rather than introduce a separate debt relief order regime. Thus, for the purposes

[49] For the effects of devolution on insolvency law generally see D. McKenzie Skene, *Corporate Insolvency* in *The Laws of Scotland: Stair Memorial Encyclopaedia* (Lexis Nexis, 2008 Reissue) at para.[3].

[50] Tribunals, Courts and Enforcement Act 2007 (Commencement No.7) Order 2009 (SI 2009/382) art.2.

[51] For commencement see the Bankruptcy and Diligence etc (Scotland) Act 2007 (Commencement No.3, Savings and Transitionals) Order 2008 (SSI 2008/115).

of CDDA s.11, it is the bankruptcy which triggers disqualification in the case of Scottish LILA debtors.

CDDA s.11(1): debt relief orders and debt relief restrictions

16–32 In the light of the legislative history outlined above, it is clear as regards persons to whom a moratorium period under a debt relief order and persons in respect of whom a debt relief restrictions order[52] is in force that the s.11(1) prohibition extends only to England and Wales. Thus, CDDA s.24 notwithstanding, the prohibition on such persons acting does not apply in Scotland. Moreover, for the prohibition to apply in Scotland, in the authors' view, it would require an amendment to the original s.11(1) which, as was seen above, remains in force in Scotland. Although, personal insolvency law is a devolved matter, there is a question as to whether amendment of the original s.11(1) is reserved to the UK Parliament, a point which is revisited below in 16–34 in relation to bankruptcy restrictions.

CDDA s.11(1): bankruptcy

16–33 The position as regards bankruptcy and BROs is even more difficult. Starting with bankruptcy, the first question is whether a person who is an undischarged bankrupt in England and Wales falls within the original s.11(1) which, since April 1, 2004, is applicable only in Scotland. The original s.11(1) prior to April 1, 2004 clearly applied to both Scottish and England and Wales bankruptcies. It is suggested that, although the original s.11(1) remains in force only in Scotland, this does not affect the construction to be given to the phrase "undischarged bankrupt" in the original s.11(1) and that it encompasses both Scottish and England and Wales bankruptcies. More problematic is the construction to be given to the term "undischarged bankrupt" as it applies in s.11(1) as substituted (and amended) and applicable solely to England and Wales. Is a Scottish undischarged bankrupt an "undischarged bankrupt" for the purposes of s.11(1)(a) as applicable in England and Wales? There is clearly a strong policy argument that, if possible, s.11(1) as applicable to England and Wales should be so construed. The obvious purpose of the amendments to s.11(1), read cumulatively, was to extend the application of s.11 to bankruptcy restrictions, debt relief orders and debt relief restrictions in England and Wales, rather than to narrow the prohibition to exclude Scottish bankruptcies. Although s.11(1) altered the layout of the wording it used exactly the same term "undischarged bankrupt" as before and s.11(2) still implies that for these purposes both Scottish and English bankruptcies are covered. On the other hand, and regrettably, there is considerable scope for an argument that, in enacting a version of s.11(1) solely applicable to England and Wales, only English and Welsh legal concepts as there set out are caught. On this basis, s.11(1), as applicable to England and Wales, applies only to English and Welsh

[52] Or undertaking. As noted in the text, such orders can currently only be imposed, and such undertakings can only be given and accepted, in England and Wales.

bankruptcies. It should no more apply to Scottish bankruptcies, the argument would run, than to Northern Ireland or, say, German bankruptcies. However, on balance, the authors suggest that the history of the matter supports the view that in s.11(1) as applied to England and Wales, the term "undischarged bankrupt" covers not only "undischarged bankrupts" who have that status in England and Wales but persons who have that status under Scots law. It is unfortunate that there is any doubt on this issue which has been created by inadequate legislative drafting. The point could be put beyond doubt if s.11(1)(a) were to be extended expressly to Scottish bankrupts. In the authors' view, such an extension could not be effected by the Secretary of State pursuant to the power in s.268 of the Enterprise Act 2002. As the s.268 power is also relevant in the context of bankruptcy restrictions, it is considered further in the next paragraph. The short point here is that the s.268 power permits the classes of bankrupts to which relevant disqualification provisions apply to be reduced not expanded.

CDDA s.11(1): bankruptcy restrictions

16–34 Dealing first with the position in Scotland, the original s.11(1), as now solely applicable to Scotland, has not been extended to encompass a person subject to bankruptcy restrictions in either England and Wales or Scotland. This is in stark contrast to, for example, s.51 of the Insolvency Act 1986 (as amended), which expressly extends the prohibition on acting as a Scottish receiver appointed by the holder of a floating charge under Scots law to persons subject to England and Wales BROs and BRUs as well as those subject to Scottish BROs or BRUs.[53] Although there is a wide power conferred on the Scottish ministers under the Bankruptcy (Scotland) Act 1985 s.71B (as inserted by the Bankruptcy and Diligence etc (Scotland) Act 2007 s.5) to amend or extend relevant disqualifications flowing from, inter alia, England and Wales BROs, BRUs and bankruptcies, there is a question as to whether the original s.11(1) is a reserved matter, meaning that s.11(1) would need to be amended by the UK Parliament (or pursuant to powers conferred by the UK Parliament) rather than by Scottish primary or delegated legislation.[54] In the authors' view, on the assumption that it is a reserved matter, the necessary amendment could be made by the Secretary of State by statutory instrument pursuant to the power in s.268 of the Enterprise Act 2002.[55] This power enables the Secretary of State to amend, or modify the effect of, a disqualification provision (being a provision which disqualifies a bankrupt or class of bankrupts from being elected or appointed to an office or position, holding an office or position, or becoming or remaining a member of a body or

[53] See especially the amendments to Insolvency Act 1986 s.51(6) and the sub-sections of s.51 effected by the Bankruptcy and Diligence etc (Scotland) Act 2007 s.3.

[54] What is devolved and what is reserved turns on interpretation of Scotland Act 1998 ss.29 and 30 and Sch.5. Sch.5, Head C1 deals with business associations and Head C2 deals with insolvency and, in each case, sets out what is reserved, with some exceptions.

[55] This provision extends to England and Wales, Scotland and Northern Ireland: see Enterprise Act 2002 s.280.

group) inter alia so as to reduce the class of bankrupts to whom the provision applies or so as to extend the provision to some or all individuals who are subject to a bankruptcy restrictions regime. For these purposes a "bankrupt" includes an individual who has been adjudged bankrupt by a court in England and Wales or in Northern Ireland or whose estate has been sequestrated in Scotland and a "bankruptcy restrictions regime" means an order or undertaking under Sch.4A to the Insolvency Act 1986 (i.e. BROs and BRUs made or accepted in England and Wales) or under any system operating in Scotland or Northern Ireland which appears to the Secretary of State to be equivalent to the system operating under that Schedule.[56] Accordingly, and subject to any devolution issues, the Secretary of State could extend the application of the original s.11(1) to persons who are subject to BROs or BRUs made or accepted anywhere in the United Kingdom. It is clear that s.268 power can be used to amend or modify disqualification provisions in primary legislation as the word "provision" in s.268(2) of the Enterprise Act is not limited to secondary legislation.[57] However, the s.268 power has not been extended by the Tribunal, Courts and Enforcement Act 2007 to encompass debt relief orders or debt relief restrictions orders.

16–35 The next question is whether, as a matter of construction of English law, the amended s.11(1)(b) as applicable in England and Wales can be construed to include persons in respect of whom a Scottish BRO[58] is in force. The view expressed in the Insolvency Service's Technical Manual is that a reference in primary legislation to a BRO or BRU being in force is capable of encompassing Scottish BROs and BRUs as exactly the same terminology ("bankruptcy restrictions orders" and "bankruptcy restrictions undertakings") used in the Insolvency Act 1986 is used in the Bankruptcy (Scotland) Act 1985. If this is correct then the reference to persons subject to bankruptcy restrictions in CDDA s.11(1)(b) should be read as extending to Scottish BROs and BRUs. However, the authors doubt that this view is correct. The s.11(1)(b) prohibition is territorially limited to England and Wales and, when enacted, it could, in any event, only have referred to BROs and BRUs under English law. The legal concepts of BROs and BRUs did not come into being under Scots law until the enactment of the Bankruptcy and Diligence etc (Scotland) Act 2007. Furthermore, the CDDA 1986 is to be read together with the Insolvency Act 1986. BROs and BRUs under that Act are solely English and Welsh BROs/BRUs and the relevant provisions, and the relevant change to s.11(1), were both inserted by the Enterprise Act 2002. It is far from obvious that a provision of English law, referring to a concept under English law, can be read as including an equivalent or analogous concept introduced subsequently in another jurisdiction even where that concept is modelled on the English concept and bears the same nomenclature. Again, the drafting of s.51 of the Insolvency Act 1986[59] is striking.

[56] Enterprise Act 1968 s.268(9), (10).

[57] Moreover, the power has been used to amend or modify several disqualification provisions found in primary legislation: see the Enterprise Act 2002 (Disqualification from Office: General) Order 2006 (SI 2006/1722) and discussion in the text from 11–28.

[58] Including, for these purposes, a BRU: see Insolvency Act 1986 Sch.4A para.8.

[59] As amended by the Bankruptcy and Diligence etc (Scotland) Act 2007 s.3.

In extending the prohibition on appointment as a receiver (by, or on the application of, a holder of a floating charge) under Scottish law to persons subject to bankruptcy restrictions, this provision of Scots law makes express and separate reference to Scottish bankruptcy restrictions and English bankruptcy restrictions rather than to a global concept of "bankruptcy restrictions". The authors consider that the better view therefore is that the amended s.11(1)(b) prohibition as applicable in England and Wales does not extend to Scottish bankruptcy restrictions and requires amendment to achieve this effect. Such amendment could be made pursuant by the Secretary of State pursuant to s.268 of the Enterprise Act 2002.[60]

16–36 A final question that arises on the assumption that the analysis in the previous paragraph is correct, and in the absence of legislative amendment along the lines suggested, is whether English bankruptcy restrictions can be extended to Scotland and vice versa by recourse to s.426(1) of the Insolvency Act 1986. This provides that an order made by a court in one part of the United Kingdom in the exercise of jurisdiction in relation to insolvency law shall be enforced in any other part of the United Kingdom as if it were made by a court exercising the corresponding jurisdiction in that other part. There is no doubt, for example, that a Scottish BRO is a court order falling within s.426(1)[61] and to this extent it is capable of being "enforced" by a court having insolvency jurisdiction in England and Wales. It is questionable whether an "order made by a court" would include a BRU as, both north and south of the border, BRUs are concluded by administrative means without the involvement of the court. Moreover, there is a more fundamental difficulty surrounding what is meant by "enforcement" for these purposes. At first sight it is not clear that "enforcement" means more than enforcing the terms of the order, for example, in the case of a Scottish BRO, by means of further injunction purporting to extend the prohibitive effect of the order to England and Wales. However, it is not clear that such "enforcement" within England and Wales could encompass the statutory consequences of breach of s.11(1) (as applicable in England and Wales) set out in CDDA ss.13 and 15, at least unless and until the English courts imposed an English BRO (if able so to do) and the breach occurred after that date. There is the further complication that the definition of "insolvency law" for these purposes specifically does not include s.11 of the CDDA.[62]

CDDA s.11: foreign companies with an established place of business in Great Britain

16–37 By virtue of the then CDDA s.22(2)(a), before October 1, 2009, the term "company" in CDDA s.11(1) included "an unregistered company and a company incorporated outside Great Britain which has an established place of business in Great Britain". From October 1, 2009, CDDA s.11(4)[63] provides that "company" in s.11 "includes a company incorporated outside Great Britain which has an established place of

[60] See, in particular, Enterprise Act 2002 s.268(5)(b), 10(b) and discussion in 16–34.
[61] See Insolvency Act 1986 s.426(1), (10)(b).
[62] Insolvency Act 1986 s.426(10)(a).
[63] Inserted by SI 2009/1941.

business in Great Britain" (i.e. the same wording as the former s.22(2)(a) omitting the reference to unregistered companies). The s.11(1) prohibitions thus extend to foreign companies.[64] The question of what constitutes an "established place of business" was considered by Hirst J. in *Cleveland Museum of Art v Capricorn Art International SA*[65] in the context of determining whether a writ had been validly served on an oversea company for the purposes of s.695 of the Companies Act 1985.[66] In summary, it appears that a company will have an established place of business within Great Britain if it has a specified or identifiable place at which it carries on business. It is not essential that there be some visible sign or physical indication of a connection with particular premises (though the absence of such factors may point against there being an established place of business). It is not necessary for the main activities of the company to be carried out at the locality in question and it is sufficient if the activities carried on at the relevant place within Great Britain are restricted to matters incidental to its main business. The term "established" connotes more than the mere setting up of a place of business at a specific location, suggesting also a degree of permanence and something that is intended to have more than a fleeting character. In the words of Oliver L.J. in *Re Oriel Ltd*, a decision relied upon by Hirst J. in the *Cleveland Museum* case:

> ". . . If for instance, agents of an overseas company conduct business from time to time by meeting clients or potential clients in the public rooms of an hotel in London, they have, no doubt, 'carried on business' in England, but I would for my part find it very difficult to persuade myself that the hotel lounge was 'an established place of business'. The concept, as it seems to me, is of some more or less permanent location, not necessarily owned or even leased by the company, but at least associated with the company and from which habitually or with some degree of regularity business is conducted."[67]

To some extent, this may not be dissimilar to the concept of "establishment" as defined in art.2(h) of the EC Regulation on Insolvency Proceedings ("any place of operations where the debtor carries out a non-transitory economic activity with human means and goods") although care is needed bearing in mind the differences in wording.[68] It appears that a place of business is capable of being sufficiently

[64] Note, however, the approach in Companies Act 2006 s.1044 where, for the purposes of the Companies Acts an "overseas company" means a company incorporated outside the UK. This is wider than the definition of "oversea company" in s.744 of the 1985 Act which it replaces. The definition in s.744 refers to companies incorporated outside Great Britain that establish a place of business in Great Britain. Under Pt 34 of the 2006 Act the Secretary of State may make provision by regulations inter alia requiring overseas companies to register particulars with the Registrar of Companies. These regulations may specify the connection with the UK that gives rise to the various disclosure obligations imposed under the 2006 Act: see, e.g. Companies Act 2006 s.1046(2). The point is now somewhat academic given that the scope of the s.11 prohibition has been widened to encompass companies that may be wound up under Pt V of the Insolvency Act 1986: see further 16–38.

[65] [1990] 2 Lloyd's Rep. 166.

[66] See now Companies Act 2006 s.1139(2).

[67] [1986] 1 W.L.R. 180 at 184.

[68] See also and compare the definition in Sch.1 to the Cross-Border Insolvency Regulations 2006 (SI 2006/1030): "any place of operations where the debtor carries out a non-transitory economic activity with human means and assets or services".

"permanent" at the moment that it is set up, so that it is not automatically the case that it will only become "established" after a passage of time.

16–38 It was unfortunate that, before October 1, 2009, the definition of a "company" for the purposes of the relevant prohibition in CDDA s.11 should have differed from that in CDDA ss.1, 1A, 9B(3), 12 and 12B. There was no good policy reason why this should have been so. It was also unfortunate that the use of the term "established" raised the possibility that an undischarged bankrupt, a person subject to a debt relief order or a person subject to insolvency restrictions would not have been barred from acting in a prohibited capacity in relation to a foreign company which had a place of business within the jurisdiction but one which had not become sufficiently "permanent" or, put another way, was so "fleeting" as to prevent it from becoming "established". In such cases, damage could still have been inflicted on the British public by the conduct of a person who was automatically disqualified under s.11, but traded with British customers or suppliers from an offshore location (for example, over the internet). The meaning of "company" in the CDDA prohibitions, including the prohibitions in s.11, is now uniformly defined in CDDA s.22(2)(b) to include companies that may be wound up under Pt V of the Insolvency Act 1986. Accordingly, the scope of the s.11 prohibition is now potentially wider than it was previously and no longer depends on there being an established place of business in Great Britain. Given the scope of the current CDDA s.22(2)(b) it is not clear to the authors why the definition in s.11(4) has been retained.

The extraterritorial reach of the CDDA arising from Council Regulation 2157/2001 on the European Company

16–39 With the coming into force of Council Regulation 2157/2001 of October 8, 2001 on October 8, 2004, it is possible to incorporate a European Company (*societas europaea*) by registration in the United Kingdom.[69] Although strictly a creature of Community Law, it is clear from arts 9, 10 and 15 of the Regulation that such a company will be treated as if it were a registered public limited company and that, accordingly, it will be a "company" falling within the scope of the CDDA prohibitions. In any event, art.47 of the Regulation provides that, as a matter of Community law, a person is prohibited from acting as a member of the management or supervisory organ of a European Company if: (a) he is disqualified under the law of the Member State in which the company's registered office is situated from serving on the corresponding organ of a public limited company governed by the law of that Member State; or (b) he is disqualified from serving on the corresponding organ of a public limited company governed by the law of a member state owing to a judicial or administrative decision in a Member State. It follows that a person disqualified under any of CDDA ss.1, 1A, 9B(3), 11, 12, 12A and 12B, which embrace all types of registered companies including public companies, will be prohibited from being a member of the organs of a European Company whether registered in the

[69] For background see DTI, *Implementation of the European Company Statute: The European Public Limited-Liability Company Regulations—A Consultative Document* (2003) and *Implementation of the European Company Statute: The European Public Limited-Liability Company Regulations—Results of Consultation* (2004).

United Kingdom or in any other Member State.[70] This appears to be the first example of provision being made in directly applicable EC law that gives disqualification provisions in the domestic law of Member States an EU-wide effect.

16–40 A further supranational corporate form, the European Private Company (*societas privata europaea*) is to be introduced and available in Member States with effect from July 1, 2010.[71] As its name suggests, the object of this proposal is to create a standard, uniform private company vehicle for small and medium-sized enterprises that wish to expand their business beyond the borders of a single Member State and provide such enterprises with an alternative to incorporating subsidiaries or establishing branches in other Member States. A European Private Company will be a creature of Community Law formed by registration in the Member State in which it has its registered office. The effect of art.30(3), (4) of the proposed Regulation is twofold. First, the disqualification of a person serving as a director of a European Private Company is to be governed by the applicable national law. It follows that where the company is registered in Great Britain, the powers to disqualify directors in the CDDA will apply. Secondly, a person who is disqualified under national law from serving as a director of a company by a judicial or administrative decision of a Member State may not become or serve as a director of a such a company. A person disqualified under any of CDDA ss.1, 1A, 9B(3), 11, 12, 12A and 12B or the equivalent provisions in Northern Ireland will therefore be prohibited from acting as a director of a European Private Company whether it is registered in the United Kingdom or in any other Member State unless he has the permission of the court.

The effect within Great Britain of bankruptcy restrictions arising from legislation other than the CDDA

16–41 The CDDA s.11 prohibition triggered by BROs and BRUs and the problems associated with the construction of that provision have been considered above.[72] BROs and BRUs made in England and Wales give rise to a range of prohibitions under the Insolvency Act 1986 and other legislation so far as those provisions apply in England and Wales.[73] In such cases the question of whether a BRO/BRU under English law will give rise to a prohibition under Scots law and the reverse question of whether a BRO/BRU under Scots law will give rise to a prohibition under English law will turn on the specific prohibition in question and how it is to be

[70] One slight doubt that arises is whether a person banned under the CDDA from acting as a director of a company would be prohibited from acting as a member of the supervisory organ of a European Company where, as is contemplated by art.8 of the Regulation, a two-tier board structure is adopted. art.47(2) refers to "the corresponding organ" but in the United Kingdom, there is no requirement for public companies to have a supervisory as well as a management board. It is suggested that art.47 will be given a generous reading in line with its obvious purpose. See now also the European Public Limited-Liability Company Regulations 2004 (SI 2004/2326), especially reg.78.

[71] See Proposal for a Council Regulation on the Statute for a European Private Company COM (2008) 396/3. For background see R. Drury, "The European Private Company" (2008) 9(1) European Business Organization L.R. 125; B. Mackowiz and F. Saifee, "Societas Privata Europaea: the European Private Company" (2009) 30(8) Co. Law. 227.

[72] See text from 16–28.

[73] See text from 11–34.

interpreted.[74] As a starting point, however, the authors would suggest that, absent specific statutory definition, under English law a reference to BROs and BRUs will be to those concepts under English law and that under Scots law a reference to BROs and BRUs will be to those concepts under Scots law. Very often there will, however, be a specific identification of BRO/BRUs by reference to the specific legislation under which they come into being.[75] The starting point in that respect is s.51 of the Insolvency Act 1986,[76] considered above in 16–34 and 16–35, which lays down a prohibition on acting as a receiver under Scots law in relation to a floating charge as appointed by or at the behest of the charge holder. That provision expressly extends the Scots law prohibition to persons subject to English BROs (and BRUs) as well as those subject to BROs (and BRUs) under Scots law.[77] Section 51 of the Insolvency Act 1986 can be contrasted with the provisions extending the prohibitions flowing from bankruptcy restrictions,[78] debt relief restrictions and moratoria under debt relief orders[79] to cover acting as receiver or manager (Insolvency Act 1986 s.31) and acting as an insolvency practitioner (Insolvency Act 1986 s.390). As regards BROs and BRUs the same arguments rehearsed above in 16–35 in relation to the CDDA s.11(1) prohibition that applies in England and Wales are also relevant. In the authors' view, such prohibitions do not extend to Scottish BROs and BRUs. It is also telling that s.390 of the Insolvency Act 1986, which applies throughout Great Britain,[80] does not yet appear to have been extended (as regards its application in either Scotland or England and Wales) so that Scottish BROs and BRUs give rise to a relevant prohibition. The authors consider that such an extension could be made by the Secretary of State pursuant to s.268 of the Enterprise Act 2002 on the same analysis set out in 16–34.[81]

[74] In some cases it is absolutely clear that Scottish (and Northern Irish) BROs/BRUs do not have a UK-wide effect as regards the relevant prohibition. Sections 426A and 427 of the Insolvency Act 1986 provide one example of a misalignment between the consequences of BROs and BRUs made in England and Wales and those made in Scotland pursuant to the Bankruptcy (Scotland) Act 1985 (as amended) and in Northern Ireland. Whereas the effect of s.426A is that a person the subject of bankruptcy restrictions in England and Wales suffers various disqualifications in connection with membership of the Westminster Parliament, s.427 currently only applies the same disqualifications to Scottish and Northern Ireland undischarged bankrupts.

[75] In Scotland, see e.g. National Health Service (General Medical Services Contracts) (Scotland) Regulations 2004 (SSI 2004/115), under which, at the time of writing, a disability arose solely from English BROs/BRUs.

[76] As amended by the Bankruptcy and Diligence etc (Scotland) Act 2007 s.3.

[77] Note also the extension of the prohibitions under the Local Government (Scotland) Act 1973 s.31 so that they are triggered by both English and Scottish BROs and BRUs, as effected by the Bankruptcy and Diligence etc (Scotland) Act 2007 s.4. Note also the wide power conferred on the Scottish Ministers under the Bankruptcy (Scotland) Act 1985 s.71B (as inserted by the Bankruptcy and Diligence etc (Scotland) Act 2007 s.5) to amend or extend relevant disqualifications flowing from, inter alia, English BROs, BRUs and bankruptcies. For a further example of drafting that makes specific reference to BROs or orders to like effect in Scotland and Northern Ireland see the Care Quality Commission (Membership) Regulations 2008 (SI 2008/2252).

[78] As introduced by Enterprise Act 2002 s.257 and Sch.21. For the territorial extent of this provision see s.280 of the 2002 Act.

[79] As inserted by the Tribunals, Courts and Enforcement Act 2007 s.108(3) and Sch.20.

[80] See Insolvency Act 1986 s.440.

[81] In this respect note that the s.268 power is not territorially limited to England and Wales: see Enterprise Act 2002 s.280. Further, regulation of insolvency practitioners is clearly a reserved matter: see Scotland Act 1998 Sch.5 para.C2.

INBOUND ISSUES

Recognition of overseas prohibitions

16–42 Recognition in the United Kingdom of disqualifications equivalent or analogous to CDDA disqualifications imposed under foreign laws is an area that, until the enactment of Pt 40 of the Companies Act 2006 has been largely unexplored and undeveloped. Even within the UK the scope for recognition and giving effect to Northern Ireland disqualifications within Great Britain and vice versa has been a comparatively recent development. There is scope for the courts in the United Kingdom having jurisdiction in relation to insolvency law to assist the courts having corresponding jurisdiction in countries or territories that have been designated for the purposes of s.426 of the Insolvency Act 1986. For these purposes, it is clear that a United Kingdom court has some jurisdiction to assist a court in a designated country or territory in relation to questions of disqualification under provisions in the law of the relevant country or territory that correspond to CDDA ss.1A, 6–10, 12–15, 19(c), 20, Sch.1 and ss.1–17 as they apply for the purposes of those provisions.[82]

16–43 The first concrete step in the recognition of overseas disqualifications was very modest. Scottish disqualifications have always been recognised and given effect to in England and Wales (and vice versa) under the CDDA as enacted, because the CDDA applies both in England and Wales and in Scotland.[83] However, Northern Ireland disqualifications were not recognised until some years after the CDDA was enacted. Recognition of Northern Ireland disqualifications under the law of England and Wales (and Scotland) was effected by the mechanism of automatically extending the effect of such disqualifications as if they were made under the law of England and Wales (and Scotland). The relevant changes were made by the insertion of ss.12A and 12B into the CDDA. These insertions were effected respectively by the Insolvency Act 2000 s.7(1) and by the Insolvency Act 2000 (Company Directors Disqualification Undertakings) Order 2004.[84] Disqualifications made under the CDDA (applicable in England and Wales and Scotland) are given recognition in Northern Ireland under art.17 of the Company Directors Disqualification (Northern Ireland) Order 2002.[85] However, the manner in which disqualifications are recognised is not symmetrical. As regards Northern Ireland disqualifications, it is the Northern Ireland High Court which retains exclusive power to grant permission to act notwithstanding disqualification, throughout the United Kingdom.[86] However, as regards Great Britain disqualifications which are recognised and given effect to within Northern Ireland, it is the Northern Ireland High Court, and not the courts of Great Britain, which is given

[82] Insolvency Act 1986 s.426(4), (5), (10).

[83] Though there are problems in relation to the applicability throughout Great Britain of the prohibitions in CDDA s.11(1): see text from 16–28 above.

[84] SI 1941/2004.

[85] SI 2002/3150 (NI 4).

[86] On the effect of Northern Ireland disqualifications in Great Britain and the retained jurisdiction of the Northern Ireland High Court to grant leave to act see CDDA 1986, ss.12A(a) and 12B(b).

the exclusive power by art.17 of the 2002 Order to grant permission to act in Northern Ireland notwithstanding disqualification.

Part 40 of the Companies Act 2006

16–44 A more far reaching change was made by Pt 40 of the Companies Act 2006 (ss.1182–1191). Pt 40 contains a series of enabling provisions which empower the Secretary of State to establish by statutory instrument a regime by which effect can be given to foreign disqualifications, or foreign restrictions as they are defined by the 2006 Act, within the United Kingdom. In particular, it will enable restrictions to be applied as regards acting in certain capacities with regard to companies registered within any part of the United Kingdom. To that extent it was enacted to "close the gap" in the law, whereby persons subject to foreign disqualification can still operate, without restriction, in relation to UK companies.[87] However, somewhat surprisingly it does not enable these restrictions to be applied to overseas companies, the conduct of the affairs of which may have an effect within the United Kingdom. Accordingly, it may be said still to have left a gap in relation to overseas companies which may have an effect within the United Kingdom.

16–45 The provision is particularly important in the EC context bearing in mind the ease with which nationals from other Member States can incorporate in the UK because of freedom of establishment.[88] The same is, of course, true regarding disqualifications imposed in the Crown Dependencies. Pt 40 came into force on October 1, 2009[89] but at the time of writing no secondary legislation required to implement the regime had been promulgated. Any such legislation is subject to the affirmative resolution procedure.[90]

16–46 Part 40 strictly falls outside the company law provisions of the 2006 Act and does not form part of the Companies Acts as defined by that legislation. This is because Pt 40 is linked to the CDDA which, as has been seen throughout this book, does not merely apply to registered companies.[91]

16–47 The central legislative concept in Pt 40 is "a person subject to foreign restrictions". Companies Act 2006 s.1182(2) provides that a person is subject to foreign restrictions if under the law of a country or territory outside the UK:

(1) he is, by reason of misconduct or unfitness, disqualified to any extent from acting in connection with the affairs of a company; or

[87] See Explanatory Notes to the Companies Act 2006 (hereafter "Explanatory Notes"), para.1506. There is similar, albeit less extensive, provision in the Australia (Corporations Act 2001 (Cth.)) s.206B, Guernsey (The Companies (Guernsey) Law, 2008 s.137(2)(c)) and Ireland (Companies Act 1990 s.160(2)(i)).

[88] See, e.g. *Centros Ltd v Erhverus-og Selskabsstyrelsen* (C-212/97) [1999] ECR I-1459.

[89] The Companies Act 2006 (Commencement No.8, Transitional Provisions and Savings) Order 2008 (SI 2008/2860).

[90] Companies Act 2006 s.1184(7).

[91] Explanatory Notes, para.1507.

(2) he is, by reason of misconduct or unfitness required either to obtain permission from a court or other authority or to meet any other condition[92] before acting in connection with the affairs of a company; or
(3) he has, by reason of misconduct or unfitness, given undertakings to a court or other authority of a country or territory outside the UK not to act in connection with the affairs of a company or restricting the extent to which, or the way in which, he may do so.

For these purposes, "acting in connection with the affairs of a company" is defined as doing any of: (a) being a director of a company; (b) acting as a receiver of a company's property; or (c) being concerned or taking part in the promotion, formation or management of a company.[93] "Company" in s.1182 is defined as "a company incorporated or formed under the law of the country or territory in question" and "director" and "receiver" are defined by reference to corresponding officers in the relevant foreign law. The purpose of s.1182 is to encompass all those who have been disqualified under, or fallen foul of, a foreign law equivalent to the CDDA.[94]

16–48 Companies Act 2006 s.1184(1) creates an enabling power in the Secretary of State and there are further supplementary provisions in ss.1184–1191 that deal with the scope of the regulations that the Secretary of State can make thereunder. Section 1184(1) states that the Secretary of State may make provision by regulations disqualifying a person subject to foreign restrictions from: (a) being a director of a UK company[95]; (b) acting as a receiver of a UK company's property; or (c) in any way, whether directly or indirectly, being concerned or taking part in the promotion, formation or management of a UK company. The regulations may provide that a person subject to foreign restrictions is disqualified automatically by virtue of the regulations or may be disqualified by order of the court on the Secretary of State's application or by the acceptance of an undertaking.[96] There is also scope for the regulations to make provision for applications to the court for permission to act notwithstanding disqualification.[97] The court for these

[92] See, for example, in Ireland the Companies Act, 1990 s.150 (as amended by the Company Law Enforcement Act 2001 s.41). Under that section a restriction may be imposed on directors of insolvent companies. The restriction relates to their acting as a director or secretary or otherwise being involved in the promotion, formation or management of a company. The restriction is that they may not so act in relation to a company unless it meets certain capitalisation requirements. For the Supreme Court of Ireland's view of this "draconian" but "largely symbolic" provision see *Re Tralee Beef and Lamb Ltd (In Liquidation), Kavanagh v Delaney* [2008] IESC 1, [2008] 3 I.R. 347. For a different view from the Irish regulator, see Office of the Director of Corporate Enforcement, *Annual Report 2008* (Dublin: The Stationary Office, 2009) available online at *http://www.odce.ie* [Accessed September 8, 2009], pp.23–24. Presumably this provision falls within both Companies Act 2006 s.1182(2)(a) and (b) (which correspond to points (1) and (2) in the text).

[93] Companies Act 2006 s.1182(3).

[94] Explanatory Notes, para.1508. However, the effect may be wider: see, in Ireland, the Companies Act 1990 s.150 referred to in footnotes above.

[95] Meaning a company registered under the Companies Act 2006: see Companies Act 2006 s.1183.

[96] Companies Act 2006 s.1184(2), (3). As regards undertakings see also s.1185(4).

[97] Companies Act 2006 s.1184(5).

purposes (and for the purposes of Pt 40 generally) means: in England and Wales, the High Court or a county court; in Scotland, the Court of Session or the sheriff court; and in Northern Ireland, the High Court.[98] It is therefore open to the Secretary of State to craft a flexible regime combining powers of disqualification, provisions for automatic disqualification and scope for the introduction of an undertakings regime. It is clear that the source of any UK disqualification will be the regulations. In other words, Pt 40 does not contemplate the automatic recognition and extension of the foreign disqualification according to its own terms.

16–49 The regulations may also make different provisions for different cases and may in particular (without this being exhaustive) distinguish between cases by reference to: (a) the conduct on the basis of which the person became subject to foreign restrictions; (b) the nature of the foreign restrictions; and/or (c) the country or territory under whose law the foreign restrictions were imposed.[99] This suggests that the regulations or the court may be required to embody or make (as the case may be) judgments about the nature, extent and operation of disqualification law in other jurisdictions. If the regulations make provision for applications to the court by the Secretary of State for a disqualification order or by the disqualified person for permission to act, they must specify the grounds on which the application may be made and may additionally specify factors to which the court shall have regard in determining an application.[100] In particular, the regulations may require the court to have regard in determining an application to the following factors[101]:

(1) Whether the conduct on the basis of which the person became subject to foreign restrictions would, if done in relation to a UK company, have led the court to make a disqualification order under the CDDA or the equivalent Northern Ireland legislation.
(2) In a case in which the conduct on the basis of which the person became subject to foreign restrictions would not be unlawful if done in relation to a UK company, the fact that the person acted unlawfully under foreign law.
(3) Whether the person's activities in relation to UK companies began after he became subject to foreign restrictions.
(4) Whether the person's activities (or proposed activities) in relation to UK companies are undertaken (or are proposed to be undertaken) outside the UK.

Thus it is envisaged that the court will make some evaluation of the extent to which the misconduct underlying the foreign disqualification makes the relevant person unfit according to UK norms and standards and possibly also a judgment about the extent to which the UK public is in need of protection. However, the question whether the misconduct would have justified a domestic disqualification order

[98] Companies Act 2006 s.1183.
[99] Companies Act 2006 s.1185(1).
[100] Companies Act 2006 s.1185(2). As regards applications for permission to act the regulations may provide for the Secretary of State to have standing to appear, give evidence and call witnesses as is the case under CDDA s.17(5): see Companies Act 2006 s.1185(5).
[101] Companies Act 2006 s.1185(3).

is merely one factor that could be taken into account.[102] The second factor suggests a concern that a person who engages in unlawful conduct in one jurisdiction that of itself would not be unlawful in the UK may be inclined to engage in unlawful conduct in the future and therefore be someone from whom the public needs protection. The third factor is presumably based on the concern that persons subject to foreign restrictions may forum shop in terms of the organisations in which they become involved, with a view to avoiding the foreign restrictions.

16–50 Regulations made under s.1184(1) must provide that a person ceases to be disqualified under Pt 40 on his ceasing to be subject to foreign restrictions. Thus, any UK disqualification imposed under Pt 40 will not be capable of continuing after the relevant foreign restrictions have lapsed. This may mean that any disqualification under Pt 40 will have to be by reference to a formula rather than a period of years to cover the possibility of the foreign disqualification being set aside by the court (e.g. on appeal or, say in Guernsey, by virtue of an order for revocation).

16–51 Companies Act 2006 ss.1186–1187 create scope for the regulations to provide for parallel criminal and civil liability along broadly similar lines to CDDA ss.13–15, where a Pt 40 disqualification is breached.

16–52 Companies Act 2006 ss.1188–1191 make provision for statements to be made by way of disclosure to the Registrar of Companies in prescribed circumstances. Section 1188 permits provision to be made in regulations requiring a person who is subject to foreign restrictions and is not disqualified under Pt 40 to send a statement to the Registrar if he does anything that, if done by a person disqualified under this Part, would be in breach of the disqualification. It is not immediately obvious how such a requirement would be enforced in practice even though, pursuant to s.1191, non-disclosure or the making of statements that are false or deceptive in a material particular may be capable of attracting criminal liability. Section 1189 permits provision to be made in regulations that would apply not only to persons disqualified under Pt 40 but also to persons disqualified under the CDDA or the equivalent Northern Ireland legislation. Under s.1189 it is open to the Secretary of State to make provision requiring a statement or notice sent to the Registrar pursuant to Companies Act 2006 s.12 (statement of company's proposed officers), s.167(2) (notice of person having become director) or s.276 (notice of person having become secretary) to be accompanied by an additional statement that the disqualified person has obtained permission from the court to act in the capacity in question. Again, the Secretary of State has the power under s.1191 to make non-disclosure or the making of statements that are false or deceptive in a material particular an offence.[103]

Selective jurisdictions with disqualification regimes

16–53 There are a number of jurisdictions, especially in the Commonwealth, that have regimes or provisions that are comparable to the CDDA. Foreign nationals who fall foul of these regimes or provisions will be susceptible to Pt 40 disqualification

[102] See further A. O'Neill, "Part 40 of the Companies Act 2006: Disqualification Orders go Global" (2007) 18(5) International Company and Commercial L.R. 166.

[103] There is also scope for regulations to be made regarding whether statements envisaged by ss.1188 and 1189 are to be documents of public record: see Companies Act 2006 s.1190.

should they become involved in the management of UK companies. Examples are: Australia (see Corporations Act (Cth.) 2001 Pt 2D.6); Hong Kong (see Companies Ordinance Pt IVA, ss.168C–168T which contains provisions that are modelled on the provisions in the CDDA); Ireland (see Companies Act 1990 ss.159–170); Singapore (see Companies Act ss.148–149A); South Africa (see Companies Act 2008 ss.69 and 162). The position in the Channel Islands and the Isle of Man is considered below given the geographical and constitutional proximity of those jurisdictions to the UK and their importance as offshore financial centres.

16–54 Some of these jurisdictions have provisions that are analogous to Pt 40. A good example is Ireland where s.160(2)(i) of the Companies Act 1990 (as inserted by s.42 of the Company Law Enforcement Act 2001) provides as follows:

> "Where the court is satisfied in any proceedings or as a result of an application under this section that . . .
>
> (i) a person is disqualified under the law of another state (whether pursuant to an order of a judge or a tribunal or otherwise) from being appointed or acting as a director or secretary of a body corporate or an undertaking and the court is satisfied that, if the conduct of the person or the circumstances otherwise affecting him that gave rise to the said order being made against him had occurred or arisen in [Ireland], it would have been proper to make a disqualification order otherwise under this subsection against him . . .
>
> the court may, of its own motion, or as a result of the application, make a disqualification order against such a person for such period as it sees fit."[104]

For these purposes, a disqualification order is an order that the person against whom the order is made shall not be appointed or act as an auditor, director or other officer, receiver, liquidator or examiner or be in any way, whether directly or indirectly, concerned or take part in the promotion, formation or management of any company, or any society registered under the Industrial and Provident Societies Acts, 1893 to 1978. By s.160(1A) of the Companies Act 1990 (as inserted by s.42 of the Company Law Enforcement Act 2001), a person is also deemed to be disqualified in Ireland where he fails to disclose in the statement to the registrar of companies on incorporation or notification of change of directors that he is disqualified in another jurisdiction or where, in purported compliance with the requirements for such a statement or notification, he permits either statement or notification to be accompanied by a statement signed by him which is false or misleading in a material respect. The period of disqualification under s.160(1A) is the unexpired period of the foreign disqualification at the date of delivery of the relevant statement or notification.

THE CROWN DEPENDENCIES

16–55 The Crown Dependencies comprise the Bailiwick of Jersey, the Bailiwick of Guernsey and the Isle of Man. The Bailiwick of Guernsey includes the separate

[104] See further A. O'Neill, "Part 40 of the Companies Act 2006: Disqualification Orders go Global" (2007) 18(5) International Company and Commercial L.R. 166.

jurisdictions of Alderney and Sark. These jurisdictions have their own separate legislative assemblies and systems of law. The Bailiwick of Guernsey is responsible for the administration of the islands of Herm, Jethou and Lihou. The island of Brecqhou is part of Sark. The Bailiwicks of Jersey and Guernsey and the Isle of Man are not part of the United Kingdom. They are self-governing dependencies of the Crown. They have their own directly elected legislative assemblies, administrative, fiscal and legal systems and their own courts of law. The Crown Dependencies are not represented in the UK Parliament. UK legislation does not normally extend to them. However, they occasionally request that UK legislation is extended to them, which can then be done by an Order in Council. As at January 1998[105] about 90,000 companies were incorporated in the Crown Dependencies. The Isle of Man had about 42,000 locally incorporated companies; Jersey, about 32,000; Guernsey, about 16,000. In all cases, the vast majority were private companies. In comparison with other offshore centres, these figures were not especially large. As at the same date Hong Kong had some 477,000 companies; the British Virgin Islands, some 302,000; Cayman, some 41,000; and Gibraltar, some 25,000. These figures are to be compared with about 1.1 million companies on the UK's registers at this time. In the late 1990s there were particular concerns about nominee directors. For various reasons, the position has greatly changed since then. It is of interest, however, that the Isle of Man courts have, in the disqualification context, expressly referred to the high standards of company directors resident on the Isle of Man.

Alderney

Disqualification orders

16–56 The disqualification of directors in Alderney is dealt with by the Companies (Alderney) Law, 1994 ("the 1994 Law"). Article 88 defines the scope of a disqualification order as an order prohibiting a person, without the leave of the court, (a) from being a director or other officer[106] of any company[107] or any specified company; (b) from participating in, or being in any way concerned in, directly or indirectly, the management, formation or promotion of any company or any specified company. It would appear from the language that the court can identify whether the prohibition related to companies is global or specific to one or more named companies but that the disqualification is one entire disqualification with no power in the court to pick between (a) and (b). A disqualification order may be renewed. The renewal may be at any time before, or within a period of one month immediately succeeding, the date of the expiration of the order. A disqualification order and any renewal thereof is to have effect for the period specified thereby which is not to exceed five years. Such order (and renewal) may

[105] The following figures are taken from *Review of Financial Regulation in the Crown Dependencies* Cmd.4109–1 (1998) which was commissioned by the UK Home Secretary and presented to Parliament by him.

[106] The term "officer" is defined as including "a director, liquidator, manager and secretary thereof": see art.163(1) of the 1994 Law.

[107] The term "company" is defined as meaning a body corporate the memorandum and articles of which are registered in the Register of Companies, and includes a "société anonyme ou à responsabilité limitée incorporated by registration under the Law of 1894": see art.163(1) of the 1994 Law.

contain such incidental and ancillary terms and conditions as the court thinks fit. Article 88 provides that an application for a disqualification order or its renewal may be made by the Committee, Her Majesty's Procureur, by any body corporate[108] of which the person is or has been an officer, or by any member or creditor of such a body corporate. Where the court considers, that by reason of a person's conduct in relation to any body corporate or otherwise, that a person is unfit to be concerned in the management of a company, the court may, if satisfied that it is desirable in the public interest to do so, make and subsequently renew (on one or more occasions) a disqualification order. In determining the question of whether a person's conduct makes him unfit, the court is directed to have regard to the matters set out in Sch.5 to the 1994 Law. Schedule 5 states that every person who is, or is to be, a director of a company shall be a fit and proper person to hold that position. In determining whether a person is a fit and proper person to hold a particular position, regard is to be had to:

> "(a) his probity, competence, solvency and soundness of judgement for fulfilling the responsibilities of that position;
> (b) the diligence with which he is fulfilling or likely to fulfil those responsibilities;
> (c) whether the interests of members or creditors or potential members or creditors of the company are, or are likely to be, in any way threatened by his holding that position;
> (d) the rules, standards and guidelines of any relevant professional, governing, regulatory or supervisory authority; and
> (e) any reports, guidelines and other documents published by the [Guernsey Financial Services] Commission."

Without prejudice to the generality of those matters:

> "... regard may be had to the previous conduct and activities in business or financial matters of the person in question and, in particular, to any evidence that he has—
>
> (a) committed an offence involving fraud or other dishonesty or violence;
> (b) contravened any provision contained in or made under the 1994 Law or any other enactment appearing to the court (having regard to the views of the [Guernsey Financial Services] Commission) to be designed for protecting members of the public against financial loss due to dishonesty, incompetence or malpractice by persons concerned in the provision of banking, insurance, investment or other financial services or the management of companies or against financial loss due to the conduct of discharged or undischarged bankrupts or persons who are otherwise insolvent;
> (c) engaged in any business practices appearing to the court (having regard to the views of the [Guernsey Financial Services] Commission) to be deceitful or oppressive or otherwise improper (whether unlawful or not) or which otherwise reflect discredit on his method of conducting business;
> (d) engaged in or been associated with any other business practices or otherwise conducted himself in such a way as to cast doubt on his competence and soundness of judgement."

[108] The term "body corporate" means a body of persons incorporated under the laws of any district, territory or place, and includes a company. A "company" for these purposes means a company incorporated under Alderney law: see art.163(1) of the 1994 Law.

16–57 Breach of a disqualification order comprises a criminal offence. In addition, the person in contravention becomes personally liable for any debts or liabilities of the company in relation to which the contravention was committed which were incurred at any time when he was acting in contravention of the disqualification order or the renewal thereof. Such personal liability is joint and several with that of the company or any other person liable in relation to that company.

Bankruptcy

16–58 It appears that Alderney bankruptcy law is largely customary law and that the position is very similar in substance to that under Guernsey law. The procedures available for dealing with individual debtors in Guernsey customary law are considered briefly in 16–64 below. None of the procedures triggers disqualification prohibitions equivalent or analogous to CDDA s.11.

Guernsey

Disqualification orders

16–59 The current law on directors' disqualification in Guernsey is contained in Part XXV of the Companies (Guernsey) Law, 2008 ("the 2008 Law").[109] Article 427 defines a disqualification order as an order made by the court[110] prohibiting a person from: (a) being a director,[111] secretary or other officer[112] of any company[113] or any specified company; (b) being a shadow director[114] of any company or any specified company; (c) participating in, or being in any way concerned in, directly or indirectly, the management, formation or promotion of any company or any specified company; (d) participating in, or being in any way concerned in, directly or indirectly, the management, formation or promotion of any overseas company[115]; (e) being an administrator of any company or any specified company; (f) being a receiver of a cell of any protected cell company or any specified protected cell company; (g) being a liquidator of any company or any specified company. A disqualification order shall have effect for the period it specifies which shall not exceed 15 years. Where a disqualification order is made against a

[109] For the previous law, see the Companies (Guernsey) Law, 1994 (as amended by the Companies (Amendment) (Guernsey) Law, 1996. These provisions were similar to those under Alderney law. The 2008 Law has effect in Guernsey, Herm and Jethou.

[110] That is, the Royal Court sitting as an Ordinary Court: see art.532 of the 2008 Law. By art.427(7), the Bailiff sits unaccompanied by the Jurats.

[111] The term "director" is defined as including an alternate director and any person occupying the position of director, by whatever name called: see arts 532 and 131 of the 2008 Law.

[112] The phrase "officer of a company" is defined as including "a director, liquidator, manager, secretary, receiver and administrator thereof": see art.532 of the 2008 Law.

[113] The term "company" is defined as including a cell company, a non cellular company or an incorporated cell of an incorporated cell company: see arts 532 and 2(3) of the 2008 Law.

[114] The phrase "shadow director", in relation to a company, is defined as a person in accordance with whose directions or instructions the directors of the company are accustomed to act. However, a person is not to be regarded as a shadow director by reason only that the directors act on advice given by him in a professional capacity: see arts 532 and 132 of the 2008 Law.

[115] The phrase "overseas company" is defined as "a body of persons registered or incorporated under the law of any district, territory or place outside Guernsey": see art.532 of the 2008 Law.

person already subject to such an order, the periods specified in the orders run concurrently unless the court orders them to run consecutively.[116] A disqualification order may contain such incidental and ancillary terms and conditions as the court thinks fit.[117]

Application for and making of disqualification orders

16–60 Disqualification orders may be made during proceedings initiated for that purpose or in the course of any other proceedings. The court can make such an order of its own motion or on application. Those who may apply for such an order are: (a) the States of Guernsey Commerce and Employment Department; (b) the Guernsey Financial Services Commission; (c) Her Majesty's Procureur; (d) the Registrar; (e) any company of which the person in question is or has been a director, shadow director, secretary, officer or is participating or has participated directly or indirectly in the management, formation or promotion thereof; (f) any liquidator, administrator, member or creditor of such a company as is mentioned in (e); (g) any receiver of a cell of a protected cell company which is such a company as is mentioned in (e); or (h) any other interested party, with the leave of the court. The court has an absolute discretion but may make a disqualification order by consent.[118]

Grounds for a disqualification order

16–61 The court has a discretion to make a disqualification order where it considers that, by reason of a person's conduct in relation to a company or otherwise, that person is unfit to be concerned in the management of a company. In determining whether a person is unfit, regard is to be had to: (a) his probity, competence, experience and soundness of judgement for fulfilling the responsibilities of a director, secretary or officer of a company; (b) the diligence with which he has fulfilled his responsibilities; (c) whether the interests of members or creditors or potential members or creditors of any company or any specified company are or are likely to be in any way threatened by his being a director, secretary or officer of a company; (d) his educational and professional qualifications, his membership of any professional or other relevant bodies and any evidence of his continuing professional education or development; (e) the rules, standards and guidelines of any relevant professional, governing, regulatory or supervisory authority; (f) his knowledge and understanding of the legal and professional obligations of directors, secretaries or officers of a company; and (g) such other matters as the court thinks fit. Without prejudice to these matters, the court may also have regard to: (a) the previous conduct and activities in business or financial matters of the person in question; (b) any convictions he has for an offence in connection with the promotion, formation, management, liquidation or striking off of a company; (c) any convictions he has for any offence and in particular any offence involving

[116] art.429 of the 2008 Law.
[117] art.427(5) of the 2008 Law.
[118] art.427(4) of the 2008 Law.

fraud or dishonesty; (d) whether he has been held liable to make contributions to a company's assets under the fraudulent and wrongful trading provisions in arts 433, 434 or 435[119]; (e) whether he has been persistently in default in relation to any provisions of the 2008 Law requiring any validation, return, account or other document to be filed with, delivered or sent, or any notice of any matter to be given, to the Registrar; (f) his conduct in connection with any company that has gone into insolvent liquidation; (g) any misfeasance or breach of any fiduciary or other duty by him in relation to a company; (h) whether he has been disqualified, by reason of misconduct or unfitness, from being concerned with the management of an overseas company under the law of any district, territory or place outside Guernsey; and (i) where he acted as a resident agent, any breach of his duties as a resident agent.

Revocation of a disqualification order

16–62 A person subject to a disqualification order may apply to the court for a revocation of the order on the ground that he is no longer unfit to be concerned in the management of a company. The court may grant the application if satisfied that: (a) it would not be contrary to the public interest to do so; and (b) the applicant is no longer unfit to be concerned in the management of a company. The revocation of a disqualification order may, with the consent of the parties and in the court's absolute discretion, be granted by consent.

Breach of a disqualification order

16–63 A breach of a disqualification order constitutes a criminal offence. In addition, it results in the person in breach incurring joint and several liability, with the company and any other person liable, for the debts and liabilities of any company in relation to which the contravention was committed which were incurred at any time when he was acting in contravention of the disqualification order.

Bankruptcy

16–64 Guernsey has old customary laws dealing with bankruptcy of individuals. There are two common law procedures for, respectively, vesting the debtor's real property in his creditors (saisie) and distributing his personal property among his creditors (désastre). However, entry into neither procedure limits the future conduct of the debtor nor does it discharge him from his debts. There is a procedure more akin to bankruptcy which involves a declaration of insolvency adjudicated by the court.[120] Such a declaration does not result in any disqualification from acting as a director. It appears that there were only a handful of such cases in the last 50 years of the twentieth century.[121]

[119] These are the wrongful and fraudulent trading provisions.
[120] Under the Law Relating to Debtors and Renunciation of 1929 and the related Ordinance.
[121] See generally, G. Dawes, *Laws of Guernsey* (Oxford: Hart Publishing), especially Ch.11 on insolvency.

Isle of Man

16–65 A significant new directors' disqualification regime came into force in the Isle of Man on June 18, 2009. The Company Officers (Disqualification) Act 2009 has largely replaced the previous statutory provisions, in particular ss.208 and 259 of the Companies Act 1931 ("CA 1931"), s.31 of the Companies Act 1982 ("CA 1982") and s.26 of the Companies Act 1992 ("CA 1992"). As regards the former provisions:

(1) CA 1931 s.208 provided a power in the court to make a disqualification order on the application of the official receiver. The jurisdiction arose where a winding up order had been made and the official receiver had made a report to the court that, in his opinion, fraud had been committed by a person in the promotion or formation of a company or by any director or other officer in relation to the company since its formation. The official receiver then had standing to apply for an order that the person, director or officer should not:

> "without leave of the court be a director of or in any way, whether directly or indirectly, be concerned or take part in the management of a company for such period not exceeding five years from the date of the report as might be specified in the order."

There was a requirement for ten days' notice of the application to be given to the prospective defendant. Any breach of a disqualification order made under this provision was a criminal offence.

(2) CA 1931 s.259 made provision for a power to disqualify in relation to fraudulent trading. If in the course of a winding up fraudulent trading was found to be established then the court had power to make an appropriate declaration on the application of the official receiver, liquidator, or any creditor or contributory. It could then go on and make a disqualification order for a period of up to five years. This power also existed (and also in the criminal court in question) where a person was convicted of fraudulent trading. Breach of an order was a criminal offence. The form of order prevented the person, without leave of the court, from being a director, or in any way, whether directly or indirectly, being concerned or taking part in the management of a company. From March 1, 2004, the Financial Supervision Commission was required to keep an index of disqualifications, open to public inspection and containing prescribed information.

(3) CA 1982 s.31 made provision for a power in the court to disqualify directors of insolvent companies. Where, on application, it appeared to the court that a person was or had been a director of a company which had at any time gone into liquidation (whether while he was a director or subsequently) and was insolvent at that time and that he was or had been a director of another company which had gone into liquidation within five years of the date of the first mentioned company going into liquidation, and that his conduct as a director of any of those companies "makes him unfit to be concerned in the management of a company" the court could make a disqualification order for a period of up to five years. The form of order was that, without leave of the court, the person

should not be a director, or in any way, whether directly or indirectly, be concerned or take part in the management of a company. Breach of an order was a criminal offence. Applications for the making of a disqualification order could be brought by the Financial Supervision Commission. A ten-day notice requirement was imposed. By amendment which took effect from March 1, 2004 the Commission was required to keep an index of disqualification orders, open to public inspection and containing prescribed particulars.

(4) CA 1992 s.26 made provision for a further a power of disqualification in the court. In sub-section (1) the power arose where a person's conduct:

"makes him unfit—(a) to be a director or secretary of a company; or (b) to be a liquidator of a company; or (c) to be a receiver or manager of a company's property; or (d) in any way, whether directly or indirectly, to be concerned or take part in the promotion, formation or management of a company."

A person subject to a disqualification order was not, without leave of the court, to undertake any of the offices and activities referred to in subs.(1)(a) to (d). The period of disqualification was to begin with the date of the order and be not less than three years nor more than 15 years. Breach of an order was a criminal offence. The power to apply for a disqualification order was vested in the Financial Supervision Commission. Without prejudice to the generality of subs.(1), subs.(3) identified certain circumstances in which the court could treat a person as "unfit" to undertake any of the relevant offices or activities referred to in subs.(1). These included cases where the person or the body corporate of which that person was a director or similar officer or the secretary:

(a) had been convicted of an offence (whether in the Isle of Man or elsewhere) involving dishonesty;
(b) had been convicted (whether in the Isle of Man or elsewhere) within the 25 years ending with the date of the application of any combination of three or more offences under the Companies Acts 1931 to 1992 or legislation having an equivalent effect in any country or territory outside the Isle of Man, whether or not convicted on the same occasion;
(c) had been convicted of any offence under the Prevention of Fraud (Investments) Act 1968, the Banking Acts 1975 to 1986, the Insurance Act 1986, the Company Securities (Insider Dealing) Act 1987, the Insider Dealing Act 1998, the Financial Supervision Act 1988 or the Investment Business Act 1991 or the Insurance Intermediaries (General Business) Act 1996 or the Corporate Services Providers Act 2000 or legislation having equivalent effect in any country or territory outside the Isle of Man; or
(d) had failed to comply with any direction of the court to remedy a default under any provision of the Companies Acts 1931 to 1992.

The section also provided for the Financial Supervision Commission to keep an index with prescribed particulars, open to inspection, of persons subject to disqualification orders.

16–66 The Company Officers (Disqualification) Act 2009 ("CO(D)A") took effect from June 18, 2009.[122] The main impetus for reform derived from an independent review, carried out by Mr Eben Hamilton Q.C., of the Commission's conduct of a disqualification case pursued under CA 1992 s.26. The review identified deficiencies in the relevant law and also in the procedures (especially in terms of delay and lack of fairness) followed by the Commission in that particular case. The key findings were set out in a public statement by the Commission of August 12, 2004. The main aims of CO(D)A were to address the independent review's recommendations and to draw together all the then current grounds of disqualification into "one stand-alone and more accessible body of law, for the purposes of clarification and transparency". The opportunity was also taken to review the grounds for disqualification "clarifying where necessary".[123] The end result is a piece of legislation which is not a thousand miles away from the CDDA. However the bill introduced in 2007, which became CO(D)A, was promulgated as a development of existing Isle of Man law rather than an attempt "to follow the UK's more prescriptive approach".[124] In addition, from September 1, 2009, new High Court rules came into force.[125] Particular provision is made in the new rules regarding the conduct of disqualification proceedings.

Disqualification orders and undertakings

16–67 The form of disqualification order is now defined for all purposes as an order that a person "must not, without leave of the High Court, be an officer of a company for a period specified in the order".[126] An officer is widely defined as a director, secretary, or registered agent; a liquidator; a receiver; a person holding an office under any relevant foreign law analogous to any of the offices previously listed or a person who, in any way, whether directly or indirectly, is concerned or takes part in the promotion, formation or management of a company. It appears from the statutory definition that there is no longer any ability in the court to "pick and choose" between the different offices in relation to which an order was made, as was the approach under CA 1992 s.26. Unless the court otherwise orders, the period of disqualification begins at the end of the period of 21 days beginning with the date of the order.[127] Where the person is already disqualified (whether by disqualification order or disqualification undertaking) the court may order the periods of disqualification to run concurrently or consecutively.[128]

16–68 For the first time, the CO(D)A introduces the concept of a disqualification undertaking. The circumstances in which such undertaking may be accepted by the Financial Supervision Commission (the "FSC") are set out below. The undertaking may be agreed to run concurrently or consecutively with any extant disqualification.

[122] Company Officers (Disqualification) Act 2009 (Appointed Day) Order 2009 (SD 325/09).

[123] See generally, Financial Supervision Commission, *Consultative Paper on the Company Officers Disqualification Bill 2007* (October 2007).

[124] Consultative Paper, p.3.

[125] As a transitional measure a new Order 43A of the rules comes into force.

[126] CO(D)A s.1(1).

[127] CO(D)A s.1(4).

[128] CO(D)A s.1(4).

For present purposes, the key difference between a disqualification order and a disqualification undertaking is that, in the case of the latter, leave to act notwithstanding disqualification may be granted by the High Court or the FSC. Otherwise a disqualification undertaking lays down a disqualification from being an officer in similar terms to a disqualification order. The FSC must prescribe the form of disqualification undertaking after consulting the Deemsters.[129]

16–69 The FSC is required to keep a disqualification register, essentially containing details of disqualification orders and undertakings and grants of leave to act notwithstanding disqualification.[130] Breach of an order is a criminal offence and the criminal court is given power to disqualify further on such a conviction if the defendant is then subject to a disqualification order or undertaking.[131] However, criminal proceedings may only be commenced by, or with the consent of, the Attorney General and must be brought no later than 12 months after the date on which evidence, sufficient in the opinion of the Attorney General to justify proceedings, came to his or her knowledge.[132] For the latter purpose, the Attorney General is empowered to provide a conclusive certificate of the relevant date.[133] In addition to criminal sanctions, CO(D)A s.12 imposes civil liability for the debts of a company on: (a) the person who acts in breach of a disqualification by acting as an officer of a company; and (b) on an officer of a company who is or is liable to be disqualified ("P") and who acts or is willing to act on instructions given by a person whom P knows to be the subject of a disqualification order or undertaking. Civil and criminal liability is also extended to cover the situation of undischarged bankrupts, who are subject to automatic disqualification under CO(D)A s.10, but who act in breach of that prohibition.[134]

Disqualification: circumstances

16–70 There are three situations in which the civil court can disqualify, two situations in which disqualification undertakings may be accepted and one situation in which the criminal court may disqualify. In addition there is an automatic disqualification in relation to undischarged bankrupts. In summary the position is as follows:

(1) Unfitness (general). The High Court may make a disqualification order for between two and 15 years if satisfied that the person in question is or has been an officer of a company and that that person's conduct renders that person unfit to be an officer of a company.[135]
(2) Unfitness (insolvency). The High Court must make a disqualification order for between two and 15 years if satisfied: (a) that the person in question is or has been an officer of a company which has at any time become insolvent

[129] CO(D)A s.6(2).
[130] CO(D)A s.13.
[131] CO(D)A s.11(1), (2), (4).
[132] CO(D)A s.11(5).
[133] CO(D)A s.15(6).
[134] CO(D)A ss.11(1), 12(1)(b).
[135] CO(D)A s.4.

(whether while the person was an officer or subsequently); and (b) that that person's conduct as an officer of the company (taken alone or taken together with his conduct as an officer of any other company or companies) makes him unfit to be an officer of a company.[136] Proceedings on this ground may only be brought within the period of two years beginning with the date that the company is wound up or dissolved unless the High Court grants leave for the application to be made later.[137] This appears to be cumulative with the time limit set out in CO(D)A s.3(3).

(3) Fraudulent trading. When making a declaration under CA 1931 s.259 regarding fraudulent trading, the court shall consider making a disqualification order for a maximum period of 15 years.[138]

(4) Undertakings. If it appears to the FSC that an offer of a disqualification undertaking has been made and that the conditions for making a disqualification order on the grounds of unfit conduct in relation to an insolvent company are satisfied,[139] then the FSC may accept the undertaking if satisfied that it is expedient in the public interest to do so (instead of applying for or proceeding with an application for a disqualification order).[140]

(5) Criminal disqualification. The criminal court may disqualify when a person is convicted for breach of a disqualification order or undertaking.[141]

(6) An undischarged bankrupt may not act as an officer of a company except with leave of the High Court.[142] For these purposes a person is "bankrupt" if he has been adjudged bankrupt by any court in the Isle of Man, England, Wales or Northern Ireland, sequestration of the person's estate has been awarded by a court in Scotland; or a court in the Republic of Ireland or any of the Channel Islands has made an order having the like effect of an adjudication of the High Court.[143]

Unfit conduct: further points

16–71 Applications for the making of a disqualification order on the grounds that a person's conduct makes him unfit to be an officer of a company may be made by: (a) the FSC (if it appears to the FSC that it is expedient in the public interest to do so); (b) the official receiver; (c) the liquidator; or (d) any past or present member or creditor of any company in relation to which the person has engaged in conduct rendering that person unfit to be an officer.[144] Twenty-eight days notice of intention to make such an application must first be given.[145] The application

136 CO(D)A s.5(1), (2), (4).
137 CO(D)A s.5(3).
138 CO(D)A s.9. There is no minimum period.
139 That is that the conditions in CO(D)A ss.4(1) or 5(1) are satisfied.
140 CO(D)A s.6.
141 CO(D)A s.11(4).
142 CO(D)A s.10.
143 CO(D)A s.10(4). The former provision was CA 1931 s.141. See also the Isle of Man Companies Act 2006 s.93(1).
144 CO(D)A s.3(1).
145 CO(D)A s.3(2).

must be brought within two years of the date on which the applicant could reasonably be expected to have sufficient evidence of knowledge to justify proceedings, unless the High Court grants leave for the application to be brought later.[146] This appears to be a cumulative requirement to that under s.5(3), which is analogous to CDDA s.7(2), and applies in the case of applications regarding insolvent companies. In most, but not necessarily all, cases however, the s.5(3) period will be determinative. In deciding whether or not a person's conduct makes him unfit, the court (and in relation to an offer of an undertaking, the FSC) must have regard to the matters set out in Sch.1, which are similar to those in Sch.1 to the CDDA.

Investigation and reporting

16–72 The CO(D)A also introduces the concept of office holder reporting, akin to that of ss.7(3) and 7(4) of the CDDA. Section 7 of the CO(D)A requires office holders to report to the FSC where they consider that the conditions of ss.4(1) or 5(1) are met. For these purposes office holders are the official receiver (compulsory winding up), the liquidator (other winding up) or the receiver. The FSC and the official receiver are also given powers in CO(D)A s.7(3), akin to those in CDDA s.7(4), to require an office holder to provide information for disqualification purposes.

16–73 In addition the CO(D)A also provides the FSC with various inspection and investigatory powers in connection with possible disqualification situations. Powers to inspect company books, accounts and documents and to investigate company transactions and to seek information from a company are conferred on the FSC where it has reasonable grounds to suspect a person of being unfit to act as an officer of the company or of acting in breach of a disqualification order or disqualification undertaking.[147] Those powers are backed up by powers to apply to a justice of the peace to investigate the affairs or aspects of the affairs of any company which, if granted, can enable the FSC to require persons to attend on the FSC and answer questions or give information or to produce documents. In addition there are various enforcement powers.

Jersey

Disqualification

16–74 The disqualification of company directors under Jersey law is currently governed by arts 78 and 79[148] of the Companies (Jersey) Law 1991.[149] Article 78 confers

[146] CO(D)A s.3(3).

[147] CO(D)A s.15, Sch.2.

[148] As substituted by Companies (Amendment No.8) (Jersey) Law 2005. See also previous art.78 as substituted by the Companies (Amendment No.6) (Jersey) Law 2002. At the time of the 1991 Law coming into force there was a separate power to disqualify conferred by art.43 of the Bankruptcy (Désastre) (Jersey) Law 1990. Article 24 of the 1990 Law now covers the position: see 16–77 below.

[149] As a matter of company law, the 1991 Law largely replaced the Loi (1861) sur les Sociétés avec Responsabilité Limitée, as amended, and the Companies (Supplementary Provisions) (Jersey) Law, 1968.

power[150] on the Minister[151] or the Jersey Financial Services Commission or the Attorney General to apply for an order to the Jersey Royal Court. If it appears[152] to such official or official body that it would be in the public interest[153] that a person should not without the leave of the court: (a) be a director of a company[154]; (b) be in any other way directly or indirectly concerned or take part in the management of a company; or (c) be in Jersey in any way whether directly or indirectly concerned or take part in the management of a body incorporated[155] outside Jersey, then such official or official body may apply to the court for an order to that effect against that person.[156] The court may make such an order[157] where satisfied that the person's conduct in relation to a body corporate (wherever incorporated and wherever it carries on business) makes the person unfit: (a) to be concerned in the management of a company; or (b) to be concerned in the management, in Jersey, of a body incorporated outside Jersey. The maximum period of such an order is now 15 years.[158] Such an order may also make further provision preventing the holding of certain offices without leave of the court. Where the application for disqualification arises in respect of a winding up of a company in the public interest or a creditors' winding up of a company of which, in either case, the relevant person was a director, there may be included in the application a recommendation that the court should include in the order a provision forbidding the person without the leave of the court from holding: (a) a private office; or (b) in an application made by the Attorney General or joined by the Attorney General for the purpose of making the recommendation, a private office, a public office or both. Where such a recommendation is made, the court may provide in the disqualification order that the person should not, without the leave of the court, hold any private office, or, as the case may be, any private or public office or any private or public office specified in the order. Where such an extra prohibition is included, the court has discretion to specify different periods for different offices. In this regard, "private office" means the office of curator, *electeur*, liquidator of a company, trustee, *tuteur*, executor or administrator of a deceased person's estate or the donee of a power of attorney. A "public office" means the office of Centenier, Vingtenier, Constable's Officer, *Procureur du Bien*

[150] Applications should be made promptly: *In re Delaney, Deltatrust (C.I.) Ltd and Sentinel Management Ltd* 1995 J.L.R. *N*-2b. For other cases where delay has been considered see *In re Dimsey* [2000] J.L.R. 401.

[151] In this context, the Minister for Economic Development.

[152] As under the CDDA, this is a matter for the official and the court does not itself have to be satisfied that the public interest justifies disqualification: see *In re Dimsey* [2000] J.L.R. 401.

[153] The previous wording used the "expedient in the public interest" formulation.

[154] The term "company" for this purpose is effectively a Jersey company, that is one registered under the 1991 Law or an "existing company", that is a company registered under the Companies (Jersey) Laws 1861 to 1968.

[155] This seems not to include a Scottish firm: see art.1(2) of the 1991 Law.

[156] This sub-paragraph effectively changes the previous law, as confirmed in *In re Dimsey* [2000] J.L.R. 401, that the conduct in question had to relate to a Jersey incorporated company.

[157] Which should not be backdated: see *In re Hay* 1996 J.L.R. *N*-1b.

[158] Prior to the amendments made in 2002, the maximum period was five years. The Jersey Royal Court expressed doubt that this was long enough for serious cases in *In re Hay* 1996 J.L.R. *N*-1b.

Public or member of an Assessment Committee constituted under the Parish Rate (Administration) (Jersey) Law 2003.

Effect of breach

16–75 Breach of an order made under art.78 amounts to an offence.[159] In addition, under art.79,[160] a person acting in contravention of an order made under art.78 is also personally responsible for liabilities of the company or other body corporate as are incurred at a time when that person was involved in its management in breach of the order. For these purposes, involvement in management includes acting as a director or being concerned, directly or indirectly, or taking part in management of a company or body corporate. The liability is joint and several with any other person liable (including any other person liable under art.79).

Disqualification and reporting duties in company insolvency

16–76 Under what is now art.43[161] of the Bankruptcy (Désastre) (Jersey) Law 1990, in the case of a "désastre", i.e. a form of bankruptcy under Jersey law, in respect of a company, there is a reporting duty on the Viscount,[162] where misconduct is identified. Where it appears to the Viscount that the company has committed a criminal offence, that a person has committed a criminal offence in relation to the company or, in the case of a director, that for any reason (whether in relation to the company or to a holding company of the company or to any subsidiary of such holding company) his or her conduct has been such that an order should be sought against him under art.78 of the Companies Law 1991, then the Viscount is required to report the matter to the Attorney General forthwith and furnish him with such information and documents as he may require. The Attorney General may, in turn, refer the matter to the Jersey Financial Services Commission or the Minister.

16–77 Prior to its amendment by the relevant 2006 Law, art.43 conferred a disqualification power on the Royal Courts of Jersey which was separate from, but additional to, that provided in art.78 of the 1991 Companies Law. As originally enacted, art.43 provided that where in the course of a désastre in respect of a company it appeared to the Attorney General expedient in the public interest that a director of a company should not be a director or, in any way, whether directly or indirectly, be concerned or take part in the management of a company, the Attorney General could apply to the court for an order to that effect. The court could make such an order for up to five years, where on such an application it was satisfied that the director's conduct "makes him unfit to be concerned in the management of a company". Breach of such an order was an offence and a person

[159] art.78(4).

[160] Substituted by the Companies (Amendment No.6) (Jersey) Law 2002.

[161] The whole of the current Part X of the 1991 Law, of which art.43 forms part, was substituted and amended by the Bankruptcy (Désastre) (Amendment No.5) (Jersey) Law 2006.

[162] A Jersey official in this context administering the "désastre". The Viscount's department is an executive arm of the Jersey Courts and of its Parliament, the States.

acting in contravention of the order was also subject to joint and several liability for the debts and liabilities of a company incurred at a time when that person was so involved in its management. Now, under the amended art.24(7), where a company is in "désastre" the court may, on the application of the Viscount, make any order in respect of a person who is or was a director of the company that it would be permitted to make under art.78 of the Companies Law in respect of such a person.

Bankruptcy

16–78 Under art.24 of the Bankruptcy (Désastre) (Jersey) Law 1990, certain persons are prohibited from acting in certain capacities. The prohibition applies to a debtor during the course of the "désastre" or a person who is or has the status of an undischarged bankrupt (by whatever name called) under the laws of any other jurisdiction. The content of the prohibition is similar to that flowing from a disqualification order under art.78 of the 1991 Law. First, the person is prohibited from holding a private office. A "private office" is, for these purposes, the office of curator, director of a company, *electeur*, liquidator of a company, trustee, *tuteur*, executor or administrator of a deceased person's estate or the donee of a power of attorney. The person is also prohibited from holding a public office. For these purposes, "public office" means the office of Connétable, Centenier, Vingtenier, Constable's Officer, "Procureur du Bien Public", and member of the Assessment Committee constituted under the Parish Rate (Administration) (Jersey) Law 2003. If holding any such office at the time of becoming an undischarged bankrupt or of entering "désastre", the person must forthwith resign from the office. Breach of such prohibition amounts to an offence.

Sark

16–79 Sark does not have any companies legislation and does not, as such, regulate directors. However, the use of Sark nominee directors became very widespread in the 1980s and 1990s. In the 1980s, it was common practice for the directors of Guernsey and Jersey companies beneficially owned overseas to have two Sark residents as directors and to hold board meetings in Sark. This was to create the fiction that the companies were managed and controlled outside Guernsey and Jersey which enabled the companies to claim tax exempt status under the Guernsey and Jersey tax rules of the time without incurring any tax liabilities elsewhere (since there was no company tax on Sark). The Guernsey and Jersey authorities effectively brought this practice to an end by establishing new rules for tax exempt companies which allowed them to hold board meetings in Guernsey or Jersey. However, by the late 1990s it was quite common for directors to be engaged in Sark or other tax-free locations so as create the fiction that the companies were controlled in such locations and hence resident there for tax purposes. In many cases the twin benefits of secrecy and tax-free status were obtained by forming non-resident companies in (say) the Isle of Man, with directors in (say) Sark. At that time the secrecy resulted from the limited disclosure requirements for non-resident companies in the Isle of Man (where there was then no requirement to declare beneficial ownership to the regulatory authorities or to make substantive reports to the tax authorities unless challenged) and the absence of any disclosure requirements in Sark (where there was no company legislation and no regulation of companies or directors). The avoidance of tax was achieved (or maintained) through the use of Sark directors to establish that the companies were resident for tax purposes in Sark, where there was no tax. Whatever the precise figures were, there was a perception that many of the directors in Sark were directors in name only, not in substance, and that the real directors (that is, the "shadow" directors in terms of UK legislation, or the beneficial owners) were other people altogether. Reports that the directors concerned sometimes assigned their powers as directors by general power of attorney to others (effectively shadow directors or beneficial owners) and provided undated letters of resignation did nothing to enhance the reputation of the practice.[163] In relation to Sark, as at Autumn 1997, when the total population was some 575, information then fairly readily publicly available indicated that: (a) total directorships held by Sark residents may have been around 15,000 or more; (b) three residents appeared to hold between 1,600 and 3,000 directorships each; (c) a further 16 residents appeared each to hold more than 135 directorships each; and (d) a further 30 residents appeared each to hold between 15 and 100 directorships. These figures were no more than "broad orders of magnitude". On the one hand, they did not include any directorships of companies incorporated in the Caribbean centres (where information was not readily available). On the other hand, they may have included some directorships in companies that had been wound up. There appeared to be a high rate of turnover in the companies concerned. Since then, the position has significantly changed, primarily as a result of new legislation adopted by the Crown Dependencies and the enforcement of higher standards of conduct through disqualification and other regimes.

[163] See *Review of Financial Regulation in the Crown Dependencies* Cmd.4109–1 (1998), Ch.11.

APPENDIX 1

Company Directors Disqualification Act 1986

CHAPTER 46

An Act to consolidate certain enactments relating to the disqualification of persons from being directors of companies, and from being otherwise concerned with a company's affairs.

[25TH JULY 1986]

BE IT ENACTED by the Queen's most Excellent Majesty, by and with the advice and consent of the Lords Spiritual and Temporal, and Commons, in this present Parliament assembled, and by the authority of the same, as follows:—

Preliminary

1 Disqualification orders: general

A1–01

(1) In the circumstances specified below in this Act a court may, and under [sections 6 and 9A][1] shall, make against a person a disqualification order, that is to say an order that [for a period specified in the order—

(a) he shall not be a director of a company, act as receiver of a company's property or in any way, whether directly or indirectly, be concerned or take part in the promotion, formation or management of a company unless (in each case) he has the leave of the court, and

(b) he shall not act as an insolvency practitioner.][2]

(2) In each section of this Act which gives to a court power or, as the case may be, imposes on it the duty to make a disqualification order there is specified the maximum (and, in section 6, the minimum) period of disqualification which may or (as the case may be) must be imposed by means of the order [and, unless the court otherwise orders, the period of disqualification so imposed shall begin at the end of the period of 21 days beginning with the date of the order][3].

(3) Where a disqualification order is made against a person who is already subject to such an order [or to a disqualification undertaking][4], the periods specified in those orders [or, as the case may be, in the order and the undertaking][5] shall run concurrently.

(4) A disqualification order may be made on grounds which are or include matters other than criminal convictions, notwithstanding that the person in respect of whom it is to be made may be criminally liable in respect of those matters.

[1] Words substituted by Enterprise Act 2002 c. 40 Pt 7 s.204(3) (June 20, 2003).
[2] Words substituted by Insolvency Act 2000 c. 39 s.5(1) (April 2, 2001).
[3] Words inserted by Insolvency Act 2000 c. 39 s.5(2) (April 2, 2001).
[4] Words inserted by Insolvency Act 2000 c. 39 Sch.4 Pt 1 para.2 (April 2, 2001).
[5] Words inserted by Insolvency Act 2000 c. 39 Sch.4 Pt 1 para.2 (April 2, 2001).

[1A Disqualification undertakings: general

A1–02 (1) In the circumstances specified in sections 7 and 8 the Secretary of State may accept a disqualification undertaking, that is to say an undertaking by any person that, for a period specified in the undertaking, the person—

(a) will not be a director of a company, act as receiver of a company's property or in any way, whether directly or indirectly, be concerned or take part in the promotion, formation or management of a company unless (in each case) he has the leave of a court, and
(b) will not act as an insolvency practitioner.

(2) The maximum period which may be specified in a disqualification undertaking is 15 years; and the minimum period which may be specified in a disqualification undertaking under section 7 is two years.
(3) Where a disqualification undertaking by a person who is already subject to such an undertaking or to a disqualification order is accepted, the periods specified in those undertakings or (as the case may be) the undertaking and the order shall run concurrently.
(4) In determining whether to accept a disqualification undertaking by any person, the Secretary of State may take account of matters other than criminal convictions, notwithstanding that the person may be criminally liable in respect of those matters.][6]

Disqualification for general misconduct in connection with companies

2 Disqualification on conviction of indictable offence

A1–03 (1) The court may make a disqualification order against a person where he is convicted of an indictable offence (whether on indictment or summarily) in connection with the promotion, formation, management [, liquidation or striking off][7] of a company [with the receivership of a company's property or with his being an administrative receiver of a company][8].
(2) "The court" for this purpose means—

(a) any court having jurisdiction to wind up the company in relation to which the offence was committed, or
(b) the court by or before which the person is convicted of the offence, or
(c) in the case of a summary conviction in England and Wales, any other magistrates' court acting [in the same local justice][9] area;

and for the purposes of this section the definition of "indictable offence" in Schedule 1 to the Interpretation Act 1978 applies for Scotland as it does for England and Wales.

(3) The maximum period of disqualification under this section is—

(a) where the disqualification order is made by a court of summary jurisdiction, 5 years, and
(b) in any other case, 15 years.

[6] Added by Insolvency Act 2000 c. 39 s.6(2) (April 2, 2001).
[7] Words substituted by Deregulation and Contracting Out Act 1994 c. 40 Sch.11 para.6 (July 1, 1995).
[8] Words substituted by Insolvency Act 2000 c. 39 Sch.4 Pt 1 para.3 (April 2, 2001).
[9] Words substituted by Courts Act 2003 c. 39 Sch.8 para.300(a) (April 1, 2005).

3 Disqualification for persistent breaches of companies legislation

A1–04

(1) The court may make a disqualification order against a person where it appears to it that he has been persistently in default in relation to provisions of the companies legislation requiring any return, account or other document to be filed with, delivered or sent, or notice of any matter to be given, to the registrar of companies.

(2) On an application to the court for an order to be made under this section, the fact that a person has been persistently in default in relation to such provisions as are mentioned above may (without prejudice to its proof in any other manner) be conclusively proved by showing that in the 5 years ending with the date of the application he has been adjudged guilty (whether or not on the same occasion) of three or more defaults in relation to those provisions.

(3) A person is to be treated under subsection (2) as being adjudged guilty of a default in relation to any provision of that legislation if—

(a) he is convicted (whether on indictment or summarily) of an offence consisting in a contravention of or failure to comply with that provision (whether on his own part or on the part of any company), or

(b) a default order is made against him, that is to say an order under any of the following provisions—

(i) [section 452 of the Companies Act 2006][10] (order requiring delivery of company accounts),

[(ia) [section 456][11] of that Act (order requiring preparation of revised accounts)][12]

(ii) [section 1113 of that Act (enforcement of company's filing obligations)][13],

(iii) section 41 of the Insolvency Act [1986][14] (enforcement of receiver's or manager's duty to make returns), or

(iv) section 170 of that Act (corresponding provision for liquidator in winding up),

in respect of any such contravention of or failure to comply with that provision (whether on his own part or on the part of any company).

(4) In this section "the court" means any court having jurisdiction to wind up any of the companies in relation to which the offence or other default has been or is alleged to have been committed.

[(4A) In this section "the companies legislation" means the Companies Acts and Parts 1 to 7 of the Insolvency Act 1986 (company insolvency and winding up).][15]

(5) The maximum period of disqualification under this section is 5 years.

4 Disqualification for fraud, etc., in winding up

A1–05

(1) The court may make a disqualification order against a person if, in the course of the winding up of a company, it appears that he—

[10] Words substituted subject to savings specified in SI 2008/948 arts 11 and 12 by Companies Act 2006 (Consequential Amendments etc) Order 2008/948 Sch.1 Pt 2 para.106(2)(a) (April 6, 2008).

[11] Words substituted subject to savings specified in SI 2008/948 arts 11 and 12 by Companies Act 2006 (Consequential Amendments etc) Order 2008/948 Sch.1 Pt 2 para.106(2)(b) (April 6, 2008).

[12] Added (subject to the transitional and savings provisions in SI 1990/2569, arts. 3, 6) by Companies Act 1989 (c. 40), s.23, Sch.10 Pt 2 para.35(2)(b).

[13] Words substituted by Companies Act 2006 (Consequential Amendments, Transitional Provisions and Savings) Order 2009/1941 Sch.1 para.85(2)(a)(i) (October 1, 2009).

[14] Word inserted by Companies Act 2006 (Consequential Amendments, Transitional Provisions and Savings) Order 2009/1941 Sch.1 para.85(2)(a)(ii) (October 1, 2009).

[15] Added by Companies Act 2006 (Consequential Amendments, Transitional Provisions and Savings) Order 2009/1941 Sch.1 para.85(2)(b) (October 1, 2009).

(a) has been guilty of an offence for which he is liable (whether he has been convicted or not) under [section 993 of the Companies Act 2006][16] (fraudulent trading), or
(b) has otherwise been guilty, while an officer or liquidator of the company [receiver of the company's property or administrative receiver of the company][17], of any fraud in relation to the company or of any breach of his duty as such officer, liquidator, [receiver or administrative receiver][18].

(2) In this section "the court" means any court having jurisdiction to wind up any of the companies in relation to which the offence or other default has been or is alleged to have been committed; and "officer" includes a shadow director.
(3) The maximum period of disqualification under this section is 15 years.

5 Disqualification on summary conviction

A1–06 (1) An offence counting for the purposes of this section is one of which a person is convicted (either on indictment or summarily) in consequence of a contravention of, or failure to comply with, any provision of the companies legislation requiring a return, account or other document to be filed with, delivered or sent, or notice of any matter to be given, to the registrar of companies (whether the contravention or failure is on the person's own part or on the part of any company).
(2) Where a person is convicted of a summary offence counting for those purposes, the court by which he is convicted (or, in England and Wales, any other magistrates' court acting [in the same local justice][19] area) may make a disqualification order against him if the circumstances specified in the next subsection are present.
(3) Those circumstances are that, during the 5 years ending with the date of the conviction, the person has had made against him, or has been convicted of, in total not less than 3 default orders and offences counting for the purposes of this section; and those offences may include that of which he is convicted as mentioned in subsection (2) and any other offence of which he is convicted on the same occasion.
(4) For the purposes of this section—

(a) the definition of "summary offence" in Schedule 1 to the Interpretation Act 1978 applies for Scotland as for England and Wales, and
(b) "default order" means the same as in section 3(3)(b).

[(4A) In this section "the companies legislation" means the Companies Acts and Parts 1 to 7 of the Insolvency Act 1986 (company insolvency and winding up).][20]
(5) The maximum period of disqualification under this section is 5 years.

Disqualification for unfitness

6 Duty of court to disqualify unfit directors of insolvent companies

A1–07 (1) The court shall make a disqualification order against a person in any case where, on an application under this section, it is satisfied—

[16] Words substituted by Companies Act 2006 (Commencement No. 3, Consequential Amendments, Transitional Provisions and Savings) Order 2007/2194 Sch.4 Pt 3 para.46 (October 1, 2007).
[17] Words substituted by Insolvency Act 2000 c. 39 Sch.4 Pt 1 para.4 (April 2, 2001).
[18] Words substituted by Insolvency Act 2000 c. 39 Sch.4 Pt 1 para.4 (April 2, 2001).
[19] Words substituted by Courts Act 2003 c. 39 Sch.8 para.300(b) (April 1, 2005).
[20] Added by Companies Act 2006 (Consequential Amendments, Transitional Provisions and Savings) Order 2009/1941 Sch.1 para.85(3) (October 1, 2009).

(a) that he is or has been a director of a company which has at any time become insolvent (whether while he was a director or subsequently), and

(b) that his conduct as a director of that company (either taken alone or taken together with his conduct as a director of any other company or companies) makes him unfit to be concerned in the management of a company.

(2) For the purposes of this section and the next, a company becomes insolvent if—

(a) the company goes into liquidation at a time when its assets are insufficient for the payment of its debts and other liabilities and the expenses of the winding up,

[(b) the company enters administration,][21]

(c) an administrative receiver of the company is appointed;

and references to a person's conduct as a director of any company or companies include, where that company or any of those companies has become insolvent, that person's conduct in relation to any matter connected with or arising out of the insolvency of that company.

[(3) In this section and section 7(2), "the court" means—

(a) where the company in question is being or has been wound up by the court, that court,

(b) where the company in question is being or has been wound up voluntarily, any court which has or (as the case may be) had jurisdiction to wind it up,

[(c) where neither paragraph (a) nor (b) applies but an administrator or administrative receiver has at any time been appointed in respect of the company in question, any court which has jurisdiction to wind it up.][22]

(3A) Sections 117 and 120 of the Insolvency Act 1986 (jurisdiction) shall apply for the purposes of subsection (3) as if the references in the definitions of "registered office" to the presentation of the petition for winding up were references—

(a) in a case within paragraph (b) of that subsection, to the passing of the resolution for voluntary winding up,

[(b) in a case within paragraph (c) of that subsection, to the appointment of the administrator or (as the case may be) administrative receiver.][23]

(3B) Nothing in subsection (3) invalidates any proceedings by reason of their being taken in the wrong court; and proceedings—

(a) for or in connection with a disqualification order under this section, or

(b) in connection with a disqualification undertaking accepted under section 7,

may be retained in the court in which the proceedings were commenced, although it may not be the court in which they ought to have been commenced.

(3C) In this section and section 7, "director" includes a shadow director.][24]

(4) Under this section the minimum period of disqualification is 2 years, and the maximum period is 15 years.

[21] Substituted subject to transitional provisions specified in SI 2003/2093 art.3 by Enterprise Act 2002 c. 40 Sch.17 para.41(a) (September 15, 2003: substitution has effect subject to transitional provisions specified in SI 2003/2093 art.3).

[22] Substituted subject to transitional provisions specified in SI 2003/2093 art.3 by Enterprise Act 2002 c. 40 Sch.17 para.41(b) (September 15, 2003: substitution has effect subject to transitional provisions specified in SI 2003/2093 art.3).

[23] Substituted subject to transitional provisions specified in SI 2003/2093 art.3 by Enterprise Act 2002 c. 40 Sch.17 para.41(c) (September 15, 2003: substitution has effect subject to transitional provisions specified in SI 2003/2093 art.3).

[24] Sections 6(3), (3A), (3B) and (3C) substituted for s.6(3) by Insolvency Act 2000 c. 39 Sch.4 Pt 1 para.5(1)(a) (April 2, 2001).

7 [Disqualification order or undertaking; and reporting provisions][25]

A1–08 (1) If it appears to the Secretary of State that it is expedient in the public interest that a disqualification order under section 6 should be made against any person, an application for the making of such an order against that person may be made—

(a) by the Secretary of State, or
(b) if the Secretary of State so directs in the case of a person who is or has been a director of a company which is being [or has been][26] wound up by the court in England and Wales, by the official receiver.

(2) Except with the leave of the court, an application for the making under that section of a disqualification order against any person shall not be made after the end of the period of 2 years beginning with the day on which the company of which that person is or has been a director became insolvent.

[(2A) If it appears to the Secretary of State that the conditions mentioned in section 6(1) are satisfied as respects any person who has offered to give him a disqualification undertaking, he may accept the undertaking if it appears to him that it is expedient in the public interest that he should do so (instead of applying, or proceeding with an application, for a disqualification order).][27]

(3) If it appears to the office-holder responsible under this section, that is to say—

(a) in the case of a company which is being wound up by the court in England and Wales, the official receiver,
(b) in the case of a company which is being wound up otherwise, the liquidator,
[(c) in the case of a company which is in administration, the administrator, or][28]
(d) in the case of a company of which there is an administrative receiver, that receiver,

that the conditions mentioned in section 6(1) are satisfied as respects a person who is or has been a director of that company, the office-holder shall forthwith report the matter to the Secretary of State.

(4) The Secretary of State or the official receiver may require the liquidator, administrator or administrative receiver of a company, or the former liquidator, administrator or administrative receiver of a company—

(a) to furnish him with such information with respect to any person's conduct as a director of the company, and
(b) to produce and permit inspection of such books, papers and other records relevant to that person's conduct as such a director,

as the Secretary of State or the official receiver may reasonably require for the purpose of determining whether to exercise, or of exercising, any function of his under this section.

8 Disqualification after investigation of company

A1–09 [(1) If it appears to the Secretary of State from investigative material that it is expedient in the public interest that a disqualification order should be made against a person who is, or has been, a director or shadow director of a company, he may apply to the court for such an order.

[25] Words substituted by Insolvency Act 2000 c. 39 Sch.4 Pt 1 para.6(b) (April 2, 2001).
[26] Words inserted by Insolvency Act 2000 c. 39 Sch.4 Pt 1 para.6(a) (April 2, 2001).
[27] Added by Insolvency Act 2000 c. 39 s.6(3) (April 2, 2001).
[28] Substituted subject to transitional provisions specified in SI 2003/2093 art.3 by Enterprise Act 2002 c. 40 Sch.17 para.42 (September 15, 2003: substitution has effect subject to transitional provisions specified in SI 2003/2093 art.3).

(1A) "Investigative material" means—

[(a) a report made by inspectors under—

(i) section 437 of the Companies Act 1985, or

(ii) section 167, 168, 169 or 284 of the Financial Services and Markets Act 2000; and

(but see section 22D(2)).][29]

(b) information or documents obtained under—

[(i) section 437, 446E, 447, 448, 451A or 453A of the Companies Act 1985;][30]

(ii) section 2 of the Criminal Justice Act 1987;

(iii) section 28 of the Criminal Law (Consolidation)(Scotland) Act 1995;

(iv) section 83 of the Companies Act 1989; or

(v) section 165, 171, 172, 173 or 175 of the Financial Services and Markets Act 2000.][31]

(2) The court may make a disqualification order against a person where, on an application under this section of that Act, it is satisfied that his conduct in relation to the company makes him unfit to be concerned in the management of a company.

[(2A) Where it appears to the Secretary of State from such report, information or documents that, in the case of a person who has offered to give him a disqualification undertaking—

(a) the conduct of the person in relation to a company of which the person is or has been a director or shadow director makes him unfit to be concerned in the management of a company, and

(b) it is expedient in the public interest that he should accept the undertaking (instead of applying, or proceeding with an application, for a disqualification order),

he may accept the undertaking.][32]

(3) In this section "the court" means the High Court or, in Scotland, the Court of Session.

(4) The maximum period of disqualification under this section is 15 years.

[8A Variation etc. of disqualification undertaking

A1–10

(1) The court may, on the application of a person who is subject to a disqualification undertaking—

(a) reduce the period for which the undertaking is to be in force, or

(b) provide for it to cease to be in force.

(2) On the hearing of an application under subsection (1), the Secretary of State shall appear and call the attention of the court to any matters which seem to him to be relevant, and may himself give evidence or call witnesses.

[(2A) Subsection (2) does not apply to an application in the case of an undertaking given under section 9B, and in such a case on the hearing of the application whichever of the OFT or a specified regulator (within the meaning of section 9E) accepted the undertaking—

[29] Substituted by Companies Act 2006 (Consequential Amendments, Transitional Provisions and Savings) Order 2009/1941 Sch.1 para.85(4) (October 1, 2009).

[30] Word inserted by Companies Act 2006 c. 46 Pt 32 s.1039(a), (b) (October 1, 2007).

[31] Sections 8(1)–(1A) are substituted for s.8(1) by Financial Services and Markets Act 2000 (Consequential Amendments and Repeals) Order 2001/3649 Pt 2 art.39 (December 1, 2001).

[32] Added by Insolvency Act 2000 c. 39 s.6(4) (April 2, 2001).

(a) must appear and call the attention of the court to any matters which appear to it or him (as the case may be) to be relevant;
(b) may give evidence or call witnesses.][33]

[(3) In this section "the court"—

(a) in the case of an undertaking given under section 9B means the High Court or (in Scotland) the Court of Session;
(b) in any other case has the same meaning as in section 7(2) or 8 (as the case may be).][34]][35]

9 Matters for determining unfitness of directors

A1–11 (1) Where it falls to a court to determine whether a person's conduct as a director [. . .][36] of any particular company or companies makes him unfit to be concerned in the management of a company, the court shall, as respects his conduct as a director of that company or, as the case may be, each of those companies, have regard in particular—

(a) to the matters mentioned in Part I of Schedule 1 to this Act, and
(b) where the company has become insolvent, to the matters mentioned in Part II of that Schedule;

and references in that Schedule to the director and the company are to be read accordingly.

[(1A) In determining whether he may accept a disqualification undertaking from any person the Secretary of State shall, as respects the person's conduct as a director of any company concerned, have regard in particular—

(a) to the matters mentioned in Part I of Schedule 1 to this Act, and
(b) where the company has become insolvent, to the matters mentioned in Part II of that Schedule;

and references in that Schedule to the director and the company are to be read accordingly.][37]

(2) Section 6(2) applies for the purposes of this section and Schedule 1 as it applies for the purposes of sections 6 and 7 [and in this section and that Schedule "director" includes a shadow director][38].
(3) [. . .][39]
(4) The Secretary of State may by order modify any of the provisions of Schedule 1; and such an order may contain such transitional provisions as may appear to the Secretary of State necessary or expedient.
(5) The power to make orders under this section is exercisable by statutory instrument subject to annulment in pursuance of a resolution of either House of Parliament.

[33] Added by Enterprise Act 2002 c. 40 Pt 7 s.204(4) (June 20, 2003). See the Enterprise Act 2002, s.276, Sch.24, paras 2–6 for transitional and transitory provisions.
[34] Substituted by Enterprise Act 2002 c. 40 Pt 7 s.204(5) (June 20, 2003). See the Enterprise Act 2002, s.276, Sch.24, paras 2–6 for transitional and transitory provisions.
[35] Added by Insolvency Act 2000 c. 39 s.6(5) (April 2, 2001).
[36] Words repealed by Insolvency Act 2000 c. 39 Sch.5 para.1 (April 2, 2001 as SI 2001/766).
[37] Added by Insolvency Act 2000 c. 39 s.6(6) (April 2, 2001).
[38] Words inserted by Insolvency Act 2000 c. 39 Sch.4 Pt 1 para.7(b) (April 2, 2001).
[39] Repealed by Companies Act 2006 (Consequential Amendments, Transitional Provisions and Savings) Order 2009/1941 Sch.1 para.85(5) (October 1, 2009).

[Disqualification for competition infringements][40]

[9A Competition disqualification order

A1–12

(1) The court must make a disqualification order against a person if the following two conditions are satisfied in relation to him.

(2) The first condition is that an undertaking which is a company of which he is a director commits a breach of competition law.

(3) The second condition is that the court considers that his conduct as a director makes him unfit to be concerned in the management of a company.

(4) An undertaking commits a breach of competition law if it engages in conduct which infringes any of the following—

(a) the Chapter 1 prohibition (within the meaning of the Competition Act 1998) (prohibition on agreements, etc. preventing, restricting or distorting competition);

(b) the Chapter 2 prohibition (within the meaning of that Act) (prohibition on abuse of a dominant position);

(c) Article 81 of the Treaty establishing the European Community (prohibition on agreements, etc. preventing, restricting or distorting competition);

(d) Article 82 of that Treaty (prohibition on abuse of a dominant position).

(5) For the purpose of deciding under subsection (3) whether a person is unfit to be concerned in the management of a company the court—

(a) must have regard to whether subsection (6) applies to him;

(b) may have regard to his conduct as a director of a company in connection with any other breach of competition law;

(c) must not have regard to the matters mentioned in Schedule 1.

(6) This subsection applies to a person if as a director of the company—

(a) his conduct contributed to the breach of competition law mentioned in subsection (2);

(b) his conduct did not contribute to the breach but he had reasonable grounds to suspect that the conduct of the undertaking constituted the breach and he took no steps to prevent it;

(c) he did not know but ought to have known that the conduct of the undertaking constituted the breach.

(7) For the purposes of subsection (6)(a) it is immaterial whether the person knew that the conduct of the undertaking constituted the breach.

(8) For the purposes of subsection (4)(a) or (c) references to the conduct of an undertaking are references to its conduct taken with the conduct of one or more other undertakings.

(9) The maximum period of disqualification under this section is 15 years.

(10) An application under this section for a disqualification order may be made by the OFT or by a specified regulator.

(11) Section 60 of the Competition Act 1998 (c. 41) (consistent treatment of questions arising under United Kingdom and Community law) applies in relation to any question arising by virtue of subsection (4)(a) or (b) above as it applies in relation to any question arising under Part 1 of that Act.][41]

[40] Added by Enterprise Act 2002 c. 40 Pt 7 s.204(2) (June 20, 2003).

[41] Added by Enterprise Act 2002 c. 40 Pt 7 s.204(2) (June 20, 2003). See the Enterprise Act 2002, s.276, Sch.24, paras 2–6 for transitional and transitory provisions.

[9B Competition undertakings

A1–13 (1) This section applies if—

(a) the OFT or a specified regulator thinks that in relation to any person an undertaking which is a company of which he is a director has committed or is committing a breach of competition law,
(b) the OFT or the specified regulator thinks that the conduct of the person as a director makes him unfit to be concerned in the management of a company, and
(c) the person offers to give the OFT or the specified regulator (as the case may be) a disqualification undertaking.

(2) The OFT or the specified regulator (as the case may be) may accept a disqualification undertaking from the person instead of applying for or proceeding with an application for a disqualification order.
(3) A disqualification undertaking is an undertaking by a person that for the period specified in the undertaking he will not—
(a) be a director of a company;
(b) act as receiver of a company's property;
(c) in any way, whether directly or indirectly, be concerned or take part in the promotion, formation or management of a company;
(d) act as an insolvency practitioner.
(4) But a disqualification undertaking may provide that a prohibition falling within subsection (3)(a) to (c) does not apply if the person obtains the leave of the court.
(5) The maximum period which may be specified in a disqualification undertaking is 15 years.
(6) If a disqualification undertaking is accepted from a person who is already subject to a disqualification undertaking under this Act or to a disqualification order the periods specified in those undertakings or the undertaking and the order (as the case may be) run concurrently.
(7) Subsections (4) to (8) of section 9A apply for the purposes of this section as they apply for the purposes of that section but in the application of subsection (5) of that section the reference to the court must be construed as a reference to the OFT or a specified regulator (as the case may be).][42]

[9C Competition investigations

A1–14 (1) If the OFT or a specified regulator has reasonable grounds for suspecting that a breach of competition law has occurred it or he (as the case may be) may carry out an investigation for the purpose of deciding whether to make an application under section 9A for a disqualification order.
(2) For the purposes of such an investigation sections 26 to 30 of the Competition Act 1998 (c. 41) apply to the OFT and the specified regulators as they apply to the OFT for the purposes of an investigation under section 25 of that Act.
(3) Subsection (4) applies if as a result of an investigation under this section the OFT or a specified regulator proposes to apply under section 9A for a disqualification order.
(4) Before making the application the OFT or regulator (as the case may be) must—

(a) give notice to the person likely to be affected by the application, and
(b) give that person an opportunity to make representations.][43]

[42] Added by Enterprise Act 2002 c. 40 Pt 7 s.204(2) (June 20, 2003). See the Enterprise Act 2002, s.276, Sch.24, paras 2–6 for transitional and transitory provisions.
[43] Added by Enterprise Act 2002 c. 40 Pt 7 s.204(2) (June 20, 2003). See the Enterprise Act 2002, s.276, Sch.24, paras 2–6 for transitional and transitory provisions.

[9D Co-ordination

A1–15

(1) The Secretary of State may make regulations for the purpose of co-ordinating the performance of functions under sections 9A to 9C (relevant functions) which are exercisable concurrently by two or more persons.
(2) Section 54(5) to (7) of the Competition Act 1998 (c. 41) applies to regulations made under this section as it applies to regulations made under that section and for that purpose in that section—

(a) references to Part 1 functions must be read as references to relevant functions,
(b) references to a regulator must be read as references to a specified regulator;
(c) a competent person also includes any of the specified regulators.

(3) The power to make regulations under this section must be exercised by statutory instrument subject to annulment in pursuance of a resolution of either House of Parliament.
(4) Such a statutory instrument may—

(a) contain such incidental, supplemental, consequential and transitional provision as the Secretary of State thinks appropriate;
(b) make different provision for different cases.][44]

[9E Interpretation

A1–16

(1) This section applies for the purposes of sections 9A to 9D.
(2) Each of the following is a specified regulator for the purposes of a breach of competition law in relation to a matter in respect of which he or it has a function—

[(a) the Office of Communications;][45]
(b) the Gas and Electricity Markets Authority;
[(c) the Water Services Regulation Authority;][46]
(d) [the Office of Rail Regulation][47];
(e) the Civil Aviation Authority.

(3) The court is the High Court or (in Scotland) the Court of Session.
(4) Conduct includes omission.
(5) Director includes shadow director.][48]

Other cases of disqualification

10 Participation in wrongful trading

A1–17

(1) Where the court makes a declaration under section 213 or 214 of the Insolvency Act [1986][49] that a person is liable to make a contribution to a company's assets, then, whether or not an application for such an order is made by any person, the court may,

[44] Added by Enterprise Act 2002 c. 40 Pt 7 s.204(2) (June 20, 2003). See the Enterprise Act 2002, s.276, Sch.24, paras 2–6 for transitional and transitory provisions.
[45] Substituted by Communications Act 2003 c. 21. See the Enterprise Act 2002, s.276, Sch.24, paras 2–6 for transitional and transitory provisions. Sch.17 para.83 (December 29, 2003).
[46] Substituted by Water Act 2003 c. 37 Sch.7 Pt 2 para.25 (April 1, 2006).
[47] Words substituted by Railways and Transport Safety Act 2003 c. 20 Sch.2 Pt 2 para.19(j) (July 5, 2004).
[48] Added by Enterprise Act 2002 c. 40 Pt 7 s.204(2) (June 20, 2003). See the Enterprise Act 2002, s.276, Sch.24, paras 2–6 for transitional and transitory provisions.
[49] Word inserted by Companies Act 2006 (Consequential Amendments, Transitional Provisions and Savings) Order 2009/1941 Sch.1 para.85(6)(a) (October 1, 2009).

if it thinks fit, also make a disqualification order against the person to whom the declaration relates.

(2) The maximum period of disqualification under this section is 15 years.

11 Undischarged bankrupts

A1–18 [(1) *It is an offence for a person who is an undischarged bankrupt to act as director of, or directly or in directly to take part in or be concerned in the promotion, formation or management of, a company, except with the leave of the court.*][50]

[(1) It is an offence for a person to act as director of a company or directly or indirectly to take part in or be concerned in the promotion, formation or management of a company, without the leave of the court, at a time when—

(a) he is an undischarged bankrupt,

[(aa) a moratorium period under a debt relief order applies in relation to him,][51] or

(b) a bankruptcy restrictions order [or a debt relief restrictions order][52] is in force in respect of him.][53]

(2) "The court" for this purpose is the court by which the person was adjudged bankrupt or, in Scotland, sequestration of his estates was awarded.

(3) In England and Wales, the leave of the court shall not be given unless notice of intention to apply for it has been served on the official receiver; and it is the latter's duty, if he is of opinion that it is contrary to the public interest that the application should be granted, to attend on the hearing of the application and oppose it.

[(4) In this section "company" includes a company incorporated outside Great Britain that has an established place of business in Great Britain.][54]

12 Failure to pay under county court administration order [*Disabilities on revocation of administration order*]

A1–19 (1) The following has effect where a court under section 429 of the Insolvency Act revokes an administration order under Part VI of the County Courts Act 1984.

(2) A person to whom [*Section 429 of the Insolvency Act 1986 applies by virtue of an order under subsection (2) of that section*] [that section applies by virtue of the order under section 429(2)(b)] shall not, except with the leave of the court which made the order, act as director or liquidator of, or directly or indirectly take part or be concerned in the promotion, formation or management of, a company.

Amendments Pending

New heading (shown italicised in square brackets) to be inserted by Tribunals, Courts and Enforcement Act 2007, s.106(2) and Sch.16, para.5(2) (date to be announced).

Section 12(1): to be repealed by Tribunals, Courts and Enforcement Act 2007, s.106(2) and Sch.16, para.5(3); s146 and Sch.23, Pt 5, para.1 (date to be announced).

[50] Section 11(1) as shown in italics continues to apply in Scotland.

[51] Inserted by the Tribunals, Courts and Enforcement Act 2007, s.108(3), Sch.20, Pt 2, para.16(1), (2) (February 24, 2009).

[52] Words in square brackets inserted by the Tribunals, Courts and Enforcement Act 2007, s.108(3), Sch.20, Pt 2, para.16(1), (3) (February 24, 2009).

[53] In relation to England and Wales, subs.(1) is substituted by the Enterprise Act 2002, s.257(3), Sch.21, para.5 (April 1, 2004). See the Enterprise Act 2002, s.256(2), Sch.19 (as amended by SI 2003/2096 art.3) for transitional provisions.

[54] Added by Companies Act 2006 (Consequential Amendments, Transitional Provisions and Savings) Order 2009/1941 Sch.1 para.85(7) (October 1, 2009).

Section 12(2): to be amended by substitution of italicised words in square brackets in place of following words in square brackets by Tribunals, Courts and Enforcement Act 2007, s.106(2) and Sch.16, para.5(4) (date to be announced).

[12A Northern Irish disqualification orders

A1–20

A person subject to a disqualification order under [the Company Directors Disqualification (Northern Ireland) Order 2002][55]—

(a) shall not be a director of a company, act as receiver of a company's property or in any way, whether directly or indirectly, be concerned or take part in the promotion, formation or management of a company unless (in each case) he has the leave of the High Court of Northern Ireland, and
(b) shall not act as an insolvency practitioner.][56]

[12B Northern Irish disqualification undertakings

A1–21

A person subject to a disqualification undertaking under the Company Directors Disqualification (Northern Ireland) Order 2002—

(a) shall not be a director of a company, act as receiver of a company's property or in any way, whether directly or indirectly, be concerned or take part in the promotion, formation or management of a company unless (in each case) he has the leave of the High Court of Northern Ireland, and
(b) shall not act as an insolvency practitioner.][57]

Consequences of contravention

13 Criminal penalties

A1–22

If a person acts in contravention of a disqualification order or [disqualification undertaking or in contravention][58] of section 12(2), [,12A or 12B][59], or is guilty of an offence under section 11, he is liable—

(a) on conviction on indictment, to imprisonment for not more than 2 years or a fine, or both; and
(b) on summary conviction, to imprisonment for not more than 6 months or a fine not exceeding the statutory maximum, or both.

[55] Words substituted by Companies Act 2006 (Consequential Amendments, Transitional Provisions and Savings) Order 2009/1941 Sch.1 para.85(8) (October 1, 2009).

[56] Inserted subject to transitional provisions in SI 2001/766, art.3(3) by Insolvency Act 2000 c. 39 s.7(1) (April 2, 2001). (except in relation to a person subject to – disqualification order under the Company (Western Ireland) Order 1989, Pt 2, SI 1989/2404 made before that date): see SI 2001/766 Arts 2(1)(a), 3(3)(a).

[57] Inserted by SI 2004/1941, art.2(1), (2) (September 1, 2004) (in relation to disqualification undertakings under the Company Directors Disqualification (Northern Ireland) Order 2002, SI 2002/3150 (NI 4) accepted on or after that date): see SI 2004/1941, art.1(2).

[58] Words inserted by Insolvency Act 2000 c. 39 Sch.4 Pt 1 para.8(a) (April 2, 2001).

[59] Words substituted by SI 2004/1941, art.2(3) (September 1, 2004) (in relation to disqualification undertakings under the Company Directors Disqualification (Northern Ireland) Order 2002, SI 2002/3150 (NI 4) accepted on or after that date): see SI 2004/1941, art.1(2).

14 Offences by body corporate

A1–23 (1) Where a body corporate is guilty of an offence of acting in contravention of a disqualification order [or disqualification undertaking or in contravention of section 12A][60] [or 12B][61], and it is proved that the offence occurred with the consent or connivance of, or was attributable to any neglect on the part of any director, manager, secretary or other similar officer of the body corporate, or any person who was purporting to act in any such capacity he, as well as the body corporate, is guilty of the offence and liable to be proceeded against and punished accordingly.

(2) Where the affairs of a body corporate are managed by its members, subsection (1) applies in relation to the acts and defaults of a member in connection with his functions of management as if he were a director of the body corporate.

15 Personal liability for company's debts where person acts while disqualified

A1–24 (1) A person is personally responsible for all the relevant debts of a company if at any time—

(a) in contravention of a disqualification order or [disqualification undertaking or in contravention][62] of section 11 [,12A or 12B][63] of this Act he is involved in the management of the company, or

[(b) as a person who is involved in the management of the company, he acts or is willing to act on instructions given without the leave of the court by a person whom he knows at that time—

(i) to be the subject of a disqualification order made or disqualification undertaking accepted under this Act or under the Company Directors Disqualification (Northern Ireland) Order 2002, or

(ii) to be an undischarged bankrupt.][64]

(2) Where a person is personally responsible under this section for the relevant debts of a company, he is jointly and severally liable in respect of those debts with the company and any other person who, whether under this section or otherwise, is so liable.

(3) For the purposes of this section the relevant debts of a company are—

(a) in relation to a person who is personally responsible under paragraph (a) of subsection (1), such debts and other liabilities of the company as are incurred at a time when that person was involved in the management of the company, and

(b) in relation to a person who is personally responsible under paragraph (b) of that subsection, such debts and other liabilities of the company as are incurred at a time when that person was acting or was willing to act on instructions given as mentioned in that paragraph.

(4) For the purposes of this section, a person is involved in the management of a company if he is a director of the company or if he is concerned, whether directly or indirectly, or takes part, in the management of the company.

[60] Words inserted subject to transitional provisions in SI 2001/766, art.3(3) by Insolvency Act 2000 c. 39 Sch.4 Pt 1 para.9 (April 2, 2001).

[61] Words inserted by SI 2004/1941, art.2(1), (4) (September 1, 2004) (in relation to disqualification undertakings under the Company Directors Disqualification (Northern Ireland) Order 2002, SI 2002/3150 (NI 4) accepted on or after that date): see SI 2004/1941, art.1(2).

[62] Words inserted subject to transitional provisions in SI 2001/766, art.3(3) by Insolvency Act 2000 c. 39 Sch.4 Pt 1 para.10(2)(a) (April 2, 2001).

[63] Words inserted by SI 2004/1941, art.2(5)(a)(i) (September 1, 2004) (in relation to disqualification undertakings under the Company Directors Disqualification (Northern Ireland) Order 2002, SI 2002/3150 (NI 4) accepted on or after that date): see SI 2004/1941, art.1(2).

[64] Substituted by Companies Act 2006 (Consequential Amendments, Transitional Provisions and Savings) Order 2009/1941 Sch.1 para.85(9)(a) (October 1, 2009).

[(5) For the purposes of this section a person who, as a person involved in the management of a company, has at any time acted on instructions given without the leave of the court by a person whom he knew at that time—

(a) to be the subject of a disqualification order made or disqualification undertaking accepted under this Act or under the Company Directors Disqualification (Northern Ireland) Order 2002, or

(b) to be an undischarged bankrupt,

is presumed, unless the contrary is shown, to have been willing at any time thereafter to act on any instructions given by that person.][65]

Supplementary provisions

16 Application for disqualification order

A1–25

(1) A person intending to apply for the making of a disqualification order by the court having jurisdiction to wind up a company shall give not less than 10 days' notice of his intention to the person against whom the order is sought; and on the hearing of the application the last-mentioned person may appear and himself give evidence or call witnesses.

(2) An application to a court with jurisdiction to wind up companies for the making against any person of a disqualification order under any of [sections 2 to 4][66] may be made by the Secretary of State or the official receiver, or by the liquidator or any past or present member or creditor of any company in relation to which that person has committed or is alleged to have committed an offence or other default.

(3) On the hearing of any application under this Act made by [a person falling within subsection (4)][67], the applicant shall appear and call the attention of the court to any matters which seem to him to be relevant, and may himself give evidence or call witnesses.

[(4) The following fall within this subsection—

(a) the Secretary of State;
(b) the official receiver;
(c) the OFT;
(d) the liquidator;
(e) a specified regulator (within the meaning of section 9E).][68]

[17 Application for leave under an order or undertaking

A1–26

(1) Where a person is subject to a disqualification order made by a court having jurisdiction to wind up companies, any application for leave for the purposes of section 1(1)(a) shall be made to that court.

(2) Where—

(a) a person is subject to a disqualification order made under section 2 by a court other than a court having jurisdiction to wind up companies, or

(b) a person is subject to a disqualification order made under section 5.

[65] Substituted by Companies Act 2006 (Consequential Amendments, Transitional Provisions and Savings) Order 2009/1941 Sch.1 para.85(9)(b) (October 1, 2009).

[66] Words substituted by Insolvency Act 2000 c. 39 Sch.4 Pt 1 para.11(1) (April 2, 2001).

[67] Words substituted by Enterprise Act 2002 c. 40 Pt 7 s.204(6) (June 20, 2003). See Enterprise Act 2002, s.276, Sch.24, paras 2–6 for transitional and transitory provisions.

[68] Added by Enterprise Act 2002 c. 40 Pt 7 s.204(7) (June 20, 2003). See Enterprise Act 2002, s.276, Sch.24, paras 2–6 for transitional and transitory provisions.

any application for leave for the purposes of section 1(1)(a) shall be made to any court which, when the order was made, had jurisdiction to wind up the company (or, if there is more than one such company, any of the companies) to which the offence (or any of the offences) in question related.

(3) Where a person is subject to a disqualification undertaking accepted at any time under section 7 or 8, any application for leave for the purposes of section 1A(1)(a) shall be made to any court to which, if the Secretary of State had applied for a disqualification order under the section in question at that time, his application could have been made.

[(3A) Where a person is subject to a disqualification undertaking accepted at any time under section 9B any application for leave for the purposes of section 9B(4) must be made to the High Court or (in Scotland) the Court of Session.][69]

(4) But where a person is subject to two or more disqualification orders or undertakings (or to one or more disqualification orders and to one or more disqualification undertakings), any application for leave for the purposes of section 1(1)(a)[, 1A(1)(a) or 9B(4)][70] shall be made to any court to which any such application relating to the latest order to be made, or undertaking to be accepted, could be made.

(5) On the hearing of an application for leave for the purposes of section 1(1)(a) or 1A(1)(a), the Secretary of State shall appear and call the attention of the court to any matters which seem to him to be relevant, and may himself give evidence or call witnesses.

(6) Subsection (5) does not apply to an application for leave for the purposes of section 1(1)(a) if the application for the disqualification order was made under section 9A.

(7) In such a case and in the case of an application for leave for the purposes of section 9B(4) on the hearing of the application whichever of the OFT or a specified regulator (within the meaning of section 9E) applied for the order or accepted the undertaking (as the case may be)—

(a) must appear and draw the attention of the court to any matters which appear to it or him (as the case may be) to be relevant;

(b) may give evidence or call witnesses.][71]][72]

18 Register of disqualification orders and undertakings[73]

A1–27 (1) The Secretary of State may make regulations requiring officers of courts to furnish him with such particulars as the regulations may specify of cases in which—

(a) a disqualification order is made, or

(b) any action is taken by a court in consequence of which such an order [or a disqualification undertaking][74] is varied or ceases to be in force, or

(c) leave is granted by a court for a person subject to such an order to do any thing which otherwise the order prohibits him from doing;[or]

[69] Added by Enterprise Act 2002 c. 40 Pt 7 s.204(8) (June 20, 2003). See Enterprise Act 2002, s.276, Sch.24, paras 2–6 for transitional and transitory provisions.

[70] Words substituted by Enterprise Act 2002 c. 40 Pt 7 s.204(9) (June 20, 2003). See Enterprise Act 2002, s.276, Sch.24, paras 2–6 for transitional and transitory provisions.

[71] Added by Enterprise Act 2002 c. 40 Pt 7 s.204(10) (June 20, 2003). See Enterprise Act 2002, s.276, Sch.24, paras 2–6 for transitional and transitory provisions.

[72] Substituted subject to transitional provisions in SI 2001/766, art.3(2) by Insolvency Act 2000 c. 39 Sch.4 Pt 1 para.12(1) (April 2, 2001) (except in relation to an application for leave of the court made before that date by a person subject to a disqualification order under the Company Directors Disqualification Act 1986 made on the application of the Secretary of State, the official receiver or the liquidator): see SI 2001/766, Arts 2(1)(a), 3(2).

[73] Words substituted by Insolvency Act 2000 c. 39 Sch.4 Pt 1 para.13(6) (April 2, 2001).

[74] Words inserted by Insolvency Act 2000 c. 39 Sch.4 Pt 1 para.13(2)(a) (April 2, 2001).

(d) leave is granted by a court for a person subject to such an undertaking to do anything which otherwise the undertaking prohibits him from doing;][75]
and the regulations may specify the time within which, and the form and manner in which, such particulars are to be furnished.

(2) The Secretary of State shall, from the particulars so furnished, continue to maintain the register of orders, and of cases in which leave has been granted as mentioned in subsection (1)(c) [. . .][76].

[(2A) The Secretary of State must include in the register such particulars as he considers appropriate of—

(a) disqualification undertakings accepted by him under section 7 or 8;
(b) disqualification undertakings accepted by the OFT or a specified regulator under section 9B;
(c) cases in which leave has been granted as mentioned in subsection (1)(d).][77]

(3) When an order [or undertaking][78] of which entry is made in the register ceases to be in force, the Secretary of State shall delete the entry from the register and all particulars relating to it which have been furnished to him under this section or any previous corresponding provision [and, in the case of a disqualification undertaking, any other particulars he has included in the register][79].

(4) The register shall be open to inspection on payment of such fee as may be specified by the Secretary of State in regulations.

[(4A) Regulations under this section may extend the preceding provisions of this section, to such extent and with such modifications as may be specified in the regulations, to disqualification orders [. . .][80].][81]

(5) Regulations under this section shall be made by statutory instrument subject to annulment in pursuance of a resolution of either House of Parliament.

19 Special savings from repealed enactments

Schedule 2 to this Act has effect— **A1–28**

(a) in connection with certain transitional cases arising under sections 93 and 94 of the Companies Act 1981, so as to limit the power to make a disqualification order, or to restrict the duration of an order, by reference to events occurring or things done before those sections came into force,
(b) to preserve orders made under section 28 of the Companies Act 1976 (repealed by the Act of 1981), and
(c) to preclude any applications for a disqualification order under section 6 or 8, where the relevant company went into liquidation before 28th April 1986.

[75] Added by Insolvency Act 2000 c. 39 Sch.4 Pt 1 para.13(2)(b) (April 2, 2001).

[76] Words repealed by Companies Act 2006 (Consequential Amendments, Transitional Provisions and Savings) Order 2009/1941 Sch.1 para.85(10)(a) (October 1, 2009).

[77] Substituted by Enterprise Act 2002 c. 40 Pt 7 s.204(11) (June 20, 2003).

[78] Words inserted by Insolvency Act 2000 c. 39 Sch.4 Pt 1 para.13(4)(a) (April 2, 2001).

[79] Words inserted by Insolvency Act 2000 c. 39 Sch.4 Pt 1 para.13(4)(b) (April 2, 2001).

[80] Words repealed by Companies Act 2006 (Consequential Amendments, Transitional Provisions and Savings) Order 2009/1941 Sch.1 para.85(10)(b) (October 1, 2009).

[81] Added by Insolvency Act 2000 c. 39 Sch.4 Pt 1 para.13(5) (April 2, 2001).

Miscellaneous and general

[20 Admissibility in evidence of statements

A1–29 (1) In any proceedings (whether or not under this Act), any statement made in pursuance of a requirement imposed by or under sections 6 to 10, 15 or 19(c) of, or Schedule 1 to, this Act, or by or under rules made for the purposes of this Act under the Insolvency Act [1986][82], may be used in evidence against any person making or concurring in making the statement.

(2) However, in criminal proceedings in which any such person is charged with an offence to which this subsection applies—

(a) no evidence relating to the statement may be adduced, and
(b) no question relating to it may be asked,

by or on behalf of the prosecution, unless evidence relating to it is adduced, or a question relating to it is asked, in the proceedings by or on behalf of that person.

(3) Subsection (2) applies to any offence other than—

(a) an offence which is—
(i) created by rules made for the purposes of this Act under the Insolvency Act [1986][83], and
(ii) designated for the purposes of this subsection by such rules or by regulations made by the Secretary of State;
(b) an offence which is—
(i) created by regulations made under any such rules, and
(ii) designated for the purposes of this subsection by such regulations;
(c) an offence under section 5 of the Perjury Act 1911 (false statements made otherwise than on oath); or
(d) an offence under section 44(2) of the Criminal Law (Consolidation) (Scotland) Act 1995 (false statements made otherwise than on oath).

(4) Regulations under subsection (3)(a)(ii) shall be made by statutory instrument and, after being made, shall be laid before each House of Parliament.][84]

[20A Legal professional privilege

A1–30 In proceedings against a person for an offence under this Act nothing in this Act is to be taken to require any person to disclose any information that he is entitled to refuse to disclose on grounds of legal professional privilege (in Scotland, confidentiality of communications).][85]

21 Interaction with Insolvency Act

A1–31 (1) References in this Act to the official receiver, in relation to the winding up of a company or the bankruptcy of an individual, are to any person who, by virtue of section 399 of the

[82] Word inserted by Companies Act 2006 (Consequential Amendments, Transitional Provisions and Savings) Order 2009/1941 Sch.1 para.85(6)(a) (October 1, 2009).
[83] Word inserted by Companies Act 2006 (Consequential Amendments, Transitional Provisions and Savings) Order 2009/1941 Sch.1 para.85(6)(a) (October 1, 2009).
[84] Existing text renumbered as s.20(1) and new s.20(2) to (4) inserted by Youth Justice and Criminal Evidence Act 1999 c. 23 Sch.3 para.8 (January 1, 2001: as SSI 2000/445).
[85] Inserted subject to savings specified in SI 2008/948 arts 11 and 12 by Companies Act 2006 (Consequential Amendments etc) Order 2008/948 Sch.1 Pt 2 para.106(3) (April 6, 2008).

Insolvency Act [1986][86], is authorised to act as the official receiver in relation to that winding up or bankruptcy; and, in accordance with section 401(2) of that Act, references in this Act to an official receiver includes a person appointed as his deputy.

(2) [Sections 1A, 6 to 10, 13, 14, 15, 19(c) and 20 of, and Schedule 1][87] to, this Act [and sections 1 and 17 of this Act as they apply for the purposes of those provisions][88] are deemed included in Parts I to VII of the Insolvency Act [1986][89] for the purposes of the following sections of that Act—

section 411 (power to make insolvency rules);
section 414 (fees orders);
section 420 (orders extending provisions about insolvent companies to insolvent partnerships);
section 422 (modification of such provisions in their application to recognised banks);
[. . .][90]
[. . .][91]

(3) Section 434 of that Act (Crown application) applies to [sections 1A, 6 to 10, 13, 14, 15, 19(c) and 20 of, and Schedule 1][92] to, this Act [and sections 1 and 17 of this Act as they apply for the purposes of those provisions][93] as it does to the provisions of that Act which are there mentioned.

[(4) For the purposes of summary proceedings in Scotland, section 431 of that Act applies to summary proceedings for an offence under section 11 or 13 of this Act as it applies to summary proceedings for an offence under Parts I to VII of the Act.][94]

[21A Bank insolvency

Section 121 of the Banking Act 2009 provides for this Act to apply in relation to bank insolvency as it applies in relation to liquidation.][95] **A1–32**

[21B Bank administration

Section 155 of the Banking Act 2009 provides for this Act to apply in relation to bank administration as it applies in relation to liquidation.][96] **A1–33**

[21C Building society insolvency and special administration

Section 90E of the Building Societies Act 1986 provides for this Act to apply in relation to building society insolvency and building society special administration as it applies in relation to liquidation.][97] **A1–34**

22 Interpretation

(1) This section has effect with respect to the meaning of expressions used in this Act, and applies unless the context otherwise requires. **A1–35**

[86] Word inserted by Companies Act 2006 (Consequential Amendments, Transitional Provisions and Savings) Order 2009/1941 Sch. Pt 2 para.85(6)(a) (October 1, 2009).
[87] Words inserted by Insolvency Act 2000 c. 39 Sch.4 Pt 1 para.14(2)(b) (April 2, 2001).
[88] Words inserted by Insolvency Act 2000 c. 39 Sch.4 Pt 1 para.14(2)(c) (April 2, 2001).
[89] Word inserted by Companies Act 2006 (Consequential Amendments, Transitional Provisions and Savings) Order 2009/1941 Sch. Pt 2 para.85(6)(a) (October 1, 2009).
[90] Words repealed by Companies Act 1989 (c. 40), ss. 212, 213(2), Sch.24.
[91] Words repealed by Companies Act 1989 (c. 40), ss. 212, 213(2), Sch.24.
[92] Words inserted by Insolvency Act 2000 c. 39 Sch.4 Pt 1 para.14(3)(b) (April 2, 2001).
[93] Words inserted by Insolvency Act 2000 c. 39 Sch.4 Pt 1 para.14(3)(c) (April 2, 2001).
[94] Added by Companies Act 1989 (c. 40), ss.208, 213(2).
[95] Added by Banking Act 2009 c. 1 Pt 2 s.121(4) (February 21, 2009).
[96] Added by Banking Act 2009 c. 1 Pt 3 s.155(4) (February 21, 2009).
[97] Added by Building Societies (Insolvency and Special Administration) Order 2009/805 art.12 (March 29, 2009).

[(2) "Company" means—

(a) a company registered under the Companies Act 2006 in Great Britain, or
(b) a company that may be wound up under Part 5 of the Insolvency Act 1986 (unregistered companies).][98]

(3) Section 247 in Part VII of the Insolvency Act [1986][99] (interpretation for the first Group of Parts of that Act) applies as regards references to a company's insolvency and to its going into liquidation; and "administrative receiver" has the meaning given by section 251 of that Act [and references to acting as an insolvency practitioner are to be read in accordance with section 388 of that Act][100].

(4) "Director" includes any person occupying the position of director, by whatever name called [. . .][101].

(5) "Shadow director", in relation to a company, means a person in accordance with whose directions or instructions the directors of the company are accustomed to act (but so that a person is not deemed a shadow director by reason only that the directors act on advice given by him in a professional capacity).

[(6) "Body corporate" and "officer" have the same meaning as in the Companies Acts (see section 1173(1) of the Companies Act 2006).][102]

[(7) "The Companies Acts" has the meaning given by section 2(1) of the Companies Act 2006.][103]

[(8) Any reference to provisions, or a particular provision, of the Companies Acts or the Insolvency Act 1986 includes the corresponding provisions or provision of corresponding earlier legislation.][104]

[(9) Subject to the provisions of this section, expressions that are defined for the purposes of the Companies Acts [(see section 1174 of, and Schedule 8 to, the Companies Act 2006)][105] have the same meaning in this Act.][106]

[(10) Any reference to acting as receiver—

(a) includes acting as manager or as both receiver and manager, but
(b) does not include acting as administrative receiver;

and "receivership" is to be read accordingly.][107]

[22A Application of Act to building societies

A1–36 (1) This Act applies to building societies as it applies to companies.

(2) References in this Act to a company, or to a director or an officer of a company include, respectively, references to a building society within the meaning of the Building Societies Act 1986 or to a director or officer, within the meaning of that Act, of a building society.

[98] Substituted by Companies Act 2006 (Consequential Amendments, Transitional Provisions and Savings) Order 2009/1941 Sch.1 para.85(11)(a) (October 1, 2009).

[99] Word inserted by Companies Act 2006 (Consequential Amendments, Transitional Provisions and Savings) Order 2009/1941 Sch.1 para.85(6)(a) (October 1, 2009).

[100] Words inserted by Insolvency Act 2000 c. 39 Sch.4 Pt 1 para.15(2) (April 2, 2001).

[101] Words repealed by Insolvency Act 2000 c. 39 Sch.5 para.1 (April 2, 2001 as SI 2001/766).

[102] Substituted by Companies Act 2006 (Consequential Amendments, Transitional Provisions and Savings) Order 2009/1941 Sch.1 para.85(11)(b) (October 1, 2009).

[103] Substituted by Companies Act 2006 (Consequential Amendments, Transitional Provisions and Savings) Order 2009/1941 Sch.1 para.85(11)(c) (October 1, 2009).

[104] Substituted by Companies Act 2006 (Consequential Amendments, Transitional Provisions and Savings) Order 2009/1941 Sch.1 para.85(11)(d) (October 1, 2009).

[105] Words inserted by Companies Act 2006 (Consequential Amendments, Transitional Provisions and Savings) Order 2009/1941 Sch.1 para.85(11)(e) (October 1, 2009).

[106] Substituted subject to savings specified in SI 2008/948 arts 11 and 12 by Companies Act 2006 (Consequential Amendments etc) Order 2008/948 Sch.1 Pt 2 para.106(4)(c) (April 6, 2008).

[107] Added by Insolvency Act 2000 c. 39 s.5(3) (April 2, 2001: commencement order SI).

(3) In relation to a building society the definition of "shadow director" in section 22(5) applies with the substitution of "building society" for "company".

(4) In the application of Schedule 1 to the directors of a building society, references to provisions of [the Companies Act 2006 or the Insolvency Act 1986][108] include references to the corresponding provisions of the Building Societies Act 1986.][109]

[22B Application of Act to incorporated friendly societies

(1) This Act applies to incorporated friendly societies as it applies to companies. **A1–37**

(2) References in this Act to a company, or to a director or an officer of a company include, respectively, references to an incorporated friendly society within the meaning of the Friendly Societies Act 1992 or to a member of the committee of management or officer, within the meaning of that Act, of an incorporated friendly society.

(3) In relation to an incorporated friendly society every reference to a shadow director shall be omitted.

(4) In the application of Schedule 1 to the members of the committee of management of an incorporated friendly society, references to provisions of [the Companies Act 2006 or the Insolvency Act 1986][110] include references to the corresponding provisions of the Friendly Societies Act 1992.][111]

[22C Application of Act to NHS foundation trusts

(1) This Act applies to NHS foundation trusts as it applies to companies within the meaning of this Act. **A1–38**

(2) References in this Act to a company, or to a director or officer of a company, include, respectively, references to an NHS foundation trust or to a director or officer of the trust; but references to shadow directors are omitted.

(3) In the application of Schedule 1 to the directors of an NHS foundation trust, references to the provisions of [the Companies Act 2006 or the Insolvency Act 1986][112] include references to the corresponding provisions of [Chapter 5 of Part 2 of the National Health Service Act 2006][113].][114]

[22D Application of Act to open-ended investment companies

(1) This Act applies to open-ended investment companies with the following modifications. **A1–39**

(2) In section 8(1) (disqualification after investigation), the reference to investigative material shall be read as including a report made by inspectors under regulations made by virtue of section 262(2)(k) of the Financial Services and Markets Act 2000.

(3) In the application of Part 1 of Schedule 1 (matters for determining unfitness of directors: matters applicable in all cases) in relation to a director of an open-ended

[108] Words substituted by Companies Act 2006 (Consequential Amendments, Transitional Provisions and Savings) Order 2009/1941 Sch.1 para.85(12) (October 1, 2009).

[109] Added by Companies Act 1989 c. 40 Pt X s.211(3) (July 31, 1990: represents law in force as at date shown).

[110] Words substituted by Companies Act 2006 (Consequential Amendments, Transitional Provisions and Savings) Order 2009/1941 Sch.1 para.85(12) (October 1, 2009).

[111] Added by Friendly Societies Act 1992 c. 40 Sch.21 Pt 1 para.8 (February 1, 1993).

[112] Words substituted by Companies Act 2006 (Consequential Amendments, Transitional Provisions and Savings) Order 2009/1941 Sch.1 para.85(12) (October 1, 2009).

[113] Words substituted by National Health Service (Consequential Provisions) Act 2006 c. 43 Sch.1 para.92 (March 1, 2007).

[114] Added by Health and Social Care (Community Health and Standards) Act 2003 c. 43 Sch.4 para.68 (April 1, 2004: November 20, 2003 for the purpose of making regulations or orders as specified in 2003 c.43 s.199(4); April 1, 2004 otherwise).

investment company, a reference to a provision of the Companies Act 2006 is to be taken to be a reference to the corresponding provision of the Open-Ended Investment Companies Regulations 2001 or of rules made under regulation 6 of those Regulations.
(4) In this section "open-ended investment company" has the meaning given by section 236 of the Financial Services and Markets Act 2000.][115]

23 Transitional provisions, savings, repeals

A1–40 (1) The transitional provisions and savings in Schedule 3 to this Act have effect, and are without prejudice to anything in the Interpretation Act 1978 with regard to the effect of repeals.
(2) The enactments specified in the second column of Schedule 4 to this Act are repealed to the extent specified in the third column of that Schedule.

24 Extent

A1–41 (1) This Act extends to England and Wales and to Scotland.
(2) Nothing in this Act extends to Northern Ireland.

25 Commencement

A1–42 This Act comes into force simultaneously with the Insolvency Act 1986.

26 Citation

A1–43 This Act may be cited as the Company Directors Disqualification Act 1986.

SCHEDULES

SCHEDULE 1
Section 9

MATTERS FOR DETERMINING UNFITNESS OF DIRECTORS

PART I

MATTERS APPLICABLE IN ALL CASES

A1–44 **1** Any misfeasance or breach of any fiduciary or other duty by the director in relation to the company [, including in particular any breach by the director of a duty under Chapter 2 of Part 10 of the Companies Act 2006 (general duties of directors) owed to the company][116].

2 Any misapplication or retention by the director of, or any conduct by the director giving rise to an obligation to account for, any money or other property of the company.

3 The extent of the director's responsibility for the company entering into any transaction liable to be set aside under Part XVI of the Insolvency Act [1986][117] (provisions against debt avoidance).

[115] Added by Companies Act 2006 (Consequential Amendments, Transitional Provisions and Savings) Order 2009/1941 Sch.1 para.85(13) (October 1, 2009).
[116] Words inserted by Companies Act 2006 (Consequential Amendments, Transitional Provisions and Savings) Order 2009/1941 Sch.1 para.85(14)(a) (October 1, 2009).
[117] Word inserted by Companies Act 2006 (Consequential Amendments, Transitional Provisions and Savings) Order 2009/1941 Sch.1 para.85(6)(b) (October 1, 2009).

[**4** The extent of the director's responsibility for any failure by the company to comply with any of the following provisions of the Companies Act 2006—

(a) section 113 (register of members);
(b) section 114 (register to be kept available for inspection);
(c) section 162 (register of directors);
(d) section 165 (register of directors' residential addresses);
(e) section 167 (duty to notify registrar of changes: directors);
(f) section 275 (register of secretaries);
(g) section 276 (duty to notify registrar of changes: secretaries);
(h) section 386 (duty to keep accounting records);
(i) section 388 (where and for how long accounting records to be kept);
(j) section 854 (duty to make annual returns);
(k) section 860 (duty to register charges);
(l) section 878 (duty to register charges: companies registered in Scotland).][118]

4A [. . .][119]

[**5** The extent of the director's responsibility for any failure by the directors of the company to comply with the following provisions of the Companies Act 2006—

(a) section 394 or 399 (duty to prepare annual accounts);
(b) section 414 or 450 (approval and signature of abbreviated accounts); or
(c) section 433 (name of signatory to be stated in published copy of accounts).][120]

5A [. . .][121]

Part II

Matters Applicable where Company has become Insolvent

6 The extent of the director's responsibility for the causes of the company becoming insolvent. **A1–45**

7 The extent of the director's responsibility for any failure by the company to supply any goods or services which have been paid for (in whole or in part).

8 The extent of the director's responsibility for the company entering into any transaction or giving any preference, being a transaction or preference—

(a) liable to be set aside under section 127 or sections 238 to 240 of the Insolvency Act [1986][122], or
(b) challengeable under section 242 or 243 of that Act or under any rule of law in Scotland.

[**8A** The extent of the member's and shadow members' responsibility for events leading to a member or shadow member, whether himself or some other member or shadow member,

[118] Sch.1 para.4 substituted for Sch. paras 4 and 4A by Companies Act 2006 (Consequential Amendments, Transitional Provisions and Savings) Order 2009/1941 Sch.1 para.85(14)(b) (October 1, 2009).

[119] Sch.1 para.4 substituted for Sch.1 paras 4 and 4A by Companies Act 2006 (Consequential Amendments, Transitional Provisions and Savings) Order 2009/1941 Sch.1 para.85(14)(b) (October 1, 2009).

[120] Substituted subject to savings specified in SI 2008/948 arts 11 and 12 by Companies Act 2006 (Consequential Amendments etc) Order 2008/948 Sch.1(2) para.106(8)(b) (April 6, 2008).

[121] Repealed by Companies Act 2006 (Consequential Amendments, Transitional Provisions and Savings) Order 2009/1941 Sch.1 para.85(14)(c) (October 1, 2009).

[122] Word inserted by Companies Act 2006 (Consequential Amendments, Transitional Provisions and Savings) Order 2009/1941 Sch.1 para.85(6)(b) (October 1, 2009).

being declared by the court to be liable to make a contribution to the assets of the limited liability partnership under section 214A of the Insolvency Act 1986.[123]][124]

9 The extent of the director's responsibility for any failure by the directors of the company to comply with section 98 of the Insolvency Act [1986][125] (duty to call creditors' meeting in creditors' voluntary winding up).

10 Any failure by the director to comply with any obligation imposed on him by or under any of the following provisions of the Insolvency Act [1986][126]—

- (a) [paragraph 47 of Schedule B1][127] (company's statement of affairs in administration);
- (b) section 47 (statement of affairs to administrative receiver);
- (c) section 66 (statement of affairs in Scottish receivership);
- (d) section 99 (directors' duty to attend meeting; statement of affairs in creditors' voluntary winding up);
- (e) section 131 (statement of affairs in winding up by the court);
- (f) section 234 (duty of any one with company property to deliver it up);
- (g) section 235 (duty to co-operate with liquidator, etc.).

SCHEDULE 2
***Section* 19**

SAVINGS FROM COMPANIES ACT 1981 SS. 93, 94, AND INSOLVENCY ACT 1985 SCHEDULE 9

A1–46 **1** Sections 2 and 4(1)(b) do not apply in relation to anything done before 15th June 1982 by a person in his capacity as liquidator of a company or as receiver or manager of a company's property.

2 Subject to paragraph 1—

- (a) section 2 applies in a case where a person is convicted on indictment of an offence which he committed (and, in the case of a continuing offence, has ceased to commit) before 15th June 1982; but in such a case a disqualification order under that section shall not be made for a period in excess of 5 years;
- (b) that section does not apply in a case where a person is convicted summarily—
  - (i) in England and Wales, if he had consented so to be tried before that date, or
  - (ii) in Scotland, if the summary proceedings commenced before that date.

3 Subject to paragraph 1, section 4 applies in relation to an offence committed or other thing done before 15th June 1982; but a disqualification order made on the grounds of such an offence or other thing done shall not be made for a period in excess of 5 years.

4 The powers of a court under section 5 are not exercisable in a case where a person is convicted of an offence which he committed (and, in the case of a continuing offence, had ceased to commit) before 15th June 1982.

[123] The insertion of Sch.1 Pt 2 para.8A is one of the modifications to the Company Directors Disqualification Act 1986 made by SI 2001/1090 in relation to Limited Liability Partnerships and is reproduced as full-text for the sake of clarity. The remaining modifications to this Act can be accessed via the Analysis Information of the relevant provisions.

[124] Added by Limited Liability Partnerships Regulations 2001/1090 Sch.2 Pt 2 para.1 (April 6, 2001).

[125] Word inserted by Companies Act 2006 (Consequential Amendments, Transitional Provisions and Savings) Order 2009/1941 Sch.1 para.85(6)(b) (October 1, 2009).

[126] Word inserted by Companies Act 2006 (Consequential Amendments, Transitional Provisions and Savings) Order 2009/1941 Sch.1 para.85(6)(b) (October 1, 2009).

[127] Words substituted by Enterprise Act 2002 (Insolvency) Order 2003/2096 Sch.1(1) para.12 (September 15, 2003).

5 For purposes of section 3(1) and section 5, no account is to be taken of any offence which was committed, or any default order which was made, before 1st June 1977.

6 An order made under section 28 of the Companies Act 1976 has effect as if made under section 3 of this Act; and an application made before 15th June 1982 for such an order is to be treated as an application for an order under the section last mentioned.

7 Where—

(a) an application is made for a disqualification order under section 6 of this Act by virtue of paragraph (a) of subsection (2) of that section, and

(b) the company in question went into liquidation before 28th April 1986 (the coming into force of the provision replaced by section 6).

the court shall not make an order under that section unless it could have made a disqualification order under section 300 of [the Companies Act 1985][128] as it had effect immediately before the date specified in sub-paragraph (b) above.

8 An application shall not be made under section 8 of this Act in relation to a report made or information or documents obtained before 28th April 1986.

SCHEDULE 3
Section 23(1)

TRANSITIONAL PROVISIONS AND SAVINGS

1 In this Schedule, "the former enactments" means so much of [the Companies Act 1985][129], and so much of [the Insolvency Act 1986][130], as is repealed and replaced by this Act; and "the appointed day" means the day on which this Act comes into force. **A1–47**

2 So far as anything done or treated as done under or for the purposes of any provision of the former enactments could have been done under or for the purposes of the corresponding provision of this Act, it is not invalidated by the repeal of that provision but has effect as if done under or for the purposes of the corresponding provision; and any order, regulation, rule or other instrument made or having effect under any provision of the former enactments shall, insofar as its effect is preserved by this paragraph, be treated for all purposes as made and having effect under the corresponding provision.

3 Where any period of time specified in a provision of the former enactments is current immediately before the appointed day, this Act has effect as if the corresponding provision had been in force when the period began to run; and (without prejudice to the foregoing) any period of time so specified and current is deemed for the purposes of this Act—

(a) to run from the date or event from which it was running immediately before the appointed day, and

(b) to expire (subject to any provision of this Act for its extension) whenever it would have expired if this Act had not been passed;

[128] Words substituted by Companies Act 2006 (Consequential Amendments, Transitional Provisions and Savings) Order 2009/1941 Sch.1 para.85(15) (October 1, 2009).

[129] Words substituted by Companies Act 2006 (Consequential Amendments, Transitional Provisions and Savings) Order 2009/1941 Sch.1 para.85(16)(a) (October 1, 2009).

[130] Words substituted by Companies Act 2006 (Consequential Amendments, Transitional Provisions and Savings) Order 2009/1941 Sch.1 para.85(16)(b) (October 1, 2009).

and any rights, priorities, liabilities, reliefs, obligations, requirements, powers, duties or exemptions dependent on the beginning, duration or end of such a period as above mentioned shall be under this Act as they were or would have been under the former enactments.

4 Where in any provision of this Act there is a reference to another such provision, and the first-mentioned provision operates, or is capable of operating, in relation to things done or omitted, or events occurring or not occurring, in the past (including in particular past acts of compliance with any enactment, failures of compliance, contraventions, offences and convictions of offences) the reference to the other provision is to be read as including a reference to the corresponding provision of the former enactments.

5 Offences committed before the appointed day under any provision of the former enactments may, notwithstanding any repeal by this Act, be prosecuted and punished after that day as if this Act had not passed.

A1–48 **6** A reference in any enactment, instrument or document (whether express or implied, and in whatever phraseology) to a provision of the former enactments (including the corresponding provision of any yet earlier enactment) is to be read, where necessary to retain for the enactment, instrument or document the same force and effect as it would have had but for the passing of this Act, as, or as including, a reference to the corresponding provision by which it is replaced in this Act.

SCHEDULE 4
Section 23(2)

REPEALS

Chapter	Short title	Extent of repeal
1985 c. 6.	The Companies Act 1985.	Section 295 to 299. Section 301. Section 302. Schedule 12. In Schedule 24, the entries relating to sections 295(7) and 302(1).
1985 c. 65.	The Insolvency Act 1985.	Sections 12 to 14. Section 16. Section 18. Section 108(2). Schedule 2. In Schedule 6, paragraphs 1, 2, 7 and 14. In Schedule 9, paragraphs 2 and 3.

APPENDIX 2

TABLE OF FORMER PROVISIONS

A2–01 This table traces the derivation and/or origin of the substantive provisions of the CDDA as originally enacted

CDDA	Insolvency Act 1985	Companies Act 1985	Companies Act 1981*	Companies Act 1976	Insolvency Act 1976	Companies Act 1948	Companies Act 1947	Companies Act 1929	Companies Act 1928
s.1(1)	ss.108(2), 109(1), Sch.6, para.1(1)	s.295(1)	s.93 (CA 1948, s.188(1B)) s.94 (IA 1976, s.9(1),(1A))	—	s.9(1)	s.188(1)	s.33(1)	s.275(4)	s.75(4)
s.1(2)	s.108(2)	s.295(2), Sch.12, para.10	s.93 (CA 1948, s.188(1C), (2), (2A)), s.94 (IA 1976, s.9(1), (1A))	—	s.9(1)	s.188(1)	s.33(1)	s.275(4)	s.75(4)
s.1(3)	ss.108(2), 109(1), Sch.6, para.1(3)	—	—	—	—	—	—	—	—
s.1(4)	s.108(2)	s.295(4)	s.93 (CA 1948, s.188(2F)) s.94 (IA 1976, s.9(7A))	—	—	s.188(5)	s.33(5)	—	—
s.2	—	ss.295(2), 296	s.93 (CA 1948, s.188(1) (a), (1C), (2), (2A)—(2B), (2D)—(2E))	—	—	s.188(1)(a), (2)	s.33(1)(a), (2)	—	—
s.3	—	ss.295(2), 297	s.93 (CA 1948, s.188(1) (b), (2B), (2C), (2D))	s.28	—	—	—	—	—
s.4	—	ss.295(2), 298	s.93 (CA 1948, s.188(1) (c), (1C), (2A), (2D))	—	—	s.188(1)(b)	s.33(1)(b)	s.275, s.217	ss.75, 76
s.5	—	ss.295(2), 299	s.93 (CA 1948, s.188(1A), (2B), (2D), (2E))	—	—	—	—	—	—
s.6(1)	s.12(1)	s.300(1)	—	—	s.9(1)	—	—	—	—
s.6(2)	s.12(7)	—	—	—	s.9(1), (9)	—	—	—	—
s.6(3)	s.12(8), (9)	s.300(2), (4)	—	—	s.9(2), (7)	—	—	—	—
s.6(4)	s.12(2), s.108(2)	s.295(2)	s.94 (IA 1976, s.9(1A))	—	s.9(1)	—	—	—	—
s.7(1)	s.12(3)	Sch.12, para.6	—	—	s.9(2)	—	—	—	—
s.7(2)	s.12(4)	—	—	—	—	—	—	—	—
s.7(3)	s.12(5)	—	—	—		—	—	—	—
s.7(4)	s.12(6)	s.300(3)	—	—	s.9(6)	—	—	—	—

CDDA	Insolvency Act 1985	Companies Act 1985	Companies Act 1981*	Companies Act 1976	Insolvency Act 1976	Companies Act 1948	Companies Act 1947	Companies Act 1929	Companies Act 1928
s.8	ss.12(9), 13, 108(2)	—	—	—	—	—	—	—	—
s.9	ss.12(9), 14	—	—	—	—	—	—	—	—
s.10	s.16, 108(2)	s.295(2)	—	—	—	s.188(1)(b)	s.33(1)(b)	s.275(1), (4)	s.75(1), (4)
s.11	—	s.302	Sch.3, para.9 (CA 1948, s.187)	—	—	s.187	—	s.142	s.84
s.12	s.221(2)	—	—	—	—	—	—	—	—
s.13	s.221(5)	ss.295(7), 302(1), Sch.24	—	s.28(7)	s.9(5)	ss.187(1), 188(6)	s.33(6)	ss.142(1), 275(4)	ss.84(1), 75(4)
s.14	Sch.6, para.7	s.733(1)–(3)	—	—	—	—	—	—	—
s.15	s.18	—	—	—	—	—	—	—	—
s.16(1)	ss.108(2), 109(1), Sched. 6, para.1(4)	s.295(6), Sched. 12, paras 1, 7	—	s.28(5)	s.9(3)	s.188(3)	s.33(3)	s.217(2)	s.76(2)
s.16(2)	ss.108(2), 109(1), Sch.6, para.1(4)	s.295(6), Sch.12, para.2	s.93(2) (CA 1948, s.188(4))	s.28(1)	s.9(2)	s.188(4)	s.33(4)	—	—
s.16(3)	ss.108(2), 109(1), Sch.6, para.1(4)	s.295(6), Sch.12, paras 3, 8	s.93(2) (CA 1948, s.188(4))	s.28(6)	s.9(4)	s.188(4)	s.33(4)	—	—
s.17(1)	ss.108(2), 109(1), Sch. 6, para.1(4), 14	s.295(6), Sch.12, para.4	—	—	—	—	—	—	—
s.17(2)	ss.108(2), 109(1), Sch.6, para.1(4)	ss.295(6), 302(3), Sch.12, paras 5, 8	s.93(2) (CA 1948, s.188(4))	s.28(6)	s.9(4)	ss.187(2), 188(4)	s.33(4)	ss.142(2), 275(7)	ss.84(2), 75(7)
s.18	ss.108(2), 109(1), Sch.6, para.2	s.301	Sch.3, para.36 (CA 1976, s.29(1))	s.29	—	—	—	—	—
s.19	—	s.295(6)	—	—	—	—	—	—	—
s.20	s.231**	—	s.636(3)	—	—	s.365***	—	—	—
s.21	ss.106, 107, 108(1)–(2), 222(1), 224(2), 227, 229, 234	—	—	—	—	—	—	—	—
s.22	s.108(1)–(4)	ss.295(3), 302(4)	s.94 (IA 1976, s.9(7))	s.28(8)	s.9(7)	s.187(3)	—	s.142(3)	s.4(3)
ss.23–26	—	—	—	—	—	—	—	—	—
Sch.1	Sch.2	—	—	—	—	—	—	—	—

* The Companies Act 1981 was an amending statute. The relevant provisions amended by the 1981 Act are referred to in parenthesis. "CA 1948" means the Companies Act, 1948: "IA 1976" means the Insolvency Act 1976; "CA 1976" means the Companies Act 1976.

** See now section 433 of the Insolvency Act 1986.

*** Section 20 has its origins in earlier provisions which dealt with the use of statement made by persons in the context of (a) winding up or (b) the exercise of the powers of investigation now contained in Part XIV of the Companies Act 1985. See also section 50 of the Companies Act 1967.

APPENDIX 3

DISQUALIFICATION STATUTORY INSTRUMENTS

The Insolvent Companies (Reports on Conduct of Directors) Rules 1996 (SI 1996/1909)

Made	*22nd July 1996*
Laid before Parliament	*24th July 1996*
Coming into force	*30th September 1996*

The Lord Chancellor, in exercise of the powers conferred on him by section 411 of the Insolvency Act 1986 and section 21(2) of the Company Directors Disqualification Act 1986[1], and of all other powers enabling him in that behalf, with the concurrence of the Secretary of State, and after consulting the committee existing for that purpose under section 413 of the Insolvency Act 1986, hereby makes the following Rules:—

1 Citation, commencement and interpretation

A3–01

(1) These Rules may be cited as the Insolvent Companies (Reports on Conduct of Directors) Rules 1996.
(2) These Rules shall come into force on 30th September 1996.
(3) In these Rules—
"the Act" means the Company Directors Disqualification Act 1986;
"the former Rules" means the Insolvent Companies (Reports on Conduct of Directors) No. 2 Rules 1986; and
"the commencement date" means 30th September 1996.

Commencement
Rule 1(1)–(3) definition of "the commencement date": September 30, 1996.

2 Revocation

A3–02

Subject to rule 7 below, the former Rules are hereby revoked.

[1] The amendment to section 21(2) made by the Companies Act 1989 (c.40) is not relevant for the purposes of these Rules.

Commencement

Rule 2: September 30, 1996.

3 Reports required under section 7(3) of the Act

A3–03 (1) This rule applies to any report made to the Secretary of State under section 7(3) of the Act by:—

(a) the liquidator of a company which the courts in England and Wales have jurisdiction to wind up which passes a resolution for voluntary winding up on or after the commencement date;

(b) an administrative receiver of a company appointed otherwise than under section 51 of the Insolvency Act 1986 (power to appoint receiver under the law of Scotland) on or after the commencement date; or

(c) the administrator of a company which the courts in England and Wales have jurisdiction to wind up [which enters administration][2] on or after the commencement date.

(2) Such a report shall be made in the Form D1 set out in the Schedule hereto, or in a form which is substantially similar, and in the manner and to the extent required by the Form D1.

Commencement

Rule 3(1)–(2): September 30, 1996.

4 Return by office-holder

A3–04 (1) This rule applies where it appears to a liquidator of a company as mentioned in rule 3(1)(a), to an administrative receiver as mentioned in rule 3(1)(b), or to an administrator as mentioned in rule 3(1)(c) (each of whom is referred to hereinafter as "an office-holder") that the company has at any time become insolvent within the meaning of section 6(2) of the Act.

(2) Subject as follows there may be furnished to the Secretary of State by an office-holder at any time during the period of 6 months from the relevant date (defined in paragraph (4) below) a return with respect to every person who:—

(a) was, on the relevant date, a director or shadow director of the company, or

(b) had been a director or shadow director of the company at any time in the 3 years immediately preceding that date.

(3) The return shall be made in the Form D2 set out in the Schedule hereto, or in a form which is substantially similar, and in the manner and to the extent required by the Form D2.

(4) For the purposes of this rule, "the relevant date" means:—

(a) in the case of a company in creditors' voluntary winding up (there having been no declaration of solvency by the directors under section 89 of the Insolvency Act 1986), the date of the passing of the resolution for voluntary winding up,

(b) in the case of a company in members' voluntary winding up, the date on which the liquidator forms the opinion that, at the time when the company went into liquidation, its assets were insufficient for the payment of its debts and other liabilities and the expenses of winding up,

[2] Words substituted by Enterprise Act 2002 (Insolvency) Order 2003/2096 Sch.1 Pt 2 para.69 (September 15, 2003).

(c) in the case of the administrative receiver, the date of his appointment,
(d) in the case of the administrator, the date [that the company enters administration][3], and for the purposes of sub-paragraph (c) above the only appointment of an administrative receiver to be taken into account in determining the relevant date shall be that appointment which is not that of a successor in office to an administrative receiver who has vacated office either by death or pursuant to section 45 of the Insolvency Act 1986.

(5) Subject to paragraph (6) below, it shall be the duty of an office-holder to furnish a return complying with the provisions of paragraphs (3) and (4) of this rule to the Secretary of State:—

(a) where he is in office in relation to the company on the day one week before the expiry of the period of 6 months from the relevant date, not later than the expiry of such period;
(b) where he vacates office (otherwise than by death) before the day one week before the expiry of the period of 6 months from the relevant date, within 14 days after his vacation of office except where he has furnished such a return on or prior to the day one week before the expiry of such period.

(6) A return need not be provided under this rule by an office-holder if he has, whilst holding that office in relation to the company, since the relevant date, made a report under rule 3 with respect to all persons falling within paragraph (2) of this rule and (apart from this paragraph) required to be the subject of a return.
(7) If an office-holder without reasonable excuse fails to comply with the duty imposed by paragraph (5) of this rule, he is guilty of an offence and—

(a) on summary conviction of the offence, is liable to a fine not exceeding level 3 on the standard scale, and
(b) after continued contravention, is liable to a daily default fine; that is to say, he is liable on a second or subsequent summary conviction of the offence to a fine of one-tenth of level 3 on the standard scale for each day on which the contravention is continued (instead of the penalty specified in sub-paragraph (a)).

(8) Section 431 of the Insolvency Act 1986 (summary proceedings), as it applies to England and Wales, has effect in relation to an offence under this rule as to offences under Parts I to VII of that Act.

Commencement

Rule 4(1)–(8): September 30, 1996.

5 Forms

A3–05 The forms referred to in rule 3(2) and rule 4(3) shall be used with such variations, if any, as the circumstances may require.

Commencement

Rule 5: September 30, 1996.

6 Enforcement of section 7(4)

A3–06 (1) This rule applies where under section 7(4) of the Act (power to call on liquidators, former liquidators and others to provide information) the Secretary of State or the official receiver requires or has required a person:—

[3] Words substituted by Enterprise Act 2002 (Insolvency) Order 2003/2096 Sch.1 Pt 2 para.70 (September 15, 2003).

(a) to furnish him with information with respect to a person's conduct as director or shadow director of a company, and
(b) to produce and permit inspection of relevant books, papers and other records.

(2) On the application of the Secretary of State or (as the case may be) the official receiver, the court may make an order directing compliance within such period as may be specified.

(3) The court's order may provide that all costs of and incidental to the application shall be borne by the person to whom the order is directed.

Commencement
Rule 6(1)–(3): September 30, 1996.

7 Transitional and saving provisions

A3–07 (1) Subject to paragraph (2) below, rules 3 and 4 of the former Rules shall continue to apply as if the former Rules had not been revoked when any of the events mentioned in sub-paragraphs (a), (b) or (c) of rule 3(1) of the former Rules (passing of resolution for voluntary winding up, appointment of administrative receiver, making of administration order) occurred on or after 29th December 1986 but before the commencement date.

(2) Until 31st December 1996—

(a) the forms contained in the Schedule to the former Rules which were required to be used for the purpose of complying with those Rules, or
(b) the Form D1 or D2 as set out in the Schedule to these Rules, as appropriate, or a form which is substantially similar thereto, with such variations, if any, as the circumstances may require,

may be used for the purpose of complying with rules 3 and 4 of the former Rules as applied by paragraph (1) above; but after that date the forms mentioned in sub-paragraph (b) of this paragraph shall be used for that purpose.

(3) When a period referred to in rule 5(2) of the former Rules is current immediately before the commencement date, these Rules have effect as if rule 6(2) of these Rules had been in force when the period began and the period is deemed to expire whenever it would have expired if these Rules had not been made and any right, obligation or power dependent on the beginning, duration or end of such period shall be under rule 6(2) of these Rules as it was or would have been under the said rule 5(2).

(4) The provisions of this rule are to be without prejudice to the operation of section 16 of the Interpretation Act 1978 (saving from repeals) as it is applied by section 23 of that Act.

Commencement
Rule 7(1)–(4): September 30, 1996.

Mackay of Clashfern, C.

17th July 1996

I concur, on behalf of the Secretary of State

Phillip Oppenheim,
Parliamentary Under Secretary of State for Company Affairs,
Department of Trade and Industry

22nd July 1996

SCHEDULE

FORMS

Rules 3(2), 4(3) and 7(2)

D1 *REPORT UNDER SECTION 7(3) OF THE COMPANY DIRECTORS DISQUALIFICATION ACT 1986.* **A3–08**

D2 *RETURN BY OFFICE-HOLDER UNDER RULE 4 OF THE INSOLVENT COMPANIES (REPORTS ON CONDUCT OF DIRECTORS) RULES 1996.*

[The Forms are not reproduced here.]

Commencement

Sch.1 para.1: September 30, 1996.

EXPLANATORY NOTE

(This note is not part of the Order)

These Rules revoke and replace the Insolvent Companies (Reports on Conduct of Directors) No. 2 Rules 1986 (SI 1986/2134) ("the 1986 Rules") subject to transitional and saving provisions. **A3–09**

The Rules make provision in relation to England and Wales for the manner in which a voluntary liquidator, administrative receiver or administrator of a company, ("the office-holder"), is to make a report to the Secretary of State, under section 7(3) of the Company Directors Disqualification Act 1986 ("the Act") in relation to any person who has been a director or shadow director of an insolvent company and whose conduct appears to the office-holder to be such that he is unfit to be concerned in the management of a company. The Rules also provide for returns to be made to the Secretary of State by office-holders, in respect of directors or shadow directors of an insolvent company, where a report has not already been made in respect of such persons under section 7(3) of the Act.

Rules 3 and 4 apply in respect of reports and returns to be made where the relevant insolvency proceedings have commenced (that is, when one of the following events has occurred: the company has passed a resolution for it to be voluntarily wound up; an administrative receiver has been appointed; or an administration order has been made) on or after 30th September 1996.

Rule 3, taken with rule 5 provides that reports under section 7(3) of the Act should be made in Form D1 set out in the Schedule or in a substantially similar form, with any necessary variations.

Rule 4, taken with rule 5, provides for a return to be made in Form D2 set out in the Schedule or in a substantially similar form, with any necessary variations, in relation to every person who has been a director or shadow director of an insolvent company on, or within the three years prior to, the commencement of the relevant insolvency proceedings. The return is required to be made by the office-holder in office one week before the end of six months after the commencement of those insolvency proceedings, and by any office-holder who vacates office during that period, except where he has made a report under rule 3 covering every such person.

Rule 6 enables the Secretary of State or the official receiver to apply to the court to enforce compliance by the office-holder with a requirement under section 7(4) of the Act to furnish information and books, papers and other records relevant to the conduct of a person as a director.

Rule 7 contains transitional and saving provisions under which rules 3 and 4 of the 1986 Rules (which made provision for purposes similar to those for which rules 3 and 4 of these Rules provide) remain in force, with modifications relating to the forms to be used, for cases where the relevant insolvency proceedings commenced on or after 29th December 1986 and before 30th September 1996.

By virtue of the operation of section 22A and 22B respectively of the Act, the Act applies to building societies within the meaning of the Building Societies Act 1986 (c. 53) and to incorporated friendly societies within the meaning of the Friendly Societies Act 1992 (c.40) as it applies to companies and these Rules apply similarly.
Important changes made by these Rules are that:

(a) only one form is now prescribed for a section 7(3) report and one for a return to be made under the Rules;
(b) every office-holder is now required by rule 4(5) to make a return to the Secretary of State in accordance with rule 4 (except where he has made a report as described under rule 4(6)).

A Compliance Cost Assessment is available copies of which have been placed in the libraries of both Houses of Parliament. Copies are also available from The Insolvency Service of the Department of Trade and Industry, P.O. Box 203, Room 5.1, 21 Bloomsbury Street, London WC1B 3QW.

The Insolvent Companies (Disqualification of Unfit Directors) Proceedings Rules 1987 (SI 1987/2023)

Made	*25th November 1987*
Laid before Parliament	*10th December 1987*
Coming into force	*11th January 1988*

The Lord Chancellor, in the exercise of his powers under section 411 of the Insolvency Act 1986 and section 21 of the Company Directors Disqualification Act 1986, with the concurrence of the Secretary of State, and after consulting the committee existing for that purpose under section 413 of the Insolvency Act 1986, hereby makes the following Rules:—

1 Citation, commencement and interpretation

A3–10 (1) These Rules may be cited as the Insolvent Companies (Disqualification of Unfit Directors) Proceedings Rules 1987 and shall come into force on 11th January 1988.

[(2) In these Rules—

(a) "the Companies Act" means the Companies Act 1985,
(b) "the Company Directors Disqualification Act" means the Company Directors Disqualification Act 1986,
(c) "CPR" followed by a Part or rule by number means that Part or rule with that number in the Civil Procedure Rules 1998[4],
(d) "practice direction" means a direction as to the practice and procedure of any court within the scope of the Civil Procedure Rules,
(e) "registrar" has the same meaning as in paragraphs (4) and (5) of rule 13.2 of the Insolvency Rules 1986[5], and
(f) "file in court" means deliver to the court for filing.][6]

[(3) These Rules apply to an application made under the Company Directors Disqualification Act on or after 6th August 2007—

[4] Amended by SI 1999/1008 (L. 8).
[5] The only relevant amending instruments are SI 1987/1919 and SI 1999/1022.
[6] Substituted by Insolvent Companies (Disqualification of Unfit Directors) Proceedings (Amendment) Rules 1999/1023 Sch.1 para.2 (April 26, 1999).

(a) for leave to commence proceedings for a disqualification order after the end of the period mentioned in section 7(2) of that Act:
(b) to enforce any duty arising under section 7(4) of that Act;
(c) for a disqualification order where made—

(i) by the Secretary of State or the official receiver under section 7(1) of that Act (disqualification of unfit directors of insolvent companies);
(ii) by the Secretary of State under section 8 of that Act (disqualification after investigation of company); or
(iii) by the Office of Fair Trading or a specified regulator under section 9A of that Act (competition disqualification order);

(d) under section 8A of that Act (variation etc. of disqualification undertaking); or—
(e) for leave to act under—

(i) section 1A(1) or 9B(4) of that Act (and section 17 of that Act as it applies for the purposes of either of those sections); or
(ii) sections 1 and 17 as they apply for the purposes of section 6, 7(1), 8, 9A or 10 of that Act.][7]

Commencement

Rule 1(1)–(3)(b): January 11, 1988.

[2 Form and conduct of applications

(1) The Civil Procedure Rules 1998, and any relevant practice direction, apply in respect of any application to which these Rules apply, except where these Rules make provision to inconsistent effect. **A3–11**

[(2) Subject to paragraph (5), an application shall be made either—

(a) by claim form as provided by the relevant practice direction and the claimant must use the CPR Part 8 (alternative procedure for claims) procedure, or
(b) by application notice as provided for by the relevant practice direction.][8]

(3) CPR rule 8.1(3) (power of the court to order the claim to continue as if the claimant had not used the Part 8 procedure), CPR rule 8.2 (contents of the claim form) and CPR rule 8.7 (Part 20 claims) do not apply.

(4) Rule 7.47 (appeals and reviews of court orders) and rule 7.49 (procedure on appeal) of the Insolvency Rules 1986 apply.

[(5) The Insolvency Rules 1986 shall apply to an application to enforce any duty arising under section 7(4) of the Company Directors Disqualification Act made against a person who at the date of the application is acting as liquidator, administrator or administrative receiver.][9]][10]

Commencement

Rule 2(a)–(b): January 11, 1988.

[7] Substituted by Insolvent Companies (Disqualification of Unfit Directors) Proceedings (Amendment) Rules 2007/1906 rule 2(2) (August 6, 2007).

[8] Substituted by Insolvent Companies (Disqualification of Unfit Directors) Proceedings (Amendment) Rules 2007/1906 rule 3(2) (August 6, 2007).

[9] Added by Insolvent Companies (Disqualification of Unfit Directors) Proceedings (Amendment) Rules 2007/1906 rule 3(3) (August 6, 2007).

[10] Substituted by Insolvent Companies (Disqualification of Unfit Directors) Proceedings (Amendment) Rules 1999/1023 Sch.1 para.3 (April 26, 1999).

[2A Application of Rules 3 to 8

A3–12 Rules 3 to 8 only apply to the types of application referred to in Rule 1(3)(c).][11]

3 The case against the [defendant][12]

A3–13 (1) There shall, at the time when the [claim form][13] is issued, be filed in court evidence in support of the application for a disqualification order; and copies of the evidence shall be served with the [claim form][14] on the [defendant][15].

(2) The evidence shall be by one or more affidavits, except where the [claimant][16] is the official receiver, in which case it may be in the form of a written report (with or without affidavits by other persons) which shall be treated as if it had been verified by affidavit by him and shall be prima facie evidence of any matter contained in it.

(3) There shall in the affidavit or affidavits or (as the case may be) the official receiver's report be included a statement of the matters by reference to which the [defendant][17] is alleged to be unfit to be concerned in the management of a company.

Commencement
Rule 3(1)–(3): January 11, 1988.

4 Endorsement on [claim form][18]

A3–14 There shall on the [claim form][19] be endorsed information to the [defendant][20] as follows—

(a) that the application is made in accordance with these Rules;

(b) that, in accordance with the relevant enactments, the court has power to impose disqualifications as follows—

(i) where the application is under section 7 of the Company Directors Disqualification Act, for a period of not less than 2, and up to 15, years; and

(ii) where the application is [under section 8 or 9A of that Act][21], for a period of up to 15 years;

(c) that the application for a disqualification order may, in accordance with these Rules, be heard and determined summarily, without further or other notice to the

[11] Added by Insolvent Companies (Disqualification of Unfit Directors) Proceedings (Amendment) Rules 2007/1906 rule 4 (August 6, 2007).

[12] Words substituted by Insolvent Companies (Disqualification of Unfit Directors) Proceedings (Amendment) Rules 1999/1023 Sch.1 para.1 (April 26, 1999).

[13] Words substituted by Insolvent Companies (Disqualification of Unfit Directors) Proceedings (Amendment) Rules 1999/1023 Sch.1 para.1 (April 26, 1999).

[14] Words substituted by Insolvent Companies (Disqualification of Unfit Directors) Proceedings (Amendment) Rules 1999/1023 Sch.1 para.1 (April 26, 1999).

[15] Words substituted by Insolvent Companies (Disqualification of Unfit Directors) Proceedings (Amendment) Rules 1999/1023 Sch.1 para.1 (April 26, 1999).

[16] Words substituted by Insolvent Companies (Disqualification of Unfit Directors) Proceedings (Amendment) Rules 1999/1023 Sch.1 para.1 (April 26, 1999).

[17] Words substituted by Insolvent Companies (Disqualification of Unfit Directors) Proceedings (Amendment) Rules 1999/1023 Sch.1 para.1 (April 26, 1999).

[18] Words substituted by Insolvent Companies (Disqualification of Unfit Directors) Proceedings (Amendment) Rules 1999/1023 Sch.1 para.1 (April 26, 1999).

[19] Words substituted by Insolvent Companies (Disqualification of Unfit Directors) Proceedings (Amendment) Rules 1999/1023 Sch.1 para.1 (April 26, 1999).

[20] Words substituted by Insolvent Companies (Disqualification of Unfit Directors) Proceedings (Amendment) Rules 1999/1023 Sch.1 para.1 (April 26, 1999).

[21] Words substituted by Insolvent Companies (Disqualification of Unfit Directors) Proceedings (Amendment) Rules 2003/1367 Sch.1 para.2(2) (June 20, 2003).

[defendant][22], and that, if it is so heard and determined, the court may impose disqualification for a period of up to 5 years;

(d) that if at the hearing of the application the court, on the evidence then before it, is minded to impose, in the [defendant][23]'s case, disqualification for any period longer than 5 years, it will not make a disqualification order on that occasion but will adjourn the application to be heard (with further evidence, if any) at a later date to be notified; and

(e) that any evidence which the [defendant][24] wishes to be taken into consideration by the court must be filed in court in accordance with the time limits imposed under Rule 6 (the provisions of which shall be set out on the [claim form][25]).

Commencement

Rule 4(a)–(c): January 11, 1988.

5 Service and acknowledgement

A3–15

(1) The [claim form][26] shall be served on the [defendant][27] by sending it by first class post to his last known address; and the date of service shall, unless the contrary is shown, be deemed to be the 7th day next following that on which the [claim form][28] was posted.

(2) Where any process or order of the court or other document is required under proceedings subject to these Rules to be served on any person who is not in England and Wales, the court may order service on him of that process or order or other document to be effected within such time and in such manner as it thinks fit, and may also require such proof of service as it thinks fit.

[(3) The claim form served on the defendant shall be accompanied by an acknowledgment of service as provided for by practice direction and CPR rule 8.3(2) (dealing with the contents of an acknowledgment of service) does not apply.][29]

(4) The [. . .][30] acknowledgement of service shall state that the [defendant][31] should indicate—

(a) whether he contests the application on the grounds that, in the case of any particular company—

[22] Words substituted by Insolvent Companies (Disqualification of Unfit Directors) Proceedings (Amendment) Rules 1999/1023 Sch.1 para.1 (April 26, 1999).

[23] Words substituted by Insolvent Companies (Disqualification of Unfit Directors) Proceedings (Amendment) Rules 1999/1023 Sch.1 para.1 (April 26, 1999).

[24] Words substituted by Insolvent Companies (Disqualification of Unfit Directors) Proceedings (Amendment) Rules 1999/1023 Sch.1 para.1 (April 26, 1999).

[25] Words substituted by Insolvent Companies (Disqualification of Unfit Directors) Proceedings (Amendment) Rules 1999/1023 Sch.1 para.1 (April 26, 1999).

[26] Words substituted by Insolvent Companies (Disqualification of Unfit Directors) Proceedings (Amendment) Rules 1999/1023 Sch.1 para.1 (April 26, 1999).

[27] Words substituted by Insolvent Companies (Disqualification of Unfit Directors) Proceedings (Amendment) Rules 1999/1023 Sch.1 para.1 (April 26, 1999).

[28] Words substituted by Insolvent Companies (Disqualification of Unfit Directors) Proceedings (Amendment) Rules 1999/1023 Sch.1 para.1 (April 26, 1999).

[29] Substituted by Insolvent Companies (Disqualification of Unfit Directors) Proceedings (Amendment) Rules 1999/1023 Sch.1 para.4(1) (April 26, 1999).

[30] Words substituted by Insolvent Companies (Disqualification of Unfit Directors) Proceedings (Amendment) Rules 1999/1023 Sch.1 para.1 (April 26, 1999).

[31] Repeal words by Insolvent Companies (Disqualification of Unfit Directors) Proceedings (Amendment) Rules 1999/1023 Sch.1 para.4(2) (April 26, 1999).

(i) he was not a director or shadow director of the company at a time when conduct of his, or of other persons, in relation to that company is in question, or

(ii) his conduct as director or shadow director of that company was not as alleged in support of the application for a disqualification order,

(b) whether, in the case of any conduct of his, he disputes the allegation that such conduct makes him unfit to be concerned in the management of a company, and

(c) whether he, while not resisting the application for a disqualification order, intends to adduce mitigating factors with a view to justifying only a short period of disqualification.

Commencement

Rule 5(1)–(4)(c): January 11, 1988.

6 Evidence

A3–16 (1) The [defendant][32] shall, within 28 days from the date of service of the [claim form][33], file in court any affidavit evidence in opposition to the application he wishes the court to take into consideration and shall forthwith serve upon the [claimant][34] a copy of such evidence.

(2) The [claimant][35] shall, within 14 days from receiving the copy of the [defendant][36]'s evidence, file in court any further evidence in reply he wishes the court to take into consideration and shall forthwith serve a copy of that evidence upon the [defendant][37].

[(3) CPR rules 8.5 (filing and serving written evidence) and 8.6(1) (requirements where written evidence is to be relied on) do not apply.][38]

Commencement

Rule 6(1)–(2): January 11, 1988.

7 The hearing of the application

A3–17 [(1) When the claim form is issued, the court will fix a date for the first hearing of the claim which shall not be less than 8 weeks from the date of issue of the claim form.][39]

(2) The hearing shall in the first instance be before the registrar in open court.

(3) The registrar shall either determine the case on the date fixed or adjourn it.

(4) The registrar shall adjourn the case for further consideration if—

(a) he forms the provisional opinion that a disqualification order ought to be made, and that a period of disqualification longer than 5 years is appropriate, or

[32] Words substituted by Insolvent Companies (Disqualification of Unfit Directors) Proceedings (Amendment) Rules 1999/1023 Sch.1 para.1 (April 26, 1999).

[33] Words substituted by Insolvent Companies (Disqualification of Unfit Directors) Proceedings (Amendment) Rules 1999/1023 Sch.1 para.1 (April 26, 1999).

[34] Words substituted by Insolvent Companies (Disqualification of Unfit Directors) Proceedings (Amendment) Rules 1999/1023 Sch.1 para.1 (April 26, 1999).

[35] Words substituted by Insolvent Companies (Disqualification of Unfit Directors) Proceedings (Amendment) Rules 1999/1023 Sch.1 para.1 (April 26, 1999).

[36] Words substituted by Insolvent Companies (Disqualification of Unfit Directors) Proceedings (Amendment) Rules 1999/1023 Sch.1 para.1 (April 26, 1999).

[37] Words substituted by Insolvent Companies (Disqualification of Unfit Directors) Proceedings (Amendment) Rules 1999/1023 Sch.1 para.1 (April 26, 1999).

[38] Added by Insolvent Companies (Disqualification of Unfit Directors) Proceedings (Amendment) Rules 1999/1023 Sch.1 para.5 (April 26, 1999).

[39] Substituted by Insolvent Companies (Disqualification of Unfit Directors) Proceedings (Amendment) Rules 1999/1023 Sch.1 para.6 (April 26, 1999).

(b) he is of opinion that questions of law or fact arise which are not suitable for summary determination.

(5) If the registrar adjourns the case for further consideration he shall—

(a) direct whether the case is to be heard by a registrar or, if he thinks it appropriate, by the judge, for determination by him;
(b) state the reasons for the adjournment; and
(c) give directions as to the following matters—

(i) the manner in which and the time within which notice of the adjournment and the reasons for it are to be given to the [defendant][40],
(ii) the filing in court and the service of further evidence (if any) by the parties,
(iii) such other matters as the registrar thinks necessary or expedient with a view to an expeditious disposal of the application, and
(iv) the time and place of the adjourned hearing.

(6) Where a case is adjourned other than to the judge, it may be heard by the registrar who originally dealt with the case or by another registrar.

Commencement

Rule 7(1)–(6): January 11, 1988.

8 Making and setting aside of disqualification order

(1) The court may make a disqualification order against the [defendant][41], whether or not the latter appears, and whether or not he has completed and returned the acknowledgement of service of the [claim form][42], or filed evidence in accordance with Rule 6. **A3–18**

(2) Any disqualification order made in the absence of the [defendant][43] may be set aside or varied by the court on such terms as it thinks just.

Commencement

Rule 8(1)–(2): January 11, 1988.

9 [. . .][44]

10 Right of audience

Official receivers and deputy official receivers have right of audience in any proceedings to which these Rules apply, whether the application is made by the Secretary of State or by the official receiver at his direction, and whether made in the High Court or a county court. **A3–19**

Commencement

Rule 10: January 11, 1988.

[40] Words substituted by Insolvent Companies (Disqualification of Unfit Directors) Proceedings (Amendment) Rules 1999/1023 Sch.1 para.1 (April 26, 1999).

[41] Words substituted by Insolvent Companies (Disqualification of Unfit Directors) Proceedings (Amendment) Rules 1999/1023 Sch.1 para.1 (April 26, 1999).

[42] Words substituted by Insolvent Companies (Disqualification of Unfit Directors) Proceedings (Amendment) Rules 1999/1023 Sch.1 para.1 (April 26, 1999).

[43] Words substituted by Insolvent Companies (Disqualification of Unfit Directors) Proceedings (Amendment) Rules 1999/1023 Sch.1 para.1 (April 26, 1999).

[44] Revoked by Insolvent Companies (Disqualification of Unfit Directors) Proceedings (Amendment) Rules 2001/765 rule 2 (April 2, 2001).

11 Revocation and saving

A3–20 (1) The Insolvent Companies (Disqualification of Unfit Directors) Proceedings Rules 1986 ("the former Rules") are hereby revoked.

(2) Notwithstanding paragraph (1) the former Rules shall continue to apply and have effect in relation to any application described in paragraph 3(a) or (b) of Rule 1 of these Rules made before the date on which these Rules come into force.

Commencement

Rule 11(1)–(2): January 11, 1988.

Mackay of Clashfern, C.

Dated 24th November 1987

I concur

Francis Maude
Parliamentary Under-Secretary of State,
Department of Trade and Industry

Dated 25th November 1987

EXPLANATORY NOTE

(This note is not part of the Order)

A3–21 These Rules set out a special code of procedure for applications by the Secretary of State or the official receiver for the disqualification of directors by the court under sections 7 and 8 of the Company Directors Disqualification Act 1986 in England and Wales.

They provide for the revocation of the Insolvent Companies (Disqualification of Unfit Directors) Proceedings Rules 1986 and the re-enactment of those Rules with amendments. These Rules provide that the application is to be by way of the originating [claim form][45] procedure where it is made in the High Court and by way of originating application where made in the County Court. In both cases these procedures are made subject to the particular provisions set out in these Rules for the purpose of section 7 and 8 applications, which will be common to the procedure in both types of court.

The amendments made to the content of the Rules revoked and re-enacted by these Rules provide for:—

(a) further matters to be endorsed upon the [claim form][46];
(b) the report of the official receiver to be prima facie evidence of the matters contained in it;
(c) the time limits on the filing of evidence in court to be mandatory;
(d) further provision in regard to the disposal of applications by the registrar;
(e) the clarification of the power of the court to make orders where the [defendant][47] does not appear, and

[45] Words substituted by Insolvent Companies (Disqualification of Unfit Directors) Proceedings (Amendment) Rules 1999/1023 Sch.1 para.1 (April 26, 1999).

[46] Words substituted by Insolvent Companies (Disqualification of Unfit Directors) Proceedings (Amendment) Rules 1999/1023 Sch.1 para.1 (April 26, 1999).

[47] Words substituted by Insolvent Companies (Disqualification of Unfit Directors) Proceedings (Amendment) Rules 1999/1023 Sch.1 para.1 (April 26, 1999).

(f) right of audience of official receivers and deputy official receivers in the High Court and the County Court.

The Companies (Disqualification Orders) Regulations 2009 (SI 2009/2471)

Made	*8th September 2009*
Laid before Parliament	*9th September 2009*
Coming into force	*1st October 2009*

The Secretary of State makes the following Regulations in exercise of the powers conferred by section 18 of the Company Directors Disqualification Act 1986[48]:

1 Citation and commencement

A3–22 These Regulations may be cited as the Companies (Disqualification Orders) Regulations 2009 and come into force on 1st October 2009.

Commencement

Regulation 1: October 1, 2009.

2 Definitions

A3–23

(1) In these Regulations—

"the Act" means the Company Directors Disqualification Act 1986;

"disqualification order" means an order of the court under any of sections 2 to 6, 8, 9A and 10 of the Act;

"disqualification undertaking" means an undertaking accepted by the Secretary of State under section 7, 8 or 9B of the Act;

"grant of leave" means a grant by the court of leave under section 17 of the Act to any person in relation to a disqualification order or a disqualification undertaking.

(2) For the purposes of regulations 5 and 9, "leave granted"—

(a) in relation to a disqualification order granted under Part 2 of the Companies (Northern Ireland) Order 1989 means leave granted by a court for a person subject to such an order to do anything which otherwise the order prohibits that person from doing; and

(b) in relation to a disqualification undertaking accepted under the Company Directors Disqualification (Northern Ireland) Order 2002 means leave granted by a court for a person subject to such an undertaking to do anything which otherwise the undertaking prohibits that person from doing.

Commencement

Regulation 2(1)–(2)(b): October 1, 2009.

[48] Section 18 has been amended by section 8 of, and Schedule 4 to, the Insolvency Act 2000 (c.39), section 204 of the Enterprise Act 2002 (c.40) and by Article 2(6) of the Insolvency Act 2000 (Company Directors Disqualification Undertakings) Order 2004 (SI 2004/1941).

3 Revocations

A3–24 The following instruments are revoked—

(a) the Companies (Disqualification Orders) Regulations 2001[49];
(b) the Companies (Disqualification Orders) (Amendment No. 2) Regulations 2002; and
(c) the Companies (Disqualification Orders) (Amendment) Regulations 2004.

Commencement
Regulation 3(a)–(c): October 1, 2009.

4 Transitional provisions

A3–25 Other than regulation 9, these Regulations apply—

(a) in relation to a disqualification order made after the coming into force of these Regulations; and
(b) in relation to—
  (i) a grant of leave made after the coming into force of these Regulations; or
  (ii) any action taken by a court after the coming into force of these Regulations in consequence of which a disqualification order or a disqualification undertaking is varied or ceases to be in force,

whether the disqualification order or disqualification undertaking to which the grant of leave or the action relates was made by the court or accepted by the Secretary of State before or after the coming into force of these Regulations.

Commencement
Regulation 4(a)–(b)(ii): October 1, 2009.

5 Regulation 9 applies to—

(a) particulars of disqualification orders made and leave granted under Part 2 of the Companies (Northern Ireland) Order 1989 received by the Secretary of State on or after 1st October 2009 other than particulars of disqualification orders made and leave granted under that Order which relate to disqualification orders made by the courts of Northern Ireland before 2nd April 2001; and
(b) particulars of undertakings accepted under the Company Directors Disqualification (Northern Ireland) Order 2002 on or after 1st October 2009, and to leave granted under that Order in relation to such undertakings.

Commencement
Regulation 5(a)–(b): October 1, 2009.

6 Particulars to be furnished by officers of the court

A3–26 (1) The following officers of the court must furnish to the Secretary of State the particulars specified in regulation 7(a) to (c) in the form and manner there specified—

(a) where a disqualification order is made by the Crown Court, the Court Manager;
(b) where a disqualification order or grant of leave is made by the High Court, the Court Manager;

[49] As amended by SI 2002/1834 and SI 2004/1940.

(c) where a disqualification order or grant of leave is made by a County Court, the Court Manager;
(d) where a disqualification order is made by a Magistrates' Court, the designated officer for a Magistrates' Court;
(e) where a disqualification order is made by the High Court of Justiciary, the Deputy Principal Clerk of Justiciary;
(f) where a disqualification order or grant of leave is made by a Sheriff Court, the Sheriff Clerk;
(g) where a disqualification order or grant of leave is made by the Court of Session, the Deputy Principal Clerk of Session;
(h) where a disqualification order or grant of leave is made by the Court of Appeal, the Court Manager; and
(i) where a disqualification order or grant of leave is made by the Supreme Court, the Registrar of the Supreme Court.

(2) Where—

(a) a disqualification order has been made by any of the courts mentioned in paragraph (1), or
(b) a disqualification undertaking has been accepted by the Secretary of State,

and subsequently any action is taken by a court in consequence of which that order or that undertaking is varied or ceases to be in force, the officer specified in paragraph (1) of the court which takes such action must furnish to the Secretary of State the particulars specified in regulation 7(d) in the form and manner there specified.

Commencement

Regulation 6(1)–(2)(b): October 1, 2009.

7 The form in which the particulars are to be furnished is—

(a) that set out in Schedule 1 to these Regulations with such variations as circumstances require when the person against whom the disqualification order is made is an individual, and the particulars contained therein are the particulars specified for that purpose;
(b) that set out in Schedule 2 to these Regulations with such variations as circumstances require when the person against whom the disqualification order is made is a body corporate, and the particulars contained therein are the particulars specified for that purpose;
(c) that set out in Schedule 3 to these Regulations with such variations as circumstances require when a grant of leave is made by the court in relation to a disqualification order or a disqualification undertaking, and the particulars contained therein are the particulars specified for that purpose;
(d) that set out in Schedule 4 to these Regulations with such variations as circumstances require when any action is taken by a court in consequence of which a disqualification order or a disqualification undertaking is varied or ceases to be in force, and the particulars contained therein are the particulars specified for that purpose.

Commencement

Regulation 7(a)–(d): October 1, 2009.

8 The time within which the officer specified in regulation 6(1) is to furnish the Secretary of State with the said particulars is the period of 14 days beginning with the day on which the disqualification order or grant of leave is made or on which action is taken by a court in consequence of which the disqualification order or disqualification undertaking is varied or ceases to be in force.

Commencement

Regulation 8: October 1, 2009.

9 Extension of certain of the provisions of section 18 of the Act to orders made, undertakings accepted and leave granted in Northern Ireland

A3–27 (1) Section 18(2) of the Act is extended to the particulars furnished to the Secretary of State of disqualification orders made and leave granted under Part 2 of the Companies (Northern Ireland) Order 1989.

(2) Section 18(2A) of the Act is extended to the particulars of disqualification undertakings accepted under and leave granted in relation to disqualification undertakings under the Company Directors Disqualification (Northern Ireland) Order 2002.

(3) Section 18(3) of the Act is extended to all entries in the register and particulars relating to them furnished to the Secretary of State in respect of orders made under Part 2 of the Companies (Northern Ireland) Order 1989 or disqualification undertakings accepted under the Company Directors Disqualification (Northern Ireland) Order 2002.

Commencement

Regulation 9(1)–(3): October 1, 2009.

SCHEDULES

Davies of Abersoch
Minister for Trade, Investment and Business
Department for Business, Innovation and Skills

8th September 2009

Regulation 7(a) SCHEDULE 1

A3–28 **DQ01** *Disqualification order against an individual*

[The Form is not reproduced here.]

Commencement

Schedule 1 para.1: October 1, 2009.

Regulation 7(b) SCHEDULE 2

A3–29 **DQ02** *Disqualification order against a corporate body or firm*

[The Form is not reproduced here.]

Commencement

Schedule 2 para.1: October 1, 2009.

Regulation 7(c) SCHEDULE 3

A3–30 **DQ03** *Grant of leave in relation to a disqualification order or disqualification undertaking*

[The Form is not reproduced here.]

Commencement

Schedule 3 para.1: October 1, 2009.

Regulation 7(d) SCHEDULE 4

DQ04 *Variation or cessation of a disqualification order or disqualification undertaking* **A3–31**

[The Form is not reproduced here.]

Commencement

Schedule 4 para.1: October 1, 2009.

EXPLANATORY NOTE

(This note is not part of the Order)

A3–32 These Regulations revoke and replace the Companies (Disqualification Orders) Regulations 2001 (SI 2001/967) as amended by SI 2002/1834 and S.I. 2004/1940 (as amended "the 2001 Regulations"). They come into force on 1st October 2009, and apply to any disqualification order made after that date, and to any grant of leave or action taken by a court after that date in consequence of which a disqualification order or undertaking (whenever made or accepted) is varied or ceases to have effect.

The Company Directors Disqualification Act 1986 (c.46) ("the CDDA") gives specified courts power to make a disqualification order against any person. As amended by the Insolvency Act 2000 (c.39), the CDDA gives the Secretary of State power to accept an undertaking from any person that, for a specified period, that person must not—

(a) without the leave of the court, be a director of a company, act as a receiver of a company's property or in any way take part in the promotion, formation or management of a company; and
(b) act as an insolvency practitioner.

These Regulations consolidate the 2001 Regulations with minor amendments.

Regulation 6 (particulars to be furnished by officers of the court) requires certain court officers to provide the Secretary of State with particulars of disqualification orders and grants of leave in relation to such orders or disqualification undertakings, and of any action taken by a court in consequence of which any such orders or undertakings are varied or cease to be in force. Section 18 of the CDDA requires that the Secretary of State must maintain a public register from the particulars so furnished.

Regulation 7 specifies the particulars mentioned in regulation 6 and the form and manner in which such particulars must be furnished to the Secretary of State. Schedules 1 to 4 contain the forms to be used when furnishing such particulars.

Regulation 9 (extension of certain of the provisions of section 18 of the Act to orders made, undertakings accepted and leave granted in Northern Ireland) places obligations on the Secretary of State regarding the retention and disposal of information furnished to the Secretary of State relating to disqualification orders made, disqualification undertakings accepted and leave granted in relation to such orders and undertakings in Northern Ireland. Key changes from the 2001 Regulations are:

(a) in regulation 2 (definitions) there is a new definition of "leave granted" for the purposes of regulation 5 (transitional provisions in relation to regulation 9) and regulation 9;
(b) in regulation 6, certain changes within the courts made by the Courts Act 2003 (c.39) and the Constitutional Reform Act 2005 (c.4) have necessitated amendments concerning the identity of certain court officers required to provide the Secretary of State with the particulars specified in regulation 7;
(c) in the form in Schedule 1, the reference to section 723B of the Companies Act 1985 (c.6) relating to confidentiality orders has been removed in the light of the repeal of that provision by the Companies Act 2006 (c.46), and alternative provision made for the provision of service addresses by directors; and

(d) the forms in Schedules 1 to 4 have been amended so as to provide for particulars of competition disqualification orders made under section 9A of the CDDA to be furnished to the Secretary of State.

An impact assessment has not been produced for this instrument as no impact on the private or voluntary sectors is foreseen.

APPENDIX 4

PRACTICE DIRECTION: DIRECTORS DISQUALIFICATION PROCEEDINGS

PART 1

1. APPLICATION AND INTERPRETATION

1.1 In this practice direction: **A4–01**

(1) "the Act" means the Company Directors Disqualification Act 1986 (as amended);
(2) "the Disqualification Rules" means the rules for the time being in force made under section 411 of the Insolvency Act 1986 in relation to disqualification proceedings[1];
(3) "the Insolvency Rules" means the rules for the time being in force made under sections 411 and 412 of the Insolvency Act 1986 in relation to insolvency proceedings;
(4) "CPR" means the Civil Procedure Rules 1998 and "CPR" followed by "Part" or "Rule" and a number means the part or Rule with that number in those Rules;
(5) "disqualification proceedings" has the meaning set out in paragraph 1.3 below;
(6) "a disqualification application" is an application under the Act for the making of a disqualification order;
(7) "registrar" means any judge of the High Court or the county court who is a registrar within the meaning of the Insolvency Rules;
(8) "companies court registrar" means any judge of the High Court sitting in the Royal Courts of Justice in London who is a registrar within the meaning of the Insolvency Rules.
(9) except where the context otherwise requires references to;
  (a) "company" or "companies" shall include references to "partnership" or "partnerships" and to "limited liability partnership" and "limited liability partnerships"
  (b) "director" shall include references to an "officer" of a partnership and to a "member" of a limited liability partnership:
  (c) "shadow director" shall include references to a "shadow member" of a limited liability partnership

[1] The current rules are the Insolvent Companies (Disqualification of Unfit Directors) Proceedings Rules 1987. For convenience relevant references to the Insolvent Companies (Disqualification of Unfit Directors) Proceedings Rules 1987, which apply to disqualification applications under sections 7, 8 and 9A of the Act (see rule 1(3)), are set out in footnotes to this Practice Direction. This Practice Direction applies certain provisions contained in the Insolvent Companies (Disqualification of Unfit Directors) Proceedings Rules 1987 to disqualification proceedings other than applications under sections 7, 8 and 9A of the Act.

and, in appropriate cases, the forms annexed to this practice direction shall be varied accordingly;

(10) "disqualification order" has the meaning set out in section 1 of the Act and "disqualification undertaking" has the meaning set out in section 1A or section 9B of the Act (as the context requires);

(11) a "Section 8A application" is an application under section 8A of the Act to reduce the period for which a disqualification undertaking is in force or to provide for it to cease to be in force;

(12) "specified regulator" has the meaning set out in section 9E(2) of the Act.

1.2 This practice direction shall come into effect on 26 April 1999 and shall replace all previous practice directions relating to disqualification proceedings.

1.3 This practice direction applies to the following proceedings ("disqualification proceedings"):

(1) disqualification applications made:

(a) under section 2(2)(a) of the Act (after the person's conviction of an indictable offence in connection with the affairs of a company);

(b) under section 3 of the Act (on the ground of persistent breaches of provisions of companies legislation);

(c) under section 4 of the Act (on the ground of fraud etc);

(d) by the Secretary of State or the official receiver under section 7(1) of the Act (on the ground that the person is or has been a director of a company which has at any time become insolvent and his conduct makes him unfit to be concerned in the management of a company);

(e) by the Secretary of State under section 8 of the Act (on it appearing to the Secretary of State from investigative material that it is expedient in the public interest that a disqualification order should be made); or

(f) by the Office of Fair Trading or a specified regulator under section 9A of the Act (on the ground of breach of competition law by an undertaking and unfitness to be concerned in the management of a company);

(2) any application made under section 7(2) or 7(4) of the Act;

(3) any application for permission to act made under section 17 of the Act for the purposes of any of sections 1(1)(a), 1A(1)(a) or 9B(4), or made under section 12(2) of the Act;

(4) any application for a court order made under CPR Part 23 in the course of any of the proceedings set out in sub-paragraphs (1) to (3) above;

(5) any application under the Act to the extent provided for by subordinate legislation[2];

(6) any section 8A application.

2. MULTI-TRACK

A4–02 **2.1** All disqualification proceedings are allocated to the multi-track. The CPR relating to allocation questionnaires and track allocation shall not apply.

3. RIGHTS OF AUDIENCE

A4–03 **3.1** Official receivers and deputy official receivers have right of audience in any proceedings to which this Practice Direction applies, including cases where a disqualification

[2] Current subordinate legislation includes the Insolvent Partnerships Order 1994 and the Limited Liability Partnerships Regulations 2001.

application is made by the Secretary of State or by the official receiver at his direction, and whether made in the High Court or a county court[3].

PART 2 DISQUALIFICATION APPLICATIONS

4. COMMENCEMENT

4.1 Sections 2(2)(a), 3(4), 4(2), 6(3), 8(3) and 9E(3) of the Act identify the civil courts which have jurisdiction to deal with disqualification applications. **A4–04**

4.1A A disqualification application must be commenced by a claim form issued:

(1) in the case of a disqualification application under section 9A of the Act, in the High Court out of the office of the companies court registrar at the Royal Courts of Justice;

(2) in any other case,

(a) in the High Court out of the office of the companies court registrar or a chancery district registry; and

(b) in the county court, out of a county court office.

4.2 Disqualification applications shall be made by the issue of a claim form in the form annexed hereto and the use of the procedure set out in CPR Part 8[4], as modified by this practice direction and (where the application is made under sections 7, 8 or 9A of the Act) the Disqualification Rules. CPR rule 8.1(3) (power of the Court to order the application to continue as if the claimant had not used the Part 8 Procedure) shall not apply.

4.3 When the claim form is issued, the claimant will be given a date for the first hearing of the disqualification application. This date is to be not less than eight weeks from the date of issue of the claim form[5]. The first hearing will be before a registrar.

5. HEADINGS

5.1 Every claim form by which a disqualification application under the Act is begun and all affidavits, notices and other documents in the proceedings must be entitled in the matter of the company or companies in question and in the matter of the Act. In the case of any disqualification application under section 7 or 9A of the Act it is not necessary to mention in the heading any company other than that referred to in section 6(1)(a) or 9A(2) of the Act (as the case may be). **A4–05**

6. THE CLAIM FORM

6.1 CPR Rule 8.2 does not apply. The claim form must state: **A4–06**

(1) that CPR Part 8 (as modified by this practice direction) applies, and (if the application is made under sections 7, 8 or 9A of the Act) that the

[3] Rule 10 of the Insolvent Companies (Disqualification of Unfit Directors) Proceedings Rules 1987.

[4] Rule 2(2) of the Insolvent Companies (Disqualification of Unfit Directors) Proceedings Rules 1987 as amended.

[5] Rule 7(1) of the Insolvent Companies (Disqualification of Unfit Directors) Proceedings Rules 1987.

disqualification application is made in accordance with the Disqualification Rules[6];

(2) that the claimant seeks a disqualification order, and the section of the Act pursuant to which the disqualification application is made;

(3) the period for which, in accordance with the Act, the court has power to impose a disqualification period.
The periods are as follows—

(a) where the application is under section 2 of the Act, for a period of up to 15 years;
(b) where the application is under section 3 of the Act, for a period of up to 5 years;
(c) where the application is under section 4 of the Act, for a period of up to 15 years;
(d) where the application is under section 7 of the Act, for a period of not less than 2, and up to 15, years[7];
(e) where the application is under section 8 or 9A of the Act, for a period of up to 15 years[8].

(4) in cases where the disqualification application is made under sections 7, 8 or 9A of the Act, that on the first hearing of the application, the court may hear and determine it summarily, without further or other notice to the defendant, and that, if the application is so determined, the court may impose a period of disqualification of up to 5 years but that if at the hearing of the application the court, on the evidence then before it, is minded to impose, in the case of any defendant, disqualification for any period longer than 5 years, it will not make a disqualification order on that occasion but will adjourn the application to be heard (with further evidence, if any) at a later date that will be notified to the defendant[9];

(5) that any evidence which the defendant wishes the court to take into consideration must be filed in court in accordance with the time limits set out in paragraph 9 below (which time limits shall be set out in the notes to the Claim Form)[10].

7. SERVICE OF THE CLAIM FORM

A4–07 **7.1** Service of claim forms in disqualification proceedings will be the responsibility of the claimant and will not be undertaken by the court.

7.2 The claim form shall be served by the claimant on the defendant. It may be served by sending it by first class post to his last known address; and the date of service shall, unless the contrary is shown, be deemed to be the 7th day following that on which the claim form was posted[11]. CPR r. 6.7(1) shall be modified accordingly. Otherwise Sections I and II of CPR Part 6 apply[12].

[6] Rule 4(a) of the Insolvent Companies (Disqualification of Unfit Directors) Proceedings Rules 1987.

[7] Rule 4(b)(i) of the Insolvent Companies (Disqualification of Unfit Directors) Proceedings Rules 1987.

[8] Rule 4(b)(ii) of the Insolvent Companies (Disqualification of Unfit Directors) Proceedings Rules 1987.

[9] Rule 4(c) and (d) of the Insolvent Companies (Disqualification of Unfit Directors) Proceedings Rules 1987.

[10] Rule 4(e) of the Insolvent Companies (Disqualification of Unfit Directors) Proceedings Rules 1987.

[11] Rule 5(1) of the Insolvent Companies (Disqualification of Unfit Directors) Proceedings Rules 1987.

[12] Attention is drawn to CPR Rule 6.14(2) regarding a certificate of service of the claim form.

7.3 Where any claim form or order of the court or other document is required under any disqualification proceedings to be served on any person who is not in England and Wales, the court may order service on him to be effected within such time and in such manner as it thinks fit, may require such proof of service as it thinks fit[13], and may give such directions as to acknowledgment of service as it thinks fit. Section III of CPR Part 6 shall not apply.

7.4 The claim form served on the defendant shall be accompanied by an acknowledgement of service.

8. ACKNOWLEDGMENT OF SERVICE

A4–08

8.1 The form of acknowledgment of service is annexed to this practice direction. CPR rules 8.3(2) and 8.3(3)(a) do not apply to disqualification applications.

8.2 In cases brought under section 7, 8 or 9A of the Act, the form of acknowledgement of service shall state that the defendant should indicate[14]:

(1) whether he contests the application on the grounds that, in the case of any particular company—

(a) he was not a director or shadow director of that company at a time when conduct of his, or of other persons, in relation to that company is in question;

(b) his conduct as director or shadow director of that company was not as alleged in support of the application for a disqualification order;

(c) in the case of an application made under section 7 of the Act, the company has at no time become insolvent within the meaning of section 6; or

(d) in the case of an application under section 9A of the Act, the undertaking which is a company did not commit a breach of competition law within the meaning of that section.

(2) whether, in the case of any conduct of his, he disputes the allegation that such conduct makes him unfit to be concerned in the management of a company; and

(3) whether he, while not resisting the application for a disqualification order, intends to adduce mitigating factors with a view to reducing the period of disqualification.

8.3 The defendant shall:

(1) (subject to any directions to the contrary given under paragraph 7.3 above) file an acknowledgment of service in the prescribed form not more than 14 days after service of the claim form; and

(2) serve a copy of the acknowledgment of service on the claimant and any other party.

8.4 Where the defendant has failed to file an acknowledgment of service and the time period for doing so has expired, the defendant may attend the hearing of the application but may not take part in the hearing unless the court gives permission.

9. EVIDENCE

A4–09

9.1 Evidence in disqualification applications shall be by affidavit, except where the official receiver is a party, in which case his evidence may be in the form of a written

[13] Rule 5(2) of the Insolvent Companies (Disqualification of Unfit Directors) Proceedings Rules 1987.

[14] Rule 5(4) of the Insolvent Companies (Disqualification of Unfit Directors) Proceedings Rules 1987.

report (with or without affidavits by other persons) which shall be treated as if it had been verified by affidavit by him and shall be prima facie evidence of any matter contained in it[15].

9.2 In the affidavits or (as the case may be) the official receiver's report in support of the application, there shall be included:

(1) a statement of the matters by reference to which it is alleged that a disqualification order should be made against the defendant[16]; and
(2) a statement of the steps taken to comply with any requirements imposed by sections 16(1) and 9C(4) of the Act

9.3 When the claim form is issued:

(1) the affidavit or report in support of the disqualification application must be filed in court;
(2) exhibits must be lodged with the court where they shall be retained until the conclusion of the proceedings; and
(3) copies of the affidavit/report and exhibits shall be served with the claim form on the defendant[17].

9.4 The defendant shall, within 28 days from the date of service of the claim form[18]:

(1) file in court any affidavit evidence in opposition to the disqualification application that he or she wishes the court to take into consideration; and
(2) lodge the exhibits with the court where they shall be retained until the conclusion of the proceedings; and
(3) at the same time, serve upon the claimant a copy of the affidavits and exhibits.

9.5 In cases where there is more than one defendant, each defendant is required to serve his evidence on the other defendants unless the court otherwise orders.

9.6 The claimant shall, within 14 days from receiving the copy of the defendant's evidence[19]:

(1) file in court any further affidavit or report in reply he wishes the court to take into consideration; and
(2) lodge the exhibits with the court where they shall be retained until the conclusion of the proceedings; and
(3) at the same time serve a copy of the affidavits/reports and exhibits upon the defendant.

9.7 Prior to the first hearing of the disqualification application, the time for serving evidence may be extended by written agreement between the parties. After the first hearing, the extension of time for serving evidence is governed by CPR rules 2.11 and 29.5.

[15] Rule 3(2) of the Insolvent Companies (Disqualification of Unfit Directors) Proceedings Rules 1987. Section 441 of the Companies Act 1985 makes provision for the admissibility in legal proceedings of a certified copy of a report of inspectors appointed under Part XIV of the Companies Act 1985. Note that the requirements of paragraph 8.1(2)(c) and (d) of this practice direction are additional to the provisions in the said rule 5(4).
[16] Rule 3(3) of the Insolvent Companies (Disqualification of Unfit Directors) Proceedings Rules 1987.
[17] Rule 3(1) of the Insolvent Companies (Disqualification of Unfit Directors) Proceedings Rules 1987.
[18] Rule 6(1) of the Insolvent Companies (Disqualification of Unfit Directors) Proceedings Rules 1987.
[19] Rule 6(2) of the Insolvent Companies (Disqualification of Unfit Directors) Proceedings Rules 1987.

9.8 So far as is possible all evidence should be filed before the first hearing of the disqualification application.

10. THE FIRST HEARING OF THE DISQUALIFICATION APPLICATION

10.1 The date fixed for the first hearing of the disqualification application shall be not less than 8 weeks from the date of issue of the claim form[20]. **A4–10**

10.2 The hearing shall in the first instance be before the registrar[21].

10.3 The registrar shall either determine the case on the date fixed or give directions and adjourn it[22].

10.4 All interim directions should insofar as possible be sought at the first hearing of the disqualification application so that the disqualification application can be determined at the earliest possible date. The parties should take all such steps as they respectively can to avoid successive directions hearings.

10.5 In the case of a disqualification application made under sections 7, 8 or 9A of the Act, the registrar shall adjourn the case for further consideration if—

(1) he forms the provisional opinion that a disqualification order ought to be made, and that a period of disqualification longer than 5 years is appropriate[23]; or
(2) he is of opinion that questions of law or fact arise which are not suitable for summary determination[24].

10.6 If the registrar adjourns the application for further consideration he shall—

(1) direct whether the application is to be heard by a registrar or by a judge[25]. This direction may at any time be varied by the court either on application or of its own initiative. If the court varies the direction in the absence of any of the parties, notice will be given to the parties;
(2) consider whether or not to adjourn the application to a judge so that the judge can give further directions;
(3) consider whether or not to make any direction with regard to fixing the trial date or a trial window;
(4) state the reasons for the adjournment[26].

11. CASE MANAGEMENT

11.1 On the first or any subsequent hearing of the disqualification application, the registrar may also give directions as to the following matters: **A4–11**

(1) the filing in court and the service of further evidence (if any) by the parties[27];
(2) the time-table for the steps to be taken between the giving of directions and the hearing of the application;

[20] Rule 7(1) of the Insolvent Companies (Disqualification of Unfit Directors) Proceedings Rules 1987.
[21] Rule 7(2) of the Insolvent Companies (Disqualification of Unfit Directors) Proceedings Rules 1987.
[22] Rule 7(3) of the Insolvent Companies (Disqualification of Unfit Directors) Proceedings Rules 1987.
[23] Rule 7(4)(a) of the Insolvent Companies (Disqualification of Unfit Directors) Proceedings Rules 1987.
[24] Rule 7(4)(b) of the Insolvent Companies (Disqualification of Unfit Directors) Proceedings Rules 1987.
[25] Rule 7(5)(a) of the Insolvent Companies (Disqualification of Unfit Directors) Proceedings Rules 1987.
[26] Rule 7(5)(b) of the Insolvent Companies (Disqualification of Unfit Directors) Proceedings Rules 1987.
[27] Rule 7(5)(c)(ii) of the Insolvent Companies (Disqualification of Unfit Directors) Proceedings Rules 1987.

(3) such other matters as the registrar thinks necessary or expedient with a view to an expeditious disposal of the application or the management of it generally[28];
(4) the time and place of the adjourned hearing[29]; and
(5) the manner in which and the time within which notice of the adjournment and the reasons for it are to be given to the parties[30].

11.2 Where a case is adjourned other than to a judge, it may be heard by the registrar who originally dealt with the case or by another registrar[31].

11.3 If the companies court registrar adjourns the application to a judge, all directions having been complied with and the evidence being complete, the application will be referred to the Listing Office and any practice direction relating to listing shall apply accordingly.

11.4 In all disqualification applications, the Court may direct a pre-trial review ("PTR"), a case management conference or pre-trial check lists (listing questionnaires) (in the form annexed to this practice direction) and will fix a trial date or trial period in accordance with the provisions of CPR Part 29: the Multi Track as modified by any relevant practice direction made thereunder.

11.5 At the hearing of the PTR, the registrar may give any further directions as appropriate and, where the application is to be heard in the Royal Courts of Justice in London, unless the trial date has already been fixed, may direct the parties (by Counsel's clerks if applicable), to attend the Registrar at a specified time and place in order solely to fix a trial date. The court will give notice of the date fixed for the trial to the parties.

11.6 In all cases, the parties must inform the court immediately of any material change to the information provided in a pre-trial check list.

12. THE TRIAL

A4–12 **12.1** Trial bundles containing copies of—

(1) the claim form;
(2) the acknowledgment of service;
(3) all evidence filed by or on behalf of each of the parties to the proceedings, together with the exhibits thereto;
(4) all relevant correspondence; and
(5) such other documents as the parties consider necessary;
shall be lodged with the court.

12.2 Skeleton arguments should be prepared by all the parties in all but the simplest cases whether the case is to be heard by a registrar or a judge. They should comply with all relevant guidelines.

12.3 The advocate for the claimant should also in all but the simplest cases provide: (a) a chronology; (b) a dramatis personae; (c) in respect of each defendant, a list of references to the relevant evidence.

28 Rule 7(5)(c)(iii) of the Insolvent Companies (Disqualification of Unfit Directors) Proceedings Rules 1987.

29 Rule 7(5)(c)(iv) of the Insolvent Companies (Disqualification of Unfit Directors) Proceedings Rules 1987.

30 Rule 7(5)(c)(i) of the Insolvent Companies (Disqualification of Unfit Directors) Proceedings Rules 1987.

31 Rule 7(6) of the Insolvent Companies (Disqualification of Unfit Directors) Proceedings Rules 1987.

12.4 The documents mentioned in paragraph 12.1–12.3 above must be delivered to the court in accordance with any order of the court and/or any relevant practice direction[32].

(1) If the case is to be heard by a judge sitting in the Royal Courts of Justice, London, but the name of the judge is not known, or the judge is a deputy judge, these documents must be delivered to the Clerk of the Lists. If the name of the judge (other than a deputy judge) is known, these documents must be delivered to the judge's clerk;

(2) If the case is to be heard by a companies court registrar, these documents must be delivered to Room 409, Thomas More Building, Royal Courts of Justice. Copies must be provided to the other party so far as possible when they are delivered to the court;

(3) If the case is to be heard in the Chancery district registries in Birmingham, Bristol, Caernarfon, Cardiff, Leeds, Liverpool, Manchester, Mold, Newcastle upon Tyne or Preston, the addresses for delivery are set out in Annex 1;

(4) If the case is to be heard in a county court, the documents should be delivered to the relevant county court office.

12.5 Copies of documents delivered to the court must, so far as possible, be provided to each of the other parties to the disqualification application.

12.6 The provisions in paragraphs 12.1 to 12.5 above are subject to any order of the court making different provision.

13. SUMMARY PROCEDURE

A4–13

13.1 If the parties decide to invite the court to deal with the disqualification application under the procedure adopted in *Re Carecraft Construction Co. Ltd.* [1994] 1 WLR 172, they should inform the court immediately and obtain a date for the hearing of the application.

13.2 Whenever the *Carecraft* procedure is adopted, the claimant must:

(1) except where the court otherwise directs, submit a written statement containing in respect of each defendant any material facts which (for the purposes of the application) are either agreed or not opposed (by either party); and

(2) specify in writing the period of disqualification which the parties accept that the agreed or unopposed facts justify or the band of years (e.g. 4 to 6 years) or bracket (i.e. 2 to 5 years; 6 to 10 years; 11 to 15 years) into which they will submit the case falls.

13.3 Paragraph 12.4 of the above applies to the documents mentioned in paragraph 13.2 above unless the court otherwise directs.

13.4 Unless the Court otherwise orders, a hearing under the Carecraft procedure will be held in private.

13.5 If the Court is minded to make a disqualification order having heard the parties' representations, it will usually give judgment and make the disqualification order in public. Unless the Court otherwise orders, the written statement referred to in paragraph 13.2 shall be annexed to the disqualification order.

[32] Attention is drawn to the provisions of the Chancery Guide. Chapter 7 of that Guide dated September 2000 provides guidance on the preparation of trial bundles and skeleton arguments. Unless the Court otherwise orders, paragraph 7.16 of the Chancery Guide requires that trial bundles be delivered to the Court 7 days before trial and paragraph 7.21 requires that skeleton arguments be delivered to the Court not less than 2 clear days before trial.

13.6 If the Court refuses to make the disqualification order under the Carecraft procedure, the Court shall give further directions for the hearing of the application.

14. MAKING AND SETTING ASIDE OF DISQUALIFICATION ORDER

A4–14 **14.1** The court may make a disqualification order against the defendant, whether or not the latter appears, and whether or not he has completed and returned the acknowledgment of service of the claim form, or filed evidence[33].

14.2 Any disqualification order made in the absence of the defendant may be set aside or varied by the court on such terms as it thinks just[34].

15. SERVICE OF DISQUALIFICATION ORDERS

A4–15 **15.1** Service of disqualification orders will be the responsibility of the claimant.

16. COMMENCEMENT OF DISQUALIFICATION ORDER

A4–16 **16.1** Unless the court otherwise orders, the period of disqualification imposed by a disqualification order shall begin at the end of the period of 21 days beginning with the date of the order[35].

PART 3 APPLICATIONS UNDER SECTIONS 7(2) AND 7(4) OF THE ACT

17. APPLICATIONS FOR PERMISSION TO MAKE A DISQUALIFICATION APPLICATION AFTER THE END OF THE PERIOD OF 2 YEARS SPECIFIED IN SECTION 7(2) OF THE ACT

A4–17 **17.1** Such applications shall be made by Practice Form N208 under CPR Part 8 save where it is sought to join a director or former director to existing proceedings, in which case such application shall be made by Application Notice under CPR Part 23, and the Part 23 Practice Direction shall apply save as modified below.

18. APPLICATIONS FOR EXTRA INFORMATION MADE UNDER SECTION 7(4) OF THE ACT

A4–18 **18.1** Such applications may be made:

(1) by Practice Form N208 under CPR Part 8;
(2) by Application Notice in existing disqualification proceedings; or
(3) by application under the Insolvency Rules in the relevant insolvency, if the insolvency practitioner against whom the application is made remains the officeholder.

19. PROVISIONS APPLICABLE TO APPLICATIONS UNDER SECTIONS 7(2) AND 7(4) OF THE ACT

A4–19 **19.1** **Headings:** Every claim form and notice by which such an application is begun and all witness statements affidavits, notices and other documents in relation thereto must be entitled in the matter of the company or companies in question and in the matter of the Act.

[33] Rule 8(1) of the Insolvent Companies (Disqualification of Unfit Directors) Proceedings Rules 1987.

[34] Rule 8(2) of the Insolvent Companies (Disqualification of Unfit Directors) Proceedings Rules 1987.

[35] Section 1(2) of the Act (as amended).

19.2 Service:

(1) Service of claim forms and application notices seeking orders under section 7(2) or 7(4) of the Act will be the responsibility of the applicant and will not be undertaken by the court.

(2) Where any claim form, application notice or order of the court or other document is required in any application under section 7(2) or section 7(4) of the Act to be served on any person who is not in England and Wales, the court may order service on him to be effected within such time and in such manner as it thinks fit, may require such proof of service as it thinks fit, and may make such directions as to acknowledgment of service as it thinks fit. Section III of CPR Part 6 does not apply.

PART 4 APPLICATIONS FOR PERMISSION TO ACT

20. COMMENCING AN APPLICATION FOR PERMISSION TO ACT

20.1 This practice direction governs applications for permission to act made under: **A4–20**

(1) section 17 of the Act for the purposes of any of sections 1(1)(a), 1A(1)(a) or 9B(4); and

(2) section 12(2) of the Act.

20.2 Sections 12 and 17 of the Act identify the courts which have jurisdiction to deal with applications for permission to act. Subject to these sections, such applications may be made:

(1) by Practice Form N208 under CPR Part 8; or

(2) by application notice in an existing disqualification application.

20.3 In the case of a person subject to disqualification under section 12A or 12B of the Act (by reason of being disqualified in Northern Ireland), permission to act notwithstanding disqualification can only be granted by the High Court of Northern Ireland.

21. HEADINGS

21.1 Every claim form by which an application for permission to act is begun, and all affidavits, notices and other documents in the application must be entitled in the matter of the company or companies in question and in the matter of the Act. **A4–21**

21.2 Every application notice by which an application for permission to act is made and all affidavits, notices and other documents in the application shall be entitled in the same manner as the heading of the claim form in the existing disqualification application.

22. EVIDENCE

22.1 Evidence in support of an application for permission to act shall be by affidavit. **A4–22**

23. SERVICE[36]

23.1 Where a disqualification application has been made under section 9A of the Act or a disqualification undertaking has been accepted under section 9B of the Act, the claim **A4–23**

[36] Addresses for service on government departments are set out in the List of Authorised Government Departments issued by the Cabinet Office under section 17 of the Crown Proceedings Act 1947, which is annexed to the Practice Direction supplementing Part 66.

form or application notice (as appropriate), together with the evidence in support thereof, must be served on the Office of Fair Trading or specified regulator which made the relevant disqualification application or accepted the disqualification undertaking (as the case may be).

23.2 In all other cases, the claim form or application notice (as appropriate), together with the evidence in support thereof, must be served on the Secretary of State.

PART 5 APPLICATIONS

24. FORM OF APPLICATION

A4–24 **24.1** CPR Part 23 and the Part 23 practice direction (General Rules about Applications for Court Orders) shall apply in relation to applications governed by this practice direction (see paragraph 1.3(4) above) save as modified below.

25. HEADINGS

A4–25 **25.1** Every notice and all witness statements and affidavits in relation thereto must be entitled in the same manner as the Claim Form in the proceedings in which the application is made.

26. SERVICE

A4–26 **26.1** Service of application notices in disqualification proceedings will be the responsibility of the parties and will not be undertaken by the court.

26.2 Where any application notice or order of the court or other document is required in any application to be served on any person who is not in England and Wales, the court may order service on him to be effected within such time and in such manner as it thinks fit, and may also require such proof of service as it thinks fit. Section III of CPR Part 6 does not apply.

PART 6 DISQUALIFICATION PROCEEDINGS OTHER THAN IN THE ROYAL COURTS OF JUSTICE

A4–27 **27.1** Where a disqualification application or a section 8A application is made by a claim form issued other than in the Royal Courts of Justice this practice direction shall apply with the following modifications

(1) Upon the issue of the claim form the court shall endorse it with the date and time for the first hearing before a district judge. The powers exercisable by a registrar under this practice direction shall be exercised by a district judge.

(2) If the district judge (either at the first hearing or at any adjourned hearing before him) directs that the disqualification claim or section 8A application is to be heard by a High Court judge or by an authorised circuit judge he will direct that the case be entered forthwith in the list for hearing by that judge and the court will allocate (i) a date for the hearing of the trial by that judge and (ii) unless the district judge directs otherwise a date for the hearing of a P.T.R. by the trial judge.

PART 7 DISQUALIFICATION UNDERTAKINGS

28. COSTS

28.1 The general rule is that the court will order the defendant to pay— **A4–28**

(1) the costs of the Secretary of State (and, in the case of a disqualification application made under section 7(1)(b) of the Act, the costs of the official receiver) if:

(a) a disqualification application under section 7 or 8 of the Act has been commenced; and

(b) that application is discontinued because the Secretary of State has accepted a disqualification undertaking under section 1A of the Act;

(2) the costs of the Office of Fair Trading or a specified regulator if:

(a) a disqualification application under section 9A of the Act has been commenced; and

(b) that application is discontinued because the Office of Fair Trading or specified regulator (as the case may be) has accepted a disqualification undertaking under section 9B of the Act.

28.2 The general rule will not apply where the court considers that the circumstances are such that it should make another order.

APPLICATIONS UNDER SECTION 8A OF THE ACT TO REDUCE THE PERIOD FOR WHICH A DISQUALIFICATION UNDERTAKING IS IN FORCE OR TO PROVIDE FOR IT TO CEASE TO BE IN FORCE

29. HEADINGS

29.1 Every claim form by which a section 8A application is begun and all affidavits, notices and other documents in the proceedings must be entitled in the matter of a disqualification undertaking and its date and in the matter of the Act. **A4–29**

30. COMMENCEMENT: THE CLAIM FORM

30.1 Section 8A(3) of the Act identifies the courts which have jurisdiction to deal with section 8A applications. **A4–30**

30.1A A section 8A application must be commenced by a claim form issued:

(1) in the case of a disqualification undertaking given under section 9B of the Act, in the High Court out of the office of the companies court registrar at the Royal Courts of Justice;

(2) in any other case,

(a) in the High Court out of the office of the companies court registrar or a chancery district registry; and

(b) in the county court, out of a county court office.

30.2 A section 8A application shall be made by the issue of a Part 8 claim form in the form annexed hereto and the use of the procedure set out in CPR Part 8, as modified by this practice direction. CPR rule 8.1 (3) (power of the Court to order the application to continue as if the claimant had not used the Part 8 procedure) shall not apply.

30.3 When the claim form is issued, the claimant will be given a date for the first hearing of the section 8A application. This date is to be not less than eight weeks from the date of issue of the claim form. The first hearing will be before registrar.

30.4 CPR Rule 8.2 does not apply. The claim form must state:

(1) that CPR Part 8 (as modified by this practice direction) applies;
(2) the form of order the claimant seeks.

30.5 In the case of a disqualification undertaking given under section 9B of the Act, the defendant to the section 8A application shall be the Office of Fair Trading or specified regulator which accepted the undertaking. In all other cases, the Secretary of State shall be made the defendant to the section 8A application.

30.6 Service of claim forms in section 8A applications will be the responsibility of the claimant and will not be undertaken by the court. The claim form may be served by sending it by first class post and the date of service shall, unless the contrary is shown, be deemed to be the 7th day following that on which the claim form was posted. CPR r. 6.7(1) shall be modified accordingly. Otherwise Sections I and II of CPR Part 6 apply[37].

30.7 Where any order of the court or other document is required to be served on any person who is not in England and Wales, the court may order service on him to be effected within such time and in such manner as it thinks fit and may require such proof of service as it thinks fit. Section III of CPR Part 6 shall not apply.

30.8 The claim form served on the defendant shall be accompanied by an acknowledgement of service in the form annexed hereto.

31. ACKOWLEDGEMENT OF SERVICE

A4–31 **31.1** The defendant shall:

(1) file an acknowledgement of service in the relevant pratice form not more than 14 days after service of the claim form; and
(2) serve a copy of the acknowledgement of service on the claimant and any other party.

31.2 Where the defendant has failed to file an acknowledgement of service and the time period for doing so has expired, the defendant may nevertheless attend the hearing of the application and take part in the hearing as provided for by section 8A(2) or (2A) of the Act. However, this is without prejudice to the Court's case management powers and its powers to make costs orders.

32. EVIDENCE

A4–32 **32.1** Evidence in section 8A applications shall be by affidavit. The undertaking (or a copy) shall be exhibited to the affidavit.

32.2 When the claim form is issued:

(1) the affidavit in support of the section 8A application must be filed in court;
(2) exhibits must be lodged with the court where they shall be retained until the conclusion of the proceedings; and
(3) copies of the affidavit and exhibits shall be served with the claim form on the defendant.

[37] Attention is drawn to CPR r 6.14(2) regarding a certificate of service of the claim form.

32.3 The defendant shall, within 28 days from the date of service of the claim form:

(1) file in court any affidavit evidence that he wishes the court to take into consideration on the application; and
(2) lodge the exhibits with the court where they shall be retained until the conclusion of the proceedings; and
(3) at the same time, serve upon the claimant a copy of the affidavits and exhibits.

32.4 The claimant shall, within 14 days from receiving the copy of the defendant's evidence:

(1) file in court any further affidavit evidence in reply he wishes the court to take into consideration; and
(2) lodge the exhibits with the court where they shall be retained until the conclusion of the proceedings; and
(3) at the same time serve a copy of the affidavits and exhibits upon the defendant.

32.5 Prior to the first hearing of the section 8A application, the time for serving evidence may be extended by written agreement between the parties. After the first hearing, the extension of time for serving evidence is governed by CPR rules 2.11 and 29.5.
32.6 So far as is possible all evidence should be filed before the first hearing of the section 8A application.

33. HEARINGS AND CASE MANAGEMENT

33.1 The date fixed for the first hearing of the section 8A application shall be not less than 8 weeks from the date of issue of the claim form. **A4–33**
33.2 The hearing shall in the first instance be before the registrar.
33.3 The registrar shall either determine the case on the date fixed or give directions and adjourn it.
33.4 All interim directions should insofar as possible be sought at the first hearing of the section 8A application so that the section 8A application can be determined at the earliest possible date. The parties should take all such steps as they respectively can to avoid successive directions hearings.
33.5 If the registrar adjourns the application for further consideration he shall:

(1) direct whether the application is to be heard by a registrar or by a judge. This direction may at any time be varied by the court either on application or of its own initiative. If the court varies the direction in the absence of any of the parties, notice will be given to the parties;
(2) consider whether or not to adjourn the application to a judge so that the judge can give further directions;
(3) consider whether or not to make any direction with regard to fixing the trial date or a trial window.

33.6 On the first or any subsequent hearing of the section 8A application, the registrar may also give directions as to the following matters:

(1) the filing in court and the service of further evidence (if any) by the parties;
(2) the time-table for the steps to be taken between the giving of directions and the hearing of the section 8A application;
(3) such other matters as the registrar thinks necessary or expedient with a view to an expeditious disposal of the section 8A application or the management of it generally;
(4) the time and place of the adjourned hearing.

33.7 Where a case is adjourned other than to a judge, it may be heard by the registrar who originally dealt with the case or by another registrar.

33.8 If the companies court registrar adjourns the application to a judge, all directions having been complied with and the evidence being complete, the application will be referred to the Listing Office and any practice direction relating to listing shall apply accordingly.

33.9 In all section 8A applications, the Court may direct a pre-trial review ("PTR"), a case management conference or pre-trial check lists (listing questionnaires) (in the form annexed to this practice direction) and will fix a trial date or trial period in accordance with the provisions of CPR Part 29: The Multi-Track, as modified by any relevant practice direction made thereunder.

33.10 At the hearing of the PTR, the registrar may give any further directions as appropriate and, where the application is to be heard in the Royal Courts of Justice in London, unless the trial date has already been fixed, may direct the parties (by Counsel's clerks, if applicable) to attend the Registrar at a specified time and place in order solely to fix a trial date. The court will give notice of the date fixed for the trial to the parties.

33.11 In all cases, the parties must inform the court immediately of any material change to the information provided in a pre-trial check list.

34. THE TRIAL

A4–34 **34.1** Trial bundles containing copies of—

(1) the claim form;
(2) the acknowledgment of service;
(3) all evidence filed by or on behalf of each of the parties to the proceedings, together with the exhibits thereto;
(4) all relevant correspondance; and
(5) such other documents as the parties consider necessary,

shall be lodged with the court.

34.2 Skeleton arguments should be prepared by all the parties in all but the simplest cases whether the case is to be heard by a registrar or a judge. They should comply with all relevant guidelines.

34.3 The advocate for the claimant should also in all but the simplest cases provide: (a) a chronology; (b) a dramatis personae.

34.4 The documents mentioned in paragraph 34.1–34.3 above must be delivered to the court in accordance with any order of the court and/or and relevant practice direction[38].

(1) If the case is to be heard by a judge sitting in the Royal Courts of Justice, London, but the name of the judge is not known, or the judge is a deputy judge, these documents must be delivered to the Clerk of the Lists. If the name of the judge (other than a deputy judge) is known, these documents must be delivered to the judge's clerk;

(2) If the case is to be heard by a companies court registrar, these documents must be delivered to Room 409, Thomas More Building, Royal Courts of Justice.

[38] Attention is drawn to the provisions of the Chancery Guide. Chapter 7 of that Guide dated September 2000 provides guidance on the preparation of trial bundles and skeleton arguments. Unless the Court otherwise orders, paragraph 7.16 of the Chancery Guide requires that trial bundles be delivered to the Court 7 days before trial and paragraph 7.21 requires that skeleton arguments be delivered to the Court not less than 2 clear days before trial. Addresses for service on government departments are set out in the List of Authorised Government Departments issued by the Cabinet Office under section 17 of the Crown Proceedings Act 1947, which is annexed to the Practice Direction supplementing Part 66.

Copies must be provided to the other party so far as possible when they are delivered to the court;

(3) If the case is to be heard in the Chancery district registries in Birmingham, Bristol, Caernarfon, Cardiff, Leeds, Liverpool, Manchester, Mold, Newcastle upon Tyne or Preston, the addresses for delivery are set out in Annex 1;

(4) If the case is to be heard in a county court, the documents should be delivered to the relevant county court office.

34.5 Copies of documents delivered to the court must, so far as possible, be provided to each of the other parties to the claim.

34.6 The provisions in paragraphs 34.1 to 34.5 above are subject to any order of the court making different provision.

35. APPEALS

35.1 Rules 7.47 and 7.49 of the Insolvency Rules, as supplemented by Part Four of the Insolvency Proceedings Practice Direction, apply to an appeal from, or review of, a decision made by the court in the course of: **A4–35**

(1) disqualification proceedings under any of sections 6 to 8A or 9A of the Act;

(2) an application made under section 17 of the Act for the purposes of any of sections 1(1)(a), 1A(1)(a) or 9B(4), for permission to act notwithstanding a disqualification order made, or a disqualification undertaking accepted, under any of sections 6 to 10.

Any such decision, and any appeal from it, constitutes "insolvency proceedings" for the purposes of the Insolvency Proceedings Practice Direction[39].

35.2 An appeal from a decision made by the court in the course of disqualification proceedings under any of sections 2(2)(a), 3 or 4 of the Act or on an application for permission to act notwithstanding a disqualification order made under any of those sections is governed by CPR Part 52 and the practice direction supplementing that Part.

ANNEX 1

Birmingham: The Chancery Listing Officer, The District Registry of the Chancery Division of the High Court, 33 Bull Street, Birmingham B4 6DS. **A4–36**

Bristol: The Chancery Listing Officer, The District Registry of the Chancery Division of the High Court, 3rd Floor, Greyfriars, Lewins Mead, Bristol BSl 2NR.

Caernarfon: The Chancery Listing Officer, The District Registry of the Chancery Division of the High Court, 1st Floor, Llanberis Road, Caernarfon, LL55 2DF.

Cardiff: The Chancery Listing Officer, The District Registry of the Chancery Division of the High Court, 1st Floor, 2 Park Street, Cardiff CFl0 1ET.

[39] CPR rule 2.1(2) and section 21(2) of the Act. See also rule 2(4) of the Insolvent Companies (Disqualification of Unfit Directors) Proceedings Rules 1987 and *Re Tasbian Limited, Official Receiver v Nixon* [1991] B.C.L.C. 59; [1990] B.C.C. 322; *Re Probe Data Systems Limited (No 3), Secretary of State for Trade and Industry v Desai* [1992] B.C.L.C. 405; [1992] BCC 110 and *Re The Premier Screw & Repetition Company Ltd, Secretary of State for Trade and Industry v Paulin* [2005] EWCH 888 (Ch).

Leeds: The Chancery Listing Officer, The District Registry of the Chancery Division of the High Court, Leeds Combined Court Centre, The Court House, 1 Oxford Row, Leeds LSl 3BG.

Liverpool and Manchester: The Chancery Listing Officer, The District Registry of the Chancery Division of the High Court, Manchester Courts of Justice, Crown Square, Manchester M60 9DJ.

Mold: The Chancery Listing Officer, The District Registry of the Chancery Division of the High Court, Law Courts, Civic Centre, Mold, CH7 1AE.

Newcastle upon Tyne: The Chancery Listing Officer, The District Registry of the Chancery Division of the High Court, The Law Courts, Quayside, Newcastle upon Tyne NEl 3LA.

Preston: The Chancery Listing Officer, The District Registry of the Chancery Division of the High Court, The Combined Court Centre, Ringway, Preston PR1 2LL.

CLAIM FORMS

Claim form
Directors disqualification application

In the	
Claim No.	

A4–37

In the matter of

SEAL

And in the matter of The Company Directors Disqualification Act 1986.

Name of Claimant

Name(s) of Defendant(s)

The hearing
(This section will be completed by the court)

The defendant(s) must attend before the (Registrar/District Judge) on

Date Time

Place

on the hearing of an application by ______________, the claimant, for a disqualification order under section __________ of the Company Directors Disqualification Act 1986 that:

The grounds upon which the claimant seeks a disqualification order are set out (in the details of claim overleaf and) in the (affidavit/report) of ______________________ (sworn/dated __________________________) a true copy of which is served herewith.

Note: If you do not attend, the court may make such order as it thinks fit

The court office at

is open between 10 am and 4 pm Monday to Friday. When corresponding with the court, please address forms or letters to the Court Manager and quote the claim number.

N500 Claim form – Directory disqualification proceedings (06.05) HMCS

Claim No.	

Does your claim include any issues under the Human Rights Act 1998? ☐ Yes ☐ No

Details of your claim

Defendant's name and address

	£
Court fee	
Solicitor's costs	
Issue date	

Endorsement

1. CPR Part 8 as modified by the Directors Disqualification Proceedings Pratice Direction applies to this claim.
2. Any evidence which the defendant wishes to be taken into consideration by the court must be filed in court within 28 days from the date of service of the claim form and copies must then be served forthwith on the claimant. The evidence must be in the form of one or more affidavits.

[3. This claim is made in accordance with the Insolvent Companies (Disqualification of Unfit Directors) Proceedings Rules 1987 (S.I. 1987/2023, as amended).]

4. The court has the power to impose a disqualification period as follows:

   where the application is under section 2 or section 4 of the Company Directors Disqualification Act, for a period of up to 15 years;

   where the application is under section 3 of the Company Directors Disqualification Act, for a period of up to 5 years;

   where the application is under section 7 of the Company Directors Disqualification Act, for a period of not less than 2 years and up to 15 years;

   where the application is under section 8 or section 9A of the Company Directors Disqualification Act, for a period of up to 15 years.

[5. On the first hearing of the claim, the court may hear and determine the claim summarily, without further or other notice to you and if it is so determined, the court may impose disqualification for a period of up to 5 years.]

[6. If at the hearing of the application the court, on the evidence then before it, is minded to impose, in the case of any defendant, disqualification for any period longer than 5 years, it will not make a disqualification order on the first hearing but will adjourn the application to be heard (with further evidence, if any) at a later date that will be notified to the defendant. At the second hearing, the court may impose disqualification period of more than 5 years without any further reference to you.]

7. Your attention is drawn to the possibility of resolving the claim by offering an undertaking pursuant to section 1A or 9B of the Company Directors Disqualification Act (as applicable) or pursuant to the summary procedure adopted in *Re Carecraft Construction Co. Ltd* [1994] 1 WLR 172 (as clarified by the decision of the Court of Appeal in *Secretary of State v Rogers* [1996] 1 WLR 1569).

Statement of Truth

*(I believe)(The claimant believes) that the facts stated in this claim form are true.
*I am duly authorised by the claimant to sign this statement.

Full name of claimant ____________________

Name of claimant's solicitor's firm ____________________

signed ____________________ position or office held ____________________
*(Claimant)(Claimant's solicitor) (if signing on behalf of firm or company)

**delete as appropriate*

Claimant's or claimant's solicitor's address to which documents should be sent if different from overleaf. If you are prepared to accept service by DX, fax or e-mail, please add details.

A4–38

Notes for claimant on completing claim form N500

Directors disqualification application

Please read all of these guidance notes before you begin completing the claim form. The notes follow the order in which information is required on the form.

- Court staff can help you fill in the claim form and give information about procedure once it has been issued. But they cannot give legal advice. If you need legal advice, for example, about the likely success of your claim or the evidence you need to prove it, you should contact a solicitor or a Citizens Advice Bureau.
- If you are filling in the claim form by hand, please use black ink and write in block capitals.
- You must file evidence to support your claim with the claim form in the form of an affidavit or affirmation or where permitted by rule 3(2) of the Insolvent Companies (Disqualification of Unfit Directors) Proceedings Rules 1986, a report by the Official Receiver.
- Copy the completed claim form, the defendant's notes for guidance and your written evidence so that you have one copy for yourself, one copy for the court and one copy for each defendant. Send or take the forms and evidence to the court office with the appropriate fee. The court will tell you how much this is.

Notes on completing the claim form

Heading

You must fill in the heading of the form to indicate whether you want the claim to be issued in a county court or in the High Court (The High Court means either a District Registry (attached to a county court) or the Companies Court at the Royal Courts of Justice in London).

Use whichever of the following is appropriate:

"In the .... county court" (inserting the name of the court)

or

"In the High Court of Justice Chancery Division .... District Registry" (inserting the name of the District Registry)

or

"In the High Court of Justice Chancery Division, Companies Court"

A disqualification application under section 9A of the Company Directors Disqualification Act must be issued in the High Court, out of the office of the Companies Court Registrar at the Royal Courts of Justice.

The section of text beginning "In the matter of . . ." is included to comply with paragraph 5.1 of the Directors Disqualification Proceedings Practice Direction. You should insert the name of the relevant company(ies) after this text.

Claimant and defendant details

As the person issuing the claim, you are called the "claimant"; the person you are suing is called the "defendant". You must provide the following information about yourself **and** the defendant according to the capacity on which you are suing and in which the defendant is being sued. When suing or being sued as:—

an individual:

All known forenames and surname (whether Mr, Mrs, Miss, Ms or Other e.g. Dr) and residential address (**including** postcode and telephone and any fax or e-mail number) in England and Wales. Where the defendant is a proprietor of a business, a partner in a firm or an individual sued in the name of a club or other unincorporated association, the address for service should be the usual or last known place of residence or principal place of business of the company, firm or club or other unincorporated association.

Where the individual is:

a firm:

Enter the name of the firm followed by the words "a firm" e.g. "Bandbow—a firm" and an address for service which is either a partner's residential address or the principal or last known place of business.

a corporation (other than a company):

Enter the full name of the corporation and the address which is either its principal office or any other place where the corporation carries on activities and which has a real connection with the claim.

N500A Notes for claimant on completing a Part 8 claim form (06.05) HMCS

a company registered in England and Wales:
Enter the name of the company and an address which is either the company's registered office or any place of business that has a real, or the most, connection with the claim e.g. the shop where the goods were bought.

an oversea company (defined by s744 of the Companies Act 1985):
Enter the name of the company and either the address registered under s691 of the Act or the address of the place of business having a real, or the most, connection with the claim.

Hearing
Paragraph 4.3 of the Practice Direction states that "When the claim form is issued, the claimant will be given a date for the first hearing of the disqualification application". Court staff will complete these details when a date for a hearing is fixed, before the claim form is served. You should fill in the blanks in the sentence below the dates with the claimant's name and the section of the Company Directors Disqualification Act 1986 under which you are seeking the defendant's disqualification. You should then complete the empty section with the details of the order you wish the court to make, and delete the sections in the following sentence as appropriate.

Details of your claim
You should set out the details of your claim here, unless you have chosen to set them out only in an attached affidavit or report.

Evidence
The evidence in support of the claim must be set out in an attached affidavit or report, which must include a statement of the matters by reference to which it is alleged that a disqualification order should be made against the defendant.

Defendant's name and address
Enter in this box the full name and address of the defendant to be served with the claim form (i.e. one claim form for each defendant). If the defendant is to be served outside England and Wales, you may need to obtain the court's permission.

Endorsement
If the claim is not brought under section 7, 8 or 9A of the Company Directors Disqualification Act 1986, paragraphs 3, 5 and 6 of the endorsement should be deleted.

Statement of truth
This must be signed by you, by your solicitor or your litigation friend, as appropriate.

Where the claimant is a registered company or a corporation the claim must be signed by either the director, treasurer, secretary, chief executive, manager or other officer of the company or (in the case of a corporation) the mayor, chairman, president or town clerk.

Address for documents
Insert in this box the address at which you wish to receive documents, if different from the address you have already given under the heading "Claimant". The address you give must be either that of your solicitors or your residential or business address and must be in England or Wales. If you live or carry on business outside of England and Wales, you can give some other address within England and Wales.

Notes for defendant
Directors disqualification application

A4–39 **Please read these notes carefully—they will help you to decide what to do about this claim.**

- You have 14 days from the date on which you were served with the claim form (see below) in which to respond to the claim by completing and returning the acknowledgment of service enclosed with this claim form. The acknowledgement of service should be completed and returned to the court office and a copy sent to the claimant named on the claim form.
- If you **do not return** the acknowledgment of service (Form N502), you will be allowed to attend any hearing of this claim but you will not be allowed to take part in the hearing unless the court gives you permission to do so.

Court staff can tell you about procedures but they cannot give legal advice. If you need legal advice, you should contact a solicitor or Citizens Advice Bureau immediately

Responding to this claim

Time for responding
The completed acknowledgment of service must be returned to the court office and a copy sent to the claimant named on the claim form within 14 days of the date on which the claim form was served on you. If the claim form was

- sent by post, the 14 days begins 7 days from the date of the postmark on the envelope.
- delivered or left at your address, the 14 days begins the day after it was delivered or left.
- handed to you personally, the 14 days begins on the day it was given to you.

Completing the acknowledgment of service (N502)
You should complete section A, B, or C as appropriate and all of section D.

Section A—contesting the claim
If you wish to contest the remedy sought by the claimant in the claim form, you should complete section A.

Section B—mitigation
If you do not wish to resist the claim for a disqualification order, but would like to offer evidence of mitigating circumstances with a view to justifying a shorter period of disqualification, you should complete section B.

Section C—disputing the court's jurisdiction
You should indicate your intention by completing section C and filing an application disputing the court's jurisdiction within 14 days of filing your acknowledgment of service at the court. The court will arrange a hearing date for the application and tell you and the claimant when and where to attend.

Section D—Statement of truth
This must be signed by you, by your solicitor or your litigation friend, as appropriate.

Where the defendant is a registered company or a corporation the claim must be signed by either the director, treasurer, secretary, chief executive, manager or other officer of the company or (in the case of a corporation) the mayor, chairman, president or town clerk.

Written evidence
Any evidence which you wish to be taken into consideration by the court must be filed in court within 28 days from the date of service of the claim form upon you. The evidence must be in the form of an affidavit.

Serving other parties
At the same time as you file your affidavit evidence with the court, you must also send copies of both the form and any written evidence to the claimant named on the claim form.

What happens next
The date of the first hearing of the claim is set out under "Hearing".

N500B Notes for defendant – Directors disqualification application (06.05) HMCS

A4–40

Claim form

Directors disqualification section 8A application

In the	
Claim No.	

In the matter of a disqualification undertaking dated

SEAL

and in the matter of the Company Directors Disqualification Act 1986.

Name of Claimant

Name of Defendant(s)

The hearing

(This section will be completed by the court)

The defendant(s) must attend before the (Registrar/District Judge) on

Date Time

Place

on the hearing of an application by______________, the claimant, for an order under Section 8A of the Company Directors Disqualification Act 1986 that:

The grounds upon which the claimant seeks the order are set out (in the details of claim overleaf and) in the affidavit of (_______) sworn on ______________ a true copy of which is served herewith.

Note: If you do not attend, the court may make such order as it thinks fit

The court office at

is open between 10 am and 4 pm Monday to Friday. When corresponding with the court, please address forms or letters to the Court Manager and quote the claim number.

N501 Claim from – Directors disqualification section 8A application (06.05) HMCS

Claim No.	

Does your claim include any issues under the Human Rights Act 1998? ☐ Yes ☐ No

Details of your claim

Defendant's(s) name(s) and address(es)

	£
Court fee	
Solicitor's costs	
Issue date	

Endorsement

1. CPR Part 8 as modified by the Directors Disqualification Proceedings Pratice Direction applies to this claim.
2. Any evidence which the defendant wishes to be taken into consideration by the court must be filed in court within 28 days from the date of service of the claim form and copies must then be served forthwith on the claimant. The evidence must be in the form of one or more affidavits.

Statement of Truth

*(I believe)(The claimant believes) that the facts stated in this claim form are true.

*I am duly authorised by the claimant to sign this statement.

Full name of claimant ____

Name of claimant's solicitor's firm ____________________________________

signed ____________________ position or office held ____________________

*(Claimant)(Litigation friend)(Claimant's solicitor) (if signing on behalf of firm or company)

delete as appropriate

Claimant's or claimant's solicitor's address to which documents should be sent if different from overleaf. If you are prepared to accept service by DX, fax or e-mail, please add details.

A4–41 Notes for claimant on completing claim form N501

Directors disqualification section 8A application

Please read all of these guidance notes before you begin completing the claim form. The notes follow the order in which information is required on the form.

- Court staff can help you fill in the claim form and give information about procedure once it has been issued. But they cannot give legal advice. If you need legal advice for example, about the likely success of your claim or the evidence you need to prove it, you should contact a solicitor or a Citizens Advice Bureau.
- If you are filling in the claim form by hand, please use black ink and write in block capitals.
- You must file evidence to support your claim with the claim form in the form of an affidavit or affirmation.
- Copy the completed claim form, the defendant's notes for guidance and your written evidence so that you have one copy for yourself, one copy for the court and one copy for each defendant. Send or take the forms and evidence to the court office with the appropriate fee. The court will tell you how much this is.

Notes on completing the claim form

Heading

You must fill in the heading of the form to indicate whether you want the claim to be issued in a county court or in the High Court (The High Court means either a District Registry (attached to a county court) or the Royal Courts of Justice in London). Section 8A(3) of the Company Directors Disqualification Act 1986 identifies the courts which have jurisdiction to deal with Section 8A applications.

An application under section 8A of the Company Directors Disqualification Act which relates to a disqualification undertaking given under section 9B of the Act must be issued in the High Court, out of the office of the Companies Court Registrar at the Royal Courts of Justice.

Use whichever of the following is appropriate:

"In the .... county court"
(inserting the court name)

or

"In the High Court of Justice Chancery Division .... District Registry"
(inserting the name of the District Registry)

or

"In the High Court of Justice Chancery Division, Companies Court"

Claimant and defendant details

As the person issuing the claim, you are called the "claimant"; the person you are suing is called the "defendant". You must provide the following information about yourself **and** the defendant according to the capacity on which you are suing and in which the defendant is being sued. When suing or being sued as:—

an individual:
All known forenames and surname (whether Mr, Mrs, Miss, Ms or Other e.g. Dr) and residential address (**including** postcode and telephone and any fax or e-mail number) in England and Wales. Where the defendant is a proprietor of a business, a partner in a firm or an individual sued in the name of a club or other unincorporated association, the address for service should be the usual or last known place of residence or principal place of business of the company, firm or club or other unincorporated association.

Where the individual is:

a firm:
Enter the name of the firm followed by the words "a firm" e.g. "Bandbow—a firm" and an address for service which is either a partner's residential address or the principal or last known place of business.

a corporation (other than a company):
Enter the full name of the corporation and the address which is either its principal office or any other place where the corporation carries on activities and which has a real connection with the claim.

N501A Notes for defendant on completing claim form N501 (06.05) HMCS

a company registered in England and Wales:
Enter the name of the company and an address which is either the company's registered office or any place of business that has a real, or the most, connection with the claim e.g. the shop where the goods were bought.

an oversea company (defined by s744 of the Companies Act 1985):
Enter the name of the company and either the address registered under s691 of the Act or the address of the place of business having a real, or the most, connection with the claim.

Hearing
Paragraph 30.3 of the Directors Disqualification Proceedings Practice Direction states that "When the claim form is issued, the claimant will be given a date for the first hearing of the section 8A application". Court staff will complete these details when a date for a hearing is fixed, before the claim form is served. However, you must complete the section below this with the details of the order you wish the court to make and fill in the details of your affidavit if you are attaching one to the form.

Details of your claim
You should set out the details of your claim here, unless you have chosen to set them out only in an attached affidavit.

Evidence
Evidence in section 8A applications must be by affidavit. The affidavit in support of the section 8A application must be filed in court at the same time as the claim form. Any exhibits to the affidavit must be lodged with the court at the same time. Copies of the affidavit and exhibits must be served with the claim form on the defendant.

Defendant's name and address
Enter in this box the full name and address of the defendant to be served with the claim form (i.e. one claim form for each defendant).

In the case of a disqualification undertaking given under section 9B of the Act, the defendant to the section 8A application shall be the Office of Fair Trading or specified regulator which accepted the undertaking. In all other cases, the defendant shall be the Secretary of State for Trade and Industry.

Addresses for service on government departments are set out in the List of Authorised government Departments issued by the Cabinet Office under section 17 of the Crown Proceedings Act 1947, which is annexed to the Practice Direction supplementing Part 66 of the Civil Procedure Rules.

Statement of truth
This must be signed by you, by your solicitor or your litigation friend, as appropriate.

Where the claimant is a registered company or a corporation the claim must be signed by either the director, treasurer, secretary, chief executive, manager or other officer of the company or (in the case of a corporation) the mayor, chairman, president or town clerk.

Address for documents
Insert in this box the address at which you wish to receive documents, if different from the address you have already given under the heading "Claimant". The address you give must be either that of your solicitors or your residential or business address and must be in England or Wales. If you live of carry on business outside of England and Wales, you can give some other address within England and Wales.

A4–42 Notes for defendant

Directors disqualification section 8A application

Please read these notes carefully—they will help you to decide what to do about this claim.

- You have 14 days from the date on which you were served with the claim form (see below) in which to respond to the claim by completing and returning the acknowledgment of service enclosed with this claim form. The acknowledgement of service should be completed and returned to the court office and a copy sent to the claimant named on the claim form.
- If you **do not return** the acknowledgment of service (Form N503), you will be allowed to attend any hearing of this claim but you will not be allowed to take part in the hearing unless the court gives you permission to do so.

Court staff can tell you about procedures but they cannot give legal advice. If you need legal advice, you should contact a solicitor or Citizens Advice Bureau immediately

Responding to this claim

Time for responding
The completed acknowledgment of service must be returned to the court office (and a copy sent to the claimant named on the claim form) within 14 days of the date on which the claim form was served on you. If the claim form was:

- sent by post, the 14 days begins 7 days from the date of the postmark on the envelope.
- delivered or left at your address, the 14 days begins the day after it was delivered.
- handed to you personally, the 14 days begins on the day it was given to you.

If the claim form was issued in the High Court in London, the acknowledgment of service should be returned to the Companies Court, General Office, Room TM 2.09, Royal Courts of Justice, The Strand, London, WC2A 2LL

Completing the acknowledgment of service (N503)
You should complete section A or B as appropriate and all of section C.

Statement of truth
This must be signed by you, your solicitor or your litigation friend, as appropriate.

Written evidence
Any evidence which you wish to be taken into consideration by the court must be filed in court within 28 days from the date of service of the claim form upon you. The evidence must be in the form of an affidavit.

Serving other parties
At the same time as you file your affidavit evidence with the court, you must also send copies of both the form and any written evidence to the claimant named on the claim form.

What happens next
The date of the first hearing of the claim is set out under "hearing".

N501B Notes for defendant – Directors disqualification section 8A application (06.05) HMCS

A4–43

Acknowledgment of service
Directors disqualification application

In the	
Claim No.	
Claimant (including ref)	
Defendant	

You should read the "notes for defendant" (Form N500B) attached to the claim form which will tell you how to complete this form, and when and where to send it.

State the full name of the defendant

Section A

☐ I intend to contest the claim on the grounds that:

☐ I was not a director or shadow director of

at the time when my conduct, or the conduct of other persons, is in question.
(Please insert the name of each of the companies concerned in the box above)

☐ My conduct as a director or shadow director was not as alleged in support of the application for a disqualification order.

☐ I dispute the allegation that my conduct makes me unfit to be involved in the management of a company.

☐ I intend to contest the claim on the grounds that:

(Only complete this if the case has been brought under section 7 of the Company Directors Disqualification Act 1986. In the box below insert the name of any company listed on the claim form after the words "In the matter of" to which this statement applies)

has at no time become insolvent within the meaning of section 6(2) of the Company Directors Disqualification Act 1986.

☐ I intend to contest the claim on the grounds that:
(Only complete this if the case has been brought under section 9A of the Company Directors Disqualification Act 1986. Please insert the name of any relevant company in the box below.)

has not committed a breach of competition law within the meaning of section 9A(4) of the Company Directors Disqualification Act 1986.

The court office at

is open between 10 am and 4 pm Monday to Friday. When corresponding with the court, please address forms or letters to the Court Manager and quote the claim number.

N502 Acknowledgment of service – Directors disqualification applications (06.05) HMCS

Section B

☐ I do not wish to dispute the claim for a disqualification order.
☐ I would like to offer evidence with a view to reducing the period of disqualification.

Section C

☐ The claim form was served outside England or Wales and I intend to dispute jurisdiction.

(You should file your application within 14 days of the date on which you file this acknowledgment of service with the court)

Section D

Statement of Truth
*(I believe)(The defendant believes) that the facts stated in this form are true.
*I am duly authorised by the defendant to sign this statement.

Full name ______________________________
Name of defendant's solicitor's firm ______________________

Signed ______________ position or office held ______________
*(Defendant)(Litigation friend)(Defendant's solicitor) (if signing on behalf of firm or company)

Dated ______________________ *delete as appropriate*

Give an address (including post code) to which notices about this case can be sent to you.

Telephone no.	

If applicable	
Ref no.	
Fax no.	
DX no.	
E-mail	

ce
Directors disqualification application

In the

Claim No.

You should read the "notes for defendant" (Form N500B) attached to the claim form which will tell you how to complete this form, and when and where to send it.

Claimant
(including ref)

Defendant

A4–44

Acknowledgment of service

Directors disqualification section 8A application

You should read the "notes for defendant" (Form N501B) attached to the claim form which will tell you how to complete this form, and when and where to send it.

In the	
Claim No.	
Claimant (including ref)	
Defendant	

Section A

☐ The defendant currently intends to appear at the hearing of the section 8A application.

☐ The defendant currently intends to file evidence on the section 8A application.

Section B

☐ The defendant intends to dispute jurisdiction

(You should file your application within 14 days of the date on which you file this acknowledgment of service with the court.)

Section C

Statement of Truth

*(I believe)(The defendant believes) that the facts stated in this form are true.
*I am duly authorised by the defendant to sign this statement.

Full name ______________________________

Name of defendant's solicitor's firm ______________________________

Signed *(Defendant)(Defendant's solicitor) position or office held (if signing on behalf of firm or company)

Dated ____________________ *delete as appropriate*

Give an address (including post code) to which notices about this case can be sent to you.

Telephone no.	

If applicable	
Ref no.	
Fax no.	
DX no.	
E-mail	

The court office at

is open between 10 am and 4 pm Monday to Friday. When corresponding with the court, please address forms or letters to the Court Manager and quote the claim number.

N503 Acknowledgment of service - Directors disqualification section 8A applications (06.05) HMCS

Pre-trial checklist
Directors disqualification

In the	
Claim no.	
Last date for filing with court office	
Date(s) fixed for trial or trial period	
Claimant	
Defendant	

To be completed by, or on behalf of,

who is [1st][2nd][3rd][ ][Claimant][Defendant] in this claim

Name of company to which claim relates

This form must be **completed** and **returned** to the court no later than the date given above. If not, your evidence may be struck out or some other sanction imposed.

If the claim has settled, or settles before the trial date, you must let the court know immediately.

Legal representatives only: You must **attach** estimates of costs incurred to date, and of your likely overall costs. In substantial cases, these should be provided in compliance with CPR Part 43.

You must also **attach** a proposed timetable for the trial itself.

A Confirmation of compliance with directions

1. I confirm that I have complied with those directions already given which require action by me. ☐Yes ☐No

   If you are unable to give confirmation, state which directions you have still to comply with and the date by which this will be done.

Directions	Date

2. I believe that additional directions are necessary before the trial takes place. ☐Yes ☐No

   If Yes, you should attach an application and a draft order.

   Include in your application all directions needed to enable the claim ***to be tried on the date, or within the trial period, already fixed.*** *These should include any issues relating to experts and their evidence, and any orders needed in respect of directions still requiring action by any other party.*

3. Have you agreed the additional directions you are seeking with the other party(ies)? ☐Yes ☐No

B Witnesses

1. How many witnesses (including yourself) will be giving evidence on your behalf at the trial? *(Do not include experts—see Section C)* ☐

Continued over

Witnesses continued

2. If the trial date is not yet fixed, are there any days within the trial period you or your witnesses would wish to avoid if possible? *(Do not include experts—see Section C)*

Please give details

Name of witness	Dates to be avoided, if possible	Reason

Please specify any special facilities or arrangements needed at court for the party or any witness (e.g. witness with a disability).

3. Will you be providing an interpreter for any of your witnesses? ☐Yes ☐No

C Experts

You are reminded that you may not use an expert's report or have your expert give oral evidence unless the court has given permission. If you do not have permission, you must make an application (see section A2 above)

1. Please give the information requested for your expert(s)

Name	Field of expertise	Joint expert?	Is report agreed?	Has permission been given for oral evidence?
		☐Yes ☐No	☐Yes ☐No	☐Yes ☐No
		☐Yes ☐No	☐Yes ☐No	☐Yes ☐No
		☐Yes ☐No	☐Yes ☐No	☐Yes ☐No

2. Has there been discussion between experts? ☐Yes ☐No

3. Have the experts signed a joint statement? ☐Yes ☐No

4. If your expert is giving oral evidence and the trial date is not yet fixed, is there any day within the trial period which the expert would wish to avoid, if possible? ☐Yes ☐No

If Yes, please give details

Name	Dates to be avoided, if possible	Reason

D Legal representation

1. Who will be presenting your case at the trial? You ☐ Solicitor ☐ Counsel ☐
2. If the trial date is not yet fixed, is there any day within the trial period that the person presenting your case would wish to avoid, if possible? ☐Yes ☐No

If Yes, please give details

Name	Dates to be avoided, if possible	Reason

E Summary disposal under the Carecraft procedure or by disqualification undertaking

1. Have you considered the possibility of resolving this case by a disqualification undertaking or under the procedure adopted in *Re Carecraft Construction Co. Ltd* [1994] 1 WLR 172 ("a Carecraft application"). If not this should be considered as soon as possible. ☐Yes ☐No
2. Please state whether the case should be listed for a Carecraft disposal or full trial at a time and date to be fixed. ☐Carecraft ☐Full trial
3. If such a Carecraft application is to be made, the agreed written statement of facts must be submitted by the claimant as set out in the Practice Direction relating to disqualification proceedings and delivered to the court not later than 2 working days before the date upon which it is intended to make the application and in any event as soon as possible.

F The trial

1. Has the estimate of the time needed for trial changed? ☐Yes ☐No

   If Yes, say how long you estimate the whole trial will take, including both parties' cross-examination and closing arguments ☐days ☐hours ☐minutes
2. If different from original estimate have you agreed with the other party(ies) that this is now the **total** time needed? ☐Yes ☐No
3. Is the timetable for trial you have attached agreed with the other party(ies)? ☐Yes ☐No

3 of 4

G Document and fee checklist

Tick as appropriate

I attach to this questionnaire—

☐ An application and fee for additional directions

☐ A proposed timetable for trial

☐ A draft order

☐ An estimate of costs

☐ Listing fee

Signed	

[Counsel][Solicitor][for the][1st][2nd][3rd][ ]
[Claimant][Defendant]

Date

Please enter your [firm's] name, reference number and full postal address including (if appropriate) details of DX, fax or e-mail

	Postcode

Tel. no.		DX no.		E-mail	
Fax no.		Ref. no.			

APPENDIX 5

INSOLVENCY RESTRICTIONS: EXTRACTS FROM INSOLVENCY ACT 1986

The Second Group of Parts

Insolvency of Individuals; Bankruptcy

[PART VIIA

DEBT RELIEF ORDERS][1]

[Preliminary][2]

[251A Debt relief orders

A5–01 (1) An individual who is unable to pay his debts may apply for an order under this Part ("a debt relief order") to be made in respect of his qualifying debts.

(2) In this Part "qualifying debt" means (subject to subsection (3)) a debt which—

(a) is for a liquidated sum payable either immediately or at some certain future time; and

(b) is not an excluded debt.

(3) A debt is not a qualifying debt to the extent that it is secured.

(4) In this Part "excluded debt" means a debt of any description prescribed for the purposes of this subsection.][3]

[1] Added by Tribunals, Courts and Enforcement Act 2007 c. 15 Sch.17 para.1 (February 24, 2009: February 24, 2009 for the purpose of making rules, regulations and orders; April 6, 2009 otherwise).

[2] Added by Tribunals, Courts and Enforcement Act 2007 c. 15 Sch.17 para.1 (February 24, 2009: February 24, 2009 for the purpose of making rules, regulations and orders; April 6, 2009 otherwise).

[3] Added by Tribunals, Courts and Enforcement Act 2007 c. 15 Sch.17 para.1 (February 24, 2009: February 24, 2009 for the purpose of making rules, regulations and orders; April 6, 2009 otherwise).

[Applications for a debt relief order][4]

[251B Making of application

A5–02

(1) An application for a debt relief order must be made to the official receiver through an approved intermediary.

(2) The application must include—

(a) a list of the debts to which the debtor is subject at the date of the application, specifying the amount of each debt (including any interest, penalty or other sum that has become payable in relation to that debt on or before that date) and the creditor to whom it is owed;

(b) details of any security held in respect of any of those debts; and

(c) such other information about the debtor's affairs (including his creditors, debts and liabilities and his income and assets) as may be prescribed.

(3) The rules may make further provision as to—

(a) the form of an application for a debt relief order;

(b) the manner in which an application is to be made; and

(c) information and documents to be supplied in support of an application.

(4) For the purposes of this Part an application is not to be regarded as having been made until—

(a) the application has been submitted to the official receiver; and

(b) any fee required in connection with the application by an order under section 415 has been paid to such person as the order may specify.][5]

[251C Duty of official receiver to consider and determine application

A5–03

(1) This section applies where an application for a debt relief order is made.

(2) The official receiver may stay consideration of the application until he has received answers to any queries raised with the debtor in relation to anything connected with the application.

(3) The official receiver must determine the application by—

(a) deciding whether to refuse the application;

(b) if he does not refuse it, by making a debt relief order in relation to the specified debts he is satisfied were qualifying debts of the debtor at the application date; but he may only refuse the application if he is authorised or required to do so by any of the following provisions of this section.

(4) The official receiver may refuse the application if he considers that—

(a) the application does not meet all the requirements imposed by or under section 251B;

(b) any queries raised with the debtor have not been answered to the satisfaction of the official receiver within such time as he may specify when they are raised;

[4] Added by Tribunals, Courts and Enforcement Act 2007 c. 15 Sch.17 para.1 (February 24, 2009: February 24, 2009 for the purpose of making rules, regulations and orders; April 6, 2009 otherwise).

[5] Added by Tribunals, Courts and Enforcement Act 2007 c. 15 Sch.17 para.1 (February 24, 2009: February 24, 2009 for the purpose of making rules, regulations and orders; April 6, 2009 otherwise).

(c) the debtor has made any false representation or omission in making the application or on supplying any information or documents in support of it.

(5) The official receiver must refuse the application if he is not satisfied that—

(a) the debtor is an individual who is unable to pay his debts;
(b) at least one of the specified debts was a qualifying debt of the debtor at the application date;
(c) each of the conditions set out in Part 1 of Schedule 4ZA is met.

(6) The official receiver may refuse the application if he is not satisfied that each condition specified in Part 2 of Schedule 4ZA is met.
(7) If the official receiver refuses an application he must give reasons for his refusal to the debtor in the prescribed manner.
(8) In this section "specified debt" means a debt specified in the application.][6]

[251D Presumptions applicable to the determination of an application

A5–04 (1) The following presumptions are to apply to the determination of an application for a debt relief order.
(2) The official receiver must presume that the debtor is an individual who is unable to pay his debts at the determination date if—

(a) that appears to the official receiver to be the case at the application date from the information supplied in the application and he has no reason to believe that the information supplied is incomplete or inaccurate; and
(b) he has no reason to believe that, by virtue of a change in the debtor's financial circumstances since the application date, the debtor may be able to pay his debts.

(3) The official receiver must presume that a specified debt (of the amount specified in the application and owed to the creditor so specified) is a qualifying debt at the application date if—

(a) that appears to him to be the case from the information supplied in the application; and
(b) he has no reason to believe that the information supplied is incomplete or inaccurate.

(4) The official receiver must presume that the condition specified in paragraph 1 of Schedule 4ZA is met if—

(a) that appears to him to be the case from the information supplied in the application;
(b) any prescribed verification checks relating to the condition have been made; and
(c) he has no reason to believe that the information supplied is incomplete or inaccurate.

(5) The official receiver must presume that any other condition specified in Part 1 or 2 of Schedule 4ZA is met if—

(a) that appears to him to have been the case as at the application date from the information supplied in the application and he has no reason to believe that the information supplied is incomplete or inaccurate;

[6] Added by Tribunals, Courts and Enforcement Act 2007 c. 15 Sch.17 para.1 (February 24, 2009: February 24, 2009 for the purpose of making rules, regulations and orders; April 6, 2009 otherwise).

(b) any prescribed verification checks relating to the condition have been made; and
(c) he has no reason to believe that, by virtue of a change in circumstances since the application date, the condition may no longer be met.

(6) References in this section to information supplied in the application include information supplied to the official receiver in support of the application.
(7) In this section "specified debt" means a debt specified in the application.][7]

[Making and effect of debt relief order][8]

[251E Making of debt relief orders

A5–05

(1) This section applies where the official receiver makes a debt relief order on determining an application under section 251C.
(2) The order must be made in the prescribed form.
(3) The order must include a list of the debts which the official receiver is satisfied were qualifying debts of the debtor at the application date, specifying the amount of the debt at that time and the creditor to whom it was then owed.
(4) The official receiver must—

(a) give a copy of the order to the debtor; and
(b) make an entry for the order in the register containing the prescribed information about the order or the debtor.

(5) The rules may make provision as to other steps to be taken by the official receiver or the debtor on the making of the order.
(6) Those steps may include in particular notifying each creditor to whom a qualifying debt specified in the order is owed of—

(a) the making of the order and its effect,
(b) the grounds on which a creditor may object under section 251K, and
(c) any other prescribed information.

(7) In this Part the date on which an entry relating to the making of a debt relief order is first made in the register is referred to as "the effective date".][9]

[251F Effect of debt relief order on other debt management arrangements

A5–06

(1) This section applies if—

(a) a debt relief order is made, and
(b) immediately before the order is made, other debt management arrangements are in force in respect of the debtor.

[7] Added by Tribunals, Courts and Enforcement Act 2007 c. 15 Sch.17 para.1 (February 24, 2009: February 24, 2009 for the purpose of making rules, regulations and orders; April 6, 2009 otherwise).
[8] Added by Tribunals, Courts and Enforcement Act 2007 c. 15 Sch.17 para.1 (February 24, 2009: February 24, 2009 for the purpose of making rules, regulations and orders; April 6, 2009 otherwise).
[9] Added by Tribunals, Courts and Enforcement Act 2007 c. 15 Sch.17 para.1 (February 24, 2009: February 24, 2009 for the purpose of making rules, regulations and orders; April 6, 2009 otherwise).

(2) The other debt management arrangements cease to be in force when the debt relief order is made.

(3) In this section "other debt management arrangements" means—

(a) an administration order under Part 6 of the County Courts Act 1984;
(b) an enforcement restriction order under Part 6A of that Act;
(c) a debt repayment plan arranged in accordance with a debt management scheme that is approved under Chapter 4 of Part 5 of the Tribunals, Courts and Enforcement Act 2007.][10]

[251G Moratorium from qualifying debts

A5–07 (1) A moratorium commences on the effective date for a debt relief order in relation to each qualifying debt specified in the order ("a specified qualifying debt").

(2) During the moratorium, the creditor to whom a specified qualifying debt is owed—

(a) has no remedy in respect of the debt, and
(b) may not—

(i) commence a creditor's petition in respect of the debt, or
(ii) otherwise commence any action or other legal proceedings against the debtor

for the debt, except with the permission of the court and on such terms as the court may impose.

(3) If on the effective date a creditor to whom a specified qualifying debt is owed has any such petition, action or other proceeding as mentioned in subsection (2)(b) pending in any court, the court may—

(a) stay the proceedings on the petition, action or other proceedings (as the case may be), or
(b) allow them to continue on such terms as the court thinks fit.

(4) In subsection (2)(a) and (b) references to the debt include a reference to any interest, penalty or other sum that becomes payable in relation to that debt after the application date.

(5) Nothing in this section affects the right of a secured creditor of the debtor to enforce his security.][11]

[251H The moratorium period

A5–08 (1) The moratorium relating to the qualifying debts specified in a debt relief order continues for the period of one year beginning with the effective date for the order, unless—

(a) the moratorium terminates early; or
(b) the moratorium period is extended by the official receiver under this section or by the court under section 251M.

[10] Added by Tribunals, Courts and Enforcement Act 2007 c. 15 Sch.17 para.1 (February 24, 2009: February 24, 2009 for the purpose of making rules, regulations and orders; April 6, 2009 otherwise).

[11] Added by Tribunals, Courts and Enforcement Act 2007 c. 15 Sch.17 para.1 (February 24, 2009: February 24, 2009 for the purpose of making rules, regulations and orders; April 6, 2009 otherwise).

(2) The official receiver may only extend the moratorium period for the purpose of—

(a) carrying out or completing an investigation under section 251K;
(b) taking any action he considers necessary (whether as a result of an investigation or otherwise) in relation to the order; or
(c) in a case where he has decided to revoke the order, providing the debtor with the opportunity to make arrangements for making payments towards his debts.

(3) The official receiver may not extend the moratorium period for the purpose mentioned in subsection (2)(a) without the permission of the court.
(4) The official receiver may not extend the moratorium period beyond the end of the period of three months beginning after the end of the initial period of one year mentioned in subsection (1).
(5) The moratorium period may be extended more than once, but any extension (whether by the official receiver or by the court) must be made before the moratorium would otherwise end.
(6) References in this Part to a moratorium terminating early are to its terminating before the end of what would otherwise be the moratorium period, whether on the revocation of the order or by virtue of any other enactment.][12]

[251M Powers of court in relation to debt relief orders

A5–09

(1) Any person may make an application to the court if he is dissatisfied by any act, omission or decision of the official receiver in connection with a debt relief order or an application for such an order.
(2) The official receiver may make an application to the court for directions or an order in relation to any matter arising in connection with a debt relief order or an application for such an order.
(3) The matters referred to in subsection (2) include, among other things, matters relating to the debtor's compliance with any duty arising under section 251J.
(4) An application under this section may, subject to anything in the rules, be made at any time.
(5) The court may extend the moratorium period applicable to a debt relief order for the purposes of determining an application under this section.
(6) On an application under this section the court may dismiss the application or do one or more of the following—

(a) quash the whole or part of any act or decision of the official receiver;
(b) give the official receiver directions (including a direction that he reconsider any matter in relation to which his act or decision has been quashed under paragraph (a));
(c) make an order for the enforcement of any obligation on the debtor arising by virtue of a duty under section 251J;
(d) extend the moratorium period applicable to the debt relief order;
(e) make an order revoking or amending the debt relief order;
(f) make an order under section 251N; or
(g) make such other order as the court thinks fit.

(7) An order under subsection (6)(e) for the revocation of a debt relief order—

(a) may be made during the moratorium period applicable to the debt relief order or at any time after that period has ended;
(b) may be made on the court's own motion if the court has made a bankruptcy order in relation to the debtor during that period;

[12] Added by Tribunals, Courts and Enforcement Act 2007 c. 15 Sch.17 para.1 (February 24, 2009: February 24, 2009 for the purpose of making rules, regulations and orders; April 6, 2009 otherwise).

(c) may provide for the revocation of the order to take effect on such terms and at such a time as the court may specify.

(8) An order under subsection (6)(e) for the amendment of a debt relief order may not add any debts that were not specified in the application for the debt relief order to the list of qualifying debts.][13]

[251N Inquiry into debtor's dealings and property

A5–10 (1) An order under this section may be made by the court on the application of the official receiver.

(2) An order under this section is an order summoning any of the following persons to appear before the court—

(a) the debtor;

(b) the debtor's spouse or former spouse or the debtor's civil partner or former civil partner;

(c) any person appearing to the court to be able to give information or assistance concerning the debtor or his dealings, affairs and property.

(3) The court may require a person falling within subsection (2)(c)—

(a) to provide a written account of his dealings with the debtor; or

(b) to produce any documents in his possession or under his control relating to the debtor or to the debtor's dealings, affairs or property.

(4) Subsection (5) applies where a person fails without reasonable excuse to appear before the court when he is summoned to do so by an order under this section.

(5) The court may cause a warrant to be issued to a constable or prescribed officer of the court—

(a) for the arrest of that person, and

(b) for the seizure of any records or other documents in that person's possession.

(6) The court may authorise a person arrested under such a warrant to be kept in custody, and anything seized under such a warrant to be held, in accordance with the rules, until that person is brought before the court under the warrant or until such other time as the court may order.][14]

[Offences][15]

[251S Obtaining credit or engaging in business

A5–11 (1) A person in respect of whom a debt relief order is made is guilty of an offence if, during the relevant period—

[13] Added by Tribunals, Courts and Enforcement Act 2007 c. 15 Sch.17 para.1 (February 24, 2009: February 24, 2009 for the purpose of making rules, regulations and orders; April 6, 2009 otherwise).

[14] Added by Tribunals, Courts and Enforcement Act 2007 c. 15 Sch.17 para.1 (February 24, 2009: February 24, 2009 for the purpose of making rules, regulations and orders; April 6, 2009 otherwise).

[15] Added by Tribunals, Courts and Enforcement Act 2007 c. 15 Sch.17 para.1 (February 24, 2009: February 24, 2009 for the purpose of making rules, regulations and orders; April 6, 2009 otherwise).

(a) he obtains credit (either alone or jointly with any other person) without giving the person from whom he obtains the credit the relevant information about his status; or
(b) he engages directly or indirectly in any business under a name other than that in which the order was made without disclosing to all persons with whom he enters into any business transaction the name in which the order was made.

(2) For the purposes of subsection (1)(a) the relevant information about a person's status is the information that—

(a) a moratorium is in force in relation to the debt relief order,
(b) a debt relief restrictions order is in force in respect of him, or
(c) both a moratorium and a debt relief restrictions order is in force, as the case may be.

(3) In subsection (1) "relevant period" means—

(a) the moratorium period relating to the debt relief order, or
(b) the period for which a debt relief restrictions order is in force in respect of the person

in respect of whom the debt relief order is made, as the case may be.

(4) Subsection (1)(a) does not apply if the amount of the credit is less than the prescribed amount (if any).

(5) The reference in subsection (1)(a) to a person obtaining credit includes the following cases—

(a) where goods are bailed to him under a hire-purchase agreement, or agreed to be sold to him under a conditional sale agreement;
(b) where he is paid in advance (in money or otherwise) for the supply of goods or services.][16]

[251V Debt relief restrictions orders and undertakings[17]

Schedule 4ZB (which makes provision about debt relief restrictions orders and debt relief restrictions undertakings) has effect.][18] **A5–12**

[251W Register of debt relief orders etc

The Secretary of State must maintain a register of matters relating to— **A5–13**

(a) debt relief orders;
(b) debt relief restrictions orders; and
(c) debt relief restrictions undertakings.][19]

[16] Added by Tribunals, Courts and Enforcement Act 2007 c. 15 Sch.17 para.1 (February 24, 2009: February 24, 2009 for the purpose of making rules, regulations and orders; April 6, 2009 otherwise).

[17] Added by Tribunals, Courts and Enforcement Act 2007 c. 15 Sch.17 para.1 (February 24, 2009: February 24, 2009 for the purpose of making rules, regulations and orders; April 6, 2009 otherwise).

[18] Added by Tribunals, Courts and Enforcement Act 2007 c. 15 Sch.17 para.1 (February 24, 2009: February 24, 2009 for the purpose of making rules, regulations and orders; April 6, 2009 otherwise).

[19] Added by Tribunals, Courts and Enforcement Act 2007 c. 15 Sch.17 para.1 (February 24, 2009: February 24, 2009 for the purpose of making rules, regulations and orders; April 6, 2009 otherwise).

[251X Interpretation

A5–14 (1) In this Part—"the application date", in relation to a debt relief order or an application for a debt relief order, means the date on which the application for the order is made to the official receiver; "approved intermediary" has the meaning given in section 251U(1); "debt relief order" means an order made by the official receiver under this Part; "debtor" means—

(a) in relation to an application for a debt relief order, the applicant; and
(b) in relation to a debt relief order, the person in relation to whom the order is

made; "debt relief restrictions order" and "debt relief restrictions undertaking" means an order made, or an undertaking accepted, under Schedule 4ZB; "the determination date", in relation to a debt relief order or an application for a debt relief order, means the date on which the application for the order is determined by the official receiver; "the effective date" has the meaning given in section 251E(7); "excluded debt" is to be construed in accordance with section 251A; "moratorium" and "moratorium period" are to be construed in accordance with sections 251G and 251H; "qualifying debt", in relation to a debtor, has the meaning given in section 251A(2); "the register" means the register maintained under section 251W; "specified qualifying debt" has the meaning given in section 251G(1).

(2) In this Part references to a creditor specified in a debt relief order as the person to whom a qualifying debt is owed by the debtor include a reference to any person to whom the right to claim the whole or any part of the debt has passed, by assignment or operation of law, after the date of the application for the order.][20]

PART IX

BANKRUPTCY

CHAPTER I

Bankruptcy petitions; bankruptcy orders

[281A Post-discharge restrictions

A5–15 Schedule 4A to this Act (bankruptcy restrictions order and bankruptcy restrictions undertaking) shall have effect.][21]

[20] Added by Tribunals, Courts and Enforcement Act 2007 c. 15 Sch.17 para.1 (February 24, 2009: February 24, 2009 for the purpose of making rules, regulations and orders; April 6, 2009 otherwise).

[21] Added subject to transitional provisions specified in SI 2003/2093 art.7 by Enterprise Act 2002 c. 40 Pt 10 s.257(1). (April 1, 2004: addition has effect subject to transitional provisions specified in SI 2003/2093 art.7).

[SCHEDULE 4ZA

CONDITIONS FOR MAKING A DEBT RELIEF ORDER][22]

[PART I

CONDITIONS WHICH MUST BE MET][23]

[Connection with England and Wales][24]

[1 (1) The debtor— **A5–16**

(a) is domiciled in England and Wales on the application date; or
(b) at any time during the period of three years ending with that date—
  (i) was ordinarily resident, or had a place of residence, in England and Wales; or
  (ii) carried on business in England and Wales.

(2) The reference in sub-paragraph (1)(b)(ii) to the debtor carrying on business includes—

(a) the carrying on of business by a firm or partnership of which he is a member;
(b) the carrying on of business by an agent or manager for him or for such a firm or partnership.][25]

[Debtor's previous insolvency history][26]

[2 The debtor is not, on the determination date— **A5–17**

(a) an undischarged bankrupt;
(b) subject to an interim order or voluntary arrangement under Part 8; or
(c) subject to a bankruptcy restrictions order or a debt relief restrictions order.][27]

[3 A debtor's petition for the debtor's bankruptcy under Part 9—

(a) has not been presented by the debtor before the determination date;

[22] Added by Tribunals, Courts and Enforcement Act 2007 c. 15 Sch.18 para.1 (February 24, 2009: February 24, 2009 for the purpose of making rules, regulations and orders; April 6, 2009 otherwise).
[23] Added by Tribunals, Courts and Enforcement Act 2007 c. 15 Sch.18 para.1 (February 24, 2009: February 24, 2009 for the purpose of making rules, regulations and orders; April 6, 2009 otherwise).
[24] Added by Tribunals, Courts and Enforcement Act 2007 c. 15 Sch.18 para.1 (February 24, 2009: February 24, 2009 for the purpose of making rules, regulations and orders; April 6, 2009 otherwise).
[25] Added by Tribunals, Courts and Enforcement Act 2007 c. 15 Sch.18 para.1 (February 24, 2009: February 24, 2009 for the purpose of making rules, regulations and orders; April 6, 2009 otherwise).
[26] Added by Tribunals, Courts and Enforcement Act 2007 c. 15 Sch.18 para.1 (February 24, 2009: February 24, 2009 for the purpose of making rules, regulations and orders; April 6, 2009 otherwise).
[27] Added by Tribunals, Courts and Enforcement Act 2007 c. 15 Sch.18 para.1 (February 24, 2009: February 24, 2009 for the purpose of making rules, regulations and orders; April 6, 2009 otherwise).

(b) has been so presented, but proceedings on the petition have been finally disposed of before that date; or
(c) has been so presented and proceedings in relation to the petition remain before the court at that date, but the court has referred the debtor under section 274A(2) for the purposes of making an application for a debt relief order.][28]

[**4** A creditor's petition for the debtor's bankruptcy under Part 9—

(a) has not been presented against the debtor at any time before the determination date;
(b) has been so presented, but proceedings on the petition have been finally disposed of before that date; or
(c) has been so presented and proceedings in relation to the petition remain before the court at that date, but the person who presented the petition has consented to the making of an application for a debt relief order.][29]

[**5** A debt relief order has not been made in relation to the debtor in the period of six years ending with the determination date.][30]

[Limit on debtor's overall indebtedness][31]

A5–18 [**6** (1) The total amount of the debtor's debts on the determination date, other than unliquidated debts and excluded debts, does not exceed the prescribed amount.
(2) For this purpose an unliquidated debt is a debt that is not for a liquidated sum payable to a creditor either immediately or at some future certain time.][32]

[Limit on debtor's monthly surplus income][33]

A5–19 [**7** (1) The debtor's monthly surplus income (if any) on the determination date does not exceed the prescribed amount.
(2) For this purpose "monthly surplus income" is the amount by which a person's monthly income exceeds the amount necessary for the reasonable domestic needs of himself and his family.
(3) The rules may—
(a) make provision as to how the debtor's monthly surplus income is to be determined;
(b) provide that particular descriptions of income are to be excluded for the purposes of this paragraph.][34]

[28] Added by Tribunals, Courts and Enforcement Act 2007 c. 15 Sch.18 para.1 (February 24, 2009: February 24, 2009 for the purpose of making rules, regulations and orders; April 6, 2009 otherwise).
[29] Added by Tribunals, Courts and Enforcement Act 2007 c. 15 Sch.18 para.1 (February 24, 2009: February 24, 2009 for the purpose of making rules, regulations and orders; April 6, 2009 otherwise).
[30] Added by Tribunals, Courts and Enforcement Act 2007 c. 15 Sch.18 para.1 (February 24, 2009: February 24, 2009 for the purpose of making rules, regulations and orders; April 6, 2009 otherwise).
[31] Added by Tribunals, Courts and Enforcement Act 2007 c. 15 Sch.18 para.1 (February 24, 2009: February 24, 2009 for the purpose of making rules, regulations and orders; April 6, 2009 otherwise).
[32] Added by Tribunals, Courts and Enforcement Act 2007 c. 15 Sch.18 para.1 (February 24, 2009: February 24, 2009 for the purpose of making rules, regulations and orders; April 6, 2009 otherwise).
[33] Added by Tribunals, Courts and Enforcement Act 2007 c. 15 Sch.18 para.1 (February 24, 2009: February 24, 2009 for the purpose of making rules, regulations and orders; April 6, 2009 otherwise).
[34] Added by Tribunals, Courts and Enforcement Act 2007 c. 15 Sch.18 para.1 (February 24, 2009: February 24, 2009 for the purpose of making rules, regulations and orders; April 6, 2009 otherwise).

[Limit on value of debtor's property][35]

A5–20

[**8** (1) The total value of the debtor's property on the determination date does not exceed the prescribed amount.

(2) The rules may—

(a) make provision as to how the value of a person's property is to be determined;
(b) provide that particular descriptions of property are to be excluded for the purposes of this paragraph.][36]

[PART 2

OTHER CONDITIONS][37]

A5–21

[**9** (1) The debtor has not entered into a transaction with any person at an undervalue during the period between—

(a) the start of the period of two years ending with the application date; and
(b) the determination date.

(2) For this purpose a debtor enters into a transaction with a person at an undervalue if—

(a) he makes a gift to that person or he otherwise enters into a transaction with that person on terms that provide for him to receive no consideration;
(b) he enters into a transaction with that person in consideration of marriage or the formation of a civil partnership; or
(c) he enters into a transaction with that person for a consideration the value of which, in money or money's worth, is significantly less than the value, in money or money's worth, of the consideration provided by the individual.][38]

[**10** (1) The debtor has not given a preference to any person during the period between—

(a) the start of the period of two years ending with the application date; and
(b) the determination date.

(2) For this purpose a debtor gives a preference to a person if—

(a) that person is one of the debtor's creditors to whom a qualifying debt is owed or is a surety or guarantor for any such debt, and
(b) the debtor does anything or suffers anything to be done which (in either case) has the effect of putting that person into a position which, in the event that a debt relief order is made in relation to the debtor, will be better than the position he would have been in if that thing had not been done.][39]

[35] Added by Tribunals, Courts and Enforcement Act 2007 c. 15 Sch.18 para.1 (February 24, 2009: February 24, 2009 for the purpose of making rules, regulations and orders; April 6, 2009 otherwise).

[36] Added by Tribunals, Courts and Enforcement Act 2007 c. 15 Sch.18 para.1 (February 24, 2009: February 24, 2009 for the purpose of making rules, regulations and orders; April 6, 2009 otherwise).

[37] Added by Tribunals, Courts and Enforcement Act 2007 c. 15 Sch.18 para.1 (February 24, 2009: February 24, 2009 for the purpose of making rules, regulations and orders; April 6, 2009 otherwise).

[38] Added by Tribunals, Courts and Enforcement Act 2007 c. 15 Sch.18 para.1 (February 24, 2009: February 24, 2009 for the purpose of making rules, regulations and orders; April 6, 2009 otherwise).

[39] Added by Tribunals, Courts and Enforcement Act 2007 c. 15 Sch.18 para.1 (February 24, 2009: February 24, 2009 for the purpose of making rules, regulations and orders; April 6, 2009 otherwise).

[SCHEDULE 4ZB

DEBT RELIEF RESTRICTIONS ORDERS AND UNDERTAKINGS][40]

[Debt relief restrictions order][41]

A5–22 **[1** (1) A debt relief restrictions order may be made by the court in relation to a person in respect of whom a debt relief order has been made.

(2) An order may be made only on the application of—

(a) the Secretary of State, or
(b) the official receiver acting on a direction of the Secretary of State.][42]

[Grounds for making order][43]

A5–23 **[2** (1) The court shall grant an application for a debt relief restrictions order if it thinks it appropriate to do so having regard to the conduct of the debtor (whether before or after the making of the debt relief order).

(2) The court shall, in particular, take into account any of the following kinds of behaviour on the part of the debtor—

(a) failing to keep records which account for a loss of property by the debtor, or by a business carried on by him, where the loss occurred in the period beginning two years before the application date for the debt relief order and ending with the date of the application for the debt relief restrictions order;
(b) failing to produce records of that kind on demand by the official receiver;
(c) entering into a transaction at an undervalue in the period beginning two years before the application date for the debt relief order and ending with the date of the determination of that application;
(d) giving a preference in the period beginning two years before the application date for the debt relief order and ending with the date of the determination of that application;
(e) making an excessive pension contribution;
(f) a failure to supply goods or services that were wholly or partly paid for;
(g) trading at a time, before the date of the determination of the application for the debt relief order, when the debtor knew or ought to have known that he was himself to be unable to pay his debts;
(h) incurring, before the date of the determination of the application for the debt relief order, a debt which the debtor had no reasonable expectation of being able to pay;
(i) failing to account satisfactorily to the court or the official receiver for a loss of property or for an insufficiency of property to meet his debts;
(j) carrying on any gambling, rash and hazardous speculation or unreasonable extravagance which may have materially contributed to or increased the extent of his inability to pay his debts before the application date for the debt relief order or which took place between that date and the date of the determination of the application for the debt relief order;

[40] Added by Tribunals, Courts and Enforcement Act 2007 c. 15 Sch.19 para.1 (February 24, 2009: February 24, 2009 for the purpose of making rules, regulations and orders; April 6, 2009 otherwise).
[41] Added by Tribunals, Courts and Enforcement Act 2007 c. 15 Sch.19 para.1 (February 24, 2009: February 24, 2009 for the purpose of making rules, regulations and orders; April 6, 2009 otherwise).
[42] Added by Tribunals, Courts and Enforcement Act 2007 c. 15 Sch.19 para.1 (February 24, 2009: February 24, 2009 for the purpose of making rules, regulations and orders; April 6, 2009 otherwise).
[43] Added by Tribunals, Courts and Enforcement Act 2007 c. 15 Sch.19 para.1 (February 24, 2009: February 24, 2009 for the purpose of making rules, regulations and orders; April 6, 2009 otherwise).

(k) neglect of business affairs of a kind which may have materially contributed to or increased the extent of his inability to pay his debts;
(l) fraud or fraudulent breach of trust;
(m) failing to co-operate with the official receiver.

(3) The court shall also, in particular, consider whether the debtor was an undischarged bankrupt at some time during the period of six years ending with the date of the application for the debt relief order.

(4) For the purposes of sub-paragraph (2)—"excessive pension contribution" shall be construed in accordance with section 342A; "preference" shall be construed in accordance with paragraph 10(2) of Schedule 4ZA; "undervalue" shall be construed in accordance with paragraph 9(2) of that Schedule.][44]

[Timing of application for order][45]

[3 An application for a debt relief restrictions order in respect of a debtor may be made— **A5–24**

(a) at any time during the moratorium period relating to the debt relief order in question, or
(b) after the end of that period, but only with the permission of the court.][46]

[Duration of order][47]

[4 (1) A debt relief restrictions order— **A5–25**

(a) comes into force when it is made, and
(b) ceases to have effect at the end of a date specified in the order.

(2) The date specified in a debt relief restrictions order under sub-paragraph (1)(b) must not be—

(a) before the end of the period of two years beginning with the date on which the order is made, or
(b) after the end of the period of 15 years beginning with that date.][48]

[Interim debt relief restrictions order][49]

[5 (1) This paragraph applies at any time between— **A5–26**

(a) the institution of an application for a debt relief restrictions order, and
(b) the determination of the application.

[44] Added by Tribunals, Courts and Enforcement Act 2007 c. 15 Sch.19 para.1 (February 24, 2009: February 24, 2009 for the purpose of making rules, regulations and orders; April 6, 2009 otherwise).
[45] Added by Tribunals, Courts and Enforcement Act 2007 c. 15 Sch.19 para.1 (February 24, 2009: February 24, 2009 for the purpose of making rules, regulations and orders; April 6, 2009 otherwise).
[46] Added by Tribunals, Courts and Enforcement Act 2007 c. 15 Sch.19 para.1 (February 24, 2009: February 24, 2009 for the purpose of making rules, regulations and orders; April 6, 2009 otherwise).
[47] Added by Tribunals, Courts and Enforcement Act 2007 c. 15 Sch.19 para.1 (February 24, 2009: February 24, 2009 for the purpose of making rules, regulations and orders; April 6, 2009 otherwise).
[48] Added by Tribunals, Courts and Enforcement Act 2007 c. 15 Sch.19 para.1 (February 24, 2009: February 24, 2009 for the purpose of making rules, regulations and orders; April 6, 2009 otherwise).
[49] Added by Tribunals, Courts and Enforcement Act 2007 c. 15 Sch.19 para.1 (February 24, 2009: February 24, 2009 for the purpose of making rules, regulations and orders; April 6, 2009 otherwise).

(2) The court may make an interim debt relief restrictions order if the court thinks that—

(a) there are prima facie grounds to suggest that the application for the debt relief restrictions order will be successful, and
(b) it is in the public interest to make an interim debt relief restrictions order.

(3) An interim debt relief restrictions order may only be made on the application of—

(a) the Secretary of State, or
(b) the official receiver acting on a direction of the Secretary of State.

(4) An interim debt relief restrictions order—

(a) has the same effect as a debt relief restrictions order, and
(b) comes into force when it is made.

(5) An interim debt relief restrictions order ceases to have effect—

(a) on the determination of the application for the debt relief restrictions order,
(b) on the acceptance of a debt relief restrictions undertaking made by the debtor, or
(c) if the court discharges the interim debt relief restrictions order on the application of the person who applied for it or of the debtor.][50]

[**6** (1) This paragraph applies to a case in which both an interim debt relief restrictions order and a debt relief restrictions order are made.
(2) Paragraph 4(2) has effect in relation to the debt relief restrictions order as if a reference to the date of that order were a reference to the date of the interim debt relief restrictions order.][51]

[Debt relief restrictions undertaking][52]

A5–27 [**7** (1) A debtor may offer a debt relief restrictions undertaking to the Secretary of State.
(2) In determining whether to accept a debt relief restrictions undertaking the Secretary of State shall have regard to the matters specified in paragraph 2(2) and (3).][53]

[**8** A reference in an enactment to a person in respect of whom a debt relief restrictions order has effect (or who is "the subject of" a debt relief restrictions order) includes a reference to a person in respect of whom a debt relief restrictions undertaking has effect.][54]

[**9** (1) A debt relief restrictions undertaking—

(a) comes into force on being accepted by the Secretary of State, and
(b) ceases to have effect at the end of a date specified in the undertaking.

[50] Added by Tribunals, Courts and Enforcement Act 2007 c. 15 Sch.19 para.1 (February 24, 2009: February 24, 2009 for the purpose of making rules, regulations and orders; April 6, 2009 otherwise).
[51] Added by Tribunals, Courts and Enforcement Act 2007 c. 15 Sch.19 para.1 (February 24, 2009: February 24, 2009 for the purpose of making rules, regulations and orders; April 6, 2009 otherwise).
[52] Added by Tribunals, Courts and Enforcement Act 2007 c. 15 Sch.19 para.1 (February 24, 2009: February 24, 2009 for the purpose of making rules, regulations and orders; April 6, 2009 otherwise).
[53] Added by Tribunals, Courts and Enforcement Act 2007 c. 15 Sch.19 para.1 (February 24, 2009: February 24, 2009 for the purpose of making rules, regulations and orders; April 6, 2009 otherwise).
[54] Added by Tribunals, Courts and Enforcement Act 2007 c. 15 Sch.19 para.1 (February 24, 2009: February 24, 2009 for the purpose of making rules, regulations and orders; April 6, 2009 otherwise).

(2) The date specified under sub-paragraph (1)(b) must not be—

(a) before the end of the period of two years beginning with the date on which the undertaking is accepted, or
(b) after the end of the period of 15 years beginning with that date.

(3) On an application by the debtor the court may—

(a) annul a debt relief restrictions undertaking;
(b) provide for a debt relief restrictions undertaking to cease to have effect before the date specified under sub-paragraph (1)(b).][55]

[Effect of revocation of debt relief order][56]

A5–28

[**10** Unless the court directs otherwise, the revocation at any time of a debt relief order does not—

(a) affect the validity of any debt relief restrictions order, interim debt relief restrictions order or debt relief restrictions undertaking which is in force in respect of the debtor;
(b) prevent the determination of any application for a debt relief restrictions order, or an interim debt relief restrictions order, in relation to the debtor that was instituted before that time;
(c) prevent the acceptance of a debt relief restrictions undertaking that was offered before that time; or
(d) prevent the institution of an application for a debt relief restrictions order or interim debt relief restrictions order in respect of the debtor, or the offer or acceptance of a debt relief restrictions undertaking by the debtor, after that time.][57]

[SCHEDULE 4A

BANKRUPTCY RESTRICTIONS ORDER AND UNDERTAKING][58]

[Bankruptcy restrictions order][59]

A5–29

[**1** (1) A bankruptcy restrictions order may be made by the court.
(2) An order may be made only on the application of—

(a) the Secretary of State, or
(b) the official receiver acting on a direction of the Secretary of State.][60]

[55] Added by Tribunals, Courts and Enforcement Act 2007 c. 15 Sch.19 para.1 (February 24, 2009: February 24, 2009 for the purpose of making rules, regulations and orders; April 6, 2009 otherwise).
[56] Added by Tribunals, Courts and Enforcement Act 2007 c. 15 Sch.19 para.1 (February 24, 2009: February 24, 2009 for the purpose of making rules, regulations and orders; April 6, 2009 otherwise).
[57] Added by Tribunals, Courts and Enforcement Act 2007 c. 15 Sch.19 para.1 (February 24, 2009: February 24, 2009 for the purpose of making rules, regulations and orders; April 6, 2009 otherwise).
[58] Added subject to transitional provisions specified in SI 2003/2093 art.7 by Enterprise Act 2002 c. 40 Sch.20 para.1 (April 1, 2004: addition has effect subject to transitional provisions specified in SI 2003/2093 art.7).
[59] Added subject to transitional provisions specified in SI 2003/2093 art.7 by Enterprise Act 2002 c. 40 Sch.20 para.1 (April 1, 2004: addition has effect subject to transitional provisions specified in SI 2003/2093 art.7).
[60] Added subject to transitional provisions specified in SI 2003/2093 art.7 by Enterprise Act 2002 c. 40 Sch.20 para.1 (April 1, 2004: addition has effect subject to transitional provisions specified in SI 2003/2093 art.7).

[Grounds for making order][61]

A5–30 [**2** (1) The court shall grant an application for a bankruptcy restrictions order if it thinks it appropriate having regard to the conduct of the bankrupt (whether before or after the making of the bankruptcy order).

(2) The court shall, in particular, take into account any of the following kinds of behaviour on the part of the bankrupt—

(a) failing to keep records which account for a loss of property by the bankrupt, or by a business carried on by him, where the loss occurred in the period beginning 2 years before petition and ending with the date of the application;
(b) failing to produce records of that kind on demand by the official receiver or the trustee;
(c) entering into a transaction at an undervalue;
(d) giving a preference;
(e) making an excessive pension contribution;
(f) a failure to supply goods or services which were wholly or partly paid for which gave rise to a claim provable in the bankruptcy;
(g) trading at a time before commencement of the bankruptcy when the bankrupt knew or ought to have known that he was himself to be unable to pay his debts;
(h) incurring, before commencement of the bankruptcy, a debt which the bankrupt had no reasonable expectation of being able to pay;
(i) failing to account satisfactorily to the court, the official receiver or the trustee for a loss of property or for an insufficiency of property to meet bankruptcy debts;
(j) carrying on any gambling, rash and hazardous speculation or unreasonable extravagance which may have materially contributed to or increased the extent of the bankruptcy or which took place between presentation of the petition and commencement of the bankruptcy;
(k) neglect of business affairs of a kind which may have materially contributed to or increased the extent of the bankruptcy;
(l) fraud or fraudulent breach of trust;
(m) failing to cooperate with the official receiver or the trustee.

(3) The court shall also, in particular, consider whether the bankrupt was an undischarged bankrupt at some time during the period of six years ending with the date of the bankruptcy to which the application relates.

(4) For the purpose of sub-paragraph (2)— "before petition" shall be construed in accordance with section 351(c), "excessive pension contribution" shall be construed in accordance with section 342A, "preference" shall be construed in accordance with section 340, and "undervalue" shall be construed in accordance with section 339.][62]

[Timing of application for order][63]

A5–31 [**3** (1) An application for a bankruptcy restrictions order in respect of a bankrupt must be made—

[61] Added subject to transitional provisions specified in SI 2003/2093 art.7 by Enterprise Act 2002 c. 40 Sch.20 para.1 (April 1, 2004: addition has effect subject to transitional provisions specified in SI 2003/2093 art.7).

[62] Added subject to transitional provisions specified in SI 2003/2093 art.7 by Enterprise Act 2002 c. 40 Sch.20 para.1 (April 1, 2004: addition has effect subject to transitional provisions specified in SI 2003/2093 art.7).

[63] Added subject to transitional provisions specified in SI 2003/2093 art.7 by Enterprise Act 2002 c. 40 Sch.20 para.1 (April 1, 2004: addition has effect subject to transitional provisions specified in SI 2003/2093 art.7).

(a) before the end of the period of one year beginning with the date on which the bankruptcy commences, or
(b) with the permission of the court.

(2) The period specified in sub-paragraph (1)(a) shall cease to run in respect of a bankrupt while the period set for his discharge is suspended under section 279(3).][64]

[Duration of order][65]

[**4** (1) A bankruptcy restrictions order— **A5–32**

(a) shall come into force when it is made, and
(b) shall cease to have effect at the end of a date specified in the order.

(2) The date specified in a bankruptcy restrictions order under sub-paragraph (1)(b) must not be—

(a) before the end of the period of two years beginning with the date on which the order is made, or
(b) after the end of the period of 15 years beginning with that date.][66]

[Interim bankruptcy restrictions order][67]

[**5** (1) This paragraph applies at any time between— **A5–33**

(a) the institution of an application for a bankruptcy restrictions order, and
(b) the determination of the application.

(2) The court may make an interim bankruptcy restrictions order if the court thinks that—

(a) there are prima facie grounds to suggest that the application for the bankruptcy restrictions order will be successful, and
(b) it is in the public interest to make an interim order.

(3) An interim order may be made only on the application of—

(a) the Secretary of State, or
(b) the official receiver acting on a direction of the Secretary of State.

(4) An interim order—

(a) shall have the same effect as a bankruptcy restrictions order, and
(b) shall come into force when it is made.

(5) An interim order shall cease to have effect—

(a) on the determination of the application for the bankruptcy restrictions order,

[64] Added subject to transitional provisions specified in SI 2003/2093 art.7 by Enterprise Act 2002 c. 40 Sch.20 para.1 (April 1, 2004: addition has effect subject to transitional provisions specified in SI 2003/2093 art.7).

[65] Added subject to transitional provisions specified in SI 2003/2093 art.7 by Enterprise Act 2002 c. 40 Sch.20 para.1 (April 1, 2004: addition has effect subject to transitional provisions specified in SI 2003/2093 art.7).

[66] Added subject to transitional provisions specified in SI 2003/2093 art.7 by Enterprise Act 2002 c. 40 Sch.20 para.1 (April 1, 2004: addition has effect subject to transitional provisions specified in SI 2003/2093 art.7).

[67] Added subject to transitional provisions specified in SI 2003/2093 art.7 by Enterprise Act 2002 c. 40 Sch.20 para.1 (April 1, 2004: addition has effect subject to transitional provisions specified in SI 2003/2093 art.7).

(b) on the acceptance of a bankruptcy restrictions undertaking made by the bankrupt, or
(c) if the court discharges the interim order on the application of the person who applied for it or of the bankrupt.][68]

[**6** (1) This paragraph applies to a case in which both an interim bankruptcy restrictions order and a bankruptcy restrictions order are made.
(2) Paragraph 4(2) shall have effect in relation to the bankruptcy restrictions order as if a reference to the date of that order were a reference to the date of the interim order.][69]

[Bankruptcy restrictions undertaking][70]

A5–34 [**7** (1) A bankrupt may offer a bankruptcy restrictions undertaking to the Secretary of State.
(2) In determining whether to accept a bankruptcy restrictions undertaking the Secretary of State shall have regard to the matters specified in paragraph 2(2) and (3).][71]

[**8** A reference in an enactment to a person in respect of whom a bankruptcy restrictions order has effect (or who is "the subject of" a bankruptcy restrictions order) includes a reference to a person in respect of whom a bankruptcy restrictions undertaking has effect.][72]

[**9** (1) A bankruptcy restrictions undertaking—

(a) shall come into force on being accepted by the Secretary of State, and
(b) shall cease to have effect at the end of a date specified in the undertaking.

(2) The date specified under sub-paragraph (1)(b) must not be—

(a) before the end of the period of two years beginning with the date on which the undertaking is accepted, or
(b) after the end of the period of 15 years beginning with that date.

(3) On an application by the bankrupt the court may—

(a) annul a bankruptcy restrictions undertaking;
(b) provide for a bankruptcy restrictions undertaking to cease to have effect before the date specified under sub-paragraph (1)(b).][73]

[68] Added subject to transitional provisions specified in SI 2003/2093 art.7 by Enterprise Act 2002 c. 40 Sch.20 para.1 (April 1, 2004: addition has effect subject to transitional provisions specified in SI 2003/2093 art.7).
[69] Added subject to transitional provisions specified in SI 2003/2093 art.7 by Enterprise Act 2002 c. 40 Sch.20 para.1 (April 1, 2004: addition has effect subject to transitional provisions specified in SI 2003/2093 art.7).
[70] Added subject to transitional provisions specified in SI 2003/2093 art.7 by Enterprise Act 2002 c. 40 Sch.20 para.1 (April 1, 2004: addition has effect subject to transitional provisions specified in SI 2003/2093 art.7).
[71] Added subject to transitional provisions specified in SI 2003/2093 art.7 by Enterprise Act 2002 c. 40 Sch.20 para.1 (April 1, 2004: addition has effect subject to transitional provisions specified in SI 2003/2093 art.7).
[72] Added subject to transitional provisions specified in SI 2003/2093 art.7 by Enterprise Act 2002 c. 40 Sch.20 para.1 (April 1, 2004: addition has effect subject to transitional provisions specified in SI 2003/2093 art.7).
[73] Added subject to transitional provisions specified in SI 2003/2093 art.7 by Enterprise Act 2002 c. 40 Sch.20 para.1 (April 1, 2004: addition has effect subject to transitional provisions specified in SI 2003/2093 art.7).

[Effect of annulment of bankruptcy order][74]

[**10** Where a bankruptcy order is annulled under section 282(1)(a) or (2)— **A5–35**

(a) any bankruptcy restrictions order, interim order or undertaking which is in force in respect of the bankrupt shall be annulled,
(b) no new bankruptcy restrictions order or interim order may be made in respect of the bankrupt, and
(c) no new bankruptcy restrictions undertaking by the bankrupt may be accepted.][75]

[**11** Where a bankruptcy order is annulled under section 261, 263D or 282(1)(b)—

(a) the annulment shall not affect any bankruptcy restrictions order, interim order or undertaking in respect of the bankrupt,
(b) the court may make a bankruptcy restrictions order in relation to the bankrupt on an application instituted before the annulment,
(c) the Secretary of State may accept a bankruptcy restrictions undertaking offered before the annulment, and
(d) an application for a bankruptcy restrictions order or interim order in respect of the bankrupt may not be instituted after the annulment.][76]

[Registration][77]

[**12** The Secretary of State shall maintain a register of— **A5–36**

(a) bankruptcy restrictions orders,
(b) interim bankruptcy restrictions orders, and
(c) bankruptcy restrictions undertakings.][78]

[74] Added subject to transitional provisions specified in SI 2003/2093 art.7 by Enterprise Act 2002 c. 40 Sch.20 para.1 (April 1, 2004: addition has effect subject to transitional provisions specified in SI 2003/2093 art.7).

[75] Added subject to transitional provisions specified in SI 2003/2093 art.7 by Enterprise Act 2002 c. 40 Sch.20 para.1 (April 1, 2004: addition has effect subject to transitional provisions specified in SI 2003/2093 art.7).

[76] Added subject to transitional provisions specified in SI 2003/2093 art.7 by Enterprise Act 2002 c. 40 Sch.20 para.1 (April 1, 2004: addition has effect subject to transitional provisions specified in SI 2003/2093 art.7).

[77] Added subject to transitional provisions specified in SI 2003/2093 art.7 by Enterprise Act 2002 c. 40 Sch.20 para.1 (April 1, 2004: addition has effect subject to transitional provisions specified in SI 2003/2093 art.7).

[78] Added subject to transitional provisions specified in SI 2003/2093 art.7 by Enterprise Act 2002 c. 40 Sch.20 para.1 (April 1, 2004: addition has effect subject to transitional provisions specified in SI 2003/2093 art.7).

APPENDIX 6

EXTRACTS FROM THE INSOLVENCY RULES 1986

The Insolvency Rules 1986 (SI 1986/1925)

MADE *[10TH NOVEMBER 1986]*

[PART 5A

DEBT RELIEF ORDERS

[5A.24 Application for leave under Company Directors Disqualification Act 1986

A6–01 (1) An application by a person—

(a) in relation to whom a moratorium period under a debt relief order applies, or
(b) in respect of whom a debt relief restrictions order or undertaking is in force, for leave ("the applicant for leave"), under section 11 of the Company Directors Disqualification Act 1986, to act as director of, or to take part or be concerned in the promotion, formation or management of a company, shall be supported by an affidavit complying with this Rule.

(2) The affidavit must identify the company and specify—

(a) the nature of its business or intended business, and the place or places where that business is, or is to be, carried on;
(b) whether it is, or is to be, a private or a public company;
(c) the persons who are, or are to be, principally responsible for the conduct of its affairs (whether as directors, shadow directors, managers or otherwise);
(d) the manner and capacity in which the applicant for leave proposes to take part or be concerned in the promotion or formation of the company or, as the case may be, its management; and
(e) the emoluments and other benefits to be obtained from the directorship.

(3) If the company is already in existence, the affidavit must specify the date of its incorporation and the amount of its nominal and issued share capital; and if not, it must specify the amount, or approximate amount, of its proposed commencing share capital, and the sources from which that capital is to be obtained.

(4) Where the applicant for leave intends to take part or be concerned in the promotion or formation of a company, the affidavit must contain an undertaking by the applicant for leave that he or she will, within not less than 7 days of the company being incorporated, file in court a copy of its memorandum of association and certificate of incorporation under [section 15][1] of the Companies Act.

(5) The court shall fix a venue for the hearing of the application, and shall give notice to the applicant for leave accordingly.][2]

[5A.25 Application for leave under Company Directors Disqualification Act 1986—report of official receiver

A6–02

(1) The applicant for leave shall, not less than 28 days before the date fixed for the hearing, give to the official receiver, notice of the venue, accompanied by copies of the application and the affidavit under Rule 5A.24.

(2) The official receiver may, not less than 14 days before the date fixed for the hearing, file in court a report of any matters which he considers ought to be drawn to the court's attention. A copy of the report shall be sent by him, as soon as reasonably practicable after it is filed, to the applicant for leave.

(3) The applicant for leave may, not later than 7 days before the date of the hearing, file in court a notice specifying any statements in the official receiver's report which he or she intends to deny or dispute.

(4) If he or she gives notice under this paragraph, he or she shall send copies of it, not less than 4 days before the date of the hearing, to the official receiver.

(5) The official receiver may appear on the hearing of the application, and may make representations and put to the applicant for leave such questions as the court may allow.][3]

[5A.26 Application for leave under Company Directors Disqualification Act 1986—court's order on application

A6–03

(1) If the court grants the application for leave under section 11 of the Company Directors Disqualification Act 1986, its order shall specify that which by virtue of the order the applicant has leave to do.

(2) The court may at the same time, having regard to any representations made by the official receiver on the hearing of the application, exercise in relation to the moratorium period or the debt relief order to which the applicant for leave is subject, any power which it has under section 251M.

(3) Whether or not the application is granted, copies of the order shall be sent by the court to the applicant and the official receiver.][4]

[1] Words substituted by Insolvency (Amendment) (No. 2) Rules 2009/2472 rule 15(2) (October 1, 2009: substitution has effect subject to transitional provisions specified in SI 2009/2472 rule 2).

[2] Added by Insolvency (Amendment) Rules 2009/642 Sch.1 para.1 (April 6, 2009).

[3] Added by Insolvency (Amendment) Rules 2009/642 Sch.1 para.1 (April 6, 2009).

[4] Added by Insolvency (Amendment) Rules 2009/642 Sch.1 para.1 (April 6, 2009).

PART VI

BANKRUPTCY

CHAPTER 20

LEAVE TO ACT AS DIRECTOR, ETC.

A6–04 **[6.202A** In this Chapter a reference to a bankrupt includes a reference to a person in respect of whom a bankruptcy restrictions order is in force.][5]

6.203 Application for leave

A6–05 (1) An application by the bankrupt for leave, under section 11 of the Company Directors Disqualification Act 1986, to act as director of, or to take part or be concerned in the promotion, formation or management of a company, shall be supported by an affidavit complying with this Rule.

(2) The affidavit must identify the company and specify—

(a) the nature of its business or intended business, and the place or places where that business is, or is to be, carried on,

(b) whether it is, or is to be, a private or a public company,

(c) the persons who are, or are to be, principally responsible for the conduct of its affairs (whether as directors, shadow directors, managers or otherwise),

(d) the manner and capacity in which the applicant proposes to take part or be concerned in the promotion or formation of the company or, as the case may be, its management, and

(e) the emoluments and other benefits to be obtained from the directorship.

(3) If the company is already in existence, the affidavit must specify the date of its incorporation and the amount of its nominal and issued share capital; and if not, it must specify the amount, or approximate amount, of its proposed commencing share capital, and the sources from which that capital is to be obtained.

(4) Where the bankrupt intends to take part or be concerned in the promotion or formation of a company, the affidavit must contain an undertaking by him that he will, within not less than 7 days of the company being incorporated, file in court a copy of its memorandum of association and certificate of incorporation under [section 15][6] of the Companies Act.

(5) The court shall fix a venue for the hearing of the bankrupt's application, and give notice to him accordingly.

Commencement
Pt 6(20) rule 6.203(1)–(5): December 29, 1986.

[5] Added by Insolvency (Amendment) Rules 2003/1730 Sch.1 Pt 6 para.40 (April 1, 2004).
[6] Words substituted by Insolvency (Amendment) (No. 2) Rules 2009/2472 rule 16(2) (October 1, 2009: substitution has effect subject to transitional provisions specified in SI 2009/2472 rule 2).

6.204 Report of official receiver

A6–06

(1) The bankrupt shall, not less than 28 days before the date fixed for the hearing, give to the official receiver and the trustee notice of the venue, accompanied by copies of the application and the affidavit under Rule 6.203.
(2) The official receiver may, not less than 14 days before the date fixed for the hearing, file in court a report of any matters which he considers ought to be drawn to the court's attention. A copy of the report shall be sent by him, [as soon as reasonably practicable][7] after it is filed, to the bankrupt and to the trustee.
(3) The bankrupt may, not later than 7 days before the date of the hearing, file in court a notice specifying any statements in the official receiver's report which he intends to deny or dispute. If he gives notice under this paragraph, he shall send copies of it, not less than 4 days before the date of the hearing, to the official receiver and the trustee.
(4) The official receiver and the trustee may appear on the hearing of the application, and may make representations and put to the bankrupt such questions as the court may allow.

Commencement
Pt 6(20) rule 6.204(1)–(4): December 29, 1986.

6.205 Court's order on application

A6–07

(1) If the court grants the bankrupt's application for leave under section 11 of the Company Directors Disqualification Act 1986, its order shall specify that which by virtue of the order the bankrupt has leave to do.
(2) The court may at the same time, having regard to any representations made by the trustee on the hearing of the application—
  (a) include in the order provision varying an income payments order [or an income payments agreement][8] already in force in respect of the bankrupt, or
  (b) if no income payments order is in force, make one.
(3) Whether or not the application is granted, copies of the order shall be sent by the court to the bankrupt, the trustee and the official receiver.

Commencement
Pt 6(20) rule 6.205(1)–(3): December 29, 1986.

[CHAPTER 28

BANKRUPTCY RESTRICTIONS ORDER][9]

A6–08

[6.240 In this and the following two Chapters, "Secretary of State" includes the official receiver acting in accordance with paragraph 1(2)(b) of Schedule 4A to the Act.][10]

[7] Word substituted by Insolvency (Amendment) Rules 2009/642 rule 5 (April 6, 2009: substitution has effect subject to transitional provisions specified in SI 2009/642 rule3(1)).
[8] Words inserted by Insolvency (Amendment) Rules 2003/1730 Sch.1 Pt 6 para.41 (April 1, 2004). (Amendment) Rules 2002/1307 rule 8(9) (May 31, 2002)
[9] Added by Insolvency (Amendment) Rules 2003/1730 Sch.1 Pt 6 para.52 (April 1, 2004).
[10] Added by Insolvency (Amendment) Rules 2003/1730 Sch.1 Pt 6 para.52 (April 1, 2004).

[6.241 Application for bankruptcy restrictions order

A6–09 (1) Where the Secretary of State applies to the court for a bankruptcy restrictions order under paragraph 1 of Schedule 4A to the Act, the application shall be supported by a report by the Secretary of State.

(2) The report shall include—

(a) a statement of the conduct by reference to which it is alleged that it is appropriate for a bankruptcy restrictions order to be made; and

(b) the evidence on which the Secretary of State relies in support of the application.

(3) Any evidence in support of an application for a bankruptcy restrictions order provided by persons other than the Secretary of State shall be by way of affidavit.

(4) The date for the hearing shall be no earlier than 8 weeks from the date when the court fixes the venue for the hearing.

(5) For the purposes of hearing an application under this Rule by a registrar, Rule 7.6(1) shall not apply and the application shall be heard in public.][11]

[6.242 Service on the defendant

A6–10 (1) The Secretary of State shall serve notice of the application and the venue fixed by the court on the bankrupt not more than 14 days after the application is made at court.

(2) Service shall be accompanied by a copy of the application, together with copies of the report by the Secretary of State, any other evidence filed with the court in support of the application, and an acknowledgement of service.

(3) The defendant shall file in court an acknowledgement of service of the application indicating whether or not he contests the application not more than 14 days after service on him of the application.

(4) Where the defendant has failed to file an acknowledgement of service and the time period for doing so has expired, the defendant may attend the hearing of the application but may not take part in the hearing unless the court gives permission.][12]

[6.243 The bankrupt's evidence

A6–11 (1) If the bankrupt wishes to oppose the application, he shall within 28 days of the service of the application and evidence of the Secretary of State, file in court any evidence which he wishes the court to take into consideration, and shall serve a copy of such evidence upon the Secretary of State within 3 days of filing it at court.

(2) The Secretary of State shall, within 14 days from receiving the copy of the bankrupt's evidence, file in court any further evidence in reply he wishes the court to take into consideration and shall as soon as reasonably practicable serve a copy of that evidence upon the bankrupt.][13]

[6.244 Making a bankruptcy restrictions order

A6–12 (1) The court may make a bankruptcy restrictions order against the bankrupt, whether or not the latter appears, and whether or not he has filed evidence in accordance with Rule 6.243.

[11] Added by Insolvency (Amendment) Rules 2003/1730 Sch.1 Pt 6 para.52 (April 1, 2004).
[12] Added by Insolvency (Amendment) Rules 2003/1730 Sch.1 Pt 6 para.52 (April 1, 2004).
[13] Added by Insolvency (Amendment) Rules 2003/1730 Sch.1 Pt 6 para.52 (April 1, 2004).

(2) Where the court makes a bankruptcy restrictions order, it shall send two sealed copies to the Secretary of State.
(3) As soon as reasonably practicable after receipt of the sealed copy of the order, the Secretary of State shall send a sealed copy of the order to the bankrupt.][14]

[CHAPTER 29

INTERIM BANKRUPTCY RESTRICTIONS ORDER][15]

[6.245 Application for interim bankruptcy restrictions order

A6–13

(1) Where the Secretary of State applies for an interim bankruptcy restrictions order under paragraph 5 of Schedule 4A to the Act, the court shall fix a venue for the hearing.
(2) Notice of an application for an interim bankruptcy restrictions order shall be given to the bankrupt at least 2 business days before the date set for the hearing unless the court directs otherwise.
(3) For the purposes of hearing an application under this Rule by a registrar, Rule 7.6(1) shall not apply and the application shall be heard in public.][16]

[6.246 The case against the defendant

A6–14

(1) The Secretary of State shall file a report in court as evidence in support of any application for an interim bankruptcy restrictions order.
(2) The report shall include evidence of the bankrupt's conduct which is alleged to constitute the grounds for the making of an interim bankruptcy restrictions order and evidence of matters which relate to the public interest in making the order.
(3) Any evidence by persons other than the Secretary of State in support of an application for an interim bankruptcy restrictions order shall be by way of affidavit.][17]

[6.247 Making an interim bankruptcy restrictions order

A6–15

(1) The bankrupt may file in court any evidence which he wishes the court to take into consideration and may appear at the hearing for an interim bankruptcy restrictions order.
(2) The court may make an interim bankruptcy restrictions order against the bankrupt, whether or not the latter appears, and whether or not he has filed evidence.
(3) Where the court makes an interim bankruptcy restrictions order, it shall send two sealed copies of the order shall be sent, as soon as reasonably practicable, to the Secretary of State.
(4) As soon as reasonably practicable after receipt of the sealed copies of the order, the Secretary of State shall send a copy of the order to the bankrupt.][18]

[14] Added by Insolvency (Amendment) Rules 2003/1730 Sch.1 Pt 6 para.52 (April 1, 2004).
[15] Added by Insolvency (Amendment) Rules 2003/1730 Sch.1 Pt 6 para.52 (April 1, 2004).
[16] Added by Insolvency (Amendment) Rules 2003/1730 Sch.1 Pt 6 para.52 (April 1, 2004).
[17] Added by Insolvency (Amendment) Rules 2003/1730 Sch.1 Pt 6 para.52 (April 1, 2004).
[18] Added by Insolvency (Amendment) Rules 2003/1730 Sch.1 Pt 6 para.52 (April 1, 2004).

[6.248 Application to set aside an interim bankruptcy restrictions order

A6–16 (1) A bankrupt may apply to the court to set aside an interim bankruptcy restrictions order.

(2) An application by the bankrupt to set aside an interim bankruptcy restrictions order shall be supported by an affidavit stating the grounds on which the application is made.

(3) Where a bankrupt applies to set aside an interim bankruptcy restrictions order under paragraph (1), he shall send to the Secretary of State, not less than 7 days before the hearing—

(a) notice of his application;
(b) notice of the venue;
(c) a copy of his application; and
(d) a copy of the supporting affidavit.

(4) The Secretary of State may attend the hearing and call the attention of the court to any matters which seem to him to be relevant, and may himself give evidence or call witnesses.

(5) Where the court sets aside an interim bankruptcy restrictions order two sealed copies of the order shall be sent, as soon as reasonably practicable, to the Secretary of State by the court.

(6) As soon as reasonably practicable after receipt of the sealed copies of the order, the Secretary of State shall send a sealed copy of the order to the bankrupt.][19]

[Chapter 30

Bankruptcy Restrictions Undertaking][20]

[6.249 Acceptance of the bankruptcy restrictions undertaking

A6–17 A bankruptcy restrictions undertaking signed by the bankrupt shall be deemed to have been accepted by the Secretary of State for the purposes of paragraph 9 of Schedule 4A of the Act when the undertaking is signed by the Secretary of State.][21]

[6.250 Notification to the court

A6–18 As soon as reasonably practicable after a bankruptcy restrictions undertaking has been accepted by the Secretary of State, a copy shall be sent to the bankrupt and filed in court and sent to the official receiver if he is not the applicant.][22]

[6.251 Application under paragraph 9(3) of Schedule 4A to the Act to annul a bankruptcy restrictions undertaking

A6–19 (1) An application under paragraphs 9(3)(a) or (b) of Schedule 4A to the Act shall be supported by an affidavit stating the grounds on which it is made.

[19] Added by Insolvency (Amendment) Rules 2003/1730 Sch.1 Pt 6 para.52 (April 1, 2004).
[20] Added by Insolvency (Amendment) Rules 2003/1730 Sch.1 Pt 6 para.52 (April 1, 2004).
[21] Added by Insolvency (Amendment) Rules 2003/1730 Sch.1 Pt 6 para.52 (April 1, 2004).
[22] Added by Insolvency (Amendment) Rules 2003/1730 Sch.1 Pt 6 para.52 (April 1, 2004).

(2) The bankrupt shall give notice of the application and the venue, together with a copy of the affidavit supporting his application to the Secretary of State at least 28 days before the date fixed for the hearing.
(3) The Secretary of State may attend the hearing and call the attention of the court to any matters which seem to him to be relevant, and may himself give evidence or call witnesses.
(4) The court shall send a sealed copy of any order annulling or varying the bankruptcy restrictions undertaking to the Secretary of State and the bankrupt.][23]

[CHAPTER 31

DEBT RELIEF RESTRICTIONS ORDER][24]

[6.252 Interpretation

In this Chapter and in Chapter 32, "Secretary of State" includes the official receiver acting in accordance with paragraph 1(2)(b) of Schedule 4ZB to the Act.][25] **A6–20**

[6.253 Application for debt relief restrictions order

(1) Where the Secretary of State applies to the court for a debt relief restrictions order to be made in relation to a person in respect of whom a debt relief order has been made under paragraph 1 of Schedule 4ZB to the Act, the application shall be supported by a report by the Secretary of State. **A6–21**
(2) The report shall include—

(a) a statement of the conduct by reference to which it is alleged that it is appropriate for a debt relief restrictions order to be made; and
(b) the evidence on which the Secretary of State relies in support of the application.

(3) Any evidence in support of an application for a debt relief restrictions order provided by persons other than the Secretary of State shall be by way of an affidavit.
(4) The date for the hearing shall be no earlier than 8 weeks from the date when the court fixes the venue for the hearing.
(5) For the purposes of hearing an application under this Rule by a registrar, Rule 7.6(1) shall not apply and the application shall be heard in public.][26]

[6.254 Service on the defendant

(1) The Secretary of State shall serve notice of the application and the venue fixed by the court on the debtor not more than 14 days after the application is made at court. **A6–22**
(2) Service shall be accompanied by a copy of the application, together with copies of the report by the Secretary of State, any other evidence filed with the court in support of the application, and an acknowledgement of service.

[23] Added by Insolvency (Amendment) Rules 2003/1730 Sch.1 Pt 6 para.52 (April 1, 2004).
[24] Added by Insolvency (Amendment) Rules 2009/642 rule 47 (April 6, 2009).
[25] Added by Insolvency (Amendment) Rules 2009/642 rule 47 (April 6, 2009).
[26] Added by Insolvency (Amendment) Rules 2009/642 rule 47 (April 6, 2009).

(3) The defendant shall file in court an acknowledgement of service of the application indicating whether or not he contests the application not more than 14 days after service on him of the application.

(4) Where the defendant has failed to file an acknowledgement of service and the time period for doing so has expired, the defendant may attend the hearing of the application but may not take part in the hearing unless the court gives permission.][27]

[6.255 The debtor's evidence

A6–23 (1) If the debtor wishes to oppose the application, he shall within 28 days of the service of the application and evidence of the Secretary of State, file in court any evidence which he wishes the court to take into consideration, and shall serve a copy of such evidence upon the Secretary of State within 3 days of filing it at court.

(2) The Secretary of State shall, within 14 days from receiving the copy of the debtor's evidence, file in court any further evidence in reply he wishes the court to take into consideration and shall as soon as reasonably practicable serve a copy of that evidence upon the debtor.][28]

[6.256 Making a debt relief restrictions order

A6–24 (1) The court may make a debt relief restrictions order against the debtor, whether or not the latter appears and whether or not he has filed evidence in accordance with Rule 6.255.

(2) Where the court makes a debt relief restrictions order, it shall send two sealed copies to the Secretary of State.

(3) As soon as reasonably practicable after receipt of the sealed copy of the order, the Secretary of State shall send a sealed copy of the order to the debtor.][29]

[CHAPTER 32

INTERIM DEBT RELIEF RESTRICTIONS ORDER][30]

[6.257 Application for interim debt relief restrictions order

A6–25 (1) Where the Secretary of State applies for an interim debt relief restrictions order under paragraph 5 of Schedule 4ZB to the Act, the court shall fix a venue for the hearing.

(2) Notice of an application for an interim debt relief restrictions order shall be given to the debtor at least 2 business days before the date set for the hearing unless the court directs otherwise.

(3) For the purposes of hearing an application under this Rule by a registrar, Rule 7.6(1) shall not apply and the application shall be heard in public.][31]

[27] Added by Insolvency (Amendment) Rules 2009/642 rule 47 (April 6, 2009).
[28] Added by Insolvency (Amendment) Rules 2009/642 rule 47 (April 6, 2009).
[29] Added by Insolvency (Amendment) Rules 2009/642 rule 47 (April 6, 2009).
[30] Added by Insolvency (Amendment) Rules 2009/642 rule 47 (April 6, 2009).
[31] Added by Insolvency (Amendment) Rules 2009/642 rule 47 (April 6, 2009).

[6.258 The case against the debtor

A6–26

(1) The Secretary of State shall file a report in court as evidence in support of any application for an interim debt relief restrictions order.
(2) The report shall include evidence of the debtor's conduct which is alleged to constitute the grounds for the making of an interim debt relief restrictions order and evidence of matters which relate to the public interest in making the order.
(3) Any evidence by persons other than the Secretary of State in support of an application for an interim debt relief restrictions order shall be by way of an affidavit.][32]

[6.259 Making an interim debt relief restrictions order

A6–27

(1) The debtor may file in court any evidence which he wishes the court to take into consideration and may appear at the hearing for an interim debt relief restrictions order.
(2) The court may make an interim debt relief restrictions order against the debtor, whether or not the latter appears, and whether or not he has filed evidence.
(3) Where the court makes an interim debt relief restrictions order, as soon as reasonably practicable, it shall send two sealed copies of the order to the Secretary of State.
(4) As soon as reasonably practicable after receipt of the sealed copies of the order, the Secretary of State shall send a copy of the order to the debtor.][33]

[6.260 Application to set aside an interim debt relief restrictions order

A6–28

(1) A person subject to an interim debt relief restrictions order may apply to the court to set the order aside.
(2) An application to set aside an interim debt relief restrictions order shall be supported by an affidavit stating the grounds on which the application is made.
(3) Where an application is made to set aside an interim debt relief restrictions order under paragraph (1), the person making the application shall send to the Secretary of State, not less than 7 days before the hearing—

(a) notice of his application;
(b) notice of the venue;
(c) a copy of his application; and
(d) a copy of the supporting affidavit.

(4) The Secretary of State may attend the hearing and call the attention of the court to any matters which seem to him to be relevant, and may himself give evidence or call witnesses.
(5) Where the court sets aside an interim debt relief restrictions order two sealed copies of the order shall be sent, as soon as reasonably practicable, to the Secretary of State by the court.
(6) As soon as reasonably practicable after receipt of the sealed copies of the order, the Secretary of State shall send a sealed copy of the order to the applicant.][34]

[32] Added by Insolvency (Amendment) Rules 2009/642 rule 47 (April 6, 2009).
[33] Added by Insolvency (Amendment) Rules 2009/642 rule 47 (April 6, 2009).
[34] Added by Insolvency (Amendment) Rules 2009/642 rule 47 (April 6, 2009).

[CHAPTER 33

DEBT RELIEF RESTRICTIONS UNDERTAKING][35]

[6.261 Acceptance of debt relief restrictions undertaking

A6–29 A debt relief restrictions undertaking signed by a person in relation to whom a debt relief order has been made shall be deemed to have been accepted by the Secretary of State for the purposes of paragraph 9 of Schedule 4ZB to the Act when the undertaking is signed by the Secretary of State.][36]

[6.262 Notification

A6–30 As soon as reasonably practicable after a debt relief restrictions undertaking has been accepted by the Secretary of State, a copy shall be sent to the person who offered the undertaking and to the official receiver.][37]

[6.263 Application under paragraph 9(3) of Schedule 4ZB to the Act to annul a debt relief restrictions undertaking.

A6–31 (1) An application under paragraph 9(3)(a) or (b) of Schedule 4ZB to the Act shall be supported by an affidavit stating the grounds on which it is made.

(2) The applicant shall give notice of the application and the venue, together with a copy of the affidavit supporting his application to the Secretary of State at least 28 days before the date fixed for the hearing.

(3) The Secretary of State may attend the hearing and call the attention of the court to matters which seem to him to be relevant, and may himself give evidence or call witnesses.

(4) The court shall send a sealed copy of any order annulling or varying the debt relief restrictions undertaking to the Secretary of State and the applicant.][38] [39]

CHAPTER 1

[GENERAL][40]

[6A.1 The individual insolvency register; the bankruptcy restrictions register

A6–32 (1) The Secretary of State shall create and maintain a register of matters relating to bankruptcies [, debt relief orders][41] and individual voluntary arrangements in accordance with the provisions of this Part (referred to in this Part as "the individual insolvency register").

[35] Added by Insolvency (Amendment) Rules 2009/642 rule 47 (April 6, 2009).
[36] Added by Insolvency (Amendment) Rules 2009/642 rule 47 (April 6, 2009).
[37] Added by Insolvency (Amendment) Rules 2009/642 rule 47 (April 6, 2009).
[38] Added by Insolvency (Amendment) Rules 2009/642 rule 47 (April 6, 2009).
[39] Added by Insolvency (Amendment) Rules 2003/1730 Sch.1 Pt 7 para.53 (April 1, 2004).
(Amendment) Rules 2003/1730 Sch.1 Pt 7 para.53 (April 1, 2004).
[40] Added by Insolvency (Amendment) Rules 2003/1730 Sch.1 Pt 7 para.53 (April 1, 2004).
[41] Words inserted by Insolvency (Amendment) Rules 2009/642 rule 48(a) (April 6, 2009).

[(2) The register—

(a) referred to in paragraph 12 of Schedule 4A to the Act (referred to in this Part as "the bankruptcy restrictions register"), and
(b) of the matters specified in paragraphs (b) and (c) of section 251W (referred to in this Part as "the debt relief restrictions register"), shall be maintained in accordance with the provisions of this Part.][42]

(3) In this Part the "registers" means the registers referred to in paragraphs (1) and (2).
(4) The registers shall be open to public inspection on any business day between the hours of 9.00 am and 5.00 pm.
(5) Where an obligation to enter information onto, or delete information from, the registers arises under this Part, that obligation shall be performed as soon as is reasonably practicable after it arises.][43]

CHAPTER 2

[INDIVIDUAL INSOLVENCY REGISTER][44]

[6A.2 Entry of information onto the individual insolvency register—individual voluntary arrangements

(1) The Secretary of State shall enter onto the individual insolvency register— **A6–33**

(a) as regards any voluntary arrangement other than a voluntary arrangement under section 263A any information—

(i) that was required to be held on the register of individual voluntary arrangements maintained by the Secretary of State immediately prior to the coming into force of this Rule and which relates to a voluntary arrangement which has not been completed or has not terminated on or before the date on which this Rule comes into force; or
(ii) that is sent to him in pursuance of Rule 5.29 or Rule 5.34; and

(b) as regards any voluntary arrangement under section 263A of which notice is given to him pursuant to Rule 5.45—

(i) the name and address of the debtor;
(ii) the date on which the arrangement was approved by the creditors; and
(iii) the court in which the official receiver's report has been filed [; and,][45]

[(c) in the circumstances set out in (a) and (b) above, the debtor's gender, date of birth and any name by which he was known, not being the name in which he has entered into the voluntary arrangement.][46]

(2) This Rule is subject to Rule 6A.3.][47]

[42] Substituted by Insolvency (Amendment) Rules 2009/642 rule 48(b) (April 6, 2009).
[43] Added by Insolvency (Amendment) Rules 2003/1730 Sch.1 Pt. 7 para.53 (April 1, 2004).
[44] Added by Insolvency (Amendment) Rules 2003/1730 Sch.1 Pt. 7 para.53 (April 1, 2004).
[45] Added by Insolvency (Amendment) Rules 2005/527 rule 41 (April 1, 2005).
[46] Added by Insolvency (Amendment) Rules 2005/527 rule 41 (April 1, 2005).
[47] Added by Insolvency (Amendment) Rules 2003/1730 Sch.1 Pt. 7 para.53 (April 1, 2004).

[6A.3 Deletion of information from the individual insolvency register—individual voluntary arrangements

A6–34 The Secretary of State shall delete from the individual insolvency register all information concerning an individual voluntary arrangement where—

(a) he receives notice under Rule 5.30(5) or Rule 5.46(4) of the making of a revocation order in respect of the arrangement; or

(b) he receives notice under Rule 5.34(3) or Rule 5.50(3) of the full implementation or termination of the arrangement.][48]

[6A.4 Entry of information onto the individual insolvency register—bankruptcy orders

A6–35 (1) The Secretary of State shall enter onto the individual insolvency register any information that was required to be held on the register of bankruptcy orders maintained by the Secretary of State immediately prior to the coming into force of this Rule and which relates to a bankrupt who—

(a) has not received his discharge on or before the date that this Rule comes into force; or

(b) was discharged in the period of 3 months immediately preceding the coming into force of this Rule.

(2) Where the official receiver receives pursuant to Rule 6.34 or Rule 6.46 a copy of a bankruptcy order from the court, he shall cause to be entered onto the individual insolvency register—

(a) the matters listed in Rules 6.7 and 6.38 with respect to the debtor as they are stated in the bankruptcy petition;

(b) the date of the making of the bankruptcy order;

(c) the name of the court that made the order; and

(d) the court reference number as stated on the order.

(3) The official receiver shall cause to be entered onto the individual insolvency register as soon as reasonably practicable after receipt by him, the following information—

(a) the name, gender, occupation (if any) and date of birth of the bankrupt;

(b) the bankrupt's last known address;

[(c) where a bankruptcy order or debt relief order has been made in the period of six years immediately prior to the day of the latest bankruptcy order made against the bankrupt (excluding for these purposes any bankruptcy order that was annulled or any debt relief order that was revoked), the date of whichever is the latest of them;][49]

(d) any name by which the bankrupt was known, not being the name in which he was adjudged bankrupt;

(e) the address of any business carried on by the bankrupt and the name in which that business was carried on if carried on in a name other than the name in which the bankrupt was adjudged bankrupt;

(f) the name and address of any insolvency practitioner appointed to act as trustee in bankruptcy;

(g) the address at which the official receiver may be contacted; and

(h) the automatic discharge date under section 279.

[48] Added by Insolvency (Amendment) Rules 2003/1730 Sch.1 Pt 7 para.53 (April 1, 2004).

[49] Substituted by Insolvency (Amendment) Rules 2009/642 rule 49 (April 6, 2009).

(4) Where pursuant to Rule 6.176(5) or Rule 6.215(8) the official receiver receives a copy of an order suspending the bankrupt's discharge he shall cause to be entered onto the individual insolvency register—

(a) the fact that such an order has been made; and
(b) the period for which the discharge has been suspended or that the relevant period has ceased to run until the fulfilment of conditions specified in the order.

(5) Where pursuant to Rule 6.216(7) a copy of a certificate certifying the discharge of an order under section 279(3) is received by the official receiver, he shall cause to be entered onto the individual insolvency register—

(a) that the court has discharged the order made under section 279(3); and
(b) the new date of discharge of the bankrupt, but where the order discharging the order under section 279(3) is subsequently rescinded by the court, the official receiver shall cause the register to be amended accordingly.

(6) Where a bankrupt is discharged from bankruptcy under section 279(1) or section 279(2), the official receiver shall cause the fact and date of such discharge to be entered in the individual insolvency register.
(7) This Rule is subject to Rule 6A.5.][50]

[6A.5 Deletion of information from the individual insolvency register—bankruptcy orders

[The][51] **A6–36**

Secretary of State shall delete from the individual insolvency register all information concerning a bankruptcy where—

(a) the bankruptcy order has been annulled pursuant to section 261(2)(a), 261(2)(b), 263D(3) or section 282(1)(b);
(b) the bankrupt has been discharged from the bankruptcy and a period of 3 months has elapsed from the date of discharge;
(c) the bankruptcy order is annulled pursuant to section 282(1)(a) and he has received notice of the annulment under Rule 6.213(2); or
(d) the bankruptcy order is rescinded by the court under section 375 and the Secretary of State has received a copy of the order made by the court.][52]

[6A.5A Entry of information onto the individual insolvency register—debt relief orders

(1) This Rule is subject to Rule 6A.5B. **A6–37**
(2) The official receiver shall cause to be entered onto the individual insolvency register as soon as reasonably practicable after the making of a debt relief order the following information relating to the order or to the debtor in respect of whom it has been made—

(a) as they are stated in the debtor's application—

(i) the name, gender, occupation (if any) and date of birth of the debtor;
(ii) the debtor's last known address;

[50] Added by Insolvency (Amendment) Rules 2003/1730 Sch.1 Pt 7 para.53 (April 1, 2004).
[51] Words repealed by Insolvency (Amendment) Rules 2004/584 rule 44 (April 1, 2004).
[52] Added by Insolvency (Amendment) Rules 2003/1730 Sch.1 Pt 7 para.53 (April 1, 2004).

(iii) the name or names in which he carries or has carried on business, if other than his true name; and

(iv) the nature of his business and the address or addresses at which he carries or has carried it on and whether alone or with others;

(b) the date of the making of the debt relief order;

(c) the reference number of the order;

(d) the date of the end of the moratorium period; and

(e) where a bankruptcy order or a debt relief order has been made in the period of six years immediately prior to the date of the latest debt relief order made against the debtor (excluding for these purposes any bankruptcy order that was annulled or any debt relief order that was revoked), the date of whichever is the latest of them.

(3) Provided that information concerning a debt relief order has not been validly deleted under Rule 6A.5B, the official receiver shall also cause to be entered on the register in relation to the order—

(a) where the moratorium period is terminated early, the fact that such has happened, the date of early termination and whether the early termination is on revocation of the debt relief order or by virtue of any other enactment;

(b) where the moratorium period is extended, the fact that such has happened, the date on which the extension was made, its duration and the date of the new anticipated end of the moratorium period; or

(c) where the debtor is discharged from all qualifying debts, the date of such discharge.][53]

[6A.5B Deletion of information from the individual insolvency register—debt relief orders

A6–38 The Secretary of State shall delete from the individual insolvency register all information concerning a debt relief order where—

(a) the debt relief order has been revoked, or

(b) the debtor has been discharged from his qualifying debts, and

a period of 3 months has elapsed from the date of revocation or discharge.][54]

CHAPTER 3

[BANKRUPTCY RESTRICTIONS REGISTER][55]

[6A.6 Bankruptcy restrictions orders and undertakings—entry of information onto the bankruptcy restrictions register

A6–39 (1) Where an interim bankruptcy restrictions order or a bankruptcy restrictions order is made against a bankrupt, the Secretary of State shall enter onto the bankruptcy restrictions register—

53 Added by Insolvency (Amendment) Rules 2009/642 rule 50 (April 6, 2009).

54 Added by Insolvency (Amendment) Rules 2009/642 rule 50 (April 6, 2009).

55 Added by Insolvency (Amendment) Rules 2003/1730 Sch.1 Pt 7 para.53 (April 1, 2004).

[(a) the name, gender, occupation (if any) and date of birth of the bankrupt;
(aa) the bankrupt's last known address;][56]
(b) a statement that an interim bankruptcy restrictions order or, as the case may be, a bankruptcy restrictions order has been made against him;
(c) the date of the making of the order, the court and the court reference number; and
(d) the duration of the order.

(2) Where a bankruptcy restrictions undertaking is given by a bankrupt, the Secretary of State shall enter onto the bankruptcy restrictions register—

[(a) the name, gender, occupation (if any) and date of birth of the bankrupt;
(aa) the bankrupt's last known address;][57]
(b) a statement that a bankruptcy restrictions undertaking has been given;
(c) the date of the acceptance of the bankruptcy restrictions undertaking by the Secretary of State; and
(d) the duration of the bankruptcy restrictions undertaking.

(3) This Rule is subject to Rule 6A.7.][58]

[6A.7 Deletion of information from the bankruptcy restrictions register—bankruptcy restrictions orders and undertakings

In any case where an interim bankruptcy restrictions order or a bankruptcy restrictions order is made or a bankruptcy restrictions undertaking has been accepted, the Secretary of State shall remove from the bankruptcy restrictions register all information regarding that order or, as the case may be, undertaking after— **A6–40**

(a) receipt of notification that the order or, as the case may be, the undertaking has ceased to have effect; or
(b) the expiry of the order or, as the case may be, undertaking.][59]

CHAPTER 3A

[DEBT RELIEF RESTRICTIONS REGISTER][60]

[6A.7A Debt relief restrictions orders and undertakings—entries of information onto the debt relief restrictions register

(1) This Rule is subject to Rule 6A.7B. **A6–41**
(2) Where an interim debt relief restrictions order or a debt relief restrictions order is made against a debtor, the Secretary of State shall enter onto the debt relief restrictions register—

[56] Rule 6A.6(1)(a)–(aa) substituted for rule 6A.6(1)(a) by Insolvency (Amendment) Rules 2004/584 rule 45(a) (April 1, 2004).
[57] Rule 6A.6(2)(a)–(aa) substituted for rule 6A.6(2)(a) by Insolvency (Amendment) Rules 2004/584 rule 45(b) (April 1, 2004).
[58] Added by Insolvency (Amendment) Rules 2003/1730 Sch.1 Pt 7 para.53 (April 1, 2004).
[59] Added by Insolvency (Amendment) Rules 2003/1730 Sch.1 Pt 7 para.53 (April 1, 2004).
[60] Added by Insolvency (Amendment) Rules 2009/642 rule 51 (April 6, 2009).

(a) the name, gender, occupation (if any) and date of birth of the debtor;
(b) the debtor's last known address;
(c) a statement that an interim debt relief restrictions order or, as the case may be, a debt relief restrictions order has been made against him;
(d) the date of the making of the order and the order reference number; and
(e) the duration of the order.

(3) Where a debt relief restrictions undertaking is given by a debtor, the Secretary of State shall enter onto the debt relief restrictions register—

(a) the name, gender, occupation (if any) and date of birth of the debtor;
(b) the debtor's last known address;
(c) a statement that a debt relief restrictions undertaking has been given;
(d) the date of the acceptance of the debt relief restrictions undertaking by the Secretary of State and reference number of the undertaking; and
(e) the duration of the debt relief restrictions undertaking.][61]

[6A.7B Deletion of information from the debt relief restrictions register—debt relief restrictions order and undertakings

A6–42 In any case where an interim debt relief restrictions order or a debt relief restrictions order is made or a debt relief restrictions undertaking has been accepted, the Secretary of State shall remove from the debt relief restrictions register all information regarding that order or, as the case may be, undertaking after—

(a) receipt of notification that the order or, as the case may be, undertaking has ceased to have effect; or
(b) the expiry of the order or, as the case may be, undertaking.][62]

CHAPTER 4

[RECTIFICATION OF REGISTERS][63]

[6A.8 Rectification of the registers

A6–43 (1) Where the Secretary of State becomes aware that there is any inaccuracy in any information maintained on the registers he shall rectify the inaccuracy as soon as reasonably practicable.

[(2) Where the Secretary of State receives notice of the date of the death of a person in respect of whom information is held on any of the registers, he shall cause the fact and date of the person's death to be entered onto the individual insolvency register and, as the case may be, the bankruptcy restrictions register or the debt relief restrictions register.][64]][65]

[61] Added by Insolvency (Amendment) Rules 2009/642 rule 51 (April 6, 2009).
[62] Added by Insolvency (Amendment) Rules 2009/642 rule 51 (April 6, 2009).
[63] Added by Insolvency (Amendment) Rules 2003/1730 Sch.1 Pt 7 para.53 (April 1, 2004).
[64] Substituted by Insolvency (Amendment) Rules 2009/642 rule 52 (April 6, 2009).
[65] Added by Insolvency (Amendment) Rules 2003/1730 Sch.1 Pt 7 para.53 (April 1, 2004).

THE THIRD GROUP OF PARTS

PART 7

COURT PROCEDURE AND PRACTICE

CHAPTER 8

APPEALS IN INSOLVENCY PROCEEDINGS

7.47 Appeals and reviews of court orders (winding up)

A6–44

(1) Every court having jurisdiction under the Act to wind up companies may review, rescind or vary any order made by it in the exercise of that jurisdiction.
(2) An appeal from a decision made in the exercise of that jurisdiction by a county court or by a registrar of the High Court lies to a single judge of the High Court; and an appeal from a decision of that judge on such an appeal lies, with the leave of that judge or the Court of Appeal, to the Court of Appeal.
(3) A county court is not, in the exercise of its jurisdiction to wind up companies, subject to be restrained by the order of any other court, and no appeal lies from its decision in the exercise of that jurisdiction except as provided by this Rule.
(4) Any application for the rescission of a winding-up order shall be made within 7 days after the date on which the order was made.

Commencement
Pt 7(8) rule 7.47(1)–(4): December 29, 1986.

7.48 Appeals in bankruptcy

A6–45

(1) In bankruptcy proceedings, an appeal lies at the instance of the Secretary of State from any order of the court made on an application for the rescission or annulment of a bankruptcy order, or for a bankrupt's discharge.
(2) In the case of an order made by a county court or by a registrar of the High Court, the appeal lies to a single judge of the High Court; and an appeal from a decision of that judge on such an appeal lies, with the leave of that judge or the Court of Appeal, to the Court of Appeal.

Commencement
Pt 7(8) rule 7.48(1)–(2): December 29, 1986.

[7.49 Procedure on appeal

A6–46

(1) Subject as follows, the procedure and practice of the Supreme Court relating to appeals to the Court of Appeal apply to appeals in insolvency proceedings.
(2) In relation to any appeal to a single judge of the High Court under section 375(2) (individual insolvency) or Rule 7.47(2) above (company insolvency), any reference in the CPR to the Court of Appeal is replaced by a reference to that judge and any reference to the registrar of civil appeals is replaced by a reference to the registrar of the High Court who deals with insolvency proceedings of the kind involved.

(3) In insolvency proceedings, the procedure under RSC Order 59 (appeals to the Court of Appeal) is by ordinary application and not by application notice.][66]

Commencement
Pt 7(8) rule 7.49(1)–(3): December 29, 1986.

7.50 Appeal against decision of Secretary of State or official receiver

A6–47 [(1) An appeal under the Act or the Rules against a decision of the Secretary of State or the official receiver shall be brought within 28 days of the notification of the decision.

(2) In respect of a decision under Rule 6.214A(5)(b), an appeal shall be brought within 14 days of the notification of the decision.][67]

Commencement
Pt 7(8) rule 7.50: December 29, 1986.

[66] Substituted by Insolvency (Amendment) (No. 2) Rules 1999/1022 Sch.1 para.4 (April 26, 1999).
[67] Existing rule 7.50 is renumbered as rule 7.50(1) and rule 7.50(2) is inserted by Insolvency (Amendment) Rules 2003/1730 Sch.1 Pt 8 para.58 (April 1, 2004).

Appendix 7

EXTRACTS FROM THE PRACTICE DIRECTION— INSOLVENCY PROCEEDINGS

PART 1

1. GENERAL

1.1 In this Practice Direction: **A7–01**

(1) 'The Act' means the Insolvency Act 1986 and includes the Act as applied to limited liability partnerships by the Limited Liability Partnerships Regulations 2001;
(2) 'The Insolvency Rules' means the rules for the time being in force and made under s.411 and s.412 of the Act in relation to insolvency proceedings;
(3) 'CPR' means the Civil Procedure Rules and 'CPR' followed by a Part or rule by number means the Part or rule with that number in those Rules;
(4) 'RSC' followed by an Order by number means the Order with that number set out in Schedule 1 to the CPR;
(5) 'Insolvency proceedings' means any proceedings under the Act, the Insolvency Rules, the Administration of Insolvent Estates of Deceased Persons Order 1986 (S.I. 1986 No. 1999), the Insolvent Partnerships Order 1986 (S.I. 1986 No. 2124), the Insolvent Partnerships Order 1994 (S.I. 1994 No 2421) or the Limited Liability Partnerships Regulations 2001
(6) References to a 'company' shall include a limited liability partnership and references to a 'contributory' shall include a member of a limited liability partnership.

. . .

16A. BANKRUPTCY RESTRICTIONS ORDERS

Making the application

16A.1 An application for a bankruptcy restrictions order is made as an ordinary application in the bankruptcy. **A7–02**

16A.2 The application must be made within one year beginning with the date of the bankruptcy order unless the court gives permission for the application to be made after that period. The one year period does not run while the bankrupt's discharge has been suspended under section 279(3) of the Insolvency Act 1986.

16A.3 An application for a bankruptcy restrictions order may be made by the Secretary of State or the Official Receiver ('the Applicant') The application must be supported by a report which must include:

(a) a statement of the conduct by reference to which it is alleged that it is appropriate for a bankruptcy restrictions order to be made; and
(b) the evidence relied on in support of the application (r. 6.241 Insolvency Rules 1986).

16A.4 The report is treated as if it were an affidavit (r. 7 9(2) Insolvency Rules 1986) and is prima facie evidence of any matter contained in it (r. 7 9(3))

16A.5 The application may be supported by evidence from other witnesses which may be given by affidavit or (by reason of r. 7.57(5) Insolvency Rules 1986) by witness statement verified by a statement of truth.

16A.6 The court will fix a first hearing which must be not less than 8 weeks from the date when the hearing is fixed (r. 6 241(4) Insolvency Rules 1986).

16A.7 Notice of the application and the venue fixed by the court must be served by the Applicant on the bankrupt not more than 14 days after the application is made. Service of notice must be accompanied by a copy of the application together with the evidence in support and a form of acknowledgment of service.

16A.8 The bankrupt must file in court an acknowledgment of service not more than 14 days after service of the application on him, indicating whether or not he contests the application. If he fails to do so he may attend the hearing of the application but may not take part in the hearing unless the court gives permission.

Opposing the Application

A7–03 **16A.9** If the bankrupt wishes to oppose the application, he must within 28 days of service on him of the application and the evidence in support (or such longer period as the court may allow) file in court and (within three days thereof) serve on the Applicant any evidence which he wishes the court to take into consideration. Such evidence should normally be in the form of an affidavit or a witness statement verified by a statement of truth.

16A.10 The Applicant must file any evidence in reply within 14 days of receiving the evidence of the bankrupt (or such longer period as the court may allow) and must serve it on the bankrupt as soon as reasonably practicable.

Hearings

A7–04 **16A.11** Any hearing of an application for a bankruptcy restrictions order must be in public (r. 6.241(5) Insolvency Rules 1986). The hearing will generally be before the registrar or district judge in the first instance who may:

(1) adjourn the application and give directions;
(2) make a bankruptcy restrictions order; or
(3) adjourn the application to the judge.

Making a bankruptcy restrictions order

A7–05 **16A.12** When the court is considering whether to make a bankruptcy restrictions order, it must not take into account any conduct of the bankrupt prior to 1 April 2004 (art. 7 Enterprise Act (Commencement No 4 and Transitional Provisions and Savings) Order 2003).

16A.13 The court may make a bankruptcy restrictions order in the absence of the bankrupt and whether or not he has filed evidence (r. 6.244 Insolvency Rules 1986).

16A.14 When a bankruptcy restrictions order is made the court must send two sealed copies of the order to the Applicant (r. 6.244(2) Insolvency Rules 1986), and as soon as reasonably practicable after receipt, the Applicant must send one sealed copy to the bankrupt (r. 6.244(3)).

16A.15 A bankruptcy restrictions order comes into force when it is made and must specify the date on which it will cease to have effect, which must be between two and 15 years from the date on which it is made.

Interim bankruptcy restriction orders

16A.16 An application for an interim bankruptcy restrictions order may be made any time between the institution of an application for a bankruptcy restrictions order and the determination of that application (Sch 4A para. 5 Insolvency Act 1986). The application is made as an ordinary application in the bankruptcy. **A7–06**

16A.17 The application must be supported by a report as evidence in support of the application (r.6.246(1) Insolvency Rules 1986) which must include evidence of the bankrupt's conduct which is alleged to constitute the grounds for making an interim bankruptcy restrictions order and evidence of matters relating to the public interest in making the order.

16A.18 Notice of the application must be given to the bankrupt at least two business days before the date fixed for the hearing unless the court directs otherwise (r.6.245).

16A.19 Any hearing of the application must be in public (r.6.245).

16A.20 The court may make an interim bankruptcy restrictions order in the absence of the bankrupt and whether or not he has filed evidence (r.6.247).

16A.21 The bankrupt may apply to the court to set aside an interim bankruptcy restrictions order. The application is made by ordinary application in the bankruptcy and must be supported by an affidavit or witness statement verified by a statement of truth stating the grounds on which the application is made (r.6.248(2)).

16A.22 The bankrupt must send the Secretary of State, not less than 7 days before the hearing, notice of his application, notice of the venue, a copy of his application and a copy of the supporting affidavit. The Secretary of State may attend the hearing and call the attention of the court to any matters which seem to him to be relevant, and may himself give evidence or call witnesses.

16A.23 Where the court sets aside an interim bankruptcy restrictions order, two sealed copies of the order must be sent by the court, as soon as reasonably practicable, to the Secretary of State.

16A.24 As soon as reasonably practicable after receipt of sealed copies of the order, the Secretary of State must send a sealed copy to the bankrupt.

Bankruptcy restrictions undertakings

16A.25 Where a bankrupt has given a bankruptcy restrictions undertaking, the Secretary of State must file a copy in court and send a copy to the bankrupt as soon as reasonably practicable (r. 6.250). **A7–07**

16A.26 The bankrupt may apply to annul a bankruptcy restrictions undertaking. The application is made as an ordinary application in the bankruptcy and must be supported by an affidavit or witness statement verified by a statement of truth stating the grounds on which it is made.

16A.27 The bankrupt must give notice of his application and the venue together with a copy of his affidavit in support to the Secretary of State at least 28 days before the date fixed for the hearing.

16A.28 The Secretary of State may attend the hearing and call the attention of the court to any matters which seem to him to be relevant and may himself give evidence of call witnesses.

16A.29 The court must send a sealed copy of any order annulling or varying the bankruptcy restrictions undertaking to the Secretary of State and the bankrupt.

PART 4

17. APPEALS IN INSOLVENCY PROCEEDINGS

A7–08

17.1 This Part shall come into effect on 2nd May 2000 and shall replace and revoke Paragraph 17 of, and be read in conjunction with the Practice Direction—Insolvency Proceedings which came into effect on 26th April 1999 as amended.

17.2

(1) An appeal from a decision of a County Court (whether made by a District Judge or a Circuit Judge) or of a Registrar of the High Court in insolvency proceedings ('a first appeal') lies to a Judge of the High Court pursuant to s 375(2) of the Act and Insolvency Rules 7.47(2) and 7.48(2) (as amended by s 55 of the Access to Justice Act 1999).

(2) The procedure and practice for a first appeal are governed by Insolvency Rule 7.49 which imports the procedure and practice of the Court of Appeal The procedure and practice of the Court of Appeal is governed by CPR Part 52 and its Practice Direction, which are subject to the provisions of the Act, the Insolvency Rules and this Practice Direction: see CPR Part 52 rule 1(4).

(3) A first appeal (as defined above) does not include an appeal from a decision of a Judge of the High Court.

17.3

(1) Section 55 of the Access to Justice Act 1999 has amended s. 375(2) of the Act and Insolvency Rules 7.47(2) and 7.48(2) so that an appeal from a decision of a Judge of the High Court made on a first appeal lies, with the permission of the Court of Appeal, to the Court of Appeal.

(2) An appeal from a Judge of the High Court in insolvency proceedings which is not a decision on a first appeal lies, with the permission of the Judge or of the Court of Appeal, to the Court of Appeal (see CPR Part 52 rule 3);

(3) The procedure and practice for appeals from a decision of a Judge of the High Court in insolvency proceedings (whether made on a first appeal or not) are also governed by Insolvency Rule 7.49 which imports the procedure and practice of the Court of Appeal as stated at Paragraph 17.2(2) above.

17.4 CPR Part 52 and its Practice Direction and Forms apply to appeals from a decision of a Judge of the High Court in insolvency proceedings.

17.5 An appeal from a decision of a Judge of the High Court in insolvency proceedings requires permission as set out in Paragraph 17.3(1) and (2) above.

17.6 A first appeal is subject to the permission requirement in CPR Part 52, rule 3

17.7 Except as provided in this Part, CPR Part 52 and its Practice Direction and Forms do not apply to first appeals, but Paragraphs 17.8 to 17.23 inclusive of this Part apply only to first appeals.

17.8 Interpretation:

(a) the expressions "appeal court", "lower court", "appellant", "respondent" and "appeal notice" have the meanings given in CPR Part 52.1(3);

(b) "Registrar of Appeals" means—

(i) in relation to an appeal filed at the Royal Courts of Justice in London, a registrar in bankruptcy; and

(ii) in relation to an appeal filed in a district registry, a district judge of that district registry.

(c) "appeal date" means the date fixed by the appeal court for the hearing of the appeal or the date fixed by the appeal court upon which the period within which the appeal will be heard commences.

17.9 An appellant's notice and a respondent's notice shall be in Form PDIP 1 and PDIP 2 set out in the Schedule hereto.

17.10

(1) An appeal from a decision of a registrar in bankruptcy must be filed at the Royal Courts of Justice in London.

(2) An appeal from a decision of a district judge sitting in a district registry may be filed—

(a) at the Royal Courts of Justice in London; or

(b) in that district registry.

(3) An appeal from a decision made in a country court may be filed—

(a) at the Royal Courts of Justice in London; or

(b) in the Chancery district registry for the area within which the county court exercises jurisdiction.

(There are Chancery district registries of the High Court at Birmingham, Bristol, Caernarfon, Cardiff, Leeds, Liverpool, Manchester, Mold, Newcastle upon Tyne and Preston. The county court districts that each district registry covers are set out in Schedule 1 to the Civil Courts Order 1983.)

17.11

(1) Where a party seeks an extension of time in which to file an appeal notice it must be requested in the appeal notice and the appeal notice should state the reason for the delay and the steps taken prior to the application being made; the court will fix a date for the hearing of the application and notify the parties of the date and place of hearing;

(2) The appellant must file the appellant's notice at the appeal court within—

(a) such period as may be directed by the lower court; or

(b) where the court makes no such direction, 21 days after the date of the decision of the lower court which the appellant wishes to appeal.

(3) Unless the appeal court orders otherwise, an appeal notice must be served by the appellant on each respondent—

(a) as soon as practicable; and

(b) in any event not later than 7 days, after it is filed.

17.12

(1) A respondent may file and serve a respondent's notice.
(2) A respondent who wishes to ask the appeal court to uphold the order of the lower court for reasons different from or additional to those given by the lower court must file a respondent's notice.
(3) A respondent's notice must be filed within—
   (a) such period as may be directed by the lower court; or
   (b) where the court makes no such direction, 14 days after the date on which the respondent is served with the appellant's notice.
(4) Unless the appeal court orders otherwise a respondent's notice must be served by the respondent on the appellant and any other respondent—
   (a) as soon as practicable; and
   (b) in any event not later than 7 days, after it is filed

17.13

(1) An application to vary the time limit for filing an appeal notice must be made to the appeal court
(2) The parties may not agree to extend any date or time limit set by—
   (a) this Practice Direction; or
   (b) an order of the appeal court or the lower court.

17.14 Unless the appeal court or the lower court orders otherwise an appeal shall not operate as a stay of any order or decision of the lower court.

17.15 An appeal notice may not be amended without the permission of the appeal court.

17.16 A Judge of the appeal court may strike out the whole or part of an appeal notice where there is compelling reason for doing so

17.17

(1) In relation to an appeal the appeal court has all the powers of the lower court.
(2) The appeal court has power to—
   (a) affirm, set aside or vary any order or judgment made or given by the lower court;
   (b) refer any claim or issue for determination by the lower court;
   (c) order a new trial or hearing;
   (d) make a costs order
(3) The appeal court may exercise its powers in relation to the whole or part of an order of the lower court.

17.18

(1) Every appeal shall be limited to a review of the decision of the lower court.
(2) Unless it orders otherwise, the appeal court will not receive—
   (a) oral evidence; or
   (b) evidence which was not before the lower court.
(3) The appeal court will allow an appeal where the decision of the lower court was—
   (a) wrong; or
   (b) unjust because of a serious procedural or other irregularity in the proceedings in the lower court
(4) The appeal court may draw any inference of fact which it considers justified on the evidence
(5) At the hearing of the appeal a party may not rely on a matter not contained in his appeal notice unless the appeal court gives permission

17.19 The following applications shall be made to a Judge of the appeal court:

(1) for injunctions pending a substantive hearing of the appeal;

(2) for expedition or vacation of the hearing date of an appeal;

(3) for an order striking out the whole or part of an appeal notice pursuant to Paragraph 17 16 above;

(4) for a final order on paper pursuant to Paragraph 17.22(8) below

17.20

(1) All other interim applications shall be made to the Registrar of Appeals in the first instance who may in his discretion either hear and determine it himself or refer it to the Judge

(2) An appeal from a decision of a Registrar of Appeals lies to a Judge of the appeal court and does not require the permission of either the Registrar of Appeals or the Judge.

17.21 The procedure for interim applications is by way of ordinary application (see Insolvency Rule 12.7 and Sch 4, Form 7.2).

17.22 The following practice applies to all first appeals to a Judge of the High Court whether filed at the Royal Courts of Justice in London, or filed at one of the other venues referred to in Paragraph 17.10 above:

(1) on filing an appellant's notice in accordance with Paragraph 17.11(2) above, the appellant must file:

(a) two copies of the appeal notice for the use of the court, one of which must be stamped with the appropriate fee, and a number of additional copies equal to the number of persons who are to be served with it pursuant to Paragraph 17.22(4) below;

(aa) an approved transcript of the judgment of the lower court or, where there is no official record of the judgment, a document referred to in paragraph 5.12 of the Practice Direction supplementing CPR Part 52.

(b) a copy of the order under appeal; and

(c) an estimate of time for the hearing

(2) the above documents may be lodged personally or by post and shall be lodged at the address of the appropriate venue listed below:

(a) if the appeal is to be heard at the Royal Courts of Justice in London the documents must be lodged at Room 110, Thomas More Building, The Royal Courts of Justice, Strand, London WC2A 2LL;

(b) if the appeal is to be heard in Birmingham, the documents must be lodged at the District Registry of the Chancery Division of the High Court, 33 Bull Street, Birmingham B4 6DS;

(c) if the appeal is to be heard in Bristol the documents must be lodged at the District Registry of the Chancery Division of the High Court, Third Floor, Greyfriars, Lewins Mead, Bristol, BSI 2NR;

(ca) if the appeal is to be heard in Caernarfon the documents must be lodged at the district registry of the Chancery Division of the High Court, Hanberis Road, Caernarfon, H55 2DF;

(d) if the appeal is to be heard in Cardiff the documents must be lodged at the District Registry in the Chancery Division of the High Court, First Floor, 2 Park Street, Cardiff, CF10 1ET;

(e) if the appeal is to be heard in Leeds the documents must be lodged at the District Registry of the Chancery Division of the High Court, The Court House, 1 Oxford Row, Leeds LS1 3BG;

(f) if the appeal is to be heard in Liverpool the documents must be lodged at the District Registry of the Chancery Division of the High Court, Liverpool Combined Court Centre, Derby Square, Liverpool L2 1XA;

(g) if the appeal is to be heard in Manchester the documents must be lodged at the District Registry of the Chancery Division of the High Court, Courts of Justice, Crown Square, Manchester, M60 9DJ;

(ga) if the appeal is to be heard in Mold the documents must be lodged at the district registry of the Chancery Division of the High Court, Law Courts, Civic Centre, Mold, CH7 1AE;

(h) if the appeal is to be heard at Newcastle Upon Tyne the documents must be lodged at the District Registry of the Chancery Division of the High Court, The Law Courts, Quayside, Newcastle Upon Tyne NE1 3LA;

(i) if the appeal is to be heard in Preston the documents must be lodged at the District Registry of the Chancery Division of the High Court, The Combined Court Centre, Ringway, Preston PR1 2LL.

(3) if the documents are correct and in order the court at which the documents are filed will fix the appeal date and will also fix the place of hearing. That court will send letters to all the parties to the appeal informing them of the appeal date and of the place of hearing and indicating the time estimate given by the appellant. The parties will be invited to notify the court of any alternative or revised time estimates. In the absence of any such notification the estimate of the appellant will be taken as agreed. The court will also send to the appellant a document setting out the court's requirement concerning the form and content of the bundle of documents for the use of the Judge Not later than 7 days before the appeal date the bundle of documents must be filed by the appellant at the address of the relevant venue as set out in sub-paragraph 17.22(2) above and a copy of it must be served by the appellant on each respondent

(4) the appeal notice must be served on all parties to the proceedings in the lower court who are directly affected by the appeal. This may include the Official Receiver, liquidator or trustee in bankruptcy.

(5) the appeal notice must be served by the appellant or by the legal representative of the appellant and may be effected by:

(a) any of the methods referred to in CPR Part 6 rule 2; or

(b) with permission of the court, an alternative method pursuant to CPR Part 6 rule 8.

(6) service of an appeal notice shall be proved by a Certificate of Service in accordance with CPR Part 6 rule 10 (CPR Form N215) which must be filed at the relevant venue referred to at Paragraph 17.22(2) above immediately after service.

(7) Subject to sub-paragraphs (7A) and (7B), the appellant's notice must be accompanied by a skeleton argument and a written chronology of events relevant to the appeal. Alternatively, the skeleton argument and chronology may be included in the appellant's notice. Where the skeleton argument and chronology are so included they do not form part of the notice for the purposes of rule 52.8

(7A) Where it is impracticable for the appellant's skeleton argument and chronology to accompany the appellant's notice they must be filed and served on all respondents within 14 days of filing the notice.

(7B) An appellant who is not represented need not file a skeleton argument nor a written chronology but is encouraged to do so since these documents may be helpful to the court.

(8) where an appeal has been settled or where an appellant does not wish to continue with the appeal, the appeal may be disposed of on paper without a hearing. It may be dismissed by consent but the appeal court will not make an order allowing an appeal unless it is satisfied that the decision of the lower court was wrong Any consent order signed by each party or letters of consent from each party must be lodged not later than 24 hours before the date fixed for the hearing of the appeal at the address of the appropriate venue as set out in sub-paragraph 17.22(2) above and will be dealt with by the Judge of the appeal court. Attention is drawn to paragraph 4.4(4) of the Practice Direction to CPR Part 44 regarding costs where an order is made by consent without attendance.

17.23 Only the following paragraphs of the Practice Direction to CPR Part 52, with any necessary modifications, shall apply to first appeals: 5.10 to 5.20 inclusive

17.24 [*This paragraph is not reproduced here.*]

17.25 [*This paragraph is not reproduced here.*]

THE SCHEDULE

[*The schedule contains forms which are not reproduced here.*] **A7–09**

APPENDIX 8

GUIDELINES FOR APPLICATIONS FOR PERMISSION TO ACT NOTWITHSTANDING DISQUALIFICATION

PERMISSION TO ACT

APPLICATIONS FOR PERMISSION TO ACT FOLLOWING A DISQUALIFICATION ORDER OR A DISQUALIFICATION UNDERTAKING

A8–01 The Secretary of State has a duty to appear on such applications and to call the attention of the court to any matters which seem to be relevant and may give evidence or call witnesses. The guidance below applies whether it is a disqualification order that has been made against you or your disqualification undertaking has been accepted.

General

A8–02 It is important that if you intend making an application for permission to act that it should be able to be considered by the Court at the same time and by the same Judge who made the disqualification order against you or before your period of disqualification has commenced.

The Secretary of State considers that an applicant for permission to act under a disqualification order or under a disqualification undertaking should:

- support the application to the court with full and particularised affidavit evidence which is supported by appropriate exhibits, and
- serve such evidence on the Secretary of State in sufficient time so as to give the Secretary of State a proper opportunity to consider it fully before the hearing of the application.

The stance taken by the Secretary of State on each application, including whether to file evidence and/or oppose the application can only be decided having regard to the facts and circumstances of each individual case.

Evidence required

A8–03 The Secretary of State considers that the information set out below should normally be included in your evidence. This list is not intended to be comprehensive and it is only a guideline. In some cases further information will be necessary and in others some of the matters listed may not be relevant.

If, having received your evidence, the Secretary of State believes that further information is needed, the Secretary of State will, as far as possible and if time allows, draw such matters to your attention. This should provide you with an opportunity to supplement your evidence and enable the Court to deal with your application with the minimum of delay and cost to you. To the extent that you do not deal with matters raised by the Secretary of State, the Court will be invited to take that into account as a factor against granting permission to act.

The information which the Secretary of State considers should normally be included in your evidence is as follows:

A. Reasons for your disqualification

A copy of the disqualification order made against you (and any available judgment) or a copy of the disqualification undertaking and any schedule thereto.

B. Details of the company in relation to which you want permission to act as a director.

The details should include:

1. The company's name, date of incorporation, registered office, paid up share capital, directors, accountants and auditor;
2. A detailed description of your current role and involvement with the company to date;
3. Your interests in the company, including share ownership;
4. An up-to-date company search, giving full details of the information filed in respect of the company with the Registrar or Companies, together with your confirmation that all statutory returns have been filed and are up to date;
5. A description of the company's performance together with copies of professionally prepared accounts of the company for the past two years if the company has been trading for that length of time and in any event up-to-date management accounts and any available financial budgets or forecasts;
6. Details of the management of the company: details of board members; board meetings and an overall description of the management structure of the company's affairs; an account of management roles and responsibilities including your role to date (if any);
7. Details of the principal activities undertaken by the company during the past [two] years and details of any proposed activities;
8. Details of any banking or other financial facilities of the company and of all securities over assets of the company and by way of guarantee for the indebtedness of the company to its bank and others;
9. Details confirming that payments to all creditors are up to date and that all returns have been made to the relevant taxing bodies;
10. Details of all actual or pending proceedings against the company, whether civil or criminal. Details of any investigations into the company's affairs by, for instance, the Inland Revenue, DTI, Office of Fair Trading or other governmental agency.

If you seek permission to act in relation to a Limited Liability Partnership equivalent information, as set out above, should be provided.

C. Your proposed role and personal factors

- A description of your proposed involvement as a director or in the management, etc, of the company and why there is a need for you to be so involved, including all the circumstances relied on by you in support of your assertion that that involvement is important to you and/or the company.
- Details of your existing (if any) and proposed remuneration, emoluments and other benefits from the company, including a copy of any service agreement or contract of employment.

- Details of any other proceedings or investigations, either civil, criminal, regulatory or by a professional body that are being, or have been, taken against you personally either in relation to any limited company (or partnership) or which otherwise bear on your application.

D. Protection of the public

Details of all steps taken and procedures put in place to protect the public including those to avoid a repetition of the acts and omissions which founded the making of the disqualification order or disqualification undertaking.

The Insolvency Service cannot give you legal advice. This guidance is designed to provide a general introduction for those seeking permission of the Court to act as a director notwithstanding their disqualification. It is not a full and authoritative statement of the law. It is not intended to provide a substitute for taking proper professional advice. The Insolvency Service cannot accept responsibility for any inaccuracies in this guidance.[1]

[1] The authors thank the Insolvency Service for permission to reproduce this guidance.

APPENDIX 9

FORMS OF ORDERS AND UNDERTAKINGS

DRAFT DISQUALIFICATION ORDER

IN THE HIGH COURT OF JUSTICE Claim No: [ ]

CHANCERY DIVISION **A9–01**

COMPANIES COURT

IN THE MATTER OF [ ] LTD

AND IN THE MATTER OF THE COMPANY DIRECTORS DISQUALIFICATION ACT 1986

MR[S] JUSTICE [ ]
[ ] DAY THE [ ] DAY OF [ ] 20 [ ]

BETWEEN:—

THE SECRETARY OF STATE FOR BUSINESS INNOVATION AND SKILLS

Claimant

AND

[ ]

Defendant

ORDER

UPON the trial of the Claimant's claim herein

AND UPON HEARING Counsel for the Claimant and for the Defendant

IT IS ORDERED AS FOLLOWS:

1. Pursuant to Sections 1 and 6 of the Company Directors Disqualification Act 1986:
   (a) the Defendant shall not be a director of a company, act as receiver of a company's property or in any way, whether directly or indirectly, be concerned or take part in the promotion, formation or management of a company, unless (in each case) he has the permission of the Court, and
   (b) the Defendant shall not act as an insolvency practitioner

   for a period of [ ] years and it is ordered that the period of disqualification shall begin [at the end of the period of [21] days beginning with [ ].] [at the end of [ ] day of [ ] [20].]
2. The Defendant do pay to the Claimant the Claimant's costs of these proceedings on the standard basis to be subject to detailed assessment if not agreed.

DRAFT ORDER FOR LEAVE TO ACT NOTWITHSTANDING DISQUALIFICATION

IN THE HIGH COURT OF JUSTICE
CHANCERY DIVISION
COMPANIES COURT

Claim No: [ ]

A9–02

IN THE MATTER OF [ ] LIMITED

AND IN THE MATTER OF THE COMPANY DIRECTORS DISQUALIFICATION ACT 1986

MR[S] JUSTICE [ ]
[ ]DAY THE [ ] DAY OF [ ] 20[10]

BETWEEN

THE SECRETARY OF STATE FOR
BUSINESS, INNOVATION AND SKILLS

Claimant

and

[ ]

Defendant

ORDER

UPON the Court having ordered on [ ] that the Defendant be disqualified pursuant to section 6 of the Company Directors Disqualification Act 1986 ("the Act") for a period of [ ] years ("the Disqualification Order")

UPON the application by the Defendant for leave pursuant to section 17 of the Act

AND UPON hearing Counsel for the Claimant and for the Defendant

AND UPON reading the evidence

IT IS ORDERED THAT:—

1. notwithstanding the Disqualification Order, the Defendant be permitted to act as a director or designated member of and to be concerned and take part in the management of each of the companies and LLPs as set out in the Schedule hereto ("the Entities") until [ ] (or further order in the meantime) for so long as and provided the conditions set out below are each complied with or met for the period of this interim leave, in respect of each of the Entities:

   (i) Income tax and VAT returns shall be prepared and filed on time with Her Majesty's Revenue and Customs and the Entity shall pay VAT, PAYE, NIC and Corporation Tax as and when due;

   (ii) [ ] shall remain as a director of each of the Entities which is a company and a designated member of each of the Entities which is a LLP;

   (iii) [ ] shall remain auditors of each of the Entities;

   (iv) provision of a copy of this Order in compliance with paragraph 2 below shall have taken place

   AND in the event of any such condition not being met or ceasing to be met in relation to any Entity then the interim leave to act in relation to such Entity shall thereupon cease with immediate effect save that in the event of the condition set out in paragraph (ii) ceasing to be met such interim leave shall cease at the expiry of the period of 14 days commencing the day after the day when such condition is not met.

2. the Defendant shall by [ ] on [ ] day [ ] [ ] [20] provide a copy of this order to [ ] and to the auditors to each Entity and each director (in the case of each company) and each designated member (in the case of an LLP) of each Entity (other than the Defendant).
3. General liberty to either party to apply.
4. the Defendant shall pay the costs of the Claimant on the standard basis to be subject of detailed assessment if not agreed.

Schedule 1

The Companies and LLPs

	Name	**Registration Number**

FORM OF DISQUALIFICATION UNDERTAKING

Warning: This is an important legal document. If you are in any doubt about signing it you should obtain legal or professional advice. **A9–03**

IN RE [name of lead company]

I. [**NAME**] of [**ADDRESS**], hereby undertake to the Secretary of State for Trade and Industry on the basis set out in the schedule attached to this disqualification undertaking, that in accordance with section 1A of the CDDA 1 WILL NOT for a period of [ ] years.

(a) *be a director of a company, act as receiver of a company's property or in any way whether directly or indirectly be concerned or take part in the promotion formation or management of a company unless (in each case) I have the leave of the court nor*

(b) *act as an insolvency practitioner.*

The scope and effect of the disqualification undertaking that I hereby give has been explained to me in the information provided by the Insolvency Service with the notice dated [ ]

In particular I understand that if I act in contravention of the above disqualification undertaking

1) I may be prosecuted for a criminal offence (Section 13 CDDA) and/or
2) I may be personally responsible for all the relevant debts of a company (Section 15 CDDA).

I confirm that before signing this undertaking I have had the opportunity of obtaining legal or professional advice on its effect.

Signed

Dated this day of

Accepted by

....

Chief Examiner

This day of

Note: The period of disqualification commences at the end of 21 days beginning with the day that the disqualification undertaking was accepted by the Secretary of State for Trade and Industry, that is Day Month Year

SCHEDULE OF UNFIT CONDUCT TO THE DISQUALIFICATION UNDERTAKING GIVEN BY [insert name of defendant]

For the purposes solely of the CDDA and for any other purposes consequential to the giving of a disqualification undertaking. I do not dispute the following matters:

- I was a director of [Limited]
- Which went into [liquidation/administration/administrative receivership] on [date]
- With assets of £ . . . .
- Liabilities of £ . . . .
- A deficiency as regards creditors in excess of £ . . . .
- And share capital of £ . . . .
- Making a total deficiency of £ . . . .

MATTERS OF UNFITNESS

(Insert summary of misconduct e.g.:

1. I paid inadequate attention to and had inadequate regard for my duties and responsibilities as director and wrongly abdicated my responsibilities as such director to [y].
2. I permitted [X Ltd] to fail to make VAT returns as required by law in the periods after [date] and permitted another director, [y], to implement a deliberate policy of not paying VAT.
3. I permitted [X Ltd] to trade at the risk of creditors, and in particular the Crown, from [date], during which period the deficiency to HM Customs & Excise increased by approximately £[ ].
4. I failed to ensure a Statement of Affairs was filed in accordance with section 47 Insolvency Act 1986.)

DRAFT BANKRUPTCY RESTRICTIONS ORDER

IN THE [HIGH COURT OF JUSTICE] [COUNTY COURT] No. [ ] of 20[ ] **A9–04**

IN BANKRUPTCY
RE: [*FULL NAME OF BANKRUPT/FORMER BANKRUPT]*
RE: BANKRUPTCY RESTRICTIONS

MR[S] [REGISTRAR/DISTRICT JUDGE] [*NAME*]
[ ]DAY THE [] DAY OF [ ] 20[]

BETWEEN

[THE OFFICIAL RECEIVER]
[THE SECRETARY OF STATE FOR BUSINESS INNOVATION AND SKILLS]
Applicant

–and–

[*FULL NAME*]
Respondent

UPON THE APPLICATION of [the Official Receiver] [the Deputy Official Receiver] [the Secretary of State for Business, Innovation and Skills] ("the Applicant") by application notice dated [*DATE*] for the making of a Bankruptcy Restrictions Order against the Respondent

AND UPON HEARING [Counsel] [the solicitor] [for] [the Applicant] [the [Deputy] Official Receiver] and [Counsel] [the Solicitor] [for] [*NAME*] ("the Respondent") [in person]

[AND the Respondent being neither present nor represented but the Court being satisfied of the service upon him of the said application notice]

AND UPON READING the evidence

THE COURT HEREBY MAKES a Bankruptcy Restrictions Order against [*NAME*], the Respondent, pursuant to section 281A of and Schedule 4A to the Insolvency Act 1986 which Order shall cease to have effect at the end of [*Date*]

AND IT IS ORDERED THAT [the [Respondent] do pay [the Applicant's] costs of the application on the standard basis, [subject to detailed assessment if not agreed] [summarily assessed in the sum of £[ ], to be paid within [ ] days]

[there be no order as to costs]

NOTES TO THE RESPONDENT

1. This Order subjects you to certain restrictions whilst it is in force.
2. The restrictions to which you are subject under this Order include (but are not limited to) the following:

(a) you must not obtain credit of the prescribed amount (currently £500) or more, either alone or with another person, from anyone without first informing that person that you are subject to a bankruptcy restrictions order (section 360(1)(a) Insolvency Act 1986);
(b) You must not carry on business (directly or indirectly) in a different name from that in which you were made bankrupt without telling all those with whom you do business the name in which you were made bankrupt (section 360(1)(b) Insolvency Act 1986);
(c) you must not act as a director of a company or (directly or indirectly) take part or be concerned in its promotion, formation or management, or act as a member of a limited liability partnership or (directly or indirectly) take part or be concerned in its promotion, formation or management, unless you are granted permission by the Court (section 11(1) Company Directors Disqualification Act 1986; Limited Liability Partnerships Regulations 2001). If you act in breach of this prohibition you commit a criminal offence and will also be personally responsible for any of the debts of the company or limited liability partnership in question.
(d) you must not act as an insolvency practitioner (sections 389 and 390(5) Insolvency Act 1986) nor as a receiver or manager of the property of a company on behalf of debenture holders (section 31 Insolvency Act 1986).

3. If you act in breach of any of the above prohibitions you will commit a criminal offence. You may be prosecuted and, if found guilty, receive a criminal penalty such as a fine or imprisonment.
4. Paragraph 2 above does not contain a complete list of everything you must not do. A wide range of restrictions on holding office is imposed under various statutes and statutory instruments. Other restrictions include (but are not limited to) being a Member of Parliament, a member of a local authority, a trustee of a charity or pension scheme and membership of, or appointment to, various other agencies, tribunals and bodies. In addition, if you are a member of a professional body this Order may have an effect on that membership.
5. It is your sole responsibility to ensure that you comply with the relevant restrictions which may apply from time to time.
6. If you are in any doubt as to how this Order affects you, you should take your own independent professional advice.

FORM OF BANKRUPTCY RESTRICTIONS UNDERTAKING

IN THE [ ] COUNTY COURT **No. of ____**

[NAME]
IN BANKRUPTCY

A9–05

Warning: This is an important legal document. If you are in any doubt about signing it you should obtain legal or professional advice.

THE INSOLVENCY ACT 1986

I, **[NAME]** of **[ADDRESS]** agree to a bankruptcy restrictions undertaking as governed by the Insolvency Act 1986 and hereby undertake to the Secretary of State for Business, Innovation and Skills, on the basis set out in the schedule of unfit conduct attached to this bankruptcy restrictions undertaking, that I will comply with the bankruptcy restrictions contained in the Insolvency Act 1986, the Company Directors Disqualification Act 1986 and any bankruptcy restrictions contained in other legislation or elsewhere, including but not limited to the governing rules of organisations, for a period of **[PERIOD]** years.

The scope and effect of the undertaking that I hereby give has been explained to me in the information provided by the Insolvency Service with the notice (BRN) sent to me and dated [DATE].

In particular, I understand that if I act in contravention of the above undertaking

1) I may be prosecuted for a criminal offence (in particular under Section 11 of the Company Directors Disqualification Act 1986, Sections 31 and 360 of the Insolvency Act 1986) and/or
2) I may be personally responsible for all the relevant debts of a company (Section 15 of the Company Directors Disqualification Act 1986).

I confirm that before signing this undertaking I have had the opportunity of obtaining legal or professional advice on its effect.

Signed:...

Date:

The above undertaking is hereby accepted by the Secretary of State for Business, Innovation and Skills.

....
Chief Examiner
For and on behalf of the Secretary of State for Business, Innovation and Skills.

Date:

Note: The period of restriction begins on the day that the bankruptcy restrictions undertaking is accepted by the Secretary of State for Business, Innovation and Skills and will last for **[PERIOD]** years from that date and the period of restriction will end on ____________.

SCHEDULE OF UNFIT CONDUCT TO THE BANKRUPTCY RESTRICTIONS UNDERTAKING GIVEN BY [NAME]

For the purposes solely of the bankruptcy restrictions undertaking given under the Insolvency Act 1986, I do not dispute the following.

- A Bankruptcy Order was made against me on **[DATE]**.
- The unpledged assets in my bankruptcy estate total £**[AMOUNT]**.
- The unsecured liabilities in my bankruptcy estate total £**[AMOUNT]**.
- The total deficiency in my bankruptcy estate is £**[AMOUNT]**.

UNFIT CONDUCT

(Insert summary of misconduct e.g.:

Between [ ] and [ ] I neglected my business affairs in a manner which had a material effect upon my insolvency, in that:

- During this time I was trading as a public house licensee at three separate public houses. I was solely responsible for the debts of my trading entities and was the sole name on the tenancy agreement and lease with the premises' owners for all three premises.
- Between [DATE] and [DATE] I allowed five separate third parties to trade at will and incur liabilities in my name from all my three public houses at various times, while failing to exercise proper control of their activities. In particular I failed to ensure that I had in place adequate financial records and systems to enable me to determine the financial performance of my business at this time. In so doing I incurred liabilities of approximately £[ ], of which the Official Receiver has been able to verify £[ ], which I could not repay. In respect of one of the public houses I had disagreements with the manager and then left him to run that public house for approximately six months without any supervision.
- The stated proportion of my liabilities directly attributable to this period during which I neglected my business affairs (of £[ ] represents [ ]% of my deficit at the date of my bankruptcy. The amount verified by the Official Receiver of £[ ] would represent [ ]% of my deficiency.)

FORM OF DEBT RELIEF RESTRICTIONS ORDER

No [ ] of 20[ ] **A9–06**

IN THE HIGH COURT OF JUSTICE

CHANCERY DIVISION

[Re DEBT RELIEF RESTRICTIONS]

RE: [FULL NAME OF DEBTOR]
IN THE MATTER OF THE INSOLVENCY ACT 1986

MR REGISTRAR [ ]
[ ] THE [ ] DAY OF [ ] 20[ ]

BETWEEN:

THE OFFICIAL RECEIVER/
THE SECRETARY OF STATE FOR BUSINESS INNOVATION AND SKILLS

Applicant

-and-

[NAME]

Respondent

ORDER

UPON THE APPLICATION of the Official Receiver ("the Applicant") by application notice dated [DATE] for the making of a Debt Relief Restrictions Order against the Respondent

AND UPON HEARING Counsel for the Applicant and for the Respondent

AND UPON READING the evidence

THE COURT HEREBY MAKES a Debt Relief Restrictions Order against [FULL NAME] pursuant to section 251V of and Schedule 4ZB to the Insolvency Act 1986 which Order shall cease to have effect at the end of [DATE]

AND IT IS ORDERED that there be no order as to costs.

NOTES TO THE RESPONDENT

1. This Order subjects you to certain restrictions whilst it is in force.
2. The restrictions to which you are subject under this Order include (but are not limited to) the following:
   (a) you must not obtain credit of the prescribed amount or more (as at 6 April 2009 the prescribed amount was £500) either alone or with another person, from anyone without first informing that person that you are subject to a debt relief restrictions order and (if applicable) a moratorium by reason of a debt relief order (section 251S Insolvency Act 1986);
   (b) you must not carry on business (directly or indirectly) in a different name from that in which the debt relief order was made against you without telling all those with whom you do business the name in which the debt relief order against you was made (section 251S Insolvency Act 1986);
   (c) you must not act as a director of a company or (directly or indirectly) take part or be concerned in its promotion, formation or management, or act as a member of a limited liability partnership or (directly or indirectly) take part or be concerned in its promotion, formation or management, unless you are granted permission by the Court (section 11 Company Directors Disqualification Act 1986; Limited Liability Partnerships Regulations 2001). If you act in breach of this prohibition you commit a criminal offence and will also be personally responsible for any of the debts of the company or limited liability partnership in question;
   (d) you must not act as an insolvency practitioner (sections 389 and 390 Insolvency Act 1986) nor as a receiver or manager of the property of a company (section 31 Insolvency Act 1986).
3. If you act in breach of any of the above prohibitions you will commit a criminal offence. You may be prosecuted and, if found guilty, receive a criminal penalty such as a fine or imprisonment.
4. Paragraph 2 above does not contain a complete list of everything you must not do. A range of restrictions on holding office is imposed under various statutes and statutory instruments. Other restrictions include (but are not limited to) Member of Parliament and other bodies. In addition, if you are a member of a professional body this Order may have an effect on that membership.
5. If you are in any doubt as to how this Order affects you, you should take your own independent professional advice.

DEBT RELIEF RESTRICTIONS UNDERTAKING

[NAME]

DEBT RELIEF RESTRICTIONS

Warning: This is an important legal document. If you are in any doubt about signing it you should obtain legal or professional advice.

THE INSOLVENCY ACT 1986

A9–07

[Note at the time of writing the precise form of DRRU that would be acceptable was under consideration by the Insolvency Service. The draft below is by way of an indication of the sort of contents that the authors consider likely such form will contain]

I, **[NAME]** of **[ADDRESS]** agree to a debt relief restrictions undertaking as governed by the Insolvency Act 1986 and hereby undertake to the Secretary of State for Business, Innovation and Skills, on the basis set out in the schedule of unfit conduct attached to this debt relief restrictions undertaking, that I will comply with the debt relief restrictions contained in the Insolvency Act 1986, the Company Directors Disqualification Act 1986 and any debt relief restrictions contained in other legislation or elsewhere, including but not limited to the governing rules of organisations, for a period of **[PERIOD]** years.

The scope and effect of the undertaking that I hereby give has been explained to me in the information provided by the Insolvency Service with the notice [ ] sent to me and dated [DATE].

In particular, I understand that if I act in contravention of the above undertaking

1) I may be prosecuted for a criminal offence (in particular under Section 11 of the Company Directors Disqualification Act 1986, Sections 31 and 251S of the Insolvency Act 1986) and/or
2) I may be personally responsible for all the relevant debts of a company (Section 15 of the Company Directors Disqualification Act 1986).

I confirm that before signing this undertaking I have had the opportunity of obtaining legal or professional advice on its effect.

Signed:...

Date:

The above undertaking is hereby accepted by the Secretary of State for Business, Innovation and Skills.

....

Chief Examiner
For and on behalf of the Secretary of State for Business, Innovation and Skills.

Date:
Note: The period of restriction begins on the day that the debt relief restrictions undertaking is accepted by the Secretary of State for Business, Innovation and Skills and will last for **[PERIOD]** years from that date and the period of restriction will end on ____________.

SCHEDULE OF UNFIT CONDUCT TO THE BANKRUPTCY RESTRICTIONS UNDERTAKING GIVEN BY [NAME]

For the purposes solely of the debt relief restrictions undertaking given under the Insolvency Act 1986, I do not dispute the following.

- A Debt Relief Order was made against me on **[DATE]**.
- The amount of the debts to which I was subject at the date of the application (including any interest, penalty or other sum that had become payable in relation to that debt on or before that date) totalled **£[AMOUNT]**.
- The total amount of qualifying debts at the application date was **£[AMOUNT]**.
- [My income and assets at the date of application were [ ] and [ ] respectively].

UNFIT CONDUCT

[DETAIL UNFIT CONDUCT AGREED FOR THE PURPOSES OF THE UNDERTAKING]

APPENDIX 10

DRAFT CARECRAFT STATEMENT

IN THE HIGH COURT OF JUSTICE NO. [ ] **A10–01**

CHANCERY DIVISION

COMPANIES COURT

IN THE MATTER OF [COMPANY NAME] LIMITED/PLC

AND IN THE MATTER OF THE COMPANY DIRECTORS DISQUALIFICATION ACT 1986

BETWEEN:

THE SECRETARY OF STATE FOR BUSINESS INNOVATION AND SKILLS

Claimant

–AND–

(1) [NAME]
(2) [NAME]
(3) [NAME]

Defendants

STATEMENT OF FACTS NOT IN DISPUTE FOR THE PURPOSES OF A "CARECRAFT" SETTLEMENT AS BETWEEN THE SECRETARY OF STATE AND THE FIRST AND SECOND DEFENDANTS

1. Introduction

A10–02

1.1 On the [date] the Secretary of State issued proceedings under Section 6 of the Company Directors Disqualification Act 1986 ("the 1986 Act") for Disqualification Orders against the Defendants in the terms of Section 1(1) of the 1986 Act.

1.2 Subject to the Court, the Secretary of State and the First and Second Defendants ("Mr. [name]" and "Mr. [name]") are willing to dispose of the proceedings by way of the shortened form of procedure sanctioned in *Re Carecraft Construction Co. Limited* [1994] 1 W.L.R. 172 as clarified by the decision of the Court of Appeal in *Secretary of State for Trade and Industry v Rogers* [1996] 4 All E.R. 854. The proceedings as against the Third Defendant ("Mr. [name]") are continuing to trial, the [hearing of which is due to start on [date]].

1.3 The purpose of this Statement is to identify, in relation to the allegations of unfitness relied on by the Secretary of State, the core material facts which (solely for the purposes of the Company Directors Disqualification Act 1986 and for any other purposes consequential to the making of a disqualification order), are not disputed by Mr. [name] and Mr. [name]. Solely for the said purposes, none of the facts set out below are disputed and it is acknowledged that there is affidavit evidence verifying each of the same.

1.4 The Secretary of State submits that by reference to the undisputed facts the conduct of Mr. [name] and Mr. [name] as directors of [company name Limited/PLC] ("the Company") has been such as to make each of them unfit to be concerned in the management of a company and that, accordingly, the Court is bound (by Section 6(1) of the 1986 Act) to make a Disqualification Order against him. It is further submitted by the Secretary of State that the conduct of Mr. [name] and Mr. [name] is such that Disqualification Orders [for a period of/within the range of [ ] to [ ]] years (which, subject to the Court, have been agreed by the parties) are appropriate.

1.5 Mr. [name] and Mr. [name] accept that, by reference to the facts which are not in dispute, the Court can be satisfied as to their unfitness to be concerned in the management of a company, and that it would be appropriate to make Orders against them [for a period of/within the range of [ ] to [ ] years. They also agree that if, pursuant to this Statement, there is a "Carecraft" disposal of these proceedings, then there should additionally be Orders that they should pay the Secretary of State's costs of these proceedings [in the sum of £].

1.6 The Secretary of State, Mr. [name] and Mr. [name] all agree that, if the Court is unwilling to approve a "Carecraft" disposal of these proceedings, then no further reference may be made by any party to this Statement, or to the fact of any proposed "Carecraft" settlement or to any admissions made herein, during the course of these proceedings. The parties agree that, in any event, they will jointly apply to the Court for a direction that a different Judge should hear the contested trial.

1.7 In the event of Disqualification Orders being made by reference to this Statement, the Secretary of State and Mr. [name] and Mr. [name] agree that they will jointly apply for a direction that this Statement be annexed to the Court's judgment.

1.8 The structure of the remainder of this Statement is as follows:

1.8.1 Section 2 contains the general background information relevant to the allegations of unfitness made against Mr. [name] and Mr. [name].

1.8.2 Sections 3, 4, 5 and 6 deal, respectively with each of the four allegations of unfitness that are made in subparagraphs [ ] of the affidavit sworn herein by Mr. [name of Claimant's deponent] on the [date].

1.8.3 Section 7 deals with an allegation of unfitness which is not contained in affidavit evidence but which has recently come to the attention of the Secretary of State. The Secretary of State and the First Defendant invite the Court to take these facts and matters into account when considering whether to approve the Carecraft disposal of these proceedings.

1.8.4 Section 8 sets out certain additional facts which the Court may wish to take into account by way of mitigation. The Secretary of State and Mr. [name] have agreed that no further facts (other than those set out in Section 8) may be adduced at the Carecraft hearing by way of mitigation.

2. General background

A10–03 2.1 The Company was incorporated and started trading in [date]. Its business was [details].

2.2 Mr. [name] and Mr. [name] founded the Company and remained its principal directors throughout. The only other director was Mr. [name] who was on the board from [date] until [date].

2.3 Mr. [name] and Mr. [name] each owned 300 of the 650 issued £1 ordinary shares in the Company.

2.4 Though Mr. [name] and Mr. [name] shared responsibility for the overall management of the Company, Mr. [name] was additionally in charge of accounting records whilst Mr. [name] had particular responsibility for arranging contracts and preparing estimates.

2.5 On the [date] Joint Administrative Receivers were appointed pursuant to the terms of a debenture dated the [date] in favour of [name].

2.6 A Statement of Affairs for the Company as at [date] sworn by Mr. [name] shows an estimated deficiency as regards creditors of [ ] this figure includes trade creditors amounting to [ ] and sums due to the Crown totalling [ ].

2.7 In the balance sheet included in the last set of audited accounts for the Company (being those for the year ending [date] the Company's excess of assets over liabilities amounted to [ ]. Accordingly, the deterioration in the net asset position on the Company going into receivership was [ ] according to the Statement of Affairs. The Statement of Affairs, however, does not make allowance for work in progress, or bad debt relief for VAT purposes.

3. Trading at the risk of the creditors

3.1 The allegation, contained in paragraph [ ] of Mr. [name of the Claimant's deponent]'s affidavit, is that Mr. [name] and Mr. [name]: **A10–04**

> ". . . caused the Company to continue to trade after [date] when they should have known that the company had no prospect of paying creditors."

3.2 In relation to the period from [date] to [date] and to the extent disclosed by the undisputed facts set out in paragraph 3.3 below, Mr. [name] and Mr. [name] admit this allegation.

3.3 The core facts material to this Allegation are the following:

3.3.1 The audited accounts for each of the years ending [date], [date] and [date] and the draft balance sheet for the year ending [date] showed that the Company had Net Current Liabilities as follows:

Year ending 31 August	Net Current Liabilities (£s)
[year]	[ ]
[year]	[ ]
[year]	[ ]
[year]	[ ]

3.3.2 As shown in paragraph 2.7 above, in the final period of trading (from the [date] being the date of the last audited accounts, to the appointment of the Joint Administrative Receivers on the [date] the Company's net asset position on going into receivership showed a deterioration of [ ] from a net asset position of [ ] to a deficit of [ ].

3.3.3 Between [date] and [date], [number] creditors took proceedings against the Company to enforce payment of debts amounting to [ ]. Of these, some were paid, leaving a net balance as at the date of the Statement of Affairs of[ ].

3.3.4 As from [date] the Company was subject to constant pressure from its bank to reduce the borrowing on its overdraft. This pressure was exacerbated by delays in payment by its own trade debtors from [date] onwards.

3.3.5 Between [date] and [date] the Company drew some [no] cheques (to the total value of approximately [ ] which were dishonoured. (Further details are to be found at paragraph 6.3.1. below).

3.3.6 By the date of the appointment of the Joint Administrative Receivers, amounts totalling [ ] for VAT and [ ] for PAYE and NIC were stated in the Statement of Affairs to be due to the relevant Crown departments. These sums included liabilities which dated back to [date].

3.3.7 In late [date] Mr. [name] and Mr. [name] consulted [name] about the continued viability of the Company following the voluntary liquidation of a major creditor. It was on [name] contacting the bank that the Receivers were appointed.

4. Crown debts

A10–05 4.1 The allegation, contained in paragraph [ ] of Mr. [name]'s affidavit, is that Mr. [name]:

"caused the Company to retain monies due to the Crown which at the date of the receivership was approximately [ ], thereby providing them with involuntary finance for the Company's continued trading".

4.2 To the extent disclosed by the undisputed facts set out in paragraph 4.3 below (and save that the amount shown in the Statement of Affairs as being due to the Crown was [ ] rather than [ ] as alleged) Mr. [name] and Mr. [name] admit this Allegation.

4.3 The core facts material to this Allegation are the following:

4.3.1 The Statement of Affairs shows the sum of [ ] as being then due to HM Customs & Excise in respect of unpaid VAT.

4.3.2 Subsequent to the swearing of the Statement of Affairs, HM Customs & Excise produced a claim to the effect:

(1) that the total debt due from the Company was [ ] which sum included [ ] by way of interest, penalties and surcharges;

(2) that the VAT of [ ] due for the quarter ended [date] and payable on [date] had not been paid, and that no VAT had been paid for the quarters ended [date] and [date].

4.3.3 The Statement of Affairs shows an overall total of [ ] as being then due to the Inland Revenue in respect of unpaid PAYE and NIC.

4.3.4 As at the date of the receivership some of the total due to the Inland Revenue dated back to [date]. (Payments had been made for PAYE and NIC for [date].

4.3.5 The Crown was treated less favourably than the Company's trade creditors as is evidenced by the fact that between the [date] and the [date] the liabilities to trade creditors decreased from [ ] to [ ] whilst in the same period the amounts due to the Crown increased from [ ] to [ ]. The increase in Crown debts was very largely due to non-payment of VAT, NIC and PAYE from [date] onwards.

5. Excessive remuneration contributing to the Company's insolvency

A10–06 5.1 The allegation, contained in paragraph [ ] of Mr. [name]'s affidavit, is that Mr. [name] and Mr. [name]

"... were responsible for the Company becoming insolvent by affording themselves a high level of remuneration".

5.2 To the extent disclosed by the undisputed facts set out in paragraph 5.3 below Mr. [name] and Mr. [name] admit this allegation.

5.3 The core facts material to this Allegation are the following:

5.3.1 The table set out below shows the total remuneration and benefits recorded in the audited accounts as having been received by Mr. [name] and Mr. [name] for each of the years ending 31st August [ ], [ ] and [ ]. Also shown are the Company's turnover and net profit (loss) for the years in question.

	Turnover £	Net Profit/Loss £	Remuneration £ (inc pension contribution)
[year]	[ ]	[ ]	[ ]
[year]	[ ]	[ ]	[ ]
[year]	[ ]	[ ]	[ ]
Totals:	[ ]	[ ]	[ ]

5.3.2 If Mr. [name] and Mr. [name] had taken more modest remuneration they would have provided the Company with a "buffer" of accumulated profits for the future. In the event, when the Company began to make losses, there was very little by way of funds available to absorb these losses; as a result the company rapidly became insolvent on a balance sheet basis.

5.3.3 When the Company started to become less successful, Mr. [name] and Mr. [name] took substantial reductions in their salaries. For the 12 months ended [date], their respective salaries were reduced to [ ] each; from the [date] to the [date] Mr. [name]'s drawings were [ ] and Mr. [name] were [ ]. Thereafter no further drawings from the Company were taken by either of them.

6. Misuse of bank account

6.1 The allegation, contained in paragraph [ ] of Mr. [name]'s affidavit, is that Mr. [name] and Mr. [name]: **A10–07**

"... were responsible for the misuse of the Company's bank account."

6.2 To the extent disclosed by the undisputed facts set out in paragraph 6.3. below, Mr. [name] and Mr. [name] admit this allegation.

6.3 The core facts material to this allegation are the following:

6.3.1 As already stated in paragraph 3.3.5 above, between [date] and [date] the Company drew some [no] cheques, to a total value of approximately [ ], which were dishonoured. Some [no] of these, to a value of [ ], were honoured on re-presentation. This left a total of [ ] cheques, to a value of approximately [ ] which were "referred to drawer" on at least one occassion; the majority of these cheques (save for those drawn in [date] and [date]) were honoured on re-presentation.

6.3.2 Mr. [name] and Mr. [name] accept that they failed adequately to monitor the fluctuations in the Company's bank account.

7. Failure to file accounts

7.1 [Because the facts and matters set out below only came to the attention of the Claimant recently they have not been verified by affidavit in these proceedings. Nevertheless these facts and matters [have been agreed/are not disputed as] between the Claimant and the First Defendant, and the Claimant is satisfied as to their veracity. Accordingly the Claimant and the First Defendant jointly invite the Court to take these facts and matters in to account when considering whether to approve the *Carecraft* disposal of these proceedings. [In the event that these proceedings are disposed of on a *Carecraft* basis. The Secretary of State expressly reserves the right to issue or cause to be issued further proceedings under the Company Directors Disqualification Act 1986 in relation to any further matters of misconduct which may come to this attention in relation to A Limited after the date of this statement]. **A10–08**

7.2 The First Defendant accepts that he failed to ensure that A Limited prepared or filed audited accounts with the Registrar of Companies contrary to the provisions of the Companies Act 1985 (as amended) to the extent disclosed by the accepted facts set out in paragraph 7.3 to 7.5 below.

7.3 A Limited ("A") was incorporated on [date]. From [date], when it was acquired from company formation agents, the First Defendant was its sole director and sole beneficial shareholder, one share being registered in his name and one share being registered in the name of [name] who held it on trust for the first Defendant.

7.4 A commenced trading on [ ]. It went into creditors' voluntary liquidation on [ ]

7.5 A failed to prepare or file audited accounts for the years ended (date), (date) (date) or (date). These accounts were due for filing on (date) and (date) respectively. The First

Defendant accepts that as sole director he was responsible for ensuring that audited accounts were prepared and filed, and he accepts that he did not do so.

8. Mitigation

A10–09

8.1 The First and Second Defendants wish the Court to have regard to the matters set out in paragraphs 8.2 to 8.3 below. No further evidence or allegations will be relied upon in mitigation other than those set out in this statement. The Claimant, whilst not accepting the truth of these matters does not object to the Court taking them into account for the purpose of disposing of this matter summarily.

8.2 The First Defendant invested £ . . . into the Company as an unsecured creditor and appears as a creditor in that sum in the Statement of Affairs. He raised this money by way of a loan from his bank secured by means of a charge on his home. He is presently repaying this loan at the rate of £ . . . per month.

8.3 The Second Defendant was ill between [date] and [date] and was not able to attend the company's premises during that period.

Signed:

. . . .
For the Secretary of State

. . . .
Defendant 1

. . . .
Defendant 2

Date: . . . .

Appendix 11

OTHER LEGISLATION

The Insolvent Partnerships Order 1994 (SI 1994/2421)

Made	*13th September 1994*
Laid before Parliament	*16th September 1994*
Coming into force	*1st December 1994*

The Lord Chancellor, in exercise of the powers conferred on him by section 420(1) and (2) of the Insolvency Act 1986 and section 21(2) of the Company Directors Disqualification Act 1986[1] and of all other powers enabling him in that behalf, with the concurrence of the Secretary of State, hereby makes the following Order.

PART VII

DISQUALIFICATION

16 Application of Company Directors Disqualification Act 1986

A11–01 Where an insolvent partnership is wound up as an unregistered company under Part V of the Act, the provisions of [sections 1, 1A, 6 to 10, 13 to 15, 17][1], 19(c) and 20 of, and Schedule 1 to, the Company Directors Disqualification Act 1986 shall apply, certain of those provisions being modified in such manner that, after modification, they are as set out in Schedule 8 to this Order.

Commencement

Pt VII art.16: December 1, 1994.

[1] Words substituted by Insolvent Partnerships (Amendment) Order 2001/767 art.2(2) (April 2, 2001).

SCHEDULE 8

Modified Provisions of Company Directors Disqualification Act 1986 for the Purposes of Article 16

Article 16

A11–02 The following provisions of the Company Directors Disqualification Act 1986 are modified so as to read as follows:—

6 "Section 6: Duty of court to disqualify unfit officers of insolvent partnerships

A11–03 (1) The court shall make a disqualification order against a person in any case where, on an application under this section, it is satisfied—

(a) that he is or has been an officer of a partnership which has at any time become insolvent (whether while he was an officer or subsequently), and
(b) that his conduct as an officer of that partnership (either taken alone or taken together with his conduct as an officer of any other partnership or partnerships, or as a director of any company or companies) makes him unfit to be concerned in the management of a company.

(2) For the purposes of this section and the next—

(a) a partnership becomes insolvent if—

(i) the court makes an order for it to be wound up as an unregistered company at a time when its assets are insufficient for the payment of its debts and other liabilities and the expenses of the winding up; or
(ii) [the partnership enters administration][2]; and

(b) a company becomes insolvent if—

(i) the company goes into liquidation at a time when its assets are insufficient for the payment of its debts and other liabilities and the expenses of the winding up,
(ii) [the company enters administration][3], or
(iii) an administrative receiver of the company is appointed.

(3) For the purposes of this section and the next, references to a person's conduct as an officer of any partnership or partnerships, or as a director of any company or companies, include, where the partnership or company concerned or any of the partnerships or companies concerned has become insolvent, that person's conduct in relation to any matter connected with or arising out of the insolvency of that partnership or company.

[(4) In this section and section 7(2), "the court" means—

(a) where the partnership in question is being or has been wound up as an unregistered company by the court, that court,
(b) where the preceding paragraph does not apply but [an administrator has at any time been appointed][4] in relation to the partnership in question, any court which has jurisdiction to wind it up.

[2] Words substituted in s.6(2)(a)(ii) by Insolvent Partnerships (Amendment) Order 2005/1516 art.11(2)(a) (July 1, 2005).

[3] Words substituted in s.6(2)(b)(ii) by Insolvent Partnerships (Amendment) Order 2005/1516 art.11(2)(b) (July 1, 2005).

[4] Words substituted in s.6 (4)(b) by Insolvent Partnerships (Amendment) Order 2005/1516 art.11(2)(c) (July 1, 2005).

(4A) Section 117 of the Insolvency Act 1986 (High Court and county court jurisdiction), as modified and set out in Schedule 5 to the 1994 Order, shall apply for the purposes of subsection (4) as if in a case within paragraph (b) of that subsection the references to the presentation of the petition for winding up in sections 117(3) and 117(4) of the Insolvency Act 1986, as modified and set out in that Schedule, were references to the making of the administration order.

(4B) Nothing in subsection (4) invalidates any proceedings by reason of their being taken in the wrong court; and proceedings—

(a) for or in connection with a disqualification order under this section, or
(b) in connection with a disqualification undertaking accepted under section 7, may be retained in the court in which the proceedings were commenced, although it may not be the court in which they ought to have been commenced.

(4C) In this section and section 7, "director" includes a shadow director.][5]

(5) Under this section the minimum period of disqualification is 2 years, and the maximum period is 15 years.

[7 Section 7: Disqualification order or undertaking; and reporting provisions

A11–04

(1) If it appears to the Secretary of State that it is expedient in the public interest that a disqualification order under section 6 should be made against any person, an application for the making of such an order against that person may be made—

(a) by the Secretary of State, or
(b) if the Secretary of State so directs in the case of a person who is or has been an officer of a partnership which is being or has been wound up by the court as an unregistered company, by the official receiver.

(2) Except with the leave of the court, an application for the making under that section of a disqualification order against any person shall not be made after the end of the period of 2 years beginning with the day on which the partnership of which that person is or has been an officer became insolvent.

(2A) If it appears to the Secretary of State that the conditions mentioned in section 6(1) are satisfied as respects any person who has offered to give him a disqualification undertaking, he may accept the undertaking if it appears to him that it is expedient in the public interest that he should do so (instead of applying, or proceeding with an application, for a disqualification order). (3) If it appears to the office-holder responsible under this section, that is to say—

(a) in the case of a partnership which is being wound up by the court as an unregistered company, the official receiver, or
(b) in the case of a partnership [which is in administration][6], the administrator, that the conditions mentioned in section 6(1) are satisfied as respects a person who is or has been an officer of that partnership, the office-holder shall forthwith report the matter to the Secretary of State.

(4) The Secretary of State or the official receiver may require any of the persons mentioned in subsection (5) below—

(a) to furnish him with such information with respect to any person's conduct as an officer of a partnership or as a director of a company, and

[5] Substituted by Insolvent Partnerships (Amendment) Order 2001/767 art.3(2) (April 2, 2001).
[6] Words substituted in s.7(3)(b) by Insolvent Partnerships (Amendment) Order 2005/1516 art.11(3) (July 1, 2005).

(b) to produce and permit inspection of such books, papers and other records relevant to that person's conduct as such an officer or director, as the Secretary of State or the official receiver may reasonably require for the purpose of determining whether to exercise, or of exercising, any function of his under this section.

(5) The persons referred to in subsection (4) are—

(a) the liquidator or administrator, or former liquidator or administrator of the partnership,

(b) the liquidator, administrator or administrative receiver, or former liquidator, administrator or administrative receiver, of the company.][7]

8 Section 8: Disqualification after investigation

A11–05 [(1) If it appears to the Secretary of State from—

(a) a report made by an inspector or person appointed to conduct an investigation under a provision mentioned in subsection (1A), or

(b) information or documents obtained under a provision mentioned in subsection (1B),

that it is expedient in the public interest that a disqualification order should be made against any person who is or has been an officer of an insolvent partnership, he may apply to the court for such an order to be made against that person.

(1B) The provisions are—

(a) section 447 or 448 of the Companies Act,
(b) section 2 of the Criminal Justice Act 1987,
(c) section 52 of the Criminal Justice (Scotland) Act 1987,
(d) section 83 of the Companies Act 1989, or
(e) section 171 or 173 of the Financial Services and Markets Act 2000.][8]

(2) The court may make a disqualification order against a person where, on an application under this section, it is satisfied that his conduct in relation to the partnership makes him unfit to be concerned in the management of a company.

[(2A) Where it appears to the Secretary of State from such report, information or documents that, in the case of a person who has offered to give him a disqualification undertaking—

(a) the conduct of the person in relation to an insolvent partnership of which the person is or has been an officer makes him unfit to be concerned in the management of a company, and

(b) it is expedient in the public interest that he should accept the undertaking (instead of applying, or proceeding with an application, for a disqualification order), he may accept the undertaking.][9]

(3) In this section "the court" means the High Court.

(4) The maximum period of disqualification under this section is 15 years.

[7] Substituted by Insolvent Partnerships (Amendment) Order 2001/767 art.3(3) (April 2, 2001).

[8] Sections 8(1)–(1B) substituted for s.8(1) by Financial Services and Markets Act 2000 (Consequential Amendments and Repeals) Order 2001/3649 Pt 9 art.470 (December 1, 2001).

[9] Added by Insolvent Partnerships (Amendment) Order 2001/767 art.3(4) (April 2, 2001).

[9 Section 9: Matters for determining unfitness of officers of partnerships

A11–06

(1) This section applies where it falls to a court to determine whether a person's conduct as an officer of a partnership (either taken alone or taken together with his conduct as an officer of any other partnership or partnerships or as a director of any company or companies) makes him unfit to be concerned in the management of a company.

(1A) In determining whether he may accept a disqualification undertaking from any person the Secretary of State shall, as respects the person's conduct as an officer of any partnership or a director of any company concerned, have regard in particular—

(a) to the matters mentioned in Part I of Schedule 1 to this Act, and

(b) where the partnership or the company (as the case may be) has become insolvent,

to the matters mentioned in Part II of that Schedule; and references in that Schedule to the officer and the partnership or, as the case may be, to the director and the company are to be read accordingly.

(2) The court shall, as respects that person's conduct as an officer of that partnership or each of those partnerships or as a director of that company or each of those companies, have regard in particular—

(a) to the matters mentioned in Part I of Schedule 1 to this Act, and

(b) where the partnership or company (as the case may be) has become insolvent,

to the matters mentioned in Part II of that Schedule; and references in that Schedule to the officer and the partnership or, as the case may be, to the director and the company, are to be read accordingly and in this section and that Schedule "director" includes a shadow director.

(3) Subsections (2) and (3) of section 6 apply for the purposes of this section and Schedule 1 as they apply for the purposes of sections 6 and 7.

(4) Subject to the next subsection, any reference in Schedule 1 to an enactment contained in the Companies Act or the Insolvency Act includes, in relation to any time before the coming into force of that enactment, the corresponding enactment in force at that time.

(5) The Secretary of State may by order modify any of the provisions of Schedule 1; and such an order may contain such transitional provisions as may appear to the Secretary of State necessary or expedient.

(6) The power to make orders under this section is exercisable by statutory instrument subject to annulment in pursuance of a resolution of either House of Parliament.][10]

[13 Section 13: Criminal penalties

A11–07

If a person acts in contravention of a disqualification order or disqualification undertaking he is liable—

(a) on conviction on indictment, to imprisonment for not more than 2 years or a fine or both; and

(b) on summary conviction, to imprisonment for not more than 6 months or a fine not exceeding the statutory maximum, or both.

14 Section 14: Offences by body corporate

A11–08

(1) Where a body corporate is guilty of an offence of acting in contravention of a disqualification order or disqualification undertaking and it is proved that the offence occurred

[10] Substituted by Insolvent Partnerships (Amendment) Order 2001/767 art.3(5) (April 2, 2001).

with the consent or connivance of, or was attributable to any neglect on the part of any director, manager, secretary or other similar officer of the body corporate, or any person who was purporting to act in any such capacity he, as well as the body corporate, is guilty of the offence and liable to be proceeded against and punished accordingly.

(2) Where the affairs of a body corporate are managed by its members, subsection (1) applies in relation to the acts and defaults of a member in connection with his functions of management as if he were a director of the body corporate.

15 Section 15: Personal liability for company's debts where person acts while disqualified

A11–09 (1) A person is personally responsible for all the relevant debts of a company if at any time—

(a) in contravention of a disqualification order or disqualification undertaking he is involved in the management of the company, or

(b) as a person who is involved in the management of the company, he acts or is willing to act on instructions given without the leave of the court by a person whom he knows at that time to be the subject of a disqualification order or disqualification undertaking or a disqualification order under Part II of the Companies (Northern Ireland) Order 1989 or to be an undischarged bankrupt.

(2) Where a person is personally responsible under this section for the relevant debts of a company, he is jointly and severally liable in respect of those debts with the company and any other person who, whether under this section or otherwise, is so liable.

(3) For the purposes of this section the relevant debts of a company are—

(a) in relation to a person who is personally responsible under paragraph (a) of subsection (1), such debts and other liabilities of the company as are incurred at a time when that person was involved in the management of the company, and

(b) in relation to a person who is personally responsible under paragraph (b) of that subsection, such debts and other liabilities of the company as are incurred at a time when that person was acting or was willing to act on instructions given as mentioned in that paragraph.

(4) For the purposes of this section, a person is involved in the management of a company if he is a director of the company or if he is concerned, whether directly or indirectly, or takes part, in the management of the company.

(5) For the purposes of this section a person who, as a person involved in the management of a company, has at any time acted on instructions given without the leave of the court by a person whom he knew at that time to be the subject of a disqualification order or disqualification undertaking or a disqualification order under Part II of the Companies (Northern Ireland) Order 1989 or to be an undischarged bankrupt is presumed, unless the contrary is shown, to have been willing at any time thereafter to act on any instructions given by that person.

17 Section 17: Application for leave under an order or undertaking

A11–10 (1) Where a person is subject to a disqualification order made by a court having jurisdiction to wind up partnerships, any application for leave for the purposes of section 1(1)(a) shall be made to that court.

(2) Where a person is subject to a disqualification undertaking accepted at any time under section 7 or 8, any application for leave for the purposes of section 1A(1)(a) shall be made to any court to which, if the Secretary of State had applied for a disqualification order under the section in question at that time, his application could have been made.

(3) But where a person is subject to two or more disqualification orders or undertakings (or to one or more disqualification orders and to one or more disqualification

undertakings), any application for leave for the purposes of section 1(1)(a) or 1A(1)(a) shall be made to any court to which any such application relating to the latest order to be made, or undertaking to be accepted, could be made.

(4) On the hearing of an application for leave for the purposes of section 1(1)(a) or 1A(1)(a), the Secretary of State shall appear and call the attention of the court to any matters which seem to him to be relevant, and may himself give evidence or call witnesses.][11]

SCHEDULE 1

Matters for Determining Unfitness of Officers of Partnerships

Section 9

Part I

Matters Applicable in All Cases

A11–11

1 Any misfeasance or breach of any fiduciary or other duty by the officer in relation to the partnership or, as the case may be, by the director in relation to the company.

2 Any misapplication or retention by the officer or the director of, or any conduct by the officer or the director giving rise to an obligation to account for, any money or other property of the partnership or, as the case may be, of the company.

3 The extent of the officer's or the director's responsibility for the partnership or, as the case may be, the company entering into any transaction liable to be set aside under Part XVI of the Insolvency Act (provisions against debt avoidance).

4 The extent of the director's responsibility for any failure by the company to comply with any of the following provisions of the Companies Act, namely—

(a) section 221 (companies to keep accounting records);
(b) section 222 (where and for how long records to be kept);
(c) section 288 (register of directors and secretaries);
(d) section 352 (obligation to keep and enter up register of members);
(e) section 353 (location of register of members);
(f) section 363 (duty of company to make annual returns); and
(g) section 399 and 415 (company's duty to register charges it creates).

5 The extent of the director's responsibility for any failure by the directors of the company to comply with—

(a) section 226 or 227 of the Companies Act (duty to prepare annual accounts), or
(b) section 233 of that Act (approval and signature of accounts).

6 Any failure by the officer to comply with any obligation imposed on him by or under any of the following provisions of the Limited Partnerships Act 1907—

(a) section 8 (registration of particulars of limited partnership);
(b) section 9 (registration of changes in particulars);
(c) section 10 (advertisement of general partner becoming limited partner and of assignment of share of limited partner).

[11] Added by Insolvent Partnerships (Amendment) Order 2001/767 art.3(6) (April 2, 2001).

PART II

MATTERS APPLICABLE WHERE PARTNERSHIP OR COMPANY HAS BECOME INSOLVENT

A11–12 **7** The extent of the officer's or the director's responsibility for the causes of the partnership or (as the case may be) the company becoming insolvent.

8 The extent of the officer's or the director's responsibility for any failure by the partnership or (as the case may be) the company to supply any goods or services which have been paid for (in whole or in part).

9 The extent of the officer's or the director's responsibility for the partnership or (as the case may be) the company entering into any transaction or giving any preference, being a transaction or preference—

(a) liable to be set aside under section 127 or sections 238 to 240 of the Insolvency Act, or
(b) challengeable under section 242 or 243 of that Act or under any rule of law in Scotland.

10 The extent of the director's responsibility for any failure by the directors of the company to comply with section 98 of the Insolvency Act (duty to call creditors' meeting in creditors' voluntary winding up).

11 Any failure by the director to comply with any obligation imposed on him by or under any of the following provisions of the Insolvency Act—

(a) section 47 (statement of affairs to administrative receiver);
(b) section 66 (statement of affairs in Scottish receivership);
(c) section 99 (directors' duty to attend meeting; statement of affairs in creditors' voluntary winding up).

12 Any failure by the officer or the director to comply with any obligation imposed on him by or under any of the following provisions of the Insolvency Act (both as they apply in relation to companies and as they apply in relation to insolvent partnerships by virtue of the provisions of the Insolvent Partnerships Order 1994)—

(a) [paragraph 48 of Schedule B1][12]
(b) section 131 (statement of affairs in winding up by the court);
(c) section 234 (duty of any one with property to deliver it up);
(d) section 235 (duty to co-operate with liquidator, etc.).".

Commencement

Schedule 8 para.1: December 1, 1994.

Limited Liability Partnerships Regulations 2001 (SI 2001/1090)

Made *19th March 2001*
Coming into force *6th April 2001*

Whereas a draft of these Regulations has been approved by a resolution of each House of Parliament pursuant to section 17(4) of the Limited Liability Partnerships Act 2000;

[12] Words substituted in Sch.1 para.12(a) by Insolvent Partnerships (Amendment) Order 2005/1516 art.11(4) (July 1, 2005).

Now, therefore, the Secretary of State, in exercise of the powers conferred on him by sections 14, 15, 16 and 17 of the Limited Liability Partnerships Act 2000 and all other powers enabling him in that behalf hereby makes the following Regulations:

PART III

COMPANIES ACT 1985 AND COMPANY DIRECTORS DISQUALIFICATION ACT 1986

4 Application of [certain provisions][13] of the 1985 Act and of the provisions of the Company Directors Disqualification Act 1986 to limited liability partnerships

A11–13

(1) The provisions of the 1985 Act specified in the first column of Part I of Schedule 2 to these Regulations shall apply to limited liability partnerships, except where the context otherwise requires, with the following modifications—

(a) references to a company shall include references to a limited liability partnership;
(b) [. . .][14]
(c) references to the Insolvency Act 1986 shall include references to that Act as it applies to limited liability partnerships by virtue of Part IV of these Regulations;
[(d) references in a provision of the 1985 Act to—
(i) other provisions of that Act, or
(ii) provisions of the Companies Act 2006, shall include references to those provisions as they apply to limited liability partnerships.][15]

(e)–(f) [. . .][16]
(g) references to a director of a company or to an officer of a company shall include references to a member of a limited liability partnership;
(h) the modifications, if any, specified in the second column of Part I of Schedule 2 opposite the provision specified in the first column; and
(i) such further modifications as the context requires for the purpose of giving effect to that legislation as applied by these Regulations.

(2) The provisions of the Company Director Disqualification Act 1986 shall apply to limited liability partnerships, except where the context otherwise requires, with the following modifications—

(a) references to a company shall include references to a limited liability partnership;
(b) references to the Companies Acts shall include references to the principal Act and regulations made thereunder and references to the companies legislation shall include references to the principal Act, regulations made thereunder and to any enactment applied by regulations to limited liability partnerships;
(d) references to the Insolvency Act 1986 shall include references to that Act as it applies to limited liability partnerships by virtue of Part IV of these Regulations;
(e) [. . .][17]

[13] Words substituted by Limited Liability Partnerships (Application of Companies Act 2006) Regulations 2009/1804 Sch.3 Pt 2 para.13(3)(a) (October 1, 2009).
[14] Revoked by Limited Liability Partnerships (Application of Companies Act 2006) Regulations 2009/1804 Sch.3 Pt 2 para.13(3)(b)(i) (October 1, 2009).
[15] Substituted by Limited Liability Partnerships (Application of Companies Act 2006) Regulations 2009/1804 Sch.3 Pt 2 para.13(3)(b)(ii) (October 1, 2009).
[16] Revoked by Limited Liability Partnerships (Application of Companies Act 2006) Regulations 2009/1804 Sch.3 Pt 2 para.13(3)(b)(i) (October 1, 2009).
[17] Revoked by Companies Act 2006 (Consequential Amendments, Transitional Provisions and Savings) Order 2009/1941 Sch.1 para.192(2) (October 1, 2009).

(f) references to a shadow director shall include references to a shadow member;
(g) references to a director of a company or to an officer of a company shall include references to a member of a limited liability partnership;
(h) the modifications, if any, specified in the second column of Part II of Schedule 2 opposite the provision specified in the first column; and
(i) such further modifications as the context requires for the purpose of giving effect to that legislation as applied by these Regulations.

Commencement

Pt III reg.4(1)–(2)(i): April 6, 2001.

SCHEDULE II

MODIFICATIONS TO THE COMPANY DIRECTORS DISQUALIFICATION ACT 1986

A11–14 Part II of Schedule I After paragraph 8 insert—

"8A

The extent of the member's and shadow members' responsibility for events leading to a member or shadow member, whether himself or some other member or shadow member, being declared by the court to be liable to make a contribution to the assets of the limited liability partnership under section 214A of the Insolvency Act 1986."

Commencement

Schedule 2(II) para.1: April 6, 2001.

Appendix 12

EXTRACTS FROM PREVIOUS LEGISLATION

Insolvency Act 1985, ss.12–16

Part II

Company Insolvency Etc.

Chapter I

Disqualification and Personal Liability of Directors and Others

Duty of court to disqualify unfit directors of insolvent companies

12 (1) The court shall make a disqualification order against a person in any case where, on an application under this section, the court is satisfied— **A12–01**

(a) that he is or has been a director of a company which has at any time become insolvent (whether while he was a director or subsequently): and

(b) that his conduct as a director of that company (either taken alone or taken together with his conduct as a director of any other company or companies) makes him unfit to be concerned in the management of a company.

(2) The period specified as the period of the disqualification in a disqualification order made under this section shall not be less than two years.

(3) If it appears to the Secretary of State that it is expedient in the public interest that a disqualification order under this section should be made against any person, an application for the making of such an order against that person may be made—

(a) by the Secretary of State; or
(b) if the Secretary of State so directs in the case of a person who is or has been a director of a company which is being wound up by the court in England and Wales, by the official receiver.

(4) Except with the leave of the court, an application for the making under this section of a disqualification order against any person shall not be made after the end of the period of two years beginning with the day on which the company of which that person is or has been a director became insolvent.

(5) If—

(a) in the case of a person who is or has been a director of a company which is being wound up by the court in England or Wales, it appears to the official receiver;
(b) in the case of a person who is or has been a director of a company which is being wound up otherwise than as mentioned in paragraph (a) above, it appears to the liquidator;
(c) in the case of a person who is or has been a director of a company in relation to which an administration order is in force, it appears to the administrator; or
(d) in the case of a person who is or has been a director of a company of which there is an administrative receiver, it appears to that receiver,

that the conditions mentioned in subsection (1) above are satisfied as respects that person, the official receiver, the liquidator, the administrator or, as the case may be, the administrative receiver, shall forthwith report the matter to the Secretary of State.

(6) The Secretary of State or the official receiver may require the liquidator, administrator or administrative receiver of a company or the former liquidator, administrator or administrative receiver of a company—

(a) to furnish him with such information with respect to any person's conduct as a director of the company; and
(b) to produce and permit inspection of such books, papers and other records relevant to that person's conduct as such a director,

as the Secretary of State or the official receiver may reasonably require for the purpose of determining whether to exercise, or of exercising, any function of his under this section.

(7) For the purposes of this section a company becomes insolvent if—

(a) the company goes into liquidation at a time when its assets are insufficient for the payment of its debts and other liabilities and the expenses of the winding up;
(b) an administration order is made in relation to the company; or
(c) an administrative receiver of the company is appointed,

and references in this section to a person's conduct as a director of any company of companies include, where that company or any of those companies has become insolvent, references to that person's conduct in relation to any matter connected with or arising out of the insolvency of that company.

(8) In this section "the court" means—

(a) in the case of a person who is or has been a director of a company which is being wound up by the court, the court by which the company is being wound up;
(b) in the case of a person who is or has been a director of a company which is being wound up voluntarily, any court having jurisdiction to wind up the company,

(c) in the case of a person who is or has been a director of a company in realtion to which an administration order is in force, the court by which that order was made; and

(d) in any other case, the High Court or, in Scotland, the Court of Session.

(9) In this section and sections 13 to 15 below "director" includes a shadow director within the meaning given by section 741(2) of the 1985 Act.

Disqualification after investigation of company

A12–02

13 (1) If it appears to the Secretary of State from a report made by inspectors under section 437 of the 1985 Act, or from information or documents obtained under section 447 or 448 of that Act, that it is expedient in the public interest that a disqualification order should be made against any person who is or has been a director of any company, he may apply to the court for such an order to be made against that person.

(2) The court may make a disqualification order against a person where, on an application under this section, the court is satisfied that his conduct in relation to the company makes him unfit to be concerned in the management of a company.

(3) In this section "the court" means the High Court or, in Scotland, the Court of Session.

Matters for determining unfitness of directors

A12–03

14 (1) Where it falls to a court to determine whether a person's conduct as a director of any particular company or companies makes him unfit as mentioned in section 12(1) or 13(2) above, the court shall, as respects his conduct as a director of that company or, as the case may be, each of those companies, have regard in particular—

(a) to the matters mentioned in Part 1 of Schedule 2 to this Act; and

(b) where the company has become insolvent, to the matters mentioned in Part II of that Schedule.

and references in that Schedule to the director and to the company shall be construed accordingly.

(2) Subsection (7) of section 12 above applies for the purposes of this section and Schedule 2 to this Act as it applies for the purposes of that section.

(3) Subject to subsection (4) below, any reference in Schedule 2 to this Act to any enactment contained in the 1985 Act or this Act shall include, in relation to any time before the coming into force of that enactment, a reference to the corresponding enactment in force at that time

(4) The Secretary of State may by order modify any of the provisions of Schedule 2 to this Act; and such an order may contain such transitional provisions as may appear to the Secretary of State necessary or expedient

(5) The power to make orders under this section shall be exercisable by statutory instrument which shall be subject to annulment in pursuance of a resolution of either House of Parliament.

Responsibility for company's wrongful trading

A12–04

15 (1) Subject to subsection (3) below, if in the course of the winding up of a company it appears that subsection (2) below applies in relation to a person who is or has been a director of the company, the court, on the application of the liquidator, may declare that this person is to be liable to make such contribution (if any) to the company's assets as the court thinks proper.

(2) This subsection applies in relation to a person if—

(a) the company has gone into insolvent liquidation;
(b) at some time before the commencement of the winding up of the company, that person knew or ought to have concluded that there was no reasonable prospect that the company would avoid going into insolvent liquidation. and
(c) that person was a director of the company at that time.

(3) The court shall make a declaration under subsection (1) above with respect to any person if it is satisfied that after the condition specified in subsection (2)(b) above was first satisfied in relation to him that person took every step with a view of minimising the potential loss to the company's creditors as (assuming him to have known that there was no reasonable prospect that the company would avoid going into insolvent liquidation) he ought to have taken.

(4) For the purposes of subsection (2) and (3) above the facts which a director of a company ought to know or ascertain, the conclusions which he ought to reach and the steps which he ought to take are those which would be known or ascertained, or reached or taken, by a reasonably diligent person having both—

(a) the general knowledge, skill and expertise that may reasonably be expected of a person carrying out the same functions as are carried out by that director in relation to the company; and
(b) the general knowledge, skill and expertise that that director has.

(5) The reference in subsection (4) above to the functions carried out in relation to a company by a director of the company includes a reference to any functions which he does not carry out but which have been entrusted to him.

(6) Subsections (3) to (6) of section 630 of the 1985 Act (responsibility for company's fraudulent trading) shall have effect in relation to a declaration under subsection (1) above as they have effect in relation to a declaration under subsection (2) of that section, and this section in without prejudice to that section.

(7) For the purposes of this section a company goes into insolvent liquidation if it goes into liquidation at a time when its assets are insufficient for the payment of its debts and other liabilities and the expenses of the winding up.

Disqualification of persons held to be liable to contribute to company's assets

A12–05 **16** Where a court makes a declaration under section 15 above or section 630 of the 1985 Act that any person is to be liable to make a contribution to a company's assets, then, whether or not an application for such an order is made by any person, the court may, if it thinks fit, also make a disqualification order against the person to whom the declaration relates.

Insolvency Act 1985, ss.108(1), (2), 109

Construction of Part II

A12–06 **108**(1) The provisions of this Part shall be construed as one with the 1985 Act and—

(a) so far as relating to the disqualification of directors and others involved in the management of companies, with Part IX of that Act;
(b) so far as relating to receivers or managers, with Part XIX of that Act; and
(c) so far as relating to the winding up of companies, with Part XX of that Act.

and references in that Act to itself and to any of those Parts of that Act shall be construed accordingly.

(2) The following provisions, namely—

(a) sections 295 and 301 of the 1985 Act (disqualification orders and register of such orders): and
(b) paragraphs 1 and 3 to 5 of Part I of Schedule 12 to that Act (procedure for applying for and obtaining disqualification orders and applications for leave under such orders).

shall apply for the purposes of sections 12, 13 and 16 above: and references in those provisions to sections 296 to 299 of that Act shall be construed accordingly.

Minor and consequential amendments of 1985 Act

A12–07

109 (1) The 1985 Act shall have effect with the amendments specified in Schedule 6 to this Act (being minor and consequential amendments relating to the disqualification of directors and others involved in the management of companies and the insolvency and winding up of companies)

(2) In the 1985 Act references to general rules under section 663(1) or (2) of that Act shall have effect as references to rules under section 106 above

(3) In the 1985 Act "administrative receiver" has the same meaning as in this Part.

Insolvency Act 1985, Schs 2 and 6

Section 14

SCHEDULE 2

Matters for Determining Unfitness of Directors

Part I

Matters Applicable in All Cases

A12–08

1 Any misfeasance or breach of any fiduciary or other duty by the director in relation to the company.

2 Any misapplication or retention by the director of, or any conduct by the director giving rise to any obligation to account for, any money or other property of the company.

3 The extent of the director's responsibility for the company entering into any transaction liable to be set aside under section 212 of this Act.

4 The extent of the director's responsibility for any failure by the company to comply with any of the following provisions of the 1985 Act, namely—

(a) section 221 (companies to keep accounting records);
(b) section 222 (where and for how long records to be kept);
(c) section 288 (register of directors and secretaries);
(d) section 352 (obligation to keep and enter up register of members);
(e) section 353 (location of register of members);
(f) sections 363 and 364 (company's duty to make annual return);
(g) section 365 (time for completion of annual return); and
(h) sections 399 and 415 (company's duty to register charges it creates).

5 The extent of the director's responsibility for any failure by the directors of the company to comply with section 227 (directors' duty to prepare annual accounts) or section 238 (signing of balance sheet and documents to be annexed) of the 1985 Act.

PART II

MATTERS APPLICABLE WHERE COMPANY HAS BECOME INSOLVENT

A12–09 **6** The extent of the director's responsibility for the causes of the company becoming insolvent.

7 The extent of the director's responsibility for any failure by the company to supply any goods or services which have been paid for (in whole or in part).

8 The extent of the director's responsibility for the company entering into any transaction or giving any preference, being a transaction or preference liable to be set aside under section 101 of this Act or section 522 of the 1985 Act or challengeable under section 615A of 615B of that Act or under any rule of law in Scotland.

9 The extent of the director's responsibility for any failure by the directors or the company to comply with section 85 of this Act.

10 Any failure by the director to comply with any obligation imposed on him by or under section 482 of the 1985 Act (company's statement of affairs) or section 39, 53, 66, 85, 98 or 99 of this Act.

Section 109 SCHEDULE 6

Amendments of 1985 Act

Disqualification etc.

A12–10 **1** (1) Section 295 (disqualification orders: introductory) shall be amended as follows.

(2) In subsection (1) after the word "liquidator" there shall be inserted the words "or administrator" and in that subsection and subsection (3) for the words "sections 296 to 300" there shall be substituted the words "sections 296 to 299".

(3) In subsection (2), at the end there shall be inserted the words—

"; and where a disqualification order is made against a person who is already subject to such an order the periods specified in those orders shall run concurrently."

(4) In subsection (6), for the words "Parts I and II of Schedule 12 have" there shall be substituted the words "Part I of Schedule 12 has".

2 In section 301(1) (register of disqualification orders), for the words "sections 296 to 300" there shall be substituted the words "sections 296 to 299".

. . .

7 (1) Section 733 (liability of directors for offences by company under certain provisions) shall be amended as follows.

(2) In subsection (1), after "216(3)" there shall be inserted "295(7)".

(3) In subsection (3), for the words "210 or 216(3)" there shall be substituted the words "210, 216(3) or 295(7)".

. . .

14 In paragraph 4(3) of Part 1 of Schedule 12 (orders under sections 296 to 299), for the words "liquidator or director" there shall be substituted the words "liquidator, administrator or director".

Companies Act 1985, ss.295–302

Disqualification

Disqualification orders: introductory

295 (1) In the circumstances specified in sections 296 to 300, a court may make against a person a disqualification order, that is to say an order that he shall not, without level of the court— **A12–11**

(a) be a director of a company, or
(b) be a liquidator of a company, or
(c) be a receiver or manager of a company's property, or
(d) in any way, whether directly or indirectly, be concerned or take part in the promotion, formation or management of a company,

for a specified period beginning with the date of the order.

(2) The maximum period to be specified is—

(a) in the case of an order made under section 297 or made by a court of summary jurisdiction, 5 years, and
(b) in any other case, 15 years.

(3) In this section and sections 296 to 300, "company" includes any company which may be wound up under Part XXI.

(4) A disqualification order may be made on grounds which are or include matters other than criminal convictions, notwithstanding that the person in respect of whom it is to be made may be criminally liable in respect of those matters.

(5) In sections 296 to 299, any reference to provisions, or to a particular provision, of this Act or the Consequential Provisions Act includes the corresponding provision or provisions of the former Companies Acts.

(6) Parts I and II of Schedule 12 have effect with regard to the procedure for obtaining a disqualification order, and to applications for leave under such an order; and Part III of that Schedule has effect—

(a) in connection with certain transitional cases arising under sections 93 and 94 of the Companies Act 1981, so as to limit the power to make a disqualification order, or to restrict the duration of an order, by reference to events occuring or things done before those sections came into force, and
(b) to preserve orders made under section 28 of the Companies Act 1976 (repealed by the Act of 1981).

(7) If a person acts in contravention of a disqualification order, he is in respect of each offence liable to imprisonment or a fine, or both.

Disqualification on conviction of indictable offence

296 (1) The court may make a disqualification order against a person where he is convicted of an indictable offence (whether on indictment or summarily) in connection with the promotion, formation, management or liquidation of a company, or with the receivership or management of a company's property. **A12–12**

(2) "The court" for this purpose means—

(a) any court having jurisdiction to wind up the company in relation to which the offence was committed, or
(b) the court by or before which the person is convicted of the offence, or
(c) in the case of a summary conviction in England and Wales, any other magistrates' court acting for the same petty sessions area:

and for purposes of this section the definition of "indictable offence" in Schedule 1 to the Interpretation Act 1978 applies in relation to Scotland as it does in relation to England and Wales.

Disqualification for persistent default under Companies Act

A12–13 **297** (1) The court may make a disqualification order against a person where it appears to it that he has been persistently in default in relation to provisions of this Act or the Consequential Provisions Act requiring any return, account or other document to be filed with, delivered or sent, or notice of any matter to be given, to the registrar of companies.

(2) On an application to the court for an order to be made under this section, the fact that a person has been persistently in default in relation to such provisions as are mentioned above may (without prejudice to its proof in any manner) be conclusively proved by showing that in the 5 years ending with the date of the application he has been adjudged guilty (whether or not on the same occasion) of three or more defaults in relation to those provisions.

(3) A person is treated under subsection (2) as being adjudged guilty of a default in relation to any such provision if—

(a) he is convicted (whether on indictment or summarily) of an offence consisting in a contravention of or failure to comply with that provision (whether on his own part or on the part of any company), or
(b) a default order is made against him, that is to say an order under—
  (i) section 244 (order requiring delivery of company accounts), or
  (ii) section 499 (enforcement of receiver's or manager's duty to make returns), or
  (iii) section 636 (corresponding provision for liquidator in winding-up), or
  (iv) section 713 (enforcement of company's duty to make returns).

in respect of any such contravention of or failure to comply with that provision (whether on his own part or on the part of any company).

(4) In this section "the court" means any court having jurisdiction to wind up any of the companies in relation to which the offence or other default has been or is alleged to have been committed.

Disqualification for fraud, etc. in winding up

A12–14 **298** (1) The court may make a disqualification order against a person if, in the course of the winding up of a company, it appears that he—

(a) has been guilty of an offence for which he is liable (whether he has been convicted or not) under section 458 (fraudulent trading), or
(b) has otherwise been guilty, while an officer or liquidator of the company or receiver or manager of its property, of any fraud in relation to the company or of any breach of his duty as such officer, liquidator, receiver or manager.

(2) In this section "the court" means the same as in section 297; and "officer" includes a shadow director.

Disqualification of summary conviction

A12–15 **299** (1) An offence counting for the purposes of this section is one of which a person is convicted (either on indictment or summarily) in consequence of a contravention of, or failure to comply with, any provision of this Act or the Consequential Provisions Act requiring a return, account or other document to be filed with, delivered or sent, or notice of any matter to be given, to the registrar of companies (whether the contravention or failure is on the person's own part or on the part of any company).

(2) Where a person is convicted of a summary offence counting for those purposes, the court by which he is convicted (or, in England and Wales, any other magistrates' court acting for the same petty sessions area) may make a disqualification order against him if the circumstances specified in the next subsection are present.

(3) Those circumstances are that, during the 5 years ending with the date of the conviction, the person has had made against him, or has been convicted of, in total not less that 3 default orders and offences counting for the purposes of this section; and those offences may include that of which he is convicted as mentioned in subsection (2) and any other offence of which he is convicted on the same occasion.

(4) For the purposes of this section—

(a) the definition of "summary offence" in Schedule 1 to the Interpretation Act 1978 applies for Scotland as for England and Wales, and
(b) "default order" means the same as in section 297(3)(b).

Disqualification by reference to association with insolvent companies

300 (1) The court may make a disqualification order against a person where, on an application under this section, it appears to it that he— **A12–16**

(a) is or has been a director of a company which has at any time gone into liquidation (whether while he was a director or subsequently) and was insolvent at that time, and
(b) is or has been a director of another such company which has gone into liquidation within 5 years of the date on which the first-mentioned company went into liquidation,

and that his conduct as director of any of those companies makes him unfit to be concerned in the management of a company.

(2) In the case of a person who is or has been a director of a company which has gone into liquidation as above-mentioned and is being wound up by the court, "the court" in subsection (1) means the court by which the company is being wound up; and in any other case it means the High Court or, in Scotland, the Court of Session.

(3) The Secretary of State may require the liquidator or former liquidator of a company—

(a) to furnish him with such information with respect to the company's affairs, and
(b) to produce and permit inspection of such books or documents of or relevant to the company,

as the Secretary of State may reasonably require for the purpose of determining whether to make an application under this section in respect of a person who is or has been a director of that company; and if a person makes default in complying with such a requirement, the court may, on the Secretary of State's application, make an order requiring that person to make good the default within such time as may be specified.

(4) For purposes of this section, a shadow director of a company is deemed a director of it; and a company goes into liquidation—

(a) if it is wound up by the court, on the date of the winding-up order, and
(b) in any other case, on the date of the passing of the resolution for voluntary winding up.

Register of disqualification orders

301 (1) The Secretary of State may make regulations requiring officers of courts to furnish him with such particulars as the regulations may specify of cases in which— **A12–17**

(a) a disqualification order is made under any of sections 296 to 300, or
(b) any action is taken by a court in consequence of which such an order is varied or ceases to be in force, or
(c) leave is granted by a court for a person subject to such an order to do any thing which otherwise the order prohibits him from doing;

and the regulations may specify the time within which, and the form and manner in which, such particulars are to be furnished.

(2) The Secretary of State shall, from the particulars so furnished, continue to maintain the register of orders, and of cases in which leave has been granted as mentioned in subsection (1)(c), which was set up by him under section 29 of the Companies Act 1976.

(3) When an order of which entry is made in the register ceases to be in force, the Secretary or State shall delete the entry from the register and all particulars relating to it which have been furnished to him under this section.

(4) The register shall be open to inspection on payment of such fee as may be specified by the Secretary of State in regulations.

(5) Regulations under this section shall be made by statutory instrument subject to annulment in pursuance of a resolution of either House of Parliament.

Provision against undischarged bankrupt acting as director, etc.

A12–18

302 (1) If any person being an undischarged bankrupt acts as director or liquidator of, or directly or indirectly takes part in or is concerned in the promotion, formation or management of, a company except with the leave of the court, he is liable to imprisonment or a fine, or both.

(2) "The court" for this purpose is the court by which the person was adjudged bankrupt or, in Scotland, sequestration of his estates was awarded.

(3) In England and Wales, the leave of the court shall not be given unless notice of intention to apply for it has been served on the official receiver in bankruptcy; and it is the latter's duty, if he is of opinion that it is contrary to the public interest that the application should be granted, to attend on the hearing of the application and oppose it.

(4) In this section "company" includes an unregistered company and a company incorporated outside Great Britain which has an established place of business in Great Britain.

Companies Act 1985, Sch.12

Section 295 SCHEDULE 12

Supplementary Provisions in Connection with Disqualification Orders

Part I

Orders under Sections 296 to 299

Application for order

A12–19

1 A person intending to apply for the making of an order under any of sections 296 to 299 by the court having jurisdiction to wind up a company shall give not less than 10 days' notice of his intention to the person against whom the order is sought; and on the hearing of the application the last-mentioned person may appear and himself give evidence or call witnesses.

2 An application to a court with jurisdiction to wind up companies for the making of such an order against any person may be made the Secretary of State or the official receiver, or by the liquidator or any past or present member or creditor of any company in relation to which that person has committed or is alleged to have committed an offence or other default.

Hearing of application

A12–20 **3** On the hearing of an application made by the Secretary of State or the official receiver or the liquidator the applicant shall appear and call the attention of the court to any matters which seem to him to be relevant, and may himself give evidence or call witnesses.

Application for leave under an order

A12–21 **4** (1) As regards the court to which application must be made for leave under a disqualification order made under any of sections 296 to 299, the following applies.

(2) Where the application is for leave to promote or form a company, it is any court with jurisdiction to wind up companies.

(3) Where the application is for leave to be a liquidator or director of, or otherwise to take part in the management of a company, or to be a receiver or manager of a company's property, it is any court having jurisdiction to wind up that company.

5 On the hearing of an application for leave made by a person against whom a disqualification order has been made on the application of the Secretary of State, the official receiver or the liquidator, the Secretary of State, official receiver or liquidator shall appear and call the attention of the court to any matters which seem to him to be relevant, and may himself give evidence or call witnesses.

Part II

Orders under Section 300

Application for order

A12–22 **6** (1) In the case of a person who is or has been a director of a company which has gone into liquidation as mentioned in section 300(1) and is being wound up by the court, any application under that section shall be made by the official receiver or, in Scotland, the Secretary of State.

(2) In any other case an application shall be made by the Secretary of State.

7 Where the official receiver or the Secretary of State intends to make an application under the section in respect of any person, he shall give not less than 10 days' notice of his intention to that person.

Hearing of application

8 On the hearing of an application under section 300 by the official receiver or the Secretary of State, or of an application for leave by a person against whom an order has been made on the application of the official receiver or Secretary of State—

(a) the official receiver of Secretary of State shall appear and call the attention of the court to any matters which seem to him to be relevant, and may himself give evidence or call witnesses, and

(b) the person against whom the order is sought may appear and himself give evidence or call witnesses

Companies Act 1981, ss.93–94

Restrictions on participation in management of companies and disclosure of directorships

Disqualification of directors and others from managing companies, etc.

A12–23

93 (1) In section 188 of the 1948 Act (orders of court restraining persons from managing companies) the following subsections shall be substituted for subsections (1) and (2)—

"(1) Where—

(a) a person is convicted of a indictable offence (whether on indictment or summarily) in connection with the promotion, formation, management or liquidation of a company or with the receivership or management of the property of a company; or

(b) it appears to the court that a person has been persistently in default in relation to the relevant requirements; or

(c) in the course of the winding up of a company it appears that a person—

(i) has been guilty of an offence for which he is liable (whether he has been convicted or not) under section 332 of this Act; or

(ii) has otherwise been guilty, while an officer or liquidator of the company or receiver or manager of the property of the company, of any fraud in relation to the company or of any breach of his duty as such officer, liquidator, receiver or manager:

the court may make a disqualification order against that person.

(1A) Where a person is convicted of a summary offence which is a relevant offence and, during the five years ending with the date of that conviction, he has had made against him or has been convicted of, in total, not less than three default orders and relevant offences (including that and any other offence of which he is convicted on the same occasion), the court by which he is convicted of that offence or, in England and Wales, any other magistrates, court acting for the same petty sessions area may make a disqualification order against that person.

(1B) For the purposes of this section, a "disqualification order" is an order that the person against whom the order is made shall not without leave of the court be a liquidator or a director or a receiver or manager of the property of a company or in any way, whether directly or indirectly, be concerned or take part in the promotion, formation or management of a company for such period, not exceeding the relevant period, as may be specified in the order.

(1C) Subsection (1)(a) and (c)(ii) of this section shall not apply in relation to anything done before the date on which section 93 of the Companies Act 1981 came into force by a person in his capacity as liquidator of a company or as receiver or manager of the property of a company.

(2) Subject to subsection (1C) of this section, subsection (1)(a) of this section—

(a) shall apply in any case where a person is convicted on indictment of an offence which he committed (and, in the case of a continuing offence, had ceased to commit) before the date on which section 93 of the Companies Act 1981 came into force but in such a case a disqualification order shall not be made for any period in excess of five years:

(b) shall not apply in any case where a person is convicted summarily—

(i) in England and Wales, if he had consented so to be tried before that date; or

(ii) in Scotland, if the summary proceedings commenced before that date.

(2A) Subject to subsection (1C) of this section, subsection (1)(c) of this section shall apply in relation to any offence committed or other thing done before the date on which section 93 of the Companies Act 1981 came into force but a disqualification order made on the grounds of such offence or other thing done shall not be made for any period in excess of five years.

(2B) The powers conferred on any court by subsection (1A) of this section shall not be exercisable in any case where a person is convicted of an offence which he committed (and, in the case of a continuing offence, had ceased to commit) before the date referred to in subsection (2)(a) of this section; and for the purposes of sub-sections (1)(b) and (1A) no account shall be taken of any offence which was committed or any default order made before 1st June 1977.

(2C) For the purposes of an application made under subsection (1)(b) of this section, the fact that a person has been persistently in default in relation to the relevant requirements may (without prejudice to its proof in any other manner) be conclusively proved by showing that in the five years ending with the date of the application he has been adjudged guilty (whether or not on the same occasion) of three or more defaults in relation to those requirements.

A person shall be treated as being adjudged guilty of a default in relation to a relevant requirement for the purposes of this subsection if he is convicted of any relevant offence or a default order is made against him.

(2D) In this section, except where the context otherwise requires—

"company" includes any company which may be wound up under Part IX of this Act:

"the court"—

(a) in relation to the making of a disqualification order under subsection (1) of this section means any court having jurisdiction to wind up any of the companies in relation to which the offence or other default has been or is alleged to have been committed;

(b) in relation to the making of a disqualification order against any person by virtue of subsection (1)(a) of this section, includes the court by or before which he is convicted of the offence there mentioned and, in the case of a summary conviction in England and Wales, any other magistrates' court acting for the same petty sessions area;

(c) in relation to the granting of leave to promote or form a company, means any court with any jurisdiction to wind up companies; and

(d) in relation to the granting of leave to be a liquidator or a director of or otherwise take part of the management of a company or to be a receiver or manager of the property of a company, means any court having jurisdiction to wind up that company;

"default order" means an order made against any person under sections 337, 375 or 428 of this Act (enforcement of duties of liquidators, receivers and managers and companies to make returns, etc.) or under section 5(1) of the Companies Act 1976 (order requiring failure to deliver accounts within required time to be made good) by virtue of any contravention of or failure to comply with any relevant requirement (whether on his own part or on the part of any company);

"officer", in relation to any company, includes any person in accordance with whose directions or instructions the directors of the company have been accustomed to act;

"petty sessions area' has the meaning given by section 150 of the Magistrates' Courts Act 1980;

"relevant offence" means an offence of which a person is convicted (whether on indictment or summarily) by virtue of any contravention of or failure to comply with any relevant requirement (whether on his own part or on the part of any company);

"the relevant period" means—

(a) in relation to an order made by a court of summary jurisdiction or an order made in pursuance of subsection (1)(b) above, five years; and

(b) in relation to any other order, fifteen years; and

"relevant requirement" means any provision of the Companies Act 1948 to 1981 which requires any return, account or other document to be filed with, delivered or sent, or notice of any matter to be given, to the registrar.

(2E) For the purposes of this section, the definitions of "indictable offence" and "summary offence" contained in Schedule 1 to the Interpretation Act 1978 shall apply in relation to Scotland as they apply in relation to England and Wales.

(2F) A disqualification order may be made on grounds which are or include matters other than criminal convictions notwithstanding that the person in respect of whom the order is to be made may be criminally liable in respect of those matters."

(2) The following subsection shall be substituted for subsection (4) of section 188—

"(4) An application to a court with jurisdiction to wind up companies for the making of a disqualification order against any person may be made by the Secretary of State or the official receiver or by the liquidator or any past or present member or creditor of any company in relation to which that person has committed or is alleged to have committed an offence or other default: and on the hearing of any such application made by the Secretary of State or the official receiver or the liquidator or of any application for leave made by a person against whom a disqualification order has been made on the application of the Secretary of State, official receiver or liquidator, the Secretary of State, official receiver or liquidator shall appear and call the attention of the court to any matters which seem to him to be relevant, and may himself give evidence or call witnesses."

(3) Subsection (5) of section 188 shall cease to have effect.

(4) After subsection (6) of section 188 there shall be inserted the following subsection—

"(7) The power under section 193(2) of the Criminal Procedure (Scotland) Act 1975 to substitute a fine for a period of imprisonment shall in relation to a conviction on indictment under subsection (6) of this section be construed as including a power to impose such fine in addition to that period of imprisonment.".

(5) Section 28 of the 1976 Act (power of High Court and Court of Session to make disqualification orders for persistent failure to comply with the relevant requirements) shall cease to have effect; but any order made under section 28 shall have effect as if made under section 188 of the 1948 Act and any application made before the appointed day for such an order shall be treated as an application for an order under section 188.

Prohibition on directors of insolvent companies from acting as liquidators, etc.

A12–24

94 (1) In subsection (1) of section 9 of the Insolvency Act 1976 (power of court to disqualify persons from acting as directors, etc.) for the words from "the court may" to the end there shall be substituted the words—

"the court may make an order that that person shall not, without the leave of the court—

(a) be a director of or in any way, whether directly or indirectly, be concerned or take part in the promotion, formation, or management of a company; or

(b) be a liquidator of a company; or
(c) be a receiver or manager of the property of a company;

for such period as may, subject to subsection (1A) below, be specified in the order.

(1A) The period which may be specified in any order under subsection (1) above shall begin with the date of the order and may not exceed five years if none of the conduct to which the court has regard under subsection (1)(b) occurred after the day appointed for the coming into force of section 94 of the Companies Act 1981, or fifteen years in any other case."

(2) In subsection (7) of that section, for the definition of "company" there shall be substituted the following definition—

" 'company' includes any company which may be wound up under Part IX of the Companies Act 1948;".

(3) The following subsection shall be inserted in that section after subsection (7)—

"(7A) An order under subsection (1) may be made on grounds which are or include matters other than criminal convictions notwithstanding that the person in respect of whom the order is to be made may be criminally liable in respect of those matters."

Companies Act 1981, Sch.3—paras 9, 36

9 In section 187 (restrictions on undischarged bankrupts acting as directors, etc.) after the words "acts as director" there shall be inserted the words "or liquidator" and after the words "is concerned in the" there shall be inserted the words "promotion, formation or". **A12–25**

Companies Act 1976 (c. 69)

36 In section 29(1) of the 1976 Act (register of disqualification orders)— **A12–26**

(a) for the words from "that a person" to "in the order" there shall be substituted the words "under section 188 of the Act of 1948 or section 9 of the Insolvency Act 1976;"; and
(b) the words from "This subsection" to the end shall cease to have effect.

Companies Act 1976, ss.28–29

Disqualification orders

Disqualification for persistent default in relation to delivery of documents to registrar

28 (1) Where, on the application of the Secretary of State, it appears to the High Court that a person has been persistently in default in relation to relevant requirements of the Companies Acts, the court may make an order that that person shall not, without the leave of the court, be a director of or in any, whether directly or indirectly, be concerned or take part in the management of a company for such period beginning with the date of the order and not exceeding five years as may be specified in the order **A12–27**

In the preceding provisions of this subsection "the court", in relation to the granting of leave, means any court having jurisdiction to wind up the company as respects which leave is sought, and in the application of this section to Scotland the references in this subsection to the High Court shall be construed as references to the Court of Session.

(2) Any provision of the Companies Acts which requires any return, account or other document to be filed with, delivered or sent, or notice of any matter to be given, to the registrar of companies is a relevant requirement of the Companies Acts for the purposes of this section.

(3) For the purposes of this section, the fact that a person has been persistently in default in relation to relevant requirements of the Companies Acts may, subject to subsection (4) below (and without prejudice to its proof in any other manner), be conclusively proved by showing that in the five years ending with the date of the application he has been adjudged guilty (whether or not on the same occasion) of three or more defaults in relation to any such requirements.

A person shall be treated as being adjudged guilty of a default in relation to a relevant requirement of the Companies Acts for the purposes of this subsection if—

(a) he is convicted of any offence by virtue of any contravention of or failure to comply with any such requirement (whether on his own part or on the part of any company); or

(b) an order is made against him under section 428 of the Act of 1948 (enforcement of duty of company to make returns to the registrar) or under section 5(1) above.

(4) No account shall be taken for the purposes of this section of any offence which was committed or, in the case of a continuing offence, began before the date on which this section comes into operation

(5) The Secretary of State shall give not less than ten days' notice of his intention to apply for an order under this section to the person against whom the order is sought, and on the hearing of the application that person may appear and himself give evidence or call witnesses.

(6) On the hearing of any application for an order under this section, or of any application for leave under this section by a person against whom an order under this section has been made, the Secretary of State shall appear and call the attention of the court to any matters which seem to him to be relevant and may himself give evidence or call witnesses.

(7) If any person acts in contravention of an order under this section he shall in respect of each offence be liable—

(a) on conviction on indictment, to imprisonment for a term not exceeding two years or to a fine or to both; or

(b) on summary conviction, to imprisonment for a term not exceeding six months or to a fine not exceeding £400 or to both.

(8) In this section "company" includes an unregistered company (wherever incorporated) within the meaning of Part IX of the Act of 1948.

Registrar of disqualification orders

A12–28 **29** (1) The prescribed officer of any court which—

(a) makes an order after the coming into operation of this section, that a person shall not, without the leave of the court, be a director of or in any way, whether directly or indirectly, be concerned or take part in the management of a company for such period as may be specified in the order, or

(b) grants leave in relation to any such order which is so made,

shall, at such time and in such manner and form as may be prescribed, furnish the Secretary of State with the prescribed particulars of the order or the grant of leave.

This subsection applies whether the order is made under section 188 of the Act of 1948, section 9 of the Insolvency Act 1976, or section 28 above.

(2) The Secretary of State shall, from the particulars with which he is furnished under subsection (1) above, maintain a register of such orders and of cases in which the court has granted leave.

(3) On the expiration of an order of which particulars are entered on the register, the Secretary of State shall delete from the register—

(a) those particulars, and
(b) any particulars of cases in which the court has granted leave in relation to that order.

(4) The register shall be open to inspection on payment of such fee as may be specified by the Secretary of State in regulations made by statutory instrument.

(5) A statutory instrument containing regulations made under subsection (4) above shall be subject to annulment in pursuance of a resolution of either House of Parliament.

Insolvency Act 1976, s.9

Disqualification of directors of insolvent companies

9 (1) Where on an application under this section it appears to the court— **A12–29**

(a) that a person—
   (i) is or has been a director of a company which has at any time gone into liquidation (whether while he was a director or subsequently) and was insolvent at that time; and
   (ii) is or has been a director of another such company which has gone into liquidation within five years of the date on which the first-mentioned company went into liquidation; and
(b) that his conduct as director of any of those companies makes him unfit to be concerned in the management of a company,

the court may make an order that that person shall not, without the leave of the court, be a director of or in any way, whether directly or indirectly, be concerned or take part in the management of a company for such period beginning with the date of the order and not exceeding five years as may be specified in the order.

(2) In the case of a person who is or has been a director of a company which has gone into liquidation as aforesaid and is being wound up by the court—

(a) any application under this section shall be made by the official receiver or, in Scotland, the Secretary of State; and
(b) the power to make an order on the application shall be exercisable by the court by which the company is being wound up;

and in any case any application under this section shall be made by the Secretary of State and the power to make an order thereon shall be exercisable by the High Court or, in Scotland, the Court of Session.

(3) Where the official receiver or Secretary of State intends to make an application under this section in respect of any person, he shall give not less than ten days' notice of his intention to that person, and on the hearing of the application that person may appear and himself give evidence or call witnesses.

(4) On the hearing of an application under this section by the official receiver or Secretary of State, or of an application for leave under this section by a person in respect of whom an order has been made on the application of the official receiver or Secretary of State, the official receiver or Secretary of State shall appear and call the attention of the court to any matters which seem to him to be relevant and may himself give evidence or call witnesses.

(5) If any person acts in contravention of an order made under subsection (1) above he shall in respect of each offence be liable—

(a) on conviction on indictment, to imprisonment for a term not exceeding two years or to a fine or to both; or
(b) on summary conviction, to imprisonment for a term not exceeding six months or to a fine not exceeding £400 or to both.

(6) The Secretary of State may require the liquidator or former liquidator of any company—

(a) to furnish him with such information with respect to the company's affairs; and
(b) to produce and permit inspection of such books or documents of or relevant to the company,

as the Secretary of State may reasonably require for the purpose of determining whether to make an application under this section in respect of any person who is or has been a director of that company; and if a person makes default in complying with any such requirement the court may, on the application of the Secretary of State, make an order requiring that person to make good the default within such time as may be specified.

(7) In this section—

"company" includes an unregistered company (wherever incorporated) within the meaning of Part IX of the Companies Act 1948;

"director", in relation to a company, includes any person in accordance with whose directions or instructions the directors of the company have been accustomed to act.

and for the purpose of this section a company goes into liquidation if it is wound up by the court, on the date of the winding up order and, in any case, on the date of the passing of the resolution for voluntary winding up.

(8) In Schedule 1 to the said Act of 1948, in regulation 88 of Part I of Table A and article 38 of Table C the references to an order under Section 188 of that Act (disqualification of directors) shall include a reference to an order under this section.

(9) Subsection (1) above does not apply unless at least one of the companies there mentioned has gone into liquidation after the date of the coming into force of this section; and the conduct to which regard may be had under paragraph (b) of that subsection does not include conduct as director of a company that has gone into liquidation before that date.

Companies Act 1948, ss.187–188

Provisions as to undischarged bankrupts acting as directors

A12–30 **187** (1) If any person being an undischarged bankrupt acts as director of, or directly or indirectly takes part in or is concerned in the management of, any company except with the leave of the court by which he was adjudged bankrupt, he shall be liable on conviction on indictment to imprisonment for a term not exceeding two years, or on summary conviction to imprisonment for a term not exceeding six months or to a fine not exceeding five hundred pounds or to both such imprisonment and fine:

Provided that a person shall not be guilty of an offence under this section by reason that he, being an undischarged bankrupt, has acted as director of, or taken part or been concerned in the management of, a company, if he was on the third day of August, nineteen hundred and twenty-eight, acting as director of, or taking part of being concerned in the management of, that company and has continuously so acted, taken part or been concerned since that date and the bankruptcy was prior to that date.

(2) In England the leave of the court for the purposes of this section shall not be given unless notice of intention to apply therefor has been served on the official receiver, and it shall be the duty of the official receiver, if he is of opinion that it is contrary to the public

interest that any such application should be granted, to attend on the hearing of and oppose the granting of the application.

(3) In this section the expression "company" includes an unregistered company and a company incorporated outside Great Britain which has an established place of business within Great Britain, and the expression "official receiver" means the official receiver in bankruptcy.

(4) Subsection (1) of this section in its application to Scotland shall have effect as if the words "sequestration of his estates was awarded" were substituted for the words "he was adjudged bankrupt".

Power to restrain fraudulent persons from managing companies

188 (1) Where— A12–31

(a) a person is convicted on indictment of any offence in connection with the promotion, formation or management of a company; or
(b) in the course of winding up a company it appears that a person—
  (i) has been guilty of any offence for which he is liable (whether he has been convicted or not) under section three hundred and thirty-two of this Act; or
  (ii) has otherwise been guilty, while an officer of the company, of any fraud in relation to the company or of any breach of his duty to the company:

the court may make an order that that person shall not, without the leave of the court, be a director of or in any way, whether directly or indirectly, be concerned or take part in the management of a company for such period not exceeding five years as may be specified in the order.

(2) In the foregoing subsection the expression "the court", in relation to the making of an order against any person by virtue of paragraph (a) thereof, includes the court before which he is convicted, as well as any court having jurisdiction to wind up the company, and in relation to the granting of leave means any court having jurisdiction to wind up the company as respects which leave is sought.

(3) A person intending to apply for the making of an order under this section by the court having jurisdiction to wind up a company shall give not less than ten days' notice of his intention to the person against whom the order is sought, and on the hearing of the application the last-mentioned person may appear and himself give evidence or call witnesses.

(4) An application for the making of an order under this section by the court having jurisdiction to wind up a company may be made by the official receiver, or by the liquidator of the company or by any person who is or has been a member or creditor of the company; and on the hearing of any application for an order under this section by the official receiver or the liquidator, or of any application for leave under this section by a person against whom an order has been made on the application of the official receiver or the liquidator, the official receiver or liquidator shall appear and call the attention of the court to any matters which seem to him to be relevant, and may himself give evidence or call witnesses.

(5) An order may be made by virtue of sub-paragraph (ii) of paragraph (b) of subsection (1) of this section notwithstanding that the person concerned may be criminally liable in respect of the matters on the ground of which the order is to be made, and for the purposes of the said sub-paragraph (ii) the expression "officer" shall include any person in accordance with whose directions or instructions the directors of the company have been accustomed to act.

(6) If any person acts in contravention of an order made under this section, he shall, in respect of each offence, be liable on conviction on indictment to imprisonment for a term not exceeding two years, or on summary conviction to imprisonment for a term not exceeding six months or to a fine not exceeding five hundred pounds or to both.

Companies Act 1947, s.33

Power to restrain fraudulent persons from managing companies

A12–32 **33** (1) Where—

(a) a person is convicted on indictment of any offence in connection with the promotion, formation or management of a company; or
(b) in the course of winding up a company it appears that a person—

(i) has been guilty of any offence for which he is liable (whether he has been convicted or not) under section two hundred and seventy-five of the principal Act (which relates to the responsibility of directors for fraudulent trading); or
(ii) has otherwise been guilty, while an officer of the company, of any fraud in relation to the company or of any breach of his duty to the company;

the court may make an order that that person shall not, without the leave of the court, be a director of or in any way, whether directly or indirectly, be concerned or take part in the management of a company for such period, not exceeding five years, as may be specified in the order.

(2) In the foregoing subsection the expression "the court", in relation to the making of an order against any person by virtue of paragraph (a) thereof, includes the court before which he is convicted, as well as any court having jurisdiction to wind up the company, and in relation to the granting of leave means any court having jurisdiction to wind up the company as respects which leave is sought.

(3) Any person intending to apply for the making of an order under this section by the court having jurisdiction to wind up a company shall give not less than ten days' notice of his intention to the person against whom the order is sought, and on the hearing of the application the last mentioned person may appear and himself give evidence or call witnesses.

(4) An application for the making of an order under this section by the court having jurisdiction to wind up a company may be made by the official receiver, or by the liquidator of the company, or by any person who is or has been a member or creditor of the company; and on the hearing of any application for an order under this section by the official receiver or the liquidator, or any application for leave under this section by a person against whom an order has been made on the application of the official receiver or the liquidator, the official receiver or liquidator shall appear and call the attention of the court to any matters which seem to him to be relevant, and may himself give evidence or call witnesses.

(5) An order may be made by virtue of sub-paragraph (ii) of paragraph (b) of subsection (1) of this section notwithstanding that the person concerned may be criminally liable in respect of the matters on the ground of which the order is to be made, and the purposes of the said sub-paragraph (ii) the expression "officer" shall include any person in accordance with whose directions or instructions the directors of the company have been accustomed to act.

(6) If any person acts in contravention of an order made under this section, he shall, in respect of each offence, be liable on conviction on indictment to imprisonment for a term not exceeding two years, or on summary conviction to imprisonment for a term not exceeding six months or to a fine not exceeding five hundred pounds or to both.

Companies Act 1929, ss.142, 217, 275

Provisions as to undischarged bankrupts acting as directors

A12–33 **142** (1) If any person being an undischarged bankrupt acts as director of, or directly or indirectly takes part in or is concerned in the management of, any company except with the leave of the court by which he was adjudged bankrupt, he shall be liable on conviction on indictment to imprisonment for a term not exceeding two years, or on summary conviction to imprisonment for a term not exceeding six months or to a fine not exceeding five hundred pounds, or to both such imprisonment and fine:

Provided that a person shall not be guilty of an offence under this section by reason that he, being an undischarged bankrupt, has acted as director of, or taken part or been concerned in the management of, a company, if he was on the third day of August, nineteen hundred and twenty-eight, acting as director of, or taking part or being concerned in the management of, that company and has continuously so acted, taken part, or been concerned since that date and the bankruptcy was prior to that date.

(2) In England the leave of the court for the purpose of this section shall not be given unless notice of intention to apply therefor has been served on the official receiver and it shall be the duty of the official receiver, if he is of opinion that it is contrary to the public interest that any such application should be granted, to attend on the hearing of and oppose the granting of the application.

(3) In this section the expression "company" includes an unregistered company and a company incorporated outside Great Britain which has an established place of business within Great Britain, and the expression "official receiver" means the official receiver in bankruptcy.

(4) Subsection (1) of this section in its application to Scotland shall have effects as if the words "sequestration of his estates was awarded" were substituted for the words "he was adjudged bankrupt."

217 (1) Where an order has been made in England for winding up a company by the court, and the official receiver has made a further report under this Act stating that, in his opinion, a fraud has been committed by a person in the promotion or formation of the company, or by any director or other officer of the company in relation to the company since its formation, the court may, on the application of the official receiver, order that that person, director or officer shall not, without the leave of the court, be a director of or in any way, whether directly or indirectly, be concerned in or take part in the management of a company for such period, not exceeding five years, from the date of the report as may be specified in the order.

(2) The official receiver shall, where he intends to make an application under the last foregoing subsection, give not less than ten days' notice of his intention to the person charged with the fraud, and on the hearing of the application that person may appear and himself give evidence or call witnesses.

(3) It shall be the duty of the official receiver to appear on the hearing of an application by him for an order under this section and on an application for leave under this section and to call the attention of the court to any matters which appear to him to be relevant, and on any such application the official receiver may himself give evidence or call witnesses.

(4) If any person acts in contravention of an order made under this section, he shall, in respect of each offence, be liable on conviction on indictment to imprisonment for a term not exceeding two years, or on summary conviction to imprisonment for a term not exceeding six months or to a fine not exceeding five hundred pounds, or to both such imprisonment and fine.

(5) The provisions of this section shall have effect notwithstanding that the person concerned may be criminally liable in respect of the matters on the ground of which the order is to be made.

Responsibility of directors for fraudulent trading

A12–34

275 (1) If in the course of the winding up of a company it appears that any business of the company has been carried on with intent to defraud creditors of the company or creditors of any other person or for any fraudulent purpose, the court, on the application of the official receiver, or the liquidator or any creditor or contributory of the company, may, if it thinks proper so to do, declare that any of the directors, whether past or present, of the company who were knowingly parties to the carrying on of the business in manner aforesaid shall be personally responsible, without any limitation of liability, for all or any of the debts or other liabilities of the company as the court may direct.

(2) Where the court makes any such declaration, it may give such further directions as it thinks proper for the purpose of giving effect to that declaration, and in particular may make provision for making the liability of any such director under the declaration a charge on any debt or obligation due from the company to him, or on any mortgage or charge or any interest in any mortgage or charge on any assets of the company held by or vested in him, or any company or person on his behalf, or any person claiming as assignee from or through the director, company or person, and may from time to time make such further order as may be necessary for the purpose of enforcing any charge imposed under this subsection.

For the purpose of this subsection, the expression "assignee" includes any person to whom or in whose favour, by the directions of the director, the debt, obligation, mortgage or charge was created, issued or transferred or the interest created, but does not include an assignee for valuable consideration (not including consideration by way of marriage) given in good faith and without notice of any of the matters on the ground of which the declaration is made.

(3) Where any business of a company is carried on with such intent or for such purpose as is mentioned in subsection (1) of this section, every director of the company who was knowingly a party to the carrying on of the business in manner aforesaid, shall be liable on conviction on indictment to imprisonment for a term not exceeding one year.

(4) The court may, in the case of any person in respect of whom a declaration has been made under subsection (1) of this section, or who has been convicted of an offence under subsection (3) of this section, order that that person shall not, without the leave of the court, be a director of or in any way, whether directly or indirectly, be concerned in or take part in the management of a company for such period, not exceeding five years, from the date of the declaration or of the conviction, as the case may be, as may be specified in the order, and if any person acts in contravention of an order made under this subsection he shall, in respect of each offence, be liable on conviction on indictment to imprisonment for a term not exceeding two years, or on summary conviction to imprisonment for a term not exceeding six months or to a fine not exceeding five hundred pounds, or to both such imprisonment and fine.

In this subsection the expression "the court" in relation to the making of an order, means the court by which the declaration was made or the court before which the person was convicted, as the case may be, and in relation to the granting of leave means any court having jurisdiction to wind up the company.

(5) For the purposes of this section, the expression "director" shall include any person in accordance with whose directions or instructions the directors of a company have been accustomed to act.

(6) The provisions of this section shall have effect notwithstanding that the person concerned may be criminally liable in respect of the matters on the ground of which the declaration is to be made and where the declaration under subsection (1) of this section is made in the case of a winding up in England, the declaration shall be deemed to be a final judgment within the meaning of paragraph (g) of subsection (1) of section one of the Bankruptcy Act, 1914.

(7) It shall be the duty of the official receiver or of the liquidator to appear on the hearing of an application for leave under subsection (4) of this section, and on the hearing of an application under that subsection or under subsection (1) of this section the official receiver or the liquidator, as the case may be, may himself give evidence or call witnesses.

Companies Act 1928, ss.75, 76, 84

Provisions with respect to fraudulent trading

75 (1) If in the course of a winding-up it appears that any business of the company has been carried on with intent to defraud creditors of the company or creditors of any other person or for any fraudulent purpose, the court, on the application of the official receiver or the liquidator, or any creditor or contributory of the company, may, it if thinks proper so do to, declare that any of the directors, whether past or present, of the company who were knowingly parties to the carrying on of the business in manner aforesaid shall be personally responsible, without any limitation of liability, for all or any of the debts or other liabilities of the company as the court may direct. **A12–35**

(2) Where the court makes any such declaration, it may give such further directions as it thinks proper for the purpose of giving effect to that declaration, and in particular may make provision for making the liability of any such director under the declaration a charge on any debt or obligation due from the company to him, or on any mortgage or charge or any interest in any mortgage or charge on any assets of the company held by or vested in him, or any company or person on his behalf, or any person claiming as assignee from or through the director, company or person, other than an assignee for valuable consideration (not including consideration by way of marriage) given in good faith and without notice of any of the matters on the ground of which the declaration is made, and may from time to time make such further order as may be necessary for the purpose of enforcing any charge imposed under this subsection.

For the purpose of the foregoing provision the expression "assignee" includes any person to whom or in whose favour by the directions of the director the debt, obligation, mortgage or charge was created issued or transferred or the interest created.

(3) Where any business of a company is carried on with such intent or such purpose as is mentioned in subsection (1) of this section, every director of the company who was knowingly a party to the carrying on of the business in manner aforesaid, shall be liable on conviction on indictment to imprisonment for a term not exceeding one year.

(4) The court may, in the case of any person in respect of whom a declaration has been made under the foregoing provisions of this section or who has been convicted of an offence under the foregoing provisions of this section, order that that person shall not, without the leave of the court, be a director of or in any way, whether directly or indirectly, be concerned in or take part in the management of a company for such period, not exceeding five years, from the date of the declaration or of the conviction, as the case may be, as may be specified in the order, and if any person acts in contravention of an order made under this subsection he shall, in respect of each offence, be liable on conviction on indictment to imprisonment for a term not exceeding two years, or on summary conviction to imprisonment for a term not exceeding six months or to a fine not exceeding five hundred pounds, or to both such imprisonment and fine.

In this subsection the expression "the court" in relation to the making of an order, means the court by which the declaration was made or the court before which the person was convicted, as the case may be, and in relation to the granting of leave means any court having jurisdiction to wind up the company.

(5) For the purposes of this section, the expression "director" shall include any person who occupies the position of a director or in accordance with whose directions or instructions the directors of a company have been accustomed to act.

(6) The provisions of this section shall have effect notwithstanding that the person concerned may be criminally liable in respect of the matters on the ground of which the declaration is to be made, and where the declaration under subsection (1) of this section is made in the case of a winding-up in England, the declaration shall be deemed to be a final judgment within the meaning of paragraph (g) of subsection (1) of section one of the Bankruptcy Act, 1914.

(7) It shall be the duty of the official receiver or of the liquidator to appear on the hearing of an application for leave under subsection (4) of this section, and on the hearing of an application under that subsection or under subsection (1) of this section the official receiver or the liquidator, as the case may be, may himself give evidence or call witnesses.

76 (1) If, where the court in England has made a winding-up order in respect of any company, the official receiver, in pursuance of subsection (2) of section one hundred and forty-eight of the principal Act, reports that, in his opinion, a fraud has been committed by any person in the promotion or formation of the company or by any director or other officer of the company in relation thereto since its formation, the court may, on the application of the official receiver, make an order under subsection (4) of the last preceding section of this Act as though the person by whom the fraud is alleged in the report to have been made were a person in respect of whom a declaration has been made under subsection (1) of that section.

(2) The official receiver shall, where he intends to make an application under this section, give not less than ten days' notice of his intention to the person charged with the fraud, and on the hearing of the application that person may appear and himself give evidence or call witnesses.

(3) It shall be the duty of the official receiver to appear on the hearing of any such application and to call the attention of the court to any matters which appear to him to be relevant, and the official receiver may on the hearing himself give evidence or call witnesses.

Provisions as to undischarged bankrupts acting as directors

A12–36

84 (1) If any person being an undischarged bankrupt acts as director of, or directly or indirectly takes part in or is concerned in the management of, any company including an unregistered company and a company incorporated outside Great Britain which has an established place of business within Great Britain except with the leave of the court by which he was adjudged bankrupt, he shall be liable on conviction on indictment to imprisonment for a term not exceeding two years or on summary conviction to imprisonment for a term not exceeding six months or to a fine not exceeding five hundred pounds or to both such imprisonment and fine.

Provided that a person shall not be guilty of an offence under this section by reason that he, being an undischarged bankrupt, has acted as director of, or taken part or been concerned in the management of, a company, if he was at the passing of this Act acting as director of, or taking part, or being concerned in the management of that company and has continuously so acted, taken part, or been concerned since the passing of this Act and the bankruptcy was prior to the passing of this Act.

(2) The leave of the court for the purposes of this section shall not be given unless notice of intention to apply therefor has been served on the official receiver and it shall be the duty of the official receiver, if he is of opinion that it is contrary to the public interest that any such application should be granted, to attend on the hearing of and oppose the granting of the application.

(3) In this section the expression "official receiver" means the official receiver in bankruptcy.

INDEX